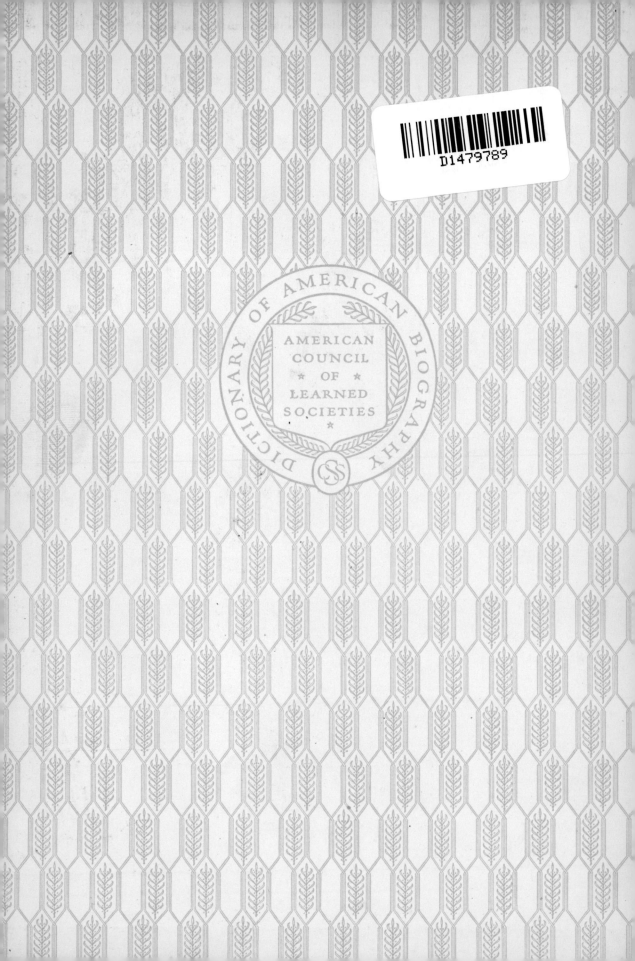

DICTIONARY OF AMERICAN BIOGRAPHY

AMERICAN
COUNCIL
* OF *
LEARNED
SOCIETIES

DICTIONARY OF
AMERICAN BIOGRAPHY

DICTIONARY OF AMERICAN BIOGRAPHY

UNDER THE AUSPICES OF THE
AMERICAN COUNCIL OF LEARNED SOCIETIES

EDITED BY
DUMAS MALONE

Larned — MacCracken

VOLUME XI

CHARLES SCRIBNER'S SONS

NEW YORK

1933

Prompted solely by a desire for public service the New York Times Company and its President, Mr. Adolph S. Ochs, have made possible the preparation of the manuscript of the Dictionary of American Biography through a subvention of more than $500,000 and with the understanding that the entire responsibility for the contents of the volumes rests with the American Council of Learned Societies.

The Dictionary of American Biography is published under the auspices of the American Council of Learned Societies and under the direction of a Committee of Management which consists of J. FRANKLIN JAMESON, *Chairman*, JOHN H. FINLEY, DUMAS MALONE, FREDERIC L. PAXSON, IPHIGENE OCHS SULZBERGER, CARL VAN DOREN, CHARLES WARREN.

The editorial staff consists of DUMAS MALONE, *Editor*; HARRIS E. STARR, *Associate Editor*; GEORGE H. GENZMER, ELEANOR R. DOBSON, MILDRED B. PALMER, *Assistant Editors.*

CONTRIBUTORS TO VOLUME XI

KATHRYN T. ABBEY	K. T. A.
THOMAS P. ABERNETHY	T. P. A.
ADELINE ADAMS	A. A.
JAMES TRUSLOW ADAMS	J. T. A.
RANDOLPH G. ADAMS	R. G. A—s.
RAYMOND ADAMS	R. A.
CYRUS ADLER	C. A.
ROBERT GREENHALGH ALBION	R. G. A—n.
CARROLL S. ALDEN	C. S. A.
EDMUND KIMBALL ALDEN	E. K. A.
JOHN LINCOLN ALGER	J. L. A.
FRANCIS G. ALLINSON	F. G. A.
WILLIAM H. ALLISON	W. H. A.
LEWIS FLINT ANDERSON	L. F. A.
JOHN CLARK ARCHER	J. C. Ar—r.
PERCY M. ASHBURN	P. M. A.
FREDERICK W. ASHLEY	F. W. A.
CHARLES B. ATWELL	C. B. A.
JOSEPH CULLEN AYER	J. C. Ay—r.
JOHN BAKELESS	J. B.
HAYES BAKER-CROTHERS	H. B–C.
THOMAS S. BARCLAY	T. S. B.
GILBERT H. BARNES	G. H. B.
CLARIBEL R. BARNETT	C. R. B.
ANNA BARROWS	A. B.
HAROLD K. BARROWS	H. K. B.
ROBERT DUNCAN BASS	R. D. B.
ERNEST SUTHERLAND BATES	E. S. B.
WILLIAM G. BEAN	W. G. B.
PERCY W. BIDWELL	P. W. B.
BRUCE M. BIGELOW	B. M. B.
FRANKLIN C. BING	F. C. B.
EDITH R. BLANCHARD	E. R. B.
ARTHUR R. BLESSING	A. R. B.
LOUISE PEARSON BLODGET	L. P. B.
LANSING B. BLOOM	L. B. B.
ROBERT W. BOLWELL	R. W. B.
WITT BOWDEN	W. B—n.
SARAH G. BOWERMAN	S. G. B.
WILLIAM K. BOYD	W. K. B.
WILLIAM BRIDGWATER	W. B—r.
W. C. BRONSON	W. C. B.
ROBERT PRESTON BROOKS	R. P. B.
ELMER ELLSWORTH BROWN	E. E. B.
MARGARET LOUISE BROWN	M. L. B.
JOHN S. BRUBACHER	J. S. B.
PAUL H. BUCK	P. H. B.
ROBERTA B. BURNET	R. B. B.
EDMUND C. BURNETT	E. C. B.
WALTER LINCOLN BURRAGE	W. L. B.
HUNTINGTON CAIRNS	H. Ca—s.
ISABEL M. CALDER	I. M. C.
JAMES M. CALLAHAN	J. M. C.
KILLIS CAMPBELL	K. C.
CHARLES F. CAREY	C. F. C.
HARRY J. CARMAN	H. J. C.
WILLIAM S. CARPENTER	W. S. C.
ARTHUR E. CASE	A. E. C.
ZECHARIAH CHAFEE, JR.	Z. C., Jr.
WILL GRANT CHAMBERS	W. G. C.
FRANCIS A. CHRISTIE	F. A. C.
GEORGE H. CLARK	G. H. C.
R. C. CLARK	R. C. C.
HARRY CLEMONS	H. Cl—s.
ORAL SUMNER COAD	O. S. C.
FREDERICK W. COBURN	F. W. C.
WILLIAM E. COLBY	W. E. C.
FANNIE L. GWINNER COLE	F. L. G. C.
ROSSETTER GLEASON COLE	R. G. C—e.
CHRISTOPHER B. COLEMAN	C. B. C.
R. V. COLEMAN	R. V. C.
THEODORE COLLIER	T. C.
JOHN R. COMMONS	J. R. C.
ROBERT SPENCER COTTERILL	R. S. C.
WALTER J. COUPER	W. J. C.
JESSE H. COURSAULT	J. H. C.
THEODORE S. COX	T. S. C.
KATHARINE ELIZABETH CRANE	K. E. C.
MERLE E. CURTI	M. E. C.
EDWARD E. CURTIS	E. E. C.
ROBERT E. CUSHMAN	R. E. C.
CHARLES WILLIAM DABNEY	C. W. D.
FRANK BURNETT DAINS	F. B. D.
EDWARD E. DALE	E. E. D.
HARRISON C. DALE	H. C. D.
RALPH DAVOL	R. D.
D. BRYSON DELAVAN	D. B. D.
WILLIAM H. S. DEMAREST	W. H. S. D.
HERMAN J. DEUTSCH	H. J. D.
IRVING DILLIARD	I. D.
A. IMRIE DIXON	A. I. D.
DOROTHY ANNE DONDORE	D. A. D.
ELIZABETH DONNAN	E. D.
WILLIAM HOWE DOWNES	W. H. D.
STELLA M. DRUMM	S. M. D.
EDWARD A. DUDDY	E. A. D.
RAYMOND S. DUGAN	R. S. D.
WALTER PRICHARD EATON	W. P. E.

Contributors to Volume XI

Contributors to Volume XI

Donald H. Menzel . . . . . D. H. M.
Robert L. Meriwether . . . R. L. M—r.
George P. Merrill . . . . . G. P. M.
Frank J. Metcalf . . . . . . F. J. M.
Carl W. Mitman . . . . . . C. W. M.
Conrad Henry Moehlman . . C. H. M.
E. V. Moffett . . . . E. V. M.
Frank Monaghan . . . . . . F. M.
Robert E. Moody . . . . . R. E. M.
Ross H. Moore . . . . . . R. H. M.
Herbert M. Morais . . . . H. M. M.
Hugh A. Moran . . . . . . H. A. M—n.
Samuel Eliot Morison . . . S. E. M.
Richard B. Morris . . . . . R. B. M.
Jarvis M. Morse . . . . . J. M. M.
Richard L. Morton . . . . R. L. M—n.
Dana C. Munro . . . . . . D. C. M.
William B. Munro . . . . . W. B. M—o.
H. Edward Nettles . . . . H. E. N.
Allan Nevins . . . . A. N.
Lyman C. Newell . . . . . L. C. N.
A. R. Newsome . . . . . . A. R. N.
Robert Hastings Nichols . R. H. N.
Roy F. Nichols . . . . . . R. F. N.
Walter B. Norris . . . . . W. B. N.
William Notz . . . . W. N.
Frank M. O'Brien . . . . . F. M. O.
Robert B. Osgood . . . . . R. B. O.
Winthrop J. V. Osterhout . W. J. V. O.
Victor H. Paltsits . . . . . V. H. P.
Henry K. Pancoast . . . . H. K. P.
John I. Parcel . . . . J. I. P.
George W. Paré . . . . . . G. W. P.
J. Parmly Paret . . . . . . J. P. P.
Stanley M. Pargellis . . . S. M. P.
John C. Parish . . . . . . J. C. P.
Frances Fenton Park . . . F. F. P.
Charles O. Paullin . . . . C. O. P.
Frederic Logan Paxson . . F. L. P.
Charles E. Payne . . . . . C. E. P.
Haywood J. Pearce, Jr. . . H. J. P., Jr.
C. C. Pearson . . . . C. C. P.
Morton E. Peck . . . . . . M. E. P.
James H. Peeling . . . . . J. H. P.
Frederick T. Persons . . . F. T. P.
A. Everett Peterson . . . . A. E. P.
James M. Phalen . . . . . J. M. P—n.
Francis S. Philbrick . . . F. S. P.
David Philipson . . . . . . D. P.
David deSola Pool . . . . D. deS. P.
John M. Poor . . . . J. M. P—r.
Charles Shirley Potts . . . C. S. P.
Anne S. Pratt . . . . A. S. P.
Julius W. Pratt . . . . . . J. W. P.
Edward Preble . . . . . . E. P.
Herbert I. Priestley . . . H. I. P.
Leon C. Prince . . . . . . L. C. P.
Richard J. Purcell . . . . R. J. P.

Lowell Joseph Ragatz . . . L. J. R.
Charles W. Ramsdell . . . C. W. R.
James G. Randall . . . . . J. G. R.
Belle Rankin . . . . B. R.
Albert G. Rau . . . . . . A. G. R.
P. O. Ray . . . . P. O. R.
John Henry Reynolds . . . J. H. R.
Charles Dudley Rhodes . . C. D. R.
George L. Richardson . . . G. L. R.
Irving B. Richman . . . . I. B. R.
David A. Robertson . . . . D. A. R.
Doane Robinson . . . . . D. R.
Edgar E. Robinson . . . . E. E. R.
William A. Robinson . . . W. A. R.
Carl B. Roden . . . . . . C. B. R.
J. Magnus Rohne . . . . . J. M. R.
Virginia Ronsaville . . . . V. R.
Marvin B. Rosenberry . . . M. B. R.
Frank Edward Ross . . . . F. E. R.
Herbert W. Schneider . . . H. W. S—r.
Montgomery Schuyler . . M. S.
Horace Wells Sellers . . . H. W. S—s.
Thorsten Sellin . . . . . . T. S.
Edwin B. Shaw . . . . . . E. B. S.
William Bristol Shaw . . . W. B. S.
Augustus H. Shearer . . . A. H. S.
Jay J. Sherman . . . . . . J. J. S.
Fred W. Shipman . . . . . F. W. S.
Lester B. Shippee . . . . . L. B. S.
George N. Shuster . . . . G. N. S.
Wilbur H. Siebert . . . . W. H. S.
David Eugene Smith . . . D. E. S.
Edgar Fahs Smith . . . . E. F. S.
Fred M. Smith . . . . . . F. M. S.
Marion Parris Smith . . . M. P. S.
William Roy Smith . . . . W. R. S.
George Franklin Smythe . G. F. S.
E. Wilder Spaulding . . . E. W. S.
Oliver L. Spaulding, Jr. . . O. L. S., Jr.
Thomas M. Spaulding . . . T. M. S.
Charles Worthen Spencer . C. W. S.
Harris Elwood Starr . . . H. E. S.
George M. Stephenson . . G. M. S.
George R. Stewart, Jr. . . G. R. S., Jr.
Witmer Stone . . . . . . W. S.
Tracy E. Strevey . . . . . T. E. S.
James Sullivan . . . . . . J. S.
William U. Swan . . . . . W. U. S.
William W. Sweet . . . . W. W. S.
Charles S. Sydnor . . . . C. S. S.
Frank A. Taylor . . . . . F. A. T.
William A. Taylor . . . . W. A. T.
Marten ten Hoor . . . . . M. ten H.
Edward Larocque Tinker . E. L. T.
Payson J. Treat . . . . . . P. J. T.
Robert B. Tunstall . . . . R. B. T.
William T. Utter . . . . . W. T. U.
John G. Van Deusen . . . . J. G. V–D.

Contributors to Volume XI

DICTIONARY OF

AMERICAN BIOGRAPHY

Larned — MacCracken

LARNED, JOSEPH GAY EATON (Apr. 29, 1819–June 3, 1870), lawyer, inventor, industrialist, was born at Thompson, Conn., the son of George and Anna Spalding (Gay) Larned, and a descendant of William and Goodith Learned who were in Charlestown, Mass., in 1632. His early education was received in the local public and preparatory schools, and he graduated from Yale College with the class of 1839, receiving the degree of B.A. He then taught the classics at Chatham Academy, Savannah, Ga., for a year, and in the fall of 1840 became a private teacher in Charleston, S. C. Early in 1841 he returned to his home and began studying law, but the following year he took charge of an academy at Waterloo, N. Y., and in November 1842 was called to a tutorship in Yale College. He continued in this capacity for some five years. In 1846 he initiated a project for raising money by subscription to purchase for the Yale law school the library of Judge Hitchcock of New Haven, then recently deceased; and during his vacations he devoted himself to this undertaking. Becoming interested in public affairs he assisted in the organization of the Free-Soil party of New Haven and published several articles in the *New Englander* (July, October 1845, April 1846) upon "Massachusetts and South Carolina." Late in 1847 he was admitted to the bar in New Haven and began the practice of law. His professional interest was gradually directed toward patent law, and thence to the financial support and development of certain inventions which came to his attention. In consequence, he withdrew from the practice of his profession about 1852, and in 1854 removed to New York City. There he soon became acquainted with Wellington Lee, who was engaged in the perfection of a steam fire en-

gine, and in 1855 they formed a partnership to manufacture steam fire engines at the Novelty Iron Works, New York. Fire engines were then looked upon as novelties merely, and to introduce them into New York City for practical use was a difficult task. Beginning in April 1856, when one of their first engines was demonstrated in City Hall Park, Lee and Larned exhibited one after another of their successively improved engines and through their perseverance were at last rewarded by having their products put into service, not only in New York but also in several other cities in the United States and Europe. In November 1858 they first demonstrated their self-propelled steam fire engine, which weighed 5½ tons, raised steam to a working pressure of 150 pounds in from six to ten minutes, and was capable of discharging over 700 gallons of water per minute through a 1⅝-inch nozzle to a horizontal distance of 267 feet and a vertical height of nearly 200 feet. The machine incorporated the rotary pump invented by J. C. Cary, driven by a reciprocating steam engine, and Lee's and Larned's patented annular boiler. For an improvement in the boiler, Larned received patent No. 23,093, on Mar. 1, 1859. The boiler then consisted of rows of upright water tubes set side by side and connected to a steam dome above the fire and to a water bottom below in such a way as to form a water-jacketed fire-box. By 1860 Lee and Larned were manufacturing and selling steam fire engines of several different sizes, the smallest being designed for hand drawing and for use in small villages and towns. One of these, however, was on duty at the Valley Forge Hose Company stationed in Thirty-seventh Street, New York. It weighed about 3,700 pounds, and was a four-wheeled affair, about ten feet long, with the vertical boiler between the rear wheels. In 1863 Lee and Larned went out of business because their enterprise ceased to be profitable. Larned thereupon became assistant inspector of ironclads for the Navy Department and had charge of work in progress at Green Point, Brooklyn, N. Y. At the close of the Civil War he returned to the practice of law in New York City. During his leisure he began to collect and compile genealogical records of his ancestors, and in 1865 he published *A Quarter-Century Record of the Class of 1839, Yale College* (1865). He was married May 9, 1859, to Helen Lee, a sister of his business partner. She survived him at the time of his sudden death in New York City.

[*Obit. Record Grads. Yale Coll.*, 1870; W. L. Learned, *The Learned Family* (1882; 2nd ed., 1898); *Scientific American*, Apr. 5, 1856, Nov. 27, 1858, Apr. 7, 1860; *Sen. Ex. Doc. No. 12*, 36 Cong., 1 Sess.; Patent Office records; *New-Eng. Hist. and Geneal. Reg.*, Oct. 1874; *N. Y. Times*, June 4, 1870.]   C. W. M.

LARNED, JOSEPHUS NELSON (May 11, 1836–Aug. 15, 1913), librarian, author, a descendant of William Learned who came to Massachusetts about 1632, was the son of Henry Sherwood and Mary Ann (Nelson) Larned. He was born in Chatham, Ont., while his parents, both citizens of the United States, were temporarily residents of Canada. During his boyhood they moved to Buffalo, where he attended public school until he was about seventeen. He was well schooled, but his further education was gained largely through his own efforts. He always regretted his lack of college training, but he appeared to his contemporaries as better informed than many college men. He became first a bookkeeper, then a clerk, and in the fall of 1857 was given a position on the Buffalo *Republic*. In 1859 he joined the editorial staff of the *Buffalo Express*, with which he remained until 1872, writing able editorials in behalf of the Union cause during the Civil War. In the office of the *Express* he was associated for about a year with Mark Twain. Larned had a financial interest in the paper from 1866 to 1877.

In the fall of 1871 Larned was elected superintendent of education, and for five years directed his efforts, unsuccessfully, toward removing the schools from politics. In 1877 he was appointed superintendent of the Buffalo Young Men's Association with the understanding that he would reorganize the library, thereafter known as the Buffalo Library. Finding the books not classified, he investigated different systems, and finally adopted Melvil Dewey's decimal classification. The Buffalo Library was the first to be completely classified under that system, since so

widely adopted. Larned planned and established a children's room, one of the first in the country. He issued free tickets to children in the schools, started a school room in the library, and established an open-shelf room. In 1886 he moved the library into a new building which it occupied jointly with other cultural organizations. He was one of the early members of the American Library Association and its president in 1893–94. After he had directed the Buffalo Library for twenty years it was taken over by the city, in 1897, as a public circulating library. Although this step was directly in line with Larned's policy, he was not in sympathy with the new board and felt compelled to resign.

Thenceforth he devoted himself to literary and civic affairs. He will perhaps be longest remembered for his *History for Ready Reference* (5 vols., 1894–95; supplements in 1901 and 1910), an alphabetical arrangement, by historical subjects, of extracts from the writings of "the best historians, biographers, and specialists." His *Primer of Right and Wrong, for Young People* appeared in 1902; his *Seventy Centuries of the Life of Mankind* (1905), was later republished as *Larned's History of the World* (1915). His *History of England* (for schools) appeared in 1900, *A History of the United States for Secondary Schools,* in 1903, and *A History of Buffalo* (2 vols.), in 1911. He edited *The Literature of American History: A Bibliographical Guide,* in 1902, for the American Library Association, and published a number of other books and papers. Larned was active in the Civil Service Reform Association, the Municipal League, the School Association, and the Buffalo Peace and Arbitration Society. He was a member of the Liberal Club, an honorary member of the Saturn Club (1897), and a member of the Thursday Club (1899). On Apr. 29, 1861, he married Frances Anne Kemble McCrea, daughter of Walter McCrea, judge of the Algoma district in Ontario. He died in 1913, survived by his wife and their three children, and was buried in Forest Lawn, Buffalo.

[*Buffalo Express*, Aug. 16, 1913; sketch by J. B. Olmsted in *Buffalo Hist. Soc. Pubs.*, XIX (1915), 3–33; bibliography of Larned's publications, *Ibid.*, 133–36; W. L. Learned, *The Learned Family* (1898); book of clippings at the Buffalo Public Library, covering the period of his connection with the library and after; interviews with associates at Buffalo Public Library and in Young Men's Association, and with members of his family.]   A. H. S.

LARNED, WILLIAM AUGUSTUS (Dec. 30, 1872–Dec. 16, 1926), lawn tennis player, seven times national champion, was born in Summit, N. J., and lived most of his life in that state and in New York. He was the son of William Zebedee and Katharine (Penniman) Larned, and a descendant of William Learned who emigrated to Massachusetts before 1632. He studied at Cornell University but did not graduate. During the Spanish-American War he was a private in Troop A of Roosevelt's "Rough Riders," and took part in the battle of San Juan Hill. For several years thereafter he suffered from the effects of West Indian fever. Soon after the United States entered the World War, having earlier learned to pilot an airplane, he was commissioned captain in the aviation section of the Signal Corps, and stationed in Washington as head of an examining board for officers in the air service. In October 1917 he sailed for France and later went to England where he was first assistant, and then aviation officer, Base Section, No. 3. He left the service in June 1919 with the rank of lieutenant-colonel.

Although he excelled at many sports, prominent among them being golf and ice-hockey, his greatest interest always centered in lawn tennis. His first big success was the winning of the intercollegiate championship in October 1892, when he represented Cornell; and during the next twenty years until his retirement in 1912 he won scores of championship titles in various sections of the country. He was officially ranked among the first ten players of the United States nineteen times within those twenty years, the only missing season being that of 1898 when he was in Cuba. During that period he was rated No. 1, eight years; No. 2 five years; No. 3 four years; No. 5 one year and No. 6 one year. In the international matches for the Davis Cup, he represented the United States on six different occasions, winning nine matches and losing five. For the famous Longwood Bowl at Boston he played seventeen years, winning twelve times. He perhaps surpassed all the other American lawn tennis players in mastery of ground-strokes, and it was his ability in this aspect of the game that gave him his fame. No player has excelled him in the ease and facility with which he executed them, particularly those on the backhand side, generally a weak point in other players; and none showed a wider range or more brilliant placing ability. In attack, he was supreme and at times invincible, but in defense his skill did not equal that of some others of his time, particularly R. D. Wrenn and the famous Doherty brothers of England. Allowed to play the game in his own way, he swept everything before him, but opposed by a perfect defense or the strategic tactics of the best court generals, he was beaten sometimes by men ranked officially below him. Furthermore, he never fully conquered an erratic

tendency to be upset by small annoyances, which would throw him off his game at times.

Larned's health was poor during the last part of his life. He suffered a nervous breakdown two years before his death, and later an attack of spinal meningitis, which compelled him to depend upon a cane. He chafed under the consequent limitation to his activities, and in a period of despondency shot himself with an army revolver at the Knickerbocker Club, New York, some time between 11 P.M., Dec. 15, and 10 A.M., Dec. 16, 1926. He was the inventor of the steel-framed racket that came into wide use. A bronze tablet dedicated to his memory has been placed in the concrete wall of the stadium of the West Side Tennis Club at Forest Hills, N. Y., where many of the Davis Cup matches have been played. He never married.

[W. L. Learned, *The Learned Family* (1898); *War Records of the Knickerbocker Club 1914–1918* (1922); *Am. Lawn Tennis*, Jan. 15, 1927; S. W. Merrihew, *The Quest of the Davis Cup* (1928); *Spalding's Official Lawn Tennis Annual* and its predecessors, 1892–1912; *Literary Digest*, Jan. 15, 1927; *N. Y. Times*, Dec. 17, 20, 1926.]   J. P. P.

LAROCHE, RENÉ (Sept. 23, 1795–Dec. 9, 1872), physician, was born in Philadelphia, the only son of René and Marie Jeanne (de la Condemine) LaRoche. His father, a graduate of the ancient school of medicine at Montpellier in France, had practised his profession in Santo Domingo before coming to Philadelphia. During his teens young LaRoche served in the War of 1812 as a captain of volunteers in Colonel Biddle's regiment. At twenty-two he entered the University of Pennsylvania, from which he was graduated with the degree of M.D. in 1820. For a short period after graduation he was a teacher in the summer school of medicine. In 1824 he was married to Mary Jane Ellis, daughter of Col. John Ellis.

LaRoche's principal contribution to medicine was in the field of medical literature. It was stated in the *Transactions of the American Medical Association,* shortly after his death, that there was scarcely a medical journal in the land which had not, at some time or other, published contributions from his pen (*Transactions,* 1873, p. 380), and an eminent contemporary, Dr. Samuel D. Gross [*q.v.*], called him "one of the most erudite medical writers which our country has produced," adding: "Simplicity and directness were among his chief excellencies" (*Autobiography,* II, 376). His best-known work, *Yellow Fever, Considered in Its Historical, Pathological, Etiological, and Therapeutical Relations* (2 vols., 1855), is a medical classic. His library on yellow fever embraced the literature of many countries and constituted an invaluable collection. When it was sold at auction, after his death, a portion was secured by the College of Physicians of Philadelphia.

He was active in professional organizations, notably in the College of Physicians, the Pathological Society of Philadelphia (of which he was an original member and at one time president), and state and county medical societies. He was one of the editors of the *North American Medical and Surgical Journal* which flourished in Philadelphia from 1826 until 1831.

LaRoche was greatly interested in music and collected a large and valuable music library, much of which ultimately passed into the hands of J. W. Drexel [*q.v.*]. Haydn's Third Mass was sung with orchestral accompaniment for the first time in Philadelphia at St. Joseph's Church, under his direction as choir-master. Gross, who knew him intimately, said: "He never seemed so happy as when he was in his library up to his elbow in his manuscripts. . . . He was a charming conversationalist, always instructive and free from affectation and pedantry" (*Ibid.*, II, 375–76). He was of frail build, and yet could endure much physical exertion.

[*Trans. Am. Medic. Asso.*, 1873; S. D. Gross, *Hist. of Am. Medic. Lit. from 1776 to the Present Time* (1876); *Autobiog. of Samuel D. Gross with Sketches of his Contemporaries* (1887), II, 374–77; *Records Am. Cath. Hist. Soc. of Phila.*, vols. III (1891), XXIX (1918); *The Biog. Encyc. of Pa.* (1874); *Pub. Ledger* (Phila.), Dec. 11, 1872.]   E. H. F.

LA RONDE, LOUIS DENIS, Sieur de (1675–March 1741), French naval officer and American prospector, was Canadian-born, son of Pierre Denis de la Ronde and Catherine Le Neuf of Quebec. At the early age of thirteen he entered the French navy and served therein for forty years as midshipman, lieutenant, and later as captain of a naval vessel. In 1689 he was a subordinate officer on the ship that carried James II to Ireland in his futile effort to regain his crown and took part in two naval contests off the Irish coast. In 1692 La Ronde cruised along the New England coast, and three years later he was captured in a sea fight and spent a year in an Irish prison. In 1697 he was with his fellow countryman Iberville [*q.v.*] on his desperate adventure in Hudson Bay and in 1700–01 accompanied his chief to Louisiana where he explored the Mississippi. In Queen Anne's War he took part in several naval battles, was wounded and shipwrecked. In 1711 he was sent on a secret mission to Boston. Twelve years later he again visited Boston as an envoy and spent the winter there. Parkman states that he spoke English and made himself agreeable to the British col-

onists. For this service he received the cross of the order of St. Louis.

In 1727 La Ronde, then captain in the Canadian army, was sent to command a post in Lake Superior on an island now called Madeline, in Chequamegon Bay. There he learned of the existence of copper mines in the vicinity and made proposals to the government to work them. It was 1733 before permission came from France and the next year La Ronde built at Sault Ste. Marie a sailing vessel of twenty-five tons, coasted along the lake shore, and sent samples of ore to Quebec. In 1736 he went thither in person to see his ore assayed and persuaded the government to send him from Europe two competent miners, who in 1739 made a favorable report of the prospects. Meanwhile at Fort La Pointe, Madeline Island, La Ronde and his sons had built a substantial log enclosure, had imported cattle and horses, and had made the beginning of a settlement. All their plans were brought to naught by an Indian war which broke out in 1740. La Ronde went to Quebec and there died. His widow, Marie Louise Chartier La Ronde, whom he had married on July 20, 1709, was granted the monopoly of Fort La Pointe and in 1744 leased it to a firm of fur-traders. La Ronde's life, full of adventure and incident, speaks of his energy and ability. At the time of his death he was senior captain in Canada and had been in the King's service over fifty years.

[See *Wis. Hist. Colls.*, XVII (1906), 299–306, 309–12; E. D. Neill, "Sieur de la Ronde, the First Navigator of Lake Superior in a Sailing Vessel, and the Pioneer in Copper Mining," *Macalester Coll. Contributions*, I ser. (1890), pp. 183–98; Cyprien Tanguay, *Dict. Geneal. des Familles Canadiennes*, vol. I (1871). See also L. P. Kellogg, *French Régime in Wis. and the Northwest* (Madison, 1925), pp. 351–57, where it is erroneously stated that La Ronde was a native of France.]   L. P. K.

LARPENTEUR, CHARLES (May 8, 1807–Nov. 15, 1872), fur-trader, author, was born near Fontainebleau, France. The earlier birthdate assumed in the inscription on his tombstone is apparently incorrect as to the year but probably correct as to the month and day. The father was a Bonapartist who fled to America and in 1818 settled with his family on a farm near Baltimore. Young Larpenteur, who seems to have been reared as a farmer's boy, probably had little schooling. At the age of twenty-one he left for the West. After working for several years in St. Louis and making a journey up the Mississippi, he engaged as a clerk with Sublette and Campbell for the Rocky Mountain Fur Company's expedition of the spring of 1833. From the Green River rendezvous, which was reached in July, he accompanied Campbell to the vicinity of the

American Fur Company's post, Fort Union, at the mouth of the Yellowstone, where Sublette and Campbell for a year attempted to maintain an opposition. On the failure of the attempt Larpenteur engaged with the dominant company. As clerk, trader, fort-builder, chief factor, sutler, and for a brief time as farmer, he spent the remainder of his life, except for occasional journeys to the settlements, on the upper and middle Missouri, and no man of his time and place had a wider range of adventurous experiences. He married an Assiniboine woman, and after her death in 1837 he married another, by whom he had several children. In 1851 he bought a land claim on the Little Sioux, in the present Harrison County, Iowa, where he developed a farm which he named "Fontainebleau." For the following twenty years, however, he lived there only at intervals; his residence shifted from post to post in the Indian country. In the winter of 1853–54 his second wife was murdered by a roving band of Omahas. On Apr. 12, 1855, he married Rebecca (White) Bingham, a white woman, who survived him by more than twenty-five years. In May 1871, ousted from a good business as a sutler at Fort Buford by the Federal law prohibiting more than one sutler at a post, he gave up the Indian country and returned to his farm. At Fort Union, in 1834, he had started a journal, which except for occasional lapses he kept until the last year of his life. On his retirement he wrote an autobiography, sending it, five months before his death, to Washington Matthews. Twenty-five years later Matthews sent it to Elliott Coues, by whom it was edited and published.

Larpenteur died at a neighbor's house, several miles from his farm. He is described as a small, spare, wiry man of distinct Gallic type, intelligent, informed, and vivacious and witty in conversation. Though in the main kindly and amiable, he was not above harboring resentments, and he writes disparagingly of many of his associates. His life was crowded with disasters, and he believed himself born under a baleful star. His autobiography, with its many inaccuracies corrected by Coues from the entries in the journal, is probably the most valuable contemporary document extant upon the fur trade of the Missouri.

[*Forty Years a Fur Trader on the Upper Mo.: The Personal Narrative of Chas. Larpenteur, 1833–72* (2 vols., 1898), ed. by Elliott Coues; A. L. Larpenteur, "Recollections of the City and People of St. Paul, 1843–98," *Colls. Minn. Hist. Soc.*, vol. IX (1901); *Annals of Iowa*, July 1902, July 1908.]   W. J. G.

LARRABEE, CHARLES HATHAWAY (Nov. 9, 1820–Jan. 20, 1883), lawyer, soldier, judge, son of Maj. Charles Larrabee of the regular army and Elizabeth (Hathaway) Larrabee,

was born at Rome, Oneida County, N. Y. His father was probably of Huguenot stock; his mother was descended from John Haynes [*q.v.*], colonial governor of Massachusetts and later of Connecticut, while Judge Joshua Hathaway, her father, at sixteen, was one of six brothers, who, with their father, carried muskets at Bennington under Gen. John Stark. Charles attended Springfield Academy and Granville College, now Denison University, Ohio, then read law in the offices of Samson Mason and W. A. Rogers in Springfield, Ohio. In 1841 he went to Pontotoc, Miss., as a civil engineer. Here he made an unsuccessful attempt at farming but was admitted to the bar. Finding the climate of Mississippi harmful to him, he removed to Chicago in July 1844, entered upon the practice of his profession, and was elected city attorney. On May 13, 1846, he was married to Minerva Norton and in March 1847, they settled at Horicon, Wis. Here Larrabee erected mills and developed a fine water power.

He was chosen in October 1847, by an overwhelming majority, one of three members to represent Dodge County in the second constitutional convention of the territory of Wisconsin. He was a strong and ardent advocate of provisions against a state debt and for a homestead exemption, both of which were embodied in the constitution. In 1848 he was chosen circuit judge of the third circuit, made up of six large counties. As a circuit judge he became, upon the adoption of the constitution, *ex officio* a member of the supreme court and served in that capacity until the separate organization of the supreme court five years later. He was a strong supporter of Stephen A. Douglas and at the latter's solicitation resigned from the bench to become a successful candidate for Congress at the fall election in 1858, overcoming a strong Republican majority in his district. He went down with Douglas, however, when in 1860 he was a candidate for reëlection. He rendered creditable service in Congress and at the close of his term offered his services in April 1861 to Gov. A. W. Randall and Gen. Rufus King. He was commissioned a major of the 5th Wisconsin Infantry May 28, 1861, and with his regiment saw much hard service in the Army of the Potomac. He proved himself to be an excellent officer but his friends felt that his chances of promotion were diminished because of his former political affiliations. On July 25, 1862, by appointment of Governor Salomon, Larrabee became colonel of the 24th Wisconsin Infantry.

As a commanding officer he rendered distinguished service but he fell a victim to a disease contracted in the swamps of the Chickahominy and on Aug. 27, 1863, he retired from the service. After leaving the army, in the hope of regaining his health, he settled in California. He lived also for a short time at Seattle and here, almost exactly thirty years after he had served as a member of the Wisconsin Constitutional Convention, he became a member of a convention to frame a constitution for Washington Territory. This constitution was, however, rejected. Subsequently he settled at San Bernardino, in Southern California, where he resumed the practice of his profession. While on his way from San Francisco to Los Angeles on Jan. 20, 1883, he was killed in a railway accident. The distinguished services which he rendered in so many fields did not win adequate recognition because of his rather nomadic life. In a letter which he wrote two or three years before his death he said: "Being born in the army, I never had a particle of State pride. All States seem to me like so many Counties. Nor have I love of locality. Cities I hate. I am happiest in building up new homes, introducing new fruits, and other light productions of the soil" (Draper, *post*, p. 388).

[Lyman C. Draper's sketch of Larrabee in *Wis. Hist. Colls.*, vol. IX (1882), is the most complete and accurate history of his life. See also: H. A. Tenney and David Atwood, *Memorial Record of the Fathers of Wis.* (1880); P. M. Reed, *The Bench and Bar of Wis.* (1882); J. R. Berryman, *Hist. of the Bench and Bar of Wis.* (2 vols., 1898); *Biog. Dir. Am. Cong.* (1928); "Biographical Sketches of the Judges of the First Supreme Court of the State of Wisconsin," 3 *Pinney's Wis. Reports*, 617; G. T. Ridlon, *Saco Valley Settlements and Families* (1895); *Daily Examiner* (San Francisco), Jan. 21, 22, 1883.]   M. B. R.

LARRABEE, WILLIAM (Jan. 20, 1832–Nov. 16, 1912), twelfth governor of Iowa, son of Capt. Adam and Hannah Gallup (Lester) Larrabee, was born at Ledyard, Conn. He was descended from Greenfield Larrabee who was in New London, Conn., in 1637. His father graduated from West Point in 1811 and served in the War of 1812. The family lived on a farm and William Larrabee received a common-school education. In 1853 he moved to Iowa, taught school for a time, and was foreman on a farm for a few years. In 1857 he bought a flour mill in the town of Clermont, in Fayette County, and remained in that business until 1874, when he sold out and went to Europe for three months. Afterward he engaged in banking and farming and became one of the largest landowners in the state. He married, on Sept. 12, 1861, Anna M. Appleton, whose family had emigrated from Connecticut to Iowa in 1854 and had settled on a farm near Clermont. During the Civil War Larrabee raised a company of soldiers, but he was not accepted for service because he had lost the sight of one eye in his youth. In 1868 he was elected to the state Senate and remained a member until he resigned to accept the nomination for governor in 1885. He was four times reëlected to the Senate without opposition in a district which sent Democrats after his retirement. During most of the time of his service in the Senate, he was chairman of the committee on ways and means.

He was elected governor by a vote of 175,504 against 168,525 for his Democratic and fusion opponent, and he was reëlected two years later by a vote of 169,595 to 153,706. These were the years when the third-party movements were reducing the Republican vote and increasing the Democratic support. The railroad question had been an active issue for a number of years. Larrabee's experience with the building of the Chicago, Milwaukee & St. Paul across the northern part of the state from 1857 to 1878 had called his attention to the need of railroad legislation. His election to the Senate was due to the long delay in railroad construction in his portion of the state. In his second inaugural address in 1888, he declared that he believed transportation charges were far too high and that they bore little relation to the cost of the service. He recommended that the railroad commission "should be authorized and required to exercise full and complete supervision over the railroads, compelling them to comply with the laws and to furnish adequate facilities at reasonable compensation." Such a message and such recommendations were far in advance of the times and his position was all the more remarkable inasmuch as he was a successful business man and a banker. In his book, *The Railroad Question* (1893), he set forth many ideas which he lived to see incorporated in state and federal legislation. His administration is generally regarded as one of the strongest in the history of the state.

Larrabee was a man of great industry, honesty and generosity. As a miller he often worked twenty hours a day for months at a time. He was a great reader. He had collected a large library and his years of retirement were occupied with the care of his estate, "Montauk," and with wide reading. He contributed to the support of the local churches, and a school building costing $100,000, the gift of the Larrabees, was almost completed at the time of his death. He had a high sense of public duty and he did not hesitate to break close friendships if he deemed it necessary. In 1906 and 1908 he supported Albert B. Cummins in his gubernatorial and senatorial campaigns, when the controversies in Iowa between the conservative and progressive wings of his party were most bitter.

[The memorial address by Wm. S. Kenyon before the legislature of Iowa, Mar. 20, 1913, printed in the Senate *Journal*, 1913, pp. 1125–39, was privately printed in pamphlet form in 1913 (*Wm. Larrabee: Memorial Address by Senator Wm. S. Kenyon*) and partially reprinted in the *Register and Leader* (Des Moines), Mar. 21, 1913. See also B. F. Shambaugh, *The Messages and Proclamations of the Governors of Iowa*, vol. VI (1904); F. E. Haynes, *Third Party Movements Since the Civil War* (1916); Cyrenus Cole, *A Hist. of the People of Iowa* (1921); B. F. Gue, *Hist. of Iowa* (1903), vols. III and IV; E. R. Harlan, *A Narrative Hist. of the People of Iowa* (1931), vol. II; G. T. Ridlon, *Saco Valley Settlements and Families* (1895); and the *Register and Leader* (Des Moines), Jan. 23, 1906, Nov. 17, 18, 19, 1912.]   F. E. H.

LARRABEE, WILLIAM CLARK (Dec. 23, 1802–May 5, 1859), Methodist Episcopal clergyman, educator, was a descendant of Stephen Larrabee, one of the pioneers of North Yarmouth, Me. William's grandparents were Jonathan and Alice (Davis) Larrabee, and he was born at Cape Elizabeth, Me., his father, a sea captain, dying soon after the boy's birth. From his seventh year, he lived with his grandparents, and with his uncle Jonathan, at Durham, Me., working on the farm and attending school. Frequenting Methodist meetings, then just being introduced into that locality, he soon professed conversion, and in June 1821 was licensed to preach. In his youth he was associated with Eliphalet Clark, who became a lifelong friend, and from whom he adopted his middle name. After being licensed, he attended New Market Academy in New Hampshire, and later, Farmingham Academy, Maine, where he was prepared to enter the sophomore class at Bowdoin College, from which he graduated in 1828. From 1828 to 1830 he was principal of Alfred Academy, Maine, and in 1830 he was appointed tutor of a preparatory school at Middletown, Conn., which was the forerunner of Wesleyan University. The next year he was made the principal of Oneida Conference Seminary, Cazenovia, N. Y., and in 1832 was admitted to membership in the Oneida Conference of the Methodist Episcopal Church. After four successful years at Cazenovia, he became the principal of Maine Wesleyan Seminary, Kents Hill, where he enlarged his reputation as an educator. In 1837–38 he also assisted in the first geological survey of the state.

He was a delegate to the General Conference of the Methodist Episcopal Church at Baltimore in 1840, and there met Matthew Simpson [*q.v.*], the young president of a new Methodist institution, Indiana Asbury University (De Pauw University), just established at Greencastle. Simpson persuaded Larrabee to accept the professorship of mathematics and natural science,

and from 1841 to 1852 he was not only a leading member of the faculty, but from 1848 to 1849, was the acting president, introducing numerous reforms in the course of study and doing much to raise educational standards. In 1848 he was one of the board of visitors at the United States Military Academy, West Point, and later was offered, but declined, several important educational positions, among them the presidency of Indiana and of Iowa universities. Elected in 1852 editor of the *Ladies' Repository*, a Methodist magazine published in Cincinnati, he soon resigned to accept nomination, on the Democratic ticket, for the superintendency of public instruction in the state of Indiana, to which he was elected. The new state constitution (1851) made provision for a uniform system of public schools, and Larrabee, the first state superintendent, was in a sense the founder of the Indiana public-school system. In 1854 he was defeated for reëlection, but in 1856 was again chosen to that office and devoted his second term to a reconstruction of the school system, the former school laws having been declared unconstitutional. He retired from office in January 1859 and died the following May.

He was married, Sept. 28, 1828, to Harriet, daughter of Col. William Dunn, and was the father of four children. He named his house at Greencastle "Rosabower" in memory of a daughter who died in infancy and was buried in the grounds, which are now a part of the campus of De Pauw University. His writings include: *Lectures on the Scientific Evidences of Natural and Revealed Religion* (1850); *Wesley and His Coadjutors* (2 vols., 1851); *Asbury and His Coadjutors* (2 vols., 1853); and a little volume of essays entitled *Rosabower* (1854), consisting of articles published in the *Ladies' Repository*. The first essay is a fanciful description of the grounds about his Indiana home and the death of his little daughter.

[*New-Eng. Hist. and Geneal. Reg.*, July 1859, reprints obituary from *Indianapolis Sentinel*, May 5, 1859; G. T. Ridlon, *Saco Valley Settlements and Families* (1895); F. C. Holliday, *Ind. Methodism* (1873); *Minutes of Conferences of the M. E. Ch.*, vols. II and III (1840); *First Fifty Years of Cazenovia Sem. 1825–1875* (n.d.); H. M. Skinner, *Biog. Sketches of the Supts. of Pub. Instruction of the State of Ind.* (1884); Logan Esarey, *A Hist. of Indiana*, vol. II (1918).]
W. W. S.

LARRAZOLO, OCTAVIANO AMBROSIO (Dec. 7, 1859–Apr. 7, 1930), jurist, governor of New Mexico, United States senator, was born at Allende in southern Chihuahua, Mexico, the son of Octaviano and Donaciana (Corral) Larrazolo. His boyhood memories were of the tragic years of the Reform and the French intervention in

Mexico. In 1870 he went to Tucson as the protégé of Bishop J. B. Salpointe, and when the latter became archbishop of Santa Fé (1875), young Larrazolo accompanied him to that city and studied at St. Michael's College. For a year he taught school in Tucson, and from 1879 to 1884 was a high-school principal in El Paso County, Tex. In the latter year he became clerk of the district at El Paso, serving until 1888, when he was admitted to the bar. He was elected district attorney for western Texas in 1890, and again in 1892. In January 1895 he moved to Las Vegas, N. Mex. During these early years he was a Democrat, and was the Democratic nominee for delegate to Congress from New Mexico in three different elections (1900, 1906, 1908). Each time he ran well but was defeated.

Throughout the Southwest, Larrazolo early came to be recognized as a brilliant orator in both English and Spanish, and also as a champion of the native people, who then constituted about half the voting population of the territory. When New Mexico was preparing for statehood (1910), he was instrumental in having written into the state constitution "strong provisions guaranteeing the rights of the Spanish-speaking voters against disfranchisement and protecting them against discrimination on account of language or racial descent. It assured the use of the Spanish language officially, together with English, for years to come" (Walter, *post*, p. 101). Hoping to better himself and his people politically, he became a Republican in 1911 and, in a dramatic speech at the party convention that fall, presented for governor a native New Mexican. His candidate was not nominated, but for the next twenty years Larrazolo was an important factor in New Mexican politics, and Spanish-Americans received greater recognition from both leading parties. Larrazolo himself was elected the first post-war governor (1918). When the coal miners' strike became general in the Rocky Mountain region in 1918, he invoked martial law and prevented the strike from spreading into New Mexico. He advocated federal aid to farmers and stockmen, and indorsed the idea of giving the public lands to the states in which they were situated, his proposal including the ownership of subsoil as well as surface. As Republican nominee for justice of the state supreme court, he was defeated in 1924; but in the fall of 1928 he was elected to the United States Senate.

Larrazolo will long be remembered as a fine example of the Spanish-American race; he was tall, of vigorous frame, and handsome, with the proud, courtly, and punctilious bearing of a Spanish gentleman. He was an ardent patriot of his adopted country and one of the most effective representatives of the native people of the Southwest. He was twice married: first in 1881 to Rosalia Cobos, who died ten years later, having borne him two children; and second, Aug. 4, 1892, to María García, by whom he had five children. His death occurred in Albuquerque.

[R. E. Twitchell, *Leading Facts of New Mexican Hist.* (1912), vol. II; *Albuquerque Morning Jour.*, Apr. 8 and 10, 1930; *Santa Fé New Mexican*, Apr. 8, May 12, 1930; P. A. F. Walter, *New Mexico Hist. Rev.*, Apr. 1932; personal acquaintance.]   L. B. B.

LARRÍNAGA, TULIO (Jan. 15, 1847–Apr. 28, 1917), second resident commissioner for Puerto Rico in the United States, was born at Trujillo Alto, Puerto Rico, and died of heart trouble at Santurce, a suburb of San Juan. He studied at the Seminario Conciliar of San Ildefonso in San Juan before coming to the United States, where he studied civil engineering at the Rensselaer Polytechnic Institute, Troy, N. Y. (1865–68). He is said to have taken part in the preparation of the topographical map of Kings County (Brooklyn) and as a member of the technical department of Badger & Company to have worked on the construction of the Grand Central Station, New York.

Returning to Puerto Rico, he was later appointed architect for the city of San Juan, and is reputed to have designed the first building with steel framework erected in that city. On June 22, 1879, he married Bertha Goyro Saint Victor, whose father was a Spaniard but whose mother was French. They had five children. In 1880 he built the first railroad in Puerto Rico, introducing American rolling stock on the island. For almost a decade (1880–89) he was engineer for the Provincial Deputation, being prominent in the construction work in San Juan harbor, and in directing the extensive road construction of the island. Under the autonomous government, granted Puerto Rico by Spain in 1898, he was sub-secretary of public works. After the American occupation, he again assumed direction of construction work in San Juan harbor. While the Foraker Bill was being discussed, he came to Washington with a political delegation, asking for home rule. In 1902 he was elected a delegate to the insular legislature for the district of Arecibo. Here he advocated important measures favoring agriculture. He was elected resident commissioner for Puerto Rico in 1904 and twice reëlected, serving from Mar. 4, 1905, to Mar. 3, 1911. In 1905 he interceded for the continuance of the Puerto Rican regiment, which was to be suppressed, and in 1906 presented a law project for the amending of the Foraker Bill. He represented the United States at the Third Pan-

American Congress in Brazil (1906) and the United States Congress at conferences of the Interparliamentary Union at Berlin (1908) and Brussels (1910). In 1905 President Wilson appointed him a member of the Executive Council of Puerto Rico.

As one of the founders of the Ateneo, which played a considerable part in the intellectual leadership of the island, as one who gave free instruction in English to poor young men, as a member of the insular library commission, and in other ways, he influenced the educational life of Puerto Rico. He was also president of the agricultural commission.

[*El Libro de Puerto Rico: The Book of Porto Rico* (1923), ed. by E. Fernandez Garcia; *Biog. Dir. Am. Cong.* (1928); *La Correspondencia de Puerto-Rico* (San Juan), Apr. 30, 1917; *La Democracia*, Apr. 30, 1917; *El Tiempo*, Apr. 30, 1917; *N. Y. Times*, May 1, 1917; information from relatives and friends.]   C. R. W.

LARSEN, PETER LAURENTIUS (Aug. 10, 1833–Mar. 1, 1915), pioneer Norwegian Lutheran clergyman and educator, was born at Christiansand, Norway, the son of Herman Larsen, an army officer, and Elen Else Marie (Oftedahl), daughter of a member of the Norwegian constitutional assembly held in 1814 at Eidsvold. When he was nine years old, the boy entered the Lancaster school at Christiansand, and in 1850, the university at Christiania (now Oslo), where he came under the influence of two of Norway's most celebrated theologians, Carl Paul Caspari and Gisle Johnson. After the completion of his studies there in 1855, when he graduated in theology, he remained in Christiania as teacher of German, French, and Hebrew.

Hearing the Macedonian call from his recently emigrated fellow countrymen in America, he went over to help them, and preached his first sermon in the United States near Rush River, Wis., on Nov. 2, 1857. Always a zealous missionary, he traveled far and wide, establishing congregations at such places as St. Paul and Red Wing, Minn. In 1859 the Norwegian Synod arranged for a theological professorship at Concordia Seminary, St. Louis, Mo., and Larsen was called to fill the position. When the Civil War broke out, he and the Norwegian students left St. Louis, whereupon the Synod established Luther College, presently located at Decorah, Iowa. Larsen was elected professor and president of the school, serving in the first capacity for fifty years and in the latter for forty-one. In 1913 he became professor emeritus. On Christmas Eve of that year he suffered a slight stroke, from which he rallied, but two years later one more severe brought on his death.

As president of a pioneer Norwegian Lutheran college, he faced many difficulties. His constituents had been in America in considerable numbers for less than twenty years when they were called upon to build a college in war times at a cost of $87,000. This expense fell upon a group which at the outset numbered seventeen pastors and sixty-nine congregations, and the successful completion of the project rested largely on the shoulders of Larsen. When fire gutted the "Old Main" on May 19, 1889, he again had to step into the breach, but by this time the idea of Christian education had been too firmly established in the people's minds for them to permit the building to lie in ruins. Other problems confronting the young American college with its somewhat European-minded constituency he met with tact and firmness. As a concession to American demands, he changed the curriculum from a six-year to an eight-year course, but the aim of the school to prepare men for the ministry always remained uppermost in his mind.

As a churchman he was a conspicuous figure. He became the center of two notable controversies, in which he himself contended that slavery is an evil rather than a sin (1861–68) and that there is powerful impartation of the forgiveness of sins in absolution (1861–1906). As editor of *Kirkelig Maanedstidende* ("Church Monthly") from 1868 to 1873, and of its successor, *Evangelisk Luthersk Kirketidende* ("Evangelical Lutheran Church Times"), from 1874 to 1889 and from 1902 to 1912, he was called upon to voice the official opinion of the Norwegian Synod on many difficult questions, chief of which were those connected with the predestination controversy. Throughout it all, Larsen succeeded in maintaining his reputation for mental and spiritual honesty, his thorough hatred of sham and subterfuge removing him from the temptations to resort to "church politics" trickery. Besides being editor and college president, he was vice-president of the Iowa district of the Norwegian Synod (1876–79), vice-president of the Norwegian Synod (1876–93), and chairman of the Lutheran Synodical Conference (1881–83). He served on many committees, being chairman of the Foreign Mission Committee for several years. From 1882 to 1884 he was also pastor of the Norwegian Lutheran congregation in Decorah.

At many Luther College banquets he was guest of honor, and tributes in verse and prose have been offered him by prominent alumni. On Oct. 22, 1884, and again in 1909, his students and fellow teachers celebrated his twenty-fifth and fiftieth anniversaries as teacher. The house which was his home for the last eighteen years of his life was a gift from former students. In 1908 he was made knight of the first class of the Order of St. Olav by King Haakon VII of Norway. He was twice married: first, July 23, 1855, to Karen Neuberg; second, Aug. 20, 1872, to Ingeborg Astrup; and he was the father of twelve children.

[O. M. Norlie, *Norsk Lutherske Prester i Amerika* (Minneapolis, 1914); L. S. Swenson, "Prof. Dr. Laur. Larsen, De Norsk-Amerikanske Skolemänds Nestor," in *Symra* (Decorah, Iowa), 5th *bind*, 4 *de hefte*, 1909; F. E. Peterson, "Presidents and Principals," in O. M. Norlie, O. A. Tingelstad, and K. T. Jacobsen, *Luther Coll. Through Sixty Years* (1922); J. M. Rohne, *Norwegian Am. Lutheranism Up To 1872* (1926); O. J. Kvale, *The Soul of Luther College* (1927); Gisle Bothne, *Det Norske Luther Coll.* (Decorah, Iowa, 1897); Karen Larsen, "A Contribution to the Study of the Adjustment of a Pioneer Pastor to American Conditions: Laur. Larsen, 1857–1880," in *Norwegian-American Hist. Asso. Studies and Records,* vol. IV (1929); Rasmus Malmin, O. M. Norlie, O. A. Tingelstad, *Who's Who Among Pastors in All the Norwegian Lutheran Synods in America 1843–1927* (1928); *Who's Who in America,* 1914–15.]   J. M. R.

LA SALLE, ROBERT CAVELIER, Sieur de (November 1643–Mar. 19, 1687), explorer, was the second son of Jean Cavelier, a wealthy burgher of Rouen, where this child was baptized in the parish church of St. Herbland, Nov. 22, 1643. His mother was Catherine Geest, and one of her relatives was the boy's godfather. His title La Salle came from a family seigniory in the neighborhood of Rouen. He studied at the Jesuit college at Rouen, which was later the Lycée Corneille, and at the urgent desire of his father entered the Society of Jesus as a novice. The training he received was antagonistic to his independent, adventurous nature, and upon his father's death, when he was twenty-two years old, he left the Jesuits, apparently without ill will on either side. Through this or other experiences, however, he had acquired a dislike for the order and all its members which often broke out into open hostility. By the law of the time, when he took his first vows he lost his share of the paternal estate, and was dependent upon the allowance his relatives chose to make him.

His elder brother, Jean Cavelier, a member of the order of St. Sulpice, before the father's death had gone to New France, where the Sulpicians held the seigniory of Montreal. Possibly the connection of an uncle with the Hundred Associates for New France had interested the Caveliers in the colony of Canada, for in the summer of 1666 Robert followed his brother thither. From the Sulpicians he received a grant of land on the western end of the island of Montreal and there he erected several buildings, traded with the natives, and lived for two years the life of a pioneer farmer. His estate afterwards received the name of "La Chine" in derision of his fruitless efforts to range from there to China.

During the winter of 1668–69 La Salle entertained at his manor house two Iroquois Indians, who informed him of westward-flowing waters and awakened in him a desire for exploration. The next summer he sold his seigniory back to the convent of St. Sulpice at Montreal and entered upon the career which brought him fame. The Sulpicians were at this time sending two members of their order to begin missions in the West; on the advice of the Superior, La Salle attached himself to this expedition, which left Montreal July 6, 1669, with seven canoes, four of them conducted for La Salle. The expedition ascended the St. Lawrence River to Lake Ontario, coasted its southern shore to Irondequoit Bay, and there beached the canoes and went into the interior to obtain guides from the Iroquois. La Salle had boasted of his knowledge of the language, but once among the Indians he could not make himself understood. By means of a Dutch interpreter, however, who spoke a little French, the explorers obtained information concerning the geography of the country west of the Iroquois villages and again skirted the lake shore to the mouth of the Niagara River, where they could hear the noise of the great falls. They did not visit the falls, but went inland, where in a village at the western end of Lake Ontario they met Louis Jolliet [*q.v.*] returning from a visit to the Ottawa country.

Jolliet's report made the Sulpicians decide to visit the Northwest, but La Salle adhered to his purpose of seeking the Ohio, the headwaters of which the Iroquois had reported to be near at hand. He had been ill and made an excuse of his illness to leave the party. Whether he at that time finally reached the Ohio and sailed down it to the falls at Louisville, as he later claimed, is a moot question. That he did not discover the Ohio and saw it for the first time when he passed its mouth in 1682 seems by far the greater probability.

What occupied the young explorer from 1669 to 1673 is not known; one narrator speaks of meeting him in 1670 hunting on the Ottawa River. Meanwhile Jolliet had discovered the upper reaches of the Mississippi and had found that it descended to the Gulf of Mexico, and a furor for western exploration was in the air. About this time a new governor arrived at Quebec who pacified the Iroquois and built a fort on the north shore of Lake Ontario to which he gave his own name of Frontenac. In the Count de Frontenac La Salle found a kindred soul; their spirits leaped together to do some great thing for France. Frontenac sent La Salle to court to obtain permission for the monopoly of the fur trade on which they hoped to build their structure of expansion.

The young Norman, bronzed by years in the open, with his imaginative description of life in the wilderness, quickly gained favor and obtained a grant of Fort Frontenac as a seigniory with exclusive permission for trade. Coming back to Canada with his future companion, Friar Louis Hennepin [*q.v.*], as a fellow passenger, La Salle made plans with Frontenac to exploit the concession and to arrange for future discovery. After three years at Fort Frontenac, during which it is probable that La Salle first visited the upper Great Lakes, he went again to France to obtain fresh privileges. Again he was successful in winning favor at court. He was granted a title of nobility and a patent permitting him to explore and exploit the regions of the West and to deal in buffalo and lesser furs, but not in beaver: an exception which he constantly ignored.

Upon his arrival in the summer of 1678 in New France, accompanied by his faithful lieutenant, Tonty of the iron hand, he and Frontenac made plans for opening the West and beginning therein an empire for Louis XIV. These plans required the building of a sailing vessel above Niagara Falls: La Salle had already two barks on Lake Ontario. A shipyard was established near Buffalo on the Niagara River and there the *Griffon* (named for Frontenac's heraldic device) was launched in the early summer of 1679. La Salle had already sent traders into the West to gather peltry for the expenses of his expedition. He also sent Tonty [*q.v.*] in advance to gather furs in the Detroit region. Thence they went together to Michilimackinac, where they arrived at the end of August. Sailing on to Green Bay, the *Griffon* awakened fear and consternation among the savages, who saw in it an emblem of the overmastering power of the white men.

At Green Bay La Salle found that his traders had gathered a great store of furs, which he loaded onto his vessel to go back to Fort Frontenac. He and his men then took canoes to continue their journey. The *Griffon* was never seen or heard from after that time; its fate has remained a mystery to this day. Advancing up Lake Michigan, the adventurers entered St. Joseph River, portaged to the Kankakee, and sailed down the Illinois to Lake Peoria, where early in January was built Fort Crèvecœur. Thence La Salle sent three men, including Father Hennepin, to explore the upper Mississippi and gather furs. He himself, leaving Tonty in charge, started overland on foot for Fort Frontenac in pursuit of some deserters and in order to settle with his creditors, who were seizing the

fort and stopping supplies. This terrible journey, during the melting weather of early spring, over an unknown route, he accomplished in sixty-five days. At the fort he was detained until late autumn, and on going back to the Illinois he found only the ruins of his enterprise; most of his men had deserted and Tonty and the missionaries had fled before an invasion of hostile Iroquois. At Mackinac in June 1680 the two explorers were reunited and returned again to the Illinois country, rebuilt their fort, this time on the upper Illinois River, on the summit of a rock near the present Ottawa. La Salle now sought to settle around his post a great confederation of western Indians, as a defense against the encroachments of the Iroquois. From this post he and Tonty set forth early in 1682 to explore the Mississippi. On their arrival at the Gulf, on Apr. 9, they took possession of all the river valley for the king of France and named it in his honor Louisiana. (*Collections of the State Historical Society of Wisconsin,* vol. XI, 1888, pp. 33–36.)

This was the climax of La Salle's career. Hitherto he had been supported by Governor Frontenac, but in 1682 Frontenac was replaced by a nominee of the Jesuit party, Antoine Lefebre, Sieur de la Barre. La Barre deprived La Salle of the command of his fort in the Illinois country and summoned him to Quebec to answer for misdemeanors. La Salle, who was on his way to Canada when he heard of this catastrophe, sent Tonty to deliver Fort St. Louis to La Barre's appointee while he continued his voyage to France, disdaining to reply to the governor's charge. In France he was at once the hero of the hour. He narrated his adventures, described the vast and wonderful country he had explored, and was restored by the King to all his commands and honors in New France.

He asked for an expedition to colonize the mouth of the Mississippi, and accordingly a fleet was prepared for this enterprise, with four ships, two hundred colonists, and many supplies. He was named viceroy of North America and given command from Illinois to the Spanish borders. The expedition sailed July 24, 1684, but by some inadvertence missed the mouth of the Mississippi and landed on the coast of Texas. The ships sailed home Mar. 12, 1685, and La Salle, now aware that he was not on the Mississippi, made heroic efforts to find it. He was on his final journey toward that river when on the Brazos River just above the mouth of the Navasota his men mutinied and shot him. His brother Jean, who had accompanied him, and his aide, Henri Joutel [*q.v.*], made their way to Tonty in the

Illinois country and thence to France without revealing the news of the death of La Salle.

La Salle's great projects and plans, his ambitious ideas and hopes, have blinded his biographers to the fact that most of his failures were due to his own defects. He was a dreamer without adequate executive power to carry out his schemes. He could not control the natives; he alienated his own men by his haughty bearing and lack of sympathy; he showed uncertainty and vacillation at critical moments. Yet his lack of success should not obscure his accomplishments both as an explorer and a publicity agent for the interior of North America. He was undoubtedly the first of the French explorers to trace the Mississippi to its mouth; he appreciated the possibilities of the Mississippi Valley, and anticipated its future greatness. In any judgment of him, his mistakes and failures must be subordinated to his vision, which encompassed an empire for France in the heart of America.

[La Salle was a voluminous writer. His many letters and journals were collected and published by Pierre Margry, in *Découvertes et Établissements des Français dans l'Ouest et dans le Sud de l'Amérique Septentrionale* (Paris, 1876–86). La Salle was Margry's hero, around the documents of whose career he built most of his six volumes. Other accounts are those of Tonty (see L. P. Kellogg, *Early Narratives of the Northwest*, 1917, pp. 283–322); Louis Hennepin, in *Description de la Louisiane* (1683), translated by J. G. Shea in 1880, and *Nouvelle Découverte* (1697), edited, in translation, by R. G. Thwaites as *A New Discovery of a Vast Country in America* (2 vols., 1903); Zénobe Membre in Chrétien Le Clercq, *Établissement de la Foy dans la Nouvelle France* (Paris, 2 vols., 1691), tr. by J. G. Shea, as *First Establishment of the Faith in New France* (2 vols., 1881). Translations of several of these accounts, including those by Jean Cavelier and Henri Joutel of the last expedition, are published in I. J. Cox, *The Journeys of René Robert Cavelier Sieur de La Salle* (2 vols., 1905). Francis Parkman, *La Salle and the Discovery of the Great West* (1879) is the best-known modern work. See also Marc de Villiers, *L'Expédition de Cavelier de La Salle dans le Golfe du Mexique, 1684–1687* (1931); Gabriel Gravier, *Découvertes et Établissements de Cavelier de La Salle de Rouen dans l'Amérique du Nord* (1870); Benjamin Sulte, "La Mort de Cavelier de La Salle," in *Proc. and Trans. Royal Soc. of Canada*, 2 ser. IV (1898). H. E. Bolton identifies the Texas sites of La Salle's colony and place of death in *Miss. Valley Hist. Rev.*, Sept. 1915.]

L. P. K.

LASATER, EDWARD CUNNINGHAM (Nov. 5, 1860–Mar. 20, 1930), cattleman, business man, and member of the United States Food Administration, was born in Goliad County, Tex. His parents, Albert H. and Sarah Jane (Cunningham) Lasater, moved to Texas from Arkansas in the late fifties. Edward's education was limited to the meager facilities of the Texas frontier, and an early ambition for law was forgotten in his love of the soil. He farmed and ranched until the drouths and depression of the early nineties left him without property and heavily involved. About this time, grasping the possibilities of the undeveloped land between the Nueces and the Rio Grande, he secured credit for the purchase of a ranch of 380,000 acres, and in time stocked it with 20,000 head of beef cattle. In anticipation of the advance of the farming settler into "the brush country," he encouraged the extension of the San Antonio & Aransas Pass Railway, founded the town of Falfurrias, and within twenty-five years sold land to more than six hundred farmers. His 2,500 Jersey cows, ranging a 40,000-acre dairy pasture, were reputed to be the largest herd of that breed in existence, and his registered stock were among the prize winners in the greatest cattle shows of the world.

Lasater was a slight, energetic, aggressive man, whose entire public enterprise was devoted to the problems of the men of the soil. He worked long and hard for clean politics on the Rio Grande, in the face of many threats against his life. In 1912 he was nominated for governor of Texas by the Progressive party. For two years, 1911–12, he served as president of the Texas and Southwestern Cattle Raisers Association. In the interests of the producers of agricultural products, he waged a long fight against various practices of the packers, the speculators, the bankers, and pernicious legislative trends.

On July 25, 1917, Herbert Hoover asked Lasater to serve with the Food Administration as chief of the department of live stock and animal food products. Lasater was soon at odds with Hoover's policies. He and Gifford Pinchot fought to remove speculation from the hog market by establishing the value of a hundred pounds of hog in its equivalent in bushels of corn. He attacked the campaign of "eat no lamb, eat no veal" as subversive of the Administration's attempt to stimulate production. Disagreeing with Hoover upon various other questions of fundamental importance to agriculture, he tendered his resignation from the Administration, Oct. 20, 1917. His published defense, including *Facts Affecting the United States Food Administration* (1917), *Reply to Mr. Hoover, U. S. Food Administrator* (1918), and a report to the Market Committee of the American National Live Stock Association, *As Showing that the Policies and Practices of Mr. Hoover, as Food Administrator are "Harmful to the Common Welfare"* (1918), alleges much floundering on the part of the Administration.

For twelve years more Lasater continued an active authority upon the problems of the range. In 1918 he published a paper on "Live Stock Marketing Conditions" in *Proceedings of the*

American National Live Stock Association, and in 1920 his testimony before the House Committee on Agriculture, under the title, *Meat Packer Legislation.* He died at Ardmore, Okla., but was buried in Texas. His first wife, Martha Noble Bennett, daughter of John M. Bennett, whom he married Dec. 28, 1892, died Aug. 19, 1900. On Oct. 29, 1902, he married Mary Gardner Miller, daughter of Garland Burleigh Miller, who survived him.

[*Who's Who in America,* 1930–31; Lasater's articles mentioned above; *N. Y. Times,* Nov. 13, 18, 1917, Jan. 27, Mar. 31, 1918, Mar. 22, 1930; *Tulsa Daily World,* Mar. 21, 1930; *Daily Oklahoman* (Oklahoma City), Mar. 21, 1930; *San Antonio Express,* Mar. 21, 1930; MSS., special articles, and memoranda in the hands of Mrs. Mary Lasater, Falfurrias, Tex.]

J. E. H.

LATHAM, MILTON SLOCUM (May 23, 1827–Mar. 4, 1882), United States senator from California, was born in Columbus, Ohio, the third son of Bela and Juliana (Sterritt) Latham. His father, a native of New Hampshire, was a practising lawyer in Ohio. The son attended schools in Ohio, and graduated in 1845 from Jefferson College, Canonsburg, Pa. He then spent some time in Russell County, Ala., where he taught school, studied law, was admitted to the bar, and served for a while as clerk of a circuit court. These experiences in the South seem to have influenced him in the friendships and opinions of later years. In 1850 he went to San Francisco, where, after holding briefly the office of district attorney for Sacramento County, he was elected to Congress, taking his seat in December 1853. He served only one term, declining renomination. By appointment of President Pierce, he became collector of the port at San Francisco (1855–57). His conduct of that office aroused considerable antagonism, partly because of the local conflicts made pointed by the activity of the Vigilance committee, partly because of the rivalry of the two factions of the Democratic party, one led by David C. Broderick and the other by William M. Gwin [*qq.v.*], both of them United States senators.

Latham was his own faction, and made a successful campaign for the governorship in 1859, winning by a large majority in spite of the savage opposition of Broderick. In his brief term as governor he transmitted to Buchanan the action of the preceding legislature agreeing to a division of the state of California, and presented at length the constitutional questions arising out of the proposal. Two days after his inauguration (Jan. 9, 1860), he was chosen by the legislature to fill the vacancy in the United States Senate created by the death of Broderick. He resigned the governorship Jan. 14, 1860, and accepted the

new position gladly—in fact he had directed the legislative canvas through his secretary. In Washington he was made much of by the administration, although his relations with his colleague Gwin were strained. On Apr. 16, he made a powerful speech on "Labor and Capital," defending slavery, and attacking the capacities of the negro, the economic motives of the North, and the morals of the Republican party. In the course of this address he said that, in the event of the dissolution of the Union, "We in California would have reasons to induce us to become members neither of the southern confederacy nor of the northern confederacy, and would be able to sustain for ourselves the relations of a free and independent state" (*Congressional Globe,* 36 Cong., 1 Sess., p. 1728). He supported Breckinridge in the presidential contest of 1860, and when later taunted with the "independent California" prophecy, denied that he was ever other than a stanch Union man. For two more years he served as a member of the helpless minority in the Senate, usually supporting the war measures, but denouncing the conduct of the administration. He was not reëlected and retired from public life, Mar. 3, 1863, upon the expiration of his term. The next twenty years were spent in Europe, in California, and in New York. He became manager of the London and San Francisco Bank (1865–78). Going to New York in 1880, he became president of the New York Mining and Stock Exchange, which occupied his attention until shortly before his death.

Sanguine in temperament, ambitious for power, Latham possessed abilities which brought him success in politics and business—for a time. Skilful in manipulation of both men and principles, he made attempts at the formulation of policies which deserved a better fate. His choice language and a strain of mysticism in his nature gave distinction and beauty to some of his addresses. He was married at San Francisco in 1853 to Sophie Birdsall, daughter of Lewis A. Birdsall. She died in 1867, and in 1870 he married Mary W. McMullin, who survived him, as did one son.

[Journal of Milton S. Latham (Jan. 1–May 6, 1860), MS. in Stanford Univ. Lib.; W. J. Davis, *Hist. of Political Conventions in Cal.* (1893); *Biog. Dir. Am. Cong.* (1928); *Biog. and Hist. Cat. of Washington and Jefferson College* (1902); *Evening Bulletin* (San Francisco), May 11, 1861, Mar. 6, 1882; *Morning Call* (San Francisco), Mar. 5, 7, 1882; *N. Y. Times,* Mar. 5, 1882].

E. E. R.

LATHBURY, MARY ARTEMISIA (Aug. 10, 1841–Oct. 20, 1913), author, hymn-writer, daughter of the Rev. John Lathbury, a Methodist minister, and Betsy Shepherd (Jones) Lathbury, was born at Manchester, N. Y. The family was of English descent. Her childhood environment was one in which religious observances had an important place and her temperament fitted the environment. She was educated first in the school at Manchester and at eighteen went to an art school at Worcester, Mass. The following year she taught drawing, painting, and French at the Methodist Conference Seminary, Newbury, Vt. For the next five years she taught at the Fort Edward (New York) Institute and for six years she was at the Drew Ladies' Seminary at Carmel, N. Y. As a child she had written poems and illustrated them and during her teaching years she wrote occasionally for her own pleasure, but her real work as an author began in 1874, when Bishop John H. Vincent engaged her as assistant editor for some Sunday School publications in connection with the Chautauqua movement, among them the *Picture Lesson Paper*. Editorial work gave her an impetus toward creative writing and she was soon producing juvenile stories and poems, usually illustrated by herself, which were published in *St. Nicholas, Harper's Young People, Wide Awake,* and various church papers and magazines. Some of these were later published in small collections, including *Fleda and the Voice* (1876), fairy tales; *Out of Darkness into Light* (1878), poems; *Idyls of the Months* (1885), poems; *The Child's Life of Christ; Stories from the Bible* (1898) ; and *The Child's Story of the Bible* (1898). Her work in connection with Chautauqua included the founding of the Chautauqua Look Up Legion, suggested by Edward Everett Hale's motto "Look Up and not Down." She and Hale were close friends and she cooperated with him in founding the Ten Times One clubs. For several years she was superintendent of a Chinese Sunday School in New York City. Her hymns are her most valuable and enduring work. Edward Everett Hale said of her as a hymn-writer: "She has marvelous lyric force which not five people in a century show." Her best-known hymns are "Day Is Dying in the West," called Chautauqua's vesper hymn, "Break Thou the Bread of Life," and "Arise and Shine." If not notable as literature, they show a deep devotional spirit and lyric quality. For the last two years of her life she was an invalid and she died at her home in East Orange, N. J.

[*Who's Who in America,* 1912–13; Frances E. Willard, sketch in *Poems of Mary Artemisia Lathbury, Chautauqua Laureate* (1915); Kate F. Kimball, article in the *Chautauquan,* Nov. 8, 1913; obituaries in the *N. Y. Times,* Oct. 21, 1913, and the *N. Y. Tribune,* Oct. 22, 1913.]   S. G. B.

LATHROP, FRANCIS AUGUSTUS (June 22, 1849–Oct. 18, 1909), mural painter, eldest son of Dr. George Alfred and Frances Maria (Smith) Lathrop, was born at sea during a voyage which his parents were making from the Atlantic coast to Honolulu by way of Cape Horn. His father, a descendant of John Lothropp and of Samuel Holden Parsons [*qq.v.*], was a young physician and had been appointed head of the then new naval hospital at Honolulu. The family remained there nine years, returning in 1858 to the mainland on the sloop-of-war *St. Mary's,* commanded by Captain Davis, afterward Admiral Davis. The voyage took three weeks owing to tempestuous weather. From San Francisco to New York the journey was continued by way of the Isthmus of Panama. In New York, Francis and his brother, George Parsons Lathrop [*q.v.*], attended a private school until 1861, when the family went to Europe and traveled for eight months. After the return the boys entered the Columbia Grammar school where Francis stood at the head of his class for three years. He entered Columbia College, but before the end of his freshman year he and his brother started for Germany with the intention of entering the University of Leipzig. They began preparatory study of the German language in Dresden. Francis then determined to begin work in the Royal Art Academy there, but James Whistler urged him to go to London and study with him; thus, after four months in Dresden, the young man went to London. He had no sooner reached that city than he was summoned to return to New York owing to his father's business reverses. For the time being study had to be abandoned and money earned, and during the ensuing year he gave lessons in drawing. When his father's circumstances had improved, he went again to London, took lodgings in Chelsea, and began work in Whistler's studio. He found, however, that his master could not give the requisite time and energy to teaching him, and it was arranged that the young man should work under Madox Brown. A little later he obtained admission to the studio of Edward Burne-Jones where he worked as assistant, making cartoons for stained-glass windows and executing other decorative work. He also worked for a time as assistant to William Morris and R. Spencer Stanhope.

After three years of this life in London he was once more recalled home in 1873 by his father whose affairs were in a critical condition. Francis found himself again obliged to be the bread-winner. He conducted a painting class at Cooper Institute; made illustrations for Clarence Cook's *House Beautiful* (1878); painted portraits; and before long obtained work as a mural painter, a specialty to which thenceforth he devoted most of his time and attention. He was one of the young men who assisted John La Farge in the interior decoration of Trinity Church, Boston, in 1878. He painted an important wall panel for the chapel of Bowdoin College, Brunswick, Me., "Moses Giving the Law to the Children of Israel," in which the figure of Aaron was a portrait of Professor Jonathan B. Sewall. This panel was given by the Bowdoin class of 1877. For the same chapel he painted copies of Raphael's "Transfiguration," "Paul at Mars Hill," "Peter and John at the Beautiful Gate," and Carlo Maratti's "Baptism of Jesus." Other decorative works are his "Light of the World" on the reredos of St. Bartholomew's Church, Madison Avenue, New York; "Apollo," over the proscenium of the Metropolitan Opera House, New York; the marble mosaic of "Widows and Orphans" in the building of the Equitable Life Assurance Company, New York; a stained-glass window representing the miracle at the pool of Bethesda, in the chancel of Bethesda Church, Saratoga, N. Y.; the Marquand memorial window in the chapel of Princeton University; the decorations in the music room of the Collis P. Huntington residence, Fifth Avenue, New York; and others. In all of his works Lathrop showed the influence of his Pre-Raphaelite masters, but aside from this there is in his decorative essays a personal stamp of imagination and an admirable instinct for design, qualities that are especially to be noticed in his Bowdoin College panel and his altarpiece in St. Bartholomew's.

Lathrop was never married. His New York studio was the tower room of the old University building in Washington Square, where S. F. B. Morse and Winslow Homer had been his illustrious predecessors. He was a charter member of the Society of American Artists, an associate of the National Academy of Design, a member of many other societies, and the recipient of a number of medals and honors. His death took place at his home at Woodcliffe Lake, N. J.

[Lathrop left an autobiographical fragment which is now in the possession of his cousin. Printed sources include: *Who's Who in America*, 1908–09; *Am. Art Annual*, 1910–11; J. D. Champlin and C. C. Perkins, *Cyc. of Painters and Paintings*, vol. III (1888); E. B. Huntington, *Geneal. Memoir of the Lo-Lathrop Family* (1884); *N. Y. Times*, Oct. 19, 1909.]

W. H. D.

LATHROP, GEORGE PARSONS (Aug. 25, 1851–Apr. 19, 1898), author and editor, was born near Honolulu, Oahu, Hawaiian Islands, the youngest son of Dr. George Alfred and Frances Maria (Smith) Lathrop, and a descendant of the Rev. John Lothropp [*q.v.*]. He was educated in private schools in New York and, from 1867 to 1870, in Dresden, Germany, where he met Rose Hawthorne, daughter of Nathaniel Hawthorne. Returning to America in 1870, he entered Columbia Law School in New York City for a term, but soon decided to leave the law for a literary career. On Sept. 11, 1871, he and Miss Hawthorne were married in St. Peter's Church, Chelsea, London. In 1875 Lathrop became associate editor of the *Atlantic Monthly* during the editorship of William Dean Howells. In 1877 he left the *Atlantic* to become editor for two years of the Boston Sunday *Courier*. In 1881, after the death of their only child, Francis Hawthorne Lathrop, he and his wife went to Europe, where he wrote "Spanish Vistas," travel essays later published in book form, for *Harper's Monthly*. Lathrop founded the American Copyright League in 1883 and acted as its secretary until the summer of 1885; later he organized as an auxiliary the Western Copyright League in Chicago. After a seven years' campaign, the international copyright law came into being, substantially as Lathrop had at first proposed it. During this time he had been literary editor of the New York *Star* and in 1887 had seen his dramatization of Tennyson's "Elaine," written in collaboration with Henry Edwards, presented in Madison Square Theatre, New York. Later in 1887 the play was presented in Boston and Chicago.

Converted to Roman Catholicism, Lathrop and his wife were received into the Church in March 1891 by the Paulist priest, Alfred Young. As a Catholic, Lathrop had an active part in two enterprises: the founding of the Catholic Summer School of America at New London, Conn., in 1892, an institution which was transferred in 1893 to its present location on Lake Champlain; and the Paulist inauguration of the Apostolate of the Press which he supported with his pen. He was the author of fifteen books of which *Rose and Roof-tree* (1875), poems; *A Study of Hawthorne* (1876); and *Spanish Vistas* (1883) are noteworthy. He edited in 1878 *A Masque of Poets* and in 1883 the Riverside edition of Hawthorne's works, with introductory notes and a biographical sketch of Hawthorne. He also adapted Hawthorne's *Scarlet Letter* for Walter Damrosch's opera of the same name, which was produced with great success in New York in 1896. With Mrs. Lathrop he wrote *A Story of Courage* (1894), a history of the Order of the Sisters of the Visitation. After his death in New York City, his widow became a nun, and as Mother Alphonsa [*q.v.*] organized a community of Dominican tertiaries, the Servants of Relief for Incurable Cancer Patients, with two hospitals in New York City.

[See "Death of George Parsons Lathrop, LL.D.," *Cath. Reading Circle Rev.*, Apr.–Sept. 1898; E. B. Huntington, *A Geneal. Memoir of the Lo-Lathrop Family* (1884); *Theatre*, Dec. 12, 1887; *N. Y. Tribune*, Apr. 29, May 1, 1887, Apr. 20, 1898.]   R. A.

LATHROP, JOHN (Jan. 13, 1772–Jan. 30, 1820), lawyer and poet, was born at Boston, Mass., the son of the Rev. John and Mary (Wheatley) Lathrop. His father was for many years the minister of the Second Church in Boston and a direct descendant of the Rev. John Lothropp [*q.v.*] who was the first minister of Scituate and later of Barnstable, Mass. At Harvard Lathrop was distinguished for his scholarship. Upon graduating in 1789 he read law in the office of Christopher Gore with considerable assiduity, but the public came to know him more as a poet than as a lawyer. At Harvard Commencement in 1792 he delivered a poem and received the degree of A.M. He practised law at Boston and also at Dedham, Mass., where he enjoyed the society of Fisher Ames. In 1798 he was appointed clerk of the courts for Norfolk County, but the work was uncongenial and he soon returned to Boston. There he became identified with the wits and versifiers of the day, notably Robert Treat Paine and Charles Prentiss. This association did not help him in the legal profession and in 1799 he embarked for India where he hoped to make a fortune. Taking up his residence in Calcutta he opened a school and wrote frequently for the newspapers, the *Hircarrah* and the *Post*. To the Marquis Wellesley, governor-general of India, he submitted a plan of an institution of learning in which the youth of India might be educated without going to England to study. He urged his cause with fervency and eloquence, but his Lordship is said to have replied, "No, no, Sir, India is and ever ought to be a Colony of Great Britain; the seeds of Independence must not be sown here. Establishing a seminary in New England at so early a period of time hastened your revolution half a century" (Knapp, *post*, p. 180).

Returning to the United States in 1809 he entertained thoughts of founding a literary journal in his native country, but the times were not favorable. There was little left for him to do except to teach. For a number of years he superintended a school in Boston, edited almanacs, delivered a course of scientific lectures, and occasionally made speeches. Later he continued some of these pursuits at Washington and Georgetown, D. C., and finally obtained a position in the post-office. He died at Georgetown in 1820. His reputation rests chiefly upon *The Speech of Caunonicus*, a poem first printed in Calcutta in 1802 and reprinted in Boston in the following year. To the *Polyanthos*, a Boston magazine, he contributed (1812–14) a series of papers under the title "The Moral Censor," and also a course of lectures on natural philosophy which he had delivered in Calcutta in 1807–08 and in Boston in 1811. Modest and affectionate by nature, Lathrop made and retained many friends who easily forgave his lack of prudence and occasional negligence of duty. He was married thrice: in 1792 to Ann Pierce; about 1801 to Jane Thompson; and about 1808 to Grace Eleanor Harrison. John Lothrop Motley [*q.v.*], the historian, was his nephew.

[The best sketch of Lathrop's life is to be found in S. L. Knapp, *Biog. Sketches of Eminent Lawyers, Statesmen, and Men of Letters* (1821). See also Samuel Kettell, *Specimens of Am. Poetry, with Critical and Biog. Notices* (1829), II, 101–08; John Lathrop, "Biographical Memoir of the Rev. John Lothropp," *Mass. Hist. Soc. Colls.*, 2 ser. I (1814); E. B. Huntington, *Geneal. Memoir of the Lo-Lathrop Family* (1884); J. T. Buckingham, *Personal Memoirs* (1852), vol. I, and Thos. Bridgman, *The Pilgrims of Boston* (1856). A poem by Lathrop delivered at Harvard Commencement in 1792 is printed in the *Mass. Mag.*, July 1792. His fourth of July orations at Boston (1796) and at Dedham (1798) were printed separately in the years in which they were pronounced.]   L. S. M.

LATHROP, JOHN HIRAM (Jan. 22, 1799–Aug. 2, 1866), pioneer in higher education in the Middle West, first and fifth president of the University of Missouri, and president of the universities of Wisconsin and Indiana, was born in Sherburne, Chenango County, N. Y. His parents, John and Prudence Elizabeth (Hatch) Lathrop were of Puritan ancestry; his father was a descendant of the Rev. John Lothropp [*q.v.*]. After preparatory study under a neighboring clergyman, he entered Hamilton College, Clinton, N. Y., in 1815, and two years later was admitted to the junior class at Yale, from which institution he was graduated in 1819. He then taught for three years, first in the grammar school at Farmington, Conn., and then in Monroe Academy at Weston. From 1822 until 1826 he was a tutor at Yale and at the same time studied law. Admitted to the bar in the latter year, he opened a law office at Middletown, Conn., but soon returned to educational work, in which he now was convinced he should make his career. He became an instructor in the Military Academy at Norwich, Vt., and later was principal of the Gardiner Lyceum at Gardiner, Me. In 1829 he became professor of mathematics and natural philosophy at Hamilton College and six years later was promoted to the Maynard professorship of law, civil polity, and political economy. He had married, in 1833, Frances E. Lothrop of Utica, N. Y.

Lathrop's career as a pioneer in higher education in the undeveloped Middle West began on Mar. 11, 1841, when, after a six weeks' journey by stage and boat to Columbia, Mo., he became the first president of the University of Missouri. His task as president was to lead in developing a university for the benefit of which Congress had appropriated land, and to which the citizens of Boone County had voluntarily given from their meager resources $117,900. The cornerstone of the first university building had been laid July 4, preceding his arrival, but the edifice was not completed until 1843. His work included overseeing the sale of lands, supervising the erection of buildings, maturing plans for curricula and teaching, and advising the legislature with regard to the nature and needs of a real university. In this work he necessarily faced difficulties arising from lack of funds, and from religious sectarianism and partisan politics. He was embarrassed, too, by the increasing controversy about slavery and could not escape the antagonism of many who knew his acceptance of the doctrine that "all men are born free."

Although the curators of the University of Missouri desired him to continue as president, he decided in 1849 to accept the chancellorship of the University of Wisconsin, where he again became a pioneer university builder for ten years. Then, after two invitations, he became president of Indiana University. When the University of Missouri was reorganized, he accepted, in 1860, a call to return to this institution as professor of English literature. His welcome was enthusiastic. During the years 1863–65, his title was chairman of the faculty and professor of moral, mental, and political philosophy. He helped to guide the university during the precarious conditions of civil war, and in 1865 he was for the second time officially made president. In the following year he died and was buried in a cemetery near the campus. He was a man of attractive personality, wide scholarship, and ability both in teaching and in educational administration. Well-grounded in the social philosophy of his time, he believed that education should be practical and that the university should provide training in agriculture and in the various professions and arts. He believed that the profession of education should be as clearly separated from that of theology as the profession of law is separated from that of medicine, and that the remuneration of the successful teacher should be equivalent to that of the successful man in other learned professions. Deeply religious, but without sectarian bias, he regularly attended and contributed to the support of church services.

Late in life he became a member of the Episcopal Church. He said that the ideal professor should be "too intensely American to be partisan, too profoundly Christian to be sectarian." This ideal was largely realized in his own life.

[See W. B. Davis and D. S. Durrie, *Illustrated Hist. of Mo.* (1876); H. L. Conard, ed., *Encyc. of the Hist. of Mo.* (1901), vol. III; W. F. Switzler, "History of the University of Missouri," in the archives of the university; Lathrop's *Address Delivered in the Chapel of the Univ. . . . of Mo. on the Occasion of the Dedication of the Edifice* (1843); *Obit. Record of the Grads. of Yale Coll. Deceased During the Academic Year Ending July 1867*; E. B. Huntington, *A Geneal. Memoir of the Lo-Lathrop Family* (1884). There is an oil portrait of Lathrop in the library of the University of Missouri, and a bronze portrait on the gateway to Francis Quadrangle.]
                                     J. H. C.

LATHROP, ROSE HAWTHORNE [See ALPHONSA, MOTHER, 1851–1926].

LATIL, ALEXANDRE (Oct. 6, 1816–March 1851), Louisiana poet, was born in New Orleans, La., of a family whose ancestors came from France and in early colonial days were sailors and *coureurs de bois.* Young Alexandre attended Les Écoles Centrale et Primaires, and later, the Collège d'Orléans. When he was only fifteen he fell in love with the pretty daughter of a Creole and they became engaged. Their families thought them too young to marry and insisted that they wait a few years. From then on Latil's life paralleled all the horrors of a Greek tragedy. He developed unmistakable signs of leprosy, which the neighbors attributed to the mating of one of his *coureur-de-bois* forebears with a *sauvagesse,* for it was then commonly believed that the mixture of French with Indian blood was responsible for this disease. In those days lepers were allowed to remain at home, so Latil continued to live with his parents. He released his fiancée from their engagement, but this did not change her devotion, for she visited him daily in an effort to bring some cheer into his hopeless situation. Finally when the ravages of his disease had become too terrible, Latil was sent to a small cabin out on Bayou St. John in the *"Terre aux Lepreux,"* where his fiancée followed him. No scandal ever attached to her name although she took entire charge of the sufferer and nursed him tenderly. So great was her love that she desired to be his wife in spite of his illness and finally succeeded in overcoming his scruples. After their marriage she continued her nursing, forced to watch the relentless progress of his disease, the repulsive scaly blanching of his face, and the torturing disintegration of his limbs.

During these years of suffering poetry had been Latil's great solace. He tried to forget his agony in reading Béranger, Barthélemy, and

Delavigne, and was finally inspired to write French verse himself. It was good and some of the verses were printed in the Creole newspapers and literary magazines. The beauty of their resigned despair impressed the local literati and they urged him to collect and publish them in book form. He did this at his own expense and in 1841 *Les Éphémères,* a small collection of twenty-four of his poems, appeared. In a pathetic foreword this boy of only twenty-five regretted that the state of his health and his failing eyesight kept him from finishing some other verses which he had wished to include. The remaining years of his life were an inferno of suffering. He became completely bedridden and blind and his fingers dropped off at the palms so he could not hold a pen. Finally, death came as a merciful release in March 1851. His wife remained with him until the end, and it seems unjust that the name of this self-sacrificing woman cannot be perpetuated; only her initials—E. T.—are known.

[E. L. Tinker, *Les Écrits de Langue Française en Louisiane au XIXe Siècle* (1932); death notice in *L'Orléanais* (New Orleans), Mar. 18, 1851; Charles Testut, "Ange et Poète," in *Veillées Louisianaises* (1849), vol. I, p. 409, and by the same author *Fleurs d'Été* (1851), containing on p. 121 a poem on Latil's death, and *Portraits Littéraires* (1850).]   E. L. T.

LATIMER, MARY ELIZABETH WORMELEY (July 26, 1822–Jan. 4, 1904), author, daughter of Rear Admiral Ralph Randolph Wormeley of the British navy and Caroline (Preble) Wormeley, was born in London, England. Her father was sixth in descent from Ralphe Wormeley, who received a grant of land in Virginia in 1649, and fourth from Ralph Wormeley of "Rosegill," Middlesex County, Va., one of the first trustees of the College of William and Mary. He was taken to England in childhood and became a British citizen. His wife was the daughter of a Boston East-India merchant and a niece of Commodore Edward Preble [*q.v.*], who won distinction in the early American navy. The childhood of the four Wormeley children was not monotonous. The family vibrated from London to Paris, to Boston, to Newport, to Virginia. Mary Elizabeth's studies were conducted in a desultory way by tutors, and she was for a time a "parlor boarder" in the school of Mrs. Cockle of Ipswich, Mass. The education of travel compensated for defects in formal study, and was of the greatest advantage to her in her career as a writer. She attended the funeral of William IV and saw Victoria enter Westminster Abbey for her coronation. She witnessed the funeral of Napoleon when his remains were brought to Paris from St. Helena, and made her début at the balls of Louis Philippe. A young man named William Makepeace Thackeray was one of the friends whom the family knew in Paris. The winter of 1842 she spent in Boston, where the families of George Ticknor, William H. Prescott, and Julia (Ward) Howe were among her friends and encouraged her to begin writing. Her first printed work was the translation of a Mexican poem for the appendix of Prescott's *History of the Conquest of Mexico* (pt. 2, vol. III, 1844). Not long after its publication the family removed permanently to the United States and thenceforth resided in Boston and in Newport, R. I.

In 1852 her father died and in the same year her first novel, *Amabel,* was published in London and New York. In 1856 she published *Our Cousin Veronica* and was married to Randolph Brandt Latimer of Baltimore. For twenty years thereafter she devoted herself to the cares of a home and three children. During the Civil War she took part in the nursing of soldiers. In 1876 she resumed writing, with the determination to make it her chief work. Though her eyes were never strong, she read and wrote indefatigably, and between 1880 and 1903 produced a large number of volumes. Her stories are not noteworthy; her best work is to be found in her series of popular histories: *France in the Nineteenth Century* (1892), and similar volumes dealing with Russia and Turkey (1893), England (1894), Europe in Africa (1895), Spain (1897); *Italy in the Nineteenth Century and the Making of Austro-Hungary and Germany* (1896); *My Scrap Book of the French Revolution* (1898); *Judea from Cyrus to Titus; 537 B.C.–70 A.D.* (1899); and *The Last Years of the Nineteenth Century* (1900). These books reveal much study and considerable understanding of national and world development. They abound in anecdotes and are written in a vivacious style. She was engaged upon a history of Germany in the nineteenth century when her own failing health and her husband's death, Dec. 24, 1903, permanently ended her work. In addition to original writing, she published the following translations: *A History of the People of Israel* (1888–96), in collaboration with J. H. Allen from the French of Ernest Renan; *The Steel Hammer* (1888) and *For Fifteen Years* (1888), from Louis Ulbach; *Nanon* (1890), from George Sand; *The Italian Republics* (1901), by J. C. L. de Sismondi; *The Love Letters of Victor Hugo, 1820–22* (1901); *Talks of Napoleon at St. Helena with General Baron Gourgaud* (1903). She died at her home in Baltimore and was buried in Greenmount Cemetery.

[Sara Andrew Shafer, in *The Dial*, Feb. 1, 1904; *Who's Who in America*, 1903–05; F. E. Willard and M. A. Livermore, *Am. Women* (1897); H. E. Hayden, *Va. Geneals.* (1891); G. H. Preble, *Geneal. Sketch of the First Three Generations of Rebels in America* (1868); *New-Eng. Hist. and Geneal. Reg.*, Oct. 1868; *Baltimore American*, Jan. 3, 4, 7, 1904; the *Sun* (Baltimore), Jan. 4, 5, 1904.]   S. G. B.

LA TOUR, LE BLOND de (d. Oct. 14, 1723), chief engineer of the French colony of Louisiana, was born in France in the latter part of the seventeenth century. During the War of the Spanish Succession, he was sent as a draftsman to Portugal in 1702, appointed engineer in 1703, and served with the army in Spain from 1704 to 1708. He was taken prisoner at Alcantara in 1705 and exchanged the next year. He participated in the siege of Marchienne and served as noncommissioned officer at the sieges of Douai, Quesnoy, and Bouchain in 1712, and of Freiburg in 1713. He was decorated with the Cross of the Royal and Military Order of St. Louis in 1715 and was named reserve captain of the Piedmont regiment and then corporal of his Majesty's Engineers. In 1720 he was appointed engineer-in-chief of the province of Louisiana which was at that time under the control of Law's Company of the West. He arrived at Old Biloxi, the capital of the province, in December of that year with a corps of assistants to superintend the construction of whatever public buildings and works might be needed. The most pressing question before the council of the province at that time was whether to rebuild Old Biloxi, which had been almost wiped out by fire the year before, or transfer the capital to some other place. Bienville [*q.v.*], the governor of the province, was very eager that the capital should be moved to New Orleans, which he had founded in 1718. But the council, acting under the advice of La Tour, decided to move the capital to a point a short distance to the west of Old Biloxi and to give it the name of New Biloxi. La Tour drew up an elaborate plan for the new capital, which included a fortress and a port on Ship Island which stood a few miles opposite in the Mississippi Sound. (The plan is reproduced in Villiers du Terrage, *Les Dernières Années de la Louisiane Française*, 1904, p. 9.) In September 1721 the transfer was made. New Biloxi developed into the Biloxi of today.

Meanwhile La Tour had been ordered to send his assistant, Adrien de Pauger [*q.v.*], to New Orleans to examine the site and transfer the settlement to a more suitable spot, if he should deem it necessary to avoid the inundations of the river. Pauger went to New Orleans in March 1721, and seeing no reason for changing the site, he surveyed the place and in a few weeks finished drawing up plans for a city of about a mile square. He sent the plans to La Tour, but instead of forwarding them to Paris, La Tour is said to have pigeonholed them for fear the capital would be moved from New Biloxi to New Orleans. Bienville had anticipated this action on the part of La Tour, and having procured a copy of Pauger's plans, he sent them on to Paris. Soon thereafter the board of liquidation, which had taken over the affairs of the company after it had collapsed in the latter part of 1720, ordered the capital of Louisiana transferred to New Orleans. Not until then did La Tour give his official approval of Pauger's plans of the city.

La Tour claimed in a letter written Dec. 9, 1721, that he had drawn up the plan of New Orleans, and most of the historians of that city, especially the earlier ones, have accepted his claim. But Villiers du Terrage (*Histoire, post,* p. 88) declares that La Tour did not see New Orleans until nearly six months after making this claim, and that probably the only part he had in the matter was to trace on paper in advance a number of little squares. He may have intended, however, that these little squares should be situated far away from the Mississippi River, probably on the Bayou St. John which flowed into Lake Ponchartrain north of New Orleans. La Tour favored establishing an inland settlement on Lake Ponchartrain rather than on the Mississippi River, on the ground that it would be easier of access from the towns along the Gulf Coast.

On June 10, 1722, La Tour and Pauger left New Biloxi for New Orleans, arriving at their destination on July 7. Other boats followed, and under La Tour's supervision the new city began to take form and shape. A church and several houses were built, a cemetery was laid out, levees were thrown up—the first on the Lower Mississippi—ditches were dug, and a canal was constructed in the rear of the city for drainage purposes. The city, as laid out by Pauger and developed by La Tour, constitutes the French Quarter or the Vieux Carré of the present city of New Orleans. (See the plan of the city in 1725, Villiers du Terrage, *Histoire, post,* facing p. 118.) Before leaving New Biloxi, La Tour was made lieutenant-general of the province, much to the disgust and chagrin of Bienville. But Bienville submitted to higher authority and formally presented La Tour in his new rôle to the troops. La Tour died in New Orleans about eighteen months after going there. As far as is known, he left no heirs or descendants.

[The best account of La Tour is contained in Baron Marc de Villiers du Terrage, *Histoire de la Fondation de la Nouvelle-Orléans (1717–22)* (Paris, 1917). A translation of this monograph appeared in the *La. Hist. Quart.*, Apr. 1920. Scattered references to him are to be found in the *Journal Historique de l'Établissement des Français à la Louisiane* (New Orleans and Paris, 1831); Pierre Heinrich, *La Louisiane sous la Compagnie des Indies, 1717–31* (n.d.), and Grace E. King, *Jean Baptiste Le Moyne, Sieur de Bienville* (1892). The brief sketches of Fort Maurepas, Fort Louis de la Mobile, and Biloxi in Alcée Fortier, *Louisiana*, vol. I (1914), are helpful in tracing the changes in the capitals of Louisiana in its earlier years.]   E. M. V.

LATROBE, BENJAMIN HENRY (May 1, 1764–Sept. 3, 1820), architect, engineer, traced the French name which marked him professionally as a "foreigner" from Henri Boneval de la Trobe, a French Protestant who, according to tradition, emigrated to Holland after the revocation of the edict of Nantes, followed the Prince of Orange to England, was wounded in the Battle of the Boyne, and settled finally in Dublin (*Brief Notices of the Latrobe Family*, London, 1864). Henry Boneval's grandson, Benjamin, joined the Moravians and was their minister at the settlement of Fulneck near Leeds. Here he married Anna Margaret Antes, who had been sent to Fulneck School. The daughter of Henry Antes [*q.v.*], of Germantown, Pa., she was related to the Rittenhouses and brought to her descendants the mathematical talent of that family. Her third child and second son, Benjamin Henry, born at Fulneck, spent his boyhood in England and his youth in Germany, where he received an excellent education. Family tradition attributes to him a service in the Prussian hussars before his return to England about 1786. In the years immediately following he printed two translations of some pretensions, the admiring *Characteristic Anecdotes, and Miscellaneous Authentic Papers, Tending to Illustrate the Character of Frederick II, Late King of Prussia* (1788) and the *Authentic Elucidation of the History of Counts Struensee and Brandt, and of the Revolution in Denmark in the Year 1772* (1789). Meanwhile he studied architecture under Samuel Pepys Cockerell, a pioneer of the Greek revival, and engineering under Smeaton, builder of the Eddystone lighthouse, for whom he investigated the scouring-works of Lincolnshire and Cambridgeshire.

His first independent work, "Hammerwood Lodge," East Grinstead, Sussex, was followed by a house at Ashdown Park, buildings at Frimley, Surrey, and the superintendence of a canal in Surrey. His father's connections and his own varied talents were bringing him influential friends, such as Sir Charles Middleton, and he was offered an appointment as surveyor of the police office of London, with bright prospects of professional advancement. In 1790 he married Lydia Sellon, daughter of the rector of St. James,

Clerkenwell, by whom he had two children, Henry and Lydia. The death of his wife in 1793, during her third confinement, was followed by a period of distress and confusion in his affairs which led him to emigrate, not without fortune, to America.

He landed in Norfolk, Va., in March 1796, with letters which assured him a friendly reception, and spent the next two and a half years in Virginia. At first, as he wrote soon after landing, he was "idly engaged . . . designing a staircase for Mr. A's new house, a house and offices for Captain P——, tuning a pianoforte for Mrs. W——, scribbling doggerel for Mrs. A——, tragedy for her mother, and Italian songs for Mrs. T——" (*Journal of Latrobe, post,* p. xv), but he was soon employed on important works. He was first consulted on improving the navigation of the Appomattox, then of the James around the falls at Richmond, then on the Dismal Swamp improvements. In 1797 his design for the penitentiary at Richmond, one of the earliest prisons on the principle of solitary confinement, was adopted, and he removed from Norfolk to Richmond to supervise its construction at a salary of £200 per annum. Here he also completed the exterior of Jefferson's Virginia state capitol, substituting for the Louis XVI ornaments of the model a more severe treatment *à l'antique* (Fiske Kimball, *Thomas Jefferson and the First Monument of the Classical Revival in America*, 1915, p. 41). Another architectural work, in 1797, was the long arcade and portico of "Greenspring," near Williamsburg (drawing at the Virginia Historical Society).

In March 1798 he went for the first time to Philadelphia, with introductions to Jefferson and others. A month before, the Bank of Pennsylvania had authorized the construction of a new banking house, which its president, Samuel M. Fox, was determined should be a handsome one. Latrobe left a sketch with Fox and went back to Richmond. It was not long before he learned that his design had been adopted, and he was pressed to return and supervise the execution. This was a principal inducement to him to wind up his Virginia affairs and remove to Philadelphia in December. A site was secured on Second Street, and the building, begun in April 1799, was occupied early in 1801. It stood until after the Civil War, when it was demolished to make room for the Appraisers' Stores. Study of the architect's drawings and of old photographs reveals what posterity has lost. The building, very simple and all of marble, was fronted with two porticoes of six Ionic columns, their details modeled on those of the Erechtheum. Although the general form was thus that of a temple, it was not a slavish imitation—less so perhaps than the classical enthusiasm of laymen on the bank board would have welcomed. The interior, vaulted throughout, had a circular banking room, crowned by a low dome and a lantern. The building was the first monument of the Greek revival in America. (Kimball, "The Bank of Pennsylvania, 1799," in *Architectural Record*, August 1918.)

Latrobe's abilities were also called into requisition in the project for a city water supply, the first in America, stimulated by the epidemic of yellow fever a few years before. His *View of the Practicability and Means of Supplying the City of Philadelphia with Wholesome Water* (published 1799) is dated Dec. 29, 1798, only a few days after his arrival in the city. It advocated the raising of water from the Schuylkill River, using pumps operated by steam-engines, to an elevated reservoir on Center Square. His plan was so practical that it led to the immediate abandonment of other schemes, and its official adoption by the City. Work was begun in March 1799, with Latrobe as engineer, under a contract which guaranteed successful operation. The engines, much the largest among the very few yet built in America, were built by Nicholas James Roosevelt [*q.v.*] at his works on the Passaic in New Jersey. Public ignorance and the delays and increased expense incident to such a pioneer undertaking had occasioned the greatest skepticism as to its success. Latrobe's son has recorded how on the night of Jan. 21, 1801, his father, "with three gentlemen, his friends, and one of his workmen, kindled a fire under the boiler, and set the ponderous machinery in motion while the city was buried in sleep," so that in the morning "the streets of Philadelphia were flowing with water from the gushing hydrants" (*Journal of Latrobe*, p. xxi). The works continued in operation until Sept. 7, 1815, when, no longer adequate, they were superseded by larger ones designed by one of Latrobe's pupils. The marble "Center House," on the general model of the *villa rotunda*, with Greek porticoes and a dome over the elevated tank, was a familiar landmark until its demolition in 1827. With William Rush's fountain, "The Nymph of the Schuylkill," it figures in John Lewis Krimmel's "Centre Square, Philadelphia, in 1812," one of the earliest American genre paintings. (Drawings by Latrobe of the house and its engines, reproduced in the *Architectural Record*, July 1927, pp. 18–22, are preserved by the Historical Society of Pennsylvania, which also has a very complete file of the early reports and pamphlets.)

In September 1801 the improvement of navigation of the Susquehanna was undertaken. The Pennsylvania portion of the survey was intrusted to Latrobe's American uncle, Col. Frederick Antes, who died at the beginning of the work. Latrobe carried it to completion, and by the end of the year had cleared the channel for downstream navigation from Columbia to tidewater. His report was published in *Report of the Governor and Directors to the Proprietors of the Susquehanna Canal* (1802). His very large and beautifully executed map is still preserved by the Maryland Historical Society, and has been authoritative in modern lawsuits. Perhaps to this period is to be referred also his undated pamphlet, *American Copper-Mines*, with its acute observations.

During these years he planned several houses in Philadelphia. "Sedgley," built for William Cramond on land acquired in March 1799 in what is now Fairmount Park, was the first design of the Gothic revival in America. Its little lodge still survives. In 1800 Latrobe designed for Robert Liston, the British minister, a house which was never built, intended for Fairmount itself. It was to be circular in plan, and represented an abstract ideal of form not realized in America until long afterwards. The Burd house at Chestnut and Ninth streets, with its broad wall surfaces and arched windows, was until its demolition a notable landmark of the city.

As early as 1800 Latrobe was at work on projects for the federal government. A design for a military academy, requested of him by the secretary of war, was furnished on Jan. 26 of that year. In November 1802, President Jefferson called him to Washington to make drawings, surveys, and estimates for a dry dock to preserve twelve frigates ready for sea. The design, dated Dec. 4, is in the possession of the Library of Congress. It shows a great vaulted hangar open at the sides and ends, and is so admirably worked out that we can well understand why the select committee of Congress was unanimous in its favor, and that this most derided of the Philosopher-President's ideas, defeated by a sectional vote, was by no means wholly impractical. (Kimball, "Benjamin Henry Latrobe and the Beginnings of Architectural and Engineering Practice in America," *Michigan Technic*, December 1917.)

When funds had been appropriated toward the completion of the federal buildings in Washington, Jefferson created for Latrobe, on Mar. 6, 1803, the post of surveyor of the public buildings. His salary was fixed at $1700 a year. The immediate task in hand was the erection of the south wing of the Capitol, to contain the Hall of Representatives. The north wing, containing the Senate Chamber, which was already complete, determined the exterior design of its fellow. Foundations had been laid, establishing an internal form for the structure in accordance with a design of William Thornton [*q.v.*], whose original plan had won the competition of 1792–93. Latrobe, like his predecessors in office, raised very sound objections to the design on both practical and artistic grounds. The old struggle between the tenacious amateur and his professional critics, in which Thornton had destroyed Hallet and George Hadfield [*qq.v.*], was renewed. It even rocked Congress, and threatened the loss of appropriations. But Jefferson, although counseling stability of plan and seeking to avoid a direct issue for political reasons, kept his architect in authority. Thornton had at last met his match. It was in the person of Jefferson himself, rather than Thornton, that the ideas of the amateur in architecture continued to embarrass Latrobe. The Roman tendencies of the pioneer of American classicism sometimes came in conflict with the Greek predilections of the younger man, and the President's orders were sometimes difficult to reconcile with structural considerations and elegancies of planning. With mutual concessions and mutual respect, however, the two men, by the close of Jefferson's administration, had brought the wings of the building to a worthy completion. (The controversial pamphlets of Thornton and Latrobe are listed by Glenn Brown, *post*, II, 225.)

In the south wing was the Hall of Representatives, with its circular ends and its twenty-four stone Corinthian columns, their capitals designed after the Greek example of the Monument of Lysicrates. For the carving two Italian sculptors, Giovanni Andrei and Giuseppi Franzoni, had been brought over in 1806. Franzoni's eagle above the speaker's desk was among the earliest American works of monumental sculpture. Many of the rooms in this wing were vaulted in masonry. In the north wing, much interior rebuilding had been undertaken, to raise the standard of construction. Here, for the east basement vestibule, Latrobe devised in 1809 his "American order" of maize, with what were promptly christened by admiring members of Congress the "corn-cob capitals."

Much other work for the federal government came meanwhile from Latrobe's hands. For the President's House he executed Jefferson's scheme of colonnaded terraces, and in 1807 made designs for the remodeling and development of the house itself (Kimball, *Thomas Jefferson,*

Architect, pp. 66–67, 175–76). These showed the semicircular portico toward the river suggested by Jefferson, and proposed the north portico, both of which were executed in the rebuilding after Latrobe's final retirement from the government service in 1817. Construction of the Washington City Canal, on which he had first advised in 1802, was actively pursued in 1803 and 1810. In 1804 he was called "engineer of the Navy Department," and in the following years he designed much work at the yards in Washington, New York, and elsewhere. In 1810 he was building fireproofs for the State Department, and, by an irony of fate, remodeling the Patent Office, presided over by his old antagonist, Thornton. In 1812 he drew plans for the Marine Hospital in Washington.

His activity was not exhausted by the labors of his official post. In 1804, he was consulted by Bishop John Carroll [*q.v.*] about the building of a cathedral in Baltimore for his diocese, which then had a national scope. Invited to submit a plan, Latrobe gave his services without any remuneration. They were to extend from 1805 to 1818, and to involve the making of seven or eight successive and distinct designs. The first two plans offered the trustees, for the first time in America, a choice between the Gothic and classic styles. One was the earliest American church design of the Gothic revival; the other was of a Roman magnificence hitherto unknown in American ecclesiastical buildings. This classical plan, which was preferred, underwent gradual transformation to its final form—a Latin cross, with a great circular crossing embracing both nave and aisles, crowned by a low Roman dome. The exterior was of broad simplicity. The portico, six columns wide, of the Greek Ionic order, was first executed in 1860–63, when the choir was also extended eastward. Building committee and builders alike were little prepared to understand or sympathize with the monumental character of the design, and many difficulties arose in its execution; but, with the support of the Bishop, Latrobe persevered, and on his final departure from Baltimore received from the trustees such a letter of testimonial as few architects could show: "It is true that objections were sometimes made to parts of your plans, the propriety and connection of which their inexperience did not permit them at the time to discern clearly, but now that the various details of the building form one grand and beautiful whole, they are fully convinced of the propriety of having on such occasions given way to your greater experience and better judgment." (Kimball, "Latrobe's Designs for the Cathedral of Baltimore," *Architectural Record,* December 1917, January 1918.)

During all these years there was an increasing flood of private commissions. In 1803 Latrobe was concerned with the reroofing of Nassau Hall at Princeton; in 1804, designing the first building, West College, for Dickinson College, Carlisle, Pa.; in 1805, the first Pennsylvania Academy of the Fine Arts, at Tenth and Chestnut streets, Philadelphia; in 1806, the additions which adapted the building once intended for the "President's House" in Philadelphia to the use of the University of Pennsylvania. Following his custom of giving gratuitous service to religious and educational institutions, he supplied the plans for these without charge. The wing of the Chestnut Street Theatre was from his design. The Bank of Philadelphia, a Gothic structure of brick and marble, was executed under the supervision of his pupil Robert Mills in 1807. That same year Latrobe built the Waln house, esteemed the finest in the city, and two years later the Markoe house—both with a rich variety of interior spatial effects. He added the portico to "Bellevue" (now Dumbarton House) in Georgetown, D. C.

His engineering work also continued. In February 1804 he was appointed engineer of the Chesapeake & Delaware Canal, for which he had made a first reconnaissance in 1799. His surveys were completed by the end of the year: a route from Welch Point on the Elk River (an arm of the Chesapeake) to Christiana Creek on the Delaware was adopted, providing for a canal twenty miles long, eighty feet wide and eight deep, fed by a branch six miles long, three and a half feet deep, and twenty-six feet wide, susceptible of extension by the valley of the Elk River and Octoraro Creek to the iron region of Pennsylvania. Work was first undertaken on the feeder, that it might be used in transportation of materials not found on the main line, and it was nearly finished in 1805, when failure of subscribers to pay caused the project to be suspended. (Documentary information regarding this project may be found in the published *Annual Reports,* and in Latrobe's letter of Jan. 4, 1808, in *Letters to the Honorable Albert Gallatin . . . and other Papers Relative to the Chesapeake and Delaware Canal,* 1808.)

Aaron Burr, in 1805, had invited Latrobe to go to Kentucky as engineer for a canal around the falls of the Ohio at Louisville, and to recruit five hundred men for the work. Latrobe's testimony to this effect was given weight by the government in Burr's trial. He was also consulted by the City of New York as to a system of drainage for the city; by the Philadelphia Chamber of Commerce in 1807 on the removal of the bar at the mouth of the Schuylkill; and by the House of Representatives as to the navigation of the Potomac. In general these projects were themselves beyond the resources of the time, and Latrobe's high standard of permanence in construction made him reluctant to employ the makeshifts by which the first of such works were later brought within the means of their proponents.

On the outbreak of the war of 1812 and the suspension of his government work, Latrobe entered partnership with Robert Fulton, Robert R. Livingston, and Nicholas J. Roosevelt, now his son-in-law, to build a steamboat adapted to navigation of the Ohio River above the falls. He removed with his family to Pittsburgh in the autumn of 1813. The war increased the costs, which the underwriters had difficulty in meeting, and the death of Fulton in 1815 brought the work to a standstill, to be finished later under other auspices. In this enterprise all Latrobe's private means were swept away. Even before going west, Latrobe had furnished designs for houses beyond the mountains, such as "Belvedere," the home of John Barker Church and his wife, Angelica Schuyler, in the upper Genesee Valley, and Henry Clay's house at Ashland, Ky. While in Pittsburgh, and later, he supplied plans for several others, the Robertson house in Pittsburgh, Governor Taylor's in Newport, Ky., the house of Governor Cass in Michigan.

On Aug. 24, 1814, following the capture of Washington by the British, the Capitol and the President's House were set on fire. The British officer charged with the task of destroying the Hall of Representatives said it was "a pity to burn anything so beautiful" (Brown, *post,* I, 39). The close of the war brought Latrobe an invitation (Mar. 14, 1815) to take charge of the rebuilding of the Capitol, and he returned to Washington in April. The external walls remained, but the interior, which had been destroyed, was now completely remodeled. The stately semicircular chambers of the House and Senate (now Statuary Hall and the Supreme Court room) were the fruit of Latrobe's activity at this time. For the vestibule of the Senate chamber he designed, as a pendant to the corn capitals, capitals composed from the flowers and leaves of the tobacco plant. Before the central Rotunda could be undertaken, difficulties had arisen with the commissioner, Samuel Lane, which made Latrobe's position insupportable, and he resigned, Nov. 20, 1817.

Among his private works in Washington during this period was St. John's Church, built originally in the form of a Greek cross. Latrobe, a member of the congregation, himself wrote the dedicatory hymn. Other works included the Van Ness house, long the finest in the city, the house of Commodore Decatur, the tower of Christ Church in Alexandria, Va., and the Court House in Hagerstown, Md. His advice had been sought by Jefferson in June 1817, in regard to the University of Virginia, and his sketches and drawings sent to Jefferson in July and October of that year were influential in the design of Pavilions V and III, and especially in the adoption, for the head of the plan, of a domed building of importance (Kimball, *Thomas Jefferson, Architect,* pp. 76–79, 187–92).

Harassed by the debts on the steamboat, he decided before leaving Washington to take advantage of the new insolvency act, the ceremony being performed, as he wrote, on Jan. 1, 1818. Penned in the margin of one of his printed notices of insolvency are the words: "Your claim on me is of a nature which no legal release can absolve . . . the field of productive activity before me is such, as to assure me,—if I live,—of the certainty of not disappointing your confidence in me" (Dreer Collection, Historical Society of Pennsylvania). With the friendly support of Gen. Robert Goodloe Harper [q.v.], he removed to Baltimore, where, besides the Cathedral, he had other important buildings under construction. He had undertaken, with Maximilian Godefroy [q.v.], designs for the Exchange in Baltimore which were adopted in February 1816, over those of Joseph Ramé. With the Exchange were incorporated the Bank of the United States and the Custom House, the whole making a large, simple, coherent building with a Roman dome some 115 feet in height. The building has been long since destroyed, but its aspect is preserved by a perspective drawing of Latrobe, belonging to the Maryland Historical Society. In the course of its execution difficulties arose between Latrobe and Godefroy which left the former arrayed against his friend, as well as his pupils, in competition for the next great prize.

The second Bank of the United States had been chartered Apr. 10, 1816, and, in anticipation of the erection of its main banking house in Philadelphia, Latrobe had made efforts, while still in the public service, to be entrusted outright with the commission. A competition was finally decided on, however, the advertisement, dated May 12, 1818, specifying that the building should be of rectangular form, with a portico on each front, "exhibiting a chaste imitation of Grecian architecture, in its simplest and least expensive form" (*United States Gazette,* July 9, 1818). Besides Latrobe, among the competitors were Mills, Strickland, Godefroy, and Hugh Bridport. Mills submitted a design fronted by six Greek Doric columns; Latrobe went further and proposed an imitation of the octastyle front of the Parthenon itself. His design, preserved in the office of the supervising architect of the Treasury, would seem to have carried the day, for there exists a later plan, reduced in size to meet the demands of the directors, who were alarmed by the threatening general financial conditions. By November a national panic had occurred, and hope for any early beginning of construction was abandoned. Thus it was only after Latrobe's final removal to New Orleans that the undertaking was resumed under the direction of Strickland. Latrobe was justified in saying that the design followed was his, but that the principal room was a departure from it. The cornerstone was laid Apr. 19, 1819; the building was occupied by the Bank from 1824 until the liquidation of 1841, and, since its purchase by the federal government in 1844, has been the Philadelphia Custom House. In it the enthusiasm of American classicism outran corresponding developments abroad. It antedated the European imitations of the Parthenon by a dozen years, and attracted an attention which was international (Kimball, "The Bank of the United States, 1818–24," *Architectural Record,* December 1925).

As early as 1809 Latrobe had been consulted in regard to a water supply for New Orleans, and the next year had sent his son Henry, who had graduated from St. Mary's College in Baltimore, to pursue the project. A year later the legislature of Louisiana granted the Latrobes exclusive privileges for twenty years from May 1813, the date at which it was thought the works could be completed. The war delayed the enterprise and Henry, who had taken part in the defense of the city and had begun the important lighthouse at Franks Island at the mouth of the Mississippi, died of yellow fever in 1817, leaving over $40,000 invested in the unfinished water works. His father determined to go himself to New Orleans. His contract successfully renewed, he brought his family overland early in 1820 and was actively pushing the work to completion when he too was attacked by yellow fever and died, on Sept. 3. As in Philadelphia, the main building of the water works was of excellent classical design, here with a pedimented portico (painting preserved in the Cabildo). Other work which he did in New Orleans included the tower of the Cathedral, erected in

1820. At the time of his death he was in negotiation with Rudolph Ackermann in London for the publication of his designs, but in the end only a single plate appeared, that of the Hall of Representatives in Washington.

Latrobe found architecture in America a polite accomplishment of the gentleman amateurs such as Jefferson, Thornton, and the young Charles Bulfinch, and a part of the business of superior builders and craftsmen such as McIntire, Hoban, and McComb. He left it a profession, with professional standards and practices, largely in the hands of his own pupils. The architect was no longer a dilettante, or a builder expected to contract for the execution of his design and tied to the building for his whole time. The foreign professionals who came before him, Hallet and Hadfield, had been borne under by existing conditions. Latrobe did not accomplish the change without bitter struggles against inertia and misunderstanding, which it took great stamina to overcome; nor without many mortifications to his proud and sensitive spirit. Few American architects before the great organizations of the past generation have had so wide and varied a practice. To compass it at that period meant constant days in the saddle, or coaching by miserable roads, and nights in more miserable ordinaries, where many of the vast mass of his drawings and letters were produced. Apprenticeship in his office constituted the first important professional training in engineering and architecture in America. Frederick Graff [q.v.], who was his pupil and assistant in the first Philadelphia water works, was in charge of their replacement by the remarkable works at Fairmount. Robert Mills and William Strickland, the principal later masters of the Greek revival, learned under him both architecture and engineering. It was his pupils who built the first American railroads. His style continued to dominate American building down to the Civil War.

He was personally accomplished and of most varied attainments. An excellent Latinist and Grecian, he knew also German, French, Spanish, and Italian, and his professional library contained works in all these languages. He drew with great facility and accuracy: many of his water colors of American scenes survive, and his rough pen sketches of important political figures, such as Washington, Edmund Randolph, and Patrick Henry, are of value as likenesses (*Magazine of American History,* August 1881). His reports on engineering and architectural projects are models of technical exposition. In design and construction he had the greatest facility and resource. During the wearisome hours of journeys or of illness—he had contracted malarial fever while on an Alpine expedition at the age of seventeen—he filled his notebooks with scientific observations, genre sketches, and fragments of romances. His scientific and artistic attainments brought him election to the American Philosophical Society (1799) and to the American Antiquarian Society (1815) as well as to the Society of Artists, before which he delivered the anniversary oration of 1811 (*Port Folio,* June 1811).

Portraits of Latrobe are reproduced in *The Journal of Latrobe* and Brown's *History of the United States Capitol (post).* His son described him as "6 feet 2 inches, of erect and military carriage" (Semmes, *post,* p. 6). By his devoted second wife, Mary Elizabeth Hazlehurst, whom he married in Philadelphia, May 2, 1800, he was the founder of a distinguished family. Of his two surviving sons, John Hazlehurst Boneval Latrobe [q.v.] became counsel of the Baltimore & Ohio Railroad, and Benjamin Henry Latrobe [q.v.] became its chief engineer.

[Latrobe's papers still remain chiefly in the hands of his descendants, the largest collection being in the possession of Ferdinand C. Latrobe. Transcripts of letters relating to the Capitol are in the MSS. Div. Lib. of Cong. Other Latrobe material is found in the Henley Smith Papers, Lib. of Cong.; the District of Columbia Papers, Dept. of State; and the papers of the Office of Public Buildings and Grounds, War Dept. (see list in Glenn Brown, *post,* II, 224). Much of this material is published in *Doc. Hist. of the Construction and Development of the U. S. Capitol* (1904). Many of Latrobe's drawings of the Capitol are preserved in the Lib. of Cong., and in the office of the superintendent of the Capitol. Extracts from his diaries and notebooks were published as *The Journal of Latrobe* (1905), with a biographical introduction by J. H. B. Latrobe, written in 1876. See also *Md. Hist. Mag.,* Sept. 1909; *Proc. Am. Inst. of Architects,* Nov. 16, 1881; *International Rev.,* Nov. 1874; *Repository of Arts,* etc. (London), Jan. 1, 1821; Wm. Dunlap, *Hist. of the Rise and Progress of the Arts of Design in the U. S.* (2 vols., 1834); *La. Courier* (New Orleans), Sept. 4, 1820; *Daily National Intelligencer* (Washington), Oct. 2, 1820; *American and Commercial Daily Advertiser* (Baltimore), Oct. 3, 1820; J. E. Semmes, *John H. B. Latrobe and His Times* (1917). Discussions of his relation to the Capitol include those of Peter B. Wight and Adolf Cluss in *Proc. Am. Inst. of Architects,* 1875 and 1876; G. A. Townsend, *Washington Outside and Inside* (1873); Glenn Brown, *Hist. of the U. S. Capitol* (2 vols., 1900–03); W. B. Bryan, *A Hist. of the National Capital* (2 vols., 1914–16); Fiske Kimball, *Thomas Jefferson, Architect* (1916).]

F. K.

LATROBE, BENJAMIN HENRY (Dec. 19, 1806–Oct. 19, 1878), civil engineer, was born at Philadelphia, Pa., the son of Benjamin Henry Latrobe [q.v.] and his second wife, Mary Elizabeth (Hazlehurst). His mother gave him his first schooling, and when he was eight he was placed with his elder brother, John H. B. Latrobe [q.v.], in Georgetown College. In 1817 the father took the family to Baltimore, and soon after that to New Orleans, where in 1820 he died. Returning with his mother to Baltimore, Latrobe attended St. Mary's College as a day student, 1821–23, taking high honors in mathematics. He then read law and practised a short time with his brother before going to Allowaystown, N. J., to act as agent for a parcel of land owned there by his mother and his uncle. Soon forced by ill health to leave Allowaystown, he returned to Baltimore, making his home with his brother and again associating with him in practice. The profession was not to his taste, however, and in 1831, through the influence of his brother, he obtained a position in the engineer corps of the Baltimore & Ohio Railroad.

Advancement was rapid on the new road for men with mathematical training and Benjamin Latrobe was soon principal assistant to Jonathan Knight [q.v.], the chief engineer. In 1832 he was in charge of the survey that located the line from Baltimore to Washington and he later designed and built the outstanding bit of construction of that branch, the Thomas Viaduct at Relay House, nine miles southwest of Baltimore. This stone-arch bridge, named for the first president of the road, was long known as "Latrobe's Folly." It has since been recognized as one of the finest pieces of railroad architecture in the country (Hungerford, *post,* I, 166), and, still in use, is now one of the oldest railroad viaducts in the world, successfully carrying modern equipment. In 1835 Latrobe left the Baltimore & Ohio to become chief engineer of the Baltimore & Port Deposit Railroad, for which he built the thirty-four difficult miles of road from Baltimore to Havre de Grace, Md. The ferries that he employed at Havre de Grace were probably the first of the present type of railroad ferries. Returning then to the Baltimore & Ohio, he directed the survey of the line from Point of Rocks to Harpers Ferry, and as engineer of location and construction (1836), built the road through the mountains from Harpers Ferry to Cumberland. Upon the completion of this part of the road, Knight resigned as chief engineer, Sept. 30, 1842, and Latrobe was appointed to his position.

In 1847 the extension to Wheeling, Va. (W. Va.), on the Ohio River was authorized, and Latrobe with three corps of engineers started in July of that year to lay out the line, completing the survey to the Ohio the next year. The construction of this road was probably his major work. With 5,000 men and 1,250 horses, drilling and loading by hand, blasting with black powder, and hauling with horses, he built 200 miles of road, including 113 bridges and eleven tunnels (one of the longest in the country at the time), in less than four years. The masonry wall construction which still carries the road along the slopes of the hills in the Cheat River Valley and the Kingswood Tunnel (4,100 feet) were the dramatic features of the task. To permit the opening of the line before the completion of the tunnel a temporary line two miles long with a grade of 10 per cent. (528 feet rise in a mile) was built and operated for passenger service for six months (T. C. Clarke, "The Building of a Railway," *Scribner's Magazine,* June 1888). Latrobe next built the Northwestern Virginia Railroad (1851–52) for the Baltimore & Ohio Railroad Company, and in 1871, as chief engineer of the Pittsburg & Connellsville Railroad, he drove the gold spike that completed this road and the Baltimore & Ohio to Pittsburgh. He originated the railroad unit of work, the "ton mile" (*Baltimore & Ohio Annual Report,* 1847), and was the authority for the maximum permissible grade of 116 feet to the mile, prescribed in the charters of the transcontinental railroads; he indorsed the proposal of the Magnetic Telegraph Company to lay the first line of the Morse telegraph along the Washington Branch of the Baltimore & Ohio; and he was a member of the committee to which Roebling submitted the plans of the Brooklyn Bridge. He retired from the railroad in 1875, and died at Baltimore three years later, after a short illness.

On Mar. 12, 1833, at Salem, N. J., he married a cousin, Maria Eleanor Hazlehurst. They were the parents of five children, one of whom, Charles Hazlehurst Latrobe [q.v.], attained distinction in his father's profession.

[J. E. Semmes, *John H. B. Latrobe and His Times* (1917); various reports by Latrobe, in Lib. of Cong.; Paul Winchester, *The Baltimore & Ohio Railroad,* vol. I (1927); Edward Hungerford, *The Story of the Baltimore & Ohio Railroad, 1827–1927* (1928), vol. I; C. B. Stuart, *Lives and Works of Civil and Military Engineers of America* (1871); *Railway Age,* Oct. 31, 1878; *Railroad Gazette,* Oct. 25, 1878; *Sun* (Baltimore), Oct. 21, 1878.]   F. A. T.

LATROBE, CHARLES HAZLEHURST (Dec. 25, 1834–Sept. 19, 1902), civil engineer, was born in Baltimore, the eldest of the five children of Benjamin Henry Latrobe, the second [q.v.], and his wife, Maria Eleanor Hazlehurst. He attended St. Mary's College, in his native city, learned the rudiments of his profession in his father's office—which was probably the best school of its kind in the United States —and graduated thence into the service of the Baltimore & Ohio Railroad. A few years later he went to Florida as the youthful but very capable chief engineer in charge of construction on the Pensacola & Georgia Railroad. Stationed at Tallahassee when the state seceded from the Union, he promptly threw in his lot with the South and, as a lieutenant of engineers in the Confederate army, completed the grading, bridge-building, and rail-laying on the last twenty miles of the Pensacola & Georgia. The road proved of considerable military use. At the close of the war Latrobe returned to Baltimore, which was his home for the rest of his life. From 1866 to 1877 he was associated with his father and with Charles Shaler Smith in the Baltimore Bridge Company. This firm erected bridges in many parts of the eastern United States. Latrobe's own work, which was of a high order, was noted especially for its structural beauty. He was appointed engineer of the Jones Falls commission in Baltimore in 1875, when his cousin, Ferdinand Claiborne Latrobe, entered on his first term as mayor of the city; and he remained in the city employ until 1889. He designed and built the great retaining walls along the Falls and designed and constructed the iron bridges across the valley at St. Paul Street, Calvert Street, and Guilford Avenue. He built a number of other bridges in Baltimore, laid out the terraced gardens along Mount Royal Avenue, and was in charge of the improvements and extensions in Mount Royal, Druid Hill, and Patterson parks. He also executed several commissions for the Peruvian government. At Arequipa he constructed an aqueduct 1,300 feet long and sixty-five feet high; and at Verrugas, on the Callao-Oroya-Huancayo railway, he built the most famous of his bridges. Spanning one of the deepest gorges in the Andes, it was 575 feet in length and had a central wrought-iron pier 252 feet high. It was said to be the tallest bridge in the world. It was framed in the United States, then taken apart for shipment, and was reërected in ninety days. During his latter years Latrobe was consulting engineer for several railroads. He was married three times: in 1861 to a widow, Letitia Breckenridge (Gamble) Holliday, who bore him two daughters and a son and died in 1867; in 1869 to Rosa Wirt Robinson, who died the next year; and in 1881 to Louise, widow of Isaac McKim. Latrobe possessed the engaging social qualities as well as the engineering and artistic genius of his family. He died in Baltimore after an illness of a year and was buried in Greenmount Cemetery.

[*Baltimore American*, Sept. 20, 22, 1902; the *Sun* (Baltimore), Sept. 20, 21, 1902; *War of the Rebellion: Official Records* (*Army*), 4 ser. I, 777–79; *Baltimore: Its Hist. and Its People* (1912), II, 400–02; J. E. Semmes, *John H. B. Latrobe and his Times 1803–91* (1917).]   G. H. G.

LATROBE, JOHN HAZLEHURST BONEVAL (May 4, 1803–Sept. 11, 1891), lawyer, inventor, public servant, was the elder son of Benjamin H. Latrobe [*q.v.*], and Mary Elizabeth (Hazlehurst) Latrobe. He was born in Philadelphia, but, with his brother Benjamin [*q.v.*], received his earlier educational training at Georgetown College in the District of Columbia and at St. Mary's College, Baltimore. Expecting to become an architect, he spent the years 1818–21 as a cadet at West Point, then the only school of engineering in the country, but resigned upon the death of his father shortly before the end of his fourth year. Returning to Baltimore, he entered the law office of Robert Goodloe Harper [*q.v.*], and was admitted to the bar in 1824. While waiting for his law practice, he pressed into service his talent as writer and artist to increase the meager income of the family. Under the pseudonym of Godfrey Wallace he made a yearly contribution to *The Atlantic Souvenir*, Mathew Carey's gift annual; in 1826 he published *The Justices' Practice under the Laws of Maryland,* begun at the suggestion of a Baltimore editor during his student days; to John Sanderson's *Biography of the Signers to the Declaration of Independence* (vol. VII, 1827) he contributed the sketch of Charles Carroll.

In 1827 he helped to draft the charter of the Baltimore & Ohio Railroad and the following year was retained by the road to secure its right of way from Point of Rocks to Williamsport, Md., services which marked his establishment in his profession. From that time until his death he was connected with the Baltimore & Ohio, and he attained wide recognition as a railroad lawyer. In 1857–58 while visiting Europe he was successful in securing from the Czar of Russia allowance for claims for a railroad from St. Petersburg to Moscow, for which he received the princely fee of $60,000. He argued many important cases in the state and federal supreme courts, and was in special demand as a patent lawyer, partly because of the engineering training he had received at West Point. His technical understanding enabled him to recognize at once the value of the Morse telegraph, and to recommend it to the president of the Baltimore & Ohio Railroad, who granted Morse the privilege of stringing the first line between Baltimore and Washington along the railroad's right of way. In response to his wife's complaint that the stoves in use claimed too much space he devised the popular Latrobe stove, to fit into the fireplace and heat not only the room in which it was installed but also the room above. It was characteristic of him that he shrank from taking credit for this useful invention, thinking it not in accord with the dignity of his profession, for although he continued to act in patent cases throughout his career, he desired to be known first as a master of legal principles. At the age of eighty-six he revised and published the eighth edition of his *Justices' Practices,* which he had begun before his admission to the bar.

Throughout his life Latrobe wielded pencil and brush with such enthusiasm that he filled his home with his works. From time to time he ventured into literature, noteworthy among his writings being *The Baltimore & Ohio Railroad: Personal Recollections* (1868); *Odds and Ends* (1876), a slight volume of poems printed for private circulation, which contained verses of grace and some merit; and *Reminiscences of West Point* (1887). In 1825 he produced the winning design for the Kościuszko monument at West Point. He also designed a number of other monuments, several structures for the Baltimore parks, and the "Baltimore Cottages" at White Sulphur Springs. It is perhaps as a patron, however, that he made a more permanent contribution to the arts. Inspired by the Franklin Institute at Philadelphia, he founded the Maryland Institute for the Promotion of the Mechanic Arts (chartered 1825), with which he kept his connection for years. He served the Academy of Art as its president before its absorption into the Peabody Institute. He was one of a committee which awarded a prize to Edgar Allan Poe for "A MS. Found in a Bottle," and a prize for a clay model to the sculptor Rinehart.

In the field of philanthropy his most conspicuous service was given to the cause of African colonization. While still in the office of General Harper he prepared the first map of Liberia for the American Colonization Society, of which his preceptor was an active leader. He was instrumental in getting a state appropriation for transportation of emigrants, helped to found the Maryland State Colonization Society, and drafted the constitution for the separate colony of Maryland in Liberia at Cape Palmas. In 1853 he was elected to succeed Henry Clay as president of the national society, in which post he continued thirty-seven years. He was one of two Americans invited by the King of the Belgians in 1876 to represent the United States at the first meeting of the International Association for the Exploration and Colonisation of Central Africa, and became the president of the American branch of that society. He rendered

other public services as member of the Board of Visitors of the United States Military Academy, regent for the University of Maryland, founder and almost life president (1871–91) of the Maryland Historical Society, member of the Park Commission to which Baltimore owes Druid Hill Park; member of the Board of the Centennial Exposition at Philadelphia. He was repeatedly selected to deliver addresses on significant public occasions.

He was married twice: on Nov. 29, 1828, to Margaret Stuart of Baltimore, who died two years later, leaving one child; and on Dec. 6, 1832, to Charlotte Virginia Claiborne of Mississippi, by whom he had seven children. His son Ferdinand Claiborne Latrobe (1833–1911) was seven times mayor of Baltimore (*Who's Who in America,* 1910–11). Latrobe's friends knew him as a gentle, courteous, wonderfully vigorous man, whose clearness of perception, versatility, systematic precision, and prodigious industry enabled him to march through his manifold labors with military discipline. Active almost to the end, he died at his home in Baltimore in his eighty-ninth year.

[See J. E. Semmes, *John H. B. Latrobe and His Times* (1917); *Baltimore American* and *Baltimore Sun,* Sept. 12, 1891; M. P. Andrews, *Tercentenary Hist. of Md.* (1925); *Baltimore: Its Hist. and Its People* (1912), vol. II; G. W. Howard, *The Monumental City* (1873); C. W. Sams and E. S. Riley, *The Bench and Bar of Md.* (1901); H. E. Shepherd, *The Representative Authors of Md.* (1911); R. H. Spencer, *Geneal. and Memorial Encyc. of the State of Md.* (1919), vol. II; *Proc. Md. Hist. Soc. in Commemoration of the Late Hon. John H. B. Latrobe* (1891); Paul Winchester, *The Baltimore and Ohio Railroad,* vol. I (1927); Edward Hungerford, *The Story of the Baltimore and Ohio Railroad* (1928), vol. I. Some of Latrobe's papers are deposited with the Md. Hist. Soc. as the Latrobe and Semmes Papers, but others are still in the possession of the family.]   E. L.

LATTA, ALEXANDER BONNER (June 11, 1821–Apr. 28, 1865), inventor, manufacturer, was born on a farm near Chillicothe, Ross County, Ohio, the youngest of the six children of John and Rebecca (Bonner) Latta. When he was five years old his father was killed in an accident, leaving his widow penniless. Consequently, after attending the country school for a few winters, the boy was obliged, at the age of ten, to go to work in a cotton factory; subsequently he became an apprentice in a machine shop. Becoming an expert machinist, he settled in Cincinnati, Ohio, in the early forties, where he was foreman in the Harkness machine shop. In 1845, under his directions, the first locomotive west of the Alleghany Mountains was built and had its trial trip from Cincinnati to Columbus and return, Latta acting as engineer. Subsequently, he designed and built a locomotive for the Boston & Maine Railroad. This machine had an extra pair of steam cylinders under the water tank, the steam being taken back and the exhaust being brought forward again through pipes fitted with ball joints. Between 1847 and the time of his death he secured a number of patents for improvements on steam engines, boilers, and locomotives, but by far his greatest inventive and manufacturing work was concerned with the development of the steam fire engine. He completed his first engine in 1852 and sold it to Cincinnati, the first city in the United States to adopt the steamer as a part of its fire-department apparatus. Latta's engines were designed to be drawn by men or horses, but he perfected, also, a self-propelled machine. One of his patents for the latter type was granted May 22, 1855, Patent No. 12,912 (*Senate Executive Document No. 20, 34* Cong., 1 Sess.). It consisted of a three-wheeled chassis, the rear wheels being connected by rods to the same steam cylinders which furnished power to the water pumps. Upon arrival at the scene of a fire the engine was raised off the ground and supported by means of screws on the sides of the boiler, so that the rear wheels might be used as flywheels. The boiler in Latta's fire engines was constructed of two square chambers, one within the other, the space between being the steam and water space. The inner chamber, which was the firebox, was filled with a series of horizontal layers of tubes arranged diagonally over each other but forming one continuous coil. The water entered this coil at the lower end and passed upward into the annular area, where it was evaporated. As his business developed, he formed a partnership with his brother, and by 1858 six out of the seven horse-drawn fire engines in Cincinnati had been made by them. They built all told about thirty, the last, in 1860, were ordered for the cities of Nashville and Memphis, Tenn. These were not delivered until the Federal troops were in full control there. For his fire-engine improvements Latta was awarded a gold medal by the Ohio Mechanics Institute Fair in 1854. He retired from active business in 1862, but was engaged in inventive work at the time of his death. He was married to Elizabeth Ann Pawson of Cincinnati in 1847, and was survived by two children. His death occurred in Ludlow, Ky.

[Patent Office records; *Scientific Artisan* (Cincinnati), Oct. 21, 1858; E. W. Byrn, *The Progress of Invention in the Nineteenth Century* (1900); H. A. and K. B. Ford, *Hist. of Cincinnati, Ohio* (1881), pp. 328, 386; *The Great Industries of the U. S.* (1872); *Cincinnati Daily Commercial*, Apr. 29, 1865; family records.]
C. W. M.

LATTIMORE, WILLIAM (Feb. 9, 1774–Apr. 3, 1843), physician, delegate to Congress from Mississippi, was born near Norfolk, Va., the son of Charles Lattimore. He and his brother, David, attended medical school and in 1801 settled at Natchez, Mississippi Territory. The brothers soon built up a thriving practice and Governor Claiborne put them in charge of the smallpox camp during the epidemic of 1801. They were able to persuade many of the people to submit to vaccination and thus soon had the malady under control. After a residence of less than a year in Natchez, William Lattimore moved to the eastern part of Wilkinson County, now known as Amite. He became interested in politics and was appointed to the territorial council by President Jefferson in 1802. The following year he was elected territorial delegate to Congress. Governor Claiborne describes him at this time as "a young man of promising Talents, & *a firm* & Genuine *republican*." In 1805 he was reëlected, but George Poindexter defeated him in 1807, and Lattimore retired to his medical practice feeling that as delegate he had received "but little of the support which I expected from the territory." In 1813 he again represented the territory in Congress, was reëlected in 1815, and served until 1817, when Mississippi became a state. He then returned to his home and represented his county in the constitutional convention.

The most important problem with which he was concerned while in Congress was the controversy over the division of the Mississippi Territory in preparation for statehood. The inhabitants along the Mississippi River wished to have the entire territory admitted as a state, while those along the Tombigbee insisted that the territory be divided into a western and an eastern state. Lattimore was at first an anti-divisionist, but when he saw that there was little possibility that the Senate would permit the creation of so large a state, he pointed out the desirability of the formation of two states and proposed that the boundary line be drawn in such a way as to give Mobile and the mouth of the Tombigbee to the western state. The inhabitants of the eastern portion of the territory strenuously objected to this and demanded the Pascagoula River as a boundary. Lattimore proposed a compromise boundary which was accepted and is the present division between Mississippi and Alabama. In this matter Lattimore had fairly represented the whole of the territory, but the people in the western section denounced the compromise, as it involved the surrender of Mobile, their only port. As a result Lattimore was not reëlected and he was never able to regain his popularity. He entered the campaign for governor against Walter Leake, in 1823, but was defeated. His last service to his state was in 1821, when he was appointed one of three commissioners to choose a site for the seat of the state government. This commission selected a location on the Pearl River near the center of the state, to which the legislature gave the name Jackson, the present capital of the state. Lattimore died at his home in Amite County, Apr. 3, 1843. He was twice married. His first wife was Cecilia (Lea) Lattimore; his second wife was Sabrina Lattimore who survived him.

[J. F. H. Claiborne, *Miss. as a Province, Territory and State*, vol. I (1880); Dunbar Rowland, ed., *Official Letter Books of W. C. C. Claiborne* (1917), vol. I, and *Miss. Territorial Archives, 1798–1803*, vol. I (1905); F. L. Riley, "Location of the Boundaries of Mississippi," *Pubs. Miss. Hist. Soc.*, vol. III (1900); newspapers in the Dept. of Archives and History of the state government, Jackson, Miss.]　　R. H. M.

LAUDONNIÈRE, RENÉ GOULAINE de (fl. 1562–1582), a French Huguenot who was sent to establish a colony in Florida, is little known except for the narratives of his expedition. He was of a noble family of Poitou and had apparently seen service in the navy (Le Moyne, Perkins translation, *post*, p. 4). In 1562, Admiral Coligny, head of the French Huguenot party, determined to found a colony in the New World. Since he was then in favor at Court, he persuaded the King to allow him to send out several shiploads of colonists under the charge of Jean Ribaut [*q.v.*], whom Laudonnière accompanied as his lieutenant. Entering St. John's River, Florida, early in June, the expedition moved up the coast and settled at the present Port Royal, S. C., naming their colony Charlesfort. Then Ribaut and Laudonnière returned to France, where they entered the port of Dieppe July 20, 1562. The religious wars in France and perhaps other matters hindered Coligny from sending aid to his colony in 1563, but in April 1564 Laudonnière was sent out with three ships and three hundred colonists. Meanwhile, however, the settlers at Charlesfort, having become discouraged, had killed their commander, built a ship, and set sail for France. Learning that the settlement was abandoned, Laudonnière decided to found a colony on St. John's River, then called Rivière de May, where he built Fort Caroline, named for King Charles IX.

Although the French were kindly received by the Indians of the region, Laudonnière forfeited the friendship of their chief by establishing relations with an enemy chief who had access to a supply of gold. Dissensions within the colony arose when rations were reduced, and when the nobles in the group protested against the labor required of them. Some threescore mutineers, with two barques, sailed for the Spanish colonies. Most of them were captured by the Spaniards; a few returned to Fort Caroline, where Laudonnière promptly hanged the ringleaders. In spite of all these difficulties, however, the fort was maintained for over a year. On Aug. 3, 1565, the fleet of Sir John Hawkins entered the river. Laudonnière, his colony sadly reduced by famine, gave Hawkins four pieces of artillery and a supply of ammunition in exchange for a vessel in which to take his people home. They were ready to sail on Aug. 15, but were delayed by contrary winds. Meanwhile Ribaut had been sent to their aid with a large fleet and many supplies. His ships were sighted Aug. 28 and arrived Aug. 29, bearing orders for Laudonnière to return to France, to reply to criticisms of his care of his colony. Before he could sail, a Spanish fleet appeared off the coast and Ribaut with most of the able-bodied men sailed in pursuit, leaving Fort Caroline almost defenseless. On Sept. 20, a Spanish force under Menendez came overland from St. Augustine, fell upon the fort, and massacred most of the inhabitants. Laudonnière, although wounded, escaped, made his way to one of Ribaut's ships, and sailed for Europe. After being wrecked and cast ashore in Wales, he finally reached France in January 1566. Coldly received by the royal authorities, he retired to his estates, where he lived quietly, engaged in writing an account of the expeditions to Florida. It was published under the title *L'Histoire notable de la Floride* (Paris, 1586), after the author's death.

In Laudonnière's company was an artist, Jacques Le Moyne, whose drawings of natives and animals are among the best and earliest made of the New World. Le Moyne thus characterizes his chief: "of varied abilities, though experienced not so much in military as in naval affairs ... a man too easily influenced by others" (Perkins translation, *post*, pp. 1, 4). His mistakes were due to his lack of judgment and the poor quality of the colonists whom he took with him; his misfortunes were the result of international jealousies, for which he was not responsible.

[Laudonnière's *Histoire notable de la Floride*, ed. in 1586 by Basanier, translated by Richard Hakluyt, and published as *A Notable Historie Containing Foure Voyages Made by Certayne French Captaynes into Florida* (1587) and reprinted in the second edition of Hakluyt's *Principal Navigations, Voyages*, etc. (vol. III, 1600). This translation appears in B. F. French, *Hist. Colls. of La. and Fla.*, n.s. I (1869), 165–362. Jacques Le Moyne's *Brevis Narratio*, etc. (1591), was published as pt. II of Theodore de Bry's series, *Collectio Peregrinationum* or Great Voyages, and has been translated into English by F. B. Perkins, under the title *Narrative of Le Moyne* (1875), and into French by C. G. M. B. de La Roncière, as *La Floride Française* (1928). Le Moyne's drawings and part of Laudonnière's text, modernized, appear in L. Ningler, *Voyages en Virginie et en Floride* (1927). The original of Le Moyne's engraving of the Indians worshiping Ribaut's column was found in 1901 in a château near Paris; the French officer is thought to be Laudonnière. See Jeannette T. Connor, in *Jean Ribaut, The Whole & True Discoverye of Terra Florida* (Fla. State Hist. Soc., 1927). A good modern account is that of Francis Parkman, in *Pioneers of France in the New World* (1865).]

L. P. K.

LAUNITZ, ROBERT EBERHARD SCHMIDT VON DER (Nov. 4, 1806–Dec. 13, 1870), sculptor, was born in Riga, Russia, and came to the United States about 1828. One of his five brothers was a bishop, one a field-marshal, and three were generals. Robert received an excellent classical and military education and was intended for the army, but his native inclination was toward art. As a young man he went to Rome, where one of his uncles, a sculptor, was employed. He studied at first with his uncle, and later, for four years, under Thorvaldsen. On arriving in New York, he was seriously handicapped. Though talented and agreeable, he was friendless. He could speak Russian, German, French, Italian, and Spanish, but knew very little English. As a result of Roman fever, he was deaf. Thus circumstanced, he was glad to work as journeyman for John Frazee [*q.v.*], then in the marble business in New York City. With far more education in art than his employer, he soon became indispensable. In 1831 they formed a partnership, and Launitz's name appeared in the city directory as sculptor, 591 Broadway. His knowledge of European languages enabled him to employ and train the best of the foreign carvers arriving as immigrants, and he therefore played an important part in developing the carving industry in this country. He turned out excellent workmen. Under him, Thomas Crawford [*q.v.*] learned to handle the chisel. After Frazee received the commission for the New York Custom House (1839), Launitz took entire charge of the Broadway shop. All his life he was artist rather than business man and in his contracts often underestimated costs. His gains were at times so meager that to eke out a living, he turned small objects in alabaster.

His gifts and training won him a welcome among the artists. In 1833 he was made a member of the National Academy of Design on his bas-relief, "Venus and Cupid." For many years his output from the marble shop was confined to mantelpieces, gravestones, and the like. His first outstanding public work, the memorial portrait statue of Charlotte Canda, in Greenwood Cemetery (1845), together with his New York Firemen's monument, also in Greenwood, brought him wide recognition. Other large cemeteries ordered his designs; these his rivals often pirated in meaner material and workmanship. In 1848 the Kentucky legislature contracted with him for a fifteen-thousand-dollar monument "to those who had fallen in defense of their country." This tribute, placed in the center of the "Bivouac of the Dead," in the State Cemetery, Frankfort, Ky., was a female figure of War, sixty-two feet high, carved in Italian marble. It cost Launitz $17,500, but with characteristic probity, he chose to abide by his contract and declined the $2,500 proffered by the legislature to reimburse him. His last important monument was the statue of Pulaski, erected in Savannah, Ga. (1854). At the close of the Civil War, Launitz found it impossible to compete successfully with the mushroom monument firms scattering stone soldiers from coast to coast, and his influence declined.

[*Coll. of Monuments and Headstones, Designed by R. E. Launitz, N. Y.* (L. Prang and Company, 1866); Truman H. Bartlett, "Early Settler Memorials," *Am. Architect and Building News*, Aug. 6, Sept. 3, 1887; Clara Erskine Clement Waters and Laurence Hutton, *Artists of the Nineteenth Century* (1885); *N. Y. Daily Tribune*, Dec. 14, 1870.]

A. A.

LAURANCE, JOHN (1750–Nov. 11, 1810), Revolutionary soldier, judge and United States senator, was born near Falmouth, England, and emigrated to New York in 1767. He studied law in the office of Lieutenant-Governor Colden and was admitted to the bar in 1772. In spite of this environment of his law-student days he married, probably in 1774 or early in 1775, Elizabeth, daughter of the flaming patriot, Alexander Macdougall [*q.v.*]. In 1775–76 he was second lieutenant in one of the regiments, raised by the Provincial Congress for Continental service, which participated in the Canada expedition. On the promotion of Macdougall to the rank of brigadier-general in August 1776, Laurance was appointed as his aide-de-camp and thus saw service in the actions in the vicinity of New York. On Apr. 11, 1777, he succeeded William Tudor as judge advocate-general on the staff of the Commander-in-Chief, and this position he held till June 1782. It was said that his record was one of "great uprightness, diligence and ability, by which he has acquired the esteem of the army and merited the consideration of his country" (*Journals of the Continental Congress*, Nov. 9, 1780). At the trial of André it was admitted by all that he combined competent performance of his duty in preparing and conducting the case against the prisoner with the dictates of "humanity and sensibility."

After the war his civil career in New York was active and varied. He made an excellent reputation for legal learning. He was associated with Robert R. Livingston in the movement to provide a water supply for the city, and in 1784 he was elected vestryman of Trinity Church and trustee of Columbia College. Political preferment also came to him. He was delegate to the Congress of the Confederation, 1785–87, and served in the state Senate, 1788–90. Owing to his handsome and dignified presence and enthusiastically Federalist sympathies, his selection, with John Cozine and Robert Troup, as bearer of the Constitution in the grand procession of July 23, 1788, preceding the ratification of that instrument, was altogether appropriate. He became New York City's "first Congressman," receiving an overwhelming vote from the city and Westchester County in the election to the House of Representatives. In the constructive activity of the First and Second congresses, 1789–93, he took a conspicuous part, to the effectiveness of which tribute was paid by the harsh comments in the diary of William Maclay. He is said to have been urged by Washington to accept the appointment, May 6, 1794, as judge of the United States district court because of his reputation in admiralty law. He held the position until Nov. 8, 1796. Upon this date he was elected to the United States Senate as successor to his friend and associate, Rufus King, retaining his seat in this body until his resignation in August 1800. The whole of his successful career in national politics is thus coincident with the period of Federalist dominance.

Laurance's first wife died on Aug. 16, 1790, and on June 30, 1791, he was married to Elizabeth Lawrence, widow of James Allen, of Philadelphia. To the children of these two marriages he left what was in those times a substantial fortune. His real estate included, besides extensive holdings in the interior of New York state, part of the D. M. Clarkson property in the city, purchased in 1784 in association with Rufus King, and a summer residence in Newark, N. J. He was reputed to be especially careful in all matters affecting title to real estate. He appears to have been a director of the Bank of the United States in 1794 (*The Life and Correspondence of Rufus King*, I, 540–41) and may also have been a director of the New York branch. After a stroke of paralysis in 1809, followed by partial recovery, he died in New York, Nov. 11, 1810.

[There is a sketch of Laurance by G. C. McWhorter in the library of the N. Y. Hist. Soc. For printed sources see: Richard Hildreth, *The Hist. of the U. S.*, 2 ser. II (1851) ; *Biog. Dir. Am. Cong.* (1928) ; E. A. Werner, *Civil List and Constitutional Hist. of the Colony and State of N. Y.* (1889) ; *N. Y. Geneal. and Biog. Record*, Jan. 1880 ; C. R. King, *The Life and Correspondence of Rufus King* (6 vols., 1894–1900), in which the subject's name is spelled *Laurance*; J. C. Hamilton, *The Works of Alexander Hamilton*, vol. VI (1851) ; C. P. Keith, *The Provincial Councillors of Pa.* (1883), p. 451 ; *Calendar of N. Y. Colonial MSS. Endorsed Land Papers* (1864) ; E. S. Maclay, *Jour. of Wm. Maclay* (1890) ; *Commercial Advertiser* (N. Y.), Nov. 12, 1810. The spelling of Laurance's name follows manuscript signatures in the Library of the N. Y. Hist. Soc.] C. W. S.

LAURENS, HENRY (Mar. 6, 1724–Dec. 8, 1792), merchant, planter, Revolutionary statesman, came from pure Huguenot stock. His grandfather, André Laurens, fled from Rochelle in 1682 at the beginning of the persecutions, settled for a while in England and Ireland, then emigrated to New York City, and finally moved to Charleston, S. C., shortly before his death about 1715. His son, Jean Samuel, later called John, married in New York Hester or Esther Grasset, who also came from a Huguenot refugee family. Henry, the third of their six children and their eldest son, was born at Charleston. John Laurens became a saddler, building up the largest business of its kind in the colony, and bequeathing a considerable estate to Henry as his residuary legatee upon his death in 1747. Henry received the best education available in the colony, deficient in the classics, but well suited to the needs of a colonial gentleman-merchant. In 1744 he was sent to London by his father, in order to receive further commercial training and to make business contacts. Three years later, a letter offering him a partnership in a London commercial house missed him by five hours at Portsmouth, perhaps thus altering his whole career. When he returned to England after settling his father's estate, the vacant position had been filled and Laurens accepted instead a Charleston partnership with George Austin, later joined by George Appleby. This firm, conducting a general commission business, became one of the most active in the important South Carolina trade, and when it was dissolved in 1762, Laurens continued alone as probably the leading merchant of Charleston.

The business consisted mainly of exporting rice, deerskins, and indigo, and importing wine, slaves, and indentured servants. Probably the most common form of trade was the exchange of rice for slaves. The firm occasionally undertook ventures of its own, but in general it handled transactions for others, charging a commission of five per cent. on all but the "Guinea business" in slaves, which paid double that amount. Laurens finally withdrew from this last phase of the business, almost apologizing for his humanitarian motives. Most of the firm's trade was with London, Liverpool, and Bristol, but from time to time, Laurens also had correspondents in Glasgow, Rotterdam, Oporto, Lisbon, Madrid, and in the British, French, and Spanish West Indies. He owned a part interest in several vessels, but the southern colonies as a whole were far behind the northern in ship-building and ship-owning. After 1764 he gradually withdrew from the commission business, though still continuing some of his mercantile operations. His interest shifted to the acquiring and managing of plantations. He doubtless hoped to strengthen his already secure social position by becoming a landed proprietor. His principal holding was "Mepkin," a beautiful three-thousand-acre estate on the Cooper River some thirty miles above Charleston, where he raised rice and indigo. He raised indigo also on his "Mt. Tacitus" and "Wambaw" estates in the Santee region. He owned several rice plantations on the Georgia coast and a large unsettled tract around Ninety Six in the back country of Carolina. His entire holdings totaled some 20,000 acres and were becoming very profitable at the outbreak of the Revolution.

The year 1764 marks a turning point in Laurens' life. The previous twenty years had been spent almost entirely in overseas commerce, a field for which he was eminently adapted; during the next twenty years, he not only became a planter, but he also became increasingly involved in the preliminaries and events of the Revolution. At forty he was one of the wealthy men of the province. Short and rather swarthy in appearance, he looked "aggressive and just a bit cock-sure." His health was good, but later he was tortured with recurrent visitations of gout. His personal morality was unquestioned and he was a strong "family man." He enjoyed a high reputation for business sagacity and honesty. He had keen insight, great ingenuity, methodical habits, and unusual industry, frequently rising before dawn to handle his correspondence. He was a merciful creditor, never imprisoning and seldom suing for debt, though he was strict with the slack and the slippery. He was a humane and considerate slave-owner. On several occasions he showed great personal courage in taking an unpopular stand. He had, however, some less fortunate qualities. He lacked a genial and expansive nature, except possibly with social intimates. He was inclined to be self-satisfied, self-righteous, and sensitive about his dignity and honor. He could be brusque and insolent on occasion. Though he generally maintained strong self-control, he sometimes showed a merciless sarcasm with tongue or pen

in debate or pamphlet dispute. More than once he became involved in duels, in which he refused to fire a shot. It was his misfortune that his public services in the Revolutionary period were more in the legislative and diplomatic field, where the less amiable qualities of his nature often handicapped him, than in executive, administrative positions for which he was so well adapted (Wallace, *post*, p. 432). His public career had started before 1764. He was elected to the provincial Commons House of Assembly in 1757 and was reëlected regularly, with one exception, from that time until the Revolution. In 1764 he declined a seat in the provincial Council on the ground that it was being degraded by the inclusion of royal placemen. He served as a lieutenant-colonel of militia against the Cherokees in 1761 and supported the colonel of British regulars in his subsequent quarrel with the militia colonel.

Laurens naturally became involved in the problems which strained Anglo-American relations in the decade before the Revolution. Then, as later, he took a middle ground between the radicals like Gadsden and the conservatives who favored little if any action. He believed in an attitude of "constitutional stubbornness" against the policy of the British ministry, but he feared the colonial mob element. This feeling was strengthened during the Stamp Act crisis when an armed mob searched his Charleston home, seeking the stamps, in spite of his contemptuous defiance. He declared that he never knowingly violated the Navigation Acts, but when the royal customs officials seized two of his vessels on frivolous technical charges, he tweaked the nose of the collector of customs and challenged Leigh, the apparently corrupt vice-admiralty judge, to a duel, justifying his conduct in a pamphlet full of incisive invective. (See *Extracts from the Proceedings of the High Court of Vice-Admiralty in Charleston, in 1767 and 1768*, 1769, and *An Appendix to the Extracts*, etc., 1769.) He approved of South Carolina's non-importation agreement of July 3, 1769, in opposition to the Townshend Acts, and supported the action of the provincial Assembly in sending money for the support of John Wilkes. He had married "the beautiful Eleanor Ball," daughter of Elias Ball, on July 6, 1750, and she had borne him at least a dozen children, only four of whom reached maturity, before her death in 1770. Their daughter Martha married David Ramsay [*q.v.*] and their daughter Eleanor married Gen. Charles Pinckney [*q.v.*]. In 1771 Laurens went to London for three years for the education of his sons John [*q.v.*] and Henry. Residing at Westminster, and associating chiefly with merchants, he used every opportunity for arguing in the interests of South Carolina and the other colonies. He became thoroughly disgusted with the corruption of the English ruling classes and removed his sons to schools in the stricter atmosphere of Geneva.

Late in 1774 he returned to America, arriving at Charleston in December. Four weeks later he was elected to the first Provincial Congress. His ability and standing gave him a commanding position in the province. He quickly became president of the executive General Committee, and in June 1775 he succeeded Charles Pinckney as president of the first Provincial Congress. In that position he boldly denounced the proposed persecution of those who would not sign the "Association." Later in June he became president of the powerful Council of Safety. In November 1775 he was in the second Provincial Congress. He was president of the second Council of Safety and a member of the so-called "dictatorship committee." In February 1776 he helped to draft South Carolina's temporary constitution and became vice-president when John Rutledge was elected president. He took a very active part in the successful defense of Charleston against the British attack in June 1776 and did what he could to avert the bitter civil war which threatened to break out in the Carolinas.

The following year, he moved from the provincial to the national sphere of politics. Elected to the Continental Congress on Jan. 10, 1777, he took his seat on July 22 and was soon actively engaged on several important committees. He was unanimously elected to succeed John Hancock as president of the Congress on Nov. 1, 1777, holding that office until Dec. 9, 1778. The Congress was at a low ebb during much of that time. The active membership at times was barely fifteen. Yet, small as it was, it was torn with factions. Laurens, racked with gout and sometimes working twenty hours a day, remained partly but not completely above these cliques, tending at times to side with the Adams-Lee group. He was active in securing the suspension of the Saratoga Convention on Jan. 8, 1778, angered at Burgoyne's charges of broken faith and hoping to force Parliament into recognizing Congress as a sovereign body. In the Conway Cabal, he exposed some of the plotting and strongly supported Washington, though he was accused, apparently falsely, of favoring Gates at the outset. He was skeptical of the motives of the French, calling them "artful specious half friends" (Wallace, *post,* p. 276), but he fully realized the value of the alliance. He did not

favor, however, leaning too heavily on French loans. When the British sent the fruitless peace commission of 1778, Laurens was unsuccessfully approached with a letter from his British merchant friend, Richard Oswald. Laurens descended to partisan levels in the controversy between Silas Deane and Arthur Lee, arising from the mission to France. He sided with Lee, supporting the recall of Deane and treating him with suspicion upon his arrival. Angered at Deane's appeal to the public, which he considered an affront to the dignity of Congress and himself, he moved to suspend hearings with Deane pending a committee investigation. The motion failed and Laurens resigned his presidency on Dec. 9, 1778, declaring his disapproval of "the manner in which business is transacted here." His friends failed to reinstate him and the presidency fell to his opponent, John Jay.

Laurens continued in Congress for another eleven months. He rose above provincial lines in 1779 when he urged continuation of the war until fishing rights off Newfoundland should be granted; and he advocated a constitutional convention. At the same time, he descended to lower partisan levels. He suspiciously investigated the semi-official commercial dealings of Robert Morris; he also quarreled with his young colleague Drayton. He barely escaped a vote of censure when the British published his captured letter to the governor of Georgia, referring to the "venality, peculation and fraud" in the government. Finally, he was elected to negotiate a loan of $10,000,000 and a treaty of amity and commerce with the Dutch. He left Congress for Charleston on Nov. 9, 1779, after more than two years in that body. The impending British attack on Charleston prevented his sailing from there, and he finally set out from Philadelphia on Aug. 13, 1780, in the little brigantine *Mercury.* Three weeks later she was captured off Newfoundland by the British, who fished out of the sea a sack of papers which Laurens had thrown overboard too late. Among these was the Lee-Van Berkel draft of a projected treaty with Holland, which served as a pretext for the British declaration of war on the Dutch (Dec. 20, 1780).

Laurens was taken to England and, after a trying meeting with the ministers, was confined in the Tower of London on Oct. 6, 1780, remaining there until Dec. 31, 1781. His claims to diplomatic immunity were ignored, and his status as a state prisoner on suspicion of high treason prevented his exchange as a military prisoner of war. His treatment seems to have been unnecessarily harsh at times; his health was poor, and he was charged for rent, living, and even for the wages of his warders. He was able to smuggle out frequent communications to the "rebel press." He resisted the efforts of British friends to seduce him from his American allegiance, in spite of threats of hanging, but he felt completely neglected by Congress. The most discreditable incident in his career was the rather subservient petition which he addressed to the three secretaries of state on June 23, 1781, with merely the request for pen and paper to write a draft and for permission to see his son. In this so-called "submission," Laurens declared that he had "never lost his affection to Great Britain" and reviewed his career, giving to almost every incident a pro-British slant, stating that he had been called a "King's Man" and that he had done what he could to avert the struggle. On Dec. 1, 1781, he made a briefer petition, in the same vein, to the Commons. In these petitions he did nothing which technically compromised his position as a citizen of the United States, but it was naturally distasteful to the Americans to see an accredited envoy and former president of the Continental Congress using so submissive a tone. Madison felt that Laurens' diplomatic commission should be annulled, but Congress on Sept. 20, 1782, refused to recall him. By that time Laurens was free. The efforts of Franklin and Burke had finally secured his release on heavy bail on Dec. 31, 1781, and he was at last cleared in exchange for Cornwallis four months later. He went to Bath for his health and later held conferences with Shelburne.

He had been appointed a peace commissioner in May 1782 but was about to return home in November when he received definite instructions to join Franklin, Adams, and Jay at Paris. He reached there only two days before the signing of the preliminary articles, but during that brief time he used his influence to secure the fishing rights and the stipulation that the British should not carry away negroes and other American property. He seems to have been more worried than Jay about making peace independently of the French. For the next year and a half he acted as a sort of unofficial minister to England, frequently crossing the Channel to confer with the ministry on commercial and other matters. He happened to be absent on one of these missions when the final peace treaty was signed. He finally arrived in New York on Aug. 3, 1784, just four years after he had left America. He reported to Congress and was mentioned for another term as president. He reached Charleston early in 1785 and retired to "Mepkin" for the remaining seven years of his life. His health had been broken by his rigorous experiences;

he was saddened by the death of his son John, one of the last casualties of the war; his property had suffered heavily, and he estimated his war losses at 40,000 guineas. He received several political honors from South Carolina, including election to the federal constitutional convention in 1787, but he remained at his estate, where he died after a prolonged period of feeble health. He was one of the first Americans to be cremated, having stipulated this disposal of his body in his will. In addition to the controversial pamphlets already mentioned, he wrote *Mr. Laurens's True State of the Case, by Which his Candor to Mr. Edmund Jennings is Manifested,* etc. (1783). Among his writings subsequently published are "A Narrative of the Capture of Henry Laurens, of his Confinement in the Tower of London" (*South Carolina Historical Society Collections,* I, 1857, pp. 18–68); *Correspondence of Henry Laurens, of South Carolina, 1776–82* (1861), and *A South Carolina Protest against Slavery* (1861).

[The best biography is D. D. Wallace, *Life of Henry Laurens* (1915), a very detailed, intimate account, thoroughly documented, and based on the several collections of Laurens papers, particularly the "Laurens Papers," in the S. C. Hist. Soc., and also those in the Library of Congress, N. Y. Public Library, Long Island Hist. Soc., and Hist. Soc. of Pa. It contains a detailed bibliography and the frontispiece is a Copley portrait of Laurens. See also: David Ramsay, *The Hist. of S. C.* (2 vols., 1809) and *Memoirs of the Life of Martha Laurens Ramsay* (1811); Freeman Hunt, *Lives of Am. Merchants* (1858), vol. I; Francis Wharton, *The Revolutionary Diplomatic Correspondence of the U. S.* (6 vols., 1889); E. C. Burnett, *Letters of Members of the Continental Cong.,* vol. I–V (1921–31); Elizabeth Donnan, "The Slave Trade into South Carolina before the Revolution," *Am. Hist. Rev.,* July 1928; *S. C. Hist. and Geneal. Mag.,* Apr. 1902–Oct. 1905, Jan. 1906–Oct. 1908, Jan. 1923–Apr. 1924, July 1927–July 1930.]

R. G. A.—n.

LAURENS, JOHN (Oct. 28, 1754–Aug. 27, 1782), Revolutionary soldier, envoy to France, was born at Charleston, S. C., the son of Henry Laurens [*q.v.*] and Eleanor Ball. He studied under several tutors in Charleston and under the Rev. Richard Clarke, of Islington, London, then attended school at Geneva, Switzerland. On Sept. 16, 1772, he was admitted to the Middle Temple (London), where he began the study of law (E. A. Jones, *American Members of the Inns of Court,* 1924, pp. 117–20. In October 1776 he married Martha, daughter of William Manning of London, a friend of his father; she died at Lille, France, in 1781. Desiring to take part in the Revolution, Laurens returned to America in 1777 and joined Washington's staff as a volunteer aide. Congress later commissioned him lieutenant-colonel. He fought at Brandywine and Monmouth and was wounded at Germantown. In addition to active service

Washington frequently detached him for secret missions. At Valley Forge he kept his father, then president of Congress, informed of the movements of the conspirators involved in the Conway Cabal. He helped to soothe D'Estaing in 1778 when the latter was piqued by Maj.-Gen. John Sullivan [q.v.]. Angered by the "constant personal abuse" of Washington by Maj.-Gen. Charles Lee [q.v.], he challenged and wounded Lee in a duel fought Dec. 23, 1778 ("The Lee Papers," *Collections of the New-York Historical Society for the Year 1873*, 1874, pp. 283–85). He was elected to the South Carolina Assembly (1779) but withdrew to resume soldiering when Prevost invaded the state, first under Brig.-Gen. William Moultrie [q.v.], then under Maj.-Gen. Benjamin Lincoln [q.v.]. With the capitulation of Charleston (1780) he became a prisoner. Paroled and exchanged, he was commissioned by Congress envoy extraordinary to France (December 1780) at the age of twenty-six. He was not intended to supersede Benjamin Franklin [q.v.], minister to France, but it was thought that a soldier "could speak knowingly of the State of the Army" and obtain much-needed money and supplies from the French government (A. H. Smyth, *The Writings of Benjamin Franklin*, VIII, 1906, p. 251). Arriving in Paris in March 1781, he at once began negotiating with the Comte de Vergennes, minister of foreign affairs. Making no headway, he presented a memorial to Louis XVI at a reception and was soon able to forward to America four transports, three of which arrived safely, loaded with money and military supplies. He then left France, as Franklin wrote, "thoroughly possess'd of my Esteem," though the good doctor added, with justice, that Laurens "*brusqu'd* the Ministers too much" (Smyth, *supra*, VIII, 251, 295; Jared Sparks, *The Writings of George Washington*, VIII, 1835, pp. 526–27). In Philadelphia Laurens reported to Congress, then rejoined the army. He stormed a British redoubt at Yorktown, and with Viscount de Noailles, negotiated the terms of capitulation, a pleasant duty inasmuch as Cornwallis was constable of the Tower of London, where the elder Laurens lay confined. Turning homeward, he sat in the Jacksonborough legislature of January 1782, but his "intrepidity bordering upon rashness," which Washington noted (Sparks, *supra*, IX, 1836, p. 100), soon manifested itself, and he recklessly engaged in the irregular warfare that still persisted in South Carolina. There he fell, on a field so unimportant and nameless that Maj.-Gen. Nathanael Greene [q.v.] wrote mournfully: "The love of military glory made him seek it

upon occasions unworthy of his rank" (William Johnson, *Sketches of the Life and Correspondence of Nathanael Greene*, 1822, II, 342).

[Sources include: Laurens MSS., L. I. Hist. Soc.; Wm. G. Simms, "The Army Correspondence of Col. John Laurens in the Year 1777–8 . . . with a Memoir," *Bradford Club Series No. 7* (1867); D. D. Wallace, *The Life of Henry Laurens, with a Sketch of the Life of Lieut.-Col. John Laurens* (1915); Laurens' reports to Congress, printed in Jared Sparks, *The Diplomatic Correspondence of the Am. Revolution*, IX (1830), 193–249; *Secret Jours. of the Acts and Proc. of Cong.*, Dec. 11, 23, 26, 27, 1780, Sept. 5, 24, 1781; "The Mission of Col. John Laurens to Europe in 1781," *S. C. Hist. and Geneal. Mag.*, Jan. 1900–Apr. 1901; Laurens letters, father and son, *Ibid.*, Apr. 1902–Oct. 1904; *Jours. of Cong.*, Nov. 5, 6, 1778, Mar. 29, Sept. 29, Dec. 15, 1779; Philip Freneau, "On the Death of Col. Laurens," *Freeman's Jour.* (Phila.), Oct. 17, 1787, reprinted in *The Miscellaneous Works of Mr. Philip Freneau* (1788); obituary in the *Royal Gazette* (Charleston), Sept. 7, 1782. The many errors in the account by Wm. Jackson, Laurens' secretary, in Alex. Garden, *Anecdotes of the Am. Revolution* (2 ser., 1828), were perpetuated by Jas. Barnes in "The Man for the Hour," *McClure's Mag.*, Dec. 1899.]

F.E.R.

LAURIE, JAMES (May 9, 1811–Mar. 16, 1875), civil engineer, was born at Bells Quarry, near Edinburgh, Scotland. At an early age he was apprenticed to a maker of mathematical and engineering instruments in his native city, with whom he remained until about 1832. He then worked for a year in the office of a civil engineer, and while thus employed became acquainted with James P. Kirkwood, whom he accompanied to Massachusetts when Kirkwood was called to the position of chief engineer of construction of the Norwich & Worcester Railroad. Laurie obtained appointment as an associate engineer with the same company and in 1835 succeeded Kirkwood as chief engineer and superintendent of construction. Upon the completion of the road, he engaged in general practice, advising railroads and canal companies on locations and directing surveys for water power and harbor developments. In July 1848 he was one of the group of engineers that founded the Boston Society of Civil Engineers. He moved his office to New York City in 1852 and in October of that year sent out letters, signed by himself and two others, inviting all engineers in the neighborhood to attend a meeting to organize a society of civil engineers in the city of New York. At this gathering, Nov. 5, 1852, the American Society of Civil Engineers was formed, with Laurie as its first president. At the first regular meeting he presented a paper, "The Relief of Broadway," proposing the use of elevated railway tracks, the discussion of which was continued in the next meeting. Interest in the Society soon flagged, however, and it did not meet during the twelve years following 1855. Laurie retained his title of president during this time, and finally called a meeting, Oct. 12, 1867, at which the Society was revived, a new president was elected, and a resolution was adopted thanking Laurie for his efforts to reëstablish the organization.

In 1855 and 1856 he was employed by the State of New York to examine railroad bridges, and in 1858 he was engaged by the government of Nova Scotia to examine and report fully on the condition of the Nova Scotia Railroad, particularly in regard to the cost of construction and operation. He then served two years as chief engineer of that road. Subsequently, he reported on the condition of the Troy & Greenfield Railroad for the State of Massachusetts and was employed for several years by that state as its consultant on the Hoosac Tunnel. He was at the same time chief engineer of the New Haven, Hartford & Springfield Railroad, and designed and built its bridge across the Connecticut River at Warehouse Point. By this time he had accumulated considerable property and thenceforth, except for one or two examinations of engineering structures, he lived in retirement at Hartford until his death. He never married.

[C. W. Hunt, *Hist. Sketch of the Am. Soc. of Civil Engrs.* (1897); *Trans. Am. Soc. Civil Engrs.*, vol. XXXVII (1897); *Railway World,* Mar. 20, 1875; *Hartford Daily Courant,* Mar. 17, 1875.]   F. A. T.

LA VÉRENDRYE, PIERRE GAULTIER DE VARENNES, Sieur de (Nov. 17, 1685–Dec. 6, 1749),

explorer, was born at Three Rivers, Canada, where his father, René Gaultier, Sieur de Varennes, was governor. His mother, Marie, was a daughter of Pierre Boucher, first historian of New France. La Vérendrye was the fourth son, and his maternal grandfather was his godfather. His father died when the boy was but four years old, and at the age of twelve he entered the colonial army. He took part in several raids, notably that at Deerfield, Mass., in 1704. Three years later he was sent to France, where as lieutenant in the Régiment de Bretagne he saw hard service, was wounded nine times, and in 1709 was left for dead on the battlefield of Malplaquet. In 1711 he returned to Canada, and the next year was commissioned ensign in the local forces. On Oct. 29, 1712, he married Marie-Anne Dandonneau du Sablé, daughter of Louis Dandonneau du Sablé, Sieur de l'Ile du Pas. She bore him four sons: Jean Baptiste, Pierre, François, and Louis Joseph.

In 1726 La Vérendrye obtained the command of a post on Lake Nipigon, north of Lake Superior, and there heard from the Indians accounts of far western regions and the routes thither. One Ochagah drew for him a map of a westward-flowing river (see *Collections of the State Historical Society of Wisconsin,* vol. XVII, 1906, pp. 102–03 and *passim*), which so impressed La Vérendrye that in 1729 he went to Quebec to obtain permission from the governor to search overland for the Western Sea. Governor Beauharnois sent him to France, where he secured permission to explore at his own expense. The promise of a monopoly of the fur trade in the regions he might discover encouraged him to attempt the exploration. In 1731 he started west with his three eldest sons and his nephew, La Jemmeraye. Pushing west from Lake Superior by the Grand Portage route, they reached Rainy Lake, where Fort St. Pierre was built. The next year they erected Fort St. Charles on Lake of the Woods. During La Vérendrye's absence in Canada, his sons penetrated further into the wilderness, and in 1734 built Fort Maurepas on Lake Winnipeg.

The year 1736 was one of disaster: in May La Jemmeraye died; and in the summer Jean Baptiste La Vérendrye, Father Aulneau, and nineteen companions were murdered by the Sioux Indians on Massacre Island, Lake of the Woods. (The site was identified in 1909.) Nevertheless, La Vérendrye continued his advance, building in 1738 Fort La Reine on Assiniboin River and Fort Rouge on the site of Winnipeg, Manitoba. From Fort La Reine the explorers made their way overland to the Mandan villages on the upper Missouri. Thence four years later two of the sons with two voyageurs pushed west to mountains, variously identified as the Black Hills and as a portion of the Rocky Mountains. On their return they buried a leaden plate, which was found in 1913 at Fort Pierre, S. D., dated to correspond with the explorers' journal (*Proceedings of the State Historical Society of Wisconsin, 1913,* 1914, pp. 146–50). In 1744 La Vérendrye for the fourth time returned to Montreal to meet his creditors and to ask aid to continue his explorations. To his disappointment, however, he was kept on duty in Canada, while his posts were assigned to another officer. In 1746 he was promoted to a captaincy and in 1749 received the cross of St. Louis for his services. In that year a new governor granted him permission to return to the west, and he was making preparations for an expedition when he died. His sons were not allowed to continue his work.

Persistence in the face of great discouragements enabled La Vérendrye to enter the far West and to be the discoverer of Manitoba, the Dakotas, the western plains of Minnesota, the northwest territories of Canada, and probably part of Montana. He and his sons were the first white men to see the Red River of the North, the Assiniboin, probably the Saskatchewan, and great stretches of the upper Missouri. His discoveries opened a vast region for the French fur trade and pointed the way to the overland route to the Pacific.

[*Journals and Letters of Pierre Gaultier de Varennes de la Vérendrye and his Sons,* edited by L. J. Burpee, is published by the Champlain Society (Toronto, 1927); the introduction contains a good biographical sketch and there is an excellent bibliography. L. J. Burpee, *Pathfinders of the Great Plains* (Chronicles of Canada, vol. XIX, 1914), epitomizes these explorations. See also *Quart. of the Ore. Hist. Soc.,* June 1925; *S. Dak. Hist. Colls.,* vol. VII (1914); L. J. Burpee, "The Lake of the Woods Tragedy," *Proc. and Trans. Royal Soc. of Canada,* 2 ser., IX (1903); L. A. Prud'Homme, "Pierre Gaultier de Varennes, Sieur de la Vérendrye," *Ibid.,* XI (1906).]   L. P. K.

LAW, ANDREW (March 1748/49–July 13, 1821), composer, compiler and pioneer teacher of sacred music, was born in Milford, Conn., the son of Jahleel and Ann (Baldwin) Hollingsworth Law. He was a grandson of Jonathan Law [*q.v.*], and Abigail Andrew, daughter of the Rev. Samuel Andrew. In 1753 the family removed to Cheshire, where the parents were admitted to the church in 1769. After graduating from Rhode Island College in 1775, Andrew studied theology with the Rev. Levi Hart of Preston, Conn., and was ordained in Hartford on Sept. 8, 1787. For a time he was connected with the presbyteries of Philadelphia and Baltimore, but preaching was not to be his life work. In 1767, when he was only nineteen years old, he had compiled *A Select Number of Plain Tunes Adapted to Congregational Worship.* By 1790 he had issued at least six books of hymns or tunes and was advertising in the *Maryland Journal* and *Baltimore Advertiser,* in November of that year, that these books could be obtained of the author who was then situated in the Maryland city. How long he remained in Baltimore is uncertain, but books of his music were printed there until 1795. In 1799 some of his books were printed in Philadelphia, and in 1814 his *Essays on Music* was printed there. In the meantime he had traveled into Vermont, where his *Christian Harmony* was printed in Windsor in 1805. From 1795 to 1797 he was in Salem and its neighborhood conducting classes in singing.

In 1781 Law petitioned the Assembly of Connecticut for the exclusive right to imprint and sell his collection of tunes. The petition was granted but the list of tunes which he proposed to publish was never used in its entirety in any one book. The patent, however, carried protection for the use of any or all of the tunes named. In 1802 he patented a new plan for printing music without the use of the staff, employing four different shapes of notes, which he afterward increased to seven different characters. In comparing his new plan with the old he pointed out that his system had only seven characters, while the old plan with its lines and spaces, and different keys, totaled 196 signs to learn. This new system, however, was not accepted by singers, and only a few of his books were published in it. His aim in teaching music was to have it very soft, slow, and solemn. For a time his music was quite popular, but most of the tunes dropped out as taste changed. "Archdale," which he believed to be his best composition, was the last to hold a place in hymn books.

Law published numerous hymnals, under varying titles. His first, the *Plain Tunes,* sixteen pages in length, contained fifty-four tunes, being those in common use at that period. In 1779 the *Select Harmony* made its appearance—one hundred pages of engraved music printed in New Haven, and containing some tunes of his own composition. *The Musical Primer* (1780) was advertised as "suitable for learners at their first setting out." *A Collection of the Best and Most Approved Tunes and Anthems* was printed in 1779. A number of his books were printed in Cheshire by his brother William. *The Art of Singing* (1792), in one volume, was made up of *The Musical Primer,* the *Christian Harmony,* and *The Musical Magazine.* Other works included *The Rudiments of Music* (1783 and later editions); *Harmonic Companion* (1807); *The Art of Playing the Organ* (1807), and *Essays on Music* (1814). According to his definition, in the first essay, the musician must be "a linguist, an orator, a poet, a painter, a mathematician, a philosopher, an architect, a christian, a friend to God and man." He died in Cheshire, Conn., at the home of his brother William. He had never married.

[N. H. Allen, "Old Time Music and Musicians," the *Conn. Quart.,* Jan.–Feb.–Mar. 1897; F. J. Metcalf, *Am. Writers and Compilers of Sacred Music* (1925); *The Diary of Wm. Bentley, D.D.,* vol. II (1907); *Musical Herald,* Aug. 1882; *Hist. Cat. of Brown Univ., 1764–1914* (1914); C. C. Baldwin, *The Baldwin Geneal. from 1500 to 1881* (1881); *Conn. Courant,* July 17, 1821; information as to certain facts from Joseph P. Beach, historian of Cheshire, Conn.]   F. J. M.

LAW, EVANDER McIVOR (Aug. 7, 1836–Oct. 31, 1920), Confederate soldier, educator, was born in Darlington, S. C., the son of E. Augustus and Elizabeth (McIvor) Law. In 1856 he was graduated from the Citadel, in Charleston, where he had been assistant professor of belles-lettres during his senior year. The following five years he spent in teaching, first at the King's Mountain Military Academy at Yorkville, S. C., and later, at the Military High School, Tuskegee,

Ala., of which he was joint-founder with Robert Parks. In 1861 he recruited a company largely from his school and as captain took it into action at Pensacola. He served in all of the most important campaigns of the war in the East including Gettysburg, where he claimed that the result might have been otherwise had Lee followed the advice of himself and of two other colleagues regarding the seizure of Round Top. After having been wounded at Cold Harbor, he transferred from the Army of Virginia to a cavalry brigade in Johnston's command. Just prior to the surrender he became major-general.

Immediately after the war he administered the estate of William A. Latta, wealthy planter and railroad man, whose daughter, Jane Elizabeth, Law had married on Mar. 9, 1863. He then lived as a planter for a while in Tuskegee and Yorkville, resumed connections with the King's Mountain Military Academy until it closed in 1884, and dabbled in engineering and newspaper work. Finally he moved to Bartow, Fla., to fulfil a long-cherished plan of opening a school modeled after the Citadel and the Virginia Military Institute. After a year's existence as a private institution, this school was established as the South Florida Military and Educational Institute and received state aid through a system of county scholarships. It was a pioneer venture; the attendance was always small and the resources meager. The students aided in the upkeep and, during the first year, no fixed salaries were guaranteed to the teachers. Nevertheless, high standards were maintained and Law exercised a lasting influence on the students. In 1903 he resigned from the Institute to devote the rest of his life to newspaper work, as editor of the *Bartow Courier-Informant* (1905-15), and to his duties as trustee of Sumerlin Institute (1905-12) and as a member of the Polk County Board of Education (1912-20). He was especially interested in all state activities commemorating the Civil War. He served as commander of the Florida division of the Confederate Veterans (1899-1903) and aided in organizing the Bartow chapter of the Daughters of the Confederacy. Several articles on the campaigns in which he fought stand to his credit. When he died he was the last of the major-generals of the Confederacy. His reputation does not rest on his military record, however, for his most lasting achievement was his part in the establishment of the foundations of the educational system of his adopted state.

[See *Who's Who in America*, 1914-15; *Confed. Mil. Hist.* (1899), VII, 422-24; *Battles and Leaders of the Civil War* (4 vols., 1887-88); T. M. Owen, *Hist. of Ala. and Dict. of Ala. Biog.*, vol. IV (1921); *Makers of America: Fla. Edition*, vol. III (1909); *Bi-ennial Reports of the Supt. of Pub. Instruction of the State of Fla.*, 1895-1903; *Acts and Resolutions Adopted by the Legislature of Fla.*, 1895, 1897, 1901; files of the *Bartow Courier-Informant*; *Pensacola Jour.*, Nov. 1, 1920; and *Confed. Veteran*, Apr. 1914. Information as to certain facts was supplied by Law's daughter, Mrs. Francis Parker Winthrop, and by former associates.]   K. T. A.

LAW, GEORGE (Oct. 25, 1806-Nov. 18, 1881), contractor, transportation promoter, was born in Jackson (now Shushan), N. Y., between Saratoga and the Vermont border, one of the five children of John Law, a native of the County Down in Ireland who had come to America in 1784 and become a dairyman-farmer. George learned the "three R's" at winter night school and became an omniverous reader. In 1824 the approaching completion of the Erie Canal tempted him away from the cows and churns. He trudged to Troy to seek his fortune. Starting as a hod-carrier, he soon learned stone-cutting and masonry. The mania for canal construction gave him a series of opportunities and he worked in turn on the Dismal Swamp, Morris, Harlem, and Delaware & Hudson canals. At the age of twenty-one he undertook his first work as a contractor, building a small lock and aqueduct. Then he constructed an inclined plane for the Lehigh Canal. By 1830 he had saved $2,800. This was increased tenfold in the next four years by successful contracting in canal and railroad construction in eastern Pennsylvania. In 1834 he married a Miss Anderson in Philadelphia. Three years later he moved to New York City, which became his home for the rest of his life. He secured two contracts for work near Tarrytown on the new Croton Water Works and in 1839 undertook his greatest piece of contracting, the High Bridge. His experience had revealed financial as well as engineering ability. Turning from contracting, he thenceforth applied his capital and skill to other fields. Elected president of the Dry Dock Bank in 1842, he rescued it from the brink of insolvency. Then, for a while, he devoted his attention to railroads. He helped to extend the Harlem Railroad twelve miles from Williamsbridge to White Plains, nearly doubling its earnings in two years and raising the value of its stock from five to seventy-five. He then took over the Mohawk & Hudson, doing away with its inclined planes, improving its roadbed and trebling the value of its stock. His next and most spectacular venture was in ocean steamships, which promised to become profitable with the federal policy of mail subsidies. In 1847, with Marshall O. Roberts and Bowes R. McIlvaine as junior partners, he formed the United States Mail Steamship Company and took over the federal contract awarded to A. G. Sloo for a biweekly mail service between New York, Havana, New Orleans, and Chagres. The company was to provide five ships and receive $290,000 annually. Their first ship reached Chagres in 1848, with passengers for California. The gold rush gave a tremendous impetus to the business; but the opposition developed when William H. Aspinwall's Pacific Mail Steamship Company started a rival line from New York to Chagres. Thereupon, Law secured four ships to compete with the Pacific Mail between Panama and San Francisco in 1850. A year later, the companies divided spheres of influence, Law keeping the Atlantic, and Aspinwall the Pacific. Law was also actively interested in the Panama Railroad. Several of his ships became involved in the Cuban troubles and in 1852 he sprang into fame. One Smith, purser of his *Crescent City,* had furnished the *New York Herald* with material which angered the captain-general of Cuba who forbade any ship bearing Smith aboard to enter Havana harbor. Though urged by President Fillmore to avoid trouble and penalized by the removal of the mails, Law sent the ship with Smith aboard into Havana time and again. This started a presidential "boom" for Law. Though only one generation removed from County Down, he was prominently associated with the Know-Nothing party and in 1855 received the support of the Pennsylvania legislature for that party's presidential nomination. When Fillmore received it instead in 1856, Law supported Frémont and attacked Fillmore in two widely circulated "North American" Letters. By that time he was a millionaire. He had sold his steamships just before the slump in the American merchant marine set in and had shifted from liners to prosaic but profitable horse cars. When the Eighth Avenue Railroad in New York City faced forfeiture of its contract in 1854 unless it completed its five miles of track within ten weeks, Law advanced some $800,000, completed the road within the given time, secured fifty cars, and then served as president of the road until his death. The road paid dividends averaging twelve per cent. during all that period. He was also promoter and president of the Ninth Avenue Railroad, started in 1859, but that line paid almost nothing. During his later years, his son took over the active management of the lines, and also of the Brooklyn and Staten Island ferries which he acquired. Law died at his home on Fifth Avenue after a period of failing health.

[The principal source is the eulogistic, anonymous campaign biography, *A Sketch of Events in the Life of Geo. Law, published in Advance of his Biog.* (1855). An uncomplimentary description of Law appeared in M. H. Smith, *Sunshine and Shadow in N. Y.* (1868). A pamphlet entitled *"North American" Docs.* (1856)

contains two of his anti-Fillmore letters. The *N. Y. Herald,* Nov. 19, 1881, contained a long obituary. Details of his steamship activities are in the lengthy *House Executive Doc. 91,* 32 Cong., 1 Sess. Results of his railroad and traction activity are in H. V. Poor, *Hist. of the Railroads and Canals of the U. S.* (1860), pp. 267, 268, 288, 291, and in the successive editions of H. V. Poor, *Manual of the Railroads of the U. S.,* 1868 ff.]   R. G. A—n.

LAW, JOHN (Oct. 28, 1796–Oct. 7, 1873), judge, congressman, son of Lyman and Elizabeth (Learned) Law, was born in New London, Conn. His paternal grandfather was Richard Law [*q.v.*], and his great-grandfather, Jonathan Law [*q.v.*]. He graduated from Yale College in 1814, read law with his father, and was admitted to the bar in 1817. The same year he went west by way of Philadelphia and the Ohio River, taking up his residence as an attorney at Vincennes, Ind. This was his home until 1851, when he moved to a tract of land near Evansville, Ind., now in the city, which he and his associates laid out as the town of Lamasco, a venture which made him at least moderately wealthy. On Nov. 24, 1822, he married Sarah, daughter of Nathaniel and Anne Ewing, of Vincennes. Thirteen children were born to them. Law was prosecuting attorney in the first judicial circuit of Indiana in 1818 and again from 1825 to 1828. In 1823–24 he served one term in the state House of Representatives. The title of judge, by which he was universally known, came from his service as judge of the seventh circuit, 1830–31, and 1844–50. He was receiver of public money at Vincennes, 1838–42, and judge of the federal court of land claims there, 1855–57, by appointment of President Pierce. By his knowledge of the law, his patience and thoroughness in dealing with the complicated land titles of the region about Vincennes, and his fairness as a judge, he made a permanent reputation in the bar of the state. A Whig from the formation of that party until the late forties, he then became, and remained till his death, a Democrat. He represented his district in the national House of Representatives in the Thirty-seventh and in the Thirty-eighth congresses (1861–65), where he supported the administration in all war measures but opposed emancipation and all steps toward "radical" reconstruction of the seceding states. In 1865 he retired from public life and from the active practice of his profession.

Law devoted much time to historical matters, especially to the history of Vincennes and to the campaigns of George Rogers Clark culminating in the capture of Fort Sackville. For fourteen years, 1859–73, he was president of the Indiana Historical Society. His *Colonial History of Vincennes, under the French, British and Ameri-*

can *Governments* (1858), which was an enlarged edition of an address published in 1839, long ranked as the most authoritative account of the subject. A lecture, "Jesuit Missionaries in the North-West," was printed in the *Third Annual Report and Collections of the State Historical Society of Wisconsin* (1857). His historical and personal interests, as well as his innate sense of justice, led him to take up the prosecution of the claims for reimbursement of Francis Vigo, whose advances of money and supplies had made George Rogers Clark's success possible, and who was a resident of Vincennes from the close of the American Revolution till his death in 1836. It has been called "a centennial law suit," for it dragged on from one hearing to another till 1876, forty years after Vigo's death in relative poverty and three years after Law himself had died, when $49,898.50 was paid to Vigo's heirs. Law was a commanding, dignified figure. His genial disposition and the charm of his conversation made him popular in social circles both in his state and in Washington. He died at Evansville, Oct. 7, 1873, and was buried in Greenlawn Cemetery, Vincennes.

[Charles Denby, "Judge John Law," *Ind. Hist. Soc. Pubs.*, vol. I, no. 7 (1897); Wm. W. Woollen, *Biog. and Hist. Sketches of Early Ind.* (1883), pp. 332–34; F. A. Myers, "John Law of Indiana," *Mag. of Am. Hist.*, May 1891; *Early Ind. Trials and Sketches; Reminiscences by Hon. O. H. Smith* (1858); F. B. Dexter, *Biog. Sketches of the Grads. of Yale Coll.*, vol. VI (1912); the *Indianapolis Sentinel*, Oct. 8, 1873; manuscript letters of Law to Lyman C. Draper, Draper MSS., 2J51–69, Wis. State Hist. Lib.]   C. B. C.

LAW, JONATHAN (Aug. 6, 1674–Nov. 6, 1750), colonial lawyer and governor, was born in Milford, Conn., the only son of Jonathan and Sarah (Clark) Law, and the grandson of Richard Law, an emigrant from England, who settled at Wethersfield in 1638 and in 1641 was one of the founders of Stamford, Conn. He was graduated from Harvard in 1695 and received the degree of A.M. from that institution in 1729. He applied himself to the practice of law, in which field he won a reputation for great skill and ability. He was one of the first men to be admitted to the Connecticut bar in 1708 after the passage of an act regulating attorneys. In the next year the Assembly appointed him justice of the peace and of the quorum for New Haven County. Except for one interval of two years he held judicial office continuously until he became governor in 1741, serving successively as judge of the county court, as assistant judge of the superior courts, and from 1725 to 1741, as chief judge of the superior courts, to which office Law like other deputy governors was annually appointed. The most important case with which he was con-

nected, as judge, as deputy governor, and as governor, was that of *Clark* vs. *Tousey*. His judgment in the case, eventually sustained by the privy council of Great Britain (1745), went far to reëstablish the validity of the Connecticut procedure with regard to intestate estates, which had been declared contrary to English law in the earlier case of *Winthrop* vs. *Lechmere*. (See C. M. Andrews, "The Connecticut Intestacy Law," *Yale Review,* November 1894, 261–94.) Law's first elective office was that of deputy to the Assembly from Milford in 1706, an office which he filled intermittently until 1717, serving occasionally as clerk or as speaker of the lower house. His continuous nomination to the magistracy from 1710 on bore fruit in his election as assistant in 1717. Thereafter he advanced rapidly in seniority until, in 1724, his name stood sixth on the lists of assistants. On the death of Gov. Gurdon Saltonstall and the advancement of Deputy-Gov. Joseph Talcott to the vacancy in 1724, Law was elected deputy governor over the heads of the five senior assistants. The choice bore striking testimony to his popularity with the voters. He was annually reëlected until October 1741, when, following the death of Talcott, he was chosen governor. He continued to hold this office until his death in 1750. As Law's governorship covered the period of the War of the Austrian Succession, he was associated with the successful Louisbourg expedition of 1745 and the abortive Canadian expeditions of 1746 and 1747, although his rôle was that of organizer and director of Connecticut's military activities rather than that of direct participant. In religious matters he was thoroughly orthodox and showed little sympathy for the "New Lights" during the period of the Great Awakening. As a public official, he was typical of the conservative governing classes of his colony and age. Little is known of his private life and personality. He was married five times: in 1698 to Ann Eliot; in 1704/05 to Abigail Arnold; in 1706 to Abigail Andrew; in 1726 to Mrs. Sarah Burr; and in 1730 to Eunice (Hall) Andrew. He was survived by his fifth wife and by seven children, one of whom was Richard Law [*q.v.*].

[See *Pub. Records of the Colony of Conn.*, vols. IV–IX (1868–76); "The Talcott Papers," *Colls. of the Conn. Hist. Soc.*, vols. IV and V (1892–96); "The Law Papers," *Colls. of the Conn. Hist. Soc.*, vols. XI (1907), XIII (1911), and XV (1914). The best sketch of Law's life is that by Albert C. Bates in "The Law Papers." See also *New-Eng. Hist. and Geneal. Reg.*, Apr. 1847, pp. 188–90, and Ezra Stiles, *Oratio Funebris pro Exequiis Celebrandis Viri Perillustris Jonathan Law* (1751).]   L. W. L.

LAW, RICHARD (Mar. 7, 1733–Jan. 26, 1806), Connecticut patriot and jurist, born in Milford,

Conn., was the son of Jonathan Law [*q.v.*] by his fifth and last wife, Eunice (Hall) Andrew Law. Richard graduated in 1751 from Yale, read law with Jared Ingersoll, was admitted to the bar in 1755, and moved two years later to New London. Here he attended the First Church (Congregational) and on Sept. 21, 1760, married Ann, the daughter of Capt. John Prentise. He seems to have been a thorough student of jurisprudence, a master of argument, if not of the art of persuasion, and a highly successful lawyer. His public career commenced in 1765 with his appointment as justice of the peace and with his election to the General Court. He was clerk of the latter during his last two years of membership and until his appointment as assistant, a position he held from 1776 to 1786. A faithful patriot, he joined in the protest against the Townshend duties and later against the Boston Port Bill, was a member of the Connecticut Council of Safety of 1776, and was one of the two delegates sent to New York to confer with Washington on the defense of the colony (1776). He was chosen a delegate to the Continental Congress in 1774, 1776, 1777, and from 1780 to 1783, but the state of his health seems to have prevented his attendance in 1774 and 1776, for he served only in the sessions of 1777, 1781, and 1782, and then without distinction.

More distinguished was his judicial career in Connecticut. In 1773 he became chief judge of the New London county court, a position that he held until 1784 when he was elevated to the bench of the superior court of which two years later he was made chief judge. In 1789 he was appointed by Washington United States district judge. Early in the Revolution the Council of Safety had requested him to compile a code of maritime law. In 1783–84 he, with the assistance of Roger Sherman, also a superior court judge, codified the statute law of the state, published as *Acts and Laws of the State of Connecticut, in America* (1784). The task brought them no little renown. In 1784 the freemen of New London unanimously elected Law the first mayor of the newly chartered city. This position, with his federal judgeship, he held until his death.

Law was generally Federalist in politics. At the Connecticut Convention of 1788 at Hartford, which so quickly ratified the federal Constitution, he spoke in favor of that document. A year later he was a member of the first electoral college from Connecticut. Yet in the spring elections of 1801 the Republicans named him their candidate for governor. Law declined the nomination, urging his age and disinclination for the office (*Connecticut Courant,* Apr. 6, 1801), but no other Republican nomination was made. Consequently he received only 1,056 votes to 11,156 for Governor Trumbull, and ran behind his own ticket. Five years later he died at his home in New London.

[F. B. Dexter, *Biog. Sketches of the Grads. of Yale Coll.,* vol. II (1896); *New-Eng. Hist. and Geneal. Reg.,* July 1847; F. M. Caulkins, *Hist. of New London, Conn.* (1852); *The Pub. Records of the Colony of Conn.,* vols. XII to XV (1881–90); *The Pub. Records of the State of Conn.,* vols. I and II (1894–95); Timothy Alden, *A Coll. of Am. Epitaphs and Inscriptions* (1814), IV, 130; the *Conn. Courant* (Hartford), Feb. 5, 1806.]

E. W. S.

LAW, SALLIE CHAPMAN GORDON (Aug. 27, 1805–June 28, 1894), "mother of the Confederacy," was born in Wilkes County, N. C., daughter of Chapman Gordon, of Virginian descent, and his wife Charity King of South Carolina. From both sides of her house she inherited martial blood, but especially from her father, who while in his teens had fought at King's Mountain and had served throughout the rest of the Revolutionary War under Generals Marion and Sumter. She married, June 28, 1825, near Eatonton, Ga., Dr. John S. Law, and settled with him in Forsythe, Ga., where they dwelt until 1834 when they removed to Columbia, Tenn. Ten years later, after her husband's death, Mrs. Law moved to Memphis in order to obtain better advantages for her seven children, and there passed the remainder of her long life.

She was self-reliant, charitable, unselfish, and devout, as her family and social relations had already proved her, and the outbreak of war offered a broader field for her executive ability and strength of will. Although she was thoroughly identified with the Confederacy by family ties, with more than two score near kinsmen—most distinguished of whom was her nephew, Gen. John B. Gordon—in the ranks and on the official list, she chafed at having only one son to lend to the Confederate armies and was quick to dedicate her own energies to the aid of her section. She was active in organizing in Memphis, in April 1861, the Southern Mothers' Hospital, which under her leadership expanded from its original twelve-bed capacity to an institution that, after the battle of Shiloh, cared for hundreds of wounded. Before this she had, at her own expense, twice journeyed to Columbus, Ky., conveying food and clothing from her hospital to the sick soldiers there. Upon the breaking up of the Memphis hospitals the money in the Southern Mothers' treasury was invested in quinine, morphine, and opium, which Mrs. Law carried into the Confederacy on her person, distributing it chiefly in the hospitals at LaGrange, Ga., where she had the compliment of having a hospital named for her. At Columbus, Ga., having learned of the destitution in Gen. Joseph E. Johnston's division at Dalton, she was instrumental in collecting hundreds of blankets, socks, and underclothing, which she went in person to see distributed to the soldiers. Officers and men idolized her for her intrepidity and cheerful confidence, and General Johnston ordered a review of thirty thousand troops in recognition of her services. After the war the hospital organization became the Southern Mothers' Association, one of the earliest memorial societies; and until shortly before her death Mrs. Law, as its only president, continued her labors in memory of the Confederacy and its sons, cooperating with other groups in erecting monuments, marking graves, and disseminating historical material about the Southern cause and its conduct. In her sixteen-page pamphlet, *Reminiscences of the War of the Sixties Between the North and South* (1892), she recounts a few of her many wartime experiences, revealing without ostentation how naturally, lovingly, and gratuitously she gave herself to the Confederacy during the war years and afterward.

[*Confed. Veteran*, Apr., July 1894; *Confederated Memorial Assos. of the South* (1904); *Memphis Commercial*, June 29, 1894; and obituary in the *Memphis Appeal-Avalanche*, June 30, 1894, reprinted in the *Southern Hist. Soc. Papers*, vol. XXII (1894).]

A. C. G., Jr.

LAWLEY, GEORGE FREDERICK (Dec. 8, 1848–Mar. 20, 1928), yacht-builder, was born in London. His father, George Lawley, had already acquired some knowledge of boat-building when he and his family emigrated to the United States in 1851, and he soon found employment in the yard of Donald McKay in East Boston. The son's earliest recollections were those of his wanderings among the chips and shavings of some of the mightiest ships of the clipper era. When he was less than twenty years old he helped his father establish a small boat yard at Scituate, where they began to build modest craft for Boston yachtsmen. Within a few years they gained a reputation for skilled and honest workmanship and established a larger yard at South Boston. World-wide fame came to them in 1885 when they built for a syndicate of Boston yachtsmen the wooden sloop *Puritan,* designed by Edward Burgess [*q.v.*], which defeated the English cutter *Genesta* in the fifth match for the *America's* Cup. The next year the firm built another cup defender, the *Mayflower,* designed by Burgess for Gen. Charles J. Paine, which defeated the British cutter *Galatea.* Although the builders had no facilities for constructing their own boats of iron, they rigged and outfitted the

third Boston yacht to contend for the cup, the iron sloop *Volunteer,* which raced successfully against the Scotch cutter *Thistle.*

Orders came to the Lawley company from all parts of the world for pleasure craft, cruisers, and racers. Among the larger craft constructed during the period of the eighties and nineties were the schooners *Sachem, Idler, Savarona, Latona,* and *Margaret.* Owing to the demand for iron and steel construction, the plant was moved to Neponset, another suburb of Boston. With this move the elder Lawley retired from the business. In the yard at Neponset some of the largest yachts flying the American ensign were fashioned, including the steel schooners *Guinevere* and *Speejacks,* the composite yacht *Sea Call,* and large power boats such as the *Taormina* and the *Athero II.* Having brought the company to a high state of efficiency George F. Lawley retired from active work in 1925 but continued his energetic interest in the plant which his son, Frederick Damon Lawley, had established in Quincy. Lawley died in his eightieth year at his home in South Boston and was survived by his wife, Hannah (Damon) Lawley.

[W. M. Thompson and T. W. Lawson, *The Lawson Hist. of the America's Cup* (1902); H. L. Stone, *The "America's" Cup Races* (1914); *Yachting* (N. Y.), May 1928; *Power Boating* (Cleveland), May 1928; *Boston Globe, Boston Herald, Boston Transcript,* Mar. 21, 1928.]

W. U. S.

LAWRANCE, JOHN [See Laurance, John, 1750–1810].

LAWRANCE, MARION [See Lawrance, Uriah Marion, 1850–1924].

LAWRANCE, URIAH MARION (Oct. 2, 1850–May 1, 1924), promoter of organized Sunday-school activity, was the son of Elonson Lawrance, a farmer and country school teacher of Winchester, Preble County, Ohio, and his wife, Amanda Melvina (Irwin). Named for the family hero, General Francis Marion, he chose to be known as Marion rather than as Uriah. In 1854 the Lawrances moved to Yellow Springs, and here the father kept the Antioch College bookstore. The enterprise proving a failure, Marion was thrown on his own resources at an early age. After experience as a farmer, storekeeper, and teacher, he entered Antioch College. At the end of a year, to his lifelong regret, ill health compelled him to give up his course. He then engaged in various business ventures till 1889, first in Syracuse, N. Y., and then in Toledo, Ohio.

At sixteen he had been an active Sunday-school worker in his family church, which was of the Christian denomination. In 1876 he became superintendent of the Sunday-school of the Washington Street Congregational Church, Toledo, which under his guidance developed into the model school of the country. Made secretary of the Ohio Sunday School Association in 1889, he brought it to a high degree of efficiency. In 1899 he became general secretary of the International Sunday School Association, which he shaped into a closely knit organization, with cooperating branches in every state. This body became affiliated with similar ones in other countries and there resulted the World's Sunday School Association, of which, also, he served as secretary from 1910 to 1914. After the latter date, he devoted his entire time to the International Association, which largely owed to him its compact organization, its use of uniform lessons, its teacher-training courses and summer conferences. In 1922 it was completely reorganized as the International Council of Religious Education, becoming broadly interdenominational. Of this new organization, for whose perfection Lawrance was largely responsible, he was made secretary emeritus. His death at Portland, Ore., resulted from over-exertion while on an extended speaking tour.

Lawrance was probably the best-known Sunday school man of his day. He was an able platform speaker and convention leader and had great skill in answering questions from the floor. He attended many world conventions and was especially prominent in those at Jerusalem, 1904, Rome, 1907, Washington, 1910, Zurich, 1913, and Tokyo, 1920. He made a speaking tour through the British Isles in 1911 as the guest of the British and World's Sunday School associations, at the close of which he was tendered a luncheon in the Parliament buildings at which many distinguished officials were present. His best-known work, *How to Conduct a Sunday-School* (1905, 1915), had a larger sale than any other work on the subject and has been translated into a dozen languages. Among his other publications are: *The Working Manual of a Successful Sunday-School* (1908); *Training the Teacher* (1908), with others; *Housing the Sunday-School* (1911); *The Sunday-School Organized for Service* (1914); *Special Days in the Sunday-School* (1916); *The Church-school Blue-Print* (1924); *My Message to Sunday-School Workers* (1924). He was also a voluminous contributor to periodicals. On Oct. 15, 1874, he was married to Flora Gaines. Their family consisted of one son and one daughter, who survived their parents.

[H. G. Lawrance, *Marion Lawrance; a Memorial Biog.* (1925); *Who's Who in America*, 1916–17; *Congregationalist*, May 15, 29, 1924; *Toledo News-Bee*, May 2, 1924; *Morning Oregonian* (Portland), May 3, 1924; information as to certain facts from son.]
F. T. P.

LAWRENCE, ABBOTT (Dec. 16, 1792–Aug. 18, 1855), merchant, manufacturer, diplomat, statesman, and philanthropist, was the seventh child and fifth son of Samuel and Susanna Parker Lawrence of Groton, Mass., where he was born and brought up on the paternal farm. Amos and William Lawrence [*qq.v.*] were his brothers. His father was of the sixth generation in descent from John Lawrence of Wisset, Suffolk County, England, who settled in Watertown, Mass., in 1635. In 1660, John Lawrence removed to Groton, then recently erected into a plantation or township by order of the General Court, and became one of its leading men. The Lawrence family continued to reside in Groton, where Samuel, the father of Abbott, was born on Apr. 24, 1754. Samuel Lawrence was one of the minute men who fought at Bunker Hill and lived to take part in the celebration there fifty years later at the laying of the corner-stone of the monument. He served through the Revolutionary War, rising to the rank of major, and, returning to Groton, settled down on his farm where he spent the rest of his life. He was a deacon of the First Congregational Church for forty years and was also one of the founders and for thirty-three years a trustee of Groton Academy. During Shays's Rebellion and all through the troubles of that period, he stood firm in support of the government, and in the advocacy of the supremacy of the laws. He is described as "a devout man, strict in all religious observances, firm, almost rigid, in the discipline of his family," and at the same time "cheerful, joyous, benignant, and given to hospitality." The mother of Abbott Lawrence was the daughter of William Parker, a Groton farmer who removed to Concord, where she witnessed the battle in 1775. She is described as having "strict notions of obedience, with deeply seated religious principles, which she succeeded in communicating to her children," and is said to have had "probably greater influence than her husband in forming their characters."

In 1808 Abbott was sent to Boston and apprenticed to his brother, Amos, who had recently established himself there as a merchant. In 1814, when he came of age, he was admitted to partnership, and the firm of A. & A. Lawrence was founded, which, as one biographer put it, "for the next half-century was to stand as a tower of strength among the business men of Boston." After the virtual retirement of the senior partner in 1831 on account of ill health,

Abbott Lawrence became the principal member of the firm and so continued until his death nearly a quarter-century later. He was quick of decision and prompt in action. To these qualities were joined a sanguine and buoyant disposition and extraordinary physical energy. In short, he was the leading Boston merchant during the period when Massachusetts enterprise and capital were turning inland from the sea, and manufacturing was supplanting trade and navigation as the leading interest of New England.

The business of A. & A. Lawrence was at first the importation of English manufactures, especially drygoods. In 1815, as soon as peace was restored, Abbott Lawrence hastened to England and purchased a large stock of goods of which there had long been a dearth in America. Through superior enterprise, he was able to get them to Boston ahead of his competitors, where they were sold at a handsome profit. For the next ten years the firm continued to be importers of English manufactures. Gradually also the partners became interested in the sale of the products of the new cotton and woolen mills which had been established in New England since the war, and eventually they became agents .exclusively for domestic manufactures. In 1830 they commenced also to be interested in manufacturing as well as selling domestic cottons and woolens. Associating themselves with the Lowells, Appletons, Jacksons, and other rising manufacturers, they presently became very active in the development of New England industry. In 1845 Abbott Lawrence took the lead in the foundation of the textile city, which bears the family name, and in the establishment of the great mills there, which soon made Lawrence the principal rival of Lowell, founded a quarter-century earlier, in the manufacture of cotton and woolen cloth.

Abbott Lawrence was also one of the first to appreciate the importance of steam railroads and to promote their construction. In 1835, in the face of widespread public indifference and scepticism, he took the lead in advocating the extension of the Boston & Worcester road over the Berkshire mountains to Albany, and the success of the Western Railroad, as it was called, presently attested the farsightedness and courage of its enterprising promoters. He took an equal interest in local improvements, where they seemed likely to be of public benefit, and gave his time and strength freely to foster promising public works in Boston. Thus in 1845 he was active in promoting the construction of municipal water works, despite the opposition of those interested in the private exploitation of the supply of water, and after a sharp contest the advocates of municipal ownership prevailed to the great gain of the city.

Abbott Lawrence's business efficiency, aptitude for affairs, and public spirit made him a favorite representative of the Boston merchants and manufacturers, whenever their special interests required the services of a business man in politics. The Lawrences, like most of the Boston merchants who turned to manufacturing in the period following the Napoleonic wars, were slow to abandon their early belief in the wisdom of a policy of freedom of trade, but after the adoption of the protective tariff act of 1824, convinced that it was useless to oppose longer what then appeared to be the favorite policy of the rest of the country, they decided to accept the system of protection and make the best of it. "The American system," Abbott Lawrence wrote long afterward, in a letter opposing the low tariff of 1846, "was forced upon us, and was adopted for the purpose of creating a home market for the products of the soil of the South and West; we resisted the adoption of a system which, we honestly believed, would greatly injure our navigation, and drive us from our accustomed employments into a business we did not understand. We came into it, however, reluctantly, and soon learned that with the transfer of our capital we acquired skill and knowledge in the use of it. . . . Those who . . . were the strongest opponents of the protective tariff among us have given up their theories. . . . We have gone forward steadily, till many descriptions of manufactures are as well settled in New England as the raising of potatoes" (Hill, *post,* p. 28).

In 1827 he was one of a delegation of seven Massachusetts business men sent to the famous Harrisburg Convention to discuss measures for promoting the interests of domestic manufactures, and in 1834 and again in 1838 he accepted election to Congress as the representative of Boston. In Congress he was an active and influential member of the committee on ways and means. He was an ardent Whig and, becoming more interested in politics, he attended the national convention of 1844 as a delegate and in 1848 was a leading candidate for the vice-presidential nomination. Taking an active part in the ensuing campaign, he was subsequently offered by President Taylor a place in his cabinet but declined both the secretaryship of the navy and that of the interior. Eventually he was prevailed upon to accept an appointment as minister to Great Britain, and for three years represented the United States at the Court of St. James's with efficiency and dignity. In 1852 he resigned in order to give more attention to his private business and did not again hold public office. He was dissatisfied with the failure of the Whig party to oppose the further extension of slavery, and, according to his biographer, would have been one of the original members of the Republican party, if death had not claimed him.

Like his brothers, Abbott Lawrence was a man of firm religious principles and became greatly interested in works of education and charity. On first going to Boston he joined one of the liberal Congregational churches and participated in the religious movement which produced New England Unitarianism. He remained to the end of his life an active member of that denomination. He was a generous benefactor of the academy at Groton, where he received his early education, and toward the close of his life he became deeply interested in the promotion of education in science, especially at Harvard College. He took a leading part in supporting the work of Louis Agassiz and in the founding of chairs at Harvard for the teaching of natural science. In 1847 he gave fifty thousand dollars to the establishment of a school of science and by his will he added another fifty thousand dollars to its endowment. This school was called in his honor the Lawrence Scientific School. Lawrence was also deeply interested in the improvement of the living conditions of the laboring population and bequeathed fifty thousand dollars for the construction of model lodging houses for wage-earners in Boston. His domestic life supported his public character as a popular and successful man of affairs. His wife, whom he married June 28, 1819, was Katherine Bigelow, the eldest daughter of Timothy Bigelow of Medford, Mass., a distinguished lawyer, who served for many years as speaker of the Massachusetts House of Representatives, and Lucy Prescott Bigelow. There were seven children, five sons and two daughters, of whom all but two sons survived their father.

[The principal life of Abbott Lawrence is Hamilton Andrews Hill, *Memoir of Abbott Lawrence* (1883). At a public memorial meeting in Boston, held immediately after his death, addresses were delivered by Edward Everett and Robert C. Winthrop, which have been preserved. Other sources include: W. H. Prescott, *Memoirs of the Hon. Abbott Lawrence* (1856); Nathan Appleton, memoir in the *Mass. Hist. Soc. Colls.*, 4 ser. IV (1858), 495–507; F. W. Ballard, *The Stewardship of Wealth, as Illustrated in the Lives of Amos and Abbott Lawrence* (1865); Freeman Hunt, *Lives of Am. Merchants*, vol. II (1858); John Lawrence, *The Geneal. of the Family of John Lawrence of Wisset, in Suffolk, England* (1869); R. M. Lawrence, *The Descendants of Maj. Samuel Lawrence* (1904); *Boston Daily Jour.*, Aug. 20, 1855. Selections from Abbott Lawrence's diplomatic correspondence were published at Boston as well as occasional pamphlets on the tariff, the currency, and other public questions. Many of these were reprinted in the Appendices of Hill's *Memoir* noted above.]   A. N. H.

LAWRENCE, AMOS (Apr. 22, 1786–Dec. 31, 1852), merchant and philanthropist, brother of Abbott and William Lawrence [*qq.v.*], was one of the leaders in the early development of the New England textile industry. He was distinguished not only for his business efficiency and success but even more for his philanthropic character and many public benefactions. He was the fourth child of Samuel and Susanna Parker Lawrence of Groton, Mass., the parents of a family of six sons and three daughters. Five of the sons grew to manhood, of whom four became successful merchants, one a successful lawyer. (See Abbott Lawrence, for account of ancestry.) Amos Lawrence was apprenticed at the age of thirteen to a merchant in Dunstable and at the age of twenty-one, having served his apprenticeship, went to Boston, where, after working a short period as a clerk, he set up in business for himself. In the following year (1808) he took in his younger brother, Abbott, as an apprentice and in 1814, when he became of age, made him a partner. The firm of A. & A. Lawrence, as it was called, soon became the most successful mercantile firm of its time.

Amos Lawrence was the head of the firm until the year 1831, when his health broke down and forced his retirement from active business. He was an invalid for the remaining twenty-one years of his life. From early youth he had been exceptionally industrious, thrifty, and temperate. Before leaving Groton for Boston, he had formed the habits of total abstinence from alcoholic liquor and tobacco, which he maintained throughout his life and, as soon as his means permitted, he showed a deep sense of the obligations of men of wealth toward the poor and needy. His invalidism in early middle life caused him to make a business of philanthropy at an age when most successful business men are still absorbed in the accumulation of wealth. It was his practice to give money, food, clothing, books, and other necessaries day by day, wherever it seemed to him that they were likely to do good. He kept a supply of such commodities always on hand in his house and devoted much time to personal supervision of their distribution. A memorandum, which he prepared in the last year of his life, shows that during the preceding ten years he had given away approximately five-sixths of his entire income during that period. The amount of these gifts, which was over half a million dollars, was exceeded by the benefactions of other rich men in his day, but in no case were more pains taken to make the gifts appropriate and helpful.

Much of Amos Lawrence's giving was in small amounts, and not a little of it anonymous. The principal recipients of the larger sums were educational institutions. He was always loyal to the academy at Groton, in which he secured his early education, and left a substantial endowment by his will in addition to many gifts during his lifetime. He was also a generous benefactor of Williams College, in which he became interested through his admiration for its president, Mark Hopkins. He took a deep interest also in the erection of Bunker Hill Monument and was the principal contributor to the building fund. Along with his benefactions went much good advice, often in the form of letters carefully written out by his own hand. After his death, those were collected by one of his sons and, at the request of members of the Boston Young Men's Christian Union and the Boston Young Men's Christian Association as well as of students at Williams College, many of them were published under the title, *Extracts from the Diary and Correspondence of the Late Amos Lawrence* (1855). This book gained wide popularity among the young men of the time.

Amos Lawrence was a man of strong religious feeling. Brought up in the old Puritan tradition, he joined the Brattle Street church on removing to Boston and always remained a member of that congregation. But he was not wholly satisfied with the rather cold and intellectual type of Unitarianism which flourished in Boston at that period, and in his benefactions he confined himself to no creed. He took much less interest in politics than in religion. He was originally a Federalist of the school of Hamilton and Jay, and in later life was a loyal Whig. Like so many Boston merchants, he was a strong admirer of Daniel Webster, whom he presented with a service of silver in evidence of his appreciation, not long after the great debate with Senator Hayne of South Carolina. But he had no desire to hold public office himself. He was a Whig presidential elector in 1852, but he refused to contribute to the campaign fund of his brother Abbott in 1848, when the latter was a candidate for the vice-presidential nomination on the ticket with General Taylor, saying that "if my vote would make my brother Vice-President, I would not give it, as I think it lowering his good name to accept office of any sort, by employing such means as are now needful to get votes." Later he rejoiced when his brother refused a place in General Taylor's cabinet, though he had supported "Old Zach" for president.

Amos Lawrence was twice married. His first wife, Sarah Richards, daughter of Giles Richards of Boston, whom he married June 6, 1811, died in 1819. Two years later he married Nancy (Means) Ellis, widow of Judge Ellis of Claremont, N. H., and daughter of Robert Means of Amherst, N. H. He had three sons and a daughter, one of whom, Amos Adams Lawrence [q.v.], also attained distinction as a merchant and philanthropist.

[The best source of information on Amos Lawrence's life and character is *Extracts from the Diary and Correspondence of the Late Amos Lawrence*, edited by his son, William R. Lawrence. See also: *Memorial Biogs. of the New-Eng. Hist. Geneal. Soc.*, vol. I (1880); Mark Hopkins, *A Discourse Commemorative of Amos Lawrence* (1853); F. W. Ballard, *The Stewardship of Wealth, as Illustrated in the Lives of Amos and Abbott Lawrence* (1865), a lecture delivered before the Y. M. C. A., New York; Chas. Adams, *Sketch of Amos Lawrence* (1883); Mary C. Crawford, *Famous Families of Mass.*, vol. II (1930); Freeman Hunt, *Lives of Am. Merchants*, vol. II (1858); John Lawrence, *The Geneal. of the Family of John Lawrence of Wisset, in Suffolk, England* (1869); *Boston Commonwealth*, Jan. 1, 3, 4, 5, 1853.]   A. N. H.

LAWRENCE, AMOS ADAMS (July 31, 1814–Aug. 22, 1886), merchant and philanthropist, was the second son of Amos Lawrence [q.v.], a leading Boston merchant and philanthropist, and Sarah (Richards) Lawrence. He was educated at Franklin Academy, North Andover, and at Harvard College, where he graduated in 1835. Entering business for himself, after graduating from college, as a commission merchant, he formed a partnership in 1843 with Robert M. Mason, under the firm name of Mason & Lawrence. Mason ceased after a few years to be active in the firm and Lawrence continued to be the principal partner for forty years. The firm was very successful, holding the selling agency for several important textile mills and eventually acquiring the selling agency for the Pacific Mills at Lawrence, which for many years was the largest plant of its kind in the United States. Lawrence also engaged independently in manufacturing textiles, his principal venture being the Ipswich Mills, which he acquired in 1860 for the manufacture of cotton hosiery and other knit goods. This was then a new industry in the United States. Although for many years he operated the mill at a loss, he ultimately succeeded in making it profitable and established the industry on a sound basis, becoming the largest manufacturer of knit goods in the country. He took an active part in promoting the interests of the textile industry, being for many years an ardent advocate of a protective tariff and in later life serving as president of the American Association of Knit Goods Manufacturers and also of the National Association of Cotton Manufacturers and Planters.

His father's philanthropic activities naturally brought the son many opportunities for charitable work. While still a young man he became a trustee of the Massachusetts General Hospital and took a great interest in the hospital and in the McLean Asylum for the Insane. He became interested also in the colonization of free negroes in Africa. With increasing years he became more and more interested in education. He established Lawrence University, named after him, in Appleton, Wis., in connection with a large real-estate speculation, in which he became a reluctant partner, and another college at Lawrence, Kan., which afterward was taken over by the state and became the nucleus of the state university. He served for several years as treasurer of Harvard College, and for many years as treasurer of the Episcopal Theological School in Cambridge. He was a generous benefactor of both institutions.

His most distinguished public service was that which he rendered in connection with the New England Emigrant Aid Company, of which he was treasurer. This company was founded in 1854 by Eli Thayer of Worcester, Mass., an ardent but impecunious anti-slavery man, for the purpose of excluding slavery from the territory of Kansas by colonizing it with freemen. Thayer's scheme was to organize a company on a strictly business basis, which would finance settlers and by their success earn profits for the stockholders. A charter was secured and funds raised by the sale of stock. Lawrence had no faith in the Emigrant Aid Company as a business venture, never regarding it in any other light than as a patriotic and charitable enterprise, and seems to have sold the stock on that basis. (See Samuel A. Johnson, "The Genesis of the New England Emigrant Aid Society," in the *New England Quarterly,* January 1930.) To his zeal, aptitude, and business efficiency the success of the enterprise must be largely ascribed. After victory was in sight for the free-state forces, he withdrew from the management of the company, though retaining his interest in the university at Lawrence and in other public institutions in Kansas.

Despite Lawrence's hostility to slavery and his strenuous efforts to keep the "peculiar institution" from spreading onto free soil, he was a conservative in politics. Brought up as a Whig, he never joined the Free Soilers and was opposed to the radical Republican party in the campaigns of 1856 and 1860. In 1856 he was nominated for the governorship of Massachusetts on the Fillmore ticket, but declined. Two years later he accepted a similar nomination and was defeated. In 1860 he was the candidate of the Constitutional Union party and ran unsuccessfully on the ticket with Bell and Everett. After the secession of South Carolina he continued to work for the maintenance of the union by peaceful means and joined Everett and Robert C. Winthrop in a trip to Washington to support the Crittenden compromise. When war broke out, he gave the Lincoln administration unwavering support to the end. He took the lead in raising a regiment of mounted troops, the 2nd Massachusetts Cavalry, but the condition of his health prevented him from taking personal command.

Like his father, Lawrence was more interested in religion than in politics. The Unitarianism which his father and uncles adopted in place of their ancestral Puritanism on moving in to the city from the country failed to satisfy the religious needs of the next generation of Lawrences, and several of them became members of the Episcopal Church. Amos Adams Lawrence was one of these and in 1842 he was confirmed at St. Paul's, together with his wife and his brother. It was his strong religious feeling rather than his politics which made him an admirer of John Brown. Brown's forceful methods he never fully approved and the raid on Harpers Ferry he condemned as the act of a lawless fanatic. The rifles which had once belonged to the Emigrant Aid Company and which were used on Brown's raid were not so used with Lawrence's consent, but Lawrence did give money to Brown and he contributed toward the purchase of the farm at North Elba for Brown's family and toward the employment of counsel at his trial after the raid on Harpers Ferry. He foresaw that Brown would be lauded by the Abolitionists as a martyr and predicted that his death would hasten the end of slavery. Lawrence died suddenly, of heart disease, in August 1886. He had married, Mar. 31, 1842, Sarah Elizabeth Appleton, daughter of William Appleton, a leading Boston merchant. She, together with six of their seven children, survived him.

[There is an excellent biography, *Life of Amos A. Lawrence with Extracts from His Diary and Correspondence* (1888), by Lawrence's son, Wm. Lawrence. Additional material of much interest will be found in the same author's *Memories of a Happy Life* (1926). An obituary appeared in the *Boston Transcript,* Aug. 23, 1886.]   A. N. H.

LAWRENCE, GEORGE NEWBOLD (Oct. 20, 1806–Jan. 17, 1895), ornithologist and wholesale druggist, was born in New York City where his entire life was spent. His parents were John Burling Lawrence and Hannah Newbold. Through his father he traced his ancestry to William Lawrence, who emigrated from Hertfordshire, England, in 1635, and settled first at Plymouth. John Burling Lawrence was engaged in the wholesale drug and chemical business, having formed a partnership with Jacob Schieffelin in 1781. George entered this establishment at the age of sixteen, later becoming a partner and in 1835 head of the firm. He had married, in 1834, Mary Ann Newbold, the daughter of George Newbold of New York City. In later life he retired in order to devote all of his time to his ornithological studies which had hitherto been a hobby to be enjoyed only as business cares permitted. From early boyhood he seems to have been interested in birds. At the age of fourteen he was allowed to have a gun and soon began collecting specimens—the nucleus of the collection of some 8,000 skins which later became the property of the American Museum of Natural History. At this time the Lawrences lived at their country home, "Forest Hill," some eight miles north of the New York City Hall, from which an unbroken forest extended to Fort Washington Point. Not far from them was the home of John James Audubon and while, at the time of young Lawrence's boyhood, the famous painter-naturalist was nearing the close of his eventful life, Lawrence became well acquainted with his sons, Victor and John, and this association doubtless stimulated his interest in ornithology.

Lawrence's early studies dealt entirely with the birds of the United States but about 1858 he turned his attention to neotropical ornithology, especially to the study of the birds of the West Indies and Central America, upon which he soon became an authority. While his knowledge was broad and comprehensive, his publications were almost entirely limited to descriptions of new species or to lists of collections submitted to him for study. In 1841 he made the acquaintance of Spencer F. Baird, the future secretary of the Smithsonian Institution, whose magnetic enthusiasm doubtless did much to clinch Lawrence's determination to devote himself to the serious study of ornithology. A little later he met John Cassin, the noted ornithologist of Philadelphia. Together they assisted Baird in the preparation of the study on North American birds published by the War Department in the series of *Reports of Explorations and Surveys*

to Ascertain the . . . Route for a Railroad from the Mississippi River to the Pacific Ocean (vol. IX, 1858). Lawrence contributed the accounts of many of the groups of water birds. In later life he became one of the founders of the American Ornithologists' Union and was soon after made an honorary member. He was similarly honored by the Zoological Society of London, the British Ornithologists' Union, and many of the scientific societies of America. He was also one of the founders of the College of Pharmacy of the City of New York. Those who knew him in the last years of his long life saw in him a typical gentleman of the old school in both manners and appearance.

[D. G. Elliot, "In Memoriam: Geo. Newbold Lawrence," *The Auk*, Jan. 1896; L. S. Foster, "The Published Writings of Geo. Newbold Lawrence," *Bull. U. S. Nat. Museum*, No. 40 (1892), with portrait and biographical sketch; Thomas Lawrence, *Hist. Geneal. of the Lawrence Family* (1858); *N. Y. Tribune*, Jan. 19, 1895; personal acquaintance.]   W. S.

LAWRENCE, JAMES (Oct. 1, 1781–June 4, 1813), naval officer, great-grandson of Elisha Lawrence, who was established as a merchant in Monmouth County, N. J., at the end of the seventeenth century, was born in Burlington, N. J. He was the son of John (or John Brown) Lawrence, a lawyer of considerable ability, and his second wife, Martha (Tallman) Lawrence. After receiving an elementary education in the grammar school of his native town, James began the study of law, but, on evincing a distaste for his father's profession, he was permitted to choose his own calling, that of the sea, and was given instruction in navigation and naval tactics. On Sept. 4, 1798, he entered the navy as a midshipman on the *Ganges* and some two years later was made acting lieutenant on the *Adams*. Retained under Jefferson's peace establishment as a midshipman, he was on Sept. 1, 1801, promoted sailing master, and some months later, lieutenant, taking rank from Apr. 6, 1802. In the war with Tripoli, 1801–05, he was, successively, first lieutenant of the *Enterprise*, commander of the same, first lieutenant of the *John Adams*, and commander of *Gunboat No. 6*. He established a reputation for gallantry as second in command in the two most daring operations of the war, Porter's boat attack on Tripoli and the burning of the *Philadelphia*. His service in connection with the first of these exploits was highly commended by Porter. Notice of the second was taken by Congress in a resolution expressing its appreciation and granting to the participants two months' extra pay. So inadequate was the pecuniary reward that Lawrence declined to receive his share of it.

He next served as first lieutenant of the *Constitution* and then commanded, successively, the *Vixen, Wasp, Argus,* and *Hornet.* He was promoted to the rank of master commandant in December 1811. Twice he carried dispatches to Europe for the State Department—on the *Wasp* in 1809, and on the *Hornet* in 1811–12. The unsatisfactory character of the messages that he brought to America in May 1812 precipitated the war of that year.

The *Hornet* was one of the vessels of the squadron of Commodore John Rodgers [*q.v.*] that put to sea from New York on the declaration of war, and she captured three of the prizes taken during this initial venture, which was on the whole rather fruitless. Lawrence's second cruise was made in company with Commodore Bainbridge in the South Atlantic Ocean. At Bahia he blockaded the British sloop of war *Bonne Citoyenne* for several days and then challenged her to single combat. For various reasons the British commander, quite properly, declined to fight. Lawrence continued the blockade until driven into port by the *Montagu,* 74 guns. Escaping under cover of darkness, he cruised to the northward, and off Pernambuco captured the merchantman *Resolution,* 10 guns. On Feb. 24, 1813, at the mouth of the Demerara River, he encountered the British brig of war *Peacock,* about the same size as the *Hornet* but with an armament only two-thirds that of the American ship. A hot, close action ensued, ending in the surrender of the *Peacock,* some fifteen minutes after the first shot was fired. She was so badly injured that she sank before all her crew could be taken off. Her loss in the fight was thirty-four, including her commander, who was killed; that of the *Hornet,* three (Mahan, *post,* II, 8). This great difference is good evidence of the superior fighting and seamanship of the Americans. The *Hornet* arrived at New York Mar. 24, 1813.

Lawrence was promoted captain Mar. 3, 1813, before news of his victory had reached America. On Mar. 31, the Common Council of New York thanked him for his victory and voted to present him with the freedom of the city, together with a piece of plate, and a week later it gave him and his crew a public dinner. On May 1, 1813, he was placed in command of the navy yard at New York. He expected next to go to sea on the *Constitution,* but on May 6 he was ordered to relieve the commander of the *Chesapeake* at Boston. His instructions were to proceed to sea as soon as the weather and the force and position of the enemy would permit and to intercept the British storeships and transports bound to Canada. This was an objective of the highest importance, but Lawrence abandoned it to fight a ship duel that could not have greatly affected the course of the war had he been successful. His judgment has been severely censured by recent naval historians (Mahan, *post,* II, 131–33; Chadwick, *post,* pp. 206–07). He took command of the *Chesapeake* on May 20 and went to sea on June 1, with the intention of fighting the British frigate *Shannon,* 38 guns, then blockading Boston. In guns the ships were well matched. In number of crew the *Chesapeake* had the advantage, but in organization, seamanship, and gunnery practice, the *Shannon* was much the superior. Even so, Lawrence had a chance of success and must be acquitted of foolhardiness. The action lasted less than fifteen minutes. Lawrence and his first lieutenant, Augustus Ludlow [*q.v.*], fell mortally wounded. The flag of the *Chesapeake* was hauled down by the enemy. Her loss was 145; that of the *Shannon,* 82.

On June 8 Lawrence was buried at Halifax with military honors. In the following August Capt. George Crowninshield [*q.v.*], a shipowner of Salem, Mass., sailing under a flag of truce, brought the body to Salem, where it was given funeral honors with a eulogy pronounced by Justice Joseph Story [*q.v.*]. Thence it was conveyed to New York, where on Sept. 16, 1813 it was buried in Trinity Churchyard. The words, "Don't give up the ship," which the mortally wounded hero is said to have uttered when carried below, became a popular rallying cry of the navy.

In 1808 Lawrence was married to Julia Montaudevert, the daughter of a New York City merchant of French descent. There were two children, a daughter who later married a naval officer, and a posthumous son who died in infancy. All recognition of Lawrence's achievements by the federal government came after his death. On July 13, 1813, in accordance with a recommendation of the President, Congress voted $25,000 to the officers and crew of the *Hornet* as prize money. In January 1814, it adopted a resolution requesting the President to present to the nearest male relative of Lawrence a gold medal as a testimony of its appreciation of his victory and to communicate to his nearest relative its sense of the loss sustained by the navy in his death.

[Record of Officers, 1798–1817, Bureau of Navigation, Navy Dept.; Albert Gleaves, *James Lawrence* (1904); articles in *Port Folio* (Philadelphia), Sept. 1813, Jan., Feb. 1817; *Biography of James Lawrence, Esq.,* etc. (1813); Thomas Lawrence, *Hist. Geneal. of the Lawrence Family* (1858); J. F. Cooper, *The Hist. of the Navy of the U. S. A.* (2 vols., 1839); A. T.

Mahan, *Sea Power in Its Relations to the War of 1812* (1919), vol. II; F. E. Chadwick, "The American Navy, 1775–1815," *Proc. Mass. Hist. Soc.*, vol. XLVI (1913).]
                       C. O. P.

LAWRENCE, RICHARD SMITH (Nov. 22, 1817–Mar. 10, 1892), inventor, gunsmith, tool-manufacturer, was the son of Richard and Susan (Smith) Lawrence, both of English descent, and was born on his father's farm in Chester, Vt. When he was two years old the family moved to Jefferson County, N. Y., and for nineteen years Lawrence lived in the vicinity of Watertown, attending school for three years, doing farm work, laboring in a wood-working shop, and spending his spare time in a custom gun shop. After serving for three months in the army during the Canadian Rebellion he went in 1838 to live with relatives in Windsor, Vt. Here he found work with N. Kendall & Company, a firm that was making guns at the Windsor prison. In six months he had so mastered the manufacturing processes that he was put in charge of the work, continuing in this capacity until 1842, when gun-making was stopped. He then remained at the prison for a time in charge of the carriage shop. In 1843, in partnership with Kendall, he opened a gun shop in Windsor. The following year, with the help of S. E. Robbins, a business man, they obtained a contract for 10,000 rifles from the federal government, and a new company, Robbins, Kendall & Lawrence, was formed and a factory built at Windsor. After three prosperous years Robbins and Lawrence purchased Kendall's holdings and for the next four years the two partners continued successfully. Lawrence supervised the design and production of the guns and was constantly improving the methods of manufacture. He devised the barrel-drilling and rifling machines, built a plain milling machine—the forerunner of the Lincoln miller—and invented the split pulley. In 1850 he introduced the practice of lubricating bullets with tallow, which made possible the success of the repeating rifle. By 1851 the partners had built up a wide reputation and were engaged to furnish all of the machinery for the Enfield Armory in England and, in addition, were awarded a large contract for British Enfield rifles. In 1852 they contracted to manufacture Sharps carbines and rifles, the former at Windsor and the latter in a new plant at Hartford, Conn. Production had hardly got under way, however, when the partners experienced serious financial difficulties induced by their unsuccessful attempt in 1850 to undertake the manufacture of railroad cars, and they failed with a loss of nearly a quarter of a million dollars. The Sharps Rifle Company thereupon bought the Robbins and Lawrence enterprise in Hartford and employed Lawrence as superintendent. He continued with the company from 1856 to 1872 when he resigned to accept a position with the city of Hartford. Until his death he served on the water board, the board of aldermen, the council board, and on the fire board. He had married Mary Ann Finney in Philadelphia on May 22, 1842, and at the time of his death in Hartford was survived by a son.

[Jos. W. Roe, *English and Am. Tool Builders* (1916, 1926); Guy Hubbard, "Development of Machine Tools in New England," *Am. Machinist*, Oct. 15, 1923, Mar. 20, 1924; *Hartford Courant*, Mar. 11, 1892; family records.]
                       C. W. M.

LAWRENCE, WILLIAM (Sept. 7, 1783–Oct. 14, 1848), merchant and philanthropist, brother of Amos and Abbott Lawrence [*qq.v.*], was one of the leaders in the early development of the New England textile industry. He was born in Groton, Mass., the third son of Samuel and Susanna Parker Lawrence, and a descendant of John Lawrence who emigrated from Suffolk County, England, and settled in Watertown, Mass., in 1635. He originally intended to be a farmer, but poor health caused him to leave home in 1809 and spend the winter with his brother, Amos, in Boston, where the latter had recently established himself in business. Finding business to his liking, William set up for himself in the following year as a commission merchant and prospered. In 1822 he took into partnership his younger brother, Samuel, forming the firm of W. & S. Lawrence. In 1825, the brothers, who had previously been chiefly importers, became interested in domestic manufactures. It was through their agency that the first incorporated company for the manufacture of woolen goods was formed, the Middlesex Manufacturing Company, with a plant at Lowell, then recently formed. Lawrence continued in active business, principally in the woolen commission business, until 1842, when he retired with what is described as "an ample fortune." His wife, Susan Ruggles Bordman, born Apr. 29, 1787, whom he married May 20, 1813, was the daughter of one of Boston's leading citizens and contributed a substantial patrimony to the family fortune. Nine children were born, of whom four survived their father.

William Lawrence's most important public service was his part in the establishment of the so-called "Suffolk Bank System." This bank, designed to put the currency of New England on a sound basis, was chartered in 1818, and Lawrence served on the board of directors from its organization to his death, thirty years later. He was also active in the promotion of public improvements in Boston, and a generous contributor to local charities. His most significant benefaction was the endowment of Groton Academy, the name of which, in recognition of his benefactions and those of his brother Amos, was changed to Lawrence Academy in 1846. One of a remarkable group of brothers, distinguished alike for their business efficiency and for their practical philanthropy, he was a leader in the generation of Boston merchants which guided New England through its industrial revolution.

[S. K. Lothrop, *Memoir of Wm. Lawrence* (1856), reprinted from the *Am. Jour. of Educ.*, July 1856; Freeman Hunt, *Lives of Am. Merchants*, vol. II (1858); Mary C. Crawford, *Famous Families of Mass.*, vol. II (1930); John Lawrence, *The Geneal. of the Family of John Lawrence of Wisset, in Suffolk, England* (1869); *Boston Transcript*, Oct. 16, 1848.]   A. N. H.

LAWRENCE, WILLIAM (June 26, 1819–May 8, 1899), jurist and Ohio congressman, the son of Joseph and Temperance (Gilchrist) Lawrence, was born in Mount Pleasant, Ohio. He received his early educational training in the village schools and in Tidball's Academy, near Steubenville. In 1838 he graduated with high honors from Franklin College at New Athens and, that autumn, entered the law office of James L. Gage of Morgan County. While pursuing his legal studies he taught school in Pennsville and at MacConnelsville, Ohio. In 1839 he entered the Cincinnati law school and the following March received his degree. In 1840 he began the practice of law, first in Zanesville, then in MacConnelsville and, the next year, settled at Bellefontaine. In 1842 he was appointed by the United States district court to be commissioner of bankruptcy for Logan County. On Dec. 20, 1843, he married Cornelia, the daughter of William Hawkins of MacConnelsville, who died three months after their marriage, and on Mar. 20, 1845, he married Caroline, the daughter of Henry Miller of Bellefontaine. In 1845 he became prosecuting attorney of Logan County and, from 1845 to 1847, was the editor of the *Logan Gazette*. He was a member of the Ohio House of Representatives in 1846 and 1847 and of the state Senate in 1849, 1850, and 1854. In the Ohio legislature he took an active part in obtaining the adoption of measures providing for reform schools for juvenile delinquents and for district school libraries. He also brought about the passage of a measure that gave greater security to real-estate interests in Ohio and was the author of the Ohio free banking law of 1851. In 1851 he was reporter for the Ohio supreme court, and he published the

twentieth volume of *Reports of Cases Argued and Determined in the Supreme Court of Ohio*, which was favorably commented upon for its logical arrangement of decisions, interspersed with the author's comments on previous cases both in Ohio and elsewhere. In 1859 he became editor of the *Western Law Monthly* and served three years. From February 1857 to September 1864 he was judge of the common-pleas court and district court. During the Civil War he was colonel, for three months, of the 84th Ohio Volunteers, serving in Maryland, and, in 1863, Lincoln appointed him district judge of Florida, but he declined to accept.

From 1865 to 1877, excluding one term from 1871 to 1873, he was a member of Congress. During his ten years' service he was an earnest advocate of all measures designed to secure civil and political equality. In 1869 he made a report on the New York election frauds, which resulted in important state and federal legislation. He was the virtual author of the law that created the Department of Justice. He also drafted the measure that gave each soldier one hundred and sixty acres of the alternate reserved sections in the railroad land grants. In the interest of the settlers, he became one of the early advocates of prohibiting the sale of public lands by authority of an Indian treaty rather than by act of Congress, and his efforts led to the passage of the act of Mar. 3, 1871. In the face of strenuous opposition, he ably defended, against the railroad attorneys before the judiciary committee, a bill requiring the Pacific railroad companies to indemnify the government to the extent of one hundred and fifty million dollars and, on July 7, 1876, carried his measure through the House of Representatives. The next year the secretary of the interior, Carl Schurz, heartily indorsed the principles of the "Lawrence Bill" in his annual report. From 1880 to 1885 Lawrence held the office of first comptroller of the United States Treasury Department and was the first of the comptrollers to print his decisions. His legal acumen won for him universal recognition. He often appeared before the United States Supreme Court in important land cases such as *Morton* vs. *Nebraska* (21 *Wall*, 660–75), *Holden* vs. *Joy* (17 *Wall*, 211–53), and *Leavenworth, Lawrence and Galveston Railroad Company* vs. *United States* (92 *U. S.*, 733–60). His firm grasp of the fundamentals of the law, his keen analysis of the salient points at issue, his quick perception of the weakness in his opponents' arguments, and his frankness made him respected and feared. In the impeachment of Johnson he prepared a brief of authorities to support the legal argument of Benjamin F. Butler (appendix to *Proceedings in the Trial of Andrew Johnson,* 1868). He appeared before the Electoral Commission in 1877 to argue the case of Oregon and South Carolina (*Congressional Record,* 44 Cong., 2 Sess., pt. 4, pp. 4, 185). He was also a recognized authority on wool and became the president of the state association of wool growers in 1891 and of the national association in 1893. He died at Kenton, Ohio.

[Files of the Congressional Joint Committee on Printing; *A Biog. Cyc. and Portrait Gallery . . . of Ohio* (1879); Henry Howe, *Hist. Colls. of Ohio,* vol. II (1891); *The Biog. Annals of Ohio,* 1902–03; *Who's Who in America,* 1899; *Biog. Dir. of the Am. Cong.* (1928); *Ohio State Journal,* May 9, 1899.] R. C. M.

LAWRENCE, WILLIAM BEACH (Oct. 23, 1800–Mar. 26, 1881), public official, writer on international law, was born in New York City, the son of Isaac and Cornelia (Beach) Lawrence. His earliest American paternal ancestor, Thomas Lawrence, emigrated from England and had settled in Newtown, L. I., by 1656. His maternal grandfather was for many years assistant rector of Trinity Church, New York. From birth he had the advantages of opulence and social station. His father was a man of wealth and influence, a presidential elector in 1820 and one-time president of the New York branch of the Bank of the United States. The boy was by nature studious and precocious, and in 1818 he was graduated with high honors from Columbia College. After graduation he studied law in the famous law school in Litchfield, Conn. During a winter in the South he spent a few days at "Monticello," as the guest of Jefferson. In 1821 he married Esther, daughter of Archibald Gracie [*q.v.*]. The years 1821–23 he spent in Europe, where he enjoyed the entrée into the most exclusive circles, thanks to letters of introduction to Lord Holland, Lafayette, and others. Few young Americans have ever been accorded a more distinguished reception abroad. In Paris he pursued studies in law at the Sorbonne and the École de Droit and attended the lectures of Say on political economy. It was at this time that he conceived the interest in international law that was to be the absorbing concern of his life and the field of his greatest achievement. For three years after his return to America he practised law in New York. In 1826 he was appointed secretary of legation in London, and in 1827, as chargé d'affaires, he conducted the correspondence regarding the northeast boundary.

For the next twenty years Lawrence lived in New York, practising his profession, pursuing his investigations in jurisprudence and public law, writing, and lecturing. Among the products of this period may be noted the *Two Lectures on Political Economy* (1831); *The Bank of the United States* (1831), an argument for its constitutionality and utility, reprinted from the *North American Review,* April 1831; *The Origin and Nature of the Representative and Federative Institutions of the United States* (1832); "The Public Distress" (*American Quarterly Review,* June 1834); a *History of the Negotiations in Reference to the Eastern and Northeastern Boundaries of the United States* (1841); an address on the *Colonisation and Subsequent History of New Jersey* (1843); and an unpublished memoir of Albert Gallatin. His celebrated argument in the case of the German Reformed Church, by which he obtained a reversal of the Chancellor's decision, was published in 1845. In 1850 he took up his residence in Newport, R. I. In 1851 he was elected lieutenant-governor of Rhode Island, and in 1852, during the administration of Philip Allen, he served as acting governor. Among other measures, he urged the abolition of imprisonment for debt and opposed, on constitutional grounds, the enactment of a law prohibiting the sale of liquor. In 1855 appeared his annotated edition of the *Elements of International Law,* by Henry Wheaton, his long-time and intimate friend, a work of extraordinary erudition, which at once took rank as a standard textbook and an authoritative commentary. Three years later he published a treatise entitled *Visitation and Search.* The political issues of the fifties also enlisted his interest. While not defending slavery, he condoned it as an economic necessity and vehemently denounced abolitionists as dangerous fanatics. He stood for state's rights, but not for secession, yet he opposed coercion and after the Civil War protested against the attempt to "hold the South in vassalage." (See his *L'Industrie Française et L'Esclavage des Nègres aux États Unis,* 1860; and two addresses: *No North, No South!,* 1856, and *The Issues of the Hour,* 1868.)

In 1863 Lawrence brought out his second edition of Wheaton. Although his learning was universally recognized, his political views gave offense in certain quarters and an attempt was made to discredit his work as "disloyal." Richard Henry Dana, Jr., 1815–1882 [*q.v.*], was engaged to prepare a "loyal" edition. Lawrence charged Dana with piracy and was sustained in his contention by an opinion of the Court to the effect that many of the notes in the Dana edition infringed his rights. In 1866 he attended the Social Science Congress at Bristol and was named a member of a commission to compile a code of international law, a project which, together with an international court, he strongly advocated. Two years later appeared the first volume of the *Commentaire sur les Éléments du Droit International.* Later three other volumes followed. Lawrence published in 1866 a pamphlet on the *Disabilities of American Women Married Abroad*; in 1871, *The Treaty of Washington; Letters from Hon. William Beach Lawrence*; and in 1874, *Administration of Equity Jurisprudence.* Meanwhile he was contributing to the *Revue de Droit International,* the *London Law Magazine,* the *Transactions of the Social Science Association,* and other periodicals, and also lecturing on international law in Columbian University, Washington. In 1873 he defended the case of the steamship *Circassian* before the Joint High Commission, obtaining a reversal of the decision of the Supreme Court. His argument, published under the title *Belligerent and Sovereign Rights as Regards Neutrals During the War of Secession* (1873), was considered both in England and America as an authoritative exposition of certain important points of public law. In temperament and manner Lawrence combined the courtliness of the aristocrat with the candor and directness of the democrat. In literary style he was inclined to be diffuse. He was an omnivorous reader and an indefatigable student. Everything that came from his pen testifies to a prodigious memory, to a penetrating mind, and to analytical and reasoning powers of the first order.

[*Biog. Cyc. of Representative Men of R. I.* (1881), I, 287–89; Chas. H. Hart, *A Discourse Commemorative of the Life and Services of the Late Wm. Beach Lawrence* (1881); J. G. Wilson, *Gov. Wm. Beach Lawrence, an Address Delivered Before the N. Y. Hist. Soc.* (1882); J. S. Hart, *Manual of Am. Lit.* (1873); Thos. Lawrence, *Hist. Geneal. of the Lawrence Family* (1858); Isaac Lawrence, memoir in *N. Y. Geneal. and Biog. Record,* Apr. 1895; *N. Y. Times,* Mar. 26, 1881.]

T.C.

LAWRIE, ALEXANDER (Feb. 25, 1828–Feb. 15, 1917), painter and crayon portrait draftsman, was born in New York City, the son of Alexander Lawrie, merchant, and his wife, Sarah Coombe. According to one account, he was apprenticed to an engraver at fifteen. He studied in the life and antique classes of the National Academy of Design, and between the years 1850 and 1854 was living in Philadelphia and showing crayon portrait heads, among them one of Thomas Sully, at the Pennsylvania Academy of the Fine Arts. In 1854 he went abroad for three years' study under E. Leutze, at Düsseldorf, under Picot in Paris, and under Greek and Italian painters in Florence. Returning to America in 1858, he opened a studio in Philadel-

phia, where he regularly exhibited work in oils —portraits, landscapes, genre—until 1864. At the outbreak of the Civil War he enlisted (Apr. 18, 1861) in the 17th Regiment, Pennsylvania Volunteer Infantry. He was discharged in August and reënlisted Sept. 5, becoming captain of Company B, 121st Pennsylvania Volunteers. Early in 1863 he was disabled and was discharged the following June.

On his recovery he again went abroad to study, but before 1866 returned to New York, where he spent the best years of his professional life. For a decade his work was a regular feature of the annual exhibitions of the Academy, to which he contributed ideal figure pieces, portraits in oil and crayon, and landscapes painted in the Adirondacks or the highlands of the Hudson. In 1868 he was elected an associate of the National Academy of Design. To the Centennial Exhibition he sent two canvases, "A Monk Playing a Violoncello," and "Autumn in the Hudson Highlands." Among the best of his crayon portraits, of which he is said to have executed "upwards of a thousand," are those of Richard Henry Stoddard, Thomas Buchanan Read, and George Henry Boker. His portraits in oil include one of Judge Sutherland painted for the American Bar Association, and one of Gen. Zealous B. Tower, for the United States Military Academy at West Point. The erroneous statement, repeated in more than one biographical work, that Lawrie did engraving is probably due to his having been confused with one Robert Lawrie, an English engraver.

Lawrie, who was unmarried, disappeared from public life about 1876. Twenty years later he was living in Chalmers, Ind., and in 1902 he was admitted to the Indiana State Soldiers' Home at Lafayette, where he remained until his death. At the age of seventy-six, he undertook the painting of a series of portraits of the generals who served in the Civil War, many of them done partly from memory. The task occupied twelve years. He completed 158 portraits, which he bequeathed to the state of Indiana. The series, now hanging in the library of the Soldiers' Home where he died, will probably in time be placed in the State House at Indianapolis.

[C. E. Clement and Laurence Hutton, *Artists of the Nineteenth Century* (2 vols., 1907); Theodore Bolton, *Early Am. Portrait Draughtsmen in Crayon* (1923); S. P. Bates, *Hist. of Pa. Volunteers,* vols. I (1869), IV (1870); *Am. Art Annual,* 1917; *Am. Art News,* Mar. 3, 1917; *Indianapolis Star,* Feb. 16, 1917; information as to certain facts from a nephew, Robert Telfer, Brookston, Ind.] M. B. H.

LAWS, SAMUEL SPAHR (Mar. 23, 1824–Jan. 9, 1921), educator, was born in Ohio County, Va., the son of James and Rachel (Spahr) Laws. His ancestors had come from England to Maryland in 1672. Having acquired the rudiments of his education in an old-field school in Virginia, he entered Miami University at Oxford, Ohio, where he was graduated in 1848 as the valedictorian of his class. He then was a student for three years in Princeton Theological Seminary, graduating in 1851 with highest honors. In the same year he was ordained and became pastor of West Church in St. Louis. His career as an educator began in 1854, when he became professor of physical science at Westminster College, Fulton, Mo. He was made president of this institution in the following year and served in this capacity until 1861, when, on account of difficulties resulting from his sympathy with the South in the Civil War, he resigned and began making a translation of Aristotle. As a Southern sympathizer he was arrested by Union authorities and confined in several prisons but eventually he was paroled. He then spent some time abroad, mostly in Paris. Before the close of the war he obtained a position as vice-president of the New York Gold Exchange, an office which he filled with recognized efficiency. After resigning this position, he invented and introduced the "ticker" by which market reports could be telegraphed simultaneously.

In New York he studied law at Columbia College and in 1870 he was granted the degree of LL.B. He had already been admitted, in 1869, to the New York bar. His interests then led him to become a student in the Bellevue Hospital Medical College, where in 1875 he received the degree of M.D. Called to the University of Missouri by unanimous action of the curators, he became on July 4, 1876, president of this institution and professor of mental and moral philosophy and of the evidences of Christianity. He served in this position until July 1, 1889. In his plans for the development of the university he displayed clear foresight. He believed that the university should be an integral part of the public-school system of the state, a fact which he forcefully brought before the legislature in 1887. After leaving the University, Laws engaged privately in scholarly work until 1893, when he accepted a position in the Presbyterian Theological Seminary, Columbia, S. C., as Perkins Professor of Natural Science in Connection with Revelation and Christian Apologetics. He retired from this position in 1898, at the age of seventy-four, moving to Richmond, Va., and later to Washington, D. C.

Laws was a solidly built man of medium height, revealing in his appearance a strong, vigorous character, tempered with geniality, but capable of brusqueness on occasion. In his inaugural address at the University of Missouri, he said: "The authority of government in a school is not derived from the pupils nor is it dependent upon them in any sense whatever. . . . It does not come up from them, but it comes down upon them. . . . The only alternative to a pupil in school is to obey or leave, willingly or by restraint. . . . Any other theory works its own inevitable destruction" (Inauguration of S. S. Laws, post, pp. 60–61). Although he was thoroughly honest in motive, his legalistic point of view, positive convictions, forceful will, and directness of word and act in discipline and in other administrative matters undoubtedly resulted in antagonisms which greater tact might have mitigated or even have avoided. His equally outstanding characteristics were his breadth of interests and his extensive and thorough scholarship. With an unusual memory, he had at command a definite, comprehensive, and well-organized stock of knowledge. A scholar in the classics and in Hebrew, he had an extensive knowledge of the sciences; an able student and writer in the field of theology, he was successful in business and made a notable mechanical invention; a teacher and investigator, he was also an educational administrator. His most profound interest appeared to be in theology, as evidenced by his teaching and writings. The latter, although brief, reveal a well-disciplined, logical mind and an extensive acquaintance with the literature in their respective fields. His published works include: A Letter by the Rev. S. S. Laws, LL.D. to the Synod of Missouri (O. S.) (1872); Metaphysics: A Lecture (1879); Life and Labors of Louis Pasteur (1886); Christianity: Its Nature (1903); Polygamy and Citizenship in Church and State (1906); and The At-onement by the Christian Trinity (1919). Laws was married, on Jan. 19, 1860, to Ann Maria (Broadwell) Doubleday, daughter of William Broadwell of Fulton, Mo. He died at Asheville, N. C., in his ninety-seventh year.

[Hist. of Boone County, Mo. (1882); Inauguration of S. S. Laws, LL.D., as President of the Univ. of Mo. (1876); brief obituary in Mo. Hist. Rev., Jan. 1921; J. M. Greenwood, sketch in Educ. Rev., Mar. 1903; Mo. Alumni Tribute to Dr. Samuel Spahr Laws (1901); Wm. F. Switzler, unpublished "History of the University of Missouri," in the archives of the University; Princeton Theol. Sem. Necrological Report, Aug. 1921; M. M. Fisher and J. J. Rice, Hist. of Westminster Coll. (1903); Testimony Taken Before the Univ. Investigating Committee, Thirty-Fifth Gen. Assembly of the State of Mo. (1889); records in the archives of the University.]   J. H. C.

LAWSON, ALEXANDER (Dec. 19, 1773–Aug. 22, 1846), line-engraver, was born on a farm at Ravenstruthers, Lanarkshire, Scotland. Leaving school at fifteen, he went to assist a brother who was in business in Liverpool, but after a year's experience, removed to Manchester. There he became interested in the prints hung in the windows of a bookseller's shop, and determined to become an engraver. He began with a penknife and a smooth halfpenny to cut designs, but the scratched result did not satisfy him, so he had a blacksmith fashion an engraver's tool for him, and with this continued his experiments. He was charmed by the French engravings of the period, and when he was twenty, determined to go to France to learn the art. Upon discovering that because of the French Revolution, then in progress, he could not go from England to France, he took passage for the United States in 1794. In Philadelphia he found employment with Thackara & Vallance, then at work upon plates for Thomas Dobson's *Encyclopaedia* (18 vols., 1790–98), which was the first American edition of the *Britannica*. While learning to engrave, he spent his free hours in the study of drawing, and after two years with his employers he set up in business for himself.

His first independent work was a series of four plates (1797) to illustrate Thomson's *Seasons*. When Joel Barlow saw Lawson's plates he expressed his regret at not having had *The Columbiad* illustrated in the United States (Ward, *post*). Lawson also engraved plates for the supplemental volumes (1803) of Dobson's *Encyclopaedia*. For a short time he was in partnership with J. J. Barralet, and engraved the plates for *The Powers of Genius* (2nd ed., 1802), by the Rev. John Blair Linn [*q.v.*], from designs by Barralet. Probably the most important incident in his career was his meeting with a fellow Scotsman, Alexander Wilson [*q.v.*], the naturalist. The friendship between the two men, begun in 1798, continued until Wilson's death. As it ripened Wilson confessed his ambition to issue a work on American birds, and Lawson finally agreed to engrave the plates for a little less than a dollar a day. He afterward explained his generosity by saying he did it "for the honor of the old country" (*Ibid.*). Wilson's *American Ornithology* was issued in nine volumes between 1808 and 1814. Lawson's plates, some of which he colored himself, attracted the attention of artists, engravers and naturalists in Europe, and the work established his reputation as an engraver. He was an industrious worker and applied himself closely, producing a great number of plates for maps, charts, and book illustrations. He engraved a portrait of Washington, after Stuart; one of Burns, after Nasmyth; and several designs after paintings by John Lewis Krimmel [*q.v.*], to whom he acted as guide and patron. His reputation was further enhanced by his plates for Charles Lucien Bonaparte's *American Ornithology; or, The Natural History of Birds Inhabiting the United States not Given by Wilson* (4 vols., 1825–33). George Ord wrote from Paris in 1830, after seeing the third volume, that the naturalists in London "united in declaring such work could not be produced in England" (Ward, *post*). Lawson was married, June 6, 1805, to Elizabeth Scaife, a native of Cumberland, England. He had a son who became an artist and two daughters who also displayed artistic talents. He continued to work until ten days before his death, which occurred in Philadelphia. In 1928 he was represented in the exhibition of one hundred notable American engravers at the New York Public Library.

[Townsend Ward, "Alexander Lawson," in *Pa. Mag. of Hist. and Biog.*, Apr. 1904; D. M. Stauffer, *Am. Engravers upon Copper and Steel* (2 vols., 1907); W. S. Baker, *Am. Engravers* (1875); Wm. Dunlap, *Hist. of the Rise and Progress of the Arts of Design in the U. S.* (2 vols., 1834), quoting an autobiographical letter from Lawson, which gives 1773 as the year of his birth, instead of 1772, the year usually given; obituary in *Pub. Ledger* (Phila.), Aug. 24, 1846.]   J. J.

LAWSON, JAMES (Nov. 9, 1799–Mar. 24, 1880), author, editor, and insurance expert, was born in Glasgow, Scotland, the son of James Lawson, a merchant of that city. Matriculating in 1812, he studied at the University of Glasgow, but late in 1815, emigrated to New York, where he worked as an accountant in the office of his uncle, Alexander Thomson, and in 1822 became a partner in the firm of Alexander Thomson & Company. Having as a young man acquired an interest in literature, in 1821 he selected American writers for representation in John Mennons' *Literary Coronal* and, later, for similar miscellanies. Duyckinck credits him with the introduction of the best American authors to the British reading public. His first small book, *Ontwa, the Son of the Forest* (1822), a verse narrative of Indian warfare, was reprinted in *The Columbian Lyre, or Specimens of Transatlantic Poetry* (1828), published in Glasgow. In this early period he formed the lasting and wide-spread contacts with men of letters which give color to his life. He contributed to the *New York Literary Gazette and American Athenaeum,* and in this weekly reviewed the first appearance of Edwin Forrest in New York (November 1826). The two men became intimate and lasting friends, and Lawson was a helpful critic and adviser to Forrest in personal as well as professional matters. (See many references in W. R. Alger's *Life of Edwin Forrest*, 1877; also in Lawrence Barrett's *Edwin Forrest*, 1881.)

About 1826 the mercantile business in which Lawson was a partner failed, and he turned to journalism. With John B. Skilman and James G. Brooks of the *Literary Gazette*, he edited the *Morning Courier* (1827–29), leaving this newspaper when it was combined with Noah's *Enquirer*. He then joined with Amos Butler in editing the *Mercantile Advertiser* until 1833. His newspaper interests did not thwart his literary activity. He wrote a romantic tragedy, *Giordano*, which was played three times at the Park Theatre (November and December 1828), with no great success (G. C. D. Odell, *Annals of the New York Stage*, vol. III, 1928, p. 384); it was published in 1832. In 1830 his *Tales and Sketches, by a Cosmopolite*, a collection of sentimental stories of Scottish background, written in stilted, formal prose, appeared. He informed his reader that "there is not a passage in them, that contains a vicious or poisonous thought." Three later volumes came from his pen, all privately printed: *Poems: Gleanings from Spare Hours of a Business Life* (1857); *Liddesdale, or the Border Chief* (Library of Congress copy, privately printed, 1874), a tragedy in blank verse, faintly reminiscent of *Macbeth*; and *The Maiden's Oath* (1877), a domestic drama. That not one of Lawson's books bore his name in print is a token of both his modesty and his literary judgment. He was one of the committee with Bryant, Halleck, and others, which selected John Augustus Stone's *Metamora* as the prize play for Forrest in 1829, and helped in the same way to bring James K. Paulding's *The Lion of the West*, with its leading character, Nimrod Wildfire, to Hackett in 1831. One of his intimate friends was William Gilmore Simms whom he introduced to the Harpers and assisted in many literary and personal matters. Simms visited him many times in New York and later in Yonkers, and Lawson in 1859 journeyed to South Carolina to see his friend, whose daughter, Mary Lawson Simms, was named for him (W. P. Trent, *William Gilmore Simms*, 1892, pp. 70 ff., 99, 154). Poe also was a friend and frequent visitor in Lawson's home and included him with affectionate comment in the series of articles on "The Literati of New York City" (*Godey's Lady's Book*, August 1846; G. E. Woodberry, *Edgar Allan Poe*, 1885, p. 258).

In 1833 Lawson entered the marine insurance business, but kept literature and its pleasant personal associations to grace his leisure hours. He became important in New York's mercantile life as an adjuster and statistician. He continued to write occasional articles and verse, however, which appeared in the *American Monthly Magazine*, the *Knickerbocker*, the *Southern Literary Messenger*, and Sargent's *New Monthly* (Duyckinck, *post*). He married Mary Eliza Donaldson (died Jan. 28, 1886), and acquired a home in Yonkers, where he continued to live after he retired from business—an esteemed and public-spirited citizen. The closing years of his long life were marred by sickness.

[E. A. and G. L. Duyckinck, *Cyc. of Am. Lit.* (2nd ed., 1875), vol. II; J. G. Wilson, *The Poets and Poetry of Scotland* (1876), vol. II; W. M. MacBean, *Biog. Reg. of St. Andrew's Soc. of the State of N. Y.*, vol. II (1925); *Notes and Queries*, Jan. 31, Mar. 13, 1880; *N. Y. Times*, Mar. 25, 1880.]   R. W. B.

LAWSON, JOHN (d. 1711), traveler, author, claims remembrance only on the authorship of one book, a so-called history of North Carolina. Nothing is known of his parentage or early life, though it has been conjectured that he was of Yorkshire descent. In 1700, being in a mood for travel, he "accidentally met with a gentleman . . . well acquainted with the ways of living in both Indies" who assured him "that Carolina was the best country to visit" (Introduction to Lawson's *History*). Immediately he took passage, and after stopping in New York, arrived in Charleston, S. C., in August. In December he started on an overland journey to the northern colony, his party consisting of six Englishmen and four Indians. The latter were soon dismissed and without guide Lawson and his comrades explored the Carolina wilderness, following Indian trails and finally taking the famous Trading Path which ran from Georgia to Bermuda Hundred, Virginia. Reaching the site of Hillsboro, N. C., the party left the Trading Path and made for the white settlements of Eastern Carolina. There Lawson remained for some years, being in 1705 one of the persons who secured the incorporation of the town of Bath. In the political dissensions of the time he took no part; apparently he was engaged in literary work, for in 1709 there appeared *A New Voyage to Carolina, Containing the Exact Description and Natural History of that Country; Together with the Present State thereof and A Journal of a Thousand Miles, traveled thro' several Nations of Indians, Giving a particular Account of their Customs, Manners; etc. By John Lawson, Gent'. Surveyor General of North Carolina*, London: Printed in the Year 1709. The book was the second volume of John

Stevens' *New Collection of Voyages and Travels.*
In 1714 and again in 1718 it was republished
with a new title, beginning *The History of Carolina.* In 1712 and 1722 German editions were
published in Hamburg from the press of M.
Vischer. Apparently the lords proprietors were
interested in the publication, for they subscribed
twenty pounds to Lawson "for maps of North
and South Carolina." The work is a vivid and
sprightly description of life on the frontier, especially valuable for its account of Indian life and
customs. For this reason Lawson is more often
cited by ethnologists than by formal historians.

It was probably while in England seeing his
book through the press that the author was made
surveyor-general of North Carolina (1708), for
which office he was recommended in a petition
of the North Carolina Assembly to the lords proprietors. In London, also, he met Christopher
de Graffenried [*q.v.*], Swiss adventurer and colo-
nizer, and joined him in the scheme to establish
in North Carolina a colony of Swiss and German
Palatines; in fact Lawson was one of three men
who supervised the migration of some six hundred Palatines, of which the direct result was the
foundation of New Bern, N. C. The new settlement soon aroused the enmity of the Indians and
in September 1711 De Graffenried and Lawson,
while on an exploring expedition, were seized by
the Tuscaroras. De Graffenried through his
power of persuasion was released, but Lawson
was put to death. His will, which was made in
1708 and probated soon after his death, left a
house, land, and one-third of his personal property to his "dearly beloved Hannah Smith," the
remainder to be divided, share alike, between his
daughter Isabella and "the brother and sister
(which her mother is with child of at present)."

[The essential facts regarding John Lawson are sum-
marized in S. B. Weeks, "Libraries and Literature in
North Carolina in the Eighteenth Century," *Ann. Re-
port of the Am. Hist. Asso.,* 1895, pp. 224–32. Con-
temporary references may be found in W. L. Saunders,
Colonial Records of N. C., vols. I and II (1886), and
H. V. Todd, *Christoph von Graffenried's Account of the
Founding of New Bern* (1920). The Sloan MSS., Brit-
ish Museum, contain three letters from Lawson to Sir
Hans Sloan. J. C. Pilling, *Bibliog. of the Iroquoian
Languages* (U. S. Bureau of American Ethnology,
Bulletin No. 6, 1888), gives the best collation of the
various editions of Lawson's *History.*]   W. K. B.

LAWSON, LEONIDAS MERION (Sept.
10, 1812–Jan. 21, 1864), physician, was born in
Nicholas Co., Ky., to the Rev. Jeremiah Lawson,
a native of Virginia, and Hannah Chancellor.
His early education was obtained from his father's instruction and from the primary school
of what afterward became Augusta College. Beginning the study of medicine at the age of eighteen under a thoroughly incompetent preceptor,

he so far overcame this handicap that two years
later he passed the examination before the licensing board of the first medical district of Ohio at
Cincinnati. He settled for practice in Mason
County, Ky., and while there took a course at the
Transylvania University and was given the degree of M.D. in 1838. He removed to Cincinnati
in 1841 and the following year he founded the
Western Lancet which he conducted until 1855.
For one year (1844) he also edited the *Journal
of Health.* Following a winter spent in study at
Guy's Hospital in London and in Paris, he moved
to Lexington in 1845 to fill a teaching appointment at Transylvania University. In 1847 he
returned to Cincinnati to accept the chair of materia medica and pathology in the Medical College of Ohio. In 1853 he was transferred to the
professorship of principles and practice of medicine. He went to Louisville in 1854 where he
gave two courses of lectures in the Kentucky
School of Medicine, returning to Cincinnati in
1856. Again in 1859 he left to fill the chair of
clinical medicine at the University of Louisiana,
but after one year he returned to the Cincinnati
school as professor of the theory and practice of
medicine, a position he occupied until his death
at the early age of fifty-one. Although he was a
subject of tuberculosis, he continued his duties
up to within a month of the end. Many of the
most profound students of tuberculosis have been
victims of the disease and the later years of Lawson's life were occupied with the preparation of
his treatise on *Phthisis Pulmonalis* which appeared in 1861. This work was as complete and
accurate as anything on the subject up to that
time, showing remarkable knowledge of the literature of the disease. It had a long and popular
vogue as a college text. Other writings include
monographs on cholera and pneumonia, and several addresses introductory to the college courses.
Lawson was a forceful and pleasing lecturer,
wholly devoted to his teaching and professional
duties. His portrait taken in his later years
shows a long thin serious face already marked
by the inroads of disease. He was twice married. His first wife was Louise Cailey of Felicity,
Ohio, who died in 1846 leaving three daughters.
He later married Eliza Robinson of Wilmington,
Del., who with two sons and five daughters survived him.

[*Trans. Ohio State Medic. Soc.,* 1865; *Cincinnati
Lancet and Observer,* Feb. 1864; H. A. Kelly and W.
L. Burrage, *Am. Medic. Biogs.* (1920); *Cincinnati
Daily Commercial,* Jan. 22, 1864.]   J. M. P—n.

LAWSON, THOMAS (*c.* 1781 or 1785–May
15, 1861), surgeon-general of the United States
army, was born in Virginia. Definite informa-

tion in regard to him begins with his appointment, from Virginia, as surgeon's mate in the navy on Mar. 11, 1809. Two years on shipboard satisfied his longings for sea life and in January 1811 he resigned. In February he was appointed garrison surgeon's mate in the army. In May 1813 he was promoted to the surgeoncy of the 6th Infantry, which position he retained throughout the War of 1812. Upon the reorganization and reduction of the army in 1815 he became surgeon of the 7th Infantry. When the medical department was reorganized in 1821 and regimental and post surgeons were placed on one list, instead of being carried separately as before, he became the senior surgeon and remained such until his appointment in 1836 as surgeon-general. Although reputed to be a "ladies' man," Lawson never married.

He was a positive character and did much for his corps. He was a good doctor, according to the standards of his day, the day of bleeding, blisters, salivation and tartar emetic. He was a good observer and wrote vigorously and forthrightly. His descriptions of "bilious intermittant" fever, which was apparently pernicious malaria, of cholera, yellow fever, and other diseases, were intelligent. He did not hesitate to point out military laxity as a cause of disease. Thus he wrote that moral as well as physical causes could be considered as having had an agency in producing the prostration of the 7th Infantry. His ability to see through theories to facts was sometimes marked, as when he wrote of cholera in New Orleans: "Whether the cause of this mysterious disease was wafted to us in a current of air down the river, or was brought among us pent up in a steamer, or whether the atmosphere of the city, which had been throughout the season very insalubrious, had reached its acme of pestilential explosion, we know not; but one thing is certain, that cholera, at least in that dreadful form which it afterwards assumed, was unknown among us until the steamer 'Constitution' arrived in port" (*Statistical Report on the Sickness and Mortality in the Army*, 1840, p. 263). Incidental to his description of this epidemic, he wrote: "The disease seized me on the third morning after its appearance among the troops. . . . On the following day the hospital steward was attacked; two acting stewards took the disease successively, and all the attendants were at one period or another affected with the disease. I am just now regaining my health; the hospital steward is not yet well, and the two acting stewards and four of the six attendants, died" (*Ibid.*, p. 265).

He was even more a soldier than a physician, and his administration was marked by concern for the military status of his department. He obtained for it military rank, two increases in numbers, proper uniform, stewards enlisted in the department, and increase of pay for other soldiers detailed to it for duty. He twice had line commands, once a regiment, and he served at other times as quartermaster and as adjutant. He was in the field in every war in which the army was engaged from 1811 to the Civil War, except the Black Hawk War. At that time he applied for field service and it was refused. In 1848 he was brevetted brigadier-general for meritorious conduct in the Mexican War. He died at Norfolk on May 15, 1861, as the result of a stroke of apoplexy. The general order announcing his death described him as "full of military fire, which not even the frosts of age could quench." He is an important figure in the history of the medical department of the army. His publication of the statistical reports on the sickness and mortality of the army (1840, 1856, 1860) and of the army meteorological registers (1840, 1851, 1855), was a service of great value.

[Jas. E. Pilcher, "Brevet Brig.-Gen. Thos. Lawson, Surgeon-Gen. of the U. S. Army, 1836–61," *Jour. Asso. Mil. Surgeons of the U. S.*, June 1904, reprinted in *The Surgeon-Generals of the U. S. Army* (1905); H. A. Kelly and W. L. Burrage, *Am. Medic. Biogs.* (1920); *Evening Star* (Wash., D. C.), May 20, 1861.]
P. M. A.

LAWSON, THOMAS WILLIAM (Feb. 26, 1857–Feb. 8, 1925), stockbroker and author, was born in Charlestown, Mass., the son of Thomas and Anna Maria (Loring) Lawson, who had emigrated from Nova Scotia a few years before. The father, a carpenter, died when young Thomas was only eight years old; and at twelve the boy, unwilling to be a burden on his mother any longer, slipped away from school one day and found work as an office boy with a brokerage firm in Boston, almost across the street from the location of his own sumptuous offices in later years. Early in his career he speculated in stocks. He made a considerable "killing" in railroad shares when he was only seventeen but lost his profits a few days later in another deal. At twenty-one he married Jeannie Augusta Goodwillie, his boyhood sweetheart, and shortly afterward became a broker on his own account. He is said to have accumulated a million dollars by the time he was thirty. He celebrated the occasion by writing a *History of the Republican Party*, which he published at his own expense, and of which he had four copies specially printed on satin. Despite his lack of formal education, he acquired by his own efforts an excellent command of English and a considerable degree of literary culture.

He spent his life in Boston, where he not only acted as agent and promoter for New York and other financiers and corporations but speculated for himself. He loved a fight when in his prime, and few men in the stock market have had so stormy a career. He assisted the Addicks interests to wrest the control of Bay State Gas from Standard Oil in 1894, though Addicks lost it again shortly afterward.

Lawson's ability was recognized by the Standard Oil magnates, and thereafter for several years he was their ally. For many years in the latter part of his life he was president of the Bay State Gas Company of Delaware. By 1900 he was worth at least fifty millions and had created a handsome estate, "Dreamwold," near Boston, which cost $6,000,000. He paid a florist $30,000 for a carnation bearing Mrs. Lawson's name. He was a lover of art, literature, and nature, and his large private office was crowded with bronzes, paintings, books, and masses of fresh flowers. These as adjuncts to the brilliant, dynamic, spectacular, faultlessly garbed but erratic personality behind the desk, rendered it unique among business offices. When Sir Thomas Lipton, the British yachtsman, challenged again for the *America's* Cup in 1901, Lawson, seeing here an opportunity for both sport and publicity, built a yacht of his own, *Independence,* to compete in the trial heats with the New York Yacht Club's two boats. But the Yacht Club practically barred his boat from competition, and he acquired a grudge against certain wealthy members of the club which long endured. He had in 1897 become connected with the promotion of Amalgamated Copper, the name under which Standard Oil capitalists reorganized the great Anaconda mine and allied properties. On this stock they now made a handsome profit, with Lawson acting as their chief broker. The stock thereafter rapidly declined in price and many holders of it suffered heavy losses.

In 1902, when Lawson, with Winfield M. Thompson, published *The Lawson History of the America's Cup,* the editor of *Everybody's Magazine,* learning of his grievance, induced him to write the allegedly true story of Amalgamated Copper, which he did under the title of "Frenzied Finance"—one of the most sensational successes in magazine history. The entire edition of the magazine containing the first instalment was exhausted in three days. To journalistic instinct, Lawson added an easy, slashing style and a knack for colorful phrasing which made his rough-and-tumble attack on the "money kings" vastly popular, even though readers regarded him as belonging in the same category. During the course

of the articles (1904–05), the writer also assailed the large insurance companies and performed a public service by bringing about the insurance investigation of 1905; but his "remedies" for the correction of stock-market gambling were not adopted. *Frenzied Finance* was published in book form and was followed by a novel, *Friday, the Thirteenth* (1907), also attacking the stock market, but this was less popular. Later books were *The Remedy* (1912); *The High Cost of Living* (1913); and *The Leak* (1919). The enmity aroused by his *Frenzied Finance* was costly to him. He lost clients and good will thereby and many serious losses were wilfully inflicted upon him by antagonists. During the last fifteen years of his life he seemed to lose his old knack for success, and his fortunes declined steadily. He lost his magnificent estate, even his automobile, and died a comparatively poor man.

[*The Lawson History of the America's Cup* (1902) and *The High Cost of Living* (1913) contain important references to the writer's history, and "Frenzied Finance" as it ran in *Everybody's* with the supplementary department, "Lawson and his Critics," has some interesting personal material. See also *Who's Who in America,* 1924–25; *Nation,* Aug. 14, 1902, Dec. 21, 1905; *Independent,* May 18, 1905; *Arena,* Sept. 1905; the *Bookman,* Apr. 1907; *Current Lit.,* Mar. 1908; *Outlook,* Sept. 5, 1908; *New Eng. Mag.,* Mar. 1909; *Boston Herald, Boston Transcript,* Feb. 9, 1925.]   A. F. H.

LAWSON, VICTOR FREEMONT (Sept. 9, 1850–Aug. 19, 1925), journalist, was born in Chicago, Ill., the son of Iver and Melinda (Nordvig) Lawson. Both parents were Norwegian, the father having been born in Norway, the mother in Illinois. Iver Lawson accumulated a considerable fortune in Chicago real estate, most of which was lost, however, in the Chicago fire of 1871. He died in 1873 leaving the residue of his estate to his son Victor. Young Lawson had been educated in the Chicago public schools and at Phillips Academy at Andover, Mass. Ill health put an end to further study. After a brief period of life in the open he returned to Chicago to take active charge of his father's estate. He inherited with other property an interest in the daily *Skandinaven* which his father and others had established. His interest in newspaper work had developed when he was employed as a boy in the circulation department of the *Chicago Evening Journal.* By a curious coincidence, the publication of a new newspaper, the *Chicago Daily News,* was begun in the same building with the *Skandinaven* in January 1876. This new publication, the first penny newspaper in the West, was sponsored by Melville E. Stone, William H. Dougherty, and Percy Meggy. Within six months the owners of the struggling paper had sold out to Lawson who retained Stone as editor and later took him into partnership. Under the efficient management of Lawson, the *Daily News* made rapid progress. In 1878 the *Evening Post* was taken over with its Associated Press franchise. In 1881 a morning edition was brought out which later became the *Chicago Record* and eventually the *Record-Herald,* when it was merged with the *Times-Herald.* The *Record-Herald* ceased publication in 1914 because of Lawson's reluctance to be connected with a paper publishing on Sunday. He had assumed editorial duties upon Stone's retirement in 1888.

At a critical moment Lawson took up the cause of the Associated Press which was rivaled by the United Press, a news service organized on a commercialized rather than a cooperative basis. As president of the organization from 1894 to 1900, he was supported by his former partner, Melville E. Stone, at this time manager of the Associated Press. He remained as director from 1893 until his death. In 1898 he turned his attention to the development of a foreign news service. The Spanish-American War had shown the need of an unbiased handling of foreign news affecting American interest. Up to this time cable news received by American newspapers was supplied by correspondents representing the British or other foreign papers. At the close of the war, Lawson placed his own correspondents in the leading European capitals and in the Orient. The example of the *Daily News* was widely followed by other papers and press associations. Another of Lawson's pioneering activities was his strong advocacy of postal savings-banks. Both by financial assistance and the use of his publishing organization, he consolidated support for the bill which was finally passed in 1910. To him, President Taft sent the pen with which the bill was signed.

The independent policy of the *Daily News* in politics and in civic reform made the paper a powerful influence in Chicago. At the same time the editor was exposed to furious attacks by corrupt agents of corporations seeking to exploit the city government. But nothing could swerve him from what he conceived to be his duty—the support of all civic reform movements. He gave generously to support a system of free lectures in public-school halls, to found a fresh air sanitarium, to maintain "better government associations," to support the Y.M.C.A., to endow the Chicago Theological Seminary, and to provide homes for the symphony orchestras, and for leading clubs of which he was a member. He was a life-time member of the New England Congregational Church of Chicago, and it was in connection with his work in the church that he met Jessie S. Bradley, daughter of W. H. Bradley of Chicago, whom he married in 1880. She it was who guided much of his humanitarian work for the relief of the poor, particularly members of the colored race. She died in 1914 leaving no children. Lawson combined the practical talents of business with ideals of good citizenship. He was religious in the strictest sense. Quiet determination, dislike of publicity, personal friendliness, and humanity marked his character and bearing. His genius as a newspaper editor consisted in making his paper a constructive force in the life of the community in which he lived and worked.

[*Who's Who in America,* 1924–25; A. N. Marquis, *The Book of Chicagoans* (1917); "Victor Freemont Lawson," *Am. Mag.,* Nov. 1909; Melville E. Stone, *Fifty Years a Journalist* (1921); *M. E. S.: His Book* (1918), a memorial to Melville E. Stone; *Chicago Daily News, Chicago Tribune,* Aug. 20, 1925.]   E. A. D.

LAWTON, ALEXANDER ROBERT (Nov. 4, 1818–July 2, 1896), Confederate soldier, lawyer, was born in St. Peter's Parish, Beaufort District, S. C. His parents were Alexander James and Martha (Mosse) Lawton. At sixteen he was appointed to the United States Military Academy, where he graduated in 1839, and was assigned as second lieutenant to the 1st Artillery. He resigned in 1841, entered the Harvard Law School, graduated in 1842, and the following year settled permanently in Savannah, Ga., where he practised his profession, with certain interludes, until his death. In 1849–54 he was president of the Augusta & Savannah Railroad; in 1855–56, a member of the Georgia House of Representatives, and in 1860, state senator.

He was a leading advocate of secession, and as a member of the state Senate supported a resolution favoring immediate withdrawal from the Union. Before the ordinance had passed, as colonel of the 1st Volunteer Regiment, acting under the orders of Governor Brown, he seized Fort Pulaski, thus committing the first overt act of war in Georgia. Commissioned brigadier-general in 1861, he was placed in charge of the Georgia coast. He organized a brigade and in June 1862 was transferred with 5,000 men to Virginia, where, under Jackson, he took part in the Valley campaigns and distinguished himself in the Seven Days' fight around Richmond. In the second battle of Manassas, when Ewell fell wounded, Lawton took charge of his division and commanded it during the advance into Maryland. At the battle of Sharpsburg he was seriously wounded, and was disabled until May 1863. In August of that year, against his own strenuous objection, he was made quartermaster-general of the Confederacy. His management of this most difficult branch of the army was highly successful (Avery, *post*, pp. 295–97).

Returning to Savannah on the close of the war, Lawton resumed his practice of law and became an important factor in politics. He entered the lower house of the legislature and served from 1870 to 1875, was chairman of the state electoral college in 1876, member and president *pro tempore* of the state constitutional convention of 1877, and leader of the Georgia delegation to the National Democratic Convention in 1880 and 1884. In 1880 he was a candidate for the United States Senate, but was defeated in a spectacular campaign by former Governor Joseph E. Brown [*q.v.*], who had become a Republican and a supporter of the congressional reconstruction policies. Brown's election was a foregone conclusion; Lawton consented to be sacrificed in order that the conservative principles for which his element stood should not appear to be acquiescing, without a struggle, in the new régime. A contemporary writer regarded this contest as "the last close struggle for supremacy between the spirit that ruled the old South and the spirit of the new South" (see Avery, *post*, p. 603).

A mere chronicle of the various public services of General Lawton fails to provide an adequate picture of the man. His erect, well-set-up figure, his intellectual force, the culture and good breeding that were evident to all, his ability as a soldier, business man, and lawyer, marked him as an eminent member of the ruling aristocracy of his time. He stood in the front rank of Southern lawyers. His high professional standing in his own state was attested by impressive tributes at the time of his death. His election as president of the American Bar Association in 1882 indicates that the bar as a whole indorsed the judgment of his fellow Georgians. His last public service was performed in the capacity of minister to Austria (1887–89), a post to which he was appointed by President Cleveland.

On Nov. 5, 1845, Lawton married Sarah Hillhouse Alexander, sister of Gen. E. P. Alexander [*q.v.*]. They had four children, and celebrated their golden wedding in 1895. Lawton died at Clifton Springs, N. Y., less than eight months later, in the seventy-eighth year of his age.

[I. W. Avery, *The Hist. of the State of Ga. from 1850 to 1881* (1881) ; memorial of the Savannah Bar Asso., *99 Ga. Reports*, 825 ; *Atlanta Constitution*, July 3, 1896 ; *Atlanta Journal*, July 2, 1896 ; L. L. Knight, *A Standard Hist. of Ga. and Georgians* (1917), vols. I, II ; C. C. Jones, Jr., and others, *Hist. of Savannah, Ga.* (1890) ; *Report of the Fourteenth Annual Session of the Ga. Bar. Asso.* (1897) ; *Report of the Nineteenth Ann. Meeting of the Am. Bar Asso.* (1896) ; *Twenty-eighth Ann. Reunion Asso. Grads. U. S. Mil. Acad.* (1897) ; C. A. Evans, *Confed. Mil. Hist.* (1899), vols. I, VI ; W. J. Northen, *Men of Mark in Ga.* (1911), III, 185–91.]

R. P. B.

LAWTON, HENRY WARE (Mar. 17, 1843–Dec. 19, 1899), soldier, was born at Manhattan, near Toledo, Ohio, a son of George and Catherine (Daley) Lawton. He received his education in the Fort Wayne Methodist Episcopal College at Fort Wayne, Ind., to which place his family had moved in his fifth year. His parents died when he was nine years old, and thereafter he lived with an uncle. At the opening of the Civil War he enlisted in the 9th Indiana Infantry, and on Aug. 20, 1861, was made first lieutenant in the newly raised 30th Indiana Infantry, with which regiment he served in the western armies throughout the war, rising to the rank of lieutenant-colonel. In the later campaigns of 1864, he commanded his regiment. On Nov. 25, 1865, he was mustered out with the brevet rank of colonel, and later was awarded the Medal of Honor for gallantry at Atlanta.

He entered upon the study of law at Harvard, but left there May 4, 1867, to accept a commission as second lieutenant in the 41st Infantry (colored), with rank from July 28, 1866. His promotion to first lieutenant came almost immediately, July 31, 1867. In 1869 his regiment was consolidated with another colored regiment and renumbered as the 24th. In 1871 he was transferred to the 4th Cavalry, and served under Gen. Ranald S. Mackenzie in the Indian wars, becoming captain Mar. 20, 1879. In 1886, under the orders of General Miles, he led the column that pursued Geronimo for thirteen hundred miles through the mountains of Arizona and Mexico, and received his surrender. On Sept. 17, 1888, he entered the Inspector-General's Department as major, was promoted lieutenant-colonel Feb. 18, 1889, and colonel July 7, 1898. During the Spanish-American War he served in Cuba as brigadier-general and major-general of volunteers, commanding the 2nd Division, V Army Corps, in the actions before Santiago. He was one of the commissioners to receive the surrender of that place, and became military governor of the city and province. Returning to the mainland, he accompanied the president in his tour of the states, and then took command of the IV Army Corps at Huntsville, Ala.

Ordered to the Philippines, he reached Manila Mar. 18, 1899, and was placed in command of the 1st Division, VIII Army Corps. On Apr. 9 he made an expedition up the Pasig River and across the Laguna de Bay to Santa Cruz. Immediately upon his return he moved upon San Isidro, on the Rio Grande de Pampanga, to break up insurgent forces which were threatening the communications of General MacArthur's division operating north of Malolos. Next, on June 1, he made a brief expedition into the district of Morong, north of the Laguna; then, on June 10, commenced his Cavite campaign, which opened with a spirited engagement at Zapote Bridge, and which pushed the "south line" far back from Manila.

In October began the decisive campaign against Aguinaldo's main force in the north. General MacArthur advanced west of Mount Arayat, to Tarlac; Lawton east of it, through San Isidro into the mountain country. Turning over his command to General Wheaton on Dec. 16, Lawton returned to Manila, and on the 18th started for the Mariquina Valley, east of the city, where the insurgents had a fortified line to keep open their communications between their northern and southern forces. On Dec. 19, while disposing his troops opposite San Mateo to force a crossing of the river, he was shot through the heart and died almost instantly.

Lawton was a striking and soldierly figure—six feet four inches tall, erect and well built. He was quick and energetic in manner and speech, a fine organizer, a thoroughly practical field soldier, and a highly competent commander, respected and loved by superiors and subordinates alike. He was married Dec. 12, 1881, to Mary Craig, daughter of Alexander and Annie (McCown) Craig of Louisville, Ky. He had seven children, three of whom died in infancy. His wife and the surviving children accompanied him to the Philippines and were in Manila at the time of his death.

[F. B. Heitman, *Hist. Reg. and Dict. U. S. Army* (1903), vol. I; O. O. Howard, "Gen. Henry W. Lawton," in *Rev. of Revs.* (N. Y.), Feb. 1900; D. C. Worcester, in *McClure's Mag.,* May 1900; R. G. Carter, *Pursuit of Kicking Bird* (1920); Otto Klemme, *General Lawton's Tod; eine Episode von den Philippinen, von Einem der dabei gewesen* (Leipzig, 1907), by a sergeant who was beside him when he fell; *Manila Times* and *N. Y. Tribune,* Dec. 20, 1899; personal and family information from Mrs. Lawton.]   O. L. S., Jr.

LAY, BENJAMIN (1677–Feb. 3, 1759), Quaker reformer, was born in Colchester, Essex, England. He was deformed, and when full grown was hump-backed and only four feet seven inches in height, with a large head and slender legs that seemed almost unequal to bearing the weight of his body. Along with his physical deficiencies went mental peculiarities which had a determining influence upon the course of his later life. As a youth, after engaging in various occupations ashore, he went to sea, and on one voyage visited Syria, but about 1710 returned to Colchester, where he married and remained for

several years. His assertiveness made him so troublesome in the affairs of the Quaker meeting that about 1717 he was removed from membership. He did not, however, either then or later, regard himself as cut off from the Society, and throughout his later life continued to be associated with the Friends. In 1718 he migrated to Barbados and engaged in business. The large black-slave population at once attracted his interest and stirred him to humanitarian efforts. He gathered the slaves about him on Sundays, feeding them and talking to them about religion. Suspicion and animosity aroused by his concern for the blacks and his constant readiness to argue on slavery caused him to leave the island in 1731 and go to Pennsylvania, where he settled near Philadelphia. In this colony he was able to bear his testimony against slavery without hindrance and it is from this period that most records of his eccentricities have come. He once attempted to imitate Christ by fasting for forty days. This act brought him near death, and only great care by friends restored his health. He feigned suicide in a Quaker meeting house, appearing to stab himself and causing a quantity of red fluid resembling blood to stream forth. Those present were greatly alarmed. He understood the value of a dramatic protest, and on one occasion stationed himself at the gateway to a meeting house with one leg bared and half buried in deep snow. To those who remonstrated he answered: "Ah, you pretend compassion for me, but you do not feel for the poor slaves in your fields, who go all winter half clad" (Vaux, *post,* p. 28). His eccentricities attracted much public attention and he was once visited by Governor Penn, Benjamin Franklin, and other gentlemen, before whom he set a plain meal of fruits and vegetables, since the use of animal products for either food or clothing was another matter upon which he bore testimony against prevailing practice. Franklin printed one of his numerous pamphlets against slavery, *All Slave-keepers that Keep the Innocent in Bondage, Apostates Pretending to Lay Claim to the Pure & Holy Christian Religion,* etc. (1737). From time to time Lay made public condemnation of the use of liquors, tobacco, and tea, and also advocated a more humane criminal code. After 1740 he lived with John Phipps near Abington Friends' meeting house, and there he died in February 1759, being buried in the Friends' burial ground. His wife, Sarah, who predeceased him, like himself was small of stature, and deformed. She is described as an intelligent and pious woman, an approved minister in the Society of Friends, who supported her husband at all times in his anti-slavery activities. Despite his eccentricities, Lay exercised considerable influence upon the Quaker attitude towards slavery and shortly before his death had the satisfaction of learning that the Society had resolved to disown slave-holding members.

[Roberts Vaux, *Memoirs of the Lives of Benjamin Lay and Ralph Sandiford* (1815); Lydia Maria (Francis) Child, *Memoir of Benjamin Lay* (1842); Benjamin Rush, "Biographical Anecdotes of Benjamin Lay," *The Annual Monitor,* vol. I (1813); Joseph Smith, *A Descriptive Cat. of Friends' Books* (1867), II, 92–93; *Biog. Cat. . . . London Friends' Institute* (1888); W. A. J. Archbold, in *Dict. Nat. Biog.*]   F. L.

LAY, HENRY CHAMPLIN (Dec. 6, 1823–Sept. 17, 1885), Protestant Episcopal bishop, was born in Richmond, Va. His father, John Olmstead Lay, was a native of Connecticut, a descendant of John Lay who was living in Lyme, Conn., as early as 1648; his mother, Lucy Anne Fitzhugh (May), was of old Virginia stock. He received his education in his native state, graduating at the University of Virginia, Charlottesville, in 1842, and at the Theological Seminary in Virginia, Alexandria, in 1846. Following his graduation in theology he was at once ordained deacon by the Rt. Rev. William Meade, bishop of Virginia. On May 13, 1847, he was married to Elizabeth Withers Atkinson. After a short pastorate at Lynnhaven Parish, Va., he removed to Huntsville, Ala., where he became rector of the Church of the Nativity. In this parish he was made priest, July 12, 1848, by the Rt. Rev. Nicholas Hamner Cobbs, bishop of Alabama. Here Lay remained as rector until made bishop. He was elected missionary bishop of the Southwest at the General Convention of 1859, held in Richmond, and immediately after the close of the convention was consecrated (Oct. 23) in Richmond. The territory to which he was appointed included Arkansas, Indian Territory, and parts adjacent. Hardly had he removed to his jurisdiction when the Civil War broke out, and the state of Arkansas soon joined the Confederacy. The Protestant Episcopal Church in the Confederate States was regarded as having ceased to be a part of the Church in the United States, and the various dioceses were organized into an entirely independent church. This was a logical application of the principle underlying the establishment of the Protestant Episcopal Church in the United States as independent of the Church of England. Further, in the application of the Southern conception of local independence, Lay became bishop of Arkansas, not missionary bishop. It was "states rights" in matters ecclesiastical. At the close of the Civil War, Lay and Bishop Atkinson of North Carolina were the first Southern bishops to join with bishops of the Northern dioceses at the General Convention held in Philadelphia 1865 in reëstablishing the unity of the denomination which had been interrupted by the war. In the reunited church he became once more missionary bishop, but with his jurisdiction limited to Arkansas. In 1868 the Eastern Shore of Maryland was established as an independent diocese and to this charge Lay was elected as bishop of Easton, assuming office Apr. 1, 1869. Here he worked until his death. He published *Letters to a Man Bewildered among Many Counselors* (1853); *Tracts for Missionary Use* (1860); *Studies in the Church* (1872); *The Church in the Nation* (1885), being the Bishop Paddock Lectures; as well as many sermons and articles on sociological topics. He died at the Church Home, Baltimore, and was buried at Easton, Md.

[*Churchman,* Sept. 26, 1885; *Sun* (Baltimore), Sept. 18, 1885; E. E. and E. M. Salisbury, *Family-Histories and Genealogies* (1892); information gathered in part from Lay's family and from Convention Journals.]
                                        J. C. Ay—r.

LAY, JOHN LOUIS (Jan. 14, 1832–Apr. 17, 1899), inventor, son of John and Frances (Atkins) Lay, was born in Buffalo, N. Y. He was descended from Robert Lay who emigrated from England to America in 1635, settling first in Lynn, Mass., and then in Saybrook, Conn. Lay's father was long a prominent business man of Buffalo, N. Y., and the boy accordingly received a well-rounded education in the city schools. He developed an especial interest in mechanics as he grew to manhood, and was engaged in various engineering enterprises in Buffalo when the Civil War began. In July 1861 he enlisted in the United States Navy as a second assistant engineer, becoming first assistant in 1863. His mechanical aptitude quickly attracted attention and he was given every opportunity to develop his inventive talents. He perfected a torpedo for offensive warfare and communicated his plan for its use to Lieut. William Barker Cushing [*q.v.*]. Shortly afterward (Oct. 27, 1864), Cushing, with a Lay torpedo aboard, succeeded in blowing up the Confederate ram *Albemarle* by driving his boat against its bow. Lay conducted further work on torpedoes at the Philadelphia Navy Yard, and on Mar. 14, 1865, he and W. W. W. Wood secured a series of four patents, Nos. 46,-850 to 46,853, describing not only apparatus for operating torpedoes but the design and equipment of a picket boat from which to discharge them. The patentees assigned these patents to Donald McKay [*q.v.*], the noted ship-builder of East Boston, Mass., but there is no record of the further development of the invention. Resigning from the navy in 1865, Lay was engaged by the Peruvian government to prepare fixed mines and place suspended torpedoes in the harbor of Callao, in order to forestall the threatened attack of a Spanish fleet. After returning to the United States in 1867, he devoted considerable time, at his home in Buffalo, to the perfection of what he called the "Lay Moveable Torpedo Submarine." He also secured a series of six patents for a steam-engine on July 23, 1867, and one for a locomotive on Oct. 29, 1867. The Lay movable torpedo was of two lengths, sixteen and twenty-three feet respectively, and consisted of a cylindrical body with conical ends, carrying in the forward end 100 to 200 pounds of explosives. It was electrically propelled and was controlled as to both direction and time of firing through a wire within a rope attached to the torpedo and paid out from its place of launching, either the shore or a vessel. The torpedo's cruising range was one and one-half miles and its speed ten to twelve miles an hour. The inventor set forth its merits in a pamphlet entitled *Submarine Warfare; Fixed Mines and Torpedos. The Lay Moveable Torpedo: Its Superiority over All other Implements of Submarine Warfare* (n.d.). Though the United States Navy purchased but two of his torpedoes, he received large sums of money from Russia and Turkey for the rights to his invention. He took up his residence in Europe about 1870, but subsequently lost his fortune, and after thirty years abroad returned to the United States in the hope of disposing of some later inventions. He died, however, homeless and penniless, in Bellevue Hospital, New York, survived by two children living in Europe.

[F. H. Severance, "The Journeys and Journals of an Early Buffalo Merchant," *Pubs. Buffalo Hist. Soc.*, vol. IV (1896); H. P. Smith, *Hist. of the City of Buffalo and Erie County* (1884), vol. II; E. A. Hill, "The Descendants of Robert Lay of Saybrook, Conn.," *New Eng. Hist. and Geneal. Reg.*, Apr., July 1908; *House Ex. Doc. No. 52*, 39 Cong., 1 Sess.; *House Ex. Doc. No. 96*, 40 Cong., 2 Sess.; *War of the Rebellion: Official Records (Navy)*, ser. 1 and 2; *N. Y. Times*, Apr. 21, 1899; *Army and Navy Jour.*, Apr. 22, 1899.]

C. W. M.

LAZARUS, EMMA (July 22, 1849–Nov. 19, 1887), poet, essayist, was born in New York City of pure Sephardic stock, the daughter of Moses and Esther (Nathan) Lazarus. A member of a large, wealthy, and devoted family, she passed a pleasant youth, with winters in New York City and summers by the sea. She was educated entirely by private tutors. Very precocious, in 1866 she had a volume entitled *Poems and Translations,* containing verses written between the ages of fourteen and sixteen, printed for private circulation. This collection, with ad-

ditions, was published in 1867. The verses were preoccupied with the conventionally romantic and vaguely melancholy themes congenial to youth, but they breathed an unusually lofty spirit and showed a pleasing fancy and considerable command of rhythm. They attracted the attention of Ralph Waldo Emerson, who became interested in the young poet, invited her to spend a week in the Emerson home at Concord, and kept up a lifelong correspondence with her. She proudly dedicated her second volume, *Admetus and Other Poems* (1871), "To my friend, Ralph Waldo Emerson." In 1874 she published her first prose work, *Alide: an Episode of Goethe's Life,* dealing with the Fredericke Brion incident, and, in 1876, *The Spagnoletto,* a five-act poetic drama with its scene laid in seventeenth-century Italy. During this decade she also contributed numerous poems to *Scribner's Monthly* and to *Lippincott's Magazine.* Thus far, she had shown little interest in the life of her own people. Although she had made a thorough study of Jewish history and literature, she was internationally minded and trained too critically to regard with great reverence the dogmas of the orthodox church to which she outwardly belonged. In declining to contribute to a Jewish hymn book, she said, "I feel no religious fervour within me" (Rachel Cohen, *post,* p. 185). Even as late as 1881, when her *Poems and Ballads of Heinrich Heine* appeared, in the introduction to this excellent translation she considered Heine as a German almost more than as a Jew. But the persecution of Russian Jews during 1879–83 turned her from a pleasing litterateur into an ardent patriot. When the refugees began to crowd into Ward's Island in 1881, she became prominent in organizing efforts for their relief. Then, the next year, in the same number of the *Century Magazine* (April 1882) which carried her critical study, "Was the Earl of Beaconsfield a Representative Jew?" there appeared an opprobrious article by a Russian journalist, Mme. Z. Ragozin, "Russian Jews and Gentiles," in which the author attempted to defend the pogroms. Miss Lazarus replied in the next number with a crushing rejoinder, "Russian Christianity *versus* Modern Judaism." Henceforth she stood as the leading American champion of her race. In 1882 she published *Songs of a Semite,* containing "The Dance to Death"—written earlier, a powerful poetic drama of fourteenth-century Jewish life—and a number of other strong and impassioned poems. In February 1883 she contributed a noteworthy article on "The Jewish Problem" to the *Century Magazine.* Later followed a series of poems in prose called "By the Waters of Babylon" (*Cen-*

tury Magazine, March 1887), and another prose series entitled "An Epistle to the Hebrews," published in the *American Hebrew.* All this work was characterized by a prophetic quality of stern moral indignation and unbending courage. Racial enthusiasm was united in Emma Lazarus with a firm faith in America as the home of the oppressed. Her sonnet to the Statue of Liberty was fittingly chosen to be placed on the pedestal of the statue in 1886. On a trip to Europe three years earlier she had been received everywhere with tokens of an international reputation. Then, at the height of her powers, she was stricken with cancer. After a second trip to Europe in 1885–87, she returned home to die at the age of thirty-eight.

[Biographical sketch and appreciation in the *Century Mag.,* Oct. 1888, reprinted as introduction to *The Poems of Emma Lazarus* (2 vols., 1889) ; Philip Cowen, "Recollections of Emma Lazarus," *Am. Hebrew,* July 5, 1929 ; Rachel Cohen, "Emma Lazarus," in *Reform Advocate,* Sept. 24, 1927, repr. from *London Jewish Chronicle* ; Mary M. Cohen, in *Poet-Lore,* June–July 1893 ; W. J. Price, in *Forum,* Mar. 1912 ; *Reflex,* Mar. 1930 ; *Am. Hebrew,* Nov. 25, Dec. 9, 1887 ; *Critic,* Dec. 10, 1887 ; *Evening Post* (N. Y.), Nov. 21, 1887 ; article in *Jewish Encyc.,* with additional references.] G. G.

LAZEAR, JESSE WILLIAM (May 2, 1866– Sept. 25, 1900), physician, who sacrificed his life in the work of the United States Army Yellow Fever Commission, was born in Baltimore County, Md. He was the son of William Lyons Lazear and Charlotte Pettigrew. After preliminary studies at Trinity Hall, a private school in Pennsylvania, he entered Johns Hopkins University, from which he was graduated with the degree of A.B. in 1889. Following three years at Columbia College, New York City, he received the degree of M.D. in 1892. After two years of internship in Bellevue Hospital and a year of European study, he settled for practice in Baltimore in 1895. While in Europe he had spent some time in the Pasteur Institute in Paris and had become especially interested in bacteriology. He was appointed to the medical staff of Johns Hopkins Hospital, while he was also assistant in clinical microscopy at the university and in the laryngological department of the hospital clinic. He displayed brilliant promise in research work and is credited with being the first in the United States to isolate the diplococcus of Neisser from the circulating blood. He was also among the first to make a study of the structure of the malarial parasite.

In February 1900 he was appointed acting assistant surgeon in the army and was assigned to laboratory duty at Columbia Barracks at Quemados near Havana, Cuba. When, later in the year, the Yellow Fever Commission was organ-

ized, he was made a member together with Maj. Walter Reed and Doctors James Carroll and Aristides Agremonte. From the time of his arrival in Cuba, he had devoted much attention to the pathology and bacteriology of yellow fever. He was able to say with confidence to the commission that research along these lines offered little promise. With the decision to investigate the possible transmission of the disease by mosquitoes, Lazear was made responsible for the care and handling of the insects, including their application to fever patients and volunteers for experimentation. He and Carroll, together with some others, allowed supposedly infected mosquitoes to bite them, but without results. Carroll later succeeded in infecting himself and suffered a sharp attack of the disease. In September, while Lazear was engaged in placing mosquitoes upon patients in a fever ward, a free mosquito alighted upon his hand and, though seen, was allowed to take its feed of blood. Five days later he was taken ill and was removed to the yellow fever hospital at Quemados, where he died September 25, after seven days' illness. His body was returned to Baltimore and lies in Loudon Park Cemetery. A memorial tablet to his memory has been placed in Johns Hopkins Hospital.

Carroll's illness and Lazear's death went far to convince the commission that they were on the right path. Their subsequent work was convincing to the world. Though Lazear's name appears on but one of the published works of the commission, Major Reed insisted that Lazear should have equal honor for whatever credit was accorded the work of the Yellow Fever Commission. In the latter's untimely death, medical research lost a man of unusual promise. With an education and mental equipment far above the average, he well might have made a high place in American medicine. He was admired by his colleagues of Johns Hopkins Hospital for his keen perception and patient industry in research, and for his simple high-minded character and likable personality. He was, however, reticent in speech and somewhat diffident in his contact with new acquaintances. He was married, in 1896, to Mabel Houston of Baltimore, who survived him with two children, one of whom he never saw.

[Obituary notices with incomplete biography appeared in the *Jour. Am. Medic. Asso.,* Oct. 6, 1900, in the *Johns Hopkins Hospital Bull.,* Nov. 1900, and in *Science,* Dec. 14, 1900. See also H. A. Kelly, *Walter Reed and Yellow Fever* (1906). The most authoritative account of the Yellow Fever Commission is found in *Senate Document 822,* 61 Cong., 3 Sess., entitled "Yellow Fever," which contains portraits of all members of the commission.] J. M. P—n.

LEA, HENRY CHARLES (Sept. 19, 1825–Oct. 24, 1909), publisher, publicist, historian, was born and died in Philadelphia. His father was Isaac Lea [*q.v.*], a descendant of John Lea, an English Quaker who came to America in 1699. His mother, Frances Anne, daughter of Mathew Carey [*q.v.*], was bred a Catholic. Henry Charles Carey [*q.v.*] and Thomas Gibson Lea were his uncles. Students of heredity and environment might note from these relationships the most striking characteristics of Henry C. Lea: love of truth, interest in science, impatience of injustice or cruelty, intense patriotism, belief in the power of the pen to influence his countrymen. At the age of six he learned the letters of the Greek alphabet at his mother's bedside. When seven he spent a short time at a school in Paris, where he laid the foundation for his mastery of French. His formal education in the classics and mathematics was directed by a certain Eugenius Nulty, to whom he recited an hour a day. He had special masters in French, Italian, drawing, and writing. He and his elder brother, Mathew Carey Lea [*q.v.*], on Saturdays tramped fifteen or twenty miles, collecting flowers which they analyzed the following day. He was interested also in conchology, his father's specialty, and when he was just past his fifteenth birthday he contributed a paper on fossil shells to Silliman's *American Journal of Science and Arts* (January 1841). This was soon followed by an article on a chemical subject in the same journal (April 1842). He was also interested in literature and, after the panic of 1837, when he could not afford to buy a copy of Anacreon he copied it in full in order to possess it.

In his eighteenth year, early in 1843, he entered his father's publishing house. He worked hard mastering the business; evenings and early mornings he still studied and wrote. Among his publications of this period are articles on conchology, on Greek epitaphs, on Tennyson, and other poets; in four years he contributed at least sixteen long articles, besides reviews. In 1844, during the Anti-Catholic riot, Lea shouldered a gun and acted as defender of the nearest Catholic church. At twenty-two his health broke down and then ensued what he described as a period of "intellectual leisure," which was to turn his attention to his life work. For a time he had to give up business and traveled. On May 27, 1850, he married his first cousin, Anna Caroline Jaudon, from Cincinnati, who was of Huguenot ancestry. During this period, for recreation he had turned to French memoirs. While reading Froissart he wondered how accurate the account was in depicting the times and sent to Paris for books which might answer his query. This was in 1849 and for the ensuing sixty years history was his chief intellectual interest. To this avocation he brought his scientific training.

His interest turned early to legal institutions and his first historical article, published in January 1859 in the *North American Review*, was later reworked as part of his first volume, *Superstition and Force* (1866). "The history of jurisprudence," he believed, "is the history of civilization. The labors of the lawgiver embody not only the manners and customs of his time, but also its innermost thoughts and beliefs, laid bare for our examination with a frankness that admits of no concealment. These afford the surest outlines for a trustworthy picture of the past, of which the details are supplied by the records of the chronicler" (*Superstition and Force,* 1878, 1892, Preface). His studies led him to realize the importance of the church, the greatest medieval institution; in 1867 he published *An Historical Sketch of Sacerdotal Celibacy,* and in 1869, *Studies in Church History*.

This fecundity was amazing since in this decade from 1860 to 1870 he was also active in his publishing business, which after 1865 he conducted alone, and deeply interested in public affairs. When the Civil War began he became one of the early members of the Union League, for which he wrote many widely circulated pamphlets. He served on its military committee, on the finance and executive committee, on the committee on colored enlistments, which raised several regiments and helped to break down the prejudice against employing colored troops, and as bounty commissioner. This was the only public office which Lea ever held, but he was constantly engaged in public affairs. In the period immediately following the war he was still an ardent Republican but as he witnessed the orgy of corruption, culminating in Philadelphia in 1870 in the creation of the Public Buildings Commission, he discarded partisanship and organized the Municipal Reform Association, of which for several years he was president. He resigned from the Union League because it refused to throw its influence on the side of reform. He was an active member of the Committee of One Hundred, formed in 1880 for the purification of politics, and president of the Reform Club. He was one of the first to support civil service reform, aiding the cause by his contributions and writings. He was the author of the Chace copyright act. Throughout his life he was interested in good government in city, state, and nation and wrote editorials, articles, and

pamphlets whenever he felt that he could contribute to the right decision of public matters.

With the formation of the firm of Henry C.
Lea's Son & Company in 1880, Lea, though remaining a special partner until 1885, in effect
retired from the publishing business. This action, which he had long contemplated, was precipitated by another breakdown due to overwork
which led to four years of comparative leisure.
In 1882 he printed privately *Translations and
Other Rhymes.* A few years later his health was
still so precarious that he consulted Dr. S. Weir
Mitchell, who prescribed a "schedule of life" to
which he conformed rigidly and thus was enabled to prolong his work for more than a score
of years. Every day he took a constitutional,
making this an opportunity to oversee his real-
estate operations, which were very extensive.
He did little traveling; during his life he made
only three short trips to Europe. Summers he
spent at Cape May, where he could, on his daily
walks, enjoy the flowers characteristic of the
seashore. The remainder of the day was spent
in revising his notes, planning his work, or
reading proof. In the late spring and early autumn he usually spent a few days at the Delaware Water Gap to enjoy the mountain flowers. Botany had been a favorite avocation from
his youth and in his later years he always had
flowers about him and frequently a rare or especially beautiful one on his desk. He was also
interested in Japanese bronzes, of which he made
a collection.

In the last twenty-five years of his life, his
chief interest was in study and writing. The
great work on which he had long been engaged,
A History of the Inquisition of the Middle Ages,
was published in three volumes in 1888. It is
still the one indispensable work on the subject.
This was followed in rapid succession by: *Chapters from the Religious History of Spain Connected with the Inquisition* (1890); *A Formu-
lary of the Papal Penitentiary in the Thirteenth
Century* (1892), edited by Lea; *A History of
Auricular Confession and Indulgences* (3 vols.,
1896); *The Moriscos of Spain, their Conversion
and Expulsion* (1901); *A History of the Inquisition of Spain* (4 vols., 1906–07); *The Inquisition in the Spanish Dependencies* (1908). At
the time of his death he was busy on a history of
witchcraft. The mass of notes which he had
copied for this work will eventually be published
and even in its incomplete form illustrates his
method of work. This method was first to collect the primary sources. In his rapidly growing library he gathered such as had been printed,
although not always in the latest and best edi-

tions. He kept copyists busy in several of the
great archives of Europe and South America,
especially in Spain. He found it necessary to
learn German at sixty, and Dutch at eighty. After collecting his material he studied it and whenever he found any passage which concerned his
subject copied it. He never employed a secretary. He was careful to include not only the
portion which he might wish to quote but all the
context, however lengthy, necessary for its elucidation. When he had exhausted all the sources
he made an analytical index of his notes. This
dictated the scope and contents of his work, as
it showed what material there was on each subject. Until this index was completed he refused
to form any judgments. When he found a dis-
proportionate amount of material on any subject
he published it in a separate article in order not
to cumber the prospective volume. Then began
the task of writing and rewriting. When he had
finished the first volume of his *History of Auricular Confession and Indulgences* and was ready
to send it to the printer he found new material
which necessitated rewriting the whole work.
In 1904 when he had finished his *History of the
Inquisition of Spain* he felt that it was too long
and rewrote it, reducing it to four volumes. His
purpose was to tell the truth exactly as he found
it from the study of the contemporary documents. He felt that "no serious historical work
is worth the writing or the reading unless it
conveys a moral, but to be useful the moral must
develop itself in the mind of the reader without
being obtruded upon him. . . . I have not
paused to moralize, but I have missed my aim
if the events narrated are not so presented as
to teach their appropriate lesson" (*A History of
the Inquisition of the Middle Ages,* Preface, p.
iv). Occasionally he did point a conclusion, as,
for example, "that the attempt of man to control
the conscience of his fellows reacts upon himself" (*A History of the Inquisition of Spain,* IV,
1907, p. 533), but in most of his later works
there is less of this tendency.

In 1899, at the time of the Dreyfus trial, liberals in France were seeking material for propaganda. Salomon Reinach asked the privilege of
translating the *History of the Inquisition of the
Middle Ages.* This had been advised by August
Molinier, the foremost French scholar on the
subject. Lea consented and revised the work, so
that the French translation (3 vols., 1900–02) is
superior to the earlier English version. This
was circulated in a cheap edition to influence
public opinion in the struggle between the
Church and State. Chapters were reprinted for
ten centimes each and were used, not only in

France, but also by the Belgian and Spanish liberals. A similar use was made of the diverting article on Leo Taxil and Diana Vaughan, which first appeared in *Lippincott's Monthly Magazine* (December 1900), and of the pamphlet, *The Dead Hand: A Brief Sketch of the Relations between Church and State with Regard to Ecclesiastical Property* (1900), which Lea wrote when the question of the disposition of the ecclesiastical properties in the Philippines was confronting the American government. Much of the latter was quoted by Waldeck-Rousseau in a speech which was published in the *Journal Officiel* and thus obtained a wide circulation. In France, references became frequent to "M. Léa, the grand old man." Many honors came to him. He received degrees from Harvard, Pennsylvania, Princeton, and was elected president of the American Historical Association. His presidential address, "Ethical Values in History," appeared in the *American Historical Review*, January, 1904. He was better known, however, to the scholars of Europe than in his own country. He received the degree of Doctor of Theology from the University of Giessen, was made a fellow of the Imperial University of Moscow, and an honorary member of learned societies in Germany, Italy, and Great Britain. His friends and correspondents included leading historians, in many countries. Bryce sought his aid in writing *The American Commonwealth*. Acton asked him to write the chapter on "The Eve of the Reformation" for the *Cambridge Modern History* (vol. I, 1902, pp. 653–92). Döllinger and Giesebrecht in Germany, Frédéricq in Belgium, Balzani and Villari in Italy, Maitland in England joined in doing him honor. There was hostile criticism, especially from some Roman Catholics in the United States, but it is significant that the most scholarly estimate of his work by a Roman Catholic abroad speaks of him as *"ce bon ouvrier de vérité"* (Alphandéry, *post*, p. 131).

Throughout, Lea remained the modest, retiring scholar. Frail in health, small in stature, kindly in nature, with a keen sense of humor, he worked on steadily. When eighty-one he wrote: "As regards an autobiography, I am like Canning's knife-grinder—'Story, Lord bless you sir, I've none to tell.' I only followed my convictions and worked as they led me. Besides, I have no time to waste. Every day shortens the little term left to me, and I have two books under way, to be finished after the Spanish Inquisition is off of my hands, and I am revising my volume on 'Celibacy' for another edition. So you see my program is a pretty full one, espe-

cially as age is beginning to tell on me, and I find that my power of labor is not what it was a half-century ago" (letter to D. C. M.). He was generous, and wise in giving. Many of the benefactions will never be known but among those which necessarily became known were the Institute of Hygiene for the University of Pennsylvania, a new wing for the Library Company building in Philadelphia, an epileptic farm, contributions to Jefferson Medical School and for the increase of salaries at the University of Pennsylvania, and finally the gift of his library with an endowment to that institution. He was always the genial host and served as dean of the Wistar Association from 1886, when he succeeded his father, until his death.

[A preliminary memoir, *Henry Charles Lea, 1825–1909* (1910), was privately printed by the family. Edward S. Bradley, *Henry C. Lea* (1931), is an authorized biography. Information may be obtained from *Proc. Am. Philosophical Soc.*, Jan.–Apr. 1911, vol. L, no. 198, reprinted as *Addresses Delivered at a Meeting Held in Memory of H. C. Lea, by E. P. Cheyney and Others* (1911); and *Proc. Mass. Hist. Soc.*, Dec. 1909 (1910), pp. 183–88, an address by C. H. Haskins. Papers and letters are in the Henry Charles Lea Lib. of the Univ. of Pa. Part of the material in this article was derived from conversations with Lea. For criticisms of his work, see Acton, in *Eng. Hist. Rev.*, Oct. 1888, pp. 773–88; Maitland, *Ibid.*, Oct. 1893, pp. 755–56; P. M. Baumgarten, *Henry Charles Lea's Hist. Writings: An Inquiry into their Method and Merit* (1909); P. M. Alphandéry, in *Revue de l'Histoire des Religions*, Jan.–Feb. 1910; Felice Tocco, *Henry Charles Lea e la Storia dell' Inquisizione Spagnuola* (Florence, 1911).]

D. C. M.

LEA, HOMER (Nov. 17, 1876–Nov. 1, 1912), soldier and author, was born at Denver, Colo., the son of Alfred Erskine and Hersa (Coberly) Lea. He was educated in public schools, the University of the Pacific, Occidental College, and at The Leland Stanford Junior University, which he attended from 1897 to 1899. As a student he studied military tactics and the principal wars of history, particularly those of Napoleon. He was wont to declare to his friends that he was destined to become a great military commander, a boast which was received with scoffing incredulity since he was an undersized and frail hunchback. In college days, also, he became deeply interested in the disturbances in China, and, in 1899, he adventurously crossed the Pacific, arriving in time to join the relief of Peking during the Boxer uprising. He never married nor developed strong ties within his own country. Instead, the rest of his life is a part of the history of the country with which he had thrown in his fortunes. So deep an impression did he make upon the Chinese with his daring persistence and obvious grasp of military science that by 1909 he rose to a generalship and became the associate of the reformer K'ang

Yu-Wei. Later, in the revolution of 1911–12, he became the confidential adviser of Sun Yat Sen. During these years he experienced extraordinary adventures and a number of almost incredible escapes from death.

In the midst of these activities he found time to write several books which created a widespread sensation at the time. These include *The Vermilion Pencil,* a novel published in 1908, *The Valor of Ignorance* (1909), a startling description of the menace of a Japanese invasion of the United States, and *The Day of the Saxon* (1912), which similarly gave warning of attacks by Oriental peoples upon the British Empire. Stricken with paralysis, he struggled to finish this last book only a few days before his death at Ocean Park, near Los Angeles. He was also engaged upon a history of politics and of the development of Chinese civilization.

The materials for the proper appraisal of his character and ability are all too meager. He has been hailed as one of the greatest military geniuses of history, and he unquestionably impressed some observers with the right to this title. No one can doubt his uncanny skill in organizing and leading the forces of the Chinese people. Opinions differ concerning his motives, and it is not easy to determine whether he was an unselfish enthusiast fascinated by the cause of Chinese freedom, or whether he seized an opportunity to satisfy his passion for military experience. At all events he is one of the most picturesque personalities of his generation and, perhaps, the most gifted American who ever joined a foreign legion.

[See *Harper's Weekly,* Jan. 4, 1913; *Literary Digest,* Nov. 16, 1912; *Who's Who in America,* 1912–13. Robert Young, "The Impudence of Charlatanism," *World Peace Foundation Pamphlet Series,* vol. II (1912), reprinted from *Japan Chronicle* (Kobe), Feb. 11, 1912, with letter from David Starr Jordan, gives the more unfavorable view of Lea's character and motives. See also *New York Times* and *New York Tribune,* Nov. 2, 1912.]   P. K.

LEA, ISAAC (Mar. 4, 1792–Dec. 8, 1886), malacologist, publisher, of Quaker stock, fifth son of James and Elizabeth (Gibson) Lea, was born at Wilmington, Del., to which place his great-great-grandfather, John Lea, had come from Gloucestershire, England, in 1699. When Isaac was fifteen the family moved to Philadelphia, and he entered the wholesale and importing establishment of his eldest brother. About this time he formed a friendship with Lardner Vanuxem [*q.v.*], with whom he made jaunts about Philadelphia, collecting minerals and rocks. Science at that day had not progressed very far, and it was difficult for the boys to obtain information about the specimens they gathered; although later they had access to a collection of minerals owned by Dr. Adam Seybert, then the only collection of its kind in the city. They were both early members (1815) of the Academy of Natural Sciences of Philadelphia. In 1814 they joined a volunteer rifle company and offered service against the British, then in possession of Washington. Although the company was not called into action, the enlistment cost Lea his birthright in the Society of Friends. In 1821 he married Frances Anne Carey, daughter of Mathew Carey [*q.v.*]. She died after a happy married life of fifty-two years, leaving two sons, Mathew Carey and Henry Charles Lea [*qq.v.*], and one daughter. Upon his marriage Lea became a member of the firm of M. Carey & Sons, the most extensive publishing house of its day in the United States. He remained with this firm and its successors until his retirement in 1851.

Lea's first scientific article (*Journal of the Academy of Natural Sciences of Philadelphia,* December 1818) was "An Account of the Minerals at Present Known to Exist in the Vicinity of Philadelphia"; his second article (*American Journal of Science and Arts,* vol. V, 1822, p. 155) was a "Notice of a Singular Impression in Sand-stone." He continued writing until 1876, his work covering a period of fifty-eight years. His style was plain but fluent; his bibliography includes 279 titles; and his papers deal with a wide range of subjects: mineralogy, hibernation, the Northwest Passage, halos with parhelia, geology, fossils, land, fresh-water, and marine *Mollusca.* After 1827 he gave most of his attention to studies of the fresh-water mollusks, becoming a recognized authority in his field. Most of his papers appeared in the *Proceedings* or *Transactions* of the American Philosophical Society, or in the *Proceedings* or *Journal* of the Academy of Natural Sciences of Philadelphia. From time to time they were republished in his *Observations on the Genus Unio,* issued between 1827 and 1874 in thirteen quarto volumes, with many lithographic plates illustrating all the species described. He described more than 1,800 species of mollusks, recent and fossil. Of pearly fresh-water mussels, the group for which he is most famous, he described 901 recent and ten fossil species. Of many he described not only the shell but also the soft parts and the glochidium (the minute embryonic shells in the gills of the mother). Among other mollusks his interest centered chiefly in fresh-water snails belonging to the genera *Melania, Goniobasis, Pleurocera, Anculosa,* and others of that group. He described a few miscellaneous fresh-water species, and about seventy-five terrestrial species.

As his studies of the *Mollusca* progressed he received specimens from correspondents in all parts of the world, who sought his aid in classifying them. Thus he acquired many species which he described as new, the types of which in most cases were retained for his collection. He received also many species already known which helped to build up his valuable series. His collections were bequeathed to the United States National Museum.

Self-confident, of strong will, successful in business, the leading authority on the fresh-water mussels, he did not take kindly to the work of Conrad and Rafinesque in this line, and his criticism of their work was sometimes very severe. In his eighty-fifth year he prepared and published *Catalogue of the Published Works of Isaac Lea, LL.D. from 1817 to 1876* (1876). Honors bestowed upon him included the presidency of the American Association for the Advancement of Science (1860); presidency of the Academy of Natural Sciences of Philadelphia (1858–63); vice-presidency of the American Philosophical Society; membership or honorary membership in numerous learned societies in America and abroad. In 1832 and again in 1853 he spent several months touring Europe and was an honored guest of many of the scientists of England, France, Germany, and other countries.

[Lea's *Catalogue of the Published Works of Isaac Lea, LL.D.* (1876); N. P. Scudder, *Published Writings of Isaac Lea, LL.D.* (Bull. 23, U. S. Nat. Museum, 1885), with a biographical sketch; *Proc. Am. Philosophical Soc.*, vol. XXIV (1887); W. H. Dall, in *Science*, Dec. 17, 1886; *Am. Jour. Sci.*, Jan. 1887; *Conchologists' Exchange*, Dec. 1886; W. J. Youmans, *Pioneers of Science in America* (1896); J. H. and G. H. Lea, *The Ancestry and Posterity of John Lea* (1906); the *Press* (Phila.), Dec. 9, 1886.]
W. B. M—l.

LEA, MATHEW CAREY (Aug. 18, 1823–Mar. 15, 1897), chemist, was born in Philadelphia, the son of Isaac Lea [q.v.] and Frances Anne (Carey) Lea, daughter of Mathew Carey [q.v.], political economist, publisher, and writer. Educated at home, he showed an especial taste for languages, literature, and mathematics. He traveled abroad with his parents during his boyhood, coming into personal contact with the European scientists of his father's acquaintance. With his younger brother, Henry Charles Lea [q.v.], he studied chemistry in the laboratory of James C. Booth [q.v.], in Philadelphia, and after devoting some time to the study of law, which he was forced to abandon on account of his health, he returned to the laboratory of

Booth, Garrett and Blair to continue work in his chosen science. His later research was done almost entirely in his private laboratory at his home, Chestnut Hill, Philadelphia.

He had a decided preference for chemical theory and speculated considerably on the properties of the atoms. Their numerical relations led him to believe that "the number 44.45 plays an important part in the science of stoichiometry," since he found this relation to extend to forty-eight of the elements ("On Numerical Relations Existing between the Equivalent Numbers of Elementary Bodies," *American Journal of Science*, 2 ser. XXIX, 1860, pp. 98, 349, quoted by Barker, *post*, p. 159). He did much in synthetic organic chemistry, and through his study of the platinum metals greatly enriched analytical chemistry, but it was in photochemistry that he was a real pioneer. Foreign chemists were the first to recognize his efforts in this new field of physico-chemical research. His published contributions, dealing with "colloid silver" and "photohaloids" were translated into European languages and were heralded as epoch-making. The beautiful forms of amorphous silver, which he discovered, continued to enkindle enthusiasm wherever and whenever exhibited.

Possessed of ample means and handicapped throughout life by precarious health, he rarely mingled with men but in quiet worked unceasingly in his private laboratory until his contributions to photographic chemistry numbered three hundred and his communications on special chemical topics more than one hundred. His papers were published chiefly in photographic journals and in the *American Journal of Science*. The only book he ever wrote, *A Manual of Photography* (1868), dealt with photochemistry. He was also active as an investigator in the domain of pure physics. He was a member of the Franklin Institute and of the National Academy of Sciences. To the Chemical Section of the Franklin Institute he bequeathed his scientific books and apparatus, together with a fund to provide for the future purchase of books on physical and chemical subjects. He was married, July 14, 1852, to his cousin Elizabeth Lea Jaudon, sister of his brother Henry's wife and widow of William Woodhouse Bakewell. She died Mar. 19, 1881, leaving him one son, and he later married Eva Lovering, daughter of Prof. Joseph Lovering [q.v.]. He died at his home in Philadelphia.

[Edgar Fahs Smith, *M. Carey Lea—Chemist* (1923); G. F. Barker, in *Nat. Acad. Sci. Biog. Memoirs*, vol. V (1905), with bibliography of Lea's most important papers; *Jour. Franklin Inst.*, Feb. 1898; *Pub. Ledger* (Phila.), Mar. 16, 1897.] E.F.S.

LEACH, ABBY (May 28, 1855–Dec. 29, 1918), classicist, was born in Brockton, Mass., the daughter of Marcus and Eliza Paris (Bourne) Leach. She was a descendant of Lawrence Leach who emigrated from England to Salem, Mass., in 1629. At a time when opportunities for the higher education of women were limited, and when courses for advanced study were for them non-existent, she went to Cambridge and induced several professors at Harvard to give her private instruction. It is difficult to realize the courage and tact then required to overcome not only masculine and even feminine prejudices against such instruction, but also the many practical difficulties which impeded liberal-minded men like William W. Goodwin and James B. Greenough [*qq.v.*] in their desire to help her. Her own belief in the necessity of such work, inherited from her New England ancestors, joined to the ability and good sense that she displayed from the beginning, had its reward. Her example inspired other young women, and her residence in Cambridge (1879–82) became the direct cause of the founding of Radcliffe College, then known popularly and somewhat derisively as "The Harvard Annex."

She was teacher of Greek and Latin languages at Vassar College in 1883 and obtained the degrees of A.B. and A.M. there in 1885. She became associate professor in 1888 and in 1889 was elected professor and chief of the newly organized department of Greek, a post which she held until her death. A teacher of force and originality, with a personal bearing and address which won a large following, she made it an object of emulation among her students to be accepted as members of her beginners' course in Greek. This was one of the first of its kind to be introduced into an American college of high rank, since she was among the first to recognize the importance of maintaining the college study of Greek literature at a period when it was declining in the preparatory schools, and she carried her classes upward through the drama and into Plato and Aristotle. Her own experience as a pioneer, and the wide acquaintance which she had formed among scholars, made her invaluable in aiding young women to satisfy their ambition for advanced work in graduate schools. Her influence thus extended far beyond her own field of Greek. Her services outside the college were numerous and notable. She was president of the American Philological Association (1899–1900); member of the Managing Committee of the American School of Classical Studies at Athens; of the Council of the Archaeological Institute of America; of the Classical Association of England and Wales, and the Classical Association of the Middle States and Maryland; and president of the Association of Collegiate Alumnae (1899–1901). In 1908 the Emperor of Japan presented her with a gold cup in recognition of her services to education. She was an occasional contributor to the *American Journal of Philology* and to the *Classical Review*; and to Lane Cooper's work on *The Greek Genius and its Influence* (1917) she contributed a chapter on "Fate and Free Will in Greek Literature."

[Samuel Chessman, *Leach Family Record* (1898); Bradford Kingman, *Hist. of Brockton, Plymouth County, Mass., 1656–1894* (1895); *Cat. of the Officers and Students of Vassar Coll.*, 1882–90; *Who's Who in America*, 1918–19; *Vassarion*, 1910; *Vassar Quart.*, Feb. 1919; *N. Y. Times*, Dec. 30, 1918; personal acquaintance.]

C. B. G.

LEACH, DANIEL DYER (June 12, 1806–May 16, 1891), Episcopal clergyman, educator, author of textbooks, one of the six children of Apollos and Chloe (Dyer) Leach, was a descendant by several lines from many of the first settlers of his birthplace, Bridgewater, Plymouth County, Mass. His father, a carpenter and builder, owned a profitable farm. Daniel's early education in the school near his home, under the direction of George Chipman, was supplemented by the varied activities presented by the home life of the period. He was a studious, self-reliant, and original boy. When sixteen years of age he left the Bridgewater Academy and engaged for a time in business in Boston. He was graduated from Brown University in 1830, studied divinity at Andover Theological Seminary, was ordained an Episcopal clergyman in 1833, preached for five years in Quincy, Mass., and retired from this parish to take up what proved to be his life work in education. From 1838 to 1842 he was principal of the Classical High School in Roxbury, Mass., and from 1842 to 1848 he conducted a private school. His interest in popular education led to his employment as an agent of the Massachusetts State Board of Education from 1848 to 1855. While holding this position he inspected more than a thousand schools and schoolhouses, noting their defects, and advising with local committees regarding ways and means for betterment. In the *Seventeenth Annual Report of the [Massachusetts] Board of Education* (1854) Leach presented plans for an improved system of ventilation which was soon widely installed. This episode emphasized one of his characteristics. To him the recognition of an undesirable condition was a direct challenge to his resourcefulness in devising means for improvement.

In 1855 he was appointed superintendent of

schools for Providence, R. I. At this time the Providence school system consisted of a committee numbering at times sixty-three, a staff of two men and one hundred women teachers, a clerk, and about seven thousand children. With his horse and chaise the superintendent was able to keep in close touch with all of his classrooms. In this little laboratory of practical pedagogy Leach dealt at first hand with the perennial problems of school administration. With insight, resource, and a rare grasp of psychological principles, he initiated experiments, created methods, and set standards that had a constructive effect upon the schools of his own and later times. His textbooks on arithmetic, geography, and spelling were widely used as standard texts for elementary schools. His reports to the Providence school committee, extending through thirty years, reveal educational insight and vision that make them profitable reading to a later generation of educators. A series of pamphlets, *Directions to Teachers* (1873), "embracing the best methods of teaching reading, spelling, object lessons, etc., with judicious counsel on the administration of discipline" contributed to the advancement of teaching over a wide area. His methods for teaching spelling resounded even in the English Parliament in the reports of an inspector sent by the British government to observe the schools of the United States and Canada (James Fraser, *Report . . . on the Common School System of the United States and . . . Upper and Lower Canada,* 1866). From 1870 to 1889 he was a member of the Rhode Island State Board of Education, and in 1877 he was elected a trustee of Brown University for life. In methods of public-school administration he was a pioneer, making his way along untried paths in a profession lacking traditions and having few precedents. In 1834 Leach married Mary H. Lawton, daughter of Capt. Robert and Penelope (Brown) Lawton, of Newport, R. I. There were three children. A memorial tablet in honor of Daniel Leach and of his brother, Col. Franklin Leach, was placed in the memorial building of the Old Bridgewater Historical Society with appropriate historical addresses of dedication on Nov. 26, 1927.

[Leach's reports to the Providence School Committee, 1855–83; files of *Providence Jour.* for June 1891; Thos. Bicknell, *Hist. of the State of R. I. and Providence Plantations* (1920); Horace S. Tarbell, address at the centennial celebration of the establishment of the public schools of Providence, R. I., printed in the *Report of the School Committee, 1899–1900 Centennial, Providence, R. I.*; F. P. Leach, *Lawrence Leach of Salem, Mass., and Some of His Descendants,* vol. II (1925); *Providence Jour.,* May 18, 1891.]

J. L. A.

LEACH, SHEPHERD (Apr. 30, 1778–Sept. 19, 1832), iron founder, capitalist, was descended in the fifth generation from Lawrence Leach who settled at Salem, Mass., in 1629 and is said to have been connected with the establishment (at Lynn, Mass.) of the first iron works in the New England colonies. The son of Abisha Leach, an iron founder and Revolutionary soldier, by his wife, Patience Woods, Shepherd Leach was born in Easton, Mass. One of the oldest and most prosperous of Easton's industries was the smelting and casting of iron, for which the local supplies of bog ore furnished the raw material and local and neighboring manufacturers of nails and kitchen ware, the market. Young Leach early displayed business ability. At twenty-four he bought his father's iron works, to which he added within a few years the furnace of his chief competitor in Easton. In the sales contract the latter agreed not to operate any iron works within a distance of twenty miles. Leach, as the agreement indicates, was ambitious to become a captain of industry. He promptly undertook to enlarge the output of the combined businesses. To supply increased power he constructed a large reservoir, and by the purchase of several hundred acres of bog land and the lease of mining privileges on other lands, secured adequate supplies of raw material.

During the decade 1820–30, increased demand for heavy castings for engines and machinery for the new textile and other factories in southern New England generated a wave of prosperity for the iron works of southern Massachusetts. Believing that this prosperity would last, Leach expanded his business still further by buying out a number of competitors in Easton and nearby towns. Soon he was operating seven furnaces in Easton alone. His profits seem to have been greater than the iron industry could absorb, for he invested in other local enterprises: spinning-mills, a gristmill, and a sawmill. In 1832 his Easton iron works employed 100 workmen, producing 200 tons of pig iron and 600 tons of castings annually.

Leach became the wealthiest man in the community, which in 1830 numbered 1,756 persons, and took a leading part in a variety of local activities. His greatest distinction, outside of business, was attained in the Massachusetts militia, in which he held a major-general's commission. On muster days he cut a fine figure. He "was large, fleshy, of a commanding appearance, a fine officer on the field, and seemed to enjoy his position as general" (Chaffin, *post,* p. 516). He was a strong supporter of the local "evangelical society" and a bosom friend of its pastor. Avoiding as far as possible the strife between opposing factions which embittered religious life in Easton as well as in many other New England communities in his day, he gave his interest in church affairs a practical turn. "On stormy Sundays he would get out an immense covered wagon that he owned, and drive from house to house until it was filled with church-goers, and then . . . to meeting. . . . Though not much of a singer himself, General Leach was very fond of singing, and would lead the choir, standing with his back to the audience and beating time in the most approved style" (*Ibid.*, 517–18). He had the reputation of being open-handed in his charities and liberal in his business dealings. His capitalistic ambitions resulted disastrously. He acquired more property than he could profitably manage, and after his death, which was the result of a fall from his chaise, his affairs were found to be in bad condition. His wife, formerly Phoebe Torrey, whom he married in 1784, survived him.

[W. L. Chaffin, *Hist. of the Town of Easton, Mass.* (1886); "Documents Relative to the Manufactures in the U. S." (2 vols., 1833), *House Doc. No. 308, 22 Cong., 1 Sess.*; F. P. Leach, *Lawrence Leach of Salem, Mass., and Some of His Descendants*, vol. I (1924).]

P. W. B.

LEAMING, JACOB SPICER (Apr. 2, 1815– May 12, 1885), Ohio farmer, producer of the famous Leaming corn, was the son of Christopher and Margaret Leaming, who, early in the nineteenth century, left Cape May, New Jersey, and moved to a farm on the Little Miami River near Madisonville, Ohio. There Leaming was born and reared. From his father he acquired an interest in corn culture, for Christopher Leaming was more than an average farmer. He raised twice as much corn per acre as his neighbors because he insisted on selection of his seed, deep planting, and careful cultivation. On Mar. 1, 1839, Leaming married Lydia Ann Van Middlesworth by whom he had nine children, seven of them boys. For sixteen years after his marriage he lived in the old homestead. A chance drive along the Bullskin Run in Hamilton County in the fall of 1855 gave him the idea which later made him famous. In need of feed for his horses, he stopped at a wayside corn field and bought some corn. Impressed by the beautiful yellow color of the corn and its early maturity, he purchased a bushel for seed. The next year he moved his family to a farm two miles from Wilmington, and here he raised corn until 1884. In the spring of 1856 he planted the corn he had bought the previous autumn and by careful attention was rewarded by a yield in excess of one hundred bushels per acre. Farmers regarded it as a phenomenal achievement and began to visit his farm to buy seed. This they planted next season and referred to it as "Leaming corn." In 1857 Leaming was advised by a country physician interested in scientific agriculture to devote his entire attention to corn cultivation. He did so, and by careful, intensive cultivation, with the aid of his sons, he began to produce superior corn. He selected his seed from the standing corn, choosing tapering ears because he believed they matured earliest. Stripped of part of the husks, these seed ears were hung in a crib to dry. The following spring a second selection was made, again from tapering ears. By this method he developed corn which matured early. Leaming was, perhaps, the first to plant corn in shallow drills, "one grain in a place, 12 to 14 inches apart in rows 4 feet apart." At the Paris Exposition in 1878, the popularity of Leaming corn was enhanced by the prizes it won. The demand for it became so pressing that Leaming advertised his seed and soon developed a flourishing seed business. The variety which he developed became well known and widely used in corn-producing sections.

[W. A. Lloyd, "J. S. Leaming and His Corn," *Ann. Report of the Ohio Corn Improvement Asso. . . . for the Year 1910* (1911), republished in *J. S. Leaming and His Corn* (n.d.); Ohio Agricultural Experiment Station, *Circular No. 117* (1911); H. A. Wallace and E. N. Bressman, *Corn and Corn-Growing* (1923).]

R. C. M.

LEAMING, JEREMIAH (1717–Sept. 15, 1804), clergyman, was the eldest son of Jeremiah and Abigail (Turner) Leaming, and the grandson of Christopher Leaming of Southampton, L. I., who settled in New Jersey. The record of his baptism on May 12, 1717, in Durham, Conn., indicates that he was born in or near that town, possibly in Middletown. Soon after his graduation from Yale College in 1745 he transferred from the Congregational to the Episcopal Church and under the direction of Dr. Samuel Johnson, minister of Stratford, Conn., he became a lay reader in Norwalk. In 1746 Trinity Church, Newport, R. I., having received a bequest from Nathaniel Kay to provide for a schoolmaster and catechist, episcopally ordained, was advised by the Society for the Propagation of the Gospel to apply to Dr. Johnson "for one of the young gentlemen educated at New Haven." As a consequence Leaming was sent to England at the expense of the Newport church, was ordained in 1748, and returned the same year to take up his work at Newport as head of the parochial school and assistant to the Rev. James Honyman. After the death of the latter in 1750 he had charge of the church until the appointment of another minister four years later. In 1758 he returned to Norwalk as minister of St. Paul's parish. At the outbreak of the Revolution he suffered severely for his Loyalist sympathies. All his considerable landed property in Connecticut was confiscated and he was for a time confined in the Fairfield county jail and so harshly treated that he contracted a rheumatic trouble which left him permanently lame. In July 1779 when British troops under General Tryon burned Norwalk, having lost all his books and household effects, Leaming decided to accompany the British to New York. He remained there until 1784, when he returned to Connecticut to become rector of the church at Stratford.

In March 1783 the clergy of Connecticut met in Woodbury to choose a presbyter who might seek Episcopal orders in England. Leaming had always been a strong advocate of a bishop for the colonies. By reason of his sufferings during the war which had gained him the reputation of a "confessor," no less than by his age and character, he was the leading presbyter among the Connecticut clergy. It was thus natural that he should be their first choice for bishop, but he declined to serve on the score of physical infirmity. In the following critical years Leaming worked effectively for the establishment of the Connecticut church and for its union with that of Pennsylvania and the other Southern dioceses. He objected (unsuccessfully) to the adoption of the word protestant by the Episcopal Church, and his Loyalist sympathies led him to protest (successfully) against the inclusion of a service for Independence Day in the new prayer-book. In 1765 he had received an honorary degree of M.A. from King's College and in 1789 the same institution conferred upon him the degree of S.T.D. In 1790 he retired from Stratford and from the active ministry and took up his residence in New York. The closing period of his life, however, was spent in New Haven at the home of the widow of James A. Hillhouse. Some years later a grand-niece, Mary Hillhouse, wrote: "He rises to my mind, the very ideal of age and decrepitude—a small, emaciated old man, very lame, his ashen and withered features surmounted sometimes by a cap, and sometimes by a small wig—always quiet and gentle in his manner, and uniformly kind and inoffensive. . . . He said little; spent most of his time in his own room, and never entertained his younger auditors with stirring tales

of his earlier manhood" (Sprague, *post,* p. 130). He was twice married: but had no children. His first wife was Ann Leaming, his second, Elizabeth (Peck) Leaming. His published works consist of various sermons and controversial theological pamphlets which have little interest today.

[See E. E. Beardsley, *The Rev. Jeremiah Leaming, His Life and Services* (1885), reprinted from the *Churchman,* Feb. 21, 28, 1885; *The Hist. of the Episc. Ch. in Conn.* (2 vols. 1866–68), and *Life and Correspondence of the Right Rev. Samuel Seabury, D.D.* (1881); F. B. Dexter, *Biog. Sketches of the Grads. of Yale Coll.,* vol. II (1896); W. B. Sprague, *Annals. Am. Pulpit,* vol. V (1859); and the *Conn. Jour.* (New Haven), Sept. 20, 1804. Many of Leaming's letters have been printed; some unpublished ones are in the possession of Dr. H. C. Robbins of New York.]

W. P. L.

LEAMING, THOMAS (Sept. 1, 1748–Oct. 29, 1797), Revolutionary patriot, soldier, lawyer, merchant, was born in Cape May County, N. J., a descendant of Christopher Leaming, an Englishman, who moved from Southampton, L. I., to Cape May in 1692, and the son of Thomas and Elizabeth (Leaming) Leaming, who owned extensive property in South Jersey. He received his education and training in Philadelphia and was associated with that city during the greater part of his career. Soon after completing his scholastic education he was placed in the office of John Dickinson [*q.v.*] to study law and was admitted to the bar of Philadelphia. His association with Dickinson made him one of the most earnest of practical patriots. He gave his time and his money to the Revolutionary cause, and, by his ardent espousal of it, exposed his estate to confiscation by the British. Early in the year 1776 he had detected the danger in which South Jersey lay from attack by the British forces, and at the expense of himself and some wealthy neighbors, he organized a battalion of militia in Cape May County. On Apr. 15, 1776, he petitioned the Continental Congress to supply powder and lead to the battalion, a prayer that was granted with the addition of the clause, "he paying for the same."

Before the Cape May Battalion was actually called into action, the Provincial Assembly of the state of New Jersey opened its sessions, June 10, 1776, and Leaming was among the deputies sent to it from his county. A week later he resigned his office as adjutant of the battalion. He remained a member of the Assembly until its sessions for the year were ended, being present on July 2, 1776, when it voted for independence. He had joined the troop of Light Horse of the City of Philadelphia, now known as the First City Troop of Philadelphia City Cavalry, in 1775, and as soon as he was relieved of his legislative duties he returned to this little command which was composed entirely of well-to-do young men who furnished their own horses and equipment. They acted as Washington's escort, and as scouts, throughout the campaigns from 1776 to 1779. Leaming was with the troop at the battles of Princeton, Trenton, Germantown, and Brandywine, and was elected to its honorary roll in 1787.

In 1777 Leaming founded the firm of Bunner, Murray & Company, which in 1780 subscribed heavily to the Pennsylvania Bank (in 1781 the Bank of North America). The firm of Thomas Leaming & Company, which may have been a branch of the same house, began in 1777 to fit out privateers, and between May of that year and 1780, eleven vessels, varying in size from eighteen-gun ships to a four-gun schooner, were put on the seas, their masters bearing letters of marque. Fifty prizes and 1,000 prisoners were taken by these privateers. The schooner *Mars,* under Capt. Yelverton Taylor, took, in three vessels which it captured, 500 British and Hessian soldiers. At the close of the war, the firm was dissolved and Leaming returned to the practice of law in Philadelphia. He married Rebecca Fisher in Christ Church, in that city, Aug. 19, 1779, and his two sons, Thomas Fisher Leaming and Jeremiah Fisher Leaming, became well-known merchants in Philadelphia. Leaming was a victim of the yellow-fever epidemic which devastated the city in 1797, dying from that disease on Oct. 29. His remains were interred in the burial ground of Christ Church.

[P. S. Howe, *Mayflower Pilgrim Descendants in Cape May County, N. J.* (1921), p. 106; *Hist. of the First Troop, Phila. City Cavalry* (1874); S. N. Winslow, *Biogs. of Successful Phila. Merchants* (1864), pp. 69–72; Henry Simpson, *Lives of Eminent Philadelphians* (1859); Maurice Beasly, "Sketch of the Early History of the County of Cape May," *Geol. of the County of Cape May, State of N. J.* (1857); E. L. Clark, *A Record of the Inscriptions . . . in the Burial-Grounds of Christ Church, Phila.* (1864), p. 605; *Jours. of the Continental Cong.,* vol. IV (1906), vol. X (1908); *Pa. Archives,* 5 ser., I (1906); *Minutes of the Provincial Cong. and the Council of Safety of the State of N. J.* (1879).]

J. J.

LEAR, TOBIAS (Sept. 19, 1762–Oct. 11, 1816), consular officer, was born at Portsmouth, N. H., the son of Col. Tobias Lear and Mary (Stilson) Lear. His father's prosperity as a shipmaster and later as a farmer enabled the son to graduate at Harvard, in 1783, and to travel and study in Europe. This preparation led to his engagement as private secretary to General Washington after his retirement to Mount Vernon in 1785. Lear held that enviable position for seven years, during which time there is every evidence that he greatly endeared

himself to Washington and his family, becoming a life-long friend as well as a valued employee. While living at Mount Vernon he published *Observations on the River Potomack, the Country Adjacent, and the City of Washington* (1793), probably the earliest separate monograph on the District of Columbia. In 1790 he had married Mary Long of Portsmouth, N. H., and after her death in 1793 he went abroad, carrying letters of introduction from Washington and Jefferson. Returning in 1794, he settled in Alexandria, Va. He was elected president of the Potomac Canal Company in 1795 and on Aug. 22 of that year married Frances (Bassett) Washington, a niece of Martha Washington and the widow of Washington's nephew, George Augustine. On her death, he married Frances Dandridge Henley, another niece of Mrs. Washington. When war was imminent in 1798 Washington appointed him his military secretary, with rank of colonel, and from that time Lear remained with him until his death. Tradition says that he was the last person to whom Washington spoke; it is certain that he received a substantial legacy from his chief in appreciation of his services.

The fact that he was honored by Washington was largely responsible for his appointment by President Jefferson, in 1801, as consul at Santo Domingo. This post presented great difficulties at that time, for Toussaint L'Ouverture was rapidly becoming independent ruler there, while Jefferson still considered the island a French possession. Faced with these conditions, Lear conducted himself with great caution and tact, and upheld with energy the rights of American citizens during a period of bloodshed and horror. His task became hopeless after the arrival of General LeClerc, sent by Napoleon to take possession of the island, preparatory to extending the empire to Louisiana. In April 1802 LeClerc declined longer to allow Lear to remain, and he was forced to return to America. Upon his arrival in Washington his conduct was commended by the President, and he was shortly afterward named consul general at Algiers, with powers to negotiate a treaty with Tripoli in cooperation with the squadron commander, also to adjust affairs with any of the Barbary rulers.

It is evident that Lear possessed the qualities necessary to deal with the vacillating potentates, for between 1803 and 1805 he assisted in making a treaty with Morocco, in keeping a precarious peace with Algiers, and in adjusting affairs in Tunis. With Tripoli, matters were complicated in many ways: by the plight of three hundred Americans imprisoned since the loss of the *Philadelphia*; by the ill-health of Commodore Barron, with whom Lear was to cooperate; by a military expedition against the de facto authorities led by William Eaton [*q.v.*], "Navy Agent to the Barbary States"; and by Lear's own ardent desire for peace. Plans for a treaty had been discussed for two years, when suddenly, on June 4, 1805, Lear signed an agreement with the Pasha which, although otherwise desirable, acceded to ransom for the prisoners. Although this treaty was upheld by the government, it became a political issue. Opponents of the administration held that in view of the fleet in the Mediterranean and the land operations in progress under Eaton, no money should have been promised. Mystery surrounds Lear's motive for making this hasty treaty: explanations that have been suggested are the seemingly groundless fear of the naval officers for the safety of the prisoners, Lear's "passion for peace," and the fact that at that time he felt certain of securing liberal terms.

Beset by many difficulties, he remained as consul in Algiers until the beginning of the War of 1812, at which time the Dey, expecting the United States to be defeated by Great Britain, gave him summary orders to leave. Arriving in Washington under the cloud of the ill-timed treaty with Tripoli, Lear found his diplomatic career at an end. He was made an accountant in the War Department, and on Oct. 11, 1816, he committed suicide, leaving no explanation of his deed.

[C. W. Brewster, *Rambles about Portsmouth, First Series* (1859); H. H. Bennett, *Vignettes of Portsmouth* (1913); T. L. Tullock, "Col. Tobias Lear," *Granite Mo.*, Oct., Nov. 1882; *Letters from George Washington to Tobias Lear* (1905); *Letters and Recollections of George Washington, Being Letters to Tobias Lear and Others* (1906); Jared Sparks, *The Writings of George Washington* (12 vols., 1834–37); J. C. Fitzpatrick, *The Diaries of George Washington* (1925), vol. IV; *Am. State Papers, Foreign Relations*, vol. II (1832); C. O. Paullin, *Commodore John Rodgers* (1910); G. W. Allen, *Our Navy and the Barbary Corsairs* (1905); R. W. Irwin, *The Diplomatic Relations of the U. S. with the Barbary Powers, 1776–1816* (1931); F. J. R. Rodd, *Gen. Wm. Eaton* (1932); *Daily National Intelligencer*, Oct. 12, 1816; manuscript material in Lib. of Cong., Dept. of State, and Navy Dept.]   R. B. B.

LEARNED, EBENEZER (Apr. 18, 1728– Apr. 1, 1801), Revolutionary soldier, was born at Oxford, Mass., the son of Col. Ebenezer Learned and his wife, Deborah Haynes. He was descended from William Learned who was admitted to the First Church in Charlestown, in 1632, and in 1640 was one of the first settlers of Woburn. During part of the French and Indian War he served as captain of a company of Oxford men in Colonel Ruggles' regiment. He was one of the leading spirits in the Revolutionary movement in his native town. On Sept. 29, 1774, he was chosen delegate to the Provincial Congress at Concord, and on Jan. 12, 1775, to that at Cambridge. Shortly after the battle of Lexington he arrived in Cambridge at the head of a body of minute-men and was assigned, Apr. 21, 1775, to the right wing of the American army. While he was not present on the field of Bunker Hill, his men were under fire at Roxbury during the course of the action. On Jan. 1, 1776, he was commissioned colonel of the 3rd Continental Infantry. He helped to arrange the understanding between Washington and Howe respecting the evacuation of Boston, and on Mar. 17, 1776, he unbarred the gates with his own hands to admit the patriot forces. While the British fleet lingered in the harbor, his men were detailed to keep nightly watch upon it with the use of whale-boats. His regiment was presently ordered to New York, but on account of ill-health he resigned in May 1776.

Returning to Oxford, he continued to render various services to the Revolutionary cause. Not content to sniff the smoke of battle from afar, he accepted a commission, voted by Congress Apr. 2, 1777, as brigadier-general, and was ordered to join the northern army under Gates and Schuyler. After collecting the militia at Fort Edward and Fort Anne, he helped to remove valuable stores from Ticonderoga to prevent them from falling into enemy hands. He accompanied Arnold on his expedition to the relief of Fort Stanwix and took a noteworthy part in the battles of Sept. 19 and Oct. 7, 1777, his brigade being publicly thanked by Gates for its valiant behavior in the first-mentioned action. After Burgoyne's surrender he was ordered to the southward. On Mar. 24, 1778, he was again forced to resign his commission by reason of physical disability. Returning to Oxford, he served the town in civil capacity, representing it at the state constitutional convention in 1779 and as member of the legislature in 1783.

Learned was twice married: on Oct. 5, 1749, to Jerusha Baker, and on May 23, 1800, to Eliphal Putnam. For a time he kept a public house on his farm. He was at one time or another selectman, assessor, justice of the peace, and moderator of town-meeting, and was active in church affairs. His courage is attested not only by the incidents of his military career but by the fact that when most of his family and neighbors espoused the cause of Daniel Shays in 1786, he supported the constituted authorities even at the risk of his life. He died at Oxford.

[G. F. Daniels, *Hist. of the Town of Oxford, Mass.* (1892); J. Wilkinson, *Memoirs of My Own Times*, 3 vols. (1816); M. de W. Freeland, *The Records of Oxford, Mass.* (1894); F. B. Heitman, *Hist. Reg. of Officers of the Continental Army* (1893); Peter Nelson, "Learned's Expedition to the Relief of Fort Stanwix," *Quart. Jour. of the N. Y. State Hist. Asso.*, Oct. 1928; W. L. Learned, *The Learned Family* (2nd ed., 1898); *Columbian Centinel* (Boston, Mass.), Apr. 11, 1801.]

E. E. C.

LEARNED, MARION DEXTER (July 10, 1857–Aug. 1, 1917), German philologist, historian, editor, was born near Dover, Del., the son of Hervey Dexter and Mary Elizabeth (Griffith) Learned. He was descended from William Learned, who was admitted to the First Church in Charlestown, Mass., in 1632. The Griffiths settled on the Eastern Shore of Maryland about 1675. Marion Dexter Learned received his college education at Dickinson College (Carlisle, Pa.), was awarded the degree of A.B. in 1880, and then taught languages in the Williamsport Dickinson Seminary from 1880 to 1884. He visited Germany in 1885 for the study of Germanic philology and completed his graduate work at the Johns Hopkins University, where he received the degree of Ph.D. in 1887. He had been appointed instructor in German in 1886 and soon advanced to the associate professorship in the same department. On June 26, 1890, he married Annie Mosser of New Cumberland, Pa.

In 1895 Learned was called to the University of Pennsylvania as head of the German department, which, during more than twenty years of devoted service, he developed into one of the leading centers of Germanic studies. The call was a recognition of the scientific value of his philological work, *The Pennsylvania German Dialect* (1889), completed while at Johns Hopkins and originally published in the *American Journal of Philology* (vols. IX–X, 1888–89). Professor Oswald Seidensticker, Learned's predecessor in the chair of German at the University of Pennsylvania, had already revealed the fact that the Pennsylvania Germans had had a history, fascinating and important in the development of the American commonwealth. Learned became the continuator of this work of historical investigation and combined with it advanced philological and literary studies that attracted graduate students of ability. Their work, with the cooperation and under the guidance of their leader, resulted in a series of publications on German and American interrelations which were a contribution of lasting value. For the advancement of such studies he founded in 1897 a quarterly called the *Americana Germanica*, which after four years appeared monthly under the new name, *German American Annals*, "devoted to the comparative study of the historical, literary, linguistic, and educational relations of Germany and America." The journal was not confined to local investigations, but invited a wide range of contributors, and aimed to be national in its interests. His own contributions to the journal were numerous, and some of his studies were republished separately, including *Philip Waldeck's Diary of the American Revolution* (1907) and *The American Ethnographical Survey* (1911), in which he attempted to catch as it were in a drag-net, all the historical and literary materials still existing in the Pennsylvania-German counties of Pennsylvania. His most elaborate work, first published in the *Annals*, was his *Life of Francis Daniel Pastorius* (1908), which was a documentary history, furnishing as nearly as possible an exhaustive collection of all the documents available on the subject after a most painstaking search in Europe and America. These materials were published verbatim, in the original languages, ancient and modern, without translation and frequently without comment. He scorned the popular demand for readable books as something unworthy, tending to lower scientific standards. He preferred to "let truth unadorned radiate from the documents."

Another work of historical value was his *Guide to the Manuscript Materials Relating to American History in the German State Archives* (1912), undertaken under the direction of the department of historical research of the Carnegie Institution. Among other works should be mentioned: *The German-American Turner Lyric* (1896); *The Saga of Walther of Aquitaine* (1892); *A New German Grammar* (1903); and *Abraham Lincoln, An American Migration, Family English not German* (1909). He continued to edit the *German American Annals* until the year of his death. By that time nineteen volumes had been published and the monographs (most of them written by his students), published separately in the series called the *Americana Germanica*, numbered thirty-two. His graduate students felt an affectionate personal regard for him. He cared for them like a father when they needed aid in securing a position, and he was eminently successful in placing his men. He had the courage of his convictions, however, was quick to give them utterance, and would grow hotly indignant if the occasion provoked it. Then his high-pitched voice would ring out like a clarion. He was president of the Modern Language Association of America in 1909, member of the American Philosophical Society, and Knight of the Royal Prussian Order of the Red Eagle.

["In Memoriam: The Late Professor Learned," *German-Am. Annals*, Sept.–Dec. 1917; "The President's Address," *Modern Language Asso. of America Pubs.*, n.s. vol. XVIII (1910), pp. xlvi–lxv; W. L. Learned, *The Learned Family* (2nd ed., 1898); *Old Penn*, Oct. 5, 1917; *Philadelphia Inquirer*, Aug. 2, 1917.]   A. B. F.

LEARY, JOHN (Nov. 1, 1837–Feb. 8, 1905), capitalist, was born at St. John, New Brunswick, Canada. As a young man he engaged successfully in shipping, lumbering, and general merchandising at St. John and Woodstock, New Brunswick, and at Houlton, Me. Business reverses, however, induced him to migrate to the Far West, and he arrived at Seattle, Washington Territory, in 1869. A couple of years later he was admitted to the bar, and, after having been associated with two law firms, he withdrew from practice in 1882. Business enterprises of most varied character, but generally identified with Seattle and the Puget Sound country, absorbed his energies for the remainder of his life. Beginning as part owner in the Talbot coal mines, he extended these interests, opening the Leary mines, and establishing his own town of Leary. From mining he turned to real estate and became one of the largest holders of real property in Seattle. His financial interests in public utilities were large; in the city gas plant, in the company to furnish the city's water, in street railway and cable lines. He was also a promoter of elevator and warehouse companies. When it seemed as if the Northern Pacific would discriminate against Seattle, Leary organized, 1873, the Seattle & Walla Walla Railroad to connect his city with the transcontinental line. In 1891, he established the Columbia River & Puget Sound Navigation Company, which soon operated a fleet of coasters and ferry boats. James P. Ludlow was enabled through Leary's aid to secure the contract to carry mail from Puget Sound to Alaska and intermediate points, a privilege formerly enjoyed by a Portland concern. This versatile individual was also part owner of the *Seattle Post*, 1882, which was amalgamated with the *Seattle Post Intelligencer*. Later he held shares in the *Morning Journal*, which in 1891 was absorbed by the *Seattle Telegraph*. He was a founder of the Seattle Chamber of Commerce (April 1882) and for two terms its president. From 1884 to 1886 he was mayor of Seattle. He strongly advocated free public education, including provision for free textbooks for all children; and he was a regent of the University of Washington. His membership in the governing council of the Irish National League of America indicated a more cosmopolitan interest. He was twice married: first to Mary Blanchard; and second, Apr. 21, 1892, to Eliza P. Ferry, daughter of Elisha P. Ferry, first governor of the state of Washington. Leary died at Riverside, Cal.

[C. B. Bagley, *Hist. of King County, Wash.* (1929), vol. II; F. J. Grant, *Hist. of Seattle, Wash., with Illustrations and Biog. Sketches of Some of its Prominent Men and Pioneers* (1891); *Seattle and Environs* (1924), vol. II; *Seattle Daily Times*, Feb. 8, 10, 13, 14, 15, 25, 1905; *Seattle Post Intelligencer*, Feb. 9, 15, 16, 1905.]   H. J. D.

LEAVENWORTH, FRANCIS PRESERVED (Sept. 3, 1858–Nov. 12, 1928), astronomer and teacher, was born at Mount Vernon, Ind., the son of Seth Marshall and Sarah (Nettleton) Leavenworth. He was a descendant of Thomas Leavenworth who emigrated from England to America after 1664 and died at Woodbury, Conn., Aug. 3, 1683. Francis had a public-school education, and entered the University of Indiana in 1876, graduating in 1880 with the degree of B.A. At the university he came into contact with Prof. Daniel Kirkwood [*q.v.*], the astronomer, and after graduation he spent a year of study under Ormond Stone at the Cincinnati Observatory. In 1881, when Stone became director of the new Leander McCormick Observatory of the University of Virginia, he took Leavenworth with him as assistant. Leavenworth held this position from 1881 to 1887, doing also some graduate work in the university. On Oct. 11, 1883, he married Jennie Campbell of Louisville, Ky. They had three children.

In 1887 he was called to Haverford College as director of the observatory, for which a 10-inch telescope had been recently acquired. From Haverford, he was called in 1892 to the University of Minnesota as professor of astronomy and director of the new observatory, which was to have, as its chief instrument, a 10½-inch telescope. Here he remained until his retirement in 1927. During the second semester of 1918 he was in Duluth on leave of absence to teach navigation in the Shipping Board's nautical school. His main career was in teaching, for which profession he was well suited. Several of his many students went on to do graduate work in other institutions and became professional astronomers. He found time, however, for some valuable research. The observation of double stars was evidently his chief interest, and this he carried on at Cincinnati, McCormick, Haverford, and Minnesota observatories, as well as at Goodsell and Yerkes, where he spent several summers. His other observations include the discovery and measurement of 250 nebulae; the visual observation of four double stars for relative parallax; photographic observation of the asteroid Eros in the 1901 campaign to determine the parallax of the sun; the observation of brightness of Nova Aquilac No. 3, and of many variable stars. His observations are published in the *Haverford College Studies,* the *Astronomical Journal,* and the *Sidereal Messenger.* He was a fellow of the Royal Astronomical Society and a member of the American Astronomical Society.

[E. W. Leavenworth, *A Geneal. of the Leavenworth Family in the U. S.* (1873); W. O. Beal, in *Popular Astronomy,* Mar. 1929; *Monthly Notices of the Royal Astronomical Soc.,* Feb. 1929; *Pubs. of the Astronomical Observatory, Univ. of Minn.,* vol. I (1930); *Who's Who in America,* 1928–29; *Minneapolis Morning Tribune* and *Minneapolis Jour.,* Nov. 13, 1928.]

R. S. D.

LEAVENWORTH, HENRY (Dec. 10, 1783–July 21, 1834), soldier, was born in New Haven, Conn., the son of Jesse and Catharine (Conkling) Frisbie Leavenworth. His father was a graduate of Yale and a Revolutionary soldier who attained the rank of colonel. The parents moved to Danville, Vt., when he was a child, and later separated, the youth accompanying his father to Delhi, N. Y. Here he studied law and in 1804 was admitted to the bar. On Apr. 25, 1812, he was made a captain of the 25th Infantry and on Aug. 15, 1813, a major in the 9th Infantry. For distinguished services at Chippewa, July 5, and at Niagara, July 25, 1814, he was brevetted respectively a lieutenant-colonel and a colonel. He was transferred to the 2nd Infantry, May 17, 1815, and on a leave of absence granted at the end of the year served a term in the New York legislature. On Feb. 10, 1818, he was made lieutenant-colonel of the 5th Infantry. With a part of his regiment he arrived at the junction of the Minnesota and the Mississippi, Aug. 14, 1819, where he at once began the building of a cantonment, later named Fort Snelling, for many years the most northerly outpost of the frontier. On Oct. 1, 1821, he was transferred to the 6th Infantry and made commandant at Fort Atkinson (Calhoun), in the present Nebraska. In the summer of 1823, following the treacherous attack on Ashley's party, he led a punitive expedition against the Arikaras, though with results so dubious that they have been a matter of controversy ever since.

On July 25 of the following year he was brevetted a brigadier-general, and on Dec. 16, was made colonel of the 3rd Infantry, then stationed at Green Bay, Wis., but in the late summer of 1826 transferred to Jefferson Barracks, near St. Louis. In the summer of 1827 he built the post

named, by the War Department, Cantonment (subsequently Fort) Leavenworth, near which the city of Leavenworth grew up. Two years later he became post commander at Jefferson Barracks. Early in 1834 he was put in command of the whole southwestern frontier, with instructions to negotiate peace among its warring tribes. With 500 troopers he set out from Fort Gibson, June 15. Illness decimated the ranks of his command, and in July he was himself stricken with a bilious fever. At Camp Smith, on the Washita near its junction with the Red, he died. The body was taken to Delhi for burial, and in 1902 was reburied at Fort Leavenworth. A monument to his memory was erected by the members of the 3rd Infantry.

Leavenworth was married three times—to Elizabeth Eunice Morrison, from whom he was divorced; at Delhi in 1810 to Electa Knapp, who died on June 12 of the following year, and in the winter of 1813–14 to Harriet Lovejoy, who accompanied him to the frontier and who survived him for twenty years. A son by his first wife, Jesse Henry Leavenworth (1807–1885), was a graduate of West Point, served for eighteen months in frontier service as a colonel in the Civil War, and for three years, 1864–67, was Indian agent for the Kiowas, Comanches, and Apaches. He was a severe critic of the military for what he termed their provocative conduct toward the Indians. Henry Leavenworth was a man of broad and varied culture. Major Davis credits him with the exercise of a profound influence upon the development of the standards of duty and discipline of the army during its formative period, and the *Military and Naval Magazine of the United States* for October 1834 pays tribute to his clearness of judgment and energy in action. In the military annals of the early frontier he holds a place second only to that of Henry Atkinson.

[F. B. Heitman, *Hist. Reg. and Dict. of the U. S. Army* (1903), vol. I; Geo. B. Davis, memoir of Leavenworth in *Jour. of the U. S. Cavalry Asso.,* Dec. 1895; V. M. Porter, "Journal of Stephen Watts Kearny," *Mo. Hist. Soc. Colls.,* vol. III, no. 2 (Apr. 1908); H. M. Chittenden, *The Am. Fur Trade of the Far West* (1902); E. W. Leavenworth, *A Geneal. of the Leavenworth Family* (1873); Thos. Forsyth, "Fort Snelling: Col. Leavenworth's Expedition to It in 1819," *Minn. Hist. Soc. Colls.,* vol. III, pt. 2 (1874); Grant Foreman, *Pioneer Days in the Early Southwest* (1926); Doane Robinson, "Official Correspondence of the Leavenworth Expedition into South Dakota in 1823," *S. D. Hist. Colls.,* I (1902), 181–256.]

W. J. G.

LEAVITT, DUDLEY (May 23, 1772–Sept. 15, 1851), almanac-maker, mathematician, author, and teacher, was born in Exeter, N. H., the eldest child of Joshua and Elizabeth (James)

Leavitt. On Apr. 7, 1795, he was married to Judith Glidden of Gilmanton, N. H., and to that place he moved in 1800. Soon afterward he began to publish a newspaper, the *Gilmanton Gazette*. He had issued his first almanac, printed by Elijah Russell at Concord, N. H., in 1797, and is said to have printed one number from his own press in Gilmanton. In 1806, having decided that he might devote summers to farming and winter evenings to teaching pupils and to making calculations for future almanacs, he bought a farm at Meredith, N. H., and thereafter made that his home. He also wrote school books and edited textbooks for publishers. From 1811 to 1817 he compiled the annual issues of the *New Hampshire Register* and for a time prepared calendars for the *Free-Will Baptist Register*.

The name of Leavitt's almanac was frequently changed. In 1815 it was called *Leavitt's Genuine, Improved New-England Farmer's Almanack, and Agricultural Register*; in 1830 it was *Leavitt's Farmer's and Scholar's Almanack*; in 1833 it was *Leavitt's the New England Farmer's and Scholar's Almanack*; and in 1850 he settled upon *Leavitt's Farmer's Almanack and Miscellaneous Year Book*. Usually he described himself as "Teacher of Mathematics and Astronomy," but sometimes as "Teacher of Mathematics and Natural Philosophy." His almanacs were usually well printed and always contained both original and reprinted articles of permanent interest, as well as mathematical problems, the solutions of which appeared the following year. In his almanac for 1847 he gave a short history of the almanac-makers of New England. Several numbers were calculated principally for amusement, and little effort was made to circulate them widely. The sale gradually increased, however, so that in 1846 60,000 copies were printed in two editions. The issue for 1853, published in Boston by Edward Livermore, was the first one printed after Leavitt's death. It carried an "Address to Patrons," in which it is stated that "at the time of his death, Mr. Leavitt had in his hands, perfectly prepared for the printer, the manuscripts of his almanac for every year up to 1857, inclusive. Besides the incalculable labor required to bring these manuscripts into their present perfect shape, Mr. Leavitt had prepared tables for his almanac from 1858 to 1899 inclusive. By so doing he has placed it in the power of those to whom he left his manuscripts to continue the publication of *Leavitt's Farmer's Almanack and Miscellaneous Year Book*, either by themselves or others to the close of this nineteenth century."

[Leavitt's *Almanacs,* of which he issued more than fifty, have been used for many of the facts, especially the issue for 1853 and the centennial number, that for 1896, which contained a sketch of Leavitt by Hon. Joseph A. Walker, and a portrait by Walter Ingalls, the original of which is in the library of the New Hampshire Historical Society. Other sources are: J. N. McClintock, *Colony: Province: State: 1623–1888. Hist. of N. H.* (1889); *New-Eng. Hist. and Geneal. Reg.,* Oct. 1851; Dean Dudley, *Hist. of the Dudley Family,* no. VII (1892), p. 802; G. W. Chamberlain and L. G. Strong, *The Descendants of Chas. Glidden of Portsmouth and Exeter, N. H.* (1925); *N. H. Statesman* (Concord), Sept. 20, 1851. Information as to certain facts was supplied by Clarence S. Brigham, librarian, American Antiquarian Society, Worcester, Mass.]

J. J.

LEAVITT, ERASMUS DARWIN (Oct. 27, 1836–Mar. 11, 1916), mechanical engineer, the son of Erasmus Darwin and Almira (Fay) Leavitt, was born in Lowell, Mass. After receiving a common-school education he entered the Lowell Machine Shop as an apprentice at the age of sixteen. Here he served three years and then was employed for one year in the firm of Corliss & Nightingale in Providence, R. I. He returned to Boston in 1856 and found employment at the City Point Works, becoming two years later an assistant foreman in charge of the construction of the engine of the United States flagship *Hartford*. In 1859 he returned to Providence as chief draftsman for Thurston, Gardner & Company, builders of high-class steam-engines, and served until the beginning of the Civil War when he entered the United States navy. Between 1861 and 1863 he was attached to the gunboat *Sagamore* in the Eastern Gulf Squadron. Later he was promoted to second assistant engineer and assigned to construction duty at Baltimore, Boston, and Brooklyn. In 1865 he was detailed to the Naval Academy at Annapolis as an instructor in steam-engineering, but he resigned in 1867 to take up the practice of mechanical engineering, specializing in pumping and mining machinery. He was recognized as an engineer of ability when, shortly thereafter, he installed the pumping engine at the waterworks of Lynn, Mass. This engine, which he designed, was of the beam compound type and its efficiency marked an advance in the economic operation of pumping engines. Following this work he designed and installed a pair of similar engines for the waterworks of Lawrence, Mass.

In 1874 Leavitt was appointed consulting and mechanical engineer for the Calumet & Hecla Mining Company, which position he held until 1904. During this connection he designed and superintended the building of the enormous equipment to be used at the company's mines in Michigan. This equipment included heavy machinery for pumping, air compression, hoisting, stamping, and general power purposes. While engaged in this work he was frequently called upon for assistance by other industrialists and municipalities as well. He advised Henry R. Worthington regarding the construction of high-duty, direct-acting pumping engines and the Bethlehem Steel Company in the introduction of the hydraulic forging process. He designed the first engines used for the cable railway of the Brooklyn Bridge, and the three great sewage pumping engines for the city of Boston. The waterworks pumping engines for Louisville, Ky., New Bedford, Boston, and Cambridge, Mass., also were designed by him. After 1888 he made frequent trips to Europe where his reputation as a consulting engineer had already spread. It is said that, as a machinery designer, he did more than any other engineer in the United States "to establish sound principles and propriety in design," and that he was "among the very first engineers . . . to appreciate the importance of weight in machinery." He was honored with the degree of Doctor of Engineering by Stevens Institute of Technology in 1884 and was the first recipient of this degree from the Institute. He was affiliated with the American Society of Mechanical Engineers (president, 1883), the American Institute of Mining and Metallurgical Engineers, the American Society of Naval Engineers, the Boston Society of Civil Engineers, and the Institution of Civil Engineers and Institution of Mechanical Engineers of Great Britain. Outside of his consulting work his chief interest lay in the Y. M. C. A. of Cambridge. He was married on June 5, 1867, to Annie Elizabeth Pettit of Philadelphia, Pa., and at the time of his death in Cambridge, Mass., was survived by three daughters.

[*Who's Who in America*, 1916–17; *Trans. Am. Soc. Mech. Engineers*, vol. XXXVIII (1917); *Boston Transcript*, Mar. 11, 1916.]   C. W. M.

LEAVITT, FRANK McDOWELL (Mar. 3, 1856–Aug. 6, 1928), mechanical engineer, inventor, was born in Athens, Ohio, the son of the Rev. John McDowell and Bithia (Brooks) Leavitt. Shortly after his birth his parents moved to New York and later to Orange, N. J., where he attended the public schools and prepared for college. He entered Stevens Institute of Technology, Hoboken, N. J., at the age of fifteen years, studied engineering, and graduated four years later with the class of 1875. His first year out of college was spent with Frederick E. Sickels in New York, working on the design of steam steering apparatus for the United States navy. He then became chief draftsman for Bliss & Williams, Brooklyn, N. Y., manufacturers of sheet-metal-working machinery. After serving five years with this company he accepted the position of master mechanic of the Texas Division of the Mexican National Railway Company, but resigned after a year to become superintendent of the Graydon & Denton Manufacturing Company in Jersey City, N. J. Two years later, in 1884, he returned to E. W. Bliss & Company, successor to Bliss & Williams, in Brooklyn, as assistant superintendent, and remained with the company, with the exception of two years, 1900–02, for the rest of his life.

From the beginning of his career Leavitt showed a marked ingenuity in conceiving and designing mechanisms to accomplish a given purpose. He possessed, too, an unusual ability to visualize a problem, so that with his great knowledge of mechanical motions and forces he could design in detail the most difficult mechanism in the simplest forms. Over three hundred patents were granted to him between 1875 and 1921. The first six years of his service with E. W. Bliss & Company were taken up chiefly with the perfection of sheet-metal-working machinery. He was the first to build a successful automatic tin-can body-making machine. He invented, too, the toggle drawing press for making kitchen utensils and other articles. This type of press was the forerunner of the huge power presses used in making automobile bodies, frames, and similar pieces of equipment produced in quantity. After he had risen to the position of superintendent of the Bliss company he was called upon to install all of the machinery in the plant of the United States Projectile Company for the manufacture of shells and other "common" projectiles. Later, as chief engineer of his company, he made an extended tour abroad visiting the British, German, and Austrian torpedo and projectile plants. While abroad he purchased the American rights to the Whitehead submarine torpedo. He did not, however, purchase any torpedo manufacturing machinery and upon his return to the United States he undertook first to design machinery of this type. He continued, too, his work in sheet-metal machinery until about 1900. From that time until his death he was concerned primarily with the improvement of torpedoes. For two years he worked independently, then he returned to the Bliss company to continue the work, becoming also director of the organization. All of his patents acquired between 1900 and 1910 were purchased by the company. They included patents for the introduction of steel for the air flask; Curtis turbines for propulsion; the combustion of fuel in the air supply and the generation of steam in connection with that combustion; a new and dependable gyroscope steering apparatus, and a host of other innovations. His improved Whitehead torpedo became known as the Bliss-Leavitt and became standard equipment in the United States navy. Under Leavitt's leadership the torpedo was still further improved in succeeding years so that at the beginning of the World War it measured twenty-one inches in diameter and more than twenty-one feet in length; possessed a reliable range of 13,500 yards; was controlled by a superheated steam and combustion gas turbine, and carried over two hundred pounds of high explosive. During the war and for two years afterward Leavitt, as "a dollar-a-year man," was in charge of the Committee on Experimental Power of the Bureau of Steam Engineering of the Navy Department at Washington and worked continuously on the problem of developing a steam plant for the propulsion of aircraft. The result of this work was the design of an aircraft steam boiler which, with all appurtenances, control apparatus and necessary water, delivered about 1,000 horse-power and weighed but a little over 2,000 pounds. This was his last engineering work. He was married on Nov. 8, 1893, to Gertrude Goodsell of New York, who with a daughter survived him at the time of his death in Scarsdale, N. Y.

[*Trans. Soc. Naval Architects and Marine Engineers*, vol. XXXVI (1928); *Who's Who in America*, 1926–27; *N. Y. Times, N. Y. Herald Tribune, Brooklyn Daily Eagle*, Aug. 7, 1928; Patent Office records.]

                                       C. W. M.

LEAVITT, HENRIETTA SWAN (July 4, 1868–Dec. 12, 1921), astronomer, was born in Lancaster, Mass. Her father was the Rev. George Roswell Leavitt, who was descended from early settlers in Hingham, Mass. Her mother was Henrietta Kendrick, who also came from colonial stock. After graduation from Radcliffe College (then the Society for the Collegiate Instruction of Women) in 1892 she spent several years in travel and teaching and as an advanced student and volunteer research assistant in the Harvard College Observatory, becoming a permanent member of the staff of the Observatory in 1902. At that time Edward Charles Pickering was directing the activities of the Observatory toward the determination of the photographic magnitudes of the stars. Assigned, as an assistant, to the study of the brightness of variable stars on the large number of photographic plates already accumulating, she soon

became, by reason of her originality and intelligent industry, the head of the department of photographic stellar photometry. Her principal achievements in this field were her determination of the magnitudes of the stars in sequences near the North Pole and in other regions; her discoveries of variable stars; and her studies of variable stars in the Magellanic Clouds which led to her discovery of the "period-luminosity" law.

The photographic study of variable stars and any attempts at a systematic photometry of the stars with photographic plates called imperatively for standards of reference. Owing to the different colors of different stars, visual magnitudes, no matter how good, would not suffice. A sequence of stars, ranging from the second magnitude to the faintest star easily photographed, was charted near the North Pole. Methods had to be developed for the determination of the photographic magnitudes of these stars. Miss Leavitt was assigned to this work. The results were published in the *Harvard College Observatory Circular 170*, Feb. 21, 1912, and in the *Annals of the Astronomical Observatory of Harvard College*, vol. LXXI (1917). They have since been in constant use by many astronomers. She followed this work with similar measurements of sequences of stars in the forty-eight "Standard Regions" (*Annals*, Vol. LXXI, 1917) and of sequences (*Annals*, Vol. LXXXV, 1919) for use in connection with the international campaign of the Astrographic Catalogue. Much of her time in her last years was devoted to the determination of standards in the Kapteyn "Selected Areas."

Miss Leavitt's discoveries include four novae and twenty-four hundred variable stars—more than half as many as are listed in the catalogue of variable stars for 1930. Her study of the light-curves of ten variables of the Algol type appeared in the *Annals* (Vol. LX, 1908). The most powerful method of measuring distance developed from her discovery that the brightest of the "cluster" variables in the Magellanic Clouds had the longest periods of variation. With the calibration of this relation between period and luminosity it has become possible to estimate distance from period and apparent brightness wherever variables of this type are found.

[Solon I. Bailey, "Henrietta Swan Leavitt," *Popular Astronomy*, Apr. 1922; *Boston Transcript*, Dec. 13, 1921.]   R. S. D.

LEAVITT, HUMPHREY HOWE (June 18, 1796–Mar. 15, 1873), Ohio congressman and jurist, was born in Suffield, Conn., the son of

John Leavitt and his wife, née Fitch. He was a distant cousin of Joshua Leavitt [*q.v.*] and a descendant of John Leavitt, of Hingham, England, who emigrated to Boston in 1628 and, later, settled in Hingham, Mass. In 1800 the Leavitts removed to Ohio and located near Warren, Trumbull County, where he spent his boyhood and received a classical education in a grammar school. For some time he attended an academy in western Pennsylvania but, at sixteen, discontinued his studies. He taught school and worked as a clerk in a retail store. In the fall of 1814 he began to study law, first, with Benjamin Ruggles of St. Clairsville, Ohio, and, later, with John C. Wright of Steubenville. Two years later he was admitted to the bar and commenced to practise in Cadiz but, in 1819, moved to Steubenville, where for four years he was the partner of John M. Goodenow. In December 1821, he married Maria Antoinette, daughter of Dr. John McDowell of Steubenville. He was appointed, by the court of common pleas, prosecutor for Jefferson County and held this office from 1823 to 1829. In 1825 he was elected to the Ohio House of Representatives. Two years later he was elected to the state Senate. His election was contested on the ground that he was disqualified for membership because he was holding the office of prosecuting attorney. With but one dissenting vote, the Senate decided, however, to allow him to take his seat. At the conclusion of his term in the Senate he was appointed clerk of the common pleas and supreme courts of Jefferson County. In 1830 he was elected to Congress, as a Jacksonian Democrat, to fill the unexpired term of his former partner, John M. Goodenow. He was one of the three Ohio representatives who voted against rechartering the Bank of the United States, because he doubted the constitutionality of the bank and also the expediency of perpetuating the institution. In later life he questioned the correctness of these views. In 1832 he was reëlected to Congress.

On June 30, 1834, Jackson appointed him federal judge of the district court for Ohio, in which capacity he continued to serve for almost forty years. When, in 1855, the state of Ohio was divided into judicial districts he was assigned to the southern district and, in April of that year, moved to Cincinnati. Many of his opinions are printed in L. H. Bond, *Reports of Cases Decided in the Circuit and District Courts of the United States within the Southern District of Ohio* (2 vols., 1852), John McLean, *Reports of Cases Argued and Decided in the Circuit Court of the United States for the Seventh Circuit* (6 vols., 1840–56), and in S. S. Fisher, *Reports of Cases arising upon Letters Patent* (6 vols., 1867–74). Although he entertained anti-slavery views he rigorously maintained the constitutionality of the Fugitive-slave Law. For this he was severely criticized by the Anti-Slavery party. In 1858 in a charge to a jury in one of these cases he said: "Christian charity was not the meaning or intent of the fugitive slave law, and it would not therefore answer as a defence for violating the law" (Howe, *post*, p. 268). His most conspicuous case was the suit of Clement L. Vallandigham [*q.v.*] in 1863. Vallandigham, found guilty by a military commission, applied for a writ of *habeas corpus.* Contrary to the usual procedure of issuing the writ as "of right" and letting General Burnside reply thereto, Leavitt at once invited Burnside to present a statement and then refused the writ upon the grounds that the arrest was legal, and that, even though it had been illegal, the writ would not be obeyed. In 1871 he resigned and moved to Springfield, where he died.

[Files of the Congressional Joint Committee on Printing; *Cincinnati, Past and Present,* pub. by Maurice Joblin (1872); J. B. Doyle, *20th Century Hist. of Steubenville and Jefferson County* (1910), p. 139; *Hist. of Cincinnati and Hamilton County* (1894); Henry Howe, *Hist. Colls. of Ohio,* vol. II (1891); J. G. Randall, *Constitutional Problems under Lincoln* (1926); J. L. Vallandigham, *A Life of Clement L. Vallandigham* (1872); H. S. Sheldon, *Documentary Hist. of Suffield* (1879); *Cincinnati Enquirer,* Mar. 17, 18, 20, 1873.] R. C. M.

LEAVITT, JOSHUA (Sept. 8, 1794–Jan. 16, 1873), clergyman, reformer, abolitionist, editor, was born at Heath, Mass., the son of Roger Smith Leavitt, a leading citizen, and Chloe Maxwell, daughter of Col. Hugh Maxwell, an Irish soldier in the American Revolution. His paternal grandfather was the Rev. Jonathan Leavitt, of Suffield, Conn. Early distinguished by good scholarship, young Leavitt entered Yale in 1810 and graduated in 1814. He then served as preceptor at Wethersfield Academy, whence he went to Northampton, Mass., to study law. He was admitted to the bar in 1819. The following year he was married to Sarah, daughter of the Rev. Solomon Williams of Northampton, Mass. He practised a short time at Heath and at Putney, Vt., but in 1823 returned to Yale and completed a two-year divinity course in a year. He was ordained and installed, February 1825, as Congregational minister at Stratford, Conn. Three years later he went to New York to be secretary of the Seamen's Friend Society and editor of the *Sailor's Magazine.* Known among New York friends as "the sturdy Puritan of New England," he entered upon strenuous lit-

erary and reformatory activities. He founded
sailors' missions in several cities, and he was
one of the first lecturers of the American Temperance Society. "Possessing," as he wrote, "no
musical skill beyond that of ordinary plain singers," he compiled an evangelical hymnal, *The
Christian Lyre,* which went into many editions.
As early as 1825 he wrote for the *Christian
Spectator* in opposition to slavery. His name
appears also in the *Journal of Public Morals* as
an editor and chairman of the executive committee of the American Seventh Commandment
Society.

Having a vigorous physique and, according
to his *Independent* associate, Henry E. Bowen,
"rare confidence in his own judgment," Leavitt
undertook publication, in 1831, of the *Evangelist,* an organ of religious revivals, temperance,
anti-slavery, and other causes. He was a member for a time of the Colonization Society, but
he differed with William Lloyd Garrison as to
its policies. When the New York Anti-Slavery
Society was founded in 1833 Leavitt was a member of its executive committee and was instrumental in merging it into the National Anti-
Slavery Society. He was among those who fled
from physical violence when Dr. Lewis Tappan's house, an abolitionist rendezvous, was
mobbed. The financial depression of 1837 forced
Leavitt to sell the *Evangelist,* but he reappeared
as editor of the *Emancipator.* Before the election of 1840 he also edited the *Ballot Box,* which
supported the party headed by J. G. Birney.
Soon after this he moved the *Emancipator* to
Boston where he opposed the Mexican War and
espoused, besides anti-slavery, many causes,
such as temperance, cheap postage, and free
trade. He wrote vigorously and sometimes
abusively. In 1848, when the pioneer work of
the abolitionists was complete, and the *Emancipator* was visibly struggling for existence,
Leavitt had an offer to return to New York as
assistant editor of the *Independent,* then about
to appear. He hesitated, but his friend, J. G.
Whittier, advised: "Not all that thee might
wish, Joshua, but a good harbor for thy old
age." Such it proved to be. As office editor of
the *Independent* for nearly twenty-five years
Leavitt disappointed the expectations of those
who predicted that he would be fiery and troublesome. He wrote millions of words of lucid
editorial comment, handled correspondence, and
won the affection and respect of his younger associates. He was in honor in Great Britain
where, in 1869, the Cobden Club awarded him
a gold medal for his work in behalf of free
trade. His editorial labor continued until a few

days before his death, which followed a stroke
of paralysis.

[The journals edited by Leavitt contain much autobiographical material, not yet collated. See F. B. Dexter, *Biog. Sketches of the Grads. of Yale Coll.,* vol. VI
(1912); obituary in *Independent,* Jan. 23, 1873; Elizur
Wright, "The Father of the Liberty Party," *Ibid.,* Jan.
30, 1873; C. G. Finney, "Dr. Leavitt's Death," *Ibid.,*
Feb. 6, 1873; Leonard Bacon, "Reminiscences of Joshua Leavitt," *Ibid.,* Feb. 13, 1873; J. P. Thompson,
"Personal Recollections of Dr. Leavitt," *Ibid.,* Mar. 6,
1873; J. P. Bretz, "The Economic Background of the
Liberty Party," *Am. Hist. Rev.,* Jan. 1929; L. H.
Everts, *Hist. of the Conn. Valley in Mass.* (1879),
vol. II; *N. Y. Geneal. and Biog. Record,* Apr. 1873;
N. Y. Times, Jan. 17, 1873. In 1916 the Massachusetts Historical Society acquired a collection of free-
soil papers assembled by Leavitt.]   F. W. C.

**LEAVITT, MARY GREENLEAF CLEM-
ENT** (Sept. 22, 1830–Feb. 5, 1912), temper-
ance advocate, was born in Hopkinton, N. H.
She was the daughter of the Rev. Joshua and
Eliza (Harvey) Clement. Her father was a
Baptist clergyman who was generally called
"Father" Clement because of his occupation,
and also because of his marked resemblance
to George Washington. Mary Greenleaf Clement attended the district schools of Hopkinton
and Thetford (Vt.) Academy, after which she
taught in country schools in Vermont and New
Hampshire. She entered the Massachusetts
State Normal School at Framingham and graduated from it in 1851, and then she taught in the
Boylston Grammar School in Boston till 1857,
when she married Thomas H. Leavitt of Greenfield, Mass., in Thetford, Vt. In 1867 she established a private school of her own in Boston
which she conducted till 1881. She was interested in the meetings held by Moody and Sankey
in Boston in 1876, and her interest in religious
and temperance work made her active in the organization of the Massachusetts W.C.T.U. In
1883 she became a traveling representative of
the national W.C.T.U. and undertook a campaign of education and organization under its
auspices. She spent nine months in the United
States and then sailed to the Sandwich Islands,
after which she visited Australia, New Zealand,
Japan, China, India, many parts of Africa (including the island of Madagascar, which she
crossed escorted only by sixteen native bearers),
the British Isles, and much of the continent of
Europe. She did not return till 1891, and many
times she spoke as often as three times a day,
employing something like 229 interpreters in
forty-seven different languages. The amount of
money she expended was extremely small, and
all but sixteen hundred dollars of it was "collected from those for whom she labored," that is,
from offerings at the meetings she addressed.
Soon after her return from her first trip, she

started on another journey through South America, and it was attended with equal success. Her activities led to the organization of the World's W.C.T.U. and it, at a meeting in Boston in 1891, made her an honorary officer for life. She died in Boston and was survived by three daughters. Her publications include only a few tracts on the liquor question, so her distinction is due to her powers as a speaker and organizer. She is credited with forming eighty-six branches of the W.C.T.U., twenty-four temperance societies, and twenty-three branches of the White Cross in her travels; but what is perhaps more significant is the fact that the motto of the W.C.T.U. was changed from "For God and Home and Native Land" to "For God and Home and Every Land" largely because of her work, thus giving a wider outlook to a movement that was at most national, if not sectarian in its inception.

[Some of the details of this account have been secured from Mrs. Leavitt's family, but there are obituary notices of her in the reports of the Massachusetts and World's W.C.T.U. for 1912, and in the *Boston Transcript* for Feb. 5, 1912. Much that she wrote or supplied the information for about foreign temperance work appeared in the *Union Signal*, the publication of the World's W.C.T.U., during the period of her activity. See also: *Who's Who in America*, 1910–11; Clara C. Chapin, *Thumb Nail Sketches of White Ribbon Women* (1895); Elizabeth Putnam Gordon, *Women Torch Bearers* (1924); and *Our Message*, the organ of the Massachusetts W.C.T.U., Mar. 1912.]   S. G.

LE BRUN, NAPOLÉON EUGÈNE HENRY CHARLES (Jan. 2, 1821–July 9, 1901), architect, was born in Philadelphia, Pa., of French ancestry, the son of Charles and Adelaide Le Brun. His father, who first came to the United States on a secret diplomatic mission while Jefferson was president, returned some years later to settle permanently. Napoléon early showed an aptitude for art and engineering and it was decided to educate him as an architect. Accordingly, he was sent in 1836 to study under Thomas U. Walter [*q.v.*], who in the fifties was architect of the Capitol extension. Walter had been the pupil of William Strickland [*q.v.*], in his day the leading architect of Philadelphia, who, in turn, had been the disciple of Benjamin H. Latrobe [*q.v.*], who came from England in 1796 and became the architect of the Capitol by appointment of Jefferson in 1803. In 1841 Le Brun began to practise for himself in Philadelphia, where he remained until he removed to New York City in 1864. On Dec. 20, 1845, he married Adèle Louise Lajus, youngest daughter of Paul Lajus, a merchant of Philadelphia. They had three sons and two daughters. The eldest and youngest sons followed their father's career and with him formed

the firm of N. Le Brun & Sons in the early eighties. Le Brun was elected a fellow of the American Institute of Architects and president of the New York Chapter. He was also president of the Willard Architectural Commission.

Among his notable contributions to the architecture of Philadelphia were the Seventh or Tabernacle Presbyterian Church on Broad Street, the Academy of Music, the Girard Estate Building, several county structures, and the interior of the Roman Catholic Cathedral of Saints Peter and Paul. The latter is noteworthy as his only application of the Renaissance style to church work. In the Romanesque style he designed the Church of the Epiphany, Second Avenue near Twenty-first Street, New York City, modeled after the church of San Zeno in Verona. The Episcopal Church of St. Mary the Virgin, in West Forty-sixth Street, New York, is an example, not wholly successful, of his work in French Gothic. When it was built, in 1895, it was called the "Chicago Church" because it was an early specimen of steel construction. A much better example of Le Brun's Gothic work was the earlier Church of St. John Baptist (1872), in West Thirtieth Street. The firm of N. Le Brun & Sons designed for the fire department of New York City the headquarters in East Sixty-seventh Street, an example of Romanesque, and the engine house in Old Slip near the foot of Wall Street, an imitation of the old Dutch Renaissance, particularly appropriate to a building within the boundaries of the Dutch town of New Amsterdam. Other engine houses by this firm were those in Eighteenth Street near Broadway and at White and Lafayette Streets, the latter in the French château style. The Home Life Insurance Building on Broadway and the San Francisco office of the Metropolitan Life Insurance Company are examples of office buildings by the firm, but its most conspicuous success was the home office building and the tower of the Metropolitan Life at Madison Square, New York (1889–1909). The main edifice constituted one of the early experiments in tall buildings and one of the early uses of the "column" for skyscraper construction; the tower and addition, designed after the elder Le Brun's death, received the award of the New York Chapter of the American Institute of Architects "for the most meritorious work of 1909" in solving "one of the most difficult problems now presented to American architects."

[*N. Y. Times*, July 10, 1901; *Am. Architect and Building News*, July 20, 1901; *Proc. of the Thirty-fifth Ann. Conv. of the Am. Inst. of Architects, 1901* (1902); Montgomery Schuyler, "The Work of N. Le Brun and Sons," *Arch. Record*, May 1910; obituary of Pierre L. Le Brun, in *The Am. Architect and the Arch. Rev.,* Apr. 9, 1924.]   M. S.

LECHFORD, THOMAS (fl. 1629–1642), was the first professional lawyer in the colony of Massachusetts Bay. The names of his parents and the details of his early life are unknown, but he was probably a member of the Lechford family of Surrey, England. At some time before 1629 he was living in London and was the auditor of Hugh Peter, lecturer at St. Sepulchre's. He was a member of Clement's Inn, and acquired some little skill in chirography. He was in Ireland with Lord Deputy Wentworth, but for how long and in what capacity are unknown. He opposed episcopacy and solicited the cause of William Prynne, for which he "suffered imprisonment, and a kind of banishment." He declined preferment at the court of George Rákóczy, prince of Transylvania and lord of lower Hungary, refused place and preferment from the Providence Company, and emigrated to New England, arriving at Boston June 27, 1638. He mentions his wife in an entry in his notebook (Trumbull, *post*) in 1639, but whether he married in England or in Massachusetts is uncertain. Her Christian name was Elizabeth, but her family name is unknown. Lechford soon found himself out of sympathy with the leaders of Massachusetts Bay. His manuscript writings, the title of only one of which, "Of Prophesie," has been preserved, were declared heretical by Deputy Governor Thomas Dudley (*Proceedings of the Massachusetts Historical Society,* III, 1859, 311–12; *Collections,* 4 ser. VII, 1865, 111–12); he was never received into church membership, and consequently could neither vote nor hold office in the colony. In the summer of 1639 he hoped to be employed as clerk and notary public by the Massachusetts General Court but, because of the distrust with which he was regarded, he was refused all preferment and forced to earn a meager living as a copyist and by drafting petty legal documents, a record of which is preserved in his notebook. For trying to influence the jury out of court in the case of William and Elizabeth Cole *vs.* Francis Doughty, Lechford in September 1639 was debarred from pleading in the courts of Massachusetts Bay. As early as July 28, 1640, he was thinking of returning to England or Ireland. In March 1640/41, he wrote to one "of no mean rank," complaining of his sufferings and asking to be sent for, and it was supposed that Prynne sent him money for his passage home. On Aug. 3, 1641, Lechford sailed from Boston, leaving his wife and household goods worth £6.13s.10d. in Massachusetts (*New-England Historical and Genealogical Register,* April 1876, pp. 201–02), and by Nov. 16, 1641, was once more at Clement's Inn, a much stronger supporter of monarchy and episcopacy than he had been before his sojourn in New England. In 1642 he published *Plain Dealing: or, Nevves from New-England,* which was reissued in 1644 under the title *New-Englands Advice of Old-England.* (It was republished under the original title in *Collections of the Massachusetts Historical Society,* 3 ser. III, 1833, and again, with an introduction and notes by J. H. Trumbull, in *Library of New England History,* No. IV, 1867). Lechford died soon after its first publication. His widow in New England married Samuel Wilbore some time before Nov. 29, 1645, and, after Wilbore's death in 1656, married Henry Bishop (*A Report of the Record Commissioners Containing Boston Births, Baptisms, Marriages and Deaths, 1630–1699,* 1883, pp. 56, 58).

["Note-Book Kept by Thomas Lechford . . . June 27, 1638, to July 29, 1641," with a sketch of his life by J. H. Trumbull, in *Trans. and Colls. Am. Antiq. Soc.,* vol. VII (1885); *Records of the Governor and Company of the Mass. Bay in New England,* vols. I and II (1853); John Cotton, *The Way of Congregational Churches Cleared* (1648).]   I.M.C.

LE CLEAR, THOMAS (Mar. 11, 1818–Nov. 26, 1882), portrait and genre painter, was born at Owego, N. Y., the son of Louis Le Clear (or Le Clere). He was a veritable infant phenomenon, for without instruction, at the age of nine, he painted acceptable portraits of his schoolmates, and at twelve he produced a surprisingly good picture of St. Matthew, of which replicas were in brisk demand at $2.50 each. In 1832 the family moved to London, Ontario, where the youth of fourteen continued to paint portraits, his most influential patron being the Hon. John Wilson, a former member of the Canadian Parliament. Two years later he was at Goderich, Ontario, painting decorative panels for a Lake Huron steamboat. Thence he found his way to Norfolk, N. Y., and after two years there to Green Bay, Wis., "sketching Indians on the way." His subsequent wanderings in search of employment took him to Elmira and Rochester, N. Y., and finally in 1839 (*ætat* twenty-one), to New York City, where he was soon able to support himself "with comfort and respectability." In 1844 he married a daughter of Russell R. Wells of Boston, Mass., and a year or more later, with his wife, he went to Buffalo, N. Y., where he worked busily on portraits and genre pieces. Returning to New York City in 1860, he passed the rest of his life there. In 1863 he was made a member of the National Academy of Design. He made two or three short trips abroad and exhibited several of his works in the Royal Academy, London, including his fine portrait of his colleague William Page (1876), now in the Corcoran Gallery, Washington, a canvas which was warmly praised by the English and American critics.

During his stay in Buffalo he had painted several successful genre pictures such as the "Marble-Players," which was bought by the Art Union, "Young America," and "The Itinerants," which was exhibited at the National Academy of 1862. These episodic canvases are well composed, agreeable in color, and manifest a distinct talent for the expression of juvenile character. But Le Clear's more significant achievements are his portraits of men, which are among the best made in America in the middle nineteenth century. Among his best-known sitters, besides Page, were Presidents Fillmore and Grant, George Bancroft, William Cullen Bryant, Bayard Taylor, Edwin Booth, Parke Godwin, Daniel S. Dickinson, and Joseph Henry, the last-named likeness belonging to the National Gallery of Art, Washington. Le Clear's first wife died in 1869 and he later married the daughter of James S. King of New York. He died at his home in Rutherford Park, N. J., in his sixty-fifth year.

[Henry T. Tuckerman's *Book of the Artists* (1867) contains the most complete account of Le Clear's life. Other sources include L. W. Kingman, *Early Owego* (1907) ; the *Art Jour.,* July 1878 ; the *Am. Art News,* Oct. 29, 1921 ; R. Rathbun, *The Nat. Gallery of Art* (1909) ; Algernon Graves, *The Royal Acad. of Arts,* vol. V (1906) ; *N. Y. Times, N. Y. Daily Tribune,* Nov. 28, 1882.]   W. H. D.

LECONTE, JOHN (Dec. 4, 1818–Apr. 29, 1891), scientist, teacher, brother of Joseph and first cousin of John Lawrence LeConte [*qq.v.*], was born in Liberty County, Ga. He was of French Huguenot descent, his earliest American ancestor being Guillaume LeConte, a native of Rouen. Louis LeConte, father of John, was a graduate of Columbia College in New York, and later a student of medicine, without, however, graduating in that profession. About 1810 he removed to Liberty County, Ga., to take possession of a plantation left him by his father. Here he married Ann Quarterman and of this marriage John was the fourth child and the second son. The father, in addition to the general management of the plantation, developed a "passionate pursuit of science," fitting up a chemical laboratory in the attic of the plantation house and setting aside a tract of land for a botanical garden. He also accumulated a large library of scientific books and periodicals. The boys of the family were trained to be naturalists and to put into organized form their knowledge of bird and animal life. John's early formal education was provided in a local private school supported by a small group of planters. One teacher only seems worthy of mention as a possible influence. This was Alexander H. Stephens [*q.v.*], who was to figure so prominently in the history of the South. In 1835 LeConte, then seventeen, was sent to Franklin College (later the University of Georgia), graduating with high honor in 1838. From Franklin he went to the College of Physicians and Surgeons in New York City. Attaining the degree of doctor of medicine in 1841, he made plans to continue his medical training at Paris; but the death of his eldest brother changed the current of events and he returned to Georgia. On July 20, 1841, he had married Eleanor Josephine Graham, whom he had met in New York. She is described as one possessed of rare intelligence, spirit, force of character, and beauty—qualities giving her assured social recognition. "No other influence," said his brother, Joseph LeConte, "so greatly affected the whole course of his life as that of his wife" ("Memoir," *post,* p. 375).

For a number of years he lived in Savannah, practising his profession but taking time to pursue scientific studies. In 1846 he became professor of physics and chemistry in Franklin College, resigning in 1855 to accept the chair of chemistry in the College of Physicians and Surgeons. His strong preferment for the subject of physics led him, within the year, to change to the professorship of physics in the South Carolina College (University of South Carolina), which he held until 1869. During the Civil War he served the Confederate government as superintendent of the niter works located in the vicinity of the college. At the time of Sherman's march through the South, LeConte witnessed not only the destruction of this plant, but the destruction of his own property. In spite of these experiences his zeal for scientific research continued and some of the more important of his studies are of this period. In 1868 he was elected to the chair of physics in the University of California, beginning work there in 1869. For the first year he acted as president of the institution in connection with his professorship. He again became president in 1875 and continued in the dual position until 1881. After that date he confined himself to the chair of physics. His contributions on scientific subjects over a period of fifty years amount to about one hundred papers. One of his earliest researches resulted in "Experiments Illustrating the Seat of Volition in the Alligator" (*New York Journal of*

Medicine and Collateral Sciences, November 1845). In 1850 he wrote a paper on the exudation of ice from the stems of certain plants and the protrusion of icy columns from certain soils (*Philosophical Magazine,* May 1850). In 1858 he developed an explanation of the phenomenon of sensitive flames, making clear the analogy of sound and light and introducing a new method of research made use of later by scientists in the study of acoustics ("On the Influence of Musical Sounds on the Flame of a Jet of Coal-gas," *American Journal of Science and Arts,* January 1858). In 1863 he wrote a paper on "The Adequacy of Laplace's Explanation to Account for the Discrepancy between the Computed and the Observed Velocity of Sound in Air and Gases" (*Philosophical Magazine,* January 1864). His paper, "On Sound Shadows in Water" (*American Journal of Science and Arts,* January 1882) contained the description and discussion of unique experiments on the propagation of vibrations through water. The results recorded attracted much attention in Europe. He wrote an exhaustive discussion of the whole subject of colored media of all kinds, under the title, "Physical Studies of Lake Tahoe" (*Overland Monthly,* November, December 1883 and January 1884). "This paper," said Joseph LeConte, "is in fact a perfect model of what a popular scientific article ought to be, for it is simple in style and yet thoroughly scientific in matter" ("Memoir," p. 383).

[Joseph LeConte, "Memoir of John LeConte 1818–1891," *Nat. Acad. Sci. Biog. Memoirs,* vol. III (1895), with list of LeConte's more important publications; Joseph LeConte, *The Autobiog. of Joseph LeConte* (1903); T. H. Hittell, "In Memory of Professor John LeConte," *Cal. Educ. Rev.,* May 1891; Frederick Slate, "In Memory of Professor John LeConte," *Ibid.*; *Popular Science Mo.,* Nov. 1889; *San Francisco Call,* Apr. 30, 1891.]   W. W. K.

LeCONTE, JOHN LAWRENCE (May 13, 1825–Nov. 15, 1883), entomologist, physician, was born in New York City, the son of John Eatton and Mary Anne H. (Lawrence) LeConte. John and Joseph LeConte [*qq.v.*] were his first cousins. They were of French Huguenot stock, being descended from Guillaume LeConte, who was born at Rouen in 1659 and migrated to Holland, and thence to America, after the peace of Ryswick in 1698. John Lawrence LeConte was educated at Mount Saint Mary's College, graduating in 1842, and at the College of Physicians and Surgeons in New York, graduating in 1846. He never practised medicine for a livelihood, since he possessed independent means. A taste for science seems to have been inherent in the family. His father, a major of engineers in the United States army, was both a zoölogist and a botanist. He seems to have been especially interested in the *Coleoptera* and published especially upon the family *Histeridae.* He was an excellent delineator of insects. It was natural, then, that John Lawrence, who was the constant companion of his father after the death of his mother in his infancy, should have shared his tastes. While at Saint Mary's College, he collected extensively, and while a medical student, at the age of nineteen, he published his first descriptive paper, on certain *Carabidae* (*Proceedings of the Academy of Natural Sciences of Philadelphia,* April 1844). He soon became interested in the subject of geographic distribution of species, and in one of his early papers wrote of the *Coleoptera* common to North America and Europe (*Annals of the Lyceum of Natural History of New York,* vol. IV, 1848, pp. 159–63). Later he studied the distribution of insects in the United States and made broad generalizations applying to other forms of life. He was the first biologist to map the faunal areas of the western part of the United States. It has been said, however, that his very important contributions to zoo-geography were "but accessories to his main work, the overflow of a mind charged with resources" (Scudder, *post*).

Although at first his taxonomic studies resulted in miscellaneous descriptions, he soon began to prepare synopses and monographs. Despite the wealth of material, he worked systematically and carefully. His patient and original investigation may be said to have culminated in his monographic revision of the *Rhynchophora* ("The *Rhynchophora* of America North of Mexico," *Proceedings of the American Philosophical Society,* vol. XV, 1876), and in his *Classification of the Coleoptera of North America* (Smithsonian Miscellaneous Collections, vol. XXVI, 1883). In both of these great undertakings he was associated with George H. Horn [*q.v.*]; but to the first Horn contributed only a single family, the *Otiorhynchidae.* In addition to studies in entomology, LeConte published essays dealing with mineralogy, geology, radiates, recent fossil mammals, and ethnology. He kept up with the advance of science, and his breadth of knowledge added authority to his special contributions to entomological science. He was recognized at home and abroad as the greatest entomologist America had produced. European entomologists visited him for consultation, and he was an honorary member of all the older and larger entomological societies in Europe. He was one of the incorporators of the National Academy of Sciences, and was president of the American Association for the Advancement of

Science in 1874. He visited Europe several times. His style was rather scholastic, and his philosophy was rather conservative, although he readily adopted evolutionary thought. During the Civil War he entered the army medical corps as surgeon of volunteers, and was promoted to the grade of lieutenant-colonel and medical inspector, in which capacity he served until the inspectors were mustered out in 1865. On Jan. 10, 1861, he married Helen S. Grier of Philadelphia. In 1878 he received strong indorsements for the post of United States commissioner of agriculture, but President Hayes chose William G. LeDuc [q.v.], giving LeConte the post of chief clerk of the United States Mint at Philadelphia, which position he held until his death.

[Memoir of LeConte by S. H. Scudder, in *Biog. Memoirs, Nat. Acad. Sci.*, vol. II (1886), repr. in *Trans. Am. Entomological Soc.*, vol. XI (1884), with a portrait and an appendix on his ancestry; *The Entomological Writings of John L. LeConte* (1878), listing his writings up to Nov. 18, 1878, published by the Cambridge Entomological Society as Dimmock's Special Bibliography, no. 1; G. H. Horn, in *Science*, Dec. 21, 1883, and in *Proc. Am. Philosophical Soc.*, vol. XXI (1884); C. V. Riley, in *Psyche*, Nov.–Dec. 1883; F. W. True, *A Hist. of the First Half Century of the Nat. Acad. of Sci.* (1913); David Sharp, in *Entomologist's Monthly Mag.* (London), Jan. 1884; the *Press* (Phila.), Nov. 16, 1883.]

L. O. H.

LeCONTE, JOSEPH (Feb. 26, 1823–July 6, 1901), geologist, the fifth child and youngest son of Louis and Ann (Quarterman) LeConte, and brother of John [q.v.], was born on the Woodmanston plantation in Liberty County, Ga. His early schooling is said to have been scanty, but among his teachers was Alexander H. Stephens [q.v.], subsequently prominent in national affairs. The boy's vacations and holidays were spent in hunting, fishing, and other sports for which the country afforded abundant facilities. In 1838 his father died and shortly afterward he entered Franklin College (later the University of Georgia) at Athens, Ga., whence he was graduated in August 1841. Accompanied by a brother and sister, he toured the northern states, but returned to spend the winter on the Georgia plantation. In the fall of 1843 he entered upon the four months' winter course at the College of Physicians and Surgeons in New York. During the following season, in company with his cousin John Lawrence LeConte [q.v.], he made an excursion into what was then the Far West, visiting the region of the headwaters of the Mississippi River by way of Niagara, Buffalo, Detroit, and the Great Lakes. Returning to New York in the fall, he resumed his medical studies and graduated in April 1845, having meanwhile made the acquaintance of Audubon, Spencer F. Baird, and

Jacob Post Girard. He spent the next two years in local travel and the carefree life of a country gentleman. In January 1847 he married Caroline Elizabeth Nisbet and settled down for a time to the practice of medicine in Macon. Concluding, after some years, that he had not yet "found himself," he went to Cambridge, Mass., in August 1850 and entered upon a course of study under Louis Agassiz which included six weeks' stay at Key West, Fla. In the following June at the suggestion of Agassiz, he presented a thesis and obtained the degree of S.B. from the newly established Lawrence Scientific School. Returning to Georgia in October 1851, he soon received a call to the professorship of all the sciences at Oglethorpe University, Midway, Ga. Here he remained but a year, resigning to accept a like position in the University of Georgia at Athens, where he remained until 1856. During this period he published a number of papers, the most important being "On the Agency of the Gulf Stream in the Formation of the Peninsula of Florida" (*Proceedings of the American Association for the Advancement of Science* for 1856, vol. X, 1857), based upon his Florida experiences with Agassiz. Administrative difficulties led him to resign his professorship at Athens, and he applied for and was elected in 1857 to the chair of geology in the College of South Carolina, Columbia, where his brother John was teaching.

LeConte remained in the South during the Civil War, although the College ceased to function in the summer of 1862. It does not appear that he took a particularly active part in the struggle, although he served for a time as chemist of the Niter and Mining Bureau, in which capacity he explored a number of "niter" caves in the Gulf States and iron deposits at Shelbyville, Ala. With the close of hostilities, he resumed his college duties and also his outside connections, in 1866–67 delivering a series of six lectures on coal and petroleum in the Peabody Institute of Baltimore. Conditions in the South were hard, at best, however, and accordingly, with the establishment of the University of California at Berkeley, he and his brother John both made successful application, in 1866, for positions on the teaching force there, and moved to California in 1869. Here, in an atmosphere that developed his full usefulness, he remained for the rest of his days, resigning from the teaching of undergraduates in 1896.

As a teacher and educator, LeConte was one of the most beloved and admired of men. Having a naturally joyous disposition, unusual talent, culture, and refinement, he possessed a rare faculty for friendship. His fecundity as a scientist is suggested by the following selection of titles (out of many) taken in the order of their appearance: "The Correlation of Physical, Chemical, and Vital Force, and the Conservation of Force in Vital Phenomena" (*Proceedings of the American Association for the Advancement of Science* for 1859, vol. XIII, 1860); "On the Law of Sexes, or the Production of the Sexes at Will" (*Nashville Journal of Medicine and Surgery*, October 1866); "On Some Phenomena of Binocular Vision" (*American Journal of Science and Arts*, 1869, 1871, 1875, 1877); "A Theory of the Formation of the Great Features of the Earth's Surface" (*Ibid.*, November, December 1872; see also June 1873); "On the Great Lava-Flood of the Northwest, and on the Structure and Age of the Cascade Mountains" (*Ibid.*, April 1874); "On the Evidences of Horizontal Crushing in the Formation of the Coast Range of California" (*Ibid.*, April 1876); "On Critical Periods in the History of the Earth and Their Relation to Evolution; and on the Quaternary as Such a Period" (*Ibid.*, August 1877), commonly considered as one of his best articles; "Some Thoughts on the Glycogenic Functions of the Liver" (*Ibid.*, February 1878); "The Genesis of Sex" (*Popular Science Monthly*, December 1879); "On the Genesis of Metalliferous Veins" (*American Journal of Science*, July 1883); *Evolution and its Relation to Religious Thought* (book, 1888); "Evolution and Human Progress" (*The Open Court*, Apr. 23, 1891); "Theories of the Origin of Mountain Ranges" (*Journal of Geology*, September-October 1893), which must be read in connection with the paper by James Dwight Dana [*q.v.*] on a similar subject for its value to be estimated; "The Ozarkian and its Significance in Theoretical Geology" (*Ibid.*, September-October 1899); "The Larynx as an Instrument of Music" (*Science*, May 17, 1901), and lastly, "What is Life?" (*Ibid.*, June 21, 1901).

From his youth LeConte was an ardent lover of camping and all sorts of outdoor sports. The experiences thus gained stood him in good stead when the pursuit of science rather than hunting or fishing brought him into similar conditions of life. He traveled widely over the Western states, often under most primitive conditions, and saw, and thought, and wrote of what he saw, with tireless energy. Passionately fond of outdoor life, he died, as he would doubtless have wished, while on a trip with the Sierra Club into the Yosemite.

[*The Autobiography of Joseph LeConte* (1903) ed. by W. D. Armes; E. W. Hilgard, memoir in *Biog. Mem-oirs Nat. Acad. Sci.*, vol. VI (1909); *San Francisco Call*, July 7, 1901; personal recollections.]

G. P. M.

LEDERER, JOHN (fl. 1669–1670), traveler and explorer, came to Virginia from Germany in 1668. Little is known about his antecedents but he must have had educational advantages, for he was familiar with several languages. From Governor Berkeley of Virginia who desired to find a passage through the mountains, he received a "commission of discovery" and the command of an expedition for that purpose. He made three marches, between March 1669 and September 1670. His first journey (Mar. 9–24, 1669), was from the head of the York River due west; he reached the top of the Blue Ridge Mountains, but did not descend their western slope. His second march (May–June 1670) was from the falls of the James River west and southwest, and through part of North Carolina; his third expedition left the falls of the Rappahannock in August 1670 and pushed westward to the mountains. Since there is no record of the visit of any white man to the upper Rappahannock after Capt. John Smith's explorations in 1608, and Smith may never have penetrated part of the region covered by his map, it is probable that Lederer entered territory never before visited by a white man. During this last expedition his companions became disheartened and deserted him. He ventured to continue his searches with only an Indian guide, who served him as an interpreter. His faithless companions did not expect him to survive and created prejudice against him by telling the people of Virginia that he had expended the public taxes of that year in his wanderings. Consequently, upon his return he was ill-treated by the inhabitants of Virginia and fled to Maryland to save his life. There he was naturalized in 1671 (*Archives of Maryland*, vol. II, 1884, pp. 282–83). He obtained a hearing from Sir William Talbot, a member of the Council, who found him a "modest ingenious person, and a pretty scholar," and determined to vindicate him by translating his account of his travels from Latin into English. Accordingly, *The Discoveries of John Lederer in Three Several Marches from Virginia, to the West of Carolina, and Other Parts of the Continent: Begun in March, 1669, and ended in September 1670, together with a General Map of the Whole Territory Which he Traversed*, was published in London in 1672. This book was the first scientific report upon the geology, botany, animals, and native tribes of the extensive district which it covered. Though Lederer appears to have reached only the "top of the Apalatæn

Mountains," he gives reasons for supposing that "they are certainly in a great errour, who imagine that the Continent of North *America* is but eight or ten days journey over from the *Atlantick* to the *Indian* Ocean." His account is generally accepted as descriptive of the Valley of Virginia, but his narrative seems apocryphal and his statements should be accepted with some reserve. The map that appeared in this volume is inaccurate, possibly because Lederer's instruments were carried off by his recreant companions.

[See *Bull. Fauquier Hist. Soc.*, Aug. 1921; *Va. Mag. of Hist. and Biog.*, Jan. 1901, April 1922; H. C. Groome, *Fauquier during the Proprietorship* (1927); Hermann Schuricht, *Hist. of the German Element in Va.*, I (1898), 40–41; H. A. Rattermann, *"Der Erste Erforscher des Alleghany Gebirges—Johannes Lederer,"* in *Der Deutsche Pionier*, Jan. 1877; F. L. Hawks, *Hist. of N. C.*, vol. II (1858); J. W. Wayland, *A Hist. of Rockingham County, Va.* (1912). Lederer's *Discoveries* was reprinted in 1891 and again in 1902, in very small editions.]   F. W. S.

LE DUC, WILLIAM GATES (Mar. 29, 1823–Oct. 30, 1917), agriculturist, soldier, railroad promoter, and United States commissioner of agriculture, was born in Wilkesville, Gallia County, Ohio, the second son of Henry Savary and Mary (Stowell) Le Duc. His father's father was Henri Duc of Lyons, France, who came to America as a young officer in the army sent with Count D'Estaing to aid the colonies in the Revolution. About 1796, after stirring adventures in Guadeloupe, he came to Middletown, Conn., where he married Lucy, daughter of Col. John Sumner of the Colonial and Continental armies. Having acquired land near Gallipolis, Ohio, he moved thither with his family about 1812 and founded the settlement of Wilkesville. His son, in 1845, changed his name to Henry Savary Le Duc, believing that his father had left off the particle when he came to America because he thought the simple Duc more democratic. In order to attend school, William went to live in Lancaster, Ohio, where he was under the care of a great-uncle. He attended the Lancaster Academy and there had among his intimate companions William T. Sherman, John Sherman, and Thomas Ewing.

In 1844 he entered Kenyon College, Gambier, Ohio, graduating in 1848. He was afterward employed for about a year in introducing school books and law publications in the South and West. Meanwhile, he studied law and on Dec. 5, 1849, was admitted to the bar. He later spent several months in Boston and edited a book by J. Stanley Grimes [*q.v.*], entitled, *Etherology and the Phreno-philosophy of Mesmerism and Magic Eloquence* (1850). In July 1850 he

moved to St. Paul, Minn., then a small village, where he opened a law office and a book and stationery store. Here, the following year, he brought his young bride, Mary Elizabeth Bronson, daughter of Rev. C. P. Bronson of Mount Vernon, Ohio, whom he had married on Mar. 25, 1851, and by whom he had four children. In connection with his book business he published the *Minnesota Yearbook* for 1851–53. He was active in the development of the region of which St. Paul was the center and in 1853 was appointed commissioner of Minnesota Territory at the exposition in New York, called the World's Fair. The display of products which he collected was largely influential in turning attention to Minnesota and the great opportunities it afforded settlers (see his article, "Minnesota at the Crystal Palace Exhibition, New York, 1853" in *Minnesota History Bulletin,* August 1916). In 1853 he secured the first charter for a railway in the territory and organized a company to build a railroad from St. Paul to Duluth. Mainly through his efforts that same year, the St. Paul Bridge Company was organized, which constructed the Wabasha Street Bridge, the first to be built over the Mississippi. Having acquired some land on the west side of the river, he laid out the town of West St. Paul. In 1856 he purchased a flour mill at Hastings, and was the first miller to manufacture and introduce upon the markets flour made from Minnesota spring wheat. Disposing of his St. Paul holdings in 1857, he moved to Hastings, which, except for the terms of his federal service and brief periods of travel, was his home during the remainder of his life.

In 1862 he entered the Union army as a captain in the quartermaster's department and was promoted to the rank of lieutenant-colonel, serving under McClellan, Hooker, Sherman, and Thomas. At the close of the war he was brevetted colonel and brigadier-general of volunteers. Returning to Hastings, he engaged in business and farming. He also projected and in part constructed the Hastings and Dakota Railroad, of which he was president until 1870. In July 1877 President Hayes appointed him United States commissioner of agriculture, which office he filled until June 30, 1881, performing its duties with conspicuous energy and ability. He established a tea farm at Summerville, S. C., to investigate the practicability of raising tea in the United States; he gave special attention to the production of sugar from sorghum and beets; and he secured a special appropriation for the investigation of animal diseases, which led to the establishment of the Bureau of Animal Industry. From 1890 to 1895 he was in Fayetteville, N. C., having been appointed by Secretary of the Treasury Windom as receiver of the national bank at that place.

He was a tall man, quick, active, and resourceful, and in his prime had great initiative and indomitable energy. He also had inventive ability (see "Genesis of the Typewriter," *Minnesota History Bulletin,* February 1916, in which he recounts his part in the development of the Remington typewriter). His personal papers and historical relics were presented to the Minnesota Historical Society, of which he was an active member for more than sixty-seven years. A paper by him on the organization and growth of the Historical Society is contained in its *Collections* (vol. IX, 1901). He died at Hastings in his ninety-fifth year.

[*Am. Ancestry,* vol. IV (1889); autobiography, typewritten copy in the U. S. Dept. of Agric. Lib.; G. S. Ives, "William Gates Le Duc," in *Minn. Hist. Bull.,* May 1919; W. H. C. Folsom, *Fifty Years in the Northwest* (1888); *Minn. Hist. Colls.,* vol. XIV (1912); D. S. Hall and R. I. Holcombe, *Hist. of the Minn. State Agric. Soc.* (1910); C. H. Greathouse, *Hist. Sketch of the U. S. Dept. of Agric.* (1898); *Who's Who in America,* 1916-17; T. M. Newson, *Pen Pictures of St. Paul* (1886); *Pioneer Press* (St. Paul), Oct. 31, 1917; *N. Y. Times,* Oct. 31, 1917.]

C. R. B.

LEDYARD, JOHN (1751-Jan. 10, 1789), explorer, was born in Groton, Conn., the son of John and Abigail (Hempstead) Ledyard and a nephew of William Ledyard [*q.v.*]. The father, a sea-captain, died at the age of thirty-five, and the mother remarried. The boy was then taken into the home of his paternal grandfather (also named John) at Hartford, where he attended grammar school. On the death of his grandfather he came under the guardianship of an uncle by marriage, Thomas Seymour, with whom for a time he studied law. In 1772, at the invitation of the Rev. Eleazar Wheelock [*q.v.*], the founder of Dartmouth College, he entered that institution with a view to becoming a missionary to the Indians; but though an apt student, he could not endure discipline, and in the following spring he returned to Hartford. Determined to see the world, he shipped as a sailor from New London for the Mediterranean. At Gibraltar he deserted and joined a British regiment, but was shortly afterward sent back to his vessel. Returning to New London, he went to New York, where he shipped for London. Here he presented himself to Capt. James Cook, then preparing for his third voyage, and as a corporal of marines sailed with the expedition that left the Thames on July 12, 1776. At Nootka Sound, which was reached in March 1778, he

began to picture the vast possibilities of the northwestern fur trade and resolved to enter it at the first opportunity.

The return voyage, on which Cook was killed at the Hawaiian Islands, Feb. 14, 1779, brought him to London late in 1780. The American Revolution was still in progress, and refusing to serve against his countrymen, Ledyard remained in barracks for two years, and was then transferred to the North American station. Obtaining shore leave on reaching the Long Island coast in December 1782, he made himself known to his mother at Southold and then escaped to Hartford. After publishing his recollections of the voyage (*A Journal of Captain Cook's Last Voyage to the Pacific Ocean,* 1783), he went to New York and later to Philadelphia, trying to obtain aid for a sailing venture to the Northwest Coast. After a year's futile efforts he sailed for Spain in June 1784, and then went to France. Though he won the regard and friendly interest of Thomas Jefferson and Commodore John Paul Jones, and though success appeared certain a number of times, all his projects failed. He then proposed walking across Siberia, and in case he found a vessel that would take him to Nootka Sound, walking over the continent to Virginia. Jefferson approved the plan and sought a passport from the Empress Catherine, who refused it. Ledyard then went to London, where he at last found a vessel getting ready for a voyage to Nootka Sound. With funds supplied him by friends, he took passage in September 1786; but the vessel had hardly left the Thames before it was overtaken by a gunboat and brought back.

Reviving his Siberian project, he went to Hamburg, and by way of Norway, Sweden, and Lapland reached St. Petersburg. Catherine was absent, and he was permitted to go on. In September 1787, at Yakutsk, officials obstructed his progress and on Feb. 24, 1788, at Irkutsk, he was arrested by order of the Empress and brought back to the Polish boundary, where he was warned not to repeat the attempt. In London again at the beginning of May, "disappointed, ragged and penniless, but with a whole heart," he at once looked about for some new adventure. At the instance of Sir Joseph Banks he was engaged by the Association for Promoting the Discovery of the Interior Parts of Africa to explore the sources of the Niger. He left London at the end of July, visited Jefferson in Paris, telling the minister that his next journey would be from Kentucky to the Pacific, and then went on to Alexandria. At Cairo he arranged to accompany a caravan to the interior. Violent rage over delay in starting after the time of departure had been fixed brought on an illness which resulted in his death.

Ledyard was somewhat under six feet tall, of "rangy" and powerful build. His personality was attractive, even to those who could give him no higher appraisal than that of "the mad, romantic, dreaming Ledyard." Jefferson characterized him as a genius and earnestly sought to further his purposes. His dream of opening up the trade of the Pacific Northwest, which he followed with an unmatched singleness of purpose and which brought him only discouragement and disaster, came true for other men within in less than a generation after his death.

[Jared Sparks, *The Life of John Ledyard* (1828); S. M. Schmucker, "John Ledyard," in *The Life of Dr. Elisha Kent Kane* (1858); *Proc. of the Asso. for Promoting the Discovery of the Interior Parts of Africa* (1810), I, 14–46; H. A. Tirrell, "Ledyard the Traveller," *Records and Papers of the New London County Hist. Soc.,* vol. III, Pt. II (1912); C. B. Moore, "John Ledyard, The Traveller," *N. Y. Geneal. and Biog. Record,* Jan. 1876; Henry Beston (Sheahan), "John Ledyard," in *The Book of Gallant Vagabonds* (1925); manuscript letter, Paine to Jefferson, June 18, 1789, Lib. of Cong.; *The Writings of Thomas Jefferson,* Memorial Ed. (1903–04), see Index.] W. J. G.

LEDYARD, WILLIAM (Dec. 6, 1738–Sept. 6, 1781), Revolutionary soldier, was born at Groton, Conn., a descendant of John Ledyard who sailed from Bristol, England, and settled in Connecticut. Ledyard's parents were John and Deborah (Youngs) Ledyard, and a nephew was the celebrated traveler John Ledyard [q.v.]. Practically nothing is known of William's early life. "Of fine form and good education for the times" is a description by N. H. Burnham (*post,* p. 32). He was married in January 1761 to Anne Williams of Stonington, by whom he had nine children. From the beginning of the Revolution he was a member of the committee of correspondence and of the military committee of his town. In 1776 he was made captain of artillery, and his command was extended to include the towns in the neighborhood. This part of the coast was exposed to British attacks, and had long been threatened. In the autumn of 1781 Benedict Arnold [q.v.], now a British general, led a raid into his native state, following a similar incursion into Virginia. He took New London, and dispatched Lieutenant-Colonel Eyre to capture Fort Griswold on Groton Heights, across the Thames River (Sept. 6, 1781). The fort was defended by Ledyard with a small body of militia, to a large degree youths, and poorly armed. The British commander, who had two battalions of regular infantry—800 men in all—demanded surrender, which Ledyard refused. Eyre then sent a second demand, stating that no quarter would be granted if resistance was made.

Ledyard again returned a spirited refusal, ordered his men to reserve fire, and inflicted a heavy loss. Eyre, who led one assaulting column, was mortally wounded; and Montgomery, who commanded the other column, was killed. Overwhelmed by numbers, Ledyard surrendered to Bromfield, who had succeeded to Eyre's place. A survivor of the conflict relates the event which followed: To Bromfield's demand: "Who commands this Fort?" Ledyard replied: "I did, but you do now," at the same moment tendering his sword (Hempstead, *post*). Ledyard was killed almost at once, apparently with his own sword, though the witnesses differ as to the British officer who was responsible for the deed. Ledyard's death was followed by a general massacre of the garrison, the odium of which has fallen upon Arnold, although he was not actually present. On the scene of the battle a monument was erected in 1830, and in 1854 Ledyard was honored by a smaller monument in the cemetery.

[C. B. Todd, "The Massacre at Fort Griswold" and J. A. Stevens, "The Ledyard Family," *Mag. of Am. Hist.,* Sept. 1881; J. A. Stevens, "The Family of Ledyard," *N. Y. Geneal. and Biog. Record,* Jan. 1876; narrative of Stephen Hempstead, a survivor of the battle, in *Missouri Republican* (St. Louis), Feb. 23, 1826; W. W. Harris, *The Battle of Groton Heights* (1870); rev. and enl. by Charles Allyn, 1882), containing narratives of Hempstead and others, but giving Ledyard's parents incorrectly; J. J. Copp, *Battle of Groton Heights* (1879); N. H. Burnham, *The Battle of Groton Heights* (1907); F. M. Caulkins, *Hist. of New London, Conn.* (1852); C. R. Stark, *Groton, Conn., 1705–1905* (1922); B. T. Marshall, *Modern Hist. of New London County* (1922).] E. K. A.

LEE, ALFRED (Sept. 9, 1807–Apr. 12, 1887), Protestant Episcopal bishop of Delaware, was born in Cambridge, Mass., and died in Wilmington, Del. His father, Benjamin Lee, was a native of Somersetshire, England, and had at one time been a midshipman in the British navy. His mother, Elizabeth (Leighton), also of English extraction, was connected with the family of William Pitt. Alfred graduated at Harvard College in 1827 and at once began the study of law. After admission to the bar he practised for two years in New London, Conn., and then entered the General Theological Seminary, New York. Graduating in 1837, he was ordered deacon on May 21, 1837, and made priest on June 12, 1838, by the Rt. Rev. Thomas Church Brownell. After a few months' service at Poquetanuck, Conn., he removed to Calvary Church, Rockdale, Pa. On Oct. 12, 1841, he was consecrated as the first bishop of Delaware in St. Paul's Chapel, New York City.

He at once removed to Wilmington, Del., where in October 1842 he became rector of St. Andrew's Church, remaining such throughout his life. It had long been the custom for bishops to be rectors of parishes, especially in the weaker dioceses, thereby securing their support in the absence of episcopal endowments; and Delaware was a weak diocese. Organized in 1786, it had no bishop until the consecration of Dr. Lee. There were in the diocese only four clergymen regularly conducting services of the Episcopal Church, and only 339 communicants. Bishop Lee was a pronounced Evangelical in his theological position and familiar with the Calvinistic theology of his school. He also had the fervor and zeal for souls likewise characteristic of Evangelicalism. Under his episcopal care new life was roused in all parts of the diocese. For a long time at least one new church was consecrated or an old one restored and opened almost every year. In 1863 he was assigned by the presiding bishop to exercise episcopal functions in Haiti, and was instrumental in establishing a mission there under the care of the American Church Missionary Society. He was also much interested in the Mexico mission, which had originated in the secession of some clergy from the Roman Catholic Church. In 1875 he was sent to Mexico to inquire into this movement and to perform episcopal duties. He confirmed over a hundred persons and ordained seven as priests. As a result of his visit the Mexican body was recognized as a foreign church under the care of the Protestant Episcopal Church (C. C. Tiffany, *History of the Protestant Episcopal Church in the United States of America,* 1895, pp. 519–20). Bishop Lee was regarded as a man of great scholarship and received honorary degrees from several institutions. His writings, however, are of the mildly edifying character common in his school of thought: *Life of the Apostle Peter in a Series of Practical Discourses* (1852); *A Life Hid in Christ with God* (1856), being a memoir of Susan Allibone; *Life of the Apostle John in a Series of Practical Discourses* (1857); *Eventful Nights in Bible History* (1886); and various sermons. He was, however, able to do more scholarly work as a member of the American committee which took part in preparing the revised version of the New Testament (1881). Here his conservative views, combined with a sound, if somewhat old-fashioned, scholarship in Greek and Hebrew, found a useful place. From May 31, 1884, to Apr. 12, 1887, he was the presiding bishop of the Protestant Episcopal Church. He married, in 1832, Julia White, daughter of Elihu White of New London, and was the father of eight children.

[Brief autobiog. sketch, privately printed; journal of Gen. Conventions of the P. E. Ch. and of the Del. Diocesan Conventions; Alfred Lee, *Memoir of Benjamin Lee* (1875); *Alfred Lee* (1888), a biography published by St. Andrew's Church, Wilmington; Heman Dyer, "Rt. Rev. Alfred Lee," in the *Churchman,* Apr. 23, 1887; *Living Ch. Ann.,* 1887; *Wilmington Daily Commercial,* Apr. 13, 1887.] J. C. Ay—r.

LEE, ANN (Feb. 29, 1736–Sept. 8, 1784), founder of the Shakers in America, was born in Manchester, England. Though she is known in Shaker history as Ann Lee, her family name was probably Lees, a common surname in Lancashire at the time of her birth. Her father, John, was a blacksmith; she had five brothers and two sisters, and with them was sent to work early, never learning to read or write. She was employed first in a cotton factory, then as cook in the Manchester Infirmary, and later as a cutter of hatter's fur. In 1758 she joined a society called the Shaking Quakers, or Shakers, which had been founded in Manchester eleven years before as a result of the revivals conducted by the exiled Camisards. The form of worship centered about an open confession of sin, and the prophecies centered about the second appearance of Christ. On Jan. 5, 1762, according to the Manchester Cathedral register (Axon, *post*), Ann Lees was married to Abraham Standerin (known in Shaker history as Stanley or Standley). He was a blacksmith, by whom she had four children who died in infancy. She became obsessed with a morbid repugnance toward marriage and a conviction of the sin of sexual relations which caused her great mental suffering. In 1770, during an imprisonment for "profanation of the Sabbath," she received such an extraordinary illumination of "the mystery of iniquity, of the root and foundation of human depravity" that she was acknowledged by the society as their leader and thereafter called Ann the Word, or, more often, Mother Ann. She began to "speak with tongues" and to preach openly against marriage and sexual intercourse, and the authorities made several attempts to quiet her. In her later life she related these persecutions to her followers in elaborate detail, with emphasis on her miraculous escapes.

A vision, in 1774, directed her to go to America; and accordingly she and her husband, her brother, William Lee (or Lees), Nancy Lee, her niece, John Hocknell (whose generosity made the expedition possible), and a few others arrived in New York on Aug. 6. John Hocknell and William Lee went up the Hudson and secured a tract of land in Niskayuna, near Albany, where the village of Watervliet later stood. Mother Ann and her husband remained in New York, where she earned what she could by washing and ironing and he was employed in a blacksmith's shop. He later became ill and they were reduced to extreme poverty. When he recovered he renounced his "Shaker principles" and went off to live with another woman. In the summer of 1776 Ann joined the group near Albany. Here for three and a half years they lived together and worked on their buildings and held their religious meetings. Mother Ann continued to have visions and revelations concerning the conduct of the "Church." Her followers called themselves "the first witnesses of the Gospel of Christ's Second Appearing," and the church which was organized after her death was called "The United Society of Believers in Christ's Second Appearing," or "The Millennial Church." Mother Ann was herself regarded as this second appearance of Christ, Jesus having been the first, and both being necessary for the complete revelation of the Father-Mother God.

The group became known through the region, and because they preached against war and would not bear arms or take oaths, they were accused of pro-British sympathies and secret correspondence. In July 1780 "Ann Standerren" and the elders were arrested by the Albany County Commissioners for Detecting Conspiracies (*Minutes, post*), and imprisoned on charges of high treason. In December she was released, her brother, William Lees [*sic*], being one of the bondsmen for her good behavior. In the following year the religious revivals continued and the number of "Believers" was greatly increased. In May 1781 Mother Ann and some of the elders started on a tour through New England where there were already scattered groups of Shakers. They held meetings in many places and endured persecutions. Mother Ann's messages on this tour seem to have been more practical than prophetic. She encouraged simple honesty, frugality, and industry; urging her hearers to "put your hands to work, and give your hearts to God." She returned to Watervliet in July 1783 literally worn out, and died there in September of the following year. After her death the little that was known of her life and her own conversations and reminiscences were elaborated by her disciples, and their "testimonies" are full of "incidents" which constitute the framework of the largely legendary biography current among Shakers.

[W. E. A. Axon, *Lancashire Gleanings* (1883), pp. 79–107; Thomas Brown, *An Account of the People Called Shakers* (1812); *Testimonies of the Life, Character, Revelations and Doctrines of Mother Ann Lee* (collected by Rufus Bishop in 1812, revised by S. Y. Wells in 1816; second edition, revised by G. B. Avery, 1888); Calvin Green and S. Y. Wells, *A Summary View of the Millennial Church* (1823); B. S. Youngs, *The Testimony of Christ's Second Appearing* (1808; rev. 1810; 4th ed., 1856, with biography of Mother Ann appended); F. W. Evans, *Shakers: Compendium of the Origin,.etc.* (1859); Charles Nordhoff, *The Communistic Societies of the U. S.* (1875); V. H. Paltsits, *Minutes of the Commissioners for Detecting and Defeating Conspiracies in the State of N. Y., Albany County Sessions, 1778–1781,* II (1909), 469–71, 504, 589, 592; Clara E. Sears, *Gleanings from Old Shaker Journals* (1916); J. P. MacLean, *A Bibliog. of Shaker Literature* (1905).]

H. W. S—r.

LEE, ARTHUR (Dec. 21, 1740–Dec. 12, 1792), diplomatist, was of the fourth generation of the Lees of Virginia, being the great-grandson of Richard Lee [*q.v.*], the first American immigrant, grandson of the second Richard and Lettice Corbin, and son of Thomas Lee, whose wife was Hannah Ludwell, daughter of Col. Philip Ludwell of "Green Spring." Born at "Stratford," the family seat in Westmoreland County, Va., built by his father, he was the eleventh child of his parents and the brother of Richard Henry, Francis Lightfoot, and William Lee [*qq.v.*]. The father having died when Arthur was only about ten years of age, the boy came under the guardianship of his eldest brother, by whom he was sent to Eton for his academic education. From Eton he passed to the University of Edinburgh, where he studied general science, polite literature, and medicine, and received in 1764 the degree of M.D. (*List of the Graduates in Medicine in the University of Edinburgh from MDCCV. to MDCCCLXVI.,* 1867, p. 8). After traveling a few months in Europe he returned to Virginia and began the practice of medicine in Williamsburg (1766). Shortly after his return to America he was elected a fellow of the Royal Society (May 29, 1766.) He did not, however, linger long at physic. America was just then deeply stirred by the Stamp Act agitation, and politics lured him with a stronger appeal. Accordingly, forsaking medicine for the law, the mounting block to politics, he returned to London in 1768, where he studied in Lincoln's Inn and the Middle Temple, subsequently establishing himself there in the practice of his new profession. His admission to the bar was in the spring of 1775, not in 1770, as usually stated (Jones, *post*, p. 123).

Whatever his other aptitudes and tastes, he soon discovered an eager pen. With the appearance of Dickinson's "Farmer's Letters," Lee set about writing a similar series, "The Monitor's Letters," designed, as he expressed it, to aid the "Farmer's Letters" in their operation "in alarming and informing" his countrymen. These, ten in number, were first printed in Rind's *Virginia Gazette* (Feb. 25–Apr. 28, 1768), at a time when Lee was in America. In London he found an alluring field for his controversial talents. At the beginning of 1769 the English political world was set agog by the "Junius Letters," and Lee, dipping his pen into the Junius bottle, proceeded to write a series of letters, some addressed to sundry British statesmen, others to the people of England, wherein, with a copious use of sarcasm and invective, he discussed American affairs, and signed himself "Junius Americanus." In some similar communications he used the signature "Raleigh." Though Jefferson, for one, had a poor opinion of the "Monitor's Letters" (P. L. Ford, *The Writings of Thomas Jefferson,* IX, 1898, p. 418), Lee's writings won him a considerable repute among political leaders in America, one consequence of which was that in 1770, mainly through the influence of Samuel Adams, he was chosen as agent of Massachusetts in London. The essay which probably deserves most consideration is *An Appeal to the Justice and Interests of the People of Great Britain,* ostensibly "By an Old Member of Parliament," published in 1774 and followed in 1775 by a *Second Appeal.*

In the meantime, Arthur Lee, together with his mercantile brother, William, plunged into London politics. In this activity he was the intimate associate as well as the political confrère of the notorious John Wilkes, for whom he conceived a great admiration. He procured the insertion in the famous Middlesex Petition of a resolution protesting against the obnoxious American measures, and the chief burden of much that he wrote was that the cause of Middlesex was the cause of Englishmen everywhere. During this period he nourished hopes that he might himself become a member of Parliament. In November 1775, he was asked by the committee of secret correspondence of the Continental Congress to become its confidential correspondent in London, and he made a characteristic beginning of his diplomatic career by casting suspicions upon some of the men who had appointed him. In October 1776, he was appointed (in place of Jefferson, who had declined) one of three commissioners, to negotiate a treaty with France and solicit aid. Joining his colleagues, Franklin and Deane, in Paris at the end of December, he found Deane, in France since July as the secret commercial agent of Congress, busily engaged in procuring supplies, and France not yet disposed to treat with the United States openly. Therefore, since he seemed not to be needed in Paris, with the advice of Franklin and Deane, he betook himself to Spain (February 1777) to see what he could do there. He was not permitted to proceed as far as Madrid, but he did succeed in obtaining through a commercial house

substantial aid from the Spanish government. He next journeyed to Berlin (May to July 1777), where also he was refused recognition and succeeded only in having his papers filched.

Returned to Paris, he resumed making complaints against his colleagues. He even had the temerity at this time (Oct. 4, 1777) to suggest to Samuel Adams and Richard Henry Lee that he be made sole minister to France and that Franklin and Deane be sent to some less important corners of Europe. The chief controversy with Deane was whether or not the supplies which France was secretly furnishing the United States through Beaumarchais and his fictitious commercial house, Roderigue Hortalez & Company, were to be paid for. On the face of the evidence they were, but Lee, on the basis of conversations with Beaumarchais before Deane's coming, asserted that they were a gift and persistently pressed this contention upon Congress. Moreover, as he viewed Deane's numerous commercial transactions, his perfervid imagination saw many instances of guilt where there was at worst only error, and accusations of fraud and peculation, mounting in virulence with each increment and repetition, were poured into the ears of his friends in Congress. His distrust of Franklin, which had had earlier beginnings, deepened, now that Franklin usually supported Deane, and the charges against him became scarcely less severe than those against Deane. Deane, Beaumarchais, Franklin, and a crew of others, he declared, were plundering the public. "I am more and more satisfied," he wrote to his brother, Richard Henry, Sept. 12, 1778, "that the old doctor is concerned in the plunder, and that in time we shall collect the proofs" (*Life,* II, p. 148, in cipher). This was characteristic: accusations following close upon the heels of suspicion; proofs to be collected in time.

While these troubles were yet in their infancy, Congress, in May 1777, selected two more commissioners, William Lee and Ralph Izard. The former was appointed to the courts of Berlin and Vienna, the latter to the court of Tuscany, but they were destined to remain for the most part in Paris to confound wisdom and to add their grumblings to the general confusion. Arthur Lee was about the same time commissioned to the court of Spain, but he also remained in Paris. Congress had sown "militia diplomacy"; it reaped what might well be called guerrilla or sniping diplomacy. Despite, however, the bickerings among the representatives of the United States at the French capital, but thanks mainly to the success of arms at Saratoga, treaties of alliance and of amity and commerce were negotiated with France and signed by all three commissioners (Feb. 6, 1778). So far as Deane was concerned, this was nearly his last diplomatic act; for, largely in consequence of Lee's charges, he had been recalled (Dec. 8, 1777), and upon his return to America was harried for several months by Congress, then dismissed. In the midst of his ordeal, however, he turned upon his arch pursuer with counter charges, out of which came at least one significant development, namely, that Arthur Lee did not have the confidence of the French minister, Vergennes. As a consequence of all this Congress was split into two hostile factions, the supporters of Lee and the supporters of Deane. After mulling over these charges and counter charges through a good many months, Congress finally came to the solemn conviction that, whatever the truth, the "suspicions and animosities" which had arisen among the commissioners were "highly prejudicial to the honor and interests of these United States" (*Journals,* Apr. 15, 1779). Then came Arthur Lee's turn to be superseded (Sept. 27, 1779). William Lee and Ralph Izard had preceded him in dismissal. Franklin alone had successfully run the gauntlet.

Lee returned to America in September 1780, was elected to the Virginia House of Delegates in 1781, then to the Continental Congress, in which he served until 1784. But he was unhappy even in Congress, where, he declared, he could only lament what he could not prevent (letter to Samuel Adams, Apr. 21, 1782, *Letters of Members of the Continental Congress,* vol. VI, forthcoming), and where it was his fate to be frustrated in his favorite objects (Madison to Randolph, Oct. 8, 1782, *Ibid.*). Under the appointment of Congress he was one of the commissioners who negotiated the Indian treaties of Fort Stanwix (Oct. 22, 1784) and Fort McIntosh (Jan. 21, 1785). In July 1785, he was appointed by Congress to the treasury board and, despite Jefferson's prediction (*Writings,* IV, 1894, p. 53), held that office until the inauguration of the new government. He opposed the adoption of the Constitution. The few remaining years of his life were spent on his estate, "Lansdowne," Middlesex County, Va. He was never married.

[See R. H. Lee, *Life of Arthur Lee* (2 vols., 1829), containing selections from his correspondence (eulogistic and inaccurate); C. H. Lee, *A Vindication of Arthur Lee* (1894); E. J. Lee, *Lee of Va., 1642–1892* (1895); Francis Wharton, *The Revolutionary Diplomatic Correspondence of the U. S.* (1889), of which Vol. I contains a discussion of his character and career; E. A. Jones, *Am. Members of the Inns of Court* (1924); E. S. Kite, *Beaumarchais and the War of Am. Independence* (2 vols., 1918); and "The Deane Papers," *N. Y. Hist. Soc. Colls.,* Publication Fund Series, vols. XIX–XXIII (1887–91), Sparks's review of the *Life,* by R. H. Lee, in the *North Am. Rev.,* Apr. 1830, is especially useful. The chief collections of MSS., aside from the official correspondence in the Library of Congress, are those in the possession of the Harvard University Library, the American Philosophical Society, the University of Virginia, and the Virginia Historical Society.]
                                                    E. C. B.

LEE, CHARLES (1731–Oct. 2, 1782), soldier of fortune, Revolutionary general, was born at Dernhall, Cheshire, England, the son of John and Isabella (Bunbury) Lee. He went to school at Bury St. Edmunds and, later, in Switzerland. In 1747 he was ensign in his father's regiment (De Fonblanque, *post,* pp. 159–60), and, on May 2, 1751, was commissioned lieutenant in the 44th Regiment. His baptism of fire occurred in 1755, when the 44th accompanied the Braddock expedition into western Pennsylvania. After the retreat from Fort Duquesne, Lee was sent to the Mohawk Valley, N. Y., where in 1756 he purchased a captaincy for £900. There he was adopted into a Mohawk tribe under an alleged Indian name, "Ounewaterika," said to mean "boiling water," and married the daughter of a Seneca chief ("Lee Papers," *post,* I, 4–5). Lee was with the 44th during Abercromby's disastrous attack on Fort Ticonderoga in July 1758. Badly wounded, he was transported back to Albany, and thence went to Long Island. Here he got into an altercation with a surgeon, whom he whipped and who afterward tried to assassinate him. Rejoining his regiment, when the tide began to turn in favor of the British, Lee was present at the capture of Fort Niagara from the French and with Amherst at the capture of Montreal, Sept. 8, 1760. In the winter of 1760–61 he returned to England. Certain controversial pamphlets of this period are attributed to him, probably incorrectly (Sparks, *post,* ch. 1).

On Aug. 10, 1761, he was appointed major in the 103rd Regiment. The next year he accompanied the British expeditionary force to Portugal, where he became lieutenant-colonel and served brilliantly under Burgoyne in the campaign of Villa Velha (De Fonblanque, p. 50). Returning peace saw him once more in England, where the 103rd was disbanded and Lee put on half pay, in November 1763. About this time, seeing no future ahead in England, he considered a plan for establishing colonies in the Illinois country. Instead of concerning himself with that project, however, he went to Poland, then under Stanislaus Poniatowski. He reached Warsaw in March 1765, and soon was on intimate terms with the pro-Russian king. Going on an embassy to Constantinople in 1766, he almost froze to death when he was snowbound in the Balkans, and he escaped with his life during the Constantinople earthquake of May 23, 1766. By December he had returned to England; he had just been granted 20,000 acres in Florida. In 1767 and 1768 he remained in England with no particular employment save playing the races and criticizing the government. Because of this latter activity, he has been identified as the author of the *Letters of Junius,* but this is a hardly tenable theory. In 1769 a civil war broke out in Poland, precipitated by the Confederation of Bar against Stanislaus, and Lee rushed back to Warsaw to take sides with his friend. This time he was made "general and adjutant" ("Lee Papers," I, 87) in the Polish service, that is, in the pro-Russian faction. He accompanied the Russian armies against Turkey in the campaign of the winter of 1769–70, fell ill, was invalided back to Hungary, and recuperated on the Mediterranean. The summer of 1771 found him again in England, but the following winter he went to France. During all this time his writings were marked by a bitter hatred of the Tory party in England and a desire to be forever fighting for "liberty"—without any very clear idea of the meaning of the term.

He returned to America in 1773 and took up land in Berkeley County, Va. (now W. Va.), in 1775. To the pamphlet controversy preceding the American Revolution he contributed *Strictures on a Pamphlet, entitled, "A Friendly Address to All Reasonable Americans"* (1774), an attack upon the conciliatory efforts of Dr. Myles Cooper. When the war broke out between Great Britain and the colonies in 1775, he was almost violently on the patriot side. His military experience and capacity for self-advertisement helped him to insinuate himself into the councils of the Continental Congress, so that when, on June 22, 1775, he renounced his half pay in the British army, he had already (June 17, 1775) been appointed second major-general of the Continental Army. In accepting this appointment he insisted upon being compensated for whatever losses he might sustain through the confiscation of his English estates, as his new holdings in Berkeley County, Va., were not yet paid for.

In July he was at the American camp at Cambridge, Mass., and served during the siege of Boston. Early in 1776 he was ordered to New York to superintend the defense of that city, where he encountered some difficulty in dealing with the state officials, not yet accustomed to a federal authority. After ordering Lee to Canada, Congress countermanded the order, and, on Mar. 1, 1776, sent him off to oppose the British in the South. He reached Williamsburg, Va., Mar. 29, and remained there until May 12, or-

ganizing a cooperative effort by Virginia and North Carolina. On June 4 he reached Charleston, where Gov. John Rutledge put the South Carolina troops under his command ("Lee Papers," II, 57). Col. William Moultrie was already at work upon the defenses of the city, particularly upon the fort on Sullivan's Island. Lee did not look with favor upon this post, and spent most of his time arranging for the retreat of Moultrie's force, when the British should attack it. The assault on Fort Moultrie finally took place on June 28, 1776, while Lee was at Heddrals Point. The British failed on both land and sea, but credit for the American victory clearly belongs to Moultrie, as Lee generously admitted in his dispatches. The rest of the summer Lee spent supervising the defenses of South Carolina and Georgia.

Upon the retirement of the British from the southern area in the late summer of 1776, Lee was ordered back to rejoin the main army. In Philadelphia, on his way north (Oct. 7, 1776), he learned that Congress had generously advanced him $30,000 to pay for his Virginia plantation. This flattery, and the exaggerated reputation for his success in the Carolinas, increased his tendency to criticize his superiors on all occasions. He reached Washington's headquarters before the battle of White Plains. After that battle, Lee's division was posted at Philipsburg, N. Y. When it became apparent that the British general, Howe, intended to pursue Washington in his retreat across New Jersey, the latter sent Lee repeated and increasingly peremptory orders to join the main army. Lee was extremely dilatory in complying with these instructions, explaining that he preferred to hang on the flank of the British and harass them. This policy was consistent with his opinion that the Americans could not stand in a pitched battle against the British but that they could best them in guerrilla warfare. It is also consistent with the theory that Lee wished to play a lone hand and gain some brilliant individual success, the credit for which he would not have to share with the Commander-in-Chief. On Dec. 12 he reached Basking Ridge, N. J., whence he wrote his famous letter to Gates condemning Washington for the loss of Fort Washington and remarking *"entre nous,* a certain great man is most damnably deficient" ("Lee Papers," II, 348). His headquarters at Basking Ridge was four miles from his division, and only twenty miles from the British under Cornwallis. On the very next day, a detachment of Colonel Harcourt's British dragoons rushed his headquarters and took Lee prisoner in a manner most humiliating to him.

He was taken to New York, where General Howe had orders from Germain to return him to England for trial as a deserter from the British army. Fortunately for the British, Howe understood that Lee had actually resigned his half pay in the British army before joining the Americans, and that therefore retaliation would ensue if the orders from London were obeyed (W. C. Ford, *The Writings of George Washington*, V, 1890, p. 168). Lee was kept for a year in close and exasperating confinement. After a winter's imprisonment, he apparently became so intimate with Howe that he drew up a document giving the British information as to how to defeat the Americans. At present it is not known for whom this was prepared, or to whom it was given. It never came to light until 1858, when it was found among the papers of Henry Strachey, who had been with the Howes in their effort to conciliate America in 1776–77 (G. H. Moore, *post*, pp. 75 ff.). Historians have since drawn the conclusion that Lee was a traitor. The document is clearly in Lee's writing and is indorsed "Mr. Lee's Plan, 29th March 1777" (*Ibid.*, facsimile). At the same time Lee was sending insistent notes to Washington and to Congress requesting that a committee of Congress be sent to confer with him and the two Howes, with veiled hints that great things might be expected from such a conference. Congress and Washington wisely refused to accede to this suggestion. It is altogether possible that Lee, with his propensity for writing familiarly to his old friends in the British army, never saw this affair as treason. It is also possible that the "Plan" was a deliberate blind, intended to mislead Howe. It is, however, extremely difficult for the historian to deny that it was giving aid and comfort to the enemies of the United States.

In April 1778 Lee was exchanged, and in May went to York, Pa., where Congress was in session. Here he had the temerity to ask why he had not been promoted during his captivity, and to criticize the promotion of others in his absence ("Lee Papers," II, 392). On May 20, 1778, he rejoined the army at Valley Forge, just as it was setting out on the Monmouth campaign. When Washington was determined to attack the British army, retreating from Philadelphia, the work of beginning that attack should, by seniority, have fallen to Lee. He declined on the ground that he did not believe the Americans could stand up against the British regulars. Lafayette was then given the honor of leading the attack, whereupon Lee reconsidered and demanded the privilege, which the Marquis surrendered with extreme generosity and courtesy.

The ensuing circumstances brought to an end Lee's career as a successful soldier of fortune. Wayne began the attack at Monmouth, and to his horror saw Lee's main body begin to retreat behind him without warning. Wayne had to fall back and the retreat of the Americans speedily took on the semblance of a rout, when Washington came up with Greene, Steuben, and the rest of the army. What actually passed between the Commander-in-Chief and the retreating Lee will probably never be known. Washington stopped the retreat, reformed the army, threw Greene, Stirling, and Wayne into the battle, and fought the British to a standstill until nightfall, when they decamped into the darkness, heading for their boats and New York (Stryker, *post*).

Without waiting for Washington's reprimand for this apparently cowardly retreat, Lee addressed an insulting letter to the Commander-in-Chief, demanding an apology for the words spoken in the heat of battle. Washington curtly refused to apologize. Demanding a court of inquiry, Lee immediately got a court martial, which sat at Brunswick from July 4 to Aug. 12, 1778. He was found guilty of disobedience of orders, misbehavior before the enemy, and disrespect to the Commander-in-Chief, and was then mildly sentenced to be suspended from the army for twelve months. He hung around the army until September, when he went to Philadelphia. Thence he wrote numerous quibbling letters to Congress, complaining of ill treatment. On Dec. 3, 1778, he published his "Vindication" (*Pennsylvania Packet*, Dec. 3, 1778; "Lee Papers," III, 255–69), which was so abusive of Washington that Col. John Laurens challenged Lee to a duel and wounded him, so that he could not take up another challenge from Anthony Wayne. By the following July Lee had retired to his estate in Virginia whence he wrote frequent and querulous letters to Congress, the newspapers, and all his friends. On Jan. 10, 1780, in consequence of an insulting letter to Congress, he was finally dismissed from the army. After living on in Virginia for two years more, he went to Philadelphia where, on Oct. 2, 1782, he died.

Lee is one of the most extraordinary and contradictory characters in American history. He had an exaggerated sense of his own ability and importance, and extraordinary luck in impressing them upon other people, until his capture by the British in 1776. His contemporaries agree that Rushbrooke's merciless caricature of him (G. H. Moore, *post*) gives a true idea of what he looked like. In anger he had little control over either his tongue or his pen. He so persistently interfered in matters which were not his business, by offering advice and criticism unasked, that one must marvel at the patience of his correspondents and particularly of his superiors. Men like John Adams and Benjamin Rush can rightly be blamed for encouraging his overweening ego. Yet British officers like Gage, Howe, and Burgoyne took his personal letters to them in all seriousness. As to whether his conduct at Monmouth was actual treason, planned ahead of time with the British commander, there may be two opinions. Clinton afterward said that Lee had to retreat. On the other hand, Washington said that Lee never should have accepted the command if he did not intend to fight; and there is ample evidence that Wayne, when he saw Lee retreating, twice sent frantic inquiries as to what to do and was never answered. It is equally clear that Lee was forgetful about sending orders, ignorant of the terrain of the battlefield, negligent in informing himself, and that he was almost crazed by the heat of June 28, 1778. But Lee had many redeeming qualities. He was extremely generous to his friends and considerate of his soldiers, and he had a genius for making loyal friends of important people.

He was buried in Christ Church graveyard in Philadelphia, despite his express desire that in death he be spared association with any church ("Lee Papers," IV, 31). His estate in Virginia was by his will divided among four loyal friends, and all his other property went to his sister in England.

[The papers left to Lee's friend, William Goddard of Baltimore, were published in 4 vols., as "The Lee Papers," *Colls. of the N. Y. Hist. Soc., for the Years 1871, 1872, 1873, 1874* (1872–75). The Lib. of Cong. has Lee's Orderly Book for 1776. Of biographies, the best is still Jared Sparks, in *Lives of Charles Lee and Joseph Reed* (1846) ; but see also Edward Langworthy, *Memoirs of the Life of the Late Charles Lee* (1792) ; and Sir Henry Bunbury, "Memoir of Charles Lee," in *The Correspondence of Sir Thomas Hanmer* (1838). All three of these have been printed in "The Lee Papers," as has Geo. H. Moore, *"Mr. Lee's Plan—Mar. 29, 1777," The Treason of Charles Lee, Major General* (1860), which considers the document found among the Strachey Papers. John Fiske, "Charles Lee," in *Essays Historical and Literary* (1902), vol. I, may also be mentioned. The best account of the end of Lee's military career is in W. S. Stryker, *The Battle of Monmouth* (1927), revised and edited by W. S. Myers. For the trial, see *Proc. of a General Court Martial . . . of Maj. Gen. Lee* (1778, 1864). The Junius question is discussed in John Almon, *The Letters of Junius* (2 vols., 1806) ; Thos. Girdlestone, *Reasons for Rejecting . . . the Presumptive Evidence of Mr. Almon* (1807), and *Facts Tending to Prove that Gen. Lee . . . was the Author of Junius* (1813). W. S. Baker has edited the MS. of Elias Boudinot, "Exchange of Major-General Charles Lee," *Pa. Mag. of Hist. and Biog.,* Apr. 1891. See also E. B. De Fonblanque, *Pol. and Mil. Episodes . . . Derived from the Life and Correspondence of the Right Hon. John Burgoyne* (1876) ; Wm. Moultrie, *Memoirs of the Am. Revolution,* etc. (2 vols.,

1802) ; H. Lee, *Memoirs of the War in the Southern Department* (1812) ; Jas. Wilkinson, *Memoirs* (3 vols., 1816) ; John Drayton, *Memoirs of the Am. Revolution,* etc. (1821) ; *The Life, Public Services, Addresses and Letters of Elias Boudinot* (2 vols., 1896), ed. by J. J. Boudinot ; *The Life and Letters of Lady Sarah Lennox* (2 vols., 1901), ed. by the Countess of Ilchester and Lord Stavordale ; the writings of contemporary statesmen, and the various collections of sources for the Revolution and the Continental Congress.]

R. G. A—s.

LEE, CHARLES (1758–June 24, 1815), jurist, attorney-general, was the second son of Henry Lee and his wife Lucy Grymes, and the brother of "Light-Horse Harry" Lee and Richard Bland Lee [*qq.v.*]. He was descended from Richard Lee [*q.v.*], the emigrant ancestor of the family. In 1770 he entered the College of New Jersey where he was commended by President Witherspoon for his "application and genius." He received the degree of A.B. in 1775. In 1777 he was serving as "naval officer of the South Potomac" and apparently retained the office until 1789, when the Virginia office ended and he applied to Washington for retention as customhouse officer. His appointment as "collector of the port of Alexandria" was confirmed by the Senate in August 1789 and he served until 1793. His friendship for Washington was rooted in early attachments. He shared Washington's political outlook, gave him constant support, and aided in the struggle in Virginia for the ratification of the Constitution. At some time he studied law in Philadelphia, where he was admitted to the bar in June 1794 (J. H. Martin, *Martin's Bench and Bar of Philadelphia,* 1883). From 1793 to 1795 he was a member of the General Assembly of Virginia for Fairfax County. He vigorously supported Washington's policies and stanchly sought to stem the enthusiasm in Virginia for Genet and France and for Thomas Jefferson. On Nov. 19, 1795, Washington offered him the appointment to the office of attorney-general of the United States to succeed William Bradford. Lee accepted the appointment on Nov. 30 and held the office until the overthrow of the Federalists in 1801. He was persistent in his opposition to a conciliatory policy toward France, advised the recall of Monroe as minister to that country in 1796, and was sympathetic in his views with his close friend John Marshall.

President Adams sought in his final appointments to take care of Charles Lee among other Federalists and on Feb. 18, 1801, nominated him as judge of one of the new circuit courts. His confirmation on Mar. 3, 1801, placed him among the so-called "midnight judges." When Congress in 1802 repealed the Judiciary Act of the previous administration Lee retired to his home in Virginia. His political fortunes fell with the defeat of the Federalist party and his remaining years were spent in private law practice in the Virginia courts and before the federal courts, especially the Supreme Court of the United States, where his friend Marshall was presiding. He served in notable cases including the celebrated case of *Marbury* vs. *Madison*. He was also one of the defense lawyers in the trial of Aaron Burr in Richmond. In the impeachment of Judge Chase by the Republicans in 1805 he was one of the defense lawyers. Lee was twice married. His first wife was Anne, daughter of Richard Henry and Anne Lee whom he married at "Chantilly," Westmoreland County, Va., on Feb. 11, 1789. She bore him six children. His second wife was Margaret C. (Scott) Peyton, widow of Yelverton Peyton and daughter of the Rev. John and Elizabeth (Gordon) Scott. Of this marriage there were three children. He spent the latter years of his life at his stone house in Fauquier County, near Warrenton, where he died on June 24, 1815.

[The best sketch of Charles Lee is given in E. J. Lee, *Lee of Va., 1642–1892* (1895). See also: Gaillard Hunt, *Calendar of Applications and Recommendations for Office During the Presidency of Geo. Washington* (1901); Geo. Gibbs, *Memoirs of the Administration of Washington and John Adams* (1846), vol. II; Jared Sparks, *The Writings of Geo. Washington*, vol. IX (1835), and XI (1836); C. F. Adams, *The Works of John Adams*, vols. VIII and IX (1853–54); A. J. Beveridge, *The Life of John Marshall* (4 vols., 1916–19); *Daily Nat. Intelligencer*, June 29, 1815.]   M. H. W.

LEE, CHARLES ALFRED (Mar. 3, 1801–Feb. 14, 1872), physician and scientist, was born at Salisbury, Conn., the son of Samuel Lee, a farmer, and Elizabeth (Brown) Lee. He was a descendant of John Lee of Essex, England, who emigrated to America in 1634. Intended for the ministry, he received a thorough education, preparing for college under his uncle, Elisha Lee of Sheffield, Mass., and at Lenox Academy. He entered Williams College in 1817 and received his degree in arts therefrom in 1822. His interest in the ministry having given way to an ambition for a medical career, he began to study under his brother-in-law, Dr. Luther Ticknor of Salisbury, and received his degree in medicine from Berkshire Medical Institution in 1826, having served incidentally as a pupil teacher in botany and anatomy. After a short sojourn in Salisbury he removed to New York City in 1827 to enter general practice. With Dr. James Stewart and others he founded the Northern Dispensary and for four years served as attending physician. In 1832 he was appointed physician to the Greenwich Cholera Hospital and in the same year physician to the New York

Orphan Asylum where he taught hygiene to the personnel. He became a frequent contributor to periodical medical literature, writing on a great variety of subjects and reporting many unusual cases; and in 1835 he issued small popular treatises on physiology and geology. He helped establish the *New York Journal of Medicine and the Collateral Sciences,* in 1843, and edited it from 1846 to 1853. He also began the publication of American editions of well-known English medical works. The first of these, A. T. Thomson's *Conspectus of the Pharmacopœias of the London, Edinburgh and Dublin Colleges of Physicians,* with which he incorporated the United States' Pharmacopœia, appeared in 1843; and in the same year he issued his edition of Jonathan Pereira's *Treatise on Food and Diet.* This was followed in 1844 by J. A. Paris's *Pharmacologia* (rewritten in 1846), and in 1845 by an edition of W. A. Guy's *Principles of Forensic Medicine.* His major effort under this head, however, was his edition of James Copland's *Dictionary of Practical Medicine* in nine volumes (1834–59). To all of these works he added much valuable original matter.

While busily engaged in New York he is said to have declined the chair of materia medica in the University of the City of New York, but in 1844 he accepted the chair of pathology and materia medica in the Geneva Medical College and in 1847 had much to do with the admission of the first woman medical student, Elizabeth Blackwell [*q.v.*], to this institution. In 1846 he also joined the faculty of the Medical School of Maine as lecturer, later becoming professor of materia medica; in 1847 he was also a member of the faculty of the Starling Medical College, Ohio; and from 1848 to 1860, professor of pathology and materia medica at the University of Buffalo. He lectured at the Vermont Medical College and declined an offer to go to Louisville, Ky. In 1850 he decided to leave the metropolis for a residence in Peekskill and to divide his time among the smaller provincial schools. During his sojourn in these medical centers he was much in demand as a consultant and to avoid friction with local men required professional ethics of the highest type. At the outbreak of the Civil War he visited Europe for the Federal government in order to study hospital construction and administration, both military and civil, and brought back plans, models, and specifications. During this trip he wrote some forty letters to the *American Medical Times* of New York (June 14, 1862–Sept. 5, 1863; see also Dec. 5, 1863). On his return he served in the sanitary department of the army. He wrote no major work and his best-known effort is his *Catalogue of Medicinal Plants . . . in the State of New York* (1848). He wrote several papers on medico-legal subjects and insanity, contributed articles on geology and mineralogy to the *American Journal of Science and Arts,* and was a militant temperance advocate, publishing in 1871 *Remarks on Wines and Alcohol.* Although one of the committee of scientific men which exposed the imposture of the Fox sisters, he became eventually an enthusiastic spiritualist. He accumulated a private library of between 3,000 and 4,000 books and his herbarium contained 1,500 specimens. In 1828 he married Hester Anna Mildeberger of New York by whom he had nine children, only three of whom survived him.

[S. M. Lee, *John Lee of Farmington, Hartford County, Conn., and His Descendants* (1878); *N. Y. Medic. Jour.,* Apr. 1872; *Trans. Am. Medic. Asso.* (1881); *Boston Medic. and Surgic. Jour.,* July 3, 1850, Feb. 29, 1872; H. A. Kelly and W. L. Burrage, *Am. Medic. Biogs.* (1920); *N. Y. Times,* Feb. 15, 1872.]
E. P.

LEE, ELIZA BUCKMINSTER (*c.* 1788–June 22, 1864), author, was born in Portsmouth, N. H., the daughter of the Rev. Joseph and Sarah (Stevens) Buckminster, both of whom were descended from Anne Bradstreet. Joseph Stevens Buckminster [*q.v.*] was her brother. Though brought up in a clergyman's family in which domestic duties were numerous and woman's position held to be subordinate, she acquired intellectual interests and considerable education from her father and brother. After her marriage in 1827 to Thomas Lee, a wealthy resident of Brookline, Mass., and a brother of Henry Lee, 1782–1867 [*q.v.*], she was able to pursue her studies and devote herself to literature. Her first work, *Sketches of a New England Village,* was published in 1838. This was followed in 1842 by her *Life of Jean Paul F. Richter,* a translation of his autobiography, to which she appended a biographical sketch. The work gave her a very considerable reputation. Her next most conspicuous work was *Memoirs of Rev. Joseph Buckminster, D.D., and of his Son, Rev. Joseph Stevens Buckminster* (1849); but she wrote much besides, including *Naomi; or Boston Two Hundred Years Ago* (1848); *Florence, the Parish Orphan* (1852); *Parthenia, or the Last Days of Paganism* (1858); and many translations from Richter, Auerbach, and other German authors, the popularity or prestige of which can be estimated from the fact that fifteen volumes of her works were included in a popular series of the seventies. The life of Richter owed some of its success to the vogue for him in particular and for German writers in general, introduced by Carlyle. A review in the *Eclectic Magazine* for November 1847 charges that it renders Richter's poetic language by dull prose, and displays such an elementary knowledge of German that the grammatical structure is not always given correctly. Carlyle's praise of her memoirs of her father and brother as revealing to him the highest aspect of New England character may also need to be discounted, as she was a disciple, or, at least, a follower of his. The fairest estimate would seem to be that she was not, according to present standards, either an accurate scholar or a writer of conspicuous creative ability or command over language. Her intellectual powers, however, were considerable, and though she had little aptitude for art, she had a strong sympathy for it, and is significant as an example of the way in which the New England intellect of her day was turning from the austerities and rigidities of Calvinism toward a more genial and tolerant philosophy.

[The details of Eliza Buckminster Lee's personal career have to be accumulated from widely scattered references. The date of her birth is established approximately by the records of Mount Auburn Cemetery. For printed references to her and to her works see: *New-Eng. Hist. and Geneal. Reg.,* Oct. 1854, Apr. 1855; *North Am. Rev.,* Oct. 1849; *Brownson's Quart. Rev.,* Oct. 1849; William Lee, *John Leigh of Agawam (Ipswich), Mass.* (1888); S. A. Allibone, *Critical Dict. of English Lit. and British and Am. Authors,* vol. III (1870).]
S. G.

LEE, FITZHUGH (Nov. 19, 1835–Apr. 28, 1905), soldier, eldest of the six sons of Sydney Smith and Anna Maria (Mason) Lee, was born at "Clermont," Fairfax County, Va. His father, a naval officer in the United States and later in the Confederate service, was an elder brother of Gen. Robert E. Lee and the second son of "Light-Horse Harry" Lee by his second marriage, to Anne Hill Carter. His mother was a grand-daughter of the Revolutionary philosopher, George Mason, and a sister of Senator James M. Mason. After preliminary education in neighborhood private schools, Fitzhugh Lee entered West Point in 1852. He was distinguished more for comradeship and horsemanship than for scholarship and narrowly escaped dismissal for his pranks, but he was graduated forty-fifth in a class of forty-nine in 1856, and served as a cavalry instructor at Carlisle Barracks, Pa., until Jan. 1, 1858, when he was ordered to Texas as second lieutenant in the 2nd Cavalry. Dangerously wounded on May 19, 1859, in Indian fighting, he recovered in time to participate in another brush with the natives, June 16, 1860. Named assistant instructor in the department of tactics at West Point, he served there from Dec. 29, 1860, to May 3, 1861, then tendered his resignation (accepted May 21, 1861) and offered his services to Virginia. As first lieutenant in the regular Confederate army, he acted as a staff-officer to Ewell and to Joseph E. Johnston during the Manassas campaign and in August 1861 was made lieutenant-colonel of the 1st Virginia Cavalry. For his participation in the Peninsular operations and in Stuart's ride around McClellan, he was promoted brigadier-general on July 25, 1862. His delay in reaching the Rapidan on Aug. 17 was one factor in postponing the offensive against General Pope, and was censured in reports by Gen. "Jeb" Stuart, but if he was at fault, which is not altogether certain, he redeemed himself the next month when his admirable delaying-tactics, covering the withdrawal from South Mountain, gained for the main army a much-needed day in which to reconcentrate at Sharpsburg.

After the Dumfries and Occoquan raids of December 1862, the shortage of horses and the lack of forage threatened the disintegration of the Confederate cavalry, but Lee contrived to subsist his men and mounts on the upper Rappahannock. He was in direct command in the battle of Kelly's Ford, Mar. 17, 1863, where his handling of his small force in dealing with the largely superior column of Gen. W. W. Averell won great praise. During the Chancellorsville campaign, he led the only complete brigade of cavalry present with the main army and performed perhaps the greatest service of his military career in guarding Jackson's march on May 2 round the exposed right wing of Hooker's army. He it was who discovered that the right of the XI Corps was "in the air," and it was on the basis of his reconnaissance that Jackson extended Rodes's division to the left for the decisive attack. He participated creditably in the remaining operations of the Army of Northern Virginia during 1863 and on Sept. 3 was made major-general. During the operations of 1864 his stand at Spotsylvania Court House on May 8 made it possible for the I Corps to seize that strategic crossroads. He was ceaselessly engaged in exhausting combat, reconnaissance, and outpost duty with the Army of Northern Virginia until August. Then he was dispatched with his cavalry division to the Shenandoah Valley to support Gen. Jubal A. Early. On Sept. 19, in the desperate fighting at Winchester, where he had three horses shot under him, he was seriously wounded and incapacitated for duty until January 1865, when he assumed command of the cavalry on the north side of James River. After Wade Hampton was sent

to North Carolina, Fitzhugh Lee became senior cavalry commander of the Army of Northern Virginia but did not operate as chief of the remnant of the cavalry corps until nearly the end of the siege of Petersburg. On Apr. 1, in his absence, his cavalry division was roughly handled at Five Forks, but during the retreat to Appomattox he kept the commanding general advised of the movements of the enemy and, when the army was surrounded and about to surrender on Apr. 9, he rode off with part of his troopers. Realizing, however, that resistance was useless, he surrendered Apr. 11 at Farmville.

While Fitzhugh Lee lacked the profound strategical sense of Forrest and made no such contributions as Stuart to the art of reconnaissance and the tactical employment of the mounted army, he was active in the field, a good tactician, hard-hitting, and not without skill in reconnaissance. He is generally ranked among the first dozen cavalry officers born in America. After spending a brief time in Richmond as a paroled prisoner of war, he went to Stafford County, where he engaged in farming. "I had been accustomed all my life," he subsequently said, "to draw corn from the quartermaster, and found it rather hard now to draw it from the obstinate soil, *but I did it!*" His historic name, his personal popularity, and his skill as a campaigner contributed to his election as governor of Virginia over John Sargent Wise by a vote of 152,544 to 136,510 in November 1885. His four-year term, though unmarked by any notable achievement, did much to secure the continued Democratic control of the state government.

Defeated for the nomination to the United States Senate in 1890, he was named consul-general to Havana, Apr. 13, 1896, which office he retained during the confused events preceding the outbreak of war in 1898. The tact and firmness which he then displayed made him a national figure, and his return to Washington on Apr. 12, 1898, took on something of the nature of a triumph. Commissioned major-general of volunteers on May 5, 1898, he was assigned the VII Army Corps, which was designed to be the chief combat-force in the occupation of Cuba. The capture of Santiago obviated the necessity of other operations, but he took his command to Cuba, established headquarters at Camp Columbia, near Havana, and was charged with the reestablishment of order. From Apr. 12, 1899, to Mar. 2, 1901, he was brigadier-general of volunteers under the act of Mar. 2, 1899, and for part of this time he commanded the Department of the Missouri. On Mar. 2, 1901, he was retired a brigadier-general. He then busied himself in planning for the Jamestown Exposition of 1907. He died in Washington and was buried in Hollywood cemetery, Richmond, Va. He had married, Apr. 19, 1871, Ellen Bernard Fowle, who with five children survived him. In physique, "Fitz" Lee, as he was always called, was about five feet ten inches in height, bearded, florid, heavy, and broad-shouldered, an admirable horseman. A facile writer, he published an address, "Chancellorsville" (*Southern Historical Society Papers,* December, 1879) and a biography, *General Lee* (1894). The latter is a standard work, though marred by many inaccuracies. His political abilities were, if anything, superior to those he displayed as a soldier, and he possessed much skill in public address. He is often confused with his first cousin, William Henry Fitzhugh Lee [*q.v.*], also a Confederate major-general of cavalry.

[The manuscript Letterbook of the superintendent of West Point contains the story of Fitz Lee's escapades as a cadet. A diverting account of some of his experiences in Texas appears in E. J. Lee, *Lee of Va., 1642–1892* (1895). G. W. Cullum, *Biog. Reg. of the Officers and Grads. of the U. S. Mil. Acad.* (3rd ed., 1891), gives his assignments in the Federal army prior to 1861. His scant correspondence and infrequent reports appear in the *War of the Rebellion: Official Records (Army).* His messages as governor of Virginia were published in the *Jour. of the House of Delegates of the State of Va.* and in the *Jour. of the Senate of the Commonwealth of Va.* Some of his dispatches as consul-general appear in *House Doc. 406, 55 Cong., 2 Sess.* Other sources include: *Who's Who in America,* 1903–05; *Confed. Mil. Hist.* (1899), III, 622–25; J. W. Jones, *Virginia's Next Gov., Gen Fitzhugh Lee* (1885); and the *Times-Dispatch* (Richmond), Apr. 29, 1905, Jan. 5, 1908. Lee left no unpublished military MSS., except for a few brief field-dispatches on the retreat to Appomattox. These are in the military papers of Gen. Robert E. Lee.]   D. S. F.

LEE, FRANCIS LIGHTFOOT (Oct. 14, 1734–Jan. 11, 1797), revolutionist and statesman, was a member of the most talented group of brothers in Virginia history, which included Richard Henry, Arthur, and William Lee [*qq.v.*]. The son of Thomas and Hannah (Ludwell) Lee, he was born at "Stratford," Westmoreland County, Va. He did not attend college but received an excellent education at the hands of tutors. Leaving the family home in early life, he settled on an estate in Loudoun County which he inherited from his father. He was widely read and deeply interested in politics and served in the House of Burgesses from Loudoun County from 1758 to 1768. On his marriage to Rebecca Tayloe in the spring of 1769, he returned to the lower country, settling in Richmond County, on a plantation called "Menokin." He had already made somewhat of a reputation as a public man, and his marriage brought him many connections in Richmond County. He was almost immediately elected a burgess for that county and served in the crucial years immediately preceding the Revolution (1769–76). He was a man of far more political influence than is generally supposed. Much less widely known than his oratorical brother, Richard Henry Lee, he was hardly inferior to him in ability and was an even more ardent revolutionist. It is doubtful whether the coterie in Virginia that was bent on resisting the British government had in it a bolder spirit. He took part in every measure of defiance to the government: he signed the Westmoreland Association against the Stamp Act on Feb. 27, 1766; he was one of the members of the House of Burgesses who threw down the gauntlet to Great Britain on June 22, 1770; in 1773 he was one of the committee that undertook to form the Virginia committee of correspondence; he signed the call for the Virginia convention of August 1774, and was a member of that convention as well as of the convention of March 1775 in which the Virginia Revolution may be said to have begun. In the same year he was chosen a delegate to the Continental Congress, in which body he continued to sit until June 1779. He was one of the Signers of the Declaration of Independence, of which he heartily approved.

Lee was an influential and useful member of Congress. With farsighted vision he insisted on securing the free navigation of the Mississippi River for American citizens. He could have remained in the Continental Congress indefinitely if his longing for a quiet country life had not prevailed over such urgings of ambition as he had, which were few. On his return to Virginia, he sat for a time in the Virginia Senate and then retired. Unlike his brother Richard Henry, he was strongly in favor of the federal Constitution. After his retirement from public office he returned to "Menokin," where he died in the winter of 1797. He would have ranked as one of the leaders of the American Revolution if he had been a good speaker and had been self-seeking. But he was shy and inarticulate in public bodies and his excellent committee work remained unknown to the general public.

[E. J. Lee, *Lee of Va., 1642–1892* (1895); *Biog. Dir. Am. Cong.* (1928); J. C. Ballagh, *The Letters of Richard Henry Lee* (2 vols., 1911–14); E. C. Burnett, *Letters of Members of the Continental Cong.,* vols. I–IV (1921–28); "The Association in Williamsburg, in 1770," *Va. Hist. Reg.,* Jan. 1850; Jared Sparks, *The Writings of Geo. Washington,* vol. IX (1853); E. G. Swem and J. W. Williams, *A Reg. of the Gen. Assembly of Va., 1776–1918* (1918).]   H. J .E.

LEE, GEORGE WASHINGTON CUSTIS (Sept. 16, 1832–Feb. 18, 1913), soldier and educator, eldest son of Gen. Robert Edward [*q.v.*]

and Mary Ann Randolph (Custis) Lee, was born at Fortress Monroe, Va. Receiving his early education in private schools of Virginia, he entered the Military Academy at West Point in 1850, from which he graduated at the head of his class in 1854. Upon graduation, he was assigned to service in the United States Army Corps of Engineers and performed work in river and harbor improvements in various sections of the country. At the outbreak of the Civil War he was on duty as assistant in the office of the chief engineer of the army at Washington. On May 2, 1861, he resigned his commission as first lieutenant in the army and offered his service to the Confederacy. His father made no effort to influence his son in his decision. "Custis," wrote the elder Lee to his wife, "must decide for himself and I shall respect his decision whatever it may be." Commissioned captain of engineers in the Confederate army, July 1, 1861, he was engaged in the construction of the fortifications of Richmond until his appointment, Aug. 31, 1861, as aide-de-camp on the staff of President Davis, with the rank of colonel of cavalry. His military ability was at once recognized by Jefferson Davis who often entrusted him with important missions. In September 1861, he was dispatched to Norfolk to examine the state of defense of that place; in October 1862, with the Federals threatening Wilmington, N. C., he was sent there to assist in the organization of the forces of resistance; and, in October 1863, his advice upon the reorganization of the Artillery Corps of the Army of Northern Virginia was sought by his father, General Lee. Although his active service on the battlefield was limited to the last months of the war, owing to the demand for his activities in other departments of the military service, his efficient and successful career won for him military advancement. He was promoted to the rank of brigadier-general, June 25, 1863, and later, on Oct. 21, 1864, to major-general.

Custis Lee longed for an active command, but President Davis was loath to part with him. "Our intercourse has been so pleasant," Davis wrote him in December 1864, "and your service so very useful to me in the relation of an Aid, that I should feel a two fold reluctance in parting from you, and should not hope to replace you by any one equally acceptable and beneficial to me. I have felt that your acquirements and natural endowments entitled you to a larger field and to better opportunities of fame than you have as a member of my staff. . . . For immediate usefulness it may well be doubted whether you are not as useful to the general service in the capacity of Aid to the Executive as you would be as

Commander of a Division" (Rowland, *post*, VI, p. 431). During the last days of the Confederacy, Lee's brigade composed of departmental clerks and mechanics of Richmond, which he had previously organized for emergency purposes in the defense of Richmond, was attached to Ewell's corps and participated in the final retreat from Petersburg. Engaged at Sailor's Creek, it displayed "a gallantry never surpassed," and Lee was commended by his superior officer for his conduct in that sanguinary battle. He, with most of his command, was captured in this engagement. The war over, he became in October 1865 professor of military and civil engineering at the Virginia Military Institute, which position he occupied until he succeeded his father, Feb. 1, 1871, as president of Washington and Lee University. The adoption of the elective system of study, the establishment of endowed scholarships, and the increase of the endowment are achievements of his long administration of twenty-six years. He was also a generous benefactor of the institution, presenting, among his gifts, portraits of Washington and Lafayette by Peale, and heirlooms of the Custis family. Resigning July 1, 1897, he retired to "Ravensworth," an ancestral home, in Fairfax County, Va. He remained unmarried.

[*Who's Who in America*, 1912–13; H. L. Abbot, *Half Century Record of the Class at West Point 1850 to 1854* (1905); R. E. Lee, *Recollections and Letters of Gen. Robert E. Lee* (1904); G. W. Cullum, *Biog. Reg. of the Officers and Grads. of the U. S. Mil. Acad.* (3rd ed., 1891); E. J. Lee, *Lee of Va., 1642–1892* (1895); Dunbar Rowland, *Jefferson Davis, Constitutionalist, His Letters, Papers, and Speeches* (10 vols., 1923); *War of the Rebellion: Official Records* (Army); *Confed. Veteran*, Apr. 1913; *Lexington Gazette*, Feb. 19, 1913; *Alexandria Gazette*, Feb. 18, 19, 1913.]

W. G. B.

LEE, HANNAH FARNHAM SAWYER (1780–Dec. 27, 1865), author, was born in Newburyport, Mass., where her baptism on Nov. 12, 1780, is recorded. Her father, Dr. Micajah Sawyer, was a well-known physician. On Jan. 20, 1807, she was married to George Gardner Lee of Boston, who had been for a time an officer in the United States navy. Her husband died in 1816 leaving her with three daughters, and she appears to have devoted herself to their upbringing till 1832, when, at the mature age of fifty-two, she began her literary career. Her first publication was an appreciation of Hannah Adams appended to the *Memoir of Hannah Adams* edited by Joseph Tuckerman. The authorship of this article was ascribed to "A Friend," and indeed none of her works was published under her own name. In 1835 she wrote a story, *Grace Seymour*, but though it was printed it was never distributed to the public, for practically the entire edition was destroyed by fire, and it was never republished. Her greatest success was achieved in 1837, when she published her *Three Experiments of Living*. This discussed living under, up to, and over one's income; and it went through thirty American and ten English editions, part of its popularity being probably due to the fact that the financial depression of 1837 made its subject timely. Taking advantage of the popularity of this work, she had bound up with some of its later editions enough of her other writings to make a fair-sized volume. These were "Elinor Fulton," "Contrast, or Modes of Education," "Rich Enough," and other rather short tract-like compositions designed to foster thrift and self-improvement. After this she began a series of educational works. In 1838 she published *Historical Sketches of Old Painters*; in 1839 *Rosanna, or Scenes in Boston*, and *The Life and Times of Martin Luther*; in 1841 *The Life and Times of Thomas Cranmer*; in 1843 *The Huguenots in France and America*; in 1844 *The Log Cabin; or, the World Before You*; in 1850 *Sketches and Stories from Life: for the Young*; in 1853 the *Memoir of Pierre Toussaint*; and in 1854 *Familiar Sketches of Sculpture and Sculptors*. These were her best-known works. None of them was very long, for she was not a voluminous writer. She seems to have outlived her fame, for no lengthy obituaries appeared at her death, and no biography or memoirs have been published; but from her first success to the early fifties she was widely read and frequently cited as an admirable and influential writer, although even in this period she was sometimes treated as superficial, as by a critic in the *New Englander* (February 1854) who dismissed her *Sketches of Sculpture* as a compilation that did not justify his notice.

[The fullest account of Mrs. Lee's career is in Sarah Josepha Hale, *Woman's Record, or Sketches of All Distinguished Women from "The Beginning" till A. D. 1850* (1853). See also the *New-Eng. Hist. and Geneal. Reg.*, Jan. 1851, Apr. 1866; Wm. Lee, *John Leigh of Agawam (Ipswich) Mass.* (1888); J. J. Currier, *Hist. of Newburyport, Mass., 1764–1909* (1909), vol. II.]
S. G.

LEE, HENRY (Jan. 29, 1756–Mar. 25, 1818), better known as "Light-Horse Harry" Lee, soldier and statesman, brother of Richard Bland and Charles Lee, 1758–1815 [*qq.v.*], was born at "Leesylvania" near Dumfries, Prince William County, Va., the son of Henry Lee, a cousin of the Lees of "Stratford," and a descendant of Richard Lee [*q.v.*]. His mother, Lucy Grymes, is claimed by tradition as one of Washington's boyhood loves. Lee graduated from the College of New Jersey in 1773 at the age of seventeen.

He was preparing to go to England to study law, having been admitted to the Middle Temple, but the impending Revolution changed his plans and his career. In 1776 he was appointed a captain in Theodorick Bland's regiment of Virginia cavalry and in April 1777 his company joined Washington's army, which was weak in horse. Lee's soldierly qualities were recognized from the first and, young as he was, he was admitted to Washington's friendship and confidence. The relations between the two men continued to be intimate until death separated them. In January 1778, Lee was promoted major and put in command of a somewhat irregular force consisting of three troops of cavalry and three companies of infantry and known as "Lee's Legion." This force, on July 19, 1779, performed one of the most brilliant feats of the war by surprising the British post at Paulus Hook near New York, in which 160 of the enemy were captured almost without loss. It was comparable to Wayne's taking of Stony Point.

In 1780, Lee, now a lieutenant-colonel, was sent south to Greene, who was in great need of a competent cavalry commander. His subsequent story is the history of the Southern campaign. In the remarkable retreat across North Carolina to Virginia, in February 1781, Lee covered the rear of Greene's army, constantly skirmishing with Tarleton's British troopers, who were unable to prevail over the American cavalry. Turning suddenly aside from the main issue, Lee cut to pieces a force of Tories on the way to join Cornwallis, thereby greatly discouraging the British faction in the Carolinas. At Guilford Courthouse, Mar. 15, 1781, he fought brilliantly but failed to keep Greene informed of his position and after a hard-fought battle he was forced to retreat.

It was Lee who gave the advice to Greene that decided the latter to march south instead of following Cornwallis into Virginia. He continued his brilliant career by capturing several British forts, among them, Augusta, Ga., and he seems to have saved the drawn battle of Eutaw Springs, Sept. 8, 1781, from being an American defeat. It was his good fortune to be present at the siege of Yorktown and to witness the surrender of Cornwallis on Oct. 19, 1781.

Lee now came to the conclusion that the war was over and resigned his commission. A hero, one of the most notable Virginia soldiers, he won the hand of his cousin, Matilda Lee, heiress of "Stratford," whom he married early in 1782. By her he had several children, of whom a son, Henry Lee, 1787–1837 [*q.v.*], and a daughter survived. Turning to politics, he entered the

House of Delegates in 1785 and in the same year was sent to the Continental Congress, where he served, with one brief interruption, until 1788. He was an active member of the Virginia convention that ratified the United States Constitution in 1788 and voted for that measure. He was always a consistent Federalist and follower of Washington. In 1790, after the death of his wife, he thought of going to France for military service, as he was still young and still enamored of war. It was unfortunate that he did not do so, for he was unfitted for civil life. He gave up this plan in order to marry, on June 18, 1793, a second wife, Anne Hill Carter, of "Shirley." The fifth child of this marriage was Robert E. Lee [q.v.]. From 1792 to 1795 he served as governor of Virginia. While still governor, in 1794, he was chosen by Washington to command the army assembled to put down the Whiskey Rebellion in Pennsylvania. Lee managed to quell this uprising without the loss of life, and enhanced his prestige. In 1799 he entered Congress. The resolutions offered by John Marshall on the death of Washington were drawn by Lee and contained the description of Washington as "first in war, first in peace and first in the hearts of his countrymen" (*Annals of Congress*, 6 Cong., 1 Sess., col. 204). Lee repeated the phrase in his memorial oration in Philadelphia on Dec. 26, 1799.

Thus far Lee's life had been prosperous and happy; it was never again to be anything but sad and troubled. For some years he lived at "Stratford," harassed by debt and besieged by creditors. One of the most dashing and capable of soldiers, a fine orator, a learned and accomplished man of letters, Lee was wanting in all the qualities of a business man. His income was small and his expenditures were enormous, and he became heavily involved in land speculations. In 1808–09 he was imprisoned for debt and engaged himself in writing his *Memoirs of the War in the Southern Department of the United States*, published in two volumes in 1812. He left "Stratford" in 1811 to live in Alexandria, where his wife and second family would have suffered want but for Mrs. Lee's own means. He was always adventurous and whimsical. While in Baltimore, in July 1812, he attempted to aid his friend, Alexander C. Hanson, in defending the press of the *Federal Republican* against a mob which threatened violence. Lee and others were taken to jail. The following night the mob was admitted to the jail and in the riot which followed he received injuries from which he never recovered. (See *A Correct Account of the Conduct of the Baltimore Mob, by Gen. Henry Lee, One of the*

Sufferers, 1814.) Handicapped now by ill health as well as by poverty, he succeeded, by the aid of the government, in reaching the West Indies, where he remained for several years, hoping for a cure. It was all in vain. Warned that death was approaching, he set sail for home but his strength gave out on the way. He was set ashore at Cumberland Island, Ga., and was tenderly cared for by the daughter of his old commander, Greene. There he died and was buried. In 1913 his remains were transferred to the Lee chapel of Washington and Lee University at Lexington, Va. Lee was not only one of the first but one of the best of American cavalry soldiers.

[Lee's *Memoirs* were republished by his son Henry Lee in 1827 and by his son Robert E. Lee in 1869. The latter edition contains a biographical sketch and letters. See also Thos. H. Boyd, *Light-Horse Harry Lee* (1931); C. B. Hartley, *Life of Maj.-Gen. Henry Lee* (1859); C. C. Jones, Jr., *Reminiscences of the Last Days, Death and Burial of Gen. Henry Lee* (1870); H. B. Grigsby, *The Hist. of the Va. Federal Convention of 1788* (2 vols., 1890–91); E. J. Lee, *Lee of Va., 1642–1892* (1895); *Daily Nat. Intelligencer* (Washington, D. C.), Apr. 8, 1818.]   H. J. E.

LEE, HENRY (Feb. 4, 1782–Feb. 6, 1867), merchant and publicist, born in Beverly, Mass., was the ninth of twelve children of Joseph and Elizabeth (Cabot) Lee. Two older brothers were educated at Harvard College, but Henry after a course at Phillips Andover Academy, decided to go at once into the business in which the Cabots and the Lees had already attained prominence, the East India trade. On June 16, 1809, he married Mary Jackson, daughter of Jonathan Jackson and sister of James (1777–1867), Charles, and Patrick Tracy Jackson [qq.v.]. They had six children; Henry Lee Higginson [q.v.] was their grandson. Lee's partnership with his brother Joseph proved successful, and in 1811 he sailed for Calcutta. Being compelled by the War of 1812 to remain in India for several years, he utilized his time in study and in making acquaintances, which afterwards proved valuable, among the trading community. Upon his return to Boston he set up as a merchant trading to the East and West Indies, Europe, and South America. Temperamentally, however, he seems to have been a scholar rather than a business man, and overconfidence resulted more than once in serious losses. On each of these occasions, with the scrupulous honesty which characterized all his dealings, he paid all his creditors in full.

His interest in commerce went far beyond the limits of his own business, and he gave much thought to the tariff question on which opinion in Massachusetts was soon to be sharply divided. In 1820 the importing merchants and shipowners were still the dominant element in the business community and in politics. They bitterly opposed the demands of the Middle and Western states for higher import duties, foreseeing increased costs of ships and a declining volume of foreign trade. In the decade 1820–30, however, manufacturing made great strides in Massachusetts and a new group of factory owners arose, demanding protective duties. The woolen manufacturers, who were suffering rather severely from foreign competition, held meetings in Boston. Their demands were opposed by a group of merchants and traders, who chose Henry Lee to set forth their views. The pamphlet of nearly two hundred pages which he prepared, *Report of a Committee of the Citizens of Boston and Vicinity, Opposed to a Further Increase of Duties on Importations* (Boston, 1827), received wide circulation, being known as the "Boston Report." Drawing liberally on his wide acquaintance with both free-trade and protectionist literature, and with a vigorous and incisive style, the author made skilful use of the scanty statistical material then available.

The Tariff of 1828 was a triumph for the protectionists, the free-traders kept up the fight. In 1831, at the Free Trade Convention in Philadelphia, Lee worked in close association with Albert Gallatin [*q.v.*], and published *An Exposition of Evidence* (1832), a sort of statistical appendix, to accompany the latter's *Memorial of the Committee Appointed by the Free Trade Convention* (1832). As a result of these activities, Lee received in 1832 the eleven electoral votes of South Carolina for vice-president. His reputation as a student of economics and statistics spread to England, and he corresponded with McCulloch, Tooke, Newmarch, and others.

He retired from business in 1840, and devoted the remainder of his life mainly to writing and study. In 1850 he emerged from his retirement to wage an unsuccessful campaign for a seat in Congress. His unconquerable shyness made it almost impossible for him to take part in politics. The nobility and honesty of his character impressed all who knew him. To his intimates he revealed himself as an accomplished conversationalist, delighting them with his genial and gay spirit.

[J. T. Morse, Jr., *Memoir of Col. Henry Lee* (1905); H. A. Hill, in *Professional and Industrial Hist. of Suffolk County, Mass.* (1894), vol. II; section on "Other Lees" in William Lee, *John Leigh of Agawam (Ipswich), Mass., 1634–1671 and His Descendants of the Name of Lee* (1888); *Boston Daily Advertiser*, Feb. 7, 1867.] P. W. B.

LEE, HENRY (May 28, 1787–Jan. 30, 1837), soldier and author, was the son of Henry, "Light-Horse Harry," Lee [*q.v.*] and his first wife, Matilda (Lee) Lee. He was born at "Stratford," Westmoreland County, Va., some twenty years before the birth of his half-brother, Robert Edward Lee [*q.v.*]. He was graduated from the College of William and Mary in 1808. Though he had early displayed keen literary interests he entered upon a political and military career. From 1810 to 1813 he represented Westmoreland County in the Virginia House of Delegates. In April 1813 he was appointed major of the 36th Infantry. Attached to the staff of Gen. James Wilkinson and later to that of Gen. George Izard, he saw active service on the Canadian border. He was married in March 1817 to Anne, daughter of Daniel McCarty of Westmoreland County. He has been described by Henry A. Wise, a contemporary, as being "rather ugly in face" but "one of the most attractive men in conversation we ever listened to" (Wise, *post*, p. 99). From 1824 to 1826 he held a minor position in the Post Office Department and was employed as a political writer by Calhoun. Adams suspected him of disloyalty to his administration and about 1826 Lee definitely went over to the Jacksonian party. He was an active pamphleteer and writer for newspapers in Jackson's behalf. During the campaign of 1828 he lived at "The Hermitage" with the General and is credited with the literary form of Jackson's inaugural which he helped to write. As a reward for his services Jackson named him consul-general to Algiers with the others in the "batch of editors" to whom he gave recess appointments in 1829. The Senate in March 1830 failed to confirm these appointments, by a unanimous negative vote in Lee's case. While his campaign writings for Jackson were offensive to some, he was also opposed because of moral charges of a personal nature.

Lee had already journeyed to his post when news of the Senate's action reached him. He spent the remaining years of his life abroad, chiefly in Paris, and died in that city on Jan. 30, 1837. He had literary talent, though his writings were tedious and have proved ephemeral because of their controversial tone. In a notice of his work, the *Southern Literary Messenger* accused him of a spirit of captiousness. His first volume, *The Campaign of 1781 in the Carolinas* (Philadelphia, 1824), was intended "to expose and to frustrate the attempts of *William Johnson of South Carolina* in his *Sketches of the Life and Correspondence of General Greene*, to defame the late General Henry Lee" (p. 2). He again wrote a lengthy volume to defend his father, this time against what he deemed the aspersions cast upon him by Jefferson on the publication of that statesman's writings (*Observations on the Writings of Thomas Jefferson,* New York, 1832, Philadelphia, 1839). He admired Napoleon extravagantly. This he evidenced by a gift to Napoleon's mother of an autograph letter that George Washington had written his father, "Light-Horse Harry" Lee, and by writing a biography of Napoleon. This too was pitched on a controversial note, as he set out to defend Napoleon's name against Walter Scott's unfavorable treatment in the latter's *Life of Napoleon Bonaparte.* He planned a two-volume work on Napoleon. The first volume, *The Life of the Emperor Napoleon,* was published in 1835, but on Lee's death in Paris in 1837 it was republished with the added material he had prepared under the title: *The Life of Napoleon Bonaparte down to the Peace of Tolentino and the Close of his First Campaign in Italy.*

[The best sketch of Henry Lee is that in E. J. Lee, *Lee of Va., 1642–1892* (1895). See also: C. G. Bowers, *The Party Battles of the Jackson Period* (1922); H. A. Wise, *Seven Decades of the Union* (1872); Jas. Parton, *Life of Andrew Jackson* (1860); P. L. Ford, *The Writings of Thos. Jefferson,* vol. X (1899); *Letters and Other Writings of Jas. Madison* (1865), vols. III and IV; C. F. Adams, *Memoirs of John Quincy Adams,* vols. VI–IX (1875–76); J. S. Bassett, *Correspondence of Andrew Jackson,* vols. III–V (1928–31); *Southern Lit. Messenger,* Apr. 1835, p. 458; *Daily Nat. Intelligencer,* Mar. 14, 1837.] M. H. W.

LEE, JAMES MELVIN (May 16, 1878–Nov. 17, 1929), author, magazine editor, and for eighteen years director of the department of journalism of New York University, was born at Port Crane, N. Y., the son of James Newell Lee, a Methodist minister, and Emma (White) Lee. Graduating from Wyoming Seminary, Kingston, Pa., in 1896, he entered Wesleyan University, Middletown, Conn., where he received the degree of A.B. in 1900. At college he was largely self-supporting, and this fact led directly to the beginning of his writing career. Among his first articles for publication were several for newspapers on the means by which other students were earning their expenses—a series so successful that he later used the material in a book *How to be Self-Supporting at College,* published in 1903.

After his graduation from Wesleyan, he joined the news staff of the *Springfield Union* (Springfield, Mass.). In 1901 he became a teacher of English in Western Reserve Seminary, West Farmington, Ohio. The next year found him back in a newspaper office as circulation manager of the *Oneonta Star* (N. Y.). Beginning in 1905, magazine work engaged his attention. In succession he was circulation manager of *Outing,* editor of *Bohemian Magazine,* literary editor of

the *Circle,* associate editor of *Leslie's Weekly,* and from 1909 to 1911, editor of *Judge.* While still with *Judge,* he became a pioneer in the teaching of journalism, being appointed a lecturer at New York University in 1910, and director of the department of journalism at that university in 1911. He held the latter position for the rest of his life.

During his association with New York University he was active in writing both books and articles, principally on topics dealing with journalism. He became an eager collector of early periodicals and of first editions in the field of American literature, especially works of Cooper and Poe. This pursuit made him a familiar figure at the bookshops near his office, in Washington Square, New York. With all this, however, he was no literary recluse. He liked people, and time and again was honored with offices in varied organizations. He spoke publicly as a champion of American journalism on many occasions. When others condemned newspapers for printing crime news and scandal, he pointed to the benefits of such publicity, adding: "It is the taste of the fish, not the fisherman, which denotes the kind of bait to be used" (*New York Times,* Dec. 1, 1925). Another saying credited to him is: "The newspaper and the cake of ice left on the back porch in the rays of the sun deteriorate at the same ratio, and when deterioration is complete you can't get much for either" (*Editor & Publisher,* Nov. 23, 1929). He called John Milton the "first copy reader," tracing the dates of his connection with *Mercurius Politicus* by the sudden improvement in its English and the later "reappearance of its former sloppy style." When the American press was stirred, in July 1926, by the cold-blooded murder of Don Mellett, youthful editor of the *Canton* (Ohio) *News,* who had attacked the vice ring of his city, Lee took the lead in establishing a fund to defray the expenses of a series of lectures on journalism in memory of the martyred editor. He also established a scholarship fund in memory of William Bradford, publisher of the first newspaper in New York. These were only two of nearly a score of such funds which he sponsored. One of his books, *History of American Journalism* (1917), has been widely used as a college reference book. Other books of his are: *Wordless Journalism in America* (1915), a book of cartoons; *Newspaper Ethics* (1915); *Instruction in Journalism in Institutions of Higher Education* (1918); *America's Oldest Daily Newspaper* (1918); *Opportunities in the Newspaper Business* (1919); *Business Writing* (1920), of which he was editor; and *Business Ethics* (1925). From 1922 until his death he was literary editor of *Editor & Publisher,* New York, conducting a weekly department in which he reviewed books and articles dealing with journalism. He edited for a time *Administration,* a business magazine, and the *Three-Em Dash,* the organ of the Newspaper Club of New York, in which he was one of the most active members. He also contributed a number of articles to the *Dictionary of American Biography.* In 1908 he married Helen Olga Wellner. They had one daughter.

[*Alumni Record of Wesleyan Univ.* (1921); *Who's Who in N. Y.,* 1924; *Who's Who in America,* 1928–29; *Independent,* Apr. 25, 1925; *Editor & Publisher,* Jan. 27, 1912, Apr. 6, 1929, Aug. 3, 1929, Nov. 23, 1929, and other issues; *N. Y. Times,* Nov. 18, 19, 1929.]
R. S. M.

LEE, JAMES WIDEMAN (Nov. 28, 1849–Oct. 4, 1919), minister, editor, author, son of Zachary J. and Emily H. (Wideman) Lee, was born at Rockbridge, Ga. In the hard times of Reconstruction he made his way, almost unaided, through Emory College, graduating in 1874; and on Dec. 26, 1875, he married Emma Eufaula Ledbetter. Having joined the North Georgia Conference of the Methodist Episcopal Church, South, in 1874, he was duly ordained and sent from place to place, according to the Methodist custom, until he reached Atlanta. Here he served the quadrennium limit first at Trinity Church and then at Park Street Church. Transferred to St. Louis in 1893, he remained there until his death save for another quadrennium (1905–09) at Trinity Church, Atlanta, and a year (1910) at Park Street Church. In St. Louis he was pastor of St. John's Church for three quadrenniums (1893–97, 1901–05, 1911–15), presiding elder of the St. Louis District (1898–1901, 1915–16), and chaplain of Barnes Hospital during his last four years. In each of his principal pastoral charges he secured the building of appropriate church auditoriums or parsonages or both; as presiding elder he raised money for the weaker churches of his district, and for the denomination's educational and benevolent enterprises, in satisfactory fashion. As a pastor he was much given to visiting and is said not only to have known every member of his church and Sunday school but also to have kept in touch with the members of past charges throughout the forty-four years of his ministry. As a preacher he was variously described by contemporaries as "eloquent and forceful," gifted with a "pungent colloquialism," of "voice high and notes a bit strident," but of "genuine spiritual insight and power." In 1892 he published *The Making of a Man,* which was at once translated into the Japanese tongue and later into the

Chinese and the Korean. Three years later he edited *The Earthly Footprints of Christ and His Apostles,* containing photographs made under his personal direction in 1894. Through the enterprise of the publishers more than a million copies were sold. He was editor of three other publications (among them *The Self-Interpreting Bible* in four volumes, 1897) and author of eight, all of them save two being religious in character. His volume, *The Geography of Genius* (1915), was made up largely of travel notes arranged to illustrate his belief that "no places are of importance . . . except such as have been made significant by association with great people, great battles or great events of some kind" (Foreword). Most important of his writings was *The Religion of Science: The Faith of the Coming Man* (1912), in which he argued for the application of the scientific method to the phenomena of the Christian religion (not its dogma) in a series of essays deemed brilliant, illuminating, and satisfying by a great many, including prominent clergymen. A good deal of a philosopher and poet as well as a preacher, Lee was most noteworthy for the diversity of the people to whom his unmistakable friendliness and persistent optimism appealed. He was a speaker much sought for special occasions; and hundreds of people of all classes and in all regions voluntarily testified to his influence on them personally. His widow, three sons, and three daughters survived him.

[Biographical sketch by Lee's son, Ivy L. Lee, in *The Geography of Genius* (edition of 1920); letters and scrapbooks in private hands; *Who's Who in America,* 1918–19; Wm. Hyde and H. L. Conard, *Encyc. of the Hist. of St. Louis* (1899), vol. III; *Wesleyan Christian Advocate* (Atlanta), Oct. 31, 1919; *Christian Advocate* (Nashville), Oct. 17, 1919; *St. Louis Globe-Democrat,* Oct. 5, 1919; *St. Louis Post-Dispatch,* Oct. 4, 5, 1919.]
C. C. P.

LEE, JASON (June 28, 1803–Mar. 12, 1845), Methodist missionary, Oregon pioneer, a descendant of John Lee who settled in Farmington, Conn., in 1641, was the son of Daniel and Sarah (Whittaker) Lee. The father was a Revolutionary soldier. In 1798 the family moved from Massachusetts to a home in the neighborhood of Stanstead, Quebec, then considered a part of Vermont, where Jason was born. Experiencing a religious conversion in his twenty-third year, he three years afterward entered Wilbraham Academy, Mass., where he won the friendly interest of its president, the Rev. Wilbur Fisk. In 1830–32 he served as a minister to the Wesleyan Methodists in Stanstead and adjoining towns. In the latter year he attended the session of the New England Conference of the Methodist Episcopal Church, by which he was ordained deacon and later elder. About the same time the missionary society of this church decided to establish a mission in the Flathead country, and on June 14, 1833, Lee was chosen as its head. Accompanied by his nephew, the Rev. Daniel Lee, and three lay assistants, he left Independence, Mo., with Nathaniel J. Wyeth's second expedition, Apr. 28, 1834. On Sept. 15 the party arrived at Fort Vancouver, where they were welcomed by Dr. John McLoughlin, the chief factor of the Hudson's Bay Company.

For various reasons the Flathead project was abandoned, and on Oct. 6 four of the missionaries settled on the Willamette, ten miles northwest of the present Salem, Ore. In a short time the little colony was securely established. In the winter of 1836–37 Lee, in association with William A. Slacum, a purser in the navy, then on a tour of investigation of the northwest coast, drew up a petition for the establishment of a territorial government, which Slacum carried to Washington. In June 1837 an additional party, including Dr. Elijah White and his wife and Anna Maria Pittman, arrived from New York by sea. On July 16 Lee was married to Miss Pittman. New missions were established in the Clatsop country and at The Dalles, on the Columbia. On Mar. 26, 1838, Lee left on an overland journey to the East. At the Shawnee Mission, near Westport, Mo., in September, he was overtaken by a messenger with the information that his wife and infant son had died on June 26. He arrived in New York at the end of October, visited Washington, where he presented a settlers' petition for territorial organization, drawn up just before his departure, and during the next year addressed many meetings in behalf of his mission.

In July 1839 he married Lucy Thomson, of Barre, Vt., and on Oct. 9, with a party of fifty— the so-called Great Reinforcement—sailed from New York for the Columbia, arriving at its mouth on May 20, 1840. In the summer of the same year he had a disagreement with Dr. White, who left the mission and returned East. His work, in spite of adverse circumstances, went energetically on. By the end of the year, however, the character of his labors was undergoing a marked change. Though the mission at The Dalles had exerted a restraining influence on the thieving of the neighborhood Indians, the hope of Christianizing the savages of the Oregon country was coming to be recognized as futile. There followed a decline of missionary work and a concentration of efforts toward the material upbuilding of the settlements and the promoting of their political interests. In all these activi-

ties, as promoter, developer, business adviser, and constant advocate of the Americanization of the country, Lee took a leading part. On Feb. 7, 1841, he presided at the preliminary meeting for territorial organization, held at Champoeg; and though the movement lapsed for a time, he was influential in reviving it in the spring of 1843 and in bringing about the completion of a provisional government on July 5 of that year. He was also the chief mover in the fostering of education. As early as January 1841, he formed the plan that resulted, the following January, in the founding of Oregon Institute, later renamed Willamette University.

New problems decided him to return East for further aid. Sailing on Feb. 3, 1844, he learned at Honolulu that various criticisms of his conduct of the mission had caused the home office to supersede him in his post. He took ship for San Blas, crossed Mexico to Vera Cruz, and by way of New Orleans hurried to New York, where he arrived late in May. A conference of the Mission Board exonerated him of blame, but he was not restored to his post. In August his health failed. He returned to his native town, where he contracted a severe cold, from the effects of which, late in the winter, he died. A daughter survived him. His second wife had died in Oregon, Mar. 20, 1842. In 1906 his remains were taken to Oregon, and on June 15, with appropriate ceremonies, were reinterred at Salem. Lee's character has been variously appraised, and his influence in the settlement and acquisition of Oregon is a theme of endless controversy.

[Daniel Lee and J. H. Frost, *Ten Years in Oregon* (1844); Gustavus Hines, *Oregon* (1851); H. H. Bancroft, *Hist. of Oregon* (1890), vol. I; "Jason Lee Memorial Addresses," *Ore. Hist. Soc. Quart.*, Sept. 1906; "Diary of Rev. Jason Lee," *Ibid.*, June, Sept., Dec. 1916; A. Atwood, *The Conquerors* (n.d.); John Parsons, *Beside the Beautiful Willamette* (1924); H. W. Scott, *Hist. of the Oregon Country* (6 vols., 1924); C. H. Carey, *Hist. of Oregon* (1922); Leonard and S. F. Lee, *John Lee of Farmington, Hartford County, Conn., and His Descendants* (1897); Leonard Lee, *Supp. to John Lee*, etc. (1900); C. J. Brosnan, *Jason Lee, Prophet of the New Oregon* (1932); Daniel Lee, "Death of the Rev. Jason Lee," in *Christian Advocate* (N. Y.), Apr. 23, 1845.]   W. J. G.

LEE, JESSE (Mar. 12, 1758–Sept. 12, 1816), pioneer Methodist preacher, born in Virginia, revered as the apostle of Methodism in New England, and noted as the earliest historian of the Methodist movement in America, was the second son of Nathaniel and Elizabeth Lee. His father owned a farm of several hundred acres in Prince George County and enough slaves to cultivate it, was three times married, had twelve children, the last born when he was in his seventy-eighth year, and at his death, aged eighty-nine, left seventy-three grandchildren and sixty-six great-grandchildren. To these descendants Jesse made no contribution; he never married. His parents attended the Church of England, and though their own rector "was but a sorry preacher and of very questionable character," under the widely felt influence of Devereux Jarrett [*q.v.*] of Bath Parish, they were brought into a vital religious experience. Jesse, a boy of high emotional sensibility, was also converted. After the introduction of Methodism into Virginia the Lees joined a Methodist Society, and their home became a regular preaching place on one of the circuits. Here Jesse got his early preparation for the ministry. His secular education had been of the limited kind which neighboring schools afforded, but included attendance at a singing school where his natural gift for song was cultivated. In the latter part of 1777 he took charge of a widowed relative's farm in North Carolina. Zealously religious, he soon became a class-leader, exhorter, and finally a local preacher. Drafted into the army in 1780, he refused to bear arms because of conscientious scruples, but professed himself ready to perform any other duty assigned. Accordingly, until he was honorably discharged after three months' service, he was first a wagon driver and later sergeant of pioneers. Unofficially, he also did the work of a chaplain.

Although urged to become a traveling preacher he long hesitated, but in the latter part of 1782 put his fitness to the test by some circuit riding in Virginia and North Carolina. In 1783 he was admitted to the Virginia Conference on trial. For the next six years he labored with marked success in North Carolina, Virginia, and Maryland. Much to his regret, notice of the "Christmas Conference" held in Baltimore in 1784, at which the Methodist Episcopal Church in the United States was organized, did not reach him in time for him to attend. The February following, Bishop Asbury took him as a helper on a tour into South Carolina, which ended at Charleston. "I was comfortable in brother Lee's company," the Bishop notes in his journal under date of Feb. 22, 1785; and for many years thereafter, though they were not always in agreement, relations between the two were intimate.

While on this tour Lee met a man from New England and through conversation with him conceived the idea of carrying Methodism into that Congregational stronghold, but Asbury was not at the time favorable. Some four years later, however, Lee was appointed to the newly formed Stamford Circuit, Connecticut. Methodist preachers had visited New England before, but Lee went in to possess the land, and it was due to his

faith and zeal, his tireless journeyings, and his evangelistic power that Methodism was everywhere planted in that unfriendly soil. Physically as well as spiritually he was well fitted for his mission. Over six feet tall, weighing more than 250 pounds, of genial countenance, he commanded attention everywhere. By his singing he could draw people about him, and by his fluent, forceful, colloquial preaching he could hold and convince them. He had the jovialness commonly attributed to fleshy persons, was somewhat of a joker, and in lively repartee was unequaled. His utterances had all the boldness of thorough-going conviction. "I did not give them velvet-mouth preaching," he said of a sermon on the loss of the soul and the torment of the damned, delivered in the meeting house at Newtown, Conn., "though I had a large velvet cushion under my hands." During the Conference year, May 1789 to October 1790, he not only labored in the principal towns of Connecticut with such effect that helpers from Maryland were sent him, but also traveled in Rhode Island, Massachusetts, Vermont, and New Hampshire. Up to 1790 he had refused ordination, but at the Conference held in New York in October of that year he was privately ordained deacon by Bishop Asbury, and the following day publicly ordained elder. He continued to labor in New England until 1797, serving as presiding elder of several districts, and carrying the conquest of Methodism as far north as Maine.

By this time the general superintendency of the work had become too onerous for even the indefatigable Asbury, upon whom, since Bishop Coke was out of the country much of the time, it largely fell. Asbury called Lee to his aid, and from September 1797 until the General Conference of 1800 he assisted Asbury as required, performing all the duties of a bishop except ordination. When at this General Conference another bishop was chosen, Lee, having been tied with Richard Whatcoat [*q.v.*] on the second ballot, was defeated on the third by four votes. Besides Whatcoat's fitness for the position, there were other reasons for this result. A few felt, or professed to feel, that the jovial Lee was not sufficiently dignified for the office. Someone started the rumor that he had forced his assistance on Asbury, and that the latter did not want him elected, a charge which Asbury denied. More effective probably in bringing about his defeat, was his independent attitude toward ecclesiastical rules and authorities, and his aggressiveness in the councils of the Church. As a youthful preacher, at the Conference in North Carolina, April 1785, he had vigorously differed with Bishop

Coke on the attitude the Methodist Church should take toward slave-holders and condemned the rules in force as ill-timed and likely to produce grave evils. Coke was so incensed that he objected to the passing of Lee's character. Lee also opposed the introduction of the "Council" into the organization of the church, and in a letter presented to its first meeting pointed out the errors of the plan. For his pains he received a reply almost insulting in tone. (See letter in L. M. Lee, *Life and Times of Rev. Jesse Lee, post.,* p. 282.) At that early date, he favored a delegated General Conference, and in 1792 submitted to Bishop Asbury a plan for such a body. Ezekiel Cooper [*q.v.*], who was associated with him in Massachusetts, wrote under date of Aug. 1, 1793, referring to Lee's policies in Lynn: "At General Conference, last November, in Baltimore, Brother Lee strove very hard to have several parts of the Discipline altered, and the bishop's power reduced, but he could not succeed. . . . Such parts of the Discipline as he favored in the General Conference . . . he was strenuous in and enforced, and required strict adherence; but such parts as he opposed in General Conference . . . he would not submit to. I told him it showed a stiff obstinacy. He wished everyone to bend to him, and would not bend to anyone, or even to the Conference." (G. A. Phoebus, *Beams of Light on Early Methodism in America,* 1887, p. 169.)

Lee accepted his defeat with good grace. He was invited to act as assistant to the bishops, but preferred to return to circuit work. After a long tour through New England he was stationed in New York until April 1801, when he was appointed presiding elder of the South District of Virginia. For the next fourteen years his labors were within the bounds of the Virginia Conference, except that in 1807 he traveled South on a roving commission as far as Savannah. In the summer of 1808 he made his last visit to New England where, while rejoicing in the great progress Methodism had made, he deplored various departures from the simplicity of early Methodism. Up to 1809 he had had no home of his own, but that year he bought a small farm near that of his father. During this period he also did some writing. His first publication was a memoir of his brother, *A Short Account of the Life and Death of the Rev. John Lee, a Methodist Minister in the United States of America* (1805). In 1810 he issued *A Short History of the Methodists in the United States of America,* the earliest written, and an invaluable compendium of facts. In 1814 he published two sermons. His *History* was criticized as lacking literary style

and not sufficiently exalting Asbury; but the Bishop said of it: "I have seen Jesse Lee's History for the first time: it is better than I expected. He has not always presented me under the most favourable aspect: we are all liable to mistakes, and I am unmoved by his" (*Journal of Rev. Francis Asbury,* 1852, III, 340). In 1809, while at Baltimore superintending the publication of his book, Lee was elected chaplain of the House of Representatives, and was reëlected at the four succeeding sessions. In 1814 he was chosen chaplain of the Senate. He was criticized by some of his brethren and attacked in the Conference for holding such office on the ground that it was incompatible with his prior engagements as an itinerant Methodist. Without his consent he was transferred from the Virginia to the Baltimore Conference in 1815, and appointed to Fredericksburg. Rightly or wrongly, he considered the transfer a political move to prevent his election to the next General Conference. He refused to go to Fredericksburg and escaped censure from the Baltimore Conference on the apparently valid plea that Fredericksburg was not within its jurisdiction. In 1816 he was appointed to Annapolis, Md. While attending a camp meeting near Hillsborough in August of that year he was taken sick and died on Sept. 12, at the age of fifty-eight. He was buried in the old Methodist burying ground, Baltimore, but his body was moved with others in 1873 to Mount Olivet Cemetery. In the extent and importance of his labors for Methodism he perhaps deserves to rank next to Asbury.

[Lee left manuscript journals which were destroyed in the burning of the Methodist Book Room, New York, in 1836. Copious extracts are preserved in Minton Thrift's *Memoir of the Rev. Jesse Lee* (1823). See also L. M. Lee, *The Life and Times of the Rev. Jesse Lee* (1848); W. H. Meredith, *Jesse Lee, A Methodist Apostle* (1909); W. B. Sprague, *Annals Am. Pulpit,* vol. VII (1859); W. W. Bennett, *Memorials of Methodism in Virginia* (1871); M. H. Moore, *Sketches of the Pioneers of Methodism in North Carolina and Virginia* (1884); G. A. Crawford, *The Centennial of New England Methodism* (1891); Stephen Allen and W. H. Pilsbury, *History of Methodism in Maine* (1887); *The Methodist Magazine,* April 1822; *Methodist Quarterly Review,* January 1850; and standard histories of the M. E. Church.]   H. E. S.

LEE, JOHN DOYLE (Sept. 6, 1812–Mar. 23, 1877), Mormon elder, notorious for his part in the Mountain Meadows Massacre, was born in Kaskaskia, Randolph County, Ill. His father, Ralph Lee, was born in Virginia and according to the son "was of the family of Lees of Revolutionary fame" (*Mormonism Unveiled,* p. 36). At the age of eight he was left an orphan among relatives, and very early learned to shift for himself. He had little formal schooling. At nineteen he saw action in the Black Hawk War.

After his marriage on July 24, 1833, to Agathe Ann Woolsey, he settled in Fayette County, Ill. He had been reared a Catholic but had always shown an interest in various religions. Upon hearing of Mormonism from missionaries, he traveled to Missouri to investigate the new sect at first hand and remained there a convert. He was soon zealous in the new church and as a member of the Mormon military organization took part in several skirmishes with the Missourians. At Nauvoo, Ill., he rose rapidly in favor with the Mormon leaders, holding important municipal and ecclesiastical offices. He twice (1839 and 1841) served as missionary. He reports a number of prophetic dreams and visions which assisted him in his conversion of others. These "spiritual" phenomena suggest that he was neurotic, which supposition is confirmed by a kind of hysterio-epileptic attack during his last imprisonment (Whitney, *post*, II, p. 786). In 1843 he became a Mason. Like many other Mormons, he spent the spring of 1844 in near-by states supporting Joseph Smith's campaign for the presidency of the United States. After the Prophet's assassination, Lee returned to Nauvoo where he soon transferred his loyalty to Brigham Young.

In 1845–46 Lee accepted the Mormon practice of polygamy and added seven more wives to his household. He informs us that altogether he had eighteen wives who bore him sixty-four children. He refused to count as a wife one elderly woman—a mother-in-law—whom he married "for her soul's sake." Upon removing to Utah he was active in colonizing outlying sections and finally settled in southern Utah not far from the Mountain Meadows. He was a fanatical mystic about his religion. Like many other Mormons he was highly aroused during the summer of 1857 over the impending invasion of Utah by federal troops under Gen. Albert Sidney Johnston and over the rumors that a company of emigrants en route from Arkansas to California was robbing Mormon settlements. Early in September 1857 a band of Indians and Mormons treacherously massacred this company at Mountain Meadows. Doubtless Lee helped to plan and execute this atrocity. The first attempt (1859) to indict the leaders in the crime was unsuccessful. Finally in 1875 Lee and others were brought to trial. Lee's first trial ended in a disagreement of the mixed jury of eight Mormons and four non-Mormons. At the second trial (1876) Lee was found guilty of murder in the first degree and sentenced to be shot. After the supreme court of Utah had upheld the original judgment, he was executed on the spot where the massacre had taken place nearly twenty years before.

Certainly Lee alone was not guilty of planning and carrying out the massacre. In his *Mormonism Unveiled* (1877), which he wrote only after being sentenced to death, he throws all the blame upon local Mormon leaders: William H. Dame, Isaac C. Haight, John M. Higbee, and Philip Klingensmith. He tried to implicate Brigham Young, but this accusation has evidently no basis in fact. However, there is no denying that Lee served as a sacrifice to appease public clamor to punish those who committed the butchery. Lee sensed this and naturally his confessions are marked by extreme bitterness against those who formerly were his friends.

[In spite of its bias, Lee's *Mormonism Unveiled* (1877) is one of the best sources. W. A. Linn, *The Story of the Mormons* (1902), follows Lee's account. O. F. Whitney, *Hist. of Utah*, vols. I and II (1892–93), gives the official Mormon account. See also: H. H. Bancroft, *Hist. of Utah* (1890); M. R. Werner, *Brigham Young* (1925); "Report of the Massacre at Mountain Meadows and other Massacres in Utah," *Senate Executive Doc. 42, 36 Cong., 1 Sess.*; *Deseret Evening News* (Salt Lake City), Mar. 23, 24, 1877:] K. Y.

LEE, LUTHER (Nov. 30, 1800–Dec. 13, 1889), clergyman, abolitionist, was a leading figure in the anti-slavery movement within the Methodist Episcopal Church. Born in Schoharie, N. Y., of humble, illiterate parents, Samuel and Hannah (Williams) Lee, he received no schooling, and from the age of thirteen was dependent on his own resources. He had a vigorous, disputatious mind, however, and as occasion offered he spoke and preached at the little Methodist churches in his community. An elder brother taught him to read, and on July 31, 1825, he married a school-teacher, Mary Miller, who gave him whatever other formal education he received. In 1827, when he was admitted to the Genesee Conference, he was too ignorant to satisfy the examining committee, but he was approved because of his power as a revivalist. After an apprenticeship on frontier circuits in New York, he transferred to the Black River Conference in 1836, where he rapidly advanced to a position of leadership. He was a fighting reformer, a powerful debater by disposition and training, and the increasing anti-slavery agitation in the Church early caught his interest. The assassination of Elijah Lovejoy [*q.v.*] at Alton, Ill., late in 1837, moved him to declare himself an abolitionist.

Most Methodists of that day did not take kindly to the official abolition organizations. Believing them "important links in the great chain of operations of the Presbyterian and Congregational churches," Methodists organized societies of their own in order to "do their benevolent works in the name of their own denomination and proper character." Accordingly, Wesleyan anti-slavery societies were formed, in the promotion of which Lee engaged with consuming zeal. His efforts were so successful that in 1838 the American Anti-Slavery Society made him their agent in western New York. Describing slavery in language "expressive of the shrieking terrors of death, the gloom of rayless despair, and the glowing fires of hell" (*Autobiography, post*, p. 210), he met with much violence, which he fronted dauntlessly. In the fall of 1839 he was employed by the Massachusetts abolitionists. He now used all his influence to further the rising agitation for political anti-slavery organization, and in 1840 he took a leading part in founding the Liberty Party.

During these critical years Lee's services were frequently required to defend Methodist clergymen in church trials for participating in abolition activity. Through the board of bishops the Church was making a determined effort to thwart such activity among its ministers; but the dual nature of Methodist polity, with authority exercised both from above through the bishops, and from below through the Conferences, made a peaceful adjustment impossible wherever the Conferences protected the abolitionists. After years of increasing friction, many abolitionists withdrew, and in 1843 they organized the Wesleyan Methodist Connection of America, without an episcopacy and on an anti-slavery basis. At the first General Conference of the new denomination, in 1844, Lee was elected president. Delegates reported fifteen thousand communicants; but the denomination never grew larger. That same year Northern Methodists precipitated a division in the Church on the slavery issue, and there were no more secessions. Lee faithfully served his Church during the two following decades, as editor of its organ, the *True Wesleyan*, as pastor in New York state, Ohio, and Michigan, and as professor on the faculty of the Wesleyan Methodist school, Adrian College, Adrian, Mich. In 1867 he returned to the Methodist Episcopal Church and after ten more years' ministry in southern Michigan, he was superannuated, dying at the age of eighty-nine at Flint, Mich. He wrote *Universalism Examined and Refuted* (1836); *Ecclesiastical Manual, or Scriptural Church Government Stated and Defended* (1850); *Slavery Examined in the Light of the Bible* (1855); *Elements of Theology* (1856); *Natural Theology* (1866). Their importance is inconsiderable.

In 1882 he published *Autobiography of the Rev. Luther Lee, D.D.*

[In addition to the above, see *Mass. Abolitionist*, 1839–1840; L. C. Matlack, *The Hist. of Am. Slavery and Methodism, from 1780 to 1849; and Hist. of the Wesleyan Meth. Connection of America* (1849); *Minutes of the Ann. Conferences of the M. E. Ch.* (1890).]
G. H. B.

LEE, RICHARD (d. 1664), statesman, was the emigrant ancestor of a noted family of Virginia. Among his descendants were Richard Henry Lee and his distinguished brothers, Henry, "Light-Horse Harry," Lee of Revolutionary fame, and Robert E. Lee [qq.v.]. He transmitted to his descendants, along with a goodly fortune, high standards of culture, morality, and a sense of public service. Of Lee's immediate parentage there is no definite information, but there is convincing evidence that he came of the Coton branch of the Shropshire Lees, an ancient and honorable English family. His coat of arms, which, carved in wood, long adorned the front door of old "Cobbs Hall," is registered in the Herald's office in London as that borne by "Colonel Richard Lee, Secretary of State in Virginia, *Anno* 1659." In legal documents he described himself as of "Stratford Laughton in the County of Essex Esquire." The name "Stratford" still remains in "Stratford Hall," birthplace of Richard Henry Lee and of Robert E. Lee. William Lee [q.v.] stated that his ancestor, Richard Lee, came to Virginia during the reign of Charles I, remained for a time, returned to England, and later made his home in Virginia. This seems true. In any event, Richard Lee emigrated in, or about, 1641 and settled in York County—in that part organized in 1651 as Gloucester County. A grant of a thousand acres of land to Richard Lee, gentleman, dated Aug. 10, 1642 (for bringing in settlers), states that it was due to him "for his own p'sonal Adventure, his wife Ann" (whose maiden name is not known), and for others. It is probable, however, that he did not live here, the "Paradise" estate, but at Gloucester Point.

About 1651 Lee removed to Northumberland County and settled on Dividing Creeks which afforded a good harbor opening into Chesapeake Bay. He was one of the first and most active pioneers of that region, acquiring tracts of land, raising large quantities of tobacco, and trading to England in ships in which he owned part interest. At one time or another he was clerk of the council, attorney-general of the colony, burgess, high sheriff of York County, councilor, and secretary of state. During the period of the Commonwealth he remained loyal to the King. A contemporary states that upon the death of

Charles I, Lee went to Europe, surrendered Sir William Berkeley's commission as governor of Virginia, and brought back a new commission from the exiled Charles II. It is said that he invited Charles to make his home in Virginia. After the subjugation of the colony, Lee acknowledged the supremacy of the Commonwealth and retained his influence in political affairs. In this he was not untrue to principle but acted in the best interests of the colony. After the Restoration he spent much of his time in England, and some of his children were educated in English universities, but he came home to die on his Dividing Creeks estate and was buried there at "Cobbs Hall." His will named eight surviving children. He has been described as "a man of good stature, comely visage, an enterprising genius, a sound head, vigorous spirit, and generous nature" (Lee, *post*, p. 245).

[The most useful work on Richard Lee and the Lee family is E. J. Lee, *Lee of Va., 1642–1892* (1895). See also: *New-Eng. Geneal. and Hist. Reg.*, Jan. 1890, Jan. 1892; and W. G. and M. N. Stanard, *The Colonial Va. Reg.* (1902). There are numerous references to Lee in the *Va. Mag. of Hist. and Biog.* and the *Wm. and Mary Coll. Quart. Hist. Mag.*]   R. L. M—n.

LEE, RICHARD BLAND (Jan. 20, 1761–Mar. 12, 1827), statesman, brother of Henry, "Light-Horse Harry," and Charles Lee [*qq.v.*], was the son of Henry and Lucy (Grymes) Lee and a descendant of Richard Lee [*q.v.*]. He was born at the family homestead, "Leesylvania," Prince William County, Va. At an early age he moved to Loudoun County, where he owned an estate inherited from his father. He became a well-to-do and influential planter with wide connections. On June 19, 1794, he was married to Elizabeth Collins of Philadelphia, the daughter of a wealthy Quaker. A member of a prominent family and a planter with sufficient means and leisure for public affairs, Lee had entered politics while still very young and represented Loudoun County in the House of Delegates from 1784 until 1788, and again in 1796. Influenced no doubt by his brother, Henry Lee, and by his wife's family, he was an ardent Federalist in a state in which the Federalist party was always weak. As one of the few prominent members of that group in the Virginia Assembly of 1788, he opposed Patrick Henry's effort to call a new convention to reconsider the United States Constitution.

In 1789 he became a member of the first Congress under the Constitution. He was not a man of great force or ability, but it was his destiny to be one of the determining factors in an event of importance to the country. Hamilton was pressing his plan for the assumption of state debts by the federal government, but he lacked a majority in the House of Representatives. He succeeded in bringing over his rival, Jefferson, to favor the assumption scheme, however, and the two leaders held a conference in July 1789, to which Alexander White and Lee, both Virginia congressmen, were invited. Lee was undoubtedly selected for his Federalist leanings, though he seemed to be committed to vote against assumption. Lee and White agreed to change their attitude on assumption, while Hamilton, for his part, consented to the choice of the Potomac River as the seat of government. In this way Hamilton secured the necessary votes to put through his assumption bill and the District of Columbia came into existence. Richard Henry Lee wrote of this episode, "It was generally supposed that the Assumption part of our Bill would be rejected by the H. R. but Messr R. B. Lee and White from our Country with Gale and Dan'l Carroll from Maryland, changing sides, the Assumption was agreed to" (*The Letters of Richard Henry Lee*, II, 535). Lee served in Congress until 1795, when he retired to his farm. In 1815 he moved to Washington. The following year he was appointed a commissioner of claims for property destroyed during the war, and from 1819 until his death he was judge of the Orphans' Court in the District of Columbia.

[See E. J. Lee, *Lee of Va., 1642–1892* (1895); J. C. Ballagh, *The Letters of Richard Henry Lee* (2 vols., 1911–14); John P. Branch Hist. Papers of Randolph-Macon Coll., June 1903; *Biog. Dir. Am. Cong.* (1928); W. H. Bryan, *A Hist. of the Nat. Capital*, vol. II (1916); E. G. Swem and J. W. Williams, *A Reg. of the Gen. Assembly of Va., 1776–1918* (1918); P. L. Ford, *The Writings of Thos. Jefferson*, I (1892), 164; and *Daily Nat. Intelligencer* (Washington, D. C.), Mar. 13, 1827.]   H. J. E.

LEE, RICHARD HENRY (Jan. 20, 1732–June 19, 1794), Revolutionary statesman, brother of Francis Lightfoot, William, and Arthur Lee [*qq.v.*], was the seventh of the eleven children of Thomas and Hannah (Ludwell) Lee and a descendant of Richard Lee [*q.v.*]. He was born at the family seat, "Stratford," in Westmoreland County, Va. Of his early life little is definitely known. He received his elementary instruction from private tutors and was sent to England to complete his education. Having finished his course at the academy at Wakefield, in Yorkshire, in 1751, he spent a few months in travel, then returned to Virginia, probably in 1752. He did not, it seems, plan a professional career, but he is said to have made a thorough study of the law and his letters reveal an acquaintance with outstanding works in history, government, and politics. Inasmuch as most of his ancestors had sat in the House of Burgesses or the council, or both, it is a natural inference that his aim from the first was a public career. His public service began in 1757, when he became a justice of the peace in his county, and in 1758 he entered the House of Burgesses. In the meantime, on Dec. 3, 1757, he had married Anne Aylett, daughter of William Aylett of Westmoreland County, and about this time he established his residence at "Chantilly," a neighboring estate to "Stratford."

It is related of Lee that in his earlier years in the House of Burgesses he took an inconspicuous, even a hesitant, part, but that once he had broken through the crust of deference to the older leaders he won the admiration of his friends and the respect of his opponents. His part in the activities of the House was one of increasing importance until he had attained a position of influence in its counsels. An aristocrat of the aristocrats, he steered from the beginning a democratic, or, perhaps more accurately, a progressive, course. One of his first speeches was in support of a measure designed to check the growth of slavery; he had a part, along with Patrick Henry, not yet a member of the House, in the matter of the so-called "Twopenny Act"; he was Henry's chief ally in the noted case of the speakership and the treasury; and he himself pushed the investigation of the treasury, winning thereby political enmities that vexed his course for a good many years. It was, however, his opposition to the Parliamentary plan of March 1764, to tax the colonies, that placed him at once in the forefront of the defenders of colonial rights. Immediately upon learning of the purpose of Parliament he declared, in a letter written to a friend in England (May 31, 1764), that "the free possession of property, the right to be governed by laws made by our representatives, and the illegality of taxation without consent" were "essential principles of the British constitution," and that colonial Britons had forfeited none of their rights and privileges, none of "the blessings of that free government of which they were members" (*The Letters of Richard Henry Lee*, I, 5–6).

When the House of Burgesses registered a protest against the proposed stamp duties, Lee was of the committee appointed on Nov. 14 to draw up an address to the King, a memorial to the Lords, and a remonstrance to the Commons, and he has been credited with the authorship of the first two of these papers. Although he was not present in the House of Burgesses when, in May 1765, Patrick Henry startled that assembly with his famous resolutions, he and Henry were in essential unison, and he shortly afterward reiterated his views in a published address to the people of Virginia. He is said to have led a "mob of gentlemen" to confront the appointed collector of stamps and compel him to promise not to serve in his official capacity. Then, in February 1766, he drew the citizens of his own county into an "association" binding themselves to import no British goods until the Stamp Act should be repealed. (See the *Virginia Historical Register*, January 1849.) This Westmoreland Association is chiefly of importance for the reason that it was the first of the numerous boycotting measures designed to bring the British government to repentance, as the Continental Association, itself promoted by Lee, was the most ambitious. It presently developed that, in November 1764, just when the House of Burgesses was uttering its protest, Lee had himself applied for appointment as collector. He was accordingly charged with inconsistency and rebuked unmercifully in the *Virginia Gazette;* but he explained that, after "reflecting seriously," he had withdrawn his application, and he pointed to his zealous works as proof of his thorough conversion.

Against the Townshend Acts he set his face even more firmly than he had done against the Stamp Act. They were "arbitrary, unjust, and destructive of that mutual beneficial connection which every good subject would wish to see preserved" (*Letters*, I, 27). The suspension of the legislature of New York, he wrote in March 1768, *"hangs like a flaming sword* over our heads and requires *by all means to be removed"* (*Ibid.*). A few months later he was urging, as a necessary means of uniting their counsels, that the several colonies set up committees for intercolonial correspondence (letter to Dickinson, July 25, 1768), an idea that was not however brought to fruition until 1773. In December 1768, his wife died, and in the following year he married Mrs. Anne Pinckard, widow of Thomas Pinckard and daughter of Col. Thomas Gaskins. During the relatively quiet period between 1768 and 1773 he engaged in shipping tobacco to his brother William in London. Yet he by no means forsook the political field, although he did, in the summer of 1770, meditate withdrawing from the popular assembly and seeking appointment as president of the council, which offered, he thought, the greater "means of doing good." Just what gave rise to this impulse it is not easy to determine. In May 1765 Patrick Henry had swept like a blazing comet across the political skies and made himself a popular idol, yet Lee was by no means eclipsed. As Henry had become the Demosthenes of Virginia, so Lee became the Cicero. He and Henry became congenial coworkers. Likewise, when Jefferson, a new luminary of liberalism, came to the House of Burgesses in 1769, Lee, Henry, and Jefferson, with a few other forward-looking men, pooled their ideas and their efforts. It was they who, in March 1773, originated the plan for intercolonial committees of correspondence, a measure which Lee declared ought to have been fixed upon from the beginning of the dispute "as leading to that union, and perfect understanding of each other, on which the political salvation of America so eminently depends" (*Letters,* I, 84) ; and it was the same group who, in May 1774, "cooked up," as Jefferson expressed it, a resolution to make the day when the port of Boston was to be closed a day of "Fasting, Humiliation, and Prayer." Lee himself had prepared a set of resolutions which included a declaration that the closing of the port of Boston was a "most violent and dangerous attempt to destroy the constitutional liberty and rights of all British America" (*Letters,* I, p. 116), and, what is of especial significance, a call for a general congress of the colonies to adopt means for securing these rights. A dissolution of the Assembly, in consequence of the fast-day resolution, prevented Lee from offering these propositions, but it did not prevent the Burgesses from gathering afterward and taking measures to the same end, including the summoning of a convention. Lee was of opinion that the action of the Burgesses was "much too feeble an opposition" to the "dangerous and alarming" despotism that was threatening. Nevertheless the past nine years had worked a great change in the minds of those elder statesmen who had long dominated the course of Virginia politics. They were at last being drawn from their long-time moorings in the quiet channels of conservatism and conciliation out into the current of revolution where Lee, Henry, and Jefferson were plying their radical oars.

Meanwhile, before the Virginia convention had assembled and voiced its demand for a general congress, Massachusetts had already sent forth the call, naming Philadelphia, September first, as the place and time. Of Virginia's seven delegates to the Congress, Peyton Randolph, speaker of the House of Burgesses and a conservative, was named first and Richard Henry Lee second. At Philadelphia Lee met with kindred spirits. John Adams pronounced him "a masterly man," and between Lee and Samuel Adams there began a lifelong friendship. As for remedies, Lee still believed that a non-importation, an enlarged form of his Westmoreland As-

sociation, would speedily and effectually accomplish the purpose, and in due time he moved it. The Continental Association, the first real step toward a federal union, was the result. The address to the King, as adopted by Congress, Lee thought was lacking in spirit.

In the Congress of 1775 Lee was active on many of the most important committees and was among the foremost proponents of strong measures. Lord North's conciliation offers, he warned, were insidious. How early he espoused the idea of independence cannot definitely be said, but in November 1775, he agreed with John Adams that it was time the colonies were adopting their own governments, and it was upon his suggestion that Adams drew up his *Thoughts on Government* (1776). Lee probably experienced no sudden change of heart, but it may have been Thomas Paine's influence that led him to join with George Wythe, in March 1776, in proposing a resolution that the King, instead of the ministry, was the "Author of our Miseries," a doctrine for which Congress was not quite ready. When presently he is discovered openly advocating independence, it is not independence as an end to be attained for its own sake that he emphasized, but rather as a necessary prerequisite to a foreign alliance. Although in this view Lee by no means stood alone, it was in no small measure in consequence of Lee's urgence that the Virginia convention, on May 15, adopted its resolutions in behalf of independence, foreign alliances, and a confederation, and it was altogether appropriate that he should be chosen to move those resolutions in Congress. By his pen they were redrawn in that compact form in which they appear in the journals of Congress (June 7, 1776).

With the presentation of the resolutions Lee's part in the Declaration of Independence, except for his subsequent signature to the finished document, was essentially ended. He had already planned to return to Virginia to take part in the formation of the new state government, and for that purpose he left Philadelphia June 13 (not on June 11, as has frequently been stated; see his *Letters,* I, 199, 201, 203). Accordingly he was not placed upon any one of the three committees to which the resolutions gave rise. Nevertheless it is to the confederation and foreign relations that the most significant phases of his career in Congress during the next two or three years appertain. In the formation of the Articles of Confederation he appears to have had but a minor part, yet no man in Congress was more concerned for the consummation of "this great bond of union" than he. When it became evident that no confederation was possible until Virginia had surrendered her claims to western lands he advocated the sacrifice and labored to that end. His connection with the problem of foreign relations became very soon anything but a happy one. Naturally, he became deeply involved in the controversy between his brother Arthur, and Silas Deane, and his vehement championship of his brother was largely instrumental in dividing Congress into two hostile factions and giving an unpleasant cast to the foreign relations of the United States for two years or more. During these years he added little to his reputation as a statesman, while his earlier buoyant hopes for the speedy triumph of the right, whether it were national or personal, were sadly dimmed. Nevertheless he continued for some time to labor zealously at his congressional tasks and in his country's cause. In May 1779, worn down in body and in spirit, he resigned his seat in Congress. In 1780 he was elected to the Virginia House of Delegates, where, strangely enough, he allied himself with the conservative forces. In 1784 he was again elected as a delegate to Congress, and by that body was chosen as its president for a year. Although handicapped by ill health and taxed by the business and the ceremonies of his office, the honor and distinction appear to have afforded him no small gratification.

Congress was at this time in a rather unstable situation. A movement essentially aimed at its dissolution had narrowly failed, and the wiser patriots, concerned for the salvation of the union, were seeking to strengthen the hands of Congress as an imperative necessity. Lee was alive to the fact that the Articles of Confederation were seriously defective, but he feared to give Congress the power of "both purse and sword." "The first maxim of a man who loves liberty," he declared, "should be never to grant to Rulers an atom of power that is not most clearly & indispensably necessary for the safety and well being of Society" (*Letters,* II, 343–44). He accordingly opposed the proposition to grant Congress a five-per-cent. impost. He was chosen as one of the delegates to the Constitutional Convention but declined on the ground that it was inconsistent that members of Congress should pass judgment in New York on their opinions in Philadelphia (*Letters,* II, 434). He did, however, while the Convention was sitting, have an important share in the creation of another great instrument of government, the Northwest Ordinance. When the Constitution was laid before Congress Lee led the opposition to it, and he was one of its most vigorous critics throughout

the campaign for its adoption. His opposition was on several grounds, chief among them, that the Convention, called only to amend the Articles of Confederation, had exceeded its powers; that the Constitution lacked a bill of rights; that it was a "consolidated," rather than a federal, government, and therefore opened the way to despotism; and that the lower house was not sufficiently democratic. His arguments were set forth in a series of "Letters of the Federal Farmer" which became a sort of textbook for the opposition. His insistence was upon amendments before rather than after adoption. Through the instrumentality of his friend Patrick Henry, also an opponent of the Constitution, Lee was chosen one of Virginia's senators in the new government, and his chief concern in the Senate was to bring to fruition the amendments which he had advocated. Some of his propositions would probably now be regarded as chimerical, but the chief of them were embodied in the first ten amendments, and the verdict of time appears to have sustained their wisdom. In October 1792, broken in health, he resigned his senatorial seat and retired to "Chantilly," where he lingered a little more than two years.

[The *Memoir of the Life of Richard Henry Lee* (2 vols., 1825), by his grandson, R. H. Lee, is unsatisfactory. There are briefer biographies, as in Charles Campbell, *Hist. of the Colony and Ancient Dominion of Va.* (1860), but they are for the most part condensations from the *Memoir*. The present sketch is based primarily on *The Letters of Richard Henry Lee* (2 vols., 1911–14), edited by J. C. Ballagh, together with the *Journals of the House of Burgesses* and the *Journals of the Continental Cong.* Genealogical facts have been drawn mainly from E. J. Lee, *Lee of Va., 1642–1892* (1895), supplemented by items in the *Va. Mag. of Hist. and Biog.* Among the works that afford helpful contributions are C. R. Lingley, *The Transition in Va. from Colony to Commonwealth* (1910); H. J. Eckenrode, *The Revolution in Va.* (1916); E. C. Burnett, *Letters of Members of the Continental Cong.,* vols. I–V (1921–31), and the writings of John Adams, Samuel Adams, and Thomas Jefferson. For the Deane-Lee episode see "The Deane Papers," *N. Y. Hist. Soc. Colls.,* Publication Fund Series, vols. XIX–XXIII (1887–91). For his senatorial career see the *Annals of Cong.,* vols. I–III, and the *Jour. of Wm. Maclay* (1890, 1927), edited by E. S. Maclay. Characterizations of Lee's person and oratory are found in Wm. Wirt, *Sketches of the Life and Character of Patrick Henry* (1817 and later editions); and H. S. Randall, *Life of Jefferson* (1858), I, 102. Lee's "Letters of the Federal Farmer to the Republican," were in two series and were printed with the title, *Observations Leading to a Fair Examination of the System of Government Proposed by the Late Convention* (1787). The second series was published separately under the title: *An Additional Number of Letters from the Federal Farmer to the Republican* (1788); the first series was reprinted by P. L. Ford in *Pamphlets on the Constitution* (1888).]
                                          E. C. B.

LEE, ROBERT EDWARD (Jan. 19, 1807–Oct. 12, 1870), soldier, the fifth child and third son of Henry, "Light-Horse Harry," Lee [*q.v.*] and Anne Hill (Carter) Lee, was born at "Stratford," Westmoreland County, Va. His father, a member of a famous Virginia family, a distinguished cavalry officer of the Revolution, and a former governor of the state, had married as his second wife a daughter of the wealthy and religious planter, Charles Carter of "Shirley." His brilliant political prospects were wrecked by a mania for speculation, and in 1811 he was forced to leave "Stratford," which belonged to Henry Lee [q.v.], a son by his first marriage. Moving to Alexandria, Va., which offered inexpensive educational facilities, the family lived modestly on the income from a trust estate left Mrs. Lee by her father. The fortunes of "Light-Horse Harry" continued to decline, and in 1813, having been badly injured in the Baltimore riot, he went to the West Indies. He died at Cumberland Island, Ga., on his way home, Mar. 25, 1818.

Diligent in his studies at the Alexandria schools and displaying marked aptitude for mathematics, Robert led a normal, outdoor life, but from boyhood he had the care of an ill mother. In 1824 the inspiration of his father's military career and the opportunity of procuring a professional education without draining the limited financial resources of the family led him to seek appointment to West Point. Entering in 1825, much more mature and better prepared than the average boy of his age, he distinguished himself alike by his scholarship and by his proficiency in military exercises, was adjutant of the corps, and was graduated number two in the class of 1829 without a demerit.

The seventeen years that followed his commission as brevet second lieutenant of engineers were such as might have been spent by any young officer of that service, who combined a fine presence with social graces, exemplary conduct, energy, and ability. After seventeen months of work on Fort Pulaski, Cockspur Island, Ga., he served as assistant engineer at Fort Monroe, Va., from May 1831 to November 1834. While stationed there, he married at "Arlington," June 30, 1831, Mary Ann Randolph Custis, only daughter of George Washington Parke Custis [q.v.], grandson of Martha Washington. Association with Custis and with the Washington traditions at "Arlington" made his father's old commander Lee's ideal, whom he seems consciously to have emulated in his bearing and in his conception of duty. His marriage was happy. Mrs. Lee was not a housekeeper, and by her tardiness habitually offended his sense of punctuality, but she was intelligent and appreciative, though strong and outspoken in her political likes and dislikes. A constant reader, she had a deeply religious nature. She held his love,

without a suggestion of wavering, through nearly forty years of married life. She bore him seven children, George Washington Custis [q.v.], Mary, William H. Fitzhugh [q.v.], Agnes, Annie, Robert Edward, and Mildred, who were reared chiefly at "Arlington." Only William H. Fitzhugh and Robert left issue. The others died unmarried.

After leaving Fort Monroe, Lee was an assistant in the chief engineer's office in Washington during the years 1834–37, and in the summer of 1835 aided in running the Ohio-Michigan boundary line. His first important independent assignment came in July 1837, as superintending engineer for St. Louis harbor and the upper Mississippi and Missouri rivers. When this work, which he performed with much success, was suspended for lack of funds in October 1841, he was transferred to Fort Hamilton, New York harbor, where he remained, with one brief stay at headquarters in Washington (1844), until Aug. 19, 1846. Then he was sent, via Washington, to San Antonio, Tex., as assistant engineer to the army under Gen. John E. Wool. He followed Wool's futile marches until the column reached Buena Vista, and won much praise by a very bold reconnaissance in front of that place. Transferred then to the Vera Cruz expedition, he immediately captivated its commander, Gen. Winfield Scott, by his diligence and capacity, and had every opportunity of winning a name for himself. At Vera Cruz, he was charged with locating the heavy land-batteries. The strategy of Cerro Gordo was largely based on reconnaissance made by him. In the advance on Mexico City he distinguished himself by two crossings of the lava field between San Augustin and Padierna in the dark, and during the battle of Churubusco he conducted the column of General Shields to the left of Scott's line. His exhausting work in placing batteries in front of Chapultepec and a slight wound received in the battle of Sept. 13, 1847, forced him to retire from the field, but he rejoined Scott in Mexico City the next day and was promptly set to work preparing maps for future operations.

Lee had been made first lieutenant of engineers in 1836 and captain in 1838; when he returned to the United States in 1848 and was placed in charge of the construction of Fort Carroll, Baltimore harbor, he had been promoted for gallantry to the rank of brevet colonel. After three years and nine months at Fort Carroll (November 1848–August 1852), he was made superintendent at West Point, much against his wishes. His term there was distinguished by a number of improvements in the plant, by changes in the curriculum, and by close attention to the individual cadets, among whom were individuals as different in taste and sympathies as James Abbott McNeill Whistler, the artist, and "Jeb" Stuart, the Confederate trooper. The social life of the academy was pleasant, but Lee was glad, with the assistance of Jefferson Davis, secretary of war, to change from the staff to the line as lieutenant-colonel of the 2nd Cavalry in March 1855. The transfer hardly fulfilled his expectations. His long absences from home became increasingly burdensome as he grew older, and were rendered more tedious by repeated details for court-martial duty. In October 1857 his father-in-law died. He was named one of the executors and had to hasten home and procure a succession of furloughs to settle a large property under a confusing testament. Mrs. Lee, meantime, had developed chronic arthritis and was fast becoming an invalid, to her husband's great distress. These circumstances kept him from active duty and made 1857–59 a dark period in his life. At one time he contemplated resigning from the army. During the time his regiment was on frontier duty in Texas, Lee was actually with it only from March 1856 to October 1857, and from February 1860 to the same month of the next year. During the last period he was in command of the Department of Texas. Prior to 1861, he had never commanded more troops in the field than four squadrons of horse, and that number only for a forty-day scout in June-July 1856. Chancing to be in Washington at the time of the John Brown raid in 1859, he was sent to Harpers Ferry to put down the "insurrection." He did so with little waste of time and life.

During the later months of his second period of duty in Texas, the secession movement began. Lee had no sympathy with it. With him, a Whig, warmly devoted to the Union, the political and economic arguments for Southern independence did not weigh. He knew little of constitutional law, and the few slaves he had owned in earlier years had died or been manumitted. The question with him—a question he hoped he would never see brought to an issue—was simply whether his first allegiance was due his state or the Union. He answered it without mental debate: in case Virginia seceded, the traditions of his family and its long association with Virginia instinctively determined him to cast in his lot with her. He stated this repeatedly before he left Texas, and said at the same time that he regarded secession as revolution. It was not until the discussions of wartime camp-fires had ac-

quainted him more fully with its constitutional basis that he accepted the doctrine of secession.

Recalled to Washington in February 1861, and placed by General Scott on waiting orders, probably with an eye to promoting him quickly in case of war, Lee watched the crisis approach, but his natural optimism led him to believe that some solution would be found before extremists, Northern and Southern, could destroy the Union. On Mar. 16, he was made colonel of the 1st Cavalry and accepted the commission without hesitation. On Mar. 15, the Confederate secretary of war wrote him offering him rank as brigadier-general in the Confederate States army, but if he ever received the letter, which shows plainly that he had not been consulted, he ignored it. Virginia, meantime, had called a constitutional convention to decide on secession. While waiting on the action of his state, Lee realized that, regardless of her decision, his conscience would not permit him to bear arms against the South. Therefore, when Francis P. Blair on Apr. 18, 1861, told him that he was authorized to offer him the field command of the United States army (Lee to Reverdy Johnson, Feb. 25, 1868, R. E. Lee, *Recollections and Letters of General Lee*, pp. 27–28), Lee declined the offer and stated his reasons for doing so. He then called on General Scott and recounted what had happened. Scott, his frank friend and admirer, told him that his position was anomalous and that he should either resign or be ready to accept any duty assigned him. Lee felt that this was true, but his affection for the army and the Union was so deep that he still hoped his honor would not compel him to dissociate himself from either. The next day he learned that the Virginia convention had voted in favor of secession. He had thereupon to decide whether he should resign immediately or await the action of the voters of the state on the ordinance of secession, which had to be submitted for their approval. The events of that single day, however, convinced him that war would not wait on a referendum. Accordingly, he submitted his resignation on Apr. 20, intending that it be effective immediately. As it was not accepted until his accounts had been checked in the routine manner, the formal date of resignation appears in official records as Apr. 25.

Lee had not communicated with the Virginia authorities, and had hoped that he would not have to participate in a war he deplored; but he considered that his sword was at the command of his native state, and when Virginia chose him as commander of her forces he accepted on Apr. 23 and threw all his energies into her defense.

After making an extraordinary record in fortifying the rivers and mobilizing the volunteers of the state, he was informally designated as military adviser to President Davis, with the rank of general (confirmed Aug. 31, 1861, to rank as of June 14, 1861). Dispatched on July 28 to the vicinity of Monterey, Va., he succeeded in halting a threatened invasion from western Virginia; but military jealousies, lack of supplies, bad weather, and over-elaborate strategy robbed him of larger results, and when he was recalled to serve again as the president's consultant his popular reputation had declined greatly. Despite some clamor against him, Davis's confidence in Lee was undiminished and he sent him, early in November, to organize the defenses of the South Atlantic seaboard. This work occupied Lee until March 1862, when he was summoned back to Richmond for a third time to assist the president, with the honorific but empty title of general in charge of military operations under the direction of the president.

The assignment was unpleasant, the duties were vague and the difficulties immense, but Lee steered a courageous course between President Davis and Gen. Joseph E. Johnston, both of them hypersensitive, and with the help of "Stonewall" Jackson [q.v.], then commanding in the Shenandoah Valley, he worked out a plan to keep the Federals in northern Virginia from reënforcing General McClellan, who was then preparing to besiege Richmond. Johnston having been wounded May 31, 1862, Lee was assigned next day to the command of the troops he promptly named "The Army of Northern Virginia." At this time, when his career as a field-commander really began, he was fifty-five years old, physically magnificent and in full vigor, five feet, ten and a half inches tall, weighing around 170 pounds, with powerful shoulders and chest, a large neck and well-moulded head, dark-brown eyes, a florid complexion, and hair that was rapidly turning gray. A short beard, which he had not worn until that spring, covered a powerful jaw, and thin, straight lips. He had never commanded in a battle. During the thirty-four months that followed he at no time had a force comparable in numbers, in artillery, or in equipment to the opposing armies. This is the fact that must constantly be remembered in any study of his campaigns. The odds against him were always three to two and sometimes three to one.

He inherited a crisis. McClellan, with nearly 100,000 men, was within seven miles of Richmond. Three separate forces were threatening Jackson in the Valley of Virginia. A large Federal army was on the Rappahannock, preparing to support McClellan. If McClellan were reenforced or permitted to bring his siege guns within range, Richmond would certainly fall. Lee hurriedly fortified the city and collected such troops as he could from the South. His problem was greatly simplified when Jackson, acting under the plan he and Lee had jointly formulated, defeated two Federal columns at Cross Keys and Port Republic, June 8–9. Lee brought Jackson's troops to Ashland, sixteen miles from Richmond, and, with the combined forces, took the offensive in what were destined to be the Seven Days' battles. At Mechanicsville on June 26, the slowness of a turning-movement that Lee entrusted to Jackson led A. P. Hill to a costly and futile attempt to storm Beaver Dam Creek; the next day at Gaines's Mill, Lee drove Fitz John Porter's corps from the north side of the Chickahominy River and forced McClellan to change his base to the James. The rearguard action at Savage Station on the 29th did little more than expedite and somewhat confuse the Federal retreat; on June 30 a mistake as to the line of the enemy's withdrawal and the non-arrival of two of the converging columns led to an indecisive battle at Frayser's Farm, where Lee had hoped to envelop and destroy McClellan; on July 1, at Malvern Hill, the inexperience of the staff prevented the massing of the whole army in a tangled terrain for a simultaneous attack on the strong Federal positions. Isolated attacks, though gallantly pressed, failed to dislodge McClellan, who withdrew that night unchallenged and took refuge under cover of his gunboats at Harrison's Landing. This campaign was the most important period in Lee's military education. Strategically sound in principle, though demanding too much of untrained officers, the campaign was tactically bad on the Southern side. It taught Lee the necessity of simpler methods and organization. It served its immediate purpose, however, in relieving the threat against Richmond, and it supplied a large part of his army with superior small-arms. Similarly it raised greatly the morale of the army and inspired confidence in Lee.

Quietly and quickly ridding himself of incompetent division commanders, Lee soon detached Jackson to the vicinity of Orange Court House to confront a new "Army of Virginia" under Maj.-Gen. John Pope. Lee had to watch both Pope and McClellan, not knowing which might strike first, but he carefully fed troops from the James to the Rapidan, and, at the first sure sign of the impending departure of McClellan to join Pope, he anticipated the actual Federal movement and soon confronted Pope with the greater part of his army. This was Lee's first display of skill in the difficult military art of troop-movement. Arriving at Gordonsville on Aug. 15, Lee determined on an immediate campaign of maneuver, in order to increase the distance between Pope and McClellan and to subsist his army in territory that otherwise would be occupied by the enemy. His initial plan of surprising Pope between the Rapidan and Rappahannock rivers was thwarted, but he crossed the Rapidan, shifted his line as far up the Rappahannock as possible, and then, boldly dividing his army, sent Jackson by roundabout roads to attack Pope's line of communication. Jackson chose to strike at Manassas Junction, Pope's advance base. Knowing that Jackson's move would force Pope to retreat at once, Lee followed Jackson's route with Longstreet's command and before noon on Aug. 29, when Jackson was fighting a defensive battle against part of the Union army, Lee concentrated his entire command in front of Pope. He encountered great unwillingness on the part of Maj.-Gen. James Longstreet [q.v.] to attack that afternoon, because Longstreet believed delay until the next morning would offer greater advantage. Lee held to the view that it was the duty of the commanding general to bring the forces together at the right moment on the chosen ground of action and to leave actual combat to the divisional and brigade commanders, and he usually contented himself with "suggestions" to competent officers. In this instance, he yielded to Longstreet's stubbornness and disclosed for the first time his one great weakness as field commander—his inability to work with unwilling tools. The general assault, thus delayed, was delivered on Aug. 30 and routed Pope in the battle of Second Manassas (Second Bull Run), but Aug. 31 was lost in reconcentrating the weary and scattered army, and a rainstorm at Chantilly (Ox Hill) on the afternoon of Sept. 1 kept Lee from overtaking his adversary.

Lee could not feed his army where it then stood. Neither could he attack the Washington fortifications, whither Pope had fled. A withdrawal would impair the morale of his army and raise that of the Federals. Accordingly, Lee determined to move into Maryland and to renew the campaign of maneuver there. Reaching Frederick on Sept. 7, he soon found that the Federals were not evacuating Harpers Ferry as he had anticipated they would be. His line of communications through the Shenandoah Valley lay close to that strongly garrisoned post, so he was forced to detach five divisions under Jackson to reduce it. After their departure, a false rumor

of a Federal advance on Hagerstown led him to direct Longstreet thither. He did so the more readily as he now planned to destroy the Baltimore & Ohio and then to advance on Harrisburg and cut the other main railway line that linked East and West. While Longstreet was on the road to Hagerstown, McClellan suddenly undertook a swift westward advance on Frederick, having received a copy of Lee's general order that had been carelessly dropped by a courier or staff-officer. Lee was caught with his forces badly divided. Hurrying Longstreet back on Sept. 14 to support the rearguard under D. H. Hill, he vainly attempted to check McClellan on South Mountain (Boonsboro) that day. Finding this impossible, he ordered a retreat to Virginia, but learning that Harpers Ferry would certainly be captured by Jackson the next day, he retreated to Sharpsburg. He miscalculated the time required for the troop-movements, his only serious blunder in logistics, and on Sept. 17, the bloodiest single day of the war, the slow arrival of troops from Harpers Ferry nearly cost him a serious defeat in the battle of Sharpsburg (Antietam). He held his ground on the 18th and then returned to Virginia, hoping soon to re-enter Maryland. Including the troops captured at Harpers Ferry, he had inflicted a loss of 27,-000 on his adversary during the Maryland expedition, but he had lost 13,000 himself, and his army was so badly shaken by straggling that he had to forego a further offensive.

Lee at once reorganized the army into two corps under Longstreet and Jackson, refitted it and restored its morale, and awaited the next move of the Army of the Potomac, which was now placed under command of Maj.-Gen. A. E. Burnside. Nearly two months passed. Then, on Nov. 14, Lee interpreted certain Federal troop-movements as indicating that Burnside was marching toward Fredericksburg. Lee would have preferred to fight on the North Anna, where he could have followed up a victory, but he could not afford to sacrifice the supplies of the lower Rappahannock valley, so he followed Burnside, accepted battle at Fredericksburg and on Dec. 13 repulsed repeated Federal assaults with bloody losses. He could not pursue the enemy because the Union artillery on the north side of the Rappahannock dominated the plain.

Food was scarce and forage almost unprocurable during the winter that followed. Most of the cavalry had to be sent to the rear, and two divisions of Longstreet's corps were dispatched to the south side of the James to meet a threatened advance against the railroad leading southward from Richmond. Lee hoped for the speedy return of these troops, but Longstreet did not take the offensive and dispersed his troops so widely, while collecting supplies in eastern North Carolina, that he could not reconcentrate quickly on receipt of orders to rejoin Lee. The Army of Northern Virginia had, therefore, been reduced to 62,500 men when, on Apr. 29, a new Federal commander, Maj.-Gen. Joseph Hooker [q.v.], launched a well-planned offensive across the Rappahannock above and below Fredericksburg. Lee was just recovering at the time from a severe illness, but he did not hesitate. Reasoning that the main attack would be west of the town, he left 9,000 troops under Early at Fredericksburg, marched with the rest to meet Hooker and, on May 1, found his adversary withdrawing to a strong line around Chancellorsville. Lee decided to turn the Federal position from the west and directed Jackson to undertake this movement. Jackson early the next morning countered with a proposal to employ all his infantry, 28,-000, with part of Stuart's cavalry, so as to roll up the whole right wing of the Federal army. Lee consented, and with 14,000 men faced the enemy's main force at Chancellorsville while Jackson marched beyond Hooker's right. Late in the day Jackson routed the XI Corps in one of the most spectacular operations of modern war. The next morning the two wings of the Army of Northern Virginia attacked the Federals, forced them into the country between Chancellorsville and the Rappahannock, and were about to deliver another assault when Lee was forced to detach troops to cope with Maj.-Gen. John Sedgwick, who had forced Early from the heights around Fredericksburg and was advancing on Lee's rear. Owing to the hesitant tactics of Maj.-Gen. Lafayette McLaws at Salem Church, it took Lee two days to dispose of Sedgwick and to reconcentrate in front of Hooker. When Lee prepared to attack again on the morning of May 6, he found that Hooker had retreated to the north bank of the Rappahannock. This, the battle of Chancellorsville, was the most brilliant of Lee's victories, but it was one of the greatest of Southern tragedies because it cost him the service of Jackson, who was wounded on May 2 and died May 10. Lee had worked in complete understanding with Jackson, whom he regarded as a perfect executive officer, and he never was able to replace him.

In the reorganization of the army that Jackson's death necessitated, Lee decided to increase the number of corps to three and to reduce their size, because he considered the old corps too large for one man to handle to the fullest advantage in a wooded country. Esteeming A. P. Hill the best division commander in the army, he named him to head the new III Corps, and for Jackson's II Corps he selected the latter's senior division commander, R. S. Ewell. This choice was dictated by sentiment, for Ewell had been associated with Jackson's most famous battles, but it placed one-third of the Army of Northern Virginia under an officer who had served only a few weeks with Lee and was unaccustomed to exercise the discretion that Lee always gave his corps commanders. The staff, of course, was reorganized at the same time, and many new officers were assigned to direct troops of whom they knew little. The result of all this was to create a new machinery of command for two-thirds of the army. Lee does not seem to have realized the dangers this change of command involved, but his decision to resume the offensive immediately and to carry the war into the enemy's country, before the new officers became familiar with their troops and their duties, must be accounted the major mistake of his entire career. It explains, more fully than anything else, the fatal lack of coördination at Gettysburg.

He was prompted to invade the North again for three reasons: first, to supply his army; secondly, to strengthen peace sentiment in the North by showing the futility of the effort to force the South into submission; and, thirdly, in the hope that he could compel Lincoln to detach troops from the far South and thereby relieve the pressure on Vicksburg. Leaving A. P. Hill with 20,000 to hold the line of the Rappahannock temporarily, he skilfully moved into the Shenandoah Valley and reëntered Maryland, with Harrisburg again his objective. On June 23 Stuart's fondness for raids around the enemy led him to exceed his orders and to separate the largest and most proficient part of the cavalry from the rest of the army at a time when Lee needed every mounted unit to watch Hooker, who was now between him and Stuart. Finding on June 28 that Hooker had crossed into Maryland on the 25th, Lee had to concentrate quickly his columns, which had been widely scattered for the collection of supplies. The advance of A. P. Hill discovered a force of unknown strength at Gettysburg on June 30. Ewell advanced promptly from the north to support him and the two, on July 1, won a stiff fight, capturing 5,000 men. Lee arrived during the afternoon and, in the language he usually employed in dealing with his corps commanders, suggested to Ewell that the advantage be pushed south of Gettysburg. In the absence of peremptory orders, Ewell delayed the attack and gave the Federals time in which to strengthen their forces on Cemetery Hill and

Culp's Hill. Lee's one chance of victory lay in striking before the Federals could concentrate all their force on the strong ground of Cemetery Ridge, but on the morning of July 2 he encountered an unexpected difficulty. Before the army had left Virginia, Longstreet had urged Lee to employ offensive strategy but defensive tactics in Pennsylvania, and he had persuaded himself that Lee had promised to do this. When he discovered that Lee was determined to attack Meade, who had now succeeded Hooker in command, Longstreet felt that Lee was courting ruin. All his pride of opinion asserted itself. He was chagrined and humiliated at the rejection of his plan, and if he did not deliberately delay in the hope of keeping Lee from what he believed would be a slaughter, he at least acted so slowly and unwillingly that Cemetery Ridge was heavily manned and its capture was almost impossible when the I Corps assaulted late in the afternoon of July 2. The movement was just successful enough to make a renewal of the attack the next morning a virtual necessity. Pickett's and Pettigrew's (Heth's) divisions charged with a valor worthy of the finest achievements of the army, but they were hurled back with dismal slaughter, and the battle was lost. Lee was forced to retreat the next day in order to reëstablish his line of communications. On the night of July 13–14 he crossed the Potomac to Virginia soil. Gettysburg was the great defeat of his military career. The caution of Ewell and the defective staff work on the two newly formed corps were responsible for some serious tactical blunders. The absence of Stuart's cavalry during the preliminaries of the battle, the strength of the Union position, and the obduracy of Longstreet explained the rest. Lee assumed full responsibility for all that had happened and sought to resign the command of the army. It was no mere gesture of humility, for however culpable Longstreet was for his behavior, Lee was to be blamed for not dealing effectively with that stubborn officer. Yet, for all of Longstreet's defects, Lee had no one in the army whom he felt justified in substituting for him. He was compelled to make the best of the personnel he had.

Despite his 20,000 casualties, Lee was anxious to resume the offensive after Gettysburg, but the detachment of two divisions of Longstreet's corps to Tennessee, the condition of the commissary, and the scarcity of replacements rendered this impossible. Only two abortive operations, one by him against Bristoe Station and one by Meade to Mine Run, occurred until May 4, 1864, when Grant crossed the Rapidan, headed for Richmond. Lee then had somewhat more than 60,-

000 men. Grant's force was almost precisely twice that. Grant's cavalry and artillery were better than they had ever been; the horses of the Army of Northern Virginia had been so close to starvation in the winter of 1863–64 that they could scarcely drag the guns or carry the men. The quartermasters' and commissary stores of the Army of the Potomac were ample and flawlessly organized; Lee's men had been subsisting on a daily ration of a pint of cornmeal and a quarter of a pound of bacon, and they had scarcely any equipment or supplies except their arms and ammunition. It was impossible from the outset, therefore, for Lee to assume the offensive against Grant on open ground where the artillery of the enemy could be used and the full Union strength be employed. He did not attempt to dispute the crossing of the Rapidan, but hurried forward to the Wilderness of Spotsylvania, in the hope of catching Grant on the move in that tangled terrain, the American counterpart of the Meuse-Argonne. On May 5 and 6 Lee repulsed Grant's attacks with heavy slaughter, and on the 6th was in the midst of a turning movement when the serious wounding of Longstreet threw the Confederate right into disorder. On May 7, Lee concluded that Grant was swinging southward, and by the dispatch of Longstreet's corps (now under R. H. Anderson) to Spotsylvania Court House, he blocked Grant's road to Richmond. Two weeks' fighting and maneuvering followed at Spotsylvania (May 8–21). Longstreet was *hors de combat*. A. P. Hill was ill and Ewell was scarcely able to keep the field. Lee had to give the closest attention to the tactical dispositions as well as to the strategy, but he constructed admirable field fortifications and beat off all Grant's assaults except that of May 12 on a salient in Ewell's front ("The Bloody Angle"). In that day's action Grant gained an early advantage because Lee, on mistaken reports from his scouts, had withdrawn the artillery supporting Edward Johnson's division; but a new line was drawn in rear of the salient and the enemy, on May 14, abandoned the captured position. Sensing on May 21 that Grant was starting another flank movement, Lee made a forced march to the North Anna and again confronted him when he arrived on May 23. The Army of Northern Virginia took up the strongest position it had yet occupied, diverted Grant's line of advance on Richmond, and effectively covered the Virginia Central railroad, though part of its track was temporarily torn up. Had Lee been able to strike either the Federal right, under Warren, or the left, under Hancock, immediately after the Union forces had crossed the river, he might have in-

flicted a severe defeat on one or the other of Grant's exposed wings; but after the Federals were entrenched, Lee's opportunity was lost. Moreover, he was stricken with a debilitating intestinal malady and before he recovered, Grant (May 27) had moved again by Lee's right, this time down the Pamunkey River. Lee marched swiftly, faced Grant on the Totopotomoy (May 28–30), and forced him to maneuver to the Confederate right for the fourth time. During the whole of this period, from the time he engaged Grant on May 4, Lee was constantly seeking an opportunity to catch Grant on the move, or to attack the Federals in detail, but he found no opening. At Cold Harbor, on June 3, Grant was repulsed with such heavy casualties that he abandoned his bludgeoning tactics. During the month that had then elapsed since Grant had crossed the Rapidan, his losses had been about 50,000, a number equal to approximately 90 per cent. of the strength of the infantry of Lee's army at the opening of the campaign. The record of Lee's losses, if ever filed, was destroyed in the evacuation of Richmond. The number was approximately half that of Grant's.

Beginning on the night of June 12–13, Grant withdrew from Cold Harbor, marched to Wilcox's Landing, and crossed the James River to destroy Lee's communications and to invest Richmond by way of Petersburg. Lee had anticipated such a move, but since the absence of his cavalry kept him from penetrating the screen Grant threw about the Army of the Potomac, and Beauregard on the south side of the river could not ascertain what part of Grant's army confronted him there, Lee was uncertain of the position of his adversary and therefore hesitated to uncover Richmond. He had been compelled to detach Breckinridge and later the II Corps (now Early's) to meet new threats in western Virginia and in the Shenandoah Valley, and for that reason, his ability to reënforce Beauregard was limited. He fed troops to the south side, however, as fast as he had assurance of a Federal concentration there and, with the help of Hoke's division, which Lee sent him promptly, Beauregard saved Petersburg. The investment of that city, which formally began on June 18, was essentially a campaign of attrition. With headquarters in or near the city, Lee had to defend a line of thirty miles, slowly lengthened to thirty-six. At the same time, he had to protect the railroads connecting Richmond with the South. He sent Early into Maryland in the hope that Grant would detach troops heavily to defend Washington, or else would be tempted to attack the strong lines in front of Petersburg. Early reached the outskirts of Washington but the diversion failed of its larger purpose. Lee's forces steadily declined through casualties and, after the winter began, through desertion, chiefly on the part of new conscripts. Every day brought starvation nearer; the exhaustion of the horse supply threatened to render the army immobile; Lee could only hold on by fortifying heavily and by using as a reserve the troops on the extreme right of the Petersburg front, where the lines of the opposing forces were not close together. The principal actions of the siege were the Crater, July 30, 1864, the battles of the Weldon railroad and Reams's Station, Aug. 19–25, 1864, and the capture of Fort Harrison, on the north side of the James, Sept. 29, 1864.

On Feb. 6, 1865, orders were issued designating Lee general-in-chief of all the Confederate armies, but the condition of his own command and the plight of operations elsewhere made it impossible for him to give more than a general strategic direction to the last-ditch battles of the exhausted Confederacy. In March the advance of Sherman's army into North Carolina made it certain that Lee would be overwhelmed if he remained at Petersburg. On the 25th he made a desperate attempt to divide the Federals by an assault on Fort Stedman, and when the repulse of this was followed by an extension of the Federal left and by a general assault on the Petersburg lines, he was forced to evacuate Petersburg and Richmond on the night of Apr. 2–3 and to begin a retreat toward the small army of Gen. Joseph E. Johnston in western North Carolina. Failure to receive supplies at Amelia Court House on Apr. 4 lost him a day and compelled him, when the Federals arrived in his front, to turn toward Lynchburg up the Southside railroad. On Apr. 6, his retreating line was struck at Sailor's Creek, and on the 9th, finding himself blocked by Sheridan, and almost surrounded at Appomattox Court House, he was forced to surrender to General Grant. Of the 35,000 troops with which he started from the Richmond-Petersburg line, only 7,800 remained with arms in their hands. When he appeared among his men after the surrender, mounted on his famous war horse, "Traveller," the veterans of the Army of Northern Virginia overwhelmed him with their regard and sympathy.

As a paroled prisoner of war, treated with great consideration by the Federal army, Lee returned to Richmond and remained there or in the vicinity until the autumn. He had no home, for "Arlington" had been sold in 1863 for nonpayment of taxes, but in September, having accepted the presidency of Washington College, he moved to Lexington, Va. He was profoundly interested in the education of the young men of the South, and, with the help of an enthusiastic faculty, he soon raised a discouraged college to a high level of scholarship and attendance, though it is not certain that all of the interesting educational innovations at the school originated with him. His supreme interest after the war was in restoring the economic, cultural, and political life of the South. Shunning all discussion of politics, and reading little about the war, though he at one time planned to write a history of the campaigns of his army, he set an example of obedience to civil authority. He applied for a pardon on June 13, 1865, and consistently urged his former soldiers to work hard, to keep the peace, and to accept the outcome of the war. Indicted for treason, he was never brought to trial. On his few lengthy journeys, especially on a tour of the South Atlantic seaboard for his health in the spring of 1870, he was welcomed with a measure of affection no other Southerner since Washington has received. His mail, which was immense, was crowded with offers of business proposals, all of which he rejected. In the midst of peaceful activities, he was stricken on Sept. 28 and died on Oct. 12, 1870, in Lexington, where he was buried. He probably had angina pectoris, and his final illness was due to some atherosclerotic process. The news of his death put every Southern community in mourning. Admiration for him, which had been almost universal in the South after 1862, found new expression in biographies, in monuments, and in countless memorial addresses. Washington College changed its name to Washington and Lee University in his honor. After sixty years, the affection and reverence of the South for him are, if anything, higher than in 1870. No American has ever had an influence on the people of the old Confederate states comparable to his. In all matters on which he expressed himself, he is still regarded as the final authority. In him the South still sees the embodiment of all its best ideals.

While Lee was distinguished as an educator, his place in American history is that of a notable Christian gentleman and a great soldier. He was confirmed in the Episcopal church in 1853, and the fundamentals of the Christian religion—humility, prayer, faith, and kindness—were his code of daily conduct. His equanimity was religious, rather than philosophical, and, though he was not a fatalist, he believed that God directed the daily affairs of man and ordered even man's adversities to his good. It was for this reason that he accepted defeat without repining. His unique relations with his soldiers, his affec-

tion for children, his dignified courtesy, and his love of animals are illustrated by a thousand anecdotes that are part of the spiritual treasury of Americans. His temper and patience seldom failed him. Self-control was second nature. His rare outbursts of wrath, usually attended by a reddening of the neck and a curious jerk of the head, were generally followed by some particularly gracious act to the object of his displeasure.

Both absolutely and in the light of the odds he faced in men and resources, Lee has been adjudged one of the greatest of modern soldiers and probably the most eminent American strategist. His achievements did not owe their brilliance to contrasted mediocrity, for most of his adversaries were able. Neither was he a great soldier because he had a great lieutenant in Jackson. Lee devised and Jackson executed. If Lee won fewer victories after Jackson's death it was not because he lacked strategical ability when acting alone but because his resources were diminished and because he found no successor to "Stonewall." His one great weakness was his inability to shape contrary minds to his purpose. Stubborn incompetents he courteously disregarded, but in dealing with Longstreet he thrice yielded to the latter's obstinacy and sought victory by assiduous pursuit of the second-best plan. Excessive consideration for the feelings of others explained this weakness. His strategical powers sprang from his extraordinary brain-power, his ability to put himself in the place of his opponents, his analysis of military intelligence, his masterful logistics, and his capacity for gauging accurately the offensive and defensive strength of given bodies of troops. These qualities and the long odds with which he had to contend in all his campaigns explain a daring that would have been rashness in a less capable leader. A desperate cause demanded desperate risks. His power to inspire confidence and to create morale was due to his record of victories, his inflexible justice, his attention to detail, his great aptitude for organization, his imperturbable presence in battle, his regard for his men, and the quality of his military material. He was less renowned as a tactician than as a strategist, because of his theory of the duties of a commanding general (outlined in the references to Second Manassas); but his facility in tactics increased steadily, especially in the employment of field fortification, which some consider his greatest contribution to the science of war. Where possible, he always reconnoitered in person, and with an unusual eye for terrain. He was wont to say that he had to see for himself. If he failed to follow up his successes, it was not for slowness or lack of dash but because the margin of superiority in combat was always so narrow that his army was usually exhausted after a victory.

Almost alone among the principal Confederate commanders he was consistently on good terms with the administration. Only on some three occasions, and these at times when President Davis was suffering to an unusual degree from the facial neuralgia that dogged him throughout the war, did he ever receive sharp messages from the chief executive. One of these he tore into bits; the others he ignored. The first reason for his success in dealing with as difficult a man as the Confederate President was his unfailing, deferential respect for constituted authority, a respect equaling that displayed by General Washington himself. The second reason was his willingness at all times to subordinate his operations to the general strategy of the administration and to explain his plans to the President. He knew Davis thoroughly, and in the urgent matter of reënforcements, which was always a subject of delicate and difficult correspondence, he usually got troops, if they were to be had, by stating frankly that if he did not receive them he might be compelled to retreat on Richmond. That never failed to arouse the President to action. Davis consulted him often regarding the enlistment and organization of the troops and about the strategy of campaigns on other fronts. Lee was prompt to answer and frank in his advice, but he was slow to impose his views on other commanders, especially on Gen. Joseph E. Johnston, whose capacities he perhaps over-valued. In nearly all his dispatches to the President, when operations elsewhere were under discussion, he explained that it was impossible to judge at a distance, when he did not know the special difficulties that had to be encountered. Consequently his influence on the "grand strategy" of the South was not great. To him, however, more than to any other military official, was due the enactment of the conscript laws.

[The major manuscript sources are as follows: Private papers, in the possession of the daughters of Capt. Robert E. Lee; engineering papers, Army Engineers' archives, Washington; educational papers, at West Point, and Washington and Lee University; military papers, War Department, Washington, and in the care of a committee of trustees for U. C. V., Richmond, Va.; field-telegrams on operations of June–Aug. 1864, Confederate Museum, Richmond, Va. His maps and military library are at the Virginia Military Institute, Lexington, Va. The greater part of his printed letters and dispatches appear in: *War of the Rebellion: Official Records* (Army); *Lee's Dispatches* (1915); J. W. Jones, *Personal Reminiscences, Anecdotes and Letters of Gen. Robert E. Lee* (1874); J. W. Jones, *Life and Letters of Robert Edward Lee* (1906); and the invaluable *Recollections and Letters of General Robert E. Lee, by his son Capt. Robert E. Lee* (2nd ed., 1924). Other important books on his life or campaigns are: E.

P. Alexander, *Military Memoirs of a Confederate* (1907); Gamaliel Bradford, *Lee the American* (1912); E. J. Lee, *Lee of Va., 1642–1892* (1895); A. L. Long, *Memoirs of Robert E. Lee* (1886); James Longstreet, *From Manassas to Appomattox* (1896); Sir Frederick Maurice, *Robert E. Lee, the Soldier* (1925); Sir Frederick Maurice, ed., *An Aide-de-Camp of Lee* (1927); Walter H. Taylor, *General Lee, His Campaigns in Virginia, 1861–65* (1906). To these may be added: *Memoirs of Lieut.-Gen. Scott* (1864); Jefferson Davis, *The Rise and Fall of the Confederate Government* (2 vols., 1881); *Battles and Leaders of the Civil War* (4 vols., 1887–88); Fitzhugh Lee, *General Lee* (1894); John Bigelow, Jr., *The Campaign of Chancellorsville* (1910). The best of the one-volume biographies, which number twenty or more, is H. A. White: *Robert E. Lee and the Southern Confederacy* (1897). The four-volume biography by the writer of this sketch will probably appear simultaneously with the publication of this work.]

D. S. F.

LEE, SAMUEL PHILLIPS (Feb. 13, 1812– June 5, 1897), naval officer, the son of Francis Lightfoot and Jane (Fitzgerald) Lee, was the grandson of Richard Henry Lee and the grandnephew of Francis Lightfoot Lee [*qq.v.*]. He was born at "Sully," Fairfax County, Va., and was appointed a midshipman in the United States navy on Nov. 22, 1825. After service on board the *Hornet* in the West Indies and on the *Delaware* and the *Java* in the Mediterranean, he was sent to the Pacific on the *Brandywine* but was later transferred to the *Vincennes* in 1834. From 1842 to 1855 he was chiefly employed in coast-survey duty. During the Mexican War he was in command of the coast-survey brig *Washington* and assisted in the capture of Tabasco on the east coast of Mexico. In 1851, in command of the *Dolphin,* he was sent to make deep-sea soundings, try currents, and search for shallow spots which had been reported by mariners. In performing this duty he cruised all over the Atlantic. His report was published by the direction of Congress and was of considerable assistance to Maury in his oceanographic work.

When news of the outbreak of the Civil War reached Lee, he was in charge of the *Vandalia* at the Cape of Good Hope, bound for the East Indies. He immediately returned without waiting for orders and was sent to the Charleston blockade. In 1862 he participated in the attack on New Orleans as commander of the *Oneida,* one of the three fast gunboats which were sent ahead to destroy the Confederate fleet above the forts. Lee drove off two rams that had attacked a Union ship, the *Varuna,* and received the surrender of Beverly Kennon, commander of the Confederate steamer *Governor Moore.* Later, in both passages of Vicksburg by the Union fleet under Farragut, the *Oneida* was second in line.

In September 1862, just after Lee had been made a captain, he was appointed an acting rear-admiral and ordered to command the North Atlantic blockading squadron off Virginia and North Carolina. He is credited with beginning the system of placing a cordon of ships far out at sea to intercept blockade runners who had escaped the ships nearer shore. As his territory included Wilmington, his prize money was considerable, and is estimated by Gideon Welles to have amounted to $150,000, the largest received by any officer. But in 1864, when the attack on Wilmington was contemplated, Welles displaced him because he did not consider him a fighting admiral or a man of prompt action. Lee was accordingly sent to command the Mississippi Squadron and did good work there on the Cumberland and Tennessee rivers in supporting Thomas against Hood and in preventing Hood from crossing the latter river at the most favorable point. After the war Lee served for a year as the head of the Signal Service, was made a rear-admiral in 1870, and commanded the North Atlantic Squadron from 1870 to 1872. He reached the retiring age in 1873 and spent the remaining years of his life in Washington, dying at Silver Spring, Md., of a stroke of paralysis. He was buried in Arlington. On Apr. 27, 1843, he had married Elizabeth, daughter of Francis P. Blair. A son (Francis Preston) Blair Lee, represented Maryland in the United States Senate from 1913 to 1917. Though never a popular hero, Lee seems to have been one of the most conscientious and efficient officers of his time.

[L. R. Hamersley, *The Records of Living Officers of the U. S. Navy and Marine Corps* (ed. 1890); Lee's *Report and Charts of the U. S. Brig Dolphin* (1854); *The Diary of Gideon Welles* (3 vols., 1911); *War of the Rebellion: Official Records* (*Navy*); E. J. Lee, *Lee of Va., 1642–1892* (1895); R. M. Thompson and Richard Wainwright, *Confidential Correspondence of Gustavus Vasa Fox, Assistant Secretary of the Navy* (2 vols., 1918–19); letter from Lee to Senator J. R. Doolittle in *Southern Hist. Asso. Pubs.*, Mar. 1905; *Army and Navy Jour.*, June 12, 1897, *Evening Star* (Washington), June 7, 1897.]   W. B. N.

LEE, STEPHEN DILL (Sept. 22, 1833–May 28, 1908), soldier and educator, at his appointment the youngest lieutenant-general in the Confederate army, was born at Charleston, S. C., the son of Thomas and Caroline (Allison) Lee, and a grandson of Thomas Lee [*q.v.*]. At seventeen he entered West Point, graduating in 1854 and being appointed second lieutenant in the 4th Artillery. After serving with his regiment on frontier duty in Texas, he was appointed first lieutenant in the fall of 1856 and during 1857 took part in the Seminole War as assistant adjutant-general of Florida. He was then appointed quartermaster of his regiment, continuing as such until the spring of 1861, during which time he saw frontier service in Kansas and Dakota.

His sympathies being with the South, he resigned from the United States Army in February 1861.

He was immediately appointed captain in the South Carolina Volunteers, and later recommissioned in the Confederate army, where his rise was not only rapid but accompanied by an unbroken series of official commendations for heroic conduct, gallantry, and technical accomplishments. As aide-de-camp to Beauregard, commanding at Charleston, S. C., he was one of the officers appointed to treat with Major Anderson, commanding Fort Sumter, prior to and following its bombardment by Confederate forces in April 1861. Following the fall of Sumter, Lee performed staff duties pertaining to the defenses of Charleston, and was appointed major of artillery in November 1861. In 1862 he was present at the battles of Seven Pines, Savage's Station, Malvern Hill, second Manassas, and Sharpsburg, being made in turn lieutenant-colonel, colonel, and brigadier-general. Except for a short period following the Seven Days' battles, he held artillery commands with distinction, particularly at Sharpsburg. His short term of command of the 4th Virginia Cavalry in July brought favorable notice. Following his appointment as brigadier-general, he was sent by President Davis to Vicksburg, Miss., where he commanded in various capacities in minor engagements during the winter of 1862–63, and participated in the repulse of Sherman at Chickasaw Bayou in December. His heroic conduct at Champion Hills, May 16, 1863, was followed by a stiff defense against the Federal forces which pierced his lines in a determined assault on May 22, but were cleared from the redoubts before dark with the loss of many men and some colors. Following the fall of Vicksburg, Lee was soon exchanged, promoted major-general, and given command of the cavalry in Mississippi.

In February 1864, he assumed command of all cavalry west of Alabama, and in March, with a small force, harassed the flanks and rear of the large force of Sherman advancing on Meridian, Miss., but was unable to stop it. In June he was appointed lieutenant-general, which appointment was later reconsidered and confirmed as temporary. The one battle under his command occurred at Tupelo, Miss., July 14, where, with a mixed force of infantry and cavalry of about 6,000 men he fought a drawn battle with the superior forces of Gen. A. J. Smith, which resulted in Smith's being forced to withdraw to Memphis. When, within a few days, Hood was put at the head of the Army of Tennessee, Lee took command of his infantry corps, leading the assault, July 28, on Ezra Church, Ga. He commanded this corps through the operations around Atlanta, and in the advance on Nashville, being severely wounded at the latter place, but refusing to give up command of his corps until a rear-guard was formed and in action. For a day at this time his was the only organized corps, and the only one commended by Hood. On Feb. 9, 1865, Lee married Regina, daughter of James Thomas and Regina (Blewett) Harrison of Columbus, Miss. He assumed command of his corps and surrendered with Johnston at High Point, N. C., Apr. 26, being paroled May 1.

His civilian career following the war was distinguished. After twelve years as a planter he entered public life, 1878, as a senator in the Mississippi legislature. In 1880 he was appointed the first president of the Mississippi Agricultural and Mechanical College, serving as such until 1899, when he resigned to accept appointment by President McKinley as a member of the commission for organizing Vicksburg Military Park. He was a member of the Mississippi constitutional convention of 1890. At the time of his death he was commander-in-chief of the United Confederate Veterans, in which organization he had long been prominent. He was the author of important articles on the Civil War, which appeared chiefly in the *Publications* of the Mississippi Historical Association, and contributed "The South Since the War" to *The Confederate Military History* (1899), edited by C. A. Evans. He died at Vicksburg.

[*War of the Rebellion: Official Records (Navy)*, vols. XII, XXIV–XXVI; *List of Staff Officers of the Confederate States Army* (1891); *Battles and Leaders of the Civil War* (1887–88), vols. I, III; M. F. Steele, *Am. Campaigns* (1909); *War of the Rebellion: Official Records (Army)*, 1 ser., I, V, XI (pts. 1–3), XII (pts. 2–3), XVII (pts. 1–2), XIX (pts. 1–2), XXIV (pts. 1, 3), XXX (pt. 4), XXXI (pt. 1), XXXII (pts. 1–3); Dabney Lipscomb, "Gen. Stephen D. Lee; His Life, Character, and Service," in the *Pubs. of the Miss. Hist. Soc.*, vol. X (1909); Dunbar Rowland, *Hist. of Miss., the Heart of the South* (1925), vols. I, II; G. W. Cullum, *Biog. Reg. Officers and Grads. U. S. Mil. Acad.* (3rd ed., 1891), vol. II; *Commercial Appeal* (Memphis), May 29, 1908.]   D. Y.

LEE, THOMAS (Dec. 1, 1769–Oct. 24, 1839), jurist and banker, was born in Charleston, S. C. His father was William Lee, a watchmaker, who as a captain in the South Carolina militia during the Revolution was exiled to St. Augustine in 1780 by the British. His mother was Anne, daughter of Jeremiah Theus [*q.v.*], the artist. Thomas attended the classical school of Thompson and Baldwin in Charleston, and after studying law under J. J. Pringle, was admitted to the bar about 1790. He made his first public appearance as an orator in 1789, at the Bastille celebration in Charleston; later he displayed a facil-

ity in French that enabled him to examine French witnesses without an interpreter. In 1791 he began his public service as associate justice or judge of the courts of sessions and of common pleas, and a few months later was elected solicitor for the southern circuit; in 1796 he was cashier of the lower house of the legislature, and in 1798, 1800, and 1802 he was its clerk; in 1804 he resigned as associate judge, but soon after was elected comptroller general, to which office he was repeatedly reëlected. He was presidential elector in 1816. He became president of the Bank of South Carolina in 1817, and six years later was appointed federal district judge for South Carolina; in both these offices he continued until his death. In politics Lee favored the principles of the Jeffersonian Republicans, but although he held public office for forty-five years, he showed too much independence ever to be rated a party man. During the nullification controversy he not only declined to contribute for the purchase of votes, but in a case involving the payment of duties under the tariff "in which it was intended to give a triumph to Nullification, by overriding the Act of Congress in the verdict of a jury" he "ruled out the defence, and thus defeated the project" (O'Neall, *post*, I, 85).

In 1817, when the pastor and certain members of the Congregational Church seceded and formed the Unitarian Church, he was chairman of the joint committee of ten that drew the articles of separation. He became a deacon, and one summer during the absence of the pastor he conducted the services. He was also identified with the rise of the temperance movement in Charleston, showing zeal without fanaticism. He was about to make a lecture tour in its interest through the upper districts of the state when he "closed his virtuous and useful life . . . after several days illness of country fever" (*Charleston Courier*, Oct. 25, 1839) and was buried in the Unitarian churchyard. The organizations with which he was identified voted formal mourning and published eulogistic tributes to his benevolence, business ability, oratorical powers, and judicial integrity (*Charleston Mercury*, Oct. 25, 28, 29, 1839). Lee is described as a man of "fine person, powerful voice, and elegant elocution" (O'Neall, *loc. cit*). He was married on Feb. 9, 1792, to Kezia, daughter of John Miles of Horse Savannah. He named her executrix of his will, suggesting that their five surviving sons dutifully counsel her. One of these sons, Thomas, became the father of Stephen Dill Lee [*q.v.*].

[Diary of Josiah Smith, Jr., 1780–81 (MS.), in S. C. Hist. Soc.; S. C. House Journals, 1791–1823; A. S. Salley, *Marriage Notices in S. C. Gazette* (1902); D. E. Huger Smith and A. S. Salley, Jr., *Register of St.*

Philip's Parish ... Charleston, S. C. (1927) ; *S. C. Hist. and Geneal. Mag.*, July 1920, p. 122, July 1923 ; Caroline Gilman, *Record of Inscriptions in the Cemetery and Building of the Unitarian ... Church, ... Charleston, S. C.* (1860) ; J. B. O'Neall, *Biog. Sketches of the Bench and Bar of S. C.* (1859), vol. I ; *Charleston Courier*, Oct. 25, 28, 29, 1839 ; Wills, 1839–45, Charleston ; epitaphs.]   A. K. G.

LEE, THOMAS SIM (Oct. 29, 1745–Nov. 9, 1819), governor of Maryland, the son of Thomas and Christiana (Sim) Lee, was born in Prince George's County, Md. He was the great-great-grandson of Richard Lee [*q.v.*] and the grandson of Philip Lee, who left Virginia to settle in Maryland in 1700. Thomas spent his early years on his father's estate and, on Oct. 27, 1771, married Mary Digges, the daughter of a wealthy Maryland landowner, a woman who was to earn distinction by her warm support of her husband's efforts in behalf of the Revolution and by mobilizing the women of Maryland for patriotic service. He began his political service in 1777 as a member of the provincial council, although he had seen military service as major of a battalion from his county. In November 1779, the legislature chose him to be governor. Unlike his predecessor, he entered upon his duties with little prestige, but his administration of difficult problems won him recognition as one of the Revolutionary leaders of his state. To his task, also, he brought unusually well-developed social talents, the exercise of which continued to add to his popularity throughout his life. When the Continental Army, weakened by hardships and desertions, was threatened with disintegration his first and most important care was furnishing troops and supplies to it. His encouragement enabled Maryland to respond to Washington's appeal for additional troops in 1780. Since such appeals for assistance were continuous throughout the remaining years of the war, his pen was constantly urging sacrifices in order to keep the state up to its requirements. As the trusted friend of Washington, he had information of the plan to trap Cornwallis at Yorktown so that, spurred by hope of victory, he strained every nerve to lend support. To him and to Maryland, it may be fairly claimed, was due much of the success of Greene, Williams, and Howard in the southern campaign.

Shortly after leaving the gubernatorial office in 1783, he was chosen a delegate to the Continental Congress, where he appeared during 1783 and 1784. Although he declined to serve in the federal convention of 1787, he consented to sit in the state convention which ratified the Constitution. In 1792, as presidential elector on the Federalist ticket, he voted for Washington for a second term. To him came the unusual honor of being recalled to the governorship after an interim of private life, when he was elected seventh governor of Maryland in 1792. In this period of service, the most important issues were the reorganization of the state militia and the aid of the federal government in crushing the Whiskey Insurrection in western Pennsylvania and Maryland. When he retired, in 1794, he established a winter home in Georgetown, near Washington, which he made a hospitable center for prominent Federalists. He declined two honors which his state would have thrust upon him : election to the United States Senate in 1794, and a third gubernatorial term, tendered him unanimously in 1798. He devoted the remainder of his life to improving his estate, "Needwood," a tract of fifteen hundred acres in Frederick County, on which he maintained two hundred slaves. Though a man of only respectable talents, his understanding and imagination rose to the challenge of a great crisis, while his social and friendly disposition won him respect and affection.

[H. E. Buchholz, *Governors of Md.* (1908) ; Folger McKinsey, *Hist. of Frederick County, Md.* (1910), vol. I ; M. P. Andrews, *Tercentenary Hist. of Md.* (1925), vols. I, IV ; J. T. Scharf, *Hist. of Md.* (1879), vol. II ; E. J. Lee, *Lee of Va.* (1895) ; *Am. and Commercial Daily Advertiser* (Baltimore), Nov. 18, 1819.]   E. L.

LEE, WILLIAM (Aug. 31, 1739–June 27, 1795), merchant, diplomat, a descendant of Richard Lee [*q.v.*], was the tenth child of Thomas Lee and his wife, Hannah Ludwell, and a brother of Richard Henry, Francis Lightfoot, and Arthur Lee [*qq.v.*]. He was born at the family seat, "Stratford," Westmoreland County, Va. Prior to 1766, when he was one of a group in Westmoreland County to adopt a vote of thanks to Lord Camden for his opposition to the Stamp Act and to subscribe for a portrait of that statesman, scarcely the vestige of a record exists concerning him. In 1768, accompanied by his brother Arthur, he went to London to engage in mercantile pursuits. There, Mar. 7, 1769, he was married to Hannah Philippa Ludwell, eldest daughter of Philip Ludwell of "Green Spring," and there, in 1770, we find him in partnership with the Dennys De Berdts (father and son) and Stephen Sayre [*q.v.*]. But he did not devote himself exclusively to business. Both he and his brother Arthur, as likewise Sayre, became deeply mersed in London politics, having thrown themselves enthusiastically into the movement of which John Wilkes was the leader. One outcome was that in 1773 William Lee and Sayre were elected sheriffs of London, and two years later Lee was chosen an alderman of the city, the only American who ever held that office.

Early in 1777 Lee was appointed by the secret committee of Congress to act jointly with Thomas Morris, sometime incumbent of the office, as commercial agent at Nantes, and in June he crossed over to France to enter upon his duties. At once he encountered a series of complications, not all of his own making, although he made some lively contributions of his own, chiefly the result of a distrust of two of the American commissioners, Franklin and Deane, a distrust sedulously fomented by Arthur Lee, the third commissioner. In short, William Lee and the commercial agency had become inextricably involved in the notorious Lee-Deane controversy. In the midst of this turmoil Congress, with characteristic ineptitude in foreign affairs, resolved to send representatives to other European courts, and in May 1777, chose William Lee to be commissioner to the courts of Berlin and Vienna. Neither of these courts was disposed to recognize the United States, and all of Lee's polite efforts through two years could not prevail upon them to change their minds. His one diplomatic accomplishment, though quite outside either of his assignments, was the negotiation with John De Neufville, an Amsterdam merchant, of a treaty of commerce between the United States and Holland. This proposed treaty, though never ratified by either party, possesses nevertheless an importance of its own (see the *American Historical Review,* April 1911, pp. 579ff.), in addition to having become the ostensible cause of war between England and Holland.

In June 1779, Lee and Izard were recalled, and in September following Arthur Lee was superseded. That William Lee's public career had been mostly a succession of failures is to be ascribed in part to defects of his own temperament, partly to circumstances beyond his control. The diplomatic missions would doubtless have proved abortive under any other person. For the next four years Lee remained abroad, making his residence at Brussels; but in September 1783, he returned to Virginia and retired to his estate at "Green Spring." His last years were saddened by almost total blindness.

[The principal printed sources for the life of Wm. Lee are: W. C. Ford, *Letters of Wm. Lee* (3 vols., 1891); Francis Wharton, *The Revolutionary Diplomatic Correspondence of the U. S.* (6 vols., 1889); "The Deane Papers," *N. Y. Hist. Soc. Colls.,* Publication Fund Series, vols. XIX–XXIII (1887–91); E. J. Lee, *Lee of Va., 1642–1892* (1895); and J. C. Ballagh, *The Letters of Richard Henry Lee* (2 vols., 1911–14). The principal manuscript sources are the Lee papers in the possession of the Virginia Historical Society, the University of Virginia, and the American Philosophical Society, and the Sparks MSS. at Harvard University.]   E. C. B.

LEE, WILLIAM GRANVILLE (Nov. 29, 1859–Nov. 2, 1929), labor leader, was born in Laprairie, Ill., the son of James W. Lee and Sylvesta Jane (Tracy) Lee. His father's family settled in Washington County, Ind., about 1790, and his mother's family near Zanesville, Ohio, some five years later. Following a grammar-school education at Bowen, Ill., he assisted his father, a carpenter and contractor, for a time. Railroad service early attracted him, however, and after doing student work on the Chicago, Burlington & Quincy, he became brakeman, in 1879, on the Atchison, Topeka & Sante Fé at Emporia, Kan. Transferred shortly to the Raton-New Mexico Division, he was promoted late in 1880 to conductor on the run between Lajunta, Colo., and Las Vegas, which position he held until 1884, when he accepted the office of deputy recorder of deeds for Ford County, Kan. Returning to railroad service four years later, he became brakeman and switchman on the Wabash and subsequently on the Missouri Pacific. On June 25, 1890, he joined the Brotherhood of Railroad Trainmen at Sedalia, Mo. Early in 1891 he secured a position as brakeman, and later as freight conductor, with the Union Pacific out of Kansas City, and promptly organized there a new lodge, which he served as master, chairman of the local committee, and member of the general committee for the Union Pacific. He became first vice-president (first vice grand master) of the Brotherhood of Railroad Trainmen on Aug. 1, 1895, was promoted to president on Jan. 1, 1909, and held that office continuously until July 1, 1928, when he was transferred to the position of general secretary and treasurer. Until 1899 his headquarters were at Peoria, Ill., but for the last thirty years of his life they were at Cleveland, Ohio. Obliged to meet many changes in conditions and in legal regulations during his long period of leadership, especially during the war and post-war years, he proved himself a shrewd, far-seeing, and energetic business executive. Under his administration the organization grew steadily in membership and secured great material benefits through collective bargains and standardized wages, through the general introduction of safety appliances, and through legislation which finally reduced the hours of railway workers to eight a day. In 1920 Lee's wisdom and courage were severely tested by a series of unauthorized strikes, and he showed himself an uncompromising upholder of the sanctity of contracts by expelling more than one-sixth of the organization's membership; in 1921 he was credited with having done more than any other man to avert the threatened nationwide strike of the railroad brotherhoods. His failure of reëlection to the presidency in 1928 was due primarily to his age and physical condition. In 1917 he was stricken with cancer, which recurred in 1923 and in 1927, perhaps as a result of his postponing a first operation in order to continue his fight for the Adamson law. Early in 1927, with his wife, Mary R. Rice, whom he had married in Chicago on Oct. 15, 1901, he sailed for a cruise on the Mediterranean. When he returned he was welcomed by a reception and dinner in New York. Later, his malady reappeared and he grew steadily worse until his death at his home in Lakewood, Cleveland. He was a Congregationalist, a Mason, and an anti-LaFollette Republican. His friendliness, sincerity, and undoubted integrity made him popular with opponents as well as with friends, and created public confidence in the Brotherhood of Railroad Trainmen as a great business organization ably and conservatively managed.

[Frequent references to Lee's work may be found in the file of *The Railroad Trainman*, and in the *N. Y. Times Index*; see also *Who's Who in America*, 1928–29; *Current Opinion*, May 1917, Sept. 1922. Information regarding certain facts has been furnished by his brother, J. C. Lee.]   H. S. W.

LEE, WILLIAM HENRY FITZHUGH (May 31, 1837–Oct. 15, 1891), Confederate soldier and congressman from Virginia, familiarly termed "Rooney" Lee to distinguish him from his first cousin, Gen. Fitzhugh Lee [*q.v.*], was born at Arlington, Va. He was the second son of Gen. Robert Edward Lee [*q.v.*] and Mary Ann Randolph (Custis) Lee, the great-granddaughter of Martha Washington by her first marriage. He was educated at Harvard where, if one may believe his classmate, Henry Adams, he showed "the Virginian habit of command" but was far from being an intellectual. Even before he left in 1857, he was, in the official language of Gen. Winfield Scott, "dying to enter the army." On Scott's recommendation he was appointed second lieutenant in the 6th Infantry and served under Col. Albert Sidney Johnston in the Mormon campaign. In 1859 he resigned his commission and became a farmer on his historic estate, the "White House," near Richmond, Va.

Upon the outbreak of hostilities in 1861, Lee, an ardent adherent of the Confederacy, organized a picked cavalry company. In May he was successively appointed captain and major of cavalry and in the West Virginia campaign served as chief of cavalry for General Loring. In the winter of 1861–62 he was ordered to Fredericksburg and was commissioned lieutenant-colonel and, shortly, colonel, of the 9th Virginia Cavalry. He

followed Stuart in all his subsequent campaigns from Yorktown to Richmond, riding with him in his first raid around McClellan's army. He fought at Second Manassas, and distinguishing himself in the rear-guard action at Turner's Pass, was unhorsed and left unconscious on the field. After making a brilliant record for bravery and leadership in Stuart's Chambersburg raid, in November 1862 he was appointed brigadier-general and commanded his brigade in the Chancellorsville, Fredericksburg, and Gettysburg campaigns. At Brandy Station, on June 9, 1863, he received a severe wound. Stuart, in his official report, deplored "the casualty which deprives us, for a short time only, it is hoped, of his valuable services." About two weeks later, while he was recuperating, he was captured and imprisoned. He was not exchanged until March 1864, when, at the age of twenty-seven, he was promoted major-general of cavalry. During the ensuing campaign of 1864, he opposed the Wilson raid in June and commanded the cavalry at Globe Tavern in August. He commanded the Confederate right at Five Forks, and during the last desperate fighting of the Appomattox campaign was second in command of the cavalry.

Had not Lee been the son of Robert E. Lee, who felt a modest hesitancy in promoting him, and had he not been so long imprisoned, his military ability probably would have won even greater recognition. He was not of the dashing type of cavalry officer, but he was a scientific fighter. Unfailingly cool, never playing for personal reputation, he held the perfect confidence and respect of his men. After the war he again became a farmer, was president of the Virginia State Agricultural Society, and served one term of four years (1875–79) in the state Senate. Elected three times to Congress, he served there from 1887 until his death in 1891. Six feet two inches in height and of powerful frame, he had pulled the stroke oar on the Harvard crew. Gen. Horace Porter, his classmate, told Lee's son that "Rooney Lee was the best oarsman I have ever seen, Fitz Lee the best horseman." But "Rooney" Lee was also a noted rider, and if possible was in the saddle every day. He was a courteous, genial gentleman and was regarded with affection by many Virginians. He was twice married: first, in 1859, to Charlotte Wickham; and in 1867 to Mary Tabb Bolling, who survived him. He died at "Ravensworth," near Alexandria, Va.

[R. E. Lee, *Recollections and Letters of Gen. Robert E. Lee* (1904); E. J. Lee, *Lee of Va., 1642–1892* (1895); *Confed. Mil. Hist.* (1899), III, 625–27; memorial addresses in Congress printed as *House Miscellaneous Doc. 320*, 52 Cong., 1 Sess.; *War of the Re-*

bellion: *Official Records* (*Army*); *Report of the Class of 1858 of Harvard Coll.* (1898); J. W. Thomason, *Jeb Stuart* (1930); the *Times-Dispatch* (Richmond), Oct. 16, 1891; information as to certain facts from members of the Lee family.]   R. D. M.

LEE, WILLIAM LITTLE (Feb. 8, 1821– May 28, 1857), jurist, son of Stephen and Mary (Little) Lee, was born at Sandy Hill, Washington County, N. Y. He graduated at Norwich University in 1842, studied in the Harvard law school, and began the practice of law in Troy, N. Y. Indications of tuberculosis determined him to seek a more favorable climate, and in February 1846 he sailed from Newburyport in the brig *Henry* to begin life anew in the Oregon country. After rounding Cape Horn, the *Henry* touched at Honolulu on Oct. 12, 1846, after a tempestuous voyage, said to be the slowest on record, and was laid up for extensive repairs. The government of Hawaii had just passed from absolute despotism to limited monarchy, the first constitution having been granted in 1840, and the machinery of administration was being laboriously set up. There were as yet few residents competent to fill public office. It was only two years since the first lawyer had arrived in the kingdom, to be immediately appointed attorney-general, and he was still the only representative of his profession. Lee's legal training brought him to the notice of the authorities, and he made so favorable an impression that before the *Henry's* repairs were completed he was invited to remain in Hawaii as head of the judicial system. An act reorganizing the courts was to be considered at the next session of the legislature, and pending its passage Lee was appointed as one of the judges for the island of Oahu. In 1847 he became chief justice of the newly created superior court of law and equity, which for practical purposes was the highest court in the kingdom, although the old supreme court consisting of the king and certain chiefs continued a nominal existence until 1852. He was also appointed to the privy council, of which he at once became one of the most influential members. He took a leading part in the action of the council which resulted in the "Great Mahele" of 1848, whereby feudal tenures were abolished and individual ownership of land was established. On request of the legislature he drafted a penal code which was enacted in 1850 and is the basis of Hawaiian criminal laws to this day. In 1851 he was elected a member of the House of Representatives, a position not then forbidden to judges, and served as speaker. The new constitution adopted in 1852 was drafted by a commission of which he was the ruling spirit, and upon its adoption he was appointed chief justice of

what was now the supreme court in name as well as fact. A great epidemic of smallpox swept the islands in 1853. Lee worked to exhaustion, assisting in the care of the sick, and his own health was never restored. That he might secure medical advice, he accepted appointment in 1855 as minister to the United States, but returned to Honolulu before his death. He was one of the little group of statesmen who were the real creators of the Hawaiian constitutional monarchy; few of them were so influential as he, and none other was so universally trusted. In 1849 he was married on shipboard in Honolulu harbor to Catherine E. Newton of Albany, N. Y., following a romantic courtship which had begun before he left Troy. After his death, she married Edward Livingston Youmans, editor of *Popular Science Monthly*.

[Article by T. M. Spaulding, in the *Honolulu Mercury*, Mar. 1930; obituaries in the *Polynesian* (Honolulu), May 30, 1857, and the *Pacific Commercial Advertiser* (Honolulu), June 11, 1857, the latter abridged in W. A. Ellis, *Norwich Univ., 1819–1911* (1911), II, 347; S. C. Damon's funeral sermon, published as *A Tribute to the Memory of Hon. William L. Lee* (1857); documents in the Hawaiian Archives in Honolulu.]   T. M. S.

LEEDS, DANIEL (1652–Sept. 28, 1720), surveyor, almanac maker, author, was born in England, probably in Nottinghamshire, and emigrated to America with his father, William, some time in the third quarter of the seventeenth century. The family may have settled first on Long Island; later they went to Shrewsbury, N. J. In 1677 Daniel Leeds removed from Shrewsbury to Burlington, and soon became a prominent figure in that town's development. He was appointed surveyor general of the Province of West Jersey in 1682, and was elected to the Assembly the same year. In 1702 he was appointed to Lord Cornbury's council, serving until 1708. As surveyor general, he made the first authorized map of Burlington, "The Streets and Lots of Land Laid in the Town of Burlington" (1696). He was also an almanac maker of note. His first almanac was issued in Philadelphia from the press of William Bradford, 1663–1752 [*q.v.*], under the title, *An Almanac for the Year of the Christian Account, 1687, Particularly Respecting the Meridian and Latitude of Burlington, but May Indifferently Serve All Places Adjacent.* The following year Bradford published a religious dissertation by Leeds entitled *The Temple of Wisdom for the Little World: In Two Parts,* etc. (1688). His second almanac, that for the year 1688, was suppressed by the Philadelphia Quarterly Meeting, because "in imitation of the Almanacs published in England, Daniel had added some light, foolish and unsavoury paragraphs, which gave great uneasiness and offence to Friends of Philadelphia" (Kite, *post*, p. 13). Bradford, the printer, was ordered by the Meeting to bring in all unsold copies of the offending almanac, and they were destroyed; although the Meeting, quite fairly, paid the printer for them.

Although he wrote a letter of apology to the Meeting after this episode, Leeds shortly withdrew from the Society of Friends, and consorted with Bradford and George Keith [*q.v.*], who had become opponents of Quakerism. Henceforth he wrote numerous pamphlets, rather recklessly accusing the founder of the Society, George Fox, of forgeries, and William Penn, of covering up the evidence of them. His pamphlets of this character, printed by Bradford, who removed to New York in 1693, include: *News of a Trumpet Sounding in the Wilderness* (1697); *A Trumpet Sounded out of the Wilderness of America* (1699); *The Rebuker Rebuked* (1703); *The Great Mistery of Fox-Craft Discovered* (1705), and *The Second Part of the Mystry of Fox-Craft* (1705). For his attacks upon the heads of Quakerdom, Leeds became a target for Quaker pamphlets. In 1700 Caleb Pusey published *Satan's Harbinger Encountered, His False News of a Trumpet Detected,* and in 1702, *Daniel Leeds Justly Rebuked for Abusing William Penn and his Foly and Fals-Hoods in His Two Printed Chalenges to Caleb Pusey*. The following year he appended "Remarks on Daniel Leeds Abusive Almanac for 1703" to his *Proteus Ecclesiasticus, or George Keith Varied in Fundamentals.* Pusey characterized Leeds as "a perverter of our Friends words," and a false citer in divers respects.

On the title-pages of his earliest almanacs Leeds described himself as a "Student of Agriculture." He passed the greater part of his life in Burlington, N. J., where he died. He was married four times: first, before he left England; second, Feb. 21, 1681, to Ann Stacy, who bore him a child and died; third, early in 1682, to Dorothy Young, who became the mother of several children; and fourth, sometime between 1700 and 1705, to a widow, Jane, *née* Revell. One of his sons, Titan Leeds (1699–1738), who computed the tables for the *American Almanac* from 1714 to 1746, is remembered as the victim of one of Benjamin Franklin's practical jokes. In his first almanac, 1733, "Poor Richard" predicted the death, "on Oct. 17, 1733, 3 hr. 29 m., P. M.," of "his good friend and fellow-student, Mr. Titan Leeds," and the next year, despite Leeds's published protest, insisted: "There is the strongest probability that my dear friend is no more," because "Mr. Leeds was too well bred to use any

man so indecently and so scurrilously" as "Poor Richard" had been used in Leeds's protest. The controversy between them went on for several years. (See P. L. Ford, *"The Sayings of Poor Richard,"* 1890.) Another son of Daniel Leeds, Felix (1687–1744), was also an almanac maker, computing almanacs for the years 1727–30.

[While no complete collection of Leeds's almanacs and pamphlets is known to exist, there are copies of his Philadelphia almanacs for 1687, 1688, and 1693; and of his New York almanacs for 1694, 1699, 1705, 1711, and 1713 in public libraries in those cities. *The Second Part of the Mystry of Fox-Craft* was reprinted in the *Mag. of Hist., Extra No. 62* (1917), and *The Great Mistery of Fox-Craft,* in *Mag. of Hist., Extra No. 96* (1923). See also Clara Louise Humeston, *Leeds: A New Jersey Family* (1905); *Memoirs of the Hist. Soc. of Pa.,* I (1826), 105; Isaiah Thomas, *The Hist. of Printing in America* (2nd ed., 2 vols., 1874); Nathan Kite, "Antiquarian Researches," in *The Friend* (Phila.), Oct. 7, 1843; M. C. Tyler, *A Hist. of Am. Lit.* (1878), vol. II; E. M. Woodward and J. F. Hageman, *Hist. of Burlington and Mercer Counties, N. J.* (1883); Joseph Smith, *Descriptive Cat. of Friends' Books* (2 vols., 1867), and *Bibliotheca Anti-Quakeriana* (1873).]

J. J.

LEEDS, JOHN (May 18, 1705–March 1790), mathematician and astronomer, was born at Bay Hundred, Talbot County, Md. He was the only child of Edward and Ruth (Ball) Leeds, both Quakers. His family was of English origin, his great-grandfather, Timothy Leeds, having come to Virginia in 1607. John's grandfather, William, removed to Maryland about 1648. John Leeds was probably self-educated and seems to have spent his entire life in Talbot County. He married Rachel, daughter of William and Elizabeth Harrison, Feb. 14, 1726, at the Choptank Meeting House, Tred Avon Parish. They had three daughters, one of them the mother of John Leeds Bozman [*q.v.*], the historian. Leeds entered public office in 1734 as one of the commissioners and justices of the peace for Talbot County. In 1738 he became county clerk, an office which he held until 1777, when he either resigned or was removed because he refused to take the oath of allegiance to the new state government.

When in 1760 Lord Baltimore signed an agreement with Thomas and Richard Penn providing for a joint commission from Maryland and Pennsylvania to mark off the long-disputed boundary between the two colonies, Governor Sharpe named Leeds as surveyor or "assistant" to the Maryland group. In 1762 he was made a regular member of the commission. Fever and ague contracted while working in the swamps, lack of proper surveying instruments, and the frequent threat of Indian attacks discouraged the commissioners and decided them, in 1763, to employ Mason and Dixon, two professional surveyors, to run the line. They completed the survey in 1767, and the final report of the commission was made the next year. Leeds's account shows that he worked 177 days at a guinea a day. In the letters of Governor Sharpe to the Proprietor he is always referred to as "the best mathematician in the province."

In June 1769, "having no other instruments . . . but a pocket watch and a reflecting telescope about twenty inches long, of Sterrup's make," Leeds observed the transit of Venus, obtaining results important enough to be published in the *Philosophical Transactions . . . for the Year 1769* (1770) of the Royal Society of London. His article shows that he was a careful reader of that early scientific journal. From April to October 1766 he served as treasurer of the Eastern Shore, and in October was appointed a justice of the Provincial Court. Partly in recognition of his services on the boundary commission, he was also appointed naval officer of Pocomoke in the same month, and shortly afterward was made surveyor general of Maryland. All of these offices, along with his county clerkship, he appears to have occupied until his Loyalist tendencies forced him out. He was frequently threatened during the Revolution, but was never harmed. Sometime after the war he was again appointed surveyor general and continued in that office until his death in 1790 at Wade's Point. To the end of his life he believed that anarchy would sooner or later follow the separation from England.

[R. H. Spencer, *Thomas Family of Talbot County, Md., and Allied Families* (1914); Oswald Tilghman, *Hist. of Talbot County, Md.* (2 vols., 1915); *Easton Ledger,* Apr. 10, 1884; "Correspondence of Governor Horatio Sharpe," in *Archives of Md.,* vols. IX (1890) and XIV (1895); "The Calvert Papers," *Md. Hist. Soc. Fund Pubs.,* nos. 28, 34, 35 (1889, 1894, 1899); Maryland Commission Book, No. 82, Tred Avon Parish Records (transcripts), and Calvert Papers, Abstracts, vols. XVII and XXI, all MSS. in Md. Hist. Soc.]
M. E. F.

LEES, ANN [See Lee, Ann, 1736–1784].

LEESER, ISAAC (Dec. 12, 1806–Feb. 1, 1868), rabbi, editor, author, was born at Neuenkirchen, in the province of Westphalia, Prussia. His father, Uri, a merchant in comfortable circumstances, died when the boy was fourteen. His mother had died when he was eight, and he was brought up by his grandmother. He attended the Gymnasium of Münster, and besides the courses there, studied Bible and Talmud privately with Abraham Sutro, chief rabbi of Münster and Mark. Sutro was an ardent traditionalist and the author of a book, *Milhamot Adonai* ("The Wars of the Lord"), directed against the Jewish Reform Movement then beginning in Germany.

In 1824, Leeser emigrated to Richmond, Va., where an uncle, Zalma Rehine, desired to adopt him. Although he worked in his uncle's store, he was also, from the beginning, a volunteer teacher of the Jewish religion; and when but twenty-two years of age published two articles in the *Richmond Whig,* replying to an attack on the Jews which had appeared in the *London Quarterly Review.* These articles attracted the attention of Jews beyond Richmond, and in 1829 the oldest Jewish congregation in Philadelphia, Mikveh Israel, which at that time required the services of a minister, elected him to the post. Thereafter he was prodigiously active. He conducted the synagogue service; he preached; he taught privately, maintaining a Jewish free school in his own home until the Jewish community in Philadelphia created a Society for this purpose. He was the inspiring force in various charitable organizations in Philadelphia. He founded *The Occident and American Jewish Advocate,* and edited it from 1843 until his death; he wrote and translated many books of instruction for Jewish schools, among them *The Jews and the Mosaic Law* (1833), a *Hebrew Spelling Book* (1838), a *Catechism for Jewish Children* (n.d.), and a *Catechism for Younger Children* (1839). He edited and translated the Prayer Book for the Portuguese Jews (1837) and for the German Jews (1848); he translated the Bible into English (1853); he edited with Joseph Jaquett a complete Hebrew Bible; he translated into English a book of Jewish travels in Palestine and Joseph Schwartz's *Descriptive Geography and Brief Historical Sketch of Palestine,* and printed no less than ten volumes of his own sermons. These publications required the printing of many thousands of pages of Hebrew, and he saw the books through the press, incidentally making Philadelphia the center of Hebrew printing in America at that time. He traveled all over the country, but especially in the South and West, speaking in synagogues, organizing them, and dedicating them. The culmination of his career was the establishment of a Jewish college, Maimonides College, of whose faculty he was the head for the last year of his life.

He remained minister of Mikveh Israel Congregation until 1850, when he retired as a result of difficulties which had developed between him and the managers, principally due to his continued refusal to sign any form of contract. In 1857, a group formed a new congregation called Beth El Emeth, in order to give him a center from which to carry on his work. During this entire period he was the stanch advocate of traditional views and the protagonist of the traditional school of Jewish doctrine and practice. Although very popular, and more widely known in his time than any other Jewish minister in America, he had some unfortunate traits which impaired his influence. In the lively letters written by Rebecca Gratz [q.v.] it appears that he was very sensitive with regard to his appearance, and this sensitiveness increased after he had a severe attack of smallpox in 1834. His warm friend, Moses A. Dropsie [q.v.], wrote of him shortly after his death: "He had an indomitable will. He was impatient and impetuous, frank and outspoken, never learned the art of disguising his thoughts." He was a pioneer in the organization of Jewish life in America, there being no phase of it in which he did not create some organized effort. Many of his creations have lived, and those that have not have been replaced by stronger institutions planned along lines similar to those that he laid down.

[Henry Englander, "Isaac Leeser," in *Central Conf. of Am. Rabbis, Year-Book*, vol. XXVIII (1918); *The Occident*, Mar. 1868; Mayer Sulzberger, in *Jewish Encyc.*; H. S. Morais, *Eminent Israelites of the Nineteenth Century* (1880), and *The Jews of Philadelphia* (1894); Peter Wiernik, *Hist. of the Jews in America* (1931); M. A. Dropsie, *Panegyric on the Life, Character and Services of Isaac Leeser* (1868), published in the appendix to *The Occident*, vol. XXV (1868); *Letters of Rebecca Gratz* (1929), ed. by David Philipson; *Jewish Exponent*, Mar. 14, 1913, Feb. 8, 1918.]
C. A.

LEETE, WILLIAM (c. 1613–Apr. 16, 1683), colonial governor, was born at Dodington, Huntingtonshire, England, the son of John and Anna (Shute) Leete, formerly of Cambridge. He was educated as a lawyer and employed as registrar in the Bishop's Court at Cambridge. Here he witnessed the persecution of the Puritans and was so touched by their fortitude that he inquired into their faith and was converted. To escape persecution, he joined the Rev. Henry Whitfield's company which sailed for America in May 1639. Before leaving England, Leete had married Anna Payne, the daughter of the Rector of Southoe (1638). During the voyage (June 1) he, together with other colonists, signed a Plantation Covenant. Upon their arrival at New Haven, they purchased land from the Indians and founded a new town, later called Guilford. Leete was chosen one of the six trustees of this land and also one of the four who were to act as a temporary government. He was town secretary or clerk from 1639 until his resignation in 1662. He was also one of the "seven pillars" who organized the Guilford church in 1643. With the establishment of a church, Guilford entered the "Combination" at New Haven and sent Leete and Desborough to represent it there, and for several years thereafter he served as one of its deputies. He was advanced to the magistracy in 1651, an office which he continued to

hold until his death. He was sent on various missions to the neighboring colonies and represented the New Haven Colony in the New England Confederation from 1655 to 1664. He was deputy governor of the New Haven Colony from 1658 to 1661 and governor from 1661 to 1664. As such, he connived at the escape of the regicides, Goffe and Whalley [qq.v.], who had sought refuge in the Colony. It was largely through his moderating influence that the New Haven Colony peaceably submitted, in 1664, to the Connecticut charter of 1662. As a reward, the Connecticut General Court chose Leete as one of its magistrates, and elected him assistant every year until 1669, when he was promoted to deputy governor of the Connecticut Colony. After serving seven years in that office and upon the death of Governor Winthrop, he was elected governor seven years in succession (1676–82) and was in office when he died. In addition, he frequently represented Connecticut in the New England Confederation, and was chosen president of the commissioners in 1673 and 1678. He died at Hartford and was buried in the cemetery of the First Church there. After the death of his first wife he was married to Sarah Rutherford, and after her death, to Mary Newman Street. He had a number of children, all by his first wife.

[Joseph Leete, *The Family of Leete* (2nd ed., renewed and enlarged, London, 1906); R. D. Smith, *Hist. of Guilford, Conn.* (1877); B. C. Steiner, *A Hist. of the Plantation of Menunkatuck* (1897); Leete's letters to John Winthrop, Jr., in *Mass. Hist. Soc. Colls.*, 4 ser. VII (1865); J. H. Trumbull, *The Public Records of the Colony of Connecticut, 1665–78* (1852); *Records of the Colony and Plantation of New Haven* (1857) and *Records of the Colony or Jurisdiction of New Haven* (1858); Ezra Stiles, *The Hist. of Three of the Judges of King Charles I* (1794); Cotton Mather, *Magnalia Christi Americana* (1702), bk. II, p. 29.]
J. H. R.

LEFEVERE, PETER PAUL (Apr. 30, 1804–Mar. 4, 1869), Roman Catholic missionary and bishop, was born in Roulers, Belgium, the son of Charles Lefevere, a farmer in easy circumstances, and his wife, Albertine-Angeline Muylle. He made his preliminary studies for the priesthood with the Lazarists in Paris, but before beginning his theological course, volunteered for service in the American missions. Destined for the diocese of St. Louis, he came to the United States in 1828, completed his studies in the diocesan seminary, and was ordained Nov. 20, 1831. Although stationed for a few months at New Madrid, Mo., his career began with his appointment to the Salt River mission in the fall of 1832. Making his headquarters in this tiny settlement in Ralls County, Mo., he ministered to the Catholic immigrant population of northeastern Missouri, southern Iowa, and western

Illinois. For some years he was the only priest on the Mississippi from St. Louis to Dubuque. Despite his utter poverty, and the appalling hardships encountered in the care of this untouched mission field, he knew no respite until his health became seriously impaired in 1840. In that year he returned to Belgium to recuperate, sailing from New York with his superior, Bishop Rosati, who was on his way to Rome. The prelate arrived while the Roman authorities were dealing with Bishop Rese's proffered resignation from the See of Detroit. They decided to appoint a coadjutor bishop to administer the diocese, and through the influence of Bishop Rosati, Father Lefevere was chosen. As titular bishop of Zela, and administrator of Detroit, he was consecrated in St. John's Church, Philadelphia, Nov. 21, 1841, by Bishop Francis Kenrick, assisted by Bishops England and Hughes.

When he entered upon his charge, he had seventeen priests, two parishes in Detroit, and sixteen more in the diocese. At his death there were eighty-eight priests, eleven parishes in the city, and 161 organized Catholic groups in the state. He was fitted to cope with this phenomenal expansion by his unlimited capacity for work, his firmness in governing, and his bent for order and discipline. The temporalities of the diocese, left in a precarious condition by his predecessor, were placed on a secure basis. He convened two diocesan synods to establish the polity which had been lacking. To supply his urgent need of priests, he became associated with Bishop Spalding of Louisville in the founding of the American College at Louvain. Its first three rectors were priests from the diocese of Detroit. In his efforts to build up a Catholic school system, he fostered the development of a diocesan community, the Sisters of the Immaculate Heart of Mary, and introduced into his diocese the Ladies of the Sacred Heart, the Sisters of Notre Dame, and the Christian Brothers. He conducted a vigorous but unsuccessful campaign in 1852–53 to obtain for his schools a proportionate share of the public funds devoted to education. To supply the lack of charitable institutions in Detroit, the Sisters of Charity were brought in, and with his help founded a hospital, an orphanage, and an asylum for the insane. He was deeply interested in the Indian population of his diocese, and strove to provide it with schools and missionaries. Personally, the Bishop was simple and unaffected in demeanor, frugal in his habits, austere in his mode of life. In protest against the drunkenness which he noticed in Detroit on his arrival, he publicly took the total-abstinence pledge. Every day at a fixed hour he could be found in his confessional. He died of erysipelas in St. Mary's Hospital in Detroit, and lies buried under the altar of the church of St. Peter and St. Paul, which he built and used as his cathedral.

[Sources include J. E. Rothensteiner, *Hist. of the Archdiocese of St. Louis* (2 vols., 1928); R. H. Clarke, *Lives of the Deceased Bishops . . . of the United States* (3 vols., 1888); *Cath. Encyc.*, IV, 759; *Detroit Free Press*, Mar. 5, 1869; other local newspaper references, and material in the diocesan archives. Lefevere's name is variously spelled in secondary accounts, but signatures in the diocesan archives testify that he himself used the spelling here given.]
G. W. P.

LEFFEL, JAMES (Apr. 19, 1806–June 11, 1866), manufacturer, inventor, was born in Botetourt County, Va., and when nine months old was taken by his parents to the Ohio country, where they settled. During his childhood and youth he experienced all of the characteristic hardships borne by pioneer families, enjoying only an occasional bit of schooling. Early in life he displayed a natural bent for mechanics, particularly in metals, and shortly after coming of age, he left his home and settled in Springfield, Ohio, then but a hamlet, hoping to engage wholly in the work he most enjoyed. He first designed, built, and operated for a number of years a waterpower sawmill just outside of Springfield on the Mad River. Foreseeing the needs of the growing town, he established an iron foundry, the first in that vicinity. It was put into operation in January 1840, and within six years its business had grown to such proportions that Leffel was compelled to erect a second and larger one. For the first few years a general foundry business only was conducted. Believing that he could improve his waterwheel, he experimented for many years, patenting his various ideas as they were perfected. The first of these waterwheels was patented May 21, 1845, and so superior was it to the regular overshot or undershot wheel that in 1846, in company with one Richards, he established and operated by water power the first cotton-mill and machine-shop in Springfield. The business of manufacturing waterwheels, however, was not lucrative, and he turned his attention to designing other and more salable foundry products. He perfected, and on Dec. 10, 1850, patented a lever jack, and on Feb. 24, 1852, two types of cooking-stoves. Subsequently he reorganized his foundry business under the name of Leffel, Cook & Blakeney, for the manufacture of his lever jack, and his "Buckeye" and "Double Oven" stoves. He then returned to his waterwheel experiments and after devoting fully ten years to the work, finally perfected the double turbine wheel. This was patented Jan. 14, 1862 (patent reissued Oct.

11, 1864), and proved to be an important step in the development of the waterwheel. For the manufacture of this new product and of an improved lever jack of his own invention patented Nov. 15, 1864, he organized a stock company known as James Leffel & Company. Hardly was this business under way, however, when Leffel died without any of the reward which his products soon reaped. His chief interest outside of his business was the breeding of fine poultry and the exhibiting of his best specimens at county fairs. On July 4, 1830, he married Mary A. Croft of Ohio and at his death, in Springfield, he was survived by his widow and two sons.

[*Hist. of Clark County, Ohio* (1881); B. F. Prince, *A Standard Hist. of Springfield and Clark County, Ohio,* vol. I (1922); Patent Office records, 1850, 1852, 1864.]

C. W. M.

LEFFERTS, GEORGE MOREWOOD (Feb. 24, 1846–Sept. 21, 1920), surgeon, laryngologist, was born in Brooklyn, the son of Marshall [*q.v.*] and Mary (Allen) Lefferts. In his fondness for discipline, his punctuality, his fastidiousness in personal attire, and other kindred qualities, he seems to have absorbed much of the military spirit of his father, who was colonel of New York's 7th Regiment at the time of the Civil War. Though he had a crippled leg, the son was naturally energetic and active, and became a proficient rider. He received his medical degree from the College of Physicians and Surgeons in 1870, and served as interne at Bellevue and St. Luke's. Attracted by the new specialty of laryngology, he then went abroad for study in the throat clinics of Europe. After attending clinics in London and Paris he went to Vienna, where he studied under two of the pioneers, Stoerk and Von Schrötter. So much was the former, Professor Karl Stoerk of the University of Vienna, impressed with his zeal and ability that he made him his chief of clinic, 1871–73, and at the completion of his term gave him a flattering certificate of service. This was a very unusual honor for a young alien.

Returning to New York in 1873, Lefferts began practice, specializing in diseases of the throat and nose. He was immediately appointed one of the laryngologists to Demilt Dispensary, sometimes styled the original school for postgraduate instruction in the United States, and in the same year was a cofounder of the New York Laryngological Society, later the Laryngological Section of the Academy of Medicine. In 1874 he was chiefly instrumental in establishing a throat clinic at the New York Eye and Ear Infirmary. In 1875, for the *New York Medical Journal,* he began an abstract department for laryngology and related subjects which was taken over in 1880 by the new *Archives of Laryngology,* which he had helped to found. In 1878 he became a cofounder of the American Laryngological Association, which he served as president in 1882.

Shortly after his return in 1873 from his European study, he began to teach his specialty at his alma mater, and in 1876 was made clinical professor there, retaining his chair until 1904, when he was given emeritus status. As a teacher he was unsurpassed and far in advance of his time. A man of large private means, he spared no expense in providing an abundance of wall charts, plates, models, and instruments. Himself a draftsman who excelled as a blackboard artist, he supervised the preparation of all exhibits. His lectures were scrupulously revised each year, and he circulated printed synopses of various kinds among his students. He was especially wedded to the idea of individual instruction, and divided his class into small groups. He is said to have disappointed his class but once in thirty years' service. His publications were few; his most pretentious work was *A Pharmacopœia for the Treatment of the Larynx, Pharynx and Nasal Passages* (2nd edition, revised and enlarged, 1884). He was married, June 11, 1891, to Annie Cuyler Van Vechten. In 1910 he gave up his extensive practice and retired to his estate at Katonah, N. Y. He died ten years later of angina pectoris.

[D. B. Delavan, *George Morewood Lefferts; A Sketch of His Life and Work* (1921), repr. in *Annals of Otology, Rhinology and Laryngology,* Mar. 1924; *Who's Who in America,* 1920–21; *Medic. Record,* Oct. 2, 1920; John Shrady, *The Coll. of Physicians and Surgeons, N. Y., . . . A Hist.* (n.d.), vol. I; *N. Y. Times,* Sept. 23, 1920; *Laryngoscope,* Aug. 1921.]

E. P.

LEFFERTS, MARSHALL (Jan. 15, 1821–July 3, 1876), engineer, builder of telegraph lines, was born in Bedford, which later became a part of Brooklyn, N. Y., the son of Leffert and Amelia Ann (Cozine) Lefferts. His father was a descendant of Leffert Pieterse who came with his father, Pieter Janse Hoogwout (or Van Haughwout), from Holland to New Amsterdam in 1660 and settled on Long Island. The next generation adopted Lefferts as a surname. Marshall had only such schooling as was available to farmers' sons in that period, although living within the bounds of what eventually became Greater New York. At fifteen he was a clerk in a hardware store. For three years he was on the staff of engineers engaged in the survey of Brooklyn. He was also employed in laying out Greenwood Cemetery, but left engineering to enter an importing house, in which he soon became a partner.

Because his firm dealt extensively in zinc wire and other commodities used in the erection of telegraph lines, he interested himself in such operations and in 1849 was president of the New York & New England and the New York State telegraph companies, which constructed lines operating on the Bain system from New York City to Boston and Buffalo. After the consolidation of the Morse and Bain interests, however, he withdrew from line management for ten years and engaged in the manufacture of iron and in perfecting the process for galvanizing that metal. By 1860 he was back in telegraph construction work, planning lines for the automatic system, and was made electrical engineer for the American Telegraph Company. His work at this time was still largely experimental, for comparatively few scientific investigations had been made in this field since the invention of the magnetic telegraph. The practical men in charge of construction had to depend on their own resourcefulness for ways and means to achieve results. Most of the makeshift devices that Lefferts employed were of course superseded within a few years; his was the trail-blazing of the pioneer—often rough and incomplete, but necessary in its day. He was the first to introduce instruments for the detection of electric faults and the first to reduce resistance of relays to common standards. As executive manager for the American Telegraph Company he built up an efficient organization, his unfailing good humor helping to make him successful in dealing with subordinates.

The Civil War put a period to Lefferts' construction activities. He was colonel of the New York 7th Regiment, a unit that had unusual prestige. It attracted the notice of the whole country when its services were offered to the government at Washington in April 1861, since it was thought significant that a body of men including so many citizens of wealth and high social position in New York should rally to the support of the Union. The regiment's service was of short duration, however, and its colonel had little opportunity to prove his military prowess. After the war, on the merging of the American Telegraph Company with the Western Union, he was put in charge of a bureau for collecting and disseminating commercial news. In 1871 he resigned his connection with the Western Union and became president and general manager of the Gold & Stock Telegraph Company. For several years, also, he was consulting engineer of the Atlantic Cable Company. He died while on his way to Philadelphia with his comrades of the 7th Regiment Veteran Corps to take part in the observance of the centennial anniversary of the Declaration of Independence. His wife, Mary Allen, whom he married June 4, 1845, with five sons and two daughters, survived him. One of his sons was George Morewood Lefferts [q.v.].

[T. G. Bergen, *Geneal. of the Lefferts Family, 1650–1878* (1878); L. M. Haughwout, "The Lefferts-Haughwout Family," *N. Y. Geneal. and Biog. Record*, Jan. 1902; James Parton and others, *Sketches of Men of Progress* (1870–71); Emmons Clark, *Hist. of the Seventh Regiment of N. Y. 1806–1889* (1890); A. P. Eastlake, "The Great Monopoly," in *Lippincott's Mag.*, Oct. 1870; *Telegrapher*, July 8, 1876; *N. Y. Times*, July 4, 1876.]   W. B. S.

LEFFLER, ISAAC (Nov. 25, 1788–Mar. 8, 1866), Virginia congressman, Iowa lawyer and legislator, brother of Shepherd Leffler [q.v.], was born on a plantation called "Silvia's Plain," in Washington County, Pa., where his grandfather, Jacob Leffler, had settled in 1774. He was the son of a second Jacob Leffler and Jane (Smith) Leffler. After studying law, he was admitted to the bar and entered upon the practice of his profession at Wheeling, Va. (now W. Va.). In 1817 he was elected to the Virginia legislature, and served during the years 1817–19, 1823–27, 1832–33. In 1827 he was elected as a member of the state board of public works. He was a representative of Virginia in the Twentieth Congress, 1827–29, but was an unsuccessful candidate for reëlection. In 1835, he removed to what is now Burlington, Iowa, but which was at that time a small settlement on the outskirts of the Territory of Michigan. Here on Apr. 15, 1835, he was admitted to the practice of law in the territorial courts. When the Territory of Michigan was divided in 1836, Isaac Leffler was elected to the legislature of the newly created Territory of Wisconsin. Reëlected for the following session, he was chosen speaker of the House. In 1836 he was the unsuccessful Whig candidate for the office of territorial delegate to Congress. He was among the first to see the importance of organizing the Iowa country into a separate territory, and on Sept. 16, 1837, was president of a meeting in Burlington at which resolutions were adopted calling for a convention to consider this subject. He also presided at the convention, which was held at Burlington Nov. 6–8, 1837, and was perhaps the most important convention in the Iowa country prior to the establishment of the Territory. In July 1838, the Territory of Iowa was created, and in 1841 Leffler was elected a member of the territorial House of Representatives to succeed his brother Shepherd, who had been elected to the territorial Council. Isaac Leffler had been recommended to President Van Buren by Daniel Webster, then secretary of state, for appointment as one of the associate justices of Iowa Territory, but did not receive the appointment. In 1843, however, he was appointed by President Tyler as United States marshal for the district of Iowa, and served until removed by President Polk on Dec. 29, 1845. At this time he resumed the practice of law at Burlington; four years later he declined appointment as register of the land office at Stillwater, Mitchell County, Iowa. In 1852 President Fillmore appointed him receiver of public moneys for the Chariton Land District of Iowa, but the following year he was removed from the office by President Pierce. Leffler was married twice: to Rebecca Forman in November 1814, and after her death, to Lethenia Mitchell in 1832. He was a man of pleasing social qualities, amiable, kind, and hospitable. In personal appearance he is said to have resembled President John Tyler. He died at Chariton, Lucas County, Iowa, and was buried in Aspen Grove Cemetery, Burlington.

[*The Hist. of Des Moines County, Iowa* (1879); *Biog. Dir. Am. Cong.* (1928); *Iowa Jour. of Hist. and Politics*, Jan. 1908, July 1911, Oct. 1922; *The Wis. Almanac and Ann. Reg.*, 1857; E. H. Stiles, *Recollections and Sketches of Notable Lawyers and Public Men of Early Iowa* (1916); L. G. Tyler, *Encyc. of Va. Biog.* (1915), vol. II; H. E. Bromwell, "Leffler" (typescript, 1920), in Lib. of Cong.]   B.E.M.

LEFFLER, SHEPHERD (Apr. 24, 1811–Sept. 7, 1879), Iowa legislator and congressman, son of Jacob and Jane (Smith) Leffler and brother of Isaac Leffler [*q.v.*], was born at "Silvia's Plain," Washington County, Pa., where his grandfather had settled a generation earlier. His early life was that of a farm boy. He attended Jefferson College at Canonsburg, Pa., graduating in 1833, studied law, and began the practice of his profession in Wheeling, Va. (now W. Va.). Deciding to seek his fortune in the West, he migrated in the spring of 1835 to what is now Burlington, Iowa. His father had preceded him to Burlington by a few weeks, and his brother Isaac also took up his residence at this place. The Leffler brothers soon became prominent in the affairs of Iowa Territory. In 1839 Shepherd Leffler was elected to the territorial House of Representatives, and in 1841, to the territorial Council; he served continuously in one house or the other of the legislature from 1839 till the admission of Iowa as a state in 1846. In public speeches and by private influence he resisted the removal of the capital from Burlington to Iowa City, but without success. He was selected as a delegate from Des Moines County to the first constitutional convention in Iowa, held at Iowa City in 1844. Although as presiding officer of

this convention he was influential in the formation of the new constitution, when Congress altered the proposed constitution by changing the boundaries of the new state so that it would be cut off from the Missouri River on the west, Leffler and other prominent Democrats broke with the party leaders and joined the Whigs in opposing its adoption. Owing in no small measure to the opposition of this group, statehood on the terms offered by Congress was rejected by the voters. Leffler also served as a member of the convention of 1846, in which a constitution was framed with the boundaries of Iowa set forth as they are today. This constitution was approved by the people of Iowa and adopted by Congress. In the first state election, Leffler was chosen one of the first two Congressmen from Iowa. He was in Washington on Dec. 28, 1846, the day that the new state was admitted; and on the following day he took his oath of office. He represented Iowa in the Twenty-ninth, Thirtieth, and Thirty-first congresses, but was defeated for reëlection in 1850 by Bernhart Henn. Upon his retirement from office, Leffler engaged in agricultural pursuits near Burlington, in real-estate operations, and in the practice of law. In 1856 he made another unsuccessful campaign for Congress. Thereafter he withdrew as far as possible from the turmoil of political strife and practically abandoned his law practice, indulging his taste for the more quiet life of the farm. In 1875 he was persuaded to make the race for governor against Samuel J. Kirkwood [*q.v.*], who had served as chief executive of Iowa during the Civil War. Leffler made a remarkable campaign but was unable to overcome the Republican majority in the state. The remaining four years of his life he spent as a country squire, undisturbed by the trend of politics. He was a good neighbor and a man of great popularity in his community. Of impressive appearance and winning manners, he made many friends. In 1840 he had married Elizabeth Parrott, and their domestic life was very happy. He died in his sixty-ninth year and was buried in Aspen Grove Cemetery, Burlington.

[*Biog. Rev. of Des Moines County, Iowa* (1905); *Hist. of Des Moines County, Iowa, and Its People* (1915), I, 396; *Iowa Official Reg.*, 1929–30; E. H. Stiles, *Recollections and Sketches of Notable Lawyers and Public Men of Early Iowa* (1916); *Biog. and Hist. Cat. of Washington and Jefferson Coll.* (1902); H. E. Bromwell, *The Bromwell Geneal.* (copr. 1910), and "Leffler" (typescript, 1920), in Lib. of Cong.; *Biog. Dir. Am. Cong.* (1928); *Dubuque Herald* and *Burlington Hawk-Eye*, Sept. 9, 1879.]   B.E.M.

LEFFMANN, HENRY (Sept. 9, 1847–Dec. 25, 1930), chemist, was born in Philadelphia, Pa. In speaking of his ancestors he once humorously said: "In these days of genetics and eugenics, it is worth while to show that a mongrel may have some merit" (LaWall, *post*, p. 113). His father, Henry Leffmann of Hamburg, Germany, was of Russian Jewish stock; his mother, Sarah Ann Paul of Doylestown, Bucks County, Pa., was a Hicksite Friend, of Welsh extraction. He was educated in the public schools, completing the four-year course at the Central High School in Philadelphia but failing to receive the degree because of illness in his last year. He was subsequently (1865) awarded the degree of A.M. (*honoris causa*). He graduated in medicine from the Jefferson Medical College in 1869, received the degree of Ph.D. from the Wagner Free Institute of Science in 1874, and that of D.D.S. from the Pennsylvania College of Dental Surgery in 1884.

Immediately after graduation from the Jefferson Medical College he began to teach chemistry there and at Central High School. He also taught toxicology in Jefferson Medical College for several years. Subsequently he became professor of chemistry in the Pennsylvania College of Dental Surgery, and in the Wagner Free Institute of Science. With the last-named institution he was actively connected for a half century. From 1888 to 1916 he occupied the chair of chemistry at the Woman's Medical College of Pennsylvania, becoming emeritus professor after his retirement from active work. At the time of his death he was lecturer on research in the Philadelphia College of Pharmacy and Science. He was an inspiring teacher, demanding industry, accuracy, and enthusiasm on the part of his students, imbuing them with the love of science and the hatred of sham, hypocrisy, and carelessness in research work. His humor, his personal charm, his encyclopedic memory, and his ability as a raconteur made him a brilliant conversationalist, and he was much in demand as a lecturer on various topics.

His contributions to chemical literature were extensive, comprising nearly five hundred papers, pamphlets, and books. *Elements of Chemistry,* issued in 1881, was followed a little later by a *Compend of Chemistry* (1882), which passed through five editions. Two books written in collaboration with William Beam, *The Examination of Water* (1889), and *Analysis of Milk and Milk Products* (1893), have gone through a number of editions; *Select Methods in Food Analysis* (1901), also in association with Beam, was favorably received and widely used. As a medical and scientific expert, testifying in courts, Leffmann was unsurpassed, and he was a master in the field of medical and legal juris-

prudence. He held a number of official positions, serving as chemist to the coroner of Philadelphia, 1875–80; chemist to the coroner and the district attorney of Philadelphia, 1885–97; and in other capacities. He was port physician of Philadelphia from 1884 to 1887, and again in 1891–92. His delightful book, *Under the Yellow Flag* (1896), is the story of this phase of his work.

He was a member of many professional and scientific organizations, served as president of the Engineers' Club of Philadelphia for one term, and in 1930 was elected to honorary membership in the Franklin Institute "in recognition of valuable services to science and research, in teaching, as former Port Physician of the City of Philadelphia, and as a discriminating but good-tempered critic." For many years he was an active member of the Society of Ethical Culture of Philadelphia. Of special interest were the Sunday evening lectures which he gave from time to time. The first of these was on "Charles Dickens' Solution of the Problem of Poverty," and some of the others were: "Primitive Man and His Work"; "The Bible and Evolution"; "The Real Thomas Paine." The last mentioned was published in 1922. Other publications of Leffmann's, outside his professional field, were *About Dickens* (1908) and *The States-Rights Fetish* (1913). He was a many-sided humanitarian, "tolerant, friendly, familiar with art, music, literature, history, science, religion and ethics" (Griffith, *post*, p. 119). Death came to him on Christmas Day, in his eighty-fourth year, after a brief illness.

On Nov. 29, 1876, he had married Fannie Frank. They had no children. Leffmann lived quietly and economically, and his testamentary benefactions emphasize his interest in science. He left generous bequests to the Wagner Free Institute of Science, in which he had established, after the death of his wife, "The Fannie Frank Leffmann Memorial Lectureship" for lectures on scientific subjects and on subjects in American colonial history. He also left trust funds for the Jefferson Medical College and the Philadelphia College of Pharmacy and Science to be used for scientific research.

[*Outline Autobiography of Henry Leffmann of Phila., with a Reference Index of Contributions to Science and Literature* (1905); papers by C. H. LaWall, Ivor Griffith, S. Solis-Cohen, Martha Tracy, and others in *Am. Jour. Pharmacy,* Mar. 1931 (Leffmann Memorial Number); *Jour. Franklin Inst.,* Feb. 1931; *Who's Who in America,* 1930–31; *Phila. Inquirer,* Dec. 26, 1930; personal acquaintance.]   W. K.

LEFLORE, GREENWOOD (June 3, 1800–Aug. 31, 1865), Choctaw chieftain, Mississippi planter, was born near the present site of the old state capitol in Jackson, Miss. He was the son of Louis LaFleur, a French-Canadian who lived among the Choctaw Indians as agent and trader, and his wife Rebecca Cravat, who was of French and Indian blood. Later, Louis LaFleur kept an inn on the Natchez Trace. Major John Donly, who handled mail along the Trace, took Greenwood, when he was about twelve years old, to his home near Nashville, Tenn. There the boy attended school for some years, and won Rosa Donly as his wife. After her death he married Elizabeth Cody (or Coody), a Cherokee, the niece of Chief Ross. His third marriage was to Priscilla James Donly, a younger sister of his first wife. There were two children of the first marriage and one of the third. In his twenties he became a chief of the Choctaws and in this capacity so vigorously encouraged education, Christianity, and law-making that the white people of Mississippi began to fear that the tribe was becoming too firmly rooted in the state. As a remedial measure the legislature, in 1830, prohibited any chieftain from executing tribal laws. Leflore appealed to the government at Washington, which, to avoid trouble, opened negotiations for the westward removal of the Choctaws. By the treaty of Dancing Rabbit Creek (signed Sept. 15, 1830; proclaimed Feb. 24, 1831), the Choctaws sold all that remained of their Mississippi lands. Rewards were allotted to the chiefs, and 640 acres were provided for each head of a family electing to remain in Mississippi and become a citizen of the United States. The treaty displeased the Choctaws, and the federal agents unduly hurried their departure. Leflore's inability to detain them, in addition to his large responsibility for the ratification of the treaty, destroyed his influence over the tribe. He therefore separated from it, remained in Mississippi, and became a citizen of the United States. In 1841–44 he was a member of the Mississippi Senate.

His rise in the economic system of the white man was remarkable. Dwelling at first in a log cabin a few miles from the city that now bears his first name, he prospered so that in 1854 he moved into a stately mansion, "Malmaison," which he began to furnish by spending $10,000 for Louis XIV furniture for a single room. His domain came to comprise 15,000 acres in Mississippi, on which were 400 slaves, and he had a part interest in 60,000 acres in Texas. Becoming dissatisfied with the way his cotton was handled at the point where it was loaded on the Yazoo River boats, he built a small town, Point Leflore, and constructed a $75,000 turnpike to divert plantation business to his town. During the Civil War his various enterprises languished and his Texas lands were lost. He had deplored secession, and remained loyal to the Union until his death at the close of the war. In accordance with his last request, his body was wrapped in the flag of the United States and was buried near his home.

[See J. F. H. Claiborne, *Miss. as a Province, Territory and State* (1880); *Pubs. Miss. Hist. Soc.*, vol. VII (1903); Dunbar Rowland, *Miss.* (1907), vol. II; *Laws of Miss.*, 1830; Florence R. Ray, *Greenwood Leflore* (pamphlet, privately printed, 1927); Robt. Lowry and W. H. McCardle, *A Hist. of Miss.* (1891), pp. 450–52; *Trans. Ala. Hist. Soc.*, vol. III (1899); *Am. State Papers, Indian Affairs*, vol. II (1834); H. B. Cushman, *Hist. of the Choctaw* (1899), pp. 400–05. A number of Leflore's letters and papers are in the possession of his great-grand-daughter, Miss Florence R. Ray, Memphis, Tenn.]   C.S.S.

LEGARÉ, HUGH SWINTON (Jan. 2, 1797–June 20, 1843), lawyer, attorney-general under President Tyler, was born in Charleston, S. C., of Huguenot descent. His parents were Solomon Legaré and his wife Mary Swinton of South Carolina, daughter of Hugh and Susannah (Splatt) Swinton. Solomon Legaré died soon after his son's birth, and the entire care of the family rested upon his widow, a woman of rare nobility and strength of character. At the age of five the son was poisoned by an inoculation with smallpox, and after a severe and protracted illness recovered slowly, though with permanently crippled limbs. This infirmity cut him off from all boyish sports and centered his attention upon intellectual pursuits. It also produced, or at least intensified, a shrinking and highly sensitive disposition. After receiving his early education from his mother, he studied at several private schools, and then for eighteen months attended the high school which later became the College of Charleston, under Mitchell King, with whom he later studied law. He spent a year under Dr. Moses Waddel at Willington, and entered the sophomore class at South Carolina College when he was fourteen. Here he was a recluse, giving three years to hard study and wide reading. He was graduated in 1814 at the head of a large class. After three years' study of law, he went to Europe in 1818, and, after a brief stay in Paris to perfect his knowledge of French, proceeded to Edinburgh, where he studied Roman law under Irving and amused himself by studying natural philosophy, mathematics, and chemistry. He returned to South Carolina in 1820 and, taking charge of the family plantation on John's Island, which had been badly managed, began to raise sea-island cotton. In the same year he was elected to the lower house of the legislature and was reëlected the next year but defeated in 1822.

The plantation was now sufficiently restored to allow him to leave, and in 1821 he moved to Charleston, where he began to practise but with almost no success. In 1824 he was sent to the legislature from Charleston and, reëlected annually, served six years. When the *Southern Review* was established in 1828, he became associated with Stephen Elliott [*q.v.*] as editor. He was also its chief contributor until it suspended, in 1832, after running through eight volumes. He was later a contributor to the *New-York Review*.

During his legislative career, Legaré was a firm believer in state's rights and a bitter opponent of the protective system, but when the issue of nullification arose he joined the Union party and fought against Calhoun's "South Carolina Exposition" in 1828. In 1830 he was elected by his political opponents to succeed James L. Petigru as attorney-general of the state and at last had an opportunity to display his legal learning and power. Arguing a case before the Supreme Court of the United States, he attracted the favorable attention of Edward Livingston, then secretary of state, and by him was offered the post of chargé d'affaires in Belgium (1832). Legaré saw in this appointment a chance to escape from the clamor and, to him, unbearable heat of the nullification controversy and also an opportunity for further study of the civil law. Accepting gratefully, he spent four years in Europe where, with light official duties at Brussels, he was able not only to study Roman and civil law under Savigny, but to learn German and Dutch. He returned to America in 1836 and was at once elected to Congress, taking his seat at the special session of 1837, called to meet the financial crisis. He took an active part in the debates, with increasing reputation, but like his friend Preston opposed the independent treasury, and this lost him reëlection. He returned to his profession and quickly built up a large practice. Identifying himself with the Whig party, he was active in the campaign of 1840, being particularly interested in the success of John Tyler, his close personal friend. When Harrison's cabinet resigned, Tyler, in September 1841, made him attorney-general. He served with distinction. In the cabinet his wide learning and his knowledge of international law made him a valuable adviser. In the technical side of his position he was no less useful. He rendered 150 opinions on a wide variety of subjects and argued a number of cases before the Supreme Court (16 *Peters*, 174–578), where his legal learning attracted admiration. When Webster resigned as secretary of state, Tyler made Legaré secretary *ad interim*. His health was failing, however, and shock caused by the deaths of his mother and sister had weakened him seriously. He accompanied Tyler to the unveiling of the Bunker Hill monument, was attacked by a chronic disease which afflicted him, and died after an illness of four days.

Those who penetrated his shell of reserve found Legaré a man of great charm. His manner was gracious and he was noted as a conversationalist who, in spite of all his learning, lacked any touch of pedantry. Gifted with a superb voice, through determined effort he became an orator of power. He was inclined to vehemence, but there was in his smooth speech little of the artificiality characteristic of American oratory of that day.

[*Writings of Hugh Swinton Legaré* (2 vols., 1845–46), ed., with a memoir, by his sister, Mary S. L. Bullen; W. C. Preston, *Eulogy on Hugh Swinton Legaré* (1843); B. J. Ramage, in *Sewanee Rev.*, Jan., Apr. 1902, reviewed and corrected in *S. C. Hist. and Geneal. Mag.*, Apr., July 1902; *Official Opinions of the Attorneys General of the United States*, vol. IV (1852); *Jour. of the Legislature of S. C.*, 1820–21, 1824–30; L. G. Tyler, *The Letters and Times of the Tylers*, vol. II (1885); *Southern Lit. Messenger*, Sept. 1843; *Southern. Quart. Rev.*, Oct. 1843; *Daily Atlas* (Boston), June 21, 1843.]
                             J. G. deR. H.

LeGENDRE, CHARLES WILLIAM (Aug. 26, 1830–Sept. 1, 1899), soldier and diplomat, was the son of Jean François and Aricie Louise Marie Gertrude (Wable) LeGendre. Born at Ouillins, France, he was educated at the University of Paris. He married, Oct. 31, 1854, at Brussels, Clara Victoria Mulock, daughter of William and Marie Guilbert Mulock, residents of New York. He thereafter emigrated to the United States and became a naturalized citizen. He helped recruit the 51st New York Volunteer Infantry, and on Oct. 29, 1861, was commissioned a major of that regiment; on Sept. 20, 1862, he was promoted to lieutenant-colonel, and on Mar. 14, 1863, to colonel. At the capture of New Bern, N. C., Mar. 14, 1862, he was cited for displaying "most conspicuous courage until he fell wounded," a ball carrying away part of his jaw. In the second battle of the Wilderness, May 6, 1864, he was again severely wounded, a ball carrying away the bridge of his nose and his left eye. By reason of such disability he was honorably discharged, Oct. 4, 1864, and the brevet title of brigadier-general, for meritorious service, was given him to date from Mar. 13, 1865.

On July 13, 1866, he was appointed American consul at Amoy, China. His district included the island of Formosa, and in March 1867, the wreck of the American bark *Rover* on the southern coast of that island gave him an opportunity to render distinguished service. Fourteen members of the crew landed on the island but were massacred by the aborigines. LeGendre requested of the Chinese authorities that a search for possible survivors be made and that a more effective occupation and control of the shores of Formosa be established, but without success. Rear Admiral Bell, of the United States Navy, then conducted a punitive expedition against the aborigines, but it ended disastrously, since the landing party fell into an ambush and was forced to retire. This misadventure, however, did not deter General LeGendre from personally leading a small party across the island. He was successful in establishing relations with the most important tribes and concluded a convention for the future protection of shipwrecked mariners.

In November 1872, he arrived in Japan en route to the United States. The American minister introduced him to the Japanese authorities, who immediately recognized in him a possibly valuable assistant in their proposed negotiations with China and their expedition against Formosa, ostensibly to protest against the massacre of some of their shipwrecked seamen. LeGendre was offered the position of counselor to the proposed mission to China, with the prospect of further advancement in the Japanese service; and this offer he accepted, resigning as American consul on Dec. 19, 1872. The mission to Peking was not an entire success, but it encouraged the Japanese to undertake the expedition against Formosa. When, however, LeGendre arrived in China on his way to the island, he was arrested by the American consul at Amoy, but was later released on order of the Department of State at Washington. He continued in the Japanese service as foreign adviser until July 1875, and received the decoration of the second class of merit (Rising Sun), being the first among either foreigners or Japanese to be admitted into the Order after its institution by the Emperor of Japan. He resided in Japan until March 1890, when he was appointed vice-president of the Korean Home Office. Upon the resignation of Judge O. N. Denny, later in that year, LeGendre became adviser to the household department of the King of Korea, holding that position until his death by apoplexy at Seoul in 1899. His influence, in those days when intrigue was so prevalent between the two opposing groups of foreign powers, was always directed to peace; and his varied experience, together with the fact that his French birth and American citizenship inspired confidence, admirably fitted him for the position of adviser.

[*War of the Rebellion: Official Records (Army)*; files of the Adjutant-General's Office, War Dept., and Pension Office; *Foreign Relations of the U. S.*, 1873; Tyler Dennett, *Americans in Eastern Asia* (1922); *N. Y. Tribune*, Sept. 3, 1899.]　　　　　A. E. I.

LEGGETT, MORTIMER DORMER (Apr. 19, 1821–Jan. 6, 1896), Union soldier, lawyer, commissioner of patents, was born on his father's farm near Ithaca, N. Y., the son of Isaac and Mary (Strong) Leggett. When he was fifteen years old his parents moved to Montville, Geauga County, Ohio. Here Leggett helped his father clear the forests to obtain a farm, studied at night, and in 1839 entered Kirtland Teachers' School at Kirtland, Ohio, where he graduated at the head of his class. With the idea of practising law and specializing in medical jurisprudence, he then attended Western Reserve College and was admitted to the bar in 1844, supplementing his previous training by a special course at Willoughby Medical School. In 1846 he moved to Akron, Ohio. Having become deeply interested in the establishment of graded schools, he engaged with a group of others in behalf of this project. As a result of the agitation, the Akron School Law was enacted by the legislature in February 1847 and Leggett was employed by Akron as superintendent to execute its provisions (S. A. Lane, *Fifty Years and Over of Akron and Summit County*, 1892, pp. 122, 124). Three years later, 1849, he was called to Warren, Ohio, for a similar purpose, and it was here in 1850 that he began his law practice. In 1856 he became professor of law and pleading in the Ohio Law College at Poland, but in 1857 removed to Zanesville, Ohio, where he continued his law practice and served as superintendent of schools as well.

At the outbreak of the Civil War Leggett joined the staff of his friend Gen. George B. McClellan, and accompanied him into West Virginia, serving without pay. Later he was designated by Gov. William Dennison of Ohio to raise a regiment, and in forty days he enrolled 1,040 men in the 78th Ohio Volunteers and was commissioned colonel. The regiment joined Grant's western army and Leggett commanded it at Fort Donelson, Corinth, and Shiloh. For his gallantry he was commissioned a brigadier-general in 1862, and during that year commanded his brigade in the fighting along the Mississippi, having had much to do with the laying of the mines in the siege of Vicksburg. Subsequently, he commanded the 3rd Division in the XVII Army Corps under Gen. John A. Logan in Tennessee. In 1863 he was brevetted major-general and in the battle of Atlanta, his division took and held Bald Hill, the key to the whole position, and now known as Leggett's Hill. He marched with Sherman to the sea and up through the Carolinas; participated in the grand review in Washington; was promoted to the grade of major-general of volunteers, and resigned his commission Sept. 28, 1866.

Returning to Zanesville, he resumed the practice of law, and became connected with several manufacturing enterprises, all of which he gave up when President Grant appointed him commissioner of patents on Jan. 16, 1871. His capacity for organization here found expression. He continued effectively the work and policies of his predecessors; had a reclassification of patents made; established the office of third assistant examiner; and by other activities concerned with its internal affairs, distinctly advanced the work and standards of the Patent Office. Following his resignation on Nov. 1, 1874, he made his residence in Cleveland, Ohio, and engaged in the practice of patent law with his sons. In 1884 he organized and was the first president of the Brush Electric Company. After a struggle, this enterprise became highly successful and was finally absorbed by the General Electric Company. He was twice married: first, on July 9, 1844, to Marilla Wells of Montville, Ohio, who died in 1876; second, in 1879, to Weltha Post of Sandusky, Ohio, who with one daughter by his first wife survived him.

[*War of the Rebellion: Official Records (Army)*; *Mil. Order of the Loyal Legion of the U. S., Commandery of the State of Ohio, Circular No. 8, Series of 1896*; C. C. Reif, in *Jour. of the Patent Office Soc.*, July 1920; T. A. Leggett and A. Hatfield, Jr., *Early Settlers of West Farms, Westchester County, N. Y.* (t.p. 1913, Foreword, 1916); W. S. Robinson, *Hist. of the City of Cleveland* (1887); *Cleveland Weekly Leader and Herald*, Jan. 11, 1896.]   C. W. M.

LEGGETT, WILLIAM (Apr. 30, 1801–May 29, 1839), journalist, descended from Gabriel Leggett, an emigrant from Essex, England, who settled in Westchester County, N. Y., about 1675, was born in New York City, son of Abraham Leggett, an officer in the Revolution, and his second wife, Catherine Wylie of New Rochelle. He attended Georgetown College for a time, but did not graduate, and in 1819 went with his parents to Illinois, where he lived a pioneer's life until his appointment as midshipman in the navy, Dec. 4, 1822. In May following, assigned to the *Cyane,* he sailed for the Mediterranean, but in 1825 he was court-martialed for a dueling affair with another midshipman at Port Mahon, was sent home, and on Apr. 17, 1826, threw up his commission. His faults were chiefly hot temper and a witty, unruly tongue—one offense was quoting passages of Shakespeare "of highly inflammatory, rancorous, and threatening import" against his captain, John Orde Creighton.

His defense (Court Martial Records, Navy Department) is an able, entertaining document. He had published some youthful verse, *Leisure Hours at Sea* (1825), and now took up journalistic writing in New York. He published a second volume of poems, *Journals of the Ocean,* in 1826, and *Tales and Sketches, by a Country Schoolmaster* in 1829; contributed "The Blockhouse" to *Tales of Glauber Spa* in 1832; and wrote constantly for the *New-York Mirror* and other periodicals. In 1828 he married Almira, daughter of John Waring of New Rochelle, and in the same year established a weekly, the *Critic,* most of which he wrote himself and which lasted only ten months.

In 1829 he became part owner and assistant editor, under William Cullen Bryant, of the *Evening Post.* Whittier's poem, "To a Poetical Trio in New York" (Haverhill, *Iris,* Sept. 29, 1832), was an appeal to Bryant, Leggett, and James Lawson [*q.v.*], another New York editor, to give up vain political debates and devote themselves to the anti-slavery cause. From June 1834 to October 1835, during Bryant's absence abroad Leggett was chief editor. He was more fluent and more of a theorist than Bryant. Though at first he had disclaimed interest in politics, he now entered warmly into political issues, adopting strong Jacksonian principles. From opposing the United States Bank he advanced to denunciation of the state banks as the worst examples of chartered monopolies and special privilege. He advocated broad suffrage and free trade. Soon he had become the oracle of the radical Democrats whose extreme wing seceded to form the Equal Rights or Locofoco party in 1835. In that year, though not yet a thoroughgoing abolitionist, he hotly attacked the administration for excluding anti-slavery propaganda from the mails, and denounced the mobs that broke up abolitionist meetings in New York. His chief characteristics as a writer were energy and absolute independence; his chief defect was violence. Combative from his backwoods and naval antecedents, he was responsible for Bryant's attempt to horsewhip Sands, editor of the *Commercial,* and later challenged Sands to a duel. This was not fought, but he had a duel with an Englishman named Banks, treasurer of the Park Theatre. Convivial in tastes, he was prominent in New York social and literary life. His severe illness in the winter of 1835–36 hastened Bryant's return from Europe, and about October 1836, he left the *Evening Post.* From December of that year to September 1837, he edited the *Plaindealer,* in which, free from the restrictions imposed by his more conservative chief on the *Post,* he continued to attack political and economic abuses and to advocate free trade, direct taxation, and the right of workingmen to organize. He also advanced from the defense of the abolitionists' right of free speech to support of their attacks on slavery. The journal was influential in shaping Democratic policies, and was fairly successful till the failure of its publishers. During part of this time Leggett also edited a daily, the *Examiner.* "How he finds time to write so much," remarked Bryant, "I know not." In 1838 he nearly secured a Democratic nomination for Congress, but, having declared himself an abolitionist and refusing to modify his declaration, he was rejected for a less radical candidate. The next year Van Buren appointed him diplomatic agent to Guatemala, his friends hoping the climate might benefit his health, but he died before sailing for the post. Though Tammany, during his attacks on the administration in 1835, had abjured Leggett and disclaimed the *Post* as a party organ, the Tammany Young Men's General Committee erected the monument over his grave in Trinity (Episcopal) Church Cemetery, New Rochelle. Whittier refers to this episode in his poem, "Leggett's Monument." Theodore Sedgwick, Jr., his friend, published in two volumes *A Collection of the Political Writings of William Leggett* (1840), remarked upon at the time as the first American attempt to establish the standing of a writer on the basis of journalistic work.

[Biographical sketch by Bryant in *U. S. Mag. and Dem. Rev.,* July 1839, and poem, *Ibid.,* Nov. 1839; *Eve. Post* (editorial), June 3, 1839; *Morning Courier and N. Y. Enquirer* and *N. Y. Daily Express,* May 31, 1839; critical estimate in *U. S. Mag. and Dem. Rev.,* Jan. 1840; J. G. Wilson, *Bryant and His Friends* (1886); Parke Godwin, *A Biog. of Wm. Cullen Bryant* (2 vols., 1883), *passim*; C. I. Bushnell, *Crumbs for Antiquarians,* vol. II (1866); J. G. Whittier, *Old Portraits and Modern Sketches* (1850); Allan Nevins, *The Evening Post, A Century of Journalism* (1922); Wm. Trimble, "Diverging Tendencies in New York Democracy in the Period of the Locofocos," *Am. Hist. Rev.,* Apr. 1919; T. A. Leggett and A. Hatfield, Jr., *Early Settlers of West Farms, Westchester County, N. Y.* (t.p. 1913, Foreword, 1916).]   A. W.

LEGLER, HENRY EDUARD (June 22, 1861–Sept. 13, 1917), librarian and author, the son of Henry and Raffaela (Messina) Legler, was a native of Palermo, Italy. His father was of Swiss-German blood and his mother Italian. Most of his early years were passed in Switzerland, whence the family emigrated to America soon after the Civil War. In 1873 they were domiciled at La Crosse, Wis., where Henry attended the public schools. In his seventeenth year, upon the death of his father, his formal education came to an end, and he began his literary career as a typesetter on the *Milwaukee Sentinel.*

He soon rose to the position of reporter and later city editor and editorial writer. In 1888 he was sent to represent his paper at the Republican National Convention at Chicago. His report was so satisfactory that he was elected that year to represent the seventh district of Milwaukee in the state Assembly. This was his only political service; he was on the committee on state affairs, but due to youth and inexperience took little part in public discussion. On Sept. 4, 1890, he was married to Nettie M. Clark of Beloit, Wis.

In that same year he was chosen secretary of the school board of Milwaukee, a position he held till 1904. It was during this time that his scholarly interests began to develop. With a number of historically minded citizens of Milwaukee he founded the Parkman Club, and to its *Publications* contributed two historical essays: "Chevalier Henry de Tonty" (1896) and "A Moses of the Mormons" (1897), both of which are lasting contributions to historical lore. In 1898 he published a small volume, *Leading Events of Wisconsin History,* which has been much used in the state schools. An essay, *James Gates Percival* (1901), and an article on "Early Wisconsin Imprints" (in the *Proceedings* for 1903 of the State Historical Society of Wisconsin) completed his literary work during his residence in Milwaukee. He subsequently published a number of papers and pamphlets on historical and bibliographical topics.

In 1895 the Wisconsin legislature passed a bill creating a Free Library Commission, and in 1904 Legler was appointed secretary of the commission with headquarters at Madison. There he continued the policy of his predecessor in providing traveling libraries for remote and isolated communities; he also arranged for a legislative reference bureau and a training school for librarians, which later became the library school of the state university. During the five years of his administration (1904–09) Wisconsin's library policy became nationally famous. In 1909 he was appointed head of the Chicago Public Library system, where, during the eight years of his administration the library grew from 1,-800,000 to 6,000,000 volumes, the branches from one to forty. Figures do not adequately represent his work in this position: he developed a staff of great ability and devotion, he aroused the reading habits of the community, he contributed to the upbuilding of every literary interest in the city, he made the library a factor in the lives of the people. The title of his volume published in 1912 by the Caxton Club is significant: *Of Much Love and Some Knowledge of Books.*

Personally Legler was very attractive. From his Sicilian mother he derived his love of beauty and his romantic disposition; but, on the other hand, he could be stern and practical. He was a loyal courageous friend, a passionate champion of humanity. He literally gave his life for his beliefs, for he died from overwork and too great devotion to the cause of learning.

[There is no adequate sketch of Legler's career; his successor Carl Roden wrote a brief biographical sketch for the Chicago Public Library *Book Bulletin*, Sept. 1917. See also *Who's Who in America*, 1916–17; *Chicago Daily Tribune*, Sept. 14, 1917.]   L. P. K.

LEHMANN, FREDERICK WILLIAM (Feb. 28, 1853–Sept. 12, 1931), lawyer, was born in Prussia, to poor parents who emigrated to Cincinnati when he was about two. Sophia, his mother, soon died, and Frederick, the cobbler father, who married again, ruled with an iron hand. The boy ran away at eight and at ten left home permanently, never again seeing any of the family. Peddling newspapers and sleeping in vacant buildings, he spent the next seven years crossing the Middle West, working on farms, herding sheep, and getting an occasional term of school. At seventeen his earnestness was rewarded by Judge Epenetus Sears of Tabor, Iowa, who sent him to Tabor College. He received the degree of A.B. in 1873 and, after brief study in his benefactor's office, was admitted to the Iowa bar. Practising first in Tabor and Sidney, Iowa, and Nebraska City, he later settled in Des Moines. There he married Nora Stark, Dec. 23, 1879, became attorney for the Wabash Railroad, and was active in politics, being instrumental in the election of a Democratic governor, Horace Boies [q.v.], on an anti-prohibition platform. His railroad practice led him to remove to St. Louis in 1890. Here, serving some causes without charge, refusing others at any price, he soon had a reputation for fair dealing such as he had enjoyed in Iowa. In 1908 he was president of the American Bar Association.

Named solicitor-general by President Taft in 1910, he accepted the appointment through professional rather than political interest. Declaring the government in error when he thought it so, and often delighting the Supreme Court by his wit, he served for two years, handling the cases which established the government's right to tax corporation incomes. He then resigned to practise with his sons. In 1914, with Joseph Rucker Lamar [q.v.], he represented the United States at the conference sponsored by Argentina, Brazil, and Chile to mediate between the United States and Mexico. His most important cases in the course of private practice were those establishing the right of the Associated Press to news as property and securing for the Southwestern Bell Telephone Company the right to earn upon valuation determined by reproduction cost less depreciation. In 1918 he was general counsel for the United States Railway Wage Commission.

Republican one election, Democrat the next, Lehmann was politically independent from his college days, when he mounted the stump for Greeley. He believed in local self-government and considered prohibition a mistake. Frequently urged to seek office, he always refused, but in 1909 was appointed chairman of the Board of Freeholders which redrafted the St. Louis charter. An omnivorous reader with a remarkable memory, a collector of books and prints, a brilliant conversationalist, he was characterized by Rabbi Leon Harrison as "the best educated man in St. Louis." He was a founder of the art museum, president of the public library, a director of the Louisiana Purchase Exposition of 1904, and active in the Missouri Historical Society. Lehmann had a physique requiring what a cartoonist labeled "the widest banquet shirt front in St. Louis." He enjoyed public speaking, for which he was in frequent demand. His published addresses include: *John Marshall* (1901); *The Lawyer in American History* (1906); *Abraham Lincoln* (1908); *Conservatism in Legal Procedure* (1909); *Prohibition* (1910); and *The Law and the Newspaper* (1917). He was also the author of articles in *Missouri Historical Society Collections* (vol. IV, 1923), and in *Messages and Proclamations of the Governors of . . . Missouri* (vol. X, 1928). On May 10, 1932, Senator Glass had printed in the *Congressional Record* an opinion of Lehmann as solicitor-general, written twenty-one years before, which held national bank affiliates to be in violation of the law. He died of the infirmities of age, survived by his wife and three sons.

[Julius Klyman, in "Interesting St. Louisans," *St. Louis Post-Dispatch*, Feb. 2, 1930; *Who's Who in America*, 1930–31; *Who's Who in Jurisprudence*, 1925; S. G. Blythe, "Lehmann the Learned," in *Sat. Eve. Post*, Mar. 4, 1911 (in error about boyhood); W. B. Stevens, *Centennial Hist. of Mo.* (1921), vol. IV; G. S. Johns, in *St. Louis Post-Dispatch*, Sept. 13, 1931; F. H. Severance, "The Peace Conference at Niagara Falls," *Buffalo Hist. Soc. Pubs.*, vol. XVIII (1914); information from Lehmann's sons, Sears and John S. Lehmann.]   I. D.

LEIB, MICHAEL (Jan. 8, 1760–Dec. 28, 1822), physician, congressman, senator, the son of Johann George Leib and Margaretha Dorothea Liebheit, was born in Philadelphia. His father, said to have been a native of Strasbourg, came to Philadelphia from Rotterdam in 1753 and served in the Philadelphia militia during the Revolution. Michael attended the common schools and studied medicine under Dr. Benjamin Rush. From Aug. 10, 1780, to the end of the war he was a surgeon in the Philadelphia militia. For the next fifteen years he was active in medical affairs, serving on the staffs of the Philadelphia Dispensary (1786–93), the Philadelphia Almshouse and Hospital (1788–90), and Bush Hill Hospital (1793). He was also a corporator of the College of Physicians of Philadelphia and a member of the Pennsylvania prison society. His activities in the Democratic Society and the German Republican Society and in the Assembly (1795–98), launched him on a political career. A rousing democratic speech of his in the legislature in 1796 moved Jefferson to predict a great future for him (*The Works of Thomas Jefferson,* edited by P. L. Ford, vol. VIII, 1904, p. 227). In 1798 he was elected to Congress. Here he distinguished himself (1799–1806) as a stanch, albeit violent, Jeffersonian. His motion to abolish the navy, subsequently withdrawn (1802), his fight for reforming the judiciary, for more liberal naturalization laws, and for reducing the marine corps, are typical of his democratic zeal. Not disposed to be "a duellist for national honor," he opposed (1806) the non-importation resolution of his colleague, Andrew Gregg [*q.v.*], convinced that the country would incur "more loss than profit by it" (*Annals of Congress,* 9 Cong., 1 Sess., p. 762). Leib collaborated with William Duane [*q.v.*] as political dictator of Philadelphia. For supporting Gov. Thomas McKean [*q.v.*] in 1799 he was rewarded with the post of physician to the Lazaretto Hospital (1800). His violence and avarice, however, soon wrecked the Republican party in Pennsylvania. Disappointed in McKean and exasperated by opposition to his candidacy for Congress in 1802 and 1804, he threw his influence with the radicals and against the Governor in 1805. The next year he resigned from Congress, reëntered the legislature (1806–08), determined to overthrow McKean, and as "the Magnus Apollo" of "the Catilinian faction" blocked the administration at every step and led the unsuccessful impeachment proceedings against the Governor. He was also a Democratic presidential elector (1808) and brigadier-general of militia (1807–11).

From 1809 to 1814 Leib was United States senator. He opposed Gallatin's taxation schemes and the recharter of the United States Bank (1811), demanded drastic measures against England (1810), but in 1812 tried to delay war, and was one of the "malcontents" whose tactics em-

barrassed the administration. On Feb. 14, 1814, he was appointed postmaster of Philadelphia, but hostile sentiment in Pennsylvania forced his removal early in 1815. His criticisms of Madison now became open denunciations. Speaking, May 13, 1816, before the St. Tammany Society, of which he formerly had been grand sachem, he asserted that the Republican party was controlled by men who had sacrificed the nation's prosperity to make war "a chess board for political gamblers to play upon" (*An Address to the St. Tammany Society,* 1816). Meanwhile his influence in state politics declined. As an old-school Democrat, he attacked the caucus nominating system, advocated a more virtuous democracy, and, curiously, by courting support from moderate Republicans and Federalists whom he earlier had abominated, was returned to the Assembly (1817–18) and to the state Senate (1818–21). From Nov. 15, 1822, to his death he was prothonotary of the district court for the city and county of Philadelphia. Keen in retort, but not a close reasoner, Leib "produced effect rather by the velocity of his missiles, than the weight of his metal" (C. F. and E. M. Richardson, *Charles Miner, a Pennsylvania Pioneer,* 1916, pp. 45–46). About 1808 he married Susan Kennedy. Two of his sons were physicians. He left an estate valued at $32,000.

[Sources, in addition to those cited above, include *Pa. Mag. of Hist. and Biog.,* Oct. 1925; Henry Adams, *The Life of Albert Gallatin* (1879); J. H. Peeling, "The Public Life of Thomas McKean, 1734–1817" (1929), typewritten Ph.D. thesis, Univ. of Chicago; J. T. Scharf and Thompson Westcott, *Hist. of Phila.* (3 vols., 1884); W. W. Harrison, *Harrison, Waples and Allied Families* (1910); *Poulson's Am. Daily Advertiser* (Phila.), Dec. 30, 1822.]   J. H. P.

LEIDY, JOSEPH (Sept. 9, 1823–Apr. 29, 1891), naturalist, third of four children of Philip and Catherine (Mellick) Leidy, was born in Philadelphia. Both his parents were of German ancestry: his father, a grandson of John Jacob Leydig who came to Pennsylvania from Wittenberg in 1729; his mother, a member of a family long settled in New Jersey. She died when Joseph was but a year and a half old, and he was brought up by her sister Christiana, his stepmother. He was sent to a private classical academy kept by a Methodist clergyman, but did not distinguish himself in his studies, preferring to wander along the banks of the Wissahickon or the Schuylkill collecting plants and minerals. A talent for drawing evinced in his early teens led his father, a prosperous hatmaker, to take the boy from school at sixteen with a view to making a sign-painter of him. Joseph's scientific predilections, however, together with his stepmother's faith and ambition, at length turned him to the study of medicine and anatomy, and in 1844 he took the degree of M.D. at the University of Pennsylvania with a thesis on "The Comparative Anatomy of the Eye of Vertebrated Animals." After serving a short time as assistant in the chemical laboratory of the University he entered upon the practice of medicine, but two years later abandoned practice for teaching, and was elected demonstrator of anatomy at the Franklin Medical College. In 1848 he visited Europe in company with Dr. W. E. Horner [*q.v.*] of the University, and after his return began, in 1849, to give a course of lectures on physiology in the Medical Institute. With Prof. George B. Wood he visited Europe again in 1850 to collect specimens for use in Dr. Wood's courses, and upon returning, resumed his lectures at the Institute. When ill health compelled Dr. Horner to retire from teaching, Leidy, who had been serving as his prosector, was appointed his substitute, and upon Horner's death in 1853, his successor in the chair of anatomy at the University of Pennsylvania. This position he continued to hold until his death, thirty-eight years later, becoming recognized as the foremost American anatomist of his time. His publications in the field of human anatomy were few, but his *Elementary Treatise on Human Anatomy* (1861, 2nd edition 1889), has been characterized as "one of the best works ever offered to the medical profession on the subject" (Chapman, *post,* p. 359). During the Civil War he served as surgeon in the Satterlee United States Army General Hospital, and in this capacity performed some sixty autopsies reported in the *Medical and Surgical History of the War of the Rebellion* (1870–88). From 1870 to 1885 he was professor of natural history at Swarthmore College, and after 1884, in addition to being professor of anatomy, he was director of the department of biology at the University of Pennsylvania.

Distinguished as he was as an anatomist, he was scarcely less so in other fields of science. His initial publications, including papers on new species of fossil shells and the anatomy of the snail, appearing in 1845 when he was in his twenty-second year, brought him election to the Boston Society of Natural History and the Academy of Natural Sciences of Philadelphia, with the second of which he was ever after closely identified. His first noteworthy contribution to vertebrate paleontology was his paper "On the Fossil Horse of America" (*Proceedings of the Academy of Natural Sciences of Philadelphia,* September 1847) in which it was shown conclusively that the horse had lived and become extinct on the American continent long before its discovery by Columbus. In this line of work Leidy became a pioneer, and before O. C. Marsh and E. D. Cope [*qq.v.*] had begun their work he had shown, through fossil remains, the one-time presence in the western United States of the lion, tiger, camel, horse, rhinoceros, and other vertebrates long since extinct or found only in milder and distant climes. Notable publications on these subjects were *The Ancient Fauna of Nebraska* (Smithsonian Contributions to Knowledge, vol. VI, 1854) and his monograph of 1869, "On the Extinct Mammalia of Dakota and Nebraska" (*Journal of the Academy of Natural Sciences of Philadelphia,* vol. VII), which last is stated by Osborn (*post,* p. 339) to be "with the possible exception of Cope's *Tertiary Vertebrata,* the most important paleontological work which America has produced." Leidy was not merely a paleontologist, however; he was a naturalist in the full meaning of the word, and continued the foremost in his line until his death, although he largely discontinued his vertebrate work when the confining duties of the university prevented his participating and competing in a field where Cope and Marsh were rapidly becoming efficient. No subject seemed too large for him to grasp, none too small to excite his interest. The wide range which he covered and his handling of it cannot be better illustrated than by comparing the works mentioned above with his *Fresh Water Rhizopods of North America* (1879), Monograph XII of the Hayden Survey, in which are shown and described forty-eight quarto plates of microscopic forms, the drawings for which were from his own hand.

Parasitology had been a favorite study of Leidy's from very early in his career and was the subject of many of his most important papers. One of his early discoveries was the identity of a minute parasitic worm in pork with the dangerous *Trichina spiralis* sometimes occurring in the muscles of the human species (*Proceedings of the Academy of Natural Sciences of Philadelphia,* October 1846). His treatise on intestinal worms, in William Pepper's *System of Practical Medicine* (vol. II, 1885), was the first comprehensive work of its kind published in America, while his *Flora and Fauna within Living Animals* (Smithsonian Contributions, vol. V, 1853) is described as epoch-making. He was the first to suggest the probability that certain parasitic forms communicated from the other animals to man might be "one of the previously unrecognized causes of pernicious anæmia" ("Remarks on Parasites and Scorpions," in

Transactions of the College of Physicians of Philadelphia, 3 ser. VIII, 1886, p. 441).

Although an indefatigable worker, Leidy is stated to have been almost wholly devoid of all ambition but that of the collection of facts. He was not given to theory, and disliked controversy on any subject. "I am too busy to theorize or make money," he is quoted as saying. The honors which came to him were of a high order. In 1881 he was unanimously elected president of the Academy of Natural Sciences of Philadelphia, an office which he continued to hold until his death. In 1885 he was made president of the Wagner Free Institute of Science. He received the Walker prize of $1,000 from the Boston Society of Natural History in 1880, the Lyell medal from the Geological Society of London in 1884, the Cuvier medal from the Institute of France in 1888, and was an original member of the National Academy of Sciences.

In August 1864, he married Anna Harden of Louisville, Ky. They had no children, but adopted a little girl, the orphaned daughter of one of Leidy's colleagues. In 1889, broken in health from constant application, he made his last trip to Europe. Returning, he resumed his teaching and other duties, but his health continued to fail and he died in 1891, at the age of sixty-eight. "Among zoölogists he was the last to treat of the whole animal world from the protozoa to man, rendering in every branch contributions of permanent value" (Osborn, p. 339). His bibliography of over six hundred titles is a telling monument to his industry.

[Sources include: H. F. Osborn, in *Nat. Acad. Sci. Biog. Memoirs,* vol. VII (1913), with bibliography; "The Joseph Leidy Commemorative Meeting Held in Philadelphia, Dec. 6, 1923," in *Proc. Acad. Nat. Sci. of Phila.,* vol. LXXV (1924); *Researches in Helminthology and Parasitology by Joseph Leidy* (1904), ed. by his nephew, Joseph Leidy, Jr., with bibliography; H. C. Chapman, in *Proc. Acad. Nat. Sci. of Phila.* (1892); Persifor Frazer, in *Am. Geologist,* Jan. 1892; C. A. Pfender, in H. A. Kelly and W. L. Burrage, *Am. Medic. Biogs.* (1920), with additional references; John Eyerman, *A Cat. of the Palaeontological Pubs. of Joseph Leidy* (1891); *Phila. Inquirer,* Apr. 30, 1891. See also list of references in Max Meisel, *A Bibliog. of Am. Nat. Hist.,* I (1924), 204–05.]   G. P. M.

LEIGH, BENJAMIN WATKINS (June 18, 1781–Feb. 2, 1849), lawyer and statesman, was born in Chesterfield County, Va. His father, Rev. William Leigh, after attending the College of William and Mary, studied theology in Edinburgh. Returning in 1772, he married Elizabeth Watkins, daughter of Benjamin Watkins and grand-daughter of Archibald Cary [*q.v.*], the two delegates from Chesterfield County to the Virginia Convention of 1776. The youthful minister was one of ten clergymen who protested against British taxation in 1774.

After receiving careful private tutelage and a course at William and Mary, Leigh began in 1802 the practice of law in Petersburg, and gained a reputation in his first case by securing the acquittal of a youth who in defense of his mother had killed his step-father. His first case in the Supreme Court of Appeals, likewise a *cause célèbre,* concerned his own admission to practice there. Having declined to take the oath against dueling required of attorneys, on the theory that they were officers of the court, he was at first denied admission; but later won over the court by a powerful argument prefaced with the statement that "he should have no doubt or apprehension which would preponderate with that tribunal, the love of justice or the pride of consistency" (*Leigh's Case,* 1 *Munford,* 468).

At the close of a brief service (1811–13) in the House of Delegates, he removed to Richmond. There he rapidly advanced in his profession and was repeatedly honored with public commissions. He supervised the preparation of the Code of 1819. In 1822 he represented Virginia in a controversy with Kentucky, whose advocate was Henry Clay, concerning lands granted as rewards for Revolutionary services. His fame reached its height in the notable Virginia convention of 1829–30, when he followed his forebears as the representative of the county of Chesterfield. In the conflict of interest between the eastern and western parts of the state, Leigh, as the representative of the wealthy, slave-holding, and conservative east, was a dominant figure; and while he was not the author of the compromise that settled the major problem, his trenchant service paved the way for its adoption. He was again a member of the House of Delegates in 1830–31. In 1833 Virginia sent him on a delicate mission to South Carolina, undertaken to secure her withdrawal of nullification—a service which had an ironic quality in its alignment of Leigh with President Jackson, whom he thoroughly disliked and distrusted.

In 1834 he was elected to the United States Senate to fill the vacancy occasioned by the resignation of W. C. Rives, who had refused to follow the instructions of the Virginia General Assembly to vote for the replacement of the government deposits in the Bank of the United States. Leigh vigorously advocated restoring the deposits, and President Jackson's protest against the resolution of censure drew from him an excoriating speech (Apr. 18, 1834). The sentiment of Virginia, however, was veering to Jackson, and Leigh was reëlected in 1835 by a majority of only two. On Feb. 20, 1836, the General Assembly, reversing its former position, instructed the Virginia senators to vote for Benton's expunging resolution. John Tyler declined and resigned, but Leigh, in a letter of noble dignity, refused either to comply or resign (*Letter from B. W. Leigh, Esq., to the General Assembly of Virginia*, 1836), and instead, on Apr. 4, 1836, made one of the greatest speeches of his career against the measure. While a member of the General Assembly in 1812 he had introduced resolutions sustaining the right of a state legislature to instruct senators, but expressly excepting a situation where the instructions required a violation of the Constitution or an act of moral turpitude. In his letter to the General Assembly, he recalled these exceptions and demonstrated that they controlled his action. The act was one of supreme courage. When on July 4, 1836, he resigned for personal reasons, he took pains to reaffirm his position. The General Assembly passed solemn resolutions of censure, which Leigh doubtless bore as unconcernedly as he had worn his honors.

He never again held public office, save, from 1829 to 1841, that of reporter of the Supreme Court of Appeals, then served by a bar of notable ability. There he was long a leader, and the court's decisions constitute the principal record of his life work. According to the lawyer's traditions, he "worked hard, lived well, and died poor." Contemporary testimony and his surviving writings and speeches reveal him as a master of the spoken and the written word. His family surroundings were distinctly intellectual. A brother, Judge William Leigh, friend and executor of John Randolph of Roanoke, was not his inferior in learning. He was thrice married: first to a cousin, Mary Selden Watkins; second, to Susan Colston, niece of Chief Justice Marshall; and third, to Julia Wickham, daughter of the eminent lawyer, John Wickham. He left numerous children.

While Leigh's services as codifier and reporter have somewhat prolonged his local reputation, even in Virginia he is to the rising generation but a name, and hardly a familiar one. An aristocrat in the best sense in a youthful and impatient democracy, of an intellectual reach far beyond most of those whose fame has outlived his own, he was forbidden, by the very clarity of his mental processes and the loftiness of his character, the compromises which the politician finds natural and the successful statesman inevitable. He chose what he believed the better way, and in maintaining his integrity, moral and intellectual, he counted as nothing the loss of present power or posthumous fame.

[See H. B. Grigsby, "The Virginia Convention of 1829–30," *Va. Hist. Reporter*, vol. I, pt. I (1854); H. R. Pleasants, "Sketches of the Virginia Convention of 1829–30," *So. Lit. Messenger*, Mar. 1851; Wm. H. MacFarland, *An Address on the Life, Character, and Public Services of the Late Hon. Benjamin Watkins Leigh* (1851), published also in *So. Lit. Messenger*, Feb. 1851; Edwin James Smith, in *The John P. Branch Hist. Papers of Randolph-Macon Coll.*, June 1904, with valuable references to sources; J. B. Dunn, in *Lib. of So. Lit.*, vol. VII (1907); H. A. Wise, *Seven Decades of the Union* (1872); L. G. Tyler, *Letters and Times of the Tylers* (3 vols., 1884–96). Leigh's own letter, *Niles' National Reg.*, Dec. 11, 1841, repr., but with important comment omitted, in *Tyler's Quart. Hist. and Geneal. Mag.*, Oct. 1927, denies the story that Leigh might have received the vice-presidential nomination in 1839, which is told in G. F. Hoar's *Autobiography* (1903), II, 402. See also *Va. Hist. Reg.*, Apr. 1849; *Va. Mag. of Hist. and Biog.*, Apr. 1921, p. 156; Wm. Meade, *Old Churches, Ministers, and Families of Va.* (2 vols., 1857); death notice in *Niles' National Reg.*, Feb. 14, 1849. A number of his letters and speeches were printed.]   R. B. T.

LEIGHTON, WILLIAM (fl. 1825–1868), glass-maker, was the most notable member of a family of glass-makers. His father, Thomas Leighton (1786–1849), was born in Birmingham, England, became foreman, or "gaffer," of a glass-house in Dublin, and was holding a similar position at the Cannongate Works in Edinburgh in 1825 when the New England Glass Company of Cambridge, Mass., contracted for his services as superintendent of its plant. Since glass-makers were forbidden to emigrate, he had to smuggle himself out of the country and was joined later by his wife Ann and their children. All seven of their sons entered the company's service: James as machinist, Oliver as cutter, the other five as blowers. John, the eldest, succeeded his father as gaffer. William learned every branch of the business and was specially interested in the chemistry of glass-manufacture. Experimenting constantly, he produced a great variety of colored glass and even made imitation jewels. In 1848 or 1849 he hit upon an original formula for ruby glass, which consisted of dropping the right number of twenty-dollar gold pieces into the mix. The resulting metal was a handsome rose-red, free from any suggestion of yellow, with a golden glint in some lights and an occasional tinge of magenta, and possessing its own characteristic weight and ring. It could stand comparison with the best European ruby glass and has always been prized. When the glass industry moved westward with the growth of the nation and the search for cheap fuel, Leighton went with it and in 1863 was taken into the firm of Hobbs, Brockunier & Company of Wheeling, W. Va. J. H. Hobbs, the senior member of the firm, was also a former employee of the New England Glass Company. Leighton now made several improvements in the technique of glass-manufacture, but his great stroke was the working out, in 1864, of a new formula for lime-flint glass. Hitherto it had been an inferior article and was little used. By substituting bicarbonate of soda for soda-ash in the batch and by determining the proportions of all the materials with greater care, he made a lime-flint glass equal in appearance to the old lead-flint, and distinguishable from it only by its weight and its lack of the resonant, metallic ring. The new glass could be manufactured for less than half the cost of the old, which it practically drove from the market. Leighton retired in 1868. He had been married, Mar. 8, 1829, to Mary Needham. His son William succeeded him as superintendent of the works of Hobbs, Brockunier & Company.

[*Vital Records of Cambridge, Mass., to the Year 1850* (2 vols., 1914–15); L. W. Watkins, *Cambridge Glass 1818–88* (1930); Deming Jarves, *Reminiscences of Glass-Making* (1865), pp. 95–96; Stephen Van Rensselaer, *Early Am. Bottles and Flasks* (Peterborough, N. H., 1926), p. 209; Jos. D. Weeks, "Report on the Manufacture of Glass," in *Report on the Manufactures of the U. S. at the Tenth Census* (1883).] G.H.G.

LEIPER, THOMAS (Dec. 15, 1745–July 6, 1825), merchant, was born at Strathaven, Lanark, Scotland, the son of Thomas and Helen (Hamilton) Leiper. He was educated in the schools of Glasgow and Edinburgh, for his parents wished him to become a minister of the Scottish Kirk. Such was not his desire, however, and in 1763, after the death of his father, he joined his brothers who had emigrated to America some years previously. Landing in Maryland in June 1763, he was first employed as a clerk in the store of John Semple at Port Tobacco. Later he went to Frederick County, and in 1765, to Philadelphia, where he entered the employ of his cousin, Gavin Hamilton, a tobacco exporter. In a few years he left his cousin and embarked in business for himself, becoming one of the leading wholesale and retail tobacco merchants of the city. He also built several large mills in Delaware County, Pa., for the manufacture of snuff and other tobacco products; and in 1780 he bought and operated stone quarries near his mills. Through the exercise of a high order of ability, energy, and business tact he soon accumulated a considerable fortune.

Some time before the Declaration of Independence he raised a fund for open resistance to the Crown, and when war was declared he contributed large sums to the cause. He was one of the original and most active members of the 1st Troop, Philadelphia City Cavalry (formed Nov. 17, 1774), taking part in the battles of Trenton, Princeton, Brandywine, and Germantown, and in several skirmishes. He was ranked as first sergeant until 1794, when he became second lieutenant, and then, treasurer of the troop. As such

he carried the last subsidies of the French to the American army at Yorktown. After the war, he acted with the troop in quelling several civil riots in Philadelphia. One of the leading Democrats in Pennsylvania, he was in strong opposition to President Washington and the Federalists; later he acted as a major of the "Horse of the Legion" raised, largely at his expense, to oppose the "Black Cockade" forces of the friends of the Adams administration.

In his business affairs he was enterprising and progressive, adopting new machines and improvements in agricultural implements. He constructed, for example, in 1809, an experimental railroad in Philadelphia, on which vehicles were drawn by horses. After various experiments he became satisfied that the principle was sound, and in 1810 he built and equipped a tramway from his quarries on Crum Creek, Delaware County, Pa., to tide-water, a distance of three-quarters of a mile. This road continued in use until 1828, when it was superseded by a canal. He also subscribed largely to the stock of various turnpikes and canals in Pennsylvania, often without hope of any immediate return. He made it a rule never to accept offices of pay or profit; but, without ever seeking them, he was elected or appointed to many of trust and distinction. He was a presidential elector in 1808, and in 1825, a director of the Bank of Pennsylvania and the Bank of the United States; commissioner for the defense of the city in the War of 1812; a member and ultimately president (1801–05, 1808–10, 1812–14), of the Common Councils of the City of Philadelphia; one of the executive committee of the St. Andrew's Society; and one of the founders and first officers (1824) of the Franklin Institute in Philadelphia. On Nov. 3, 1778, he married Elizabeth Coultas Gray, and to them were born thirteen children. He died at his country estate, "Avondale," in Delaware County, Pa.

[Henry Simpson, *The Lives of Eminent Philadelphians now Deceased* (1859); J. T. Scharf and T. Westcott, *Hist. of Phila.* (1884), vol. I; E. P. Oberholtzer, *Phila., A Hist. of the City and Its People* (1912), vol. I; J. L. Wilson, *Book of the First Troop Phila. City Cavalry 1774–1914* (1915); L. B. Thomas, *The Thomas Book* (1896); A. Ritter, *Phila. and Her Merchants* (1860); *Aurora and Franklin Gazette* (Phila.), July 8, 1825.] J.H.F.

LEIPZIGER, HENRY MARCUS (Dec. 29, 1854–Dec. 1, 1917), educator and lecturer, was born in Manchester, England, the son of Marcus and Martha (Samuel) Leipziger. The family emigrated to the United States early in the boy's life and settled in New York City. He attended the public schools there, and entered the College of the City of New York, from which he received the degrees of A.B. and B.S. in 1873. He distinguished himself in history, literature, English composition, oratory, and debating. Entering the law school of Columbia College, he received the degree of LL.B. in 1875, and was admitted to the bar. He opened an office, but soon determined to return to teaching, a profession which he had been following in the evening schools of New York while pursuing his law studies.

He suffered a complete nervous breakdown in 1881 and from then until 1883 traveled widely and read extensively. In 1884 he persuaded a group of Jewish philanthropists to establish the Hebrew Technical Institute, of which he became the superintendent. In it he organized courses to train Jewish youths in the trades and crafts so as to fit them for special callings. The reputation which he won for this work led, in 1891, to his appointment as assistant superintendent of schools in New York City, a position which he held until 1896. During this period he laid the plans for a system of public lectures to be given evenings in different school centers, under the auspices of the board of education. That which was a small experiment at first soon grew into one of the largest organized lecture systems of the country, if not of the world. He himself used to call it "The People's University." Hundreds of lecturers were employed, thousands of lectures were given, and audiences numbering more than a million a year were in attendance. So heavy became the work that a special position of supervisor of public lectures was created, and this office Leipziger filled up to the day of his death. Thereafter the work gradually disintegrated, not primarily because of faulty foundations, but from various causes—evening extension courses in colleges and schools, and more particularly, the phonograph and the moving pictures. For twenty years, however, it had been one of the greatest forces for adult education in New York City, and as a result of it Leipziger became one of the best-known educators there.

Outside of his regular work he interested himself in various Hebrew charities, in libraries, and in historical societies. In personal appearance he was a most distinguished figure despite his medium stature and somewhat frail body. The best likeness of him in the form of an oil painting now hangs in the College of the City of New York.

[*Who's Who in America*, 1916–17; G. W. Harris, "Apostle of the Open Schoolhouse," in the *Independent* (N. Y.), Aug. 19, 1915; *City Coll. Quart.*, Mar. 1918; *N. Y. Times* and *Tribune*, Dec. 2, 1917.]   J. S.

LEISHMAN, JOHN G. A. (Mar. 28, 1857–Mar. 27, 1924), steel-manufacturer, diplomat,

was born in Pittsburgh, Pa. His father died when the boy was quite young, and in March 1865 his mother, whose health was poor, placed John and his sister Martha in the Protestant Orphan Asylum in Pittsburgh. Though Martha was soon given a foster home with a friend of the family, John remained in the Orphan Asylum until 1869, when a Miss E. Smith of Dunningsville, Washington County, applied for a boy "to take on trial." In the secretary's report book for that year the incident is recorded with the conclusion: "Resolved with his Mother's consent to give John Leishman." In September of that year, according to the same records, "his Mother came to Pittsburgh . . . in improved health and brought John to the City to work for himself." There is added the comment, "He is a bright good boy." His first job was that of office boy in the iron and steel works of Schoenberger & Company. Here he worked twelve years. The author of *The Romance of Steel* pictures him as "undersized," adding that "when he got his first job . . . he looked as if he had escaped from a kindergarten" (*post*, p. 149). He later rose to the position of "mud-clerk," with an office in a little shanty on the river bank, and the task of supervising the unloading of barges. Having accumulated a little money, he started a furnace of his own, but abandoned it after a time to form an iron and steel brokerage firm known as Leishman & Snyder. In this work he won the regard of Andrew Carnegie who employed the firm to obtain orders for him. Leishman dissolved the partnership in 1886, when, at the age of twenty-nine, he became vice-president of Carnegie Brothers, Limited. When this organization united with other interests in the formation of the Carnegie Steel Company, he was elected president.

In June 1897 President McKinley appointed him envoy extraordinary and minister plenipotentiary to Switzerland. He thereupon resigned from the steel company, and devoted the rest of his active life to public service in the diplomatic field. His next post was that of minister to Turkey, which he entered upon in 1900. Six years later he became the first ambassador to that country. During this time he had the opportunity to show his patience and tactfulness in the face of very trying circumstances. His principal task was to present to the Turkish government the demands of the United States for the same protection to American schools and American property that was accorded the schools and property of other nations. In April 1909 he was transferred to Rome as ambassador to Italy, and from 1911 to 1913 was in Berlin as ambassador to Germany. He died at Nice, France, on the eve of his sixty-seventh birthday. On Sept. 9, 1880, while still in the office of Schoenberger & Company, Leishman married Julia Crawford, daughter of Edward Crawford, a manufacturer. Of the three children born to them, one, Nancy, became the Duchess of Croy.

[*Palmer's Pictorial Pittsburgh and Prominent Pittsburghers* (1905); *Who's Who in America*, 1922–23; *Reg. of the Dept. of State*, Oct. 15, 1912 (1912); *Foreign Relations of the U. S.*, 1897–1913; H. N. Casson, *The Romance of Steel* (1907); records of the Protestant Orphan Asylum of Pittsburgh; *Pittsburgh Post*, Feb. 20, June 10, 1897, Mar. 28, 1924.]   A. I.

LEISLER, JACOB (1640–May 16, 1691), *de facto* lieutenant-governor of New York, was born in Frankfort, Germany, and baptized on Mar. 31, 1640. He was the son of a Calvinist pastor of Bockenheim, Jacob Victorius Leyssler, and his wife Susanna. In 1660 young Jacob came to New Amsterdam a penniless soldier in the Dutch West India Company. Three years later, Apr. 11, 1663, his marriage with Elsje Tymens, the rich widow of Pieter van der Veen, and a step-daughter of Govert Loockermans, connected him with leading Dutch families, among them the Bayards and Van Cortlandts, and provided him the capital to engage in the fur and tobacco, and later, in the wine, trade. He was soon numbered among the richest merchants of the colony. Until 1689 he played little part in the troubled affairs of New York. An arbitrator of various legal disputes, the mouthpiece of Suffolk country petitioners, a captain in the militia, and a deacon in the Dutch Reformed Church, he emerged from comparative obscurity only when, with Jacob Milborne, he attacked as a violation of ecclesiastical liberty the appointment to his church of the Anglican Dominie Nicholas van Rensselaer [*q.v.*]. In several suits brought against him he betrayed an unconsidered obstinacy of temper, while his own suit for a share of Govert Loockerman's estate changed the scorn with which his aristocratic kinsmen regarded his plebeian origin and his uncouthness of manner into bitter personal enmity.

Since Nicholas Bayard [*q.v.*] and Van Cortlandt were on the council, these personal feelings added a special vehemence to the course of the Revolution of 1689 in New York, caused there as elsewhere by fear of French invasion, suspicion of papists in the administration, and agitation for representative government. The overthrow at Boston of Sir Edmund Andros [*q.v.*], governor general of the Dominion of New England, of which New York was a part, left Lieutenant-Governor Francis Nicholson [*q.v.*] to continue alone at New York. It is uncertain what part Leisler played in instigating the first overt act against Nicholson, which was the seizure by his trainband of the fort at New York, but he soon emerged as leader of the various discontented elements, which numbered important Dutchmen and Englishmen as well as the mob. Nicholson fled the country in June, his council proved incapable of continuing the government, and Leisler on his own authority proclaimed William and Mary. In June a committee of safety representing his faction in six New York counties named him as captain of the fort, and in August, as commander-in-chief. In December he seized letters addressed to Nicholson or to "such as for the time being take care for Preserving the Peace and administring the laws," interpreted them as justifying his assumption of authority, and styled himself lieutenant-governor. He was, therefore, a revolutionary usurper, and was never sanctioned by the British government, which, in August 1689, selected a new governor, Sloughter, and authorized the raising of regular troops to restore order in New York. Nevertheless, during twenty months, Leisler filled the post of executive as well as the high feeling and disorder of the times permitted. Governing by military force, with his own supporters in administrative positions, he suppressed riots, constituted courts, struck a seal, signed commissions, collected taxes, and called an assembly composed of his partisans from a part of the province only. Albany recognized his authority early in 1690, largely because of Indian dangers, and his principal concern was thenceforth the French War, to which he devoted himself with vigor. His enthusiasm was responsible for the first attempt to create a military union of the colonies, though his quick temper, and that of his chief lieutenant and son-in-law, Milborne, contributed to the disastrous failure of the joint expedition which resulted.

Administrative difficulties delayed in England the sailing of Sloughter and the two companies of regulars. The latter, without Sloughter, arrived in January 1691, under Capt. Richard Ingoldesby, who, with no further authority than his own military commission and the knowledge that all the members of the new council were Leisler's enemies, demanded the surrender of the fort. Leisler refused, for acquiescence would have been an admission that his government had no shadow of legality. For nearly two months New York hovered on the brink of civil war, with Leisler's adherents in the fort, and Ingoldesby's, reinforced by militia from the countryside, in the town. Shots were exchanged on Mar. 17, and two of the king's soldiers were killed. Sloughter arrived two days later, proclaimed his commission, and again demanded the surrender. Reluctant to lose his power, Leisler hesitated too long, and so gave his enemies colorable grounds for bringing charges of treason against him. At his trial he refused to plead until the question of the legal basis of his authority was settled; he was condemned to death, and Sloughter was prevailed upon to sign the death-warrant. Both Leisler and Milborne were hanged. Leisler's career divided New York into two camps, and lent a peculiar passion to political controversies until well into the eighteenth century. In 1695 Parliament reversed his attainder and restored to his family confiscated property; in 1702 the New York Assembly voted an indemnity of £2,700 to his heirs.

[Berthold Fernow, *The Records of New Amsterdam* (1897); E. B. O'Callaghan, *Calendar of Hist. MSS. in the Office of the Secretary of State, Albany, N. Y., Pt. I, Dutch MSS.* (1865); E. R. Purple, *Geneal. Notes Relating to Lt. Gov. Jacob Leisler . . .* (1877); E. B. O'Callaghan, *Docs. Rel. to the Colonial Hist. of the State of N. Y.*, vol. III (1853); *Doc. Hist. of the State of N. Y.*, vol. II (1849); *Colls. of the N. Y. Hist. Soc.*, Pub. Fund Series, vol. I (1868); *Calendar of State Papers, Colonial, 1689–1692*; L. F. Stock, *Proc. and Debates of the British Parliaments Respecting North America*, vol. II (1927); C. M. Andrews, *Narratives of the Insurrections 1675–1690* (1915); A. B. Faust, *The German Element in the U. S.* (1927), violently pro-Leislerian; Mrs. Schuyler van Rensselaer, *Hist. of the City of N. Y.* (1909), sympathetic; H. L. Osgood, *The Am. Colonies in the Seventeenth Century*, vol. III (1907), tends to be hostile.]   S. M. P.

LEITER, LEVI ZEIGLER (Nov. 2, 1834–June 9, 1904), merchant, was a descendant of James Van Leiter, a Dutch Calvinist who came from Amsterdam to Baltimore in 1760. In the village of Leitersburg on the tract which his ancestor had purchased from Lord Craven in Western Maryland, Levi Leiter was born, the son of Joseph and Anne (Zeigler) Leiter. He served his mercantile apprenticeship as clerk in the village store, until he was twenty years of age. Filled with the "Greeley spirit," he started West in 1854, worked for a year in the store of Peter Murray at Springfield, Ohio, and the following year arrived in Chicago, where he found employment as a clerk in the firm of Downs & Van Wyck. In 1856 he took a similar position with Cooley, Wadsworth & Company, wholesale dry-goods merchants. At the same time Marshall Field [*q.v.*] also joined the firm as a clerk and salesman and a strong friendship developed between the two young men. Later, both became partners in the concern.

Potter Palmer [*q.v.*] had already established himself as a dry-goods merchant on Lake Street, and, being desirous of retiring from this business, he interested Field and Leiter in the purchase of a controlling interest. Selling their interest in Cooley, Wadsworth & Company, to John V. Farwell [*q.v.*] in 1865, they established the firm of Field, Palmer & Leiter. At the end of two years Palmer withdrew. The others carried on the business for fourteen years, Field as merchant, Leiter as credit manager. The latter was a prodigious worker, with sound judgment and unquestioned integrity. He led the way in reducing the credit period for the purchase of goods at wholesale from four months to sixty days. Under Field's leadership, with a credit policy that greatly decreased losses, the firm prospered remarkably.

Leiter did not have Field's vision nor his boldness in projecting new plans. Furthermore, he had become interested in real estate, and in 1881 retired from the firm, already a very wealthy man. His good judgment and his faith in the future of Chicago induced him to risk his fortune on the city's continued growth, and as a result he greatly increased his already large fortune. To his credit it must be said that his success was in large part the consequence of his constructive leadership in aiding the recovery of the city from the consequences of the disastrous fire of 1871. As a director he induced the Liverpool & London & Globe Insurance Company to locate its office in the city and thus encouraged the return of other insurance companies. He had early given his support to the Chicago Art Institute, becoming its second president. In 1877 he took the lead in providing a new building for the Chicago Historical Society, which had suffered greatly in the fire. The founding of the Chicago Public Library had his financial support. As director of the Chicago Relief and Aid Society (1874–80), he was active in the work of philanthropy. He was a leader in his own group of business men and first president of the Chicago Commercial Club.

In October 1866 he married Mary Theresa Carver, daughter of Benjamin Carver of Chicago, by whom he had four children. One of them, Mary, married Lord Curzon, viceroy of India, and the family became socially prominent in England. Joseph, Leiter's one son, brought about the most dramatic episode in his father's life, when in 1897–98, he tried to "corner" the wheat market. The "corner" was unsuccessful and the older Leiter, who stood behind his son, is said to have lost $9,750,000. At the conclusion of this event, the Leiters withdrew from speculation and Levi busied himself with art, literature, the collection of Americana, and foreign travel. He lived in his latter years at Washington, where he collected a valuable library of early American history and literature.

[Who's Who in America, 1903–05; Chicago Daily News, June 9, 1904; Chicago Daily Tribune, June 10, 1904; The Leiter Library, a Cat. of the Books and Maps Relating Principally to America, Collected by Levi Z. Leiter. With Collations and Bibliog. Notes by Hugh Alexander Morrison (privately printed, Washington, 1907).]   E. A. D.

LE JAU, FRANCIS (1665–Sept. 15, 1717), clergyman, teacher, first rector of the Goose Creek Anglican parish, South Carolina, was born in Angers, France, of Huguenot parents. Early in life he must have had educational advantages and cultural contacts, for he was master of at least six languages and displayed habitual inclination toward the fine arts. About 1685, probably under stress of persecution, he fled with others to England, where he embraced Anglicanism. He graduated from Trinity College, Dublin, receiving the degree of M.A. in 1693, and of B.D. in 1696; the degree of D.D. was conferred upon him, Jan. 24, 1700. Before 1700 he was canon in St. Paul's Cathedral, London, but though established in this influential parish, he decided in that year, because of ill health, to go to Antigua, West Indies, as a missionary. There he and his family lived nearly six years and laid the foundations for the social and moral uplift of 2,000 negro slaves who were under his immediate care. In 1706, after a brief return to the British Isles, he emigrated to Goose Creek, South Carolina, eighteen miles from Charles Town. At intervals, during the absence of the Commissary, he served St. Philip's Church, Charles Town. In addition to his regular work among the whites, he interested himself in the education of negroes and Indian slaves; and the work he did in their behalf constitutes an important chapter in the history of the province. Generations of them were taught to read and write when there was as yet no school in the parish. Despite long-continued resistance on the part of their owners, he established the family relation among the slaves, and composed ritual pledges adapted to their peculiar needs, to which they made public avowal at baptism, marriage, and reception into his church. He concerned himself, also, with their physical and social welfare, denouncing the brutal treatment accorded them, and publicly condemning the law that provided for physical mutilation of runaway slaves. He exposed cruel practices in letters to the British authorities and called upon them to put slavery upon a more humane basis.

Despite his wide learning Le Jau reflected some of the superstitions of his time. He found in cruelties practised on slaves the cause for epidemics of fever and smallpox, as well as of Indian wars; in the "dying of much cattle" he discerned a punishment of heaven for the laziness of the people. Until his death he defended the specifications of his creed and resisted all encroachments upon the Anglican liturgy. The luster of his pulpit, however, must have been a subject of frequent comment among visitors to Charles Town and Goose Creek. His letters contain references to large congregations, and indicate that it was common for the church building to be filled with white people, while negro slaves and Indians crowded the open windows and doorway.

Shortly before his death he was appointed to the pulpit of St. Philip's Church, Charles Town. Simultaneously he became Commissary of the Bishop of London. His appointment is dated July 31, 1717; but before this he had been attacked by a lingering illness, which caused a paralysis of his lower limbs and affected his speech. He died in poverty. His first marriage was with Jeanne Antoinette Huguenin, Apr. 13, 1690. She bore him four children and died Christmas day, 1700. Elizabeth Harrison, of Westminster, his second wife, bore him two children.

[The little that is obtainable about Le Jau's family is gleaned from the family record owned by the Rev. Francis Le Jau Frost, New Brighton, Staten Island, N. Y. The material pertaining to his life and work consists chiefly of letters in the archives of the Society for the Propagation of the Gospel in Foreign Parts, London, the Bodleian Library, Oxford, and Fulham Palace. There are transcripts of some of these in the Library of Congress and in the archives of the National Council of the Protestant Episcopal Church, New York City. See also Frederick Dalcho, An Hist. Account of the Protestant Episcopal Ch. in S. C. (1820); Pubs. Huguenot Soc. of London, VII (1893), 140, 142; C. P. Pascoe, Two Hundred Years of the S. P. G. (1901); Alumni Dublinenses (1924); A. H. Hirsch, The Huguenots of Colonial S. C. (1928), and in Trans. of the Huguenot Soc. of S. C., No. 34 (1929); J. I. Waring, St. James Ch., Goose Creek, S. C., a Sketch of the Parish from 1706 to 1909 (n.d.).]   A. H. H.

LELAND, CHARLES GODFREY (Aug. 15, 1824–Mar. 20, 1903), writer, was born in Philadelphia, the eldest child of a commission merchant, Charles Leland, and his wife, Charlotte (Godfrey). On his father's side he was of Massachusetts, and on his mother's of Rhode Island stock. He received his early schooling at Jamaica Plain, Mass., and in Philadelphia, where Bronson Alcott was one of his teachers. At the age of nine Leland was already reading with the voracity of Macaulay. From 1841 to 1845 he attended the College of New Jersey, where "piety and mathematics rated extravagantly high in the course," but despite serious deficiencies in those subjects he not only graduated in due course but won the regard of his teachers, especially of Albert Baldwin Dod, of whom he has left a beautiful account in his *Memoirs* (1893). After graduating, he went to Germany, by way of Italy, and studied for two years at the universities of Heidelberg and Munich. By "incredible labour" he learned the German language, but learned it thoroughly, and meanwhile changed from an overgrown, delicate boy into a burly, genial giant of a man, with a beard like Charlemagne's and a Gargantuan appetite for food, drink, and tobacco. Germany he learned to love as he loved no other country but his own. In 1848 he migrated from the University of Munich to the Sorbonne in time to be a captain on the barricades for three days and to serve on a committee of Americans that congratulated the revolutionists on their successful coup.

Returning to Philadelphia, he studied law in the office of John Cadwalader, was called to the bar, but soon turned to journalism. For the next twenty-one years journalism and authorship, varied by forays into politics, war, and western exploration, were his vocation. In 1849 he began contributing articles on art to John Sartain's *Union Magazine*. A little later he became Rufus Griswold's assistant on P. T. Barnum's *Illustrated News* in New York. He next joined the staff of the Philadelphia *Evening Bulletin*. By this time the growing prosperity of his father made him only partially dependent on his writing, and on Jan. 17, 1856, he married Eliza Bella Fisher, daughter of Rodney Fisher of Philadelphia. Meanwhile he had published his first book, *Meister Karl's Sketch-Book* (1855), a volume of essays and sketches in the tradition established by Washington Irving but quite Lelandesque in style and flavor. He was also engaged at this time in translating Heine and in writing for various magazines. He was a master of literary journalism, always fluent, entertaining, good-humored, and well informed. He could acquit himself well on almost any subject, in prose or verse. From January to May 1857 he edited *Graham's Magazine* and contributed to the May number his famous "Hans Breitmann's Barty," the popularity of which has only been equaled by Bret Harte's "Heathen Chinee." He wrote other Breitmann ballads, which were published as pamphlets and were widely read both in America and England. They were finally collected in *The Breitmann Ballads* (London, 1871) and *Hans Breitmann's Ballads* (Cambridge, Mass., 1914). Many of them are merely humorous, but the best of them, in their wealth of parody and literary allusion, their rich humor, metrical skill, and poetic feeling, are unique creations of the comic spirit. Though Leland himself enjoyed them, he never realized that they

are the best proof of his genius. In 1862 he became editor of the *Continental Monthly* in Boston, an organ of the Union cause and, according to his own story, coined the term *emancipation* as a substitute for the disreputable *abolition*. In 1863 he enlisted in a Philadelphia artillery company and saw, rather than participated in, the battle of Gettysburg. There followed a period of travel in Tennessee and the West and then, in 1866, he became managing editor of John W. Forney's Philadelphia *Press*.

His father having died, Leland gave up active newspaper work and went to Europe in 1869, settling finally in London, where he remained until 1879. By this time he had an international reputation as a humorist, poet, and essayist; he was socially one of the most agreeable of men; and in consequence he became very popular. He and Walter Besant founded the short-lived but famous Rabelais Club. Leland devoted himself to the study of gipsy lore and language and became a master of Romany, which he delighted in speaking. Becoming interested in the industrial arts, characteristically he began to think them of the utmost importance in education and returned to Philadelphia in order to introduce them into the public schools. He gave time and money without stint to the project, wrote a whole series of textbooks, and worked indefatigably. He achieved a certain measure of success, but in 1884, somewhat weary of the subject, he returned to London. During all these years he was publishing a number of books, the more important being: *The Music Lesson of Confucius* (1872); *The English Gipsies* (1873); *The Gypsies* (1882); *The Algonquin Legends* (1884); *A Dictionary of Slang* (1889, 1897), with Albert Barrere; *Etruscan-Roman Remains in Popular Tradition* (1892); *Memoirs* (1893); *Legends of Florence* (1895-96); and *The Unpublished Legends of Virgil* (1901). He prided himself especially on the discovery of Shelta, a dialect, of ancient descent, spoken by some Irish and Welsh gipsies. He had an extraordinary faculty for languages, and to the end of his life, was a student of anything mysterious or occult. During his later years he lived much in Florence and never ventured further north than Homburg, his favorite among the health resorts of Germany. He died in Florence and was buried in Laurel Hill Cemetery, Philadelphia.

[Leland MSS. in library of the Hist. Soc. of Pa. and of Princeton Univ.; C. G. Leland, *Memoirs* (1893); E. R. Pennell, *Charles Godfrey Leland* (1906), reviewed in the *Nation* (New York), Sept. 27, 1906, and the *Athenaeum* (London), Dec. 1, 1906; Joseph Jackson, *A Bibliog. of the Works of Charles Godfrey Leland* (1927), repr. from the *Pa. Mag.*, July 1925-Jan. 1927; Sherman Leland, *The Leland Mag.* (1850); A. W.

Smith, *Geneal. of the Fisher Family 1682–1896* (1896); *Pa. Mag.*, Apr. 1925; "American Humour," *British Quart. Rev.*, Oct. 1870; *Revue des Deux Mondes*, Aug. 15, 1872; *Academy*, Apr. 4, 1903; *Jour. Gypsy Lore Soc.*, vol. III, no. 3 (1924); *Who's Who in America*, 1899–1902; the *Press* (Phila.), Mar. 21, 1903.]

G. H. G.

LELAND, GEORGE ADAMS (Sept. 7, 1850–Mar. 17, 1924), physician, otologist, educator, was born in Boston, a son of Joseph Daniels and Mary Plimpton (Adams) Leland, and a descendant of Henry Leland who came to Massachusetts in 1652. He was educated at the Boston Latin School and at Amherst College, graduating with the degree of A.B. in 1874. At Amherst, which was the first American college to establish a department of physical education, he came under the influence of its first professor, Edward Hitchcock, 1828–1911 [*q.v.*], and acquired such an interest in the subject that after graduation he established a cash prize for excellence in gymnastics which was awarded annually for some forty years. Completing the course at the Harvard Medical School in 1877, he received the degree of M.D. in 1878, after eighteen months' service as interne in the Boston City Hospital. In July 1878, he married Alice Pierce Higgins of Boston. Recommended by President Seelye of Amherst to introduce a system of physical education into the schools of Japan, he took his bride to Tokio, where he remained until 1881, having charge of physical culture in the National Education Department, leading the classes in the normal schools and some in the preparatory department of the University, and thus training about one hundred young men to become teachers in all grades of the schools throughout the Empire. For this service he was awarded the Fourth Order of Merit of the Sacred Treasure of Japan. He was the author of works on Japanese anthropometry and on physical education and gymnastics (1881), published in Tokio in Japanese, as well as a volume on medical gymnastics published in Chinese.

In 1881 he went to Vienna, where he began the study of laryngology and otology with Von Schroetter and other well-known specialists, thence to Heidelberg and other German cities, returning to Boston in 1883. In 1885 he was appointed otologist to the Boston Dispensary. He was also assistant for diseases of the throat at the City Hospital Out Patient Department, with Drs. Hooper, De Blois, and Farlow. His most important appointment was as otologist to the City Hospital. This he retained throughout his life. He gave courses in otology and rhinology at the Boston Polyclinic, and was professor of laryngology at the Dartmouth Medical School from 1893 to 1914, when he became professor emeritus. His ideas upon physical development directed his attention to the need of free nasal respiration. His operations upon the deformed nasal septum were original, ingenious, and successful. They well deserved recognition. He was also expert in the treatment of tonsils. He was a fellow of the American Otological Society and of the American Laryngological Association, and in 1912 was president of the latter organization. He was also a member of the American Rhinological, Laryngological, and Otological Society; and of the New England Otological and Laryngological Society, of which he was president for two years. A man of rugged honesty, he was devoted to his profession, and though he had a keen sense of humor, had few outside interests. He died in Boston in his seventy-fourth year.

[J. W. Farlow, *George Adams Leland* (1924), repr. from *Trans. Am. Laryngol. Asso.*, vol. XLVI (1924); *Who's Who in America*, 1920–21; *Obit. Record Grads. and Non-Grads. Amherst Coll.*, 1924; *Amherst Coll. Biog. Record* (1927); Sherman Leland, *The Leland Mag., or a Geneal. Record of Henry Leland and His Descendants* (1850); *Jour. Am. Medic. Asso.*, Apr. 5, 1924; *Boston Transcript*, Mar. 17, 1924; personal acquaintance.]

D. B. D.

LELAND, JOHN (May 14, 1754–Jan. 14, 1841), Baptist clergyman, the son of James and Lucy (Warren) Leland and a descendant of Henry Leland who came to America in 1652, was born at Grafton, Mass. His early education was limited to the elementary training of the common schools. At eighteen, having received "a sign from God," he decided to forsake worldly pleasures and devote himself to the ministry. In 1774, he obtained a Baptist preacher's license, and two years later, with his bride Sarah Divine (or Devine), whom he married Sept. 30, 1776, he started for Virginia. There, after a temporary ministerial assignment at Mount Poney, he established himself at Orange. During his fourteen-year residence here, leading the Baptist forces, he played a prominent part in the disestablishment of the Episcopal Church and in the ratification of the Constitution. As an exponent of religious liberty, he was instrumental in the repeal of the incorporation act and began the successful fight to regain the glebe lands held by the clergy. While engaged in this work, he was nominated by the Baptists of Orange County as a delegate to the Virginia convention of 1788, to oppose the Constitution. Convinced by his opponent, James Madison, that the federal instrument would not interfere with religious freedom, he campaigned for his rival, who was consequently elected. On Aug. 8, 1789, at a meeting of the Baptist General Committee at Richmond, Leland proposed the abolition of slavery. Taking an active part in the revival of 1787, he was regarded as one of the most popular preachers in the "Old Dominion." His *Virginia Chronicle* (1790) added to his renown, since it became the basis of R. B. Semple's *History of the Rise and Progress of the Baptists in Virginia* (1810).

In 1791, Leland moved to Cheshire, Mass., where he resided for fifty years. In his native commonwealth, as well as in Connecticut, he fought diligently for the complete disestablishment of the Congregational Standing Order. As leader of the Connecticut Baptists, in his tract *Van Tromp* (1806), he suggested that a constitutional convention be called to adopt a new organic instrument providing for religious liberty. Twelve years later his suggestion was adopted. When a constitutional convention was held in his own state in 1820, Leland in his *Short Essays on Government,* published that year, proposed an amendment to separate church and state. In 1833, his hopes were realized with the final overthrow of the Congregational system in Massachusetts. An advocate of political as well as religious liberalism, he was at first a Jeffersonian Republican and later a Jacksonian Democrat. Enthusiastic over the election of Jefferson, in 1801 he traveled to Washington to present his hero with an enormous cheese, made by the women of Cheshire. For this incident he was dubbed the "Mammoth Priest." In 1811, he was elected on the Republican ticket to the Massachusetts legislature. Although engaged in these temporal pursuits, during his fifty-year abode in Massachusetts he took an active part in missionary work, in defending the Christian revelation against deism, and in composing popular hymns. In 1838 he published *Some Events in the Life of John Leland, Written by Himself.* When he was eighty-three, death claimed his wife, the mother of his nine children. Three years later he was buried by her side in the cemetery of Cheshire.

[L. F. Greene, *Writings of Elder John Leland* (1845), which contains Leland's autobiography, letters, and most important writings ; H. M. Morais, "Life and Work of Elder John Leland" (master's thesis in the Faculty of Political Science, Columbia Univ., 1928) ; F. F. Petitcler, "Recollections of Elder John Leland," in *Berkshire Hist. and Sci. Soc., Berkshire Book,* 1892, I, pt. 2, 269–90 ; J. T. Smith, "Life and Times of Rev. John Leland," *Bapt. Quart.,* Apr. 1871 ; Sherman Leland, *The Leland Mag., or a Geneal. Record of Henry Leland and His Descendants* (1850) ; R. J. Purcell, *Conn. in Transition* (1918) ; W. B. Sprague, *Annals Am. Pulpit,* vol. VI (1856) ; *Boston Transcript,* Jan. 21, 1841.]　　　　　　　　　　　H. M. M.

LEMKE, PETER HENRY (July 27, 1796– Nov. 29, 1882), Roman Catholic missionary, was born in Rhena, Mecklenburg, where his father

was a magistrate. Privately tutored, he entered the Gymnasium at Schwerin in 1810, paying his own way by giving music lessons. Three years later, he joined the army of liberation and after campaigning against Napoleon and the Danes entered Paris in 1814. During the "Hundred Days" he was again in service and fought at Waterloo under Blücher. He then matriculated at the University of Rostock. Reacting against the riotous student life there and the rationalist philosophy which he encountered, he entered the Lutheran ministry, in 1819. While preaching at Dassow, he studied the writings of Luther and through Adler, a student at Ratisbon, and Melchior Diepenbrock, later cardinal of Breslau, he grew interested in the Roman Catholic Church, which he joined in 1824. On the completion of his theological studies, he was ordained, Apr. 11, 1826, and assigned to a curacy at Ratisbon, where he preached to the garrison, gave religious instructions in the state school, and served as Cardinal Diepenbrock's vicar general. In 1831, he was called as a private chaplain by Frederick Schlosser, a nephew of Goethe and a book collector, who maintained an estate near Heidelberg. Here Lemke busied himself with agriculture, riding, and lectures at the University. A robust man of action, he tired of this sinecure; and on learning of the demand for German priests in Pennsylvania, volunteered for the American missions and eventually took passage, landing in New York, Aug. 20, 1834. He hurried to present himself to Bishop F. P. Kenrick [*q.v.*] of Philadelphia, who assigned him to the German parish of Holy Trinity and tutored him in English. Finding that he had annoyed the trustees of Holy Trinity by a sermon on Luther, he asked to be transferred to the missions of Demetrius Augustine Gallitzin [*q.v.*]. Journeying on horseback through the woods from Munster to Loretto, he met the aged Gallitzin bundled up in a sleigh, on his way to a mass-station, and was appointed to a log chapel at Ebensburg (1834), from which he attended the countryside.

Like his superior, he became enthusiastic over colonization projects, and in 1837 he purchased land at Hart's Sleeping Place which he farmed in model fashion. Three years later, he founded Carrolltown, where he erected a rude chapel. Though injured in felling a tree in this year, he followed the trail to Loretto to attend the dying Gallitzin, whose place he filled for four years on Bishop Kenrick's insistence. He had hardly returned to his beloved settlement at Carrolltown when he set out for Germany, where he collected vestments, books, and money, even from Louis of Bavaria. Proud of his American citizenship, he refused all posts offered him by Cardinal Diepenbrock. In Munich, he inspired Dom Boniface Wimmer [*q.v.*] to lead a colony of Benedictines to Pennsylvania, thus bringing to a successful conclusion a project which he had outlined as early as 1835 in the pages of *Der Katholik* of Mainz. In 1846, he met Wimmer's party in New York, but to his disappointment, the Benedictine abbey was built at Beatty on the Sportsman's Hall Property instead of at Carrolltown. Later, however, Lemke's Carrolltown acreage was used for a priory. Thereafter, he attended churches at Reading and Philadelphia until 1851, when he joined the Benedictines.

Somewhat too settled in habits to accommodate himself to the discipline of a religious, Father Lemke departed for "bleeding Kansas" without his superior's permission (1855). As soon as difficulties with the Abbot were compromised he was assigned to a congregation at Doniphan by Bishop J. B. Minge. He then took up land near Atchison, where eventually there was established the Abbey of St. Benedict. After complete reconciliation, he returned to Pennsylvania (1858) and then toured Germany in the interest of American missions. During a sojourn in Vienna, he wrote his *Leben und Werken des Prinzen Demetrius Augustin Gallitzin* (Münster, 1861) in an effort to stimulate missionary zeal. Upon his return from Europe, he acted as pastor of St. Michael's Church at Elizabeth, N. J. (1861–71), where he established a Benedictine academy. In 1871, he built St. Henry's Church, which he served until his retirement, soon after the celebration of his golden jubilee in the priesthood. His last years were spent in the Carrolltown priory among his aged colonists. During this period he wrote for the *Northern Cambria News* a serial memoir of early days in Cambria County.

[See F. Kittell, *Souvenir of Loretto Centenary* (1899); A. A. Lambing, *Hist. of the Cath. Ch. in the Dioceses of Pittsburg and Allegheny* (1880), and memoir of Lemke in *Ave Maria,* Jan. 20–Feb. 24, 1883; *Cath. Encyc.,* IX, 146; *Sadlier's Cath. Directory,* 1883; sketch by L. F. Flick, in *Records Am. Cath. Hist. Soc.,* IX (1898), 129–92; Oswald Moosmüler, *Bonifaz Wimmer* (1891). Although Lemke's name is sometimes spelled Lemcke, according to Flick, *ante,* he himself always spelled it without the "c."]   R. J. P.

LEMMON, JOHN GILL (Jan. 2, 1832–Nov. 24, 1908), botanist, was born at Lima, Mich., the son of William and Amila (Hudson) Lemmon. He attended the common schools and, for a time, the University of Michigan. Enlisting in the Union army in 1862, he was captured in 1864 and held in Andersonville Prison until the end of the war. In 1866, his health broken, he emigrated to Sierra Valley, California. Here, for a period of eight years, he wrote almost weekly letters to California newspapers, detailing in a fluent style his embittered recollections of the Civil War. Then one day a group of native herbs in the dooryard of his cabin attracted his attention and, recalling an early training in botany, he sent specimens of them to Asa Gray [*q.v.*]. Two of these were new species and one was named for him. He was of a highly enthusiastic temperament, and the incident changed the current of his life. His health partially restored by the new interest which meant to him undying fame, he eagerly set about the botanical exploration of wide untouched areas in California, Nevada, and finally Arizona, meanwhile keeping up for two decades a spirited correspondence with his botanical patron at Harvard. Highly successful in his herbarizings, he gratified his appetite for publicity by furnishing the newspaper public well-written articles on the wonders of California's vegetation and his own numerous discoveries at almost weekly intervals for a period of over twenty years. More than any other man of his time he acquainted the people of his adopted state with the existence of a science of botany.

Meantime he earned his living by keeping a small private school, and by reason of this occupation, assumed the title, professor. When Asa Gray came to California in 1876, Lemmon, ardent hero-worshiper, went to meet him, thrilled but with a secret fear that Gray would regard his professorship as irregular. The story of their meeting has been preserved: Gray, who was a little man, laid his hand with understanding kindness on the shoulder of the tall ungainly Lemmon and assured him that he was more of a professor than many of greater pretensions. Lemmon, glorified by the benediction, wore proudly to the end of his life the title thus confirmed by the great Harvard botanist.

In 1880 he married Sara Allen Plummer. He was gentle and she firm, but the two by their interests and instincts were admirably suited to each other; and they agreed to dedicate their lives to botanical science and to all altruistic movements. Their lack of money, however, tangled the skein of all their activities and efforts. Income derived from the collection and sale of botanical specimens proved insufficient for their needs, and Lemmon secured appointment to superintend California's exhibit in forestry and botany at the Cotton Centennial Exposition in New Orleans in 1884. He next promoted the movement to create a state board of forestry and was appointed its botanist in 1888. He made two reports on the forest trees of California,

"Pines of the Pacific Slope" (1888) and "Cone-bearers of California" (1890), in the biennial reports of the California State Board of Forestry. These volumes, the first attempt to undertake an account of the Pacific Coast forests from the standpoint of forestry, had high value and attracted world-wide attention. Though they are now forty years old, foresters of the present day recognize the similarity of Lemmon's canons of forest management to those of present-day practice. As botanist to the state board he served four years. California was still too backward to understand the need of scientific forestry, however, and the political causes which had set up the forestry board soon brought about its end. By way of popular education, Lemmon now issued a number of booklets and pamphlets on the trees, such as *Hand-book of West-American Cone-bearers* (1892) and *How to Tell the Trees; and Forest Endowment of the Pacific Slope* (1902), thus diffusing among the people a knowledge of the state's forests and helping to prepare public opinion for the established forestry policy which came after his death.

For the last twenty-eight years of his life he was a resident of Oakland, where he and his wife busied themselves with many civic and reform activities. He died in his seventy-seventh year, survived by the helpmeet who had energized his life. Mount Lemmon, a fine peak in the Tucson Range of Arizona, where he did valuable field work, was named for him.

[This sketch is based chiefly on MSS., including the abundant Lemmon correspondence. Exaggerated accounts of Lemmon and his wife have appeared in the ephemeral press. An obituary of Lemmon appeared in the *Examiner* (San Francisco), Nov. 25, 1908. The sketch by George Wharton James, in his *Heroes of California* (1910), is highly colored and somewhat exaggerated; it relates mainly to the field work of the Lemmons in Arizona. See also J. M. Guinn, *Hist. of the State of Cal. and Biog. Record of Oakland* (1907), vol. II.]   W. L. J.

LEMOYNE, FRANCIS JULIUS (Sept. 4, 1798–Oct. 14, 1879), physician, abolitionist, advocate of cremation, was the son and grandson of Parisian physicians. His father, John Julius LeMoyne de Villiers, came to America with French colonists, among whom he practised his profession for four years at Gallipolis, Ohio. In 1797 he married Nancy McCully, lately arrived from Ireland, and they removed to Washington, Pa., where Francis Julius was born. After graduating at Washington College in 1815, he studied medicine first with his father and later at Jefferson Medical College in Philadelphia. Returning homeward across the Alleghanies in 1822, he encountered a great snowstorm. The party in the stagecoach were unable to find ac-

commodation at the crowded taverns along the way and so all night pushed forward through intense cold. Reaching Pittsburgh, Francis procured a horse and rode on to Washington. Although he was of robust constitution, after this experience he suffered from chronic rheumatism that did not allow him a night's repose in bed through twenty-nine years.

In 1823 he married Madeleine Romaine Bureau, whom he met at his father's house, whither she had brought a sister from Gallipolis for medical treatment. They had three sons and five daughters. About the time of his marriage, LeMoyne's father in helping others became bankrupt, so that to the physical handicap of the young doctor was added a burden of debt. From friends he was able to borrow money and recover the fine homestead built by his father in 1813, which with its old garden is still a point of interest in Washington. By hard work and frugal living he succeeded in restoring the family fortune after several years. In the decade of the thirties he was an intrepid supporter of the anti-slavery movement, and an able debater in its cause, showing much physical courage in opposing the American Colonization Society, which he believed to be founded in the interests of slavery. He was the candidate of the Liberty Party for the vice-presidency of the United States in 1840, and the candidate of the Abolitionists for the governorship of Pennsylvania in 1841, 1844, and 1847. Later his house became one of the stations of the "Underground Railway," enabling slaves to reach freedom in the North.

When he was about fifty-five, the condition of his health made the active practice of medicine no longer possible for him, and he turned to scientific farming, introducing improved strains of sheep, cattle, and horses into the county. He donated $10,000 to the founding of a public library in his town, and for many years catalogued the books as they were acquired. Deeply concerned in the cause of education, he became in 1830 a trustee of Washington College (after 1865 Washington and Jefferson College) and in 1836, of the Washington Female Seminary at its founding. He gave the American Missionary Association $20,000 for the endowment and erection, on a bluff near Memphis, Tenn., of the LeMoyne Normal Institute for colored people, still a successful enterprise. Later he added $5,000 for its equipment. He established two professorships of $20,000 each at Washington and Jefferson College, one in agriculture and correlative branches (1872), the other in applied mathematics (1879). These donations were prompted by the conviction that for students not entering the learned professions more profit was to be derived from the physical sciences than from Latin and Greek.

About 1874, in France and Italy, there was a sudden rise of interest in favor of cremation as a means of disposing of the dead, and LeMoyne became its first prominent advocate in America. In 1876 he erected the first crematory in the United States, situated on his own property on a hill overlooking Washington, where it stands today. The first public cremation took place there on Dec. 6, 1876. It was that of a Bavarian nobleman, Baron Joseph Henry Louis de Palm who had come to America in 1862 and had died in New York. The event aroused much comment at the time. The body of LeMoyne himself was the third to be cremated, and up to the year 1900 there had been forty-one cremations in that place; since then none have occurred.

[*Commemorative Biographical Record of Washington County, Pa.* (1893); Alfred Creigh, *Hist. of Washington County, Pa.* (2nd ed., 1871); Boyd Crumrine, *Hist. of Washington County, Pa.* (1882); E. R. Forrest, *Hist. of Washington County, Pa.* (1926); *Phila. Record*, Oct. 15, 1879; information from LeMoyne's daughter, Mrs. George W. Reed of Washington, Pa.] E. M. W.

LE MOYNE, JEAN BAPTISTE [See BIENVILLE, JEAN BAPTISTE LE MOYNE, Sieur de, 1680–1768].

LE MOYNE, PIERRE [See IBERVILLE, PIERRE LE MOYNE, Sieur d', 1661–1706].

LE MOYNE, WILLIAM J. (Apr. 29, 1831–Nov. 6, 1905), actor, began his career in the theatre as a member of one of the numerous amateur dramatic clubs that flourished in Boston during the middle nineteenth century. He was born in that city, probably the son of Thomas and Elizabeth (Cody) Le Moyne, and after appearances with the Aurora Dramatic Club, of which he was a founder, at the Howard Athenæum and elsewhere in Boston, he went to Portland, Me., as a minor member of the company in which Catherine Norton Sinclair, the recently divorced wife of Edwin Forrest, was starring under the tutelage and with the support of George Vandenhoff. There he made his professional début, on May 10, 1852, as one of the officers in *The Lady of Lyons.* During that engagement he also played Friar Lawrence in *Romeo and Juliet,* Sir Oliver Surface in *The School for Scandal,* and Polydor in *Ingomar.* From that time onward he was continuously active in his profession for almost fifty years, with the exception of his period of service in the Union army during the Civil War. Going to Troy, N. Y., he joined the stock company under the management of George C. Howard, acting Deacon Parry in the first dra-

matic version of *Uncle Tom's Cabin.* He was for several seasons in Montreal, Philadelphia, Charleston, and Boston, being at the Howard Athenæum, Boston, in 1859–60 when that historic playhouse was under the management of Edward L. Davenport [*q.v.*]. In October 1861 he enlisted in Company B, 28th Massachusetts Regiment, being first lieutenant while Lawrence Barrett [*q.v.*] was captain, and succeeding Barrett when the latter resigned. He took part in the battles of James Island, second Bull Run, Chantilly, and South Mountain, where he was wounded. Permanently incapacitated for further service, he was honorably discharged. In after years he was wont to tell stories of picturesque and exciting incidents of his life as a soldier.

Returning to the stage upon his recovery, he began, after several seasons of desultory tours, an engagement with the stock company at Selwyn's Theatre in Boston which continued three successive seasons. Beginning in the fall of 1871, he was a member for two seasons of Augustin Daly's company at the Fifth Avenue Theatre in New York, his first part there being Burrit in *Divorce.* This rôle was followed by a number of others, which included Rocket Rural in *Old Heads and Young Hearts,* Moody in *The Provoked Husband,* Sir Harcourt Courtley in *London Assurance,* Simon in *Article 47,* Silky in *The Road to Ruin,* Dr. Caius in *Merry Wives of Windsor,* and Lord Durly in *Madeline Morel.* By the historian of that company, Edward A. Dithmar (*post*), he is described as "a natural humorist and a master of the art of make-up." He was at the Boston Museum for three seasons thereafter, and during this decade acquired a considerable fame on tour in a group of plays that gave him opportunity to interpret such divergent Dickens characters as Caleb Plummer, Captain Cuttle, Uriah Heep, Squeers, Fagin, and Dick Swiveller. From the beginning of the season of 1877–78 he was associated almost continuously for nearly twenty years with one or another of the leading New York stock companies, at the Union Square, Daly's, the Madison Square, and the Lyceum, the cast of practically every play given at the last mentioned theatre, during his ten years there, containing his name in an important rôle. He was the first Dick Phenyl in the United States in Pinero's comedy, *Sweet Lavender,* and among the many parts he acted at the Lyceum Theatre were Major Homer Q. Putnam in *The Wife,* Judge Knox in *The Charity Ball,* and Sir Joseph Darby in *The Case of Rebellious Susan.* The annual tours of the Lyceum company made his acting familiar to large numbers of playgoers in all the important cities of the United States. He

Leney

supported Julia Marlowe in *Barbara Frietchie* in 1899–1900, but after a few other engagements was compelled to retire from the stage on account of ill health. William Winter (*post*, I, 286) says he was "an actor of rare talent and remarkable versatility. His impersonations of eccentric, humorous, peppery old gentlemen were among the finest and most amusing that our stage has known." He died at Inwood-on-Hudson, N. Y., where he had been living since his retirement. He was divorced from his first wife. His second wife was an actress, first known on the stage as Sarah Cowell, and after her marriage as Sarah Cowell Le Moyne, under which name she starred in *The Greatest Thing in the World* and other plays.

[J. B. Clapp and E. F. Edgett, *Players of the Present* (1899); W. F. Gilchrest, in F. E. McKay and C. E. L. Wingate, *Famous Am. Actors of Today* (1896); E. A. Dithmar, *Memories of Daly's Theatres* (privately printed, 1897); T. A. Brown, *A Hist. of the N. Y. Stage* (1903); Kate Ryan, *Old Boston Museum Days* (1915); J. F. Daly, *The Life of Augustin Daly* (1917); William Winter, *The Life of David Belasco* (1918), vol. I; Arthur Hornblow, *A Hist. of the Theatre in America* (1919); *N. Y. Dramatic Mirror*, Mar. 23, 1895, Nov. 11, 1905; *The Sun* (N. Y.), Aug. 31, 1902; *Boston Transcript*, Nov. 6, 1905; *N. Y. Tribune*, *N. Y. Times*, Nov. 7, 1905.]   E. F. E.

LENEY, WILLIAM SATCHWELL (Jan. 16, 1769–Nov. 26, 1831), engraver, born in London of Scotch lineage, was the son of Alexander and Susanna Leney. As a youth he was articled to a clever, original artist, Peltro W. Tompkins, who held an appointment as historical engraver to Queen Charlotte and as drawing-master to the royal princesses. Tompkins executed considerable imaginative work as well as portraits of dignitaries, and young Leney, well-trained in the practice of both line and stipple engraving, "a smooth and dextrous worker" (Weitenkampf), followed his master into both fields. He was engraving over his own name for London publishers when he had little more than attained his majority. During his English career he executed numerous portraits, magazine illustrations, a series of small line plates portraying scenes from stage plays for John Bell's *British Theatre* (1791–97), and six large plates after Fuseli and others, for Boydell's Shakespeare. He also engraved a large plate of Rubens' "Descent from the Cross," of such merit that it won him a gold medal.

Leney was about thirty-six when, with his wife, Sarah (White) Leney, he left England for America, settling in New York. The directory for 1806–07 shows him established as an historical engraver in Greenwich Street, "near the Market." The New York of the opening century offered a promising field to a skilled engraver.

L'Enfant

America, beginning to take account of its assets in public men and natural beauty, was demanding portraits of the one and scenic "views" of the other, and developing an appetite for illustrated books and magazines. Leney engraved several large plates for Collins' Quarto Bible (1807), executed portrait plates for *Delaplaine's Repository* (1815) and the *Analectic Magazine,* and also a series of large plates of scenery, mostly in and about New York. Among his more important portraits are Trumbull's DeWitt Clinton, Stuart's Captain Lawrence and John Jay, West's Robert Fulton, Sully's Patrick Henry, Copley's John Adams, and Washington after Stuart and Houdon. His work commanded large prices for that early day, as is shown by entries in his account-book indicating that he received as much as $100 to $150 for engraving an octavo portrait. In 1812 he threw in his lot with William Rollinson [*q.v.*], banknote engraver, for whom he executed portrait vignettes. Rollinson's prospectus characterizes his partner as "the first artist in America and of very respectable rank in life." About 1820 Leney, with his wife and nine children, retired to a farm on the St. Lawrence at Longue Pointe, near Montreal, where he passed the rest of his life. For some years he continued to engrave, executing the first banknotes for the Bank of Montreal and a series of large views of Quebec and the Montreal region, which are now rare. He left numerous descendants in Canada.

[Frank Weitenkampf, *Am. Graphic Art* (1912); W. S. Baker, *The Engraved Portraits of Washington* (1880), and *Am. Engravers* (1875); *One Hundred Notable Engravers* (N. Y. Pub. Lib., 1928); D. M. Stauffer, *Am. Engravers* (1907), vol. I; G. C. Williamson, *Bryan's Dict. of Painters and Engravers*, vol. III (1927).]   M. B. H.

L'ENFANT, PIERRE CHARLES (Aug. 2, 1754–June 14, 1825), soldier, engineer, was born in Paris. His father was Pierre L'Enfant, one of the "painters in ordinary to the King in his Manufacture of the Gobelins"; his mother was Marie Charlotte Leullier. Many of his father's paintings, battle scenes and landscapes, are preserved, several at the Musée de Versailles. The son apparently had received some instruction in engineering and architecture before his enthusiasm took him, at twenty-three, to fight for the independence of the United States. He served as a volunteer at his own expense, and spent his modest means freely in the enterprise. Accorded the brevet of lieutenant in the French colonial forces, he was promised by Silas Deane [*q.v.*] and later received, through resolutions of Congress, a commission as first lieutenant of engineers, with rank from Dec. 1, 1776. On Feb. 14,

1777, he sailed from L'Orient with Colonel du Coudray, a month ahead of Lafayette, and spent the winter at Valley Forge. On Feb. 18, 1778, he was commissioned captain of engineers, attached to the inspector-general, Steuben [*q.v.*]. A letter of his as published in translation in Rivington's *Gazette* contained some expressions which L'Enfant felt impelled to repudiate in a letter to Washington from White Plains, Sept. 4, 1778 (Library of Congress, Washington Papers, XXV, 337), leaving Washington's regard for his services unimpaired.

Seeing no prospect of action in the North he secured his transfer to the Southern army where he served under Laurens. In the assault on Savannah, Oct. 9, 1779, he was wounded while leading the advance guard of an American column. Still using a crutch when the enemy invested Charleston, he was made a prisoner in the capitulation of the city in May, and was not exchanged until January 1782. Returning to Philadelphia, he was promoted major by special resolution of Congress May 2, 1783, and on June 13 received a French pension of three hundred livres and was presented for a captaincy in the French provincial forces. In July and August he was with Steuben in his journey to secure the British evacuation of the posts on the northern frontier. Following leave to go to France, he was honorably retired from the American service in January 1784.

During the war his artistic abilities had been called into service on more than one occasion. In response to a request from Lafayette, Washington sat to L'Enfant for his portrait, an outline sketch only, which has not survived. At West Point is a sketch of the encampment of the Revolutionary army in the Highlands of the Hudson with an inscription by General Knox: "By Major L'Enfant, Engineer, 1780." Of his authorship there can be no doubt, but the date must be placed after his return to the North. He designed a pavilion for the fête given in Philadelphia July 15, 1782, by the French minister, to celebrate the birth of the Dauphin (*Pennsylvania Magazine,* vol. XXI, 1897, pp. 257 ff.).

He was one of the early members of the Society of the Cincinnati and, submitting by request a design for a medal, he proposed the wearing of an eagle instead. The eagle, which was adopted, and the diploma of the Society were both of his design (B. J. Lossing, *The Pictorial Field Book of the Revolution,* vol. II, 1852, p. 126 n.; L'Enfant's original drawings are in the archives of the Society in New York). He was asked to have these designs executed abroad, and late in 1783 sailed for France, charged by Washington

with copies of the constitution of the Society and communications to the leading French officers.

Soon he showed the defects of his fine qualities of imagination and enthusiasm. He had undertaken to go at his own expense. "The reception which the Cincinnati met with," he wrote Hamilton, "soon induced me to appear in that country in a manner consistent with the dignity of the society of which I was regarded as the representative. . . . My abode at court produced expenses far beyond the sums I at first thought of" (Jusserand, *post,* p. 148). For the eagles ordered from Duval and Francastel, the large sum of 22,303 livres had to be carried on credit and was still unpaid three years later. Such financial difficulties caused L'Enfant to hasten back to New York, where he arrived Apr. 29, 1784. Fortunately the Society was appreciative of his efforts, and ultimately reimbursed him in part for his expenses.

Living in New York, he found occasional and increasing occupation for his talents. When in the autumn of 1787 Caffieri's monument to General Montgomery found its resting place under the portico of St. Paul's, facing Broadway, L'Enfant was asked to devise a means of concealing the rough stonework of the back which was visible from within through the great east window behind the altar. Accordingly, he designed the reredos still existing, a typical Louis XV composition of clouds and sunburst, with the tables of the Mosaic law. An altar rail was added in the same style, unique in America (Morgan Dix, *A History of the Parish of Trinity Church,* vol. II, 1901, pp. 141–42). The following July, he assisted in devising the pageantry of the procession in favor of New York's adopting the Constitution. At the banquet afterwards, the President and members of Congress sat under a dome of his design, surmounted by a figure of Fame proclaiming the new era. (A contemporary drawing and a description are given in the *New York Historical Society Quarterly Bulletin,* July 1925.) It was a fitting prelude to his next work, the first capitol of the young republic.

A large sum was subscribed to provide suitable accommodation for the new government in New York, its temporary seat, and L'Enfant was entrusted with the task of converting the old Jacobean City Hall at the head of Wall Street, on the site of the present Sub-Treasury, into Federal Hall. Here Congress met Mar. 4, 1789, and on the balcony, the railing of which is preserved by the New York Historical Society, Washington was inaugurated on Apr. 30. The building was indeed worthy of the occasion, both in form and symbolism. The House of Representatives, adorned with niches, occupied the rear portion of the lower story; the Senate chamber, over the foyer, had chimney pieces of American marble; the pilasters had American emblems; the thirteen metopes of the frieze without were each adorned with a star. The front, with a tall colonnaded loggia over a high basement, was illustrated in the *Massachusetts Magazine* (June 1789) and the *Columbia Magazine or Monthly Miscellany* (August 1789). It was the inspiration of James Hoban [*q.v.*] in the front of his South Carolina Capitol at Columbia. The cost, indeed, ran far beyond the funds subscribed, but the New Yorkers, hoping the handsome building would help them to retain the capital permanently, were reconciled; and, besides a handsome testimonial, they offered L'Enfant ten acres of land near Provost Lane. Feeling it less than his deserts, L'Enfant declined this gift. A decade later, when in financial distress, he made a request for payment in money instead, but again declined the $750 which was tendered.

L'Enfant now had his great opportunity, and proved himself worthy of it in imagination and prophetic foresight, if not in discretion. He was called on by Washington to survey the site and make the plan for the new Federal City. He stimulated Washington to enlarge the size of the area acquired to make it "proportioned to the greatness which . . . the Capitale of a powerfull Empire ought to manifest" (document in Kite, *post*, p. 47). For the site of the Capitol he urged the choice of Jenkins' Heights, which "stand as a pedestal waiting for a monument"; for the President's house, a lower eminence with a broad sweeping view southward toward the Potomac. He rejected the suggestion of a merely rectangular street plan, as "but a mean continance of some cool imagination, wanting a sense of the real grand and truly beautiful." "Having first determined," he writes, "some principal points to which I wished making the rest subordinate I next made the distribution regular with streets at right angle, *north-south* and *east-west,* but afterwards I opened others on various directions, as avenues to and from every principal places . . . menaging a reisprocity of sight." On these principles he produced by June 22 the essential features of his design. (See Memoir of June 22, 1791, printed in *Records of the Columbia Historical Society,* vol. II, 1899.) The more complete plan submitted to the President in August is preserved in the Library of Congress.

Although L'Enfant, in asking Jefferson for the plans of various European cities for reference (Apr. 4, 1791, see Kite, p. 42), emphasized that "it is my wish and shall be my endeavor to delineate on a new and original way the plan," and gives no hint which would diminish his own originality or arouse republican hostility, there can be no doubt that he was greatly influenced by the plan of what was then the French capital, Versailles (Fiske Kimball: "The Origin of the Plan of Washington, D. C.," *Architectural Review,* September 1918; Elbert Peets, "The Genealogy of L'Enfant's Washington," *Journal of the American Institute of Architects,* April-June 1927). The Capitol corresponds in position to the palace, the President's house to the Grand Trianon, the Mall to the *parc,* East Capitol Street, Pennsylvania and Maryland avenues on the east to the Avenues de Paris, de Sceaux, and de St. Cloud. On the west, Pennsylvania Avenue corresponds essentially with the Avenue de Trianon. L'Enfant was far, however, from forcing this analogy, and gave constant consideration to the nature of the ground.

Setting to work with the greatest energy, he cleared the principal sites and avenues, eager to establish their full extent at once, and even to begin the public buildings, plans for which he had not yet submitted. Difficulties soon arose through his unwillingness to submit to the authority of the Commissioners of the Federal District, or even to that of the President. He opposed the immediate sale of lots, withholding his plan at the sale itself even from members of Congress; and before the plan had been legally adopted or even completed on paper, forcibly tore down a house, previously begun by a powerful land-owner, which was found to lie within a street. To Washington's successive gentle "admonition," kindly "reprehension," and later reproof, he merely returned his own justifications and reasons. They might indeed have been convincing under other circumstances. Certainly it would have been desirable, abstractly, to postpone sales until the public itself, rather than speculators, should receive the increment of value on its lots; to push the work rapidly with a great force; to begin simultaneously the canals, wharves, bridges, aqueducts, the terracing and grading and quarrying operations, all of which he proposed to undertake in 1792 and some of which, without consultation, he had already begun before winter. It was natural, too, that the original proprietors, who later signed a testimonial to L'Enfant (Mar. 9, 1792), should be pleased with such a program of activity, which promised a rapid increase of value to their own lots. But this program left the Commissioners, the Secretary of State, and the President aghast, involving as it did more in the first year than the entire sum available for all the work, and necessitating an immediate borrowing of a million dollars, at a time when the hostility of many states made the whole Federal City project extremely precarious. Convinced of L'Enfant's genius, Washington and Jefferson exhausted every means of securing due subordination through official instructions and friendly private explanations, but L'Enfant was impervious to all. On Feb. 27 he was instructed that his services were at an end.

Among those interested in the Federal City who preserved their faith in L'Enfant were Hamilton and Robert Morris. Hamilton was the moving spirit in the Society for Establishing Useful Manufactures, which proposed to use the power of the falls of the Passaic, at Paterson, N. J. In July 1792, on Hamilton's recommendation, the Society employed L'Enfant at a salary of $1500 to lay out the "capital scene of manufactures." On Sept. 22 he laid before the directors "a plan of the town, which far exceeds anything of the kind yet seen in this country," and was pushing work on the first buildings and on the power canal. By 1793 it was evident that L'Enfant's plans and beginnings were over-sanguine, and he was at odds with the other executive officers of the corporation. In June he was even summarily suspended by some of the directors, but Hamilton intervened and L'Enfant continued at work with some measure of authority until September, when, having secured new employment, he accepted an honorable discharge. His expense accounts caused some demur, and in October he refused to give up certain plans. The differences between his employers' view of him and his own view of himself as an independent professional man were here as elsewhere, irreconcilable. (The whole affair is best covered by J. S. Davis, *Essays in the Earlier History of American Corporations,* 1917, I, 349–493.)

Morris and his associates, who were the principal speculators in lots in Washington, recognized in L'Enfant a man who could minister also to their tastes for elegance of life. John Nicholson, Morris's partner, employed him on his house on Ridge Avenue, reputed to have been built in 1791 at a cost of $50,000. Old views make it seem probable that L'Enfant's agency was confined to the interior. He also designed rooms for the Philadelphia Assembly. The project for a separate building proving abortive, a room was decorated at Oeller's Hotel—"most elegant, . . . with a handsome music gallery at one end . . . papered after the French taste, with the Pantheon figures in compartments . . ." (Wansey's *Excursion to the United States,* 1794, cited by T. W. Balch in

The Philadelphia Assemblies, 1916, p. 100). His chief undertaking in Philadelphia, however, was Morris's famous house on Chestnut Street between Seventh and Eighth streets. It followed the style of L'Enfant's youth in Paris, untouched by the mounting classical tide of intervening years. Like the Hotel Moras (Biron), it had bowed pavilions at either end. A colonnade was to run between; the exterior, by L'Enfant's insistence, was to be faced with marble. In the fall of 1793 L'Enfant was actively at work, but his plans were so ambitious that the cost was multiplied by ten, and two years later Morris was begging that at least the west wing could be covered before winter (E. P. Oberholtzer, *Robert Morris,* 1903, pp. 298, 331). The financial embarrassments which crowded on Morris brought the work, little further advanced, to a standstill in 1797, and his complete bankruptcy in 1798 left promissory notes for large sums in L'Enfant's hands. The unfinished house, as depicted in Birch's well-known engraving, was set down as "Morris's Folly," and a larger share in his ruin was attributed to it than it deserved. Across the account of his property Morris wrote: "A much more magnificent house than I ever intended to have built." It was sold by the sheriff in 1797 and its ruins were demolished in 1801. There survive today only two bas-reliefs carved by the sculptor Jardella, one incorporated at the time in one of the Drayton tombs in South Carolina; the other, formerly at Harmonville, recently built into the house at "Olney," Harford County, Md.

The federal government, not averse to indicating that it still respected L'Enfant's abilities, on Apr. 3, 1794, appointed him temporary engineer at Fort Mifflin on Mud Island in the Delaware, charging him with the duty of strengthening the defenses. The fort had been first built by the British officer Montresor, and, until attacked from the rear, had made an excellent resistance against the British in their approach to Philadelphia. A plan designed by L'Enfant (now lost) was submitted to Congress by the Secretary of War, Dec. 19, 1794 (*American State Papers, Military Affairs,* vol. I, 1832, pp. 82–86), but little actual construction was done by L'Enfant, and we may assume that once more his proposals were too extensive for the means available at the time. After 1800 he appears chiefly as a claimant against the federal government, haunting the halls of Congress. His compensation for the work at Washington had not been fixed in advance. His claims for services ultimately rose to the fantastic amount of $95,500, as against the sum of $2,500 to $3,000 which Washington and the Commissioners had thought he would consider liberal. On two occasions Congress did vote certain grants to him which went to his creditors, leaving him still unsatisfied. That the administration remained well disposed was proved on two occasions: In 1812 he was tendered appointment as professor of civil and military engineering in the new Military Academy at West Point, but the entreaties of Monroe, then secretary of state, could not prevail on him to accept. The War of 1812 again brought him employment, in work on Fort Washington on the Potomac (*Ibid.*, pp. 587–88), but the old story of disappointed hopes and claims was here once more repeated.

Of his last years we have a picture in a letter of Thomas Digges, whose hospitable roof near Fort Washington furnished him a friendly asylum. "The old Major is still intimate with me—quiet, harmless and unoffending as usual—I fear from symptoms of broken shoes, rent pantaloons, out at elbows, &c &c that he is not well off—manifestly disturbed at his getting *the go by* . . . never facing toward the Fort, tho' frequently dipping into the eastern ravines and hills of the plantation—picking up fossils and periwinkles—early to bed and rising—working hard with his instruments on paper eight or ten hours every day as if to give full and complete surveys of his works &c . . ." (Library of Congress, L'Enfant-Digges-Morgan Papers, Oct. 26, 1816). He remained with the Digges family, removing finally to "Green Hill," the estate of William Dudley Digges in Prince George's County, where he laid out the grounds and gardens, and where he died June 14, 1825. His personal effects, a few surveying instruments, books, and maps, were valued at $45.

His aspect in somewhat earlier days, as reported from the recollections of W. W. Corcoran, was that of "a tall, erect man, fully six feet in height, finely proportioned, nose prominent, of military bearing, courtly air and polite manners, his figure usually enveloped in a long overcoat and surmounted by a bell-crowned hat—a man who would attract attention in any assembly" (*Records of the Columbia Historical Society*, II, 216).

L'Enfant was a hundred years ahead of his time. Through the decades of the nineteenth century the city of Washington was slowly growing up to his plan, and its wide dispersion over a large area prompted many a gibe at its chimerical designer. In the age of romanticism and formlessness, numerous and serious departures were made from it. The Mall was planted as an informal park, instead of a great *allée*. The Washington Monument was located neither quite on one of the chief axes, nor on the other. But a glorious resurrection awaited the design; and an apotheosis, its maker. The Park Commission of 1901 recognized all its merits, and recommended its restoration and extension. In letter and spirit it governs the development of the capital of today. L'Enfant's remains, disinterred from their unmarked grave, lay in state in the Capitol and were honored by the President and a great concourse (Apr. 28, 1909). They found a final resting place at Arlington, among the soldier dead, overlooking the city he had designed, and with its plan, his greatest title to fame, graved on the slab above.

[The chief manuscript sources are the L'Enfant-Digges-Morgan Papers, Washington Papers, Jefferson Papers, Hamilton Papers, and District of Columbia Papers from the Dept. of State, all in the MSS. Div., Lib. of Cong. The Taggart Papers in the same repository contain many clippings and transcripts regarding L'Enfant. The fullest publication of documents (some fully emended) pertaining to his connection with the Federal City is Elizabeth S. Kite, "L'Enfant and Washington," *Hist. Docs.: Institut Français de Washington,* cahier III (1929). This does not entirely supersede the earlier and more exact publication of documents in the *Records of the Columbia Hist. Soc.*, vols. II (1899), XI (1908), XIII (1910), and XVII (1914). The fullest and most judicious notice of his life is that of J. J. Jusserand in his *With Americans of Past and Present Days* (1916), reprinted as an introduction to "L'Enfant and Washington," cited above. Further details of his military career are given by Thomas Balch in *The French in America during the War of Independence*, vol. II (1895) and by A. B. Gardiner in *The Order of the Cincinnati in France* (1905). An obituary appeared in the *Daily National Intelligencer* (Washington), June 25, 1825.]
F. K.

LENKER, JOHN NICHOLAS (Nov. 28, 1858–May 16, 1929), Lutheran clergyman, historian, and translator, was born at Sunbury, Pa., the son of John Bobb and Mary Ann (Gearhart) Lenker. He attended Wittenberg College in Springfield, Ohio, where he received the degrees of A.B. and A.M. in 1879 and 1880, and in 1881 he received the candidate of theology degree from Hamma Divinity School in Springfield. The next year he spent in graduate study at the University of Leipzig, Germany. He was ordained in 1880 but did not enter the active ministry until two years later when he was called to Grand Island, Nebr. After four years there he was called to work for the Board of Church Extension of the General Synod of the Evangelical Lutheran Church in the United States and in eight years raised $400,000 for this cause. He then turned his attention to the virgin field of Pan-Lutheranism. During his student days in Germany he had traveled at his own expense in Denmark, Norway, Sweden, Finland, Russia, the Baltic Provinces, and in Austria and Germany. Everywhere he tried to arouse the churches to a "Lutheran consciousness," and everywhere he sought to persuade the churches in the older lands to take a conciliatory attitude toward the daughter churches in the "diaspora." To bridge the gap between the old and the new lands, Lenker joined Dr. Luthardt of Leipzig University and Pastor Medem of Magdeburg in publishing three pamphlets *Kirchliches Addressbuch fuer Auswanderer nach Nordamerika* (1882), *Blank Letters of Recommendation* (1882?), and *Dringende Bitte fuer Auswanderer* (1882). But the seeds of Pan-Lutheranism were most effectively sowed and disseminated in the epochal and prophetic Lutherans in All Lands Series.

In 1893 Lenker published a book, built largely of the materials that he had collected in his travels and from first-hand correspondence with leaders in various lands, which he called *Lutherans in All Lands*. The first edition of more than eight hundred pages was supplemented by other editions, the most notable being the supplemented edition of 1919. In 1901 the book appeared in German under the title *Die Lutherische Kirche der Welt*. A Lutherans in All Lands Company was formed at Grand Island, Nebr., and later at Minneapolis, Minn.; both of these were superseded by the Luther Press at Minneapolis. From these presses came the *Lutherans in All Lands Quarterly* and the *Northern Review*, both under the editorship of Lenker.

From 1900 to 1904 Lenker was at the Danish-American Lutheran institution, Trinity Seminary, Blair, Nebr., where he taught church history, Old Testament exegesis, Hebrew, and German. Again straining at the leash of routine, he set about to make another dream come true. Some years earlier he had resolved that he would issue a standard edition of Luther's works for the English-speaking people. The first volume, *Luther's Commentary on the First Twenty-two Psalms*, translated by Henry Cole, was issued in 1903. *Luther on the Creation* was published in 1904, supplemented in 1910 by a second volume: *Luther on Sin and the Flood. The Epistles of St. Peter and St. Jude* also appeared in 1904. Of "Luther's Church Postil Gospels," one volume appeared in 1904, two in 1905, one in 1906, and one in 1907. *Luther on Christian Education* was published in 1907. "Luther's Epistle Sermons" were published in three volumes (1908–09). These thirteen volumes were all issued from Lenker's two Minneapolis presses. At his death he had nine other volumes of Luther's works ready for the press. Lenker was president of the General Lutheran Missionary Conference; vice-president of the American Lutheran Mission for Russia; secretary of the American Lutheran Sta-

tistical Association; and founder of the students' missionary societies of Norway, Sweden, and Finland. On Sept. 18, 1919, he was married to Nora Cecelia Walsted of Christiania (Oslo), Norway. After 1904 he made his home in Minneapolis.

[See *Who's Who in America,* 1928–29; J. C. Jenssen (Roseland), *Am. Luth. Biogs.* (1890); *Luth. Church Herald,* June 11, 1929; the *Lutheran,* June 13, 1929; *Minneapolis Morning Tribune,* May 17, 1929. Information as to certain facts has been supplied by Lenker's friends and by Mrs. John Nicholas Lenker.]

J. M. R.

LENNON, JOHN BROWN (Oct. 12, 1850– Jan. 17, 1923), for twenty-seven years treasurer of the American Federation of Labor, was born in Lafayette County, Wis. When he was two years old his parents, John Alexander and Elizabeth Fletcher (Brown) Lennon, moved to Hannibal, Mo., where the boy attended the public schools. After his father entered the Union army in 1861, John, at the age of eleven, was obliged to assist his mother with the responsibility of their small farm. His father was a tailor by trade and after the war reopened his shop in Hannibal, where John served four years' apprenticeship. In 1869 he went West, settling in Denver, Colo., where he set himself up as merchant tailor. The next year he was joined by his parents and sisters, his father took charge of the shop, and young Lennon became a journeyman for various merchant tailors of Denver. On Apr. 5, 1871, he married Juna J. Allen of Hannibal.

Lennon was instrumental in organizing a Tailor's Union in Denver, of which he became secretary. Before the end of the convention year 1883, the Denver union became affiliated with the new national organization, the Journeyman Tailors' Union of America. The following year, while acting as president of his local union, Lennon was appointed as a delegate to the convention of the national union at Chicago. Here he was chosen national president, and in 1885 became one of the vice-presidents. Elected general secretary in 1887, he moved to New York, the seat of the national headquarters. At this time he also became first editor of *The Tailor,* the official journal of the organization. In 1896 the general office was removed to Bloomington, Ill., which was Lennon's home thenceforth until his death. He continued as general secretary until July 1910.

A delegate from the Tailors' Union to the convention of the American Federation of Labor for the first time in 1889, he was elected treasurer of the latter organization in 1890 and served continuously until 1917. As a member of the executive council he was closely associated with

Samuel Gompers [*q.v.*] and others prominent in the Labor Movement. In his later years he became well known as a public speaker, delivering numerous addresses upon the church and labor, and the anti-saloon movement before considerable gatherings in various parts of the country. He was a leader in organizing the forces arrayed against the liquor traffic and a member of the committee on social service of the Federal Council of Churches of Christ in America. In 1913 he was appointed by President Wilson as one of the three labor members representing the conservative traditions of the American Federation of Labor on the Commission on Industrial Relations, whose report was published in 1915. In 1917 he became a member of the board of mediators of the United States Department of Labor.

[*Who's Who in America*, 1922–23; *The Tailor*, Jan. 23, Feb. 5, 1923; P. U. Kellogg, in *Rev. of Revs.* (N. Y.), Sept. 1913; *Am. Federationist*, Mar. 1923; *N. Y. Times*, Jan. 19, 1923; *Daily Bulletin* (Bloomington, Ill.), Jan. 18, 1923.] 　　　　J. R. C.

LENNOX, CHARLOTTE RAMSAY (1720– Jan. 4, 1804), novelist, dramatist, and translator, was born in New York, possibly in Albany where she spent most of her girlhood. Her father, James Ramsay, an army officer, is said (with no evidence) to have been lieutenant-governor of the province. Her childhood in New York was not happy, judging from a satire in her poems. At about the age of fifteen she was sent to England to be educated by a wealthy aunt, but on her arrival she found the lady incurably insane. Shortly after this her father died, leaving his widow and Charlotte unprovided for. At the age of twenty-seven she published her first book, *Poems on Several Occasions*, which was dedicated to Lady Isabella Finch, who probably had befriended the young woman. A year later (1748) she played in comedies at Richmond, where Garrick went to find some promising actors. Horace Walpole said that she was a "deplorable actress" (*Letters, post,* II, 126). On Oct. 6, 1747, she was married to Alexander Lennox who was in the printing shop of Strachan in Cornhill, and who was later employed in the Customs Office as tide-waiter. She had a daughter who died in 1802 and a son who was forced to leave the country, after committing an offense, and came to America. Her husband died about 1797, but for several years he had had nothing to do with his family.

Perhaps the most pleasant and valuable friendship in her life was with Samuel Johnson. He encouraged and advised her in her writing, introduced her to his friends and to other literary men who could help her, wrote favorable reviews of her books, quoted her in the *Dictionary,* and wrote dedications and other items for her. When her novel *Harriot Stuart* appeared he gave an all-night party to some twenty guests in celebration. His admiration seems to have aroused the jealousy of the other bluestockings in his circle. "Mrs. Thrale says that though her books are generally approved, nobody likes her" (*Diary and Letters of Madame D'Arblay,* I, 1842, p. 68). Johnson introduced her to Samuel Richardson and she likewise won his favor; she was a frequent visitor at his house and was admitted to his readings. In several places in her books she paid homage to these friends. Fielding also was an admirer and wrote enthusiastically of her work.

Mrs. Lennox's literary reputation depends chiefly upon her novels, a mixture of sentimental romance and the novel of manners combining in a strong feminine appeal. Her first, *The Life of Harriot Stuart* (1750), was in part autobiographical—an unorganized account of the heroine's misfortunes, adventures, and love affairs. Her most famous was *The Female Quixote, or the Adventures of Arabella* (1752), which burlesqued the old French romances of Scudéry in the story of a girl who formed her notions of life and love from such reading. A more exciting plot is in *The History of Henrietta* (1758), which she later dramatized. Her most sentimental and least effective work, *Sophia* (1762), was regretted even by her friendly critics. Her late novel, *Euphemia* (1790), written in old age, with feeble morality and delicate sensibility, was kindly reviewed and generally ignored. She was unsuccessful in her association with the theatre, both as an actress and as a dramatist. A poetic pastoral, *Philander* (1758), was not produced; nor was *Angelica, or Quixote in Petticoats* (1758), which was based on the theme of her novel, *The Female Quixote*. Garrick said that it too closely resembled Steele's *Tender Husband*. A hostile group hissed her best play, *The Sister* (1769), and it was withdrawn from Covent Garden after one performance. This comedy used the main theme of her novel *Henrietta,* and Burgoyne's *Heiress* is indebted to it for its best parts. At Garrick's suggestion she modernized *Eastward Hoe* under the title *Old City Manners* (1775), produced at the Theatre-Royal—introducing elegance at the expense of the vitality of the Elizabethan classic. Another division of her literary work is the translations from the French. These include *The Memoirs of M. de Bethune, Duke of Sully* (1756); *The Memoirs of the Countess of Berci* (1756), a romance nearly as absurd as those she burlesqued in *The Female Quixote; Memoirs for the History of Madame de Maintenon, and of the Last Age* (1757), translated from the French of Angliviel de la Baumelle; *The Greek Theatre of Father Brumoy* (1759), from the French of Pierre Brumoy, to which Dr. Johnson and others contributed; and *Meditations and Penitential Prayers Written by the Duchess de la Vallière* (1774). She wrote *Shakespear Illustrated* (1753) to show the sources of the plays, and generally condemned Shakespeare for a lack of originality, morality, and artistry, quoting much from Johnson, and following Rymer's lead. In 1760–61 she published *The Lady's Museum*, a periodical described by Nichols as "consisting of a Course of Female Education and variety of other Particulars for the Information and Amusement of the Ladies" (*Literary Anecdotes*, VIII, 1814, p. 497). Her books brought her very little income and her old age was "clouded by penury and sickness" (Nichols, *post*, III, p. 201). At the close of her life she received a pension from the Royal Literary Fund and was befriended by the Rt. Hon. George Rose and the Rev. William Beloe. She died on Jan. 4, 1804, at Dean's Yard, Westminster, and "was buried with the common soldiery in the further burying-ground of Broad Chapel" (*Ibid.*). Reynolds painted her portrait in 1761, of which an engraving by Bartolozzi was printed in Hardinge's *Shakespeare,* and one by Cooke accompanied the sketch of Mrs. Lennox in the *Lady's Monthly Museum* for June 1813.

[There is a biography of Charlotte Lennox in the *Dict. of Nat. Biog.* See also: John Nichols, *Lit. Anecdotes of the Eighteenth Century,* vol. III (1812), and *Illustrations of the Lit. Hist. of the Eighteenth Century,* vol. III (1818); G. B. Hill, *Boswell's Life of Johnson* (1887), vols. I–IV; Sir John Hawkins, *Life of Samuel Johnson* (1787); Peter Cunningham, *The Letters of Horace Walpole,* vol. II (1857); Austin Dobson, *Samuel Richardson* (1902), and *The Journal of a Voyage to Lisbon by Henry Fielding* (1892); *Gentleman's Mag.,* Dec. 1750, Mar. 1758, June 1762, Jan. 1804. Information as to certain facts was supplied by Miss Miriam R. Small, of Wells College, who is preparing a monograph of Mrs. Lennox for publication. On some points, however, the contributor's opinion differs from that of Miss Small.]   R. W. B.

LENOX, JAMES (Aug. 19, 1800–Feb. 17, 1880), book-collector and philanthropist, was born at 59 Broadway, New York City, the third son of a family of nine children. His father, Robert, born in Kirkcudbright, Scotland, in 1759, had married Rachel Carmer in New York in 1783. He was a merchant, a heavy investor in New York City real estate, and when he died in 1839 was ranked as one of the five richest men of the city. From 1819 to 1826 he was vice-president of the Chamber of Commerce and served as president from the latter date until his

death. He was a trustee of the College of New Jersey and according to Maclean (*post,* II, p. 308) "for many years all investments of College money were made under his direction." James Lenox received the degree of A.B. from Columbia College in 1818 and was admitted to the New York bar on Jan. 18, 1822. He took the usual European tours common to youths of his station, then settled down as partner in his father's business. Soon after his father's death he retired to give the rest of his life to the care of his investments, to the purchase of books and objects of art, and to an active but unobtrusive participation in the philanthropic life of the city.

Considering his Scotch-Presbyterian ancestry, it is not surprising that he collected Bibles. When he died he had brought together one of the great collections of the Bible in English. From Bibles his interest extended to works of the early printers, and for books printed in the fifteenth century his library ranked among the most important in the country at that time. It was for him that the first copy of the Gutenberg Bible was sent to the United States. Milton, Bunyan, the Roman Index Expurgatorius, and Shakespeare also appealed to him. His books soon came to fill the great house at 53 Fifth Avenue and to offer a serious problem, which he solved by giving books and objects of art to the Lenox Library, incorporated in 1870. To this corporation he gave also the entire block on Fifth Avenue between Seventieth and Seventy-first streets, and for it he erected a building designed by Richard Morris Hunt. He lived to see the collection opened to the public, with George Henry Moore its superintendent and Samuel Austin Allibone librarian. The library site was part of a thirty-acre tract originally owned by his father. With the opening of streets and the development of Central Park Lenox began to sell portions of the farm about 1864. The block between Seventieth and Seventy-first streets, and Madison and Park Avenues, he gave to the Presbyterian Hospital. He gave land also for the Presbyterian Home for Aged Women, land for churches and chapels, and continued his active part in the work of the "Old First" Presbyterian Church on Fifth Avenue opposite his home. In the last twelve years of his life it is estimated that he gave over three million dollars to charitable uses. The College of New Jersey received benefactions from him throughout his life.

Lenox has been characterized as "a man of few words and few intimate friends, but of varied information, much studious reading, extensive correspondence and many books. . . . He possessed an extraordinary aptitude for sticking to and finishing up any work he had in hand" (Stevens, *post*, pp. 2, 43). With John Carter Brown of Providence and George Brinley of Hartford he ranks as a pioneer in the field of American history. He published *Washington's Farewell Address to the People of the United States* (1850); *Nicolaus Syllacius De Insulis Meridiani atque Indici Maris Nuper Inventis* (1859), with a translation into English by the Rev. John Mulligan; *Shakespeare's Plays in Folio* (1861); *The Early Editions of King James' Bible in Folio* (1861); *Letter of Columbus to Luis de Santangel* (1864); and "Bibliographical Account of the Voyages of Columbus" (*Historical Magazine*, February 1861). Lenox died at 53 Fifth Avenue and was buried in the New York City Marble Cemetery on Second Street.

[The best account of Lenox as a book-collector is Henry Stevens, *Recollections of Mr. James Lenox of N. Y. and the Formation of his Lib.* (1886). See also D. B. Delavan, *Early Days of the Presbyterian Hospital in the City of N. Y.* (1926); John Maclean, *Hist. of the Coll. of N. J.* (2 vols., 1877); and the *N. Y. Times*, Feb. 19, 1880. For a sketch of his father see W. M. MacBean, *Biog. Reg. of Saint Andrew's Soc.* (1922), vol. I. The New York Public Library has also several collections of Lenox's letters and interleaved copies of such printed catalogues as Rich, Ternaux-Compans, and Lea Wilson, checked by him to show the progress of additions to his collections.] H.M.L.

LENTHALL, JOHN (Sept. 16, 1807–Apr. 11, 1882), naval architect, who was chiefly responsible for the wooden warships of the Union navy in the Civil War, was a native of the District of Columbia. His father, also John Lenthall, was an Englishman who while acting as Latrobe's superintendent in the building of the Capitol was killed on Sept. 19, 1808, by the fall of a vaulting in the north wing. His mother, Jane Lenthall, survived till 1852. The son is said to have learned shipbuilding from his father and from Samuel Humphreys. During several years of study in Europe he prepared drafts of 300 different ships in European navies. He entered the naval service on May 1, 1835, was appointed chief naval constructor in 1849, and chief of the bureau of construction in 1853, the first professional naval architect to occupy that post if the few months' occupancy by Samuel Hartt is excepted. Before entering this position he had served at the Portsmouth and Philadelphia navy yards. While at these places and in Washington from 1849 on, he was chiefly responsible for the design of the class of wooden, steam frigates represented by the *Merrimac* and including such ships as the *Wabash, Niagara, Roanoke, Colorado,* and *Minnesota.* They were recognized as the best ships of their kind before iron vessels appeared.

During the Civil War Lenthall remained as chief of the bureau of construction. Gideon Welles, who called him "honest John Lenthall," said of him: "He has not much pliability or affability, but, though attacked and denounced as corrupt and dishonest, I have never detected any obliquity or wrong in him. His sternness and uprightness disappointed the jobbers and the corrupt, and his unaffected manner has offended others" (Welles, *post,* I, p. 74). As a master of wooden shipbuilding, Lenthall was naturally a conservative regarding ironclads and the new monitors. Accordingly he seems to have let others, especially Fox and Stimers, go ahead with the building of light-draft monitors and iron gunboats without taking much interest in them, with the result that many of the ships built turned out to be deficient in some respects. Lenthall continued as head of his bureau till January 1871, although he had reached retiring age earlier. He continued to make his home in Washington and as late as 1881 was a member of an advisory board on new construction. Thus he had a hand in the building of the new navy that began at that time. He died suddenly in the Baltimore & Ohio railroad station in Washington as he was boarding a train for New York. A General Order from the secretary of the navy, W. H. Hunt, announced his death and commended his life and services. He was buried in Rock Creek Parish Cemetery, Washington, where his father, mother, and sister also lie.

[Besides the records of the Navy Department, the chief data about Lenthall can be secured from an obituary notice in the *Army and Navy Reg.*, Apr. 15, 1882. The General Order of Secretary Hunt is in the issue of Apr. 22. See also the *Diary of Gideon Welles* (3 vols., 1911), Latrobe's sketch of Lenthall's father in the *Nat. Intelligencer* (Washington), Sept. 23, 1808, and the *Washington Post*, Apr. 12, 1882. An interesting sidelight on Lenthall is found in R. P. Meade, *Life of Hiram Paulding* (1910), p. 237.] W.B.N.

LEONARD, CHARLES LESTER (Dec. 29, 1861–Sept. 22, 1913), physician, pioneer in the medical use of X-rays, came of old New England ancestry, being directly descended from John Leonard who settled in Springfield, Mass., in 1632. His parents were M. Hayden Leonard and Harriet E. (Moore) Leonard of Easthampton, Mass., where he was born. He graduated from the University of Pennsylvania in 1885 (A.B.), from Harvard in 1886 (A.B.), and from the Medical School of the University of Pennsylvania in 1889 (M.D.). He studied abroad from 1889 to 1892 and received the degree of master of arts from his Alma Mater in the latter year. After beginning his medical practice he inclined toward surgery and was connected with the surgical staff of the University Hospital, Philadelphia, mainly as anesthetist. He married Ruth Hodgson, by whom he had one daughter.

Leonard will always be remembered as one of the pioneer Roentgenologists of the United States. Possessed of a scientific and technical mind, he became intensely interested in the X-rays in 1896, very soon after their discovery and announcement by Roentgen ("Cases Illustrative of the Practical Application of the Roentgen Rays in Surgery," in collaboration with J. W. White and A. W. Goodspeed, *American Journal of the Medical Sciences,* August 1896). At the time, the X-rays were regarded as of service only in the detection of fractures and opaque foreign bodies such as bullets. Leonard was the first, in America, at least, to demonstrate the presence of stones in the kidney and other portions of the urinary tract by means of this agent (1898). This demonstration at once gave him world-wide publicity in the medical profession, especially among those beginning to specialize in this new branch of medicine. His ability to detect stones and his powers of observation and interpretation at that time were almost uncanny. He saw what others could not see, even when it was pointed out to them, and he was usually correct in his deductions. Throughout the early years of his experience he worked with small and what now seems most inefficient apparatus, but he was able to do more with little than almost any other man in his specialty. He was, indeed, a master of his art.

Leonard was a prolific writer, an untiring student, and a generous teacher of pleasing personality who was always ready to share his knowledge with his professional colleagues. In the thirteen years of his practice of Roentgenology he published forty-four articles on the diagnostic uses of X-rays and their application in the treatment of cancer and other conditions. He was an active member of the American Roentgen Ray Society and its president in 1904 and 1905, and was the founder of the Philadelphia Roentgen Ray Society. He was keenly interested in many other medical societies and a frequent contributor to their scientific programs. In 1902, he resigned from the University of Pennsylvania and engaged thereafter in the private practice of his specialty. As a result of excessive exposure to X-rays from the unprotected tubes of the early years and the frequent use of the fluoroscope to test the tubes and to demonstrate his hands to those interested, he soon developed the chronic skin affections which attacked the hands of so many of the early workers who knew nothing of the dangers of the rays. He refused surgical treatment until it was too late, largely because, like so many others then, he regarded the condition as harmless and likely to heal after protective measures were devised. In the latter years of his life he was a constant but uncomplaining sufferer, never allowing his affliction to interfere with his duties. Those who knew him well marveled at his fortitude. Some of the chronic ulcers on his hands eventually induced cancer, which spread to other parts of his body, and from which he died—a martyr. His last paper, "Radiography of the Stomach and Intestines," was a review of all the literature on the X-ray examination of the stomach and intestinal tract, up to 1913, prepared for the International Congress of Medicine, London, August 1913. Since he was unable to attend, it was read for him by a colleague, and was published in the *American Journal of Roentgenology,* November 1913, after his death.

[*Am. Jour. Roentgenology,* Nov. 1913, with bibliography; *Am. Jour. Roentgenology and Radium Therapy,* Aug. 1928; *Archives of the Roentgen Ray* (London), Sept. 1913; *Lancet* (London), Oct. 1913; H. A. Kelly and W. L. Burrage, *Am. Medic. Biogs.* (1920); *N. Y. Times,* Sept. 24, 1913; records of the Univ. of Pa.; personal recollections.]   H. K. P.

LEONARD, DANIEL (May 18, 1740–June 27, 1829), lawyer, Loyalist, chief justice of Bermuda, was born in Norton, Mass., the son of Ephraim and Judith (Perkins) Leonard. Ephraim Leonard, an iron-monger, was fourth in descent from James, who with a brother came to America from Pontypool, Wales, and erected the first successful iron foundry at Saugus, Mass. In 1652 the Leonard brothers removed to Taunton, Mass., and set up their "bloomery" where bog ore was plentiful. For two hundred years Leonards were identified with the iron industry. During King Philip's War (1676) the family was immune from attack because they had supplied iron arrow-heads to appreciative Indians. The Leonards of New England belonged to the provincial aristocracy, and for more than a century the family dominated Southern Massachusetts socially and politically. John Adams was accustomed to refer to this region as the "Land of the Leonards." Brought up in what, for rural New England, was baronial style—in a spacious mansion with deer-park and family coach—Daniel had social prestige and was ranked second upon entering Harvard College with the class of 1760. At Commencement he delivered, in Latin, the salutatory address. Entering law practice at Taunton, he hung his shingle under that of Samuel White, speaker of the Massachusetts Assembly, whose daughter, Anna, he married in 1767. He succeeded his father-in-law as King's attorney for Bristol County in 1769 and was elected the following year to the General Court where at first he spoke with zeal in opposition to King George. As lieutenant-colonel of the 3rd Bristol County Regiment he was one of the Young Bloods of Massachusetts. Trumbull, in his satirical poem, "M'Fingal," refers to Leonard as one who would

> "Scrawl every moment he could spare
> From cards and barbers and the fair."

Governor Hutchinson, attracted by Leonard's ability and popularity, came to Taunton and, after a lengthy discussion under a pear tree (thereafter famous as the "Tory pear tree") persuaded Leonard to espouse the cause of the Crown and secured his appointment in 1774 as mandamus councilor. This so enraged his rebellious Whig neighbors that Leonard was subjected to indignities, his home at Taunton Green was fired upon, and he was forced to flee to Boston. Within British lines he was placed on the payroll as solicitor to customs commissioners. He then wrote a series of seventeen articles in defense of the Crown policies, published in the *Massachusetts Gazette* (1774–75) over the signature "Massachusettensis." To these, John Adams replied over the signature "Novanglus." Leonard's papers were published in England as the ablest exposition of Royal policy written in America.

When the Declaration of Independence was signed, Leonard was proscribed, his property confiscated, and he was forbidden to return on penalty of death. When British troops were dislodged from Boston he sailed away to Halifax and on to England, where he was admitted to the bar and, upon separation from the colonies, secured the post of chief justice of Bermuda, which he held from 1782 to 1806. He revisited Massachusetts in 1799 and again in 1808. About 1815 he returned to London to practise law and eventually became dean of English barristers, presiding at the quarterly dinners in the Inner Temple. Leonard's first wife died in 1768 on the birth of a daughter. In 1770 he was married to Sarah Hammock of Boston by whom he had two daughters and a son, Charles, who remained in America to inherit his grandfather's estate. His second wife died at sea on the way from England to Bermuda in 1806. In his ninetieth year, while living with his daughter Harriet, in London, Leonard died as the result of a pistol wound. The family insisted he was not of a temperament to commit suicide. He was buried in St. Pancras cemetery.

[See E. A. Jones, *The Loyalists of Mass.* (1930) and *Am. Members of the Inns of Court* (1924); Ralph Davol, *Two Men of Taunton* (1912); W. R. Deane, *A Geneal. Memoir of the Leonard Family* (1851); M. C. Tyler, *The Lit. Hist. of the Am. Revolution* (1897), vol. I; C. F. Adams, *The Works of John Adams* (10 vols., 1850–56); H. E. Egerton and D. P. Coke, *The Royal Commission on the Losses and Services of the Am. Loyalists, 1783–85* (1915); *Proc. Mass. Hist. Soc.*, 1 ser. XIII (1875), 2 ser. VI (1891); *Times* (London), June 30, 1829. The authorship of the "Massachusettensis" papers was questioned by John Adams, who attributed them to Jonathan Sewall. Leonard's authorship is confirmed in a letter by Gov. Hutchinson to Leonard from London, Apr. 8, 1776; in an affidavit by Ward Chipman, who testified in 1822 that he copied the letters for Leonard while a clerk in Leonard's Boston office; in a statement by Francis Baylies, a nephew of Leonard, in discussion with L. M. Sargent (see the *Boston Transcript*, Apr. 15, 18, 1851); and in an acknowledgment by Leonard himself in a reprint of the letters, London, 1821.]   R. D.

LEONARD, GEORGE (Nov. 23, 1742–Apr. 1, 1826), Loyalist, was born at Plymouth, Mass., the son of the Rev. Nathaniel and Priscilla (Rogers) Leonard, and the nephew of Major, later Colonel, George Leonard, a judge and member of the Council of the province. He was descended from James Leonard who emigrated from Pontypool, Wales, in the seventeenth century. His marriage to Sarah Thacher, a native of Boston, occurred on Oct. 14, 1765. During the blockade of Boston he served as a lieutenant of the Associated Loyalists, besides fitting out ten vessels to aid the British. In March 1776 he accompanied the Loyalists to Halifax and was not overlooked in the Banishment Act. In the spring of 1778 he was with the troops in Rhode Island. He left Newport to receive Burgoyne's army but was forced into Plymouth Harbor by bad weather. Soon he sailed for Boston with a fleet of provisions. As navy agent and contractor for the Associated Refugees in Rhode Island he furnished the vessels for their expeditions on Long Island Sound in 1779, being given £2,000 in advance. At Martha's Vineyard in September of the same year he had the tax collector seized by one of his naval officers and permitted the inhabitants to send a representative to Boston who obtained a suspension by the Assembly of the payment of taxes. He also destroyed eleven American vessels and exacted from the Islanders provisions and fuel for the garrison at Newport. With Col. Edward Winslow he warned the people of Nantucket that the renewal of their hostile activities would be punished.

At the end of 1780 Leonard was appointed one of eight directors of the recently revived Associated Loyalists, who thereafter carried on privateering operations from Manhattan, Long Island, and Staten Island. Resigning in September 1782, he was granted an allowance of £200 a year. In the following April he wrote from Brooklyn requesting a six months' advance of his annuity in order to remove to Nova Scotia with his family of fifteen persons, including servants. He was next named one of five agents to distribute lands at the mouth of the River St. John to the inpouring refugees. Remonstrances against these agents, including Leonard, who had drawn a large lot on the harbor, led them to submit voluntarily to a trial at Halifax before the governor and Council, who decided on Aug. 3, 1784, that they had been fair and impartial in their dealings. When Parr Town was incorporated in May 1785 as the city of St. John, Leonard was appointed by the governor of New Brunswick alderman and chamberlain.

In 1786 he was made superintendent of trade and fisheries for the coasts of the Maritime Provinces and neighboring islands. In this office he was energetic in suppressing illicit trade in Passamaquoddy Bay and asserting British rights to its islands. In 1790 he was appointed to the Council, in which he served thirty-six years. He labored for the education and conversion of the Indians to the Protestant faith and built the Indian Academy at Sussex Vale, where he lived. As senior councilor Leonard would have succeeded to the government on the death of Lieut.-Gov. George B. Smyth in April 1823, but he declined on account of his infirmities. He died on Apr. 1, 1826, surviving his wife scarcely two months. Both were buried at Sussex Vale, where their monument still stands.

[J. W. Lawrence, *The Judges of New Brunswick, and Their Times* (n.d.); W. O. Raymond, ed., *Winslow Papers, A.D. 1776–1826* (1901); Hist. MSS. Commission, *Report on Am. MSS. in the Royal Institution of Great Britain*, vols. II–IV (1906–09); Thos. Jones, *Hist. of N. Y. During the Revolutionary War* (1879), vol. II; J. H. Stark, *The Loyalists of Mass.* (1910); E. A. Jones, *The Loyalists of Mass.* (1930); W. R. Deane, *A Geneal. Memoir of the Leonard Family* (1851); *New-Eng. Hist. and Geneal. Reg.*, Oct. 1858; the *Quebec Gazette*, May 1, 1826.]   W. H. S.

LEONARD, HARRY WARD (Feb. 8, 1861–Feb. 18, 1915), electrical engineer and inventor, was born at Cincinnati, Ohio, the son of Ezra George Leonard, a merchant, and Henrietta Dana (Ward). He was a descendant of Solomon Leonard, a native of Monmouthshire, England, who emigrated to Leyden, Holland, and thence, not long after 1630, to Massachusetts, where he lived successively at Plymouth, Duxbury, and Bridgewater. General Artemas Ward [*q.v.*] was an ancestor. Leonard attended grammar and high school at Cincinnati, and entered the Massachusetts Institute of Technology in 1879. He graduated in 1883 with the degree of electrical engineer, and the next year became associated with Thomas A. Edison as one of a staff of four employed by him to introduce the central-station system into the major cities of

the country. When only twenty-six (1888), he became superintendent of the Western Electric Light Company at Chicago, and the next year was head of the firm of Leonard & Izard of that city, one of the first organizations in the United States to engage in central-station and electric-railway construction. In 1889 the firm was purchased by the Edison General Electric Company and Leonard became general manager for the United States and Canada of the light and power departments of the combined Edison interests. Resigning this position in 1894 he established a business of his own at Bronxville, N. Y., the Ward Leonard Electric Company, for the manufacture of electrical equipment, principally of his own invention. In 1889 he patented the first electric train-lighting system (patents 405895, 405896, 405897), the elements of which are in use today. He had this system in operation on two trains between Chicago and Milwaukee in 1888. The best-known of his inventions is the Ward Leonard system of motor control (patent 463802, Nov. 24, 1891, and many others), which provides a method of varying the speed of direct-current motors over a wide range without the use of a starting resistance, by applying a variable voltage to the motor armature. This system not only furnishes a very flexible and rapid control of heavy machinery, but also eliminates power loss in rheostats. It is estimated that fifteen percent. of the cost of rolling steel has been saved by replacing steam engines with electric motors equipped with the Ward Leonard system. An electric elevator-control device (patent 468100, Feb. 2, 1892) used by the Otis Elevator Company on the first electric elevators installed in the New York Athletic Club and the *Times* Building, New York City, the double-arm circuit breaker (patent 705102, July 22, 1902), a system of multiple voltage motor control (patent 478344, July 5, 1892), were important inventions of his and were incorporated by license rights in equipment manufactured by most of the leading electrical firms of the country. Other inventions of interest for which he was responsible are a system of regenerative braking for railroad trains and mine hoists, an incandescent-lamp socket, the "compound controller" for machine tool motors, and the four-speed-change gear that was used on several of the higher-priced automobiles. Leonard was interested also in the electric lighting and starting of automobiles, and designed one of the first of the simple and efficient systems of the modern type. He contributed many articles to the technical press, and papers and addresses of his appear in the *Transactions of the American Insti-*

tute of Electrical Engineers. He was a fellow, a vice-president (1893–95), and a manager (1890–93) of this Institute and received the John Scott Medal award of the Franklin Institute for his contributions to electrical development. He was president of the Inventor's Guild (1913–14), which was one of his hobbies, as was also the development of the village of Bronxville, N. Y., of which he was president. In 1895 he married Carolyn Good of New York; there were no children. He died suddenly while attending the annual dinner of the American Institute of Electrical Engineers in New York.

[*Ann. Report of the Commissioner of Patents*, 1889–1915; *Proc. Am. Inst. Electrical Engineers*, Mar. 1915 (vol. XXXIV); *Technology Rev.*, Apr. 1915; *Electrical Trades' Directory and Handbook* (London, 1899); Manning Leonard, *Memorial: Geneal., Hist. and Biog., of Solomon Leonard* (1896); *N. Y. Times*, Feb. 19, 28, 1915.]
F. A. T.

LEONARD, HELEN LOUISE [See RUSSELL, LILLIAN, 1861–1922].

LEONARD, LEVI WASHBURN (June 1, 1790–Dec. 12, 1864), Unitarian clergyman, educator, the eldest of the three sons of Jacob and Mary (Swift) Leonard, was born in the South Parish of Bridgewater, Mass., where his family had been rooted for five generations. His father was a farmer and had been an ensign in the Revolution. He was a descendant of Solomon Leonard of Monmouthshire, England, who went to Holland, and thence, about 1633, came to America. Leonard graduated from Harvard College in 1815 and from the Divinity School in 1818, taught for two years in the Bridgewater Academy, and was ordained Sept. 6, 1820, as pastor of the First Congregational (Unitarian) Society of Dublin, N. H. There, in the shadow of Monadnock, he spent most of his active life, exerting over the whole town a strong, beneficent, and lasting influence. To a remarkable extent he molded the very character of the community. He organized its lyceum, established its library, superintended its schools, shaped the measures approved in its town meeting, and was the adored pastor of its principal church. He had a genius for the pastoral office and developed in his people a rare devotional spirit. Although, like so many of the Unitarian clergymen of his day, he was conservative in temper and chary of controversy, he could not hold the stanch Trinitarians of his parish, who withdrew amicably in 1827 and formed the Second Congregational Society. As an educator his influence was more than local. His plans for school buildings and his methods of teaching were widely copied; his textbooks were popular and long-lived. Besides two sermons, a tract, and a lec-

ture, his publications, which were usually issued at Keene, N. H., include: *The Literary and Scientific Classbook* (1826); *Sequel to Easy Lessons* (1830); *Selections of Reading Lessons for Common Schools* (1830); *The North American Spelling Book* (1835); *Modes of Instruction in Common Schools* (1844); *Analysis of the Elementary Sounds of the English Language* (1848); and *The History of Dublin, N. H.* (1855). He was the chief compiler for the Cheshire Pastoral Association of *Christian Hymns* (1845). Among his interests were genealogy, mathematics, and entomology; in this last department he aided his classmate, Thaddeus William Harris [*q.v.*], who named *Hesperia Leonardus* for him. He was twice married: in 1830 to Elizabeth Morison Smith of Peterboro, N. H., who died in 1848; in 1851 to Elizabeth (Dow) Smith of Exeter, the widow of his first wife's brother. At her behest he moved to Exeter in 1853, but his congregation would not allow the pastoral connection to be dissolved. In 1855 William Frederick Bridge was installed as his colleague pastor, and Leonard continued to preach occasionally, as his failing health would permit. Meanwhile he edited for eight years the weekly *Exeter News-Letter*. He died in Exeter and was buried in Dublin.

[Manning Leonard, *Memorial: Geneal., Hist., and Biog. of Solomon Leonard* (1896); L. W. Leonard and S. A. Smith, *Geneal. of the Family of Wm. Smith of Peterborough, N. H.* (1852); L. W. Leonard and J. L. Seward, *Hist. of Dublin, N. H.* (1920); *New-Eng. Hist. and Geneal. Reg.*, July 1865; *Exeter News-Letter*, Jan. 2, 1865; *Gen. Cat. Harvard Divinity School*, 1910; S. A. Eliot, *Heralds of a Liberal Faith*, vol. III (1910).]
G. H. G.

LEONARD, ROBERT JOSSELYN (Feb. 5, 1885–Feb. 9, 1929), educator, was born in San José, Cal., son of Joseph Howland and Ella Isabelle (Clark) Leonard. He was a descendant of James Leonard who came from Monmouthshire, England, in 1638, at the request of the Massachusetts Bay Colony, to survey the hills for iron; and settled in Taunton, Mass., where he set up an iron forge. Robert's father received the degree of M.D. at the University of Vermont (1861). Returning to his home in California, he lost everything in real-estate deals, retaining, however, his library, which included rarities like a complete file of the first San Francisco newspaper. After his death, Robert and his brother cared for their mother and sister. "Even so," he wrote later, "I have not known the 'pinch' of poverty, due to a well-educated, loving and helpful mother who never let us feel poor. We had a wealth of good books, left from more prosperous times, 'freedom of spirit' . . . and good companions." Following a year at the San José

High School, he entered the State Normal School in San José, from which he was graduated in 1904. Drawing and manual training engrossed him. Drawing he continued throughout his life; manual training gave him a lifelong interest in automobiles—his hobby; proficiency in manual arts gave him an opportunity to teach in Belmont School and later in Fresno. In after years he introduced industrial education into the Berkeley schools and into the Horace Mann School of Columbia University. From Columbia he received his academic degrees: B.S., 1912; A.M., 1914; Ph.D., 1923. On Aug. 13, 1912, he was married to Eugenie Ann Andruss of Seattle, Wash., by whom he had a daughter and a son.

In 1914 he was appointed to the chair of vocational education at the University of Indiana, the first such professorship ever established. That same year he analyzed the paper-box industry of New York City, making the first extensive occupational study with a view to determining the kind of education required for a specific industry. In 1915 he surveyed occupations in the state of Indiana and also in the cities of Hammond and Richmond. These studies resulted in his publishing several books: *An Investigation of the Paper Box Industry to Determine the Possibility of Vocational Training* (1915); *A Study of the People of Indiana and Their Occupations* (1915); *Some Facts Concerning the People, Industries and Schools of Hammond, Indiana* (1915); and *Report of the Richmond, Indiana, Survey for Vocational Education* (1916). In 1917–18 he was special agent of the Federal Board for Vocational Education; and as supervisor for the central states he traveled constantly, inaugurating and supervising schools for training teachers for the army, navy, and marine corps. This work was his contribution to the national defense.

From 1918 to 1923 at the University of California he was professor of education, director of the division of vocational education, acting dean of the school of education (1921–23), and University representative in educational relations (1921–23). In this last capacity he advised the president and regents on matters of policy in all parts of the institution and proposed a plan for the reorganization of the University. From 1923 to 1929 he was professor of education and director of the school of education in Teachers College, Columbia University, where he organized the first course in college administration. He directed surveys of the colleges of Maine, Florida, and the United Lutheran Church in America, as well as of many individual institu-

tions. Believing profoundly in continuing education for all, he was one of the founders of the American Association for Adult Education, and during the last ten years of his life its object absorbed much of his interest. His addresses show that he was not in sympathy with much that is current in so-called progressive education, particularly in the elementary school, believing that it sugar-coated experience and cheapened real life values. A memorial volume containing some of his discourses, *An Outlook on Education,* was published in 1930. He was the author, also, with others, of *An Introductory Course on Part-time Education* (1920); *Data Sheets for Teachers' Course on Part-time Education* (1920); and *The Co-ordination of State Institutions for Higher Education Through Supplementary Curricula Boards* (1923). After a severe attack of influenza he returned to his work too soon, suffered a relapse, and in a delirium fell from the window of his apartment.

[*Who's Who in America,* 1928–29, which is incorrect in some details; unpublished notes by R. J. Leonard; information as to certain facts from his widow; *Industrial Educational Mag.,* Mar. 1929; *Kadelphian Rev.,* Mar. 1929; *Evening Star* (Washington, D. C.), Feb. 9, 1929; *N. Y. Times,* Feb. 10, 1929.] D.A.R.

LEONARD, STERLING ANDRUS (Apr. 23, 1888–May 15, 1931), educator, author, was born in National City, Cal., only child of Cyreno N., a dentist, and Eva (Andrus) Leonard, both of colonial New England stock. At his father's death his mother became a teacher in the public schools of Indianola, Iowa, where for a decade after his eighth year he attended school and college (Simpson), the relations between mother and son being particularly close, especially through their interest in great literature, from which they read aloud to each other. He received the degree of A.B. at the University of Michigan in 1908; that of M.A. in 1909, while an assistant in the English Department; and that of Ph.D. at Columbia in 1928, while on leave of absence from his professorship of English at Wisconsin, to which he was appointed in 1920. Previously, he had been experimenting pedagogically in the Milwaukee Normal School, in the Horace Mann School of New York, and, as exchange teacher, 1911–12, in the Gymnasium at Danzig, Germany, thus preparing himself for leadership in the National Council of the Teachers of English, of which he was president in 1926. At his untimely death he had already achieved much, while promising much more, by writing, by lecturing, and by training secondary-school teachers at his university. In 1913 he had married Minnetta F. Sammis of Terre Haute, Ind., a graduate of Teachers College, Columbia, who shared his educational ideals; and intimate association with their one child unquestionably stimulated his already shrewd and humane insight into the growth of mind and character and the objectives and methods of training them.

He was the author of *English Composition as a Social Problem* (1917); *Essential Principles of Teaching Reading and Literature* (1922); *General Language* (1925); and *The Doctrine of Correctness in English Usage, 1700–1800* (1928); and the editor of *Poems of the War and the Peace* (1920); Melville's *Typee* (1920); *Atlantic Book of Modern Plays* (1922); and, with W. W. Theisen, of a graded series of literature-readers, lively and fresh in substance. He left several almost completed manuscripts chiefly on English usage.

In an age of muddling transitions, ingenious fads, and noisy charlatanry in secondary education, Leonard was peculiarly serviceable by his sound scholarship, by his clear realization of life as changing in form and method while unchanging in essential values, by his scientific sense of observed and tested facts, by his resourceful and untiring energy, and by the fearless integrity of a cultured, witty, kindly, just, and lovable gentleman. He revealed the same balanced, alert, and genial radicalism in his active interest in social, economic, ethical, and political problems of the day.

A lover of good music and an excellent amateur with both violin and viola, he was for years an outstanding member of the Madison Civic Orchestra. He could swing a tennis racket. He loved to look at sunsets from a hill, to paddle a canoe through a forest stream, or to tack in the breezes of Lake Mendota. He did not play golf and belonged to no country club. He was of medium height, ruddy and round-faced with expression playing back and forth between quizzical and grave, wiry in frame, impetuous in gait, gesture, and speech, and fond of an evening of playful intellectual give-and-take with one or two or three friends on diverse themes, both within and outside his professional interests. He died, sinking numb with cold and exhaustion, in the late afternoon waters of Mendota, after clinging for an hour and a half to his over-turned sailing canoe, jesting to his companion, while the University crew rowed by with its launch in the sunny distance and the University life-saving station towered empty in plain sight across the waves a mile to the south.

[*Who's Who in America*, 1930–31; *Am. Speech*, June 1931; *Elementary Eng. Rev.*, June 1931; *Eng. Jour.*, Sept. 1931; *Capital Times* (Madison, Wis.), May 16, 1931; and, for a moving account of his drowning in Mendota, the letter by his rescued companion, Prof. I. A. Richards of Cambridge Univ., England, published in the *Capital Times*, July 17, 1931.]   W. E. L.

LEONARD, WILLIAM ANDREW (July 15, 1848–Sept. 21, 1930), bishop of the Protestant Episcopal Church, was born at Southport, Conn., and died at Gambier, Ohio. His father was William Boardman Leonard, a banker, of Brooklyn, N. Y.; his mother, Louisa Dimon Bulkley. The Leonards were among the earliest settlers of Taunton, Mass., where they carried on the smelting of iron from local ores; the Bulkleys were descended from Peter Bulkeley [*q.v.*], a noted non-conformist divine who came to America in 1635 and founded Concord, Mass. William received his academic education at Phillips Academy, Andover, and at St. Stephen's College, Annandale, N. Y. During the Civil War he enlisted in the Union army, but, being under military age, was withdrawn by his father. He graduated at the Berkeley Divinity School in 1871, was ordained deacon of the Protestant Episcopal Church on May 31 of that year, and was advanced to the priesthood, July 21, 1872. In 1873 he married Sarah Louisa Sullivan, of Brooklyn, who died in 1916. He was assistant minister in Holy Trinity Church, Brooklyn, 1871–72, and rector of the Church of the Redeemer, Brooklyn, 1872–80. He founded the Brooklyn Free Library, and was chaplain of the 23rd Regiment, New York National Guard. From 1880 to 1889 he was rector of St. John's Church, Washington, where he became a near friend of many men of national prominence. He declined elections as bishop of Washington Territory, 1880, and as assistant bishop of Southern Ohio, 1889; but in the latter year accepted election as assistant bishop of Ohio, and was consecrated Oct. 12, 1889. Six days later, upon the resignation of Bishop Bedell, he became bishop of that diocese.

His most prominent achievements in Ohio were the building of the cathedral in Cleveland, which was consecrated in 1907, and the strengthening of Kenyon College and its divinity school, Bexley Hall, at Gambier, which institutions he found in a feeble condition financially and administratively. He was in charge of the Protestant Episcopal churches in Europe from 1897 to 1906, and was president of the Fifth Province of the Episcopal Church for ten years (1914–24). Upon the death of the presiding bishop, J. G. Murray, in October 1929, he became by seniority acting presiding bishop until the election of Bishop C. P. Anderson to that office in the following November; and again, upon the death of Bishop Anderson in January

1930, he became acting presiding bishop until the election of Bishop James De Wolf Perry in March following. For many years he was a trustee of Western Reserve University, Cleveland, and of Lake Erie College, Painesville, Ohio. Among his published works are: *Via Sacra* (1875); *History of the Christian Church* (1878), for Sunday Schools; *A Faithful Life* (1888); *New York Church Club Lectures* (1893); *Witness of the American Church to Pure Christianity* (1894); and a life of his grandfather, *Stephen Banks Leonard* (1909). He was devoutly religious, conservative in his views of theology and ritual, yet widely tolerant of differences of opinion and practice among his clergy; under him the diocese was singularly united and at peace. A man of great personal dignity, he was yet exceedingly genial and hospitable.

[L. E. Daniels, *William Andrew Leonard* (1930); G. F. Smythe, *A Hist. of the Diocese of Ohio Until the Year 1918* (1931); *Cleveland Plain Dealer*, Sept. 22, 1930; *Christian Century*, Oct. 1, 1930; *Who's Who in America*, 1930–31; letters and papers in Kenyon Coll. Lib.]

G. F. S.

LEONARD, ZENAS (Mar. 19, 1809–July 14, 1857), trapper, author, was born near Clearfield, Pa., the son of Abraham and Elizabeth (Armstrong) Leonard. His schooling, described by his publisher as "a common school education," appears to have been meager. He worked on his father's farm until the day he was twenty-one, when he announced his intention of striking out for himself. At Pittsburgh he found employment in the store of an uncle, remaining there several months. Determined to be a trapper in the Far West, he went to St. Louis, and in April 1831, as a clerk, left for the mountains with the party of Gantt and Blackwell. He was at the rendezvous in Pierre's Hole, Idaho, in the summer of 1832, and took part in the famous battle of July 18, of which he has left an account.

At the Green River rendezvous of 1833 he met Bonneville and was engaged as a member of Walker's California expedition. With this party, which after great privations and several bloody encounters with Indians, crossed the Utah and Nevada deserts and scaled the Sierras, and which was probably the first company of American whites to see the Yosemite Valley and the giant Merced sequoias, he reached the coast in November. Returning by a more southern route, and traversing what has since been known as Walker's Pass, the expedition reached Bonneville's camp on Bear River in July 1834. For another year Leonard remained in the mountains, trapping in various directions and undergoing many perilous experiences. In the summer of 1835 he returned with Bonneville and in the fall reached his old home. After a few months he returned to the West, settling in Sibley, Mo., on the site of Old Fort Osage, and engaging in the Indian and Santa Fé trade. He married Isabelle Harrelson, by whom he had two children. He died in Sibley.

It was in Clearfield that he wrote the account of his travels, which was published in part in the *Clearfield Republican,* and as a whole in book form under the title, *Narrative of the Adventures of Zenas Leonard* (1839). In 1904 it was republished, with an introduction and notes by W. F. Wagner, under the title, *Leonard's Narrative; Adventures of Zenas Leonard, Fur Trader and Trapper, 1831–1836.* Though, owing to the theft or loss of a part of his journal, Leonard is sometimes faulty as to incident and oftener faulty as to dates, his work is highly valued, and as a contemporary depiction of the daily life of the trapper is surpassed only by the *Journal . . . 1834–1843* (1914) of Osborne Russell. Of Leonard's personality little is known.

[*Leonard's Narrative: Adventures of Zenas Leonard* (1904), ed. by W. F. Wagner; Allen Glenn, *Hist. of Cass County, Mo.* (1917); information from F. C. Shoemaker, Columbia, Mo., and W. D. Leonard, Kansas City, Mo.]

W. J. G.

LE PAGE DU PRATZ, ANTOINE SIMON [See DUPRATZ, ANTOINE SIMON LE PAGE, fl. 1718–1758].

LE ROUX, BARTHOLOMEW (*c.* 1665–July 1713), New York gold and silversmith, is said to have been born in Amsterdam, Holland, between 1660 and 1665, the eldest son of Pierre and Jane Le Roux, who were of French Huguenot descent. The family emigrated to London, and the father became a naturalized English subject in 1681; the mother, in 1685/86 (*New York Genealogical and Biographical Record,* April 1919, pp. 151–53). Bartholomew evidently learned his trade from his father, who was a member of the Goldsmiths' Company of London. Young Le Roux emigrated to America some time prior to June 6, 1687, on which date he was made a freeman of the city of New York (*Collections of the New York Historical Society, Publication Fund Series,* vol. XVIII, 1886, p. 53). A year and a half later, Dec. 14, 1688, he married Gertrude Van Rollegom, the record describing him as "young man from London" (S. S. Purple, *Records of the Reformed Dutch Church, . . . Marriages,* 1890). They had eleven children; the eldest son, Charles [*q.v.*], became in after years the official silversmith of New York.

In 1689, at the outbreak of the rebellion led by

Jacob Leisler [*q.v.*], Le Roux was a member of the city militia company commanded by Capt. Gabriel Minvielle. He and his fellow soldiers supported Leisler by insisting that the whole company be on guard at the fort, in spite of regulations which permitted only half a company to be in arms at one time. Lieutenant-Governor Nicholson and Col. Nicholas Bayard, a member of the council, demanded an explanation for this action, and Le Roux, as spokesman for the company, declared that they feared an attack by Papists from Staten Island and Boston, and, as many of the soldiers already in the fort were Papists, they "thought themselves not secure to be so guarded" (E. B. O'Callaghan, *The Documentary History of the State of New York*, 8vo ed., vol. II, 1849, pp. 17–18). Le Roux disapproved of Leisler's subsequent political activities, however, for he seems to have taken no further part in the rebellion, and some years later when Governor Bellomont favored the Leisler faction and removed their opponents from office, Le Roux joined with Nicholas Bayard and several hundred other Protestants in an address of protest to William III.

As a silversmith he was a good craftsman and prospered, becoming well-known and trusted in the community. On Dec. 30, 1693, he purchased a house and lot at the corner of Broadway and Morris Street (Conveyances, XVIII, 268, in Hall of Records, New York City), and when he died he owned "Goods Chattels & Creditts In diverse places within this province" (Record of Wills, VII, 194–98, Hall of Records, New York). He was elected to several city offices—constable in 1691, collector in 1699, assessor in 1707, and assistant alderman in 1702–04 and 1708–13. He was often asked to be a sponsor at baptisms, a witness or executor of wills, and to make inventories of estates. He died in 1713, some time between July 10, when he made his will, and July 28, when the common council ordered the election of an assistant alderman "in the Room of Mʳ Bartholomew Le Roux deceased" (*Minutes, post*, III, 40). The School of Fine Arts, Yale University, owns a large two-handled bowl made by Le Roux, one of the most elaborate and ornate pieces in its collection.

[In addition to references given above, see: R. T. H. Halsey, *The Metropolitan Museum of Art: Cat. of an Exhibition of Silver Used in N. Y., N. J., and the South* (1911), pp. xx–xxi; *Minutes of the Common Council of the City of N. Y.* (1905), vols. I–III; E. B. O'Callaghan, *Docs. Relating to the Colonial Hist. of N. Y.*, vol. IV (1854); *Colls. of the N. Y. Hist. Soc., Pub. Fund Ser.*, vols. XXV, XXVI (1893–94); C. L. Avery, *Early Am. Silver* (copr. 1930).]   A. E. P.

LE ROUX, CHARLES (December 1689– Mar. 22, 1745), engraver and silversmith, the eldest son of Bartholomew [*q.v.*] and Gertrude (Van Rollegom) Le Roux, was born in New York City and baptized there Dec. 22, 1689. He learned the gold and silversmith's trade from his father, and after the latter's death in 1713 he successfully carried on the business which the elder Le Roux had founded. In 1715 he married Catherine, daughter of Dr. Gerardus Beekman, and his connection with this well-known family added to his prestige and influence in the community. As a craftsman he excelled his father and for many years was the official silversmith of New York City. The records show that to him alone, from 1720 to 1743, was entrusted the making of the gold and silver boxes which enclosed the seal accompanying the engrossed freedom of the city granted by the common council for noteworthy service or to distinguished visitors. One of these boxes was presented to Andrew Hamilton [*q.v.*], the eminent Philadelphia lawyer who defended John Peter Zenger in the famous trial which established the freedom of the press (I. N. P. Stokes, *The Iconography of Manhattan Island, 1498–1909*, vol. IV, 1922, plate 33). Le Roux also engraved the plates for several of the series of bills of credit issued by the city and colony (*New York State Library . . . Calendar of Council Minutes, 1668–1783*, 1902, pp. 260–61), and in 1735, when there was a controversy between Mayor Richard and the common council as to the custody of the city seal, the goldsmith was directed to make and engrave a separate seal for the mayor's use, for which he received £5:9:3 (Stokes, *ante*, vol. IV, plate 31).

Like his father, Charles was also active in the civic and religious affairs of the city; and in the factional strife which prevailed during the administration of Governor Cosby he sided with the popular party. In 1734 he was chosen an assistant alderman on a ticket nominated by "an Interest opposite to the Governour's" (*New York Weekly Journal*, Oct. 7, 1734), and three years later, in a contested assembly election, he signed a petition protesting against the "Barefaced Villany" of the sheriff in certifying the election of the candidate of the "court faction" (E. B. O'Callaghan, *The Documentary History of the State of New York*, 4to ed., vol. III, 1850, pp. 292–94). As a member of the common council from 1734 to 1739 his activities were extensive, including the auditing of the treasurer's accounts, investigating land titles, having lots surveyed, superintending repairs to the City Hall and to the fire engines, drafting new laws, and suppressing nuisances. He held the offices of church warden and deacon in the Reformed Dutch Church. In April 1738, he was captain of one of the city military companies, and on Aug. 15 of that year he was promoted to the rank of major (*Ibid.*, IV, 1851, pp. 139–40, 147). During the so-called Negro Plot of 1741–42 he was sworn as a member of the grand jury, and when one of his own negroes was accused of being a party to the conspiracy, he entered into a recognizance to have the slave transported (Daniel Horsmanden, *A Journal of the Proceedings in the Detection of the Conspiracy . . . ,* 1744, pp. 137, 139, 150, 154).

[In addition to references given above, see: R. T. H. Halsey, *The Metropolitan Museum of Art: Cat. of an Exhibition of Silver Used in N.Y., N.J., and the South* (1911); *N.Y. Geneal. and Biog. Record,* Apr. 1919; *Minutes of the Common Council of the City of N.Y., 1675–1776* (8 vols., 1905), vols. III–V and index; *Colls. of the N.Y. Geneal. and Biog. Soc.,* vols. II, III (1901–02); *Colls. of the N.Y. Hist. Soc., Pub. Fund Ser.,* XLII (1910), 122; J. G. Wilson, *The Memorial Hist. of the City of N.Y.,* II (1892), 161–62; and *Ecclesiastical Records of the State of N.Y.,* vols. III, IV (1902).]   A. E. P.

LÉRY, JOSEPH GASPARD CHAUSSE-GROS de (July 20, 1721–Dec. 11, 1797), was an engineer of New France who made several journeys to the Great Lakes and the Mississippi Valley and laid out several forts in these regions. His father, Gaspard Chaussegros de Léry (1682–1756), a pupil of Vauban, was sent to Canada in 1716 to superintend its fortifications, and erected the defenses of Quebec and Montreal. He married Marie-Renée le Gardeur de Beauvais, of the Canadian *noblesse.* Their son Joseph entered Quebec Seminary at the age of ten and when only thirteen applied for the position of assistant engineer. He was then considered too young for such an office, but it was granted to him early in 1739. That same year he accompanied the expedition from Canada to Louisiana, which took part in the war against the Chickasaw Indians. With the Louisiana troops was the engineer Broutin, whom Léry assisted in reconnoitring the route to the Chickasaw villages. At the close of this campaign he was commissioned ensign and in 1743 went to Crown Point on Lake Champlain to complete the defenses of Fort Saint Frédéric. In 1748 he was commissioned first ensign and the following year was sent by the governor to Detroit to survey the route and to report on the fortifications. His account of this voyage is the first of the nine journals which he wrote that are still extant. In 1751 he was promoted to a lieutenancy and employed on forts in Acadia. The governor then sent him to France to explain the necessity of such posts, the existence of which had been declared by the English a violation of neutrality. After his return to Canada he married in 1753 Louise Martel de Brouague.

The journals of the years 1754–55 are the longest and most important of his diaries, for during those years he again visited Detroit, aided in erecting the forts along the Allegheny River, and made plans and sketches of routes, which he introduced into the text. In the French and Indian War he took part in the campaign against Oswego, was made captain in 1757, served in Montcalm's army, and was wounded on the Plains of Abraham. After the capitulation he and his wife visited France and England. In the latter country George III so admired Madame de Léry that he said to her: "Madame, if all the Canadian ladies are like you, I have truly made a conquest" (Lindsay, *post,* p. 373). In 1764 Léry returned to Canada, where in 1778 he was chosen a member of the legislative council of Quebec and in 1791 was member of the same council for Lower Canada. He died at Quebec and was buried in the Cathedral.

[The journals of Léry are published in *Rapport de l'Archiviste de La Province de Quebec* for 1926–29. There are nine, eight of which belong to the Quebec Archives; the ninth (1759), to the Canadian Archives, having been obtained from England. A translation of the journal of 1754–55, with a sketch by Col. Crawford Lindsay, is in the *Ohio Archæol. and Hist. Quart.,* Oct. 1908. The most complete account is in François Daniel, *Le Vicomte C. de Léry et sa famille* (1867). W. S. Wallace, *Dict. of Canadian Biog.* (1926), gives Léry's name as Joseph Gaspard (or Gaspard Joseph) and his father's name as Joseph Gaspard; sources also differ as to the spelling of the name of Léry's wife.]

L. P. K.

LESCHI (d. Feb. 19, 1858), a Nisqualli chief, the son of a Nisqualli warrior and a Klikitat squaw, was born and lived within his father's tribe on the Nisqually River, in the present state of Washington. He joined the Indian uprising in 1855, became a chief, and commanded the forces west of the Cascades, while Kamaiakan [*q.v.*] led the resistance to the east of the mountains. Perhaps his chief exploit was the attack on the little village of Seattle, in January 1856, when he is said to have led a thousand warriors and to have been repulsed only with the aid of a ship in the harbor. After the failure of the outbreak he gave himself up to the army officer commanding in the Yakima country and received amnesty. Nevertheless Gov. Isaac I. Stevens [*q.v.*] did not relax his efforts to bring him to trial for murders committed during the uprising, and, by the promise of fifty blankets, bribed one of his own tribe to betray him to the civil authority. During his spectacular trial the rivalries and animosities of the frontier territory flamed. The influence of the United States army and the sympathy of the Hudson's Bay Company, as well as the interest of certain citizens, united to defend Leschi on the ground that he had not been present on the occasion in question and, furthermore, that such acts were acts of war for which he could not be answerable to any civil authority. At the first trial, held immediately after his surrender in November 1856, the jury disagreed. After the court was moved to the capital at Olympia a second trial was held in March 1857 and a conviction was obtained. On appeal to the state supreme court Leschi was sentenced to be hanged on Jan. 22, 1858. When the arrest of the sheriff on a charge of selling liquor to the Indians prevented the execution on the day named, mass meetings of angry settlers protested against a further stay of sentence. A special session of the territorial supreme court ordered him to be resentenced and, before a possible pardon could be obtained from the federal capital, he was hanged according to the law.

[*Pioneer and Democrat* (Olympia, Wash. Territory), especially issues of Jan. 29, Feb. 5, 26, 1858; Ezra Meeker, *Pioneer Reminiscences of Puget Sound: The Tragedy of Leschi* (1905); C. A. Snowden, *Hist. of Wash.* (1909), vols. III and IV; H. H. Bancroft, *Hist. of Wash., Idaho, and Mont.* (1890); Hazard Stevens, *The Life of Isaac Ingalls Stevens* (2 vols., 1900).]

K. E. C.

LESLEY, J. PETER [See LESLEY, PETER, 1819–1903].

LESLEY, PETER (Sept. 17, 1819–June 1, 1903), geologist, third child but first son of Peter and Elizabeth Oswald (Allen) Lesley, was born in Philadelphia, Pa. The fourth Peter Lesley in direct succession, he was known at first as Peter Lesley, Jr., but disliking his first name, in early manhood transferred the "J" from Junior, and adopted the signature of J. P. Lesley. His grandfather, a cabinet maker, came to America from Aberdeenshire, Scotland, and, landing in Boston, walked thence to Philadelphia where he settled. A few years later he saw service in the Revolution. His son, Peter's father, was also a cabinet maker. Young Peter was a nervous, timid child, extremely near-sighted. At the age of six he was sent to a private school where he developed into a bright pupil, fond of his books. At fifteen he entered the University of Pennsylvania, graduating with the degree of A.B. in 1838, but with health so impaired that on the advice of his physicians he discontinued his studies and sought outdoor employment with the state geological survey. For this line of work he had shown no predilection, but he was appointed and made such creditable progress as to win special commendation from Henry Darwin Rogers [*q.v.*], the director.

For political reasons the survey was discontinued in 1841, and Lesley returned to his books, attending the Theological Seminary at Princeton, 1841–44. During his vacations, he continued to assist Rogers in editing the reports of the unfinished survey. In this work, particularly in the drawing of maps and sections, it is said he showed great skill. After being licensed as a preacher by the Philadelphia Presbytery in 1844, he sailed for a year in Europe, where he spent several months touring on foot, and several months studying at Halle. Returning to Philadelphia in May 1845, he took a position as colporteur for the American Tract Society, preaching and distributing tracts through the northern and central parts of Pennsylvania. This work taxed his strength too severely, however, and in 1846 he once more entered the service of Rogers, who was then located in Boston, aiding him as before in the preparation of his maps and sections. Late in 1847 he was called to act as pastor of a Congregational church at Milton, Mass. Here, Feb. 13, 1849, he married Susan Inches Lyman, daughter of Judge Joseph Lyman, a young woman whose religious affiliations were Unitarian. This step caused discord in Lesley's church, particularly since the young minister himself was quite liberal in his views, and in 1852 he formally abandoned pastoral work and turned once more to geology. The year before the Pennsylvania legislature had furnished funds for the completion of the state survey, on which he was again employed.

He subsequently surveyed coal and iron fields for various corporations in various parts of the country. His first book, *A Manual of Coal and Its Topography* (1856), confirmed his reputation as a geologist of the first rank. From 1856 to 1864 he served as secretary of the American Iron Association, and during this period published, in addition to several geological pamphlets, a volume of nearly eight hundred pages entitled *The Iron Manufacturer's Guide* (1859) which brought him no inconsiderable reputation. In 1859 he became professor of mining in the University of Pennsylvania, and with its growth became successively dean of the Science Department (1872) and dean of the newly established Towne Scientific School (1875), retiring, as professor emeritus, in 1883. In 1859 also he was made librarian and secretary of the American Philosophical Society, holding the former position until 1885 and the latter until 1887, when he became vice-president. In 1863 he was sent to Europe by the Pennsylvania Railroad to study rail manufacture and the Bessemer steel process. This year marked the beginning of the great petroleum excitement, which caused such a demand for his services as to bring about a nervous breakdown and forced him in 1866 to make another trip to Europe for rest and recreation.

Returning, two years later, he became in 1869 the editor of a weekly newspaper, *The United States Railroad and Mining Register*, which he conducted until the end of 1873.

In this year, in response to the clamor of the oil men, there was authorized a second geological survey of Pennsylvania, with Lesley as state geologist. He was at this time fifty-four years of age and at the height of his career. He continued as state geologist throughout the thirteen years of the survey's existence, or until 1887. From this organization there emanated the most remarkable series of reports ever published by any survey. Up to and including 1887, when all field work was discontinued, there were issued seventy-seven octavo volumes of text with thirty-three atlases and a Grand Atlas. These were followed in 1892 and 1895 by the three octavo volumes constituting the final report. The magnitude of the task was too great for Lesley's strength, and he again broke down in 1893—so completely, this time, that his summary and final reports were left for others to finish. Though for a time after this last breakdown his health caused his friends no great anxiety, he slowly weakened, and in 1903 he had a stroke of apoplexy, from which he died, in his eighty-fourth year. His wife and two daughters survived him.

The quantity of Lesley's work was enormous; that much of it was not of as high order as he could wish was not his fault, but that of a legislature crying for immediate benefits. He was a man of tall, lank, but commanding, figure, of an impressionable and emotional nature, endowed with tremendous nervous energy, aggressive and outspoken, an enthusiast and optimist, but at times lamentably melancholy. "His writings are full of expressions which for terseness and unpolished emphasis are unequalled" (Merrill, *post*). Nor were his writings limited to scientific subjects. He was a philologist of considerable repute; he wrote poetry; delivered a series of Lowell Lectures in 1865–66, published under the title, *Man's Origin and Destiny* (1868); under the pseudonym, John W. Allen, Jr., brought out a work of fiction, *Paul Dreifuss, His Holiday Abroad* (1882), a "photographically minute account of a holiday trip in the winter of 1881, 1882"; and contributed many articles to magazines and encyclopedias. As editor of the *Railroad and Mining Register* his paragraphs were well nigh numberless. He was an original member of the National Academy of Sciences, and a member or honorary member of many other scientific organizations.

[*Life and Letters of Peter and Susan Lesley* (2 vols., 1909), ed. by their daughter, Mary Lesley Ames, re- prints as appendices the biographical notices from *Am. Geologist*, Sept. 1903; *Mines and Minerals*, July 1903; *Bull. Geol. Soc. of America*, vol. XV (1904); *Quart. Jour. Geol. Soc. of London*, May 14, 1904; *Proc. Am. Philosophical Soc.*, vol. XLV (1906); *Trans. Am. Inst. Mining Engineers*, vol. XXXIV (1904). See also W. M. Davis, in *Biog. Memoirs Nat. Acad. Sci.*, vol. VIII (1919); G. P. Merrill, *The First One Hundred Years of American Geology* (1924); *Phila. Inquirer*, June 3, 1903.]

G. P. M.

LESLIE, CHARLES ROBERT (Oct. 19, 1794–May 5, 1859), painter and author, was born in London, but his parents, Robert and Lydia (Baker) Leslie, were Americans, natives of Maryland, where their ancestors had settled early in the eighteenth century. In 1786 the family had moved to Philadelphia, where Robert Leslie established a clock and watch store. He found it expedient in 1793 to go to London for the purpose of buying goods for the establishment, taking his family with him. Thus both of his sons were born during the London sojourn. He already had three daughters, one of whom was Eliza Leslie [*q.v.*]. In the autumn of 1799 the family sailed for America from Gravesend in the American ship *Washington*, which, though a merchantman, was heavily armed, for France and the United States were at war. Only a few days after leaving England the *Washington* was attacked by a French man-of-war, *La Bellone*. After a brisk duel the latter was driven off, but the damage sustained by the American ship was so serious that her commander was forced to make for Lisbon, the nearest port, five hundred miles away, for repairs. On Mar. 31, 1800, the ship again put to sea, but it was forty-two days later when she finally dropped anchor at Philadelphia—nearly eight months from the time she left Gravesend.

Robert Leslie died a few years later, leaving so little property that his widow was obliged to open a boarding-house. Charles and his brother were sent to school at the University of Pennsylvania. In 1808, Charles was apprenticed to Bradford & Inskeep, booksellers. He now began to make sketches at every opportunity and haunted the theatre, making friends with the actors, drawing their portraits, and painting scenery. His likeness of George Frederick Cooke, the actor, made quite a hit, and convinced Bradford, his employer, that the youth's artistic talent was well worth cultivating. Consequently the boy was sent to London in 1811 to take up the serious study of painting. From the day of his arrival his choice of a vocation was justified and his career was successful almost from the start. He made a host of influential friends; worked assiduously in the school of the Royal Academy under Fuseli; sat at the feet of Benjamin West and Washington Allston; and roomed with Samuel F. B. Morse. His London life was interesting, and his autobiography is full of amusing anecdotes and genial personal gossip relating to such personages as Coleridge, Scott, Lamb, Irving, Sidney Smith, Wilkie, Landseer, Constable, Turner, Flaxman, and others equally eminent. But there is not a trace of egotism. Leslie's character was evidently modest and amiable in an exceptional degree.

After some early attempts at historical painting on a large scale, he wisely turned to anecdotic genre, a class of subjects far better adapted to his talents, in which for many years he had no superior. He took his motives from the works of Shakespeare, Sterne, Addison, Pope, Goldsmith, Fielding, and Smollett; he also illustrated many familiar scenes from the comedies of Molière, from *Don Quixote, Gil Blas,* and other works. His "Slender, Shallow and Anne Page," "Sir Roger de Coverley Going to Church," "May Day in the Time of Queen Elizabeth," and other early paintings of the sort established his reputation, and within a few years he was made an associate and then a member of the Royal Academy. In 1833 he accepted the appointment of teacher of drawing in the United States Military Academy at West Point, but after discharging the duties of the office for a few months he returned to England, where the rest of his life was passed. In 1847 he became professor of painting in the Royal Academy, and the substance of his lectures to the students during the four years that he held the office was published later under the title of *A Handbook for Young Painters* (1855). He wrote *Memoirs of the Life of John Constable, Esq., R.A.* (1843), and began a biography of Sir Joshua Reynolds which was completed by his literary executor, Tom Taylor (*Life and Times of Sir Joshua Reynolds,* 1865). Leslie's style is simple, clear, and pithy, and his writings form a valuable contribution to the literature of art. His biographer in the *Dictionary of National Biography* states that his principal defect as a painter was his use of color, which was at times harsh. The Pennsylvania Academy of the Fine Arts owns eleven of his early works, including his "Murder of Rutland by Lord Clifford," "Touchstone," "Audrey and William," "Olivia," and "Sophia Western." Leslie married Harriet Stone of London in 1825; he died in London at the age of sixty-five.

[Charles Robert Leslie, *Autobiog. Recollections* (1860), edited, with an essay on Leslie as an artist and selections from his correspondence, by Tom Taylor; Geo. Johnston, *Hist. of Cecil County, Md.* (1881); *Dict. Nat. Biog.*; Wm. Dunlap, *Hist. of the Rise and Progress of the Arts of Design in the U. S.* (3 vols., 1918); H. T. Tuckerman, *Book of the Artists* (1867); Samuel Isham, *Hist. of Am. Painting* (1905); P. G. Hamerton, article in *Fortnightly Rev.,* Jan. 1866; H. T. Tuckerman, article in *Christian Examiner,* Sept. 1860; R. C. Waterston, article in *North Am. Rev.,* Jan. 1861; *Living Age,* July 9, 1859, June 2, 1860; *Art Journal,* vol. XII (1860), LIV (1902); *Chambers's Jour.,* July 28, 1860; *Quart. Rev.* (London), Apr. 1860; *Temple Bar,* Mar. 1896; *Century Illustrated Monthly Mag.,* Dec. 1900.]

W. H. D.

LESLIE, ELIZA (Nov. 15, 1787–Jan. 1, 1858), author, sister of Charles Robert Leslie [*q.v.*], was born in Philadelphia, Pa., the daughter of Robert and Lydia (Baker) Leslie. Her great-grandfather, Robert Leslie, had emigrated from Scotland to the Maryland colony about 1745 and had bought a farm. Her grandparents and her parents were natives of Cecil County, Md. Soon after their marriage her parents removed to Philadelphia, where her father was a watchmaker. He seems to have been an unusual man, a self-taught mathematician and draftsman, a fair performer on the flute and violin, and enough of a scientist to be elected to the American Philosophical Society, where he was the friend of Thomas Jefferson and Benjamin Franklin. When Eliza was five, Robert Leslie took his family to England, where they remained over six years, while he was in the business of exporting clocks. A few years after their return to Philadelphia he died, leaving his family very poor; but, as Eliza Leslie said, they kept their difficulties to themselves, asked no assistance, and incurred no debts.

Eliza's education had been carried on chiefly at home, by reading and by private lessons in French and music, but she had had three months in a London school of needlework and had taken a course in the cooking school of Mrs. Goodfellow in Philadelphia. Recipes learned at this school she was in the habit of copying for friends, until one of her brothers suggested that it would save trouble to publish a book. This resulted in her first publication, *Seventy-Five Receipts for Pastry, Cakes, and Sweetmeats* (1837). Her only writing previous to this had been verses, with soldiers, sailors, and shepherds for heroes, which she herself estimated as foolish after seeing a real English shepherd. The publisher of the cook book urged her to write juvenile stories and she then began to publish the Mirror Series. Her literary success was now assured and cook books and stories continued to win for her popularity and a good income for the remainder of her life. Her story "Mrs. Washington Potts" won a prize from *Godey's Lady's Book* and three other prizes came to her from periodicals. She contributed frequently to the *Lady's Book* and *Graham's Magazine* and edited *The Gift,* an annual, and *The Violet,* a juvenile "souvenir."

Her only novel, *Amelia, or a Young Lady's Vicissitudes* (1848), was first published in the *Lady's Book*. Her other works include: *The American Girl's Book* (1831); *Pencil Sketches* (three series, 1833, 1835, 1837); *The Domestic Cookery Book* (1837), which went through thirty-eight editions by 1851; *Althea Vernon; or, The Embroidered Handkerchief* (1838); *The House-Book* (1840); *The Young Revolutionists* (1845), hero stories, chiefly of the American Revolution; *The Lady's Receipt Book* (1846); *The Dennings and Their Beaux* (1851); and *The Behaviour Book* (1853). As a story writer Eliza Leslie had an easy narrative style and a taste for satire, which was criticized by one contemporary reviewer as depriving her work of any "lasting attraction." Another critic considered her characters "perfect daguerreotypes of real life." Her contributions were said always to increase the circulation of periodicals. Her books on domestic economy were the most popular and brought in the largest financial returns. She lived for some years at the United States Hotel, Philadelphia, where she was visited by many of her own countrymen and travelers from abroad. She had a reputation for a remarkable memory, original ideas, and an unfailing supply of apt anecdote. During the last ten years of her life she was working on a biography of John Fitch, the inventor, who was a friend of her father. She died at Gloucester, N. J.

[Eliza Leslie's autobiography was published in John S. Hart, *Female Prose Writers of America* (1852). See also R. W. Griswold, *The Prose Writers of America* (1847); Sarah Josepha Hale, *Biog. of Distinguished Women* (ed. 1876); review of *Pencil Sketches in North Am. Rev.*, Oct. 1833; E. A. and G. L. Duyckinck, *Cyc. of Am. Lit.* (ed. 1875); *Godey's Lady's Book*, Apr. 1858; Geo. Johnston, *Hist. of Cecil County, Md.* (1881); *N. Y. Times*, Jan. 4, 1858.]   S.G.B.

LESLIE, FRANK (Mar. 29, 1821–Jan. 10, 1880), wood-engraver, pioneer publisher of illustrated journals, born in Ipswich, England, was the son of Joseph Leslie and Mary Elliston Carter and was named Henry. His father, a glove-manufacturer, urged the boy to enter his business, but he preferred to carve wood and at the age of thirteen astonished his elders by making a wood-engraving of the coat-of-arms of the town of Ipswich (*Frank Leslie's Illustrated Newspaper*, Feb. 7, 1880). "Frank Leslie" was at first a pseudonym which he employed on sketches and engravings submitted surreptitiously to various publications. His work attracted the attention of the *Illustrated London News* and at twenty-one he was employed in that journal's engraving department. Firm in the belief that there was a wider field in the United States for his art he emigrated to New York in 1848.

His name appears in the directory of the following year as "Leslie, F., engraver, 98 Broadway," although his name was not legally changed until 1857 (*Laws of the State of New York*, 1857, Chapter 205). In 1852 he was employed in Boston on *Gleason's Pictorial*, in which many of his full-page engravings appeared, but at the end of the year he returned to New York to become superintendent of the engraving department of a new publication, the *Illustrated News*, which was first issued on Jan. 1, 1853. The issue of July 30, 1853, carried a double-page engraving bearing Leslie's name and entitled "Inauguration Ceremonies of the Crystal Palace." An engraving of this size ordinarily required four months' time to complete, but through Leslie's ingenuity, this picture was completed in three days. After the drawing had been made, he had divided it into thirty-four blocks and had set as many engravers to work, thus accomplishing the feat. Using the same device subsequently in his own papers Leslie was able to picture events the day following their occurrence.

Before the end of 1853 the *Illustrated News* had merged with *Gleason's Pictorial* and Leslie had started the first publication of his own, *Frank Leslie's Ladies' Gazette of Paris, London, and New York Fashions*, first issued in January 1854. About a year later he bought out an unsuccessful publication, the *New York Journal*, which appeared under a new name, *Frank Leslie's New York Journal*, in January 1855. His next publication, *Frank Leslie's Illustrated Newspaper*, which was to give him enduring fame, was first issued on Dec. 15, 1855. In his initial editorial he declared that the earlier illustrated newspapers, such as *Gleason's Pictorial*, lacked "the artistic facilities for seizing promptly and illustrating the passing events of the day." Leslie had discovered how to succeed where others had failed. Beginning Aug. 15, 1857, he pleased the German-reading population by printing each weekly issue in German under the title *Illustrirte Zeitung*. *Frank Leslie's Monthly*, at first known as *Frank Leslie's New Family Magazine*, was started in September 1857, absorbing the earlier *Gazette of Fashion*.

During the Civil War Leslie's profits increased at a rapid rate. His artists were found wherever the campaigns were hottest. As his revenues increased, so did the number of his publications. They included the *Chimney Corner, Lady's Magazine, Lady's Journal, Boy's and Girl's Weekly, Sunday Magazine, Chatterbox, Pleasant Hours, Boys of America, Jolly Joker, Illustrated Almanac, Comic Almanac,* all bearing the name of Frank Leslie. It was his desire to provide "mental pabulum" for all classes of society. To one publication, the *Day's Doings,* "Illustrating Extraordinary Events of the Day, Police Reports, Important Trials, and Sporting News," he did not attach his name. When the *Times* editor called it "a most wicked and disgusting sheet" (*New York Times,* July 3, 1872), Leslie merely stated that he was indebted to the *Times* for the news items on which the pictures were based. Leslie greatly prized a gold medal presented to him by Napoleon III *"pour services rendus"* as a United States commissioner to the Exposition Universelle of 1867 at Paris. He also took great satisfaction, as a member of the New York state board of managers for the Centennial at Philadelphia, in producing a magnificently illustrated volume: *Frank Leslie's Historical Register of the United States Centennial Exposition, 1776* (1777). This was a distinct financial loss, however, and, coupled with colossal expenditures in connection with his estate "Interlaken," at Saratoga, and a pleasure trip to California, and with the general financial depression of 1877, brought him to bankruptcy. He left to his widow liabilities aggregating $300,000.

Until Frank Leslie was married a second time, July 13, 1874, to Mrs. Miriam Florence Squier [see Leslie, Miriam Florence Folline] his domestic life was particularly unhappy. By his first wife, whom he married in England, he had three sons. Litigation attending his divorce extended over several years. His death was undoubtedly hastened by additional litigation which he felt constrained to undertake against his two surviving sons in 1879 because they used the name "Frank Leslie" in connection with a journal they were publishing.

["Frank Leslie," in *Frank Leslie's Sunday Mag.,* Mar. 1880; *Frank Leslie's Illustrated Newspaper,* Jan. 24, 1880; obituaries in New York papers of Jan. 11, 1880, particularly the *World*; *Territorial Enterprise,* Extra (Virginia City, Nev.), July 14, 1878; *Harper's Weekly,* Jan. 31, 1880; Frederic Hudson, *Journalism in the U. S. from 1690 to 1872* (1873); A. B. Paine, *Th. Nast, His Period and Pictures* (1904); vital statistics, N. Y. City; court records, N. Y. county.]
           A. E. P.

LESLIE, MIRIAM FLORENCE FOLLINE (*c.* 1836–Sept. 18, 1914), wife and successor of Frank Leslie [*q.v.*], daughter of Charles and Susan Danforth Follin, was born in New Orleans, La. She apparently changed the spelling of her last name. The date of her birth she successfully concealed. Her girlhood appears to be linked with New York City and she seems to have acquired a good education in the French, Spanish, and Italian languages. Her marriage to David Charles Peacock on Mar. 27, 1854, was annulled on Mar. 22, 1856. About two years later she was married to Ephraim George Squier

[*q.v.*], diplomat and journalist, who during the early years of the Civil War was a member of Frank Leslie's editorial staff. It is probable that she was an assistant in the publisher's office in the late sixties. When *Frank Leslie's Lady's Journal* was issued on Nov. 18, 1871, it was "conducted by Miriam F. Squier." It was a weekly "Devoted to Fashion and Choice Literature," and each issue contained a leading article entitled "What New Yorkers are Wearing." With alternate numbers subscribers received a large colored fashion plate. The publisher, long estranged from his wife, became enamoured of his capable and comely editress who reciprocated his affection and divorced Squier, May 31, 1873 (*Superior Court Judgments,* New York County, vol. XXXV). Her married life with Leslie she spoke of as "her one happy matrimonial experience." She entertained lavishly both in the metropolis and at the Leslie Saratoga estate "Interlaken." She and Leslie took a trip across the continent in 1877 in sumptuous train accommodations and with a considerable retinue of friends and servants. In *California: A Pleasure Trip From Gotham to the Golden Gate* (1877) she wrote an account of the trip. Because of some uncomplimentary statements she made about Virginia City, Nev., both she and her husband were scored ruthlessly by the local news sheet, the *Territorial Enterprise,* Extra, July 14, 1878.

Days of adversity followed which culminated in her husband's death in 1880. She resolutely assumed the management of the business with its $300,000 deficit, knowing for a time what it meant to live "in a carpetless flat." A curious but undoubtedly advantageous move in 1882 was to have her name changed to Frank Leslie by court order. For fifteen years continuously she was her own manager and editor and was highly successful. This success she always claimed was due to her "ability to deal with and judge the value of news" (*New York Tribune,* May 20, 1895). Others said her charming and magnetic personality was a large factor. With ample income to retire she leased the business in 1895 to a syndicate for five years, but after three years she felt it necessary to occupy once again the editor's chair of *Frank Leslie's Popular Monthly* and resurrect the business. Her written works extended over several years and touched a variety of subjects. In 1871 she published *Travels in Central America,* from the French of Arthur Morelet. Later works included *Rents in Our Robes* (1888); *Beautiful Women of Twelve Epochs* (1890); *Are Men Gay Deceivers* (1893); and *A Social Mirage* (1899). On Oct.

4, 1891, Mrs. Leslie was married to the English art and dramatic critic, Wm. C. Kingsbury Wilde ("Willie" Wilde), a brother of Oscar Wilde, but a divorce followed two years later. After one of her many trips to France she returned in 1901 claiming to have succeeded to the title "Baroness de Bazus." An ardent feminist, she was a vice-president and generous benefactor of the Women's Press Club (*New York Tribune*, Nov. 29, 1903), and she willed the bulk of her fortune to the cause of woman's suffrage. She had no children.

[*Who's Who in America*, 1912–13; *Who's Who in N. Y. City and State* (1904); Rose Young, *The Record of the Leslie Woman Suffrage Commission, Inc.*, 1917–29 (1929); *Frank Leslie's Popular Monthly*, Nov. 1898; *Leslie's Illustrated Weekly Newspaper*, Oct. 1, 1914; *Daily Picayune* (New Orleans), July 31, 1898; *N. Y. Tribune*, May 22, 1894, May 20, 1895; Oct. 2, 1900, July 18, 1901; *N. Y. Times*, Sept. 19, 21, 1914; vital statistics, N. Y. City; court records, N. Y. County.]
A. E. P.

LESQUEREUX, LEO (Nov. 18, 1806–Oct. 25, 1889), paleobotanist, son of V. Aimé and Marie Anne Lesquereux, was born in the village of Fleurier, in the canton of Neuchâtel, Switzerland. His ancestors were French Huguenots—victims of the edict of Nantes. His father was a manufacturer of watchsprings; his mother, a woman of education who aspired to see her son a minister in the Lutheran church and to this end persisted in attempting to make him a classical scholar. In this effort she failed. The boy could not and would not confine himself to his books, but early developed an almost uncontrollable enthusiasm for outdoor life and natural history. In one of his early mountain-climbing expeditions, when he was about ten years old, he fell from a high crag and was so badly injured that for days his life was despaired of, though he ultimately recovered with only the partial loss of hearing in one ear as a permanent result. When he was thirteen, at his mother's earnest solicitation he went to Neuchâtel to study, but though he did well in arithmetic and French, in Latin and Greek he failed.

By the age of nineteen, however, he was fitted for the University. Since his father was unable to bear the expense of maintaining him there, he accepted a position at Eisenach, Saxony, as professor of French, expecting to earn enough to pay his own expenses. Here he met Sophia von Wolffskeel von Reichenberg, the daughter of General von Wolffskeel, and despite the discrepancy in their respective stations, between Lesquereux and this young woman a mutual attachment developed which was ultimately allowed to culminate in marriage. Increasing deafness forced Lesquereux to give up teaching a year

or two after his marriage. For a while he eked out a somewhat scanty living for his wife and children by engraving watchcases, and in time formed a partnership with his father in the manufacture of watchsprings. During his prolonged incapacity from a serious illness, his wife learned a branch of the trade and supported the family until his recovery.

Cut off almost completely from social intercourse by his deafness, he turned his attention back once more to nature, particularly to the mosses and lower forms of plant life, quickly mastering his subject and constituting himself a recognized authority. About this time, the Swiss government, in view of the increasing scarcity of fuel, offered a prize for the best essay on the formation and preservation of the peat bogs, which had become the chief source of supply. Lesquereux won the prize with his *Recherches sur les Tourbières du Jura* (1844). Furthermore, the essay brought him in touch with Jean Louis Rodolphe Agassiz [*q.v.*], Arnold Henry Guyot [*q.v.*], his former classmate, and other scientific men of the day. The episode proved a turning point in his career. The Swiss government next employed him to prepare a small textbook on peat for use in the schools, and created for his especial benefit the office of director of peat bogs. He was also—through the social influence of his wife, it is said—employed to report upon the peat bogs of Germany, Sweden, Denmark, and France. Unfortunately, while he was engaged in these congenial tasks the political revolutions of 1847–48 came about, and all employees of the existing government were ousted. Agassiz had gone to America in 1846, and Lesquereux and his friend Guyot followed, landing in Boston in September 1848. Lesquereux was at this time in his forty-second year, "stone deaf," and unable to speak English. Nevertheless he triumphed over his handicap by learning to read lip movements, and ultimately was able to carry on conversation with three persons at once, speaking English, French, and German in turn, although it was necessary in such case that he be told in advance the language each individual was to speak. Since his own speaking knowledge of English was gained after he reached America, his vocalization was bad, as with deaf mutes in general.

His first scientific work in the United States was the classification of the plant collection made during the Agassiz expedition of 1848 to Lake Superior. Later he moved to Columbus, Ohio, where he became associated with the eminent cryptogamic botanist, William Starling Sullivant [*q.v.*], in his bryological work. He then turned to a systematic study of the coal plants and quickly became the recognized authority on matters relating to the entire Appalachian coal field, with the literature of which his name must be forever associated. His most valued single contribution is his "Description of the Coal Flora of the Carboniferous Formation in Pennsylvania and Throughout the United States" (*Second Geological Survey of Pennsylvania: Report of Progress, P.*, 3 vols. in 2, 1880–84), but he is to be credited also with the determinations of the coal plants for the Kentucky survey of 1860, the Illinois survey of 1866 and 1870, the Indiana survey of 1876 and 1884, as well as the Tertiary plants of the Hilgard survey of Mississippi and the Cretaceous and Tertiary plants of the Hayden survey of the Dakotas.

Lesquereux's deafness cut him off from all attendance on society meetings and he was known intimately to few. He had a very modest opinion of his own merits. He "was a devout Christian believer. . . . He extended his creed to take in all scientific discoveries, but he did not count any of its essentials disturbed thereby. He seems never to have been reached by the currents of modern thought which have overflowed the old foundations for so many" (Orton, *post*, p. 294). His friend and colleague, Peter Lesley, writes: "A homelier, a more beautiful face I never saw. The homeliness was in the flesh; the beauty was the varying expression of a perfectly lovely spirit. He was a little man with inexhaustible powers of life. His eyes were limpid; his smile heavenly; his gratitude for the smallest favors from men and his childlike confidence in the care of God, unbounded. Everybody trusted and loved him" (*post*, p. 210). He was honored by membership in the leading scientific societies of Europe and was the first member to be elected to the National Academy of Sciences after its organization. He died in Columbus, Ohio, in his eighty-third year.

[See autobiographical letter from Lesquereux in his posthumous monograph, *The Flora of the Dakota Group* (1891), also pub. as *Monographs of the U. S. Geol. Survey*, vol. XVII (1892); brief notice in *Am. Jour. Sci.*, Dec. 1889; memoir by Peter Lesley, based on material from Lesquereux himself, in *Biog. Memoirs Nat. Acad. Sci.*, vol. III (1895); memoir by Edward Orton, in *Am. Geologist*, May 1890; W. J. Youmans, *Pioneers of Science in America* (1896); *Pop. Sci. Mo.*, Apr. 1887; *Proc. Am. Philosophical Soc.*, vol. XXVIII (1890); C. R. Barnes, in *Botanical Gazette*, Jan. 1890; frequent references in M. L. Ames, *Life and Letters of Peter and Susan Lesley* (2 vols., 1909); *Cincinnati Commercial Gazette*, Oct. 26, 1889. J. C. Poggendorff, in *Biographisch-literarisches Handwörterbuch zur Geschichte der Exacten Wissenschaften* (1898), gives Lesquereux's name as Charles Leo, but he seems never to have used the Charles.]   G. P. M.

LESTER, CHARLES EDWARDS (July 15, 1815–Jan. 29, 1890), author, was born at Griswold, Conn., of New England ancestry, son of Moses Lester and Sarah Woodbridge, a granddaughter of Jonathan Edwards. Following his schooldays in Connecticut he traveled in the Southwest, descending the Mississippi in the winter of 1834–35, and studied law at Natchez, Miss., under the Democratic leader, Robert J. Walker [*q.v.*], later secretary of the treasury under Polk. Lester, who, though an anti-slavery man, was always an ardent Democrat, afterward warmly acknowledged Walker's influence on his character and political views. He was admitted to the bar, but subsequently attended Auburn (N. Y.) Theological Seminary, 1835–36, and became a Presbyterian minister, holding several charges in northern New York. His interest in the anti-slavery movement appears in his book *Chains and Freedom* (1839), the life of a runaway slave. Compelled by ill health to leave the ministry, he visited England in 1840 as a delegate to the World Anti-Slavery Convention, held in Exeter Hall, London, where he met Campbell, Beatty, Dickens, and other British writers. His book *The Glory and the Shame of England* (2 vols., 1841), published upon his return, attracted much attention as an exposure of the hardships of British labor in factories and mines. To a defense by Peter Brown entitled *The Fame and Glory of England Vindicated* (1842), Lester replied in *The Condition and Fate of England* (1842). During Polk's administration he was consul at Genoa, 1842–47, an account of his service appearing in *My Consulship* (1853). His residence abroad gave opportunity for much study and writing, including translations from Machiavelli, Ceba, Alfieri, and Azeglio, all published in 1845. Following his return, he lived chiefly in the vicinity of New York, engaged in varied literary work, served as correspondent of the London *Times*, and was a prolific popular writer in biography, history, and allied fields. His *Life and Voyages of Americus Vespucius*, in collaboration with Andrew Foster, based partly on research in Italy and perhaps his best piece of investigation, was published in 1846 and passed through many editions, the last in 1903. Among his other books may be noted *Artists of America* (1846); *The Napoleonic Dynasty* (1852), with Edwin Williams; *Our First Hundred Years* (1874–75); *America's Advancement* (1876); and lives of Sam Houston (1855), Charles Sumner (1874), Tilden and Hendricks (1876), and Peter Cooper (1883). A complete list would number twenty-seven works, some in two volumes, and many of them republished. Though popular rather than erudite, and often compilations designed to meet demands of the hour, his books are generally clear and vigorous, showing genuine interest in the spread of knowledge and liberal ideas. During the Civil War he worked in Washington hospitals, recording his experiences in *The Light and Dark of the Rebellion* (1863). His wife, who survived him, was Ellen, daughter of Capt. Haley Brown of Sackett's Harbor, N. Y., whom he married Aug. 8, 1837. He had one child, Ellen Salisbury, who married Col. Sylvester Larned, and at whose home in Detroit Lester died of consumption after several years of increasing ill health. He was then engaged on a work to be called "The Great Explorers." In person he was of commanding presence, standing over six feet, possessed of unusual range of knowledge and gifts of conversation. During his long career he had known intimately Webster, Sumner, Frémont, Greeley, Tilden, the elder Bennett, and many other distinguished figures in public life.

[Sources include family material and Lester's writings; *Gen. Biog. Cat. of Auburn Theolog. Sem.* (1918); D. L. Phillips, *Griswold—A Hist.* (1929); *No. Am. Rev.*, Apr. 1846; *Detroit Free Press*, Jan. 30, 1890; *Sou. Quart. Rev.*, Jan. 1854; Lester in *Our First Hundred Years* quotes frequently from "My Life Note-Book, MS.," but this is not possessed by the family and if published has not been located.]   A. W.

LESUEUR, CHARLES ALEXANDRE (Jan. 1, 1778–Dec. 12, 1846), artist, naturalist, distinguished in both France and the United States, was born at Le Havre, France, the son of Jean-Baptiste Denis Lesueur, an officer of the Admiralty, and his wife, Charlotte Geneviève Thieullent. He attended the Royal Military School at Beaumont-en-Auge from 1787 to 1796, and at eighteen was assigned to the dispatch boat *Le Hardi* for brief service in the English Channel. In his twenty-third year he secured through competitive examination a humble post with the scientific expedition sent out in 1800 by order of the First Consul to explore the coasts of Australia. His skill as an artist soon won him a place on the scientific staff, and with the young naturalist François Péron, his companion in the corvette *Géographe,* he formed an intimate friendship. The two remained with the expedition through hardships which decimated both scientific force and crew, and when they returned to France in 1804 brought to the Museum of Natural History at Paris a collection of more than 100,000 zoölogical specimens, including some 2,500 new species. A report by Cuvier credited Péron and Lesueur themselves with discovering more new species than all the other naturalists of the modern era up to their time. Lesueur collaborated at first with Péron and later with Louis Desaulx Freycinet, in preparing an account of the expedition, *Voyage de découvertes aux Terres Australes* (vols. I and II, 1807–16).

The death of Péron in 1810 and the final downfall of Napoleon in 1815 brought him sorrow and discouragement, and he welcomed the opportunity to become the traveling companion and coworker of William Maclure [*q.v.*], wealthy philanthropist and amateur geologist, with whom he left France in August 1815. After a survey of the West Indies in the winter of 1815–16, they reached New York May 10, 1816, proceeded thence to Philadelphia, and almost immediately set out on a tour of the interior. Their route took them through Delaware and a part of Maryland, to Mercersburg, Pa., across the mountains to Pittsburgh, north to Lake Erie, to Niagara Falls, thence across New York state past the Finger Lakes, and down the Mohawk Valley to Albany. They explored the shores of Lake George and Lake Champlain, went over into the Connecticut Valley, followed the river to the coast and the coast to Boston and Newburyport. Returning overland from Newburyport to Albany, they descended the Hudson by steamboat to Newburgh, and thence went by road to Philadelphia, arriving late in October. During the journey, while Maclure was making his geological observations, Lesueur sketched and painted, collected shells and fossils, and made notes for a work he hoped to produce on the fishes of North America.

In the following spring, after a brief field-trip into New Jersey, the period of his contract with Maclure expired, and for the next nine years he maintained himself in Philadelphia, by engraving and printing his own plates and by teaching drawing and painting. He was soon elected to membership in the American Philosophical Society and the Academy of Natural Sciences of Philadelphia, and was a frequent contributor to their publications. From 1817 to 1825 he was a curator of the Academy. In 1819 he worked for a time on the mapping of the northeast boundary between the United States and Canada; he visited Kentucky in 1821, and the upper Hudson in 1822 and 1823.

Maclure, meantime, had become interested in Robert Owen's projected community at New Harmony, Ind., and in 1825 Lesueur yielded to his persuasion and consented to join the venture. By the keel-boat *Philanthropist* from Pittsburgh, in which Thomas Say [*q.v.*], who became his close friend, Gerard Troost [*q.v.*], the mineralogist, Robert Owen, the founder, and his son, Robert Dale Owen [*q.v.*], were fellow passengers, he arrived in New Harmony in January 1826.

Here for twelve years he taught drawing in the community school, engraved plates for Say's important works on conchology and entomology, and produced several for his own *American Ichthyology,* which was abandoned after the publication of five plates in 1827. Traveling sometimes with Troost or Say, sometimes alone, from New Harmony as a base, he visited St. Louis in 1826, New Orleans repeatedly, Nashville, and the mountains of Tennessee, making notes, drawings, and sketches of the specimens he gathered, the geological formations he studied, the country itself, and the manners of the people.

In 1837 the gradual decline of the New Harmony community, his loneliness since the death of Say in 1834, and the warning that if he remained abroad his meager pension would cease, decided him to return to France, and for the next eight years he was in Paris, spending most of his time in the library or the museum, at work on his manuscripts and sketches. While here he also tried his hand at lithography. In 1845 he was called to Le Havre to become director of the newly founded Museum of Natural History there, and the last two years of his life were thus passed in his native city.

Lesueur was the first to study the fishes of the Great Lakes of North America. In addition to several papers on reptiles, crustaceans, and other subjects, he published twenty-nine papers on American fishes which are listed in Bashford Dean's bibliography (*post*). The most notable of all his American contributions is a monographic review of the family of suckers or *Catostomidae* (*Journal of the Academy of Natural Sciences of Philadelphia,* vol. I, 1817). He was one of the first in America of the school of systematic zoölogy which regards no fact as so unimportant that it need not be correctly ascertained and stated. "In showing his drawings," wrote a former pupil, "Lesueur generally offered a lens, that you might see every hair delineated." The same pupil, Prof. Richard Owen, also wrote (letter to D. S. J., Dec. 14, 1886), "In conversation with me, Agassiz once paid a high compliment to Lesueur's accomplishments in ichthyology, considering him then (as I inferred) the next best to himself in the United States."

[*Am. Jour. Sci. and Arts,* Sept. 1849; E. T. Hamy, *Les Voyages du Naturaliste Ch. Alex. Lesueur dans l'Amérique du Nord* (1904), and Mme. Adrien Loir, *Charles Alexandre Lesueur, Artiste et Savant Français* (1920), both based on Lesueur's MSS. and drawings in the Muséums d'Histoire Naturelle of Le Havre and Paris; D. S. Jordan, in *Pop. Sci. Mo.,* Feb. 1895; G. B. Lockwood, *The New Harmony Movement* (1905); Bashford Dean, *A Bibliog. of Fishes,* vol. II (1917); *Bull. Soc. Philomathique de Paris,* 8 ser. VIII (1896), pp. 15–33; G. B. Goode, in *Report of the U. S. Nat. Museum, 1897,* pt. II (1901); W. J. Youmans, *Pioneers of Science in America* (1896).]   D. S. J.

LE SUEUR, PIERRE (*c.* 1657–*c.* 1705), explorer and trader, was one of the enterprising Frenchmen who opened up the Northwest and by his diplomacy with the Indians checked intertribal war and rapine. He was born in Artois, France, the son of Victor and Anne (Honneur) le Sueur. In 1679 or earlier he came to Canada as a servant or *donné* for the Jesuit missionaries. In this capacity he was sent to Sault Ste. Marie, where the lure of the fur trade tempted him to abandon the religious profession. As early as 1681 he was denounced as a *coureur de bois* and subjected to a fine; nevertheless he persisted in his adventures and by 1682 was among the Sioux Indians on the upper Mississippi. The early name for the Minnesota River —the St. Pierre—is believed to have been assigned in his honor.

Not much is known of Le Sueur's movements for six years after 1683; in 1689 he was with Perrot on the upper Mississippi, when possession of all Sioux territory was taken for France. The next year at Boucherville, Canada, Mar. 29, 1690, he married Marguerite Messier. When Duluth [*q.v.*] was recalled from the West, Le Sueur was sent in 1693 to negotiate with the Sioux and to persuade them to keep peace with the Chippewa. To further this end he built a fort on Madeline Island and in 1695 one at the end of the Brulé– St. Croix portage, Prairie Island, Mississippi River. Some time earlier he had built a fort on the west shore of Lake Pepin, opposite the mouth of Chippewa River. In 1695 he achieved his greatest diplomatic triumph: bringing to Canada a Sioux chief and his wife together with a Chippewa chief, so that the former might make an alliance with Governor Frontenac, and peace between the hereditary enemies might be publicly ratified.

Le Sueur next went to France to obtain permission to work a mine he thought he had discovered, but on the return voyage was captured by an English vessel off Newfoundland. Held prisoner for a time, he was released by the Peace of Ryswick, and made a second attempt to reach his mine, but before he succeeded his permit was confiscated and he was recalled. In 1700 he made a new effort to open his supposed mine; he joined Iberville [*q.v.*] in Louisiana and, going up the Mississippi in a sailing vessel, built Fort l'Huillier on a branch of the St. Pierre River, and left there a company to continue mining. The enterprise failed; the ore proved to be only colored earths, and Le Sueur's men abandoned the fort when attacked by hostile tribesmen. The site of this fort was marked in 1926 by the Minnesota Historical Society. In April 1702 Le Sueur returned to France to obtain new concessions. On his way back to Louisiana some years later he died on shipboard. His widow was living in Louisiana in May 1706.

[Little has been written on Le Sueur's career. The best outline is in *Bulletin des Recherches Historiques,* Mar. 1904; see also L. P. Kellogg, *The French Régime in Wis. and the Northwest* (1925), *passim*; W. W. Folwell, *A Hist. of Minn.*, I (1921), 38–42; his Mississippi voyage is narrated in Bénard de la Harpe, *Journal Historique de l'Établissement des Français à la Louisiane* (Paris, 1831), translated in J. G. Shea, *Early Voyages up and down the Mississippi* (1861). See also *Wis. Hist. Colls.*, XVI (1902), 177–93.]   L. P. K.

LETCHER, JOHN (Mar. 29, 1813–Jan. 26, 1884), congressman and governor of Virginia, was born at Lexington, Rockbridge County, Va., the son of William Houston and Elizabeth (Davidson) Letcher and a great-grandson of Giles Letcher who emigrated to Virginia and settled in Goochland County. His father was first cousin to Gen. Sam Houston [*q.v.*]. He attended Washington College (later Washington and Lee University), graduating in 1833, and subsequently studied law. In 1839 he established himself in practice in Lexington and in the same year became editor of the *Valley Star,* a Democratic paper, recently established to promote the cause of Jacksonian Democracy in the Whig stronghold of Rockbridge County. From 1840 to 1844 he retired from his editorial duties to devote his time to law and politics, but from 1844 to 1850 he was again with the paper. In 1840, 1844, and 1848, he was active in the presidential campaigns, serving as a Democratic elector in 1848. He signed in 1847 the noted Ruffner pamphlet which advocated the abolition of slavery in that part of Virginia west of the Blue Ridge. He was a member of the state constitutional convention of 1850–51 and was a vigorous advocate of the white basis of representation in both houses of the legislature.

As a Democrat, he represented the eleventh Virginia district ("tenth legion of Democracy") in Congress from 1851 to 1859. A member of the committee on ways and means, he was a vigilant opponent of governmental extravagance, earning for himself the sobriquet of "Honest John Letcher, Watchdog of the Treasury." His views upon slavery had changed since 1847; in a public letter of 1858, he wrote: "At the time of the publication of that address [the Ruffner pamphlet] . . . I did regard slavery as a social and political evil. I did not regard it then or since as a moral evil for I was at that time, have been ever since, and am now the owner of slave property, by purchase, and, not by inheritance."

Since 1851 he had convinced himself that his former views of the social and political evils of slavery were erroneous (*Valley Star,* July 15, 1858). In Congress he always upheld the rights of the South against Northern interference, though he never glorified slavery as an institution. Nominated by the Democratic party of Virginia, in 1859, for the governorship, he was elected by a small majority after a spirited campaign. His Whig opponents stigmatized him as an abolitionist; the *Lexington Gazette* referred to him as the candidate of the "free soil democracy of Virginia." In the presidential election of 1860, Letcher supported Stephen A. Douglas, and after the secession of the states of the lower South, he lent his support to the peace movement. He opposed the secession of Virginia until Lincoln called for troops to coerce the seceding states.

To the requisition upon Virginia for her quota of troops, Letcher replied to Secretary of War Cameron: "I have only to say that the militia of Virginia will not be furnished to the powers at Washington for any such use or purpose. . . . You have chosen to inaugurate civil war, and having done so we will meet it in a spirit as determined as the Administration has exhibited toward the South" (Munford, *post,* p. 282). As war governor he was a zealous supporter of the Confederacy and advocated the vigorous prosecution of the struggle until Southern independence should be won. At the close of the war he was confined for several months in the Old Capitol prison at Washington. Despite the fact that his private residence in Lexington was burned by Hunter's raiders in 1864, he advised the South to accept the results of the contest in good faith. Speaking to the cadets of the Virginia Military Institute, September 1866, he said: "Let the passions, the prejudices, and revengeful feelings . . . between the sections . . . be consigned, in solemn silence, to a common grave, there to sleep forever. . . . The past is gone and should be forgotten" (*Address . . . at the Virginia Military Institute,* 1866, pp. 11–12). After the war Letcher resumed his practice of law at Lexington and served two terms in the House of Delegates, 1875–76 and 1876–77. In early manhood, he had married Mary S. Holt of Augusta County, Va., and to them were born nine children.

[Oren F. Morton, *A Hist. of Rockbridge County* (1920); Beverley B. Munford, *Virginia's Attitude Toward Slavery and Secession* (1909); L. G. Tyler, *Hist. of Va.* (1924), vols. II and III; M. V. Smith, *Virginia . . . a Hist. of the Executives* (1893); S. R. Houston, *Brief Biog. Accounts of Many Members of the Houston Family* (1882), pp. 22, 47, 58–61; *Biog. Dir. Am. Cong.* (1928); *Valley Star,* July 15, 1858; *Lexington Gazette,* Mar. 10, 1859; *Richmond Dispatch,* Jan. 27, 1884.]   W. G. B.

LETCHER, ROBERT PERKINS (Feb. 10, 1788–Jan. 24, 1861), Kentucky congressman, governor, was born in Goochland County, Va., the seventh of the twelve children of Stephen Giles and Betsey (Perkins) Letcher. His grandfather, Giles Letcher, was the first of the line in America. He was of Welsh descent, but at the time of his emigration the family was living in Ireland. About 1800 Stephen Giles Letcher moved his family to Kentucky, settling first near Harrodsburg and shortly afterward in Garrard County (M. B. Buford, *The Buford Family in America*, 1903, p. 116). The elder Letcher was a brick-maker and his sons worked with him in that trade. Robert Perkins attended the academy conducted by Joshua Fry, one of the most noted of the teachers of early Kentucky, and later studied law in the office of Humphrey Marshall. During the War of 1812 he saw a brief service as judge advocate in the regiment of Kentucky Mounted Volunteer Militia commanded by Lieut.-Col. James Allen (*Report of the Adjutant General of the State of Kentucky: Soldiers of the War of 1812*, 1891, p. 248). His term of enlistment came to an end in October 1812 and he did not reënlist. Instead of pursuing a military career he turned to politics and in 1813 was elected to represent Garrard County in the lower house of the state legislature. He was a representative in 1813, 1814, 1815, and 1817. In 1822 he was elected to Congress and was continuously reëlected till 1835. His influence in Congress was considerable, but it was due rather to his genial personality and to his intimacy with Henry Clay than to his own talents as a lawmaker. He had a prominent part in bringing about the Clay-Adams combination in the presidential election of 1825. Adams described him as a man of "moderate talents, good temper, playful wit, and shrewd sagacity" (C. F. Adams, *Memoirs of John Quincy Adams*, VIII, 1876, p. 336). In his last term in the House he was a member of the committee on foreign affairs.

Upon his return to Kentucky Letcher was elected to the state House of Representatives and continued to represent Garrard County in that body during 1836, 1837, and 1838. In December 1837 he was elected speaker of the House by a small majority and only after prolonged balloting. One year later he was unanimously reëlected to the same office. In 1840 he was elected governor of Kentucky on the Whig ticket. His chief service in this position consisted in halting, although he could not wholly stop, the ruinous policy of internal improvements on which the state was embarked. After the ex-piration of his term as governor in 1844, he remained a resident of Frankfort until August 1849 when he was appointed minister to Mexico. In this office he acquitted himself satisfactorily. Upon his return to Kentucky in 1852 he became again a candidate for Congress but was beaten by J. C. Breckinridge, his Democratic opponent. This was the end of his political career and thereafter he lived quietly in retirement until his death. Letcher was twice married: his first wife was Mary Oden Epps, his second, Charlotte Robertson who survived him. There were no children of either marriage.

[There is a sketch of Letcher in Alice E. Trabue, *A Corner in Celebrities* (1923), and one by Jennie C. Morton, in the *Reg. of Ky. State Hist. Soc.*, Jan. 1905. See also: Lewis and R. H. Collins, *Hist. of Ky.* (2 vols., 1874); *The Biog. Encyc. of Ky.* (1878); W. E. Connelley and E. M. Coulter, *Hist. of Ky.* (1922), vol. II; and the Kentucky legislative journals.]   R. S. C.

LETCHWORTH, WILLIAM PRYOR (May 26, 1823–Dec. 1, 1910), philanthropist, was born in Brownville, N. Y., of Quaker ancestry, the son of Josiah and Ann (Hance) Letchworth and the great-grandson of John Letchworth who came to America from England in 1766. At the age of fifteen, after a common-school education, he began a business career, and ten years later was junior partner in the hardware firm of Pratt & Letchworth, Buffalo. He prospered and built up a comfortable fortune. In 1859 he purchased a large estate known as "Glen Iris," at Portage, N. Y. Rejected for the army during the Civil War, he allowed the New York volunteers to use his estate for a training camp. For some years history and archeology —especially the archeology of the Indians— were among his hobbies. In this connection he had the remains of Mary Jemison [*q.v.*], "the White Woman of the Genesee," removed in 1874 from the old Buffalo Creek Reservation to his estate. His collection of Indian antiquities eventually became the Genesee Valley Museum. He was an early member of the Buffalo Historical Society. He was also much interested in the fine arts and in 1871 was president of the Buffalo Academy of Fine Arts.

In 1869 he retired from business to devote himself to philanthropy. He refused to run for Congress as a Republican, although assured of election, but accepted a commissionership on the state board of charities. In this capacity his initial effort was directed toward removing normal children from the Erie County Poorhouse. After agitating the subject in the press, he succeeded by 1874 in having many of them interned temporarily in local asylums, and was largely instrumental in securing legislation (1875, 1876) prohibiting the confinement of normal children between the ages of three and sixteen in the state almshouses. This movement was later extended to promote the adoption of such children by private families, and became widely known as the Erie County System. In 1878 Letchworth was made president of the state board of charities.

With the problem of the dependent child on the way to solution, he now turned his attention to the delinquent child and the insane poor, and in 1880 began an extensive tour of Europe to study European methods of dealing with these problems. His copious findings on the second subject were published in 1889 under the title, *The Insane in Foreign Countries*. In 1883 he read a paper before the Tenth Annual National Conference of Charities and Corrections on the proper grouping of dependent and incorrigible children and was elected as president of the following conference (October 1884). In 1884, as a result of his efforts, manual training was introduced into the Western House of Refuge at Rochester, the name of the institution being changed to State Industrial School. In his work for the insane poor, also, he brought about several innovations. He pointed out some superiorities of European institutions, worked to secure state control of all insane persons and to establish farm colonies, and in 1886 aided in the addition of a new state insane asylum at Ogdensburg to the seven already established. In the early nineties he changed his objective from the insane to the epileptic, and in 1893, through his initiative, the tract of land known as Sonyea owned by the Shakers near Mount Morris was purchased by the state as a colony for epileptics. It was opened formally in 1896, as Craig Colony. In 1900 he published *Care and Treatment of Epileptics*. A stroke of apoplexy in 1903 made him an invalid for the rest of his life. When "Glen Iris" was threatened by the demands of electric power companies in 1906 he deeded the tract to the State of New York, and it was henceforth known as Letchworth Park. In 1909 the new Eastern New York State Custodial Asylum in Rockland County was renamed Letchworth Village. In addition to some sixty-five papers or reports on matters connected with charities and corrections, he published a *Sketch of the Life of Samuel F. Pratt* (1874), and issued an edition (1898) of James E. Seaver's *Narrative of the Life of Mary Jemison* with illustrations and supplementary material collected by himself.

[J. N. Larned, *The Life and Work of William Pryor Letchworth* (1912); Stephen Smith, *An Appreciation of the Life of William Pryor Letchworth* (1911); *Twelfth Ann. Report, 1907, of the Am. Scenic and Hist. Preservation Soc.* (1907); *Who's Who in America,* 1910–11; *Who's Who in N. Y.,* 1909; *N. Y. Times,* Dec. 3, 1910.] E. P.

LETTERMAN, JONATHAN (Dec. 11, 1824–Mar. 15, 1872), organizer of the field medical service of the Union Army in the Civil War, was born in Canonsburg, Washington County, Pa. His father was Jonathan Letterman, a physician, and his mother was a daughter of Craig Ritchie of Canonsburg. His early education, by a private tutor, was followed by a course in Jefferson College in his native town, from which he was graduated in 1845. He received his medical education at Jefferson Medical College, Philadelphia, where, in 1849, he received the degree of M.D. Immediately following his graduation he passed the examination before the United States Army examining board in New York and was appointed assistant surgeon.

During the following twelve years his service was largely on the western and southwestern frontiers, with troops engaged in intermittent warfare with Seminoles, Navajos, Apaches, and Utes. The ingenuity and the improvisations necessary in the treatment, care, and transportation of the wounded under the difficult conditions incident to such warfare was an excellent training for the larger problems which were to confront him later. At the outbreak of the Civil War in 1861 he was assigned to duty with the Army of the Potomac; in June 1862 he was promoted to major and surgeon and was appointed medical director of that army, then under the command of Major-General McClellan. In this position he displayed a remarkable degree of administrative ability. He completely reorganized the field medical service, created an effective mobile hospital organization, and instituted an ambulance service for the evacuation of battle casualties. This organization functioned so effectively at Chancellorsville and later at Antietam and Gettysburg that it was adopted for use throughout the Union army; in fact, the basic plan of field hospitalization and evacuation devised by Letterman has influenced that service in every modern army. He spent the latter part of the war as inspector of hospitals in the department of the Susquehanna. Resigning his army commission in December 1864, he took up his residence in San Francisco, Cal. In 1866 he published his *Medical Recollections of the Army of the Potomac*.

Letterman was married in October 1863 to Mary Lee, of Maryland, to whose home he came, worn from the fatigue of the battlefield of Antietam. Her sudden death in November 1867 was a crushing blow from which he never fully recovered. The consequent mental depression, coupled with a chronic intestinal trouble, kept him a semi-invalid until his death in his forty-eighth year. By a general order of the War Department, Nov. 13, 1911, the large military hospital in the Presidio of San Francisco was designated the Letterman General Hospital, in honor of the man who revolutionized the system of care of the wounded upon the battlefield.

[B. A. Clements, *Memoir of Jonathan Letterman* (1883), reprinted from *Jour. Military Service Inst.,* New York, Sept. 1883; J. T. Smith, "Review of Life and Work of Jonathan Letterman," *Johns Hopkins Hospital Bull.,* Aug. 1916; H. A. Kelly and W. L. Burrage, *Am. Medic. Biogs.* (1920); *Daily Morning Bull.* and *Daily Alta California* (San Francisco), Mar. 16, 1872.]   J. M. P—n.

LEUPP, FRANCIS ELLINGTON (Jan. 2, 1849–Nov. 19, 1918), journalist, was born in New York City, the son of John P. and Emeline M. (Loop) Leupp. Graduating from Williams College in 1870 and from the Columbia Law School in 1872, he served under Bryant and Parke Godwin as assistant editor of the New York *Evening Post* till Bryant's death in 1878. After editing a memorial volume upon Bryant, in that same year he bought an interest in the Syracuse *Herald* and became its editor. In 1885 he removed to Washington to become a freelance contributor to the *Evening Post,* and upon the death of its regular correspondent, E. B. Wright, in 1889, was placed in charge of its Washington bureau, representing at the same time the *Nation.* This post he held till 1904. From 1892 to 1895 he also edited *Good Government,* the official organ of the National Civil Service Reform League.

Leupp's chief reputation was made by his articles for the *Evening Post* and the *Nation,* which gave him for some years an almost unrivaled reputation among Washington correspondents for expertness, alertness, and honesty. A man of culture and breeding, he gained the confidence of leading public men, to whom he often supplied facts or advice of value. His habit was to make a daily round of the departments, Congress, and the White House. He gathered his material with great thoroughness, and he was painstaking in his verification of statements and in buttressing his opinions. Till the Venezuelan message brought a rupture of their close relations he was regarded as Cleveland's mouthpiece, often quoting him on public questions; and later he was intimate with Roosevelt, his book *The Man Roosevelt* (1904) being a record of their friendship. He particularly liked to write compressed, pungent sketches of public men, often spending six months on an essay. Frequently he expressed opinions at variance with those of the *Evening*

Post's editorial page. As the years passed and his background of knowledge grew his articles became more philosophical and he dealt more fully with the play and counter-play of forces behind the scenes in Washington. Even after his retirement from the *Evening Post* he contributed occasionally to it and to the *Nation,* and his "National Miniatures" (1918) was a final compilation of *Nation* vignettes. He wrote also for the *Outlook,* and in the last week of 1911 published in it the most important interview which William Howard Taft gave out while president.

From early manhood Leupp took a keen interest in the Indians, visiting the reservations in New York state and mastering the literature upon Indian life. In 1886 he made an extended Western trip, visiting reservations as far as the Pacific Coast and spending several months with different tribes; and he repeated this excursion in 1889. He was frequently consulted by members of Congress on the Indian question. In 1895, during consideration of a treaty with the Utes for opening their land to settlement, Secretary Hoke Smith sent him to the Southern Ute reservation as confidential agent. In 1896–97 he was a member of the Board of Indian Commissioners and made repeated trips to visit Western tribes and schools and to talk with Indian chiefs. Roosevelt sent him in 1902 to investigate accusations against the officials in charge of the Kiowa, Comanche, and Apache Indians, and his report was printed as a public document (*Senate Document 26,* 58 Cong., 2 Sess.). His years as Indian Commissioner, 1903–09, witnessed much constructive work for Indian betterment. The aims and spirit of his labors are reflected in *The Indian and His Problem* (1910), which deals with the larger relations of the Indian to legislation and administration, and *In Red Man's Land* (1914), which treats of the Indian as an individual. On his retirement he devoted himself to general literary work. His habit of exploring little-known corners of the capital gave him materials for his *Walks About Washington* (1915). He had married Ada Lewis Murdock of New York City on Oct. 13, 1874, and on his death in Washington left three daughters and one son.

[*Who's Who in America,* 1918–19; "Washington Correspondents," the *Nation,* Nov. 30, 1918; *Evening Post* (N. Y.), *N. Y. Times,* Nov. 20, 1918.]   A. N.

LEUTZE, EMANUEL (May 24, 1816–July 18, 1868), historical and portrait painter, was born at Gmünd, Württemberg; but his family moved to the United States soon after his birth and settled in Fredericksburg, Va. His father was "an honest but stern mechanic," whose prime motive in leaving his native land was political discontent. The family shortly moved from Virginia to Philadelphia, where Emanuel received his first instruction in drawing. His early work in painting, done at about twenty-one, consisted of portraits and figure-pieces. In 1840 his work gained for him the patronage and encouragement of Edward L. Carey and other influential Philadelphians, and he was thus enabled to go to Europe for further training in painting. He proceeded to Düsseldorf in 1841 and became a pupil of Karl Friedrich Lessing. His attention was now turned to historical painting, and his first serious essay in this line was "Columbus Before the Council of Salamanca," which was so well received by the authorities of the academy that at their instance it was bought by the Art Union of Düsseldorf. After this success he made a trip to the Swabian Alps, the Tyrol, and Italy. Returning to Düsseldorf, he married the daughter of a German officer and remained there for nearly twenty years. In 1859 he returned to the United States, where an important government commission and numerous private orders awaited him, and where he resided for the rest of his life, dividing his time between New York and Washington.

He had begun in Germany and continued in America a long series of large historical compositions, for the most part dealing with American subjects. The best-known and most important of these are his "Washington Crossing the Delaware," in the Metropolitan Museum of Art, New York, and "Westward the Course of Empire Takes its Way," on the wall of the west staircase of the House of Representatives in the Capitol at Washington. Among many other historical paintings may be mentioned "Washington at Monmouth," "The Landing of the Norsemen," "The Settlement of Maryland," "The Storming of Teocalli, Mexico," and "Cromwell and Milton," the last-named piece belonging to the Corcoran Gallery, Washington.

In common with most historical paintings, Leutze's work is labored, conventional, and in some cases stilted. The immense panel in the Capitol, illustrating the pioneering spirit and the conquering of the Far West, is a failure from the decorative point of view. Its color is dry and disagreeable. The painter had spared no pains, however, to make it veracious and spirited; he had traveled to the Far West to study the scenery and to Germany to consult Kaulbach on the best technical methods to employ in executing a mural painting. His effort to combine history and allegory in the one composition

resulted in inevitable confusion, which was increased by the hard realism of the landscape setting, and the circumstance that the view embraced the Rocky Mountains on the one hand and the Pacific Ocean on the other. The method employed in the execution of the panel is interesting. The painting was done directly on the wall, on a thin layer of cement composed of crushed stone and lime. The watercolor was applied to this ground and fixed by a spray of water-glass solution. The artist received $20,000 for the work.

His most famous painting, "Washington Crossing the Delaware," has been extensively reproduced in school textbooks. The studies for the floating ice on the river, however, were made in the painter's Düsseldorf studio overlooking the Rhine. An ironical article in a newspaper referred to the work as "Washington Crossing the Rhine" (*St. Louis Globe-Democrat*, Mar. 3, 1918). The pose of Washington is undeniably theatrical. Moreover, to stand up in a small craft making its way through formidable ice floes would appear to be a needless invitation to disaster. The flag is an anachronism. Few modern historical pictures are more tumid and few have been more popular in this country. Among Leutze's portraits may be mentioned those of General Grant, Nathaniel Hawthorne, General Burnside, and the artist himself. The Hawthorne was painted in Washington in 1862 and now belongs to the Thomas B. Clarke collection. Leutze died in Washington.

[H. T. Tuckerman, *Book of the Artists* (1867); Samuel Isham, *Hist. of Am. Painting* (1905); Charles E. Fairman, *Art and Artists of the Capitol of the U. S. of America* (1927); Helen W. Henderson, *The Art Treasures of Washington* (1912); Lorinda M. Bryant, *Am. Pictures and their Painters* (1917); Charles H. Caffin, *The Story of Am. Painting* (1907); Jas. T. Fields, *Yesterdays with Authors* (1872); *Lit. Digest*, Mar. 16, 1918; *Mentor*, July 1926; *Lippincott's Mag.*, Nov. 1868; *Evening Star* (Washington), July 20, 1868].
W. H. D.

LEVERETT, JOHN (1616–Mar. 16, 1679), governor of Massachusetts, was the son of Thomas and Anne (Fisher) Leverett and was baptized July 7, 1616, in St. Botolph's Parish, Boston, England. The family appears to have been of fair social rank and to have had some property. In 1629 Thomas received a grant of land on the Muscongus in New England, and in 1633 he emigrated with his wife and three children to Massachusetts. He had occupied various offices in old Boston, being alderman when he left. John became a freeman May 13, 1640. Sometime previous to that he had married Hannah Hudson who reached Boston with her parents in 1635. By her he had four children. She died in 1646 and in 1647 he married Sarah Sedgwick, who survived him and by whom he had fourteen children. He appears to have been prosperous and to have been engaged in foreign trade, for in 1646 it was noted that he and Edward Gibbons had lost a ship off Virginia valued at £2,000. He had also become interested in public affairs and soon after he became a freeman he was sent with Edward Hutchinson on a mission to the Indian chief Miantonomo. In 1644 he went to England and took part in the war, receiving a command in the Parliamentary army and gaining distinction. He had returned to Boston, Mass., by 1648, and from 1651 to 1653 he was a member of the General Court. In 1652 he was one of the commissioners sent to Maine to proclaim the settlements there subject to the jurisdiction of Massachusetts. He was also in 1651 one of the selectmen for the town of Boston. In 1653 he was appointed colonial agent in England and sailed sometime before 1655, remaining in London until 1662. On his return he was again elected to the General Court for the years 1663–65, being speaker of the House for a part of that time. From 1665 to 1670 he was a member of the Council, and from 1671 to 1673 deputy governor.

Leverett had always liked military life and in 1639 had joined the Ancient and Honorable Artillery Company of which he was a member for thirty-two years. In 1663 he was made major-general of all the Massachusetts forces and so remained until elected governor of the colony in 1673. He continued to be annually elected to the governorship until his death in 1679. His tenure as governor is noteworthy as including the period of King Philip's War, in which he rendered excellent service. It is also of importance as marking the beginning of the activities of Edward Randolph who was sent from England to enforce the laws of trade. Leverett refused to take the oath to administer them and had a long struggle with the royal official. Throughout his career he was constantly called upon for special services: he was one of the commissioners sent to confer with Stuyvesant at New York over the difficulties with the Dutch (1653); he led the force which expelled the French from the Penobscot (1654); and he was one of the four to whom was confided the custody of the colony charter in the troubled year 1664. It has always been claimed that he was knighted, though there is much confusion as to why and when (*Memoir, post,* pp. 81ff.). The date agreed upon by the family historians is 1676 and the reason, his services in the Indian War, though it seems odd that Charles II should thus honor the governor of the recalci-

trant Massachusetts. It is said he never used the title, and in the long epitaph on his tomb he is described as "Esquire."

[Chas. E. Leverett, *A Memoir . . . of Sir John Leverett, Knt., Gov. of Mass., 1673–79* (1856); N. B. Shurtleff, *A Geneal. Memoir of the Family of Elder Thos. Leverett of Boston* (1850), and *Records of the Gov. and Company of the Mass. Bay in New Eng.* (5 vols., 1853–54); J. B. Moore, *Memoirs of Am. Govs.,* vol. I (1846); Samuel Waldo, *A Defense of the title of . . . John Leverett . . . to a Tract of Land in the Eastern Parts of the Province of the Mass. Bay, Commonly called Muscongus Lands* (1736); R. N. Tappan, "Edward Randolph," *Prince Soc. Pubs.,* vols. XXIV–XXVIII (1898–99); *Mass. Hist. Soc. Colls.,* 4 ser. II (1854).]   J. T. A.

LEVERETT, JOHN (Aug. 25, 1662–May 3, 1724), president of Harvard College, was the eldest son of Hudson Leverett, a disreputable attorney who was the eldest son of Gov. John Leverett [*q.v.*]. His mother was Sarah Peyton (or Payton). From the Boston Latin School John entered Harvard College, graduated A.B. in 1680, and A.M. in 1683. His student notebook includes selections from the Anacreontics of Cowley, a Latin salutatory oration to Governor Andros, and syllogistic disputations. In 1685 he was chosen fellow and tutor of the College, which during the next fifteen years (President Mather being an absentee) was governed and instructed largely by Leverett and William Brattle [*q.v.*]. These young men, while insisting on "Righteousness, Faith and Charity," were less concerned with religious forms of polity (Nathanael Appleton, funeral sermon, *A Great Man Fallen in Israel,* 1724, p. 30), than with preparing students for life. One pupil afterward declared that they had "made more Proselytes to the Church of England than any 2 men ever did that liv'd in America" (Henry Newman to Mr. Taylor, Mar. 29, 1714, S. P. C. K. MSS., London); and another spoke of the "enlarged catholic Spirit" cherished in him by Mr. Leverett (Ebenezer Turell, *The Life and Character of the Rev. Benjamin Colman,* 1749, p. 123). Hence the tutors were accused of subversive teaching. Leverett's support of his former pupil Benjamin Colman [*q.v.*] opened a breach between him and the Mathers; and in a shake-up of the college government, occurring in 1700, he was dropped out.

Leverett had already prepared for this eventuality by studying law, and by entering politics as representative from Cambridge, in 1696–97. One of his pupils complained of being obliged to recite "at five o'clock in the winter mornings that Mr. L. might seasonably attend the General Court at Boston" (Sibley, *post,* III, 183). In 1699 he was appointed justice of the peace (W. H. Whitmore, *The Massachusetts Civil List,*

1870, p. 138), and began practising as attorney (Samuel Sewall, *Diary*, I, 495); in 1700 he was chosen speaker of the House. Gov. Joseph Dudley [*q.v.*], an old friend, appointed him in 1702 judge of the superior court, and judge of probate for Middlesex County. Leverett was elected to the Provincial Council in 1706, as of Eastern Maine, where he had inherited a great land grant, the Muscongus Patent of 1630; in order to procure capital for settling this tract, he organized the Lincolnshire Company in 1719. Governor Dudley sent him on three missions: in 1704 to the Iroquois; down East in 1707 to rally the dispirited Port Royal expedition—a forlorn hope indeed; and to Governor Lovelace at New York in 1709. In the meantime Leverett's friends had recovered control of the Harvard Corporation, which on Oct. 28, 1707, elected him president, eight votes to five. This choice provoked a political commotion. Governor Dudley only obtained the customary legislative grant of £150 for the president's salary, by reviving the supposedly defunct College Charter of 1650, which flattered the legislature and eliminated from the Corporation those fellows opposed to Leverett. After the deal went through, he was inaugurated president Jan. 14, 1707/08.

Leverett was the first lawyer and judge to hold the Harvard presidency. Widely cultivated, comparatively broad-minded, and impressive in person, he governed the College "with great Sweetness and Candor . . . tempered with Convenient Severity" (S. Sewall, in Sibley, *post*, III, 191). Few alterations were made in the formal curriculum; but students were introduced to recent Anglican divinity, to Henry More's *Enchiridion Ethicum;* and were offered instruction in French. Colman wrote that after residing at Oxford and Cambridge he could assert that "no Place of Education can well boast a more free air than our little *College* may" (Turell, *op. cit.,* p. 123). Student life grew gayer, the first college club and periodical were started, and Commencements became uproarious. These tendencies raised a cry of idleness and extravagance against the students, in which young Benjamin Franklin joined (*New England Courant*, Nos. 41 and 44, 1722). Cotton Mather, who called Leverett the "pretended president," and the *"infamous drone"* (Quincy, I, 523–24, 343), accused the students of reading "plays, novels, empty and vicious pieces of poetry, and even Ovid's Epistles, which have a vile tendency to corrupt good manners" (Quincy, *post,* I, 559). Numbers increased so that Massachusetts Hall had to be built. President Leverett was elected in 1713 fellow of the Royal Society (Thomas Thomson, *History of the*

Royal Society, 1812, p. xxxiii), to which Thomas Robie, one of the tutors, contributed astronomical and other scientific observations. Leverett was energetic in securing to the College former benefactions which had been neglected by his predecessors, and in procuring new ones: notably those of Thomas Hollis, whose professorship of divinity (1721) was kept free from religious tests by the determined stand of the president and fellows.

From 1713, when the College Corporation refused to appoint Governor Dudley's son to the vacant treasurership (Quincy, I, 206–07), Leverett had a clerico-political fight on his hands. Judge Sewall accused him of neglecting religious exercises (*Diary*, III, 202–03); Cotton Mather instigated an investigation of the College in 1723. The Corporation, in order to protect themselves, had coöpted liberal divines to vacancies in their fellowship, instead of following the ancient custom of admitting college tutors to the governing body. This gave the Mather and Dudley factions a popular political issue which they improved against the College, and only by subtle politics and the support of Governor Shute was Leverett able to prevent a complete shake-up. He died suddenly on May 3, 1724 (Samuel Sewall, *Diary*, III, 336–37). Benjamin Wadsworth succeeded to the presidency, and continued the liberal policy inaugurated by Leverett. "To his firmness, and that of his associates . . . the institution is probably in a great measure indebted for its religious freedom at this day" (Quincy, *post*, I, 324). Leverett married first, in 1697, the widow Margaret Berry, daughter of President Rogers (most of their children died young); and second, the widow Sarah (Crisp) Harris, who bore him no children but lived to have two more husbands.

[See J. L. Sibley, *Biog. Sketches of Grads. of Harvard Univ.*, III (1885), 180–98, where references to funeral sermons and other sources will be found; Josiah Quincy, *The Hist. of Harvard Univ.* (1840); Harvard Corporation Records, in *Colonial Soc. of Mass., Pubs.*, vols. XV and XVI (1925); *Diary of Samuel Sewall 1674–1729* (3 vols., 1878–82); *Journals* of the House of Representatives of Massachusetts, vols. I–VI; manuscript Commonplace book in Massachusetts Historical Society; Colman MSS., *Ibid.*; manuscript Diary (so-called, really his private record of Corporation meetings, 1707–23), in University Archives; a remnant of Leverett's personal papers in Vol. I of the Ewer MSS., New-England Historic Genealogical Society; Henry Newman's Letters in Archives of the Society for Propagation of Christian Knowledge, London. Leverett left no published works, and no portrait of him has been traced.]   S. E. M.

LEVERING, JOSEPH MORTIMER (Feb. 20, 1849–Apr. 4, 1908), Moravian bishop, historian, son of Lewis Alexander and Sophia (Hauser) Levering, was born in Hardin County, Tenn. On his father's side he was descended from a line of Moravian missionaries, settled in America during the eighteenth century. In 1852 his family moved to West Salem, Ill., and in 1856 to Olney, where he attended private school and prepared for college. In 1870 he entered the Moravian College and Theological Seminary at Bethlehem, Pa., where he distinguished himself for unusual ability, receiving both the arts and divinity degrees in 1874. After teaching for a few months at Nazareth Hall, Nazareth, Pa., he was ordained deacon (Dec. 20, 1874) and in January 1875 assumed the pastorate of the new congregation at Uhrichsville, Ohio. On May 21, 1876, he was ordained presbyter and three years later was called to the pastorate at Lakemills, Wis. He remained there until 1883 and then entered upon the pastorate of the church at Bethlehem, Pa., the largest congregation of his denomination in the United States. On Sept. 30, 1888, he was consecrated bishop at Bethlehem by Bishops A. A. Reinke and H. J. Van Vleck. In 1901 continued ill health forced him to retire temporarily from active work, but he devoted his leisure to an intensive study of the Moravians in America, and in 1903 published *A History of Bethlehem, Pennsylvania, 1741–1892,* in commemoration of the sesqui-centennial of the leading Moravian settlement in America. This huge volume of over eight hundred pages is far more than an ordinary town history. It is a cross-section of the whole story of the growth of the United States as revealed in the wealth of manuscript letters and reports of Moravian agents and missionaries preserved in the Archives of the Bethlehem church. It is especially strong in its revelation of the social and economic forces that were at work in the land. The author's distaste for the flimsy and trivial led him to avoid the pitfall that traps so many local historians—he included in the book no notices of individuals, as such, apart from the exposition of his theme. He prepared, also, many articles and papers for special occasions and anniversaries, most of them published in the proceedings of the Moravian Historical Society, of which, from 1895 to 1908, he was president. In 1903 he was elected president of the governing board of the Moravian Church, and in that capacity won distinction for his executive ability and tact. He died suddenly, Apr. 4, 1908. He was married, June 6, 1876, to Martha Augusta Whitesell of Bethlehem, who, with two daughters, survived him.

[Manuscript obituary, Moravian Archives, Bethlehem, Pa.; *Trans. Moravian Hist. Soc.*, vol. VIII (1909); John Levering, *Levering Family Hist. and Geneal.* (1897); *Bethlehem Daily Times*, Apr. 4, 1908; *Pub. Ledger* (Phila.), Apr. 5, 1908; *The Moravian,* Apr. 8, 1908.]
A. G. R.

LEVERMORE, CHARLES HERBERT (Oct 15, 1856–Oct. 20, 1927), educator and peace advocate, was born in Mansfield, Conn., the son of a Congregational clergyman, Rev. Aaron Russell Livermore, and his wife, Mary Gay (Skinner). His family in both branches was deep-rooted in the soil of his native state, his father being a direct descendant of John Livermore, who emigrated from Ipswich, England, to Boston and was one of the first proprietors of the town of Wethersfield, Conn.; and his mother, from Henry Wolcott, one of the first settlers in Hartford. Shortly after his graduation from college Charles adopted the early spelling of the family name. Educated as a boy at the Hopkins Grammar School, New Haven, he went to Yale, where he received the degree of A.B. in 1879. He then entered upon thirty years of teaching and study, serving as principal of Guilford Institute (1879–83), doing graduate work at Johns Hopkins University (1883–85), teaching history in the Hopkins Grammar School (1885–86), in the Massachusetts Institute of Technology (1888–93), and holding the position of principal in Adelphi Academy, Brooklyn, N. Y. (1893–96). He then became president of Adelphi College, Brooklyn, which he founded in 1896 and served until 1912.

His retirement from Adelphi, which was followed by a year of rest and recuperation in the South, marked his withdrawal from the field of education, and his definite entrance into activities in behalf of world peace, which became henceforth the work, almost the passion, of his life. For four years (1913–17) he was associated with the World Peace Foundation in Boston, during the last two, as acting director. In 1917 he became secretary of the New York Peace Society; in 1919, of the World Court and the League of Nations Union; and in 1922, of the American Association for International Co-operation. In 1923 he joined with other distinguished peace leaders in organizing the League of Nations Non-Partisan Association, which he served as vice-president until his death. During this period, after the establishment of the League of Nations, he prepared and published annually a complete survey of the work of the League for each current year, thorough, critical, and extremely useful. His learning, skill, devotion, and high statesmanship as a peace worker earned dramatic and distinguished recognition in 1924, when he won the American Peace Award of $50,000 offered by Edward W. Bok for "the best practicable plan by which the United States may co-operate with other nations to achieve and preserve the peace of the world." Several hundred thousand plans were submitted in this contest, of which 22,165 met the conditions and were considered by the judges. Levermore's plan emphasized the two "substantial provisions" that (1) the United States should adhere to the Permanent Court of International Justice, and (2) should extend its cooperation with the League of Nations, "without becoming a member of the League . . . as at present constituted." He received the prize from Hon. John W. Davis at a great mass meeting in Philadelphia, on Feb. 4, 1924. The enormous publicity which accompanied the granting of this award brought its winner fame and acclaim throughout the world. Invitations for articles and addresses were showered upon him; but a long-postponed dream of seeing Europe and studying peace in the area of war took him abroad, and he spent two years in England, France, Italy, and Switzerland, with visits to Athens, Constantinople, and North Africa. On his return, he went to California, in anticipation of a journey to the Orient, and stopped for a short stay in Berkeley. Here he died suddenly of arteriosclerosis of the brain. He was survived by his wife, Mettie Norton Tuttle, whom he married Sept. 4, 1884, two sons, and three daughters.

Zealous and thorough study made him a scholar of first-class attainment in many fields. Special knowledge of history and politics, coupled with utter devotion to his task, and a fine dignity and power of personality, constituted his equipment for success as a leader in the cause of peace. His publications disclose the avocations as well as the vocations of his life: *The Republic of New Haven* (1886); *Political History Since 1815* (1889, revised edition 1893), with D. R. Dewey; *The Academy Song Book* (1895); *The Students' Hymnal* (1911); *Forerunners and Competitors of the Pilgrims and Puritans* (2 vols., 1912), *The American Song Book* (1917); *Life of Samuel Train Dutton* (1922); and numerous magazine articles and reviews.

[W. E. Thwing, *The Livermore Family of America* (1902); *Yale Univ. Obit. Record*, 1928; F. W. Williams, *A Hist. of the Class of Seventy-nine, Yale College* (1906); *The Winning Plan Selected by the Jury of the Am. Peace Award* (1924); *N. Y. Times*, Feb. 4, 1924; *Who's Who in America*, 1926–27; *Boston Transcript*, Nov. 4, 1927; *San Francisco Examiner*, Oct. 21, 1927; *San Francisco Chronicle*, Oct. 22, 1927.]
J. H. H.

LEVIN, LEWIS CHARLES (Nov. 10, 1808– Mar. 14, 1860), lawyer, editor, congressman, was born in Charleston, S. C. He attended South Carolina College at Columbia until 1827 and about 1828 removed to Woodville, Miss., where he taught school and read law. After being wounded in a duel he left Woodville, became a "peripatetic law practitioner" in Maryland, Kentucky, and Louisiana, and in 1838 settled in Philadelphia where he was admitted to the bar. There he was first conspicuous as a temperance speaker and as editor of the *Temperance Advocate*. Next attracted to the Native-American movement, he took a prominent part in the formation of that party in Philadelphia (1843) and edited and published the *Sun,* a penny daily and Native-American organ. In the Philadelphia riots of 1844 he counseled moderation and respect for the property rights of Catholics, in order to maintain the honor of the party. In both the state convention at Harrisburg (Feb. 22, 1845) and the first Native-American national convention at Philadelphia (1845) he was untiring in his efforts to extend the party organization.

The high feeling against Catholics and the foreign-born crystallized by the riots of 1844 carried Levin into Congress where for three terms (1845–51) he preached nativism with almost fanatical zeal. Envisaging the country "on the very verge of overthrow by the impetuous force of invading foreigners" (Dec. 18, 1845), he pleaded for restricted immigration and stricter naturalization laws (*Congressional Globe,* 29 Cong., 1 Sess., App., pp. 46–50). Nativism seems to have been an obsession which colored his views on every question before the House. The Oregon struggle represented an attempt by England to implant feudalism on American soil. The sending of a chargé to Rome was "a proposition to unite this free Republic with absolute Rome" (*Ibid.,* 30 Cong., 1 Sess., App., p. 438). He would have none but native Americans serve in a proposed regiment of riflemen, and he opposed discontinuing the recruiting service because of the nation's internal enemies. He was a high-tariff advocate, a rabid expansionist, and as chairman of the committee on naval affairs labored indefatigably for the dry dock at Philadelphia. Although he was popular in his congressional district and supported by the Whigs for Congress in 1848, the disgruntled Native Americans took enough votes from the combined Whig-Native-American ticket in 1850 to defeat him. After leaving Congress he continued his law practice. Always loyal to nativism, in a broadside, *To the Americans of Pennsylvania* (1856), he urged the electorate to vote "a pure, unadulterated American Fillmore ticket," and to wash its hands of Black Republicanism, the instrument of the Pope. Before the next presidential campaign he was in his grave, a victim of insanity. A contemporary, not overly sympathetic, regarded Levin as "one of the most brilliant and unscrupulous orators" he had ever heard and doubted "whether during his day any person in either party of the State surpassed him on the hustings" (A. K. McClure, *Old Time Notes of Pennsylvania*, 1905, I, pp. 89, 90). He was married twice: first, to Anne Hays of Kentucky, and after her death to Julia Gist, a widow, of Philadelphia.

[Nothing is known of Levin's ancestry, though there is a reference to a Lewis Levin, Sr., in B. A. Elzas, *The Old Jewish Cemeteries at Charleston, S. C.* (1903). Family records were destroyed in the Charleston earthquake of 1886. See *Biog. Dir. Am. Cong.* (1928); H. S. Morais, *The Jews of Phila.* (1894); B. A. Elzas, *The Jews of S. C.* (1905); J. T. Scharf and Thompson Westcott, *Hist. of Phila.* (3 vols., 1884); *Niles' Nat. Reg.*, July 13, 1844; *Proc. of the Native Am. State Convention Held at Harrisburg, Pa., Feb. 22, 1845; Pub. Ledger* (Phila.), and *Phila. Daily News*, Mar. 15, 1860.]   J. H. P.

LEVINS, THOMAS C. (Mar. 14, 1789–May 5, 1843), Roman Catholic priest, was born in ancient Drogheda, Ireland, the son of Patrick and Margaret Levins. He studied at the famous Jesuit institutions of Clongowes, Dublin, and Stonyhurst, Lancashire, England, a fact which in itself indicated that his family was comfortably circumstanced. Joining the Society of Jesus, he was apparently further trained on the Continent before being ordered to Georgetown College, Georgetown, D. C., where for three years he taught natural philosophy and mathematics (1822–25). Withdrawing from the Society, he accepted the invitation of Dr. John Power [*q.v.*] to enter the diocese of New York, where he served as an assistant at St. Peter's Church and as pastor of old St. Patrick's. A writer of ability with a Celtic taste for journalism, he associated himself with the newly founded *Truth Teller* and later (1833) became a joint editor with Rev. J. A. Schneller of the *New York Weekly Register and Catholic Diary*, a position which he held until the publication was merged with the Philadelphia *Catholic Herald* in 1836. Irreproachable in character but of a sour, critical disposition, he ran afoul of Bishop John Dubois [*q.v.*] who in 1834 suspended him for technical disobedience. Apparently a leader of the Irish faction, he resented a Frenchman as his ordinary. He was popular in the diocese, however, and with the trustees, who appointed him principal of the school and even threatened to cut off the bishop's income; but Dubois stood firmly for ecclesiastical discipline, and Levins as an orthodox priest soon severed his connections with the trustees and lived a model life as a lay Catholic. He now gave his attention to journalism, founding the ephemeral

Green Banner and writing for the *Catholic Register*. Something of a mineralogist and an excellent mathematician when scientists were rare in New York, he acted twice on the board of examiners for West Point (see *Truth Teller*, Mar. 24, 1827) and was retained as an engineer on the Croton aqueduct. The plans for the high bridge are said to have been his work. Restored to his priestly office in 1841, he was assigned by Bishop John Hughes to the rectorship of St. John's Church, Albany, but owing to failing sight and threatened paralysis, he was unable to assume active duty. Levins was a versatile man and a capable controversialist, but his career was marred by his inability to fit into an organization.

[Archbishop Corrigan in *U. S. Cath. Hist. Soc., Hist. Records and Studies*, vol. II, pt. I, Oct. 1900; P. J. Foik, *Pioneer Cath. Journalism* (1930), in *U. S. Cath. Hist. Soc. Monograph Ser.*, vol. XI; J. H. Smith, *The Cath. Ch. in N. Y.* (1905), vol. I; J. G. Shea, *Hist. of the Cath. Church in the U. S.*, vol. III (1890); *Freeman's Jour.*, May 6, 1843; *Cath. Herald*, May 11, 1843; *Cath. Mag.*, June 1843; *Metropolitan Cath. Directory* (1844); *N. Y. Tribune*, May 6, 1843.]   R. J. P.

LEVY, JOSEPH LEONARD (Nov. 24, 1865–Apr. 26, 1917), rabbi, was born in London, England, the son of the Rev. Solomon and Elizabeth (Cohen) Levy. He received his Jewish training at Jews' College, London, and his secular education at the universities of London (B.A. with honors, 1884), and Bristol (1885–86). In Bristol on Dec. 26, 1888, he was married to Henrietta Platnauer. Two daughters were born to the union. At the early age of twenty he assumed his first clerical charge at Bristol. After four years, in 1889, he came to America, called by the Synagogue at Sacramento, Cal. From 1893 to 1901 he was associated with Joseph Krauskopf [*q.v.*] as rabbi of Temple Keneseth Israel of Philadelphia. From there he was called to Temple Rodeph Shalom of Pittsburgh in 1901, of which he was the rabbi for the rest of his life. Though orthodox in training and early inclination, in America he identified himself with reform Judaism, becoming one of its leaders. Gaining national fame as a preacher and orator, he attracted large congregations of both Jews and Christians. He frequently exchanged pulpits with preachers of Christian denominations, and in 1908 he introduced in Pittsburgh interdenominational services for Thanksgiving day.

Levy was a man of wide interests. He was a governor of the Hebrew Union College of Cincinnati, and a trustee of the University of Pittsburgh. He was especially active in spreading propaganda and in raising funds for the Department of Synagogue Extension of the Central

Conference of American Rabbis. As an earnest peace advocate, he was affiliated as founder, trustee, or officer, with several local, state, and world peace societies. He opposed the manufacture of military toys for children, and he advocated that Palestine be neutralized as the center of a world peace council empowered by an international force to prevent war. He aided in founding (1894), the Philadelphia Sterilized Milk, Ice and Coal Society and (1895) the Home of Delight Settlement, was a founder of the Pennsylvania Anti-Tuberculosis League, and a trustee of the Denver National Hospital for Consumptives. He took an active interest in the solution of the vice problem, urging the building of model tenement houses. He advocated pensions for widowed mothers, higher education for negroes, and the settlement of Jews in farming districts. In Pittsburgh he was active in virtually every public-welfare movement in the city. In the literary field, Levy was editor of the *Atlantic Coast Jewish Annual* (1896), editor (1901–05) and contributing editor (1905–10) of *The Jewish Criterion,* and author of *A Book of Prayer* (1902), *Questions for Our Consideration* (1898), *Nineteenth Century Prophets* (1907), *Founders of the Faiths* (1908), *Old Arrows from New Quivers* (1909), some sixteen volumes of sermons, and a number of prayer manuals and textbooks for Jewish religious schools. His special contribution to American Judaism was his success in correlating the Synagogue with the forces of social welfare.

[*Who's Who in America,* 1916–17; R. I. Coffee, article in *Central Conference of Am. Rabbis, Twenty-eighth Ann. Convention* (1917); the *Jewish Criterion* (Pittsburgh, Pa.), Apr. 27, May 5, 11, 1917; the *Reform Advocate* (Chicago), May 5, 1917; *Am. Jewish Year Book,* 1903–04.]   D. deS. P.

LEVY, LOUIS EDWARD (Oct. 12, 1846–Feb. 16, 1919), photo-chemist, inventor, author, was born at Stenowitz, Bohemia, the son of Leopold and Wilhelmina (Fisher) Levy. When he was nine years old his parents emigrated to the United States and settled in Detroit, where he attended school. In 1861 he entered the employ of Louis Black & Company, opticians, and at the same time studied optics, the microscope, and surveying. He gained sufficient knowledge of the mariner's compass to correct the compasses of lake pilots. In 1866 he made observations in Detroit for the United States Meteorological Service and studied wet-plate photography to record his researches with the microscope. Photography fascinated him, and it was in this branch of science that he made his most notable achievements. At twenty-three he was given the management of the branch office of Louis Black & Company in Milwaukee. He continued his studies and experimented in methods of photo-engraving. In 1873 he accepted the invitation of David Bachrach, Jr., to use the facilities of the latter's photographic studio in Baltimore. The two worked together and invented a photo-chemical engraving process which they called the "levytype," and which they patented in January 1875. In the same year Levy organized the Levy Photo-Engraving Company in Baltimore and took into the business his brothers Max [q.v.] and Joseph. In 1877, believing that Philadelphia offered better opportunities for them, the brothers moved there and established the Levytype Company. Later Max and Joseph established similar plants in Chicago and Cincinnati.

About 1889 Max Levy returned to Philadelphia and worked with his brother Louis in an effort to develop better methods of half-tone reproduction. They invented the Levy half-tone screen—an etched glass grating—which they patented in Europe and America in 1893. For this invention they received the John Scott Legacy Medal. Louis Levy later invented an etching machine by which etchings could be produced by the application of a spray of acid forced upward against a horizontal metal plate by an air blast. For this invention he received the Elliott Cresson Medal of the Franklin Institute in 1899 and recognition from other sources. His last invention was a device for applying powdered resin to plates preparatory to the etching process. For this invention he received the Elliott Cresson Medal in 1907.

After the Levytype Company was established in Philadelphia a publishing department was added to the business. In 1887 Louis Levy purchased the *Evening Herald,* a Democratic daily which he published until July 1890, and the *Sunday Mercury.* He used these papers to demonstrate his inventions and to prove that his company could produce engravings of current events promptly. He was the author of several works, including *The Jewish Year* (1895); *The Jewish Refugees in the United States* (1895), and his own reminiscences, *Recollections of Forty Years: A Photo-Engraving Retrospect* (1912). Among the works which he edited are *The American Jew as Patriot, Soldier and Citizen* (1895), by Simon Wolf, and *Cuba and the Cubans* (1896), by Raimundo Cabrera. In his later years he gave much time to philanthropic work. He was one of the founders and for many years president of the Association for the Relief and Protection of Jewish Immigrants and served as president of the Jewish Community (Kehillah) in Philadelphia. He had married, on Jan. 9, 1881, Pauline Dalsheimer of Baltimore. She with two sons survived him.

[See *Specifications and Drawings of Patents issued from the U. S. Patent Office*, Jan. 1875, Feb. 1893, June 1899, Sept. 1905, Aug. 1906, May 1909; *Official Gazette of the U. S. Patent Office*, Apr. 27, Dec. 28, 1915; memoir of Levy in *Jour. of the Franklin Institute*, May 1919; *Who's Who in America*, 1918–19; *Photo-Engravers Bull.* (Chicago), Apr. 1926; *Jewish Exponent* (Phila.), Feb. 21, 1919; *Bull. of Photography* (Phila.), Mar. 5, 1919; and the *Press* (Phila.), Feb. 18, 1919. Information as to certain facts was supplied by Levy's sons; the author also had a long personal acquaintance with Levy.]   S. H. H.

LEVY, MAX (Mar. 9, 1857–July 31, 1926), photo-engraver, inventor, was the son of Leopold and Wilhelmina (Fisher) Levy and was born in Detroit, Mich. At an early age he showed a distinct talent for drawing. During the course of his schooling in the Detroit public schools he decided to make architecture his life work and upon completing school in 1875 he entered an architect's office in Detroit. About this time his brother Louis [*q.v.*] patented a new photo-relief process which he called "levytype," for producing photo-relief plates for printing, and had established a successful photo-engraving business using the "levytype" process in Baltimore, Md. In need of assistance to carry it on, Louis induced his brothers Max and Joseph to join him, the former as draftsman and the latter as photographer. Max therefore gave up his architectural work and never returned to it. In the belief that Philadelphia offered a larger field of opportunity than Baltimore, the three brothers moved their photo-engraving plant to that city early in 1877. Success followed them and three years later Max and Joseph went to Chicago, Ill., and there opened the first photo-engraving enterprise in that city. A year or two later Max established Cincinnati's first photo-engraving plant and continued with the management of these two organizations for several years. About 1889 he returned to Philadelphia to work with his brother Louis on improvements in the process of half-tone reproduction. They concentrated their attention on making a perfect screen of lines used in the process between the camera and copy. Louis conceived the idea of etching the lines on glass and blackening the depressions and Max worked on the design and construction of the delicate machinery to make such screens absolutely accurate. After two years of tedious experimentation the screen was perfected in 1891 and patents were secured both in the United States and Europe in 1893. Max then gave up the photo-engraving business to engage in the manufacture of half-tone screens.

His first place of business was established in Philadelphia but in 1902 he built a new plant in the suburb of Germantown.

Levy not only managed this business but also continued making improvements in his manufacturing methods, resulting in the production of screens of better quality. Before he died 25,000 were in use the world over. With his delicate machinery as many as four hundred perfect lines to the inch could be ruled and etched on glass, and diffraction gratings could be produced containing thousands of lines to the inch. In addition to making screens, Levy also manufactured photographic plate-holders and camera diaphragms of his own invention for photo-engravers' use. Although at the time of the World War Levy had retired, he engaged in work for the War Department and ruled the graticules used in the eyepieces of range-finders. He never gave up entirely his inventive work, and in 1917 patented the hemocytometer, a microscopic measuring machine used in blood-counting which has been adopted by the United States army and by many medical institutions. During his active career Levy wrote many articles for the technical press and trade journals and became widely known for his contributions to the advance of half-tone illustration. During the last ten or more years of his life he devoted much of his time to painting. For his contributions to half-tone illustration the Franklin Institute, Philadelphia, awarded him the John Scott Legacy Medal, and the Royal Cornwall Polytechnic Institute presented him with a silver medal. The Franklin Institute awarded him also the Edward Longstreth medal for his invention of the hemocytometer. Levy married Diana Franklin in Baltimore, Md., on Sept. 22, 1885, and at the time of his death in Allenhurst, N. J., he was survived by his widow and three sons.

[*Specifications and Drawings of Patents Issued from the U. S. Patent Office*, Feb. 1893, June 1894, Jan. 1895, Jan. 1896, Feb., Oct., 1897, May 1898, Aug. 1901, Dec. 1907, May 1909; *Official Gazette of the U. S. Patent Office*, Jan. 30, 1917, Oct. 8, 1918, Apr. 25, 1922; L. E. Levy, *Recollections of Forty Years: A Photo-Engraving Retrospect* (1912); F. E. Ives, *Autobiog. of an Amateur Inventor* (1928); *Who's Who in America*, 1926–27; *Jewish Exponent* (Phila.), Aug. 6, 1926; *Inland Printer* (Chicago), Sept. 1926; *Process Monthly* (London), Sept. 1926; *N. Y. Times*, Aug. 1, 1926.]   C. W. M.

LEVY, URIAH PHILLIPS (Apr. 22, 1792– Mar. 22, 1862), sailor and patriot, born in Philadelphia, Pa., was the son of Michael and Rachel (Phillips) Levy. Between the ages of ten and twelve, Levy served, without his parents' consent, as a cabin boy on coasting vessels. In 1806 he began a four-year apprenticeship under John Coulter, Philadelphia merchant and shipowner, who placed Levy in the "best naval school" of Philadelphia for nine months during the 1808 embargo. Serving as first mate after his apprenticeship, Levy made enough money by October 1811 to become part owner of a schooner, the *George Washington*, of which he took command as master. The schooner was lost the following January through a mutiny off the Isle of May (*United States* vs. *Tully, 28 Fed., 226*), and, war against England having been declared, Levy applied for a position in the United States navy. He was commissioned sailing master, Oct. 21, 1812, and served on harbor duty until the following June, when, as volunteer acting lieutenant, he joined the *Argus*, then about to transport the American minister to France. In August 1813, just before the *Argus'* encounter with the *Pelican*, Levy was transferred to a prize vessel, was captured, and spent sixteen months in England.

Returning to naval duty, for the next ten years his quarrelsome pride, his shipmates' contempt for his having risen from the ranks, and a prejudice against his Jewish ancestry involved him in a series of broils, most of them petty, but one of them culminating in a duel, fatal to his opponent. Six times court-martialed, he was twice dismissed from the service: the first time (1819) for contempt, but after nearly two years President Monroe's disapproval of the sentence reinstated him; the second time (1842) he was cashiered for the infliction of a bizarre punishment on a subordinate, but the sentence was commuted to twelve months' suspension by President Tyler. Levy's steady rise in rank during these years was evidence both of the pettiness of his squabbles and of his relentless energy, but his appointment as captain (1844) was followed by a decade of vain endeavor to obtain a command, his public service at this period being confined chiefly to an unofficial and indirect assistance in the abolition of flogging from the navy. In 1855 the newly created "Board of Fifteen" dropped him from the navy's rolls. He protested to Congress in a *Memorial* (New York, 1855), and defended himself before the Court of Inquiry in 1857, with the result that his rank was restored. He received a command, became flag officer of the Mediterranean Squadron in 1860, returned to his New York home, and died there. He had married rather late in life and was survived by his widow, Virginia Levy. Despite his sensitiveness, vanity, and occasional insubordination, he was a courageous and humane officer and a fervid patriot. His admiration for Jefferson led him to purchase "Monticello," which unforeseen litigation after his death prevented from becoming a public shrine (*Public Ownership of Monticello: Hearings Before the Committee on Rules of the House of Representatives . . . July 24, 1912*; 33 *N. Y. Reports*, 97; 40 *Barbour's Supreme Court Reports*, N. Y., 585) ; and at the outbreak of the Civil War he offered his fortune to President Lincoln for his country's use (Isaac Markens, "Lincoln and the Jews," *American Jewish Historical Society Publications*, 1909, no. 17, p. 158).

[Autobiographical data in Levy's *Defence . . . Before the Court of Inquiry, Held at Washington City, November and December, 1857* (1858); G. A. Townsend, *Monticello and Its Preservation* (1902); *Am. Jewish Hist. Soc. Pubs.*, *passim*; *N. Y. Herald*, Mar. 26, 1862.]
J. C. W.

LEWELLING, HENDERSON [See LUELLING, HENDERSON, 1809–1878].

LEWELLING, LORENZO DOW (Dec. 21, 1846–Sept. 3, 1900), reformer, governor of Kansas, was born in Salem, Iowa, the youngest son of William and Cyrena (Wilson) Lewelling and a nephew of Henderson Luelling [*q.v.*], who retained the earlier spelling of the name. The family was originally Welsh. Lorenzo's grandfather moved from North Carolina to Indiana in 1825 and with his sons engaged in the nursery business there. When promising reports came to them of opportunities in Iowa several of the sons moved on and established themselves in Salem in the same business. William Lewelling became a minister in the Society of Friends, but he died when his son was only two years old, leaving a family of small children to be brought up by the widow and, after her death, by relatives. Young Lewelling worked for neighboring farmers and attended country school until he was sixteen. On the outbreak of the Civil War he attempted to enlist, but on account of his youth and their Quaker faith his relatives protested. He then engaged in several forms of non-military service in the Federal army, and after various experiences, returned to Iowa and entered Whittier College at Salem. Later he taught in the Iowa State Reform School for Boys. In 1870 he married Angie Cook, a school teacher, whom he had known in college. In 1873 they became the first superintendent and matron of the State Reform School for Girls, where they remained until the death of Mrs. Lewelling in 1885. During this period Lewelling became a member of the first board of the Iowa State Normal School at Cedar Falls, and later was president of the board. He also published for a time, beginning in 1880, the *Des Moines Capital*, an anti-administration paper in opposition to the Republican organization.

After his first wife's death he was married to Ida Bishop.

About 1887 Lewelling settled in Wichita, Kan., where he engaged in business. These were years in which the Populist movement was developing and Lewelling became known as a public speaker and as a reformer in politics. In 1892 he was the fusion candidate of the Democrats and Populists for governor and was elected, serving from 1893 to 1895. The Senate was controlled by the Populists, but in the lower house the vote was almost evenly divided. A legislative struggle resulted, two bodies were organized, each claiming to be the constitutional House of Representatives. In the course of this controversy open hostilities were narrowly avoided, and the Governor, to avert bloodshed, agreed to submit the decision to the supreme court, which decided in favor of the Republican House. Differences of opinion naturally developed in regard to the way in which the situation had been handled. An anti-administration group was formed, but Lewelling was renominated by the Populist party. The Democrats put a separate ticket in the field and the Republican candidate was elected. In 1896 and again in 1898 Lewelling was elected a member of the state Senate, and his death occurred while he was holding this office. He was a representative Quaker. He and his family were opposed to slavery and he taught in a school for negroes in Missouri after the close of the Civil War when it was necessary to have friends guard the door to protect him from the threatened assaults of the people of the neighborhood. His ancestry and life experience prepared him for his most striking rôle as the Populist governor of Kansas. Perhaps his Quaker aversion to the use of force led to his concessions in the legislative war, which featured his administration as governor.

[The principal sources of information are O. A. Garretson, "The Lewelling Family—Pioneers," in the *Iowa Jour. of Hist. and Pol.*, Oct. 1929; Clarence R. Aurner, *Hist. of Educ. in Iowa* (1920), vol. V; W. J. Costigan, "Lorenzo D. Lewelling," *Trans. Kan. State Hist. Soc.*, vol. VIII (1902); W. E. Connelley, *A Standard Hist. of Kan. and Kansans*, vol. II (1918); W. P. Harrington, *The Populist Party in Kan.* (n.d.) reprinted from the *Kan. State Hist. Soc. Colls.*, vol. XVI (1923–25); *Who's Who in America*, 1899–1900; *The Kan. Blue Book* (1899); B. F. Gue, *Hist. of Iowa* (1903), vol. IV; *Topeka Daily Capital*, Sept. 4, 1900; *Iowa State Reg.*, Sept. 5, 1900.]   F. E. H.

LEWIS, ALFRED HENRY (c. 1858–Dec. 23, 1914), journalist, author, was born in Cleveland, Ohio, the son of Isaac J. Lewis, a carpenter, and his wife, Harriet Tracy. He was admitted to the bar as soon as he came of age, hung out his shingle, dabbled in politics while waiting for clients, and served as prosecuting attorney, 1880–81, in the city police court. Then with his family he went West, and for the next few years he was a hobo cowboy. He worked on the ranches of Senator S. W. Dorsey and Col. O. M. Oviatt in Meade County, Kan., in the Cimarron country, helped drive cattle to Dodge City and other shipping points, rode down into the Texas Panhandle, gained a little newspaper experience of a kind in New Mexico on the *Las Vegas Optic,* and wandered into southeastern Arizona. It was a happy, carefree period, but by 1885 he was living once more with his parents in Kansas City, Mo., and was trying to build up a law practice. Clients were few and far apart, and in his leisure he turned again to politics and journalism. About this time, too, he married Alice Ewing of Richfield, Ohio, who outlived him. One of his brothers was city editor of the *Kansas City Times,* and in 1890 Lewis contributed to it an imaginary interview with an old cattleman domiciled at the St. James' Hotel. The story was copied far and wide; Lewis had not received a dollar for it, but for his next "Old Cattleman" story he was paid $360. He joined the staff of the *Kansas City Star,* was sent to Washington the next year as correspondent of the *Chicago Times,* and when that paper died in 1894 became head of William Randolph Hearst's Washington bureau. His political articles were trenchant and partisan, often bitter; he was regarded as one of Hearst's ablest men. For the last sixteen or seventeen years of his life he lived in New York, devoting himself to writing magazine articles and fiction for the Hearst magazines, chiefly for the *Cosmopolitan.* From Dec. 19, 1898, to Nov. 12, 1900, he edited a weekly Democratic sheet, the *Verdict,* which was sponsored by O. H. P. Belmont. Most of his work was strictly ephemeral—fictionized biographies of John Paul Jones (1906), Andrew Jackson (1907), and Aaron Burr (1908); novels of political life such as *The Boss* (1903) and *The President* (1904); stories of the police and the underworld such as *Confessions of a Detective* (1906) and *The Apaches of New York* (1912). Of the eighteen books that he published in the last fifteen years of his activity, only his Wolfville stories of cowboy life are likely to be remembered. Of these there were, in all, six volumes: *Wolfville* (1897); *Sandburrs* (1900); *Wolfville Days* (1902); *Wolfville Nights* (1902); *Wolfville Folks* (1908); and *Faro Nell and her Friends* (1913). At the time of their publication they were immensely popular. They are all put into the mouth of the "Old Cattleman," a gentleman of infinite leisure, a tolerant philosophy, and a language all his own. Though containing little that is original, they belong to the best tradition of American humorous story-telling. Probably thousands of readers have been disappointed to find that Wolfville and its rival settlement of Red Dog are not on the map of Arizona, so real do they become in the discursive, drawling reminiscences of the "Old Cattleman." Lewis himself had many of the qualities of this, his chief character. He died in New York after a short illness.

[*Who's Who in America*, 1899–1915; *N. Y. Times*, Dec. 23, 24, 1914; *N. Y. Morning Telegraph*, Dec. 24, 25, 1914; *Kansas City Star*, Dec. 23, 1914; *Editor and Publisher*, Dec. 26, 1914; W. R. Coates, *A Hist. of Cuyahoga County and the City of Cleveland* (1924), vol. I; J. K. Winkler, *W. R. Hearst: An American Phenomenon* (1928); Cleveland and Kansas City directories.]   G. H. G.

LEWIS, ANDREW (1720–Sept. 26, 1781), soldier, Revolutionary patriot, was born in Ireland. His parents, John and Margaret (Lynn) Lewis, came of Scotch-Irish or of Welsh stock, with a possible admixture of Huguenot blood. John Lewis killed his Irish landlord in self-defense and fled to America, finally settling in 1732 at "Bellefonte," near Staunton, Va. He was one of the first and most influential settlers in the Valley of Virginia. He fixed the location of Staunton, and aided in organizing Augusta County. Andrew and his wife, Elizabeth Givens, followed the retreating frontier and settled on the upper Roanoke River near the present site of Salem, Va. He was county lieutenant of Augusta, and justice of the peace and representative in the legislature from the county of Botetourt a few years after its creation. He was also a member of the Revolutionary colonial conventions of March and of December 1775. His life presents a chronicle of border warfare and of peaceful missions to Indian nations. Yet he found time to accumulate a considerable fortune which he bequeathed to his wife, five sons, a daughter, and three grandsons. He was upwards of six feet tall, agile, uncommonly strong, and possessed of a "reserved and distant deportment." He served in the Augusta militia and surrendered with Washington at Fort Necessity. He was in Braddock's army but was not present at its defeat. During General Forbes's campaign of 1758, Lewis was taken prisoner in Major Grant's unfortunate reconnaissance. He was later released and aided in making the Indian Treaty of Fort Stanwix (1768), one of the several important treaties which he helped to frame.

Lewis' chief claim to fame was his victory over the Indians in the battle of Point Pleasant, the outstanding event in Lord Dunmore's War. In 1774, when numerous Indian forays brought death and terror to the whole border country,

Governor Dunmore of Virginia quickly organized two forces to attack the Indians northwest of the Ohio River. He placed Lewis in command of the force from the southwestern counties. Lewis' men left Camp Union (site of Lewisburg, W. Va.), and marched in nineteen days to Point Pleasant, just above the confluence of the Ohio and Kanawha rivers, a distance of 160 miles across the Alleghany Mountains. Here the army of more than 800 men was attacked at daybreak, Oct. 10, by an Indian force of about equal size. The ensuing battle was one of the fiercest and most bloody in the annals of Indian warfare. Lewis led his men with uncommon skill and courage. Eighty-one Virginians were killed and 140 wounded. About two hundred Indians were killed. The victory was the determining factor in this war, which brought far-reaching consequences. It gave peace with the Indians along the whole American frontier during the first three years of the Revolutionary War, practically nullified the Quebec Act of 1774, led to rapid westward expansion, and prepared the way for George Rogers Clark's great campaign of 1778–79. On Mar. 1, 1776, Congress commissioned Lewis brigadier-general, though Washington wished a higher command for him. He assumed command of the American forces stationed at Williamsburg. In July 1776 he drove Governor Dunmore from Gwynn's island. He resigned his commission in the Continental Army Apr. 15, 1777, but continued to serve his state in the military forces and in Gov. Thomas Jefferson's executive council until his death.

[The fullest account of Dunmore's War is Virgil A. Lewis, *Hist. of the Battle of Point Pleasant* (1909), which contains a useful bibliography. See also: Justin Winsor, *Narrative and Critical History of America*, vol. VI (1888); F. B. Heitman, *Hist. Reg. of Officers of the Continental Army* (1914); Louise P. Kellogg, *Frontier Advance on the Upper Ohio* (1916); *Va. Mag. of Hist. and Biog.*, July 1905, Apr. 1910, Oct. 1911, Apr. 1916; R. A. Brock, *The Official Records of Robt. Dinwiddie, Lieut.-Gov. of the Colony of Va.* (2 vols., 1883–84); Lyman Chalkley, *Chronicles of the Scotch-Irish Settlement in Va.* (3 vols., 1912–13); J. A. Waddell, *Annals of Augusta County, Va.* (ed. 1902); J. L. Peyton, *Hist. of Augusta County, Va.* (1882); *Orderly Book . . . of Gen. Andrew Lewis* (1860), ed. by Chas. Campbell; *Official Letters of the Govs. of Va.*, vol. II (1928), vol. III (1929).]   R. L. M—n.

LEWIS, ARTHUR (Aug. 19, 1846–June 13, 1930), actor, manager, was born in the Hampstead section of London, the son of James Frederic and Françoise (Upward) Lewis, the latter of French birth and ancestry. He was the nephew of Sir George Lewis, an eminent solicitor, by whom he would have been trained for the legal profession but for the opposition of his father, who chose the physician's career for him. After studying in Edinburgh and London, he gladly renounced all thought of medicine for the stage, and on Dec. 27, 1868, acted his first rôle, a minor character in the Christmas pantomime of *Bluebeard* at the Drury Lane Theatre. He was so pleased at the opportunity to engage in congenial work that he exclaimed impetuously to a friend: "They are actually paying me for something I like to do."

Except for two brief intermissions, the rest of his life was passed on the stage, or in connection with the theatre in various capacities, although the testimony of his friends and associates bears witness to the fact that throughout his long life he was a man of more diverse interests than the average actor. During the Franco-Prussian War he left the stage temporarily to become a war correspondent, and in 1880 he interrupted his work in the theatre to visit the United States, unsuccessfully seeking rubies on the island of Santa Catalina. Returning to London, he became a member of Mary Anderson's company. He acted with her at intervals between 1882 and 1889 and accompanied her on her farewell tour of the United States, playing at the Lyceum Theatre in London and during her American engagements such characters as Mimos in *Pygmalion and Galatea,* De la Feste in *Comedy and Tragedy,* Benvolio in *Romeo and Juliet,* Lord Tinsel in *The Hunchback,* and Cleomenes in *The Winter's Tale.* For a time he was a manager, and had the direction of engagements and tours of Coquelin, Sarah Bernhardt, Mme. Rejane, and M. Antoine. Among the many parts he played in later years were the Marquis de Mirepoix in *Monsieur Beaucaire* (1902), Count Ivan Pavlovic in *Hawthorne of the U. S. A.* (1905), Mr. Viveash in *The Hypocrites* (1907), Huzar in *The Lily* (1911), Father Roubier in *The Garden of Allah* (1911), Mr. Justice Grimdyke, with Maude Adams, in *The Legend of Leonora* (1914), Dr. Stetson and Mr. Stapleton in *The Great Lover* (1915–16), and Dr. Dickinson in *The Camel's Back* (1923). His last rôle was that of Manuel in *A Hundred Years Old,* with Otis Skinner. In the autumn of 1929 illness compelled him to leave the stage, and he died the following year at the Home for Incurables in Bronx Borough, New York City.

In the course of an interview not long before his death, he said: "I have had the variety I was seeking in life. I never liked doctoring. That is a life that is too hard and confining for me, but I've always thought it ridiculous that I became an actor. I should never have done that, although I have enjoyed it thoroughly. What I should really have liked to be is a lawyer and a judge. Often, very often, I've played the part of a judge.

I've worn the white curled wig and black gown of the English magistrates and felt very important and impressive. That's what we all like to feel, like someone who counts, isn't it?" (*Evening World,* New York, Dec. 27, 1928). Although he thus felt that he would have been happier in another walk of life, he was far from being a failure in the profession he served faithfully for nearly sixty years. He was survived by his widow, Essex Dane, actress and playwright.

[T. A. Brown, *A Hist. of the N. Y. Stage* (1903), vol. III; John Parker, *Who's Who in the Theatre,* 1925; *N. Y. Times* and *Sun* (N. Y.), June 14, 1930; *Billboard* (Cincinnati), June 21, 1930; personal information from Mrs. Lewis.]   E. F. E.

LEWIS, CHARLES BERTRAND (Feb. 15, 1842–Aug. 21, 1924), humorist who wrote under the pseudonym "M. Quad," was born in Liverpool, Ohio, the son of a contractor and builder. His formal education included a course at the Michigan State Agricultural College, but like many other Middle Western writers of the period following the Civil War, Lewis gained his essential training in the composing rooms of small-town newspapers. He began to learn the printer's trade at the age of fourteen and served a thorough apprenticeship as journeyman printer and foreman on newspapers at Pontiac and Lansing, Mich. Some years as a private in the Union army further familiarized him with the rank-and-file American audience for which he was later to provide entertainment. After working for some time as a compositor on the *Lansing Jacksonian,* Lewis accepted the offer of a newspaper editorship in Jonesboro, Tenn., but while traveling on the Ohio River he was seriously injured by a boiler explosion during a steamboat race and spent many weeks recuperating in Cincinnati. He then returned to his old position at Lansing. Later, while in temporary charge of the paper, he printed a humorous account of the accident, entitled, "How It Feels to be Blown Up." This widely copied piece started him on his career as a professional "funny man."

In 1869 Lewis joined the staff of the *Detroit Free Press* as legislative reporter. Between sessions of the law-makers he wrote a variety of descriptive and humorous sketches which gained for his paper an enlarged circulation and a national renown. Similar work was being done by Robert J. Burdette of the *Burlington* (Iowa) *Daily Hawkeye* and James M. Bailey of the *Danbury* (Conn.) *News;* but the public demand for burlesque and verbal caricature was unlimited and was profitably exploited by a host of paragraphers. Among Lewis' most popular inventions was the negro organization known as **the**

Lime Kiln Club, presided over by a philosophic and pretentious negro called Brother Gardner. He also parodied Western journalism in imaginary items from the *Arizona Kicker* and developed a vein of domestic humor in describing the comic tribulations of the Bowser family. The production of these specialties soon became Lewis' main business, but he also found time to write several popular books on the Civil War besides a number of dime novels and plays. One of the plays, called *Yakie*, came on the stage in 1884. Lewis' profits as a commercial writer would seem to have been substantial. During the greater part of his twenty-two years on the *Free Press* he held a proprietary interest in the paper.

The last phase of Lewis' life added little or nothing to his reputation. In May 1891 he went to New York as a staff contributor on the *World* and the *Evening World,* for which he regularly wrote six columns of humor a week. Nearly all that he did, except for occasional magazine stories, was in continuation of the type of writing begun early in his career. During the last twelve years of his life he was crippled by rheumatism but persisted in his work to the end. His books, of which *Brother Gardner's Lime Kiln Club* (1882) and *The Life and Troubles of Mr. Bowser* (1902) are favorable examples, entitle him to a minor position in the school of Western humorists headed by Artemus Ward, Bill Nye, and Eugene Field. When he died in Brooklyn in his eighty-third year, he was the last representative of the group and his work was even then all but forgotten.

[*Who's Who in America,* 1920–21; *N. Y. Times, World* (N. Y.), Aug. 23, 1924; *Detroit Free Press,* Aug. 23, 24, 1924; *Lit. Digest,* July 29, 1922.]

G. F. W.

LEWIS, CHARLTON THOMAS (Feb. 25, 1834–May 26, 1904), classicist, editor, lawyer and publicist, was born in West Chester, Pa., the son of Joseph J. and Mary (Miner) Lewis and the grandson of Enoch Lewis and Charles Miner [*qq.v.*]. He was educated in West Chester and at Yale College, where he ranked high in the class of 1853, displaying special proficiency in the classics and in mathematics, and holding the office of class poet. A tabulation of his later occupations will suffice to show his extraordinary versatility. For a year after his graduation he studied law, the profession of his father. In 1854 he was admitted on trial, and in 1856 admitted into full connection by the Philadelphia Conference of the Methodist Episcopal Church, serving on the Newark circuit, in Wilmington, and in Philadelphia. In 1857–58 he was professor of languages in the Normal University of Illinois at Bloomington. From 1859 to 1862 he taught in Troy University, Troy, N. Y., first as professor of mathematics and later as professor of Greek; during 1862 he was also the acting president of the university. In the winter of 1862–63 he returned to the ministry of the Methodist Episcopal Church, at Cincinnati, but soon put this occupation aside to become deputy commissioner under his father, who had been made commissioner of internal revenue by President Lincoln. In 1864 he took up the practice of law in New York, and this was the chief occupation of the remainder of his life, with the exception of the years 1868–71, during which he was an editor of the New York *Evening Post.*

In all of his fields of endeavor Lewis was successful, and to most of them he made some permanent contribution. Among his published works were an English edition, in collaboration with M. R. Vincent, of *John Albert Bengel's Gnomon of the Greek Testament* (2 vols., 1860–62), and *A History of Germany, from the Earliest Times* (1874), founded on David Müller's *Geschichte des Deutschen Volkes* (1872). Other writings of his dealt with the law of insurance, in which he specialized and on which he was recognized as an authority. He was counsel to the Mutual Life Insurance Company of New York and in 1898–99 lectured on life insurance at Cornell, Harvard, and Columbia universities. His most important book was *Harper's Latin Dictionary,* prepared in collaboration with Charles Shore, which was published in 1879 and fifty years later had not been superseded in its field. It was followed by *A Latin Dictionary for Schools* in 1889, and by *An Elementary Latin Dictionary* in 1891.

Lewis was active in politics and in other public affairs. In 1896 he was a delegate to the convention of Gold Democrats at Indianapolis, serving as a member of the committee on platform. During much of his life he was intensely interested in organized charities and in prison reform. He was president of the Prison Association of New York, 1893–1904, delegate of the United States to the International Prison Congress at Paris in 1895, and vice-president of the National Prison Association in 1897, and supplemented his personal efforts with pamphlets and articles. His work in this field, and his Latin dictionary, are the outstanding accomplishments of a career that was as unselfish as it was varied.

On July 25, 1861, he married Nancy D. McKeen of Brunswick, Me., who died Aug. 19, 1883. She was a grand-daughter of Joseph McKeen [*q.v.*], first president of Bowdoin College; one of her children was Charlton Miner Lewis (1866–1923), who as professor of English at Yale carried on the scholarly tradition of the family. Lewis' second wife, whom he married June 30, 1885, was Margaret P. Sherrard, of Michigan. He died at the age of seventy, in Morristown, N. J., which had been his home for a number of years.

[Records of the class of 1853 of Yale College, including *Yale College: Class of 1853* (1883) and *Supp. Hist. of the Yale Class of 1853* (1903), which contains bibliography of Lewis' writings; *Obit. Record Grads. Yale Univ.*, 1904; *Fifty-ninth Ann. Report of the Prison Asso. of N. Y., for the Year 1903* (1904); *Who's Who in America*, 1903–05; *Evening Post* (N. Y.), May 27, 1904; collection of newspaper articles in the possession of Mrs. Charlton Thomas Lewis, who has corrected and supplemented the information which they contain.]

A. E. C.

LEWIS, DIOCLESIAN (Mar. 3, 1823–May 21, 1886), temperance reformer and pioneer in physical culture, was born near Auburn, N. Y., the son of John C. and Delecta (Barbour) Lewis. His family, of Welsh descent, were farmers and home-builders. A younger brother, Loran L. Lewis, became a justice of the supreme court of New York and another brother, George Washington Lewis, a physician in Buffalo. Dio Lewis, as he was always called, left school at the age of twelve and, after a period of work and teaching, established a private school in Lower Sandusky (now Fremont), Ohio. After a year he returned to New York, studied medicine with a physician in Auburn, spent the year 1845–46 at the Harvard Medical School in Boston, and began practice, without a degree, in Port Byron, N. Y. In 1849 he was married to Helen Cecilia Clarke, daughter of Dr. Peter Clarke of New York, and began practice again in Buffalo. In this city he published the *Homœopathist*, a monthly magazine, and started gymnasium classes for women. He worked out a system of "free gymnastics," exercises to be performed without apparatus. Setting this idea aside temporarily, he embarked on a series of temperance lectures, based on the "Washingtonian movement" begun in 1840, and traveled throughout the South and later the Middle West and Canada. In 1851 he received an honorary degree of M.D. from the Homœopathic Hospital College, Cleveland, Ohio.

In 1860 he went to Boston, where he began to organize gymnasium classes. The work soon extended to private schools and to the hospitals in the vicinity of Boston. Lewis incorporated the Boston Normal Institute for Physical Education in 1861, with many prominent persons on the board of directors, and, during the next seven years, over four hundred men and women were graduated from his school. In 1862 he published

his most important book, *New Gymnastics,* which had a large sale and served to make his name known in both the United States and Great Britain. From 1864 to 1868 he also conducted a sanitarium and gymnasium in Lexington, Mass., a large girls' school, with Theodore D. Weld [*q.v.*] as head-master, in the same town, and a private family hotel, the "Bellevue," in Boston.

After 1871 he again turned his attention to temperance reform and carried out an extensive program of lectures and campaigns throughout the country in aid of the Woman's Christian Temperance Union. In Boston and elsewhere he found considerable opposition to his views, for he always stoutly held that the cause of prohibition would never be advanced through legal methods but rather through a campaign of moral suasion. His appearance on the lecture platform is said to have been striking and dramatic. Quick of wit, pleasant and sympathetic, he usually won over his vast audiences. For a brief period before his death he again conducted a sanitarium near Boston; but in 1881 he removed to New York, giving up his practice and lecturing, although continuing his literary work. His publications, mostly books on gymnastics or health, were ephemeral in character.

[The best source of information is the laudatory *Biog. of Dio Lewis* (1891), by Mary F. Eastman. See also: H. A. Kelly and W. L. Burrage, *Am. Medic. Biogs.* (1920); *Boston Transcript*, May 21, 1886; *N. Y. Tribune*, May 22, 1886.]

H. R. V.

LEWIS, DIXON HALL (Aug. 10, 1802–Oct. 25, 1848), Alabama congressman and senator, was descended from Robert Lewis, a native of Brecon, Wales, who settled in what is now Gloucester County, Va., about 1635. The son of Francis Lewis and his wife, Mary Dixon (Hall), who was related to the Bolling and Randolph families of Virginia, Dixon Hall Lewis was born probably in Dinwiddie County, Va., but throughout most of his childhood lived in Hancock County, Ga. He attended the famous Mount Zion Academy conducted by Rev. Nathan S. S. Beman [*q.v.*], step-father of William Lowndes Yancey, and went thence to South Carolina College. Going to Alabama after his graduation in 1820 (LaBorde, *post,* p. 441), he studied law under Judge Henry Hitchcock in Cahawba, then the capital, and was admitted to the bar in 1823. Two years later he opened an office in Montgomery. Though he showed unusual capacity in his profession, the call of politics in the new state drew him to devote all his energies to government service. His political philosophy was largely influenced by his uncle, Bolling Hall, sometime representative in Congress from

Georgia, a supporter of William H. Crawford, and a member of the so-called "Georgia faction" in Alabama politics. Hall was an intimate of the leaders of the extreme state-rights viewpoint in Virginia and Georgia and he strongly indoctrinated his nephew with that political philosophy.

Lewis was elected to the lower house of the Alabama legislature in 1826 as an ardent advocate of state-rights principles, and during his service of three terms (1826–28) came to be recognized as the leader of the faction in the Democratic party in Alabama which was opposed to every tendency towards centralization. He was foremost in the organization of the State-Rights group. His outstanding career in the legislature earned for him an election to Congress in 1829, at the early age of twenty-seven, and he continued in Washington till his death in 1848. In Congress he soon became recognized as one of the chief supporters of the state-rights doctrines. He vigorously opposed, on constitutional grounds, the United States Bank, the high protective tariff, and internal improvements by the federal government. He served in the House from 1829 to 1844, became chairman of the committee on ways and means, and in 1839 lost the speakership by four votes in a bitter contest with the Benton faction (*Congressional Globe*, 26 Cong., 1 Sess., p. 56). When William R. D. King [*q.v.*], leader of the Union Democrats in Alabama, resigned from the Senate in 1844 to become minister to France, Lewis was appointed senator in his stead by Gov. Benjamin Fitzpatrick [*q.v.*], his wife's brother-in-law. At the regular election in 1847 he defeated King, again a candidate, and Arthur Francis Hopkins [*q.v.*], Whig leader, for the full term. In the Senate he continued to promote the principles he had advocated in the House. After a short time he was made chairman of the committee on finance and was instrumental in framing and passing the Walker Tariff of 1846. Though he seldom spoke in Congress, he was commonly considered one of the most influential men in party councils and was exceedingly popular.

He was married, Mar. 11, 1823, to Susan Elizabeth, daughter of Gen. John A. Elmore and sister of Franklin Harper Elmore [*q.v.*]. To them were born seven children. All his life Lewis was afflicted with excessive flesh and in his later years weighed 450 pounds. His huge bulk necessitated special arrangements on stage-coaches, in the legislative chambers, and in the halls of Congress. He died in New York, whither he had gone to address a free-trade organization, and

was buried with civic honors in Greenwood Cemetery on Long Island.

[Yancey and Bolling Hall papers in the Dept. of Archives and Hist. of Ala.; T. P. Abernethy, *The Formative Period in Ala., 1815–1828* (1922); T. H. Jack, *Sectionalism and Party Politics in Ala., 1819–1842* (1919); T. M. Williams, *Dixon H. Lewis* (1910), in Ala. Polytechnic Inst. Hist. Studies, 4 ser.; W. Garrett, *Reminiscences of Public Men in Ala.* (1872); Willis Brewer, *Ala.: Her Hist.* (1872); T. M. Owen, *Hist. of Ala.* (1921), vol. IV; *Biog. Dir. Am. Cong.* (1928); "Calhoun as Seen by His Political Friends: Letters of Duff Green, Dixon H. Lewis, Richard K. Crallé, during the Period from 1831 to 1848," *Southern Hist. Asso. Pubs.*, vol. VII (1903); J. M. McAllister and L. B. Tandy, *Geneal. of the Lewis and Kindred Families* (1906); Maximilian LaBorde, *Hist. of the S. C. Coll.* (1859); newspaper files in Ala. Dept. of Archives and Hist.]   T. H. J.

LEWIS, EDMUND DARCH (Oct. 17, 1835–Aug. 12, 1910), landscape painter and collector, son of David and Camilla (Phillips) Lewis, was born in Philadelphia, Pa., where the family had been identified with the social and business life of the city since 1708, when Ellis Lewis, a native of Wales, came to America and settled in Kennett Township, Pa. David Lewis was a trustee of the University of Pennsylvania and an official of two Philadelphia insurance companies, but by temperament was a reader and a man of letters rather than a business man. From his mother's side of the family Edmund derived an artistic bent and a lifelong ardor for collecting. The Phillipses for generations had been collecting old china, furniture, curios, and prints; John Phillips, Edmund's uncle, left a collection of 40,000 prints to the Pennsylvania Academy of the Fine Arts.

Edmund Lewis had only a private school education. While still a youth he began the study of art under Paul Weber, with whom he remained for about five years. His success as a landscape painter was almost instantaneous; he soon became the favorite painter of Philadelphia, and although his facility and industry were phenomenal, the demand for his work exceeded the supply. Many exaggerated accounts have been given of his facility in turning out pictures. At one time it was stated that he painted his landscapes by the yard and cut them into strips of the desired size and shape. It is, however, true that he often duplicated his stock subjects. The result of this commercialization of his art was that in his later years the vogue for his work diminished sensibly. "Mr. Lewis," said a writer for the Philadelphia *Public Ledger*, "set a pace in pot-boiling such as the world of art had never before seen." He had a keen business sense and invested his savings so well that at the time of his death his estate amounted to about $300,000. Excepting a relatively small legacy from his father in 1895, this sum had been obtained entirely from the sale of his pictures.

His ruling passion, however, was his collection, on which he expended large amounts. He was a born collector, and his talent as a painter simply enabled him to satisfy this hobby. His residence, 30 South Twenty-second St., Philadelphia, consisted of two city houses thrown into one, with one room built especially for tapestries, and with a large ballroom constructed as an addition at the rear. This mansion became a veritable museum of period furniture, tapestries, old silver, porcelain and pottery, bric-a-brac and curios. Special rooms were devoted to exhibits of Empire furniture, Dresden china, Oriental art, and Colonial objects of household art. In the nineties many notable receptions and musicales were given by the owner, who was glad to share his enjoyment of his treasures with his friends. He died unmarried, and his collection, intact, passed into the hands of a nephew.

[An interesting account of Lewis' methods is given in a long article published by the Philadelphia *Public Ledger,* Aug. 28, 1910. Obituaries appeared in the *Public Ledger* and the *N. Y. Times,* Aug. 13, 1910, and a criticism in *Am. Art News,* Sept. 17, 1910. Most of the information in this sketch was supplied by Lewis' nephew, Clifford Lewis, Jr.]   W. H. D.

LEWIS, ELLIS (May 16, 1798–Mar. 19, 1871), Pennsylvania jurist, was born at Lewisberry, Pa., the youngest of eight children of Maj. Eli and Pamela (Webster) Lewis. He was descended from Ellis Lewis, originally from Wales, who emigrated to Pennsylvania from Ireland in 1708. Though orphaned at the age of nine, he was well cared for by his brothers, sisters, and guardian, who gave attention to his early education. At twelve he was apprenticed for seven years to John Wyeth in Harrisburg to learn "the art and mystery of a Printer." There his work and the library facilities provided him an excellent chance to learn. After five years he tired of this life and ran away to New York City under an assumed name. In 1818 he returned to Pennsylvania to the town of Williamsport and engaged in the newspaper business, which brought him favorably before the public. In 1821 he began the study of law and was admitted to the bar the following year at the age of twenty-four. On Nov. 21, 1822, he was married to Josephine Wallis.

Lewis was a stanch Democrat throughout his career. In 1824 he was appointed deputy attorney-general of Lycoming and Tioga counties and in 1832 he was sent as a delegate to the state Democratic convention. His work showed his legal ability and judicial temperament, and in 1833 Governor Wolf appointed him attorney-

general of the state. He retained at the same time his seat in the legislature, to which he had been elected previously, and was instrumental in abolishing imprisonment for debt, which did much to make him popular. After but a few months as attorney-general he succeeded to the office of president judge of the eighth judicial district. His opinion in the case of *Commonwealth* vs. *Armstrong* (reprinted in 1 *Pennsylvania Law Journal,* 1842, p. 393) against clerical interference with a parent's right to educate his child was published throughout the country. In 1843 he became president judge of the second district. In 1848 he published *An Abridgment of the Criminal Law of the United States.* Elected in 1851 to the supreme bench for the six-year term, he devoted himself to his duties with tremendous energy. In 1854 he automatically became chief justice. All his expositions were exact, direct, and luminous; and his technical mastery, his wide learning, and his conciliatory spirit had a great influence in the court's decisions. At the end of his term on Dec. 7, 1857, he retired to private life, after declining a unanimous renomination for the chief justiceship. It was said of him in the *Daily Pennsylvanian* (Mar. 27, 1857): "No man within our Commonwealth has had the judicial experience of the present Chief Justice, and no Judge has labored more zealously to free the docket of the Supreme Court of the accumulated litigation of ages. . . . We doubt much whether Judge Lewis has ever been equalled in industry on the Bench." His last years he spent in quiet retirement.

[B. A. Konkle, *The Life of Chief Justice Ellis Lewis, 1798–1871* (1907); *U. S. Mag. and Democratic Rev.* (N. Y.), Apr. 1847; Ellis Lewis, *Hist. of Eli Lewis and Family* (1925); the *Press* (Phila.), Mar. 21, 1871.]
E. B. S.

LEWIS, ENOCH (Jan. 29, 1776–July 14, 1856), mathematician, educator, publicist, and editor, was born on a farm in Radnor, Pa., near Philadelphia, and spent almost the whole of his life within twenty miles of his birthplace. His parents, Evan and Jane (Meredith) Lewis, were descended from Welsh Friends who had settled the neighborhood nearly a century earlier; his paternal ancestor was another Evan Lewis who came from Pembrokeshire, South Wales, to Pennsylvania in 1682. Enoch, a serious-minded and precocious boy, rapidly exhausted the educational facilities of the Radnor school, of which he was himself made master at the age of fifteen. Thereafter he was almost entirely self-educated, feeling himself debarred, as a conscientious member of the Society of Friends, from attending the University of Pennsylvania, the only easily accessible institution of higher learning. Despite this handicap he became eminent in mathematics, a study for which he inherited an aptitude from his mother. From his fifteenth to his fifty-first year his chief occupation was teaching, in Philadelphia, in Westtown, or as head of his own school, which he opened in 1808 at New Garden, Pa., and later moved to Wilmington, Del. He combined or varied the scholastic life with farming and surveying, and for a time held the post of city regulator of Philadelphia.

Lewis began writing early in his career, and his literary activities increased as he grew older. He was the author of a large number of books, pamphlets, and articles on a wide variety of subjects. His textbooks on arithmetic, algebra, trigonometry, and grammar were the direct outcome of his profession. His devotion to the principles of his sect (which he defended in *A Vindication of the Society of Friends,* 1834) was responsible for the greater part of his published work. He wrote for the Society "Memoirs of the Life of William Penn" (*The Friends' Library,* vol. V, 1841), and nearly completed the first volume of a history of North America which was to emphasize the social and economic progress of the continent and to make plain the misery and folly of war. Although he sometimes dealt with purely doctrinal questions, his keenest interest was in moral and political issues, such as the abandonment of compulsory military service, the protection of the Indians, and the abolition of slavery. He believed that this last problem could best be solved by convincing the South that slavery was economically unsound, and to propagate this idea he founded in 1827 a monthly magazine, the *African Observer,* the failure of which after one year of life was due in part to its editor's moderation. In 1847, he founded, in Philadelphia, the *Friends' Review* (first issue, Sept. 4, 1847), a weekly journal which he edited until a few weeks before his death. In its pages he found an outlet for the expression of his views on all the wide range of subjects in which he was interested; he himself wrote most of the original material which it contained.

Lewis' mind was remarkable for its .ngenuity and its lucidity; his character, for its consistency. If he convinced himself that a course of action was right he adopted it forthwith and held himself to it strictly, although with other people he was much more lenient. His personal efforts in behalf of the causes he supported were as persistent and as effective as his writings. He was twice married, first, on May 9, 1799, to Alice Jackson of New Garden, who died Dec. 13, 1813; second, in May 1815, to Lydia Jackson of Lon-

dongrove, Pa., a cousin of his first wife. Charlton Thomas Lewis [*q.v.*] was his grandson.

[The authoritative source for the facts of Lewis' life is the *Memoir of Enoch Lewis* (1882), by his son, Joseph J. Lewis, privately printed at West Chester, Pa. It contains no formal list of Lewis' writings, but many of them are mentioned in the text, pp. 77–100. See also J. S. Futhey and Gilbert Cope, *Hist. of Chester County, Pa.* (1881); *Friends' Intelligencer* (Phila.), 7th mo. 26, 1856; *Daily News* (Phila.), July 16, 1856.]
A. E. C.

LEWIS, ESTELLE ANNA BLANCHE ROBINSON (April 1824–Nov. 24, 1880), author, was the daughter of John N. Robinson and was born at her father's country home near Baltimore, Md. Her father, who died while his daughter was an infant, was a Cuban by birth, of Anglo-Spanish descent, a man of means, culture, and social prestige. His wife was the daughter of an officer in the American Revolution. Estelle was educated at Emma Willard's Female Seminary, Troy, N. Y., and remained a student throughout life. She became proficient in classical and modern languages and acquired some knowledge of the sciences and of law. While still in school she made translations from the *Æneid* into English verse and published stories in the *Family Magazine,* edited by Solomon Southwick, at Albany, N. Y. Soon after leaving school, she was married, in 1841, to Sylvanus D. Lewis, an attorney. They made their home in Brooklyn, N. Y., but were divorced about 1858 and after that Mrs. Lewis resided chiefly abroad.

Mrs. Lewis always devoted the greater part of her time to literary work. She contributed, under the name "Stella," poems, stories, translations, and articles on art, literature, and travel to the *Democratic Review,* the *American Review,* the *Spirit of the Nineteenth Century, Graham's Magazine, Godey's Lady's Book,* the *Home Journal,* and the *Literary World.* Public attention was first attracted to her poetry by the romantic poem, "The Ruins of Palenque," which appeared in the *New World.* In 1844 her first volume of poems, *Records of the Heart,* was published under the pen-name Sarah Anna Lewis. Included in her later works are *Child of the Sea and Other Poems* (1848); *Myths of the Minstrel* (1852); *Sappho; a Tragedy, in Five Acts* (1875); and *The King's Stratagem; or, the Pearl of Poland; a Tragedy in Five Acts* (1869). She was extravagently praised in her own time but the sincerity of some of the eulogy has since been called into question. It has been said that Poe, who was a friend of the Lewises, at a time of financial need accepted money from Sylvanus Lewis to revise and write flattering reviews of his wife's poetry. He is also said to have written the sketch of Mrs. Lewis which appeared in

Rufus Wilmot Guswold's *Female Poets of America.* Her best longer poems are generally conceded to be "Child of the Sea," a tale of sea adventure in the style of Byron, and *Sappho,* which, translated into modern Greek, was staged at Athens. Of her minor poems, perhaps the best are "Lament of La Vega in Captivity," "The Angel's Visit," and "The Forsaken." Her poetry is always somewhat stiff and over-regular in meter and rhyme, but it has emotional appeal. Her favorite type was the narrative poem of romance and heroic passion. Her last work was a sonnet series eulogizing Poe. She died in London, but her body was later removed to the United States for burial.

[See E. A. and G. L. Duyckinck, *Cyc. of Am. Lit.* (ed. 1875) ; Mary E. Phillips, *Edgar Allan Poe, The Man* (1926), vol. II ; *Appletons' Ann. Cyc.,* 1881 ; Sarah Josepha Hale, *Biog. of Distinguished Women* (1876) ; *Pall Mall Gazette* (London), Nov. 25, 1880 ; *London Daily News,* Nov. 26, 1880. For Poe's criticisms, to be discounted, see *The Literati* (1850) and notices in the *U. S. Mag. and Democratic Rev.,* Aug. 1848, and *Southern Lit. Messenger,* Sept. 1848.]　　　S. G. B.

LEWIS, EXUM PERCIVAL (Sept. 15, 1863–Nov. 17, 1926), physicist, educator, was born in Edgecombe County, N. C., the son of Henry Exum Lewis, a physician, and Emma (Haughton) Lewis. Educational facilities were meager in the rural community in which the Lewis family was settled. Privations that arose from the Civil War and the untimely death of his father when Lewis was only seven prevented his attending any elementary school whatever. His early education was obtained almost entirely by his own efforts, through reading and association with a country clergyman who gave him the freedom of his library. When he was yet a boy he went to West Chester, Pa., where he worked as a printer's apprentice. His service in this office stood him in good stead. No doubt it contributed greatly to his accuracy in spelling and his ability to read rapidly—habits that were valuable assets to him in the occupation he eventually adopted. His scientific training began a few years later when, as a young man, he accepted a position as clerk in the War Department, in Washington, D. C. While thus employed, he attended night classes at Columbian University (the present George Washington University) and received the degree of B.S. in 1888. Three years later he entered Johns Hopkins University as a graduate student in physics. There he came in contact with Professor H. A. Rowland [*q.v.*], the famous spectroscopist. Rowland was an inspiring teacher; his enthusiasm and idealism were a strong influence in Lewis' career, for he, too, adopted the study of spectroscopy as his life work.

In 1895, after receiving the degree of Ph.D. from Johns Hopkins, he went to the University of California as instructor in physics. Promotion to the grade of assistant professor came the following year, partly because a physicist was desired who could cooperate with the Lick Observatory in the field of astrophysics and spectroscopy. The period 1898–1900 Lewis spent abroad, as Whiting fellow, at the Physical Institute of the University of Berlin. He then returned to the University of California, where he became successively associate professor of physics (1902), professor (1908), and chairman of the department (1918) ; the last two positions he held until his death. In 1901 he was married to Louise Sheppard of San Francisco. They had two children—a son and a daughter. He was a member of expeditions to observe the eclipse of the sun in the South Seas, 1908, at Goldendale, Wash., June 1918, and at Ensenada, Lower California, in 1923. His chief studies in this connection were of the flash and the coronal spectrum. Although Lewis published no books, he was the author of papers on many diverse subjects, in the *Astrophysical Journal* and other scientific periodicals, and at the time of his death was working on the manuscript of a textbook of spectroscopy.

In the field of his major activity, his chief contributions related to the spectra of gases under various conditions of excitation, purity, etc. During his residence in Berlin he made the first systematic investigation of the influence of small quantities of a foreign substance on the character of the spectra of hydrogen, oxygen, and nitrogen. While he was engaged in studying the latter gas, he discovered a peculiar fluorescent afterglow that persists in the nitrogen discharge tube when a trace of oxygen or water vapor is present. Lord Rayleigh, inspired by these observations, discovered the chemical substance he termed "active nitrogen," which, he showed, was capable of exciting fluorescence in other vapors than oxygen or water. Lewis investigated the band spectra of many substances. He was a pioneer in the very difficult fields of infra-red and far ultra-violet spectroscopy. He studied the continuous spectrum of hydrogen in the Schuman region, its intensity and extent, and the conditions most favorable to its appearance. He measured the wave-lengths of several hundred new lines in the ultra-violet spectra of the rare gases krypton and xenon. Among his extensive researches in fields other than spectroscopy, were his investigations of ionization and electrical conductivity of gases. He devised a most ingenious method of determining the amplitude of sound waves by observation of illuminated ultra-microscopic particles set into forced vibration by the waves. He also studied various phenomena accompanying magnetic hysteresis.

Lewis was more than an able teacher. He possessed a rare ability to divest a complex subject of its difficulty. His lectures on spectroscopy were models of clarity. An idealist and a philosopher, he was distinguished by great simplicity of character and singleness of purpose. His devotion to the study of scientific truth made him uncompromising in dealing with civic or political questions. He was an early advocate of equal suffrage and was generous in support of projects for the improvement of political conditions.

[*Who's Who in America*, 1926–27; J. H. Moore, in *Pubs. Astron. Soc. of the Pacific*, Apr. 1927; E. E. Hall, in *Science*, May 6, 1927; *San Francisco Chronicle*, Nov. 18, 1926; informaton as to certain facts from Mrs. E. P. Lewis.]   D. H. M.

LEWIS, FIELDING (July 7, 1725–c. Jan. 1, 1782), Revolutionary patriot, brother-in-law of George Washington, and builder of "Kenmore" at Fredericksburg, Va., was probably a descendant of Robert Lewis, a native of Brecon, Wales, who settled in what is now Gloucester County, Va., about 1635. Fielding's immediate forebears were cultivated, wealthy, and influential. He was the son of John Lewis, member of the Virginia Council, and of Frances, daughter of Henry Fielding, gentleman, of King and Queen County, Va.; his grandfather, John Lewis—also a Councillor—had married Elizabeth Warner, daughter of Col. Augustine Warner of "Warner Hall," in Gloucester County, and of Mildred Reade, his wife. In this way, it is said, there came into possession of the Lewis family the old mansion, "Warner Hall," in which Fielding was born.

His association with George Washington was long and intimate. On Oct. 18, 1746, he married Washington's cousin, Catherine Washington, by whom he had three children. After her death, he married, May 7, 1750, Washington's sister, Betty. There were eleven children of this union. The letters and diaries of Washington show that he was a frequent visitor at "Kenmore," and was much attached to the family there. It was after his marriage to Betty that Lewis built "Kenmore." The house is constructed of brick, with walls two feet thick. The woodwork in its spacious rooms is fashioned in exquisite detail. Washington was much interested in its building and aided in designing its interior decorations. During the Revolution he sent two Hessian artisans, captured at Trenton, to adorn the mansion with elaborately decorated

mantels and ceilings. Lewis was also associated with Washington, in 1761, in the organization of the Dismal Swamp Company, formed to build a canal through that swamp and to drain its lands. Beginning in 1760, Lewis served for almost a decade as burgess from Spotsylvania County.

From the beginning of the struggle with Great Britain he was an ardent patriot. On June 1, 1774, he joined with a group of citizens of Fredericksburg, who adopted a resolution pledging themselves to concur in whatever the colonies should do respecting the "hostile invasions of the rights and liberties of the town of Boston." He was chosen a member of a committee to correspond with neighboring towns and counties. The Revolutionary county committee of Spotsylvania, of which Lewis was chairman, adopted, on May 9, 1775, resolutions thanking "Capt. Patrick Henry for the part which he played in the gunpowder affair." Ill health excluded Lewis from military service; but he spent his strength and fortune in the cause of liberty. In July 1775 the General Assembly decided to establish a factory at Fredericksburg for the making of small arms for the state troops, and appointed Lewis chief commissioner to superintend the undertaking. Early in 1776 operations were begun. Lewis remained in charge of the factory until 1781, when he was forced by sickness to resign. When necessary funds for this vital work could not be secured by the state, he advanced seven thousand pounds of his own money, thereby saving the enterprise. This generous action left him in very straitened circumstances at the end of his life. His death occurred sometime between Dec. 10, 1781, when he added a codicil to his will, and Jan. 17, 1782, when the will was probated.

[J. M. McAllister and L. B. Tandy, *Geneals. of the Lewis and Kindred Families* (1906); *William and Mary Coll. Quart. Hist. Mag.*, Apr. 1897, Jan., Apr., July, 1901, Oct. 1918, Jan., Apr. 1919; *Va. Mag. of Hist. and Biog.*, Jan. 1898, July 1922, July 1924; *Official Letters of the Governors of the State of Va.*, vol. II (1928); *Calendar of Va. State Papers*, vol. I (1875), ed. by W. P. Palmer; *The Diaries of George Washington, 1748–1799* (4 vols., 1925), ed. by J. C. Fitzpatrick; *Va. County Records—Spotsylvania County*, vol. I (1905), ed. by W. A. Crozier; V. M. Fleming, *The Story of Kenmore* (1924).]   R. L. M—n.

LEWIS, FRANCIS (Mar. 21, 1713–Dec. 31, 1802), New York merchant and signer of the Declaration of Independence, was the only child of the Rev. Francis Lewis, rector of Llandaff, Glamorganshire, Wales, and Amy Pettingal of Caernarvon. Left an orphan at an early age, he spent his childhood and youth, under the care of his mother's relatives, in Wales and at Westminster School and in a mercantile house in

London. Thus soundly and prudently prepared he came to New York in 1738 and began a career in trade which was distinguished for activity and finally by success. He carried on business for a time in New York and Philadelphia, returned to England for two years, and made voyages between America and northern European ports in the course of which he twice suffered shipwreck. During this period of adventure he was captured by Indians in 1756 after the fall of Oswego, where he was present as friend of the English commander and as clothing contractor for the troops. He was sent to France for exchange and afterward received from the colonial government a grant of land in acknowledgment of his military services. He had married, on June 15, 1745, Elizabeth Annesley of New York. In 1765, having accumulated a considerable fortune and attained a position of influence in New York, he retired to Whitestone, Long Island, but in 1771 he returned to the city for a time to help establish his son, Francis, in business, even making a journey with him to England to form commercial connections there. After his return he was completely occupied with public affairs.

In the Revolutionary agitations in New York after 1774 his participation was continuous and occasionally conspicuous. In 1774 he was a delegate to the Provincial Convention and a member of the Committee of Fifty-one and the Committee of Sixty. In July of that year he was one of the eleven who resigned from the former in protest against what seemed excessive caution in opposing Parliamentary legislation. Throughout the exciting events of 1775 and 1776 he was active both in the proceedings of the Continental Congress and in the critically deliberate process of forming a government for the new state of New York. Increasingly identified with "continental" affairs, he was a delegate to Congress from May 1775 till November 1779 and served thereafter till July 1781 as one of the commissioners of the Board of Admiralty. He took no part in debate but was indefatigable in committee work. His long experience, orderly disposition, and practical sagacity made him a valued member of such semi-administrative bodies as the Marine, the Secret, and the Commercial committees, and finally of the Admiralty Board. He was frequently charged with duties in connection with the supply of the army and was a strong supporter of Washington at the time of the intrigues against his leadership.

With the rest of the New York delegation he was precluded by instructions from voting for the Declaration of Independence on July 4, 1776, but he was one of those whose signatures were appended to the document, probably on Aug. 2, 1776. A little more than a month later Lewis' house in Whitestone was destroyed by the British army and his wife was made prisoner. The rigorous conditions of her captivity during the months before she could be exchanged undermined her health and hastened her death (1779). The Revolution deprived Lewis of his home and, because of his expenditures in the cause, of most of his wealth. He lived in retirement with the families of his sons until his death in his ninetieth year.

[There is a sketch of Lewis by Robert Waln, Jr., in John Sanderson, *Biog. of the Signers to the Declaration of Independence*, vol. VI (1825). His career in Congress can be traced in the *Journals* and in E. C. Burnett, *Letters of Members of the Continental Cong.*, vols. I–V (1921–31). The account of him in Thos. Jones, *Hist. of N. Y. During the Revolutionary War* (2 vols., 1879), ed. by E. F. de Lancey, is hostile, while that in Julia Delafield, *Biogs. of Francis Lewis and Morgan Lewis* (2 vols., 1877), is strongly eulogistic. Some, though not all, of Jones's errors are corrected in the Editor's Note LIV. An inaccurate but vivid sketch is that in J. A. Scoville, *The Old Merchants of N. Y. City*, vol. III (1865). Notices of his death appeared in the N. Y. *Evening Post*, Jan. 3, 1803, and the *Spectator*, Jan. 5, 1803. The date of Lewis' birth and the names of his parents were supplied by one of his descendants.]   C. W. S.

LEWIS, ISAAC NEWTON (Oct. 12, 1858–Nov. 9, 1931), soldier, inventor, son of James H. and Anne (Kendall) Lewis, was born in New Salem, Fayette County, Pa. In 1880 he was appointed from Kansas to the United States Military Academy, and upon his graduation in 1884 was commissioned second lieutenant in the 2nd Artillery. He was married, Oct. 21, 1886, to Mary, daughter of the Rev. Richard Wheatley of New York City, and had four children. He was promoted through the grades to colonel, which grade he reached Aug. 27, 1913, and on Sept. 20 of the same year he was retired from active service on account of disability incurred in line of duty. He graduated from the Torpedo School in 1886, and during the subsequent years of his service devoted himself to further technical study and experimentation. He was signally successful in perfecting and inventing a number of devices, notably the Lewis depression position finder (patent no. 447,335, Mar. 3, 1891), and the Lewis machine gun (patent no. 1,004,666, Oct. 3, 1911). He also invented a plotting and relocating system for seacoast batteries, a time-interval clock and bell system of signals for artillery fire control, a quick-firing field gun and mount, quick-reading mechanical verniers, an electric car lighting system (patent no. 504,681, Sept. 5, 1893), a windmill electric lighting system and a gas-propelled torpedo (patent no. 933,086, Sept. 7, 1909). During his service Lewis was entrusted with many important assignments, particularly along scientific lines in connection with artillery and ordnance. He served as a member of the board of regulation of coast artillery fire, New York Harbor (1894–98); recorder of the board of ordnance and fortification, Washington (1898–1902); instructor in electricity and power; director of the department of enlisted specialists; acting commandant of the Coast Artillery School at Fortress Monroe, Va.; commander of the post of Fortress Monroe and the Artillery District of the Chesapeake (1904–11). He also devised a system of fire control for San Francisco harbor, which he demonstrated in France, Germany, Austria, and Russia, and which the last-named country adopted. In 1900, under special instructions of the Secretary of War, he visited several European countries and made a study of their methods of manufacturing and supplying ordnance material. He was the originator of the modern corps organization of artillery which was adopted in 1902.

Immediately upon his retirement from active service he proceeded to Liège, Belgium, to build a factory for the development and manufacture of the Lewis machine gun in Europe, having failed to secure the approval of the War Department in Washington for the trial and development of the gun for the United States service. After the outbreak of the World War, he moved to England, and was connected with the Birmingham Small Arms Company. In 1916 tests were conducted in the United States for the purpose of selecting a machine gun for the United States service. The Lewis gun was submitted with others, and was rejected by the War Department board, because of the large number of malfunctions and stoppages during the firing test. Its rejection started a controversy, which raged for some time in the service and the press and finally reached a stage where open letters from high-ranking officers of the army were published. In order to settle the technical questions involved, a board was constituted, and the inspector-general of the army was ordered to investigate other aspects of the case. The findings of the board (see *New York Times,* Nov. 11, 1916), and of the inspector-general were approved by the Secretary of War, who ordered that further controversy on this subject cease (*Ibid.,* Dec. 18, 1916). After certain requirements had been complied with, the gun was accepted by the government and large numbers were used by the army in arming airplanes. Lewis remained in Europe throughout the war, in personal contact with the French, British,

and Belgian field armies. Lewis guns were delivered to the Allies at the front at the rate of 3,500 complete gun units per week, and a total of over 100,000 guns were used by them. He was technical director of the Lewis Machine Gun Company of London; president of the Lewis Machine Gun Company and director of the Automatic Arms Company of Cleveland, Ohio; technical director and manager of the *Armes Automatique Lewis* of Belgium; and director of the *Société des Armes Lewis,* of Paris. Possessing a profound knowledge of mechanical and electrical engineering and thoroughly conversant with all phases of coast artillery construction and equipment, he earned an enviable reputation in his profession. At the close of his life his home was in Montclair, N. J.; his death occurred suddenly in a railroad station at Hoboken.

[G. W. Cullum, *Biog. Reg. Officers and Grads. U. S. Mil. Acad.* (3rd ed., 1891); record in the Adjutant General's Office, Washington; *Army Ordnance,* Dec.–Jan. 1931–32; *Specifications and Drawings of Patents Issued from the U. S. Patent Office,* Mar. 1891, Aug. 1892, Sept., Oct. 1893, Mar. 1894, Mar. 1898, Aug. 1902, Sept., Dec. 1909, Oct. 1911; *Official Gazette of the U. S. Patent Office,* Aug. 13, 1912, Aug. 18, 1914, June 15, 1915, Aug. 22 1916, Oct. 3, Dec. 26, 1922; *Who's Who in America,* 1930–31; C. H. Claudy, in *Sci. Am.,* Feb. 14, 1920; *Army and Navy Jour.,* Dec. 23, 1916, Jan. 6, June 30, 1917; *N. Y. Times,* July 1, 2, 1917, Nov. 10, 1931.]   C. F. C.

LEWIS, JAMES (Oct. 5, 1837–Sept. 10, 1896), actor, whose real name was James Lewis Deming, was born in Troy, N. Y., the son of William Hoadley and Arabella (Benson) Deming. When he was seventeen years old and was employed as a clerk in a store in Troy, an actor who wished to look for a better engagement persuaded him to play a part in *The Writing on the Wall* for one night with the stock company at the Troy Museum. Although his part was a small one, he scored such a hit that he was offered an engagement for the remainder of the season, and this circumstance determined his choice of a career. From Troy he worked his way west and south, barnstorming, playing sometimes in tavern dining-rooms and even in churches. When the Civil War broke out he was playing in Montgomery, Ala., in a company in which John Wilkes Booth was leading man. He hastened to Savannah in time to catch the last steamer that sailed north before the blockade. Then came several seasons of "stock" in Rochester, Cleveland, and Pittsburgh, successively. In 1865 he was engaged as low comedian at the Olympic Theatre, in New York City. Here he acted in a great variety of farces and dramas. Later he was low comedian of the stock company at the Continental Theatre, Boston. During this engagement he was praised by the critics for his Dick Swiveller in *The Old Curiosity Shop.*

The popularity of burlesque at this time led Lewis into this field. His droll portrayals of the burlesque Lucretia Borgia, and Rebecca in *Ivanhoe* at the Waverly Theatre, New York, attracted the attention of the young Augustin Daly. Daly engaged Lewis for his stock company at the Fifth Avenue Theatre on West Twenty-fourth Street. Lewis first appeared there at the beginning of the third week of the Daly season, Sept. 6, 1869, as John Hibbs in *Dreams,* receiving very flattering notices from the press. He acted in many rôles, constantly gaining in artistic technique. His most notable success was as Bob Sackett in the five-act comedy *Saratoga* by Bronson Howard, which enjoyed a long run. In the second Fifth Avenue Theatre, at Broadway and Twenty-eighth Street, Lewis added still further to his reputation. It was here in *The Big Bonanza* (Feb. 17, 1875) that he and Mrs. George H. Gilbert [see Gilbert, Anne Hartley] had two of those parts which made the Daly Stock Company famous.

While Daly was in temporary retirement, Lewis, with Mrs. Gilbert, joined a company organized by Henry E. Abbey to play comedy in New York and on tour, but he rejoined the Daly company at Daly's Theatre, New York, in its second season, 1880–81, and continued as one of the shining lights of this organization of brilliant artists. With John Drew, Mrs. Gilbert, and Ada Rehan [*qq.v.*] he was one of the "Big Four" of the company, appearing several times with them in London and on the Continent and winning very favorable recognition from the critics. In old and modern comedy, especially in adaptations from the German, he excelled in the portrayal of comic old men. He was also very successful in his characterizations of blasé and worldly types. His outstanding characteristic as a comedian was his dryness, leading a Harvard professor to say, "Lewis is so dry he crackles." He died suddenly at West Hampton, Long Island. His first wife was a native of Cleveland, Ohio. His second wife, Medora Frances Herbert, whom he married on May 8, 1871, survived him.

[See J. F. Daly, *The Life of Augustin Daly* (1917); Wm. Winter, *Wallet of Time,* vol. I (1913); Laurence Hutton, *Curiosities of the Am. Stage* (1891) and *Plays and Players* (1875); Arthur Hornblow, *Hist. of the Theatre in America,* vol. II (1919); J. R. Towse, *Sixty Years of the Theatre* (1916); clippings on James Lewis in the Robinson Locke Collection in the N. Y. Pub. Lib.; *N. Y. Dramatic Mirror,* Sept. 19, 1896; *N. Y. Herald,* Sept. 7, 1869, Dec. 22, 1870; *N. Y. Tribune,* Dec. 22, 1870, Sept. 11, 1896; *Boston Herald,* Sept. 11, 1896; *N. Y. Times,* Sept. 11, 1896. Lewis was extremely reticent about his birth and family. A sketch of him in the *Troy Northern Budget,* Sept. 13, 1896, mentions his parents, and he appears in J. K. Deming, *A Geneal. of the Descendants of John Deming* (1904).]   L. H. F.

LEWIS, JOHN FRANCIS (Mar. 1, 1818–Sept. 2, 1895), Virginia Unionist and United States senator, was born near Port Republic, Rockingham County, Va., son of Gen. Samuel Hance and Nancy (Lewis) Lewis. Both parents were descended from John Lewis, an Irish immigrant "Who slew the Irish lord, settled Augusta County, Located the town of Staunton And furnished five sons to fight the battles of the American Revolution" (epitaph, printed in L. G. Tyler, *Encyclopedia of Virginia Biography,* 1915, V, 576). Lewis' formal education was meager. Management of the family plantation, along with some practice of law, was normally his chief occupation. In 1842 he married Serena Helen, daughter of Daniel Sheffey. Though both his father and his father-in-law were prominent public men and he himself professed ardent Whig sympathies, not until 1859 did he approach active politics. Having then expressed in the local newspaper his opposition to secession as a theory and as a policy, he was elected to the state convention of 1861. Here he offered no resolution, made no report, seems not even to have spoken; but he persistently voted against secession and ultimately refused to sign the ordinance. The coming of the Civil War prevented, it is said, his acceptance of President Lincoln's tender of the marshalship of western Virginia. During the war his rôle was that of a peaceful Unionist; it has been asserted, however, without recorded contradiction, that he also "manufactured large quantities of iron for the Confederacy, under special contracts with it" (A. F. Robertson, *Alexander Hugh Holmes Stuart,* 1925, p. 249). In 1865 he was a candidate for Congress against A. H. H. Stuart [*q.v.*], but was badly beaten. Lewis seems to have followed the lead of his friend John Minor Botts [*q.v.*] during the early part of the Reconstruction period (Botts, *The Great Rebellion,* 1866, p. 192), attending the various meetings which led to the formation of the Republican party in Virginia, appearing before the congressional investigating committee, endeavoring to build a strong and liberal party and to secure a place of prominence in it. Later he joined the combination with the Conservatives and was, in consequence, elected lieutenant-governor in 1869. The same combination (apparently much influenced by railroad and bond-holding interests) elected him to the federal Senate for the short term, John W. Johnston of the Southwest being the Conservative (Democratic) selection for the full term. In the Senate (January 1870–March 1875) he was chairman of the committee on the District of Columbia, but otherwise obtained no particular recognition. After the expiration of his term he was appointed marshal by President Grant, and served 1875–81. When the Republican-Readjuster combination was being effected, he was of much assistance and in consequence was again elected lieutenant-governor (1881). "There's Cameron, he's for the Democrats; and there's Lewis, he's for the negroes . . .," was the hostile comment of the *Richmond Dispatch* on the combination (June 4, 1881, p. 2, cited in Pearson, *post*, p. 139). In 1889 he broke with Gen. William Mahone [*q.v.*], head of the combination, and materially aided in his overthrow by working for a Straight-Out Republican movement. His last years were spent at "Lynwood," the family estate in Rockingham County, where he died of cancer after a long, brave fight. Three sons and four daughters survived him. The Democratic press noted that though his independence of thought and impulsiveness of action had often led him into disagreements with his friends and neighbors, these had never doubted his integrity, and even his political opponents credited him with robust, manly virtues.

[Obituaries and estimates appeared in the *Richmond Dispatch*, Sept. 3, and the *Rockingham Register*, Sept. 6, 1895. H. J. Eckenrode, *The Political Hist. of Va. during the Reconstruction* (1904), and C. C. Pearson, *Readjuster Movement in Va.* (1917), give the political background in detail.]   C. C. P.

LEWIS, JOSEPH HORACE (Oct. 29, 1824–July 6, 1904), Confederate soldier, congressman, Kentucky jurist, was the son of John and Eliza Martz (Reed) Lewis. His father was a prominent and prosperous citizen of southern Barren County, Ky., and it was there, near Glasgow, that the younger Lewis was born. His early education was sufficient to secure him admission to Centre College which in the days before the Civil War was one of the leading educational institutions in the West. He was graduated from Centre in 1843, then began the study of law in the office of Judge C. C. Tompkins of Glasgow. He was admitted to the bar in 1845 and began the practice of law at Glasgow. His later career as a jurist and the high preferment he attained in that field would indicate, even if other testimony were lacking, that his law training was not insufficient nor his legal ability of a low order. For the time being, however, his law practice was subordinated to politics. In 1850 he was elected to the state House of Representatives. He was reëlected in 1851 and in 1853. The *Journals* of the House for these years do not indicate that he was active as a legislator.

Lewis found it necessary in the troubled years before the war to reconstruct his principles. He had been elected to the legislature as a Whig but upon the collapse of that party he transferred his loyalty to the Democratic party to which he afterward steadily adhered. He was the Democratic candidate for Congress in 1857 and again in 1861 but was defeated on both occasions. He was ardent in his Southern sympathies and in 1860 was active in his support of Breckinridge for the presidency. When war came it found him with his mind made up. Upon the establishment of Camp Dick Robinson he began recruiting in Kentucky for the Confederate army, and in September 1861 he was commissioned colonel of the 6th Regiment of Kentucky Infantry. He fought throughout the war and was frequently cited for his bravery in action, notably at Shiloh. In September 1863, as a result of his part in the battle of Chickamauga, he was made brigadier-general (Thompson, *post*, p. 391). With that rank he commanded the famous "Orphan Brigade" for the remainder of the war. He opposed Sherman in his march across Georgia and the Carolinas and surrendered with the Confederate forces at Washington Court House.

At the close of the war Lewis returned to Kentucky and resumed the practice of law at Glasgow. In the general reaction toward the Confederates in Kentucky he was elected to the state legislature in 1868. In 1870 he was elected to Congress to fill a vacancy and the next year was elected for a full term. After a few years spent in the practice of law he was elected circuit judge in 1880 but resigned in 1881 to seek election to a vacancy on the court of appeals. In 1882 he was reëlected for a term of eight years and in 1890 again elected for eight years (Z. F. Smith, *The History of Kentucky,* 1895, pp. 776, 778, and 817). It was these seventeen years of continuous service on the court of appeals (for four years of which he was chief-justice) that constituted the most valuable contribution made by Lewis to the state. His probity gave authority to his decisions and contributed no little to the high respect accorded to the court. Upon the expiration of his term in 1899 Lewis retired to his farm in Scott County and engaged in no further public activity beyond serving as chairman of the Goebel Reward Commission after 1900 (Louisville *Courier-Journal,* July 7, 1904). Lewis had married, on Nov. 29, 1845, Sarah H. Rogers of Glasgow, who died in 1858 leaving two children. After the war he was married to Cassandra (Flournoy) Johnson, widow of Jilson P. Johnson of Louisville.

[The best account of Lewis as a lawyer and as a legislator is given in H. Levin, *The Lawyers and Lawmakers of Ky.* (n.d.). Further sources include: E. P. Thompson, *Hist. of the Orphan Brigade* (1898); Lewis and Richard H. Collins, *Hist. of Ky.* (2 vols., 1874); *Biog. Cyc. of the Commonwealth of Ky.* (1896); *War of the Rebellion: Official Records (Army)*; and J. M. McAllister and L. B. Tandy, *Geneals. of the Lewis and Kindred Families* (1906), p. 60.] R. S. C.

LEWIS, LAWRENCE (June 20, 1856–Sept. 2, 1890), lawyer, author, was born in Philadelphia, the son of Robert Morton and Anna Elizabeth (Shippen) Lewis. Named for an uncle, he was known to his contemporaries as Lawrence Lewis, Jr. He was educated at Episcopal Academy and at the University of Pennsylvania, where he graduated in 1876 with the degree of A.B. and later secured the master's degree. After studying law in the office of William Henry Rawle, he was admitted to the bar in 1879, and was made a member and for a time secretary of the Law Academy of Philadelphia. In 1883 he married Dora Kelly. His earliest notable achievements were in the field of historical and legal literature. In 1880 he published *An Essay on Original Land Titles in Philadelphia,* which was awarded the Duponceau Prize Medal by the Law Academy. It was a product of genuine historical and legal scholarship. In 1881 he published another work showing remarkable powers of research and synthesis for so young a scholar—*The Constitution, Jurisdiction and Practice of the Courts of Pennsylvania in the Seventeenth Century* (reprinted from *Pennsylvania Magazine of History and Biography,* vol. V, no. 2). This was followed in 1882 by *A History of the Bank of North America,* a study prepared at the request of the president and the directors of the bank: a laudatory account from the Hamiltonian point of view, but valuable because of its portraits, facsimiles, letters, and list of subscribers and directors. He also published *Memoir of Edward Shippen, Chief Justice of Pennsylvania* (1883; reprinted from *Pennsylvania Magazine* for April 1883), and *A Brief Statement of the Origin, Nature, and History of the French Spoliation Claims* (n.d.). He annotated *The American and English Railroad Cases,* volumes X–XX (1883–85) and *American and English Corporation Cases,* volumes I–VIII (1884–85), edited *Weekly Notes of Cases,* 1879–90, and contributed to periodicals.

He early established himself as a practising attorney, winning his outstanding success as attorney for claimants under the Act of Congress of 1885 by which claims arising out of French actions prior to July 31, 1801, were to be adjudicated in the United States Court of Claims. As counsel for the defendant in the case of *Fore-paugh* vs. *Delaware, Lackawanna & Western Railroad Company,* which involved the important new legal principle of limited liability of business associates, he secured a verdict validating contracts which limited the liability of the company. Because of his study of land titles and of legal procedure he was called upon to draft for the state a new law of escheats greatly simplifying complicated legal processes. His career was cut short by his death in a railroad accident near West Chester.

[See *Legal Intelligencer,* Sept. 12, 1890; *Meeting in Memory of Lawrence Lewis, Jr.* (Law Academy of Phila., 1890); *The Press* and *Public Ledger* (Phila.), Sept. 3, 1890. The various French spoliation cases in which Lewis was counsel may be studied in the appropriate volumes of the Court of Claims *Reports* and in the voluminous periodical literature of the time. See "French Spoliations," a bibliography, in *Boston Pub. Lib. Bull.,* Spring No., 1885.] W. B—n.

LEWIS, MERIWETHER (Aug. 18, 1774–Oct. 11, 1809), explorer and governor, was a native of that cradle of noted Americans, Albemarle County, Va., where he was a neighbor of the Jeffersons, Randolphs, and other prominent families. He was named for his mother, Lucy Meriwether, and was the eldest child of her marriage with her cousin, William Lewis. Both families were among the élite of their region; William Lewis, a cousin of Fielding Lewis [*q.v.*], served in the Continental Army and died soon after the surrender at Yorktown, leaving a considerable estate. Within a brief time his widow married John Marks, and when Meriwether was about ten years old the family removed with a large group of kinsfolk to upper Georgia, where they had plantations on the Broad River in the present Oglethorpe County. Here young Lewis grew up amid pleasant surroundings. Much of his time was spent in the open, and he became an expert hunter. He also took note of the fauna and flora of the vicinity and early showed both scientific and literary tastes. It is said that when told by his schoolmaster that the earth turned around he jumped high in the air and was disappointed that he came down in the same place, until it was proved to him that he moved with the moving earth. He also showed great presence of mind during danger; when a group of women and children, gathered about a bonfire, were frightened at an alarm supposed to be caused by Indians, it was Meriwether Lewis who dashed a bucket of water on the flames, leaving the group to grateful darkness (manuscript letter, Draper MSS., 15DD32 Wisconsin Historical Library).

At the age of thirteen Lewis returned to Virginia to study under the Rev. Matthew Maury, who grounded him well in Latin and also taught him mathematics and the rudiments of science. He continued his studies under private tutors for five years, planning to attend William and Mary College, but when he was eighteen years old his step-father died, his mother returned to the Virginia plantation, "Locust Hill," on Ivy Creek near Charlottesville, and Meriwether as the eldest son felt it his duty to remain at home and manage the estate. He also took great interest in the education of his brother, Reuben Lewis, and his young half-brother and sister, John and Mary Marks.

Lewis was twenty when the president called for troops to suppress the Whisky Rebellion; as a member of the local militia he went into camp first at Winchester, then across the mountains near Pittsburgh. There early in 1795 he wrote to his mother that he was "quite delighted with a soldier's life." In consequence, May 1, 1795, he enlisted in the regular army, being commissioned ensign in the 2nd Legion. That year he marched to Greenville, Ohio, where he attended the treaty made by Anthony Wayne [q.v.] with the northern Indians, which ended the wars in the Northwest Territory. During this campaign he was one of the subordinates of William Clark [q.v.], his future companion in exploring the West.

On Nov. 1, 1796, Lewis was transferred to the 1st Infantry and in 1799, commissioned lieutenant. During the last years of the eighteenth century he was stationed in turn at several cantonments. His honesty and industry were so noted that he was chosen paymaster for his regiment. In 1797 he obtained a furlough, visited his home, and later journeyed to Kentucky on business, for his own and the family estate (manuscript letters in Wisconsin Historical Library). Late in the summer of 1797 he was on active duty in command of a company at Fort Pickering, a newly erected fortification near the site of Memphis, built after the evacuation of that region by the Spanish. This fort was in Chickasaw Indian Territory and here Lewis learned the language and the customs of these Indians. Thence he was ordered to Detroit and was stationed at that outpost in 1801 when his friend and neighbor, Thomas Jefferson, was elected president.

In the first week after his election Jefferson wrote to Lewis, offering him the post of private secretary. The letter was couched in flattering terms. In selecting a secretary, said Jefferson, "I thought it important to respect not only his capacity to aid in the private concerns of the household, but also to contribute to the mass of information which it is interesting to the admin-

istration to acquire. Your knowledge of the Western country, of the Army and of all its interests and relations has rendered it desirable for public as well as private purposes that you should be engaged in that office." The salary would be only five hundred dollars, but Lewis would live in the executive mansion, and could retain his military rank. The letter concluded, "It has been solicited by several who will have no answer till I hear from you" (Jefferson Papers, Library of Congress).

Lewis received Jefferson's letter at Pittsburgh, en route from Detroit. He immediately accepted the offer it contained, and, acting on the President-Elect's suggestions, obtained leave of absence from his military superior, Gen. James Wilkinson. He was in Washington about the time of the inauguration, and shortly afterwards removed with the President to the White House. There he was expected to oversee the domestic arrangements, since Jefferson's daughters were both married and could stay with their father only occasionally. The establishment was served by eleven servants brought from Monticello; hospitality was lavish and democratic; Jefferson kept open house for diplomats, congressmen, and friends. Dinner was served at four o'clock and the table was surrounded by men of note, who often continued the conversation until midnight. Thomas Paine and Joel Barlow, Jefferson's former companions in Paris, were in Washington that winter, and the discussion and councils must have been a liberal education for the President's young friend and secretary. He was also employed in affairs of state. On Dec. 8, 1801, Jefferson sent Lewis to convey his annual message to the Senate, not wishing to appear and to read it in person as his predecessors had done.

During Lewis's two years at the White House, the matter of exploring for a land route to the Pacific Ocean was frequently discussed. It was a project which had occupied Jefferson's thought for twenty years, and Lewis had long cherished the wish to be chosen leader of such an expedition. In 1792 when but eighteen years of age he had importuned Jefferson, then secretary of state, to permit him to undertake the journey. It was deemed premature at that time, but the plan had never been abandoned by either Jefferson or Lewis. Now the time seemed ripe for carrying it into execution. On Jan. 18, 1803, Jefferson sent to Congress a private message concerning Indian trading houses; in it he discussed the advisability of learning something of the far western Indians, and proposed an appropriation for a journey of discovery. Lewis himself had made the estimate of the necessary expenses, and Congress quickly appropriated the $2,500 he desired.

Jefferson considered Lewis's qualifications for the leadership of such an expedition unsurpassed: "Of courage undaunted; possessing a firmness and perseverance of purpose which nothing but impossibilities could divert from its direction; careful as a father of those committed to his charge, yet steady in the maintenance of order and discipline; intimate with the Indian characters, customs, and principles; habituated to the hunting life; guarded by exact observations of the vegetables and animals of his own country against losing time in the description of objects already possessed; honest, disinterested, liberal, of sound understanding, and a fidelity to truth so scrupulous that whatever he should report would be as certain as seen by ourselves; with all these qualifications as if selected and implanted by nature in one body for this express purpose" (memoir by Jefferson in *History of the Expedition*, 1814). All he lacked, in Jefferson's opinion, was scientific knowledge—methods of taking latitude and longitude and the use of astronomical instruments. Jefferson therefore sent him to Philadelphia to study with the scientists there; afterwards, at Lancaster, Andrew Ellicott [*q.v.*] gave him advice on astronomy and map-making.

Jefferson had prepared instructions of a detailed nature for Lewis's conduct on the journey; these he sent him June 30, 1803, and with them his passports through French territory. Before his departure, however, news reached Washington of the purchase of Louisiana, which made it possible for the expedition to pass through territory belonging to the United States. At the instance of Jefferson, Lewis was to choose a companion officer; he offered the position to William Clark of Louisville, and the names and fame of Lewis and Clark are inseparably united.

The expedition mustered in Illinois, not far from the mouth of the Missouri; there during the winter of 1803–04 the men were enlisted and drilled. In the spring of 1804 Lewis assisted in the transfer at St. Louis of upper Louisiana to the United States, while Clark brought on the men and was joined by Lewis at St. Charles, Mo. The route was to follow the Missouri to its source. The chief difficulty apprehended was the enmity of some of the upper river tribes, especially the Sioux. A band of these Indians attempted to arrest the passage of the expedition, but the leaders' firmness and tact prevailed and they reached the Mandan villages in North Dakota late in the fall. There the men wintered and prepared for the further journey. Thence

Lewis sent letters to his family and the President which were the last messages from him for eighteen months. As guides for the upper river a French-Canadian and his Shoshone wife, Sacajawea [*q.v.*], were taken from the Mandans, when, on Apr. 7, 1805, the voyage was resumed. By July they reached the falls, where a long portage was made; by August the explorers came to the end of navigation. Sacajawea here found relatives from whom horses were obtained to cross the divide. Arrived at the Columbia, the expedition built canoes and descended that river to the ocean. The continent had at last been crossed by means of its two great rivers.

Fort Clatsop was built, not far from Astoria, to house the party for the winter and the rainy seasons. Since no ships came to this port in the spring, it was determined to recross the continent by the route the party followed coming out. The explorers returned over another pass to the place where they had cached their canoes the previous autumn. Lewis determined to make a detour along Maria's River, which he had named on the outward journey for his cousin, Maria Wood. It appeared that this tributary went farther north than any other and might interlock with higher branches of the Columbia. On this stream he had a hostile encounter with a band of Indians, the only serious skirmish on the trip. Some days later he was accidentally wounded by one of his men, who mistook him for a deer. By the time they reached the Mandans Lewis was in bad condition, but with rest and care he made a quick recovery. The captains persuaded a Mandan chief to accompany them to St. Louis, where they arrived on Sept. 23, 1806, to the great joy of the entire nation, who had long given them up for lost.

The success of the expedition was due to the combined abilities of the two leaders, Lewis and Clark. Lewis, however, was the true chief, the ultimate authority on every question. His journals show that he was deeply impressed with his responsibility; they show also his intellectual ardor and scientific spirit, and his humane feeling for man and nature. The two chiefs at once began to plan for a published account of their adventures. In November 1806 they started for Washington. There Lewis resigned from the army and Jefferson appointed him governor of Louisiana, the territory embracing all the province north of the present state of that name.

On returning to St. Louis in the summer of 1807, he found much to do in pacifying factions and reconciling feuds. His services as governor were brief but useful. His even-handed justice, his humanity and honesty gave the province the administration it needed. He organized the militia, had the laws codified, and aided Clark, who had been appointed superintendent of Indian affairs, in negotiating with the Indians. In the summer of 1809 he learned with distress that because of some technicality some of the bills he had issued on the government had been repudiated. He decided to go to Washington to investigate, and left St. Louis intending to go by way of New Orleans and the ocean. At Chickasaw Bluffs (now Memphis), however, he changed his plan and went overland, striking the Natchez Trace at the crossing of the Tennessee below Muscle Shoals. He had with him two servants, a negro and a half-breed Spaniard. On the night of Oct. 11, at a rude inn in central Tennessee, he died. Jefferson later assumed it was by his own hand. His family and the people of the locality where his death occurred believed he was murdered, and the weight of evidence seems to be with this surmise. No money was found on his body and his watch was later recovered in New Orleans. In 1848 the state of Tennessee erected a monument to him, in the county which now bears his name, but his best monument is the Lewis and Clark expedition and the accounts thereof prepared by his own pen.

[The best brief biography of Lewis is that written by Jefferson for inclusion in the first edition of the *Hist. of the Expedition under the Command of Captains Lewis and Clark* (2 vols., Phila., 1814), prepared for the press by Nicholas Biddle and Paul Allen from material left by Lewis and lent by Clark. This account was published in London in 1814 under the title, *Travels to the Source of the Missouri River*. An edition was prepared by Elliott Coues (4 vols., 1893), and another by J. B. McMaster (3 vols., 1904). The first report of the expedition appeared as *Message from the President of the United States, Communicating Discoveries Made . . . by Captains Lewis and Clark . . . Feb. 19, 1806* (1806). The original journals remain in the Am. Phil. Soc., Philadelphia. R. G. Thwaites edited *Original Journals of the Lewis and Clark Expedition* (8 vols., 1904–05). An additional Lewis journal of his trip down the Ohio was edited by M. M. Quaife, in *Wis. Hist. Soc. Colls.*, vol. XXII (1916). G. R. Gilmer, *Sketches of Some of the First Settlers of Upper Georgia* (1855), describes the conditions of Lewis's boyhood. John Swain, in "The Natchez Trace," *Everybody's Mag.*, Sept. 1905, describes a visit to his grave in central Tennessee. On his government of Louisiana see Louis Houck, *A Hist. of Missouri* (1908), II, 408. For genealogy see W. T. Lewis, *Geneal. of the Lewis Family* (1893) and L. H. A. Minor, *The Meriwethers and their Connections* (1892).]   L. P. K.

LEWIS, MORGAN (Oct. 16, 1754–Apr. 7, 1844), soldier, jurist, governor of New York, was the second son of Francis Lewis [*q.v.*] and Elizabeth Annesley, of New York. His early schooling was at home and in Elizabethtown, N. J., and he was graduated at the College of New Jersey (Princeton) in 1773. He was studying law at the time of the outbreak of the Revolution.

After a summer of volunteer service in 1775 at Cambridge, Mass., and in New York, he was in the winter and spring of 1776, major in the 2nd Regiment of the "New York Line." From June 1776 till the end of the war he was deputy quartermaster-general for the New York Department and was chief of staff with Gates at Ticonderoga and at Saratoga. Resuming his legal studies at the close of the war he was admitted to the bar, and he also took his first steps in politics by successfully running for the Assembly in 1789–90 and in 1792. He had married, May 11, 1779, Gertrude, daughter of Robert R. and Margaret Beekman Livingston of Clermont. This alliance with the "Livingston interest," coupled with his honorable, if hardly brilliant, military record, practically set the conditions of his public career. For a considerable period he profited extensively at the hands of the Clinton-Livingston combination in the Anti-Federalist and Republican parties. He was attorney-general from November 1791 to Dec. 24, 1792, and third justice of the supreme court of New York from the latter date to Oct. 28, 1801, when he was promoted to the chief-justiceship. In the discharge of the duties of these offices his record was perhaps not especially distinguished, but certainly respectable.

In 1804 his nomination to the governorship by the Republicans (practically dictated by DeWitt Clinton) projected Lewis into quite a different scene. The exceptional situations both of the Federalists and of Aaron Burr enabled him, it is true, to win decisively over the latter after a campaign of unexampled virulence. But for vigorous exercise of a governor's power and the development and maintenance of party leadership, the sinuosities and the ruthlessness of New York politics at that period called for a disposition and for capacities which apparently Lewis did not possess. Clinton turned against him. Both factions, the Lewisites, or "Quids," and the Clintonians toyed with Federalist support, and each in turn captured the council of appointment and used its powers in savagely proscriptive fashion. As it proved, Lewis's tenderness for the Livingstons in patronage matters and his deposition of Clinton from the New York City mayoralty were acts of rashness; and the victory of Tompkins in the gubernatorial campaign of 1807 crowned Clinton's determination to subjugate the Livingston influence. As the War of 1812 approached Lewis was enabled to return to politics for terms in the state Senate and for a seat on the council of appointment. During the war he was quartermaster-general and in 1813 major-general in service on the Niagara frontier. In this campaign his age and, above all, the conditions of intrigue in the high command, forbade his winning distinction, and in 1814 he was in command of the region about New York City.

Whatever the extent or consequences of his errors or misfortunes in the field of party warfare, Lewis took an enlightened and frequently generous view of the duties and privileges of one in public station. During the war he advanced funds for the discharge of American prisoners of war and remitted rents on his estates for tenants who had rendered military service. His later years were filled with activities of a more or less public character. As landlord on the Livingston estates he took action characterized by enlightened foresight and to a large degree avoided the troubles of the anti-rent disturbances. He was a pillar of Masonry in the period of strong agitation against the order. He was also president of the New York Historical Society, 1832–36, president-general of the Society of the Cincinnati, 1839–44, and one of the founders of New York University. He died in his ninetieth year in New York City.

[Julia Delafield's *Biogs. of Francis Lewis and Morgan Lewis* (2 vols., 1877) gives much personal and family detail. See also: J. D. Hammond, *The Hist. of Pol. Parties in the State of N. Y.* (2 vols., 1842); D. S. Alexander, *A Pol. Hist. of the State of N. Y.*, vol. I (1906); Henry Adams, *Hist. of the U. S. of America During the Administration of James Madison*, vol. I (1891); J. S. Jenkins, *Lives of the Govs. of the State of N. Y.* (1851); *N. Y. Tribune*, Apr. 8, 9, 10, 1844.]

C. W. S.

LEWIS, ORLANDO FAULKLAND (Sept. 5, 1873–Feb. 24, 1922), social worker, penologist, and author, born at Boston, Mass., was the younger son of John Jay Lewis and Abbie Goodwin (Davis) Lewis. On his father's side, he was a descendant of George Lewis, who came from East Greenwich, England, to Plymouth, Mass., about 1630; on his mother's, of William Davis who, according to family tradition, emigrated to Massachusetts from Wales about 1635. His father was a Universalist minister, who, about 1890, gave up his pastorate for the lecture platform; his mother was a successful writer for children's magazines. Both were energetic and had many affiliations with religious, social, and civic undertakings.

Lewis was educated in the Boston schools but spent the last two years before entering college in Munich, Germany, where his brother was enrolled in the Royal Conservatory. In 1892 he matriculated at Tufts College, from which he received the degree of A.B. in 1895, and a master's degree after two years as a graduate student and instructor in modern languages. A brief period of foreign study in Munich and at the Sorbonne was followed by graduate work at the University of Pennsylvania, where, in 1900, he was granted a doctorate in Germanic languages. Five years of modern language teaching at the University of Maine did not give him the stimulus and the mental satisfaction which he craved. A summer course under the sociologist Charles R. Henderson [*q.v.*] at the University of Chicago interested him in the work of social betterment, and in 1905 he became superintendent of the Joint Application Bureau of the Charity Organization Society in New York City. Articles published by him subsequently show that he was profoundly interested at this time in the vagrant, in the child laborer, and in health problems. In 1908 he joined the faculty of the School of Philanthropy, and on Apr. 20 of the same year he married Edith Schieffelin Sabine, of New York City.

In 1910 he was elected general secretary of the Prison Association of New York, and in the work of aiding confined or released prisoners and their families and in the struggle for the application of modern penological principles, his sympathetic personality reached its full expression. Out of the studies to which this interest led him grew his most scholarly work: *The Development of American Prisons and Prison Customs, 1776–1845* (1922), unequaled by any other publication for the period it covers. From 1911 to 1918 he also issued a monthly journal, *The Delinquent*.

Excursions into the field of politics convinced him that he was temperamentally unfit to "play the game." Toward the end of his life he became aware of a talent which gave him, perhaps, as much pleasure as did his vocation, the writing of short stories. His products won immediate acceptance, and several found a place in anthologies of "best stories," among them "Alma Mater" and "The Get Away" (*O. Henry Memorial Award: Prize Stories of 1920* and *of 1921*).

[*Who's Who in America*, 1920–21; *N. Y. Times*, Feb. 25, 1922; E. R. Cass, in *The Seventy-Eighth Ann. Report of the Prison Asso. of N. Y. . . . 1922* (1923); H. S. Braucher, in *The Survey*, Mar. 4, 1922; *Lewisiana* (17 vols., 1887–1907), bk. XXIV; G. L. Davis, *Samuel Davis, of Oxford, Mass., and Joseph Davis, of Dudley, Mass., and Their Descendants* (1884).]

T. S.

LEWIS, SAMUEL (Mar. 17, 1799–July 28, 1854), first state superintendent of common schools in Ohio and one of the most influential of the founders of the free public school system of that state, was born in Falmouth, Mass., son of Samuel Lewis, a sea-captain, and of Abigail (Tolman) Lewis. Unlike his contemporary, Horace Mann, whose career presents many interesting parallels, he was almost entirely self-educated, having left school at the age of ten. In 1813 his family, impoverished by losses at sea, removed to the neighborhood of Cincinnati, where, after working as farm-laborer, mail-carrier, and surveyor's assistant, he achieved a local reputation as a skilled carpenter. His keen and active mind sought a more intellectual occupation, however; and in 1819 he turned to the study of law, supporting himself and aiding his parents meanwhile by working in the office of the clerk of the court of common pleas. Here his ability, his indefatigable industry, and his uprightness of character won for him the favor and support of some of the leading citizens of Cincinnati. In 1822 he was admitted to the bar, where his devotion to the interests of his clients, together with the above-mentioned qualities, contributed to his marked success. During the following year he married Charlotte Goforth, daughter of Dr. William Goforth [q.v.], a well-known physician of Cincinnati.

Ever a champion of the weak and oppressed, he early became an advocate of a public system of education which should be "free to all, rich and poor, on equal terms" (First Annual Report, 1838, p. 8). His first successful stroke on behalf of this cause was made in 1826 when he advised and induced his friend and client, William Woodward, to establish the endowment which, through the agency of the magnificently housed and equipped Woodward High School, has exercised a beneficent cultural influence upon thousands of the youth of Cincinnati, poor as well as rich. The same purpose led Lewis to take an active part in the proceedings of the College of Teachers, a body organized in 1831 to promote the interests of education. In 1837, largely in consequence of an agitation inaugurated by this organization, the Ohio legislature created the office of state superintendent of common schools and appointed Lewis as the first incumbent. Impressed by the opportunities for public service which the position seemed to offer, he devoted himself to its duties with characteristic zeal and loftiness of purpose. To acquaint himself with the educational situation he traveled over twelve hundred miles, largely on horseback, visiting some sixty-five counties and over three hundred schools. Nearly all the recommendations of his first annual report, including a state school fund of $200,000, authority for districts to borrow money for schoolhouses and for city boards to establish schools of higher grade, and provision for evening schools, were enacted into law Apr. 7, 1838. This legislation proved, however, to be in advance of the public

opinion of the time. Numerous memorials were presented urging its repeal and the abolition of the state superintendency. Lewis vigorously opposed this reactionary movement, but his health was already impaired by his strenuous labors, and in 1839 he resigned.

Soon after his return to private life he became actively interested in the anti-slavery movement. In 1841, in cooperation with Salmon P. Chase and others, he organized the Liberty Party, which nominated him for Congress in 1843 and 1848 and for the governorship in 1846, 1851, and 1853. His last campaign for the governorship greatly overtaxed his strength and helped to hasten his death, which occurred the following year.

[Biog. of Samuel Lewis (1857), by his son W. G. W. Lewis; J. W. Taylor, A Manual of the Ohio School System (1857); C. B. Galbreath, Samuel Lewis, Ohio's Militant Educator and Reformer (1904); First, Second, and Third Annual Report of the Supt. of Common Schools . . . of Ohio (1838–39); Am. Jour. of Educ., Dec. 1858, Mar. 1859, p. 85; Sept. 1868, p. 793.]

L. F. A.

LEWIS, TAYLER (Mar. 27, 1802–May 11, 1877), Orientalist, was born in the village of Northumberland, Saratoga County, N. Y. His father, Samuel Lewis, had been an officer in the Revolutionary War; his mother, Sarah Van Valkenburg, was of Dutch descent; and he was named after her uncle, John Tayler, former lieutenant-governor of the state. He went to school in Northumberland and at Fort Miller, where the associations seem to have made a deep impression upon him, for he used to go back to the school and later to the school site year after year. He was prepared for college by Dr. Proudfit at Salem, N. Y., and entered Union College in 1816, graduating in the class of 1820. He studied in the law office of Judge S. A. Foote at Albany, was admitted to the Saratoga bar in 1825, and began to practise at Fort Miller. Here he joined the Dutch Reformed Church, was chosen to the consistory, and took up the study of Hebrew.

Dissatisfied with the law, he began to teach, as principal of the academy at Waterford (1833–35), then at Ogdensburg (1833–37), and in 1838 at Waterford again. A Phi Beta Kappa oration, "Faith, the Life of Science," which he delivered at Union College in 1838, aroused a good deal of attention, and that year he was appointed professor of Greek in the University of the City of New York. He now wrote and studied much; and his Plato contra Atheos: Plato against the Atheists (1845), may still be read with interest by Grecians. In 1850 he became professor of Greek at Union College, and later professor of Oriental languages and Biblical literature. He was a hard student and mastered (besides Latin and Greek) Syriac, Koptic, Arabic, and Chaldaic, and read widely in mathematics, music, astronomy, and history. He was also deeply interested in current events at an exciting time in the national history. A strong anti-slavery man, he contributed to the propaganda of the Civil War *State Rights: a Photograph from the Ruins of Ancient Greece* (1864). The chief interest of his life, however, was the study of religion, and his main purpose was to show that revelation and scientific knowledge are not merely consistent but interdependent. Among his more important publications are *The Six Days of Creation* (1855), *The Bible and Science, or the World Problem* (1856), and *The Divine Human in the Scriptures* (1860). He was a representative American student and contributed to the American edition of J. P. Lange's *Commentary on the Holy Scriptures* (1865–80) and was on the American board of the Committee for the Revision of the Old Testament. In 1833 he married Jane Keziah, daughter of Daniel Payn, by whom he had six children. He was of slight and fragile figure, which contrasted strikingly with the vigor of his controversial energy and the power of his scholarship. His portraits present a severe countenance, but those who remember him think of a very fine and gentle expression and beautiful silver hair. His students had a great affection for him, though in later years they took advantage of his deafness to say dreadful things in his classroom or when they met him on the campus.

[*Gen. Cat. of the Officers, Grads. and Students of Union Coll., 1795–1868* (1868); E. N. Potter, *Discourses Commemorative of Prof. Tayler Lewis, LL.D., L.H.D. . . .* (1878); Wm. Wells, "Tayler Lewis: In Memoriam," *Meth. Quart. Rev.,* Oct. 1878; Homer Gage, "Tayler Lewis," *Union Alumni Mo.,* Apr. 1930; A. V. V. Raymond, *Union Univ.* (1907), vol. II; "Univ. of the State of N. Y. Ninety-First Ann. Report of the Regents," *Docs. of the Assembly of the State of N. Y.,* 1878, no. 58; R. B. Welch, in *House Ex. Doc. No. 1, Pt. 5,* 45 Cong., 2 Sess.; *New Eng. Jour. of Educ.,* June 7, 1877; *N. Y. Tribune,* May 14, 1877.]
E. E. H.

LEWIS, WILLIAM (Feb. 2, 1751 o.s.–Aug. 16, 1819), lawyer, of Quaker stock, the son of Josiah Lewis and his wife, who was probably Martha Allen, was born on his father's farm near Edgemont, Chester (now Delaware) County, Pa. He attended a country school near his home and afterwards entered a seminary established by the Society of Friends at Willistown, Pa., where he made rapid progress. Although from early boyhood he wished to become a lawyer and was supported in this ambition by his father, his mother did not give her consent to the plan until his seventeenth year. He was then placed in the Friends' Public School in Philadelphia to receive instruction in Latin. In 1770 he commenced the study of law under Nicholas Waln of West Chester and Philadelphia. He was admitted to the bar in November 1773 and again in 1776, after the adoption of the state constitution, and became one of the leading Quaker lawyers of Pennsylvania. He attracted especial attention by his success as counsel for the defense in many of the treason cases which arose in Philadelphia during the Revolution and afterward. One of the most famous treason cases with which he was connected was that of the Northampton Insurgents in 1799, when he was one of the counsel for John Fries [*q.v.*], a defendant. In this case his client was pronounced guilty and sentenced to death, but was later pardoned by President Adams (see Francis Wharton, *State Trials of the United States during the Administration of Washington and Adams,* 1849, pp. 458–648; and *The Two Trials of John Fries,* 1800).

He was elected a member of the Pennsylvania legislature in 1787 and again in 1789, when he was also chosen a member of the state constitutional convention. On Oct. 6, 1789, he was appointed attorney of the United States for the district of Pennsylvania and on July 20, 1791, accepted appointment as judge of the federal district court for the eastern district of Pennsylvania, in which capacity he served until Apr. 11, 1792. He then returned to his more lucrative private practice, which he continued until two years before his death. In February 1794 he was employed as counsel by the petitioners against the election of Albert Gallatin to the United States Senate. In this capacity he addressed that body in the Senate chamber, the first time professional counsel had spoken from the Senate floor. In politics he was a thorough Federalist and was frequently consulted on legal matters by government officials. He was much interested in the abolition of slavery within the state of Pennsylvania and is credited with having been instrumental in securing the passage of the act of Mar. 1, 1780, "for the gradual abolition of slavery in Pennsylvania." Learned in the law, clear and logical in argument, he was admitted to be one of the leading lawyers of his generation. He sometimes procrastinated in preparing his cases, and then made use of many ingenious devices for gaining time. His annoying habit of studying his case while it was in progress and introducing new points when he had the closing argument led the court to make a general rule prohibiting new points by concluding counsel (Binney, *post,* p. 43). He was twice married: first to Rosanna Lort by whom he had three children, and second to Frances Durdin. He died in Philadelphia after a short illness.

[Wm. Primrose, "Biography of William Lewis" (written 1820), *Pa. Mag. of Hist. and Biog.*, Apr. 1896; J. S. Futhey and Gilbert Cope, *Hist. of Chester County, Pa.* (1881); Horace Binney, *The Leaders of the Old Bar of Philadelphia* (1859), repr. in *Pa. Mag.*, Apr. 1890; E. P. Oberholtzer, *Phila., A Hist. of the City and Its People* (n.d.), vol. I; J. T. Scharf and Thompson Westcott, *Hist. of Phila.* (1884), II, 1527–28; J. H. Martin, *Martin's Bench and Bar of Phila.* (1883); *Poulson's Am. Daily Advertiser*, Aug. 17, 19, 1819.]
                                         J. H. F.

LEWIS, WILLIAM BERKELEY (1784– Nov. 12, 1866), planter, politician, was the son of John Lewis of Loudoun County, Va., whose wife was a Berkeley. At an early age he went to Nashville, Tenn., then a frontier village. The years of his youth are obscure, but his fortune was made when he eloped with the young daughter of William Terrell Lewis, a prominent planter and land speculator of the neighborhood. This marriage made him a brother-in-law of John H. Eaton [q.v.]. The bride, Margaret, and her husband were received into the home of James Jackson, a leading merchant of Nashville. The two Lewis families were not related by blood, nor was James Jackson related to Andrew Jackson, but the young couple was soon invited to "The Hermitage," where a life-long friendship between Lewis and the future President was cemented. The elder Lewis having died, his home, "Fairfield," near "The Hermitage," became the abode of the younger Lewises for the remainder of their lives.

During Jackson's Natchez campaign of 1812 and his Creek campaign of the next year, Lewis served as his quartermaster, and his efficient work during these trying times secured his place in the affections of the General. After the battle of New Orleans, Lewis was one of a small coterie of friends who recognized Jackson's availability for the presidency. The correspondence of 1816–17 between Jackson and Monroe, which later served a valuable political purpose, may not have been intended for such use, but it was Lewis who manipulated it and it was he who later capitalized it (Parton, *post*, II, 356–71), thus showing himself doubtless a man of keen foresight and consummate tact. When the time arrived, in 1821, for Jackson's presidential campaign to assume definite shape, it was Lewis, along with a few other Nashville friends, who busied himself in putting the cause before the people. His first wife having died, he had married Mrs. Adelaide Stokes Chambers, daughter of Gov. Montfort Stokes [q.v.] of North Carolina. The Monroe correspondence was now used to bring Stokes to Jackson's support. In such

ways did the subtle Lewis work. When, during the campaign of 1828, charges were made concerning the legality of Jackson's marriage, Lewis was assigned the congenial task of investigating and reporting on the matter. His version was that adopted by Jackson's biographer, Parton, and by posterity. Upon Jackson's elevation to the presidency, Lewis became second auditor of the treasury, a resident of the White House, and a member of the "Kitchen Cabinet." He took a leading part in trying to conciliate the warring factions during the Eaton controversy, and on many other occasions acted as the personal agent of the President. He had early allied himself with the Van Buren forces and worked consistently to promote the cause of the New Yorker. He disagreed with Jackson on the spoils system and the bank question, but he never put himself in opposition to the President, and the two remained firm friends to the end.

After Jackson's retirement, Lewis retained his post as auditor. Van Buren, however, showed little gratitude for the faithful services rendered in his behalf, and Lewis had no influence with the new administration. In 1845 he retired to his home near Nashville in time to attend at the bedside of the dying Jackson. For the remainder of his days he lived in comparative seclusion, emerging, however, to furnish Parton with information which put numerous incidents concerning Jackson in the most favorable light. During the Civil War his sympathies were with the Union. He died shortly after its close, and lies in an unmarked grave in Mount Olivet cemetery at Nashville.

[J. T. Moore and A. P. Foster, *Tennessee, The Volunteer State* (1923); James Parton, *Life of Andrew Jackson* (1885); J. S. Bassett, *The Life of Andrew Jackson* (1911); and *Correspondence of Andrew Jackson* (vols. I–V, 1926–31); W. T. Lewis, *Geneal. of the Lewis Family* (1893); M. S. Asher, "Major William B. Lewis, of Fairfield," clipping from Nashville *American*, 1905, in book of clippings in State Lib., Nashville; *Republican Banner* (Nashville), Nov. 13, 1866.]
                                         T. P. A.

LEWIS, WILLIAM DAVID (Sept. 22, 1792– Apr. 1, 1881), merchant, banker, was born at Christiana, New Castle County, Del., the son of Joel Lewis, who married a Miss Hughes. Both parents were Welsh Quakers. He attended Clermont Seminary and Lower Dublin Academy and at the age of seventeen was apprenticed to the house of Samuel Archer & Company, Philadelphia merchants in the East India and China trade. Four years later he was invited by his brother, John D. Lewis, who was a commission merchant in Russia, to join him at St. Petersburg. Unable to obtain passage because of the war between the United States and Great Britain, he called upon Henry Clay in Washington, procured an appointment as one of the private secretaries to the peace commission, and sailed from New York on the *John Adams* under a flag of truce (Feb. 27, 1814). At Gothenburg he left the commissioners and, continuing his journey, arrived at the Russian capital in the midst of the excitement aroused by the Allied triumphs over the Emperor Napoleon. He spent some months learning the Russian language, then entered his brother's employ, and lived in Russia until August 1824, during this period making two voyages to the United States for the house and a tour of western Europe. In Russia his genial personality and constant good humor won him many friends, including Count Nesselrode, the Tsar's Minister of Foreign Affairs, Platov, hetman of the Cossacks, the Nikolai Ivanovich Grech, editor of the *Syn Otechestva* (a weekly magazine), who introduced him into the literary group that met at the home of the poet Derzhavin. Much later, his metrical translation of Russian poems (*The Bokchesarian Fountain, by Alexander Pooshkeen, and other Poems by Various Authors,* privately printed, Philadelphia, 1849) was enthusiastically greeted by his friend Grech in the *Sievernaia Pchela* (St. Petersburg, July 18, 1851). In July 1817 Lewis was thrown into prison at the instance of John Leavitt Harris, United States consul at St. Petersburg, with whom he had a personal quarrel. He was soon released, and, returning to the United States in November 1819, was immediately challenged by Harris. Lewis promptly accepted and shot his opponent in the thigh when they met at Red Bank, on the Delaware. Shortly thereafter, Leavitt Harris, uncle of the duellist, who had also been consul at St. Petersburg, sued Lewis for slander, the latter having accused the elder Harris of corruption so gross that John Quincy Adams, secretary of state, characterized it as "unprincipled rapacity" (*Memoirs,* IV, 284). In St. Petersburg both parties sought documentary aid from the government of the Tsar, and after seven years of litigation, which involved Secretary Adams, President Monroe, and eminent legal counsel, a Philadelphia jury awarded Harris $100 (Feb. 15, 1827). On June 28, 1825, Lewis married Sarah Claypoole of Philadelphia and established himself as an importer and commission merchant in that city. He was for ten years cashier of the Girard Bank (1832–42) and helped finance a number of the early Pennsylvania railroads, including the New Castle & Frenchtown Railroad (1831–32), the Philadelphia, Germantown & Norristown Railroad, and the Philadelphia, Wilmington & Baltimore Rail-

road. He then became president of the Pennsylvania Academy of the Fine Arts, president of the Catawissa Railroad Company, and collector of customs for the Port of Philadelphia (1849–53). He was a life-long friend of Henry Clay, who procured confirmation by the Senate of his nomination to the collectorship in September 1850 after it had been blocked for months by Senator James Cooper of Pennsylvania. After he retired from business (about 1855) he lived on his estate near Florence, N. J., where he died in April 1881.

[Biog. memoirs of Lewis by J. W. Forney, in *Progress* (Phila.), Dec. 21, 1878, Apr. 9, 1881; *Memoirs of John Quincy Adams* (12 vols., 1874–77), ed. by C. F. Adams; *Writings of John Quincy Adams,* VI (1916), VII (1917), ed. by W. C. Ford; *Biog. Encyc. of Pa. of the Nineteenth Century* (1874); S. A. Allibone, *A Critical Dict. of Eng. Lit. and British and Am. Authors,* vol. II (1870); *The Charges against the Collector and Surveyor of the Port of Phila.; Reply of Chas. Gibbons to the Argument of David Paul Brown* (n.d.); W. D. Lewis, *A Brief Account of the Efforts of Senator Cooper of Pa. and Chas. Gibbons and their Associates* (1851); Rebecca I. Graff, *Geneal. of the Claypoole Family of Phila.* (1893); the *Press* (Phila.), *Phila. Inquirer,* and *Phila. Record,* all Apr. 2, 1881.]

F. E. R.

LEWIS, WILLIAM GASTON (Sept. 3, 1835–Jan. 7, 1901), soldier, engineer, was born at Rocky Mount, N. C., of Revolutionary stock, the son of Dr. John Wesley and Catharine Ann (Battle) Lewis, and the grandson of Exum and Ann (Harrison) Lewis. As a boy he attended Lovejoy's Military School at Raleigh and graduated from the University of North Carolina in the year 1855. Later he taught school at Chapel Hill, N. C., and in Jackson County, Fla. During 1857–58 he served as a government surveyor in Minnesota, and from 1858 to 1861 as assistant engineer on the Tarboro branch of the Wilmington & Weldon Railroad. The Civil War found him a member of the Edgecombe Guards, from which he received appointment as ensign and lieutenant in the newly organized 1st North Carolina Regiment, Apr. 21, 1861, and after creditable service in the battle of Big Bethel, he was promoted major of the 33rd North Carolina Infantry. For meritorious services at New Bern, he won additional promotion to lieutenant-colonel, 43rd North Carolina, and in June 1863 participated in Ewell's Shenandoah Valley campaign. He took part in the battle of Malvern Hill, and at Gettysburg received special commendation from his brigade commander. Subsequently he took part in the battles of Bristow Station, Mine Run, and in April 1864, in the capture of Plymouth, N. C. He was promoted to the colonelcy of his regiment, and at Drewry's Bluff, May 16, 1864, he received official praise from General Ransom for skilful construction of the outer works. For this he was promoted brigadier-general, June 2, 1864, as of May 31, 1864. As a brigade commander, Lewis was with Early in his engagements with Sheridan in the latter part of the year 1864, and in the battles around Petersburg (A. A. Humphreys, *The Virginia Campaign of '64 and '65*, 1883). He participated in the final retirement of the Confederate army westward, and at Farmville, Va., Apr. 7, 1865, was severely wounded and taken prisoner. It is of record that throughout the war, he took part in some thirty-seven battles and engagements (*Confederate Military History*, 1899, vol. IV, pp. 328–30).

After the close of the war, Lewis resumed practice as a civil engineer. He became agent of the state board for swamp lands, was state engineer for some thirteen years, was appointed chief engineer of the Albany & Raleigh Railroad in 1899, and was for an extended period chief of engineers of the North Carolina National Guard. He died suddenly of pneumonia at his home in Goldsboro, N. C., in his sixty-sixth year, and was survived by his widow, Martha E. (Pender) Lewis of Edgecombe County, N. C., to whom he had been married on Mar. 15, 1864. Two sons and four daughters also survived him. He was interred with military honors at Goldsboro.

[See Walter Clark, *Hist. of the Several Regiments and Battalions from N. C. in the Great War, 1861–'65* (1901); *Battles and Leaders of the Civil War* (4 vols., 1887–88); *War of the Rebellion: Official Records* (Army); *Alumni Hist. of the Univ. of N. C.* (ed. 1924); W. J. Battle, *The Battle Book* (1930); *Charlotte Daily Observer*, Jan. 9, 1901; *Confed. Veteran*, Jan. 1901. There is a valuable sketch of Lewis in the possession of his son, Jas. S. Lewis, Rocky Mount, N. C.]   C. D. R.

LEWIS, WINSLOW (May 11, 1770–May 19, 1850), sailor, lighthouse builder, was born in Wellfleet, Mass., the son of Winslow and Mary (Knowles) Lewis and a descendant of Kenelm Winslow, brother of Gov. Edward Winslow of the Plymouth Colony. He married Elizabeth Greenough, Nov. 7, 1793, and after her death in 1842, married Martha S. Hurlburt, Nov. 22, 1843. There were no children by the second wife, and of those by the first, only Dr. Winslow Lewis of Boston survived him or left descendants. He was "bred to the sea," and had attained the rank of captain and made several voyages as a commander before retiring to engage in business in Boston. He left the sea before 1810, and in the War of 1812 he commanded the Boston Sea Fencibles, a volunteer organization of seamen. He was captured by the British in this war, but it was while he was on his way to inspect a lighthouse, and he was soon released on parole. He was a member of the first Common Council of the City of Boston in 1822; an alderman of the same city in 1829, 1830, 1835, and 1836; and a member of the lower house of the Massachusetts legislature from 1828 to 1833. He was president of the Boston Marine Society, a semi-official organization of shipmasters, from 1818 to 1820; and he was a member and officer of the Ancient and Honorable Artillery Company.

His chief business was as a contractor and builder, though he also manufactured rope and cotton duck; but his nautical experience probably led him to specialize in designing and building lighthouses and providing equipment for them. On June 8, 1810, he obtained a patent for a "lantern, reflecting and magnifying" for illuminating lighthouses, and in 1811 it was installed in Boston Light for trial. It proved satisfactory, and Secretary Gallatin contracted with him to put his lamps and reflectors in all the United States lighthouses, then forty-nine in number, Lewis giving a bond for $60,000 to save half the previous consumption of oil. When this work was completed in 1815, he entered into another agreement to supply all lighthouses with the best sperm oil for seven years, and to visit each of them annually and report its condition, "in consideration being allowed one-half the oil consumed under the old plan." On its expiration, this contract was renewed for one-third of the oil. He also built about a hundred structures for the lighthouse service. Some of these, like the beacon on Romer Shoal, New York Harbor, have been replaced; but others, like the beacon on Bowditch's Ridge in Salem (Mass.) Harbor, still stand (1933). On June 24, 1808, he had received a patent for a binnacle light and on Jan. 23, 1818, received another patent for lamps. In his lifetime he was charged with both fraud and incompetence, but rivalry for government contracts or for professional prestige seems to have been responsible for the accusations. Prior to 1852, the United States Lighthouse Service was undoubtedly badly organized and poorly equipped, but Lewis seems to have done a great deal to make it more effective and economical.

[The chief sources of information, not all of which is accurate, are the following publications: *New-Eng. Hist. and Geneal. Reg.*, Jan. 1863; O. A. Roberts, *Hist. of the Mil. Company of the Massachusetts, now Called The Ancient and Honorable Artillery Company*, vol. II (1897); David Melville, *An Exposé of the Facts Respectfully Submitted to the Govt. and Citizens of the U. S. Relating to the Conduct of Winslow Lewis of Boston* (Providence, 1819), copies in Mass. State House Lib. and Boston Athenæum; Winslow Lewis, *Review of the Report of I. W. P. Lewis on the State of the Light Houses on the Coast of Me. and Mass.*

Sent to the House of Representatives by the Hon. Walter Forward, Secretary of the Treasury, Feb. 24,1842 (Boston, 1843), copy in Boston Athenæum; M. F. Willoughby, *Lighthouses of New England* (1929); Fitz-Henry Smith, Jr., *The Story of Boston Light* (1911); *A Digest of Patents . . .* (1840); *Boston Jour.*, May 20, 1850.]   S. G.

LEXOW, CLARENCE (Sept. 16, 1852–Dec. 30, 1910), lawyer and politician, was born in Brooklyn, N. Y., a son of Rudolph and Caroline (King) Lexow. His father was editor of the *Belletristisches Journal,* a German-language periodical published in New York. For his secondary schooling Clarence attended the German-American Collegiate Institute of Brooklyn and at sixteen went with a brother to Germany, where both boys spent several years in study at the universities of Bonn and Jena. The father had counted on his training as a preparation for journalism, but the sons were attracted to the law as a profession. Returning to New York, Clarence Lexow was graduated from Columbia University Law School in 1874. He was admitted to the bar and practised in the city until 1881, when he removed to Nyack, Rockland County, N. Y., largely for reasons of health. After a time he began to take a modest part in up-state politics and rapidly developed into an organization Republican in the period of Thomas C. Platt's dominance. After an unsuccessful attempt to obtain a seat in Congress, he was chosen a state senator in 1893.

During his first term, the revelations of police corruption in the City of New York made by the Rev. Dr. Charles H. Parkhurst [*q.v.*] led the Chamber of Commerce to ask the legislature for an investigation. The leaders of the Republican majority in that body acceded to the demand, less with the intention of reforming conditions than with the view of exposing Tammany Hall's control of the ballot-box. Lexow moved for the appointment of a Senate special committee and was named as chairman. The matter seems to have been to him only a tactical move in partisan politics, though it may be set down to his credit that in a period marked for political hypocrisy he made no hollow profession of loftier aims. He and his committee were quite unprepared to deal with the mass of evidence of police extortion and blackmail that was marshaled by John W. Goff [*q.v.*] as counsel. Lexow and his colleagues, however, in the words of Dr. Parkhurst (*post,* p. 144), "in time became disciplined to a receptive attitude of mind." Police captains broke down and confessed their guilt on the witness stand; scores of indictments and dismissals from the force followed; a city administration pledged to reform was elected. Throughout the investigation, Lexow took only a perfunctory part. A leader of vision, with a similar opportunity, might have headed a triumphant crusade for civic decency. Failing that, he might at least have secured for himself an independent position as a legislator. Lexow did neither the one thing nor the other. Although his name was long a reminder of one of the most dramatic episodes in New York municipal history, the man himself never rose above the confines of narrow partisanship. In his report as committee chairman the outstanding feature was a recommendation for a bi-partisan board of police commissioners. This suggestion was opposed by the enlightened public opinion of the city and was rejected in later legislation.

As head of the Senate committee on cities Lexow had charge of the Greater New York charter, enacted in 1897. His own account of that law, as it appears in *The Autobiography of Thomas Collier Platt* (1910), gives the major part of the credit for the measure to Platt. For two years Lexow had been recognized as one of the group of senators who could be depended on to block reform bills at Platt's behest (*New-York Tribune,* Apr. 3, 1895). He was the author of a report on trusts and unlawful combinations and in 1898 his service in the Senate ended. He was chairman of the New York Republican convention of 1895, and a presidential elector in 1900. The remainder of his life was devoted to his law practice. He was survived by his wife, Katherine M. Ferris, whom he had married Feb. 3, 1881, together with a son and two daughters.

[*Who's Who in America,* 1910–11; E. L. Murlin, *An Illustrated Legislative Manual: The N. Y. Red Book,* 1898; E. B. Andrews, *The U. S. in Our Own Time* (1903); J. D. Townsend, *N. Y. in Bondage* (1901); C. H. Parkhurst, *My Forty Years in N. Y.* (1923); obituaries in N. Y. papers, notably *The Sun,* Dec. 31, 1910.]   W. B. S.

LEYNER, JOHN GEORGE (Aug. 26, 1860–Aug. 5, 1920), inventor, manufacturer, the second white male child born in Colorado, was born on his father's ranch in Left Hand Creek Canyon, Boulder County. He was the eldest son of Peter A. Leyner, of German birth, and Maria A. Dock, of Dutch ancestry, who as bride and groom "went West" by ox-team from Des Moines, Iowa. His education was limited to that afforded by the public school in his district. Until he was nineteen years old he remained on his father's ranch, always more interested in machinery than in tilling the soil. After engaging for four years, 1879–83, in threshing grain for the farmers in his neighborhood and working for two more as engineer, first for a mining and milling company in Jackson, and then for a flour-milling company in Canfield, Colo., he established in 1886 a machine shop and foundry in Longmont, Colo. After a year or two, however, he sold this business and purchased an interest in a machine shop in Denver, of which he later acquired full ownership. The experience gained in repairing mining machinery here gave Leyner an insight into the mechanical needs of the mining industry and the opportunity to exercise his inventive talents. Accordingly he devised many improvements in the machinery then used, and in 1893 perfected a compressed air rock-drilling machine of the piston type in which the drilling steel is attached to and oscillates with the piston. In an endeavor to improve on this first machine he developed a means of supporting the drill loosely in the rock-drilling engine in position to be struck by a rapidly oscillating piston of light weight. After nine years of constant effort the new engine was perfected and patented June 13, 1899 (patent no. 626,761). It was far superior to any rock-drilling machine then made, for it not only increased by 100 per cent. the number of blows struck by the piston but also reduced the weight of the latter from sixty to sixteen pounds. Not content with this achievement, Leyner next devised the hollow drill, through which he forced air and water to the bottom of the drill hole to expel the rock cuttings while drilling. The resulting Water Leyner Rock Drill or "jackhammer," as it is popularly called, was adopted the world over, and in 1902, to supply the demand, Leyner organized the J. George Leyner Engineering Works Company and erected an extensive manufacturing plant at Littleton, Colo. Continuing his inventive work, he perfected, after seven years of effort, a drill-sharpening machine incorporating many radical improvements. He secured patent 917,777 for this invention, engaged in its manufacture, and was soon handling 80 per cent. of the drill-sharpening business of the world. He also made many novel improvements in the air compressor, for the most important of which he received patent no. 938,004, dated Oct. 26, 1909. All of his patented machines and other mining machinery were manufactured in his plant at Littleton until 1911, when he disposed of the entire establishment to the Ingersoll-Rand Company of New York. Instead of retiring, he began working in 1913 on a farm tractor of the caterpillar type. Receiving a patent for this device on Jan. 29, 1918, he organized a manufacturing company and had constructed two experimental machines when he was injured in an automobile accident and died, at Littleton. He was married twice: first, in 1883 to Fanny Bat-

terson; and after her death, to Lina M. Brooks, on June 3, 1912. His widow survived him.

[*Specifications and Drawings of Patents Issued from the U. S. Patent Office*, May, Nov. 1893, June–Sept. 1896, July 1897, May, Aug., Sept. 1898, June 1899, June 1900, Sept. 1902, Sept. 1903, Apr. 1904, Feb., Aug., Nov. 1905, Mar. 1906, Feb., Apr., Dec. 1907, July, Oct. 1908, Mar., May, Aug., Oct. 1909, May 1910, Aug. 1911, May 1912; *Official Gazette of the U. S. Patent Office*, Oct. 1, 1912, Apr. 8, June 17, Sept. 9, Nov. 11, Dec. 23, 1913, May 12, Aug. 4, 1914, Jan. 12, 1915, Jan. 29, 1918; W. B. Kaempffert, *A Popular Hist. of Am. Invention* (1924); *Rocky Mt. News* (Denver), Aug. 6, 1920; data furnished by Ingersoll-Rand Company, N. Y., and J. Ditson, Littleton, Colo.]
C. W. M.

LEYPOLDT, FREDERICK (Nov. 17, 1835–Mar. 31, 1884), publisher, bibliographer, was born in Stuttgart, Germany, the son of Michael Friedrich and Christiane Magdalene (Deihle) Leypoldt. He was originally named Jakob Friedrich Ferdinand, but after he came to America was known as Frederick Leypoldt. Of a literary inclination and reluctant to follow his father's trade, he left his native land in 1854, and eventually became a naturalized citizen of the United States. In New York he obtained employment in the foreign bookstore of F. W. Christern, who in 1859 helped him to establish in Philadelphia a bookstore dealing in books in all languages. This store, with its reading-room of foreign periodicals and its circulating library, became a literary center. While the Civil War prevented the importation of books, Leypoldt extended his interests to publishing. His initial venture, *The Ice-Maiden* by Hans Christian Andersen, translated by Fanny Fuller, appeared in 1863 and was followed by other publications, at first translations, later textbooks for the study of modern languages. He opened a branch office in New York in 1864, soon giving up the bookstore to concentrate his interest on the New York office. In 1865 Henry Holt [*q.v.*], afterward his lifelong friend, joined him in business; and in January 1866 the firm of Leypoldt & Holt was formed. It continued the policy of publishing translations and textbooks, of which Leypoldt wrote several under the anagram, L. Pylodet. On Sept. 27, 1867, he married Augusta Harriet Garrigue, who survived him thirty-five years.

In 1868 he relinquished the publishing side of the business and began his career as a bibliographer by taking charge of the firm's *Literary Bulletin, a Monthly Record of Current Literature*. This bulletin formed the beginning of a series of publications of varying titles which, after absorbing by purchase from George W. Childs [*q.v.*] the *American Literary Gazette and Publishers' Circular*, became, in January 1873, *The Publishers' Weekly*. Leypoldt was sole editor and publisher from 1871 until Jan. 5, 1879; Richard Rogers Bowker then became proprietor, but Leypoldt was again editor and publisher from July 5, 1879, until his death. Many features of the present *Publishers' Weekly* owe their origin to him. In 1880 he established the monthly *Literary News,* which, after his death, was edited by his widow until its cessation in 1904.

As early as 1862 he felt the lack of trade bibliographies, and in the *Publishers' Weekly* he endeavored to provide current lists. No annual catalogue had been published in America since 1856. In the issue of his *Literary Bulletin* for January 1869 appeared the forerunner of his effort to supply the lack. Beginning in 1870, he issued a series of three such annuals: *The American Catalogue of Books for 1869* (1870), *The Trade Circular Annual for 1871 including The American Catalogue of Books Published in the United States during 1870* (1871), and *The Annual American Catalogue, 1871* (1872), the last prefaced by the statement that the work was to be discontinued because of "great obstacles and discouragements." The following year (1873), however, *The Uniform Trade List Annual* anticipated in form by the appendix to his second annual catalogue, and by similar publications by Howard Challen, made its first appearance. It consisted of catalogues of 101 publishers bound in alphabetical order. This project for the book trade was so successful that the idea was adopted in other countries and the American publication, under the revised title, *The Publishers' Trade List Annual,* has continued without interruption.

Work on *The American Catalogue,* under consideration since 1872, the culmination of the series of book-trade aids designed by Leypoldt, was begun in 1876. The compilation of this list of books in print July 1, 1876, proved so costly an undertaking that Leypoldt was obliged to make a financial arrangement with A. C. Armstrong, under whose imprint the volumes were issued in 1880 and 1881. Leypoldt was one of the founders of the *Library Journal* in 1876, and its publisher until his death. When in June 1880 the *Journal,* then published at a loss, was about to discontinue, he personally assumed the responsibility for its continuance. He was interested in the founding of the American Library Association in 1876, and published several library aids for others, compiling and issuing *A Reading Diary of Modern Fiction* (1881) and, with Lynds E. Jones, *The Books of All Time* (1882). In 1879 he undertook the publication of the *Index Medicus,* which, though it brought

him a financial loss, proved so valuable that it was continued until the end of his life and afterward. In June 1927 it combined with the *Quarterly Cumulative Index* to form the *Quarterly Cumulative Index Medicus.* With his high ideals and scholarly standards Leypoldt made an important contribution to American bibliography. He died of cerebral fever in the spring of 1884.

[R. R. Bowker, "Frederick Leypoldt," *Publishers' Weekly,* Memorial Number, Apr. 5, 1884; A. Growoll, *Book-trade Bibliog. in the U. S. in the XIXth Century* (1898); R. R. Bowker, "Augusta H. Leypoldt, 1849–1919," *Publishers' Weekly,* June 14, 1919; *Am. Bookseller,* Apr. 15, 1884; S. S. Green, *The Public Library Movement in the U. S., 1853–1893* (1913); *N. Y. Tribune,* Apr. 1, 1884, *N. Y. Evening Post,* Mar. 31, 1884, *N. Y. Times,* Apr. 1 1884; personal communications from R. R. Bowker, Marian A. (Leypoldt) Osborne, Henry Holt & Company.]   A. S. P.

L'HALLE, CONSTANTIN de (d. June 6, 1706), Recollect priest, was an early chaplain at Detroit. He is said to have been of distinguished family, but nothing is known of his life before his arrival, June 1, 1696, in Canada. For the next five years he served as parish priest in several localities. IIe was for a time at Longueuil and in November 1701 signed the register at Batiscan. Meanwhile Antoine de la Mothe, Sieur Cadillac [*q.v.*], had founded under a grant from the King a new colony on the strait that lies between Lake Erie and Lake St. Clair. Cadillac, who had served some time previously as commandant at Mackinac, had a strong dislike for the Jesuit missionaries and chose that his new colony of Detroit should be served only by Recollects. At just what time Father Constantin became chaplain for the garrison is not definitely established, because the earliest records of the parish church of Ste. Anne, Detroit, were destroyed by fire; he is said to have accompanied Cadillac to Detroit in June 1701 but his signature on the register at Batiscan shows that he was in Canada in November of that year. The first entry on the Ste. Anne parish record is by Father Constantin, the baptism in 1703 of Cadillac's daughter. From then on the records of this mother church of the Northwest are extant.

Father Constantin is said to have promoted the interests of religion in the infant colony. Cadillac wrote that he was well satisfied with him (*Michigan Pioneer and Historical Collections,* vol. XXXIII, 1904, p. 150). Although his mission was for Europeans, he often ministered to the neighboring Indians, many of whom had been baptized by the Jesuits at Mackinac. In 1706, however, a revolt broke out among the Ottawa, led by the renegade known as Le Pesant. The Indians rushed through the town, found the missionary in his garden, seized and bound him. He was loosed by a friendly Indian, and sent towards the fort, but the rebels, seeing him escaping, shot and killed him. He was found to have received several knife and gunshot wounds. His body was buried beneath the church of Ste. Anne; it has been several times removed; the first time, in 1723, it was identified by the vestments. Although he was not a martyr in the strict sense of the word, Father Constantin's sad fate and untimely death have kept his memory alive. His handwriting in the earliest records of the parish shows him to have been a man of refinement and culture.

[See J. G. Shea, *Hist. of the Cath. Ch. in the U. S.*, vol. I (1886); *Mich. Pioneer and Hist. Colls.*, especially the volume mentioned above, containing the Cadillac papers; Silas Farmer, *The Hist. of Detroit and Mich.* (1884); *Am. Cath Hist. Researches*, vol. XIII (1896); A. C. Laut, *Cadillac* (1931). The form of Father Constantin's name given above is taken from a signature. Several secondary accounts give Nicolas Bénoit Constantin de L'Halle as his full name.]   L. P. K.

L'HALLE, NICOLAS BÉNOIT CONSTANTIN de [See L'HALLE, CONSTANTIN DE, d. 1706].

L'HOMMEDIEU, EZRA (Aug. 30, 1734–Sept. 27, 1811), lawyer, legislator, agriculturist, was born at Southold, Long Island, the son of Benjamin L'Hommedieu and his wife, Martha Bourne, daughter of Ezra Bourne of Sandwich, Mass. His grandfather, Benjamin L'Hommedieu, a French Huguenot (born at La Rochelle), came to America about 1686, settled at Southold in 1690, and died there in 1748 at the age of ninety-two. Graduating from Yale in 1754, Ezra studied law and was admitted to the bar, but he appears to have occupied himself chiefly in administering his own affairs. In 1765 he married Charity Floyd, sister of William Floyd [q.v.] and of the wife of Gen. Nathaniel Woodhull [q.v.]. It has been said that in politics he consistently furthered Floyd's interests in preference to his own.

From 1775 until his death L'Hommedieu was continuously in public service, his local, state, and national services often overlapping, since there was no "self-denying ordinance" to forbid. He was a member of all the New York provincial congresses, and accordingly was one of the framers of the constitution of 1777, then a member of the Assembly until 1783, and thereafter until 1809 (excepting the year 1792–93) of the state Senate. Twice (1784, 1799) he served on that curious New York body, the council of appointment, and again in the interpretative constitutional convention of 1801. Meanwhile he had been sent for four successive terms (1779–

83) as a delegate to the Continental Congress, and once more in 1788. In January 1784 he became clerk of Suffolk County, an office which he held, except for one year (March 1810–March 1811), for the remainder of his life.

As a legislator, whether in the Assembly or Senate of his state or in Congress, his career is marked by an active though unobtrusive participation in proceedings, particularly in the important labors of committees, whose reports he often drew. In Congress, whilst closely cooperating with his colleagues in all matters affecting his own state, as was customary in the New York delegation, on other questions he showed an independent mind, not always following the lead of his persuasive colleague, Duane, or of that other dominating character, Robert R. Livingston. Faithful to his instructions, he nevertheless did not hesitate to point out to his own government what he conceived to be errors of counsel. His letters to Governor Clinton are a valuable source of information upon proceedings in Congress. As in Congress he consistently supported measures looking toward governmental efficiency, so in the Constitutional period he was a Federalist.

L'Hommedieu's chief title to fame is as the principal author of the University of the State of New York as reconstituted in 1787. Tradition has ascribed the fatherhood of the institution to Hamilton, but legislative records seem to show conclusively that it was the measure fathered by L'Hommedieu, leader of the "country party," rather than that proposed by Hamilton, sponsor for the Columbia College group, that constitutes the foundation of the university, although the Hamiltonian party eventually succeeded in effecting important modifications of L'Hommedieu's plan. He was a regent of the university from its first establishment in 1784 until his death. In his later years he interested himself largely in agricultural experiments and wrote numerous papers upon agricultural subjects for the Transactions of the New York Society for the Promotion of Agriculture, Arts, and Manufactures, of which he was for a number of years vice-president. His wife having died in 1785, in 1803 he married Mary Catharine, daughter of Nicoll Havens of Shelter Island. His death occurred at the family seat at Southold, and his monument stands near the Founders' Monument in the Presbyterian cemetery.

[Consult C. B. Moore, "Biography of Ezra L'Hommedieu," *N. Y. Geneal. and Biog. Record*, Jan. 1871; E. Whitaker, "The Founders of Southold," *Ibid.*, July 1895; "Salmon Records," *Ibid.*, Oct. 1916–July 1918; B. F. Thompson, *Hist. of L. I.* (1839); E. Whitaker,

History of Southold, L. I. (1881); R. H. Gabriel, *The Evolution of L. I.* (1921); *Southold Town Records*, vol. II (1884); C. Z. Lincoln, *The Constitutional Hist. of N. Y.* (1906), vol. I; Sidney Sherwood, "University of the State of N. Y.: Origin, History, and Present Organization," *Regents' Bull.*, no. 11 (1893), reprinted in U. S. Bureau of Educ., *Circular of Information*, no. 3 (1900); *Pub. Papers of Geo. Clinton* (10 vols., 1899–1914); *Journals of the Provincial Cong. . . . of N. Y.* (2 vols., 1842); *Journals of the Continental Cong.*; and F. B. Dexter, *Biog. Sketches of the Grads. of Yale Coll.*, vol. II (1896). The date of L'Hommedieu's death, given in this sketch, is taken from his tombstone.]   E. C. B.

LIBBEY, EDWARD DRUMMOND (Apr. 17, 1854–Nov. 13, 1925), glass-manufacturer, philanthropist, patron of art, was born at Chelsea, Mass., the son of William L. and Julia (Miller) Libbey. He received his education in Boston and later attended lectures at Boston University. In 1874 he entered the factory of the New England Glass Company, East Cambridge, Mass., of which his father was general manager, and worked in all branches of it to learn every detail in the manufacture and marketing of glass. In 1883, upon the death of his father, who had bought the business some years before, he became sole proprietor. In 1886, a strike by the workmen for higher wages, which conditions could not justify, made it necessary to close the plant permanently.

Libbey then went to Toledo, Ohio, attracted by the ample supply of natural gas and good glass sand, and in 1888 began operations there under the name of the Libbey Glass Company. In 1893 he erected a building at the World's Columbian Exposition, Chicago, in which he operated a demonstration glass plant throughout the period of the fair. Becoming interested in the development of automatic machinery for the manufacture of table tumblers, the invention of Michael J. Owens [*q.v.*], he organized the Toledo Glass Company (1894) and in the plant which was constructed for it carried on the manufacture of table tumblers until 1899, when the plant was acquired by the American Lamp Chimney Company of which Libbey was president. This company was soon consolidated with the Macbeth-Evans Glass Company of Pittsburgh, Pa., and the Toledo plant operated as a branch factory.

In 1899 Owens developed a machine for blowing bottles, perhaps the most revolutionary contribution to the glass industry since the invention of the blowing iron. In 1903, the machine having been perfected, Libbey organized and became president of the Owens Bottle Machine Company (reorganized in 1919 as the Owens Bottle Company), which took an exclusive license from the Toledo Glass Company for the manufacture in the United States of the bottle machine and all kinds of bottles. The Owens European Bottle Machine Company was organized in 1905. In 1912 Libbey purchased for the Toledo Glass Company the Colburn patents for the manufacture of sheet glass, and after the process had been further developed by Owens and the original inventor, he organized and became president in 1916 of the Libbey-Owens Sheet Glass Company, which purchased these patents and embarked upon the manufacture of sheet and plate glass, at Charleston, W. Va.

Libbey was intensely interested in civic, philanthropic, and educational work. He served on the Toledo board of education and, as its president, began a notable building program. For many years he supplied scholarships through which the teachers of the public schools could continue their higher education, and by his will provided for the perpetual maintenance of a scholarship fund. He was also a member of the City Plan Commission. In company with other citizens, he organized, in 1901, the Toledo Museum of Art, of which he was president until his death. In his first annual report, 1902, he advocated a policy of education as well as conservation, foreseeing for the institution a future in which it should take its place as an educational factor along with the public schools, colleges, and universities. He made possible the erection of the first unit of the museum building, opened in 1912, and later gave an addition, dedicated in 1926, which more than doubled its size. He made frequent trips abroad and with his wife Florence (Scott) Libbey, whom he had married in 1890, formed a collection of paintings, including work of Holbein, Hals, Rembrandt, Velasquez, De Hoog, Van Cleef, Reynolds, Gainsborough, and Raeburn, which he gave to the Toledo Museum. He also presented to the Museum a collection of Egyptian antiquities and a unique collection of glass, and by bequest left it the bulk of his estate, providing funds for additions to its building, for the maintenance and operation of the Museum and its educational program, and for the acquisition of works of art for its permanent collections. In 1922, in recognition of his services to industry, commerce, and art, King Albert conferred upon him the Belgian Order of the Crown with the rank of Commander.

[Harvey Scribner, *Memoirs of Lucas County and the City of Toledo* (1910), vol. II; J. M. Killits, *Toledo and Lucas County, Ohio* (1923), vol. III and supp., *Hist. of Toledo* (1923); N. O. Winter, *A Hist. of Northwest Ohio* (1917), vol. III; *Who's Who in America*, 1924–25; T. F. MacManus, *A Century of Glass Manufacture* (1918), published by Libbey Glass Company; *System*, June 1919; A. E. Fowle, *Flat Glass*

(1924); *The Glass Container*, Dec. 1925; *Museum News* (Toledo), Mar. 1926; Libbey's will; newspaper articles, Nov. and Dec. 1925, esp. *Toledo News Bee*, Nov. 13–15, 17, 20, 1925, and *The Sun* (N. Y.), Nov. 18, 1925, editorial.]　　　　　　　　　B–M. G.

LICK, JAMES (Aug. 21, 1796–Oct. 1, 1876), philanthropist, born of German ancestry in Fredericksburg, Lebanon County, Pa., was the eldest son of John and Sarah (Long) Lick. His grandfather, William Lick (Lük), had served as a soldier in the war of the Revolution, and at the time of his death in 1819 had reached the age of 104. Shortly before this event, possibly as early as the autumn of 1817, the grandson, after snatches of an elementary education and a short apprenticeship as a carpenter and joiner, went to Baltimore, where for a year or more he worked as a piano-maker in the employ of Joseph Hiskey. In 1820 he went to South America, and lived there for seventeen years, first in Buenos Aires, later in Valparaiso and Lima. He came back to the United States once, probably in 1832, and considered for a time remaining in Philadelphia or New York. He seems to have been engaged in piano and organ making during these years, but apparently had other interests and derived a very considerable income from them, for when he arrived in San Francisco, Cal., on the eve of the discovery of gold, he brought with him a large sum of money, which in later years was estimated at $30,000. He commenced at once the purchase of real estate in San Francisco, the greatest amount of his acquisitions being made in the year 1848. His property came to include large holdings in the Santa Clara Valley, smaller amounts on the shores of Lake Tahoe, in Virginia City, Nev., and on the "Isla de Santa Catalina," off the coast of southern California. Near San José he built a flour mill at great cost. In this venture and in others he revealed extreme eccentricity in his choice of materials, in his treatment of workmen, and in the objects of his interest. In San Francisco at the corner of Montgomery and Sutter streets he built a hotel which bore his name. Here he spent his later years.

As his fortune grew he seems to have given more and more thought to its disposal. In 1874 he prepared an elaborate deed in trust, naming a board of seven trustees who were to carry out his plans. The program was changed a year later and again shortly before his death. The chief beneficiaries were to be the Society of California Pioneers, of which he was president at the time, and the California Academy of Sciences, but the bequest which came to be of greatest significance was that providing $700,000 for "a powerful telescope, superior to and more powerful than any telescope ever yet made." It is not definitely known just when Lick fixed upon this idea. It is clear that it was modified by others before it took final form. He left more than a third of a million dollars to various charities in San Francisco and San José. Not a religious man, and for a time actively interested in the memory of Thomas Paine, he had at one time elaborate plans for perpetuating in this world the name of his family and his own name in particular. These took the form of monuments to be erected in San Francisco. In the final deed of trust, $20,000 was set aside for the monument and commemorative tablets at his birthplace. This sum and $150,000 left to John H. Lick (born to Barbara Snavely, in Fredericksburg, in 1818), whom he had recognized as his son, together with some small bequests, were all that he reserved for his family from a fortune well above three million. He never married.

On the occasion of his funeral in San Francisco the editor of the *Daily Evening Bulletin* wrote: "So long as San Francisco and the state of California shall endure the name of James Lick will be associated with them" (*Bulletin*, Oct. 2, 1876). Horatio Stebbins [*q.v.*], who preached the funeral sermon, summed up the life of this "man of property" as "without romantic incident or exploit," and anticipated the biographer in saying that his benefactions would "encircle the name of our citizen with a quiet, steady lustre of beneficence" (*Ibid.*, Oct. 4, 1876). The Lick Observatory, built upon Mount Hamilton, Santa Clara County (thirteen miles east of San José), was completed and placed in the hands of the regents of the University of California in June 1888. Eighteen months earlier, on Jan. 9, 1887, the body of James Lick had been brought from the Masonic cemetery in San Francisco and placed in the pier which now supports the great telescope.

[Sources include: *Cal. Mail Bag* (San Francisco), Aug. 1874; *Daily Evening Bulletin* (San Francisco), Oct. 2, 3, 4, 1876; S. C. Upham, *Notes of a Voyage to Cal. via Cape Horn, together with Scenes in El Dorado in the Years 1849–50* (1878); E. T. Sawyer, *Hist. of Santa Clara County, Cal.* (1922); H. S. Foote, *Pen Pictures from the Garden of the World or Santa Clara County, Cal.* (1888); E. S. Holden, *A Brief Account of the Lick Observatory* (1894); *Quart. of the Soc. of Cal. Pioneers*, June 30, 1924. The director of the Lick Observatory gives date of birth as Aug. 25; the date here given was obtained from the baptismal records of St. John's Lutheran Church, Fredericksburg, Lebanon County, Pa., through the aid of a "half-nephew" of James Lick.]　　　　　　　　　　　　　E. E. R.

LIEB, JOHN WILLIAM (Feb. 12, 1860–Nov. 1, 1929), mechanical engineer, son of John William and Christina (Zens) Lieb, was born in Newark, N. J. His father, a native of Württemberg, Germany, had emigrated to the United States in 1846, and was an especially skilled mechanical craftsman and inventor. At the age of sixteen, after attending Newark Academy and Stevens High School, Hoboken, young Lieb entered Stevens Institute of Technology, from which he graduated with the degree of M.E. in 1880. For six months after leaving the Institute, he worked as a draftsman for the Brush Electric Company, Cleveland, Ohio; then, in January 1881, he obtained similar employment in the engineering department of the newly organized Edison Electric Light Company in New York. Here he assisted in making plans for the dynamos and other electrical equipment of a proposed central electric lighting plant; but, before the year closed, he was transferred to the Edison Machine Works in New York, where the equipment was being prepared, to assist Thomas A. Edison in the experimental researches involved. No central lighting plants existed at that time, so that the work of Edison and Lieb was of a pioneering character. When the plant, called the Pearl Street Station, was put into regular operation in New York on Sept. 4, 1882, under the auspices of the Edison Electric Illuminating Company, Lieb was made electrician in charge. Two months later he was selected by Edison to go to Milan, Italy, as his representative in connection with the design, installation, and operation of the Edison underground electrical system for the Italian Edison Company. Lieb remained in Italy for the succeeding twelve years: serving, first, as chief electrician of the Milan Edison Station; then, as chief engineer; and finally, as other electrical stations were erected and the activities of the Italian Edison Company expanded, as manager and technical director, not only of the power plants, but also of the manufacture of incandescent lamps, dynamos, and other electrical equipment. The Milan station began regular service early in 1883, and was, at that time, the largest and most successful electric light and power station in Europe. Under Lieb's direction some of the earliest experiments were undertaken at Milan, in the parallel operation of large direct-driven alternators, in the operation of large synchronous motors, and in the long-distance transmission of high-tension alternating current by underground cables. In 1893, he installed, also, an electric trolley car system in Milan, which was one of the earliest in Italy. Returning to the United States in 1894, he was made assistant to the vice-president of the Edison Electric Illuminating Company. Later he was made vice-president and general manager, serv-

ing in this capacity until the company's reorganization as the New York Edison Company in 1901. Subsequently, he became successively associate general manager, vice-president and general manager, and finally, senior vice-president, which position he held at the time of his death. In this last capacity he was in general charge of the installation and operation of the company's power plants and of the transmission systems, and directed all research and development work. He served in a like capacity for all of the affiliated electric companies in the metropolitan area. From 1900 until his death he was president of the Electrical Testing Laboratories in New York, which organization, through his influence and direction, made many important contributions in the electrical field. He was a member and officer of many technical and scientific societies both in the United States and Europe, a lecturer on engineering, industrial, and economic subjects in many of the leading universities and technical schools of the United States, and a contributor to the transactions of professional and learned societies. His work was recognized the world over and he was signally honored both at home and abroad, being made a Grand Officer of the Royal Society of the Crown of Italy, an *ufficiale* of the order of St. Maurizio e Lazzaro, and an officer of the Legion of Honor. The American Institute of Electrical Engineers in 1924 awarded him the Edison Medal for his work in connection with "the development and operation of electric central stations for illumination and power." During the World War he was chairman of the National Committee on Gas and Electric Service; adviser to the Federal, New York State, and New York City Fuel Administrations; and chairman of the Joint Fuel Committee of the National Public Utility Association.

As a recreation, he engaged for many years in a critical study of the manuscripts of Leonardo da Vinci, investigating and translating sketches and texts covering his researches and observations, particularly in natural science and engineering. He possessed one of the largest libraries of Vinciana in existence, was a corresponding member of the Raccolta Vinciana of Milan, Italy, and published "Leonardo da Vinci —Natural Philosopher and Engineer" (*Journal of the Franklin Institute*, June, July 1921). On July 29, 1886, he married Minnie F. Engler of New York City, who with two daughters and a son survived him at the time of his death in New York.

[*Jour. Am. Inst. of Electrical Engineers*, Dec. 1929; F. D. Furman, *Morton Memorial: A Hist. of the*

Stevens Institute of Technology (1905); *Who's Who in America*, 1928–29; obituary sketch printed and circulated by the Edison Pioneers; *Trans. Am. Soc. Civil Engineers*, vol. XCIV (1930); *Mechanical Engineering*, Dec. 1929; *Electrical World*, Nov. 9, 1929; *N. Y. Times*, Nov. 2, 1929.]
                                  C. W. M.

LIEBER, FRANCIS (Mar. 18, 1800–Oct. 2, 1872), political scientist, educator, was born in Berlin, Germany, the tenth child of Friedrich Wilhelm Lieber in a family of nine sons and three daughters. His boyhood was spent amid the turmoils of the Napoleonic conquest when family and friends were charged with patriotic emotions. His elder brothers enlisted in the war of 1813, but Francis had to wait impatiently till 1815 upon the return of the emperor from Elba. With two brothers he joined the army under Blücher and fought through the campaign of Waterloo, receiving at the battle of Namur wounds which nearly cost him his life. As a schoolboy he was somewhat wayward and inattentive to formal instruction, but possessed of an ardent desire to become famous in some way.

About 1811 he had come under the influence of Friedrich Ludwig Jahn, the great German teacher and founder of societies for the cultivation of gymnastics and patriotism, and for eight years as pupil and companion was closely associated with him in awakening the youth of the Fatherland. After Waterloo Lieber resumed his studies, but the governmental reaction which ensued had a serious effect upon the young men who followed the teachings of Jahn. In 1819 he was arrested as a dangerous character and when released after four months was forbidden to study at any university except Jena, a decree which ended any hope of advancement in his native province. At Jena he received the degree of Ph.D. in 1820, but was immediately ordered away and spent the following year in the study of surveying at Halle and Dresden. Just then the war of liberation in Greece broke out and roused the enthusiasm of the oppressed German liberals. Lieber at once enlisted and, making his way with difficulty to Marseilles, sailed for Greece in January 1822, with a mixed crowd of foreign recruits. The experiences of these enthusiasts were bitter. Refused food and shelter, robbed by bandits, and finding only cowardice and incapacity among the supposed Greek patriots, they were soon disillusioned and Lieber with much difficulty made his way back to Italy. Eventually he reached Rome and in his ragged and penniless condition approached the German ambassador, Niebuhr. His intelligence as well as his misfortunes made such an impression that he was taken in as a tutor to the ambassador's son and for a year enjoyed the society and the inspiration of the great historian of Rome while in the midst of the art and antiquities of the ancient capital. At Niebuhr's suggestion he wrote his first book, *Tagebuch Meines Aufenthaltes in Griechenland* (Leipzig, 1823), which was published also in Dutch as *De Duitsche Anacharsis* (1823). In his *Reminiscences of an Intercourse with Mr. Niebuhr the Historian* (1835), Lieber refers to this period as the most instructive of his life. Following Niebuhr's resignation, Lieber returned to Berlin in the summer of 1823 and sought a revocation of the order which prevented him from study or preferment in Prussia. After much difficulty this was obtained with a small subsidy now needed because his father, an iron merchant, had lost his fortune and could no longer assist. He pursued mathematics at Berlin and Halle until August 1824, when the government in its fear of liberal conspiracies arrested a group of young men, including Lieber, and placed them in prison in Köpenick. Detained ostensibly only as a witness, he was threatened by the police with life imprisonment because he would neither give evidence nor confess, but after six months he was released on the petition of Niebuhr and returned to Berlin to find livelihood difficult. A request for a government position, even with Niebuhr's recommendation, came to nought, and Lieber in 1826 made his way secretly to England.

A year of uncertainty occupied with teaching languages, writing for German periodicals, and less congenial tasks, ended with a call to Boston, Mass., where he landed in June 1827, to take charge of a gymnasium and swimming school. Here he acquired influential friends and continued literary work, though with meager returns, until he hit upon a plan for an encyclopædia modeled after Brockhaus' *Conversations Lexikon*. This was the foundation of the *Encyclopædia Americana* (13 vols., 1829–33), and the work found immediate acceptance. Many distinguished Americans contributed to its pages and Lieber made acquaintances which were mutually helpful throughout his career. He married upon her arrival in New York Sept. 21, 1829, Matilda Oppenheimer, to whom he had been a tutor in England, and returned with her to Boston. To facilitate his literary work he moved to Philadelphia in 1834 and among other activities prepared the elaborate constitution and regulations of Girard College (*A Constitution and Plan of Education for Girard College . . . with an Introductory Report*, 1834). His growing reputation led to his election in 1835 to the chair of history and political economy in South Carolina College (now University of South

Carolina). In the latter subject he was the successor of Thomas Cooper [*q.v.*]. Remaining there twenty-one years, he gained a great reputation as a teacher but had difficulties as a disciplinarian and was viewed with some suspicion because of his sympathy for the abolitionists, though he owned slaves while in the state. His resignation was thought to have been due to his disappointment at his failure to be elected president in 1855. (E. L. Green, *A History of the University of South Carolina*, 1916, pp. 60–61).

Although he complained of the distance from his former friends and regarded himself as an exile, this period was decidedly fruitful, for in the course of it Lieber produced the works which eventually made him famous. These were his *Manual of Political Ethics* (2 vols., 1838–39), *Legal and Political Hermeneutics* (1839), and *On Civil Liberty and Self-Government* (2 vols., 1853). Numerous shorter essays and a wide correspondence with public men on both sides of the Atlantic contributed further to a marked influence upon American thought. The object of his *Political Ethics* is indicated by a sub-title which he once proposed, namely, "the Citizen considered with regard to his Moral Obligations arising from his Participation in Government" (Perry, *post*, p. 106), and the solution lay in the repeated injunction "no right without its duties, no duty without its rights" (*Ibid.*, p. 416). The work is a theory of the State, but includes many practical topics of extra-constitutional character, such as public opinion, parties, obligation to vote, influence in voting, friendship in politics, newspaper publicity, and the respective duties of representatives, judges, advocates, and officeholders. He reversed the usual order by discussing the natural rights of man, not as a creature in a primitive state, but in his present highly civilized condition. Viewing the State as founded upon the relation of right he coined the term "a jural society" (*Manual of Political Ethics*, p. 171), a condition not based on contract, but aboriginal with man. Sovereignty to him is an attribute of society expressed through public opinion, law, and power, definitions which Lieber claimed to be the first to employ. In general his system endeavors to reconcile the differences between the philosophical idealists and the historical school which taught that whatever is is right. His many personal experiences with governments came to the assistance of his learning. The *Hermeneutics* was intended as a chapter of his *Political Ethics,* but became so extended that it was published separately. His distinction between interpretation and construction had great influence among legal writers of his day. The first is "the art of finding out the true sense of any form of words" (*Legal and Political Hermeneutics,* p. 23) in the sense which the author intended to convey, while construction is the drawing of conclusions respecting subjects that lie outside the direct expression of the text. Constitutions should be construed closely, he holds, since their words have been carefully weighed. The treatise received high commendation from Chancellor Kent, Henry Clay, Rufus Choate, and others. *On Civil Liberty and Self-Government* is the best known of Lieber's works, as it was widely read and adopted as a college textbook. He discusses historically the various elements of freedom in their relation to law and government and defines liberty as the protection or check against undue interference, either from individuals, from masses, or from government. His treatment of Anglican liberty was new, dealing with the elements and actual amount of guaranteed freedom rather than the terms of the constitution. Originality lay also in his valuation of social institutions as invincible protectors of political liberty. In these volumes Lieber presented the first systematic works on political science that appeared in America. Political writing had been voluminous, but the contents had been confined to concrete legal or political controversy with no complete philosophy of the State. Later writers have observed that he falls into some confusion of state with government, and that his learned but diffuse illustrations obscure his argument, but he retains credit as a notable pioneer with wide influence in more than one generation. Along with theoretical studies Lieber maintained a lifelong interest in the special field of penal law. In 1833 he translated with notes Beaumont and De Tocqueville, *On the Penitentiary System in the United States.* His own views were published in 1838 in *A Popular Essay on Subjects of Penal Law,* containing forty-one rules based on the fundamental principles of "mild laws, firm judges, calm punishments" (*Miscellaneous Writings,* II, 471). In 1848 he prepared a report later published as a document by the legislature of New York and reprinted by him as "Abuse of the Pardoning Power," as an appendix to *On Civil Liberty.* Some of his suggestions for reform were embodied in later state constitutions.

In 1857 he was appointed to a chair in Columbia College, New York, from which he was transferred in 1865 to the law school, where he remained for the rest of his life. His personal characteristics doubtless contributed to his reputation and influence. He was of medium stature with refined features, somewhat stout in body, but muscular and abounding in energy, and his physical vigor permitted him to work long hours at his desk. His cheerful disposition, ready conversational powers and sprightly wit, coupled with extensive learning, made him a delightful companion to young or old. Possessed of deep religious sentiment he worshipped as a liberal Episcopalian, though with dislike for the then new theories of Darwin. At Columbia he became more than ever a prominent figure among political philosophers and extended his attention into international relations. After the outbreak of the Civil War he was much consulted by the Union government. Among other papers and opinions he wrote *Guerrilla Parties Considered with Reference to the Laws and Usages of War* (1862), and *A Code for the Government of Armies* (1863), which was issued by the War Department in revised form as *Instructions for the Government of Armies in the Field, General Orders No. 100.* No work of this kind was in existence at that time in any language. It was accepted as standard by writers on military law, was adopted by Germany in the conflict of 1870, and has continued to be the basis of international understanding on the conduct of war. Lieber was also the first to propose an unofficial congress of political savants to codify the existing rules of international law, a project recognized soon after his death by the founders of the Institut de Droit International. The public services of his later life included a government appointment as keeper of the Confederate records captured during the war, and another in 1870 as umpire to the Mexican Claims Commission. With this last he was occupied at the time of his death.

The children of Francis and Matilda Lieber included a daughter who died in infancy and three sons: Oscar Montgomery, who became a prominent geologist in the South and died of wounds received while in the Confederate army; Hamilton, who volunteered in the Union army, lost an arm at Fort Donelson, and subsequently filled various military positions; Guido Norman, who fought in the Federal infantry and eventually became judge advocate-general of the United States.

[The most important sources of information are: T. S. Perry, ed., *The Life and Letters of Francis Lieber* (1882); Lewis R. Harley, *Francis Lieber: His Life and Pol. Philosophy* (1899); Daniel C. Gilman, ed., *Reminiscences, Addresses, and Essays by Francis Lieber ... Being Vol I of His Miscellaneous Writings; Contributions to Pol. Science, ... by Francis Lieber ... Being Vol. II of His Miscellaneous Writings* (1881), the latter containing a bibliography; Elihu Root, "Francis Lieber," *Am. Jour. of International Law*, July 1913, giving an estimate of Lieber's contributions to inter-national law, which may be compared with a similar tribute by Bluntschli in *Miscellaneous Writings*, vol. II; C. S. Phinney, *Francis Lieber's Influence on American Thought and Some of His Unpublished Letters* (1918). At the Johns Hopkins University a collection of his manuscripts consisting of lectures, annotated copies of his works, legal opinions, is displayed with similar relics of his colleagues Bluntschli and Laboulaye in memory of their "international cloverleaf." For an account of this, see *Bluntschli, Lieber, and Laboulaye* (privately printed, 1884). In the Huntington Library, San Marino, Cal., a large body of MSS. includes his diaries, many letters from prominent men, and material connected with the *Encyclopædia Americana.*]

J. M. V.

LIEBLING, EMIL (Apr. 12, 1851–Jan. 20, 1914), pianist, teacher, and composer, the second son of Jacob and Henriette (Mosler) Liebling, was born in Pless, Germany. His brothers Max, Saul, and Georg also became well-known musicians. Their father was a church singer and he gave all of his children their first musical training. Emil emigrated to America in 1867 at the age of sixteen and taught first in and about Covington, Ky., and later in Cincinnati, Ohio. He was fond of relating his early experiences in Kentucky, where, after buying a saddle-horse, he rode horseback across the country, stopping at every house in which he heard a piano or learned of there being one. After introducing himself as a pianist, he would offer to play and he generally emerged with one or more pupils to add to his growing class. In 1872 he settled in Chicago as a private teacher but soon returned to Germany to study. He first went to Berlin where he was a student of Kullak and Ehrlich in piano and of Dorn in composition. From Berlin he went to Vienna to study piano with Dachs, and finally he became a student of Liszt at Weimar. During his entire stay abroad, he taught part of the time, first in the Kullak Conservatory at Berlin, later in Vienna and Weimar, evidently earning his own way.

He did not confine his study to music but acquired a large literary knowledge and became a proficient linguist. During his sojourn in Europe he enjoyed the friendship of Sherwood, Von Sternberg, and Moszkowski, the first two of whom later became prominent in America. He returned to America in 1876 and immediately won recognition as a pianist and composer. While he was considered an especially fine Bach player, he was equally brilliant as an interpreter of Liszt, Chopin, Beethoven, and Schumann. In 1877 he appeared as soloist with the Theodore Thomas Orchestra and he made many successful appearances with the violinist August Wilhelmj, both as soloist and accompanist. He was greater as a pianist than as a composer; many of his compositions were fashioned on the popular order of his period. Among the best are the following: "Gavotte Moderne," *opus* 11, "Florence Valse," *opus* 12, "Feu Follet," *opus* 17, "Albumblatt," *opus* 18, "Cradle Song," *opus* 23, and "Menuetto Scherzoso," *opus* 28. With W. S. B. Mathews he compiled the *Pronouncing and Defining Dictionary of Music* (1896) and he edited the last volume, "Essentials of Music" (1910), of *The American History and Encyclopedia of Music* (12 vols., 1908–10). He also contributed many articles to musical magazines. An outstanding personal characteristic was his generosity, and many an indigent student and fellow musician received help from him. He was married to Mrs. Florence Jones who survived him by a few years.

[See W. S. B. Mathews, *The Great in Music* (1900); G. L. Howe and W. S. B. Mathews, *A Hundred Years of Music in America* (1889); Albert Payne, *Celebrated Pianists of the Past and Present* (Am. ed., 1894); *Who's Who in America*, 1912–13; and obituaries in the *Musical Courier*, Jan. 28, 1914, and in the *Chicago Daily Tribune*, Jan. 21, 1914. Information as to certain facts was supplied by Liebling's nephew, Leonard Liebling, editor of the *Musical Courier*, and from his friend, Mr. D. A. Clippinger.]   F. L. G. C.

LIGHTBURN, JOSEPH ANDREW JACKSON (Sept. 21, 1824–May 17, 1901), soldier, Baptist preacher, son of Benjamin and Rebecca (Fell) Lightburn, came of backwoods stock, his Scotch grandfather having migrated in 1774 to the transmontane region on the Youghiogheny River near West Newton, Westmoreland County, Pa. Here Joseph was born and spent his earlier years, and at Mount Pleasant, in the same county, he obtained the rudiments of an education. In 1840 he removed to western Virginia with his father, who in 1841 acquired 600 acres of land on Broad Run in Lewis County. He helped his father build an overshot grist mill on the West Fork of the Monongahela River near the boyhood home of Thomas Jackson, later famous as "Stonewall," against whom, in 1842, Joseph Lightburn competed unsuccessfully for a cadetship at West Point. Near his home he gained such further education as was provided by the schools of the period, and attended the local Broad Run Baptist Church. In 1846, during the Mexican War, he enlisted in the regular army and was assigned to the recruiting service. He remained in the army as a non-commissioned officer till 1851, then returned to milling and farming. In October 1855 he married his stepsister, Harriet Ellen Whittlesey. Her father, Stephen Whittlesey, a graduate of Williams College, had been a Baptist minister. Her widowed mother, Nancy Anne Whittlesey, had become the second wife of Benjamin Lightburn in 1852. To Joseph and Harriet Lightburn were born five children.

In 1861, Lightburn, a stanch Union man, was selected as delegate to the Wheeling conventions of May 13 and June 11 which established the "Reorganized Government of Virginia"—a step toward the formation of the separate state of West Virginia. On Aug. 14, 1861, he received from Gov. Francis H. Pierpont [*q.v.*] a commission as colonel of the 4th Regiment of Virginia (West Virginia) Volunteers (Union forces) and participated in the battles of Charleston and Gauley Bridge. Placed in general command of the forces in the Kanawha Valley on Aug. 17, 1862, following the transfer of General Cox to Washington, he conducted a successful retreat down the Kanawha to Point Pleasant before the superior force of General Loring. Early in 1863 he was ordered to the Mississippi near Vicksburg, and attached to the Army of the Tennessee under General Grant. In March he was promoted to be brigadier-general and in May assumed command of a brigade in F. P. Blair's division, XV Army Corps. His command led the first assault on Vicksburg and subsequently participated in engagements at Jackson, Chickamauga, and Missionary Ridge, and in Sherman's advance on Atlanta. After recovering from a gunshot wound in the head, which he received in August 1864, he was transferred to the Shenandoah Valley, where he participated in several engagements. He was a warm friend of Gen. Lew Wallace.

In 1867 he represented Lewis County in the legislature of West Virginia. Before the war he had served irregularly as a Baptist minister, and in 1868 was ordained by the Broad Run Baptist Association. He became a leader of his denomination in the state and continued in active service until his death. He was a man of fine physique and striking military bearing, and as a preacher was strong and effective.

[R. B. Cook, *Lewis County in the Civil War* (1924); T. F. Lang, *Loyal W. Va. from 1861 to 1865* (1895); E. C. Smith, *A Hist. of Lewis County, W. Va.* (1920); C. B. Whittelsey, *Geneal. of the Whittelsey-Whittlesey Family* (1898); *War of the Rebellion: Official Records* (*Army*), esp. 1 ser. XIX (pts. 1, 2), XXIV (pt. 2), XXV (pts. 2, 3), XXXVIII (pts. 3, 5), XLIII (pt. 2), XLVI (pt. 2); *Exponent Telegram* (Clarksburg, W. Va.), Mar. 4, 1928, Nov. 11, 1928.]   J. M. C.

LIGON, THOMAS WATKINS (May 1, 1810–Jan. 12, 1881), congressman, governor of Maryland, was born on a farm in Prince Edward County, Va., the son of Thomas D. Ligon and his wife, Martha, daughter of Thomas Watkins, a Revolutionary officer. His father died while young Thomas was still a boy and his mother was married again, to Jack Vaughan of Prince Edward County, by whom she had six children. Thomas was educated at Hampden-Sydney College (where he graduated in 1830), at the University of Virginia, and at the Yale Law School (1831–32). He passed the examination for the bar in his native state but felt obliged to turn elsewhere for an opportunity to practise law. His choice fell on Baltimore, whither he repaired in 1833. In 1840 he married Sallie Dorsey and established his residence permanently near Ellicott City, although he maintained his office in Baltimore. After the death of his first wife he married her sister, Mary.

Immediately after his arrival in Baltimore he entered heartily into politics, vigorously sustaining the Jacksonian policies. In 1843 he became the Democratic candidate for the Maryland House of Delegates and was elected. The following year he was a successful candidate for Congress, where he served two terms (1845–49), being invariably arrayed with the strict constructionists. Winning the Democratic nomination for governor of Maryland in 1853, he was elected by a small majority. During his entire administration he was involved in a bitter struggle with the Know-Nothing party, which dominated both houses of the Assembly. During this period the Baltimore elections were characterized by open street fights around the markets and Monument square: awls became weapons and policemen remained mere spectators of violence. Although Governor Ligon undoubtedly realized how bitterly his antagonists would defend themselves, he opened an attack in his annual message of 1856 on "the formation and encouragement of secret political societies" (*Message of the Executive of Maryland, to the General Assembly*, 1856, p. 28). Fire drew fire: a special committee on the message produced a partisan report which was largely an attack on the governor for his "ill-timed and undeserved discourtesy" (Appendix to *Journal of the Proceedings of the House of Delegates of the State of Maryland, January Session,* 1856). Ligon's determination to interpose the militia to preserve order in Baltimore during the election of 1857 brought him to the verge of an open conflict with the mayor. The Governor yielded when a citizens' committee secured precautionary measures from the mayor, but he showed battle to the end by boldly devoting eleven pages of his last annual message to a discussion of "lawlessness in Baltimore." By giving his address to the newspapers before presenting it to the Assembly he further antagonized that august body, which at first refused to accept his communication.

Kindly and courteous, but reserved and simple, Ligon failed to awaken the personal enthusiasm which rallies followers in a battle, but although he retired under apparent defeat, his struggle encouraged a reform movement which bore fruit within less than three years. He spent the remainder of his long life quietly at his beautiful residence, "Chatham," where he died at the age of seventy. He was buried in the old family plot near his dwelling with the unostentatiousness which marked his entire life. though his body has since been removed to St. John's Cemetery, Ellicott City.

[H. E. Buchholz, *Governors of Md.* (1908); J. T. Scharf, *Hist. of Md.* (1879), vol. III; L. F. Schmeckebier, "History of the Know Nothing Party in Maryland," in *Johns Hopkins Univ. Studies in Hist. and Pol. Sci.,* ser. XVII, nos. 4–5 (Apr.–May 1899); Baltimore *Sun* and *Baltimore American*, 1854–60; M. P. Andrews, *Hist. of Md.* (1929); F. N. Watkins, *A Cat. of the Descendants of Thomas Watkins of Chickahomony, Va.* (1852); obituaries in the *Sun* and *Baltimore American,* Jan. 13, 1881.]   E. L.

LILIENTHAL, MAX (Oct. 16, 1815–Apr. 5, 1882), rabbi, was born in Munich, Bavaria, the son of Loew Seligmann and Dina (Lichtenstein) Lilienthal. The father was one of the leading members of the small Jewish community of the Bavarian capital. Max Lilienthal was among the few young Jews of his generation who matriculated in the University of Munich. He graduated in 1837, receiving the degree of doctor of philosophy. His brilliant showing in his final examination attracted the attention of government officials and he was offered a position in the diplomatic service, which he declined when he found that to hold a government appointment he would be obliged to accept Christianity.

While waiting for an opening elsewhere he continued his studies in the royal library of Munich, and contributed a series of bibliographical notices of the Hebrew manuscripts in its possession to the literary supplement of *Die Allgemeine Zeitung des Judenthums.* As a contributor he came into close relation with the editor, Dr. Ludwig Philippson, the best-known rabbi in Europe, who was at that time in correspondence with Uwaroff, the minister of education of the Russian Empire. A plan was afoot to modernize the Jewish schools in Russia, and a beginning was to be made in Riga, where a new school was to be established. When Uwaroff applied to Philippson to recommend a superintendent for this new school, Philippson suggested Lilienthal, who accepted the appointment. He remained in Russia five years, but the governmental attempt to establish modern schools failed, notably when it appeared that this policy was a part of a proselytizing plan. Disheartened and disillusioned, Lilienthal left Russia, determined to seek asylum in a free land. He stopped en route at his birthplace to marry his fiancée,

Babette Nettre. With his bride he landed at New York in November 1845.

Lilienthal was the first rabbi with a European reputation to settle in the United States. Shortly after his arrival he was elected chief rabbi of three congregations in New York. He established also a day school for boys which attracted the attention of fathers not only in New York but also in other parts of the country. Among them were some Jewish residents of Cincinnati, Ohio, who urged the selection of Lilienthal for the vacant pulpit of the Bene Israel Congregation of that city. He was elected to the post, preached his inaugural sermon on July 14, 1855, and soon became one of the leading citizens of Cincinnati. He served as a member of the board of education, 1860–69; he was elected a member of the union board of high schools in 1861 and of the board of directors of the University of Cincinnati in 1872, holding the latter place until his death. The keynote of his activity was his intense Americanism. He contested with all his power every attempt of sectarian religionists to encroach upon the American principle of the separation of church and state. He opposed in burning words the attempt to introduce Bible reading into the public schools. This Cincinnati "Bible in the Schools" case, which was argued before the courts in 1870 (*Cincinnati Board of Education* vs. *John D. Minor, 23 Ohio,* 211), became a *cause célèbre* in the educational annals of the country.

Lilienthal took an active part in the establishment of the Union of American Hebrew Congregations in 1873 and the foundation of the Hebrew Union College at Cincinnati in 1875. He served as associate editor of the *American Israelite,* to which he contributed articles on "My Travels in Russia" (1854–56), and as editor of the first Jewish juvenile weekly published in the United States, the *Sabbath School Visitor.* He published a volume of German poems, *Frühling, Freiheit und Liebe,* in 1857, and in that same year, a *Synopsis of the History of the Israelites from the time of Alexander the Macedonian to the Present Age* (Cincinnati, 1857). He organized the Rabbinical Literary Association in 1879 and was elected its first president. He edited two volumes of the quarterly journal issued by this organization, the *Hebrew Review,* which ceased publication after his death.

Possibly his greatest service lay in the promotion of good will between Christians and Jews. He was the first rabbi to preach frequently from Christian pulpits. He was a real ambassador of religious amity. The closing years of his life were saddened by the virulent outburst of anti-Semitism in Germany and by the anti-Jewish persecutions in Russia, but even these inhumanities could not quench his optimistic hope of the coming of the better day of human brotherhood and universal peace. Indeed, this was the leading motif of his activity.

[David Philipson, *Max Lilienthal, American Rabbi* (1915), and memoir in *Central Conf. of Am. Rabbis, Yearbook,* vol. XXV (1915); Sophie Lilienthal, *The Lilienthal Family Record* (privately printed, San Francisco, 1930); R. J. Wunderbar, *Geschichte der Juden in den Provinzen Liv-und Kurland* (1853); Pauline Wengeroff, *Memoiren einer Grossmutter* (Berlin, 1908), I, 118–37; Leon Scheinhaus, *"Ein deutscher Pionier,"* in *Allgemeine Zeitung des Judenthums,* Aug. 25, 1911; J. S. Raisin, *The Haskalah Movement in Russia* (1913); *Jewish Encyc.* (ed. of 1925), vol. VIII; *Cincinnati Enquirer,* Apr. 6, 7, 8, 10, 1882.]   D. P.

LINCECUM, GIDEON (Apr. 22, 1793–Nov. 28, 1874), frontier physician, naturalist, son of Hezekiah and Sally (Hickman) Lincecum, was born in Hancock County, Ga., and died near Long Point, Washington County, Tex. He was a grandson of Gideon, born in France, who came to America with his father, Paschal, and settled in Maryland. The boy's early years were spent in restless wanderings with his family through Georgia and western South Carolina, and up to the time he was fourteen years old he had obtained only five months' formal schooling. For eight months during the War of 1812 he served as a volunteer Georgia militiaman. On Oct. 25, 1814, he married, near Eatonsville, Ga., Sarah Bryan, daughter of Robert Bryan. After some years spent in the private study of medicine, and an experience in teaching in Georgia, he became a merchant at the frontier settlement of Columbus, Miss. In 1821 he was appointed by the Mississippi legislature commissioner to organize Monroe County. After the region had become settled, he was for several years an Indian trader in the Choctaw country of central Mississippi, and became familiar with the languages and legends of the Choctaw and Chickasaw tribes, which knowledge he used later in his "Life of Apushimataha" (*Mississippi Historical Society Publications,* vol. IX, 1906) and "Choctaw Traditions about Their Settlement in Mississippi and the Origin of Their Mounds" (*Ibid.,* vol. VIII, 1904). Becoming a physician (in the frontier manner of getting a stock of drugs and hanging out a shingle), he practised medicine with unusual success in the towns of Cotton Gin Port and Columbus from 1830 to 1848. In the latter year he went to Texas, where he settled at Long Point, on a tract of land that he had chosen while exploring Texas thirteen years before.

Lincecum was a true frontiersman, impatient of inaction and restraint. Passionately fond of nature from his boyhood, he improved his leisure hours during his first fourteen years in Texas in making a series of extensive studies of the agricultural or mound-building ants, which were published in the *Journal of the Proceedings of the Linnean Society; Zoology,* vol. VI (London, 1852); and later in the *Proceedings of the Academy of Natural Sciences of Philadelphia,* second series, vol. X (1866). Because of Lincecum's unfortunate tendency to personalize animal behavior, his conclusions, although sponsored by Charles Darwin, met with incredulity on the part of savants such as Forel; but his observations have been verified in the main by later workers (see H. C. McCook, *The Natural History of the Agricultural Ant of Texas,* 1879, pp. 12-13; W. M. Wheeler, *Ants . . .,* 1913, pp. 286-90). He maintained a wide correspondence with naturalists in Europe and America, and sent rich collections from Texas and Mexico to the Smithsonian Institution, the Academy of Natural Sciences of Philadelphia, and the Jardin des Plantes of Paris. He was gifted with an acute, independent, and observant mind, but being self-taught and isolated from other workers, he at first lacked the precision of the trained naturalist—a defect that he later largely overcame by diligence and persistence in observation. In addition to the works already mentioned, his publications include papers on natural-history subjects, chiefly insects, and his posthumously printed "Autobiography."

["Autobiography," *Miss. Hist. Soc. Pubs.,* vol. VIII (1904); *Southwest Rev.,* Autumn, 1929; *Dallas Daily Herald,* Dec. 12, 1874; original materials in the possession of S. W. Geiser, and in the archives of the University of Texas Library.]   S. W. G.

LINCOLN, ABRAHAM (Feb. 12, 1809-Apr. 15, 1865), sixteenth president of the United States, was, to use his own words, born "in the most humble walks of life" (*Works,* I, 8). His birthplace was a log-cabin about three miles south of Hodgen's mill on what was known as the "Sinking Spring Farm" in Hardin (now Larue) County, Ky. Lincoln himself could trace his line no farther back than to certain ancestors in Berks County, Pa., whom he vaguely described as Quakers; but research has disclosed a lineage reaching back to Samuel Lincoln who came from Hingham, England, and settled in Hingham, Mass., in 1637. On the Lincoln side the descent was as follows: Samuel Lincoln (d. 1690); Mordecai Lincoln of Hingham and Scituate, Mass. (d. 1727); Mordecai Lincoln of Berks County, Pa. (d. 1736); John Lincoln of Berks County, Pa., and Rockingham County, Va. (d. 1788); Abraham Lincoln of Rockingham County, Va., and later of Kentucky; Thom-

as Lincoln, father of the President. The merging of the Lincolns with the migratory streams of pioneer America is illustrated by the progeny of John Lincoln mentioned above—"Virginia John" as he was called. Of his five sons, whose names were reminiscent of ancient Israel, Jacob alone remained in Virginia, while Abraham, Isaac, John, and Thomas removed to Kentucky, eastern Tennessee, or Ohio. Abraham Lincoln, grandfather of the President, emigrated from Rockingham County, Va., to Green River, Lincoln County, Ky., about 1782; but was killed about 1786 by Indians while opening a farm in the forest (Beveridge, *post,* I, 11, note 2).

Thomas Lincoln (1778-1851) was large, powerful, and compactly built. According to his distinguished son, he was "a wandering laboring-boy," and "grew up literally without education" (*Works,* VI, 25), and in mature life was barely able to write his name. Born in Rockingham County, Va., he went with his father to Lincoln County, Ky., roved about for some years, married and settled in Elizabethtown, Hardin County, after which he pursued the occupations of carpenter and farmer, changing his residence frequently, making nothing of his poorly chosen farms, avoiding contacts with "society" in town, and bequeathing little besides life itself to his son. Thomas' first wife, Nancy Hanks, was the mother of Abraham. According to the best available authority, she was the natural child of Lucy Hanks; and her paternity is unknown, the date of her birth being a matter of conjecture. Some years after the birth of Nancy, Lucy Hanks married Henry Sparrow in Mercer County, Ky.; and Nancy was reared by her aunt, Betsy Hanks (Mrs. Thomas Sparrow). Though many tender eulogies of Lincoln's mother have been written, there is little reliable evidence concerning her. She seems to have been superior to the general Hanks level in intellectual vigor, and was described as spiritually inclined, affectionate, amiable, cool, and heroic (Herndon and Weik, *post,* I, 10). Whatever her natural endowments, she was "absolutely illiterate" (Beveridge, I, 16) and was throughout life identified with lowly people. Her marriage to Thomas Lincoln occurred on June 12, 1806, the backwoods ceremony being performed in the cabin of a friend in Washington County, Ky., by Jesse Head, a Methodist parson. On the Hanks side the ancestry of Lincoln is beclouded in a maze of misinformation; and much of the data presented by earlier biographers on this subject must be rejected, including unreliable accounts of a mythical Nancy Shipley Hanks, sometimes erroneously mentioned as Lincoln's maternal grandmother, and of various alleged Hankses whose real name was Hawks. According to W. E. Barton (*Lineage of Lincoln,* pp. 186, 210), the parents of Lincoln's grandmother, Lucy, were Joseph and Ann (Lee) Hanks of Hampshire County, Va., and Nelson County, Ky.; and one finds Hankses in the seventeenth and eighteenth centuries living on the Rappahannock as close neighbors of various Lees with whom at times they intermarried. It is only by conjecture as to several links, however, that Barton argues a connection between Lincoln's line and that of Robert E. Lee (*Ibid.,* pp. 208–11).

Without following all the migrations of "Thomas the unstable," it may be noted that during the years of Abraham's early boyhood the family lived in a picturesque spot on Knob Creek about eight miles from his birthplace—a spot of natural beauty, of peace and grandeur, in a region of rocky cliffs, noble trees, and clear streams. Throughout life Lincoln carried fresh recollections of his Kentucky home—of the backwoods school where he was taught to read, write, and "cipher to the rule of three," of fishing and hunting adventures, of boyish escapades, of the old stone house on Nolin Creek where the young people gathered for dances, and of the mill to which as a child he carried the family grist. When the boy was seven the family was again on the move, this time for the Indiana woods. With their sorry stock of household goods they "packed through" to the Ohio River, ferried across, and followed a newly blazed trail to the home in the brush which Thomas had selected. This home, in which the Lincolns were at first but squatters, was located in the Pigeon Creek neighborhood in what is now Spencer County, Ind. The first winter they had not even a cabin —merely a rude shelter of poles, brush, and leaves enclosed on three sides and called a "half-faced camp." Their cabin, when Thomas got round to building it, had at first neither floor, door, nor window; and the family fare was a matter of game animals, honey, birds, nuts, and wild fruit. The family of Thomas and Nancy Lincoln, with their two children, Sarah and Abraham, was soon joined by Nancy's foster parents, Betsy and Thomas Sparrow, with the colorful Dennis Hanks, who was as essential a part of this backwoods picture as "that Darne Little half face camp," as Dennis called it, which the Sparrows used after the Lincolns had discarded it. Tragedy soon descended upon Pigeon Creek. Thomas Sparrow and Betsy his wife were stricken with what the settlers called the "milk sick," and were laid away in coffins fashioned by Thomas Lincoln. To these and other sufferers Nancy Lincoln had generously ministered. She soon fell ill, lingered without medical help for a week, and died (October 1818) with words of pious admonition for her children. In life and death her brief story was that of the American pioneer woman.

Thomas Lincoln soon found another wife in Sarah (Bush) Johnston of Elizabethtown, Ky., widow of Daniel Johnston, who came with her three children to the Indiana cabin; and with the addition in 1823 of John Hanks there were nine persons in this narrow abode. The household equipment was now improved; and the stepmother became an important factor in the boy's rearing. From the Weik manuscripts—memories of Lincoln's early associates recorded after many years—we may reconstruct, through Beveridge's pages, a fairly definite picture of Lincoln as an easy-going backwoods youth who did his stint of hard labor on the homestead, performed odd jobs for neighbors, shunned the vociferous camp-meetings of the time, avoided membership in the church, and used his leisure for self-improvement by the reading of a few good books. The Bible, *Robinson Crusoe, Pilgrim's Progress,* Aesop's *Fables,* William Grimshaw's *History of the United States,* the *Kentucky Preceptor,* Weems's *Life of Washington,* and various other biographies and books of verse were the principal works known to have been used by Lincoln at this period. As to formal schooling, there was very little. While living in the Knob Creek home in Kentucky, Abraham and his sister Sarah had attended country schools for some weeks; now in Indiana he sat for brief periods under several schoolmasters (Andrew Crawford, Azel W. Dorsey, and William Sweeney by name) to whose log schools he had to walk long distances; but, in all, his attendance at school did not exceed one year. Out of school his vigor for reading and study was probably less a matter of ambition than of healthy intellectual interest. It was his stepmother who told the familiar story of his ciphering on boards which he shaved off with a drawing-knife to prepare for fresh efforts. His readiness to walk many miles for books is well attested, as is also his fondness for speech-making and for mimicking the preachers and orators who penetrated to the rough creekside. He somehow grew up without the frontier vices, avoiding liquor and being wholly free from dissoluteness and profanity. Though avoiding girls, he was uncommonly sociable; and the nearby country store at Gentryville held for him an unfailing fascination. The river attracted him powerfully and entered largely into his early life. He earned a few dollars by rowing passengers from the shore to passing steamers; and in the year 1828 he made the trip from Gentry's landing on the Ohio to New Orleans. Though stirred with the ambition to become "a steamboat man," he returned to the monotony of Pigeon Creek, where his father had a claim upon his labor. As the boy emerged from his teens he was tall, powerful, muscular, ungainly, tender toward animals, a recounter of robust stories, mighty with the axe, and not without a certain latent poetry in his nature. His relations with his father seem not to have been happy, and he welcomed the day when he could shift for himself.

In the year of Abraham's coming of age (1830) the Lincolns were again on the move. Having sold his Indiana holdings, Thomas set out with his family to Macon County, Ill., whither John Hanks had preceded them. With ox-drawn wagons they trekked through forest and prairie, crossed the Wabash, and settled on the Sangamon River not far from Decatur. At first Abraham remained with the family, helping to build the new cabin, splitting fence rails, planting corn, and assisting in the rough tasks of the following winter. In the service of one Denton Offutt he assisted in building and navigating a flatboat from a point on the Sangamon River near Springfield to New Orleans; but the story that "the iron entered his soul" on seeing the New Orleans slave auction, and that he vowed if he ever had a chance to "hit that thing" he would "hit it hard," is untrustworthy (Beveridge, I, 107). Returning from the southern mart on a steamer, Lincoln, then only a drifter, selected as his home the village of New Salem, about twenty miles northwest of Springfield— a remote hamlet set high on a bluff overlooking the Sangamon.

Here he spent six picturesque and formative years (1831–37), working in the store of Denton Offutt till it "petered out"; managing a mill; conducting a store with W. F. Berry, who died leaving a heavy debt ($1,100) all of which Lincoln finally paid; splitting rails and doing odd jobs to earn a scant living; acting as village postmaster; traversing the county as deputy surveyor; and all the while reading law, studying grammar, widening his acquaintance, following the trends of national politics, and laying the foundations for a wide personal influence. It was during this period that he served in the Black Hawk War, being unanimously elected captain by the men of his company. Another gauge to measure his stature is the devotion of the "Clary Grove Boys"—stalwart rowdies to whom hero worship was as natural as swearing,

drinking, and fighting. This tribute to Lincoln's manhood, which came in spite of his freedom from the vices of the gang, seems to have been in part a recognition of his prowess in competitive sport, especially wrestling, and in part a pure matter of personal attachment.

In 1834 Lincoln was chosen to the state legislature; and he served during four successive terms (1834–41), first at Vandalia, the old capital, and later at Springfield. It was a frontier legislature, but its party maneuvers were spirited, and it offered Lincoln his first political training. Being a Clay Whig in a Democratic body, he belonged to the minority; but he became Whig floor leader and directed the fortunes of his party in the lower house, receiving in several sessions the full party vote for the speakership. On national issues, which were necessarily of concern to him as a prominent party worker, he acted as a regular Whig, supporting the Bank of the United States, opposing the leading measures of Jackson and Van Buren, and attacking the independent treasury. He studiously avoided association with abolitionists, but he did not want this attitude construed as positive support of slavery. Consequently, when the legislature in 1837 passed resolutions severely condemning abolition societies, Lincoln and his colleague Dan Stone from Sangamon County entered a protest, asserting that slavery was "founded on both injustice and bad policy, but that the promulgation of abolition doctrines tends rather to increase than abate its evils" (*Works*, I, 52).

In 1837 Lincoln left New Salem, which was soon thereafter abandoned, later to be rebuilt as a memorial to him, and made his home in Springfield. So poor was he at this time that his surveying instruments had been attached to pay a debt; he rode into town on a borrowed horse carrying his possessions in two saddle-bags, and was glad to make arrangements with friends for free lodging and board. He was now a practising lawyer, having been licensed as an attorney Sept. 9, 1836; and he formed a partnership with J. T. Stuart, a man of influential family, able in the law, and prominent in Whig circles. While in New Salem, Lincoln had paid court to Ann Rutledge whose father kept the rude inn where he boarded. Though the girl's attractions and tragic death have inspired an extravagant amount of sentimental fiction, actual evidence on the matter is scant. She was engaged to a man named John McNamar, but his long absence suggested desertion. Her engagement to Lincoln seems to have been conditional upon honorable release from her absent lover. That Ann preferred Lincoln in case her lover should return and renew his suit seems doubtful; and on both sides there were reasons for deferring marriage. With matters in this unsettled state, Ann died of "brain fever," Aug. 25, 1835. Lincoln's proposal to Mary Owens, whom he met through the kindness of her sister at New Salem, need not be treated here; nor is there room to analyze the confused testimony that surrounds his troubled courtship of Mary Todd.

Herndon's sensational story of Lincoln's failure to appear at his wedding, said to have been set for Jan. 1, 1841, has produced a mass of contradictory discussion. In the best treatment of the subject (Sandburg and Angle, *Mary Lincoln, Wife and Widow*, 1932, pp. 40–60, 174–185, 330), the conclusion is reached that there was no defaulting bridegroom at a wedding, but that some violent emotional disturbance did occur; indeed, no one can read Lincoln's correspondence of the period without being impressed with his excessive morbidity. After a series of breaks and reconciliations, complicated by Mary's rumored flirtations with other men, the disturbed lovers were finally brought together; and they were married in some haste on Nov. 4, 1842. As to the degree of happiness that attended their married life it is equally difficult to reach a fully rounded conclusion (see Lincoln, Mary Todd). On Lincoln's side there was indifference to domestic niceties and a certain untidiness and lack of dignity that grated upon the sensibilities of a proudly reared woman; on the other hand, the domestic atmosphere was not improved by Mary's bursts of temper. Their first son, Robert Todd [*q.v.*], was born Aug. 1, 1843; he alone grew to manhood. The other children were: Edward Baker (Mar. 10, 1846–Feb. 1, 1850), William Wallace (Dec. 21, 1850–Feb. 20, 1862), and Thomas or "Tad" (Apr. 4, 1853–July 15, 1871).

In the years 1847–49 Lincoln served one term in Congress, where he had the distinction of being the only Whig from Illinois. His election with more than 1,500 majority over the doughty backwoods preacher, Peter Cartwright, was a significant personal triumph, for Cartwright was himself a man of great popularity. In his undistinguished career as congressman the matters most worthy of comment are those which pertain to the Mexican War and to slavery. Lincoln had not opposed the war while campaigning as a candidate; but when his party sought political advantage by denouncing the conflict as a Democratic war unjustly begun by Polk, Lincoln joined aggressively in this party attack. He voted (Jan. 3, 1848) that the war was "unnecessarily ... begun by the President"; and on Dec.

22, 1847, he introduced his "spot resolutions" (*Congressional Globe,* 30 Cong., 1 Sess., p. 64), which were so worded as to imply that the "spot" on which had occurred the shedding of American blood, which Polk had interpreted as Mexican aggression, was in fact an unoffending settlement of Mexican people, outside American jurisdiction, against which an American force had been unnecessarily sent contrary to General Taylor's advice. On Jan. 12, 1848, he made a striking speech on his resolutions—a Whig speech in which he subjected the President's evidence to cold analysis, accused him of befogging the issue, and questioned the purposes of the administration as to the duration of the war and the terms of peace (*Ibid.,* pp. 154–56). In this speech Lincoln made a declaration which hardly comported with his later declarations against Southern secession; for he asserted the right of "any people," or of "a majority of any portion of such people," to "shake off the existing government, and form a new one" (*Works,* I, 338–39). Though Lincoln had voted to grant supplies to sustain the war, and though his anti-war speech made but slight impression generally, he had deeply offended the people of his state. His attitude was denounced in Illinois as unpatriotic; he was described as a "second Benedict Arnold," and was accused of having plead the cause of the enemy (Beveridge, I, 432). On various occasions Lincoln voted for the Wilmot proviso; and on Jan. 10, 1849, he read a proposal to abolish slavery in the national capital (*Congressional Globe,* 30 Cong., 2 Sess., p. 212). It is characteristic of his conservatism that he proposed such abolition only in case three conditions should be met: emancipation was to be gradual; compensation was to be made to slaveholders; and the proposed act was not to go into force unless approved by the citizens of the District at a special election.

Lincoln did not move among the great in Washington, nor did he rise above the obscurity of the average congressman. He amused a small circle by his camaraderie and droll stories, but the more brilliant social life of the capital was closed to him. Vigorous anti-slavery men were not his associates, but he formed a real friendship with Alexander H. Stephens of Georgia. Party affairs took much of his energy. He spent weary hours addressing documents to voters; wrote numerous letters; served as the Illinois member of the Whig national committee; delivered a rollicking speech against Cass which was essentially a campaign document (July 27, 1848, *Works,* II, 59–88); and participated in the Whig convention at Philadelphia in 1848, laboring hard for the inexperienced Zachary Taylor and against his former hero, Henry Clay. In the campaign of 1848 his services on the stump were not eagerly sought, least of all in Illinois; but he visited Massachusetts, speaking at Worcester, Chelsea, Dedham, Cambridge, Lowell, and Boston. One misses in these speeches the resonant tone of Lincoln's later declarations. Antislavery as he was at heart, he counseled against voting for the Free-Soil candidate, Van Buren, since such action would help to elect Cass. Though the Whigs were nationally successful in this election, Lincoln had the humiliation of seeing his party lose his own district, where the defeat of S. T. Logan for Congress might be interpreted as a repudiation of Lincoln's record by his neighbors. With a sense of futility he bade goodbye to Washington; and, while the thunders of the mid-century slavery crisis were shaking the country, he renounced politics, returned to the obscurity of Springfield, and sadly resumed his law practice.

As a lawyer Lincoln rose to front rank in his own state. He was associated with capable partners—at first John Todd Stuart, then Stephen T. Logan, and finally William H. Herndon. His practice was important and extensive in the state supreme court and also in the federal courts. After Illinois was divided into two federal judicial districts, Lincoln attended the sessions of the United States courts in Chicago with increasing frequency. In his circuit practice, where cases had to be quickly whipped into shape, he was not more than ordinarily successful; but in the higher courts, where careful study served to bring into play the sureness of his matured judgments, his record was outstanding (Paul M. Angle, in *Lincoln Centennial Association Papers,* 1928, esp. pp. 38–41). It is true that Lincoln is chiefly remembered as a luminous figure among the circuit-riding lawyers who traveled the judicial circuit presided over by Judge David Davis. He thoroughly enjoyed this picturesque life, jogging over the prairies in his rickety buggy, meeting the country folk on their own level, and joining the happy migratory life of judge and attorneys as they lodged two in a bed and eight in a room, swapped stories, and made the taverns resound with hilarity. During court week the lawyers were in demand for political speeches, and Lincoln's popularity was enhanced by his aptness on these occasions. It was here that his humor and story telling showed at their best; and to the stories themselves must be added the wizardry of Lincoln's quaint manner and the charm of his smile. Some of the specific cases of this circuit-riding phase have received undue emphasis, such as the Wright case in which Lincoln represented the widow of a Revolutionary soldier and recovered an exorbitant fee which a grasping pension agent had charged, and that of "Duff" Armstrong whom Lincoln successfully defended on a murder charge, making use of an almanac to refute testimony as to moonlight on the night of the murder. The human interest of these smaller cases has served to obscure the really important litigation with which Lincoln was connected. His services were enlisted in determining such important matters as the right of a county to tax the Illinois Central Railroad (17 *Illinois,* 291–99), the right to bridge a navigable stream (the *Effie Afton* case, Beveridge, I, 598–605), and the protection of the McCormick Reaper Company against infringement of its patents (*Ibid.,* I, 575–83). In this McCormick case, which was tried before a federal court at Cincinnati, Lincoln suppressed his feelings when snubbed by eastern attorneys; and later as president he appointed one of these lawyers, Stanton, to his cabinet. A study of his whole legal career shows that he was more than a country lawyer; and to those factors which gave him fair success in the rural county seats— his common sense, his shrewdness, his effectiveness before a jury, his strong invective, and his reputation for honesty—one must add further qualities that mark the outstanding attorney: a searching thoroughness of investigation (Beveridge, I, 573–74), a familiarity with pertinent judicial doctrines, and a knack of so stating a legal question as to brush away its technicalities and get at the core of the controversy. There are instances of his declining to receive excessive fees, refusing questionable cases, and even withdrawing from a case on discovering during the trial that his client's cause was unjust. In fragmentary notes for a law lecture he stated his conception of professional standards (*Works,* II, 140–43). A successful lawyer, he said, must stress diligence, attend promptly to the preparation of documents, and cultivate extemporaneous speaking as the "lawyer's avenue to the public." He should discourage litigation and choose honesty above professional success. "Work, work, work," he said, "is the main thing" (*Ibid.,* VI, 59).

The Lincoln of the prairies was a man of marked individuality. Standing six feet four, with uncommon length of arms and legs, his figure loomed in any crowd, while the rugged face bespoke a pioneer origin and an early life of toil and poverty. In a head not over large each feature was rough and prominent. In contrast to the round, full-cheeked Douglas, Lincoln's face showed deep hollows and heavy shadows. The craggy brow, tousled hair, drooping eyelids, melancholy gray eyes, large nose and chin, heavy lips, and sunken, wrinkled cheeks produced an effect not easily forgotten. A wide variety of qualities is revealed in his portraits, which give the impression of a character whose depth is not readily sounded—a personality in which conflicting hereditary strains were peculiarly blended. Those who have described him from life dwell upon the contrast between the seeming listlessness of the face in repose and the warmth of the countenance when animated with conversation or public speech. The trappings of the man intensified the effect of crudeness. In a day of grandiloquent male adornment Lincoln's habiliments departed as far from the Godey fashion plate as did his mid-western speech from the sophisticated accent of the East. The battered stovepipe hat stuffed with papers, the rusty ill-fitting coat, the ready-made trousers too short for the legs, the unpolished boots, the soiled stock at the neck, the circular cloak in winter or linen duster in summer, the bulging umbrella and hard-used carpet-bag, gave an entirely unpremeditated effect of oddity, the man's appearance being apparently of no more concern to him than the food which he seemed to eat without tasting.

Few men could match Lincoln as a stump-speaker. Beginning with apparent diffidence he gained composure and assurance as he proceeded, speaking with freedom, naturalness, and convincing power. In impassioned periods the gaunt figure, despite the sunken chest, became "splendid and imposing" (Herndon and Weik, II, 77); and in the directness of his intense passages the tall form seemed to gain in height. His mind had that tenacity and steadfastness of logic that goes with slowness in forming conclusions. There is a clarity and compactness in his writings which is in pleasing contrast to the verbosity so common in his day. Never descending to triteness or banality, his papers show careful composition and abound in epigrams and pithy phrases. This power of written and spoken utterance must be reckoned high among his qualities as a statesman. His political philosophy revealed a democratic liberalism closely resembling the creed of Thomas Jefferson. Anglo-Saxon principles of civil liberty were fundamental in his thinking (A. C. Cole, in *Journal of the Illinois State Historical Society*, Oct. 1926–Jan. 1927, pp. 102–14); he advocated the broadening of political rights, even favoring woman suffrage far ahead of his time; and the leveling doctrines of the Declaration of Independence became a

kind of religion with him. Laborers and the less favored classes generally found in him an earnest champion. Though never identifying himself with any ecclesiastical denomination, he was not lacking in the religious sense; and in his public papers he expressed with sincerity the spiritual aspirations of his people.

In the agitation that swept the country with the repeal of the Missouri Compromise Lincoln emerged from political inactivity and launched upon the larger career which occupied the coming years. From 1854 on there appeared a new tone in his speeches, a notable earnestness combined with adroitness in narrowing the contest to one phase of the slavery question, thus making it a suitable party issue. In a speech at Springfield, Oct. 4, 1854, repeated at Peoria on Oct. 16 (*Works*, II, 190–262), Lincoln answered Douglas, who had spoken in the same hall the previous day. His reasoned appeals to the Declaration of Independence, his sarcasm, his searching questions, and his shrewdness in avoiding pitfalls, indicated that he had now struck his stride as a leader. Still calling himself a Whig, though events were drawing him toward the new Republican party, he worked hard for the senatorship from Illinois in 1855; but, after successive ballots in the legislature indicated his dwindling strength, he aided the cause of the Anti-Nebraska fusionists against the Democrats by throwing his support to Trumbull.

The next year Lincoln became definitely identified with the new party; and at the Republican state convention at Bloomington he delivered, on May 29, 1856, what some have called his greatest speech (*Works*, II, 308 note). In a time of high excitement over the Kansas struggle, when radicals were trying to capture the Republican party, Lincoln's task was to make a fighting speech which would have enough boldness to inspire the crusading abolitionists and yet so define the issue as to keep the support of moderates. Herndon exhausted his adjectives in describing the speech and declared that on that occasion his partner was seven feet tall. Lincoln soon became active in the new party, attending every meeting he could reach, speaking frequently, managing the details of party machinery, and carrying on an extensive correspondence with voters. He was now the leading Republican as he had been the leading Whig of Illinois. At the time of Frémont's nomination for the presidency at Philadelphia in 1856 he received 110 votes for the vice-presidential nomination; and in this way his name was widely advertised in the North. He campaigned for Frémont in this election, though McLean had been his choice; but he had only partial success in winning Whig support for the Republican cause.

Successfully seeking the Republican senatorial nomination in 1858, Lincoln delivered a carefully prepared speech on June 16 before the state Republican convention at Springfield. "A house divided against itself cannot stand," said he. "I believe this government cannot endure permanently, half slave and half free. I do not expect the Union to be dissolved—I do not expect the house to fall—but I do expect it will cease to be divided. It will become all one thing, or all the other" (*Works,* III, 2). In this speech, as elsewhere, Lincoln denounced the Dred Scott decision of 1857 as part of a pro-slavery conspiracy which, unless thwarted, would one day legalize slavery even in the free states. In the campaign with Douglas for the senatorship, Lincoln at first trailed his opponent, speaking at Chicago on July 10 just after his antagonist had spoken at the same place, and repeating the performance at Bloomington and elsewhere. On July 24, 1858, he challenged Douglas [*q.v.*] to a series of debates; and the acceptance of the challenge gave Lincoln the advantage of being matched against the outstanding leader of the Democratic party. Beginning at Ottawa, Aug. 21, reaching an early climax at Freeport, Aug. 27, and closing at Alton on Oct. 15, the seven "joint debates" were but the most striking incident of a long duel between Lincoln and Douglas. It was indeed a memorable contest. The emotion of cheering crowds, the clack and rattle of western campaigning, the sporting spectacle of contestants facing each other in successive forensic rounds, the physical disparity between the candidates, the contrast between Douglas' private railroad car and the crowded coach or freight caboose in which Lincoln, not without an eye to political effect, lumbered into town to be fetched to his lodging in a hay-wagon—these features lent a picturesque interest to a contest in which the importance of the stakes far exceeded the realization of participants or spectators. Each candidate showed respect for the other, and the discussions were conducted on a high plane, albeit with a deadly earnestness. In the speeches there were few elements that were new. Lincoln shrewdly capitalized the growing split in the Democratic ranks; he denounced Douglas' indifference as to the right or wrong of slavery; and he used with telling effect the inconsistency between "popular sovereignty" and the doctrine of the Dred Scott decision, both of which Douglas favored. At·Freeport, by a question as to whether the people of a territory could exclude slavery, he forced Douglas to compromise himself as presidential candidate in 1860

by taking a position which offended the South, though gaining votes for the senatorial contest in Illinois.

Once and again in the debates Lincoln disavowed abolitionist doctrines and stressed the conservative note. He did not advocate the unconditional repeal of fugitive-slave laws nor oppose the admission of states in which slavery might be established by constitutions honestly adopted. Negro citizenship did not receive his indorsement, nor did he urge political or social equality for the races. His advocacy of abolition in the District of Columbia was again qualified by those safeguarding conditions which he had previously proposed as congressman. With the politician's eye for vote-getting and for uniting the incongruous elements of his nascent party, he avoided the language of the anti-slavery crusader and narrowed the issue to the clear-cut doctrine of freedom in the territories. The effectiveness of his campaign was shown in the election returns. His party carried districts containing a larger population than those carried by the Democrats, but inequitable apportionment gave Douglas a majority in the legislature, insuring his election. The contest lifted Lincoln into national prominence; and in 1859 he made many speeches in Ohio, Indiana, Iowa, Wisconsin, and Kansas, impressing his ideas upon the people of important doubtful states.

His name was now being mentioned for the presidency, and it was as a presidential possibility that he delivered on Feb. 27, 1860, his Cooper Institute speech in New York (*Works,* V, 293–328). This was a notable formulation of the issues on which the new party could do battle. Exclusion of slavery from the territories as the doctrine of the fathers was the keynote of the address, which was delivered in Lincoln's best style and with a dignity in keeping with the occasion. Decrying the efforts to discredit the Republican party by identifying it with the radicalism of John Brown or the abusiveness of Helper's *Impending Crisis,* he spoke for an attitude of understanding and friendliness toward the Southern people. He urged his party to "yield to them if . . . we possibly can," doing "nothing through passion and ill temper"; and he denounced efforts to destroy the Union.

Lincoln was named in state convention as the choice of Illinois Republicans for the presidency; and a combination of factors led to his success in the national convention at Chicago. Seward was considered too radical and was injured by the powerful opposition of Greeley. Other candidates had weak points; Bates could not carry the Germans; Chase could not muster his own state.

The moderate element was growing in the new party, and in certain "battle-ground states"—Illinois, Indiana, Pennsylvania, and New Jersey, which had supported Buchanan in 1856—it was vitally important to nominate a conservative candidate. Lincoln had steadily counseled moderation; he had avoided connection with the Know-Nothings, had pleased the Germans by his opposition to measures directed against foreigners, and had made himself highly acceptable as a second choice in case Seward could not be named. In short, Lincoln was so free from radicalism, so careful to avoid offense, and yet withal so skilful in inspiring enthusiasts that he proved to be precisely the type of candidate to which a convention turns after the luminous stars of the pre-convention canvass have proved unavailable. The atmosphere of the wigwam at Chicago was favorable to the "rail splitter," opposition within the state having been skilfully sidetracked. O. H. Browning, for instance, who favored Bates because of his strength with the old Whigs, was a member of the Illinois delegation pledged to Lincoln; and he labored loyally for him at the convention. David Davis, in charge of the Lincoln forces at Chicago, worked tirelessly and did his part well, though his bargaining in cabinet positions was contrary to Lincoln's instructions. With 465 delegates present and 233 necessary to a choice, the first ballot stood: Seward 173½, Lincoln 102, Cameron 50½, Chase 49, Bates 48, the rest scattered. On the second ballot Cameron's name was withdrawn to Lincoln's advantage, Seward receiving 184½ votes, Lincoln 181, Chase 42½, Bates 35. On the third ballot the change of four Ohio votes during the count precipitated a stampede to Lincoln, who became the convention's choice amid scenes of wild excitement.

In the fury of the ensuing campaign, with the Democratic party split between North and South and disunion threatened in case of Republican success, Lincoln remained quietly at Springfield. He conferred with leaders, received delegations, wrote letters, and prepared a short autobiography for campaign purposes; but he avoided political speeches. While the people of the South were expecting the worst from him, he did but little to reassure them. In the election of Nov. 6, 1860, he was chosen president by pluralities in enough states to give him a considerable electoral majority; but as regards the whole popular vote he was a minority president. There were ten Southern states in which not a single popular vote had been cast for him; and, strangely enough, his own county in Illinois voted against him. Lincoln carried every Northern free state except New Jersey. His vote in New England was nearly three times that of Douglas; elsewhere in the East his vote stood to that of Douglas as 7 to 4; in the Western states the contest was closer, the ratio being 8 to 7. Lincoln's total in the popular vote was 1,866,452 as compared to 1,376,957 for Douglas, 849,781 for Breckinridge, and 588,879 for Bell (Edward Stanwood, *A History of the Presidency,* 1924, I, 297). The electoral vote stood: Lincoln 180, Breckinridge 72, Bell 39, Douglas 12.

In the critical interval between his election and his inauguration Lincoln continued his policy of silence, making no speeches and avoiding public statements as to his policy. While events were moving rapidly in the lower South and disunion was consummated by the formation of a Southern Confederacy without hindrance from Washington, the President-Elect, though never doubting that the government possessed the authority to maintain itself, remained passive and quiet at Springfield. Matters of patronage, cabinet making, the preparation of his inaugural address, conferences, and correspondence occupied his attention. He found time for a trip to Coles County where he visited his aged stepmother, directing that the grave of his father be suitably marked, and for one to Chicago to meet Hannibal Hamlin, Nov. 21-26, 1860. To the measures of compromise proposed in Congress he gave scant encouragement. The Crittenden proposal to avert disunion was shattered by Lincoln's inflexible refusal to countenance the territorial extension of slavery. He requested General Scott to be ready to "hold or retake" the forts in the South as the case might require; and he did little to allay Southern fears as to his policy. He assured John A. Gilmer of North Carolina (Dec. 15, 1860, *Works,* VI, 81) that he would not discriminate against the South in appointments and that the only substantial difference between the Southern people and himself was in the matter of slavery extension. To another Southerner, Samuel Haycraft, he wrote that the "good people of the South" would find in him "no cause to complain" (Nov. 13, 1860, *Ibid.,* VI, 69-70). These and other similar letters, however, were confidential, and the pacific nature of his intentions was not appreciated. The pliable Seward, during these days, was more prominent as Republican spokesman than the President-Elect. A survey of the Southern press in this crisis shows a division of sentiment between those who recognized Lincoln's election as legal and would await an "overt act" before embarking upon disunion and those who asserted that abolition had swept the North and that the "cause of the South" had no

future except by separation. (See D. L. Dumond, *Southern Editorials on Secession*, 1931,
esp. pp. 221–223, 304–06; see also A. C. Cole in
American Historical Review, July 1931, pp. 740–
67.) It was not long before the men who held
the latter view seized the reins in the lower
South; and fast-moving events made theirs the
controlling policy for the South in general.
(Much light is thrown on Lincoln as president-
elect by the colorful letters of Henry Villard to
the *New York Herald*, November 1860 to February 1861). In the matter of cabinet making
the inclusion of Seward, Chase, and Bates was
a recognition of rivals, while Welles was chosen
as a New Englander and a former Democrat who
had turned Republican. Lincoln had wished to
include some representative of the South (as
distinguished from the border states) and had
approached John A. Gilmer of North Carolina
on this subject, but his efforts to this end proved
unsuccessful. Bargains in the nominating convention were kept by the appointment of Caleb B.
Smith of Indiana and Simon Cameron of Pennsylvania.

On Feb. 11, 1861, with words of restrained
emotion, Lincoln left Springfield for Washington. His speeches en route did little to reassure
the skeptical East, but they made it clear that
the government would resist secession. The effect of these speeches in the South was distinctly
unfavorable (D. L. Dumond, *The Secession
Movement*, 1931, pp. 258–60). Newspapers carried full accounts of the journey, and unfortunate
publicity was given to trivial incidents, as when
Lincoln, whose chin was now marred by a new-
grown beard, publicly kissed a little girl for
whom he inquired as his train stopped at her
town, and explained that the facial adornment
had been assumed at her request. His secret
night ride to Washington, occasioned by detective reports of assassination plots, was a humiliation to his friends and a subject of ridicule by
his opponents. In a conciliatory inaugural address Lincoln again disclaimed any intention to
interfere with slavery in the states, counseled
observance of all federal laws (not excepting the
Fugitive-slave Law), and plead earnestly for
the preservation of the Union, which he declared
to be perpetual (*Works*, VI, 169–85). Denouncing secession as anarchy he announced that the
national power would be used to "hold, occupy,
and possess" (he did not say "repossess") federal "property and places." Declaring that
"physically speaking, we cannot separate," he
asked his countrymen "one and all" to "think
calmly," pledging that the government would
not assail them, and closed with a poetic remind-

er of those "mystic chords of memory" which he
hoped would yet "swell the chorus of the Union."

Inexperienced as he was in the management
of great affairs, untrained in executive functions
requiring vigorous action, the new President
found himself borne down by a cruel pressure of
miscellaneous duties, overwhelmed by a horde of
office seekers, and embarrassed by unfamiliar
social exactions, while through it all the Sumter
crisis, involving the momentous issue of civil
war, was pressing for a solution. With the eyes
of the nation on the fort at Charleston as a test
of the new administration, with Major Anderson
reporting that in a few weeks the garrison must
surrender unless provisioned, and with informal
negotiations in progress between Union leaders
and Southern commissioners concerning the relation of the Washington government to the
Confederacy, events were pushing the new executive to a decision. Meanwhile his very position
as leader was at stake. Seward had begun by
supposing that he would be premier, and had
fatuously proposed a startling program of foreign aggression as a means of reuniting the
country. Lincoln's answer to his secretary left
no doubt as to who was president, but his words
left no sting. If a certain thing must be done,
said he simply, "I must do it" (*Works*, VI, 237).
As to Sumter, Lincoln took advice but made his
own decision, not, however, without a certain
laxness in his control of the situation which unfortunately gave Southern leaders the impression
of bad faith; for Seward, without Lincoln's authority, had made virtual promises which the
administration could not keep. Lincoln asked
his cabinet to submit written advice as to pro-
visioning Sumter. Only two members, Chase
hesitatingly and Blair emphatically, favored it.
Seward, Cameron, Welles, Smith, and Bates
counseled evacuation, though some of the secretaries later changed their positions. Having already committed himself to the general policy of
holding federal property, and feeling that evacuation would be tantamount to surrender, Lincoln
ultimately decided to provision the fort. Yet
Seward assured the Confederate commissioners
that the fort would be evacuated; and Lincoln
himself was willing to evacuate it if by this
means the secession of Virginia could be averted.
"A State for a fort," he is reported to have said,
"is no bad business" (*Annual Report of the
American Historical Association for the Year
1915*, 1917, p. 211). Late in March he sent Ward
H. Lamon [*q.v.*] to Charleston, primarily to investigate and report; but Lamon unfortunately
gave Anderson, Beauregard, and Governor Pickens the impression that the garrison would be

withdrawn (*War of the Rebellion: Official Records,* ser. I, vol. I, 1880, pp. 222, 230, 237, 294). In all this there was considerable muddling, though without bad faith on Lincoln's part; and the confusion was increased by a bungling of orders due to Seward's interference with arrangements made by Lincoln and Welles, as a result of which the Sumter expedition was crippled by the detachment of the powerful *Powhatan.* The pacific attitude of the President was manifest in the purpose of the expedition (to convey food to the garrison and to land reënforcements only in case of attack), and also in the care which he took to notify the governor of South Carolina of his action, thus removing the element of hostile surprise.

Diverse interpretations have been placed upon Lincoln's action, and the whole subject has occasioned a flood of controversy. There are many threads to the story; and to the perplexities of conflicting evidence must be added the difficulties of reading thoughts and assessing motives in a field where violent misunderstandings were inevitable. Under the onslaught of opposing forces, with the border states and upper South on the brink of secession and the war clouds gathering, Lincoln himself seems to have vacillated, to have pondered evacuation, meanwhile testing its possible consequences and even giving hints that such a course was under consideration without committing himself to it (a process to which statesmen must often resort), and in the end to have concluded that, in view of the uncertainty of compensating benefits accruing to the cause of union, the fort should not be surrendered. As the exhaustion of supplies made some change inevitable, the closest approximation to the preservation of the status quo was what Lincoln decided to do—to feed the garrison without aggressively strengthening it.

When the war came, Lincoln met the issue with a series of purely executive measures, for Congress was not convened until July 1861. He treated the conflict as a huge "insurrection"; and before Congress, on July 13, 1861, recognized a state of war, he had summoned the militia, proclaimed a blockade, expanded the regular army beyond the legal limit, suspended the *habeas corpus* privilege, directed governmental expenditures in advance of congressional appropriation, and in cooperation with his cabinet and the state governments had launched a multifold series of military measures. In a masterly message to Congress on July 4, 1861, he explained his Sumter policy, recounted the steps that led to war, stated the issue as between separation and union, commented on the world significance of

the struggle, and appealed for ratification of previous acts as well as for future cooperation (*Works,* VI, 297-325). This legislative ratification of the president's irregular acts was soon given (*United States Statutes at Large,* XII, 326); and the Supreme Court added its sanction by deciding in the Prize Cases (67 *U. S.,* 635-99), though not without vigorous dissent, that executive proclamations were adequate for the inauguration of maritime war.

As the war progressed, Lincoln extended his executive powers until, man of peace that he was, he was called a dictator. In dealing with disloyal activities—a serious problem because of pro-Southern activity in the North—he urged no special laws against treason, he but slightly used such laws as existed, and he had no system of nation-wide prosecutions; but, under his suspension of the *habeas corpus* privilege, thousands of persons were arrested on suspicion, after which, usually without trial, they were kept in prison for a time and then released. In this his purpose was precautionary and preventive, not punitive or vindictive. When confronted with anti-war or anti-administration agitation in speech or press, Lincoln usually showed toleration; and throughout the war "Copperhead" meetings were common and opposition newspapers persisted in their attacks upon the President and his party. The case of C. L. Vallandigham [*q.v.*], arrested for an anti-war speech of May 1, 1863, by order of General Burnside, was a familiar theme of denunciation by Lincoln's opponents; but the facts show leniency and tact in him rather than severity. He and all the cabinet regretted the arrest; and when a military commission condemned the agitator to imprisonment during the war, Lincoln commuted the sentence to banishment within the Confederate lines. Later, when Vallandigham escaped from the South and conducted a violent agitation in Ohio, Lincoln left him unmolested. There were, it is true, instances of newspaper suppression, as in the case of the *Chicago Times* in June 1863 (in which case Burnside's suspension order was promptly revoked); but in general Lincoln advised military restraint and counseled the suppression of assemblies or newspapers only when they were working "palpable injury" to the military (*Works,* IX, 148).

Looking broadly at his administration, one is impressed with the many difficulties that beset Lincoln's path. He had a rival for the presidency (Chase) in his cabinet. Within his own party the "Jacobins," a group which seemed at times a cabal of congressional leaders but which became the dominant element, tried his patience with their radicalism, their defiant opposition, and their interference in the conduct of the war. Abolition demands required his utmost tact; for the outcries of such men as Wendell Phillips reached at times an almost hysterical pitch. Always he had the activities of anti-war leaders to deal with. Though bringing Democrats within his cabinet and appointing many of them to civil and military positions, he was unable to carry through his "all parties program"; and he found it necessary to function as leader of one party, the Republican or "Union" party. Scheming men imposed on his generosity and a constant stream of people clamored at his doors. He had the defeatists to deal with—men who demanded peace first and union afterward; while he had the equally hard problem of keeping the Union cause clear of abuse, so that victory, when achieved, would not itself become a curse. The maladjustment of governmental activities, state and federal, military and civil, made his tasks needlessly hard; while the profiteering, plunder, and graft that came in the wake of war wounded his honest soul. A group of senators, partisans of Chase [q.v.], descended upon him in December 1862, demanding the removal of Seward and threatening to take important matters of policy out of his hands. Though inwardly suffering bitter distress (*Diary of O. H. Browning*, I, 601), Lincoln received the intriguing senators with calm, rode the storm by shrewd steering, kept both Seward and Chase in his cabinet, silenced his critics, and reassured the public. Often he faced a hostile and meddling Congress, and at times he seemed almost deserted. Favoring a war policy with as little of vengeance as possible, always remembering that the people of the South were to be respected, he encountered the opposition of the vindictive element which ultimately seized the Republican party and overthrew his policy in reconstruction days. It is in his reaction to these difficult circumstances that we find the measure of Lincoln's qualities as president: his unaffected kindness, his poise, his humor, his largeness of soul, his fairness toward opponents, his refusal to get angry, his steadiness, his ability to maintain that well-tempered morale which is so indispensable in a desperate war. There was also the notable trait of selflessness; for if Lincoln suffered when his pride was pierced, such was the temper of his self-control (which must not be misunderstood as mere humility) that no outward reaction of irrascibility, peevishness, or ungenerous conduct resulted.

In his cabinet Lincoln found an ill-assorted group. Welles inwardly denounced Seward; Bates distrusted Stanton, Seward, and Chase;

Stanton and Seward were uncongenial; and Chase, though never actually disloyal to Lincoln, was a constant source of discord. Yet Lincoln, lax as he was in administrative methods, maintained an attitude of cooperation in his official family. Such changes as occurred in his cabinet were of a sort to strengthen the President's position, the vigorous Stanton displacing the incompetent Cameron, Chase being shrewdly kept in the cabinet until after the renomination of Lincoln when he gave way to the more pliable Fessenden, Speed and Dennison serving as acceptable substitutes for Bates and Blair.

In the military phases of his task Lincoln was sorely beset. Governmental organization for war purposes was ill suited to the emergency and seemed at times formless. Some of the state governors embarrassed him by over-activity that trenched upon the duties of the secretary of war; others caused trouble by sheer recalcitrancy. Military efficiency was subordinated to personal ambition; there was a superfluity of political generals; and there was confusion and experimentation in the central control of the army. Troops when brought into the field were often unreliable; "some of the brigadier-generals," wrote Halleck (*Works of Lincoln,* VII, 77), were "entirely ignorant of their duties and unfit for any command." The war machine suffered from an ill-advised system of conscription, from undue state control of military matters, from widespread desertion and "bounty jumping," and from harmful newspaper activity, which betrayed military secrets, discredited the government, defamed generals, fomented antagonism among officers, and weakened the morale of soldier and citizen. Congressional interference was evident in the Committee on the Conduct of the War (W. W. Pierson, in *American Historical Review,* April 1918, pp. 550–76), which investigated Union disasters, held protracted conferences with the President, and considered themselves "a sort of Aulic Council clothed with authority to supervise the plans of commanders in the field, to make military suggestions, and to dictate military appointments" (*Ibid.,* p. 566, citing W. H. Hurlbert, *General McClellan and the Conduct of the War,* 1864, p. 160). That Lincoln listened patiently to the committee and yet never permitted them to take the wheel from his hand, is evidence at once of his tact and his shrewdness.

With his burning sense of the issues at stake and his pathetic eagerness for one battle to end it all, Lincoln was subjected to repeated humiliation in the defeat of Union arms. His reaction to defeat is illustrated in his memorandum of

July 23, 1861, following the first Bull Run, in which he outlined a comprehensive plan for pushing the blockade, drilling the forces, discharging "three-months men" who would not reënlist, bringing forward new volunteer units, protecting Washington against attack, and formulating a joint forward movement in the West (*Works*, VI, 331–32). The pressure of military duties upon Lincoln was more than any president of a republic should bear. He pored over books on strategy; scanned the military map; prepared orders for the army; gave counsel concerning such details as the acquisition of horses and the price of guns; outlined plans of campaign, not forgetting, however, the hazard of binding a distant commander to specific lines and operations; directed the allocation of supplies; attended war councils; and devoted constant attention to military appointments. He assumed a special degree of military responsibility at the time of McClellan's illness in January 1862; and he had to make those repeated calls for troops which intensified the depression of the country. In his experimentation with men he expressed a whimsical wish for a "school of events"—mimic situations in which men might be tried (F. B. Carpenter, *Six Months at the White House*, p. 225); and he even contemplated taking the field himself (*Diary of O. H. Browning*, I, 523).

Kindness and forbearance, mingled at times with fatherly admonition, characterized his attitude toward his generals. When Frémont issued impossible orders in the West without consulting the President, Lincoln sent him a word of "caution, and not of censure," directed that certain orders be "modified," sent Blair from his cabinet for a friendly conference, and finally removed the General only when his insubordinate conduct left no alternative. Lincoln's search for a winning general is a painful story. McClellan snubbed him, differed with him as to plans, wrote complaining letters, and fell short in the business of fighting. Lincoln ignored the snubs with the remark that it were better "not to be making points of . . . personal dignity" (*Letters of John Hay and Extracts from Diary*, I, 53); and on the retirement of Scott in November 1861 he made McClellan general-in-chief of all the armies. The President's plans, beset as he was by boards, senators, councils, military "experts," and clamoring editors, proved hopelessly at variance with McClellan's performance. In January 1862 the perplexed President issued a peremptory "war order" directing a "general movement of all the land and naval forces of the United States against the insurgent forces" for Feb. 22 (*Works*, VII, 89). This order was ignored, and Lincoln acquiesced in McClellan's oblique movement against Richmond via the peninsula. At the outset of the peninsular campaign, however, Lincoln relieved McClellan of supreme command; and he modified the latter's plan for the concentration of Union forces against Richmond by retaining McDowell's corps near Washington, while he also decreased McClellan's importance by reorganizing the army under corps commanders. McClellan's ineffectiveness caused Lincoln to put Pope in command of a separate Army of Virginia; but on Pope's failure at the second battle of Bull Run the President dropped him and ordered a reconsolidation of forces under McClellan, who was thus given a new opportunity. Then came McClellan's failure to pursue Lee after Antietam, upon which Lincoln finally removed him from command. The failure of McClellan's successors—of Burnside at Fredericksburg and Hooker at Chancellorsville—added to Lincoln's perplexity and tended to discredit his ability in military matters; while Meade's success at Gettysburg was marred by another failure to pursue and crush Lee's army, and even under Grant, whom Lincoln brought to the East in 1864, there were months of sanguinary fighting with hope deferred. Lincoln's blunders in military matters, which are not to be denied, were largely attributable to political pressure or to unsatisfactory human material, and were partly offset by constructive factors such as his guarding of Washington, his attention to the western phases of the war, and his final support of Grant in the face of bitter criticism.

Cautious in his dealings with Congress, Lincoln seldom seized the initiative in the framing of legislation. He went his own way by a remarkable assumption of executive authority; and on the few occasions when he sought to direct important legislation he was usually unsuccessful. The congressional election of 1862 was unfavorable to him; and elements out of sympathy with Lincoln were often dominant in Congress, which sought to curb the president's power of arrest, passed measures which he disapproved, and came to an *impasse* with him as to reconstruction. Though the reconstruction issue is a notable exception, Lincoln usually yielded when Congress enacted measures distasteful to him, as in the case of the West Virginia bill and the second confiscation act. Moderates were disappointed in this pliancy, which they described as "going over to the radicals"; yet the radicals themselves were far from capturing Lincoln, and at the time of his death in office an open break such as that which occurred under Johnson seemed probable.

Though the issuing of the Emancipation Proclamation is the most memorable of Lincoln's acts, the stereotyped picture of the emancipator suddenly striking the shackles from millions of slaves by a stroke of the pen is unhistorical. Lincoln's policy touching slavery was a matter of slow development. Throughout the struggle he held that Congress did not have the power to abolish slavery in the South; and in keeping with his "border-state policy" he resisted for many months the clamors of abolitionists. When Union generals, notably Frémont in Missouri and Hunter in the lower South, attempted emancipation by military edict, Lincoln overruled them; and he said to a religious group: "I do not want to issue a document that . . . must . . . be inoperative, like the Pope's bull against the comet" (*Works*, VIII, 30). Answering Greeley's anti-slavery appeal on Aug. 22, 1862, he wrote, though with the proclamation already in his drawer, that his "paramount object" was to "save the Union," and was not "either to save or to destroy slavery" (*Ibid.*, VIII, 16). It was found, however, that war over a vastly extended front with a slave-holding power forced the government either to take steps toward emancipation or to become both its own enemy and a promoter of slavery. By July 1862, therefore, Congress had, at least on paper, provided as much as the Emancipation Proclamation involved, by freeing slaves coming within Union military lines, emancipating slave-soldiers, and decreeing liberation generally as to all "rebel-owned" slaves in the sweeping though ineffectual confiscation act of July 17, 1862. In addition, Congress had by this time prohibited slavery in the territories and in the District of Columbia.

Meanwhile, from Lincoln's pondering of the slavery problem there had emerged a plan of constructive statesmanship. Recognizing state authority in the premises, mindful of Southern property rights, and moved by the conviction that the North ought equitably to share the financial burden of emancipation, since it must share the guilt of slavery, Lincoln had urged Congress to launch a scheme of gradual emancipation by voluntary action of the states, with federal compensation to slave-holders. This plan, however, as well as the scheme of deportation and colonization in Africa, had broken down; and in July 1862 Lincoln reached the decision to issue his edict of liberation. By this time the increasing radicalism of the war mind, the indifference of the border states to his compensation scheme, and the realization that foreign sympathy could

not be obtained for a government which "sought to put down the rebellion with the left hand, while supporting slavery with the right hand" (Chase Manuscripts, Library of Congress, vol. LXII, no. 1989) had done their work. On July 22, 1862, Lincoln summoned his cabinet and read aloud the first draft of the Emancipation Proclamation. His decision was now made; he was not asking advice "about the main matter." Rather he was announcing his course and taking counsel about incidental questions pertaining to its execution. Accepting Seward's suggestion that the measure would gain force if issued on the morrow of victory, he waited until Lee had been fought off at Antietam and gave out his preliminary proclamation on Sept. 22, 1862 (*Works*, VIII, 36–41). In this edict he gave warning that on Jan. 1, 1863, all slaves in rebellious districts would be made free; but the proclamation was far from an abolition document, for the President emphasized the restoration of the Union as the object of the war, and pledged further efforts to provide compensation to slaveholders. By common usage, the term "Emancipation Proclamation" applies to the edict of Jan. 1, 1863, that of Sept. 22, 1862, being but a warning. The Proclamation of Jan. 1, 1863, contained no general declaration against slavery as an evil (*Ibid.*, VIII, 161–64). The Union slave states were naturally not affected; and important districts of the South (the whole state of Tennessee as well as portions of Virginia and Louisiana) were excluded from the terms of the proclamation. The most curious fact about the whole matter was that the proclamation applied only to regions under Confederate control; and Lincoln was denounced for freeing slaves only on paper in districts where his power could not extend. It is hard to put in a word the actual effect of the Proclamation. Preservation of slavery in non-rebellious districts was clearly implied; and if the Southern states had done all Lincoln asked in September 1862, thus obviating the necessity of the final proclamation, there was nothing in the preliminary document to prevent the war from ending with slavery still maintained. Yet the President's stroke at slavery did somehow change the character of the war; and its moral effect was great, albeit somewhat offset by the displeasure of those who opposed a "war to free the negroes." Military emancipation extended as the armies advanced in the South; but as to the legal potency of the Proclamation Lincoln himself had grave doubts. Effective liberation, in fact, came through state action in the border states and more notably through the anti-slavery amendment to the Constitution. Perhaps the chief importance of the Proclamation was in paving the way for these final measures. Lincoln's part in the whole matter was necessarily central. It was he who determined the time, circumstances, and manner of the proclamation; and it was his conviction that, had it been issued six months earlier, public sentiment would not have sustained it (F. B. Carpenter, *Six Months at the White House*, p. 77).

In spite of serious complications with France and Great Britain, Lincoln gave little direct attention to foreign affairs. He brushed aside Seward's bellicose foreign program of Apr. 1, 1861; and he materially assisted in the preservation of peace by softening Seward's instructions of May 21, 1861, to Charles Francis Adams on the general question of Great Britain's attitude toward the war and by directing that Adams treat the whole dispatch as confidential. In the *Trent* affair the influence of Sumner, Seward, and Bright contributed powerfully toward peace with Great Britain, the threads being in Seward's hands; but Lincoln's moderation, though at first he seems to have supposed that Mason and Slidell ought not to be released (Frederic Bancroft, *The Life of W. H. Seward*, 1900, II, 234), was an important factor. His restraint in international dealings is shown by a "paper" which he prepared, advocating that the *Trent* case be arbitrated (*Diary of O. H. Browning*, I, 517). On such questions as the French proposal for mediation, French intervention in Mexico, and the protests against British aid in the building and equipment of Confederate warships, the course of the administration was successfully directed by Seward, to whom Lincoln wisely delegated foreign affairs with the minimum of presidential interference.

While preserving the dignity of his high position, Lincoln's manners as president were unconventional and his habits irregular. Often his meals, when carried upstairs, would be left untouched for hours. He took no regular exercise, his chief relaxation being found in the summer evenings at the Soldiers' Home. During the first week of the battle of the Wilderness, says Carpenter (*Six Months at the White House*, p. 30), he "scarcely slept at all"; and the black rings under his eyes bespoke the strain under which he labored. In his last year his friends all noted his mental weariness; as he expressed it, the remedy "seemed never to reach the *tired* spot" (*Ibid.*, p. 217). Despite this strain there was always a readiness to shake hands with a casual visitor and to receive the humblest citizen or soldier. In reviewing the death penalty for desertion or sleeping on sentinel duty, he eagerly

sought excuses for clemency; yet his mercy was not mere weakness, and at times he did confirm the death sentence. He read the newspapers but little, for news reached him through more direct channels. Day and night his familiar form was seen in the telegraph office of the War Department across from the White House. In humorous stories and the repetition of favorite literary passages he found mental relaxation. The poem "Oh Why Should the Spirit of Mortal Be Proud" had a peculiar fascination for him, and his familiarity with Shakespeare was often a matter of surprise. Laughter was an absolute need of his harassed mind and he habitually thought in terms of parable, his anecdotes usually having a backwoods flavor and a tang of the pioneer West. His enjoyment of rough jest is shown in his fondness for such humorists as Nasby and Artemus Ward; his matter-of-fact secretaries had to endure a chapter from Ward as a preface to his reading of the Emancipation Proclamation in cabinet meeting. The melancholy of the earlier Lincoln deepened under the pressure of war. Not alone did the nation's woes bear heavily upon him, but the death of his son Willie in February 1862, following nightly vigils at the bedside, added a personal bereavement which would have come nigh to prostration but for the pressure of public duties.

Though a ready speech-maker, Lincoln as president made very few public addresses, the chief examples being his inaugurals, his Gettysburg address, and his last speech, Apr. 11, 1865, which dealt with reconstruction (*Works*, XI, 84–92). In lieu of the "White House publicity" of later presidents, he made use of the art of correspondence. When answering criticism or appealing to the people, he would prepare a careful letter which, while addressed to an individual or delegation, would be intended for the nation's ear. When a meeting of citizens protested against the arrest of an agitator, Lincoln wrote an elaborate letter (to E. Corning and others, June 12, 1863) explaining his policy of arbitrary arrests and pointing out the inability of the courts to deal with rebellion. Referring to the death penalty for desertion he asked, "Must I shoot a simple-minded soldier boy who deserts, while I must not touch a hair of a wily agitator who induces him to desert?" (*Works*, VIII, 308). Writing to Cuthbert Bullitt, July 28, 1862, he raised the question whether Southern unionists should be "merely passengers . . . to be carried snug and dry throughout the storm, and safely landed right side up" (*Ibid.*, VII, 296). On finding it impossible to attend a meeting of "unconditional Union men," at Springfield, Ill., he wrote an important letter to J. C. Conkling (*Works*, IX, 95–102) in which he defended the Emancipation Proclamation as a measure for saving the Union. In this letter he paid tribute to the men of Antietam, Murfreesboro, and Gettysburg, not forgetting "Uncle Sam's web-feet," for whose noble work "at all the watery margins" he expressed deep thanks. Of like importance were his letter to Greeley on the slavery question (Aug. 22, 1862), to Raymond of the *Times* regarding compensated emancipation, to Governor Seymour concerning the opposition of New York to the conscription law, and to Mrs. Bixby, whom he beautifully consoled for the loss of her sons in battle. On Nov. 19, 1863, in dedicating a soldiers' cemetery at Gettysburg, Lincoln lifted the nation's thoughts from the hatreds and imminent horrors of war in a brief address which is recognized as his most famous speech (*Works*, IX, 209–10). In his few simple words of dedication the factor of enmity toward the South was notably lacking; and the prevailing note was Lincoln's central idea of the broad significance of the Civil War as a vindication of popular rule.

The story of the campaign and election of 1864 has never been fully told. In an atmosphere of national depression and war-weariness, with prominent men denouncing the "imbecility" of the administration at Washington, with victory deferred after three years of terrible losses, with financial credit at low ebb, and with defeatists demanding peace on the ground that the war was a failure, the President faced the hazard of a popular election. Though the presidential boom of Salmon P. Chase [*q.v.*], to which Lincoln closed his ears, soon collapsed, Frémont accepted nomination from an anti-Lincoln group; and the Democrats ominously gathered their forces while at the same time postponing their nomination until August. Such Republicans as Greeley, H. W. Davis, Beecher, Bryant, Whitelaw Reid, and many others, were minded to drop Lincoln; but Republican managers set an early date for the party convention (June 7), Lincoln meanwhile keeping Chase in the cabinet, and there was little difficulty in obtaining the President's renomination when the convention met at Baltimore. The renomination was in fact unanimous; but in the months that followed, the military outlook became still gloomier; and when McClellan was nominated by the Democrats in August on a peace platform his strength seemed truly formidable. At this juncture a surprising movement developed—nothing less than an effort to supplant Lincoln with a "more vigorous leader" and force his withdrawal (New York *Sun,* June 30, 1889, p. 3). A plan was laid for a

convention to meet at Cincinnati, Ohio, on Sept. 28 "to concentrate the union strength on some one candidate, who commands the confidence of the country, even by a new nomination if necessary" (*Ibid.*). At this time Greeley wrote that Lincoln was "already beaten," and that only "another ticket" could save the party from "utter overthrow." As late as Aug. 25, H. W. Davis wrote: "My letters from Maryland say Lincoln can do nothing there, even where the Union party is most vigorous, and everybody is looking for a new candidate from somewhere." These extracts will serve to suggest the active opposition to Lincoln within his own party, which was due to such factors as the lack of Union success in battle, the conservatism of Lincoln, his leniency toward the South which ran counter to the radical plan of reconstruction, his call of July 18, 1864, for 500,000 volunteers, and the feeling that the President under Seward's influence was an opportunist and compromiser rather than a vigorous executive. The real strength of the anti-Lincoln movement is difficult to gauge because a favorable turn in the administration's fortunes occurred in September with the fall of Atlanta and Republican electoral successes in Vermont and Maine, after which, for the sake of party harmony, various anti-Lincoln men such as Wade and Greeley gave him their support. With this turn of the tide the demand for Lincoln's withdrawal lost its point and the Cincinnati convention was never held. Efforts were put forth to include certain states of the Confederacy in the election, and the President carried Louisiana and Tennessee where reorganized "loyal" governments had been set up; but the votes of these states, being unnecessary, were not recognized by Congress in the electoral count. Thus only the Union states were counted; and all of them except Kentucky, Delaware, and New Jersey gave Lincoln their electoral vote. This electoral sweep, together with Lincoln's popular majority of more than 400,000 over McClellan, gave the election somewhat the appearance of a Lincoln landslide; there were, however, powerful McClellan minorities in Illinois, Indiana, Ohio, New York, and Pennsylvania. (H. M. Dudley, "The Election of 1864," *Mississippi Valley Historical Review,* March 1932.) In the event of McClellan's election Lincoln had resolved "to so cooperate with the President-elect as to save the Union between the election and the inauguration." As his secretaries record, it was the President's intention to "talk matters over" with McClellan and say to him: "Now let us together, you with your influence and I with all the executive power of the Government, try to save the country." At the time when this patriotic resolve to cooperate with a victorious opponent was made (Aug. 23, 1864), the President considered his own defeat "exceedingly probable" (Nicolay and Hay, *Lincoln,* IX, 251–52).

At his second inauguration, Mar. 4, 1865, Lincoln made no effort to review the events of his administration, but delivered a brief address which, for loftiness of tone, ranks among his greatest state papers (*Works,* XI, 44–47). Breathing a spirit of friendliness toward the enemy, he refused to blame the South for the war, and counseled his countrymen to "judge not, that we be not judged." "With malice toward none; with charity for all," he concluded, "let us strive on to finish the work we are in; to bind up the nation's wounds; . . . to do all which may achieve and cherish a just and lasting peace. . . ." There were few Northern leaders who manifested as fair an understanding of the Southern people as Lincoln (A. C. Cole, in *Lincoln Centennial Association Papers,* 1928, pp. 47–78); and he devoted careful thought and labor to the restoration of the Southern states to the Union. In his proclamation of Dec. 8, 1863, he pardoned (with certain exceptions) those Confederates who would swear allegiance to the Union; and he vigorously promoted the organization of "loyal" governments in the Southern states, requiring that they abolish slavery, and standing ready to welcome them into the Union though the loyal nucleus be no more than ten per cent. of the voters of 1860. When Congress, on July 2, 1864, passed the Wade-Davis bill providing a severe plan that would hinder reconstruction, Lincoln applied the "pocket" veto, and announced his reasons in a "proclamation" of July 8 (*Works,* X, 152–54), upon which the authors of the bill, with an eye to the President's embarrassment in the campaign for reëlection, severely attacked him in an address to the people known as the Wade-Davis manifesto. The details of Lincoln's further efforts toward reconstruction are too elaborate to be recounted here. His scheme was carried through to his own satisfaction in Tennessee, Louisiana, Arkansas, and Virginia; but Congress never recognized any of these "Lincoln governments" of the South.

As to peace negotiations with the Confederacy, Lincoln insisted upon reunion and the abolition of slavery, but manifested a generous disposition on collateral issues. This was his attitude in connection with the peace efforts of Horace Greeley [*q.v.*] in 1864; and the same moderate attitude was manifested in connection with Blair's mission to Richmond (see Blair, Francis Preston, 1791–1876) and in the Hampton Roads Conference of February 1865. In this conference Lincoln, in company with Seward, conferred on board a warship with three Confederate commissioners (J. A. Campbell, A. H. Stephens, and R. M. T. Hunter); and accounts agree that, while the President again insisted upon reunion and emancipation, he showed willingness to use the pardoning power freely in the South, to allow self-government to the returning states, and even to recommend liberal compensation to slave-holders. On the fall of Richmond Lincoln visited the Confederate capital, where he walked the streets unmolested, and advised with Southern leaders, notably J. A. Campbell. He expressed a desire to permit the "rebel" legislature of Virginia to return and reorganize the state; but this purpose, as well as his other plans for the South, was defeated.

He gave the closest attention to the final military phase of the war, visiting the army and remaining with Grant at City Point from Mar. 24 until Apr. 9, except for his two-day visit to Richmond on the 4th and 5th. His return to Washington coincided with Lee's surrender, an event which gave added significance to the President's last speech, which was a statesmanlike paper read to a cheering crowd at the White House on the night of Apr. 11. Returning to the subject of reconstruction, he appealed to a divided North to let the South come back to the Union. Casting theories aside, he said: "We all agree that the seceded States . . . are out of their proper practical relation with the Union, and that the . . . object of the government . . . is to again get them into that proper practical relation" (*Works,* XI, 88). "Concede," he said, "that the new government of Louisiana is . . . as the egg is to the fowl, we shall sooner have the fowl by hatching the egg than by smashing it" (*Ibid.,* XI, 91). On the last day of Lincoln's life the subject of reconstruction was discussed at length in cabinet meeting; and a project was considered which resembled the plan later announced by President Johnson on May 29, 1865 (40 Cong., 1 sess., *Report of Committees of the House of Representatives,* no. 7, pp. 78–79). Again Lincoln expressed the wish that all vindictiveness be laid aside and that the Southern people be leniently treated (F. W. Seward, *Reminiscences,* 1916, p. 254). With opposition growing within his own party and threatening the ruin of his generous plans had he lived, he was removed by assassination, which silenced criticism and conferred the martyr's crown. At Ford's Theatre on the night of Apr. 14, 1865, he was shot by John Wilkes Booth [*q.v.*]. After lying unconscious through the

Lincoln

Lincoln

night he died the following morning. The state rites over, the funeral train moved west with frequent stops; and amid fulminations of vindictive oratory, with people and soldiers mourning their beloved Chief, the body was laid to rest at Springfield.

The early crystallization of the enduring Lincoln tradition was illustrated by Stanton's comment, "Now he belongs to the ages." That he was among the "consummate masters of statecraft" may be disputed, but such was the impression he left that this distinction has been accorded him. In the shortest list of American liberal leaders he takes eminent place: liberalism with him was no garment; it was of the fiber of his mind. His hold upon the affections of his own people has not been due merely to the fact that he, a backwoods lad, rose to the highest office in the land. It is doubtful whether any other leader of the North could have matched him in dramatizing the war to the popular mind, in shaping language to his purpose, in smoothing personal difficulties by a magnanimous touch or a tactful gesture, in avoiding domestic and international complications, in courageously persisting in the face of almost unendurable discouragements, in maintaining war morale while refusing to harbor personal malice against the South. Not inappropriately, he has become a symbol both of American democracy and the Union.

[For bibliographies, see Daniel Fish, *Lincoln Bibliography* (1906), also in *Complete Works*, XI, 135–380; Jos. B. Oakleaf, *Lincoln Bibliography* (1925); W. E. Barton, "The Lincoln of the Biographers," *Trans. Ill. State Hist. Soc. for the Year 1929* (1929), pp. 58–116. The most important edition of the writings and speeches is J. G. Nicolay and John Hay, *Complete Works of Abraham Lincoln* (Gettysburg ed., 12 vols., 1905), and it is to this edition that the foregoing references are made. Additional writings are to be found in G. A. Tracy, *Uncollected Letters of Abraham Lincoln* (1917); *Lincoln Letters, Hitherto Unpublished, in the Library of Brown Univ. and other Providence Libraries* (1929); P. M. Angle, *New Letters and Papers of Lincoln* (1930). The best edition of the Lincoln-Douglas debates is that of E. E. Sparks in *Colls. of the Ill. State Hist. Lib.*, vol. III (1908). Of manuscript collections the most important are the Weik MSS. (preserved by J. W. Weik, collaborator with Herndon), and the voluminous Lincoln papers deposited in the Lib. of Cong., but withheld from investigators for many years. Certain alleged Lincoln documents have proved to be forgeries, such as the letters to Senator Crittenden, Dec. 22, 1859, and to A. H. Stephens, Jan. 19, 1860 (see W. C. Ford in *Mass. Hist. Soc. Proc.*, May 1928), the letter to an Italian named Melloni, alleged to have been written in 1853 (*N. Y. Times*, Nov. 20, 23, 24, 1931, May 8, 1932), and the fantastic collection of Lincoln and Ann Rutledge letters published in the *Atlantic Monthly*, Dec. 1928–Feb. 1929 (see P. M. Angle, "The Minor Collection: A Criticism," *Ibid.*, Apr. 1929). Autobiographical portions of Lincoln's utterances have been collected in *An Autobiography of Abraham Lincoln* (1926), by N. W. Stephenson.
Campaign biographies were issued by J. L. Scripps, J. H. Barrett, and J. Q. Howard in 1860, and by H. J. Raymond, W. M. Thayer, and J. H. Barrett again in 1864. After Lincoln's death there appeared a number

of biographies by men who had known him more or less closely. Ward H. Lamon [*q.v.*] brought out *The Life of Abraham Lincoln from his Birth to his Inauguration as President* (1872). This work, which gives a realistic and partly unfavorable picture of Lincoln, was written not by Lamon but by Chauncey F. Black. Isaac N. Arnold of Chicago, from years of association with Lincoln, published studies in 1866 and 1869, and *The Life of Abraham Lincoln* (1885). J. G. Holland, *Life of Abraham Lincoln* (1866), though produced too soon to permit of historical perspective, was a work of merit, compiled with discrimination and attractively written. In 1889 appeared *Herndon's Lincoln: The True Story of a Great Life*, by W. H. Herndon and J. W. Weik, which should be used in the edition of P. M. Angle (1930). With all its limitations, this biography is a classic. It presents Lincoln without the halo, giving a view of the every-day life of the man with a wealth of anecdote and a power of portrayal which has caused it to be extensively used by later biographers. Herndon substituted "for Lincoln's aureole the battered tall hat, with valuable papers stuck in its lining, which he had long contemplated with reverent irritation" (Charnwood, *Abraham Lincoln* p. 102). It is, however, the Lincoln of the prairies whom Herndon and Weik present; their account of the presidency is wholly inadequate. Many years later Weik returned over the same trail and published *The Real Lincoln* (1922), reaffirming certain disputed statements in the Herndon work and adding minor details. The monumental work by Lincoln's secretaries, J. G. Nicolay and John Hay, *Abraham Lincoln: A History* (10 vols., 1890), inaugurated a new era of Lincoln historiography. It is a voluminous history as well as a biography, for the authors attempted to include everything. Approved by Robert Lincoln, it possesses both the advantages and the defects of an authorized biography. From their daily contact with the President, Nicolay and Hay had an inside acquaintance with his administration; and they made use of a vast range of material, including papers which have been used by no other writers. Their uniform tendency, however, to treat everything from the point of view of Lincoln, their unsympathetic attitude toward his opponents, and their partiality for the Republican party, made it impossible for them to produce the definitive biography.

Since Nicolay and Hay, the Lincoln bibliography has reached tremendous dimensions, and a full list would comprise thousands of items. The activity of collectors and dealers in Lincolniana has magnified the importance of every trivial item; and the yearly output of Lincoln addresses and articles, tinctured with the political or social predilections of the authors, is of staggering proportions. Only a few outstanding titles can be mentioned here. At the forefront of recent biographies is Albert J. Beveridge, *Abraham Lincoln, 1809–1858* (2 vols., 1928). This great work is not as readable as certain other biographies, for the author has presented his material as he found it with the minimum of literary coloring; its high value derives from its soundness and thoroughness of historical investigation. Ida M. Tarbell, *The Life of Abraham Lincoln* (2 vols., 1900), is based on material collected by the author in the service of *McClure's Mag.*, and was first published serially in that periodical in 1895–96. It has merit as a popular "life," but some of its statements, *e.g.*, those concerning the parentage of Nancy Hanks, have been disproved. *Abraham Lincoln* (1917), by Lord Charnwood, is an excellent one-volume biography. Though he conducted but little original research and used easily available published sources, Charnwood has produced a well-proportioned narrative which gains much by being addressed to an English audience. Another short biography of high merit is *Lincoln: An Account of His Personal Life*, etc. (1924), by N. W. Stephenson. With rare literary artistry Stephenson treats the "emergence" of Lincoln's character from its earlier hesitances into the "final Lincoln," whom he places among the "consummate masters of statecraft." W. E. Barton has been tireless in his researches and has produced a great many books on Lincoln, among which are: *Life of Abraham Lincoln* (2 vols., 1925); *The Pa-*

ternity of Abraham Lincoln (1920); *The Soul of Abraham Lincoln* (1920); *The Women Lincoln Loved* (1927); *The Lineage of Lincoln* (1929); *Lincoln at Gettysburg* (1930). Carl Sandburg, *Abraham Lincoln: The Prairie Years* (2 vols., 1926), though attempting no elaborate documentation or critical evaluation of sources, is extraordinarily vivid and has a remarkable pictorial quality in its portrayal of the rough American pioneer life out of which Lincoln came. Emil Ludwig, *Lincoln* (1930), translated from the German by Eden and Cedar Paul, though of slight importance as a historical contribution, is dramatic and readable, conforming to the new biographical vogue. Edgar Lee Masters, *Lincoln the Man* (1931) is almost alone in its devastating treatment. The following biographies should also be mentioned: Carl Schurz, *Abraham Lincoln* (1891); E. P. Oberholtzer, *Abraham Lincoln* (1904); J. T. Morse, *Abraham Lincoln* (2 vols., 1893); J. G. Nicolay, *A Short Life of Abraham Lincoln* (1902).

Certain works of reminiscence give special emphasis to Lincoln, such as: H. C. Whitney, *Life on the Circuit with Lincoln* (1892); U. F. Linder, *Reminiscences of the Early Bench and Bar of Illinois* (1879); A. K. McClure, *Abraham Lincoln and Men of War-Times* (1892); H. B. Rankin, *Intimate Character Sketches of Abraham Lincoln* (1924); A. T. Rice, ed., *Reminiscences of Abraham Lincoln by Distinguished Men of His Time* (1886); Joshua F. Speed, *Reminiscences of Abraham Lincoln* (1884); James Speed, *James Speed; A Personality* (1914); and W. O. Stoddard, *Inside the White House in War Times* (1890). The following diaries are of special note: *Letters of John Hay and Extracts from Diary* (3 vols., p.p., 1908, with omissions and with personal names reduced to initials); *Diary of Gideon Welles*, ed. by J. T. Morse, Jr. (3 vols. 1911), a voluminous and valuable record for the presidency containing many devastating statements concerning members of Lincoln's cabinet (critically analyzed, especially as to Welles's numerous emendations, by H. K. Beale in *Am. Hist. Rev.*, Apr. 1925, pp. 547–52); "Diary and Correspondence of Salmon P. Chase" (*Annual Report of the Am. Hist. Asso. for the Year 1902*, vol. II, 1903); "The Diary of Edward Bates," ed. by H. K. Beale, *Annual Report of the Am. Hist. Asso. for the Year 1930*, vol. IV (1932); *The Diary of Orville Hickman Browning*, ed. by T. C. Pease and J. G. Randall (3 vols. 1927–33, in the *Ill. Hist. Colls.*). Various problems of Lincoln's presidency are treated by J. G. Randall in *Constitutional Problems Under Lincoln* (1926).

The following are special studies of particular phases of Lincoln's career: C. F. Adams, "President Lincoln's Offer to Garibaldi," *Mass. Hist. Soc. Proc.*, 3rd ser., vol. I (1908), pp. 319–25; P. M. Angle, "Abraham Lincoln: Circuit Lawyer," *Lincoln Cent. Asso. Papers . . . 1928* (1928); D. H. Bates, *Lincoln in the Telegraph Office* (1907); F. B. Carpenter, *Six Months at the White House with Abraham Lincoln: The Story of a Picture* (1866); A. C. Cole, *Lincoln's "House Divided" Speech* (1923), "Lincoln and the American Tradition of Civil Liberty," in *Jour. Ill. State Hist. Soc.*, Oct. 1926–Jan. 1927, pp. 102–14, "Abraham Lincoln and the South," in *Lincoln Cent. Asso. Papers . . . 1928* (1928), "President Lincoln and the Illinois Radical Republicans," in *Miss. Valley Hist. Rev.*, March 1918, pp. 417–36, and "Lincoln's Election an Immediate Menace to Slavery in the States?", *Amer. Hist. Rev.*, July 1931, pp. 740–67; W. E. Dodd, *Lincoln or Lee* (1928); D. K. Dodge, *Abraham Lincoln, Master of Words* (1924); J. T. Dorris, "President Lincoln's Clemency," *Jour. Ill. State Hist. Soc.*, Jan. 1928, pp. 547–68; John Eaton, *Grant, Lincoln and the Freedmen* (1907); C. R. Fish, "Lincoln and the Patronage," *Am. Hist. Rev.*, Oct. 1902, pp. 53–69, and "Lincoln and Catholicism," *Ibid.*, July 1924, pp. 723–24 (a rebuke to those who by spurious quotations have falsified Lincoln's attitude toward the Catholics); F. I. Herriott, "Memories of the Chicago Convention of 1860," *Annals of Iowa*, Oct. 1920, and "The Conference in the Deutsches Haus, Chicago, May 14–15, 1860," *Trans. Ill. State Hist. Soc. . . . 1928* (1928); Frederick T. Hill, *Lincoln the Lawyer* (1906); Caroline Hanks Hitchcock, *Nancy Hanks:*

The Story of Abraham Lincoln's Mother (1899), an unreliable work, unfortunately followed by certain biographers; E. C. Kirkland, *The Peacemakers of 1864* (1927); J. H. Lea and J. R. Hutchinson, *The Ancestry of Abraham Lincoln* (1909), useful as to the English Lincolns but unreliable as to the American line; M. D. Learned, *Abraham Lincoln, An American Migration* (1909), useful in proving that the origin of the Lincoln family was English, not German, and in tracing the movements of the Lincolns as a "typical American migration"; Waldo Lincoln, *History of the Lincoln Family* (1923), a valuable genealogical contribution; C. H. McCarthy, *Lincoln's Plan of Reconstruction* (1901); J. B. McMaster, *A Hist. of the People of the U. S. during Lincoln's Administration* (1927); Charles Moore, compiler, *Lincoln's Gettysburg Address and Second Inaugural* (1927); Mary L. Miles, "The Fatal First of January, 1841," *Jour. Ill. State Hist. Soc.*, Apr. 1927, pp. 13–48; Rexford Newcomb, *In the Lincoln Country* (1928); C. O. Paullin, "President Lincoln and the Navy," *Am. Hist. Rev.*, Jan. 1909, pp. 284–303, and "Abraham Lincoln in Congress, 1847–1849," *Jour. Ill. State Hist. Soc.*, Apr.–July 1921, pp. 85–89; J. G. Randall, "Lincoln in the Rôle of Dictator," *So. Atl. Quar.*, July 1929, and "Lincoln's Task and Wilson's," *Ibid.*, Oct. 1930; P. O. Ray, *The Convention that Nominated Lincoln* (1916); J. F. Rhodes, "Lincoln in Some Phases of the Civil War," *Harvard Graduates' Mag.*, Sept. 1915, pp. 1–19; J. T. Richards, *Abraham Lincoln, the Lawyer-Statesman* (1916); Don C. Seitz, *Lincoln the Politician* (1931); Albert Shaw, *Abraham Lincoln* (2 vols., 1929), a "cartoon history" with hundreds of contemporary drawings; J. W. Starr, Jr., *Lincoln & the Railroads* (1927); N. W. Stephenson, "Lincoln and the Progress of Nationality in the North," *Annual Report of the Am. Hist. Asso. for the Year 1919*, vol. I (1923), pp. 353–63; Ida M. Tarbell, *In the Footsteps of the Lincolns* (1924), a somewhat inaccurate book; W. H. Townsend, *Lincoln the Litigant* (1925), and *Lincoln and His Wife's Home Town* (1929); L. A. Warren, *Lincoln's Parentage and Childhood* (1926), a most valuable and scholarly work. For references on the assassination, see Booth, John Wilkes.]

J. G. R.

LINCOLN, BENJAMIN (Jan. 24, 1733–May 9, 1810), Revolutionary soldier, was the descendant of a simple yeoman family which had lived in Hingham, Mass., since the settlement of that town, where he himself was born. His father, Benjamin, a maltster and farmer who had accumulated a modest property, was an officer in the local militia and represented his town in the General Court. He married Elizabeth Thaxter, widow of Capt. John Norton, and she became the mother of the younger Benjamin. The boy received only a common-school education at Hingham, but he had a good mind and wrote English well, as his numerous letters and dispatches show. On Jan. 15, 1756, he married Mary Cushing, daughter of Elijah and Elizabeth (Barker) Cushing, of Pembroke, Mass. They lived together over fifty-four years and had six sons and five daughters. In 1757 Lincoln was chosen town clerk, and in 1762, justice of the peace. He had apparently settled down to the life of a moderately prosperous small-town farmer, when with the increasing excitement over the political difficulties between the colonies and the mother country he began to take a more prominent part in public affairs. He was a member of the legislature in 1772 and 1773, and during the next two years sat in the Provincial Congress. He was elected secretary of that body and a member of the committee on supplies, and for a short time in 1775, during the absence of Joseph Warren, he acted as its president.

His military career had begun some years before. In July 1755 he had been made adjutant of the 3rd Regiment of Suffolk County; he was commissioned major in June 1763, and lieutenant-colonel in January 1772. In February 1776 he was appointed brigadier-general by the Council and became known to Washington. Promoted to third major-general the following May, he was given command, Aug. 2, 1776, of the Massachusetts troops stationed near Boston and in September was chosen to command the militia regiments raised to reinforce the army at New York. He took part in the operations in that section and won Washington's good opinion.

On Feb. 19, 1777, he was appointed major-general in the Continental service, and the next summer was ordered to command the militia in Vermont. Here his common sense and knowledge of local conditions were of great assistance to Stark, whom he aided by reinforcements in the defense of Bennington. Operating on Burgoyne's flank, he prepared the way for the victory at Saratoga by breaking the enemy's line of communication with Canada. During the last fighting against Burgoyne he was severely wounded in the leg, and returned to Hingham, where he remained for some ten months. In August 1778 he was declared fit for duty and rejoined Washington. Because of a controversy over seniority occasioned by the promotion of Benedict Arnold [q.v.], Lincoln had considered resigning, but was prevailed upon not to do so, and on Sept. 25, 1778, he was appointed to the command of the American army in the Southern department.

After being detained ten days at Philadelphia by Congress, he finally reached Charleston, S. C., on Dec. 4. He had gathered laurels in his northern campaign and much was expected of him in the South. He had, however, the usual troubles of the Revolutionary commander with undisciplined troops and short-time patriots, and although he was able to force Prevost to let go his hold on Charleston, he could not turn the enemy out of Savannah. D'Estaing, with the French fleet, attempted to cooperate with him in the Savannah River, but the operation was a failure and D'Estaing sailed away. This left the sea open to Clinton at New York, who sailed for South Carolina with 7,000 troops. He landed at

a short distance from Charleston, marched his troops overland, and attacked the city. Lincoln, instead of retreating into the back country, shut himself up in the town and in May 1779 was captured with his whole army by Clinton. In extenuation of his blunder it must be said that the civil authorities had strongly objected to the evacuation of the town and a considerable part of Lincoln's force was made up of Carolina militiamen who might not have followed him had he abandoned the city. He was granted unusually good terms by the British, but his surrender was a severe blow to the American cause. When the news was received in the North the task of retrieving the Southern situation was given to Horatio Gates [q.v.].

Lincoln was paroled and allowed to proceed north, but there were delays and he did not reach Philadelphia until July. He asked for a court of inquiry to investigate his conduct at Charleston, but the court was never held and no charges were ever pressed. Returning to his home at Hingham, he anxiously awaited exchange so that he might join the army again. In November he was formally exchanged for the British general, Phillips. During the winter he remained in Massachusetts raising recruits and supplies, but the following summer he was once more in the field, operating under Washington in the neighborhood of New York. Commanding the troops which at the end of August 1781 marched southward to join in the Yorktown campaign, he took part in that last fighting of the war. On Oct. 30, 1781, he was made secretary of war by Congress, an office which he held until his resignation just two years later, after the signing of the Treaty of Peace.

Lincoln now returned to his farm at Hingham. It was many years before he could realize upon the certificates of pay which he had received for his service, and in the meantime he engaged in speculation in wild lands in Maine, a venture which nearly brought him to financial ruin. He made frequent trips to the Province and in 1784 and 1786 was one of the Massachusetts commissioners to treat with the Penobscot Indians concerning land purchases. About Jan. 1, 1787, he was appointed to lead the state troops to suppress Shays's Rebellion. The legislature had planned to raise some five thousand men but had provided no money for expenses, and Lincoln personally raised about twenty thousand dollars among some citizens of Boston to finance the campaign. He then marched to Worcester, where trouble was expected at the next session of the court, but no violence occurred, and he went on to the assistance of General Shepherd who was defending the federal arsenal at Springfield. Within a month the two insurgent forces under Day and Shays had been dispersed. On the night of Feb. 2, Lincoln made his famous night march through a terrible snow storm to Petersham, where he captured 150 men, the remnant of Shays's band, and brought the rebellion to an end. He now proved his statesmanship by urging the legislature to be lenient with the rebels, making an example of a few ringleaders only, but his advice was not accepted.

In 1788 he was chosen a member of the convention to consider the new Federal Constitution, and worked for its ratification. That same year he ran for the office of lieutenant-governor and, when no candidate received the majority necessary to a choice, was elected by the legislature. Defeated the next year, he was appointed to the federal office of collector of the port of Boston, a post accompanied by a salary which was most welcome in his now straitened circumstances. In 1789, also, he was one of the federal commissioners appointed to treat with the Creek Indians on the borders of the Southern states, and four years later (1793), was a member of a similar commission to negotiate with the Indians north of the Ohio. In this connection he kept a journal, published in the *Collections of the Massachusetts Historical Society* (3 ser. V) in 1836. His "Observations on the Climate, Soil, and Value of the Eastern Counties, in the District of Maine: Written in the Year 1789" appeared in the same *Collections* (1 ser.) in 1795. He retired from the collectorship at Boston Mar. 1, 1809, and died the following year.

[The longest account of Lincoln is that by Francis Bowen, in Jared Sparks, *The Lib. of Am. Biog.*, 2 ser. XIII (1847). There is some material in the *Hist. of the Town of Hingham* (1893), vol. III; a number of references to him appear in *Am. Hist. Asso. Report for 1896*, vol. I, *passim*; see also *Mass. Hist. Soc. Colls.*, 2 ser. III (1846), 233–55; letters regarding the Burgoyne campaign in *New-Eng. Hist. and Geneal. Reg.*, Oct. 1920; F. S. Drake, *Memorials of the Soc. of the Cincinnati of Mass.* (1873). Citations of certain manuscript and other material relating to his part in Shays's Rebellion are given by J. T. Adams, *New England in the Republic* (1926), pp. 159–63, notes. A. J. Bowden, *Fifty-five Letters of George Washington to Benjamin Lincoln, 1777–1799* (1907), a calendar, and *N. Y. Pub. Lib., Calendar of the Emmet Coll. of MSS., etc., Relating to Am. Hist.* (1900), also point the way to manuscript material. *Year Book, 1897, City of Charleston, S. C.* (n.d.), contains documents on the siege of Charleston. An obituary appeared in the *Columbian Centinel* (Boston), May 12, 1810.]   J. T. A.

LINCOLN, ENOCH (Dec. 28, 1788–Oct. 8, 1829), lawyer and politician, fourth son of Levi [*q.v.*] and Martha (Waldo) Lincoln, and brother of the younger Levi [*q.v.*], was born at Worcester, Mass. He attended Harvard College for a short time but left without taking a degree.

Having studied law in Worcester, he was admitted to the bar in 1811 and began practising at Salem, but moved, in 1812, to Fryeburg in the District of Maine, still a part of Massachusetts. Fryeburg was then a center of considerable importance and he spent five years in practice there, moving to Paris, Me., in 1819. He was assistant United States district attorney, 1815–18. Although a young lawyer of promise, he soon devoted most of his time and energy to politics, his affiliations being with the Jeffersonian Republicans. On Mar. 16, 1818, he was elected to the federal House of Representatives to serve the unexpired term of Albion K. Parris [*q.v.*], recently appointed to the federal bench, and took his seat in the second session of the Fifteenth Congress, Nov. 16, 1818. He was reëlected to the four following Congresses, his total service covering the period 1818–26. Maine had, in the meantime, 1820, been admitted to the Union as a separate state. He rarely spoke and his congressional career was without special distinction.

Resigning from the House in 1826, he was elected governor of Maine that same year, and was reëlected in 1827 and 1828. He was a popular and successful executive and encountered little opposition. His messages to the legislature, which show considerable literary ability, dealt with problems of the new state, then essentially a frontier community. The fact that the dispute with Great Britain over the Northeastern Boundary was becoming serious probably accounts for his emphasis on the need of protection for the state's long maritime and inland frontiers. He insisted on the validity of Maine's title to the entire area in dispute and stated emphatically his belief that the federal government had no right, without the consent of a state, to cede the property of that state. The portions of his messages dealing with the boundary question are important items in the documentary history of that protracted diplomatic controversy, which remained unsettled long after his death. He had been influential in the selection of Augusta as the state capital and his death occurred in that place a few days after he had participated in the ceremonies attending the laying of the cornerstone of a new academy for young women. His health had been failing for some time and he had declined another nomination, hoping to devote himself to literary work in Scarborough, where he had lately established a residence. He never married. He had several avocations which throw considerable light on his character and temperament. In 1816 he published a poem, *The Village* (printed by Edward Little & Company, Portland), evidently based on his observation of life in Fryeburg. More important was his interest in Indian languages and tribal institutions in Maine, which led him to carry on investigations there and in neighboring British territory. This study naturally brought him into contact with the earlier history of the white settlements in Maine. From his unfinished work in this connection, two studies were afterwards printed, "Remarks on the Indian Languages" and "Some Account of the Catholic Missions in Maine" (*Collections of the Maine Historical Society,* I ser., vol. I, 1831; 2nd ed., annotated, 1865, pp. 412–17 and 428–46, respectively).

[William Lincoln, *Hist. of Worcester, Mass.* (1837); Waldo Lincoln, *Hist. of the Lincoln Family* (1923); E. H. Elwell, "Enoch Lincoln," *Colls. Me. Hist. Soc.,* 2 ser., vol. I (1890); *Me. Hist. and Geneal. Recorder,* vol. III, no. 3 (1886); "The Late Governor of Maine," in *The Yankee and Boston Literary Gazette,* Nov. 1829; L. C. Hatch, *Maine, A Hist.* (1919); *Kennebec Jour.* (Augusta), Oct. 9, 16, 1829; MSS. in the Am. Antiq. Soc.]   W. A. R.

LINCOLN, JOHN LARKIN (Feb. 23, 1817–Oct. 17, 1891), university professor, Latinist, author, teacher, was born in Boston, Mass. He was of English stock, sixth in descent from Stephen Lincoln, husbandman, who emigrated from Windham, England, in the seventeenth century. His maternal great-grandfather, Samuel Larkin, also came from England in the seventeenth century. He was himself the son of Ensign and Sophia Oliver (Larkin) Lincoln. His father, printer and publisher in Boston, was a man of strong religious convictions and similar convictions his son always held. Trained for four years in the Boston Latin School young Lincoln was ready for college at thirteen but, "to fill in the time," remained at school, graduating as valedictorian and entering Brown University at fifteen. He was graduated with honors from Brown in 1836 and for one year was tutor in Columbian College, Washington, D. C. During the years 1837–39 he studied at Newton Theological Institution but nevertheless chose a collegiate career. After acting as tutor in Greek at Brown for two years, he spent three years in Europe, where he studied philology and theology at the universities of Halle and Berlin (1841–43). Among his distinguished classical teachers were Bernhardy and Böckh. He spent the year 1843–44 in travel and study, mainly in Geneva and Rome. Returning to Brown University he was for one year assistant professor, then in 1845 he was made full professor of the Latin language and literature. In 1857, and again in 1887, he refreshed and increased his equipment by travel and study in Greece, Germany, and Italy. He had married, in 1846, Laura E. Pearce of Providence.

From 1859 to 1867 the University granted Lincoln part-time absence to conduct a school for young women. He was a born teacher. He twice refused to leave his life work for a college presidency elsewhere. He made his teaching of Latin a medium for the appreciation of beauty in all literatures and was "quick to feel and to point out the deeper philosophical ethical lesson" in a given text. His unfailing wit and humor relieved his indefatigable demands for exactitude in scholarship and he was one of the best-loved men on the teaching staff. Significant evidence of this affection was the gift of $100,000—at that time a large sum—collected by grateful graduates and friends in order that Lincoln "whether teaching or not," might always receive his full salary. His human interest in student life is also reflected in the name, "Lincoln Field," given to the old athletic grounds.

Lincoln's published works include *Titus Livius: Selections from the First Five Books, Together with the Twenty-first and Twenty-second Books Entire* (1847, 1871); *The Works of Horace* (1851, 1882); and *Selections from the Poems of Ovid* (1882, 1884). He also contributed many articles to the *North American Review,* the *Christian Review,* the *Baptist Quarterly,* and *Bibliotheca Sacra.* The clarity of his commentaries gave perspective to the study of Latin by many thousands of American students outside of Brown University. From his numerous essays some of the more characteristic on classical subjects are reprinted in the memorial volume published in 1894. He was an early member of the American Philological Association. There is an admirable portrait of Lincoln by Herbert Herkomer at Brown University. It reveals a face of spiritual beauty, intellectual vigor, and human kindliness.

[Wm. E. Lincoln, *In Memoriam: John Larkin Lincoln* (1894); W. C. Bronson, *The Hist. of Brown Univ., 1764–1914* (1914); *Hist. Cat. of Brown Univ., 1764–1904* (1905); obituary and editorial in the *Providence Daily Jour.,* Oct. 17, 1891.]   F. G. A.

LINCOLN, LEVI (May 15, 1749–Apr. 14, 1820), lawyer and politician, was born at Hingham, Mass., the son of Enoch and Rachel (Fearing) Lincoln. His father was the great-grandson of Samuel Lincoln who emigrated from England to the Colonies in 1637 and settled at Hingham. Levi was apprenticed to a blacksmith in his youth, but when friends discovered the boy's ability and fondness for study, they persuaded his father to permit him to continue his education. Having graduated from Harvard College in 1772, he began the study of law in Newburyport, continuing it later in Northampton. At the outbreak of the

Revolution he performed a brief tour of duty with the militia. He began the practice of law in Worcester, and maintained a residence there throughout the remainder of his life. He immediately became prominent in local affairs, holding various civil offices during the remainder of the war and serving as judge of probate from 1777 to 1781. In 1779 he was elected to the convention which drew up the first state constitution and two years later declined an election to the Continental Congress. His services during these years gave him a share in the important work of establishing the civil institutions of the new state.

In the meantime his legal practice had been growing rapidly and he had become widely known as a successful trial lawyer. In 1781, together with several eminent members of the Massachusetts bar, he shared in one of the most famous litigations in the history of the state, although its importance was not fully realized until later years. Three cases came before the courts, *Quork* (spelling varies) *Walker* vs. *Nathaniel Jenison, Nathaniel Jenison* vs. *John Caldwell and Seth Caldwell,* and *The Commonwealth* vs. *Nathaniel Jenison,* which involved the question of the right to hold a negro in slavery in view of the Bill of Rights in the constitution of 1780. Lincoln, and Caleb Strong [*q.v.*], who afterwards was one of his bitter political opponents, appeared as counsel for the Caldwells, and argued against the legality of slavery in Massachusetts. The decision of the supreme court, upholding their contentions, was afterwards regarded as a landmark in the long struggle against slavery. (For details of these cases see Emory Washburn, "The Extinction of Slavery in Massachusetts," *Collections of the Massachusetts Historical Society,* 4 ser. IV, 1858, pp. 337–44.)

In the gradual development of the Republican-Federalist alignment, Lincoln became a leader of the former party in Massachusetts, despite the fact that members of his profession and social class were generally Federalists. He served a term in the state House of Representatives and another in the Senate, 1796–97, and in 1800, after a bitter campaign involving, under the existing law which required a majority, three special elections, he was chosen, Dec. 19, to serve the remainder of the unexpired term of Dwight Foster, resigned, in the Sixth Congress. In the meantime, Nov. 3, he had also been elected a member of the Seventh Congress; but before he could take his seat in the latter he was appointed attorney-general of the United States by President Jefferson. For some months he also acted

as secretary of state, pending James Madison's arrival in Washington. He served creditably as attorney-general from Mar. 5, 1801, to Dec. 31, 1804, but the office at this time offered no particular opportunities for distinction. Meantime, he was active in party politics and was the object of a vast amount of abuse by Federalist newspapers, clergymen, and campaign orators. He did not tamely submit and in his *Letters to the People, by a Farmer* (Salem, 1802) he assailed the political activity of the clergy. "The blow," records Rev. William Bentley, "is serious, & the more the Clergy & their friends attempt to defend themselves, the more severe are the strokes upon them. This subject never was so freely handled in New England & never did the Clergy suffer a more serious diminution of their influence & of their power" (*Diary,* II, 1907, p. 407). Jefferson's letters show that Lincoln was firmly established in the President's confidence and entrusted with important responsibilities in the Republican "regeneration" of New England, including distribution of the patronage by which that process was expedited (P. L. Ford, *The Writings of Thomas Jefferson,* VIII, 1897).

Lincoln gave up his federal post, greatly to President Jefferson's regret and soon resumed his political activity in Massachusetts, being elected to the Governor's Council in 1806, and lieutenant-governor in 1807 and 1808, when the Republicans succeeded in getting control of the governorship for the first time. He served as governor following the death in office of James Sullivan, but was an unsuccessful candidate in 1809, when the reaction caused by the Embargo gave the state to the Federalists. He served two terms on the Governor's Council, 1810–12, and in the latter year was offered a place on the United States Supreme Court by President Madison. Justice Cushing, a stalwart Federalist, had recently died, an event described by Jefferson as "another circumstance of congratulation," inasmuch as it offered opportunity to establish a Republican majority in that tribunal. Jefferson's letters to Madison describe Lincoln as an eminently desirable appointee because of his legal attainments, equal to those of any other New England Republican, his integrity, political firmness, and unimpeachable character (P. L. Ford, *Ibid.,* IX, 1898, pp. 282–84, *passim*). Lincoln declined, however, for his eyesight was failing rapidly. He spent his remaining years on his farm in Worcester. A life-long friend of one of his sons many years later described "this home, so like an English manor in its dignity and hospitality and the variety and extent of its occupations, so like a New England farm in the homeliness of its daily employments" (Alonzo Hill, *Memorial Address on Levi Lincoln, Jr.,* 1868). It is probably not a mere coincidence that from it two of his sons, Levi and Enoch [*qq.v.*], went forth to distinguished political careers. He had married, Nov. 23, 1781, at Lancaster, Mass., Martha, daughter of Daniel and Rebecca (Salisbury) Waldo, by whom he had nine children.

[William Lincoln, *Hist. of Worcester, Mass.* (1837); Waldo Lincoln, *Hist. of the Lincoln Family* (1923); C. F. Aldrich, "The Bench and Bar," in D. H. Hurd, *Hist. of Worcester County* (1889), vol. I; *National Aegis* (Worcester), Apr. 19, 26, 1820; letters of Levi Lincoln, Sr., in the possession of the Mass. Hist. Soc. and Am. Antiquarian Soc.]   W. A. R.

LINCOLN, LEVI (Oct. 25, 1782–May 29, 1868), lawyer and politician, eldest son of Levi [*q.v.*] and Martha (Waldo) Lincoln, was born and spent his life, except when absent on public service, in Worcester, Mass. He graduated from Harvard College in 1802, was admitted to the bar in 1805, and began practice in his native town. A Jeffersonian Republican by inheritance and belief, he was soon active in politics. It was in this field, rather than at the bar, that he was destined to achieve distinction. In 1812 he was elected to the Massachusetts Senate, beginning a public career which lasted for about thirty-five years. Between 1814 and 1822 he served several terms in the state House of Representatives, opposing there the policy of Gov. Caleb Strong during the second war with Great Britain, and especially the state's participation in the Hartford Convention in 1814. With the subsidence of party acrimony after the war, his influence grew, and he served as speaker during his last term, although the House majority was nominally Federalist.

In 1820–21, as a member of the state constitutional convention, he delivered speeches on elections (*Journal of Debates and Proceedings, 1821,* pp. 265–66) and on the judiciary (*Ibid.,* p. 216) which show that he was still a Jeffersonian, but he soon began to move toward the National Republican position and in 1824 supported John Quincy Adams for the presidency. Meantime, he had seen service as lieutenant-governor (1823) and, briefly, as a member of the Massachusetts supreme court. In 1825 he was elected to the governorship, the first incumbent of that position, as he stated in his message to the legislature, June 2, 1825, "whose whole experience is more recent than the adoption of the Frame of Government which he is called to participate in administering" (*New England Palladium & Commercial Advertiser,* Boston, June 3, 1825). In many respects a new

era was beginning in Massachusetts history, and party activity was temporarily quiescent. Lincoln was reëlected annually until 1834, with a measure of unanimity never attained by his successors in office.

Like other members of the family, he had notable executive capacity, though perhaps his greatest service as governor was his appointment, in 1830, of Lemuel Shaw [*q.v.*] as chief justice of the state supreme court, in defiance of the precedent which called for the promotion of the senior associate justice. Rev. Alonzo Hill declared, after Lincoln's decease, that, unlike his father, he was "no classical scholar nor profound metaphysician," no great reader, but a man of sound common sense, "whose gifts were eminently practical" (*Memorial Address on Levi Lincoln, Jr.,* 1868). An examination of his semi-annual messages to the legislature confirms the truth of this estimate. Among the problems discussed were such eminently practical matters as a topographical survey of the state, an investigation of its geological resources, improvement in the administration of justice by elimination of obsolete common law provisions, amelioration of the laws of debt and insolvency, and proper methods of assuring the medical profession an adequate supply of anatomical material. His comments on the problem of penitentiary administration constitute an interesting contribution to the history of American penology. In his first message he urged that the corporation laws be amended in order to limit the liability of shareholders for corporate debts, and, reverting to the same subject on Jan. 6, 1830, he showed that, as a consequence of existing business depression, the principle of holding shareholders liable to the full extent of their property, had "brought irretrievable ruin to individuals" and had fatally impaired "that confidence in property, upon which alone, credit can be obtained." He was insistent that the state assume broader educational functions and in 1826 urged the establishment of "a Seminary of practical Arts and Sciences." He likewise emphasized the need of better professional training for teachers. His later messages as governor contained numerous disquisitions on the nature of the Union, provoked by the South Carolina nullification movement. "Opposition, by force, to the laws of the General Government, is Rebellion, from which the only escape is in Revolution," he declared on Jan. 8, 1833 (*Boston Daily Advertiser & Patriot,* Jan. 9, 1833).

He could, apparently, have had an indefinite tenure of the governorship but gave up the post in order to enter national politics. On Feb. 17,

1834, he began service in the House of Representatives in place of John Davis [*q.v.*], who had resigned to succeed Lincoln as governor. He was elected to the three succeeding Congresses, his service extending from Feb. 17, 1834, to his resignation on Mar. 16, 1841. He was a constant participant in debate but hardly an outstanding figure in Washington. Following his withdrawal from Congress, he served as collector of the Port of Boston, 1841–43, until removed by President Tyler. He also served two more terms in the state Senate, 1844–45, the last one as president of that body. He then retired to his home in Worcester, where he spent the rest of his life. He had always been active in local affairs and his name appears in a wide variety of social and business activities in that community. He served as mayor of Worcester in 1848, after its incorporation that year as a city. He was one of the founders of the American Antiquarian Society. His interest in educational matters is indicated by his long service on the governing boards of Leicester Academy and Harvard University. He was an enthusiastic promoter of agricultural improvement and a successful practical farmer; a number of his addresses on agricultural topics were printed. In person he is described as erect and dignified in carriage, retaining the manners of the first part of the century, and being regarded by neighbors and associates as "a gentleman of the old school." He married, Sept. 6, 1807, Penelope Winslow, daughter of William and Mary (Chandler) Sever, by whom he had eight children.

[Waldo Lincoln, *Hist. of the Lincoln Family* (1923); *A Memorial of Levi Lincoln the Gov. of Mass. from 1825–34* (privately printed, Boston, 1868); D. H. Hurd, *Hist. of Worcester County, Mass.* (1889); Emory Washburn, in *Proc. Mass. Hist. Soc.*, vol. XI (1871); *Proc. Am. Antiq. Soc.* (1868); MSS. in Am. Antiq. Soc. including "Life, Services and Character of Hon. Levi Lincoln of Worcester, Mass.," by Charles Hudson; Joseph Palmer, in *Boston Daily Advertiser*, supplement to issue of July 15, 1868; *Worcester Daily Spy*, May 30, June 3, 1868; *Worcester Palladium*, June 3, 1868.]
W. A. R.

LINCOLN, MARY JOHNSON BAILEY (July 8, 1844–Dec. 2, 1921), teacher, author of the "Boston Cook Book," was born in South Attleboro, Mass., the daughter of a Congregational minister, Rev. John Milton Bailey and his wife Sarah Morgan Johnson Bailey. After the death of her father in her seventh year, the mother and three children had little for support beyond their own earnings; and they moved to Norton so that the two daughters might have the benefit of Wheaton Female Seminary (later Wheaton College). After her graduation from Wheaton in 1864, Mary taught a country school in Vermont

for one term and then married David A. Lincoln of Norton on June 21, 1865. Some years later business reverses made it desirable that she should be an earner as well as her husband. At about this time, 1879, the Boston Cooking School was being organized, and through the aid of her elder sister, who as a kindergarten teacher had been associated with some of its founders, she was invited to assume direction of it. After a few lessons in fancy cookery from Miss Sweeney, who had been a pupil of Pierre Blot, a famous French teacher of cookery of the sixties in New York and Boston, and after observing Maria Parloa's methods, Mrs. Lincoln agreed to undertake this new work. From 1879 to 1885, as the first principal of this novel school, she shaped its general plan and indirectly shaped the course of much later work in domestic science in grade and normal schools. After her resignation from the Boston Cooking School she was busy with lectures before schools, clubs, and some of the leading food fairs.

Mrs. Lincoln's Boston Cook Book, published in 1884, grew out of her experience as housekeeper and teacher. It marked a change in culinary literature, for most of the earlier works lacked the orderly plan which the application of school-room methods had given to this work. In 1885 Mrs. Lincoln published the *Peerless Cookbook,* followed in 1886 by *Carving and Serving* and in 1887 by the *Boston School Kitchen Textbook* (1887), which was the model for many later editions. *What to Have for Luncheon* was published in 1904. For ten years (1894–1904) Mrs. Lincoln was culinary editor of the *American Kitchen Magazine* and her department "From Day to Day" was read by thousands of housekeepers and teachers. She combined in rare fashion the direct methods of the teacher with her long experiences as housekeeper. Understanding the needs of home women, she used words they could quickly grasp. Thus she accomplished more in her period than more scientifically trained women have done in a later day, in attracting attention to household science.

[Mary J. B. Lincoln, "How I Was Led to Teach Cookery," the *New Eng. Kitchen*, May 1894; *Who's Who in America*, 1920–21; *N. Y. Herald*, Dec. 4, 1921; *Evening Post* (N. Y.), Dec. 5, 1921; personal acquaintance.]
A. B.

LINCOLN, MARY TODD (Dec. 13, 1818–July 16, 1882), wife of Abraham Lincoln, was born in Lexington, Ky., of distinguished ancestry and was reared amid genteel surroundings. Her great-grandfather, Gen. Andrew Porter, was prominent in the Revolution; her great-uncle, John Todd, accompanied George Rogers Clark, serving as county lieutenant of

Illinois; and her grandfather, Levi Todd, participated in the battle of Blue Licks, served as major-general of militia, and lived in a proud estate called "Ellerslie" close by the home of Henry Clay. Her parents, Robert S. and Eliza (Parker) Todd, had six children that survived infancy; by a second marriage to Betsy Humphreys her father had eight others that reached maturity. Of the six Todd-Parker children four are said to have had "abnormal personalities" (Evans, *post,* p. 51). Lexington was a cultural center and distinguished guests entered the Todd home. Mary was carefully educated at an academy kept by Dr. John Ward and in the select school of Mme. Mentelle where she learned French and was instructed in the social graces. In 1837 she visited Springfield, Ill.; and two years later she made the Illinois capital her home, living with her sister, Mrs. Ninian W. Edwards, daughter-in-law of Gov. Ninian Edwards. Favored by the prominence of the Edwards home, and aided by her own accomplishments, she became a belle in the fashionable society of Springfield; and her acquaintance among people of political importance was extensive. Her engagement to Lincoln and the discredited story of the defaulting bridegroom have been treated above (see Lincoln, Abraham). One of the factors in the renewal of the interrupted courtship was Mary's complicity in the Lincoln-Shields duel, an affair in which Lincoln assumed blame for certain newspaper skits which she wrote in ridicule of Shields. On Nov. 4, 1842, the pair were married after hasty preparations, and Springfield remained their home until 1861. Despite Lincoln's awkwardness they moved in the best of local society; but in their own home there was a limited hospitality. Unfavorable things were said of their domestic life, and even her friends admitted that Mary's temperament was difficult; while her background and outlook differed markedly from those of her husband, toward whose family she was unsympathetic. Within the limitations of her unstable and tempestuous temperament, however, she was a devoted wife and mother. Her reputation has suffered much from the Ann Rutledge legend and from the ungracious writings of Herndon; but it is hard to believe that the Lincoln home was as thoroughly unhappy as Herndon has pictured it. Lincoln's home letters show an affectionate regard for his wife and a playful delight in their four boys.

During the presidency of her husband, Mrs. Lincoln, in what Stoddard called her "somewhat authoritative" way, gave special attention to levees and other social affairs. A Southern lady in the White House, she was subjected to criticism, much of which was gossip and malicious slander; certainly the imputations of disloyalty were unfounded. Even the touches of social gayety with which she relieved the strain of wartime anxiety were criticized as inappropriate. She suffered during the war by reason of divisions in her own family (her sister's husband, Ben. H. Helm, being a Confederate general), and by the crushing bereavement of her son Willie's death. From the terrible moment when her husband was assassinated at her side, troubles multiplied upon her head. The death of "Tad" in 1871 left only one of her four sons. A certain mental instability now became more pronounced; she was adjudged insane and spent some months in a private sanitarium at Batavia, Ill. (1875), after which, on second trial, she was declared to be sane and again capable of managing her estate. In 1870 Congress tardily granted her an annual pension of $3,000. This was increased in 1882 to $5,000, at which time an additional gift of $15,000 was voted. After some years of foreign travel she spent her last clouded days in the home of Mrs. Edwards at Springfield, where she died of paralysis, July 16, 1882.

A short, plump brunette, Mrs. Lincoln had a certain formal beauty and was described as vivacious and apt in conversation. Accounts of her extravagance combined with penuriousness, her interference in politics, her irritable temper, and her concealment of expenditures from her husband are too numerous and authoritative to be ignored; but on the other side of the picture one finds kindlier testimony such as that of W. O. Stoddard who found her, in spite of varying moods, an agreeable mistress in the White House and a ministering friend to soldiers in Washington hospitals.

[A. J. Beveridge, *Abraham Lincoln, 1809–1858* (2 vols., 1928); W. E. Barton, *Life of Abraham Lincoln* (2 vols., 1925); Katherine Helm, *The True Story of Mary, Wife of Lincoln* (1928), based on diaries, letters, and recollections of Mrs. Ben H. Helm; Honoré W. Morrow, *Mary Todd Lincoln* (1928), a novelist's book, of little historical value; Elizabeth H. Keckley, *Behind the Scenes, or Thirty Years a Slave and Four Years in the White House* (1868), intimate, revealing comment by Mrs. Lincoln's colored seamstress; Gamaliel Bradford, *Wives* (1925), a well considered portrait; W. O. Stoddard, *Inside the White House in War Times* (1890); W. H. Townsend, *Lincoln and His Wife's Home Town* (1929); W. A. Evans, *Mrs. Abraham Lincoln: A Study of Her Personality and Her Influence on Lincoln* (1932), a full-length treatment, from the medical and scientific viewpoints; Carl Sandburg and P. M. Angle, *Mary Lincoln, Wife and Widow* (1932), especially significant for its documentary study of the Lincoln-Todd courtship and wedding.] J. G. R.

LINCOLN, ROBERT TODD (Aug. 1, 1843–July 26, 1926), secretary of war and minister to England, devoted most of his life to private and personal affairs, and sedulously avoided the appearance of capitalizing the reputation of his father. He was the eldest and the only surviving child of Abraham and Mary (Todd) Lincoln and was born in Springfield, Ill. During his boyhood his father rose from insignificance to national importance, and every effort was made to give to Robert the educational advantages that Abraham was conscious of having missed. He attended the Springfield schools, and then Phillips Exeter Academy in New Hampshire. He was sent on to Harvard in the fall of 1859, carrying to the president a note of introduction from Stephen A. Douglas, which characterized him as the son of his friend, "with whom I have lately been canvassing the State of Illinois" (J. S. Currey, *Chicago: Its History and Its Builders*, 1912, II, p. 82). He was kept in college while his associates entered the army, for his father, as he wrote to Grant, did not "wish to put him in the ranks" (*New York Times*, July 27, 1926). After graduating in 1864 he spent four months in the Harvard Law School but left when he was given an appointment on the staff of General Grant. He was married on Sept. 24, 1868, to Mary, the daughter of Senator James Harlan of Iowa (Johnson Brigham, *James Harlan*, 1913, p. 238). Of the three children of this marriage, two daughters survived him.

On leaving the army Lincoln studied law in Chicago and was admitted to the bar in 1867. He gained profitable clients among the railroad and corporate interests, and his name appears as a charter member of the Chicago Bar Association (1874). He was often mentioned by political leaders, who were not averse to profiting by his name, but he generally kept aloof. He went to the state Republican convention, however, in 1880, at the head of a Grant delegation from Chicago, and was in close sympathy with the effort of Senator Logan to procure a third term for Grant. Logan repaid him, when he had himself accepted defeat and had switched his allegiance to Garfield, by inducing Garfield to summon Lincoln to the War Department. Lincoln became secretary of war without enthusiasm and had an uneventful term of office, with the army dominated by his father's old generals, and with the Grant retirement bill as the most important controversial matter save for the perennial case of Gen. Fitz-John Porter. His management of the relief of the Greely Expedition evoked a public criticism from his subordinate, the chief signal officer, Gen. W. B. Hazen [*q.v.*]. He felt impelled to support Arthur for renomination in 1884, to the disappointment of Logan. He resumed the practice of law in

1885 but was recalled to public service in 1889 by President Harrison who sent him to London as minister. Here the name did him good service, and he withstood the charms of British society so well as to earn the encomium of Theodore Roosevelt, who characterized "all of our ministers to England [as] pro-British except Bob Lincoln" (M. A. DeW. Howe, *James Ford Rhodes*, 1929, p. 121). He continued, however, to keep his name out of the papers and gained none of the distinction as spokesman for the people of the United States that has come to many of the ministers at the Court of St. James's.

For nearly twenty years after his return from England, Lincoln continued in his work as counsel for great business interests, and in his semi-seclusion upon which he would permit no intrusion. Among his chief clients was the Pullman Company; and when the founder of this company, George M. Pullman, died in 1897, he became first its acting executive and then its president. After the Pullman strike of 1894, and the use of the injunction in connection with this, it became common for radicals to compare adversely his apparent lack of interest in the common man and his father's humanity in the emancipation of the slaves, but he paid no attention to the criticisms. In 1911 he was forced to resign the presidency on account of his health though he retained a connection with the company as chairman of the board of directors. In 1912 he moved to Washington, D. C. He remained almost unknown as he advanced in years. He had acquired a summer home, "Hildene," at Manchester, N. H., and there he found seclusion and the golf that he thought kept him alive. He was interested in astronomy and found pleasure in the solution of algebraic problems. His father's papers, which Hay and Nicolay had worked over in the eighties, remained in his possession until near the end of his life when he deposited them in the Library of Congress to be sealed for twenty-one years after his death.

[*Harvard Coll. Class of 1864: Secretary's Report*, no. 8 (1914); the *Harvard Grads.' Mag.*, Sept. 1926; *Ill. State Hist. Lib. Pub.*, no. 11 (1906); *Lit. Digest*, Aug. 14, 1926; *Rev. of Revs.*, Sept. 1926; *Outlook*, Aug. 4, 1926; *N. Y. Herald-Tribune* and *N. Y. Times*, Sept. 27, 1926.]
F.L.P.

LINCOLN, RUFUS PRATT (Apr. 27, 1840–Nov. 27, 1900), physician, laryngologist, and intranasal surgeon, was born at Belchertown, Mass., the son of Rufus S. and Lydia (Baggs) Lincoln. He studied at Williston Seminary, Easthampton, Mass., and at Phillips Exeter Academy, from which he graduated in 1858. He then entered Amherst College, where he received the degree of A.B. in 1862. Following his graduation, he enlisted in the 37th Massachusetts Volunteers as second lieutenant and was promoted to a captaincy after two months. He served through the Civil War, was in many battles, and was twice wounded. He rose to the rank of colonel and toward the close of the war was made inspector-general of the VI Corps, Army of the Potomac.

As soon as he was mustered out of the army he began the study of medicine, attending the College of Physicians and Surgeons, New York, for one year and Harvard Medical School for two more years, and received from the latter institution in 1868 his medical degree. Settling in New York, he formed a partnership with the well-known surgeon Willard Parker [q.v.], but was soon attracted to the then new specialty of laryngology, which included intranasal surgery. He leased the house which had been presented to Gen. George B. McClellan, where for thirty-two years, without interruption, he was entirely occupied with the duties of a practice which was enormous. His career was almost unique, since patients came to him solely because of his merit. He acquired no prestige from post-graduate study in Europe, he declined to associate himself with any college faculty, hospital, or clinic, and he did little writing. In the belief of good judges he stood at the head of his special field, an estimate which seems to be borne out by the fact that his opinion was sought by Morell-Mackenzie in the case of Emperor Frederick of Germany. He was distinguished especially for his technic in the removal of retronasal growths by means of the electric snare, and here he seems to have had no peers or successors. These formations are semi-malignant and, in theory at least, should be extirpated by a bloody and mutilating intervention; but Lincoln succeeded in removing many of them by the bloodless and painless method. One of his earliest patients with this trouble is said to have been General Judson Kilpatrick, and the renown of his cure had much to do with Lincoln's early vogue as an intranasal surgeon. Of the few papers contributed by Lincoln to medical literature the majority were devoted to the removal of retronasal growths. He was a cofounder and past president of the New York Laryngological Society —later the Laryngological Section of the Academy of Medicine—and was also a past president of the American Laryngological Association. In 1869 he married Caroline C. Tyler; his only son, Rufus Tyler Lincoln, died of appendicitis at the age of sixteen. Lincoln's own death was premature, for he was stricken in the midst of apparent health with appendicitis. At the operation Dr. Charles B. McBurney [q.v.] found an anomalous congenital formation which made it impossible to locate the appendix, so that after much effort it was finally necessary to abandon the operation, and the patient succumbed to exhaustion; at an autopsy the suppurating organ was found in an inaccessible position.

[The date of birth is that given in *Amherst Coll. Biog. Record of the Graduates and Non-Graduates* (1927); T. F. Harrington, *The Harvard Medic. School* (1905), vol. III, gives Apr. 27, 1841 and some other sources give Apr. 17, 1841. See also *Boston Medic. and Surgic. Jour.*, Dec. 6, 1900; *Medic. Record*, Dec. 8, 1900; *N. Y. Medic. Jour.*, Dec. 1, 1900; H. A. Kelly and W. L. Burrage, *Am. Medic. Biogs.* (1920); *N. Y. Times*, Nov. 28, 1900; personal knowledge.] E. P.

LIND, JOHN (Mar. 25, 1854–Sept. 18, 1930), lawyer, congressman, governor, diplomat, was born in Kånna, Småland, Sweden, the son of Gustav and Catherine (Jonason) Lind. His family came to the United States in 1867 and settled in Goodhue County, Minn., and Lind remained a resident of that state throughout his life. He attended the schools of his native and adopted countries and became sufficiently proficient in the use of English to teach in a district school in Sibley County in 1872–73, after which he set himself to the task of studying law. He was admitted to the bar in 1877, and while he was gaining experience as a lawyer he served for two years as superintendent of schools in Brown County and for four years as receiver of the United States land office at Tracy, Lyon County. His election to Congress in 1886 marked the inception of three successive terms as a Republican (1887–93) and one as a Democrat (1903–05). He had already won a reputation for simplicity of manner and directness of speech and as a legislator showed a disposition to belittle extreme partisanship and to shy at blind party loyalty. Although regarded as a "good" Republican during his first three terms, he was a believer in the free coinage of silver, tempering his course, however, with a statement on the floor of the House that something ought to be yielded to expediency and that the Sherman Silver Purchase Act for the time being was an effective substitute (*Congressional Record,* 51 Cong., 1 Sess., p. 5696).

In 1896 he was the gubernatorial candidate of the Silver Republicans, Democrats, and Populists but was defeated. In 1898, speaking as the nominee of the Democrats and their allies, he undoubtedly gave an accurate statement of his political faith when he said: "I have not been a Populist, and I cannot say that I have become a Populist. To be frank with you, my friends, I will say to you that I don't know that I have any party. Perhaps it might be said of me that I am a political orphan" (*Minneapolis Tribune*, Oct. 11, 1898). As governor (1899–1901) Lind was the first to interrupt the succession of Republican incumbents since 1859. He remained until his death a leader and oracle of independent and progressive thought. He was an admirer of William Jennings Bryan, and he gave support to the foreign and domestic policies of Woodrow Wilson. In 1924, however, he deserted the Democratic party in favor of the Progressive candidate, Robert M. LaFollette, and in 1928 he refused to support Alfred E. Smith. In 1910 he declined the Democratic nomination for the governorship.

During the first days of August 1913, the country was surprised at the appointment of Lind to be the personal representative of President Wilson in Mexico. The object of his mission was to help effect the peaceful overthrow of Huerta and the return of stable government (Baker, *post*, p. 267). He remained in Mexico for several months but was unable to accomplish the object of his mission. From the beginning of December 1913 he consistently advocated the recognition of Carranza and after his return was active and influential in his favor. Probably his greatest contribution was his influence upon progressive legislation affecting his state—in railroad regulation, taxation, legal reform, and public education. During the interim in his political career he served in the Spanish-American War. The pension which he received from this service formed the basis of a trust fund to be used to aid crippled students at the University of Minnesota, an act prompted, perhaps, by the fact that he had lost his left hand in his youth. Physically he was unmistakably Swedish, tall, wiry, sandy-haired, and blue-eyed. He possessed the industry, initiative, bent for controversy, and facility of expression of his race, but he was intensely American and in the heat of political campaigns made no appeal to racial or nationalistic prejudice. In his declining years he interested himself in ancient Scandinavian history, but he never identified himself with the activities of the Swedish-Americans as a group. His liberal point of view in religion and his defection from orthodox Republicanism explains the lukewarm, not to say hostile, attitude of the Swedish-American clergy toward him. Lind married, on Sept. 1, 1879, Alice A. Shepard of Mankato, Minn.

[W. W. Folwell, *A Hist. of Minn.*, vol. III (1926), has a chapter on "Lind and his Times, 1899–1901," with ample citations. Ray S. Baker, *Woodrow Wilson: Life and Letters*, vol. IV (1931), is the best printed source for Lind's mission to Mexico. Other sources include: A. E. Strand, *A Hist. of the Swedish-Americans in Minn.* (1910), vol. I; J. H. Baker, *Lives of the Govs. of Minn.* (1908); Edith L. O'Shaughnessy, *A Diplomat's Wife in Mexico* (1916); *Minneapolis Tribune*, Sept. 19, 1930. The author of this sketch made use of Lind's papers, some of which are in the possession of the Minn. Hist. Soc.]   G. M. S.

LINDABURY, RICHARD VLIET (Oct. 13, 1850–July 15, 1925), lawyer, was born on a farm near Peapack, Somerset County, N. J. His father, Jacob H. Lindabury, was of English descent while his mother, Mary Ann Vliet, was of Holland-Dutch parentage. His boyhood was spent in farm work and in rather irregular attendance at the district school. An apt pupil, he enlisted the interest of his teacher and through him of the local pastor of the Dutch Reformed Church with the result that the latter secured permission to teach the boy in preparation for Rutgers College and ultimately for the ministry. Thus some three years largely devoted to the evening study of Greek and Latin ensued. A serious illness which made the boy an invalid for two years prevented the consummation of these plans. In 1870, however, young Lindabury was offered the opportunity to take up the study of law in the office of Alvah A. Clark, of Somerville, N. J., a relative, and a former member of Congress. Supporting himself by teaching a local school he was able to be admitted to the bar in 1874 and opened an office in Bound Brook. In 1878 he moved to Elizabeth where he made his first and last effort to enter politics by seeking the post of city attorney, an effort which was unsuccessful.

For several years Lindabury engaged in general practice. He was counsel for the Anti-Race-Track Gambling League and made speeches widely against gambling. Though a Democrat he opposed his party in this situation since he believed they had been corrupted by the gambling interests. In 1892 he defended the Singer Manufacturing Company against the payment of a tax from which the company claimed it was immune under its charter. Losing the case in the lower court he retained Joseph H. Choate to aid him on appeal and won the case in the court of errors and appeals. The next year the state's effort to collect the tax was renewed and again, with Choate's aid, he won a decision. This began his career as a corporation lawyer. His next important case was his defense of the American Tobacco Company against an action brought by the state of New Jersey to dissolve it as an illegal combination in restraint of trade. Choate, as counsel for the tobacco company, retained Lindabury as associate counsel and allowed him to handle the case on appeal. He won a significant victory which firmly established his reputation and brought him all the business he could manage.

In 1896 Lindabury moved his office to Newark where he remained for the rest of his life. After two years alone he became senior partner of the firm of Lindabury, Depue & Faulks. His practice was tremendous in scope and lucrative in character. After his death one of the leaders of the bar said of him: "No other American lawyer ever represented and counseled so large an aggregate of capital investment as Lindabury represented and counseled" (Guthrie, *post*, p. 48). In 1905 he represented the Metropolitan and Prudential Life Insurance companies in the Armstrong investigation in New York. He headed the distinguished group of lawyers which defended the United States Steel Corporation against the dissolution suit brought against it by the federal government in 1911 and won a decisive victory in the Supreme Court's decision in 1920 (251 *U. S.*, 417). In 1912 and 1913 he appeared for J. P. Morgan and other financial interests before the Pujo committee in Congress which was investigating the so-called "money trust." Besides those mentioned he had as clients such business interests as the Standard Oil Company of New Jersey, the Central Railroad of New Jersey, the International Harvester Company, the United States Rubber Company, Bethlehem Steel Company, American Sugar Refining Company, the Pennsylvania Railroad Company, and many others.

Lindabury could never be persuaded to enter politics although he was many times sought by the leaders of his party for public office. Nor would he accept judicial appointment though this was twice tendered him. He was, however, a member of the New Jersey Palisades Interstate Park Board and a trustee of Stevens Institute of Technology. He retained an interest in farming and lived on a six-hundred-acre farm at Bernardsville, which he called "Meadowbrook" and which he operated on a paying basis. He was a tall handsome man, fond of riding and outdoor life. On July 8, 1892, he was married to Lillian (Van Saun) Dinger, who had one daughter and by whom he had a son and a daughter. He died from apoplexy after a fall from his horse.

[Wm. D. Guthrie, "Richard V. Lindabury," *Am. Bar Asso. Jour.*, Jan. 1926; *Who's Who in America*, 1924–25; *N. J. Law Jour.*, Sept. 1925; the *Jour. of Commerce* (N. Y.) and *N. Y. Times*, July 16, 1925.]   R. E. C.

LINDBERG, CONRAD EMIL (June 9, 1852–Aug. 2, 1930), Lutheran clergyman, was born in Jönköping, Sweden, where he received his early schooling in the Gymnasium. At eighteen he began to preach, and in 1871, with the aid of friends, he came to the United States to study at Augustana College and Theological Seminary, then located at Paxton, Ill. In two years he completed the theological course, but being too young to be ordained he continued his studies at Mount Airy Lutheran Theological Seminary, Philadelphia, where he remained until 1876. In 1874 he was ordained to the Lutheran ministry by the Augustana Synod, and while under its charge he also managed to study at the University of Pennsylvania. In 1879 he was called to the Gustavus Adolphus Church in New York City, where for eleven years he served as pastor and as president of the New York Conference of the Augustana Synod. In 1890 he was called to be professor of systematic theology at the Augustana College and Theological Seminary, which had been removed to Rock Island, Ill. From 1901 to 1910 he was vice-president, and from 1920 until his death, dean of the institution. He was also vice-president of the Augustana Synod (1899–1907), and a member of the Augustana Synod Home and Foreign Mission Board (1899–1913). In 1901 he was made Knight of the Royal Order of the North Star by the King of Sweden and in 1924, Commander of the Royal Order of Vasa.

He was a diligent student throughout his whole life, and the fact that he was a bachelor rendered it possible for him to adhere closely to a fixed schedule of devotions and study; his whole life, as well as his theology, was pervaded by a spirit of deep mysticism and reverence. Although at different times, he taught in practically every theological field, his chief work was done in dogmatics and apologetics. In 1898 he published *Encheiridion I Dogmatik Jämte Dogmhistoriska Anmärkninger*. This was later expanded into a larger book, *Christian Dogmatics and Notes on the History of Dogma,* which in 1922 was issued in an English translation by Rev. C. E. Hoffsten. It was adopted as a textbook in Lutheran theological seminaries both in America and Europe, and attained a position of established authority. In 1928 a revised edition appeared.

In the field of apologetics, he wrote *Apologetics, or a System of Christian Evidence* (1917, 1926). Unlike Lutheran theologians who have come to America in their maturity, Lindberg apparently had no fear of issuing his works in the English language. Besides these major productions, he also wrote a number of smaller books, and articles and reviews in church magazines. He was chief editor of the *Augustana Theological Quarterly* from 1900 to 1902, and after his retirement from the editorship, due to other pressing duties, he still continued to contribute to the publication. He died just as he had finished his last book, *Beacon Lights of Prophecy in the Latter Days,* issued posthumously in 1930.

[*Augustana Alumni Reg.* (1924); *Who's Who in America,* 1930–31; *Tidskrift: Augustana Theological Quarterly,* vol. X, no. 1; *Lutheran Companion,* Aug. 16, 1927; *Augustana,* vol. LXXV, no. 33 (1930); *Lutheran Church Herald,* Aug. 26, 1930; J. C. Jensson (Roseland), *Am. Lutheran Biogs.* (copr. 1890).]   J. M. R.

LINDBERGH, CHARLES AUGUSTUS (Jan. 20, 1859–May 24, 1924), congressman and leader in the Non-Partisan League, was born in Stockholm, Sweden, the son of August and Louise (Carline) Lindbergh. His parents emigrated to the United States in 1859 and settled on a farm near Melrose, Stearns County, Minn. The son, after some preliminary education, attended the law school of the University of Michigan and graduated in 1883. He began the practice of law in Little Falls, Minn., where he made his home for the remainder of his life. In 1906 he was elected as a Republican to Congress and served for five successive terms (1907–17). In 1916 he was defeated by Frank B. Kellogg in the primary election for United States senator. Two years later, as a Progressive Republican with Non-Partisan League indorsement, he was defeated for the governorship of Minnesota. He entered the primary for the same office on the Farmer-Labor ticket in 1924, but his death occurred before the election.

The name Lindbergh did not have the ring in Minnesota in 1917–18 that it had ten years later when his only son, of the same name, electrified the world by his transatlantic flight. The elder Lindbergh was of the type to whom statues are erected only after the lapse of many years. Starting his congressional career as a Rooseveltian, when the West was infatuated with progressive policies that brought Republican "insurgency" against "standpat" leadership, Lindbergh was always in the first rank of "reformers." His praise for Roosevelt's attacks on the methods of big business, following the panic of 1907; his vote against the Payne-Aldrich tariff; his vote to declare the office of speaker vacant, despite the unwillingness of some of the leaders of the revolt against "Cannonism" to go to that length; his commendation of the moral influence of Wilson in framing the Underwood tariff, including the income tax provision; his espousal of rural credits and postal savings banks; his resolution which inspired the Pujo investigation of the "money trust"; his advocacy of the repeal of the canal tolls exemption; his indorsement of Wilson's Mexican policy; his statement that the Socialists' view of war was correct; and his de-

nunciation of "war propaganda—dollar plutocracy versus patriotic America" and a "nation muzzled by false national honor"—all reacted favorably upon his constituency and the people of his state. It was not long after the United States declared war on Germany, however, that his prophecy (Mar. 1, 1917) was strikingly fulfilled: "The man who reasons and exercises good sense to-day may be hung in effigy tomorrow by the jingoes" ('(*Congressional Record,* 64 Cong., 2 Sess., App. p. 701).

Lindbergh's interest in financial reform prompted his volume entitled *Banking and Currency and the Money Trust,* published in 1913. In July 1917 he published *Why is Your Country at War, and What Happens to you After the War,* purporting to analyze the causes of the war. The book was used against him in the following year, when his candidacy threatened to plunge the Republican party down to defeat by the Non-Partisan League. The press vilified him, his meetings were broken up, and he was threatened with violence. His defeat was hailed as a victory for "loyalty." His appointment to the War Industries Board was greeted with such a storm of protest that Lindbergh resigned in order not to obstruct the cooperation of certain elements in the prosecution of the war. His last work was *The Economic Pinch* (1923), which explained further his social and economic ideas. Although he was generous, honest, and a champion of the common people, he had few personal friends. After his death his name gained increased respect. Lindbergh married, soon after he settled in Little Falls, Mary Lafond. After her death he married Evangeline Lodge Land, who became the mother of Charles Augustus Lindbergh, Jr.

[Lynn and Dora B. Haines, *The Lindberghs* (1931); *Biog. Dir. Am. Cong.* (1928); Margaret S. Ernst, "Lindbergh's 'Bolshevik' Father," the *Nation,* June 15, 1927; *Lit. Digest,* June 11, 1927; the *Minneapolis Tribune* and *N. Y. Times,* May 25, 1924.]   G. M. S.

LINDE, CHRISTIAN (Feb. 19, 1817–Nov. 24, 1887), pioneer Wisconsin physician, was born on the family estate near Copenhagen, Denmark. He was of a noble Danish family and his full name was Christian Lemvigh Paul Lövenörn de Linde-Freidenreich. He was educated in the Royal University of Copenhagen, from which he graduated in 1837. After his graduation, while working in the hospitals of the Danish capital, he became involved in the political troubles that were disturbing all Europe and in 1842 he emigrated to America. He chose the vicinity of Oshkosh, Wis., where there was good hunting, as the place to establish a landed estate and live the life of a country gentleman. In a new community, where medical knowledge was at a premium, he was called upon to treat neighboring settlers and Indians, among whom he quickly established a wide reputation as a healer. Many local traditions are current regarding his early professional work among the Indians of the Fox River valley. Possessed of great physical strength and courage, qualities strongly appealing to the Indian mind, he was highly regarded as a mighty hunter and medicine man. In adopting him into their life and confidence they gave him the name of Muckwa (White Bear), a tribute to his size and blonde complexion. A campaign of vaccination which he was compelled to institute against a smallpox outbreak put to a severe test the Indians' confidence and the doctor's tact and ingenuity. Insistent demands for his professional services compelled him to give up his country home and to settle for practice, first in Green Bay, then in Fond du Lac, and finally in Oshkosh, where he made his home for the remainder of his life. He was the pioneer surgeon of that section of the state, a skilful operator, of sound judgment and original ideas. He is credited with having discovered the value of animal tendons for surgical suture material and with having first applied them to the treatment of wounds. Specialization in medicine was hardly known in the pioneer community in which he lived and he was always a busy general practitioner. He was a member of county, state, and national medical societies, serving as president of the Winnebago County society and vice-president of the Wisconsin organization. His writings, mainly on surgical subjects, were presented before meetings of these societies. In addition to his medical attainments, he was a classical scholar and a linguist, able to converse in seven languages, though he never achieved any great mastery of the English tongue. Exposure incident to country practice in the inclement winters of Wisconsin made him a chronic sufferer from bronchitis, which caused his death, in Oshkosh. He was married three times: to Sarah Dickinson in 1843, to Sarah Davis in 1852, and to Mrs. Huldah Henning Volner in 1858. A son, Fred, issue of the first marriage, studied medicine, and until his death in 1880, was associated with his father in practice. Two daughters survived him.

[H. A. Kelly and W. L. Burrage, *Am. Medic. Biogs.* (1920); *The U. S. Biog. Dict.,* Wis. Vol. (1877); R. J. Harney, *Hist. of Winnebago County, Wis.* (1880); *Wis. State Jour.* (Madison), Nov. 25, 1887; information from the family.]   J. M. P—n.

LINDENKOHL, ADOLPH (Mar. 6, 1833–June 22, 1904), cartographer, oceanographer, was born at Niederkaufungen, Hesse Cassel,

Germany, fifth of the nine children of George C. F. Lindenkohl and Anna Elizabeth (Krug). At Cassel he received the thorough education of the Realschule and later of the Polytechnische Schule, graduating from the latter in 1852. That same year he came to the United States with an elder sister and engaged in teaching in private schools, first in York, Pa., and then in Washington, D. C. In 1854 he joined the United States Coast and Geodetic Survey as cartographic draftsman, and here he labored for practically half a century, rising step by step to the position of senior cartographic draftsman. He became a citizen of the United States in 1857, and at different times during the Civil War was assigned to duty with the army, serving as a topographer on the defenses of Baltimore, and assisting in a topographic survey of the Potomac River and in the compilation of cartographic data for the department of West Virginia. In 1872 he married Pauline Praeger of Baltimore; three boys and three girls were born to them between the years 1873 and 1883.

Lindenkohl's official duties were wholly of a technical nature, connected with the production of hydrographic charts; and his charts published by the Coast and Geodetic Survey are notable examples of high technique in engraving, etching, and lithography. His map of New York City and environs, printed privately in New York City in 1860 and engraved by his brother, Henry Lindenkohl, is an outstanding example of cartographic art of that day. Being possessed of a scientific bent of mind, he went behind the data shown on the charts and related them to the broader fields of scientific inquiry. He mastered the mathematical principles of projections and became recognized as a leading authority on the subject. He made the first transverse polyconic map of the United States; he pointed out the advantages of the transverse polyconic projection for reducing scale error for mapping regions of considerable extension in longitude; and he directed attention to the advantages of the transverse mercator projection in the solution of certain cartographic problems. In the field of oceanography, the submarine channel of the Hudson River, which can be followed clearly on a hydrographic chart for a number of miles out into the open sea, was a problem that early engaged his attention. In the *Report,* 1884, of the Coast and Geodetic Survey, and in the *American Journal of Science,* June 1885, he presents a careful study of this channel, tracing its connection with the geological features of the adjacent coastal region, and concluding that it was brought about by glacial action. Other papers, which appeared in the annual reports of the Coast and Geodetic Survey, in *Petermann's Mitteilungen,* and in various other journals, dealt with the Gulf Stream, the circulation in the Gulf of Mexico, and with the temperature and salinity of the North Pacific Ocean. He was not a prolific writer, but each of his publications is a carefully prepared paper, informed by broad scholarship. These papers stimulated interest and encouraged discussion in the field of oceanography, which at that time counted but few active workers in this country.

[*Bull. Philosophical Soc. of Washington,* Aug. 1905; *Proc. Washington Acad. of Sci.,* vol. X (1908); *Evening Star* (Washington, D. C.), June 23, 1904; Coast and Geodetic Survey records; family records.]

H. A. M—r.

LINDERMAN, HENRY RICHARD (Dec. 26, 1825–Jan. 27, 1879), director of the mint, was born in Lehman township, Pike County, Pa., son of Dr. John Jordan and Rachel (Brodhead) Linderman. After studying medicine with his father, and also probably in New York City, he practised for several years in Pennsylvania. In 1853 he was made chief clerk in the mint at Philadelphia, and served in that capacity for twelve years, resigning to enter private business. On Mar. 4, 1867, President Johnson appointed him director of the Philadelphia mint, where he remained for two years. Removed by President Grant in April 1869, he was thereafter associated with various governmental activities for which his experience and ability fitted him. In 1869–70 he assisted Comptroller John Jay Knox [*q.v.*] in drafting the coinage act of 1873. Among other provisions of this important measure was one combining the mint and assay offices into a bureau administered as a unit of the Treasury Department. In 1872 Secretary Boutwell authorized Linderman to conduct an examination of the Western mints. When the coinage act took effect, on Apr. 1, 1873, President Grant appointed him the first director of the Bureau of the Mint.

On Nov. 19, 1872, Linderman made a detailed report to the secretary of the treasury, urging certain monetary changes. One of these was the establishment of a true par of exchange with Great Britain, to replace the inaccurate technical par which dated from colonial times; accordingly, an act was passed, effective Jan. 1, 1874, which correctly expressed the relation between the legal moneys of the two countries. In the same report he had proposed the coinage of a silver "trade dollar" of 420 grains, designed to supersede the popular Mexican silver dollar in Oriental trade, but not to be used as a medium of domestic exchange. This anomalous coin had a short and unhappy history. Authorization for its coinage was included in the act of Feb. 12, 1873; its limited legal-tender status was revoked and power to suspend coinage given in 1876; finally, in 1887, the right to coin it was repealed. One writer says of this fiscal experiment, "Its creation was a misfortune, its existence a failure, and its retirement a necessity" (Watson, *post,* p. 207). In general, however, Linderman had sound ideas on questions of coinage. His annual reports are full of valuable information ably presented, especially that of 1876, which contains a "Review of the Several Propositions for the Coinage of Legal Tender Silver Dollars under a Double Standard." In 1877 he published his *Money and Legal Tender in the United States,* a concise and accurate handbook since superseded by more extensive treatments, to which the agitation about silver gave a timely significance. "As to merely technical matters . . . ," a reviewer declared, "nothing could be more lucid and methodical" (*The Nation,* Jan. 10, 1878, p. 30).

Because of criticism of its management, Linderman conducted an exhaustive investigation into the San Francisco mint, making a report of his findings, dated October 1877. Less than a year later the Bureau of the Mint itself was under fire, and specific charges of misconduct in office were made against Linderman by a congressional sub-committee. These were categorically denied by him (*New York Tribune,* June 17, 18, 1878). The anxiety caused by these investigations, after the strenuous work of the year before, proved too much for his health; he was not on duty after November, and his death followed in January. No conclusive report on the investigations exists, but there is no question as to Linderman's personal integrity. He was an exceptionally able director of the mint at a period when efficient conduct of the office was particularly difficult.

[*The Biog. Encyc. of Pa. of the Nineteenth Century* (1874); *Frank Leslie's Illustrated Newspaper,* Nov. 20, 1875; J. P. Watson, *The Bureau of the Mint. Its Hist., Activities and Organization* (1926); *Ann. Reports of the Director of the Mint,* 1867, 1868, 1873–78; information from the Bureau of the Mint, Treasury Department; *Evening Star* (Washington, D. C.), *N. Y. Tribune,* Jan. 28, 1879; D. K. Watson, *Hist. of Am. Coinage* (1899); A. B. Hepburn, *Hist. of Coinage and Currency in the U. S.* (1903).]

L. P. B.

LINDHEIMER, FERDINAND JACOB (May 21, 1801–Dec. 2, 1879), botanist, was born in Frankfurt-am-Main, Germany, and died in New Braunfels, Comal County, Tex. He was the son of a well-to-do merchant of Frankfurt, Johan H. Lindheimer. He attended the universities of Wiesbaden and Bonn, but left the latter without a degree in 1827. He taught in Georg Bunsen's *Erziehungsanstalt* in Frankfurt until the institute was closed by the government in the spring of 1834, because of revolutionary activities. He then accompanied Bunsen and another colleague to America and lived for a few months in the famous German "Latin-farmer" community at Belleville, St. Clair County, Ill. In the fall of 1834, with five companions, he went to Mexico by way of New Orleans, but after a sojourn of sixteen months he returned to New Orleans to enlist in the ranks of the Texans in their war for independence (*Aufsätze, post,* pp. 78–144). After the war he tried farming near Houston, but he was unsuccessful. Then, encouraged by his old university friend and fellow-student, George Engelmann [*q.v.*], he undertook the systematic collection of botanical specimens in Texas. He succeeded in interesting Asa Gray of Harvard College in this work, and for nine years made most extensive collections of Texan plants. These were described in the work entitled *"Plantæ Lindheimerianæ,"* published in Volumes V (October 1845) and VI (no. 1, 1850) of the *Boston Journal of Natural History.* He was a man of unusual will, determination, and devotion to science. Completely fearless, he spent months at a time in the wilderness, without seeing a white man. The Indians came to look upon him with a deep reverence as a great medicine man (*Aufsätze,* pp. 63–78).

In 1846, at San Antonio, Lindheimer had married Eleonore Reinarz, the daughter of a recently arrived immigrant from Aachen. She was of great assistance to him in the preparation of his specimens. In 1847 he took part in the "Darmstädter Kolonie," or the "Communistic colony of Bettina," occupying a tract of land between the Llano and the San Saba rivers. The colony lasted but little more than six months. In 1852 he became editor of the *Neu Braunfelser Zeitung,* which he conducted for eighteen years. The paper was nominally Democratic, but independent. During the fifties Lindheimer opposed the German agitation for abolition and himself supported the Southern cause during the Civil War. Aside from wielding a political influence through his paper, he published in it and in the *Neu Yorker Staats-Zeitung* valuable scientific, philosophical, and historical essays. An appreciative former student, Gustav Passavant, collected and published a number of these in 1879, at Frankfurt, under the title, *Aufsätze und Abhandlungen von Ferdinand Lindheimer in Texas.* Lindheimer also conducted a free private school and served as superintendent of public instruc-

tion in the county and as justice of the peace. He is described as quiet and deliberate, and temperate in his habits. He was a freethinker in his opinions, but he never antagonized religious institutions and he valued nothing more than freedom and independence.

[*Allgemeine Deutsche Biog.,* Band XVIII (1883); Ferdinand Roemer, *Texas* (1849); R. L. Biesele, *The Hist. of the German Settlements in Tex., 1831–61* (1930); *Der Deutsche Pionier,* Jan. 1880; C. H. Winkler, "The Botany of Tex.," *Bull. of the Univ. of Tex.,* no. 18 (1915); J. W. Blankinship, "Plantæ Lindheimerianæ, Part III," *Mo. Botanical Garden, Eighteenth Ann. Report* (1907); files of the *Neu Braunfelser Zeitung*; S. W. Geiser, "Ferdinand Jacob Lindheimer," *Southwest Rev.,* Winter 1930.]   S. W. G.

LINDLEY, CURTIS HOLBROOK (Dec. 14, 1850–Nov. 20, 1920), lawyer, jurist, was born in Marysville, Cal., a descendant of John Lindley, an early settler in Guilford, Conn. Charles Lindley, his father, who studied at the Yale Law School, went to California in 1849, with his wife, Ann Eliza Downey, a native of Newtown, Conn. In 1865–66 young Lindley attended the Eagleswood Military Academy at Perth Amboy, N. J., and at the age of sixteen enlisted in the regular army. His father secured his release before the full term of his enlistment and he returned to study. He attended the San Francisco High School, 1868–70, and spent the next two years at the University of California. Military instruction in the University was organized at this time, and Lindley became ranking captain of the cadets and the first commissioned officer. Meanwhile, when he was seventeen, he started out with companions on a prospecting expedition in Nevada. He ran a stationary engine on the Comstock Lode and just before practising law was stationary engineer at the Union Works. He firmly believed that every lawyer should take some sort of an engineering course, and himself studied mining engineering to aid him in the practice of mining law.

He was admitted to practise in May 1872 and within a short time was appointed secretary of the California Code Commission, of which his father was a member. On June 19, 1872, he was married to Elizabeth Mendenhall. He practised law in Stockton, being appointed to fill a vacancy as superior judge of Amador County. Failing of election to the same office, he moved to San Francisco, forming, in 1890, a partnership with Henry Eickhoff. While on the bench in Amador County, Lindley had occasion to decide several mining cases. He began to specialize in this branch of the law and ultimately published a treatise on the subject (*A Treatise on the Amer-*

ican Law Relating to Mines and Mineral Lands, 1897). His work, familiarly known as "Lindley on Mines" quickly took rank as the leading text on the subject and became recognized as the most authoritative text on mining law in the United States. It gives evidence of painstaking research and philosophic insight far beyond that of the average legal textbook. Rossiter W. Raymond, the eminent mining engineer, refers to the three-volume third edition as "truly an imposing *magnum opus.*"

Before the war Lindley had delivered lectures on mining law at the Leland Stanford, Jr., University and at the University of California. Among his Stanford students was Herbert Hoover, and from that contact a lasting friendship was formed. Upon Hoover's appointment as head of the Food Administration, he called Lindley to Washington as a "dollar-a-year" man to assist in organizing its legal department. Standing out from the infinite detail and perplexing problems of this organization which had sprung up on a moment's notice was the creation of the United States Grain Corporation. Lindley carefully drafted a proposed charter for this corporation and submitted it to President Wilson as a "tentative draft." It was a matter of pride to him that the President penned out the words "tentative draft," and, without delay, signed the proclamation making the charter effective. Despite the fact that his special field was mining law, he was able to turn at once to problems of commercial and constitutional law, and to matters concerning which there were no precedents, but his judgments proved eminently sound. Finding the climate of Washington a severe drain upon his vitality, Lindley returned to California to build up his health and his practice. He died, as he had so often expressed a wish to die, "in the harness," being stricken, an hour after the conclusion of a most trying mining case, with the illness that resulted in his death five days later.

[See *Who's Who in America,* 1920–21; W. E. Colby, "Curtis Holbrook Lindley, 1850–1920," *Cal. Law Rev.,* Jan. 1921; the *Engineering and Mining Jour.,* Apr. 18, 1914; *Econ. Geology,* Sept. 1914; J. M. Lindly, *The Hist. of the Lindley-Lindsley-Linsley Families in America,* vol. I (1930), vol. II (1924); *San Francisco Chronicle,* Nov. 22, 1920. Information as to certain facts was supplied by Lindley's son, Curtis Lindley.]
W. E. C.

LINDLEY, JACOB (June 13, 1774–Jan. 29, 1857), a leader among the founders of Ohio University, was born in the Blockhouse or Lindley Fort near the site of Prosperity Town, in Washington County, Pa., the seventh son of Demas Lindley. At the age of eighteen he was sent to an academy in Canonsburg, Pa., which subse-quently became Jefferson College. A few years later he entered the College of New Jersey, having traveled the entire distance from the Monongahela River by the "ride and tie" method in company with James Carnahan, destined to become the ninth president of that institution. In 1800 he graduated, married Hannah Dickey, and was licensed to preach by the Washington County Presbytery. In 1803 he settled as pastor of the church at Waterford, Ohio. Two years later he was appointed trustee of the, as yet, nonexistent Ohio University. Unlike some of his fellow appointees he took from the first an active interest in the affairs of the prospective institution. On Apr. 2, 1806, he was made member of a committee "to contract with some person or persons for building a house in the town of Athens for the purpose of an academy on the credit of rents that will hereafter become due" (from the two townships of land granted to the University). On the completion of this building Lindley was appointed to a committee "to report a plan for opening and conducting an academy and providing a preceptor." A few days later he was himself elected preceptor and entered upon his duties in the spring of the same year, 1808. For the first four years he was the sole instructor in the only department of the University then existing, the preparatory department.

By 1822 the institution was in a position financially to make possible the provision for instruction of college grade. A college faculty was organized in which Lindley was assigned to the chair of mental and moral philosophy and belles-lettres. Two years later, in 1824, he was transferred to the chair of mathematics, which position he held until 1826. With his scholastic duties he apparently combined those of pastor of a Presbyterian church established there in 1809 largely through his influence. Although there is no evidence that he possessed unusual talent as teacher, administrator, or scholar, he seems nevertheless to have been the moving spirit in inaugurating the activities of the first university to be founded on a grant made by the federal government. In 1828 he took charge of a church at Walnut Hills, near Cincinnati, but in 1829 he removed to Grave Creek in Virginia and shortly afterward to Pennsylvania. After he had left the state, the legislature appointed Thomas Bryce to his seat on the board of trustees of the university. Lindley contested the action (1836) and won his suit, but he resigned from the board two years later upon removing to the South. Finally he returned to Connellsville, Pa., where he died at the residence of his son, Dr. Lutellus Lindley, in 1857. At the solicitation of his daughters and some other young mothers Lindley published at Uniontown, Pa., in 1846, a little treatise on the training of children entitled *Infant Philosophy*. The work is characterized chiefly by the importance it attaches to the education of children while still very young, below three years of age, and by its vigorous attack on Locke's *"tabula rasa"* theory.

[In preparing this sketch, the author made use of an unpublished biographical sketch of Lindley by Emma C. McVay, a grand-niece. Printed sources include: C. M. Walker, *Hist. of Athens County, Ohio* (1869); W. E. Peters, *Legal Hist. of the Ohio Univ.* (1910); C. W. Super, *A Pioneer Coll. and Its Background* (1924); C. L. Martzolff, *Ohio Univ.* (1910); *Gen. Cat. of Ohio Univ., 1804–57*.]   L.F.A.

LINDSAY, NICHOLAS VACHEL (Nov. 10, 1879–Dec. 5, 1931), poet, known as Vachel Lindsay, was born in Springfield, Ill. His paternal ancestry was Kentuckian, his maternal Virginian, and on both sides it was Scotch. His father, Vachel Thomas Lindsay, one of the pioneer settlers in the Springfield region, was a physician; his mother, Catharine (Frazee) Lindsay, possessed some literary talent and was an ardent member of the Christian Church. Their son early developed the combined interest in religion, poetry, and art, which was to dominate his entire life. After graduation from the local high school in 1897, he attended Hiram College in Ohio for three years with the thought of entering the ministry. This aim was then abandoned for the study of art, pursued under difficulties, while working in Marshall Field's wholesale department, at the Chicago Art Institute night school, 1900–03, and later continued at the New York School of Art, 1904–05, where he worked under William M. Chase and Robert Henri, also lecturing on art at the West Side Y. M. C. A. in the winter of 1905–06. Meanwhile, beginning at the age of eighteen, he had written a few intermittent poems, and, in the spring of 1906, being without funds and unable to obtain work, he started on his famous walking trip through the South, distributing a poem, "The Tree of Laughing Bells," in exchange for bed and board (Lindsay, *A Handy Guide for Beggars, . . . Being Sundry Explorations Made . . . in Florida, Georgia, North Carolina, Tennessee, Kentucky, New Jersey, and Pennsylvania*, 1916). After further Y. M. C. A. lecturing in New York City, he drifted back to Illinois in 1908, where in the course of the winter he appeared on Y. M. C. A. programs at Springfield and during the next two years stumped the state on behalf of the Anti-Saloon League. In the spring of 1912 he attempted to repeat his Southern ad-

venture on a walking trip to the Pacific Coast, but he found the Western ranchmen less hospitable to the claims of poetry and his journey came to a sudden end in New Mexico (Lindsay, *Adventures while Preaching the Gospel of Beauty*, 1914).

His first volume of poetry, *General William Booth Enters into Heaven and Other Poems* (1913), attracted little attention, but its successor, *The Congo and Other Poems* (1914), met with wide popular acclaim. The title-poem started a whole school of literature devoted to the negro; its striking originality of conception, its imaginative reach, and its infectious, insistent rhythms ensure its literary immortality. In it Lindsay created a new poetic music of ragtime and echolalia, a blend of speech and song, clattering but impassioned, that well expressed the hurtling energy of America. His new technique was exercised with almost equal felicity in "A Negro Sermon: Simon Legree" and "John Brown," while in the more conventional verse of "The Eagle that is Forgotten" (in honor of Altgeld) and of "Abraham Lincoln Walks at Midnight" he achieved high dignity and prophetic power. His unusual temperament, that of a revivalist preacher poetically inspired, and devoted to the political liberalism of the West, enabled him for a time to realize in his poetry a Messianic quality that responded to the hopes of the hour. The lyrical impact of his style, united with its whimsicality and colloquial phrasing, seemed to infuse a new note of aspiration into everyday existence. His remarkable chanting of his own verses was in these first years an unforgettable experience for his auditors, and he became in the popular mind a romantic modern analogue of the medieval troubadour. (Thirty phonograph records of his chantings, not made, unfortunately, until late in his career, are in the possession of the library of Barnard College.)

Unquestionably, Lindsay's influence counted greatly in the contemporary revival of American poetry. But his genius early began to show signs of exhaustion. *The Chinese Nightingale and Other Poems* (1917) was notably uneven, and *The Golden Whales of California and Other Rhymes* (1920) was, for the most part, labored and artificial. When he was invited in 1920 to recite his poems at Oxford University—the first American poet to be so honored—Lindsay's creative work was already definitely over; the season of British lionizing that followed marked the high point of his public recognition which henceforth steadily declined. Essentially intuitive, and almost totally devoid of critical ability—his prose works, *The Art of the Moving Picture*

(1915) and *The Golden Book of Springfield* (1920) show the extravagance of his generous enthusiasms—he became in his later years a formalized echo of himself. As his creative power lessened, his manner grew steadily more pompous and hieratic. Of his later volumes, *Going-to-the-Sun* (1923) is chiefly interesting because of its bizarre illustrations by the author; *Going-to-the-Stars* (1926) and *The Candle in the Cabin* (1926) are both quite negligible; while *The Litany of Washington Street* (1929), a prose collection of orations on an imaginary highway stretching from California to India, though better than the later poetry, expresses little more than a vague emotional idealism. His personal eccentricities, such as his habit of dining publicly with a number of huge dolls set up at his table, continued to attract local attention wherever he sojourned, but in the literary world at large he had already become a legend rather than a living reality long before his death. He was married on May 19, 1925, to Elizabeth Conner of Spokane, Wash., where he resided for a time, but his last days were spent in his native town of Springfield. They were ended, suddenly and unexpectedly, by heart failure on Dec. 5, 1931. There were two children, a son and a daughter.

[There are good obituaries in the *N. Y. Herald-Tribune*, Dec. 6, 1931, *Boston Evening Transcript*, Dec. 5, 1931, and the *Ill. State Register* (Springfield), Dec. 5, 6, 1931; there are interesting personal reminiscences in Stephen Graham, *Tramping with a Poet in the Rockies* (1922), and Christopher Morley, *Ex Libris Carissimis* (1932), pp. 90–98. An excellent biographical-critical sketch by Louis Untermeyer is prefixed to the selections in his anthology, *Modern American Poetry* (3rd ed., 1925). A. E. Trombly, *Vachel Lindsay, Adventurer* (1929), contains a bibliography. For various estimates see Edward Davison, *Some Modern Poets* (1928); Alfred Kreymborg, *Our Singing Strength* (1929), pp. 368–78; Edgar Lee Masters, "Vachel Lindsay," *Bookman*, Oct. 1926; "A Letter from Vachel Lindsay," *Ibid.*, Mar. 1932; H. M. Robinson, "The Ordeal of Vachel Lindsay: A Critical Reconstruction," *Ibid.*, Apr. 1932; Ludwig Lewisohn, *Expression in America* (1932), pp. 569–74; Stephen Graham, "Vachel Lindsay," *Spectator* (London), Jan. 23, 1932; Hazleton Spencer, "The Life and Death of a Bard," *Am. Mercury*, Apr. 1932.]   E. S. B.

LINDSAY, VACHEL [See Lindsay, Nicholas Vachel, 1879–1931].

LINDSAY, WILLIAM (Sept. 4, 1835–Oct. 15, 1909), jurist and senator, was born near Lexington, Va., the son of Andrew and Sallie (Davidson) Lindsay, and the grandson of James Lindsay, who emigrated from Scotland and settled in Rockbridge County, Va., before 1795. He attended the common schools and the high school at Lexington and then began to study law with Judge John W. Brockenborough. In 1854 he moved to Clinton, Ky., where he continued reading law with Judge Edward Crossland while he taught school, was admitted to the bar in 1858, and began to build up a successful practice. At the outbreak of the Civil War, with a group of Kentuckians, he enlisted as a private in the Confederate service, became lieutenant of Company B, 22nd Tennessee Infantry, and, on Feb. 23, 1862, captain of the company. After the battles of Belmont and Shiloh, his company was transferred to the 3rd Kentucky Regiment, in which he was captain of Company M, but soon resigned to become assistant quartermaster of the 7th Kentucky Infantry in Preston's brigade of Breckinridge's division. Having taken part in the battles around Vicksburg, his regiment was mounted in 1864 and acted with Forrest's cavalry under Abraham Buford. After the surrender of General Taylor, he was paroled at Columbus, Miss., in May 1865 and resumed practice at Clinton, Ky., where, the year before, he had married Swann Semple, who died in 1867. The next year he married her sister, Hattie Semple.

Lindsay was a member of the Kentucky Senate from 1867 to 1870. In 1870 he was elected to the court of appeals, of which he became chief justice in 1876. He soon established a reputation as a clear and able jurist, and his opinions were widely quoted as authoritative. His opinion in *Douglass* vs. *Cline* (75 *Ky.*, 608–10) established a precedent in regard to the nature of mortgages and the extent of judicial discretion in appointing receivers. His opinion denying the right to try an extradited person for an offense not named in the extradition proceedings (*Commonwealth* vs. *Hawes, 76 Ky.*, 697–98), the first decision of the kind, was upheld by the United States Supreme Court and was called "very able" by Justice Samuel Freeman Miller (*U. S.* vs. *Rauscher*, 119 *U. S.*, 428). Having declined reëlection, in 1878 he retired from the bench and soon built up a lucrative practice in Frankfort. In 1883 he married as his third wife, Eleanor Holmes. He was again a member of the state Senate from 1889 to 1893; in the latter year he was chosen to fill a vacancy in the national Senate and, in 1894, to serve a full term. At Washington he was a friend and supporter of Cleveland. In 1896 he indorsed the sound-money Democrats and supported their ticket by speeches. Not seeking reëlection, he established a law firm in New York City, the firm of Lindsay, Kremer, Kalish, and Palmer. He was also a trustee of the Carnegie Institution and commissioner of the Columbian Exposition and of the Louisiana Purchase Exposition. His last years were spent in Frankfort, Ky.

[*The Biog. Encyc. of Ky.* (1878); *Biog. Cyc. of the Commonwealth of Ky.* (1896); H. Levin, *The Lawyers* and Lawmakers of Ky. (1897); Rept. of the Adj.-Gen. of the State of Ky. Confederate Ky. Volunteers, War 1861–65, vol. I (1915); War of the Rebellion: Official Records (Army), ser. I, III (1881); Who's Who in America, 1908–09; Green Bag, July 1897, Sept. 1900; M. I. Lindsay, The Lindsays of America (1889), pp. 243–45; The Courier-Journal (Louisville), Oct. 16, 1909, Aug. 21, 1896.]   W.C.M.

LINDSEY, WILLIAM (Aug. 12, 1858–Nov. 25, 1922), manufacturer, author, playwright, was born in Fall River, Mass., the son of William and Maria (Lovell) Lindsey. After completing his education in the public schools of Fall River, he was employed or engaged there in a number of businesses, for the most part connected with or dependent upon cotton manufacturing. In 1886 he moved to Boston and became a salesman for establishments dealing in textile products. He was to those who knew him intimately at this time a rather unusual person, for though he possessed both aptitude and enthusiasm for business, he also displayed literary tastes and ambitions not usually associated with ability in practical affairs. He accumulated a considerable and choice collection of books for a man of his means, and he tried his hand at authorship, publishing a book of poems, The Apples of Istakhar, in 1895, and a collection of short stories dealing with athletics, Cinder Path Tales, in 1896. But he did not neglect money making. In 1899 he succeeded in securing the adoption by the British government of a fabric belt for carrying ammunition, and he established factories in England, France, and Germany to supply the demand created by the outbreak of the Boer War. In 1904 he retired and returned to Boston to live on the considerable fortune thus created, which was to be increased by the World War.

His circumstances now permitted him to devote himself more completely to literature, and in 1909 he published in London and Boston The Severed Mantle, a romance of medieval Provence. This was followed in 1915 by The Red Wine of Roussillon, a blank-verse drama having Southern France in the Middle Ages for its setting. Under the title of Seremonda, it was performed in New York from Jan. 1 to Feb. 10, 1917, and afterward in Boston and Chicago, with Julia Arthur in the title rôle. Although the New York Times review of Seremonda dismissed the play as the work of an uninspired amateur, it probably brought him more public notice than any of his other works, despite the fact that in England there had been some spontaneous appreciation of his Provençal romance by persons sharing his enthusiasm for the place and period it depicted. His next work was a novel having the region of the Adirondacks for its setting. Called The Backsliders, it appeared in 1922, fol-

lowed in 1923 by a posthumous volume, The Curtain of Forgetfulness, a sonnet sequence. In general, his literary works reflect books more than they do life.

In 1915 one of Lindsey's daughters, who was on her way to England with her husband immediately after their marriage, lost her life in the sinking of the Lusitania. As a memorial to her, her parents erected a chapel adjoining Emmanuel Church in Boston which has come to be recognized as a structure of architectural and artistic distinction. Lindsey either conceived or approved of practically everything in this building, showing he had a genuine instinct for refinement. He died in Boston, his wife, Annie Hawthorne Sheen, whom he had married on Dec. 16, 1884, and a son and daughter surviving him.

[See Who's Who in America, 1922–23; Elwood Worcester, Life's Adventure (1932); Boston Transcript, Nov. 25, 1922; Fall River Globe, Nov. 27, 1922. For reviews of Seremonda, see the N. Y. Times, Jan. 2, 14, 1917.]   S.G.

LINDSLEY, JOHN BERRIEN (Oct. 24, 1822–Dec. 7, 1897), physician, clergyman, educator, was born at Princeton, N. J., the son of Rev. Philip Lindsley [q.v.], professor in the College of New Jersey, and Margaret, daughter of Nathaniel Lawrence, attorney-general of New York. He was named for his mother's grandfather, John Berrien, a Huguenot, chief justice of the province of New Jersey. Having been the pupil of his father, who had become president of the University of Nashville, he graduated from that institution in 1839, and then took two years of further work there. He studied medicine in Louisville and Philadelphia, and received the degree of M.D. at the University of Pennsylvania in 1843. Turning to theological study, he was ordained in 1846 by the Presbytery of Nashville. During the next two years he served churches near that city, and also ministered to colored people, under appointment from the Presbyterian Board of Domestic Missions. Another important part of his education was acquired in his close association with the eminent geologist Gerard Troost [q.v.], begun in college and continued till Troost's death in 1850.

His principal interest, medical education, developed in 1849. Having spent a winter in studying facilities for such education in other institutions, he organized, in 1850, the medical department of the University of Nashville, the first school of its kind south of the Ohio River. He was its dean for six years at the end of which time there were four hundred students, and professor of chemistry and pharmacy for twenty-three years. Becoming chancellor of the University in 1855, he brought about the merger of the collegiate department, which had been closed since 1850, with the Western Military Institute, and the adoption of a military organization. In this form the college flourished till 1861. During the Civil War he cared vigilantly for the university's interests, the medical department continuing while the college was closed. The Confederate hospitals in Nashville, one of which occupied the university buildings, were in his charge till the Federal occupation in 1862. After the war he was again dean of the medical school for four years. In 1867 he organized Montgomery Bell Academy as a preparatory school. His proposal that the college be made a school for teachers in connection with the Peabody Education Fund was realized in 1875, when the Peabody Normal College was opened, in the university buildings. He resigned his chancellorship in 1870, but taught in the medical school till 1873. In this year he took part in the organization of the Tennessee College of Pharmacy, in which later he was professor of materia medica.

His energy, public spirit, and power of leadership impelled him to activity in many social concerns. He devoted himself especially to public health, serving through four cholera epidemics in Nashville, and from 1876 to 1880 occupying the position of health officer, in which capacity he brought about important improvements in sanitation. During these years he was also secretary of the state board of health. As a member of the board of education of Nashville (1856–60) he had much to do with the establishment of a school system of high rank. In 1866 he was superintendent of schools, and at a critical time effectively defended them against political attacks. He was secretary of the state board of education from 1875 to 1887. His pamphlet, *Our Ruin: Its Cause and Cure* (1868), provoked a movement which resulted in a change of officials in Nashville in 1869. A pamphlet, *On Prison Discipline and Penal Legislation* (1874), was widely circulated. He was a member of many medical and learned societies and organizations for social progress. After he had been a minister of the Presbyterian Church in the United States of America for twenty-four years, in 1870 he joined the Cumberland Presbyterian Church, because he considered its theological spirit more liberal; subsequently he made important contributions to the history of this denomination. His writings were chiefly articles, pamphlets, and reports. For many years he collected materials for a history of his state, and in 1886 published *The Military Annals of Tennessee, Confederate, Series I.* He was married, Feb. 9,

1857, to Sarah, daughter of Jacob McGavock of Nashville, and grand-daughter of Felix Grundy [*q.v.*]; they had six children. His death occurred in Nashville.

[J. M. Lindly, *The Hist. of the Lindley-Lindsley-Linsley Families in America*, vol. II (1924); *Ann. Report of Am. Hist. Asso. for the Year 1889* and *1892*, for bibliog. of Lindsley's publications; W. W. Clayton, *Hist. of Davidson County, Tenn.* (1880); I. A. Watson, *Physicians and Surgeons of America* (1896); records of Univ. of Nashville; *Minutes Gen. Assembly Presbyt. Ch. U. S. A.*, passim; *Nashville American*, Dec. 8, 1897; information from a daughter, Louise L. Lindsley.]
R. H. N.

LINDSLEY, PHILIP (Dec. 21, 1786–May 25, 1855), educator, Presbyterian clergyman, was a descendant of Francis Linley, who was in New Haven, Conn., as early as 1645, and settled in New Jersey in 1666. The Lindsleys (the name was variously spelled) were important supporters of the American cause during the Revolution and were strongly attached to Presbyterianism. Philip was born near Morristown, N. J., the son of Isaac and Phebe (Condict) Lindsley. At thirteen he entered the school of Robert Finley [*q.v.*] at Basking Ridge and in 1802 was admitted to the junior class of the College of New Jersey, from which he graduated in 1804. After teaching in Morristown and in Finley's school, he returned to the college in 1807 as tutor and to study theology under President Samuel Stanhope Smith [*q.v.*], who deeply influenced him. On Apr. 24, 1810, he was licensed to preach by the Presbytery of New Brunswick. During the next two years he preached for a time at Newton, Long Island, and later continued his theological studies under Rev. Matthew La Rue Perrine. Appointed senior tutor at Princeton in 1812, the next year he became professor of languages, and later also librarian. In June of 1817 he was ordained by the Presbytery of New Brunswick, and that year became vice-president of the College. After a year's service as acting president, in 1823, he declined an election to the presidency. During his Princeton teaching he declined also the presidencies of Transylvania University in Kentucky, Ohio University, and Cumberland College at Nashville. In 1824, however, he yielded to the importunities of Cumberland College, which had just been chartered as the University of Nashville.

He gave up a secure place in the East to take charge of a struggling school in Tennessee, because he saw the possibilities of the Southwest, and its educational needs appealed to him. "Throughout the immense valley of the lower Mississippi, containing at least a million of inhabitants," he wrote in a circular letter to his friends, "there exists not a single college"

(*Works*, III, 25). At his ceremonious inauguration in January 1825, he already held the largest conceptions for the future. "Provision should be made," he said, "for instruction in all the sciences and in every department of philosophy and literature" (*An Address, Delivered . . . at the Inauguration of the President of Cumberland College*, 1825, p. 34), and he soon announced a splendid scheme of buildings. His hope of aid from the state government was short-lived, and since he planned an institution which should be positively religious, but not denominational, he could not seek church support; private gifts were disappointing; yet after twelve years he proclaimed undiminished ambitions for the University. Neither impossibly magnificent ideals nor difficulties, however, kept him from working effectively toward what was practicable, an undergraduate college. To the building up of this he devoted himself steadfastly for a quarter of a century, refusing six academic presidencies and the provostship of the University of Pennsylvania. He gathered an able faculty and a growing body of students, and brought into being a strong and useful institution, the foundation of the educational eminence of Nashville.

Meanwhile he was a powerful educational missionary. His baccalaureate addresses were widely circulated in the state. In these and other speeches and in many newspaper articles he preached the value of education, particularly higher education, and the need of colleges and schools. His effect on public opinion appeared in the fact that by 1848 there were twenty colleges in Tennessee. He was a man of wide reading—in history, literature, contemporary politics, theology, church affairs, and social reform. Though he had not been active in ecclesiastical matters, his work in education brought him in 1834 the moderatorship of the Presbyterian General Assembly. In 1850 he resigned his office as president to become professor in New Albany Theological Seminary at New Albany, Ind. There he spent his last five years, resigning his professorship in 1853. He died at Nashville, whither he had gone to attend the General Assembly. He was married in October 1813 to Margaret Elizabeth, daughter of Nathaniel Lawrence, attorney-general of New York; and on Apr. 19, 1849, to Mrs. Mary Ann (Silliman) Ayers, a niece of Benjamin Silliman [*q.v.*]. One of his sons, John Berrien Lindsley [*q.v.*], was also head of the University of Nashville. Lindsley's publications were chiefly addresses on educational subjects and sermons; his complete *Works* in three volumes, edited by L. J. Halsey, were issued in 1866.

[L. J. Halsey, introduction and supplementary biographical sketch in *Works of Philip Lindsley* (1866); J. M. Lindly, *The Hist. of the Lindley-Lindsley-Linsley Families in America*, vol. I (1930); *Gen. Cat. of the Coll. of N. J., 1746–1896* (1896); John MacLean, *Hist. of the Coll. of N. J.* (1877), vol. II; W. B. Sprague, *Annals Am. Pulpit*, vol. IV (1859); *Am. Jour. of Educ.*, Sept. 1859; W. W. Clayton, *Hist. of Davidson County, Tenn.* (1880); *Nashville Union and American*, May 26, 1855.]

                                        R. H. N.

LINING, JOHN (1708–Sept. 21, 1760), physician, pioneer physiologist, experimenter in electricity, came to Charles-Town in the Province of South Carolina when he was twenty-two years old. He brought with him from Scotland an excellent training in medicine and a scientific zeal that only intensive research could satisfy. His attention was first directed to those epidemic diseases, "which," he wrote, "as regularly return at their stated Seasons, as a good Clock strikes Twelve when the Sun is in the Meridian" (*Philosophical Transactions of the Royal Society of London*, vol. XLII, 1743, p. 492). He had many occasions to treat yellow fever, particularly during the epidemics of 1732 and 1748. During the latter year, especially, he made a thorough study of this disease, and sent to Europe the earliest account, from America, of its symptoms and pathology. This description was in the form of a letter to Dr. Robert Whytt, professor of medicine at the University of Edinburgh. It was published in an Edinburgh medical journal in 1753 and reprinted many years later both separately and as a supplement to Colin Chisolm's *An Essay on the Malignant Pestilential Fever* (1799).

The warm weather of South Carolina, contrasted with the rugged climate of the Scotland of his boyhood, particularly impressed the young physician and led him to study the effects of climatic conditions upon his own metabolism. This celebrated experiment, which extended over one year, was reported in the *Philosophical Transactions of the Royal Society of London* (vols. XLII and XLIII) in 1743 and 1745. Each day he noted the temperature, using Fahrenheit's newly devised thermometer, and recorded the humidity, the extent of cloudiness, the amount of rainfall, and the force of the wind. These observations were the first published records of the weather in America. At the same time he recorded his weight both morning and night, his pulse rate, the daily intake of food and water, and the weight of his excretions. This experiment yielded important data on the variations in the amount of the so-called insensible perspiration under different conditions of temperature and extended the observations made by the illustrious Sanctorius many years before. While Lining's results are now mainly of historical interest, the plan of his experiment and the faithful performing of the tedious measurements still arouse admiration.

Lining extended his meteorological observations over several years, and his accounts of Charleston weather were published in communications to the secretary of the Royal Society in 1754 (*Philosophical Transactions,* vol. XLVIII, pt. 1). He corresponded with Benjamin Franklin and upon one occasion asked the Philadelphia sage how he had arrived at the "out-of-the-way notion" of the identity of lightning and electricity. Franklin answered with a detailed account of the reasons that had led him to perform his famous kite experiment. Lining repeated Franklin's experiment, and he, too, soon gained a not inconsiderable renown as an investigator of electricity. A London inquirer sought information from him about the possible danger to the observer in conducting such investigations. His reply, published in the *Philosophical Transactions of the Royal Society* (vol. XLVIII, pt. 2) in 1755, in which he emphasized the necessity of proper grounding and insulation of the apparatus, was very practical and quite indicative of his skill. He died in 1760. In 1739, according to data obtained by Dr. Robert Wilson, he had married Sarah Hill of Hillsboro, N. C., but left no children. Contemporary writers referred to him as "the celebrated Dr. Lining" or "the ingenious Dr. Lining." Today he holds a secure position in the history of science as a distinguished member of that group of intellectual Americans who played a leading part in the early development of science and medicine in this country.

[David Ramsay, *The Hist. of S. C.,* vol. II (1808); F. C. Bing, "John Lining, an Early American Scientist," in *Scientific Monthly,* Mar. 1928; Robert Wilson, in H. A. Kelly and W. L. Burrage, *Am. Medic. Biogs.* (1920); letter from Benjamin Franklin to John Lining in Jared Sparks, *The Works of Benjamin Franklin,* V (1837), 347–55.]   F.C.B.

LINN, JOHN BLAIR (Mar. 14, 1777–Aug. 30, 1804), poet, clergyman, was born in Shippensburg, Pa., of an ancestry distinguished for learning and piety. His grandfather and great-grandfather emigrated from the north of Ireland to Chester County, Pa., in 1732. His father, William Linn, was an eminent Presbyterian clergyman, and his mother, Rebecca, was the daughter of the Rev. John Blair, whose brother and son were likewise clergymen. When John was nine years old, the family removed to New York City, and in 1795 he graduated from Columbia College. While still an undergraduate, he wrote both verse and prose, some of which he collected and published in two volumes: *Miscellaneous Works, Prose and Poetical; By a Young Gentleman of New-York* (1795) and *The Poetical Wanderer* (1796). After his graduation, he began the study of law under the direction of Alexander Hamilton, who was a friend of his father, and who had recently resigned as Secretary of the Treasury and resumed his legal practice in New York. While he was a law student he wrote at least two plays, neither of which is extant. One of these, *Bourville Castle, or the Gallic Orphan,* was first presented at the John Street Theatre, New York, Jan. 16, 1797. Charles Brockden Brown and William Dunlap [*qq.v.*] "corrected the manuscript and wrote out the parts for the performers" (William Dunlap, *post,* p. 157). "Its success," says Brown, "was such as had been sufficient to have fixed the literary destiny of some minds" (*Valerian, post,* p. viii).

Linn, however, soon abandoned both the writing of plays and the study of law to prepare himself for the ministry. He studied theology in Schenectady under the Rev. Dirick Romeyn and while there wrote prose and verse for Schenectady newspapers. He received a license to preach from the classis of Albany in 1798, and soon afterwards accepted a call from the First Presbyterian Church of Philadelphia. In 1799 he married Hester Bailey, daughter of Col. John Bailey, of Poughkeepsie, N. Y. Of the three sons that were born to them the two youngest survived their father. In Philadelphia, despite ill health and heavy parochial duties, he wrote much and planned much that he was unable to write. His first volume after he entered the ministry was *The Death of George Washington: a Poem in Imitation of the Manner of Ossian* (1800). Next appeared *The Powers of Genius* (1801, 1802; London, 1804), a long poem reminiscent of Shenstone and Akenside. In 1802 came *A Discourse Occasioned by the Death of the Reverend Jong Ewing.* In the summer of 1802 Linn was overcome by the heat, and during the two remaining years of his life he never recovered his health. In 1803, however, he published in Philadelphia two letters written in reply to Unitarian tracts by Dr. Joseph Priestley. At the time of his death he was writing a narrative poem which was published in imperfect form in 1805 under the title *Valerian, a Narrative Poem, Intended, in Part, to Describe the Early Persecutions of Christians, and Rapidly to Illustrate the Influence of Christianity on the Manners of Nations.*

Charles Brockden Brown, who in 1804 married Linn's sister, Elizabeth, and who wrote for *Valerian* a biographical sketch of the author, praised his ability as a preacher: "It is well known, that few persons in America, though assisted by age and experience, have ever attained so great a popularity as he acquired before his twenty-third year." Brown's less laudatory judgment of his poetry is indubitably correct: "All his performances . . . candour compels us to consider as preludes to future exertions, and indications of future exccllence" (*Valerian*, p. xxi).

[William Dunlap, *A Hist. of the Am. Theatre* (1832); B. F. French, *Biographia Americana* (1825); W. B. Sprague, *Annals Am. Pulpit*, vol. IV (1858); Henry Simpson, *The Lives of Eminent Philadelphians Now Deceased* (1859); Linn's manuscript letters in the collection of the Hist. Soc. of Pa.; *Poulson's Am. Daily Advertiser*, Sept. 1, 1804.]   N. E. M.

LINN, LEWIS FIELDS (Nov. 5, 1795–Oct. 3, 1843), physician, senator, was born near Louisville, the grandson of Col. William Linn, a Kentucky pioneer and one of the favorite officers of George Rogers Clark; the son of Asahel Linn and Nancy Ann Hunter, who was the widow of Israel Dodge and the mother of Henry Dodge [*q.v.*]. Left an orphan at the age of twelve and equipped only with the meager educational advantages of the frontier, he decided to study medicine. Despite interruptions caused by ill health and by participation in the War of 1812 as the "surgeon" attached to Dodge's troops, Linn completed his professional training at Philadelphia in 1816. Removing to Sainte Genevieve, Mo., he commenced immediately the arduous life of a frontier physician; he loved his profession and soon had an extensive practice in southeastern Missouri. He was an authority on Asiatic cholera and rendered inestimable professional services in combating that desolating scourge through two epidemics. A man of fine presence and bearing, with a personal charm and professional skill that won for him many devoted friends, Linn was urged frequently to run for Congress. Although interested in public affairs and in the Democratic party, he refused to abandon his professional obligations except for one term during the late twenties in the state Senate. In 1833 he became a commissioner to settle French land claims, and, upon the death of Alexander Buckner, Governor Dunklin appointed him to the United States Senate, many Whigs urging his selection as the most preferable Democrat. He entered the Senate as an ardent admirer of Jackson, "the hero of his heart's warmest admiration."

Linn's ten years of service, 1833–43, fall naturally into two divisions. During the first few sessions he was primarily a representative of his section, pressing with marked success numerous private claims of his constituents, keeping in active touch with an incredible number of them, instituting public surveys of the iron and lead resources, and assisting the infant glass industry of Missouri. He rarely addressed the Senate, but his invariable friendliness toward his colleagues and his moderation of speech and action, in a day of intense partisanship, brought him the almost universal esteem of his associates. "He had political opponents in the Senate, but not one enemy" (*Congressional Globe*, 28 Cong., 1 Sess., p. 29). He had none of the arrogance and pomposity of his colleague, Benton; they were a strangely mated but effective pair. Linn was a strong political and personal supporter of the measures of the second Jackson administration and an able exponent of the self-conscious Jacksonian Democracy (*Letter to Constituents*, 1840). He maintained his position in Missouri, being easily reëlected in 1837 and in 1843, with practically no opposition from the Whigs. During Van Buren's administration Linn became a leader in the revival at Washington of interest in Oregon. Benton long had been a vehement advocate of extension to the Pacific; Linn shared his views, indorsed by the economic interests of Missouri, that the Oregon territory must be "saved" from the English (Benton, *post*, II, pp. 468ff.).

Following the Slacum report of December 1837, Linn, chairman of the committee on territories, began persistently to press the issue. He introduced in 1838 a bill to "reoccupy" the territory and to establish a government with military protection. For five years he continued to urge upon an indifferent Senate the protection of American interests there, and in every session of several congresses he sponsored without success legislation providing for the occupation and settlement of Oregon, against the "daring designs of England." In the early forties, two powerful economic factors, free land and the lure of trade, forced new interest. Following a prolonged and spirited debate Linn's Oregon Bill, with its governmental, military defense, and liberal land-grant policies, passed the Senate on Feb. 28, 1843, by a vote of twenty-four to twenty-two (*Congressional Globe*, 27 Cong., 3 Sess., App., *passim*). His effort on this occasion was the final act of his public life as he died suddenly in Missouri in October 1843. His wife, Elizabeth A. Relfe, whom he married in 1818, survived him. He was a representative product of the new West, a sincere exponent of Manifest Destiny, and a devoted friend of the adventurous and aggressive frontier.

[The *Cong. Globe*, 25 Cong., 2 and 3 Sess., 26 Cong., 1 Sess., 27 Cong., 3 Sess., and *Senate Executive Doc. 470*, 25 Cong., 2 Sess., are valuable. E. Linn and N. Sargent, *Life and Pub. Services of Dr. Lewis F. Linn*

(1857) is useful, but laudatory and uncritical. J. M. Greenwood, *Lewis Fields Linn* (1900), and W. F. Switzler, *The Father of Ore.* (1899), contain much information. The Oregon issue is treated in T. H. Benton, *Thirty Years' View* (2 vols., 1854–56), in W. I. Marshall, *Acquisition of Ore.* (2 vols., 1911), and in Cardinal Goodwin, *The Trans-Mississippi West* (1922). The *St. Louis New Era*, Oct. 11, 12, 1843, reflects significant contemporary opinion, and J. H. Linn, *A Funeral Discourse on the Life and Character of the Hon. Lewis Field* [sic] *Linn* (1844), gives a good account of Linn's charitable work in connection with his medical activities.]

T. S. B.

LINN, WILLIAM ALEXANDER (Sept. 4, 1846–Feb. 23, 1917), newspaper editor, author, son of Dr. Alexander and Julia (Vibbert) Linn, was born at Deckertown, now Sussex, N. J. After preparatory schooling at Deckertown and Andover, Mass., he entered Yale College, where he became an editor of the *Yale Literary Magazine* and graduated in 1868 as class poet. He next joined the staff of Horace Greeley as a reporter and served the *New York Tribune* for three years, then became city editor of the *Evening Post* of William Cullen Bryant in 1871. From July 1872 to May 1873 he edited the *Morning Whig,* Troy, N. Y., but it was not successful financially and he returned to the *Evening Post.* He was made news editor in 1883, after the accession to the editorship of Edwin Lawrence Godkin [*q.v.*], and managing editor in 1891. His worth as a first-rate news editor and as a journalist of the highest professional standards became speedily apparent. The *Evening Post* of this period never sought popular favor, but because of the brilliancy of the editorial page of Godkin and the complete reliability and trustworthiness of the news columns under Linn, was considered almost unique in the journalism of that time.

Eager as he was for news promptness, Linn never permitted his news sense to interfere with the kindliness and consideration which should be foremost in the calendar of a journalist who is also a gentleman. Nevertheless, he shared to the full Godkin's capacity for wrath at injustice. "Fiery in rebuke and cutting in contempt," as the *Evening Post* described him at the time of his death (Feb. 24, 1917, p. 7), he was also tender-hearted, thoroughly just, of an impeccable intellectual honesty, and possessed of unusual executive power. As a master of the details of his profession he was unexcelled. His highest journalistic achievement was his refusal after the election of 1884 to accept the returns from New York State disseminated by the Associated Press, with their insistence that Blaine was elected. The returns extended over several days because of the difficulty of getting news from remote counties. In the *Evening Post's* first issue

the day after the election, Linn insisted that Cleveland had "probably" won and set himself to the task of obtaining from every disputed county a separate, trustworthy report. The result was that the *Evening Post* announced on the second day: "Cleveland President—New York Gives Him Her Vote," although the Associated Press (not to be confused with the existing organization of that name) still insisted on the third day that Blaine had carried New York by 1,000 votes.

After retiring from the *Evening Post* in 1900, because of ill-health, Linn gave considerable time to independent writing. His most ambitious literary work, *The Story of the Mormons* (1902), a volume of 637 pages, was the first to make use of the extensive Helen Gould collection of materials on the Mormon Church. It was admittedly the most authoritative treatment until recent years. A biography, *Horace Greeley* (1903), was less successful. *Rob and His Gun* (1902), four valuable historical monographs published in the *Papers and Proceedings of the Bergen County Historical Society* (1905, 1908, 1915, 1917), and numerous articles on the building-and-loan movement are among the products of his pen. For many years he was a resident of Hackensack, N. J., where he was a founder of the Johnson Public Library, the Historical Society, the Hackensack Mutual Building and Loan Association (a pioneer enterprise over which he presided thirty years with remarkable efficiency and success), and the Peoples National Bank, of which he was president for a dozen years. He was county collector (1915–17), and a member of the Palisades Park Commission, which created the New York and New Jersey Interstate Park. On Jan. 31, 1871, he married Margaret A. Martin, who died in 1897. They had no children.

[*The Evening Post Hundredth Anniversary, Nov. 16, 1801–1901* (1902); Allan Nevins, *The Evening Post: A Century of Journalism* (1922); *Papers and Proc. Bergen County Hist. Soc., 1916–17,* no. 12 (1917); *Who's Who in America,* 1916–17; H. P. Wright, *Hist. of the Class of 1868, Yale Coll.* (1914); *Obit. Record Grads. Yale Univ.,* 1917; *Evening Post* (N. Y.), Feb. 24, 1917.]

O. G. V.

LINTNER, JOSEPH ALBERT (Feb. 8, 1822–May 5, 1898), entomologist, was born in Schoharie, N. Y., the son of Rev. George Ames Lintner and his wife, Maria Wagner. He graduated from Schoharie Academy in 1837, then entered business in New York City, continuing his studies in the Mercantile Library and contributing occasional scientific articles to the *New York Tribune.* In 1848 he returned to Schoharie, where he remained in business until 1860, when he moved to Utica and was there for some years as a manufacturer of woolens. During this business career he continued his scientific studies. He began collecting insects in 1853, and published his first article in 1862. In 1856 he married Frances C. Hutchinson of Utica. In 1868 he abandoned his business to become assistant in zoölogy in the State Museum. He was placed in charge of the entomological department in 1874 and in 1880 was appointed state entomologist. For the last thirty-six years of his life he was occupied almost solely in work with insects. He published over nine hundred separate articles, and, in addition to these, thirteen annual reports and four numbers of a pamphlet entitled *Entomological Contributions* (1872–79). He wrote extensively for the agricultural press, especially for the *Country Gentleman,* and for twenty-five years was the entomological editor of this journal. His articles were always of a practical character. His annual reports were prepared with extreme care and were models of their kind. His style was simple, dignified and concise, and his treatment of his topics was extremely thorough. The regents of the University of the State of New York awarded him the degree of Ph.D. He was president of the Association of Economic Entomologists in 1892, and was a member of many American scientific societies. His chief claim to distinction rests in his thirteen annual reports, which are worthy successors to the reports of his predecessor, Asa Fitch [*q.v.*]. He died in Rome, Italy.

[*N. Y. State Museum Bulletin,* May 1899; *Entomological News,* June 1898, with portrait; *N. Y. Tribune,* May 7, 1898.]   L. O. H.

LINTON, WILLIAM JAMES (Dec. 7, 1812– Dec. 29, 1897), wood-engraver, political reformer, poet, and printer, was born in London, the grandson of an Aberdeen ship-carpenter who had settled in London as a builder. From him, says Linton, "I perhaps inherited some tendency to radicalism" (*Memories,* 1895, p. 16). He was educated under Dr. Burford at Stratford, was apprenticed in 1828 to George Wilmot Bonner, wood-engraver, and later worked for John Orrin Smith, whose partner he became in 1842. About this time he did much engraving for the *Illustrated London News.* Meanwhile he espoused the cause of personal liberty, going into the Chartist movement, and, says Richard Garnett, "beyond it in professing himself a republican" (*post*). In close contact with Henry Hetherington, he edited the *Odd Fellow* (April 1841–August 1842), opposed the "laws then gagging the press," became deeply interested in the plans of Mazzini, was the friend of Italian and Polish reformers, and was concerned in the publication

of the *National* (1839), the *Leader* (1850), the *English Republic* (1851–55) and the *Northern Tribune* (1854). He engaged also in purely literary activities, was intimate with the group of R. H. Horne, succeeded Douglas Jerrold as editor of the *Illuminated Magazine* (1845), and wrote a *Life of Paine* (1839), *To the Future* (1848), *The Plaint of Freedom* (1852), and *Claribel and Other Poems* (1865). In addition, he established his reputation as a wood-engraver, doing notable work for the Moxon Tennyson (1857) and Milton's *L'Allegro* (1859). He married, about 1836, a sister of Thomas Wade, the poet; after her death, another sister (d. 1855); and in 1858, Eliza Lynn, the novelist. The last marriage was ended by amicable separation. "In 1866," he wrote, "I had little occupation in England. . . . So in November of that year I crossed the ocean to New York" (*Memories,* pp. 204, 205).

Here he taught wood-engraving at the Cooper Union (1868–70) and worked for Frank Leslie's *Illustrated News.* Among American books illustrated with his engravings, many after his own designs, were Whittier's *Snow-Bound* (1868); J. G. Holland's *Kathrina* (1869); Longfellow's *Building of the Ship* (1870), and *Edwin Booth in Twelve Dramatic Characters* (1872), both from drawings by W. J. Hennessy; W. C. Bryant's *Thanatopsis* (1878) and *The Flood of Years* (1878). The last-named included his "most ambitious pieces of imaginative work" (Parkes, "Wood-Engravings," *post,* p. 178), and occasioned his own poetical *Interpretations* of the designs, printed by him in three copies. He also contributed to other books and to *Scribner's* and *The Century.* He became an academician of the National Academy of Design in 1882 and received an honorary A.M. degree from Yale in 1891. His engravings have distinction, and show that firmness and honesty which he himself called "the first qualification of an engraver." He was an adherent of the "white line," and believed that the engraver should draw with the graver and be an interpreting artist. About 1877 there arose the "new school" of American wood-engravers, finding first vigorous expression in the blocks by Frederick Juengling [*q.v.*] after James E. Kelly. The work of this school showed some vagaries, especially a sometimes slavish devotion to the rendering of details in texture. Linton's warning against a tendency to give substance rather than spirit was denounced. Thereupon he wrote *Some Practical Hints on Wood-Engraving for the Instruction of Reviewers and the Public* (1879) and *The History of Wood-Engraving in America* (1882). In the latter indispensable reference book, commenting critically on the "new school," he ends: "Notwithstanding all my censures, the revival of wood-engraving is in their hands. They will outgrow their mistakes." In 1884 he also published *Wood-Engraving: A Manual of Instruction.*

Linton removed, probably in the early seventies, to Hamden, near New Haven, Conn., established the Appledore Press, and from 1878 on issued books, pamphlets, and leaflets in limited editions. The two most noteworthy were *The Golden Apples of Hesperus: Poems not in the Collections* (1882)—"the whole of it, drawing, engraving, composition, and printing the work of my own hands"—and *Masters of Wood-Engraving.* The latter was printed, in three copies, to serve as a model for the London publication of 1889. Other products of this press were *Translations* (1881); *Rare Poems of the Sixteenth and Seventeenth Centuries* (5 copies, 1882), later issued in trade editions in Boston and London; *In Dispraise of a Woman—Catullus with Variations* (1886), and *Love Lore* (1887), a collection of his own poems. He also edited *The Poetry of America, 1776–1876* (London, 1878) and, with R. H. Stoddard, *English Verse* (1883, 5 vols.), and wrote *The Flower and the Star* (1868), with illustrations drawn and engraved by himself; *Poems and Translations* (London, 1889); *European Republicans* (1892); *The Life of John Greenleaf Whittier* (London, 1893); and *Memories* (1895), first issued as *Threescore and Ten Years* (1894). His last publication was *Darwin's Probabilities: A Review of his Descent of Man* (1896). He was aggressively vigorous in asserting his beliefs, "amiable and helpful, full of kind actions and generous enthusiasms" (Garnett, *post*); "obstinate and affectionate, and intolerant of interference" (Parkes, *op. cit.,* p. 176). He died in New Haven, at the house of Thomas W. Mather, who had married his daughter Margaret in February 1875.

[Examples of Linton's work are in the British Museum, the Victoria and Albert Museum, the New York Public Library, and Yale University; the large collection in the last-named institution includes books by Linton, letters, manuscripts, and drawings. An idea of his enormous production in wood-engraving is given in Kineton Parkes, "The Wood-Engravings of W. J. Linton," in *Bookman's Jour. and Print Collector,* July 8, 1921, and his work on wood, as well as his relations to the "new school" of American wood-engravers, is discussed by S. R. Koehler, in *Vervielfältigende Kunst der Gegenwart,* vol. I (Vienna, 1887) and in Frank Weitenkampf, *American Graphic Art* (1924); the Appledore publications are described by Howard Mansfield, from copies in his own possession, in the *Gazette of the Grolier Club,* no. 2, November 1921, by A. H. Bullen in *The Library,* February 1889, and by Kineton Parkes in *Bookman's Jour.,* Aug. 12, 1921; his place at Hamden is minutely described by Linton himself in "An Artist's Habitat," in *Lippincott's Monthly Mag.,* May

1895; see also his *Memories*; G. S. Layard, *Mrs. Lynn Linton, Her Life, Letters, and Opinions* (1901); sketch by Richard Garnett in Supplement (1901) to *Dict. Nat. Biog.*; *Report . . . of the Century Asso. for the Year 1897* (1898); *N. Y. Times, Evening Post* (N. Y.), Dec. 30, 1897.]

F. W.

LIPPARD, GEORGE (Apr. 10, 1822–Feb. 9, 1854), novelist, founder of the Brotherhood of the Union, the son of Daniel B. Lippard, once county treasurer of Philadelphia, and of Jemima Ford, was born on his father's farm in West Nantmeal township, Chester County, Pa. When he was two years old his parents removed to Philadelphia, where his father opened a grocery and later became a constable. George was sent to a public school, where he developed so rapidly that at fourteen he attracted the attention of members of his church and was sent to the Classical Academy, Rhinebeck, N. Y., to prepare for college, and eventually for the ministry of the Methodist Church. It is said (Elliott, *post,* p. 14) that "in disgust at the contradiction between theory and practice" of Christianity which he observed, he left his studies, determined to renounce the sacred calling. He then spent four years reading law, but abandoned that profession also, as not according with his ideas of human justice. Toward the close of the year 1841 he was given a place on the staff of the *Spirit of the Times,* an energetic, even sensational, Democratic daily then published in Philadelphia. He began his journalistic career by reporting police-court hearings in an original, sympathetic, and humorous way which attracted readers and resulted in an increase in the circulation of the paper. He then wrote for its columns a series of sketches under the general title, "Our Talisman," which in character were not unlike some of the "Sketches by Boz." When Dickens visited Philadelphia in 1842, Lippard wrote an impression of the historic "levee" held in the novelist's honor. Soon afterward, he produced a series called "Bread Crust Papers," in which Henry B. Hirst [*q.v.*] was satirized as "Henry Bread Crust" and Thomas Dunn English [*q.v.*], as "Thomas Done Brown," a title Poe later saw fit to revive.

Lippard worked so industriously that his health began to fail, and he retired from journalism determined to become an author. For his first story, "Philippe de Agramont," which appeared in the *Saturday Evening Post,* July 9, 1842, the young author received fifteen dollars. A more lengthy romance, "Herbert Tracy; or, the Legend of the Black Rangers," was begun in the same weekly, Oct. 22, 1842. At the beginning of 1843, Lippard became connected with *The Citizen Soldier,* a new weekly, to which he contributed "The

Lippard

Battle Day of Germantown," "The Ladye Annabel," and "Adrian, the Neophyte," all immediately republished in pamphlet form. Early in 1844 he began *The Monks of Monk Hall,* published in ten semi-monthly parts. This story, subsequently called *The Quaker City,* was an exposé of vice in Philadelphia, and upon being reprinted with additions (1845) had an enormous sale throughout the United States, was reprinted in England, and translated into German. Lippard dramatized it, and in December 1844 it was announced for representation in the Chestnut Street Theatre, Philadelphia, but was withdrawn by order of the mayor, who feared a mob would destroy the playhouse. The play, much altered for the worse, was performed at the Chatham Theatre, New York, in January 1845. Lippard wrote another play, *Coro, the Priest Robber,* which was not printed; but the story appears in the posthumous volume, *Legends of Florence* (1864).

In 1844 he began his career as a lecturer, his subjects being what he termed "legends" of the Revolution. During one of these lectures he defended *The Quaker City* against the charge of immorality. By this time it had reached a sale of 4,000 copies, and the author's popularity was very great. He was engaged by the *Saturday Courier* of Philadelphia to contribute to its pages a series of "Legends of the Revolution," and before the series was completed that weekly's circulation had increased from 30,000 to 70,000 copies. The "Legends" were copied by newspapers all over the United States. His lectures, usually upon Revolutionary characters and incidents, became so popular that he was invited to speak in many parts of the country, and became as widely known for his platform appearances as for his romances.

Meantime, books were coming from his pen in rapid succession: in 1846 he published *The Nazarene* and *Blanche of Brandywine*; in 1847, *Legends of Mexico* and *Washington and His Generals: or, Legends of the Revolution*; in 1848, *Paul Ardenheim* and *Bel of Prairie Eden*. During this year he contributed articles to *The Nineteenth Century,* a quarterly. In 1849 he published a weekly, *The Quaker City,* which contained few contributions that he did not write. In 1850 appeared *Washington and His Men—Second Series of Legends of the Revolution*; and in 1851, *Adonai, the Pilgrim of Eternity* and one number only of *The White Banner,* launched as a quarterly, which he wrote entirely himself. These were followed by *Mysteries of the Pulpit* (1852), *The Man with the Mask* (1852), *The Empire City* (1853); *New York: Its Upper-Ten and Lower Million* (1854); and *Eleanor; or,*

Slave Catching in Philadelphia (1854). For several years before his death he was a regular contributor to the *Sunday Mercury* and *Scott's Weekly* of Philadelphia, in which some of his later romances and essays originally appeared.

Disgusted with all conventions of his time, Lippard originated a philosophy and a religion of his own. On May 14, 1847, he married Rose Newman by the simple ceremony of taking her hand, the event occurring upon a high rock (Mom Rinker's Rock) of the romantic Wissahickon. In 1850 he organized the Brotherhood of the Union, of which he constituted himself the "Supreme Washington," or head. This organization was an effort to carry into effect his idea of a brotherhood of man, and at the time of his death there were circles, or lodges, of the order in twenty-three states. He was an enemy of capital and, in his own undisciplined manner, had developed a Marxian theory while Karl Marx was still an unknown schoolboy. As a novelist he was ignored by the recognized American critics. He wrote hurriedly and almost constantly, and declared he appealed to the worker and not to the literary man. There are many poetical passages in his novels, however, and he really became the poet of the proletariat. After the death of his wife in 1851 he traveled a great deal in the interest of the Brotherhood of the Union, and lived for a while in Cleveland. In 1853 he returned to Philadelphia, where he died of consumption the following year. His grave in Odd Fellows Cemetery there is marked by a symbolic monument of granite, erected in 1886 by the Brotherhood he founded, now known as the Brotherhood of America.

[Lippard's autobiography appeared in the *Saturday Courier,* Jan. 15, 1848; a sketch and critique by C. C. Burr is prefixed to *Washington and His Generals* (1847), and a sketch by J. B. Elliott to the reprint (1894) of Lippard's lecture, *Thomas Paine: Author-Soldier of the Revolution.* See also E. W. C. Greene, in *Sunday Mercury* (Phila.), Feb. 12, 1854; *The Life and Choice Writings of George Lippard* (1855); E. P. Oberholtzer, *The Lit. Hist. of Phila.* (1906); *Daily News* (Phila.), Feb. 10, 1854; *Official Souvenir Fiftieth Annual Session Supreme Council, Brotherhood of the Union* (Phila., 1900); *The Brotherhood,* Dec. 1900. Further material for a biography and bibliography of Lippard has been gathered by the author of this sketch, who contributed "A Bibliography of the Works of George Lippard" to the *Pa. Mag. of Hist. and Biog.,* Apr.–Oct. 1930.]
J. J.

Lippincott

LIPPINCOTT, JAMES STARR (Apr. 12, 1819–Mar. 17, 1885), horticulturist and meteorologist, was born in Philadelphia, Pa. He was the son of John and Sarah West (Starr) Lippincott, and a lineal descendant of Richard Lippincott, who had emigrated from Devonshire, England, and about 1665 moved from New England to Shrewsbury, N. J. James attended Haverford

College, Haverford, Pa., in 1834–35. He began his career as a teacher, but later changed to farming, first establishing himself at Cole's Landing near Haddonfield, N. J. Soon, however, he became interested in the science rather than the practice of farming and in 1868 removed to Haddonfield where he continued to study and write on agricultural subjects. While living on the farm, he invented a "vapor index" for measuring the humidity of the air. He kept meteorological instruments outside of his Haddonfield house, and took accurate records of the weather and climate. He tabulated and reduced observations made by Benjamin Sheppard near Greenwich, Cumberland County, N. J., from March 1856 to June 1861, for the Smithsonian Institution, and was its observer at Cole's Landing from 1864 to 1866, and from 1869 to 1870 at Haddonfield. He visited Europe twice, once, in 1850, as a delegate to the World's Peace Congress in Frankfort, Germany. On these trips he made extensive observations which he recorded in letters to his friends and to the press.

His literary activities were directed to the collection of a large and select library, containing rare books on a wide variety of subjects, and to writing on genealogical, biographical, and agricultural matters. He did much work on Lippincott's *Universal Pronouncing Dictionary of Biography and Mythology* (1870) and wrote a series of papers which were published in the *Reports of the Commissioners of Agriculture*: "Climatology of American Grape Vines," 1862; "Geography of Plants," 1863; "Market Products of West New Jersey," 1865; "Observations on Atmospheric Humidity," 1865; "The Fruit Regions of the Northern United States and Their Local Climates," 1866. He contributed various shorter articles to *The Gardener's Monthly and Historical Advertiser,* later, *the Gardener's Monthly and Horticulturist,* and other agricultural periodicals. He was much interested in the Society of Friends, of which he was a member, and he prepared an index to forty volumes of their journal, *The Friend.* He compiled also a catalogue of the books belonging to the library of the four Monthly Meetings of Friends of Philadelphia (1853). At the time of his death he had collected a great deal of genealogical data relating to both the Lippincott and Starr families, a considerable portion of which was published later. He was a man of wide learning and a kindly critic, able to give constructive assistance on nearly all subjects. He was married twice: first, in 1857, to Susan Haworth Ecroyd, of Muncy, Pa.; and, in 1861, to Anne E. Sheppard. He had no children by either marriage. His death occurred at Greenwich, Cumberland County, N. J.

[*The Lippincotts in England and America* (1909), ed. from his genealogical papers; Chas. Lippincott, *A Geneal. Tree of the Lippincott Family* (1880); *Biog. Cat. of the Matriculates of Haverford Coll. . . . 1833–1922* (1922); *Ann. Reports of the Board of Regents of the Smithsonian Institution,* 1863, 1868–72; G. R. Prowell, *The Hist. of Camden County, N. J.* (1886); *The Friend,* Apr. 4, 1885; information from George P. Lippincott, Jr., Marlton, N. J.]   W. B. M—k.

LIPPINCOTT, JOSHUA BALLINGER (Mar. 18, 1813–Jan. 5, 1886), publisher, the only child of Jacob and Sarah (Ballinger) Lippincott, was born in Juliustown, Burlington County, N. J. He was descended from Richard Lippincott who moved from New England to Shrewsbury, N. J., about 1665. After receiving a common-school education he went to Philadelphia between 1827 and 1830 and entered the employ of Clarke, the bookseller. He applied himself to this business and mastered its details sufficiently so that when his employer became financially embarrassed and the stock was purchased by creditors, he was continued in sole charge of the business although he was but eighteen years of age. He remained in this position until 1836 when he began business on his own account at Clarke's old location under the name of J. B. Lippincott & Company. At first he published principally Bibles and prayer books, then religious works. He was ambitious to place himself at the head of the Philadelphia book trade, and with this end in view, in 1849 he bought the firm of Grigg, Elliot, & Company, which was then the largest and most prosperous publishing house in the city. His firm was reorganized, Jan. 1, 1850, and became Lippincott, Grambo & Company. In 1851, while on a trip to Europe, he laid the foundations for the extensive book-importing business in which his firm later engaged. On June 30, 1855, with the retirement of Grambo, the firm resumed the name J. B. Lippincott & Company and Lippincott became the acknowledged head of the publishing business in Philadelphia. In 1865 he again visited Europe and entered into business relations with nearly all the leading publishing houses in London. His foreign business increased and in 1876 he established a London agency.

In 1855 Lippincott published the first edition of *Lippincott's Pronouncing Gazetteer,* under the editorship of Joseph Thomas and Thomas Baldwin, which was accepted as a standard reference and went through several editions. In the sixties he took over the publication of Prescott's histories. In 1870, having delegated Thomas to head a companion work to the *Gazetteer,* he published in two volumes the *Universal Pronouncing Dictionary of Biography and Mythol-*

ogy. In 1870 and 1871 he published the second and third volumes of Samuel Austin Allibone's _Critical Dictionary of English Literature and British and American Authors._ He also published successive editions of the _Dispensatory of the United States,_ some of Bulwer's novels, Worcester's dictionaries, and numerous other works of reference. Not confining himself to the printing of books, he put out the _North American Medico-Chirurgical Review,_ edited by Samuel D. Gross, which was suspended after the outbreak of the Civil War, established _Lippincott's Magazine_ in 1868, and in 1870 began the publication of the _Medical Times._

Lippincott's eminence as a business man led him into many connections. In 1854 he was elected a director of the Farmers' & Mechanics' Bank of Philadelphia, in 1861 a member of the board of managers of the Philadelphia Savings Fund Society, and in 1862 a director of the Pennsylvania Company for Insurance on Lives and Granting Annuities. In 1874 he was chosen a member of the board of trustees of Jefferson Medical College, and in 1876 he was elected to the board of trustees of the University of Pennsylvania. Besides these positions, most of which he held until his death, he was for many years a member of the board of directors of the Philadelphia & Reading Railroad Company. He was a lover of animals and for some time was president of the Society for the Prevention of Cruelty to Animals. He was also a generous donor to the department of veterinary medicine of the University of Pennsylvania, of which he was regarded as one of the founders. In February 1885 he incorporated his firm as the J. B. Lippincott Publishing Company and retired from business because of ill health. He had married Josephine Craige on Oct. 16, 1845, and they had four children. He died in Philadelphia, leaving an estate valued at several million dollars.

[_Joshua B. Lippincott: A Memorial Sketch_ (1888); J. T. Scharf and Thompson Westcott, _Hist. of Phila., 1609–1884_ (1884), vol. III; Geo. Morgan, _The City of Firsts_ (1926); Henry Hall, _America's Successful Men of Affairs,_ vol. II (1896); J. L. Chamberlain, ed., _Universities and Their Sons: Univ. of Pa.,_ vol. I (1901); Chas. Lippincott, _A Geneal. Tree of the Lippincott Family_ (1880); the _Pennsylvanian_ (Phila.), Oct. 20, 1845; _Publishers' Weekly,_ Jan. 9, 1886.]   J. H. F.

LIPPINCOTT, SARA JANE CLARKE (Sept. 23, 1823–Apr. 20, 1904), author, better known as "Grace Greenwood," was the youngest daughter and one of eleven children of Dr. Thaddeus and Deborah Clarke and was born in Pompey, Onondaga County, N. Y. Dr. Clarke, a physician of some prominence, was born in Lebanon, Conn., of Puritan ancestry. His wife, of Huguenot descent, came from Brooklyn, Conn. Sara Jane's childhood was passed in Pompey, in the neighboring town of Fabius, and chiefly in Rochester, N. Y., where she was educated in public and private schools. In 1842 the family removed to New Brighton, Pa., near Pittsburgh. Here, in 1844, she began her prose writing under the pseudonym "Grace Greenwood" in some articles contributed to the _New Mirror._ She had in her girlhood published some verse under her own name. Several volumes of prose and verse appeared during her years at New Brighton: _Greenwood Leaves; a Collection of Sketches and Letters_ (1850); _History of My Pets_ (1850); _Poems_ (1851); _Greenwood Leaves: Second Series_ (1852); and _Recollections of My Childhood, and Other Stories_ (1852). After spending fifteen months in Europe, 1852–53, she published _Haps and Mishaps of a Tour in Europe_ (1854), which was unfavorably reviewed in the London _Athenæum,_ Nov. 18, 1854.

In October 1853 Sara Jane Clarke was married to Leander K. Lippincott of Philadelphia and with him undertook the editorship of the _Little Pilgrim,_ a juvenile monthly. From this time her writing was continuous and included contributions to _Hearth and Home,_ the _Atlantic Monthly, Harper's New Monthly Magazine,_ the _New York Independent,_ the _New York Times,_ the _New York Tribune,_ and the English magazines _Household Words_ and _All the Year Round._ She was one of the earliest women in the United States to become a regular newspaper correspondent and her letters from Washington and Europe, which she often visited, to leading New York, Chicago, and California papers were very popular. Her place of residence was sometimes Philadelphia, sometimes Washington, sometimes New York City. During this period her writings included _Merrie England: Travels, Descriptions, Tales, and Historical Sketches_ (1855); _A Forest Tragedy and Other Tales_ (1856); _Bonnie Scotland: Tales of Her History, Heroes, and Poets_ (1861); _Stories and Sights of France and Italy_ (1867); _New Life in New Lands: Notes of Travel_ (1873); _Heads and Tails: Studies and Stories of Pets_ (1875); and _Queen Victoria: Her Girlhood and Womanhood_ (1883), published also in London.

During the Civil War Mrs. Lippincott visited many camps and hospitals, talking and reading to the soldiers. President Lincoln spoke of her as "Grace Greenwood the patriot." She was actively interested, though not a vigorous propagandist, in all movements for the advancement of women. A contemporary critic, John S. Hart, said of Mrs. Lippincott that her life was so full of pleasant social relations, variety, and excitement that she was never able to concentrate on any important work but contented herself with "light critiques, and lighter letters." It is probable, however, that her popularity was greater because of the lightness of her work, and her style does not indicate capacity for more serious productions. Her most representative and best-liked volumes are *Greenwood Leaves* and *Haps and Mishaps of a Tour in Europe.* Her best poems are probably "Ariadne," a stiff classical imitation, and "Darkened Hours," a conventional lament over unattained ambition. Neither her prose nor her poetry is much read today. Mrs. Lippincott was the mother of one daughter in whose home in New Rochelle, N. Y., she spent the last four years of her life.

[*Who's Who in America,* 1903–05; Frances E. Willard and Mary A. Livermore, *A Woman of the Century* (1893); E. P. Oberholtzer, *The Lit. Hist. of Phila.* (1906); J. S. Hart, *The Female Prose Writers of America* (ed. 1855); Stanley Waterloo and J. W. Hanson, Jr., *Famous Am. Men and Women* (1895); R. W. Griswold, *The Female Poets of America* (1849); Chas. Lippincott, *A Geneal. Tree of the Lippincott Family* (1880); obituaries in the *N. Y. Times,* and the *N. Y. Daily Tribune,* Apr. 21, 1904.]   S. G. B.

LIPPITT, HENRY (Oct. 9, 1818–June 5, 1891), manufacturer, governor of Rhode Island, was a member of a family long associated with industrial interests. His first American ancestor was John Lippitt who settled in Rhode Island in 1638. John's great-grandsons, Charles and Christopher, organized in 1809 one of the pioneer cotton-mills of the state. Warren, son of Charles, followed the sea for a time and rose to the rank of captain, but later in life he became a cotton merchant in Providence and Savannah. He married Eliza Seamans and their son Henry was born in Providence. The boy was educated at the academy at Kingston, R. I., and shortly after his graduation began his business career. He first worked as a clerk, and then as a bookkeeper, for merchants in Warren and Providence, entering into a partnership in a commission business in 1838. In 1848 with his father and brother he became part owner of a cotton mill, the first of those with which he was later to be connected. The Tiffany Mill at Danielson, Conn., and in Rhode Island the Coddington Mill at Newport, the Social and Harrison Mills and the Globe Mill at Woonsocket, and the Manville Mills at Lincoln, came successively under Lippitt's control between 1848 and 1862. His position as a leader in the manufacturing world naturally drew him into other important connections also. He was president of two of its banks, and of corporations controlling its leading hotel and its opera house. With others he organized the

Providence Board of Trade, acting as its presiding officer for three years.

As a young man, Lippitt was one of those who organized the Providence Marine Corps of Artillery in 1840. He eventually became lieutenant-colonel of this company and in the Dorr War of 1842 took an active part against Dorr and his party. During the Civil War he served on a commission for enrolling and drafting men under the call for soldiers in 1862. In 1875 he ran for the governorship of the state. Upon the failure of any of the candidates to obtain a majority of the votes the election was carried to the General Assembly, where Lippitt was elected. He retained the office for a second year, having been chosen in the same manner. He proved a competent executive. Lippitt had married, in 1845, Mary Ann Balch of Providence. They had eleven children, one of whom, Charles Warren, later became governor.

[*Biog. Cyc. of Representative Men of R. I.* (1881); T. W. Bicknell, *The Hist. of the State of R. I. and Providence Plantations* (1920), vol. III; *Proc. of the R. I. Hist. Soc., 1891–92* (1892); *Providence Daily Jour.,* June 5, 1891.]   E. R. B.

LIPSCOMB, ABNER SMITH (Feb. 10, 1789–Dec. 8, 1856), lawyer, jurist, was born in Abbeville District, S. C. His parents, Elizabeth Chiles and Joel Lipscomb, were both natives of Virginia. His father early removed to South Carolina and there bore a part in the American Revolution. During his boyhood young Lipscomb attended the rural schools of Abbeville District, which were then extremely poor. Later he studied law in the office of John C. Calhoun and was admitted to the bar in 1811. He moved west and settled at St. Stephens on the Tombigbee River, in what was then the Mississippi Territory, afterward a part of Alabama. Here he rose rapidly in his profession and in 1819, at the age of thirty, was appointed one of the circuit judges, who, sitting *in banc,* constituted the supreme court. Four years later he became chief justice of the supreme court, a position he held for twelve years. His opinions are to be found in the first ten volumes of the *Alabama Reports.*

In 1835 he resigned from the supreme court and opened a law office in Mobile. Three years later, upon the unsolicited nomination of his party, he became a candidate and was elected to the legislature as a Democrat in a district overwhelmingly Whig in sentiment. As a member of the legislature and chairman of the judiciary committee he did much to simplify the system of pleading and practice in use in the state. The next year, resigning his seat in the legislature, he once more heeded the call of the frontier and removed to Texas where he speedily acquired a large law practice. He had resolved to stay out of public life, for which he had undoubted talent but little taste, but within a year after his arrival he had allowed President Mirabeau B. Lamar to persuade him to accept the office of secretary of state of the young Republic of Texas. In this capacity he became a warm advocate of annexation and as a member of the Convention of 1845 introduced the resolutions accepting the terms of annexation proposed by the United States. He also had a conspicuous part in framing the constitution for the new state, and to him have been attributed the provisions for homestead exemption and marital rights which have won admiration from statesmen in other lands. After annexation, the new governor, J. Pinckney Henderson, appointed him a justice of the supreme court. This position he filled most acceptably until his death in 1856, having twice been elected to the office by popular vote. His opinions, which are to be found in the first seventeen volumes of the *Texas Reports,* were usually short and to the point, and were generally couched in the forceful language of the frontier. Law books were almost non-existent, both in Alabama and in Texas, and the opinions of the courts were largely the product of the logic and sense of justice of the judges who composed them. Nearly half of the opinions handed down by the supreme court of Texas from 1845 to 1856, including most of those dealing with questions of procedure, were written by Lipscomb. Thus it was that he had a conspicuous part in laying the foundations of the jurisprudence of two important Southern states. He was twice married: on Apr. 13, 1813, to Elizabeth Gaines, the daughter of a planter of St. Stephens, Ala., who died in 1841; and on May 10, 1843, to Mary P. Bullock, daughter of Dr. Thomas Hunt, of Austin, Tex., who survived him.

[J. D. Lynch, *The Bench and Bar of Tex.* (1885); 17 *Tex. Reports,* iii–vi; 19 *Tex. Reports,* iii–ix; H. S. Thrall, *A Pictorial Hist. of Tex.* (1879); W. A. Garrett, *Reminiscences of Pub. Men in Ala.* (1872); *State Gazette* (Austin), Dec. 13, 1856; *Dallas Morning News,* Sept. 1, 1929, Feature Section, p. 3.] C. S. P.

LIPSCOMB, ANDREW ADGATE (Sept. 16, 1816–Nov. 23, 1890), minister, college president, son of William Corrie and Phoebe (Adgate) Lipscomb, was born in Georgetown, D. C., and died in Athens, Ga. His father, who had withdrawn from the Methodist Episcopal Church because it seemed to him autocratic, was a minister in the Methodist Protestant Church. At eighteen, the son followed the father into that ministry and preached subsequently in several places—in Baltimore and Washington, and in

Alexandria, the girlhood home of his mother. In 1839 he published a small *Life of Rev. Charles W. Jacobs,* a fellow denominationalist. At about that time also he married Henrietta Blanche Richardson of Baltimore, and in 1840, or soon afterward, he went to preach in Montgomery, Ala. There he was ordained a Methodist Episcopal minister. He soon resigned his pastorate to found a school called the Metropolitan Institute for Young Ladies. In 1844 he won second prize in a contest promulgated by the American Protestant Society in New York in an attempt to show the menace of Romanism to America. This thesis, published as *Our Country, its Danger and its Duty* (1844), was republished ten years later. In 1845 his interest in psychology, which later caused him to write at length on Hamlet, led him to deliver before the University of Alabama an address on the "Morbid Exhibitions of the Human Mind." The next year in his *Social Spirit of Christianity,* he noted and approved the rising disposition to consider religion as more social than individual. In 1853, probably as the result of a recent trip, he published in Mobile a pamphlet called *Impressions of Northern Society upon a Southerner.* The following year he published *Studies in the Forty Days Between Christ's Resurrection and Ascension,* and later he wrote *Studies Supplementary to the Studies in the Forty Days.* About 1855 he left Montgomery to become president of the Female College at Tuskegee. His wife died soon afterward, and he subsequently married a former Alabama student of his, Susan Dowdell.

In 1860 the chancellorship of the University of Georgia, at Athens, became vacant, and Lipscomb was advanced as a candidate. Elected, he assumed the office and retained it till the death of his son in 1874, when he resigned. He was considered an innovator in his day because of his substitution of moral suasion for force as a means of discipline, and the affectionate veneration in which he was held contributed to the success of his administration. After a brief interval he went to Vanderbilt University to teach esthetics, but after a few years he resigned on account of his health and went back to Athens to live in retirement. There he continued to contribute to religious periodicals; published a booklet, *Lessons from the Life of St. Peter* (1882); and wrote sermons and hymns and many lectures on Shakespeare. But the main interest of his life was always teaching.

[M. L. Rutherford, *The South in Hist. and Lit.* (1907); A. L. Hull, *A Hist. Sketch of the Univ. of Ga.* (1894); E. M. Coulter, *College Life in the Old South* (1928); *Atlanta Constitution,* Nov. 24, 25, 1890.]

J. D. W.

LISA, MANUEL (Sept. 8, 1772–Aug. 12, 1820), fur trader, was born at New Orleans, the son of Christopher de Lisa, a native of Murcia in Spain, who came to America about the time the Spanish took possession of Louisiana, and of María Ignacia Rodríguez, a native of St. Augustine, Florida. Probably not later than 1790, Manuel Lisa went to St. Louis, where during the next ten years he became well established in the fur trade. The Spanish government awarded him a patent entitling him to a monopoly of trade with the Osage Indians. About 1806 he formed relations with a group of St. Louis traders, and on Apr. 19, 1807, headed an expedition of forty-two men up the Missouri River with the purpose of erecting trading posts and forts where furs might be stored and exchanged and from which watch might be kept upon the Indians. On Nov. 21 he placed a trading house at the mouth of the Big Horn River and during the following spring built near it a fort which he called Fort Raymond in honor of his son. This post, later known as Fort Manuel, was the first structure of its kind on the upper Missouri. Upon his return in the summer of 1808 he joined with Andrew Henry, Pierre Chouteau [*qq.v.*], and others in forming the Missouri Fur Company, of which William Clark [*q.v.*], who with Meriwether Lewis had ascended the Missouri in 1804, was to be resident agent at St. Louis. In June 1809, the company sent forth from St. Louis its first expedition, 350 men, half of them Americans and half French Canadians and Creoles, with Lisa as one of the leaders. About twelve miles above the mouth of the Big Knife River, in what is now North Dakota, they erected Fort Lisa. It had been Lisa's intention to proceed to the Three Forks of the Missouri, but he sent Pierre Ménard [*q.v.*] and Andrew Henry instead, and in October 1809 himself returned to St. Louis. In the spring of 1811 he led a search party of twenty-five men, sent out from St. Louis to look for Henry and his command. The trip of 1811 is famous in Missouri River annals for a race between the barge of the Lisa party and a flotilla belonging to the John Jacob Astor interests which was on its way to the Columbia River under the command of Wilson Price Hunt [*q.v.*]. Hunt had about three weeks' start of Lisa, but, on the second of June, was overtaken by the latter, just beyond the mouth of the Niobrara River. Here the two expeditions fraternized, and, when the Astorians, through Lisa's help, had secured horses from the Arikara and Mandan Indians, took their departure overland. Lisa, together with Andrew Henry, who had arrived at the Niobrara, returned to St. Louis in October. In the summer of 1814 he was appointed by William Clark, now governor of Missouri Territory, to the post of sub-agent for the Indian tribes on the Missouri above the mouth of the Kansas River.

Lisa's travels on the Missouri took him vast distances. Between 1807 and his death he made twelve or thirteen trips, performing some 26,000 miles of river travel. His trade was profitable, amounting sometimes to as much as $35,000 in one season. He was three times married. His first wife was Mary (or Polly) Charles, by whom he had three children, all of whom died when young. While his first wife was still living he married, in 1814, Mitain, an Omaha woman, daughter of one of the leading families of the Omaha tribe. By Mitain he had two children, who survived him. In 1819, on his last trip up the Missouri, he took with him his third bride, who had been Mrs. Mary (Hempstead) Keeney; she was a daughter of Stephen Hempstead, a prominent figure in the early history of St. Louis. They spent the winter at Fort Lisa, a post erected in 1812 a few miles above the site of the present Omaha. At this post Lisa entertained members of the famous expedition led by Maj. Stephen H. Long [*q.v.*] into the region beyond the Missouri. He died at St. Louis in the following summer, and was buried in Bellefontaine Cemetery, where a shaft marks his grave.

[H. M. Chittenden, *The Am. Fur Trade of the Far West* (1902) vol. I; W. B. Douglas, "Manuel Lisa," in *Mo. Hist. Soc. Colls.,* vol. III, nos. 3, 4 (1911); Kathryn M. French, in *S. Dak. Hist. Colls.,* vol. IV (1908); G. F. Robeson, in *Palimpsest* (Iowa City), Jan. 1925; F. L. Billon, *Annals of St. Louis in Its Territorial Days* (1888); *Missouri Gazette & Public Advertiser* (St. Louis), Aug. 16, 1820.]   I. B. R.

LIST, GEORG FRIEDRICH (Aug. 6, 1789–Nov. 30, 1846), economist, journalist, was born in the free imperial city of Reutlingen in Württemberg, Germany, the youngest child of a prosperous tanner, Johannes List. His mother's family name was Schäfer. He attended the local Latin school and in 1806 entered the public service of Württemberg, rising to the rank of ministerial undersecretary. Having rounded out his education by extensive reading and study at the University of Tübingen, he was appointed professor of administration and politics there, during the ministry of his friend Von Wangenheim (1817). When the succeeding reactionary government took exception to his affiliation with the *Handelsverein,* an association of merchants seeking the abolition of internal duties, List resigned his professorship, became secretary of the association and editor of its journal, and as such took a leading part in the movement which culminated in the German Customs Union (*Zollverein*).

During his professorship he married Catherine Neidhard, a beautiful young widow, daughter of Professor Seybold.

In 1819 he was elected to the Diet of Württemberg from Reutlingen, but his liberal ideas and his advocacy of economic reforms (aid to industry, equitable taxes, and a budget system) incurred the enmity of the bureaucratic government. He was indicted for sedition and sentenced to ten months' imprisonment. Eluding arrest by flight, he spent the four years following in exile. In Paris he met Lafayette, who invited him to accompany him on his proposed visit to America. During a visit to England in 1823 he made his first acquaintance with railroads. On the advice of friends, he returned to Württemberg in May 1824, but was arrested and taken to the fortress Asperg. In the following January he was released on condition that he leave the country. Finding his further stay on the Continent impossible, he emigrated, with his wife and four children, to the United States, arriving in New York June 10, 1825.

Having accepted the invitation of Lafayette—with whom and his son, Georges, he kept up a life-long friendship—to accompany him on his tour of the Atlantic states, List met many of the leading men in American public life. After a temporary sojourn on a farm near Harrisburg, he moved to Reading, Pa., in 1826. There he became editor of the *Readinger Adler,* a German-American weekly founded in 1796. His versatility, his intimate knowledge of international affairs, and the patriotic spirit which animated his writings soon made the *Adler* one of the most influential papers in Pennsylvania. It was popularly styled "the Berks County Bible." During the presidential campaign of 1828 List's influence among Pennsylvania Germans had much to do with swinging Pennsylvania to Andrew Jackson.

His interest in economics, and especially in questions of commercial policy, brought him into close contact with Charles Jared Ingersoll, Pierre Du Ponceau, Mathew Carey [*qq.v.*], Redwood Fisher, and other leaders of the Pennsylvania Society for the Encouragement of Manufactures and the Mechanic Arts, which was then the center of the protectionist movement; and List soon became one of its foremost literary exponents. His *Outlines of American Political Economy* (1827), *Observations on the Report of the Committee of Ways and Means* (1828), address, *On the Boston Report, and Particularly on Its Principles Respecting the Landed Interest of Pennsylvania,* delivered in 1828 before the Pennsylvania legislature, and his controversy with Gov. W. B. Giles [*q.v.*] of Virginia made

him known throughout the country as one of the ablest advocates of the "American System." As a tribute to his effective work, the Pennsylvania Society gave a banquet in his honor at Philadelphia, Nov. 3, 1827, and requested him to write under its auspices a college textbook on political economy. The presidency of Lafayette College was offered to him about the same time. List, however, turned his attention to business projects. These included the development of rich anthracite deposits which he had discovered near Tamaqua, and the building of a railroad from that point to Port Clinton. In 1828 he organized the Little Schuylkill Navigation, Railroad & Coal Company, the progenitor of the modern Reading System, and successfully initiated the building of its line, which was opened to traffic in 1831.

In the same year, as an executive agent of the Department of State, he went to Europe, where he planned to introduce Pennsylvania anthracite. Having become naturalized, he was appointed United States consul at Hamburg by President Jackson in 1831, and, failing of confirmation by the Senate, was given the consulate at Baden. From 1834 to 1837 he was United States consul at Leipzig and from 1843 to 1845 at Stuttgart. After his return to Europe he divided his energies mainly between literary work and the promotion of a German railway system. In pursuance of a long-cherished plan he founded, jointly with Rotteck and Welcker, the *Staats-Lexikon* in 1835, to which he contributed several noteworthy articles on American institutions, including railway transportation. In furtherance of the latter he founded the *Eisenbahn-Journal* (1835), and with indomitable energy and in the face of obstacles of all kinds successfully championed the building of a railroad from Leipzig to Dresden. His epochal brochure, *Über ein sächsisches Eisenbahn-System,* appeared in 1833.

Continued persecutions by Metternich and his agents caused him to leave Germany once more, in 1837, and he spent the next three years in research and literary work in Paris. There he wrote a prize essay, *Système naturel d'économie politique* (1837), on the most feasible method of changing from protection to free trade, which was adjudged an *"ouvrage remarquable"* by the French Academy. Returning to Germany in 1840, he again took up his studies on commercial policy, and in 1841 published his *opus magnum,* under the title, *Das Nationale System der Politischen Ökonomie.* In the *Zollvereinsblatt* (1843-46) he founded an organ through which he created a popular interest in questions of political economy and helped to lay the economic foundation of modern Germany as brought about later by Bismarck. He was for many years a leading contributor to the *Augsburger Allgemeine Zeitung.*

On a visit to Austria and Hungary in 1844 as a missionary of protection to domestic industry, he met a cordial welcome; but a visit to England in 1846, where he hoped to prepare the way for a commercial alliance between Great Britain and Germany, proved a disappointment; and he returned to his home in Augsburg broken in health and spirits. He sought relief in a journey to the Tyrol, where, in a moment of despondency, he ended his life.

List was one of the leading economists of the nineteenth century. His theory of productive forces, of the economic importance of nations as against the individualism and cosmopolitanism of Adam Smith, and his application of the historical method fructified and advanced the study of economics. His *National System* (translated into French in 1851; into English, 1856), while in the main a defense of protectionism, upholds it not as an end unto itself but rather as a temporary means of nursing infant industries, his ultimate goal being universal free trade. In American tariff history he was, next to Alexander Hamilton, the most constructive among the early advocates of protection.

[The two best German biographies of List are Ludwig Häusser's *Friedrich List's gesammelte Schriften* (3 vols., 1850–51), and Karl Jentsch's *Friedrich List* (1901). Margaret E. Hirst, *Life of Friedrich List* (1909), contains selections from his writings, including his *Outlines of American Political Economy.* The most recent noteworthy biography is K. A. Meissinger, *Friedrich List der tragische Deutsche* (1930). Walter von Molo, *Ein Deutscher ohne Deutschland* (1931), is a historical novel based on List's career. His life in the United States is discussed by William Notz in *Weltwirtschaftliches Archiv,* Kiel, April and July 1925, and in the *Am. Econ. Rev.,* June 1926. The 8th German edition (Stuttgart, 1925) of his *Das Nationale System der politischen Okonomie* contains a historical and critical introduction by K. Th. Eheberg and an elaborate bibliography by Max Hoeltzel. A new English edition of the *National System,* with an introduction by J. S. Nicholson, appeared in 1904. The Friedrich List-Gesellschaft, E. V., Stuttgart, in cooperation with the German Academy, is publishing a complete critical edition of List's works: *Friedrich List, Schriften-Reden-Briefe* (9 vols., Berlin, 1927–33), of which vol. II, *Friedrich List: Grundlinien einer politischen Okonomie und andere Beiträge der amerikanischen Zeit, 1825–1832, herausgegeben von William Notz* (1931), contains his American writings.] W. N.

LISTEMANN, BERNHARD (Aug. 28, 1841– Feb. 11, 1917), violinist, conductor, educator, was born at Schlotheim, Thuringia, Germany, the son of Wilhelm and Henrietta Listemann. His father was a merchant. Bernhard, who early showed exceptional musical ability, had instruction at the Leipzig Conservatory from Ferdinand David and at Vienna from Joseph Joachim and Henry Vieuxtemps. With his brother Fritz, also a violinist, he went on one occasion to Weimar to give a recital when both were so poor as to seek out necessarily the cheapest lodging house. Bernhard was fortunate in attracting the attention of Franz Liszt who gave him a private hearing and aided him in obtaining engagements. From 1858 to 1867 Listemann was concert master at the residence of the Prince of Schwarzburg-Rudolstadt. In the latter year he came with his brother Fritz to the United States. He spent a year in New York and then joined the orchestra of the Harvard Musical Association in Boston. Finding that "the programs were very conservative in character and reflected . . . the conservatism of the patrons of the concerts," he presently secured employment as concert master of the Theodore Thomas Orchestra during the seasons from 1871 to 1874. Both he and Thomas were enthusiastic pioneers in introducing Wagner to American audiences. Listemann had previously, while briefly revisiting Germany, married, July 25, 1870, Sophie Sungershausen.

In 1875 Listemann founded the Boston Philharmonic Club which gave many concerts, local and national. From this nucleus grew the Boston Philharmonic Orchestra, which, without financial guaranty, engaged famous artists and presented notable programs. In 1880 Listemann produced for the first time in Boston both the "Faust" and the "Dante" of Abbe Liszt. When, a year later, the Boston Symphony Orchestra, founded by Maj. Henry L. Higginson [*q.v.*], gave its first concert with Georg Henschel as conductor, Listemann was concert master. His musicianship contributed toward the initial successes of the orchestra, but he remained with it only four seasons. He is described by the Symphony's historian, M. A. DeWolfe Howe, as "a very superior artist in his way," but "a man of too much impulsive initiative to follow any one's beat implicitly." He was one of several musicians who left the Symphony when Wilhelm Gericke began his first conductorship; "whether they were dismissed for musical or disciplinary reasons, the public knew only that they were gone" (Howe, *post,* p. 71).

Listemann remained for a time in Boston where he taught, served as conductor of the Boston Amateur Orchestral Club and directed a string quartet. He accepted in 1893 an offer to head the violin department of the Chicago Musical College, founded by Florenz Ziegfeld, Sr. The rest of his career was that of a successful instructor and performer at Chicago. He had hundreds of pupils; among the most distinguished were Francis Macmillan and Benjamin

Cutter. His quartet was active down to the period of the World War and he often appeared as a soloist. His death was caused by heart disease. Surviving him were his widow, four sons, and a daughter. Among his professional publications was his *Method of Modern Violin Playing*, brought out by Oliver Ditson & Company in 1869.

[For references to Listemann's achievements with the Boston Philharmonic see *Dwight's Jour. of Music*, Aug. 16, Oct. 11, Nov. 8, Dec. 6, Dec. 20, 1879. Brief but revealing characterizations appear in M. A. DeW. Howe, *The Boston Symphony Orchestra* (rev. ed., 1931). See also: the *Musician*, July 1908; *Musical America*, Feb. 17, 1917; the *Boston Transcript* and the *Chicago Tribune*, Feb. 12, 1917. A manuscript by Listemann's widow, prepared for the author of this sketch in 1929, is now in the library of the New England Conservatory of Music.]   F. W. C.

LITCHFIELD, ELECTUS BACKUS (Feb. 15, 1813–May 12, 1889), railroad builder, was born in Delphi Falls, N. Y., to which place his parents, Elisha and Percy (Tiffany) Litchfield had removed in 1812 from Connecticut. Both families were of early Massachusetts stock. The father served at Sacketts Harbor during the War of 1812 under Gen. Electus Backus, for whom the son was named. He afterward became prominent in local and state politics, serving five terms in the state Assembly and two in Congress. Electus began business as a merchant in Cazenovia but in 1844 moved to New York City where for ten years he conducted a wholesale grocery business. His younger brothers, E. Darwin Litchfield and Edwin C. Litchfield, soon followed him to the metropolis, and through Edwin, who, as a member of the law firm of Litchfield & Tracy, handled much legal work for railroads, all the brothers were drawn into the railroad business.

The state of Michigan in 1846 sold its uncompleted Michigan Southern railroad to a firm in which the engineer, John B. Jervis, and Edwin Litchfield were the leading members. By uniting it with the Northern Indiana Railroad and completing the construction on both lines they secured by May 1852 a through route from Lake Erie to Chicago. Meanwhile Electus was treasurer, and later president, of the Toledo & Cleveland, a portion of which the Litchfields built. They constructed also a Toledo-Detroit line, the Air Line from Toledo to Elkhart, Ind., and minor branches, all of which formed a well-knit system. They allied themselves with the Chicago & Rock Island, then building west to the Mississippi, of which Jervis was president and Elisha C. Litchfield, another brother, a director. They were interested in the construction of the Terre Haute & Alton, and Litchfield, Ill., on this line was named for them. East of Cleveland an understanding was reached with the new roads along the south shore of the lake to Buffalo, thence across New York state, and with the Hudson River Railroad, which resulted in connecting interests from New York to Chicago. The meager facts available do not reveal any one author of this remarkable network of interests, the most impressive before the Civil War, but the Litchfields contributed much to bring it within the realm of possibility, and would have profited immensely had not the panic of 1857 broken it up for a time. Caught with interests too far extended, they could not hold their control in the reorganizations.

For several years afterward Electus Litchfield busied himself with building the Fifth Avenue and Atlantic Avenue street railways, the Coney Island Plank Road, and other enterprises in Brooklyn, of which city, after 1846, he was a leading resident. With his brother Edwin he developed the old Cortelyou farm which they had purchased south of the expanding city. Needing money after the panic he successfully urged the city to buy a large part of this area for park purposes, and to this combination of self-interest and vision Brooklyn owes her famous Prospect Park. Much later he purchased and renovated the Brooklyn, Bath & West End Railroad which did much to develop West Brooklyn and the New Utrecht sections. Meanwhile, in 1862, E. B. Litchfield & Company contracted with the St. Paul & Pacific to build their lines in Minnesota, taking stock and bonds in pay. Financial difficulties soon landed the road in Litchfield's hands, and to complete enough construction to obtain the appertaining land grants he organized the "First Division of the St. Paul & Pacific Railroad," sold bonds in Holland to finance the work, and finished the main line west to Breckenridge and the branch north to St. Cloud. Litchfield, Minn., received its name at this time. In 1870 the Litchfields sold to the Northern Pacific, then booming under Jay Cooke's control, but when that road collapsed in 1873 the stock came back to them. They attempted a reorganization in 1875, but failed, and in 1879 sold their remaining holdings to James J. Hill [q.v.] who made their lines the nucleus of his Great Northern system. Curiously, it was E. B. Litchfield's son, W. B. Litchfield, and a half-brother, E. S. Litchfield, who had helped Hill to a start when in 1867 they became silent partners with him in his warehouse business on the St. Paul levee.

During most of this time the Litchfields had been bankers, brokers, and agents for railroad loans in New York City and had been interested in various minor undertakings. Electus married Hannah Maria Breed, daughter of Elias Breed of Norwich, N. Y., in 1836. Five children were born to them. He was a man of ingratiating personality and of vision, but his enterprises were characterized by the extravagant financing of boom periods.

[See W. W. Folwell, *A Hist. of Minn.* (1926), III, 441–61; J. G. Pyle, *Life of Jas. J. Hill* (2 vols., 1917); Abner Morse, "Geneal. of the Descendants of Lawrence Litchfield," *New-Eng. Hist. and Geneal. Reg.,* Apr., July 1855; N. O. Tiffany, *The Tiffanys of America* (1901); *Railroad Gazette* (N. Y.), May 17, 1899; and annual reports of the railroads concerned. Information as to certain facts was supplied for this sketch by Litchfield's grandsons, Electus D. and Percy Litchfield of New York City.]   O. W. H.

LITTELL, ELIAKIM (Jan. 2, 1797–May 17, 1870), editor and publisher, was born at Burlington, N. J., grandson of a Revolutionary officer, Eliakim Littell, for whom he was named, and son of Stephen and Susan (Gardner) Littell. He attended a grammar school at Haddonfield, N. J., but his formal education was limited. By reading the works of standard authors, however, he acquired a sound literary judgment. After serving an apprenticeship in a bookstore he ventured into publishing. Soon he began editing reprint periodicals of a high literary and intellectual quality and to this work practically his whole life was given. His first periodical was the *Philadelphia Register and National Recorder,* a sixteen-page weekly, of which he was editor and joint publisher, the first number appearing on Jan. 2, 1819. In July following, it became the *National Recorder.* It consisted at first largely of American newspaper reprint, interspersed with a little original copy, but on July 7, 1821, it was renamed the *Saturday Magazine,* and consisted thereafter "principally of selections from the most celebrated British reviews, magazines, and scientific journals." The size was increased to twenty-four pages. A year later it became a ninety-six-page monthly, as the *Museum of Foreign Literature and Science* and was edited for more than a year by Robert Walsh [*q.v.*], who combined this work with his duties as editor of the Philadelphia *National Gazette.* After Walsh's departure, Littell assumed editorial responsibility, except during 1835, with the occasional assistance of his brother, Dr. Squier Littell [*q.v.*]. The *Museum* began to experiment with illustrations in 1826 and soon made them a regular feature. In 1843 it was united with the *American Eclectic* as the *Eclectic Museum of Foreign Literature, Science, and Art,* published in New York and Philadelphia, with John Holmes Agnew as editor.

In 1844 Littell sold out his interest in the *Eclectic Museum* and went to Boston, where in April this "indefatigable caterer for the public mind" founded *Littell's Living Age,* consisting mainly of reprints from the British press. The *Museum* had had a circulation of 2,000, but under Littell the *Living Age* reached 5,000—a respectable figure for the time. His chief successes were with magazines which he himself both edited and published. The *Journal of Foreign Medical Science and Literature,* which he began to publish in 1824 as the continuation of an earlier journal, soon merged with the *American Medical Recorder.* The *Religious Magazine and Spirit of the Foreign Theological Journals,* founded in 1828 with the Rev. George Weller as editor, survived only four volumes before it was discontinued—"very much liked but did not pay." In 1855 Littell founded still another periodical, the *Panorama of Life and Literature,* a 144-page monthly, which he announced as "not so comprehensive in its scope; so redundant in its fulness, or so complete in all its parts" as the *Living Age.* He continued in active direction of his business until his death, which occurred at his home in Brookline, Mass.

He was remarkable for his business acumen, wide reading in ancient and modern literature, a somewhat irascible temper, and a clever pen. His editorial duties did not prevent his occasional production of graceful prose and verse, and he was a sprightly correspondent. He is especially significant for his service in bringing foreign thought to the attention of Americans during the early development of the national culture. During his lifetime, no cultivated American home was complete without at least one of his publications. He took a lively interest in national affairs and was a stanch supporter of the Union during the Civil War, contributing particularly to the discussion of financial questions. On Feb. 12, 1882, he married Mary Frazee Smith, by whom he had six children, two of whom died in infancy. His son, Robert Smith Littell, succeeded him as editor of the *Living Age.*

[Family records and the files of Littell's various periodicals; John Littell, *Family Records: or Geneals. of the First Settlers of Passaic Valley* (1852); G. T. Little, *The Descendants of George Little* (1882); S. A. Allibone, *A Critical Dict. of English Literature and British and Am. Authors* (1870), vol. II; Algernon Tassin, *The Mag. in America* (1916); A. H. Smyth, *The Phila. Mags. and Their Contributors, 1741–1850* (1892); F. L. Mott, *A Hist. of Am. Mags., 1741–1850* (1930); *Littell's Living Age,* June 18, 1870; *New-England Hist. and Geneal. Reg.,* Apr. 1875; *Memorial Biogs. of the New-England Historic Geneal. Soc.,* vol. VI (1905).]   J. B.

LITTELL, SQUIER (Dec. 9, 1803–July 4, 1886), physician, was born in Burlington, N. J., the son of Stephen and Susan (Gardner) Littell. Losing both parents very early in his childhood, he was adopted by his uncle Squier Littell of Butler, Ohio, and received his early education in schools near Lebanon, Ohio. Association with his uncle, who had a large practice, inspired him to study medicine, and after a period of apprenticeship at home he went to Philadelphia in 1821 and continued his studies under the guidance of Joseph Parrish. He matriculated at the medical school of the University of Pennsylvania and received the degree of M.D. in 1824, his graduating thesis being entitled "Theory of Inflammation." Lured by youthful love of adventure and the prospect of a medical appointment there, he went to South America. On arriving in Buenos Aires he was amazed at the degree of learning possessed by the medical men, and though he missed the appointment he sought, he became by examination a licentiate of the Academy of Medicine. Four months' effort convinced him that Buenos Aires was not a suitable field for him and he embarked on a journey toward the United States, rounding the Horn and stopping at Valparaiso, Lima, and other Pacific ports. Thinking that Guayaquil, Ecuador, offered opportunities for one of his calling, he sojourned there for a while; but ultimately he continued his trip to Philadelphia by way of the Isthmus of Panama and Cartagena.

In Philadelphia he renewed his former acquaintances and contacts and engaged in general practice. He had long nourished an ambition to teach anatomy, but an impediment in his speech discouraged him. In Philadelphia his success was progressive, and about 1834 he married Mary Graff Emlin, daughter of Caleb Emlin, by whom he had one son and one daughter. His wife died shortly after the birth of the second child. His medical activities for a long while were of a general character, but with the development of especial skill in ophthalmic surgery he came to be prominently identified with that specialty. When Wills Hospital, founded for the treatment of the lame, the halt, and the blind, was organized in 1834, he became one of its first surgeons. He served in this capacity for some thirty years, thus aiding materially in creating the reputation that has made the ophthalmic work of the hospital internationally famous. He was elected a fellow of the College of Physicians in 1836 and later became one of its councilors. It is an interesting fact that, despite his skill as an ophthalmic surgeon, he learned the use of the ophthalmoscope late in life and with some difficulty.

His literary efforts were many and varied. He edited the *Monthly Journal of Foreign Medi-*

cine (January 1828–June 1829), and he contributed over many years articles to various medical journals, particularly on ophthalmological subjects. From time to time he assisted his brother, Eliakim Littell [q.v.], in the editing of the *Museum of Foreign Literature and Science*. In 1837 he wrote *A Manual of Diseases of the Eye* which was favorably received abroad, although it was one of the earliest American books on this subject. He was active in all the organizations with which he was affiliated and wrote many memoirs of distinguished members of the College of Physicians of Philadelphia. He was also active in the affairs of the Episcopal Church and from January 1839 to May 1841 edited *The Banner of the Cross,* one of the most influential of the church papers of that period. He also wrote poetry and arranged no less than twelve metrical translations of the medieval hymn *"Dies Irae."* He succumbed at the age of eighty-three to what would now be designated as cardio-renal disease, his death occurring at Bay Head, N. J.

[John Littell, *Family Records, or the Geneals. of the First Settlers of Passaic Valley* (1852); T. H. Shastid, in C. A. Wood, *The Am. Encyc. of Ophthalmology,* vol. X (1917); H. A. Kelly and W. L. Burrage, *Am. Medic. Biogs.* (1920); A. D. Hall, in *Trans. Coll. of Physicians of Phila.,* vol. IX (1887); *Phila. Press,* July 7, 1886.]
L. W. F.

LITTELL, WILLIAM (1768–Sept. 26, 1824), lawyer and author, was a native of New Jersey, but removed with his father when very young to the western part of Pennsylvania, where he remained, "it is believed," until he emigrated to Kentucky about the year 1801. In "early life" he studied "Physics and Divinity." (*The Argus of Western America,* Frankfort, Ky., Sept. 29, 1824.) These facts, given in his obituary, represent all that seems to be known of the first thirty years of his life. Whatever career he may have had as a divine was probably limited to Pennsylvania, but he practised medicine for a short time at Mount Sterling, Ky. (Statement of Col. William Sudduth in Shane MSS., 12CC64, State Historical Society of Wisconsin.) He gave up medicine for law and it is a matter of record that Transylvania conferred the degree of LL.D. upon him in 1810 (Robert and Johanna Peter, *Transylvania University,* Filson Club Publications No. 11, 1896, pp. 90, 125).

In 1805, presumably while engaged in the practice of law at Frankfort, he contracted with the state to publish the *Statute Law of Kentucky.* This work appeared in five volumes, 1809–19. In 1806, however, before the first volume appeared, he published three books at Frankfort. The first was styled *Epistles of William, Surnamed Littell, to the People of the Realm of Ken-*

tucky and consisted largely of satirical essays dealing with the prominent men of his time, the second was *A Narrative of the Settlement of Kentucky,* and the third the well-known and meritorious *Political Transactions in and Concerning Kentucky.* From these adventures in politics and history he turned to the writing of law books, beginning in 1808 with his *Principles of Law and Equity.* There ensued a period of six years while he practised law and devoted himself to the compilation of his *Statute Law,* but in 1814 he had a relapse into frivolity with the publication of his *Festoons of Fancy, Consisting of Compositions Amatory, Sentimental and Humorous in Verse and Prose.* In 1822 he issued, in association with Jacob Swigert, *A Digest of the Statute Law of Kentucky,* in two volumes; and, in 1823–24, *Reports of Cases at Common Law and in Chancery, Decided by the Court of Appeals of the Commonwealth of Kentucky.* In 1824 his last book appeared, *Cases Selected from the Decisions of the Court of Appeals of Kentucky Not Hitherto Reported.* Littell's fame rests on his work as a compiler of law books. His *Epistles* was of such a character as to bring him into disrepute and to give him a reputation for flippancy and scurrility that he never succeeded in living down.

He was twice married; first, on Jan. 22, 1816, to Martha Irwin McCracken, daughter of William Irwin of Fayette County and widow of Capt. Virgil McCracken of Woodford County (Fayette County Marriage Records, vol. I, p. 58). They had one son, William, who died Aug. 30, 1824 (*Western Statesman,* Sept. 1, 1824). After the death of his first wife, Littell married, Dec. 9, 1823, Eliza P. Hickman, widow of Capt. Paschal Hickman of Franklin County (Franklin County Deed Book L, pp. 71–73), who, with a son, survived him. According to the tax lists he died possessed of some five thousand acres of land, but he was heavily in debt—probably as a penalty of authorship—and the General Assembly at its next session provided that his lands should be sold by a special official instead of at a forced sale (*Session Acts,* 1824–25, ch. 91, pp. 98–99). A Kentucky historian writing from material no longer available characterizes him as a man of bad morals, of great eccentricity, and of no particular ability except as a land lawyer (Lewis and Richard H. Collins, *History of Kentucky,* 1874, I, 412). The evidence is too scanty to allow a judgment as to his legal abilities, but is overwhelming as to his eccentricities. He had a reputation for immorality; his will hints at domestic unhappiness. The fact that he named a prominent Episcopal minister as one of the two guardians of his sons indicates that he was not without respect for the clergy and the preface to his *Statute Law* indicates his religious belief.

[Littell's will is recorded in Franklin County Will Book, no. 2, p. 1; his *Political Transactions* has been republished as Filson Club Pubs., No. 31 (1926); a poem, "Rapture," from his *Festoons* is included in F. P. Dickey, *Blades o' Bluegrass* (Louisville, 1892), p. 287.]   R. S. C.

LITTLE, CHARLES COFFIN (July 25, 1799–Aug. 9, 1869), publisher, was born in Kennebunk, Me., the son of David and Sarah (Chase) Little and a descendant of George Little who came to Newbury, Mass., in 1640. He left Maine as a youth and secured employment in a Boston shipping house, but in 1821, when the small bookstore of Carter, Hilliard & Company advertised for a clerk, he obtained the position. In 1827 the firm was reorganized as Hilliard, Gray & Company, with Little as a member, and in 1837 he became its senior partner. His chief associate thenceforth was James Brown, 1800–1855 [*q.v.*], formerly an employee of Hilliard. After being known as Charles C. Little & Company for a time, the firm adopted the title of Little & Brown, which in 1847 was changed to Little, Brown & Company.

The business had been greatly increased during Little's connection with it as employee and junior partner, and it continued to grow in importance after he became its head. His particular responsibility was the supervision of the legal publications of the firm, and in a few years his house became the foremost in America in this field. In 1843 and again in 1846 it issued *A Catalogue of Law Books Published and For Sale by Charles C. Little and James Brown,* and though this list included many imported English works, the number of the firm's own publications was large. Little continued as the principal partner and general manager of the business throughout his life. At his death, the house retained its leadership in the publishing of legal works and was prominent among American publishers of books of a general nature.

Little was active as a capitalist, and to some extent in public affairs. He was selectman of Cambridge in 1836 and 1841, in the lower house of the Massachusetts legislature in 1836 and 1837, and was for many years president of a Cambridge bank, besides being an active director of a gas company and a street railroad. Since he employed a considerable part of his personal fortune in the erection of buildings that did much to introduce a more convenient type of structure for both residential and business purposes, his influence on the economic and material development of his community was widely recognized. The day after his death the "booksellers of Boston" held a special meeting in recognition of his services as a publisher and as a citizen.

Little was married on Jan. 1, 1829, to Sarah Anne Hilliard, daughter of his partner, William Hilliard, and sister of Francis Hilliard [*q.v.*]. After her death on Aug. 29, 1848, he was married, Jan. 18, 1854, to Abby, daughter of Henry Wheaton of Providence, R. I. He left four sons and one daughter, all by the first marriage.

[G. T. Little, *The Descendants of George Little* (1882); *Books from Beacon Hill* (1927), pub. by Little, Brown & Co.; L. R. Paige, *Hist. of Cambridge* (1877); *New-Eng. Hist. and Geneal. Reg.*, Oct. 1869; *Proc. Am. Antiquarian Soc.*, vol. LIII (1869); *Boston Transcript*, Aug. 9, 1869; *Boston Post* and *Boston Traveler*, Aug. 10, 1869; *Boston Daily Advertiser*, Aug. 11, 1869; *Cambridge Press*, Aug. 14, 1869.]   S. G.

LITTLE, CHARLES JOSEPH (Sept. 21, 1840–Mar. 11, 1911), theologian, was born in Philadelphia, Pa., the son of Thomas Rowell and Ann (Zimmermann) Little. On his father's side he was descended from George Little who came from England to Massachusetts in 1640. Though in his boyhood his health was frail, he spent his days in manual work and studied at night by lamp and candle light. He had a double endowment in American and German opportunities in his home and in time became a linguist of unusual skill in Greek, Latin, Italian, and French. When he was twenty-one he graduated from the University of Pennsylvania, and in 1862 was admitted to the Philadelphia Conference of the Methodist Episcopal Church. He served pastorates at Newark, Del., Saint James and Spring Garden Street, Philadelphia; Springfield, Pa., and Chestnut Hill, Philadelphia. His exceptional abilities were soon recognized and he was called from the pastorate into the educational field, becoming teacher of mathematics in Dickinson Seminary in 1867. He studied in Europe, 1869–72, and in the latter year married Anna Marina Elizabeth Bahn, daughter of Dr. Carl Bahn. Returning to the United States, he spent two years in the pastorate of Christ Church, Philadelphia, and then became professor of philosophy and history in Dickinson College. In 1885 he was made professor of logic and history in Syracuse University, and in 1891 was elected to the chair of church history in Garrett Biblical Institute. He became president of the Institute in 1895 and held that position to the day of his death.

Little believed in a thoroughgoing theological education in the old-time essentials. His administration covered the years of transition in higher criticism, and while the battle raged most fiercely he was steady as a rock, holding fast to old truths and welcoming all new light. He was a member of the General Conferences of the Methodist Episcopal Church in 1888, 1892, 1896, 1900, 1904, and 1908. He was a man of power and influence in his church, and in every community of which he became a part, and an orator of great impressiveness upon special occasions. As a delegate to the Methodist Centennial Conference at Baltimore in 1884 he made one of the notable addresses, and at the British Wesleyan Conference in 1900 he delivered the Fernley Lecture, *Christianity and the Nineteenth Century* (1900). It was a strong presentation of the value and permanence of an experimental religion, maintaining itself against all the reactions of rationalism.

He appeared to be an inexhaustible fountain of information, giving the impression of encyclopaedic knowledge available at a moment's notice. Some of his greatest efforts seemed to be the product of immediate inspiration. He was extraordinarily versatile and a remarkable conversationalist; his phenomenal memory seemed to retain all he had read. He had a temperamental aversion to the publishing of books. The conditions of the Fernley lectureship necessitated the publication of that lecture, but *The Angel in the Flame* (1904), a series of sermons preached in First Church, Evanston, was published only at the solicitation of the Methodist Book Concern. These sermons, while they illustrate Little's power of clear thinking and vivid expression, hardly show him at his best. A volume entitled *Biographical and Literary Studies* (1916), brought out some five years after his death, is more representative of his finest work. The papers and addresses here gathered together suggest the wide range of his interests and his grasp on many subjects, literary, historical, and religious. The memorial volume of 1912 (*post*) contains eight of his addresses and essays.

[*In Memoriam, Charles Joseph Little* (1912), ed. by C. M. Stuart; *Who's Who in America*, 1910–11; Matthew Simpson, *Cyc. of Methodism* (1882); histories of Northwestern University and Garrett Biblical Institute; G. T. Little, *The Descendants of George Little* (1882); obituaries of Anna (Bahn) Little, in *Christian Advocate* (N. Y.) Nov. 24, 1904, and *Minutes of the Rock River Conference*, 1905; *Northwestern Christian Advocate*, Mar. 15, 1911; *Christian Advocate* (N. Y.), Mar. 16, 1911; *Chicago Tribune*, Mar. 12, 1911; *Journals* of the General Conferences named above.]
                                         D. A. H.

LITTLE, GEORGE (Apr. 15, 1754–July 22, 1809), naval officer, was born in Marshfield, Mass., the son of Lemuel and Penelope (Eames or Ames) Little. He was descended from Thomas Little who emigrated to Plymouth from Devonshire, England, in 1630, and from Lieut. William Fobes, second in command in King

Philip's war. Nothing is known of Little's first service in the American Revolution beyond the information that he landed at Bristol, R. I., on Mar. 7, 1778, after a period of confinement on board the British prisonship *Lord Sandwich* at Newport. Later in that year he served in the Massachusetts navy, successively, as second lieutenant of the brigantine *Active* and master of the brigantine *Hazard*. On May 3, 1779, he was commissioned first lieutenant, and as first officer on the *Hazard* participated in the unfortunate Penobscot expedition. He was first lieutenant on the state ship *Protector* when on June 9, 1780, that vessel captured the British privateer *Admiral Duff,* thirty-two guns, in one of the severest naval engagements of the Revolution. In the following year when the *Protector* surrendered to his Majesty's ships *Roebuck* and *Medea* he was taken prisoner and was for a time confined in Mill Prison, England. Bribing a sentry, he, with several other American officers, made his escape, crossed the channel to France, and with the aid of Franklin returned to Massachusetts. In 1782 he was promoted to a captaincy, given command of the sloop *Winthrop,* and ordered on a cruise along the Eastern Coast. He had the good fortune to capture nearly the whole of the armed British force at Penobscot, thereby retrieving somewhat the naval honor of his state, lost in the Penobscot expedition of 1779. A voyage that he made in the *Winthrop* during the winter of 1782–83 was the last cruise in the war of the Massachusetts navy.

After his discharge on June 23, 1783, Little returned to Marshfield where he owned a farm. From Mar. 4, 1799, he served by appointment of President Adams as captain in the new federal navy, then undergoing expansion on account of the naval war with France. His part in this desultory conflict was, with the exception of Commodore Truxtun [*q.v.*], exceeded by no other officer. He was appropriately given command of the frigate *Boston,* a gift of the Bostonians to the federal government. On July 24 he put to sea under orders to proceed to Cape François and to cruise off the northern coast of Santo Domingo for the protection of American trade. In December while in company with the *General Greene* he captured the Danish brig *Flying Fish*. Notwithstanding the fact that the taking of this prize was plainly authorized by the orders of the Navy Department, the Supreme Court which finally passed upon the case held Little liable for damages. In 1800, the last year of the war, Little captured several ships, including the *Deux Anges,* a letter of marque of twenty guns, and the *Berceau,* a naval vessel of twenty-four guns,

next to the largest prize made by the Americans. It was taken after a severe action, as the *Berceau,* although inferior to the *Boston,* made a strong resistance. With the arrival of the two vessels in Boston in November 1800, Little's active part in the war came to an end. Under Jefferson the navy was greatly reduced and Little was discharged from the service on Oct. 20, 1801. He died suddenly in Weymouth, Mass., at the age of fifty-five. On June 24, 1779, he was married to Rachel Rogers (1758–1838) of Marshfield. Their son Edward Preble Little, who was named for Commodore Preble and was a midshipman on the *Boston,* was a member of the United States House of Representatives, 1852–53.

[*Mass. Soldiers and Sailors of the Revolutionary War,* IX (1902), 868; L. S. Richards, *Hist. of Marshfield,* vol. II (1905); C. O. Paullin, *The Navy of the Am. Revolution* (1906); G. W. Allen, *Our Naval War with France* (1909); *Mass. Hist. Soc. Proc.,* vol. XX (1884); *New-England Palladium* (Boston), July 28, 1809.]   C. O. P.

LITTLE CROW V (*c.* 1803–July 3, 1863), Indian chief, was the son of Little Crow IV. The name Little Crow, Chetan-wakan-mani, "the sacred pigeon-hawk that comes walking," was held in succession by several chiefs of the Kapoja band of Mdewakanton Sioux, in southeastern Minnesota. The Little Crow who appears in Pike's journal (1805–06) and who signed the treaty ceding the ground on which Fort Snelling was built, is generally accounted the third of the dynasty. Wabasha [*q.v.*], the head chief, told Pike that Little Crow III was "the man of most sense in their nation." He appears frequently in the accounts of travelers of the time and always with praise. In 1824 he visited Washington. He was succeeded by Little Crow IV, known also as Big Thunder and Big Eagle. The accounts of his life are hopelessly conflicting. It is agreed that he died of an accidentally self-inflicted wound, but the dates given are widely divergent. Gen. H. H. Sibley, who was present at the death of the chief, says that he died in 1834, and that he was a good and wise man who taught his people agriculture and as an example to them worked in his own fields. On his deathbed he called in his eldest son and after reproving the young man for his evil ways and telling him that another son, recently killed by the Chippewas, had been intended for the succession, reluctantly gave him the chieftainship.

Little Crow V, according to Sibley, paid little heed to his father's reproof. He was a drunkard and a confirmed liar, with few redeeming qualities. He signed the treaty of Mendota, Aug. 5, 1851, by which the Mdewakanton Sioux ceded most of their lands and withdrew to the upper

Minnesota River, but he afterward used this treaty as an argument for stirring up antagonism to the whites. A persuasive orator, he was chiefly responsible for the outbreak which followed eleven years later. On Aug. 18, 1862, incensed because of the non-arrival of the annuities provided for in the treaty and deluded by the belief that because of the Civil War no soldiers would be available for the defense of the settlements, the Sioux rose in revolt. Along a stretch of the frontier for more than two hundred miles they pillaged and burned the farm houses and villages and with an unparalleled ferocity tortured and massacred the inhabitants, nearly a thousand of whom are estimated to have perished. Little Crow commanded the force which unsuccessfully attacked Fort Ridgely, Aug. 20–22, and also the force which was routed by General Sibley at Wood Lake, Sept. 23. After this decisive action he fled to his kinfolk farther west, but in the following year, with a young son, again ventured into the devastated territory, to which many of the settlers had returned. On the evening of July 3, while prowling about a farm near Hutchinson, McLeod County, he was shot and killed.

Despite his dissoluteness, Little Crow V was a man of energy and determination. He possessed, however, no military talents, and he held power solely through his oratorical abilities. Though he is said to have had twenty-two children, the issue of six wives, the dynasty ended with his death.

[Cyrus Thomas, *Handbook of Am. Indians*, vol. I (1907); H. H. Sibley, "Reminiscences of the Early Days of Minn.," *Minn. Hist. Soc. Colls.*, vol. III (1880); W. W. Folwell, *Hist. of Minn.* (4 vols., 1921–30); Elliott Coues, *The Expeditions of Zebulon Montgomery Pike* (3 vols., 1895); H. R. Schoolcraft, *Summary Narrative of an Exploratory Expedition . . . in 1820* (1855).]

W. J. G.

LITTLE TURTLE (*c.* 1752–July 14, 1812), Miami chief, whose Indian name was Michikinikwa, was born in a Miami village on Eel River, twenty miles northwest of Fort Wayne, Ind. His father was a Miami chief and his mother is said to have been a Mahican. Of his early life little is known. He was on good terms with the British and rendered some service to them in the American Revolution. He took part in the massacre of De La Balme's forces, at Aboite River, in 1780. In the troublous years that followed, when the early Ohio settlements were being made, Little Turtle grew no more friendly toward Americans. His skill in war and his oratorical powers made him one of the most important chiefs in the old Northwest. With great military shrewdness he acted as one of the principal leaders of the Indians at the de-

feat of Harmar, in 1790, and of St. Clair, in 1791. In the autumn of 1792 he commanded the Indian forces in a skirmish with a company of Kentuckians. When General Anthony Wayne marched his troops into the Northwest, Little Turtle led the attack on Fort Recovery in 1794 and sought British aid against the Americans, but, later, counseled peace. His advice was not taken by the other chiefs, who were elated over their former successes; he lost his leadership in council and was not in command at Fallen Timbers. He signed the Treaty of Greenville in 1795 and many subsequent treaties with the United States. When William Henry Harrison [*q.v.*] undertook the rapid acquisition of title to Indian lands, Little Turtle was granted a special annuity by the United States (Indian Office Letter Book, A, pp. 144, 205, 233) and, with his son-in-law, William Wells, was sent to obtain Indian support for the cession; but his activities failed to satisfy Harrison. Nevertheless, in 1805 his annuity was increased by fifty dollars and he was given a negro slave (*American State Papers, post*, p. 702).

He visited the cities of the United States several times and became a popular Indian hero to the Americans. He met the French philosopher, Volney, who questioned him about the native races, and he received gifts from the great Kościuszko. In 1801 he delivered, before a committee of Friends in Baltimore, a speech against the introduction of whiskey into the Indian country (*Memorial of Evan Thomas, and others, a Committee Appointed for Indian Affairs by the Yearly Meeting . . . 1802*, 1802, pp. 5–10). The United States built him a house at his village. He adopted some American ways and acquired a white man's disease, gout. Among his own people his prestige declined sharply, but he is credited with keeping the Miami from joining the confederacy of Tecumseh. A frequent visitor at Fort Wayne, he received medical attention from the army surgeon and died there shortly after the beginning of the second war with England.

[C. M. Young, *Little Turtle* (1917); C. F. Chasseboeuf, Comte de Volney, *Tableau du Climat et du Sol des États-Unis* (1803), vol. II; "Governors Messages and Letters. Messages and Letters of Wm. H. Harrison," *Ind. Hist. Colls.* (2 vols., 1922); *Am. State Papers, Indian Affairs*, vol. I (1832); E. D. Mansfield, *Personal Memories* (1879); J. P. Dunn, *True Indian Stories* (1908).]

W. B—r.

LITTLEFIELD, GEORGE WASHINGTON (June 21, 1842–Nov. 10, 1920), cowman, banker, and patron of higher education, was born in Panola County, Miss., the child of Fleming and Mildred M. (Satterwhite) Littlefield. His father, a cotton planter, emigrated to Texas to settle in Gonzales County in 1850. Three years later he died and left the problems of an extensive plantation and two hundred slaves to the management of his capable wife. In August 1861 George W. Littlefield enlisted in Company I of the 8th Texas Cavalry, known to fame as Terry's Texas Rangers, and served until the Civil War was almost over. As a lieutenant he fought at Shiloh, where his company lost one-third of its men; as a captain he experienced heavy fighting under Bragg. He fought at Chickamauga and at the battle of Lookout Mountain. During a furlough, Jan. 14, 1863, he married Alice P. Tiller of Houston, Tex. Late in December 1863, while he held the brevet rank of major, he suffered a severe wound; and several months afterward was mustered from service and returned to Texas apparently a hopeless invalid.

His health improved, however, while he was managing a family plantation and operating a small country store, and when the floods of the San Marcos and Guadalupe rivers destroyed the local crops in 1871, he retrieved the family fortune by driving a herd of Texas cattle over the trail to Abilene, Kan. Seeing the possibilities of driving cattle from the over-crowded ranges of Texas to the markets of the Middle West, he formed a mercantile and trail-driving partnership which lasted seven years and proved very profitable. In 1877 he established a cattle ranch on the free, open ranges of the Panhandle near Tascosa which in 1881 he sold to a Scotch company for $253,000. Another ranch which he located on the Pecos River in New Mexico in 1882 soon ranged 40,000 head of cattle and spread the fame of Littlefield's LFD brand the length of the West. In 1883 he moved from Gonzales to Austin, where in 1890 he organized the American National Bank. Its growth was rapid, and he served as its president until his death. The great bronze doors of its present building, embossed with herds of LFD cattle, still suggest the basis of its origin. In time murals were painted upon the walls depicting the work of handling approximately 70,000 cattle upon 450,000 acres in the Littlefield name.

In 1912 Littlefield's attention was attracted to the need of a great depository of Southern historical source material, and two years later he established the Littlefield Fund for Southern History at the University of Texas, an endowment which he later enlarged to $125,000, the income from which was to be used "for the full and impartial study of the South and its part in American History." The interest thus encouraged led him to make further gifts and bequests: $225,000 for the purchase of the Wrenn Library,

$350,000 for the Alice Littlefield Dormitory, $250,000 for an entrance to the University commemorating great Southern statesmen, $500,000 to apply on the construction of a main building, besides other generous donations.

Littlefield had the traditional characteristics of the Western man in that he was easily approached and generous hearted. He was of heavy, medium stature, while his ruddy complexion suggested the man of the open rather than the office. He was a strong supporter of the Democratic party, a Mason, and an adherent of the Southern Presbyterian Church. At his death in his seventy-ninth year he was survived by his wife, but he left no children.

[E. C. Barker, "Southern History in the South," *Nation* (N. Y.), July 2, 1914; letters from E. C. Barker suggesting a Southern History fund, and replies in decision by Geo. W. Littlefield, 1912–14, in the Archives of the Univ. of Texas; L. E. Daniell, *Types of Successful Men of Texas* (1890); J. M. Hunter, *The Trail Drivers of Texas*, vol. II (1923); *The Alcalde* (Austin), X, 1513; *Who's Who in America*, 1918–19; *Austin American*, Jan. 6, 1918; *Dallas Morning News*, Nov. 11, 1920.]   J. E. H.

LITTLEJOHN, ABRAM NEWKIRK (Dec. 13, 1824–Aug. 3, 1901), Protestant Episcopal bishop of Long Island, was born in Florida, Montgomery County, N. Y., where his maternal grandfather, Abram Newkirk, was among the early settlers of the region. Soon after his birth his parents, John and Eleanor (Newkirk) Littlejohn, removed to Johnstown, N. Y. After graduating with high standing from Union College in 1845, he studied privately for the ministry of the Episcopal Church and was ordained deacon Mar. 19, 1848, by Bishop William Heathcote DeLancey of Western New York. After a brief ministry in St. Ann's Church, Amsterdam, N. Y., he removed to St. Andrew's Church, Meriden, Conn., and was ordained to the priesthood by Bishop Thomas C. Brownell in Christ Church, Hartford, June 12, 1849. In 1850–51 he was in charge of Christ Church, Springfield, Mass., and then became rector of St. Paul's Church, New Haven, Conn., where his successful ministry brought him into prominence. He served as lecturer in pastoral theology at the Berkeley Divinity School during most of his rectorship at St. Paul's. In 1858 he was elected president of Geneva (now Hobart) College, Geneva, N. Y., but declined the office. He was called in 1860 to the Church of the Holy Trinity, Brooklyn, N. Y., where both as a preacher and pastor he attained notable success. When, in 1868, two new dioceses, those of Central New York and Long Island, were created in the state of New York, he had the honor of being elected simultaneously by both to the office of bishop.

He chose Long Island, and was consecrated to the episcopate in his own church on Jan. 27, 1869.

Bishop Littlejohn was one of the earliest members of the American episcopate to press for the erection of a cathedral. He interested Alexander T. Stewart [q.v.], the New York merchant, and his wife, and through their donations the Cathedral Church of the Incarnation was erected at Garden City, Long Island, in 1885. After Stewart's death his widow gave a large sum for the endowment of the work, and the Cathedral Schools, St. Paul's for boys and St. Mary's for girls, were erected on the same foundation. Littlejohn was in charge of the American Episcopal churches in Europe from 1874 to 1885. He officiated at the consecration of the American Church of St. Paul at Rome and was instrumental in establishing the present Church of the Holy Trinity in Paris. In the field of literature he attained a considerable reputation and contributed articles on literary, philosophical, and religious topics to American and English reviews. He was invited in 1880 by the University of Cambridge, England, to deliver a course of lectures, which were afterward published under the title, *Individualism: Its Growth and Tendencies, with Some Suggestions as to the Remedy for Its Evils* (1881); and in 1884 he delivered the Paddock Lectures at the General Theological Seminary, published that year as *The Christian Ministry at the Close of the Nineteenth Century*. He was married to Jane Armstrong, in June 1851, and had two daughters. He died suddenly, in his seventy-seventh year, while visiting in Williamstown, Mass.

[W. S. Perry, *The Episcopate in America* (1895); F. S. Lowndes, *Bishops of the Day* (1897); *Lloyd's Clerical Directory*, 1898; *Am. Church Almanac*, 1902; *Churchman, Church Standard*, and *Living Church*, all of Aug. 10, 1901; *N. Y. Tribune*, Aug. 4, 1901; information from Mrs. Harry Hart, Pelham, N. Y., and from the vital records of New Haven, Conn.]   G. L. R.

LITTLEPAGE, LEWIS (Dec. 19, 1762–July 19, 1802), soldier of fortune, born in Hanover County, Va., was the son of Col. James Littlepage by his second wife, Elizabeth Lewis. His paternal ancestors had been settled in Virginia since 1660. In 1778 he entered the College of William and Mary, but, eager for a diplomatic career, in which ambition his uncle and guardian, Col. Benjamin Lewis, supported him, he was accepted as a protégé, after solicitation, by John Jay [q.v.], recently appointed minister to Spain. He sailed for Bordeaux late in 1779, remained many months in Nantes learning French, and arrived at Madrid in November 1780, when Jay took him into his family. By petty intrigues with William Carmichael, Jay's secretary, and

Henry Brockholst Livingston, Jay's brother-in-law, he contributed to dissensions in the Jay household. Meanwhile Jay advanced him numerous sums of money, amounting to more than a thousand dollars. In June 1781, despite the pointed advice of Jay, he turned from diplomacy to war and joined the staff of the Duc de Crillon. Jay refused to advance him further moneys, whereupon the posts were filled with insulting letters from the youthful warrior. To these Jay replied in patient, conciliatory spirit. At the siege of Port Mahon Littlepage was wounded. Jay demanded in March 1782 that he return to Madrid; he replied that his "military Quixotism is not yet abated" and joined the Duc de Crillon in the disastrous siege of Gibraltar. He was on a floating battery which was blown up, but he escaped and won a reputation for gallantry and the praises of the King of Spain. At Gibraltar he formed a friendship with Lafayette and the Prince of Nassau.

In the fall of 1783 he was in Paris, where he attempted to secure the appointment to carry the definitive treaty of peace to Congress. His failure he unjustly attributed to the machinations of Jay, from whom he was now completely estranged. In December 1783 he accompanied the Prince of Nassau to Constantinople; the following year, at the Diet of Grodno, he met Stanislaus Augustus, King of Poland, and agreed, when once he had settled his affairs in the United States, to enter his service.

He arrived in Virginia in July 1785; in November he went to New York to secure from Congress a letter of recommendation to the King of Poland. He transmitted to Jay, then secretary for foreign affairs, letters from various European worthies. When Congress adjourned on Dec. 2 without having considered his petition, Littlepage suspected another of Jay's machinations. Jay meanwhile began suit to collect the moneys due him. Littlepage, encouraged by the French minister, prepared a vituperative attack upon Jay which was published in the *New York Daily Advertiser* for Dec. 6, 7, and 10. Littlepage had been given money by the State of Virginia to settle accounts with Houdon; this money he deposited as a bond to settle the debt, and sailed for France. Jay, to contradict "this Young Man's Ebullitions," early in 1786, published a lengthy pamphlet, *Letters, Being the Whole of the Correspondence between the Hon. John Jay, Esquire and Mr. Lewis Littlepage,* later republished with additional material. Littlepage, from Warsaw, replied with his *Answer to a Pamphlet . . .* (1786), which did little more than confirm his vituperative abilities.

On Mar. 2, 1786, he became chamberlain to the King of Poland and during the next several years negotiated a successful treaty with the Empress of Russia and another with the court of Spain. He traveled in Italy and was employed as a secret envoy to the French court. He participated, in 1788, in the naval victory over the Turks at Oczacow and from 1792 to 1794 he fought against the Russian invasion of Poland. When in February 1798 his friend King Stanislaus died, the Emperor of Russia paid him almost £10,000 sterling promised him by Stanislaus. He remained in Warsaw until early in 1801 when he went to Hamburg. Here his life and fortune were threatened by numerous plots; and he became involved in difficulties with England and France. Wearied by European intrigues, he returned to Virginia. His health had been shattered by the active life of court and camp, and he died in Fredericksburg at the age of thirty-nine. In accordance with his request, his papers were destroyed by his executors.

[Jay's pamphlet, collated with the original letters, is an exact printing of the correspondence between Jay and Littlepage while they were in Spain; H. E. Hayden's *Va. Geneals.* (1891; repr. 1931), pp. 395-420, contains a valuable and sympathetic sketch, with important letters to and from Littlepage; see also the *New York Daily Advertiser* (*ante*); William Jay, *Life of John Jay* (1833), I, 204-29; and *Va. Herald* (Fredericksburg), July 20, 1802.]   F.M.

LIVERMORE, ABIEL ABBOT (Oct. 30, 1811–Nov. 28, 1892), Unitarian clergyman, author, president of the Meadville Theological School, was a descendant of John Livermore who in 1634 came to Watertown, Mass., from Ipswich, England. He was the grandson of the Rev. Jonathan Livermore, pastor of the Congregational Church in Wilton, N. H., and son of Jonathan Livermore, a Wilton farmer of high repute, who married Abigail Abbot, daughter of Maj. Abiel Abbot, a Revolutionary patriot. The son Abiel, after early years of farm employment and district schooling, was for six months, at the age of fifteen, a student in an academy in Chelmsford, Mass., and thereafter in Phillips Exeter Academy until in 1830 he was admitted to the sophomore class of Harvard College. In Harvard he roomed with Francis Bowen, the later philosopher, was active in college societies, supported himself by tutoring boys for college entrance, and won high standing for scholarship. After theological study (1833–36) in the Cambridge Divinity School, he was ordained, Nov. 2, 1836, as pastor of the Congregational Church in Keene, N. H. During this congenial pastorate he was a community leader in the promotion of culture. He served on the school committee, was a trustee of Cheshire Academy, founded a flourishing book and periodical club, stimulated interest in foreign literature, and edited a *Social Gazette* for the publication of the literary efforts of local young people. In 1841 he published a commentary on Matthew's Gospel which in three years had four editions and was reissued in Belfast, Ireland. By 1844 the work covered four Gospels and the Book of Acts, and in this form was republished in London, 1846. In 1854 he added a volume on Romans, and in 1881 two more on the rest of the New Testament. The work afforded a moderate liberal interpretation on principles learned in the Cambridge school. At this time he shared in the anti-slavery movement and successfully competed for a prize of five hundred dollars offered by the American Peace Society by a work entitled *The War with Mexico Reviewed* (1850). This historical discussion shows a mastery of many original sources and skilfully exhibits the social psychology of the country in that period.

Seeking a milder climate Livermore accepted a call to the Unitarian Church in Cincinnati, serving there from May 26, 1850, to July 6, 1856. To this troubled church he brought stability by his tolerant, inclusive, fraternal spirit, his talent for organization, and the sustained high thinking and literary charm of his preaching. To unite and increase the liberal churches he organized in 1852 the Western Unitarian Conference, serving it as corresponding secretary. The publication of his elevated *Discourses* in 1854 and articles in the *North American Review* (July 1855) and the *Christian Examiner* (January 1856) made him widely known and led to an appointment as editor of the *Christian Inquirer,* necessitating a removal to New York in July 1856. Aiding in the organization of a Unitarian Church in Yonkers, N. Y. (1857), he became its settled pastor in June 1859. In addition to these two offices he served as non-resident lecturer for brief annual periods in the Theological School of Meadville, Pa., and in 1863 relinquished other duties to become the president of that institution.

Conservative as he was by temperament, his new administrative career showed open-minded hospitality to new policies and progressive thought. In 1864 the school was opened to women students. In the autumn of that year he gave twelve lectures in the Lowell Institute in Boston upon Christianity as related to an environment of general religious development and in the following he gave in Meadville a course on comparative religion, sharing with Bouvier of Geneva and James Freeman Clarke of Harvard the distinction of first introducing the subject into the academic curriculum. He made some adjustment of his Biblical teaching to the modern critical views of Kuenen and in his course in ethics dealt with modern social problems. From 1881 there was a rapid development of courses in practical and theoretical sociology in the curriculum. While president he published *Lectures to Young Men on Their Moral Dangers and Duties* (1864), completed his New Testament commentary (1881), collaborated with Sewall Putnam in a *History of the Town of Wilton* (1888), and wrote varied articles for the *Unitarian Review* (1874–91). On May 17, 1838, he married his cousin Elizabeth Dorcas Abbot of Windham, N. H., a woman of poetic gift, author of a novel, *Zoe, or the Octaroon's Triumph*. She died Sept. 13, 1879. On June 18, 1883, he married Mary A. (Keating) Moore of Meadville who survived him. He had no children. Resigning his presidency in 1890 he retired to the ancient hillside home in Wilton and there he died. An oil portrait of Livermore is preserved in the Meadville School, now situated in Chicago.

[For biographical details see: W. E. Thwing, *The Livermore Family of America* (1902); S. G. Griffin, *Hist. of the Town of Keene* (1904); G. A. Thayer, *The First Cong. Ch. of Cincinnati: A Hist. Sketch* (1917), and the *Hist. of the Town of Wilton* (1888), mentioned above. For characterizations see: F. A. Christie, *Makers of the Meadville Theol. School* (1927); F. L. Phalen, "Abiel Abbot Livermore," in *Heralds of a Liberal Faith* (1910), vol. III, ed. by S. A. Eliot; and J. H. Morison, article in the *Christian Reg.*, Dec. 2, 1892. Livermore's diary for the years 1836–48, with notes by J. H. Wilson, is in the possession of the N. H. Hist. Soc., Concord, N. H. That for earlier and later years is in the possession of the Rev. John Henry Wilson, Littleton, Mass.]   F. A. C.

LIVERMORE, ARTHUR (July 29, 1766–July 1, 1853), chief justice of New Hampshire, congressman, third son of Judge Samuel Livermore, 1732–1803 [*q.v.*], and Jane, daughter of the Rev. Arthur Browne of Portsmouth, was born in Londonderry (now Derry), N. H. His early education was begun at a school in Portsmouth and was continued after 1775 at Holderness by his father and by Dr. John Porter. He was sent when about fifteen to a school in Concord, and here he later studied law in the office of his brother, Edward St. Loe Livermore [*q.v.*]. Admitted to the bar in 1791, he practised in Concord till 1793, and then in Chester. Already he was showing signs of both the ability and the fiery temper which distinguished him in later life, for besides building up a practice, he was elected a representative to the legislature (1794–95), was commissioned solicitor of Rockingham County (1796–98), and gave a thrashing to the notorious "Lord" Timothy Dexter [*q.v.*], then living in Chester. In 1798 he was appointed a judge of the superior court of New Hampshire, and in

1809 he was made chief justice. When the courts were reorganized in 1813 he was appointed associate justice of the supreme court. This court, however, was dissolved in 1816, and Livermore, for a time, exchanged the bench for the floor of Congress, to which he was three times elected a representative, in 1816, 1818, and 1822. In 1820 he was elected to the Senate of New Hampshire, and in 1822 he was made judge of probate in Grafton County, but he resigned the next year. At the expiration of his third term in Congress, in 1825, he returned to the bench as chief justice of the New Hampshire court of common pleas, but in 1832 this court was abolished, and he retired from public life, after thirty-eight years of continuous service. He had married, on Mar. 27, 1810, Louisa Bliss, daughter of Joseph Bliss of Haverhill, N. H. There were eight children, six of whom were sons.

Livermore was an able member of the state legislature and of Congress, where he was known as a strong opponent of the extension of slavery in general, and of the Missouri Compromise in particular. Despite this attitude, he numbered prominent Southerners among his friends, even including John Randolph of Roanoke. He was not a great speaker, but he effectively employed his sarcastic wit. As a judge he was guided by honesty and common sense rather than by precedents, and he refused to allow the discussion of technicalities to obscure justice. He was never a rich man, but he was always generous. Soon after his father's death (1803), he purchased from his elder brother the family estate at Holderness. Here there was always hospitality for the poor. Obliged to sell the Holderness property, he retired in 1832 to a small farm, "Craigie Burn," in the neighboring township of Campton, where he spent the last twenty years of his life. He lies buried in the old churchyard at Holderness.

[The most interesting biographical material is contained in unsigned manuscript notes now known to be by Livermore's son, Arthur, and preserved in the library of the N. H. Hist. Soc. at Concord. These are partially reproduced in an address by E. S. Stearns, printed in the *Proc. Grafton and Coos County Bar Asso.*, vol. II (1893). Additional material is found in letters from Arthur Livermore, Jr., in *Ibid.*, vol. III (1897). The manuscript copies of the records of Trinity Church, Holderness, now in the library of the N. H. Hist. Soc., are of some value. See also: *Annals of Cong.*, 1817–21, 1823–25; C. H. Bell, *The Bench and Bar of N. H.* (1894); W. E. Thwing, *The Livermore Family of America* (1902); E. S. Stackpole, *Hist. of N. H.* (1916), vol. II; and the *Portsmouth Jour. of Lit. and Pol.*, July 9, 1853. Two portraits are reproduced in the *Proc. Grafton and Coos County Bar Asso.*, II, 434, 439, and a copy of one of these hangs in the court-room in the State Library at Concord.] E. V. M.

LIVERMORE, EDWARD ST. LOE (Apr. 5, 1762–Sept. 15, 1832), lawyer, congressman, was born in Portsmouth, N. H., the eldest son of Samuel Livermore, 1732–1803 [*q.v.*] and Jane Browne. His early youth was passed during the critical years preceding the American war for independence. His father, who held the office of King's attorney for New Hampshire, withdrew with his family from Portsmouth to Londonderry (now Derry) and later (1775) to Holderness, then a frontier settlement with no roads and little communication with the world. As there was no school, Edward, now thirteen, and his younger brothers, George and Arthur [*q.v.*], were taught by their parents and by Dr. John Porter and his wife, who had accompanied the Livermore family to Holderness. Porter was a Harvard graduate and his wife a woman of culture, and Edward and his brothers were given the foundation of a classical education. This seems to have been the only academic training he had, but it was sufficient to give him the polished speech, which later distinguished him, and to prepare him for the study of law. The latter he pursued in the office of Chief Justice Theophilus Parsons, at Newburyport, Mass., and at the age of twenty-one he began to practise in Concord, N. H. A few years later he returned to his birthplace, Portsmouth, where he soon entered public life.

In 1791 Livermore was elected to the convention (of which his father was president) assembled to revise the constitution of New Hampshire and he served on several important committees. He was also appointed during this period solicitor of Rockingham County (1791–93) and United States district attorney in New Hampshire, 1794–97. He resigned the latter office when the governor made him judge of the superior court, and a year later he resigned this position also because of its meager salary of only eight hundred dollars. On Sept. 20, 1798, President Adams appointed him naval officer for the port of Portsmouth, but Jefferson removed him in 1802 for party reasons. Livermore appears after this as an ardent Federalist. Having moved to Newburyport, Mass., he was elected (1807) to represent Essex County in Congress, where he served for four years, proving himself an able speaker and a strong opponent of measures favored by Jefferson and Madison, especially the Embargo, against which he spoke frequently and forcefully. In 1811 he took up his residence in Boston. Here he became prominent as a sharp critic of the War of 1812. In 1815 he removed with his family to Zanesville, Ohio, then considered "the West," where he expected to settle, but he soon returned to New England and purchased a farm near the confluence of the Con-

cord and the Merrimac rivers, in that part of Tewksbury, Mass., which was later included in Lowell. Here he died, at the age of seventy. He was buried in Boston in the Old Granary Burying-ground. Livermore was twice married: on Aug. 7, 1784, to Mehitable, daughter of Robert Harris of Concord, by whom he had five children; and on May 2, 1799, to Sarah, daughter of William Stackpole of Boston, by whom he had seven children. Samuel Livermore, 1786–1833 [*q.v.*], a son by the first marriage, distinguished himself in the law; Harriet Livermore, a daughter by the first marriage, became well known as an evangelist. Quick of temper, proud, impatient of contradiction, and intellectually keen, he was respected and admired, but he did not attain the popularity or prominence of his father.

[See C. H. Bell, *The Bench and Bar of N. H.* (1894); E. S. Stackpole, *Hist. of N. H.* (1916); W. E. Thwing, *The Livermore Family of America* (1902), which reproduces a portrait; the memoir by C. L. A. Read in *Contributions of the Old Residents' Hist. Asso. of Lowell, Mass.*, vol. II (1883); and the obituary in the *Boston Daily Advertiser & Patriot*, Sept. 21, 1832. There are personal references to him in some manuscript notes furnished by his nephew, Arthur, to E. S. Stearns, and now in the library of the N. H. Hist. Soc. at Concord. *The N. H. Provincial and State Papers*, vols. X (1877) and XXII (1893), and the *Annals of Cong.*, 1807–11, contain the official record of his public service and his speeches in Congress.]   E. V. M.

LIVERMORE, GEORGE (July 10, 1809–Aug. 30, 1865), antiquarian, was the son of Deacon Nathaniel and Elizabeth (Gleason) Livermore and a descendant of John Livermore who emigrated to Massachusetts from Ipswich, England, in 1634. Born in Cambridge, Mass., he attended public and private schools in the town until he was fourteen years old and then went to work in a store kept by his brothers. College was denied him because of his frail constitution. In 1834 he entered the shoe and leather business and four years later he became a wool merchant, but his great interest was in books and reading. Biblical works were his specialty, and as his collection of Bibles and related material grew, be became recognized as an authority in that field. In 1845 he traveled abroad and met, among other distinguished men, Dibdin, the bibliographer, and the poets Rogers and Wordsworth. Upon landing at Liverpool, and again upon leaving England, he visited the grave of William Roscoe, for whose achievements and character he had great admiration. In 1849 he wrote a series of eight articles for the *Cambridge Chronicle* (Apr. 5–May 24), signed "The Antiquary," reprinted in a thin volume entitled *The Origin, History, and Character of the New-England Primer* (1849) which attracted considerable attention. He was elected a member of the American Antiquarian Society and of the Massachusetts Historical Society in the autumn of that year. At Commencement in 1850 Harvard conferred upon him the honorary degree of master of arts. In 1855 he became a member of the American Academy of Arts and Sciences and was the treasurer of that institution at the time of his death.

When the Civil War broke out Livermore threw himself whole-heartedly into the cause of the Union. The question whether the government should accept colored troops evoked from him a work of over two hundred pages entitled *An Historical Research Respecting the Opinions of the Founders of the Republic, on Negroes as Slaves, as Citizens, and as Soldiers* (1862). His thesis was that the leaders of the American Revolution regarded negroes as men capable of bearing arms and of being citizens, and that the same attitude should prevail in the current crisis. President Lincoln consulted the book when preparing the Emancipation Proclamation and later gave Livermore the pen with which he signed that document. Livermore survived the Civil War, but the excitement of Lee's surrender and the shock of Lincoln's death were more than his delicate constitution could bear. He died less than six months after these events occurred and was survived by his wife, Elizabeth Cunningham (Odiorne) Livermore, and three sons. Although his nature was sensitive, intense, and sometimes intolerant, his outstanding qualities were simplicity, modesty, and conscientiousness. As an antiquarian and scholar he was remarkable for his accuracy.

[The *Memoir of Geo. Livermore* (1869), by Chas. Deane, is the best account, but good side-lights are thrown on his career by the tributes of contemporaries in the *Proc. Mass. Hist. Soc.*, vol. VIII (1866) ; *Boston Daily Advertiser*, Sept. 2, 1865 ; H. C. Badger, *The Consecrated Life* (1865) ; and E. E. Hale, *The Pub. Duty of a Private Citizen* (1865). For genealogical details see W. E. Thwing, *The Livermore Family of America* (1902).]   L. S. M.

LIVERMORE, MARY ASHTON RICE (Dec. 19, 1820–May 23, 1905), reformer, suffragist, author, was the fourth child of Timothy and Zebiah Vose Glover (Ashton) Rice. Her father was descended from Edmund Rice, who came to Massachusetts in 1638; her mother's father was born in London. In her parents' Boston home on Salem Street, not far from the Old North Church, Mary Rice passed most of her childhood. Here she was indoctrinated with the tenets of Calvinistic religion and with high ethical standards, while she received the education provided for girls by the public and private schools of Boston. Her New England schooling was once interrupted, when her father, infected with the western fever of the thirties, moved to a frontier section of New York state, only to return to Boston two years later, convinced that pioneer farming had few attractions.

Mary, having completed the work of the Hancock Grammar School at fourteen, entered the Female Seminary of Charlestown, where, before the end of her first year, she was teaching as well as studying. After graduation, she remained here as an instructor in French and Latin until an opportunity came to teach on a Virginia plantation. From this experience she later drew the picture of plantation life which is to be found in her *Story of my Life*. After her return to Massachusetts, while teaching at Duxbury, she met and married (May 1845) the Rev. Daniel Parker Livermore, of the Universalist Church. They lived together fifty-four years, until the death of Livermore on July 5, 1899. The first pastorate served by the young couple after their marriage was at Fall River, where they were indefatigable in their labors with reading and study groups, one of which was made up of factory operatives. Here Mary Livermore's first published work, a temperance story, was written. The next post, at Stafford, Conn., was resigned because of Daniel Livermore's advocacy of the temperance cause, in opposition to the majority of his congregation. After serving pastorates in Weymouth and Malden, Mass., they started for Kansas in 1857, but abandoned their intention to settle there and remained in Chicago. Here Daniel Livermore became editor and proprietor of a church periodical, the *New Covenant,* which he conducted from 1857 to 1869, his wife serving as associate editor. At the same time she cared for her two children, took a lively interest in local charities, and did much miscellaneous writing. She was the only woman to report the convention which nominated Lincoln.

With the outbreak of the Civil War, she devoted her extraordinary energy to the work of the Northwestern Branch of the United States Sanitary Commission. Up to this time she had given scant attention to the extension of the suffrage to women, believing that desirable social reforms could be accomplished by other methods than the vote. Her war experience seems to have convinced her that woman's suffrage would be the most direct route to the curtailing of the liquor traffic, improvements in public education, and the alleviation of many problems of poverty; and at the close of hostilities she directed all her efforts to the enfranchisement of women. At the first woman's suffrage convention in Chicago she delivered the opening address, and was elected president of the Illinois Woman's Suffrage

Association. In 1869 she established *The Agitator*, a paper devoted to the cause. A few months later, *The Agitator* was merged with the *Woman's Journal*, just established in Boston, and she undertook the editorship of the new periodical. The family then moved from Chicago, and for the remainder of her life she lived in Melrose, Mass.

In 1872 she gave up her editorial work to devote her time to public lecturing, and for the last twenty-five years of the century she was a well-known platform speaker, on social questions and topics of history, biography, politics, and education. The lecture she most frequently delivered was probably, "What Shall We Do with Our Daughters?" a plea for the higher education and the professional training of women. The two subjects in which she was most interested and in which her influence was most largely felt were the education of women and the cause of temperance. For ten years she was president of the Massachusetts Women's Christian Temperance Union; she was also president of the Massachusetts Woman's Suffrage Association, and was connected with the Women's Educational and Industrial Union and the National Conference of Charities and Corrections. Notable among her later publications are her two autobiographical volumes, *My Story of the War: A Woman's Narrative of Four Years Personal Experience* (1888) and *The Story of My Life, or, The Sunshine and Shadow of Seventy Years* (1897). In 1893 her name appeared, with that of Frances E. Willard [*q.v.*], as joint editor of *A Woman of the Century*, a compilation of biographical sketches, which went through a number of editions, under other titles. Throughout her life her vigor rarely failed, and she spoke from a public platform after she had passed her eighty-third birthday.

[Works mentioned above; *Arena*, Aug. 1892; Lilian Whiting, *Women Who Have Ennobled Life* (1915); E. S. Phelps, in *Our Famous Women* (1884); Mrs. J. A. Logan, *The Part Taken by Women in Am. Hist.* (1912); E. L. Didier, in *The Chautauquan*, July 1906; E. C. Stanton, S. B. Anthony, and M. J. Gage, *Hist. of Woman Suffrage* (6 vols., 1881–1922); W. E. Thwing, *The Livermore Family of America* (1902); *Woman's Jour.*, May 27, June 10, 1905; *Outlook*, June 3, 1905; *Boston Transcript*, May 23, 1905.]   E. D.

LIVERMORE, SAMUEL (May 25, 1732– May 18, 1803), jurist, congressman, senator, was the third son and fourth child of Deacon Samuel Livermore and Hannah Brown, daughter of Deacon William Brown of Waltham, Mass. The Livermore family in America descended from John Livermore (Leathermore or Lithermore), a potter by trade, who left England in 1634 and was admitted the following year as

freeman in Watertown, Mass. His descendants became people of substance and of importance. His great-grandson, Deacon Samuel, inherited from an uncle a farm in the township of Waltham, where he took up his residence and held various offices. Here his son Samuel was born. Nothing is known of the boy's early education, but at eighteen he was teaching in Chelsea, Mass., and at nineteen he entered the College of New Jersey (later Princeton), where he expected to fit himself for the ministry. He took his degree in one year, after which he returned to his teaching, at the same time studying law in the office of Edmund Trowbridge. At the age of twenty-four he was admitted to the bar and began to practise in Waltham, but he soon moved to Portsmouth, N. H., where he established his reputation as an energetic and fearless lawyer. He also became the warm friend of the royal agent, Governor Wentworth.

When trouble was brewing between the colony and the mother country, Livermore withdrew from Portsmouth to the Scotch-Irish settlement of Londonderry (now Derry), N. H. He was elected to represent the township in the General Assembly of 1768–70 but was recalled to Portsmouth in 1769 when Wentworth appointed him judge-advocate in the Admiralty court, and attorney-general. Five years later, however, he returned to Londonderry, and the next year (1775) he pushed farther still into the wilds to Holderness, at that time accessible only in winter, when vehicles could travel over the snow. Here he made his home, acquiring by grant and purchase more than two-thirds of the whole township, over which he practically ruled as "squire," building a dignified residence, a church, and a gristmill, and personally superintending both farm and mill when the break with England prevented the fulfilment of his duties as King's attorney-general. Despite his apparent withdrawal from the Revolutionary conflict, popular confidence in him led to his election in 1776 as attorney-general, and from this time almost until his death he held office under the state practically continuously, sometimes, indeed, filling two offices at once.

In 1779 he was elected by the General Court as commissioner to the Continental Congress to represent the interests of the state in the controversy over the "New Hampshire Grants" on the west side of the Connecticut River. His services as commissioner led to his being chosen again as a representative to Congress in 1785, 1789, and in 1791. At the end of the last term (1793), he was elected to the United States Senate, and at the end of the six-year term, he was reëlected for another six years but resigned in 1801 because of failing health. Twice he was chosen president of the Senate, *pro tempore*, and as such signed the address to the President on the death of Washington. Meantime, he had also been holding other state offices, the most important being that of chief justice of the superior court (1782–90). Thus he did not at first resign when elected to Congress, for there was then no law requiring it. When the Constitution of the United States was being debated, and the vote of New Hampshire hung in the balance, Livermore as a member of the convention of 1788 did great service in bringing about ratification, thus securing the ninth state and ensuring the acceptance of the Constitution. In 1791 he was president of the New Hampshire constitutional convention.

On Sept. 23, 1759, Livermore married Jane, daughter of the Rev. Arthur Browne of Portsmouth, the first minister of the Church of England to settle in New Hampshire. There were five children, the eldest of whom died in infancy. Of his surviving sons, Edward St. Loe and Arthur [qq.v.] both became distinguished lawyers, and George Williamson (1764–1805) held for many years the office of clerk of the court and register of deeds at Holderness. Few more picturesque or important figures than Samuel Livermore are found in early New Hampshire history. Homely and sometimes harsh of speech, he possessed a frankness and kindness of heart which atoned for his brusqueness, while his honesty and common sense as a judge made amends for his contempt for precedents and for his sometimes inconsistent decisions. He died at his home in Holderness and was buried there in the cemetery of Trinity Church.

[A part of Livermore's journal, telling of his journey to college in 1751, is quoted in a manuscript sketch of him (140 pp., undated) by his grandson, in the library of the N. H. Hist. Soc. at Concord. This manuscript also contains copies of letters and other memoranda. The journal has been printed in part in *Putnam's Mag.*, June 1857, pp. 631–35. The *N. H. Provincial and State Papers*, vols. VII, VIII, X, XXII (1873–1893), contain the records of his activities in the state, and the *Jours. of Cong.* and *Annals of Cong.* give his congressional service. A good sketch of his life by C. R. Corning may be found in the *Proc. Grafton and Coos County Bar Asso.*, vol. I (1888), and there are also sketches in C. H. Bell, *The Bench and Bar of N. H.* (1894); E. S. Stackpole, *Hist. of N. H.* (1916), vol. II; and the *N. H. Hist. Soc. Colls.*, vol. V (1837). More of his personality is given in the chapter devoted to him by Geo. Hodges in *Holderness* (1907). For the family genealogy, see Henry Bond, *Geneals. of the Families and Descendants of the Early Settlers of Watertown, Mass.* (1855), and W. E. Thwing, *The Livermore Family of America* (1902). See also F. M. Colby, "Holderness and the Livermores," *Granite Monthly*, Feb. 1881. A copy of a portrait by Trumbull hangs in the courtroom in the State Library at Concord and is reproduced in the *Proc. of the Grafton and Coos County Bar Asso.*, vol. II, and by Hodges, who also reproduces a portrait of Mrs. Livermore, attributed to Copley.]
                                                E. V. M.

LIVERMORE, SAMUEL (Aug. 26, 1786–July 11, 1833), lawyer and legal writer, was born in Concord, N. H., the son of Edward St. Loe Livermore [q.v.], by his first wife, Mehitable Harris. He graduated from Harvard College in 1804, studied law, and was admitted to the Essex County bar. After his admission to the bar he moved to Boston, where he practised law for several years. During the War of 1812 he served as a volunteer on board the *Chesapeake* and was wounded in the engagement with the *Shannon*. After the war he moved to Baltimore and with others assisted Alexander C. Hanson [q.v.] in the publication of the *Federal Republican*. From Baltimore he moved to New Orleans, where his name appears in the city directory for 1822. Within a few years he had achieved distinction as a lawyer.

In 1811 Livermore published in Boston *A Treatise on the Law Relative to Principals, Agents, Factors, Auctioneers, and Brokers,* the first American work of its kind (Charles Warren, *A History of the American Bar*, 1911, p. 337). A second edition of this work in two volumes, entitled *A Treatise on the Law of Principal and Agent: and of Sales by Auction*, was published in Baltimore in 1818. In 1828 he published in New Orleans *Dissertations on the Questions which Arise from the Contrariety of the Positive Laws of Different States and Nations,* the first American work on the conflict of laws. The book has been described as "a forceful but belated attempt to reinstate the statutory theory of the mediaeval commentators" (J. H. Beale, *post*, part I, par. 38, p. 49). His doctrines, however, "could not be applied in a country where both commercial and social intercourse between all parts of it are constant and continuous." Livermore influenced Story and other American lawyers by calling attention to the works of medieval authors. He presented to the Harvard Law School his collection of medieval works, containing 400 volumes and including the writers of the sixteenth, seventeenth, and eighteenth centuries on the conflict of laws. This collection "formed the basis of the large apparatus which Story's bibliography describes" (*Ibid.*). Livermore died at Florence, Ala., while he was on his way from New Orleans to New England to visit his relatives.

[For biographical data see W. E. Thwing, *The Livermore Family of America* (1902); W. T. Davis, *Bench and Bar of the Commonwealth of Mass.* (1895), vol. I; *Quinquennial Cat. of the Officers and Grads. of Harvard Univ.* (1915); and the *Florence* (Ala.) *Gazette*, July 12, 1833. For his legal writings consult J. G. Marvin, *Legal Bibliog.* (1847), and J. H. Beale, *A Treatise* on the *Conflict of Laws, or Private Internat. Law,* vol. I, pt. 1 (1916). References to his gift of books to the Harvard Law School appear in *The Centennial Hist. of the Harvard Law School* (1918).]   M. J. W.

LIVINGSTON, EDWARD (May 28, 1764–May 23, 1836), statesman, was born at "Clermont," Columbia County, N. Y., the youngest son of Robert R. Livingston the elder [*q.v.*] and Margaret Beekman. His eldest brother was the distinguished Chancellor Robert R. Livingston [*q.v.*], and his sisters, by their marriages, added notable names to the family connection. Upon the death of his father in 1775, Edward Livingston was sent to school in Albany but he soon transferred to the school of Dominie Doll at Esopus (now Kingston) where he prepared for the College of New Jersey (Princeton), entering the junior class in 1779. He subsequently declared that at college he had been an indifferent scholar, learning only so much as was absolutely necessary to obtain his degree, which was granted in 1781. But he was already proficient in languages and his interest in philosophy and poetry was sufficient to attract the attention of John Jay. From Princeton he returned to "Clermont" to spend a year in the study of French under a Mr. Tetard and German under a refugee minister to whom his mother had given shelter. In 1782 he began the study of law at Albany in the office of John Lansing [*q.v.*] where he found as fellow students Alexander Hamilton, Aaron Burr, and James Kent. The removal of the British troops from New York City in November 1783 permitted the Livingston family to reoccupy their town house and there Edward continued his studies until his admission to the bar in January 1785. Moving freely in the society of New York, he acquired the title of "Beau Ned" on account of his habits of dress. While engaged in the practice of law he married, on Apr. 10, 1788, Mary, eldest daughter of Charles McEvers, a New York merchant. Three children were born to them before Mrs. Livingston contracted scarlet fever and died, Mar. 13, 1801.

The political career of Edward Livingston began with his election to Congress in 1794. The Livingstons had joined with the Schuylers in the movement for the ratification of the Constitution. They were, however, overlooked by Washington in the distribution of patronage and, almost in a body, they went over to the Clintons and the party of Thomas Jefferson. Taking his seat in the House of Representatives on Dec. 7, 1795, Edward Livingston moved on Dec. 15 to revise the penal code of the United States, which he said was in general too sanguinary and very badly proportioned. Nothing came of this effort in behalf of what was already a pet measure with him, but in March 1796 he secured the enactment of a measure for the relief of American seamen who were impressed or abandoned destitute on foreign shores. In the same month the House was called upon for appropriations to carry out Jay's treaty of 1794 with England. Although the treaty had been ratified, it was still opposed by the Republicans, and Livingston introduced a resolution calling for all the papers from the President, except those which any existing negotiation might render improper to be disclosed (*Annals of Congress,* 4 Cong., 1 Sess., p. 426). Representing the Republican stronghold of New York City, Livingston was reëlected in 1796 and again in 1798. He was, therefore, a member of the House of Representatives in 1801 when the failure of the electoral college to choose a president threw the election into that body. In the ensuing contest between Aaron Burr and Thomas Jefferson, there were rumors, not entirely groundless, that Livingston was favorable to the candidacy of Burr (Hunt, *post,* p. 86; D. S. Alexander, *Political History of The State of New York,* 1906, I, 103; Edward Livingston Manuscripts). The two men came from the same social class in New York and were personal friends. Nevertheless, Livingston was one of the six New York members who voted consistently for Jefferson, although it was believed he did so without enthusiasm.

Livingston had refused to run again for Congress in 1800 but the success of the Republicans in the election led to his appointment as United States attorney for the District of New York. Almost simultaneously he was appointed mayor of New York, a post estimated to be worth $10,000 a year. He collected and published *Judicial Opinions Delivered in the Mayor's Court of the City of New York in the Year 1802* (1803). While carrying the burden of both offices, he fell a victim to the yellow fever which raged in New York during the summer of 1803. He recovered to find that during his illness one of his agents, in the collection of custom house bonds sent him by the Treasury, had absconded with the funds. Livingston immediately resigned his offices and turned over his property to trustees to be sold in payment of his debts. "I can show, however, upwards of $100,000 in property at a very moderate valuation above my debts," he wrote his sister, Mrs. Montgomery, Aug. 24, 1803. "I shall with the close of this year begin the world anew and have serious thoughts of doing so at New Orleans" (Edward Livingston Manuscripts). Without waiting for an adjustment of his accounts, he voluntarily confessed judgment in favor of the United States for $100,000 although the sum actually due turned out to be $43,666.21. In December he started for New Orleans, arriving there in the middle of February. Immediately he began the practice of the law, appearing in thirty-five cases during the spring of 1804 and receiving payments chiefly in the form of land. That he was desperately in need of money soon became apparent. His brother, who had been left in charge of his affairs in New York, found that Livingston's private debts amounted to $195,-000. This sum, added to the debt due the United States, exceeded the value of his property. When all his property had been sold, he still owed $18,-000 on his private debts as well as the debt due the government.

Determination to pay his debts soon brought him into difficulties. Among his creditors was Aaron Burr [q.v.], who had embarked upon his famous "conspiracy." Burr, on July 26, 1806, transferred his debt to Dr. Justus E. Bollman [q.v.], who presented a draft upon Livingston in New Orleans. Payment had scarcely been made when General Wilkinson [q.v.], who had originally been a confederate of Burr but who had betrayed him and was energetically striving to bring him to punishment, accused Livingston in open court of connection with the "conspiracy" (Hunt, pp. 126–33; account by Livingston in Edward Livingston Manuscripts). The only ground of this accusation was the payment of the draft to Dr. Bollman. Livingston had just cleared himself of the calumny when the famous Batture controversy brought him into conflict with President Jefferson. Certain alluvial lands at New Orleans had passed by descent to John Gravier who, in 1803, fenced a portion of them which had long been used by the people for the anchorage of their ships. Gravier brought suit against the city to confirm his title and engaged Livingston as his attorney. When judgment for the plaintiff was secured in 1807, Livingston received half the property as his fee. Livingston believed he was now within immediate reach of great wealth, for he observed that the improvement of the property would provide wharfage and warehousing facilities for the growing city. But the improvements were hindered by popular disturbances and the grand jury declared the work a nuisance. Appeal to Governor Claiborne led to the reference of the matter to Washington. But Jefferson was angry because Livingston in his conduct of the office of United States attorney had given ground for criticism of his party and its appointments. The Attorney-General ruled against Livingston and the United States marshal was directed to dispossess him on the ground that the land belonged to the United States as sovereign of the soil. The dispossession was carried out in contravention of an injunction from the territorial court, whereupon Livingston brought an action against the marshal in the United States court at New Orleans to recover damages, according to the forms of the civil law, for his expulsion and a restoration to possession, and, a little later, an action for damages against Thomas Jefferson. Meanwhile, he published pamphlets upon the subject and made the halls of Congress ring with his complaints, but all his labors were without fruit, so far as the action of any branch of the government was concerned. (The documents in the case are collected in *American State Papers, Public Lands,* vol. II, 1834.)

Since coming to New Orleans, Livingston had been separated from his children. One son had died in 1802 and the daughter and remaining son had been confided to the care of relatives. On June 3, 1805, Livingston married Madame Louise Moreau de Lassy, widow of a French officer and the daughter of Jean D'Avezac de Castera, a rich planter of Santo Domingo, who with her mother had been forced to flee during the negro insurrection on the island. She was the sister of Auguste D'Avezac [q.v.]. To Livingston and his wife a daughter was born in October 1806, who proved to be the only one of his children to live to maturity. In January 1809, Livingston, accompanied by his wife and daughter, went to Washington where he remained to fight for his Batture property while they proceeded to "Clermont." While pressing his claims before Congress, he was encouraged by the news that title to the property had been denied the city of New Orleans. At the same time the suit against the marshal was pending in the court at New Orleans and thither Livingston returned. In 1813 the news that his daughter Julia was dying of consumption obliged him once more to take the long journey to New York. He arrived to hear that she had been buried the day before he landed.

The outbreak of war with Great Britain in 1812 afforded Livingston an opportunity to reduce his debt to the United States by supplying live-oak to the government for the construction of frigates. The autumn of 1814 saw the war carried into Louisiana. Livingston, who had been the friend of Andrew Jackson since they had served together in Congress, asked an appointment as aide-de-camp. This Jackson refused in kindly fashion, but requested Livingston to give him information about the country. As chairman of the committee on public defense, Livingston not only organized the people of Louisiana to resist the British but also brought to his support the brothers Laffite (see Laffite, Jean). At the battle of New Orleans, he served Jackson as aide-de-camp, military secretary, interpreter, and confidential adviser upon all subjects. He not only drafted the various orders and proclamations of the General but also undertook the negotiations with the British for the exchange of prisoners. Before leaving New Orleans, General Jackson sat for his miniature, painted on ivory, which he presented to Livingston. (Hunt, ch. x; Jackson to Livingston, Sept. 30, 1814, and Oct. 23, 1814, Livingston to Mrs. Montgomery, Jan. 20, 1815, Edward Livingston Manuscripts.)

The close of the war left Livingston free to struggle again with his debts. His project to sell timber to the government was no longer feasible and he returned to his law practice. In 1820 he was elected a member of the Louisiana legislature and the following year was commissioned to revise the penal law of the state. His early interest in penal legislation had increased as he studied the writings of Bentham, which came to him in the French of Dumont in 1802. "Although strongly impressed with the defects of our actual system of penal law," Livingston wrote to Bentham, "yet the perusal of your works first gave method to my ideas, and taught me to consider legislation as a science governed by certain principles" (*Works of Jeremy Bentham*, 1843, XI, 51). The task of compiling the penal law of Louisiana was almost completed when the results of his labors were destroyed by fire. The work had to be done again, and in 1825 the finished code was presented to the legislature. It was divided into a Code of Crimes and Punishments, a Code of Procedure, a Code of Evidence, and a Code of Reform and Prison Discipline, besides a Book of Definitions. The machinery proposed for the working of the system included a house of detention, a penitentiary, a house of refuge and industry, and a school of reform; all under the superintendence and conduct of one board of inspectors. Every part of the work evinces the most elaborate attention to the preservation of a complete unity of design and aims at the prevention rather than the avenging of crime. Although it was not adopted, the publication of the code brought Livingston immediate and wide fame. (It can be most conveniently consulted in *The Complete Works of Edward Livingston on Criminal Jurisprudence*, 2 vols., 1873.) He was chosen foreign associate of the Institute of France and was later described by Sir Henry Maine as "the first legal genius of modern times" (*Cambridge Essays, Contributed by Members of the University, 1856*, n.d., p. 17).

Meantime, Livingston was unanimously chosen in July 1822 to represent the New Orleans district in Congress. He was afterward twice reelected, and gave as his chief reason for desiring to remain in the House of Representatives the hope that he might adapt his penal code to the use of the United States. In 1826 he paid his long-standing debt to the government, which, with accumulated interest, amounted to $100,014.89. The means of discharging the debt was afforded by a court decision which gave him title to a portion of the Batture property, although the larger part continued in dispute. Released from financial worry, he became less interested in Louisiana, where he had always regarded himself as in exile. He was attentive to the interests of his constituents but failed to visit his district and spent much of his time in New York. Popular favor deserted him and he was defeated for reëlection in 1828 but was immediately chosen by the legislature to represent Louisiana in the United States Senate. Livingston entered the Senate at the same time that Andrew Jackson became president. The two men had continued firm friends; Livingston had voted for Jackson in the contested election of 1824 and worked for his election in 1828. The President wished to employ his friend in the administration, and Livingston would have accepted the post of minister to France. His private affairs, however, were not in condition to permit him to depart at once and Jackson was obliged to make another appointment. Livingston presented to the Senate his *System of Penal Laws for the United States of America* (1828), but no action was taken on it. He continued in the Senate, firmly attached to the party of Jackson, until the spring of 1831, when he was appointed secretary of state.

In 1828 his sister, Mrs. Montgomery, died, bequeathing to him the bulk of her fortune, including her home at "Montgomery Place." He was therefore able to maintain a large establishment and "his manner of living and of entertaining guests was not excelled, if equalled, at Washington" (Hunt, p. 365). At the same time, he had not sought the office and would have preferred the cultivation of roses at "Montgomery Place." Among the more important matters which came before him as secretary of state was a treaty with France whereby the government of that country agreed to pay the claims of United States citizens for spoliations suffered under the Berlin and Milan decrees. He also drafted in 1832 the celebrated proclamation to the nullifiers of South Carolina. On May 29, 1833, he resigned as secretary of state to become minister to France. As secretary of the legation Jackson appointed Thomas P. Barton, who had married the daughter and only surviving child of Livingston.

The appointment of Livingston to the French mission was made in an effort to bring about the payment of the claims of American citizens for spoliations during the Napoleonic wars which the French government had admitted in the treaty of July 4, 1831. The agreement was to pay twenty-five million francs in six yearly instalments, but no payments had been made, the Chamber of Deputies having failed to make the necessary appropriations. Although Livingston was courteously received in France, a year of negotiations failed to secure action. Jackson became thoroughly angry, and in his message of December 1834 suggested that Congress authorize reprisals upon French property in case no provision should be made for the payment of the debt at the next session of the Chamber of Deputies. This suggestion produced great public excitement in France but, through further pressure from Livingston, the Chamber of Deputies, in April 1835, determined to appropriate the money. At the same time it was provided that payment should not be made until satisfactory explanations were given of the terms used in the presidential message. Livingston felt that he could no longer remain at his post and, with a conciliatory message to the French government, he handed over the business of his office to Barton as chargé d'affaires and returned home. Retiring to "Montgomery Place" in the late summer of 1835, he found that public opinion in the United States approved of his conduct in France. In January 1836, he visited Washington to argue a case before the Supreme Court. While there he counseled the President on the pending negotiations with France, which were soon to be brought to a favorable conclusion through the friendly mediation of England. This visit to Washington was Livingston's last absence from his family. He passed the remainder of the winter in New York, and early in the spring was once more at "Montgomery Place." Taken suddenly and violently ill with bilious colic on May 21, he died two days later and was buried in the family vault at "Clermont." Later, his remains were removed to the tomb of his second wife at Rhinebeck, N. Y.

"The pursuit of honest fame, the desire to serve your country," were once extolled as virtues by Edward Livingston in a letter to his young son (Hunt, p. 236). In reality they were his own ideals. Utterly lacking in ability to manage his own financial affairs, he possessed great power as a lawyer and a statesman. His services to mankind were remarked in the many tributes paid to his memory. The common council of the city of New York declared that he had been "a leader in every enterprise calculated to improve or adorn society" (Hunt, p. 433). In his oration delivered before the Academy of the Institute of France, François Mignet, the historian, said: "By the death of Mr. Livingston, America has lost her most powerful intellect, the Academy one of its most illustrious members, and Humanity one of her most zealous benefactors" (*Ibid.*, p. 434).

[The MSS. of Edward Livingston are privately owned; they include about 2,500 letters and documents. Among printed sources, the following may be cited: C. H. Hunt, *Life of Edward Livingston* (1864); E. B. Livingston, *The Livingstons of Livingston Manor* (1910); H. D. Gilpin, "Biog. Notice of Edward Livingston," in *Trans. of the Hist. and Lit. Committee of the Am. Philosophical Soc.*, vol. III, part 1 (1843); C. H. Peck, "Edward Livingston," in *The Conservative Review*, June 1900; Carleton Hunt, "Life and Services of Edward Livingston," in *Proc. of the La. Bar Asso.*, May 9, 1903 (1903); S. Lewis, *Strictures on Dr. Livingston's System of Penal Laws* (1825), and *Remarks on the Hon. Edward Livingston's Introductory Report to His System of Penal Law* (1831); "Two Letters of Chancellor Kent," *Am. Law Review*, Apr. 1878, pp. 479–90; Eugene Smith, "Edward Livingston and the La. Codes," *Columbia Law Review*, Jan. 1902, pp. 25–36; E. H. Moore, "The Livingston Code," *Jour. of the Am. Inst. of Criminal Law and Criminology*, Nov. 1928, pp. 344–63, with an excellent bibliography; Francis Rawle, "Edward Livingston," and E. I. McCormac, "Louis McLane" and "John Forsyth," in S. F. Bemis, ed., *The Am. Secretaries of State and Their Diplomacy*, vol. IV (1928).]
W. S. C.

LIVINGSTON, HENRY BROCKHOLST (Nov. 25, 1757–Mar. 18, 1823), jurist, was born in New York City. His father was William Livingston [*q.v.*], a governor of New Jersey, and his mother was Susanna French. He graduated from the College of New Jersey (Princeton) in 1774, James Madison being a fellow student. At the outbreak of the war he entered the Continental Army with a captain's commission. He served as aide, with the rank of major, to Gen. Philip Schuyler, and also to General St. Clair. He took part in the siege of Ticonderoga, and was a member of Benedict Arnold's staff during the Saratoga campaign and at the surrender of Burgoyne. He later returned to Schuyler and left the service with the rank of lieutenant-colonel. In 1779 he went to Spain as private secretary to John Jay, his brother-in-law, who was sent as minister to that country. On his return voyage in 1782 he was captured by the British, taken to New York, and imprisoned there until the arrival of Sir Guy Carleton who released him on parole. Barred from further military activity he went to Albany and studied law under Peter Yates and in 1783 was admitted to the bar. He returned to New York in that year, after its evacuation by the British, and began the practice of his profession. At this time he abandoned his first name and was thereafter known merely as Brockholst Livingston. He rapidly rose to a position of prominence at the bar. He developed a violent antagonism to Federalism under the new constitution and cast in his lot with Jefferson's party. In spite of his close relationship with Jay he bitterly opposed the Jay Treaty, being present at the riot at which Hamilton was wounded by a stone, and also at the burning of Jay in effigy.

In 1802 Livingston was appointed a judge of the supreme court of New York, on which James Kent was one of his colleagues. His appointment to the Supreme Court of the United States was seriously considered by Jefferson in 1804, and he was strongly recommended by Albert Gallatin, secretary of the treasury, but the appointment went to William Johnson [q.v.]. On Nov. 10, 1806, however, upon the death of Justice William Paterson, Jefferson nominated Livingston to the Supreme Court and the appointment was confirmed in December of that year. He took his seat at the ensuing February term. Owing to the practice of Chief Justice Marshall of writing most of the opinions of the court himself, especially in cases of importance, it is not easy to identify the individual contributions or views of the associate justices in the early period. During the seventeen years that Livingston sat on the Supreme Court he wrote the opinion of the majority in only thirty-eight cases. Not one of these involved any constitutional problem; they dealt rather with questions of maritime and commercial law in which he was deeply interested and highly trained. He dissented in eight cases and either wrote or joined in six concurring opinions. He is said to have been in great doubt as to the proper decision in the Dartmouth College Case, after hearing the arguments, but was won over to Marshall's position, partly through his respect for the expressed opinion of Kent. His decisions on the circuit court were more noteworthy than those on the Supreme Court. In 1808 he clarified the law of treason by holding that resistance, even violent resistance, to the Embargo acts could not be held to be treason if the intention of the accused was private gain (I *Paine's Circuit Court Reports,* 265). In 1810 he attracted notice by an opinion on the circuit court indicating his belief in the constitutionality of the Embargo acts, a point upon which the Supreme Court never squarely passed. In 1817 he held, also in the circuit court, that the power of Congress to enact bankruptcy laws was not exclusive and that the bankruptcy law of New York was valid (I *Paine's Circuit Court Reports,* 79).

Livingston died in Washington in his sixty-sixth year. He was married three times: to Catharine Keteltas, to Ann Ludlow, and to Catharine (Seaman) Kortright. He had a keen interest in history and was chosen one of the vice-presidents of the New York Historical Society when it was founded in 1805. He also helped in the organization of the public school system of New York. Justice Joseph Story, describing him in 1808, wrote: "Livingston has a fine Roman face; an aquiline nose, high forehead, bald head, and projecting chin, indicate deep research, strength, and quickness of mind. I have no hesitation in pronouncing him a very able and independent Judge. He evidently thinks with great solidity and seizes on the strong points of argument. He is luminous, decisive, earnest and impressive on the bench. In private society he is accessible and easy, and enjoys with great good humor the vivacities, if I may coin a word, of the wit and moralist" (W. W. Story, *Life and Letters of Joseph Story,* 1851, I, p. 167).

[See Alden Chester, *Courts and Lawyers of N. Y.* (1925), vol. III; E. B. Livingston, *The Livingstons of Livingston Manor* (1910); Charles Warren, *The Supreme Court in U. S. Hist.* (1922), vol. I; D. S. Alexander, *A Pol. Hist. of the State of N. Y.,* vol. I (1906); H. L. Carson, *The Supreme Court of the U. S.* (1891); *Daily Nat. Intelligencer* (Washington, D. C.), Mar. 19, 1823. Livingston's opinions on the Supreme Court can be found in 4 *Cranch* (U. S.) to 8 *Wheaton* (U. S.). His circuit court opinions appear mainly in *Paine's Circuit Court Reports* (2 vols., 1810–23).] R. E. C.

LIVINGSTON, JAMES (Mar. 27, 1747–Nov. 29, 1832), Revolutionary soldier, was probably born in Montreal, where his father, John Livingston, the grand-nephew of Robert Livingston [q.v.], had settled soon after his marriage to Catryna Ten Broeck. At the outbreak of the American Revolution his parents returned to Saratoga County, N. Y., while Livingston, with two of his brothers, joined the invading army of Gen. Richard Montgomery, their kinsman by marriage. In 1775 Livingston raised and commanded a regiment of Canadian refugees. During the siege of St. John's, Quebec, he led 300 of his Canadians, supported by fifty Americans under Maj. John Brown, 1744–1780 [q.v.], against Fort Chambly, which he captured with eighty prisoners and important stores of munitions and foodstuffs. His possession of this fort materially reduced the strength of the defenses of St. John's, and his prisoners provided a useful threat of retaliation to any measure that the British might take against such prisoners as Ethan Allen and his comrades. At the close of the unsuccessful siege of Quebec he found himself without a command, but, on Jan. 8, 1776, the Continental Congress commissioned him colonel and shortly afterwards he was in command of an additional battalion of the New York line. He served under Benedict Arnold [q.v.] on the expedition to relieve Fort Stanwix and fought in both battles of Saratoga. In 1780, he was in command at Stony Point and Verplanck's Point when the *Vulture* brought André up the Hudson to arrange with Arnold for the betrayal of West Point. Suspicious of the circumstances, he fired on the British vessel, caused her to drop down the river instead of waiting for André, and thus prevented the safe return of André to the British lines. When his regiment was reduced in 1781, he resigned from the army.

Under the act of 1784 he became a member of the first board of regents of the University of the State of New York and continued to be a member after the reorganization of 1787. In 1786 and 1787 he was a member of the New York Assembly from Montgomery County, and he sat in that body again from 1789 to 1791. He died at Schuylerville in Saratoga County. He married, probably about 1771, Elizabeth Simpson of Montreal. They had nine children; of these the first was Elizabeth, the mother of Gerrit Smith [q.v.], and the sixth was Margaret, the wife of Daniel Cady and the mother of Elizabeth Cady Stanton [qq.v.].

[Most authorities give Nov. 29 as date of death although *Daily Albany Argus,* Dec. 8, 1832, gives Nov. 20; see John Schuyler, *Institution of the Soc. of the Cincinnati* (1886), pp. 251–53; J. H. Smith, *Our Struggle for the Fourteenth Colony* (2 vols., 1907); E. A. Werner, *Civil List and Constitutional Hist. . . . of N. Y.* (1889); Peter Force, *Am. Archives,* 4 ser., IV (1843), col. 1636; E. B. Livingston, *The Livingstons of Livingston Manor* (1910); E. Ten B. Runk, *The Ten Broeck Genealogy* (1897).]   K. E. C.

LIVINGSTON, JOHN HENRY (May 30, 1746–Jan. 20, 1825), Dutch Reformed clergyman, educator, was born near Poughkeepsie, N. Y., the son of Henry and Susanna (Conklin) Livingston. His father, Henry, was the son of Gilbert, a younger son of Robert Livingston [q.v.], first lord of Livingston Manor. John Henry was taught at home by his parents and by a private tutor, then studied under Rev. Chauncey Graham at Fishkill and Rev. Nathaniel Taylor at New Milford, Conn. Ready for Yale at twelve years of age, he was graduated there in 1762 and began the study of law at Poughkeepsie. After two years, his health impaired, he gave himself to personal reflections, came to a positive religious experience, and felt himself called to the Christian ministry. His family was of the Dutch Reformed Church and the circumstance of the church at the time appealed to him. The English language was just finding place in its pulpits, a movement was afoot for the education of ministers in America, and independence from the rule of the church in Holland was increasing; controversy on these matters divided the church into two parties.

Going to Holland to study theology, as was then the custom, he remained there from 1766 to 1770. He was examined by the Classis of Amsterdam, June, 1769, was licensed, and in April 1770, was ordained; he passed a vigorous examination at the University of Utrecht, May 16, 1770, and received the degree of doctor of theology. His distinction in family, education, and personal gifts was such that a call was sent to him by the church in New York to be one of its ministers, to preach chiefly in English, occasionally in Dutch. Accepting, he served this charge for forty years. On Nov. 26, 1775, he married his second cousin, Sarah, daughter of Philip Livingston [q.v.]. She died Dec. 29, 1814. They had one child.

Upon returning to New York Livingston became almost immediately an effectual influence in the church at large. Though so young, he set forth a plan of union, brought from Holland, which in about two years united the two opposing factions. The American party had secured from George III, in 1766, the charter for Queen's College, at New Brunswick, N. J., where in 1771 work was commenced. In 1774 the faculty at Utrecht recommended Livingston for the office of president and professor of theology, but because of the war no appointment was made. The British occupied New York, and Livingston, a Patriot, left the city. Until the close of hostilities he was in the Hudson River country, serving successively the churches of Kingston, Albany, Livingston Manor, and the two charges of Poughkeepsie and Red Hook. In 1783 he resumed his ministry in New York. The following year the General Synod of the Dutch Reformed Church elected him its professor of theology, establishing by this appointment the first theological seminary in the United States. Thenceforth he held the professorship in addition to his pastorate. He taught his students in New York and at times at Flatbush, Long Island. During this period he was also very active in the further organizing of the united church. He prepared its *Psalm Book* (1789), *The Psalms of David, with Hymns and Spiritual Songs . . . For the Use of the Reformed Dutch Church in North America* (1796), and also *The Constitution of the Reformed Dutch Church, in the United States of America,* accepted by the Synod in 1792 and published in 1793, a compilation of the church's law, worship, and doctrinal standards. He was zealous in communication with other church bodies in America and in the Old World, and zealous in the cause of foreign missions.

In 1810 he was chosen president of Queen's College (now Rutgers University), with the understanding that his duties in this office would be only formal, that his professorship of theology would continue and be his chief concern. He brought to New Brunswick his five theological students of that time. The college continued small and without adequate resources, and after a time its classes were omitted for some years. The theological classes continued, however, and other professors were associated with Livingston. After fifteen years in his new home and his twofold office, active to the end, he died in his sleep, at the age of seventy-nine.

Livingston published a number of sermons and addresses, including: *Oratio Inauguralis de Veritate Religionis Christianae* (1785); *The Glory of the Redeemer* (1799); *An Address Delivered at the Commencement Held at Queen's College in New-Jersey, Sept. 25, 1810* (1810); *A Funeral Service, or Meditations Adapted to Funeral Addresses* (1812); and *A Dissertation on the Marriage of a Man with his Sister-in-law* (1816). He had a fine physical presence; he was tall, of dignified bearing, and impressive public address. With high attainments in the classics and in theology and unusual spiritual qualities he combined a practical understanding of church affairs. He was the accepted leader who guided the Dutch Reformed Church, now the Reformed Church in America, to its complete and independent American organization.

[Alexander Gunn, *Memoirs of the Rev. John Henry Livingston* (1856); W. B. Sprague, *Annals Am. Pulpit*, vol. IX (1869); E. T. Corwin, *A Manual of the Ref. Ch. in America* (3rd ed., 1879); F. B. Dexter, *Biog. Sketches Grads. Yale Coll.* vol. II (1896); D. D. Demarest, *Hist. and Characteristics of the Ref. Prot. Dutch Church* (4th ed., 1889); W. H. S. Demarest, *A Hist. of Rutgers College* (1924); *Centennial of the Theol. Sem. of the Ref. Ch. in America* (1885); *Eccl. Records, State of N. Y.*, vol. VI (1905); *The Acts and Proc. of the Gen. Synod of the Ref. Prot. Ch. in North America*, vol. I (1859); C. C. Cuyler, *A Sermon Occasioned by the Death of the Rev. John H. Livingston* (1825); N. J. Marsellus, *A Sermon . . . on . . . the Death of the Rev. John H. Livingston* (1825); John De Witt, *The Path of the Just as the Shining Light; a Funeral Discourse* (1825).]   W. H. S. D.

LIVINGSTON, JOHN WILLIAM (May 22, 1804–Sept. 10, 1885), naval officer, the son of Eliza (Livingston) and William Turk, a surgeon in the United States navy, was born in New York City. In 1843, by act of the New York legislature, he and his wife, Mary A. (Livingston) Turk, changed their name to Livingston. Livingston, then John William Turk, was appointed a midshipman on Mar. 4, 1823. In his early years of service he was on the *Ontario*,

Delaware, and *Constitution* in the Mediterranean, and on the *Constellation* during the later years of the campaign against pirates in the West Indies. After being promoted to a lieutenancy in 1832, he cruised in the Pacific in the *Dolphin* and the *Fairchild* and returned to the United States in the frigate *Columbia*. On the voyage the *Columbia* proceeded to Muckie in the northern part of Sumatra, and, on New Year's Day of 1839, bombarded the village in punishment for outrages committed upon American ships and seamen trading for pepper on that coast. The *Columbia* then proceeded to China and the Sandwich Islands and home around Cape Horn.

During the Mexican War Livingston was executive officer of the *Congress* on the west coast of Mexico, and took part in several attacks on Mexican towns, especially Mazatlán, where he commanded the artillery division. Later he served in the East India Squadron. When he became a commander, in 1855, he was given the *St. Louis* on the coast of Africa, where he served from 1856 to 1858. Early in the Civil War he was in command of the steamer *Penguin* operating on the blockade of Wilmington and Hampton Roads and, later, of the steamer *Bienville*. He commanded the sailing frigate *Cumberland* but had left her, on account of sickness, before she was sunk by the *Merrimac*. After the recapture of the Norfolk navy yard in May 1862, he was made its commandant. From this duty he was detached in 1864 and sent to command the naval station at Mound City, Ill. In 1861 he had been commissioned captain and, in 1862, commodore. Although he held no other important post and had been retired in 1866 he was promoted rear admiral in 1868. He died in New York City.

[Files of the Bureau of Navigation in Washington; L. R. Hamersly, *The Records of Living Officers of the U. S. Navy*, 4th ed. (1890); *War of the Rebellion: Official Records* (Navy), esp. ser. 1, IV, V, VI, XXVII (1896–1917); for cruise of the *Columbia*, F. W. Taylor, *The Flagship* (1840), vol. I, esp. pp. 364, 387; for capture of Mazatlán, *U. S. Naval Institute Proc.*, May–June, 1915, pp. 894–95; *Jour. of the Assembly of the State of N. Y. . . . 1843* (1843), p. 155; *Army and Navy Jour.*, Sept. 12, 1885; *N. Y. Tribune*, Sept. 11, 1885.]   W. B. N.

LIVINGSTON, PETER VAN BRUGH (October 1710–Dec. 28, 1792), merchant, brother of Philip and William Livingston [*qq.v.*], was born at Albany, N. Y., and baptized Nov. 3, 1710. He was a grandson of Robert Livingston [*q.v.*], and the son of Philip Livingston, second lord of the manor, and of Catharine (Van Brugh). Most of his boyhood was spent in Albany, where his father served as secretary of Indian affairs during the latter years of Robert Livingston's life. He was educated at Yale, graduating in the class of 1731. Shortly after receiving his degree, he settled in New York City, and joined the mercantile interests of the little port. On Nov. 3, 1739, he married Mary Alexander, daughter of James Alexander [q.v.], a member of the council and surveyor-general of New Jersey, and sister of William [q.v.], who later married Livingston's sister Sarah. His business ventures prospered sufficiently to enable him to build a mansion in the Dutch tradition on Princess Street. During the French wars he accumulated a small fortune from government contracts for supplying various military expeditions. His privateering enterprises were likewise fortunate and profitable. Having formed a business arrangement with his brother-in-law, Alexander, he secured through his partner a commission from Governor Shirley to supply the army which was being equipped for an assault on Fort Niagara in 1755. The profits from this contract were partially dissipated during a protracted suit in chancery between Alexander and Livingston over the precise terms of their agreement. In his extensive mercantile operations Livingston was judged, even by his political foes, to belong to that group known as "fair traders and honest men" (Jones, post, II, 321). He found time during the busiest years of his career to serve from 1748 to 1761 as a trustee of the College of New Jersey, later Princeton. After the death of his first wife, in 1767, he married Elizabeth, widow of William Ricketts.

In provincial politics he was generally found on the side of the popular party, which was strongly Presbyterian in its religious preferences. For a time he was an able lieutenant in carrying out the plans of the Whig triumvirate consisting of his brother William, John Morin Scott, and William Smith, Jr. [qq.v.]. He heartily indorsed the merchants' memorials in 1763 and 1764 against Grenville's projects to raise a revenue in America and he seems to have been less alarmed than his wealthy colleagues by the high-handed tactics of the mechanics and small shopkeepers in the year of the Stamp Act. At any rate, in 1774 he took his stand with the radical wing of the Whig faction. A member of the Committee of Fifty-One, organized to choose delegates to the First Continental Congress, he protested against the attempt of the conservative merchants to dominate the committee and resigned in company with such radicals as Alexander MacDougall and Isaac Sears in order to give point to his protest. When John Adams stopped in New York on his way to the First Continental Congress he dined with Livingston and found him "an old man, extremely staunch

in the cause, and very sensible," who was not afraid of the extremists in New England. "He has been in trade," wrote Adams, "is rich, and now lives upon his income" (The Works of John Adams, vol. II, 1850, pp. 348, 351).

Livingston was a member of the Committee of Sixty organized in November 1774 to enforce the "Association" entered into by the Continental Congress and to assume such governmental powers as seemed necessary in the emergency. In this group the radicals had a clear majority, which they used to create the Committee of One Hundred, an extra-legal body charged with the responsibility for provincial affairs until the opening of the first provincial congress in 1775; Livingston was a member of this committee and was sent to the provincial congress, which promptly named him its presiding officer. In the summer of 1775 he was designated treasurer, but withdrew in August on the plea of ill-health and thereafter took no active part in provincial affairs. "With a continual slow fever," he wrote, "a reluctance to food, and a constant vigilance or want of sleep, I find myself reduced to the necessity of taking some measures to preserve life" (American Archives, 4 ser. III, 559). That the measures were efficacious is evident from the fact that he lived to be eighty-two, the last sixteen years of his life, if one may judge by the absence of his name from the public records, being spent in retirement. He died at Elizabethtown, N. J.

[E. B. Livingston, The Livingstons of Livingston Manor (1910); F. B. Dexter, Biog. Sketches Grads. Yale Coll., vol. I (1885); E. B. O'Callaghan, Docs. Relative to the Colonial History of the State of N. Y., vol. VI (1855); Peter Force, Am. Archives, 4 ser. III–V (1840–44), 5 ser. I–III (1848–53); C. L. Becker, The Hist. of Political Parties in the Province of N. Y. (1909); Wm. Smith, The Hist. of the Late Province of N. Y. (2 vols., 1829); Thomas Jones, Hist. of N. Y. during the Revolutionary War (2 vols., 1879), ed. by E. F. de Lancey; New-Jersey Journal (Elizabethtown), Jan. 2, 1793.]   J. A. K.

LIVINGSTON, PHILIP (Jan. 15, 1716–June 12, 1778), merchant, signer of the Declaration of Independence, gave generously of his time and money to a wide variety of philanthropic enterprises. Born at Albany, fifth son of Philip and Catharine (Van Brugh) Livingston, he was reared in the well-nigh princely style affected by his father, the second lord of the manor. He was awarded the degree of A.B. at Yale in 1737, thus entering the select company of less than a score in the province who had received collegiate training. He established himself as an importer in New York City and like his elder brother, Peter Van Brugh Livingston [q.v.], became closely identified with the commercial progress of the seaport. Understanding the devious ways of trade during the French wars, he realized handsomely upon his ventures, especially his privateering expeditions. Having married Christina, daughter of Col. Dirck Ten Broeck of Albany, on Apr. 14, 1740, he established his family in a comfortable town house on Duke Street and maintained a beautiful country seat on Brooklyn Heights, overlooking the harbor into which his ships brought his increasing wealth. In 1755 Sir Charles Hardy, then governor of the province, wrote: "Among the considerable merchants in this city no one is more esteemed for energy, promptness and public spirit than Philip Livingston" (Livingston, *post*, p. 170).

Livingston's subsequent career marked him as unique in his concern over civic affairs. He early deplored the province's lack of a collegiate establishment and was one of the first to advocate the founding of King's College, now Columbia. Though the Episcopalian control of the institution was not to his liking, he contributed to its support. Indeed, for his day there was a remarkable catholicity about his benefactions. Anglicans as well as the Presbyterians with whom he worshipped received his bounty. In 1746 he set aside a sum for the establishment at Yale of a professorship of divinity which still bears his name. He bore a hand in the building of the stone meeting house in John Street which housed the first Methodist society in America. Every sort of public enterprise was apt to arouse his enthusiasm. Recognizing the increased taste for good reading within the province, he helped to organize the New York Society Library in 1754 along the lines outlined by Benjamin Franklin and his colleagues in Philadelphia. About the same time he assumed the presidency (1756–57) of the newly established St. Andrew's Society, the earliest benevolent institution in New York City. With Leonard Lispenard, John Cruger, and others, in 1768 he collaborated in the organization of the New York Chamber of Commerce. When the New York Hospital was incorporated in 1771 he became a member of the first board of governors.

His civic interests gradually led him into politics, his apprenticeship being served in the board of aldermen, where he sat for nine years after 1754 as representative for the East Ward. In the developing struggle between the De Lanceys and the Livingstons, he supported the family whose name he bore, but his partisanship was never as intense as that of his younger brother, William [*q.v.*]. In his view the Whig faction, or popular party, was essentially a protest against the political ascendancy of certain groups whom

he did not like and a means of voicing in dignified fashion his belief that the province should enjoy a large measure of local autonomy. His religious nonconformity undoubtedly helped him to see the errors of the Anglican supporters of the De Lanceys. When the Livingstons achieved their first important victory, in the election of 1758, Philip was swept into the Assembly on a wave of anti-De Lancey votes. During his service in the lower house he was a determined foe of the financial policy brought forward by Grenville and other imperial administrators. In 1764 he helped phrase the address of the Assembly to Lieutenant-Governor Colden [*q.v.*], calling upon him to join in an endeavor to secure that "great badge of English liberty," the right of His Majesty's subjects everywhere to be taxed only with their own consent. When the Stamp Act became a reality, Livingston frowned upon the rioting of the "Sons of Liberty," but joined in the more dignified protests of lawyers and merchants. He was a member of the New York delegation which attended the Stamp Act Congress, spending most of his time apparently in consultation with the committee which drafted the protest to the House of Lords.

As the rift between the "Sons of Liberty" and the aristocratic leaders of the popular party widened, Livingston was inclined to favor a truce with the De Lanceys, that factional quarrels might be forgotten in the common cause of merchants and gentry against Parliamentary interference. He was elected to the Assembly for the third time in 1768 and on Oct. 27 was chosen speaker of the House. When the governor dissolved the Assembly in January 1769, Livingston hoped to win the support of moderate men in both the De Lancey and Livingston factions. Failing in this conciliatory gesture, he was defeated in New York City. Thereupon his nephew, Peter R. Livingston, withdrew and allowed him to be returned from the manor. The majority in the Assembly, refusing to recognize his right to sit for a "pocket borough" in which he did not reside, declared his seat vacant. Undismayed by this turn of events, he remained active in politics, emerging as one of the forceful but conservative leaders of the opposition to the "Intolerable Acts." In 1774 he served on the Committee of Fifty-One which named the New York delegates to the First Continental Congress and he was one of the five selected to attend the sessions at Philadelphia. At the moment he was in a distinctly conservative mood, weighing carefully the cost to colonial merchants of any disruption of normal trade with Great Britain. John Adams found him disinclined to listen to radical proposals. "Philip Livingston," he wrote, "is a great, rough rapid mortal. There is no holding any conversation with him. He blusters away; says if England should turn us adrift, we should instantly go to civil wars among ourselves" (*Works, post*, II, 351). Livingston became a member of the Committee of Sixty to enforce the terms of the "Association" and was placed on the Committee of One Hundred to carry forward provincial affairs until the meeting of the first provincial congress in 1775. He and his cousin, the second Robert R. Livingston [*q.v.*], were members both of the New York congress and the Second Continental Congress. They apparently had an arrangement whereby one would be in New York while the other was attending sessions in Philadelphia. It thus happened that Philip was in New York when the vote on Richard Henry Lee's historic resolution was taken, but he signed the Declaration of Independence in August 1776. He cannot, however, be regarded as one who forced an affirmative answer when the question of independence was raised.

Both in New York and in Philadelphia he rendered conscientious service on important committees. For his province he sat upon the committee "for the hearing and trial of disaffected persons of equivocal character." In the Continental Congress he was in turn a member of the Committee on Indian Affairs, the Treasury Board, the Marine Committee, the Committee on Commerce, and the board of commissioners to inspect the army under the command of Washington. His duties in Continental affairs were constantly interrupted by the demands of the province. In 1777 he was chosen by the convention of the state of New York as one of the senators from the southern district in the upper house of the new legislature. He attended the first meetings of this body and then, despite ill health and the protests of his family, he returned to the Continental Congress, then sitting at York, Pa. There he continued in the public service until his death in June 1778.

Philip Livingston's career as philanthropist and statesman was an interesting contrast to that of his acquisitive grandfather, Robert [*q.v.*], the founder of the family in America. He gave generously of his private fortune, pledging his personal credit without hope of future profit to maintain confidence in the Continental Congress. Honored by his generation for probity and ability, he was too dignified in bearing to win popularity and too austere in temper to arouse warm personal friendships. His intimate associates found behind his austerity and somewhat forbidding manner an affectionate disposition and a kindliness which constantly responded to urgent public appeals.

[E. B. Livingston, *The Livingstons of Livingston Manor* (1910); C. L. Becker, *The Hist. of Political Parties in the Province of N. Y.* (1909); Thomas Jones, *Hist. of N. Y. during the Revolutionary War* (2 vols., 1879), ed. by E. F. de Lancey; Martha J. Lamb, *Hist. of the City of N. Y.* (2 vols., 1877–81); Theodore Sedgwick, Jr., *A Memoir of the Life of William Livingston* (1833); *The Works of John Adams*, ed. by C. F. Adams, vol. II (1850); *Am. Archives*, 4 ser. III–V (1840–44), 5 ser. I–III (1848–53); *Journal of the Provincial Congress . . . of N. Y.* (1842); *Journal of the Votes and Proc. of the General Assembly of the Province of N. Y.* (1766); F. B. Dexter, *Biog. Sketches Grads. Yale Coll.*, vol. I (1885); John Sanderson, *Biog. of the Signers to the Declaration of Independence*, vol. III (1823).]

J.A.K.

LIVINGSTON, ROBERT (Dec. 13, 1654–Oct. 1, 1728), first lord of the manor of Livingston in New York, was born at Ancrum, Roxburghshire, Scotland, the son of John Livingston, a vigorous preacher of the Scottish church, and Janet Fleming, daughter of an Edinburgh merchant. His father belonged to a younger branch of the Livingstons of Callendar, who as earls of Linlithgow were important courtiers at Holyrood. When his son was nine years old, to avoid the displeasure of the episcopal party in Scotland after the Stuart restoration, Rev. John Livingston took his family to Rotterdam, where he became pastor of a Presbyterian congregation. Robert's boyhood was spent among the Scottish refugees whose children easily adopted the speech, manners, and customs of their Dutch neighbors. In April 1673, one year after his father's death, he sailed for New England, but his ultimate destination was the frontier village of Albany, where he appeared in 1674, the year that the province of New York was returned to the British by the Treaty of Westminster. The following year the young Scot, who was equally fluent in Dutch and English, was appointed town clerk of Albany and secretary of the board of commissioners for Indian affairs. He soon transformed the latter office from a mere clerkship to a position of control and direction; his reports and recommendations on Indian relations were of great importance to the successive governors of the province, with whom he came, consequently, to have considerable influence.

Both this influence and the knowledge of the Indian trade gained in his official position helped him to advance his larger plans to acquire wealth and standing in the community. Within five years of his coming to Albany he had purchased the Indian claims to choice tracts along the Hudson and had married (July 9, 1679) Alida Van Rensselaer, widow of Domine Nicholas Van Rensselaer and sister of Peter Schuyler [*qq.v.*]. This marriage brought him social connection with two of the most important families in the province, aristocratic landholders who expected and received favors from the Proprietor and the Crown. In 1686, by reason of his friendship with Governor Dongan, he secured a patent erecting his landholdings into the manor and lordship of Livingston. As later confirmed by a charter of George I, the manor consisted of more than 160,000 acres in the present counties of Dutchess and Columbia. This princely domain was made possible by income from public office carefully invested, by profits from governmental contracts, by interest on large sums advanced to the governor in anticipation of the collection of the provincial taxes, and by many pounds sterling drawn from private trade with the Indians and the French.

Though a supporter of the Stuarts, Livingston discreetly acknowledged the result of the Revolution of 1688 in England, but vigorously repudiated Jacob Leisler [q.v.] and his followers in New York. The aftermath of his opposition to the Leislerians was a series of attempts on the part of his political foes to deprive him of his offices and estates. Twice within ten years he visited England to defend his interests. On his first mission, in 1694–95, he made the acquaintance of the Earl of Bellomont [q.v.], to whom he recommended Capt. William Kidd [q.v.] as a suitable commander of a privateer to be fitted out against the pirates preying on British commerce. He returned to the colony as secretary of Indian affairs for life. Prior to the failure of the privateering venture through Kidd's treachery in turning pirate himself, Bellomont and Livingston were close friends, and when the former became governor he showered the Albany official with favors and summoned him to the Council. After Bellomont's death in 1701 Livingston's enemies persuaded the Assembly to sequestrate his estates. Again he sought help in England, remaining until 1705, when he returned to the province armed with a royal commission confirming him in all his offices and property. The provincial governors now turned to him for advice. Lord Cornbury [q.v.] leaned upon him heavily and Gov. Robert Hunter [q.v.] used his extensive knowledge of the fur trade and frontier conditions. The latter rewarded him with valuable contracts, notably in connection with the supply of provisions to the Palatine refugees, who were settled on land purchased from Livingston.

From 1709 to 1711 he was sent to the provincial Assembly from the Albany district, and five years later his manor returned him as its representative. Elected speaker in 1718, he displayed a marked tendency to support the Assembly in its frequent quarrels with the governor, a tendency which in his descendants took the form of more serious political nonconformity. Retiring from office in 1725 because of ill health, he died three years later. He left the manor to his son Philip, who in 1721 had become his deputy as secretary for Indian affairs and succeeded him in that office and on the Council. A younger son, Robert, received 13,000 acres at "Clermont."

To the end of his days Livingston persisted in his efforts to draw a considerable income from public office. Governor Fletcher wrote of him in 1696: "He has made a considerable fortune . . ., never disbursing six pence but with the expectation of twelve pence, his beginning being a little Book keeper, he has screwed himself into one of the most considerable estates in the province . . . he had rather be called knave Livingston then poor Livingston" (Documents, post, IV, 251), while in a moment of anger over army contracts Bellomont charged that he had "pinched an estate out of the poor soldiers' bellies" (Ibid., IV, 720). In him was a curious mixture of the steadfast courage of the Covenanter and the grasping shrewdness of the trader. His success in winning the support of the British government for his private ventures marked him as a courtier and diplomat of no mean ability. In some measure that success was probably due to his genial presence and courtly manner, which easily won him friends who quickly discerned his intelligence and resourcefulness.

[E. B. O'Callaghan, Docs. Relative to the Colonial Hist. of the State of N. Y., vols. III–V (1853–55), and The Doc. Hist. of the State of N. Y., vols. I–III, 8vo. ed. (1849–50); Wm. Smith, The Hist. of the Late Province of N. Y. (2 vols., 1829); E. B. Livingston, The Livingstons of Livingston Manor (1910); W. L. Fleming, "The Public Career of Robert Livingston," a scholarly article in N. Y. Geneal. and Biog. Record, July–Oct., 1901; Peter Wraxall, An Abridgement of the Indian Affairs . . . Transacted in the Colony of N. Y., from the Year 1678 to the Year 1751 (1915), ed. by C. H. McIlwain.]   J.A.K.

LIVINGSTON, ROBERT R. (August 1718–Dec. 9, 1775), jurist, Revolutionary patriot, baptized Aug. 30, 1718, was the only son of Robert Livingston of "Clermont," who was a younger son of Robert [q.v.], first lord of Livingston Manor in New York; his mother, Margaret Howarden, was of English ancestry. In accordance with a custom common in New York families at that time, he was known as Robert R., to distinguish him, as Robert son of Robert, from other Roberts in the family. On Dec. 8, 1742, he married Margaret Beekman, only daughter of Col. Henry Beekman of Rhinebeck and his wife, Janet Livingston, who was a daughter of Robert Livingston (nephew of the first lord) and of Margaretta Schuyler. His wife's rich inheritance, added to "Clermont," made him one of the greatest landholders of the province. Of his four sons, two, Robert R. and Edward [*qq.v.*], took conspicuous part in public life, while four of his five daughters made notable marriages, bringing into the family connection Gen. Richard Montgomery, Freeborn Garrettson, the Methodist preacher, Morgan Lewis, later governor of the state, and John Armstrong, 1758–1843, soldier, diplomat, and secretary of war.

Livingston applied himself early to legal studies and devoted himself all his life to the law and politics. In 1756 he was recommended to the Board of Trade by Governor Hardy to fill a vacancy in the Council, but was not appointed. From 1758 to 1768 he served as member of the Assembly from Dutchess County and in 1762 promoted a compromise whereby a loan was made to Parliament to pay bounties for volunteers requisitioned by Sir Jeffery Amherst. He was appointed judge of the Admiralty court in 1759 and in January 1763 was made puisne judge of the supreme court of the Colony. The acceptance at this time by Livingston and the other judges of commissions on tenure of the King's will marked the cessation of a bitter struggle over the independence of the judiciary. When in 1764 the question arose of the right to appeal from the courts to the governor and Council, Livingston, being one of the judges who refused to allow appeal, became one of the leading antagonists of Lieutenant-Governor Cadwallader Colden [*q.v.*] in his effort to establish that right, and Colden, in letters to the Lords of Trade and to the Earl of Halifax (Jan. 22, 23, 1765), sought his removal from the bench, but without success.

Livingston was chairman of the New York committee of correspondence appointed to concert measures with the other colonies in opposition to the execution of the Stamp Act, and was one of the earliest promoters of the movement which culminated in the Stamp Act Congress. As a member of that body his most important service was the drafting of the address to the King, but he was also a leader in debate. He proposed a series of resolves which embodied a plan of confederation providing a permanent congress to assign to each colony a quota to be raised for imperial purposes by each colony in its own way. Although these resolves were couched in mild language, they referred to the possibility that "the wish to retain" the Mother Country might be weakened. Ten years later, writing to his son in the Continental Congress, Livingston displayed similar views: he still op-

posed independence, favoring conciliation, yet recognized that conditions might in time require more aggressive tactics.

In 1768 he lost his seat in the Assembly. The following year, when his cousin Philip [*q.v.*], elected from Livingston Manor, was refused admittance, Robert R. Livingston was chosen in his stead. The now conservative Assembly, however, anticipating his election, had passed a resolution that henceforth no judge should be allowed to take a seat. He was therefore rejected, but continued the struggle, and when he finally relinquished his claim in favor of Philip's nephew, Peter R. Livingston, who became a member in February 1774, he had been five times elected by the manor and as many times rejected by the Assembly. In April 1768 he had been named for the Council a second time, by Governor Moore, but his previous political activity made his appointment out of the question. In 1767 and again in 1773 he was one of the commissioners to settle the New York–Massachusetts boundary, which the Livingston lands adjoined. Amiable, admired by a wide circle of personal friends, social in disposition, he had a career illustrative of many phases of the conditions and conflicts of pre-Revolutionary New York. Though an Anglican and a great landholder, he was a leader of the "Whig" interest: in imperial problems he was ready to go as far as necessary to assure the colonies' economic welfare; little influenced by the philosophy of revolution, he was opposed to going further merely for the sake of principle.

[Published material includes: E. B. Livingston, *The Livingstons of Livingston Manor* (1910); T. S. Clarkson, *A Biog. Hist. of Clermont* (1869); A. M. Keys, *Cadwallader Colden* (1906); C. L. Becker, *The Hist. of Political Parties in the Province of N. Y. 1760–76* (1909); E. B. O'Callaghan, *Docs. Relative to the Colonial Hist. of the State of N. Y.*, vols. VII, VIII (1856–57); *Journal . . . of the Gen. Assembly of the Colony of N. Y.*, vol. II (1766); *Journal of the First Congress of the American Colonies in Opposition to the Tyrannical Acts of the British Parliament* (1845), ed. by Lewis Cruger; *The Address of Mr. Justice Livingston to the House of Assembly of N. Y. in Support of his Right to a Seat* (1769). Manuscript material is found in the Olin Collection, Bancroft Transcripts, and William Smith Papers in N. Y. Pub. Lib.; John Ross Delafield, Johnston Redmond, and L. W. Smith collections in private hands; and in the MSS. Div., Lib. of Cong.]
R. C. H.

LIVINGSTON, ROBERT R. (Nov. 27, 1746–Feb. 26, 1813), chancellor of New York, statesman, diplomat, farmer, experimenter, was born in New York City, the second child and eldest son of Judge Robert R. Livingston [*q.v.*] and Margaret Beekman his wife. He was a brother of Edward Livingston [*q.v.*]. Many were his relatives in public life, notably, the Revolutionary leaders Philip, William, and Peter Van

Brugh Livingston [*qq.v.*], his cousins, and John Armstrong, Richard Montgomery, and Morgan Lewis [*qq.v.*], his brothers-in-law. Much of his significance as an historical figure is due to the unofficial and largely unchronicled influence he wielded after becoming the most important member of the family group. His formal education was acquired at King's College, where he graduated with the class of 1765. At the college Commencement in Trinity Church he delivered a speech (as did each of his classmates) which was reported by the uniformly appreciative *New York Mercury* (May 27, 1765) as "a spirited Oration in Praise of Liberty. . . . The graceful young speaker, animated with his noble subject, gave the highest satisfaction." When he left college he studied law, as his father and grandfather had done, at first in the office of his cousin, William Livingston, then with William Smith, Jr., the colonial judge. Admitted to the bar in 1770, he practised for a time in partnership with John Jay. On Sept. 9, 1770, he married Mary, daughter of John Stevens and sister of John Stevens, the inventor [*q.v.*]. Of this marriage two daughters were born. In 1773 he received his first political office, the only one he held under the Crown, recorder of the City of New York, by virtue of which he presided over certain criminal trials. In 1775, his revolutionary sympathies having made him no longer acceptable, he was replaced.

In the same year he was elected delegate to the Continental Congress, in which he served during 1775–76, 1779–81, and 1784–85. The best-known but least important of his activities during his first period of service in this body was his membership in the committee of five appointed to draft a declaration of independence. Probably the chief motive of his appointment was a politic attempt to gain for the idea of independence the support of the hesitating province of New York. His personal opinion was that independence was inevitable and necessary, but at that time inexpedient, and in debate he was, according to Jefferson, one of the chief speakers for a postponement of the issue. When independence was considered on July 2 every colony voted affirmatively except New York, whose delegation was excused from voting because it was not authorized to do so by the New York convention. On the 9th a newly elected convention declared for independence. On July 15 Livingston left for New York to take a seat in that body, and was therefore absent when the signing of the engrossed copy of the Declaration began on Aug. 2. Thus it happened that, although a member of the drafting committee, he neither voted for nor signed the Declaration of Independence.

Far more important, although not spectacular, was his other work in Congress. He served on the committees to draft an address to the people of Great Britain, to confer with the New York convention regarding the defense of the Hudson, to confer with Washington and Schuyler on military affairs, to investigate the powder supply; on the committee of ways and means, and as the representative of New York on the committee to draw up a plan of confederation. During his second period of attendance on Congress (1779–81) he was even busier. He was an active member of committees on financial affairs, supplies, legal organization, foreign affairs, military problems, and special correspondence. In the dispatch book of Congress, listing committees, reports, and commitments, his name often appears three or four times on a page, increasing steadily in frequency until 1781. Few other members were more indefatigable or more in demand as committee members, and probably no one else showed a greater versatility in the variety of work in which he engaged. Notable in this activity was his membership on committees for establishing a court of appeals, drafting commissions for its judges, and preparing their instructions. Early in 1780 he was nominated as judge of this court, but he apparently declined to be considered for the position (Burnett, *post*, V, 12). He wrote many reports, of which perhaps the most important was that adopted by Congress, Dec. 14, 1779, describing the financial exigencies of the general government and recommending methods of meeting them. In August of the following year he was added to the ways and means committee and later was one of those with whom Robert Morris corresponded on financial matters.

On Jan. 10, 1781, Congress by resolve established a department of foreign affairs; on Aug. 10, Livingston, then enjoying at "Clermont" a brief respite from public affairs, was elected secretary of this department, having at different times been nominated by both Lloyd and Varnum. Various other leaders and local favorites had been nominated, but only Arthur Lee made a real attempt to secure the office. Livingston was the candidate most acceptable to France, and Luzerne claimed that he influenced the election in his behalf. The most important of Livingston's diplomatic correspondence while secretary related to the negotiations of peace with Great Britain. He approved the instructions to the American commissioners at Paris, directing them to act with the knowledge and concurrence of France, and did not share Jay's suspicions, which were intensified by Marbois' famous letter recommending that the United States be excluded from the fisheries. This was, he held, the unauthorized expression of a subordinate, not that of the French court whose interests, in his opinion, coincided with those of the United States. He deplored the secret article relating to the Florida boundary and communicated it to Luzerne, with explanations designed to prevent a sense of injury on the part of France. When the treaty was submitted by the commissioners, he approved it as a whole, but reprimanded them for their manner of negotiating without the full concurrence of France, eliciting a defense of their conduct in which even Franklin joined. During the negotiations he sent quantities of ammunition for the diplomatic battle: arguments for extended boundaries, for fishing rights, and against the repatriation of Loyalists; discussions of Western territories and West Indian trade; and warnings that the boundary of Florida, if held by Spain, should be definitely specified. He recommended minor improvements in the provisional treaty which were incorporated in the definitive treaty.

He ended the practice, which had been followed by countries that had not recognized American independence, of treating with Franklin at Paris through the agency of France instead of directly as the representative of a free nation. He limited his dealings with Rendon, the unofficial Spanish agent in the United States, because the latter was without full credentials; and he approved Jay's dignified course at Madrid, recommending that Jay, when Aranda wished to treat in 1782, repay the latter for Spain's previous hauteur "with all the delays we can interpose" (to Jay, Dec. 30, 1782, Wharton, *post,* IV, 176). He advocated the appointment of Americans only to diplomatic and consular posts, opposing accordingly Adams' proposal to appoint R. F. W. Dumas as chargé d'affaires, and his policy was subsequently adopted by Congress. Strongly adverse to Congress' unfortunate practice of sending diplomats to many European courts, he expedited the recall of Francis Dana from Russia and prevented the establishment of diplomatic agents in Lisbon and in Brussels.

The establishment of the department of foreign affairs marked an advance in the development of American executive machinery. The enterprising, painstaking, and systematic, but not unimaginative way in which Livingston proceeded in the securing of quarters and assistants, the filing of correspondence and reports, and the establishing of routine practices did much to combat the vagueness of the methods of Congress. He kept the military leaders informed of political developments; sent to the state governments circular letters, foreign-news dispatches, and information as to the bearing of state activity on the foreign prestige and obligations of the Republic; and made digests of European news for the information of Congress. He resigned, on Dec. 2, 1782, because of the inadequacy of his salary, which, he reported, was $3,000 a year less than the expenses of the office. His resignation may also have been due in part to the inconsistent and, according to Madison, "frequently improper" actions of Congress. He was twice induced by Congress to prolong his stay, first until Jan. 1, 1783, and thereafter until May. It was June when he finally left for "Clermont." Unfortunately the office thereafter became for a time practically non-existent and a large part of Livingston's work of organization was undone. The noteworthy events of his third period of attendance upon Congress (1784–85) were his motion to appoint a minister to Great Britain, the adoption of which created the post to which Adams was elected in 1785; his membership on the committee to define such duties of the court of appeals as related to matters referred to it by the secretary for foreign affairs; his candidacy, never resulting in election, for the posts of minister to Great Britain, Spain, and the Netherlands; and his activity on several committees.

Far from being engrossed in federal concerns, Livingston was deeply involved in the public affairs of his state. He was a leader in the successive Revolutionary organizations that replaced the imperial governmental machinery: the New York congress and committee of safety of 1776; the council of safety of 1777; and the commission to carry on the government during the interval between the adoption of a state constitution and the time when it began to function. After the war he was a member of the commission to govern New York following the British evacuation, and of the commissions to fix on a boundary with Massachusetts in 1784, and with Vermont in 1790. In 1811 he was on the first canal commission, which projected plans that were later realized in the Erie Canal. More important was his membership on the committee to draft the first New York constitution, drawn up in 1777. His principal contribution to this instrument was the council of revision, consisting of the governor, the chancellor and the justices of the supreme court, which should exercise the veto power.

Although he is usually identified by the title,

"Chancellor," "the one undisputed fact in his Chancellorship is that he held the position from 1777 to 1801" (James Brown Scott, *post*), for there were no chancery reports in his time. He drew up "Rules in Chancery" to guide the court, but Chancellor Kent later wrote that there was not a single dictum of his predecessors to guide him. According to Chancellor Jones, this court "never boasted a more prompt, more able or more faithful officer" (*Albany Law Journal*, Apr. 9, 1881, quoting J. W. Francis), and Jefferson described him as "one of the ablest of American lawyers." Noteworthy among his opinions in the records of the council of revision are those opposing the confiscation and alienation laws directed against the Loyalists, laws granting special powers to the magistracy (lest the freedom of the citizenry be endangered), special taxes, the paper money bill of 1786, and the bill of 1785 to abolish slavery in New York. By virtue of his office as chancellor he administered the oath to President Washington in 1789.

In the New York ratifying convention he not only led the influential Livingston factions in support of the federal Constitution but was also one of the most frequent speakers. He proposed and carried a resolution that only after the whole of the Constitution had been considered, each part in turn, should any vote be put on any clause or amendment, thus preventing the possible rejection of the whole by an adverse vote on the most criticized part, and forestalling attempts at obstruction by multiplying amendments. Excepting Hamilton, possibly no individual at this time contributed more toward the success of Federalism in New York. Nevertheless, in the distribution of patronage Livingston was entirely overlooked by the new government. Carrying with him the numerous family group, he became a Republican some time before 1791, when he successfully supported Burr for Philip Schuyler's place in the United States Senate. He disagreed with Hamilton's financial plans, especially the plan for funding the debt. Washington's offer, in 1794, of the ministry to France, in succession to Morris, seemed an afterthought and was declined. He became one of the leading opponents of Jay's treaty, publishing against it, as "Cato," *Examination of the Treaty of Amity, Commerce, and Navigation, Between the United States and Great Britain* (1795). In the first election for governor he had received an unsolicited nominal vote. In 1795 he ran for the office, but was defeated by Jay. In 1800 Jefferson offered him the secretaryship of the navy, which he declined, but early the following year he accepted the appointment as minister to France.

In October 1801, a year after the treaty of San Ildefonso, he sailed with two principal objectives: first, to prevent the rumored retrocession of Louisiana to France, and if too late for that, to acquire West Florida for the United States; second, to negotiate for the payment of American claims arising from French spoliations. Soon suspecting, in spite of the repeated denials of French officials, that the delivery of Louisiana to France had already been made, he decided that it would be fruitless to raise objections to this at Paris (to Madison, Jan. 13, 1802, *American State Papers, Foreign Relations*, II, 1832, p. 513). Nevertheless, he sought through Rufus King in London to induce Great Britain, during the peace negotiations at Amiens, to put obstacles in the way of the cession (to King, Mar. 10, 1802, *Ibid.*, II, 515). In his representations to the French court Livingston was met by Talleyrand with a policy of silence and inattention; and he finally sent a strong note of remonstrance to that minister, who was obliged to make a verbal apology and, through Marbois, a written explanation (Livingston to Madison, Nov. 2, 1802, State Department Archives). Subsequently, Livingston repeatedly assured his friends that his treatment was better than that of other diplomatic representatives in Paris.

Of his policy in the negotiations leading to the Louisiana purchase he has left his own account: "I had long forseen that the possession of the East bank of the Mississippi . . . would be insufficient. . . . I therefore (though without powers) . . . endeavored to satisfy the people in power here, that . . . it was proper to give us all the country above the Arkansas. . . . In March I ventured upon what was here considered as a bold and hazardous measure a direct and forcible address to him [Napoleon] personally on the subject of our claims upon which having received from him a positive assurance that they should be fully and promptly paid, I began to look forward to this as a means of accomplishing my other object because I was sure he could not, . . . in case of a war, . . . find any other means of discharging it" (Livingston to Mitchell, July 13, 1803, Columbia University Library, "Letters to Clinton, Miscellaneous 34"). Livingston took advantage of the excitement in the United States following the closing of the Mississippi by transmitting to Talleyrand as soon as he received it (Apr. 8, 1803), Senator James Ross's resolution for an armed expedition against New Orleans (*American State Papers, Foreign Relations*, II, 552), with a note expressing his expectation that the threat would be fulfilled. When Napoleon, foreseeing the difficulty of retaining Louisiana during the impending war with Great Britain, suddenly offered to sell the whole, Livingston after waiting in order to act concurrently with Monroe, who was on his way to join him, seized the opportunity; and after some profitable haggling over the price, sixty million francs and payment of the spoliation claims by the United States was agreed upon (May 2, antedated to Apr. 30). This was, according to Henry Adams, "the greatest diplomatic success recorded in American history" (*History of the United States,* II, 48). "From this day," said Livingston as he signed the treaty, "the United States take their place among the powers of the first rank" (E. B. Livingston, *post,* p. 372). He believed that the treaty would "forever exclude us from the politics of this stormy quarter of the globe" (to Madison, June 3, 1803, *American State Papers, Foreign Relations,* II, 563).

Talleyrand refused to say whether West Florida was included in the purchase, in spite of repeated questions and even threats. Although Livingston previously held that Florida was not so included, shortly after the treaty was signed he formulated the theory that the treaty of retrocession, based on the original session of 1762, indicated that West Florida was a part of the purchase. This theory later became the basis of American policy. Another qualification of his success lay in the faults of the claims convention which later caused Livingston much bitterness. As a minister, Livingston displayed great pertinacity and the courage to undertake firm measures, as well as capacity to overcome the handicaps of deafness and imperfect command of French. While often deploring the lack of instructions, he did not hesitate to act boldly without them. By the French he was regarded as a "most importunate" negotiator and some of his arguments seemed "almost menacing." He hated a quarrel but, even more, he hated degrading submission which never prevents one. Tact also he showed, as, for example, when on his arrival he allayed the fears that he was a "violent democrat" and "on every occasion . . . carefully avoided entering into any party matters" (Livingston to Janet Montgomery, May 9, 1802, John Ross Delafield Manuscripts).

Livingston resigned in the autumn of 1804. He was given a cordial leave-taking by Napoleon, and after a visit to London and several months' travel with his family in Europe he returned to "Clermont," where he lived the rest of his life in political retirement. He devoted his leisure to a wide range of intellectual interests and hobbies. He had designed and built near "Clermont" a beautiful house which he embellished with the many fine things he brought from France—books, paintings, furniture, silver, Gobelin tapestries. Much of his time he occupied with the study of agriculture, corresponding with Washington, Jefferson, and his friends abroad in the interest of scientific methods. He was a pioneer in the importation of Merino sheep and in the use of gypsum as fertilizer. He was one of the organizers, in 1791, of a society subsequently called the Society for the Promotion of Useful Arts, served as president from 1791 to his death, and contributed to its publications. (There is "An Eulogium" upon him in the *Transactions,* vol. III, 1814.) His scientific curiosity expressed itself also in his interest in paleontology.

He had been associated with the attempts in steam navigation of Fitch, Morey, Stevens, and Nicholas Roosevelt, and in 1798 had undertaken the construction of a steamboat. His aid, which was technical as well as financial, made possible the experiment of Robert Fulton [*q.v.*] on the Seine and later the success of the *Clermont* on the Hudson. "It is doubtful whether Fulton would have done anything in steam navigation . . . had it not been for the arrival [of Livingston] in France . . ." (H. W. Dickinson, *Robert Fulton, Engineer and Artist,* 1913, p. 134). From the beginning, he sought exclusive rights in steam navigation. His great political influence enabled him to secure the grant of a New York monopoly in 1798 (on conditions, however, which his boat failed to fulfill), the renewal of this monopoly in 1803 in his and Fulton's joint interest, and supplementary laws in 1808 and 1811. The monopoly was popularly felt to be onerous, New Jersey, Connecticut, and Ohio all passing retaliatory laws relating to navigation on interjacent waters, but Livingston turned his earnings back into the business, and the money from the monopoly was partly responsible for the rapidity with which the steamboat was developed (*Ibid.,* p. 267). The difficulty of maintaining the monopoly was great, and in the consequent litigation and pamphlet warfare Livingston was personally very active, visiting the Assembly to urge legislation, outlining argument for counsel, and maintaining the right of the state to erect a monopoly in a correspondence with his brother-in-law and rival, John Stevens [*q.v.*]. Undaunted by competition, the partners extended their operations to the Mississippi, and petitioned the legislature of Virginia for a monopoly on the James River. Legal conflict over the New York monopoly continued after Livingston's death and was ended only by the decision in the case of *Gibbons* vs. *Ogden*.

Livingston was founder and first president of the American Academy of Fine Arts, and trustee of the New York Society Library. As a versatile intellectual luminary, a jurist, and a political leader, he occupied a higher place in the esteem of his contemporaries than it has been his lot to retain in the memory of his countrymen.

[Date of death here given is from E. B. Livingston, *post*, and *Albany Argus*, Mar. 2, 1813; the *Albany Reg.*, and the N. Y. *Evening Post*, Mar. 2, and other papers, give Feb. 25. Good biographical sketches are M. L. Bonham, Jr., "Robert Livingston," in S. F. Bemis, ed., *The Am. Secretaries of State and Their Diplomacy*, vol. I (1927); E. B. Livingston, *The Livingstons of Livingston Manor* (1910); J. L. Delafield, "Chancellor Robert R. Livingston of New York and His Family," in *Sixteenth Annual Report, 1911, of the Am. Scenic and Historic Preservation Soc.* (1911). Other sketches of some value are Frederic DePeyster, *A Biog. Sketch of Robert R. Livingston* (1876); James Brown Scott, in *Great Am. Lawyers*, ed. by W. D. Lewis, vol. I (1907), and John Bassett Moore, "Robert R. Livingston and the La. Purchase," *Columbia Univ. Quart.*, June 1904; D. S. Alexander, "Robert R. Livingston, the Author of the La. Purchase," in *Proc. N. Y. State Hist. Asso., the Seventh Ann. Meeting* (1906). Also to be consulted are Theodore Sedgwick, Jr., *A Memoir of the Life of William Livingston* (1833); C. H. Hunt, *Life of Edward Livingston* (1864); T. S. Clarkson, *A Biog. Hist. of Clermont* (1869); Henry Adams, *Hist. of the U. S.* (9 vols., 1889–90); D. S. Alexander, *A Pol. Hist. of the State of N. Y.*, vol. I (1906); J. D. Hammond, *The Hist. of Pol. Parties in the State of New-York*, vol. I (1842); C. E. Hill, "James Madison," in S. F. Bemis, ed., *The Am. Secretaries of State and Their Diplomacy*, vol. III (1927). Much of the information available in printed form is in published collections of documents: W. C. Ford and Gaillard Hunt, *Jours. of the Continental Cong.* (27 vols., 1904–28); E. C. Burnett, *Letters of Members of the Continental Cong.*, vols. I–V (1921–31); Jonathan Elliot, *The Debates in the Several State Conventions, on the Adoption of the Federal Constitution*, vol. II (1836); Peter Force, *Am. Archives* (9 vols., 1837–53); Francis Wharton, *The Revolutionary Dipl. Correspondence of the U. S.* (6 vols., 1889); *Am. State Papers, Foreign Relations*, vol. II (1832); "State Papers and Correspondence bearing on the Purchase of La.," *House Doc. 431, 57 Cong., 2 Sess.*; A. B. Street, *The Council of Revision of the State of N. Y.* (1859). The manuscript sources are scattered among public repositories, family archives, and private collections. The Lib. of Cong. has the papers of the Continental Congress, including letters of Livingston and the committee for foreign affairs, and pertinent material in the papers of Livingston's contemporaries and in the British transcripts. The N. Y. Public Lib. has a box of Livingston papers and pertinent material in the Emmett, Olin, and Bancroft papers; the Department of State has Livingston's official correspondence while minister; the N. Y. Hist. Soc. has his minutes of the debates in the ratifying convention, his account books, and other material; the Columbia Univ. Library, the Pa. Hist. Soc., the Huntington Library, the Mass. Hist. Soc., each has from a few to several dozen Livingston papers.]   R. C. H.

LIVINGSTON, WILLIAM (November 1723–July 25, 1790), lawyer, first governor of the state of New Jersey, grandson of Robert and brother of Philip and Peter Van Brugh Livingston [*qq.v.*], was in many ways the ablest of the

sons of Philip and Catharine (Van Brugh) Livingston. He was born at Albany (baptized Dec. 8, 1723), and spent his childhood there under the indulgent care of his maternal grandmother, Sarah Van Brugh. At the age of fourteen he lived for a year with a missionary among the friendly Mohawks, an experience which his family felt would be valuable if the lad turned his attention later to the fur trade or the possibilities of land speculation on the frontier. The following year he was sent to New Haven to follow the path chosen by his three elder brothers. He graduated from Yale in the class of 1741. While in college he decided that law had a larger claim than mercantile affairs upon his interest. Accordingly, he avoided his brothers' counting-houses in New York City and entered the law office of James Alexander [*q.v.*], who had been a vigorous champion of the freedom of the press in connection with the Zenger trial. Under such preceptors as Alexander and William Smith, 1697–1769 [*q.v.*], both veteran advocates of Whiggish tendencies, Livingston became confirmed in political views distinctly liberal for his generation. His intimate associates among the younger men were John Morin Scott [*q.v.*], William Peartree Smith, and William Smith, Jr. [*q.v.*], the historian, with whom he prepared a digest of the provincial laws (1752, 1762). Around these three gathered a group of sturdy Calvinists who courageously objected to the dominant position of the Anglican gentry and their allies in provincial politics. About 1745, before he had completed his legal studies, Livingston married Susanna French, the daughter of a wealthy New Jersey landholder. Henry Brockholst Livingston [*q.v.*] was their son; their daughter Susanna married John Cleves Symmes [*q.v.*], their daughter Sarah became the wife of John Jay [*q.v.*].

From the day of his admission to the bar in 1748 Livingston was a leader among those of assured position who liked to be known as supporters of the popular cause. Petulant and impatient of restraint, he soon aroused the resentment of the conservatives by his sweeping criticism of established institutions. Always more facile in writing than in speech, he delighted to compose satirical verse and witty broadsides which earned him a greater reputation as a censor than as a satirist. A young lady of his acquaintance, alluding to his tall, slender, and graceless figure, named him the "whipping-post."

In 1751 the controversy over the establishment of a college in the province became a focal point in his developing political philosophy. Although anxious to promote a collegiate foundation, he protested against the plan to place the institution in the hands of a board of trustees dominated by the Episcopalians and refused to serve as a representative of the Presbyterians on the board. To him the proposal appeared as the first step toward establishing the Anglican Church in New York and giving it general supervision of educational matters. His views were ably presented in the *Independent Reflector,* a weekly which his friends inaugurated in 1752 "to oppose superstition, bigotry, priestcraft, tyranny, servitude, public mismanagement and dishonesty in office" and to teach the "inestimable value of liberty." On the question of the college he took the stand that the institution should be non-sectarian and catholic, that it should be established not by royal charter but by act of the Assembly, and that the trustees and faculty should be subject to no religious or political tests. Though he failed to prevent the chartering of King's College by George II, his efforts were responsible for the diversion of half of the "college fund" to the building of a jail and pest house.

His contributions to the *Independent Reflector* and the "Watch Tower" column in the *New York Mercury* violently attacked the movement to establish an Anglican episcopacy in America and accused the faction, headed by Lieutenant-Governor James De Lancey [*q.v.*], of favoring the union of church and state. His appeals on this issue aroused the nonconformists and strengthened the liberal party, which was rapidly becoming a Livingston faction in provincial politics. The first important victory of the Livingstons at the polls resulted in driving the De Lanceys from their control of the Assembly in 1758. William Livingston was accorded a position of leadership not only in the councils of the party but also in its tactics in the legislative body. He was determined in his opposition to Parliamentary interference in provincial affairs. Convinced of the desirability of provincial home rule, he was equally persuaded of the necessity of the wealthy liberals continuing to rule at home. As the issues raised by Grenville's tax program reached a crisis, the unity of the Livingston forces was seriously threatened, for the patrician elements in the party were troubled by the violent reaction of the plebeian groups to the Stamp Act. Livingston labored hard to reconcile the "Sons of Liberty" and other radicals to the moderate leadership which his family represented, but the masses were dissatisfied with the temporizing Whigs. Even the attack on the Anglicans, which he renewed in his *Letter to the Right Reverend Father in God, John, Lord Bishop of Landaff* (1768), no longer aroused the voters.

In the election of 1769 the De Lanceys won a decisive victory and secured a majority in the Assembly. William Livingston's power was gone for the moment. In disappointment he penned *A Soliloquy* (1770), purporting to be a meditation of Lieutenant-Governor Colden, which beneath a thin veneer of satire was an unsparing invective against the provincial representatives of British authority.

Never entirely happy in his legal work and temporarily dispirited by the turn of his political fortunes, Livingston determined to retire to his country estate near Elizabethtown, N. J. Years earlier, in his *Philosophic Solitude* (1747), he had ventured to reveal in verse his longing for the quiet of the countryside. In May 1772 he laid out pretentious grounds, planted an extensive orchard, and erected a mansion known as "Liberty Hall." There he began life anew as a gentleman farmer, but he did not find solitude. The removal to New Jersey was merely a prelude to a career more illustrious than the one just finished in New York politics. Becoming a member of the Essex County Committee of Correspondence, he quickly rose to a position of leadership and was one of the province's delegates to the First Continental Congress. There he served on the committee with his son-in-law, John Jay, and Richard Henry Lee [*qq.v.*] to draft an address to the people of British America. He was returned as a deputy to the Second Continental Congress, serving until June 5, 1776, when he assumed command of the New Jersey militia. It was a responsibility extremely irksome to him, yet he discharged his duties with his usual conscientiousness until the legislature under the new constitution elected him first governor of the state. For the next fourteen years he bore the responsibilities of the governorship during the extraordinary conditions of war and reconstruction. The multitudinous duties, civil and military, the threats of the enemy, and the disloyalty of friends harassed his nervous and excitable temper but failed to overcome his spirited support of the patriot cause. Rivington's *Royal Gazette* dubbed him the "Don Quixote of the Jerseys."

His boundless energy was an incalculable asset during the gloomiest period of the war. When peace came his messages to the legislature dealt discriminatingly and comprehensively with the problems of reconstruction. He opposed the cheapening of the currency by unrestricted issues of paper money, counseled moderation in dealing with the Loyalists and their property, and looked forward to the day when the question of slavery would be settled on the basis of gradual emancipation. As authority slipped out of the hands of Congress, he called for a revision of the Articles of Confederation, in which he was privileged to participate at the Federal Convention of 1787. Though he was not conspicuous in debate, he ably supported the New Jersey plan and worked for a compromise that would mean success. His influence was largely responsible for the alacrity and unanimity with which the state convention ratified the Constitution. Two years later, while he was resting at Elizabethtown, his years of public service came to an end.

Though his life was spent in the excitement of political strife and affairs of state, he longed for the quieter routine of the farmer. After his removal to New Jersey he managed to devote some time to experiments in gardening, becoming an active member of the Philadelphia Society for the Promotion of Agriculture. It was his pleasure to show his friends his vegetables at "Liberty Hall." Among his intimates and in an ever-widening circle of acquaintances he was honored for his high moral courage and his fine sense of social responsibility. The confidential agents of the French government reported to Paris that he was a man who preferred the public good to personal popularity. No better estimate in brief compass remains in the writings of his colleagues than the sketch penned by William Pierce in 1787 (Farrand, *post*, III, 90). "Governor Livingston," wrote the Georgian, "is confessedly a man of the first rate talents, but he appears to me rather to indulge a sportiveness of wit than a strength of thinking. He is, however, equal to anything, from the extensiveness of his education and genius. His writings teem with satyr and a neatness of style. But he is no Orator, and seems little acquainted with the guiles of policy."

[A body of papers of William Livingston, containing many letters and extensive records of his legal practice, was presented to the Mass. Hist. Soc. by Charles L. Nichols in 1922, and some additional MSS. were given to the society in 1923. Theodore Sedgwick, Jr.'s *A Memoir of the Life of William Livingston* (1833), was written from materials in possession of Livingston's descendants, but contains numerous inaccuracies. C. H. Levermore, "The Whigs of Colonial New York," in *Am. Hist. Rev.*, Jan. 1896, is valuable, and there are important references in C. L. Becker, *The Hist. of Political Parties in the Province of N. Y.* (1909) and E. B. Livingston, *The Livingstons of Livingston Manor* (1910). See also Max Farrand, *The Records of the Federal Convention of 1787* (1911); L. Q. C. Elmer, in *Colls. N. J. Hist. Soc.*, vol. VII (1872); F. B. Dexter, *Biog. Sketches Grads. Yale Coll.*, vol. I (1885); and M. C. Tyler, *The Lit. Hist. of the Am. Rev.* (1897), esp. II, 17–20.]   J. A. K.

LIVINGSTONE, WILLIAM (Jan. 21, 1844– Oct. 17, 1925), lake carrier, newspaper owner, banker, was born at Dundas, Ontario. His parents, William Livingstone, a ship's carpenter, and Helen (Stevenson) Livingstone, moved to Detroit while he was a child. Here he completed a common-school education, learned the machinist's trade, and began his career with the lake merchant marine, a career which lasted more than sixty years and included all grades of service and all types of shipping. "Sailor Bill," as he was known, mastered each step of ship operation and carrier management. In 1864 he was in partnership with Robert Downie as ship chandler and general merchant. Two years later, in June 1866, he married his partner's daughter, Susan. He owned a line of tugs which assisted sailing freighters between Lake Erie and Lake Huron. Later, as general manager of the Percheron Steam Navigation Company and of the Michigan Navigation Company, he was responsible for the construction of the steamships *Palmer* and *Livingstone*, 297 feet in length. These, the largest ships then on the Great Lakes, were too large, his associates felt, to be practical, yet Livingstone lived to see 600 feet a common length for freighters.

A Republican in politics, he early became a party leader. He served for many years as chairman of the Republican State Central Committee. He represented his district in the Michigan legislature in 1875, was collector of revenue for the port of Detroit under President Arthur, and chairman of the Michigan delegation to the National Convention in 1896. In 1892, with Senator Thomas W. Palmer, he purchased the defunct *Detroit Journal*. This paper he made a respected organ of the Republican party and a financial success. He was proud of his capabilities as a newspaper writer and later wrote and printed privately *Livingstone's History of the Republican Party* (1900), in two volumes. In 1884 he helped organize the Dime Savings Bank (now the Bank of Michigan), which he served as vice-president, 1884–1900, and as president from 1900 to his death. He was president of the American Bankers Association and of the Detroit Clearing House Association.

Throughout his career he was a force among the lake carriers. It was he who saw the possibilities of consolidating into a single body the voluntary associations of shippers. From its incorporation in 1902 until his death he was president of the Lake Carriers' Association. In this capacity he was influential in getting the federal government to construct the Davis and Sabin locks at Sault Ste. Marie and the Livingstone Channel in the Detroit River. As president of the Lake Carriers' Association he personally took charge of the relief work during the memorable storms of 1917, and succeeded in freeing many ships and in saving immense sums in ships and cargoes.

Active in social and philanthropic circles, he was a member of more than one hundred clubs and societies and possessed a host of friends among owners, seamen, statesmen, and politicians. From all walks of life men came to seek his counsel, and although both stern and busy, he was always ready to aid and advise the sailor, the captain, or the bank employee who asked his help. Tall, lean, broad-shouldered, "straight as an arrow," he was a figure to be remembered. Untiring physically, mentally alert, efficient and self-sufficient, he overcame all odds and made a success of each activity. Yet the thing in which he took most pride was his license testifying to his fitness as a pilot for ships of all tonnage. Death came to him suddenly one afternoon, while he was at work in the office of the Lake Carriers' Association. A lighthouse designed by Giza Maroti and completed in 1930 was erected at the east end of Belle Isle by the Lake Carriers' Association and other friends as a memorial to his life and work.

[*Livingstone's Hist of the Republican Party* (2 vols., 1900); *Cyc. of Mich.* (2nd ed., 1900); *Mich. Biogs.* (1924), vol. II; *Early Hist. of Mich. with Biogs.* (1888); *Am. Mag.*, Jan. 1923; *Ann. Report of the Lake Carriers' Asso.*, 1902–25; esp. that for 1925; *Who's Who in America*, 1924–25; G. N. Fuller, *Historic Mich.* (1928), III, 397; A. N. Marquis, *The Book of Detroiters* (1914); *N. Y. Times*, Oct. 18, 1925.]   J. J. S.

LLOYD, ALFRED HENRY (Jan. 3, 1864– May 11, 1927), philosopher, was born in Montclair, N. J., the son of Henry H. and Anna (Badger) Lloyd. The death of Henry Lloyd in 1868 left his widow and five children in financial difficulties, from which they were temporarily saved by the assistance of her father, Daniel Badger. Upon his death in 1874, the family sank to the brink of penury. Alfred and his twin brother, Arthur, were sent to their uncle, Myrom Lloyd, principal of a school in Westfield, Mass. Later the twins attended high school in Andover, Mass., whither their mother had removed, and still later they completed their preparatory work at St. Johnsbury Academy. At this time Alfred intended to enter the Congregational ministry and a friend offered to pay his expenses through Dartmouth if he would pledge himself to do so, but the lad refused to mortgage his right to change his mind. Instead, he virtually worked his own way through Harvard by means of tutoring and scholarships. Elected president of the college Young Men's Christian Association, he resigned because of the organization's refusal to admit Unitarians. This experience, and similar ones, revealing the narrowness of many devout Christians, along with a growing interest in philosophy, finally dissuaded him from entering the ministry. He graduated from Harvard in 1886, and after a year of teaching at Phillips Academy, Andover, he returned to the college for graduate work in philosophy. In 1889 he gained the Walker Fellowship, which took him abroad for two years of study at Göttingen, Berlin, and Heidelberg. He became instructor in the department of philosophy under John Dewey at the University of Michigan in 1891. Here he remained for the rest of his life, as assistant professor from 1894 until 1899, associate professor until 1906, and full professor thereafter. In 1915 he became dean of the graduate school, and on the death of President Marion L. Burton [*q.v.*] in February 1925 he was made acting president, in which capacity he served during the trying period that preceded the coming of President Clarence C. Little in October 1925. His sound judgment, unfailing tact, and irenic disposition caused him to be pushed inevitably into the administrative work for which he was so well fitted. Nevertheless this work equally inevitably deflected him from his even more important productive work as a philosopher. In his early books, *Citizenship and Salvation* (1897), *Dynamic Idealism* (1898), and *Philosophy of History* (1899) he laid the foundations of an activist idealism, which in many respects foreshadowed the famous *filosofia del atto* of Croce and Gentile, although Lloyd's method was at once more cursory and more objective than that of either of the great Italians. He concerned himself almost entirely with the implications of relationship, in which he found proof of the activity, intelligibility, and ultimate intelligence of the universe. His highly original dialectic of the categories, influenced but not governed by Hegel, brought time, space, and causality into a thorough-going dynamic monism. With a Spinoza-like aloofness and high serenity, from the vantage-point of reason he accepted the necessary involution of evil with good and found no need to take refuge in mere faith. *The Will to Doubt*, which he published in 1907, may be taken as an impersonal answer to William James's *The Will to Believe*, but, though much more profound, it never obtained a fraction of the influence of that far-reaching essay. Both Lloyd's thought and terminology were too original to be easily grasped, his reasoning was difficult to follow, and his fondness for paradox often rendered him obscure. His one easily understood work was the least important, *Leadership and Progress* (1922), a study of the post-war psychology from the standpoint of a political liberal. He was married, Dec. 28, 1892, to Margaret E. Crocker of Springfield, Mass.

[*Jour. of Philosophy*, Mar. 1, 1928; *Philosophical Rev.*, Nov. 1927; *Mich. Alumnus*, May 21, Dec. 24, 1927; *Science*, July 1, 1927; *Who's Who in America*, 1926–27; *Detroit News*, May 11, 1927; personal acquaintance.]   E. S. B.

LLOYD, DAVID (*c.* 1656–Apr. 6, 1731 o.s.), lawyer, politician, chief justice of Pennsylvania, was born in the parish of Manafon, Montgomeryshire, Wales. Nothing is known about his family, but he was probably a relative of Thomas Lloyd [*q.v.*]. They came from the same county in Wales, and Thomas, in his will, refers to David as his kinsman. He may have lived for a time at Cirencester in Gloucestershire, for it was there that he married his first wife. He studied law and on Apr. 24, 1686, received a commission from William Penn as attorney-general of Pennsylvania. He and his family arrived in Philadelphia on July 11 and he was shortly afterward appointed clerk of the county court, clerk of the provincial court, and deputy master of the rolls. He was closely associated with Thomas Lloyd, who was at that time master of the rolls, in his controversy with deputy-governor Blackwell. For refusing the demand of the provincial council to produce the court records, he was removed from the clerkship of the provincial court on Feb. 25, 1689, but the post was apparently restored after Blackwell's recall (*Minutes of the Provincial Council of Pennsylvania*, 1838 edition, I, pp. 202, 347). He served in the Assembly as a representative from Chester County, where he had landed interests, 1693–95, and began his long intermittent career as speaker of the Assembly in 1694. He was a member of the provincial council from Chester in 1695–96 and again from 1698 to 1700.

In 1698, Lloyd became involved in a quarrel with Robert Quarry, the judge of the newly created court of vice-admiralty. He was accused of advising the magistrates to take goods by force out of the King's warehouse at Newcastle and of otherwise resisting the enforcement of the acts of trade and navigation. On one occasion, when the marshal of the court produced his commission, Lloyd held it aloft and pointing to the picture of his Majesty which adorned it, is said to have exclaimed: "Here is a fine baby, a pretty baby, but we are not to be frightened with babies" (Root, *post*, p. 100). As a result of Quarry's complaints, Lloyd was rebuked by Penn, removed from his post as attorney-general, and suspended from the council in 1700.

This was the turning point of Lloyd's career. He became an almost lifelong enemy of Penn and of James Logan [*q.v.*], secretary of the prov-

ince and the chief representative of the proprietary interests in Pennsylvania. His first reaction was to join forces with Quarry, who appointed him deputy judge and advocate to the admiralty. But this was only a passing phase. He was elected to the Assembly from Philadelphia County in 1703 and almost immediately became the recognized leader of the democratic or anti-proprietary party. He was reëlected annually from either the county or the city of Philadelphia until 1710 and was speaker in 1704–05 and from 1706 to 1709. During these years he was constantly in conflict, not only with Logan, but also with the deputy governors, John Evans [*q.v.*] and Charles Gookin. As an orthodox Quaker, he advocated the right of affirmation for jurors and witnesses and opposed the appropriation of public funds for military purposes. Supplies were to be voted only on condition that they "should not be dipt in blood." As a democrat, he insisted upon constitutional reform, upon the right of the Assembly to meet and adjourn at its own pleasure, and upon the popular control of the judiciary. He was the author of the famous remonstrance or list of grievances sent to William Penn in 1704 and the prime mover in the attempt to impeach Logan in 1707. The people finally became tired of the eternal bickering and Lloyd and nearly all of his partisans were defeated in 1710. He soon regained his popularity, however, and was reëlected to the Assembly, but not to the speakership, in the following year. He removed from Philadelphia to Chester, in 1711, and represented Chester County in the Assembly in the years 1712–14, 1715–18, 1723–24, and 1725–29. He was again chosen speaker for the sessions 1714–15, 1723–24, and 1725–29. He was recorder of the city court of Philadelphia from 1702 to 1708 and chief justice of the province from 1717 until his death, which occurred at Chester on Apr. 6, 1731.

It is difficult to analyze Lloyd's character and assess the value of his work because the records of the time were written almost entirely by his enemies. According to their view, his ethical standards as a lawyer were questionable and he was vindictive and unscrupulous as a politician. He is said to have ante-dated the remonstrance that was sent to Penn in 1704 and to have signed it as speaker, although the Assembly had adjourned. James Logan says that he was a man "of a sound judgment, and a good lawyer, but extremely pertinacious and somewhat revengeful" (Penn and Logan Correspondence, vol. I, p. 18). Proud and other early historians of Pennsylvania followed this lead and Lloyd was long regarded as a quarrelsome demagogue. He has been rehabilitated, however, in recent years, and the tendency now is to represent him as a pioneer in the fight for democratic principles in America. He helped to organize the forces of popular opinion which resulted in the issue of Markham's "Frame of Government" in 1696 and Penn's "Charter of Privileges" in 1701 and it is believed that the abolition of the legislative powers of the council was due to his influence. He steadily resisted the efforts of the governor and council to control the judiciary and to encroach upon the functions of the Assembly. Members of the Society of Friends are grateful to him for the struggle that he made to secure the right of affirmation and to oppose the establishment of a military force. He was probably also responsible for the vigorous protests against the slave trade that came so frequently from the Chester Monthly Meeting between 1711 and 1731. He was the greatest lawyer of colonial Pennsylvania and he probably exerted the greatest single influence on the character of its early legislation. Although he was obstinate and vindictive during the active period of his life, he mellowed in his later years, signed an affectionate and loyal tribute to the memory of Penn, and was even known to cooperate with Logan. Lloyd was married twice. His first wife, whose name was Sarah, lived at Cirencester in Gloucestershire, England. His second wife was Grace Growden, daughter of Joseph Growden of Bucks County, Pa. They were married in 1697 and she was still living at the time of his death.

[The traditional view of Lloyd's life and work is based on the Penn MSS. in the Hist. Soc. of Pa. and the "Correspondence Between Wm. Penn and Jas. Logan," in the *Memoirs of the Hist. Soc. of Pa.*, vols. IX and X (1870–72). There is also considerable source material in the *Minutes of the Provincial Council of Pa.*, vols. I and II (1838). For a favorable account, see Isaac Sharpless, *Pol. Leaders of Provincial Pa.* (1919), and Frank M. Eastman, *Courts and Lawyers of Pa.* (1922), vol. I. For the controversy with Robert Quarry, see W. T. Root, *The Relations of Pa. with the British Govt., 1696–1765* (1912). See also: Robert Proud, *The Hist. of Pa., 1681–1742* (2 vols., 1797–98); Lawrence Lewis, Jr., "The Courts of Pa. in the Seventeenth Century," *Pa. Mag. of Hist. and Biog.*, vol. V, no. 2 (1881); John H. Martin, *Martin's Bench and Bar of Phila.* (1883); W. R. Shepherd, *Hist. of Proprietary Govt. in Pa.* (1896); and C. H. Browning, *Welsh Settlement of Pa.* (1912). Lloyd himself published two small treatises, *A Vindication of the Legislative Powers* (1725), and *A Defense of the Legislative Constitution of the Province of Pa.* (1728). An answer to the *Vindication*, written by Logan (1725), is reprinted in the *Pa. Mag. of Hist. and Biog.*, Oct. 1914. The inscription on Lloyd's tombstone in the Friends' Burial Ground in Chester states that he was seventy-five years old at the time of his death. A book by B. A. Konkle, "David Lloyd and the First Half-Century of Pa.," is now in preparation.]　　　　　　　　　　　　　　　　　W. R. S.

LLOYD, EDWARD (Nov. 15, 1744–July 8, 1796), Maryland official, was designated "the Patriot" because of his eminent services during the Revolutionary period, in order to distinguish him from others of the family succession. He was the eldest son of Edward Lloyd, III, and Ann (Rousby) Lloyd and was descended from an Edward Lloyd who emigrated to Lower Norfolk, Va., in 1623 and later moved to Maryland. Edward Lloyd, 1779–1834 [*q.v.*], was his son. Nothing definite is known of his formal training but he acquired a library of over a thousand volumes of luxurious editions. His public service, which began with his election in 1771 as burgess for Talbot County, continued under provincial, state, and federal governments until his death. He was elected because of his acknowledged hostility to Gov. Robert Eden's proclamation, fixing fees of certain officers in opposition to legislative desires. He naturally joined in a remonstrance to the governor, protesting against the usurpation of legislative prerogative. The election of 1773 returned him to his seat, which he held till the overthrow of the colonial government.

Lloyd was made a member of the Committee of Correspondence for Talbot County to attend a gathering of similar committees at Annapolis in June 1774. This body created the responsible Council of Safety, of which Lloyd was made a member, charged with executive control during legislative adjournment. It also authorized an election of delegates to a convention to be held at Annapolis. Although Lloyd was not originally returned to this body, he took his seat in January 1776 after the expulsion of one of the members. He was returned to the lower house at the first election held under the new state constitution and there elected early in 1777, by joint legislative ballot, to the executive council, a post to which he was twice successively reëlected. In November 1779, when the Assembly balloted for governor, Lloyd was defeated by Thomas Sim Lee [*q.v.*]. After one more year of service in the lower house, he was chosen in 1781 by the state electoral college senator for the Eastern Shore, winning reëlection at the end of his five-year term and again in 1791, though he did not live to complete his third term. He had already rendered national service by acting as one of the two Maryland delegates in the Congress of the Confederation during 1783–84, participating in the vote on the peace treaty with Great Britain. As a delegate from Talbot County in the state convention, he voted for the ratification of the new federal Constitution.

After his marriage on Nov. 19, 1767, to Elizabeth Tayloe of Virginia, Lloyd had settled down to the management of his vast landed estate. He lived a life of splendor and of lavish hospitality, ordering luxuries prodigally from London—clothes, wines, plate, coaches, a pleasure-boat—and maintaining a large deer-park for his guests' pleasure. As a member of the Maryland Jockey Club he kept and raced pedigreed horses. He prided himself on being one of the largest wheat growers in America. The burning and looting of "Wye House" late in the war has usually been ascribed to a military expedition from the British fleet, but may well have been the act of a predatory band. The despoiled owner lost no time in erecting an imposing mansion near the original site and also erected a town house in Annapolis for his greater comfort during legislative sessions. In view of his monetary interests his public activities may be regarded as indicating real public spirit.

[See Oswald Tilghman, *Hist. of Talbot County, Md., 1661–1861* (2 vols., 1915); Christopher Johnston, "Lloyd Family," *Md. Hist. Mag.*, Dec. 1912; Rebecca L. P. Shippen, "The Lloyds of 'Wye House,' Talbot County, Md.," *Md. Original Research Soc. of Baltimore, Bulletin*, June 1906; *Archives of Md.*, vols. XI (1892), XVI (1897), XXI (1901); *Proc. of the Conventions of the Province of Md. Held at . . . Annapolis in 1774, 1775, and 1776* (1836); legislative journals. The date of birth is taken from Lloyd's tombstone.]

E. L.

LLOYD, EDWARD (July 22, 1779–June 2, 1834), congressman, governor of Maryland, was born at "Wye House," the only son of Edward Lloyd, 1744–1796 [*q.v.*], and Elizabeth (Tayloe) Lloyd. His formal training, gained from tutors, was supplemented by his contact with the political thinkers who were constant guests at his father's home. Probably owing to his family connections, he entered public service young and was sent as a delegate to the state legislature in 1800 when he had barely reached his majority. His chief service during this period was the promotion of the constitutional amendment providing for the removal of the property qualification from the franchise, an action which undoubtedly increased his popularity with the mass of his constituents. From the state Assembly he passed to the national House of Representatives in 1806 to fill a vacancy in the Ninth Congress. He was reëlected to the Tenth Congress, but his congressional career was terminated abruptly by his election by the legislature (June 1809) to the governorship, left vacant by the resignation of Governor Wright. This unexpired term ended the following November, but Lloyd was twice reëlected for one-year terms. Republicanism scored a significant victory under his benevolent direction: the free ballot act repealed the last remaining property qualification—that for holding office. The two parties were so evenly balanced in Maryland at that time that though the

Republicans controlled the executive post, the Federalists regained the speakership in the House with resulting friction between administrative and legislative branches.

Lloyd left the governorship in 1811 to enter the state Senate, where he heartily supported President Madison in his attitude toward England, and where he served until his resignation in January 1815. When another turn of the political wheel restored the Republicans to power toward the close of the second decade of the century, Lloyd was sent to the United States Senate. Reëlected in 1825, he found himself obliged, owing to constant attacks of gout, to resign in January 1826, and to retire temporarily to private life. He was drawn forth for a final service in the Maryland Senate for the period 1826–31, part of the time as its presiding officer. Lloyd had married on Nov. 30, 1797, Sally Scott Murray, the daughter of an Annapolis physician. He died at Annapolis in his fifty-fifth year and was buried in the family burying-ground at "Wye." He lived the life of the typical Maryland gentleman, characterized by a genuine enthusiasm for agricultural interests, by munificent private hospitality, and by humanitarian interests. In the midst of luxurious surroundings he moved with simplicity and dignity of manner, while his advocacy of democratic legislation attested his devotion to patriotic principles.

[Oswald Tilghman, *Hist. of Talbot County, Md., 1661–1861* (2 vols., 1915); Christopher Johnston, "Lloyd Family," *Md. Hist. Mag.*, Dec. 1912; Rebecca L. P. Shippen, "The Lloyds of 'Wye House,' Talbot County, Md.," *Md. Original Research Soc. of Baltimore, Bulletin*, June 1906; H. E. Buchholz, *Governors of Md. from the Revolution to the Year 1908* (1908); M. P. Andrews, *Tercentenary Hist. of Md.* (1925), vol. I; *The Biog. Cyc. of Representative Men of Md. and the District of Columbia* (1879); *Republican Star* (Easton), June 21, 1803; *Baltimore Patriot and Mercantile Advertiser*, June 3, 1834; *Baltimore Republican*, June 4, 1834; *Easton Gazette*, June 7, 1834; legislative journals.]

E. L.

LLOYD, HENRY DEMAREST (May 1, 1847–Sept. 28, 1903), journalist, author, born in New York City, was the eldest child of Aaron and Maria Christie Demarest Lloyd. He inherited from both sides of the family a long pioneer and dissenting tradition and was brought up by his father, a penurious minister of the Dutch Reformed Church, in a rigidly Calvinistic atmosphere against which in later life he definitely reacted. He was granted the degree of A.M. from Columbia College in 1869 and in the same year was admitted to the New York bar. Three years of youthful reform activity followed. In 1871 with the Young Men's Municipal Reform Association he contributed to the defeat of Tammany Hall. In 1872, in accordance with his enthusiastic free-trade principles, he vigorously opposed Greeley's nomination at the Liberal Republican Convention. Disappointed in politics, he turned to journalism, accepted a position with the *Chicago Tribune,* and settled in Chicago where, in 1873, he married Jessie Bross, the daughter of William Bross, formerly lieutenant-governor of Illinois.

As financial editor and editorial writer, he familiarized himself with the growing trust and labor movements and started, if one excepts his college oration against monopoly, the campaign that was his life. In 1881 his "Story of a Great Monopoly" so vividly exposed the methods of the railroads and the Standard Oil Company that the *Atlantic Monthly* (March 1881), in which Howells had had the courage to publish it, ran to seven editions. With this article he became the first, as he remained perhaps the greatest, of the new "muck-rakers." He perceived the dangers of the rising monopolies and became the untiring champion of the independent competitor, the consumer, and the worker. In succeeding articles he attacked the classical political economy, with its reliance upon competition, the abuses of grain speculation, the financial machinations and rebate practices of the railroads, and monopoly in all its guises.

In 1885 he decided to devote his whole time to public welfare. He left the *Tribune,* and, in the course of a European trip, made invigorating contacts with English leaders in politics and industry. He returned with renewed interest in problems of labor which was rapidly intensified by succeeding events. The current depression was accompanied by increasing industrial unrest which culminated in the Haymarket "massacre" of 1886. In defiance of the dominant opinion of the time, Lloyd, who had no sympathy with anarchism or violence, espoused the cause of the convicted anarchists and assisted in having two death sentences commuted. This experience of legal oppression was complemented by his investigation of industrial oppression in the Spring Valley coal strike. His first book, *A Strike of Millionaires against Miners* (1890), was a characteristically dramatic plea for industrial justice. He continued this direct interest in the industrial conflict by acting in 1893 as an unofficial organizer of the Milwaukee street-car workers and by defending Debs for his conduct of the Pullman Strike of 1894. All this contributed to the writing of his most important book, *Wealth against Commonwealth* (1894), five hundred pages of denunciation of monopolies, especially the Standard Oil Company, distilled from the records of court and legislative

inquiries. It was widely read but stimulated no such uprising of an informed public as his faith in democracy had led him to expect.

The growth of the National People's party temporarily restored his hopes of an independent political party, and after playing an influential rôle in its conventions, he reluctantly accepted its nomination for Congress in 1894 but was, of course, overwhelmingly defeated in his corporation-controlled Chicago district. Two years later, the narrowing of the platform to the remonetization of silver, which he regarded as necessary but not sufficient, and the absorption of the party by the Democrats, so disappointed him that he withdrew from active participation in national political life. He continued, however, to play an active and frequently official rôle in the progressive politics of his home suburban village, Winnetka. He did not formally join the Socialist party until 1903, but he meanwhile supported the Socialists because they alone seemed to have a program designed to achieve the abolition of monopolistic power and the emancipation of the working class. His democratic idealism led him independently to the advocacy of "Social Democracy" and to occasional support of a communistic or cooperative experiment.

These interests hungered for an outlet more constructive than mere denunciation. After elaborating his semi-religious philosophy in the "Manuscript of 1896" and other essays, published in *Man, the Social Creator* (1906), he spent the years 1897–1901 in travel for the purpose of observing social experiments. From England he brought back the message of labor copartnership (*Labour Copartnership,* 1898; *Newest England,* 1900) and from New Zealand, a profound enthusiasm for compulsory arbitration of industrial disputes (*A Country without Strikes,* 1900), an enthusiasm that to his deep regret failed to convert the American Federation of Labor. His last trip was to Switzerland to study the initiative and referendum (*A Sovereign People,* 1907). During the long anthracite strike of 1902, Lloyd was active in attacking the operators' policy and in promoting relief work. When the owners finally agreed to arbitrate he was the principle associate of Mitchell and Darrow in presenting the miners' case. Before recovering from this strain, he entered in 1903 an equally exhausting campaign for the municipal ownership of street railways in Chicago, at the height of which he died.

[Caro Lloyd's *Henry Demarest Lloyd* (1912), a laudatory but reliable biography by his sister, contains a full bibliography of his writings. Shorter notices appear in the *Winnetka Town Meeting: Memorial Meeting in Honor of Henry Demarest Lloyd* (1903); *Chi-*

cago Daily Tribune, Sept. 29, 1903; Chicago Daily News, Sept. 28, 1903; Arena, December 1903. Lloyd's more important addresses and articles have been reprinted in Men, the Workers (1909); Mazzini and Other Essays (1910); and Lords of Industry (1910).]

W. J. C.

LLOYD, JAMES (Mar. 24, 1728–Mar. 14, 1810), pioneer obstetrician and surgeon, was born at Oyster Bay, Long Island, the youngest of ten children of Henry and Rebecca (Nelson) Lloyd. His grandfather, James Lloyd, emigrated to Boston, Mass., about 1670 from Somersetshire, England, and became an important colonial merchant. His father, who had a large estate on Long Island, N. Y., was also a Boston merchant. After a preliminary education in a private school at New Haven, Conn., young Lloyd was apprenticed in medicine for five years to Dr. William Clark, one of the leading practitioners of Boston. He then went to England and spent two years in London, listening to lectures on midwifery by the first "man-midwife," William Smellie, attending the demonstrations of the leading London surgeon of the time, William Cheselden, then at the height of his career, acting as a "dresser" at Guy's Hospital, and meeting and perhaps working with two young men, the brothers William and John Hunter, who were destined to revolutionize obstetrics and surgery even more completely than Smellie and Cheselden. Both were great influences in Lloyd's life, then and later.

Lloyd returned in 1752 to Boston, where he began the practice of surgery. Success came rapidly and completely; his practice became extensive and he was considered in consultation "one of the most useful and intelligent physicians in the State" (Gardiner, post, p. 17). He introduced the new methods of surgery to New England and was the first physician to practise midwifery in America, thus taking obstetrics away from the hands of midwives and putting it upon a scientific basis. He made no contributions to medical literature; he was eminently a practitioner, not a scholar, although he had many pupils. His handsome home was the center of fashionable Boston; his garden was noted, for he was somewhat of a practical as well as a scientific horticulturist; he was fond of sports; he numbered among his intimate friends, as well as patients, General Howe and Lord Percy. When war came, greatly to his credit, he remained in Boston as a physician; his only important medical contemporary, Silvester Gardiner [q.v.], retired to Halifax. He rendered good service to both the remaining English, after the evacuation, and to the Americans; and Gen. Israel Putnam is said to have made his home with him on en-

tering the town. He was, however, greatly shaken by the war; many of his more well-to-do patients had left Boston, his Long-Island estate, inherited from his father, had been partially destroyed by the British troops, who had cut down his woodland; and he was somewhat broken in health. He made a half-hearted attempt to obtain compensation for the loss of his woodland and even went to London (1789) for the purpose. His claim was refused, unless he would become a British subject; this he steadfastly refused to do and, with his self-respect unimpaired, he returned home the same year empty-handed. He lived through the reconstruction period after the Revolution, although life must have lost much of its zest. His wife, Sarah Corwin, died in 1797. When Dr. Benjamin Waterhouse [q.v.] began vaccination for smallpox in Boston in 1800, by the Jennerian method, Lloyd saw the significance of the discovery and became an ardent advocate of it. After a long illness, Lloyd died at the age of eighty-two. A son, James Lloyd, became United States senator from Massachusetts.

[J. S. J. Gardiner, Sermon . . . on the Decease of Dr. Jas. Lloyd (1810); Jas. Thacher, Am. Med. Biog. (1828), pp. 359–76; Lorenzo Sabine, Biog. Sketches of Loyalists of the Am. Revolution (2 vols., 1864), II, 23; S. A. Green, Hist. of Medicine in Mass. (1881); Ephraim Eliot, "Account of the Physicians of Boston," Proc. Mass. Hist. Soc., vol. VII (1864); New Eng. Jour. Medicine and Surgery, Apr. 1813; Am. Ancestry, vol. III (1893); W. L. Burrage, Hist. Mass. Medic. Soc. (1923); Lawrence Park, Gilbert Stuart (1926), vol. I; Boston Gazette, Mar. 15, 1810.]

H. R. V.

LLOYD, MARSHALL BURNS (Mar. 10, 1858–Aug. 10, 1927), inventor, manufacturer, was born in St. Paul, Minn., the son of John and Margaret (Conmee) Lloyd. His father was an Englishman who had emigrated to Canada in 1832 and in the early fifties had settled in St. Paul with his bride. While Lloyd was still an infant, however, his parents returned to Canada to live and settled on a farm at Meaford on Georgian Bay. Here young Lloyd obtained a bit of an education and at the age of fourteen went to work in the village store. Possessing unusual initiative and aggressiveness he soon gave up this work to sell fish, catching his own fish and peddling them from door to door. At sixteen he went alone to Toronto and for two years worked in a grocery store and also peddled soap. At eighteen he became a rural mail-carrier on the sixty-five-mile route between Port Arthur and Pidgeon River, and while so engaged he joined the rush of settlers and real-estate speculators to Winnipeg. For a living he worked as a waiter, and by shrewd purchases of land with his meager savings he accumulated several thousand dollars within a few months. With this fund he went to North Dakota, bought a farm at Grafton, and brought to it his parents and brothers and sisters. He soon discovered that he did not like farming and went alone again to St. Thomas, N. Dak., where he engaged in the insurance business. While thus employed he patented a weighing scale for the use of farmers and undertook to manufacture the article in St. Thomas. Shortly after getting under way, however, the factory was completely destroyed by fire and Lloyd lost everything. In the hope of securing financial aid to rebuild his plant he went to Minneapolis, Minn., but was not successful. In order to live he became a shoe salesman and in his spare time worked on other inventions.

After more than ten years Lloyd was eventually rewarded when the C. O. White Manufacturing Company of Minneapolis gave him an interest in the company in exchange for the right to use a machine he had patented for weaving wire door and table mats. He then patented a machine for weaving wire spring mattresses. With this invention he was able to buy out the White Company in 1900 and to found the Lloyd Manufacturing Company. The success of his woven-wire bed spring was immediate and he sold manufacturing rights not only to American industrialists but also to manufacturers in Europe, Australia, New Zealand, and South Africa. Following this venture he perfected a machine to make wire wheels for baby carriages and began their manufacture first in Minneapolis and then in Menominee, Mich., where his plant was permanently established. His next successful invention was the machinery for manufacturing thin tubing out of ribbons of steel of any width, and the machinery to weave wicker-ware of other than flat surfaces. He changed the time-honored method of weaving, and instead of attaching the weft or warp to the frame of the article desired, he found a way of weaving the wicker independently of the frame and attaching it afterward. He then devised a loom to weave wicker in the new way. This machine, capable of weaving wicker-ware more exactly and in one-thirtieth of the time required by the expert hand-weaver, revolutionized the wicker-manufacturing industry.

In addition to his activities in the several manufacturing companies which he founded, Lloyd, a few years before his death, successfully organized a community cooperative department store and theatre in Menominee. He was also mayor of Menominee for two terms from 1913 to 1917. He was married three times but there were no children from any of the marriages.

His third wife, Mrs. Henriette Hammer Pollen of Orange, N. J., whom he married on Apr. 11, 1922, survived him at the time of his death in Menominee.

[*Who's Who in America*, 1926–27; *Ann. Report of the Commissioner of Patents*, 1888 and years following; *Menominee Herald-Leader*, Aug. 10, 1927; information as to certain facts from the Lloyd Manufacturing Company.]

                             C. W. M.

LLOYD, THOMAS (Apr. 17, 1640 o.s.–Sept. 10, 1694 o.s.), physician, deputy governor of Pennsylvania, was the son of Charles Lloyd of Dolobran, Meifod parish, Montgomeryshire, Wales, and Elizabeth Stanley of neighboring Shropshire. He was born at Dolobran and was educated at Jesus College, Oxford; he is probably the Thomas Lloyd who graduated in January 1661/62. After leaving college, he studied medicine and managed the estate of his brother Charles, who had been imprisoned as a Quaker. He also joined the Society of Friends and was interned at Welshpool near Dolobran from 1665 until 1672, but was allowed considerable freedom to practise his profession. He arrived in Philadelphia Aug. 20, 1683, was appointed master of the rolls in December, and was elected to the provincial council early in 1684. The council acted as chief executive of the province from Penn's departure to England in August 1684 until it was replaced by an executive commission of five members in February 1688. Lloyd was president of the council during this period and was the most influential member of the executive commission which served until the arrival of deputy-governor John Blackwell in December 1688. He also received a commission from Penn (August 1684) as keeper of the great seal of the province. The appointment of Blackwell, who was not a Quaker, was displeasing to Lloyd and he refused to affix the great seal to certain commissions which Blackwell had prepared. His attitude was insolent and the legality of his conduct was doubtful, but he had popular support and, in spite of Blackwell's opposition, was reëlected to the council in 1689. The quarrel lasted for more than a year and was finally settled by the proprietor himself, who removed Blackwell and restored the council's executive powers. Lloyd was again chosen president of the council and served in that capacity until March 1691, when Pennsylvania was temporarily separated from the three lower counties on the Delaware. He was then appointed deputy governor of the province, while William Markham [*q.v.*] was made deputy governor of the lower counties. When Pennsylvania became a royal province, Governor Fletcher requested Lloyd to remain in office as deputy or lieutenant governor, but he refused and was superseded by Markham in April 1693. He died in Philadelphia.

Lloyd married Mary Jones of Welshpool, Montgomeryshire, Wales, Nov. 9, 1665. They had a large family. After the death of his first wife he was married, possibly in 1684, to Patience Story (née Gardiner), the widow of Robert Story of New York. The dominating factors of his career were his love of democracy and his loyalty to the principles of the Society of Friends. His controversy with Blackwell involved the right of the executive to organize the judiciary and to interfere with the legislative branch of the government. He and his Quaker friends were also offended by Blackwell's efforts to establish a militia force for the defense of the province against the French and the Indians. His orthodoxy was likewise reflected in his opposition to George Keith [q.v.] and the so-called Christian Quakers. He was the ablest and most popular political leader in Pennsylvania from 1684 to 1693, a worthy predecessor of his "kinsman" David Lloyd [q.v.].

[For a sympathetic account of Lloyd's political career see Isaac Sharpless, *Pol. Leaders of Provincial Pa.* (1919), pp. 55–83. The controversy with George Keith is discussed in Rufus M. Jones, *The Quakers in the Am. Colonies* (1911), pp. 437–58. See also W. R. Shepherd, *Hist. of Proprietary Govt. in Pa.* (1896); C. H. Browning, *Welsh Settlement of Pa.* (1912); Robert Proud, *The Hist. of Pa., 1681–1742*, vol. I (1797); Mrs. R. H. Lloyd, *The Pedigree of the Lloyds of Dolobran* (p.p. 1877); C. P. Smith, *Lineage of the Lloyd and Carpenter Family* (1870), sometimes inaccurate; and T. A. Glenn, *Geneal. Notes Relating to the Families of Lloyd, Pemberton, Hutchinson, Hudson, and Parke* (1898). There is considerable source material in the *Minutes of the Provincial Council of Pa.*, vol. I (1838). Two pamphlets written by Lloyd himself in 1682 have been published: *An Epistle to my Dear and Well Beloved Friends of Dolobran* (1788) and *A Letter to John Eccles and Wife* (1805).]

W. R. S.

LOCHMAN, JOHN GEORGE (Dec. 2, 1773–July 10, 1826), Lutheran clergyman, was born in Philadelphia, the son of Nicolaus and Anna Maria (Schneider) Lochman. As a catechumen he impressed J. H. C. Helmuth [q.v.], who urged the boy's parents to stint themselves if necessary in order to educate their son for the ministry. Upon his graduation in 1789 from the University of Pennsylvania Lochman took up the study of theology under Helmuth's direction, supporting himself meanwhile by teaching, was licensed by the Ministerium of Pennsylvania at Reading in 1794, and was ordained at Hanover in 1800. He was married twice: on Sept. 7, 1795, to Mary Magdalena Grotz of Philadelphia, who died, leaving him with two children; and on June 3, 1799, to Susan Hoffman of Philadelphia, who bore him thirteen children and outlived him by fifteen years. One of his sons, Augustus Hoff-

man Lochman (1802–1891), was a prominent clergyman of the next generation. Lochman was a man of solid though probably not extensive attainments, humane and charitable in disposition, modest and dignified in manner, industrious and wise in the discharge of his duties. As pastor at Lebanon 1794–1815 and at Harrisburg 1815–26, he was respected and even venerated by his parishioners. His theological opinions were distinctly Lutheran though not rigidly orthodox; like his preceptor Helmuth he saw little value in precise theological definitions and had a warm appreciation for the work of other denominations. He was the author of *Haupt-Inhalt der Christlichen Lehre* (Lebanon, 1808); *A Valedictory Sermon Preached at Lebanon* (1815); *An Inaugural Sermon Preached at Harrisburg* (Harrisburg, 1815); *The History, Doctrine, and Discipline of the Evangelical Lutheran Church* (1818); *Principles of the Christian Religion, in Questions and Answers, Designed for the Instruction of Youth in Evangelical Churches* (1822; 4th ed., 1834); and *Hinterlassene Predigten* (1828). He trained about thirty candidates for the ministry. One of his greatest services to the Church was his share in the formation of the General Synod, which was designed to bind all the Lutheran congregations of the United States into a general organization for the administration of common enterprises and the maintenance of educational and doctrinal standards. As president in 1818 of the Ministerium of Pennsylvania he took the leading part in the negotiations with the Lutherans of the South and West, and when the General Synod was organized at Frederick, Md., Oct. 21–23, 1821, he was chosen president. But among the rural congregations of the Ministerium of Pennsylvania opposition to the General Synod was stubborn and united; and Lochman had the bitter disappointment of seeing the Ministerium deny the General Synod its support. Five years later, as a result probably of overwork, he suffered an apoplectic stroke. After months of invalidism he died at Harrisburg while the bells of his church were tolling for the deaths of Jefferson and Adams.

[C. A. Hay, *Memoirs of Rev. Jacob Goering, Rev. Geo. Lochman, D.D., and Rev. Benj. Kurtz, D.D., LL.D.* (1887); *Univ. of Pa. Biog. Cat. Matriculates of the Coll., 1749–1893* (1894); D. M. Gilbert, *Services Commemorative of the 100th Anniversary of Zion Evangelical Luth. Ch., Harrisburg, Pa., Nov. 10–11, 1895* (1896); T. E. Schmauk, *Old Salem in Lebanon* (1898); G. F. Krotel, "The Gen. Synod and the Pa. Synod: A Few Chapters of History," *Luth. and Missionary*, Nov. 9, 16, 23, 1865; *Documentary Hist. of the Evangelical Luth. Ministerium of Pa., ... 1748 to 1821* (1898); Lochman's diary (Luth. Hist. Soc., Gettysburg, Pa.); W. B. Sprague, *Annals Am. Pulpit*, vol.

IX (1869); *Pa. Intelligencer* (Harrisburg), July 14, 1826.]
                                        G. H. G.

LOCKE, DAVID ROSS (Sept. 20, 1833–Feb. 15, 1888), journalist and political satirist, who, under the pseudonym of Petroleum V. Nasby, achieved fame during the Civil War, was born at Vestal, Broome County, near Binghamton, N. Y., the son of Nathaniel Reed and Hester (Ross) Locke. His grandfather, John, had been a minute man in the Revolution; his father, a soldier in the War of 1812; while his mother, daughter of Dr. William Ross, was a granddaughter of Joshua Mersereau, who in various capacities saw service during the Revolution.

David's academic education ended when he was ten years old, and he went directly into newspaper work, from which he was never afterwards dissociated. After a fourteen-mile walk he presented himself at the office of the Cortland *Democrat* and made overtures for a job. He was a little too short to have full command of a type-case at the time, but was, nevertheless, apprenticed for a period of seven years. The *Democrat* was a vigorous political organ. Locke was connected with it until he reached the age of seventeen, when he became an itinerant printer and was employed successively in a number of cities of the North and South.

In 1852 he formed a partnership with a young man by the name of James G. Robinson. Together they founded at Plymouth, Richland County, Ohio, the *Plymouth Advertiser*. There he married Martha H. Bodine, who bore him three sons. Though the newspaper prospered after a fashion, Locke left it and, seeking better opportunities, was located afterwards in various Ohio towns. He was editor of the *Jeffersonian* at Findlay when he wrote the first letter signed with the name of Petroleum V. Nasby. It bore the date of Mar. 21, 1861. Locke had followed his father in his opposition to slavery, and his travels through the South had served to deepen the conviction that it was an evil for which the best remedy was extermination. His newspaper experience had sharpened his conviction to a cutting edge. The device to which he resorted in his newspaper attacks was a common and popular one. His creation, Petroleum V. Nasby, for whom Thomas Nast later created a pictorial embodiment, was an overdrawn but effective caricature of the Copperhead. Locke made Nasby in the image of an illiterate, hypocritical, cowardly, loafing, lying, dissolute country preacher, whose orthographical atrocities were fashioned after the style of his predecessor, Artemus Ward. Nasby sponsors slavery and the Democratic party, and thus condemns them; he is not only foolish but corrupt, the necessary inference being that the Copperheads and the Democrats were as foolish in their opinions and as corrupt in their practices; and his "advenchers" were always so invented as to make the Democratic or Southern side of an argument appear ludicrously inept. The letters were marked by a rich humor, aggressive maliciousness, skilful caricature, sustained resourcefulness, and a merciless insistence. They brought Locke fame and a fortune. In 1865 he took editorial charge of the *Toledo Blade* and in a few years owned a controlling interest in it. In 1871 he went to New York as managing editor of the *Evening Mail*, but later returned to Ohio. He continued the Nasby letters in the *Blade* almost until the time of his death, the last one appearing Dec. 26, 1887. Under his editorship the paper attained immense popularity. During his later years he espoused the cause of prohibition and carried on a campaign against the liquor traffic under the flaunting banner line, "Pulverize the Rum Power." Abraham Lincoln was one of Locke's most unreserved admirers, and on more than one occasion he was known to hold up business of state in order to read his visitors a few of the Nasby letters. Lincoln, and later Grant, offered Locke political opportunities, but he declined them all. The only office he ever aspired to was that of alderman from the third ward in Toledo, and it was with considerable difficulty that he secured his election to this post. He held the office when he died in 1888.

Beginning with *The Nasby Papers* (1864), numerous collections of the letters appeared in book form. Locke wrote other published works, including *The Morals of Abou Ben Adhem* (1875) and *The Demagogue* (1891), a political novel, and he was a popular lecturer, but the letters alone constitute the fame which he achieved and which died with him. He was the most powerful political satirist of his day and country. "Wat posterity will say, I don't know; neither do I care," said Nasby. ". . . It's this generashen I'm going for." The succeeding generation has treated him accordingly.

[Robert Ford, *Am. Humourists, Recent and Living* (1897); *The Nasby Letters* (1893); G. L. Faxon, *The Hist. of the Faxon Family* (1880); H. L. Mersereau, "Mersereau Family Geneal.," in *N. Y. Geneal. and Biog. Record*, Oct. 1896, Jan. 1897; A. B. Paine, *Th. Nast, His Period and His Pictures* (1904); J. B. Pond, *Eccentricities of Genius, Memories of Famous Men and Women of the Platform and Stage* (1900); H. P. Smith, *Hist. of Broome County, N. Y.* (1885), and *Hist. of Cortland County, N. Y.* (1885); J. M. Killits, *Toledo and Lucas County, Ohio 1623–1923* (1923); *Toledo Blade*, Feb. 15, 1888; *N. Y. Herald*, Feb. 16, 1888; clippings and information furnished by relatives.]
                                        J. A. E.

LOCKE, JOHN (Feb. 19, 1792–July 10, 1856), physician, scientist, inventor, was born at Lempster, N. H., the son of Samuel Barron Locke and his first wife, Hannah Russell. He was descended from William Locke who emigrated to Massachusetts from England in 1635, settling first at Charlestown, and then at Woburn. For the first few years of his life Locke lived in a number of places but in 1796 his father settled on a large tract near Bethel, Me., and in connection with his home and farm, built saw and grist mills, a Methodist meeting house, and other establishments. In time the settlement came to be known as Locke's Mills. Here young Locke received his early schooling which was augmented by the books of his father's large library. He became intensely interested in botany, learned as much as he could locally, and then by working in the mills and by teaching school earned enough money to attend intermittently an academy at Bridgeport, Conn. The smattering of additional knowledge of the natural sciences he received only made him more desirous for an education, but his father opposed his ambitions. In the summer of 1815, following a bitter religious quarrel with his father, Locke left home and worked his way to Yale College. There he attended Silliman's lectures on chemistry and for a while was an assistant in his laboratory. Then from 1816 to 1818 he studied medicine under several doctors in Keene, N. H., and at the same time continued his studies in botany, delivering lectures on the subject in various schools and colleges of New England.

In the autumn of 1818 Locke received an appointment of assistant surgeon in the United States navy and was assigned to the frigate *Macedonian* under special order to explore the Columbia River. A storm wrecked the ship, however, and the expedition was abandoned. Locke then went to Boston, where he wrote and published in 1819 his *Outlines of Botany*. It contained over two hundred illustrations, all drawn and engraved by himself. In the same year he obtained the degree of M.D. at Yale. For a time then he was curator of botany at Harvard College, but in 1821 he seized the opportunity of getting away from New England, which he felt was dominated by religious intolerance, and accepted a teaching position in a girls' school in Lexington, Ky. After a year he resigned this position and went to Cincinnati, Ohio, and established there the Cincinnati Female Academy which he conducted until 1835. He then was appointed professor of chemistry and pharmacy in the Medical College of Ohio in Cincinnati and very successfully occupied this chair for eighteen years, resigning

in 1853, just three years before his death. By far the most productive years of his life were those from 1835 onward. In this period his interests and his researches gradually changed from the natural to the physical sciences and it was in the latter field that he did his foremost work.

Between 1835 and 1840 he engaged in some private geologic and paleontologic studies, publishing the results in scientific journals. These studies included observations on the characteristics of certain species of fossil trilobites and on the occurrence of certain unusual ore deposits. Locke was employed, too, for geological survey work by both the state of Ohio and the federal government. One of his subsequent reports on the mineral lands of Iowa, Illinois, and Wisconsin was published by Congress in 1840 (*House Executive Document 239,* 26 Cong., 1 Sess.) and republished in enlarged form in 1844 (*Senate Document 407,* 28 Cong., 1 Sess.). After 1840 his attention was directed to the study of terrestrial magnetism and electricity. He contributed over fifteen papers on these and allied subjects to the *American Journal of Science and Arts,* to the *Transactions* of the American Philosophical Society, and to the *Smithsonian Contributions to Knowledge*. He also lectured both in the United States and in England, using for illustration scientific apparatus of his own and his son's design and construction. He invented several valuable instruments including a surveyor's compass, level, an orrery, and his so-called electromagnetic chronograph (see the *American Journal of Science and Arts,* September 1849). This instrument, devised between 1844 and 1848, at the request of the United States Coast Survey, completely changed the art of determining longitudes, for it recorded on a time scale, automatically printed by a clock, the occurrence of an event to within one one-hundredth of a second. Furthermore it could be connected with the nation's telegraph system so that an observer of an astronomical event anywhere, by the simple depression of a key, could record the time of the event as indicated by the clock to which the instrument was attached. Locke's instruments and system were installed in the Naval Observatory, Washington, in 1848, with wonderful results, and for his invention Congress awarded him $10,000 in February 1849. Locke married Mary Morris of Newark, N. J., on Oct. 25, 1825, in Cincinnati, and at the time of his death there, was survived by his widow and a number of children.

[G. M. Roe, *Cincinnati: The Queen City of the West* (1895); J. G. Locke, *Book of the Lockes* (1853); M. B. Wright, *An Address on the Life and Character of the Late Prof. John Locke* (1857); E. H. Knight, *Knight's*

Am. Mech. Dict. (3 vols., 1874–76) ; *Am. Jour. of Sci.*, 2 ser. VIII (1849) ; *Cincinnati Daily Enquirer,* July 11, 1856 ; Patent Office records.]   C. W. M.

LOCKE, MATTHEW (1730–Sept. 7, 1801), Revolutionary soldier and congressman, son of John and Elizabeth Locke, went from Pennsylvania to piedmont North Carolina about 1752 and settled near the present city of Salisbury, Rowan County. In 1749 he was married to Mary Elizabeth Brandon, and in later life to Mrs. Elizabeth Gostelowe of Philadelphia. Before the Revolution he achieved local prominence as justice of the peace, vestryman, and member of the House of Commons, 1770–71, and 1773–75. In the Regulator disturbance he was a moderate, apparently preserving the confidence of both parties; in January 1771 he favored the legislative regulation of official fees and in the following March was a representative of the county officials on a joint committee for the final determination of disputed cases involving fees, arising between the Regulators and the county officials, one of whom (Francis Locke) was his brother.

He was active in the patriot cause before and during the Revolution, as an agent and member of the Rowan Committee of Safety (1774–76) in its execution of the resolves of the Continental and Provincial congresses and its discipline of Loyalists; as a delegate to the Third (August 1775), Fourth (April 1776), and Fifth (November 1776) Provincial congresses; as paymaster, brigadier-general, and auditor for the district of Salisbury; and as a member of the state House of Commons (1777–81, 1783–84, and 1789–92) and of the Senate (1781–82, and 1784). His stubborn hostility to the adoption of the federal Constitution is shown by his votes in the Hillsborough Convention of 1788 and in the Fayetteville Convention of the next year, and by his selection in 1788 as a North Carolina delegate to a projected second federal convention. Numerous important committee assignments attest his influence in the colonial and state political bodies of which he was a member.

From 1793 to 1799 Locke represented the Salisbury district in the national House of Representatives. So far as the records show, he never participated in the debates of Congress and he usually cast a negative vote. Rural, provincial, uneducated, religious, with little knowledge of statecraft and international relations, he was an extreme Jeffersonian Republican who believed that the best government is the one which governs least and most economically. He was hostile to the Federalist policies of the administrations of Washington and Adams and was one of the twelve radical Republicans in the House who voted against the complimentary reply to Washington's message of Dec. 7, 1796 (*Annals of Congress,* 4 Cong., 2 Sess., cols. 1667–68). His opposition to the popular measures for national defense in the spring of 1798, when war with France was impending, brought about his crushing defeat in August (3,131 votes to 231) by Archibald Henderson [*q.v.*] of Salisbury. "The Election of Mr. Henderson is very honourable to him and his Constituents," wrote President Adams (Wagstaff, *post,* I, p. 161). But the Federalist excesses of 1798 and the passing of the French crisis strengthened Republicanism in North Carolina; and Locke, though defeated by Henderson in the congressional election of 1800, polled a larger vote than in 1798 and was mentioned as a senatorial candidate in the Republican General Assembly of 1800 (*North-Carolina Mercury and Salisbury Advertiser,* Aug. 21, 1800).

At the opening of the Revolution, he was operating a wagon line between points in piedmont North Carolina and Charleston, S. C., but agriculture was his chief occupation. He acquired considerable landholdings in Rowan and Iredell counties and in Tennessee, and was the sixth largest slaveholder in his county in 1790. He was a trustee of Salisbury Academy, incorporated in 1784. His common sense, character, and faithfulness to the will of his rural constituents kept him in public life almost steadily for thirty years. On Sept. 7, 1801, at his home near Salisbury, he "breathed his last, a firm and fixed Republican."

[*Colonial Records of N. C.* (10 vols., 1886–90) ; *State Records of N. C.* (16 vols., 1895–1905) ; A. L. Fries, ed., *Records of the Moravians in N. C.* (4 vols., 1922–30) ; H. M. Wagstaff, ed., *The Papers of John Steele* (2 vols., 1924) ; *Annals of Cong.,* 1793–99 ; *Raleigh Reg. and N.-C. State Gazette,* Oct. 13, 1801 ; *N.-C. Jour.* (Halifax), Sept. 10, 1798 ; Rowan County Wills, in N. C. Hist. Commission, Raleigh ; Jethro Rumple, *A Hist. of Rowan County, N. C.* (rev. ed., 1916) ; J. H. Wheeler, *Reminiscences and Memoirs of N. C. and Eminent North Carolinians* (1884) ; W. E. Dodd, *The Life of Nathaniel Macon* (1903) ; George McCorkle, "Sketch of Col. Francis Locke," in *N. C. Booklet,* July 1910.]   A. R. N.

LOCKE, RICHARD ADAMS (Sept. 22, 1800–Feb. 16, 1871), journalist, was born in England, at East Brent, Somersetshire. Some works of biography have given New York as his birthplace. In his early career in America, realizing the prejudice which then existed against British writers, he did not emphasize the fact that he was not a native American. He was not, as Edgar Allan Poe wrote of him, a lineal descendant of John Locke. The descent was collateral, through the philosopher's uncle, Louis

Locke. Their common ancestor first mentioned in the written pedigree was John Locke, sheriff of London in 1460. The father of Richard Adams Locke was Richard Locke of Highbridge House, Burnham, and of East Brent, Somersetshire, a land surveyor entered as "gentleman" in the College of Arms pedigree; the grant of arms to the Lockes was made by Queen Mary in 1555 (*An Account of the Locke Family, East Brent,* 1792). His mother was Anne Adams of East Brent. He married Esther Bowering of East Brent, probably in 1826.

After leaving Cambridge University Locke started the London *Republican,* an organ of democracy. This and his second literary venture, the *Cornucopia,* were failures. In 1832 he emigrated to New York City with his wife and infant daughter Adelaide and became a reporter on the *Courier and Enquirer.* In the summer of 1835 he joined the *Sun,* then a struggling penny paper, at a salary of twelve dollars a week. He was taken on by the founder of the paper, Benjamin H. Day [*q.v.*], and not, as Edgar Allan Poe says (*post,* p. 120), by Moses Yale Beach, the second owner. In August 1835 Locke wrote for the *Sun* the celebrated "Moon Hoax," which purported to reveal the discovery, by Sir John Herschel with his new telescope at the Cape of Good Hope, of men and animals on the moon. The revelations pretended to be reprinted from the Edinburgh *Journal of Science,* although that periodical was then defunct. Locke peopled the moon with winged humans and invented a variety of animals, including biped beavers from whose houses smoke issued. The hoax was so well written and so sprinkled with astronomical terms as to deceive most of the *Sun's* readers. A delegation came from Yale College to ask to see the original *Journal of Science.* The hoax increased the *Sun's* circulation to more than nineteen thousand, the largest of any daily of that time. The articles were reprinted in pamphlet form in Paris, London, Edinburgh, and Glasgow. Poe wrote that, having found the hoax anticipative of all the main points of his own "Hans Phaall," he let that tale remain unfinished. It has been suggested—Augustus De Morgan took it for granted in his *Budget of Paradoxes* (1872) —that the hoax was the work of Jean Nicolas Nicollet, French astronomer who, like Locke, came to America in 1832. There is no real evidence to support the suggestion. Locke resigned from the *Sun* in the autumn of 1836 and, with Joseph Price, started the *New Era,* a penny daily. In this he attempted to duplicate the success of the "Moon Hoax" with "The Lost Manuscript of Mungo Park," a fabrication which pur-

ported to tell hitherto unrelated adventures of the Scottish explorer. The public, knowing Locke, was not again deceived. When the *New Era* failed Locke became an editorial writer on the *Brooklyn Daily Eagle.* Later he was employed in the New York custom house. He died at his home on Staten Island at the age of seventy years. He is thus described by his friend Poe (*post,* p. 127): "Like most men of *true* imagination, Mr. Locke is a seemingly paradoxical compound of coolness and excitability. He is about five feet seven inches in height, symmetrically formed; there is an air of distinction about his whole person—the *air noble* of genius. His face is strongly pitted by the smallpox and, perhaps from the same cause, there is a marked obliquity in the eyes; a certain calm, clear *luminousness,* however, about these latter amply compensates for the defect, and the forehead is truly beautiful in its intellectuality. I am acquainted with no person possessing so fine a forehead as Mr. Locke."

[F. M. O'Brien, *The Story of The Sun* (1918); Edgar Allan Poe, *The Literati* (1850); Frederic Hudson, *Journalism in the U. S. from 1690 to 1872* (1873); *N. Y. Herald,* Feb. 18, 1871; information as to certain facts from Locke's grand-daughter, Mrs. F. Winthrop White, New Brighton, Staten Island, N. Y.]   F. M. O.

LOCKHART, CHARLES (Aug. 2, 1818–Jan. 26, 1905), pioneer oil producer, refiner, and one of the early promoters of the Standard Oil Trust, was born at Cairn Heads, Wigtownshire, Scotland. His father, John, and his mother, Sarah (Walker)—the latter a daughter of a noted linen manufacturer in Sorbie—brought their seven children to the United States in 1836. In Scotland Charles had received an elementary education, and, while working for an uncle, a rudimentary business training. During the first nineteen years after his arrival he was in Pittsburgh as errand boy and later clerk for James McCully, a wholesale grocer and dealer in produce and flour, beginning at a wage of seventy-five cents a week and working fourteen hours a day. In 1855, however, he and William Frew, a fellow clerk, were taken into partnership under the firm name of James McCully & Company and during the Civil War the concern enjoyed unusual prosperity.

Lockhart's first interest in oil was awakened in 1852 upon meeting one Isaac Huff, who had come to Pittsburgh with three barrels of oil that had been taken out of his salt well near Tarentum, Pa. The latter could find no purchaser for this then little-used product, but Lockhart agreed, as a speculation, to take all that was produced during a period of five years at 31¼ cents per gallon. He then made a fortunate bargain to sell this oil to Samuel M. Kier [*q.v.*] during the same period at twice the amount. In the following year he bought the well, which was one of the first in the state, and assumed active direction. In 1859, the year oil was discovered in Titusville, Lockhart and four associates organized a firm under the name of Phillips, Frew & Company, and leased the land on Oil Creek. The first well yielded forty-five barrels a day. In 1860, filling a couple of gallon oyster cans, one with crude and the other with distilled oil (refining was not yet generally practised), he took them to England, and lighted the first petroleum lamp. Upon the basis of these samples he was able to build up a considerable export trade in oil. Lockhart and Frew soon bought out their partners' interests and built the Brilliant refinery, the first important refinery erected. This was followed by the building of the Atlantic refinery in Philadelphia. He was prominent in the rapidly extending activities of the Standard Oil Company. In 1872 he became a stockholder in the South Improvement Company, and in 1874, at a meeting with John D. Rockefeller, William G. Warden, and Henry M. Flagler [*q.v.*], he helped to lay the foundation of the Standard Oil Trust, transferring his refineries to the Standard Oil Company and taking stock in return. He had agreed to absorb as rapidly as possible the other refineries in the neighborhood of Pittsburgh, and in 1874 he became president of a newly organized concern, called the Standard Oil Company of Pittsburgh, which began to lease or buy these refineries. In 1879, at the instigation of the Petroleum Producers' Union, he was indicted with other officials of the Standard Oil group, on the charge of conspiracy to effect various illegal ends (Tarbell, *post*, I, 239, 393ff.). A compromise was achieved the following year, however, and the case did not come to trial (*Ibid.*, I, ch. viii and p. 401). When the Standard Oil Trust was incorporated he became one of its directors, and at its dissolution in 1892 he became president of the Atlantic Refining Company.

He was also engaged in the manufacture of saws, axes, shovels, iron and steel, and locomotives, and had timber, farming, and gold mining interests in Colorado and Idaho. He was also among the founders of the American and Red Star steamship lines. He retired from active direction of his interests in 1900 and died five years later. In his will he gave generously of his fortune to the four leading hospitals of Pittsburgh and to various welfare organizations. In June 1862 he married Jane Walker, by whom he had five children.

[Erasmus Wilson, *Standard Hist. of Pittsburg, Pa.* (1898); I. M. Tarbell, *The Hist. of the Standard Oil Company* (2 vols., 1904); *Biog. Rev.*, vol. XXIV (1897); *Pittsburg Post, Pittsburg Dispatch,* and *Pittsburg Press,* Jan. 27, 1905.]   A.I.

LOCKREY, SARAH HUNT (Apr. 21, 1863– Nov. 8, 1929), surgeon, suffragist, was born in Philadelphia, Pa., the daughter of Charles and Martha Jane Wisner Lockrey. Her father had been left an orphan at the age of six when all the others of his immediate family died during a yellow fever epidemic in Philadelphia. He was cared for by a neighbor, learned the carpenter's trade, and became a successful business man. Her mother's ancestors were Scotch Covenanters. She graduated from the Girls' Normal School and began teaching at the age of seventeen. Although a shy girl who preferred books to other companions, she early showed the conscientiousness that later made her a courageous leader. In her longing to be of service to others she was active in religious organizations and wished to be a missionary, but finally she turned to medicine as a career. While a medical student she taught in the night schools of Philadelphia and tutored in physiology. She graduated from the Woman's Medical College of Pennsylvania in 1888 and then served as an interne at the Woman's Hospital. With the rapid growth of her practice she became a specialist in abdominal surgery. In 1895 she was appointed assistant to Dr. A. E. Broomall at the Woman's Hospital and later became chief of the gynecological staff, soon after which the West Philadelphia Hospital for Women made her a visiting chief on its surgical staff. These positions, which she held until her death, gave her constant opportunity to exercise her skill as a surgeon. She was consultant to the Elwyn school for the feeble-minded and for over twenty-five years physician to the Methodist Episcopal Deaconess Home, where she was instrumental in starting a daily clinic.

Notwithstanding her very active professional life, Dr. Lockrey always found time for church work. For a number of years she served on the board of the Methodist Collegiate Institute, a school for girls, and was president of the board of trustees of the Thirteenth Street Methodist Episcopal Church, an unusual position for a woman to hold at that time. In 1921 she became a Presbyterian. One of her keenest interests was the advancement of women. Years before woman's suffrage became popular she worked and sacrificed to bring about the political equality of women. She gave generously of her time and money, took part in pageants and parades, and developed ability as a public speaker. Dr. Anna Howard Shaw found in her a faithful and active supporter. Later she worked with Mrs. Lawrence Lewis and Alice Paul, went frequently to Washington, and was among the delegates who presented the subject to President Wilson and to members of Congress shortly before the passage of the Nineteenth Amendment. Finally she was one of those imprisoned for suffrage activities. With a number of others, mostly professional women, she received a jail sentence in August 1918 for taking part in the Lafayette Square meeting in Washington, but the sentence was remitted.

[*Jour. Am. Medic. Asso.*, Dec. 7, 1929; *Medic. Woman's Jour.*, Dec. 1929; *Weekly Roster and Medic. Digest*, Nov. 23, 1929; the *Pa. Medic. Jour.*, Dec. 1929; *Bull. of the Medic. Women's Nat. Asso.*, Jan. 1930; *Equal Rights*, Nov. 16, 1929; *Pub. Ledger* (Phila.), Nov. 9, 1929; information as to certain facts from Dr. Lockrey's associate, Dr. Miriam M. Butt.]   A. L. L.

LOCKWOOD, BELVA ANN BENNETT (Oct. 24, 1830–May 19, 1917), teacher, lecturer, lawyer, suffragist, daughter of Lewis Johnson and Hannah (Green) Bennett, was born in Royalton, Niagara County, N. Y. She was educated in the public schools there, and in the Genesee Wesleyan Seminary. In 1848, at the age of eighteen, she married a farmer, Uriah H. McNall, and was left a widow at twenty-four with one child. After her husband's death she taught at Royalton, but finding that she received only half the salary granted to men she went to Genesee College for further training, graduating (A.M.) in 1857. She taught at Lockport, at the Gainesville Seminary, and was principal of the McNall Seminary in Oswego, N. Y. After the Civil War she moved to Washington, D. C., and there began the study of law. On Mar. 11, 1868, she was married to Dr. Ezekiel Lockwood, a dentist and claim agent, who died in 1877. She graduated from the National University Law School in 1873 at the age of forty-three and was admitted to the Washington bar. In her practice she specialized in cases of claims against the government. She was the first woman admitted to practice before the Supreme Court of the United States, and she began to plead before this court at the age of forty-nine. Her activities centered about a lifelong struggle for women's rights, and she made her law office in her own house the meeting place for national leaders in the struggle to improve conditions for women. In her capacity as lawyer she helped to secure for the women of the District of Columbia equal property rights and equal guardianship of children. She also prepared an amendment to the statehood bill granting suffrage to women in Oklahoma, Arizona, and New Mexico. For eight years she lectured successfully and was prominent both nationally and internationally in promoting women's rights, temperance, peace, and arbitration. She was the first woman candidate for president of the United States, receiving twice, in 1884 and 1888, the nomination of the National Equal Rights party of the Pacific Coast ("How I Ran for the Presidency," *National Magazine*, March 1903). In 1886 she contested the election of Cleveland in the electoral college. She was a delegate from the State Department to the International Congress of Charities, Correction, and Philanthropy in Geneva in 1886 and a delegate to the Universal Peace Congress in Paris in 1889. In 1892 she was made a member of the International Peace Bureau in Berne and was secretary of the American Branch of the Bureau. She was also one of the nominating committee for the Nobel Peace Prize. A few of her papers on peace and arbitration have been published. A life-size oil portrait of her was unveiled by the women of the District of Columbia in 1913 and is now in the gallery of the National Museum. She is on the state honor roll of New York of the National League of Women Voters. She was a vigorous, persistent, aggressive personality, and she fought incessantly for fifty years for women's rights, using all the legal weapons at her command. An eloquent advocate, she made some of the most effective speeches heard in the long suffrage campaign.

[*Who's Who in America*, 1916–17; Frances E. Willard and Mary A. Livermore, *A Woman of the Century* (1893); the *Lit. Digest*, June 16, 1917; the *Woman Citizen*, June 2, 1917; the *Suffragist*, May 26, 1917; *Case and Comment*, Aug. 1917; the *Evening Star* (Washington), May 19, 1917; *N. Y. Times*, May 20, 1917.]   F. F. P.

LOCKWOOD, JAMES BOOTH (Oct. 9, 1852–Apr. 9, 1884), army officer and Arctic explorer, was descended from Richard Lockwood, who settled on the Eastern Shore of Maryland about the beginning of the eighteenth century. The son of Henry Hayes Lockwood, artillerist and brigadier-general of volunteers during the Civil War, and Anna (Booth) Lockwood of Delaware, he was born at Annapolis, Md., where his father was serving as professor in the Naval Academy. After attending a private school at Bethlehem, Pa., and St. John's College, Annapolis, he entered the army in 1873, as second lieutenant, 23rd United States Infantry. He served with his regiment at various posts in the Trans-Mississippi region until he volunteered in June 1881 for duty with the Lady Franklin Bay Arctic Expedition, under the command of Lieut. A. W. Greely. During the autumn of 1881 he made scientific observations at the headquarters, Lady Franklin Bay, Grant Land, and was engaged in preliminary field work for future explorations. In March 1882 he crossed Kennedy Channel to Greenland, visited the observatory and grave of Charles F. Hall [*q.v.*], examined caches, and explored the various routes in northwest Greenland to the Polar Ocean which might be used for future travel. This journey of ten days, covering a distance of 135 miles, was made in temperatures seventy-four degrees below freezing, without injuries of any kind.

On Apr. 3, 1882, Lockwood started again, under orders charging him with "the full control and arrangement of the most important sledging and geographical work of this expedition, the exploration of the northeastern coast of Greenland . . . [and] the extension of knowledge regarding lands in the Polar circle" (*Report, post,* I, 182–83). Supported by a man-drawn-sledge party to Cape Bryant, he left that point with a dog sledge, accompanied by Sergeant D. L. Brainard and Christiansen, the Eskimo, and, traveling entirely over the ice-floes of the Arctic Ocean, after incredible efforts and great suffering, reached his farthest, Lockwood Island, 83° 24′ N., 40° 46′ W., on May 13. From a mountain top his vision reached Cape Washington, nine miles south of the northernmost land of the world. This expedition, also, returned without injury, although the journey out and back involved travel of 1,070 statute miles, in average temperatures below zero for sixty days and at times eighty-one degrees below freezing. The journey gained the honors of the highest north, held continuously by England for three centuries. It proved that extreme north Greenland was a mountainous, glacier-covered region; the 124 miles of new coast was indented by eight inlets of unknown depth; the main ice of the Arctic Ocean was marked by a tidal crack, sometimes a hundred feet wide, through which a sounding of 840 feet failed to reach bottom.

An attempt to surpass this northing in 1883 was prevented by Lockwood's finding extensive open water at Black Horn Cliffs, Greenland, which his orders forbade his passing. This trip failing, he was ordered to attempt the crossing of Grant Land to the western ocean, whose indistinct limits had been seen from Mount Arthur by Greely in 1882, crossing from the head of Archer Fiord. With Brainard, Christiansen, and a dog team, Lockwood started on Apr. 25, 1883, and on May 15, after an extraordinarily difficult journey overland, discovered and camped in a great inlet of the western ocean (Greely Fiord), in 80° 48.5′ N., 78° 26′ W., making in his two trips one-eighth the way around the world north of the eightieth degree. The divide between the

two oceans was 2,600 feet, and from a mountain over 4,400 feet high Lockwood discovered the remarkable configuration of Grant Land. It is an ice-free, vegetation-covered region, bounded on the north by the mountains discovered by Greely in 1882, and by similar mountain peaks to the south, which were fronted for a hundred miles by an unbroken glacial front varying from 140 to 200 feet in perpendicular height. Greely Fiord was about sixty miles long, and from ten to fifteen miles broad. One mountain was called Fossil from the great quantities of fossils found there—petrified wood, shells, and fish. Seals were seen in Greely Fiord and much game abounded in the country, and the extended trip was only possible because game supplied food after the rations gave out.

Following his return to headquarters, Lockwood was ordered, June 1, 1883, to take over the duties of naturalist of the expedition, and he prepared an inventory of the specimens collected. During the boat retreat, beginning in August, and the starvation winter at Cape Sabine, 1883–84, he distinguished himself by his manly attitude, and when the crossing of Smith Sound was considered, asked that in his weak state he be left behind so as not to lessen any other comrade's chance of life. He died at Cape Sabine some two months before the survivors of the party were rescued.

[F. A. Holden and E. D. Lockwood, *Descendants of Robert Lockwood* (1889); Charles Lanman, *Farthest North; or, The Life and Explorations of Lieut. James Booth Lockwood, of the Greely Arctic Expedition* (1885); A. W. Greely, *Three Years of Arctic Service: An Account of the Lady Franklin Bay Expedition of 1881–84* (2 vols., 1886), and *International Polar Expedition: Report of the Proc. of the U. S. Expedition to Lady Franklin Bay, Grinnell Land* (2 vols., 1888), which contains Lockwood's journal (App. No. 122, in vol. I).]　　　　　　　　　　　　A. W. G.

LOCKWOOD, RALPH INGERSOLL (July 8, 1798–Apr. 12, 1858?), lawyer, author, was born at Greenwich, Conn., the son of Stephen and Sarah (Ingersoll) Lockwood. Although members of the family held no positions of national importance, it was, nevertheless, a distinguished one. Robert, the founder of the family in America, emigrated from England about 1630 and settled first in Watertown, Mass., and later in Fairfield, Conn. During Colonial and Revolutionary times, many of his descendants held military offices, and by the year 1834 eleven had graduated from Yale College. Ralph was the fourth of a family of eight children. In March 1821, his parents moved to Mount Pleasant, now Ossining, Westchester County, N. Y., where the father purchased a farm of 100 acres.

Ralph and two younger brothers, Albert and

Munson, studied law and became members of the bar. Albert and Munson practised in Westchester County—Albert eventually becoming county judge—but Ralph moved to New York City and there practised for the remainder of his life. His wit and eloquence attracted attention, and he soon became one of the well-known lawyers of the city. When he was twenty-seven years old he published a vigorous analysis of the problems confronting Congress in the enactment of a national bankruptcy act (*Essay on a National Bankrupt Law,* 1825) in which he discussed the mooted question as to whether the benefits of the law should be extended to all classes or confined solely to the trading class, himself advocating a middle course. In December 1838, he was elected a member of the New York Law Library, later the New York Law Institute. He was severely critical of what he termed "the faults and absurdities of the English common law." His interest lay in the field of equity and he became, in time, one of the leading chancery lawyers of the state. Reverence for the courts he did not regard as a duty and his attacks upon the decisions of the court of chancery were distinguished for their vigor and fearlessness. In addition to his capabilities as a lawyer he had a natural interest in literature and was an excellent French scholar. He visited France upon two occasions and for a number of years acted as counsel for the leading French citizens of New York City. In 1848 he published *Analytical and Practical Synopsis of All the Cases Argued and Reversed, in Law and Equity, in the Court for the Correction of Errors, of New York, 1799 to 1847;* he also edited the American edition of J. E. Bright's *A Treatise on the Law of Husband and Wife* (2 vols., 1850).

Lockwood was the author of two novels, *Rosine Laval* (1833) and *The Insurgents* (2 vols., 1835). Both were published anonymously, *Rosine Laval* appeared under the pseudonym, "Mr. Smith." He had long cherished an ambition to write fiction, and when forced to leave New York temporarily to escape a plague of the cholera he found himself with sufficient leisure to gratify it. In thirty minutes the plot was conceived and in six weeks *Rosine Laval* was finished. A nervous breakdown, induced by overwork, gave him the leisure to write *The Insurgents,* which was completed in three months. Neither of the two, from the literary point of view, is valuable and only in the most exhaustive histories of American literature is it possible to find any mention of them. *Rosine Laval* was intended to be a light novel, but its humor is of a past generation, and the swoonings and the harrowing death, which

seemed to the author necessary occurrences before the love problem could be resolved, are unconvincing. *The Insurgents,* a novel of Shays's Rebellion, was a more serious undertaking. The same faults which mar *Rosine Laval* are present, however, and reveal that Lockwood, whatever his accomplishments as a lawyer, was not possessed of marked aptitude for the writing of fiction. In the preface to his first novel he wrote that he had for several years threatened to fall seriously in love and to marry, but when he died he was still a bachelor.

[F. A. Holden and E. D. Lockwood, *Descendants of Robert Lockwood, Colonial and Revolutionary Hist. of the Lockwood Family in America* (1889), which gives date of death as Apr. 12, 1858, and also as 1855; information from J. F. Conillon, Librarian, N. Y. Law Institute; biog. material in his works.]   H. Ca—s.

LOCKWOOD, ROBERT WILTON (Sept. 12, 1861–Mar. 20, 1914), painter, known as Wilton Lockwood, was born at Wilton, Conn., a town for which he was named by his parents, John Lewis and Emily Waldon (Middlebrook) Lockwood. He was descended from Robert Lockwood who emigrated to Massachusetts in 1630 and ultimately settled in Fairfield, Conn. His mother died in 1865 and the father removed the household to New York, but the boy showed distaste for city life and was sent to the home of his aunts at Rowayton, Conn. He worked on their farm and attended school in winter. Later he was employed in a New York broker's office where his ability to draw attracted some attention and led to his introduction to John La Farge [*q.v.*], at whose studio he had instruction. He also attended classes at the Art Students' League of New York, whence he went to Paris to draw at Julian's under Benjamin Constant. He returned to New York, painted several portraits, and, with the money thus earned, resumed his studies at Munich, a city which Frank Duveneck had made popular with American art students. He lived also for several years at Paris where his style matured and his personality, that of a tall, rufous American, of courteous bearing and sharp repartee, made him a marked figure among artists. A group of his portraits at the New Salon in 1895 won special encomia. He married at London, England, in 1892, Ethel Whiton of Boston.

Returning to the United States in 1896 the Lockwoods settled in Boston. Whether this was a wise choice of location for an artist of Lockwood's talent and temperament is debatable. Working quietly at his Boylston Street studio in the winter, and in the summer at South Orleans, Cape Cod, he lived a life outwardly uneventful but always actively creative. His portraiture was penetrating, searching, and psychologically profound, some of his likenesses being almost uncanny in revealing a personality. Among his notable sitters were John La Farge, the canvas now at the Boston Museum of Fine Arts; Grover Cleveland, for Princeton University; Justice Oliver Wendell Holmes, for the Massachusetts Bar Association; President Francis A. Walker, of the Massachusetts Institute of Technology, for the St. Botolph Club; and Otto Roth, violinist, a work awarded the Temple Gold Medal at the Pennsylvania Academy of the Fine Arts in 1898. Other portraits won for Lockwood silver medals at Paris in 1900, Buffalo in 1901, and St. Louis in 1904.

Lockwood's flower paintings grew out of his enthusiastic gardening. As a peony grower he was nationally known and won several prizes for his flowers. His paintings were exquisitely subtle and still quite objective apparitions of the choicest blooms at his Cape Cod home. They were painted against a thinly toned background, usually on the reverse side of a primed canvas. Some of these are owned by the Metropolitan and Worcester Art museums, and the Corcoran Gallery of Art in Washington. After the artist's death, the St. Botolph Club, Boston, of which he was long a member, held a memorial exhibition of his works. The catalogue's foreword, by a brother painter, acclaimed him as "one of the ablest artists Boston has ever had—perhaps the most subtle and sensitive."

[See especially the biographical sketch by Charles Hovey Pepper in the memorial exhibition catalogue, Dec. 19, 1914. The *Boston Evening Transcript* and *Boston Herald*, Mar. 21, 1914, printed long obituaries by William H. Downes and F. W. Coburn. Other sources include: T. R. Sullivan, article in *Scribner's*, Feb. 1898; Samuel Isham and Royal Cortissoz, *The Hist. of Am. Painting* (1927); *The Artists' Year Book*, 1905–06; *Time and the Hour*, Mar. 5, 1898; F. A. Holden and E. D. Lockwood, *Descendants of Robert Lockwood: Colonial and Revolutionary Hist. of the Lockwood Family in America* (1889); L. F. Middlebrook, *Reg. of the Middlebrook Family* (1909).]   F. W. C.

LOCKWOOD, SAMUEL DRAKE (Aug. 2, 1789–Apr. 23, 1874), jurist, was born in Poundridge, N. Y., the son of Joseph and Mary (Drake) Lockwood, and a descendant of Robert Lockwood who emigrated to Watertown, Mass., in 1630 and later settled in Fairfield, Conn. His schooling was very scanty. From 1803 to 1811 he lived and studied law with an uncle, Francis Drake, in Waterford, N. Y. Licensed in February 1811, he practised in Batavia, Sempronius, and Auburn until he started for Illinois in October 1818. Meanwhile he had evinced unusual maturity. He served as sergeant major (1808) and paymaster (1811) of a militia regiment, as a justice of the peace and master in chancery

(1812 only), became a trustee of his church (Presbyterian, 1812), and participated in organizing (1815) New York's first Bible society. He carried to the West commendatory letters that assured him immediate recognition. Like other ambitious settlers in the new state, he was a candidate for political office. On Feb. 6, 1821, he was elected by the legislature attorney-general. Next an unsuccessful candidate for election to the United States Senate, in the autumn of 1822, he was appointed, before that ambition was disappointed, secretary of state (Dec. 28, 1822), thereupon resigning the attorney-generalship; only to resign the secretaryship when confirmed (Jan. 28, 1823) receiver of the Edwardsville land-office. He remained for some years somewhat ambitious and influential in politics. In the passionate struggle in the years 1822–24 over the calling of a constitutional convention (to make Illinois a slave state), he was active and powerful in behalf of the anti-slavery cause, which he aided, particularly, by editing one anti-convention newspaper and contributing to others. The next legislature elected him an associate justice of the state supreme court (commissioned Jan. 19, 1825), which office he filled with exceeding success and honor until Dec. 4, 1848, when a new constitution, framed by a convention in which he was an active delegate, went into effect, making the judges elective by the people. He did not seek popular indorsement.

Through his twenty-four years of service, Lockwood bore the heaviest burden in the labors of the court. His, also, was the greatest individual contribution to the notable revision of the Illinois statutes prepared in the years 1826–29 by the judges and the legislature. He was an excellent and a learned lawyer; a judge characterized by intelligence, urbanity, and social wisdom; a kindly man, of pure character, somewhat austere in his unbending rectitude, of marked modesty, yet equally of marked energy and determination. His reputation in the state was notable, and his influence continually exercised for good causes. At various times and in various capacities he was active in fostering public education, and in promoting measures for the care of mental and physical defectives. He was a charter trustee of each of the state institutions established for the care of the insane, deaf mutes, and blind. From 1851 until his death he was a legislative trustee of the land-department of the Illinois Central Railroad. Originally a Whig, he acted after 1855 with the Republican party. On Oct. 3, 1826, he married Mary Virginia Stith Nash of St. Louis. The last years of his life he spent in Batavia, Ill., where he died.

[See Wm. Coffin, *Life and Times of Hon. Samuel D. Lockwood* (1889) ; *The Biog. Encyc. of Ill. of the Nineteenth Cent.* (1875) ; J. M. Palmer, *The Bench and Bar of Ill.* (1899), vol. I ; Thos. Ford, *A Hist. of Ill.* (1854) ; T. C. Pease, "The Frontier State, 1818–48," *The Centennial Hist. of Ill.*, vol. II (1918) ; F. A. Holden and E. D. Lockwood, *Descendants of Robt. Lockwood : Colonial and Revolutionary Hist. of the Lockwood Family in America* (1889) ; F. W. Scott, "Newspapers and Periodicals of Ill., 1814–79," *Ill. State Hist. Lib. Colls.*, vol. VI (1910) ; *Trans. Ill. State Hist. Soc. . . . 1903* (1904), pp. 213–14 ; *Chicago Legal News*, Apr. 20, 1889 ; *Chicago Tribune*, Apr. 25, 1874. Lockwood's opinions, so far as they survive, appear in 1–9 *Illinois Reports*.]   F. S. P.

LOCKWOOD, WILTON [See LOCKWOOD, ROBERT WILTON, 1861–1914].

LOCY, WILLIAM ALBERT (Sept. 14, 1857–Oct. 9, 1924), zoologist, teacher, historian of the development of biological science, came of Dutch ancestry, his forefathers having emigrated from Holland in 1651. Born at Troy, Mich., son of Lorenzo Dow and Sarah (Kingsbury) Locy, he grew up in a home that provided education in music, science, and the humanities. His father was a dentist. Having received the degree of B.S. from the University of Michigan in 1881, he continued his studies in biology there during 1881–82 and received the degree of M.S. in 1884. During 1884–85, under a fellowship at Harvard University, he completed a noteworthy embryological investigation on the development of *Agelena naevia* (a spider), in the laboratory of Prof. Edward Laurens Mark. The year 1891 he spent at the University of Berlin. Under an honorary fellowship at the University of Chicago in 1894, he prosecuted studies upon the structure and development of the vertebrate head, in the laboratories of Prof. Charles O. Whitman, producing a thesis on this subject which was accepted for the degree of Ph.D. in 1895 (*Journal of Morphology*, May 1895). For several summers he was occupied in research at the Marine Biological Laboratories at Woods Hole, Mass.

After an experience of three years' teaching in secondary schools, in 1887 he became professor of biology in Lake Forest University, Illinois, his title being changed in 1889 to professor of animal morphology. While at Lake Forest he also served one year as professor of physiology at the Rush Medical College, Chicago. In January 1896 he went to Northwestern University, Evanston, Ill., as professor of zoology and director of the zoological laboratories, in which capacity he remained for twenty-eight years. During this time fifty-four advanced degrees were given by the university for work done under his direction and supervision.

He produced no less than fifty-six scientific papers, some of which are regarded as landmarks in their fields. "His study of the embryonic neuromeres of the fore and mid-brain of fishes stands in the fore-front of investigation on neural metamerism"; while "his study of the *nervus terminalis* (accessory cranial nerve) in Elasmobranchs . . . was so thorough as to dominate and become the standard for all later investigations" (Crew and Lillie, *post*, p. 492). Other highly valued papers concern the embryonic development of elasmobranchs (sharks), and the derivation of the pineal eye.

During the later years of his career he gave his attention more and more to developing a general interest in the early history of the sciences of biology and medicine, and his devotion to this field of research is marked by a series of brief, valuable, historical, non-technical papers ; among them, *Malpighi, Swammerdam and Leeuwenhoek* (1901) ; "Service of Zoology to Intellectual Progress" (*Popular Science*, October 1909) ; "Earliest Printed Illustrations of Natural History" (*Scientific Monthly*, September 1921) ; "Wilhelm Hofmeister" (*Ibid.*, October 1924). In 1911 appeared a more extended paper upon "Anatomical Illustrations Before Vesalius" covering forty-four pages, with twenty-three figures, and appearing in the Whitman memorial number of the *Journal of Morphology* (December 1911). The final outcome of his zeal in the study of the historical development of biology took the form of three books : *Biology and Its Makers* (1908, 3rd ed. 1915, German ed., Jena, 1915) ; *The Main Currents of Zoology* (1918) ; and, his last work, completed a few days before his death, *Growth of Biology* (1925). He was editor in charge of zoological articles for the *New American Supplement to the Encyclopaedia Britannica* (5 vols., 1897), writing several of them himself ; and he held a membership in many scientific societies. On June 26, 1883, he married Ellen Eastman, daughter of Dr. Joseph and Nancy McAllister Eastman of Flint, Mich., by whom he had two sons.

[Henry Crew and F. R. Lillie, "William A. Locy, 1857–1924," *Science*, Nov. 28, 1924 ; F. H. Garrison, "William A. Locy, In Memoriam," *Annals of Medic. Hist.*, June 1925 ; C. E. Tharaldsen, "William A. Locy, Zoologist and Historian of Biological Science," *Scientific Mo.*, Nov. 1925 ; J. McK. Cattell and D. R. Brimhall, *Am. Men of Science* (3rd ed., 1921) ; *Who's Who in America*, 1924–25 ; *Chicago Daily Tribune*, Oct. 11, 1924.]   C. B. A.

LODGE, GEORGE CABOT (Oct. 10, 1873–Aug. 21, 1909), poet, was born at Boston, Mass., the son of Henry Cabot Lodge [*q.v.*] and Anna Cabot Mills (Davis) Lodge. His childhood was spent in his father's home on the windy peninsula of Nahant; and as he grew older he became the protégé of that charmed circle which included Henry Adams, Edith Wharton, Sturgis Bigelow, John Hay, Cecil Spring-Rice, and Theodore Roosevelt. At the age of eighteen he entered Harvard. In college he passed four studious and thoughtful years, read Leconte de Lisle, Renan, Schopenhauer, and the Upanishads, and developed a mood of poetic pessimism which sat oddly upon his perfect health and joyous vitality. The winter of 1895–96 was spent with his friend Joseph Trumbull Stickney at the Sorbonne in Paris, observing the humors of the Boulevards and reading the Italian and Greek poets. The next year at the University of Berlin he mastered the German language, frequented the productions of classic drama, took courses in philosophy, and digested the initiation into esoteric Buddhism which he had received the previous summer at Tuckanuck from his life-long mentor Dr. Bigelow. In the autumn of 1897 he settled in Washington as his father's secretary. His first volume *The Song of the Wave, and Other Poems* was published in the spring of 1898. Here, along with echoes of Whitman, Browning, Swinburne, Leconte de Lisle, and Leopardi, were found his characteristic elevation of thought and sonorous melody of verse, culminating in the fine sonnet "To Silence" beginning:

"Lord of the deserts 'twixt a million spheres."

The year 1898 brought the Spanish-American War, a vivid episode in his life. As ensign on the *Dixie,* under his uncle, Capt. Charles H. Davis [*q.v.*], he commanded a gun crew, fought two minor engagements, was of the landing party that demanded the surrender of Ponce, Porto Rico, and with his own hands raised the American flag over the city hall. Theodore Roosevelt states: "He made an admirable officer, training his men with unwearied care and handling them with cool readiness under fire" (*post,* pp. xiv, xv). After the war Lodge resumed his duties as secretary of a Senate committee, yet, as always, reading omnivorously and writing copiously. Several novels and plays were written and destroyed, but his sonnets began to meet a welcome from the editors of *Scribner's,* the *Century,* and the *Atlantic Monthly.* On Aug. 18, 1900, he married Matilda Elizabeth Frelinghuysen Davis, by whom he had two sons and a daughter. After a winter in Paris the remaining eight years of his life were passed at Washington, with summers at Tuckanuck, in domestic happiness, numerous friendships, vigorous open-air life by day, and, unfortunately for his health, constant poetic composition far into the night. He died of heart failure following an attack of ptomaine poisoning, at Tuckanuck.

The brief years of Lodge's poetic activity produced a remarkable body of published work. Following *The Song of the Wave* in 1898 came *Poems (1899–1902)* in 1902, *Cain, a Drama* in 1904, *The Great Adventure,* inspired by the death of Trumbull Stickney, in 1905, and *Herakles* in 1908. *The Soul's Inheritance, and Other Poems* appeared in 1909 after his death. In 1911 his *Poems and Dramas* were published in two volumes with an introduction by Theodore Roosevelt, companioned by a third containing an intimate and perceptive biography by Henry Adams. Lodge was a sound scholar in the fields of philosophy, and of classic and contemporary literature. His early work was academic, a little rhetorical, more than a little metaphysical, but with each succeeding volume he came nearer to the poignant realities of modern life. He fell, however, upon a barren time in English poetry, and died before the first stirrings of the poetic renaissance which preceded the Great War. During his lifetime both the production of poetry and public interest in it were at lowest ebb. Outside of the circle of his friends he had small appreciation while living and has found few readers since his death. Yet his two poetic dramas, *Cain,* presenting the eternal foe of compromise, and *Herakles,* the vicarious savior of mankind, do not suffer in comparison with any others in American literature. A half-dozen of his sonnets belong with the best in our language.

[*The Life of George Cabot Lodge* (1911), published anonymously but written by Henry Adams; Edith Wharton, "George Cabot Lodge," in *Scribner's Mag.,* Feb. 1910; Theodore Roosevelt, introduction to *Poems and Dramas of George Cabot Lodge* (1911); *Living Age,* May 17, 1913; *Who's Who in America,* 1908–09; *Washington Times,* and *Evening Star* (Washington), Aug. 23, 1909; personal acquaintance.]   F.G.

LODGE, HENRY CABOT (May 12, 1850– Nov. 9, 1924), senator, author, was born in Boston. He was the only son of John Ellerton Lodge, a prosperous merchant and owner of swift clipper-ships engaged in commerce with China. His mother was Anna Cabot, grand-daughter of George Cabot [*q.v.*], the Federalist sage. After an early education in E. S. Dixwell's Latin School, Boston, he entered Harvard College and graduated in 1871 near the middle of his class without having distinguished himself either in his studies or in any of the outside activities. Immediately after graduation Lodge married his cousin, Anna Cabot Davis, daughter of Rear Admiral Charles H. Davis [*q.v.*], and went to Europe for a year, spending most of the time in Rome. He had, as he later wrote, "no definite plan; no taste, no aptitude, no mastering passion" so far as the choice of a life career was concerned. Returning to Boston in 1872 without having formed any definite plans for the future, he decided to study law as a presumably useful preparation for whatever vocation he might ultimately enter. Accordingly, he spent the next two years at the Harvard Law School, from which he graduated in 1874, again without any special distinction, and in April 1875 he was admitted to the Boston bar.

Meanwhile, Henry Adams, his former teacher of history at Harvard, offered Lodge the assistant editorship of the *North American Review* and this opportunity was eagerly accepted (1873–76). All thought of following the active practice of law was forthwith cast aside, and for the next few years Lodge devoted himself with great zest to various literary pursuits. In addition to routine editorial work he wrote articles for various periodicals and at the same time completed his work for the first degree of Ph.D. (1876) ever obtained in political science at Harvard. His thesis was published as "The Anglo-Saxon Land-Law," in *Essays in Anglo-Saxon Law* (1876). In the following year appeared his *Life and Letters of George Cabot,* still the standard biography of his great-grandfather. Lectures given by Lodge at Harvard (1876–79) formed the substance of his book, *A Short History of the English Colonies in America* (1881). His most notable historical work is represented by his contributions to the American Statesman Series, edited by his cousin, John T. Morse, Jr.: *Alexander Hamilton* (1882), *Daniel Webster* (1882), and *George Washington* (2 vols., 1888). These readable biographies, however, are colored by his political predilections, and as time went on his writings were marred by increasing partisanship. Books of less consequence in the field of history are his *Historical and Political Essays* (1892), and *The Story of the Revolution* (2 vols., 1898). In the course of his career he published several collections of essays and speeches.

Lodge's interest in history inspired him to an initial participation in public affairs, and the thrust of his ancestry also impelled him to take some part in the politics of his own neighborhood. His first venture into the arena of partisanship was made in 1879 when he became a candidate for the Massachusetts House of Representatives from the district which included the town of Nahant, near Boston, where he maintained his legal residence. This district being strongly Republican, he was elected. In the following year, shortly after his thirtieth birthday,

he went as a delegate to the Republican National Convention which nominated Garfield for the presidency. He was reëlected to the lower branch of the state legislature in the same autumn; but in 1881 he sought promotion to the state Senate and failed. Turning to national politics, he then tried to secure the Republican nomination for Congress from his district in 1882, but here again he was unsuccessful. Lodge was much discouraged by these two reverses, but a chance to regain self-confidence came in 1883 when he was chosen to manage the Republican campaign for governor against the redoubtable Gen. Benjamin F. Butler. In this fight Lodge displayed political generalship of a high order, and an adroitness which surprised even his own friends. His candidate won, and the prestige which came to the campaign manager from the victory enabled Lodge to get himself chosen as delegate-at-large to the Republican National Convention which nominated Blaine in 1884. Along with Theodore Roosevelt at that convention he worked strenuously against the selection of Blaine, but unlike most of his own intimates Lodge did not desert the ranks of Republican regulars. He not only supported the national ticket in the campaign but put himself forward as the regular Republican candidate for Congress in his own district. By reason of the Mugwump defection he was badly defeated, but by staying regular he placed himself in line for another nomination in 1886, and was then elected to Congress by a narrow margin.

Although Lodge was not yet thirty-seven years of age when he entered Congress he soon became known to the entire membership because he took the floor often and effectively. The clarity with which he presented his arguments gained attention and made him one of the notable figures in the House, even before his first term was finished. The most conspicuous measure with which he closely associated himself during his career in the House was the so-called "Force Bill," which aimed to establish federal supervision over all polling places at national elections, and thus to prevent the exclusion of colored voters in the Southern states. The debates on this bill stirred up a vast amount of sectional bitterness, much of which recoiled on Lodge as the reputed author of the proposal. In his own district, however, his attitude proved to be a political asset of direct value, and he had no difficulty in securing reëlection by increased majorities in 1888 and 1890. He served six years in the House (1887–1893). Besides stirring up the South he ran foul of the practical politicians in all parts of the country by his championship of civil-service reform. His sturdy defense of the civil-service laws was of the utmost value to the cause at a critical juncture. Moreover, it was on his recommendation that Theodore Roosevelt became a member of the national Civil Service Commission and proceeded to make the system function.

From the time of his first venture into politics Lodge nurtured an ambition to become a senator from Massachusetts. In January 1893 the two chambers of the legislature agreed upon him as a successor to Senator Dawes, who declined to be a candidate for reëlection. To the end of his life, his hold on his seat in the Senate was never seriously in doubt save on one occasion: in January 1911, during the Progressive upheaval, he was reëlected by the Massachusetts legislature by a majority of only six votes. During his career of thirty-seven years in the House and Senate Lodge had to do with the framing of many important measures. He helped to draft the Sherman Anti-Trust Law of 1890, the Pure Food and Drugs Law, and several tariff measures, especially the one of 1909. On tariff matters he proved himself a thorough-going protectionist at all times. He was in the forefront of the fight against free silver during the years 1894 to 1900. He was a consistent strong-navy man, viewed all proposals for compulsory international arbitration or disarmament with suspicion, approved the Venezuela message of 1895, supported the acquisition of the Philippines, and abetted Roosevelt's successful intrigue in Panama. He voted against the proposal for direct election of senators, opposed woman suffrage, voted against the adoption of the Eighteenth Amendment, and helped to pass the soldiers' bonus measure over President Coolidge's veto.

Lodge always regarded the field of international affairs as his sphere of special competence. He read widely on this subject and his speeches in the Senate disclosed a thorough familiarity with international law and precedents. He was restrained by no ingrowing conscience in dealing with the rights or claims of countries other than his own. Roosevelt set a high value on Lodge's judgment on international matters of every sort and during the years 1901–09 the latter became one of the President's closest advisers in this field of executive policy. He was selected as one of the American representatives on the Alaskan Boundary Commission of 1903, despite the fact that the commission was required to be made up of "impartial jurists." Lodge was neither impartial nor a jurist. His mind was thoroughly made up and closed before he started for

London on this mission. Lodge soon found a place on the Foreign Relations Committee, and helped draft the resolutions which led to the war with Spain; he reported the Hay-Pauncefote treaty as well as the Alaskan Boundary agreement with Great Britain. But it was not until late in his senatorial career that the rule of seniority gave him the chairmanship. Almost immediately thereafter he was thrown into the thick of the most important controversy which the Senate had waged in more than a half century. His leadership of the fight against the ratification of the Peace Treaty and the Covenant made him in 1919 a national figure and the acknowledged leader of those who desired to keep the United States out of the League of Nations.

Before the peace conference began, Lodge had expressed himself as favorable to the imposition of harsh terms and a heavy indemnity on Germany, and as opposed to the coupling of the League of Nations, which in principle he approved, with the treaty of peace (*Congressional Record*, 65 Cong., 2 Sess., pp. 9392–93, Aug. 23, 1918; memorandum to White, Dec. 2, 1918, Allan Nevins, *Henry White: Thirty Years of American Diplomacy*, 1930, pp. 352–55). Convinced that his own ideas rather than Wilson's represented American opinion, he even suggested that Henry White [*q.v.*] show to certain leaders of the Allies his (Lodge's) memorandum, and thus strengthen the hands of those opposed to Wilson. This White did not do. In the course of the negotiations, however, certain of Lodge's speeches, widely quoted in the European press, served to make his hostility to Wilson's plans well known. The differences between the two men were not composed by the White House dinner, after Wilson's first return, and in March 1919 Lodge submitted in the Senate a resolution signed by himself and thirty-six other Republican senators which set forth their objections to the combination of the Treaty and the Covenant in a single document. Under the rules of the Senate this resolution could not be formally received, but it served notice that more than one-third of the senators were not prepared to accept the Covenant in the form proposed. In July 1919 the Treaty and Covenant, now somewhat modified, were officially transmitted to the Senate in their final form. After prolonged deliberation the Foreign Relations Committee, through Lodge as its chairman, reported them with a series of reservations. After a lengthy debate these were adopted by a majority vote; but in the end the two documents (with the reservations added) were rejected, chiefly by the votes of Democratic senators at the behest of Wilson, to whom the reservations were objectionable. Much of the bitterness that was engendered might have been avoided if both sides to the controversy had disclosed a spirit of compromise at an earlier stage. Lodge's action gained for him at the time warm admiration and bitter resentment in about equal measure. His own account of the controversy may be seen in his posthumously published book, *The Senate and the League of Nations* (1925).

In the presidential election of 1920 the issue of the entry of the United States into the League of Nations became an outstanding one and the result was regarded by Lodge as a complete vindication of his course. He was one of those who had been chiefly responsible for the nomination of Harding, and with the latter's election Lodge's influence in the field of foreign relations became greater than it had been at any previous time, even in Roosevelt's day. With the inauguration of President Harding in 1921, negotiations for a separate treaty with Germany were begun and this treaty in due course received ratification. Lodge was now the senior member of the Senate, titular leader of the Republican majority there, and chairman of the Foreign Relations Committee. He served as one of the four American Representatives at the Washington Conference of 1921. His leadership was also demonstrated by the action of the Senate on the World Court reservations a little later. During the next year or two, however, failing health impaired his work. In the end it became necessary for him to undergo a severe surgical operation from which he never fully recovered. He died at the Charlesgate Hospital in Cambridge on Nov. 9, 1924. A son, George Cabot Lodge [*q.v.*], had died in 1909; his other children, a daughter and a son, survived him.

Lodge was unquestionably a man of acute intellect, a wide reader with a retentive memory, and was endowed with literary skill of a high order. A diligent worker, he was in addition an adept in the art of getting others to work for him. As a practical politician he was equal to the best, nor was he always scrupulous in his choice of the means, provided they served the end. Conservative in temperament, he revered the ancient landmarks in government, and was rarely receptive to reform proposals of any sort. His diction was distinguished and his eloquence persuasive, especially when he put himself forward as the valiant defender of American rights, claims, or aspirations, as he so often did. Lodge was loyal to his friends, but ruthlessly vindictive toward those whom he disliked or opposed. His breadth of view was frequently warped by per-

sonal grudges. He was not always frank and sometimes took refuge in sophistry. Hence even those who admired him greatly often did so with reservations.

[Lodge's autobiographical volume, *Early Memories* (1913), does not deal with his political career. William Lawrence, *Henry Cabot Lodge* (1925), is an intimate biographical sketch. C. S. Groves, *Henry Cabot Lodge, the Statesman* (1925), deals more fully with political activities. See also *Mass. Hist. Soc. Proc.*, vol. LVIII (1925), pp. 99–110, 324–76; *Memorial Addresses Delivered in the Senate and House of Representatives ... in Memory of Henry Cabot Lodge* (1925); *Eleventh Report of the Class of 1871 of Harvard Coll.* (1921); *Who's Who in America*, 1924–25; and articles or notices in the following: *Outlook*, Nov. 19, Dec. 10, 1924; *Nation*, Nov. 19, 1924, Nov. 4, 1925; *Living Age*, Dec. 20, 1924; *Literary Digest*, Nov. 29, 1924, Nov. 7, 1925; *Boston Evening Transcript*, Nov. 10, 1924; *N. Y. Times*, Nov. 10, 11, 16, 1924.]   W. B. M—o.

LOEB, JACQUES (Apr. 7, 1859–Feb. 11, 1924), physiologist, the son of Benedict and Barbara (Isay) Loeb, was born at Mayen in the Rhine province. His parents died in his youth. He attended the Askanisches Gymnasium in Berlin, the universities of Berlin, Munich, and Strassburg, receiving a medical degree in 1884 and passing the *Staatsexamen* in 1885. He returned to Berlin and in 1886 went to Würzburg as assistant to Fick. Two years later he became assistant to Goltz in Strassburg. The winters of 1889–90 and 1890–91 he spent at Naples, carrying on experiments in heteromorphosis. In 1891 he accepted a position at Bryn Mawr and a year later went to the University of Chicago. He remained until 1902 when he accepted a call to the University of California. In 1910 he became a member of the Rockefeller Institute for Medical Research and remained there until his death. He was married, in October 1890, to Anne L. Leonard.

Loeb's original bent was toward philosophy but he was not satisfied with metaphysics: rather he demanded that the great questions of philosophy be put to experimental test. One of the most fundamental of these questions which had a special fascination for him was the freedom of the will. Could this be tested experimentally? In the universities of Berlin and Munich, and in the laboratory of Goltz at Strassburg, he found no answer though Goltz was then experimenting on the brains of dogs by a method which at first seemed promising. At last from Julius von Sachs, the famous botanist of Würzburg, he obtained a clue. Sachs controlled the behavior of plants with great precision on the assumption that plants are simple machines. Loeb tried similar experiments on animals and found that in many cases they reacted with the same machine-like regularity as plants. He called such reactions tropisms. Before the age of thirty he published the "tropism theory" which was destined to make him famous.

An illustration of his method of thought is apparent in the study of the behavior of certain caterpillars which emerge from the ground in spring and climb up trees to the tips of the branches where the opening buds furnish food. What leads them to do this, in some cases before the buds have started to open? The current answer was: A marvellous instinct which directs them to their food without any apparent cause and which is inherited from generation to generation. Not satisfied with this explanation, Loeb made the following experiment. He placed some of the caterpillars in a test-tube in a darkened room and directed the closed end toward the light. The caterpillars crawled to this end and there remained. Food was then pushed along the tube until it almost touched them but, as Loeb expressed it, they were slaves to the light, just as plants are; they could not turn around to take the food which was beside them and they starved to death within easy reach of it. The reason for their climbing trees was now clear: they were attracted by the light and the only assumption needed in regard to heredity was that they inherited some substance which made them sensitive to the light. To this extent they were mechanisms, completely under the control of the experimenter.

Thus at the outset of his career Loeb concluded that certain instincts may be resolved into tropisms. He subsequently developed these ideas. Eventually he was able, by adding carbonic acid to water, to produce in an aquatic animal, ordinarily indifferent to the light, a reaction drawing it irresistibly toward a source of illumination. This led him to question whether certain psychological problems might be placed upon a physico-chemical basis. If behavior might be changed by the addition of an acid why not by the secretions of a gland? "Might not this idea be applied to attraction between the sexes, which may involve a change from a selfish to an altruistic attitude? And why limit the consideration to glandular products? Since Pawlow [the Russian physiologist] and his pupils have produced a salivary secretion in dogs by means of optical or auditory signals it no longer appears strange that what we call an idea should bring about chemical changes in the body" (*Journal of General Physiology*, vol. VIII, Sept. 15, 1928, p. xxiii).

Relating these considerations to the nature of ethics, Loeb stated his theory in the following terms: "If our existence is based on the play of blind forces and only a matter of chance; if we ourselves are only chemical mechanisms—how can there be an ethics for us? The answer is, that our instincts are the root of our ethics and that the instincts are just as hereditary as is the form of our body. We eat, drink, and reproduce not because mankind has reached an agreement that this is desirable, but because, machine-like, we are compelled to do so. We are active, because we are compelled to be so by processes in our central nervous system; and as long as human beings are not economic slaves the instinct of successful work or of workmanship determines the direction of their action. The mother loves and cares for her children, not because metaphysicians had the idea that this was desirable, but because the instinct of taking care of the young is inherited just as distinctly as the morphological characters of the female body. We seek and enjoy the fellowship of human beings because hereditary conditions compel us to do so. We struggle for justice and truth since we are instinctively compelled to see our fellow beings happy. Economic, social, and political conditions, or ignorance and superstition, may warp and inhibit the inherited instincts and thus create a civilization with a faulty or low development of ethics. Individual mutants may arise in which one or the other desirable instinct is lost, just as individual mutants without pigment may arise in animals; and the offspring of such mutants may, if numerous enough, lower the ethical status of a community. Not only is the mechanistic conception of life compatible with ethics: it seems the only conception of life which can lead to an understanding of the source of ethics" (*The Mechanistic Conception of Life*, p. 31).

Loeb believed that a fixed idea may produce a sort of tropism to which the mind mechanically responds without any such process as deliberate choice and this may happen over and over again until deliberate choice is almost or quite impossible. He even believed that much which appears to be deliberate choice is really largely mechanical and that in ordinary human actions there is far less freedom of the will than would appear at first sight. When he first announced his ideas in the nineties they created a sensation. They came at a time when the trend toward anthropomorphic thinking was very strong and they had a marked influence upon philosophy, psychology, sociology, and kindred disciplines.

But Loeb was not content merely to influence the will of the animal; he wished also to control the entire process of life, the whole course of development from beginning to end, and his experiments in these directions led to some brilliant discoveries. Development usually commences with the fertilization of the egg. This was regarded as the most mysterious of life processes. The way in which Loeb set to work to solve the mystery is characteristic. He reasoned that the sperm carries into the egg something which starts its development. In an effort to discover whether he could introduce this substance without using sperm, he subjected the egg to treatment of the most varied sort and discovered a number of methods, both chemical and physical, of starting development without the aid of sperm. He found that in some cases these parthenogenetic animals, as they are called, could be raised to full and normal maturity. He also found means of bringing about fertilization between different species and of thus producing hybrids not occurring in nature. From this beginning he found means of controlling generation in such a way as to produce at will all sorts of things not ordinarily found in nature, such as Siamese twins and triplets, and two-headed animals. He believed that in this way he could lay the foundation for a theory of development.

From this standpoint he studied regeneration, a field which attracted him because it was so long a stronghold of mysticism. It had often been assumed that when a missing part of the organism is replaced, there must be a "directive force" which ensures that the regenerated part shall be exactly what is needed to complete the organism. Loeb found that this is not always so; under some conditions a hydroid instead of regenerating a lost stolon produces a polyp "so that we have an animal terminating at both ends of its body in a head." Such cases are difficult to explain on the basis of a "directive force" which operates to supply the needs of the animal; they are less difficult to explain if it is assumed that the formation of organs is due to the accumulation of specific substances (as had been postulated in the case of plants) at the place where the organ in question is to be formed. Such an accumulation of substances can be controlled to a certain extent by the experimenter.

Loeb went on to examine from a mechanistic approach the equally important question of adaptation. He found that many characteristics of the organism which are regarded as adaptive may be explained on a mechanistic basis. The reactions of animals to light depend on a photochemical substance which may arise without reference to adaptation. It is not necessary to suppose that heliotropism can arise only in response to a need or under the guidance of a "directive force." Loeb emphasized the fact that in many cases what are called "adaptations" arose without any "directive force" before they could possibly have been useful. Where adaptations really exist they can often be explained on a physicochemical basis so that the assumption of a directive force is not necessary.

The process of death, which in higher animals terminates development after a longer or shorter interval, had a great fascination for Loeb. He made experiments which showed that in certain animals death could be postponed by keeping the temperature sufficiently low. He also called attention to the fact that by means of his method of artificial parthenogenesis the life of the egg can be indefinitely prolonged. His brother Leo Loeb, by means of transplantation and tissue culture, had succeeded in doing the same thing for the ordinary cells of the body.

Back of his desire to control life processes was his profound belief that the ills of mankind are largely due to ignorance and superstition and that if some of the mysteries of biology could be cleared up the greatest possible good to mankind would result. His own words were: "What progress humanity has made, not only in physical welfare but also in the conquest of superstition and hatred, and in the formation of a correct view of life, it owes directly or indirectly to mechanistic science" (*Yale Review,* July 1915, p. 785). He believed that the development of scientific knowledge could lead to a philosophy free from mysticism by which the human being could achieve a lasting harmony with itself and its environment. Such a goal he believed could be reached only by research, which would eventually reveal altruism as an innate property of human nature, just as the tropisms and instincts are inherent in lower organisms. To establish such a conception he exerted his utmost effort. The great driving force of his life lay not only in a powerful intellectual urge, but also in profound emotion. He spared no effort in his attempt to reduce life processes to mechanism. It may be added that he was often rewarded with startling success.

In making his experiments Loeb believed that the only satisfactory method was to follow the procedure of the exact sciences and to try to express all the observed phenomena by equations containing no arbitrary constants. He followed the progress of physics and chemistry with the closest attention and seized upon all that could be made useful in solving his own problems. Thus he made extensive use of the dissociation theory of Arrhenius which led him to discover artificial parthenogenesis and the action of balanced solutions, that is, solutions like blood and sea water, in which a salt, which is toxic by itself, serves as an antidote to other toxic salts so that when mixed in proper proportions a non-toxic mixture is obtained. So also he found in the principle of the Donnan equilibrium a clue to unraveling certain puzzling features in the behavior of colloids, the study of which is so important for biology. He was actively engaged in this work when, during a visit to Bermuda, he was overtaken by death.

Loeb was above all an idealist. Protected by academic life, and by a devoted wife, he lived largely in a world of ideals which dominated his life. He embodied Pasteur's profession of faith before the Academy, in the words now graven on his tomb: "Heureux celui qui porte en soi un dieu, un idéal de beauté, et qui lui obéit." He possessed the austerity which goes naturally with high ideals, and the temper of the aristocrat, but he had also a tender heart which responded to the sorrows of all who suffered and a sympathy for the masses who struggle against oppression, whether economic or spiritual. His temperament was that of an artist, running the gamut of the creative imagination, its brooding depression, its rare exaltation. He could not remain on the level of mediocrity. The outstanding feature of his intellectual equipment was his creative faculty. But fortunately his imagination was associated with a keen critical sense. The more audacious the conception, the more rigorously he tested it: he repeated his experiments over and over again. Few of his observations of fact had subsequently to be modified. He published only a small part of his experimental work, and few of his many ideas found their way into print. He would often think aloud in the course of a lecture, making and discarding one hypothesis after another. Ideas came to him so rapidly that often he did not know which to follow, but when he had singled one out he was not satisfied until he had thoroughly tested it. To him research was a happy adventure, however much it involved what might be called drudgery. He selected problems on the basis of their importance, and his mind gloried in difficult problems. It was always alert, poised to turn easily in any direction.

He had supreme confidence in the cause to which he consecrated his life: a conviction that mechanism could explain the most baffling mysteries. It almost approached a dogma. It was a militant faith which grew firmer with each new discovery, and if a philosophy be judged by its fruits, his convictions justified themselves. The emotional character of his thought, in conversation, was sometimes bewildering to more phlegmatic natures. A visitor to his laboratory was quite likely to leave in a somewhat breath-

less state. The rapidity with which he evolved, examined, and rejected ideas was astonishing. But the conceptions that survived were thought through and worked over under an emotional stress which is often evident in his writing. This emotional urge seemed to be capable of lifting him above personal considerations to levels of complete objectivity. And this seemed to him the true scientific attitude. Inspired by a militant idealism, he revolutionized more than one field of thought and made contributions which constitute an epoch in the progress of biology.

Aside from his numerous papers, Loeb published the following books: *Der Heliotropismus der Tiere und seine Übereinstimmung mit dem Heliotropismus der Pflanzen* (1890); *Untersuchungen zur physiologischen Morphologie der Tiere*, Volume I, *Über Heteromorphose*, Volume II, *"Organbildung und Wachstum"* (1891–92); *Comparative Physiology of the Brain and Comparative Psychology* (1900); *Studies in General Physiology* (1905), containing reprints of several papers previously published; *The Dynamics of Living Matter* (1906); *Untersuchungen über künstliche Parthenogenese und das Wesen des Befruchtungsvorgangs* (1906); *The Mechanistic Conception of Life* (1912); *Artificial Parthenogenesis and Fertilization* (1913); *The Organism as a Whole* (1916); *Forced Movements, Tropisms, and Animal Conduct* (1918); *Proteins and the Theory of Colloidal Behavior* (1922); and *Regeneration* (1924). He also founded and edited, in collaboration with W. J. V. Osterhout, the *Journal of General Physiology*, and in collaboration with Osterhout and T. H. Morgan, edited the Monographs on Experimental Biology.

[A biographical sketch by W. J. V. Osterhout, with a complete bibliography, printed in the *Jour. of Gen. Physiol.*, vol. VIII, Sept. 15, 1928, was reprinted in the *Nat. Acad. Sci. Biog. Memoirs*, vol. XIII (1930). See also: R. L. Duffus, "Jacques Loeb: Mechanist," *Century Mag.*, July 1924; Simon Flexner, "Jacques Loeb and His Period," *Science*, Oct. 14, 1927; T. B. Robertson, "The Life and Work of a Mechanistic Philosopher, Jacques Loeb," *Science Progress* (London), July 1926; P. H. DeKruif, "Jacques Loeb, the Mechanist," *Harper's Mag.*, Jan. 1923; *Science*, May 16, 1924; *N. Y. Times*, Feb. 13, 14, 24, 1924.]   W.J.V.O.

LOEB, LOUIS (Nov. 7, 1866–July 12, 1909), painter and illustrator, was born in Cleveland, Ohio. His parents were Alexander and Sarah (Ehrman) Loeb. At the age of thirteen he found employment in a lithographing establishment where he obtained his first instruction in drawing. He then went to New York and entered the Art Students' League, of which he was later to become the president. The next logical step was Paris, where he was a pupil of J. L. Gérôme. He soon began to send his works to the exhibitions, but the first official recognition he received was an honorable mention at the Salon of 1895, when he was almost thirty, for his "Dreamer" and a portrait. In 1897 he received the third-class medal of the Salon for his "Woman with Poppies" and "Fireflies." The former canvas was subsequently shown at the Society of American Artists' exhibition and at the Pennsylvania Academy. It was also in the nineties that he began to come before the public as an illustrator for magazines and books. He illustrated for the *Century* Mark Twain's "Pudd'nhead Wilson" (beginning November 1893); John Fox's "Cumberland Vendetta" (beginning June 1894); Langdon E. Mitchell's "Lucinda" (May 1895); Francis Marion Crawford's "Via Crucis" (beginning November 1898); two or three papers by Thomas A. Janvier; and many other single pieces or series.

After his return to America in 1896 he took a studio in New York where the rest of his life was passed. He was made an associate of the National Academy of Design in 1901 and became an academician in 1906. He was a member of the Society of American Artists, the Society of Illustrators, the Architectural League of New York; and he conducted antique and life classes in the Art Students' League. Between 1901 and 1906 he received eight medals for his paintings and drawings. His "Temple of the Winds" was acquired by the Metropolitan Museum, New York, and "The Siren" (1904) became the property of the National Gallery of Art, Washington. The former, a characteristic classical theme, is the most widely known of his pictures. Isham found his paintings academic, and a little oversweet; but that criticism does not apply to his black-and-white works. Interesting testimony as to his practice is supplied by William A. Coffin, who states that Loeb never placed his works before the public until he believed he had expressed in them the last word he was capable of in thought and execution. None of his illustrations give the measure of his imaginative power quite so well as the drawings he made to accompany Thomas A. Janvier's paper on "The Comédie Française at Orange," in the *Century* for June 1895. The event was of singular artistic interest. The leading actors of the Théâtre Français presented *Œdipus* and *Antigone* in the majestic Roman theatre at Orange. Loeb's nocturnal motives, especially his "Mademoiselle Bréval Singing the 'Hymn to Pallas Athene'" and his "Entrance of the Upper Tier," are uncommonly impressive in their light-and-shade effects, and have something of grandeur and mystery which

one does not often meet with in illustrations. Loeb's brief but brilliant career came to an untimely end at Canterbury, N. H., in 1909.

[*Century*, Nov. 1909; *Bookman*, Feb. 1900; *Outlook*, Aug. 14, 1909; *Harper's Monthly Mag.*, June 1907; *Harper's Weekly*, July 31, 1909; *Am. Art Ann.*, 1909–10; Samuel Isham, *Hist. of Am. Painting* (1905); the *Am. Hebrew*, July 16, 1909; *N. Y. Times*, July 14, 1909.]   W. H. D.

LOEB, MORRIS (May 23, 1863–Oct. 8, 1912), chemist, son of Solomon and Betty (Gallenberg) Loeb, was born at Cincinnati, Ohio. While he was still a lad, his parents moved to New York, where his father cooperated in establishing the banking firm of Kuhn, Loeb & Company. After extended study at Julius Sachs's school, he entered Harvard University in 1879. Early in his course his interest in chemistry was awakened by Charles L. Jackson and stimulated by other teachers. At his graduation in 1882 he received honorable mention in this subject, and *magna cum laude* for his general work. He continued his study of chemistry in Germany under the foremost teachers, including A. W. von Hofmann, and received the degree of Ph.D. at the University of Berlin in 1887. Anticipating the significance of the new field called physical chemistry, he studied this branch first at Heidelberg and later at Leipzig under Ostwald and Nernst. Upon his return to the United States in the fall of 1888, he declined the inviting career of a banker and adopted chemistry as his life work. After spending a year as an assistant in the private laboratory of Wolcott Gibbs [*q.v.*] at Newport, R. I., he went to Clark University, Worcester, Mass., as a docent in physical chemistry, and thereby became one of the American pioneers in this branch. In 1891 he was elected professor of chemistry in New York University, where he remained until 1906, having served as director of the laboratory during the eleven years preceding his resignation.

Being naturally sympathetic and generous, he really severed his formal connection with the University in order to devote himself unreservedly to the needs of charitable and scientific organizations. This service, which was continued throughout the remainder of his life, was not restricted to his own race, indeed it was limited only by his resources, time, and strength. One of his major interests was the Chemists' Club of New York. Of this he was a founder and patron, and its successful establishment as a meeting place of American chemists, its growth as a center of chemical interests, and its permanency as a depository of chemical literature and memorabilia are due in largest measure to his wise counsel, executive service, and generous gifts. He contributed liberally to the building fund, was personally interested in the construction of the building, and in his will left all his holdings of stock to the Chemists' Building Company for cancellation. In 1908 he was appointed on the committee to visit the chemical laboratory of Harvard University. He met his responsibilities with faithfulness and generosity. His early interest in chemistry at Harvard, deepened by years of study and research, soon found expression in a gift of $50,000 (jointly with his brother James) to the fund for founding the Wolcott Gibbs Memorial Laboratory for research in physical and inorganic chemistry. He was a founder and promoter of the Association of Harvard Chemists.

During the twenty-five or more years of his activity as a chemist, he published about thirty articles, including essays, lectures, and research papers, in foreign and domestic journals. The earlier contributions are on organic chemistry; many, from 1888 onward, are on physical chemistry (especially on the determination of molecular weights); and several, scattered through the entire period, relate to various aspects of chemical education and similar interests. Three of his early scientific papers, which were found in manuscript form after his death, were condensed and edited by Theodore W. Richards because they were the first presentation of physical chemistry in America; in this condensed form they are included under the title "Fundamental Ideas of Physical Chemistry" in *The Scientific Work of Morris Loeb* (1913). He also wrote a *Laboratory Manual Prepared for Students in Elementary Inorganic Chemistry at New York University* (1900). Although prepared for his students at New York University, the book was so clear and concise that it found its way into other institutions. An unusually helpful feature of this book was a set of laboratory maxims at the end; two reflect the methods of the author, *viz.,* "Note-books have good memories; jottings on loose paper are useful when you can find them," and "An unrecorded experiment was never begun." He was a member of the American Chemical Society and other important chemical organizations, and was an enthusiastic worker in these societies and in the meetings sponsored by them, a notable example being the Eighth International Congress of Applied Chemistry held in New York, 1912. At this congress he read a significant paper on "Studies in the Speed of Reductions" (published in *The Scientific Work of Morris Loeb*). From 1911 until his death he was a member of the New York City

Board of Education. On Apr. 3, 1895, he married Eda Kuhn who shared his manifold interests. His death occurred in New York; among his bequests was a fund of $500,000 to be used eventually by Harvard University for the furtherance of the science of chemistry and physics.

[T. W. Richards, *The Scientific Work of Morris Loeb* (1913), includes a chronological list of his papers and a brief biog.; see also *Morris Loeb, 1863–1912, Memorial Vol.* (1913), privately printed for the Chemists' Club; *Jour. of Industrial and Engineering Chemistry,* Nov. 1912; *Science,* Nov. 15, 1912; *Am. Hebrew,* Oct. 11, 18, 1912; *Survey,* Oct. 26, 1912; *Harvard Graduates' Mag.,* Dec. 1912; *Who's Who in America,* 1912–13; *N. Y. Times,* Oct. 9, 1912.]   L. C. N.

LOEB, SOPHIE IRENE SIMON (July 4, 1876–Jan. 18, 1929), social worker, journalist, author, is credited with having secured more constructive welfare legislation than any other woman in America. She was born in Rovno, Russia, in a Jewish home. The eldest child of Samuel and Mary (Carey) Simon, she was descended from generations of rabbis and scholars. Brought to the United States by her parents at the age of six, she grew up in McKeesport, Pa. When she was sixteen her father, a watchmaker and jeweler, died, leaving his widow practically penniless. Her mother's bitter struggle to keep the home together and educate six children fixed Sophie's determination from girlhood to do something to help the widowed mothers and fatherless children of America. After graduation from high school she taught, devoting her leisure to social work. At twenty she married Anselm Loeb, of Pittsburgh. The union proved an unhappy one, and on recovering her legal freedom she called herself "Miss Loeb." For some years she supported herself in Pittsburgh by teaching china painting and by newspaper writing.

In 1910, unknown, and without means, she removed to New York to launch a crusade for legislation providing aid for mothers with dependent children. As a reporter on the *Evening World,* she sought assignments in the slums in order to get facts at firsthand, and wrote a series of compelling "human-interest stories." From the platform, too, she plead the case for subsidized mother-care as against orphanage care. Within a year she had the backing of influential people and was making headway with her first bill at Albany. Three years of work, "educating legislators," secured the appointment in 1913 of a commission for the relief of widowed mothers. As a member of this commission she went abroad to study conditions in the six European countries most advanced in child-conservation, and later rendered an exhaustive report. She headed the hard-fought campaign which secured in 1915 the passage of the initial mothers' pension act in accordance with which the New York Child Welfare Board was appointed with Miss Loeb as president. During her seven years' tenure of this unsalaried post, appropriations for mothers' aid rose from $100,000 to over $5,000,000, largely through her unremitting fight to liberalize the application of the law. Other crusades for housing relief, model tenements, cheaper milk, cheaper gas, public baths, play streets, maternity care, school centers, and safer movie-theatres, she carried through by newspaper publicity plus direct legislative campaigning. Single-handed she waged a fight for low taxi fares and bonded drivers. In 1917 she settled a strike of taxi drivers in seven hours. During wartime coal shortage she stimulated Congressional inquiry, spending six months among the miners to ascertain facts. In 1920 she served on the commission appointed by Gov. Alfred E. Smith to codify the child-welfare laws of the state. In 1924, as first president of the Child Welfare Committee of America, founded largely through her determination, she carried her campaign to the nation, addressing many of the state legislatures. She toured Palestine in 1925, interviewing dignitaries—Arab, Jewish, and Christian, and embodied the results in a series of articles, afterward put into book form. In 1926 the International Child Welfare Congress at Geneva indorsed her anti-orphanage resolution. The League of Nations, 1927, solicited her aid as adviser on Child Welfare, requesting a report on blind children in America, which she completed. Beside her regular work for the *World,* carried on for eighteen years, she wrote syndicate articles, plays, and moving-picture features of humanitarian interest. Among her several books are *Epigrams of Eve* (1913), *Everyman's Child* (1920), and *Palestine Awake* (1926).

She was a little woman, endowed with tremendous driving power, courage, and tenacity of purpose. For herself she wanted nothing, least of all concessions to the fact that she was a woman. She organized her work like a man of affairs, fought in the open, and took hard knocks with impersonal unconcern. In quickness of mind and a certain intolerance of slower thinking, she was wholly feminine. When she died in New York, a thousand people attended her funeral.

[N. Y. *Evening World,* Jan. 19, 1929; *World* (N. Y.), Jan. 19, 22, 1929; *N. Y. Times,* Jan. 19, 21, 1929; *National Mag.,* Dec. 1923; *Survey,* Feb. 15, 1929; *Jewish Tribune,* Jan. 25, 1929; *Am. Hebrew,* Jan. 25, 1929; *Woman's Jour.,* Feb. 1929; *Who's Who in N. Y.,* 1924; *Who's Who in America,* 1924–25; information as to certain facts from a brother, A. M. Simon, McKeesport, Pa.]   M. B. H.

LOEW, MARCUS (May 7, 1870–Sept. 5, 1927), theatre owner and motion-picture producer, was born on New York's East Side. His parents, Herman L. and Ida (Lewinstein) Loew, were Austrian Jews who had recently emigrated from Vienna. The family was in humble circumstances and the boy's formal schooling ended at about his tenth year. Even at that early age he was employed by a map-coloring firm and later, with another boy, started a job-printing business and issued a weekly paper. When this venture proved unprofitable, he found employment with a fur company and at eighteen was in business on his own account. There followed six or seven years of ups and downs, including bankruptcy succeeded by a full discharge of obligations to which he could not have been legally held. In 1895 he made an investment that opened to him the gate to prosperity and by the turn of the century he was well established, with a portion of his capital invested in New York apartment houses. His real-estate investments led incidentally to his acquaintance with David Warfield, the actor, and the two men, by the merest chance, had their attention directed to the profitable business being done in New York by the so-called penny arcades, or peep shows. They joined Adolph Zukor in promoting that form of popular amusement but after a time withdrew from partnership with him and in 1904 formed a company of their own with a capital of $100,000.

The moving picture was just beginning to give some promise of its power to entertain the public. Loew and Warfield were among the first to sense its possibilities. At Cincinnati they made their first serious effort to "bring the movies to the arcades." Then they opened picture houses—usually remodeled stores—in New York. These were soon as great money-makers as the penny arcades had been. In Brooklyn Loew took over a real playhouse and by the time the film producers had turned out actual photoplays he was ready to show them to his public, at the same time presenting vaudeville features to offer variety. That was a program which quickly appealed to popular audiences and within a few years Loew was operating scores of small theatres in New York and other cities. At his death in 1927 there were about three hundred amusement places under his control. Until 1920 Loew had no part in the production of film plays, but in that year he bought the Metro Film Corporation and in 1924 the Goldwyn Pictures and the Louis B. Mayer Company. Loew's Incorporated, with about a hundred subsidiary companies, was capitalized at $100,000,000, with 10,000 stockholders.

His brilliant success as a showman was ascribed by Loew himself largely to good fortune.

His associates found him a genial and witty companion, whose early experiences had left him not unwilling to make ventures. By some he was credited with a genuine esthetic sense. His mistakes, from a business standpoint, were remarkably few, considering the magnitude of his operations. In 1894 he married Caroline Rosenheim. She with twin sons, Arthur and David, survived him.

[C. D. Fox and M. L. Silver, *Who's Who on the Screen*, 1920; *Lit. Digest*, Sept. 24, 1927; Will Irwin, *The House that Shadows Built* (1928); B. B. Hampton, *A Hist. of the Movies* (1931); Terry Ramsaye, "Little Journeys to the Homes of Famous Film Magnates," *Photoplay Mag.*, Aug. 1927; the *Am. Hebrew*, Sept. 16, 1927; *N. Y. Times*, Sept. 6, 1927.]   W.B.S.

LOEWENTHAL, ISIDOR (*c.* 1827–Apr. 27, 1864), Presbyterian missionary, the son of Jewish parents, was born in Posen, Prussia (now Poznan, Poland). He received at home and at school the early education of the orthodox Jewish boy, chiefly in the Hebrew language, literature, and religion. Later he attended a gymnasium where he studied with great success classical literature, modern languages, science, philosophy, and music. After graduation at seventeen from the gymnasium, he engaged for a time in clerical service in a mercantile house, continuing his studies meanwhile with a view to entering one of the German universities. He shared the liberal political opinions of a growing number of young men of his day and associated with certain of them in their agitation for governmental reform. He published anonymously in the summer of 1846 a poem adverse to the State. His authorship thereof was soon detected by the police, and he chose to flee from Posen to escape arrest. He secured at Hamburg passage on an English ship bound for America and landed at New York in the fall of the year. Finding no other employment, he took to peddling "notions" throughout the countryside about Philadelphia. Chance took him to the home of the Rev. S. M. Gayley, a minister of Wilmington, Del., who saw in the peddler a man of extraordinary qualities. Through the good offices of this clergyman and his son in Lafayette College, Loewenthal secured a post on the college faculty. Beginning in January 1847, he taught Hebrew and German, and pursued courses toward a degree. He was tutor in Latin, also, during the year 1847–48. He received from Lafayette College in 1848 the degree of B.A., and later that of M.A. In the spring of 1847 his mind turned favorably toward Christianity. In the autumn he professed conversion, was baptized by the Rev. Mr. Gayley, and was received into membership in the Rockland, N. J., Presbyterian

Church, of which Gayley was then the minister. After spending the years 1848–50 as a teacher of languages in the collegiate school at Mount Holly, Pa., he entered Princeton Theological Seminary. He distinguished himself as a theological student. Articles of his were published in the *Biblical Repository,* and at graduation in 1851 he read a paper on "India as a Field of Missions." He served during 1854–55 as a tutor in Princeton College. On Apr. 18, 1855, he was ordained by the Presbytery of New York, and in the following August he sailed from New York for a missionary career in India under the auspices of his Church. His first year in India was spent in language study at Rawal Pindi. Thereafter he worked at Peshawar among the Afghans in particular.

Although frequently in danger both to property and life, in this turbulent northwestern region, he gave diligent and effective attention to evangelism and translation. He preached in Pashtu, Persian, and Urdu, and knew other tongues, also, including Arabic. He made at least one tour in Kashmir and familiarized himself with Kashmiri. By the spring of 1863 he had completed and published (in Great Britain) a Pashtu version of the New Testament. Before his untimely death he had nearly finished a Pashtu dictionary. He died at the age of thirty-eight—shot in his own garden after midnight by his watchman who may have mistaken him for a robber. He left certain unpublished manuscripts, including Pashtu translations of portions of the Hebrew Old Testament. He had contributed articles to British and American periodicals, including the *Foreign Missionary* magazine of his own Board.

[See the *Twenty-Third Ann. Report of the Lodiana Mission* (1857); the *Foreign Missionary*, July, Oct. 1863, Feb., Sept. 1864; J. C. Lowrie, *A Manual of the Foreign Missions of the Presbyt. Ch.* (1868); B. H. Badley, *Indian Missionary Directory and Memorial Vol.* (Lucknow, 1876); *Missionary Review of the World*, Aug. 1891; Wm. Rankin, *Memorials of Foreign Missionaries of the Presbyt. Ch.* (1895); H. H. Holcomb, *Men of Might in India Missions* (1901); the *Jewish Era*, Apr. 1902; *Encyc. of Missions* (1904); and E. M. Wherry, *Our Missions in India* (1926).]   J. C. Ar—r.

LOGAN, BENJAMIN (*c.* 1743–Dec. 11, 1802), Kentucky pioneer, was born in Augusta County, Va., whither his parents, David and Jane Logan, had come from West Pennsborough Township, Cumberland County, Pa., in 1740. The Logan family, originally of Scotch stock, had settled in northern Ireland and emigrated from that country to Pennsylvania early in the eighteenth century. Benjamin, the eldest of six children, was left by the death of his father in 1757 the head of the family. Under the Virginia law of primogeniture he was sole heir of the estate, which seems to have been of respectable proportions. In 1764 he accompanied Bouquet's expedition with the rank of sergeant. Upon his return he and his brother John removed to the Holston region where Benjamin bought a farm and, in 1773 or 1774, married Ann Montgomery. He held the rank of lieutenant in a company of Virginia militia which accompanied the Governor in Dunmore's War against the Ohio Indians in 1774 (R. G. Thwaites and L. P. Kellogg, *Documentary History of Dunmore's War, 1774*, 1905, p. 82, note). His importance in Western history began in 1775 when with other frontiersmen of southwest Virginia he joined Richard Henderson who was going out to settle his Transylvania colony. Logan established a fort within the limits of the present Stanford and called it St. Asaph's. The coming of the Revolution brought incessant Indian warfare to Kentucky and gave Logan many opportunities to show his worth. His chief service in the war was as a leader of the retaliatory expeditions against the Indians in Ohio after their invasions of Kentucky in 1778, 1780, and 1782. In 1781 he was appointed county lieutenant of Lincoln County and as such was the ranking militia officer of the district. He was also a member of the Virginia General Assembly from Lincoln County for three terms, 1781–82, and 1785–87. Throughout the Revolution he was the most influential and the most trusted of the Kentucky leaders.

With the transition from war to peace in Kentucky Logan failed to hold his dominant position. His education had been so imperfect as probably to be a handicap to him even on the frontier, and he was temperamentally more a man of action than a politician. Yet he represented his county in the various conventions which marked the "struggle for autonomy" in Kentucky, he was a member of the convention (1792) which made the first constitution of Kentucky, and he was a member of the electoral college which made Isaac Shelby the first governor of the state. He was a presidential elector in 1792 and a member of the electoral college which chose the first Senate of the Kentucky legislature. During these years his military exploits were few, although in 1788 he led the Kentucky troops in the expedition against the Indians of the Northwest. In 1790 Washington appointed him a member of the Board of War in the West and Governor Shelby subsequently made him brigadier-general of state militia. In 1793 and 1794 he represented Lincoln County in the Kentucky House of Representatives, and in 1795 he was elected a representative from Shelby County, to which place he

had removed. In 1796 he was a candidate for governor, receiving a plurality of votes on the first ballot of the electoral college but being beaten on the second by James Garrard. His death in 1802 was the result of apoplexy; he was buried near the present Shelbyville, Ky. He had eight children, one of whom, William Logan, later was United States senator from Kentucky. Logan was of giant physique and was renowned throughout the West for his great strength and courage. He had more worldly wisdom than was usual with frontiersmen and at his death possessed one of the largest estates in Kentucky.

[J. A. Waddell, *Annals of Augusta County, Va.*, vol. II (1888); Lewis and R. H. Collins, *Hist. of Ky.* (1874); W. H. Egle, *Notes and Queries, Ann. Vol.*, 1900 (1901), p. 209; Lyman Chalkley, *Chronicles of the Scotch-Irish Settlement in Va.* (3 vols., 1912); T. M. Green, *Hist. Families of Ky.* (1889); L. D. V. Harper, *Colonial Men and Times; Containing the Jour. of Col. Daniel Trabue* (1916); B. T. Conkwright, "A Sketch of the Life and Times of Gen. Benj. Logan," *Reg. of the Ky. State Hist. Soc.*, May 1916; J. A. McClung, *Sketches of Western Adventure* (1832); C. C. Graham, "Pioneer Life," *Louisville Monthly Mag.*, vol. I (1879).]   R. S. C.

LOGAN, CORNELIUS AMBROSE (Aug. 24, 1832–Jan. 30, 1899), physician, politician, was born at Deerfield, Mass., the son of Cornelius Ambrosius [*q.v.*] and Eliza (Akeley) Logan. His father was a distinguished actor and theatrical manager. Olive Logan [*q.v.*] was his sister. The home of the family after 1840 was Cincinnati, Ohio. Logan was educated at Auburn Academy and later entered the medical profession. In 1854 he was married to Zoe Shaw. For a time he was medical superintendent of St. John's Hospital, Cincinnati, but in February 1857 he emigrated to Leavenworth, Kan. During the Civil War he was commissioned (June 29, 1864) surgeon of the first regiment of Kansas state militia. After the war he was active in the medical profession. As botanist of the state geological corps in charge of sanitary relations he made a study published under the title: *Report on Sanitary Relations of the State of Kansas* (1866). When the Kansas State Medical Society (chartered 1859) was reorganized in 1866 he was elected its first president and, for several years thereafter, served on one or more of its committees. His presidential address, delivered Apr. 3, 1867, sounded the keynote of his medical activity in the state: first, the strengthening of the medical society; second, the raising of the standards of the profession and the eliminating of quacks; third, the establishing of regular medical instruction at the state university. In June 1867, in association with Tiffin Sinks, M.D., he established the *Leavenworth Medical Herald*, a monthly magazine, and conducted the editorial section until April 1871. He published a book, *Physics of the Infectious Diseases* (1878), and wrote several articles for professional periodicals. No great scientific attainments and no important scientific discoveries can be attributed to him. Kansas was a frontier community and its greatest need was the establishment of stabilized institutions, and in medicine as in politics, the elimination of incompetents and impostors who were particularly numerous as a result of some two decades of disorder.

The lure of politics eventually drew Logan into the two contests for United States senatorships in 1873, but he was defeated in the first contest, and in consequence of the exigencies of both local and national politics, he was removed from the second by his appointment as envoy extraordinary and minister plenipotentiary to Chile. The Senate confirmed the appointment Mar. 17, 1873, and he held the position until 1877. During 1874 he arbitrated differences between Chile and Peru, arising out of the alliance of 1865, and also handled early stages of the Tacna dispute. In 1879 he was appointed from Illinois, to which state he had removed from Kansas, to the post of minister resident to the Central American states and was confirmed by the Senate Apr. 1. This position was held until 1882 when he was transferred to his former post in Chile, the new appointment being confirmed Mar. 15. The outstanding problem of this second Chile mission was the Tacna-Arica controversy. Aside from his political and professional activities he was a devoted Odd Fellow. He held high offices in the Grand Lodge of Kansas and during his residence in Chile established the order there. Subsequent to his return to the United States in 1885 Logan became the literary executor of his cousin, Gen. John A. Logan of Illinois. In this capacity he published the latter's book: *The Volunteer Soldier of America* (1887), together with a biographical memoir. Later he removed to California where after a long illness he died in Los Angeles at the home of his daughter, Celia Logan Waterous.

[There is no biography of Logan and such sketches as appear in encyclopedias are inaccurate. The library of the Kansas State Historical Society (Topeka) has a limited amount of manuscript and printed material pertaining to the Kansas phase of Logan's career. Such diplomatic correspondence as is in print is contained in *The Papers Relating to the Foreign Relations of the U. S.*, 1874, 1875, 1883. W. R. Sherman, *The Diplomatic and Commercial Relations of the U. S. and Chile, 1820–1914* (1926), gives a bare skeleton of a part of the period of Logan's diplomatic career. See also: H. A. Kelly and W. L. Burrage, *Am. Medic. Biogs.* (1920); D. W. Wilder, *The Annals of Kan., 1541–1885* (1886); memoir in *Jour. of Proc. of the Seventy-Fifth Ann. Communication of the Sovereign Grand Lodge, I.O.O.F.*, 1899; *Evening Standard* (Leavenworth, Kan.), Jan. 31, 1899. Available information seems to indicate that Logan was named *Cornelius Ambrosius* but later adopted the simpler form for the middle name.]

J. C. M.

LOGAN, CORNELIUS AMBROSIUS (May 4, 1806–Feb. 22, 1853), actor, dramatist, manager, was of Irish parentage, the son of a farmer who was killed by British troops while working on his farm near Baltimore, Sept. 12, 1814. He was one of a large family of children, and during his boyhood and early youth he sang as a church choir boy, began to study for the priesthood at St. Mary's College, worked in a shipping house, and made several voyages across the Atlantic as sailor and supercargo. Reaching New York on one of his return trips, he abandoned the sea and engaged in newspaper work there. Removing to Philadelphia, he began his connection with the theatre which continued for the rest of his life. One of his earliest appearances as an actor was made at the Tivoli Garden, Philadelphia, in July 1825, as Bertram in Maturin's tragedy of that name, and he afterward acted at the Walnut Street Theatre and other playhouses in that city. The records of the New York stage reveal him at the Bowery Theatre in 1826, announced as "a new actor from Philadelphia," and playing Smith in *The Road to Ruin*, Claudio in *Much Ado About Nothing*, and Trip in *The School for Scandal*. Moving from Philadelphia to Pittsburgh with his family, he became manager of the theatre there and later embarked on a wandering career that carried him through the central West, encountering the precarious hazards of theatrical fortune by traveling with his company, baggage, scenery, and properties, by canal-boat, steamboat, and wagon.

Despite his labors as manager and writer of plays, Logan never gave up acting, and his name is frequently found on the playbills of Cincinnati, where he lived for some years, and in the records of many other cities. He acted Sir Peter Teazle in *The School for Scandal* and Peter Simpson in *Simpson & Co.* so often that he was called Peter Logan in private life by many who supposed that it was his real name. At one time he managed a theatre in Albany, and on May 24, 1849, he returned to New York, after an absence of many years, and at Burton's Chambers Street Theatre took the part of Aminadab Slocum in his own play, *Chloroform, or New York a Hundred Years Hence*. It was played for eight successive nights, a remarkable run in those days. As an actor, he is reported by one who saw him many times to be full of an innate and quiet humor that was in no degree dependent upon physical action or facial grimace. He was one of the earliest dramatists to capitalize Yankee eccentricities for comedy purposes, among his numerous plays being *Yankee Land, or the Foundling of the Apple Orchard, The Wag of Maine,* and *The Vermont Wool Dealer,* a farce in one act popularized by Dan Marble. His daughter Celia declares that he was the author of *The People's Lawyer,* famous for its central character of Solon Shingle, and that Dr. Joseph Stevens Jones, to whom its authorship is accredited, merely revised it. His three daughters, all of considerable prominence on the stage, were Eliza, Celia, and Olive [*q.v.*], and his son, Cornelius Ambrose Logan [*q.v.*], was well known in the triple capacity of physician, journalist, and author. He died suddenly of apoplexy near Marietta, Ohio, while on a steamboat, accompanied by his daughter Eliza, on his way from Cincinnati to Pittsburgh. His wife, Eliza (Akeley) Logan, survived him.

[J. N. Ireland, *Records of the N. Y. Stage* (2 vols., 1866–67); H. P. Phelps, *Players of a Century* (1880); T. A. Brown, *A Hist. of the N. Y. Stage* (1903), vol. III; Arthur Hornblow, *A Hist. of the Theatre in America* (1919), vol. II; A. H. Quinn, *A Hist. of the Am. Drama from the Beginning to the Civil War* (1923); Montrose J. Moses, *The Am. Dramatist* (1925); G. C. D. Odell, *Annals of the N. Y. Stage,* vol. III (1928); J. T. Scharf, *Hist. of Baltimore City and County* (1881); *Cincinnati Daily Enquirer,* Feb. 25, 1853; article by Celia Logan in an unidentified newspaper, embodying personal reminiscences by James Rees; records of the Cemetery of Spring Grove, Cincinnati, Ohio.]   E. F. E.

LOGAN, DEBORAH NORRIS (Oct. 19, 1761–Feb. 2, 1839), historian, was the daughter of Charles and Mary (Parker) Norris and a grand-daughter of Isaac Norris [*q.v.*], chief justice of Pennsylvania. As "saucy Debby Norris" she attended the school of Anthony Benezet [*q.v.*], who found that her sense of fun could be restrained only by her sense of honor. Though female education was then held of little importance, she continued her studies at home through self-imposed courses of reading and formed lasting habits of literary work. Her father's "palatial" residence, then in the outskirts of Philadelphia, on Chestnut Street near Fifth, and her grandfather's at Fairhill, were both centers of hospitality in which the girl received social training and formed a wide acquaintance with the leaders of the time. On Sept. 6, 1781, she became the wife of George Logan [*q.v.*]; of their three children—all sons—one survived her. Through nearly forty years of happy marriage she was devoted to her husband and his interests. He trusted her judgment fully, and gave her unlimited control of his property during his absence from the country in 1798. After his death she prepared a *Memoir of Dr. George Logan of Stenton,* which was published by her great-grand-daughter in 1899.

In all the relations of life her contemporaries credit her with exemplary conduct and great personal charm. Her extensive family connections gave her a close acquaintance with the leading men of the place and time; her beauty, ability, and goodness attracted to "Stenton" eminent Philadelphians and the most distinguished visitors to the city. To her clear memory and graphic description in the memoir of her husband we owe some of the most vivid accounts of the Revolutionary and early Republican city. When John F. Watson was writing his *Annals of Philadelphia* (1830) he found her a source of invaluable information. Her greatest service to history, however, was in recognizing the value of the family papers at "Stenton." In spite of the current lack of interest in colonial history, she preserved them for posterity. Large quantities of these papers were stored in the garrets, mouldy, worm-eaten, and tattered, literally perishing from neglect. Beginning in 1814, she deciphered, copied, and annotated thousands of pages that eventually constituted eleven quarto manuscript volumes. These were given to the American Philosophical Society and were later published by the Historical Society of Pennsylvania ("Correspondence between William Penn and James Logan," being vols. IX and X of its *Memoirs,* 1870–72). Deborah Logan survived her husband nearly eighteen years. She was buried in the little family cemetery at "Stenton."

[Sarah Butler Wister and Agnes Irwin, *Worthy Women of Our First Century* (1877); Deborah Norris Logan, *The Norris House* (1867); *Sally Wister's Journal* (1902), ed. by A. C. Myers; *Poulson's Am. Daily Advertiser,* Feb. 4, 1839.]   A. L. L.

LOGAN, GEORGE (Sept. 9, 1753–Apr. 9, 1821), physician, United States senator, was the son of William and Hannah (Emlen) Logan. He was born at "Stenton," the home established near Germantown, Pa., by his grandfather, James Logan [*q.v.*], in 1728. His father was a wealthy merchant in Philadelphia until 1751, when he inherited "Stenton"; subsequently he devoted himself to the cultivation of its 500 acres. A strict Quaker and a leader of the conscientious objectors to war, he was a loyal supporter of the Penn family, whom he represented in America after 1741. George was sent to school in England for a time and then continued his studies under Robert Proud [*q.v.*]. In spite of the boy's predilection for medicine, his father apprenticed him to a Philadelphia merchant. In the counting-house, however, he had time to read much from the fine collection of medical books that had come to the library at "Stenton" through the death of Dr. William Logan of Bristol, England, a brother of James Logan. At the end of his apprenticeship, he was able to turn to medicine as a profession, went to England, and lived for some months in the home of Dr. Simms, in Essex, compounding prescriptions and studying pharmacy. He entered the University of Edinburgh, and after graduating in medicine in 1779, traveled in England and on the Continent, spending some time in Paris studying anatomy and enjoying a close friendship with Benjamin Franklin that continued until the latter's death.

When Logan returned to Philadelphia in 1780 his parents and brother were dead and his inheritance was seriously impaired by the war. Except for "Stenton," which had escaped destruction, there remained to him only "wasted estates and piles of utterly depreciated paper currency" (*Memoir, post,* p. 41). Reluctantly abandoning the idea of practising medicine, he moved to "Stenton" soon after his marriage, Sept. 6, 1781, to Deborah Norris [see Deborah Norris Logan], and applied himself enthusiastically to the study of improved methods of farming. He was elected a member of the American Philosophical Society in 1793, and was a founder of the Philadelphia Society for the Promotion of Agriculture.

In 1785 he was elected to the Pennsylvania Assembly, and during three successive years was reëlected. A friend of Jefferson, who often visited him, he became a Republican and as such was elected to the legislature in 1795, 1796, and 1799. While there he advocated the encouragement of agriculture, domestic manufacture, and popular education. Like his father a devoted friend to peace, he determined to bring about a better understanding with France in order to avert the war that threatened in 1798. In spite of bitter opposition from the Federalists to his generous project—opposition that even caused him to be put under surveillance—he sold some land to pay his expenses and, equipped with a letter of introduction from Jefferson, sailed for Hamburg. There, through the influence of Lafayette, who was living in exile nearby, he obtained papers from the French legation which permitted him to enter France. Reaching Paris, Aug. 7, soon after the departure of Elbridge Gerry [*q.v.*], the last of the American commissioners, he endeavored to impress Talleyrand with the disastrous effect that the recent French policy had had upon public opinion in the United States. Treated with respect by Talleyrand and with cordiality by Merlin, head of the Directory, he eventually secured the release of imprisoned American seamen, had the pleasure of seeing the embargo raised on American ships, and was given assurances that a minister from the United

States would be favorably received. His mission was the object of much hostile criticism; upon his return to America he was accorded icy contempt by Washington, while on Jan. 30, 1799, Congress passed the so-called "Logan Act" (1 *Statutes at Large,* 613), forbidding a private citizen to undertake diplomatic negotiations without official sanction. President Adams was more friendly, however, and Logan's unofficial messages from Talleyrand, though anticipated by a communication through William Vans Murray [*q.v.*], United States minister to the Netherlands, doubtless helped to modify the general bitterness toward France.

Popular approval of Logan was shown, meanwhile, by his appointment, and later election, to the United States Senate in 1801 after the resignation of Peter Muhlenberg [*q.v.*]. He served until 1807, when he declined reëlection. Despite the "Logan Act" of 1799, he went to England in 1810 in an unsuccessful attempt to prevent the war of 1812. During his visit he received much social consideration and established pleasant relations with Englishmen interested in agriculture and negro emancipation. His last years were spent quietly at "Stenton," where he died and was buried. Much in his life suggests the influence of Franklin. That he habitually wore homespun to encourage domestic manufacture indicates his sincerity and disinterestedness. His courage was undaunted by bitter political rancor; his humane spirit was often ahead of his time. He is said to have been the only strict Quaker who ever sat in the United States Senate.

[*Memoir of Dr. George Logan of Stenton by his Widow, Deborah Norris Logan: With Selections from his Correspondence* (1899), ed. by his great-granddaughter, Frances A. Logan; J. W. Jordan, *Colonial Families of Phila.* (1911), vol. I; J. F. Watson, *Annals of Phila.,* enlarged by W. P. Hazard (3 vols., 1898); *The Quid Mirror* (1806); P. L. Ford, *The Writings of Thomas Jefferson,* vol. VII (1896); C. F. Adams, *The Works of John Adams,* vols. VIII, IX (1853–54); J. S. Bassett, *The Federalist System* (1906); "Correspondence between William Penn and James Logan," vol. I, being *Memoirs of the Hist. Soc. of Pa.,* vol. IX (1870); Charles Warren, *Memorandum on the Hist. and Scope of the Laws Prohibiting Correspondence with a Foreign Govt.* (1915); *Nat. Gazette and Lit. Reg.* (Phila.), Apr. 10, 1821; Logan Papers and Norris Papers (MSS.), Hist. Soc. of Pa.]   A. L. L.

LOGAN, JAMES (Oct. 20, 1674–Oct. 31, 1751), colonial statesman and scholar, founder of a prominent Pennsylvania family, was of Scottish ancestry on both sides. His father, Patrick Logan of East Lothian, was a master of arts of the University of Edinburgh and a clergyman in the Established Church until his conversion to Quakerism in 1671; his mother, Isabel (Hume), came of a noble family connected with the Lairds of Dundas. His father was master of a Latin school in Lurgan, County Armagh, Ireland, when James was born, and later was master of a school in Bristol, England, where his eldest son, William (1686–1757), became a distinguished physician. James, the second son, early showed a scholarly aptitude. Before he was thirteen he had received from his father a creditable knowledge of Greek, Latin, and Hebrew, and at nineteen, upon his father's return to Ireland, he was left in charge of the school at Bristol. James continued his studies until 1697. He then wished to go to Jamaica, but since his mother opposed this desire, he engaged in the shipping trade between Dublin and Bristol. At about this time he made the acquaintance of William Penn, who was impressed with the young man's ability and learning. He became Penn's secretary in 1699, and was his confidential adviser and friend and the counselor of his sons and grandsons, for half a century.

In September 1699 he sailed with Penn on the *Canterbury* for Pennsylvania. The persistent anecdote survives that on the voyage the ship was attacked by pirates; Logan took a spirited part in the defense of the ship, while Penn, the pacifist, retired below. On being reproved by Penn for resorting to arms, Logan retorted: "I being thy servant, why did thee not order me to come down?" (A. H. Smyth, *The Writings of Benjamin Franklin*, vol. I, 1905, pp. 366–67). Though the legend may be apocryphal, question and answer are characteristic of the attitudes and policies of the two men. Logan, who later declared that he was not a "strict professor," believed defensive war justifiable. In 1741 he suggested that Friends who could not conscientiously vote for measures of defense should refrain from seeking election to the legislature (*To Robert Jordan and Others*, 1741, reprinted in *Pennsylvania Magazine of History and Biography*, vol. VI, no. 4, 1882).

His career of fifty-two years in Pennsylvania was one of increasing responsibility and honor. Penn made him secretary of the Province and clerk of the Provincial Council, in which capacities he served from 1701 to 1717. When the Proprietor returned to England, he made Logan commissioner of property and receiver general, an office which involved issuing titles to lands, collecting quit rents, and the general supervision of the Penn family interests in the colony. On Apr. 21, 1702, Logan was made a voting member of the Council, and on the arrival of Governor Evans (Feb. 8, 1703/4) a fully qualified member, which he remained until his retirement on May 29, 1747. He became in time president and senior member of the Council, and, as such, was

chief executive of the Province from Aug. 4, 1736, to June 1, 1738 (after the retirement of Governor Gordon), during which interval the "Border War" between Maryland and Pennsylvania took place. He was elected to the board of aldermen of Philadelphia on Oct. 17, 1717, and mayor of the city on Oct. 2, 1722.

In politics Logan represented the Proprietary party, made up mostly of wealthy Philadelphia Quakers and supporters of the Penn family, all with strong aristocratic interests. Opposed to this faction was the democratic party led by David Lloyd [*q.v.*], speaker of the Assembly, a member of the Society of Friends, but opposed to the increase or even to the maintenance of the proprietary authority. Lloyd's support came from the country Friends and from the people of small means. It was inevitable that Logan and Lloyd should come into conflict. Technical charges of usurpation of authority were lodged against the Secretary. These were drawn up as articles and first presented to the Council in February 1706/7, but were defeated by adjournment. When they were revived in September 1709 Logan carried the case to England, and upon his return in March 1711/12, completely vindicated, all impeachment proceedings were dropped.

Logan's judicial career began with his appointment, Aug. 25, 1726, by Governor Gordon, as one of the justices of Philadelphia County. On Sept. 2, 1727, he was re-commissioned and made a judge of the court of common pleas, and on Aug. 25, 1731, he was appointed chief justice of the supreme court, to succeed his old enemy David Lloyd, who had recently died. This post he held until Aug. 9, 1739. His *Charge Delivered from the Bench to the Grand Inquest . . . 1736* (Philadelphia, 1736; London, 1737) dealt with the duties of man in society, a subject upon which he began a treatise which was apparently never completed.

Apart from his official duties, he made a fortune in land investment and in trade with the Indians. He was a voracious reader and collected a library of over three thousand books which he left to the city of Philadelphia. He corresponded with many of the eminent men of his time. On Dec. 9, 1714, he married, at the Friends' Meeting House in Philadelphia, Sarah Read, the daughter of Charles Read, a prominent merchant. By this marriage he had five children. James, his eldest son, became the first librarian of the Loganian Library, which was formed into the Library Company of Philadelphia in 1792. Logan was also at one time a suitor for the hand of the beautiful Anne Shippen, who eventually married Thomas Story.

Logan established a family seat at "Stenton," an estate of 500 acres near Germantown, where he is recorded as living in "princely style" and keeping open house. He was always successful in his relations with the Indians, and the accounts of the ceremonial visits of delegations of Indians to "Stenton," and of the hospitality they enjoyed there give a pleasant picture of a phase of pioneer America which disappeared all too quickly. After his retirement from the Council in 1747, he spent most of his time at his estate, and devoted himself to study. Natural science was his absorbing interest and botany his special field. He was a friend of John Bartram [q.v.] and a correspondent of Peter Collinson, and his botanical investigations received recognition from Linnæus, who named the *Loganiaceae* for him, an order with thirty genera and over three hundred species. His most important scientific work was a series of "Experiments Concerning the Impregnation of the Seeds of Plants," the results of which he reported to his friend Peter Collinson in London and to the Royal Society (1736; see Charles Hutton and others, *Philosophical Transactions . . . Abridged,* 1809, VII, 669). His conclusions he later published in a Latin treatise, *Experimenta et Meletemata de Plantarum Generatione* (Leyden, 1739). Translated into English by Dr. John Fothergill, the celebrated Quaker physician, it was published in London in 1747. Other papers contributed by Logan to the Royal Society of London include "An Account of Mr. T. Godfrey's Improvement of Davis' Quadrant" (*Philosophical Transactions, Abridged,* VII, 669) ; "Some Thoughts on the Sun and Moon, When Near the Horizon Appearing Larger than When Near the Zenith" (*Ibid.,* VIII, 112) ; "Concerning the Crooked or Angular Appearance of the Streaks or Darts of Lightning in Thunderstorms" (*Ibid.,* VIII, 68). He also published two translations : *Cato's Moral Distiches, Englished in Couplets* (1735), and *M. T. Cicero's Cato Major; or His Discourse of Old Age* (1744), the latter said by Charles Evans (*American Bibliography,* II, 1904, p. 258) to be generally considered the best specimen of printing from Franklin's press.

Portraits of Logan reveal a man of aristocratic bearing and commanding presence. He has been described as "scholarly and genial among his friends, but harsh and unfair in his judgment of his enemies" (R. M. Jones, *The Quakers in the American Colonies,* 1911, p. 483). In his politics, his manner of life, and his tastes, he represented the aristocracy of the intellect, the antithesis of the democracy that was soon to be dominant.

[Logan Papers (45 vols.), Logan Letter Books (7 vols.), Deborah Logan's Selections (5 vols.), all in Hist. Soc. of Pa.; "Correspondence between William Penn and James Logan," ed. by Edward Armstrong, in *Memoirs of the Hist. Soc. of Pa.,* vols. IX, X (1870–72) ; Norman Penney, *The Correspondence of James Logan and Thomas Story* (copr. 1927) ; A. C. Myers, *Immigration of the Irish Quakers into Pa., 1682–1750* (1902), containing, pp. 238–40, an autobiog. sketch of Logan; Wilson Armistead, *Memoirs of James Logan* (1851) ; Irma Jane Cooper, *The Life and Public Services of James Logan* (1921) ; Isaac Sharpless, *Political Leaders of Provincial Pa.* (1919) ; Wm. Darlington, *Memorials of John Bartram and Humphry Marshall* (1849) ; J. W. Harshberger, *The Botanists of Phila.* (1899) ; R. H. Fox, *Dr. John Fothergill and His Friends* (1919) ; J. F. Watson, *Annals of Phila.* (2 vols., 1830), enlarged, etc., by W. P. Hazard (3 vols., 1898) ; J. W. Jordan, *Colonial Families of Phila.* (1911), vol. I.]

M. P. S.

LOGAN, JAMES (*c.* 1725–1780), a Mingo leader and orator, sometimes called John Logan, the son of Shikellamy [q.v.], was probably born at Shamokin, now Sunbury, Pa. He was named Tahgahjute, but rather early in life he began to be called Logan, probably in honor of the secretary of Pennsylvania, James Logan [q.v.]. His elder brother, John Shikellamy, or Taghneghdoarus, after their father's death, became sachem of the Iroquois and their agent at Shamokin, while James Logan, "the lame Son of Shick Calamys" (*Minutes of the Provincial Council, post,* VI, p. 35), continued to maintain a close and serviceable association with the Pennsylvania authorities. Probably it was this James Logan who became conspicuous in the Ohio country in the decade between 1770 and 1780, though in the accounts of him dating from that period there occurs no reference to his lameness, and in a document of the time, not now extant in its original form, his name seems to have been signed for him as "Capt. John Logan."

Though he does not appear in contemporary records as chief or sachem, he occupied a position of prominence among the Mingo bands on the Ohio and Scioto rivers, and, after the Yellow Creek massacre of April 1774 in which certain members of his family were slaughtered, he was the leader of small detachments engaged in retaliatory forays against the settlements. Though far from being the cause of Dunmore's War, as sometimes asserted, this cruel massacre certainly provided the occasion for its outbreak. It was also the incident that changed to hatred Logan's friendship for the colonists and set him upon the path of vengeance. He was more successful in his campaign than were Cornstalk [q.v.] and his warriors, and when, in November 1774 after the battle of Point Pleasant, the defeated Indians gathered at Chillicothe to make a treaty, Logan refused to become reconciled even though he was said to have taken already some thirty scalps in his private quarrel. His reply to John Gibson [*q.v.*], who had been sent by Dunmore to obtain his presence at the making of the treaty, was that "morsel of eloquence" which was read at the conference, was copied in many colonial newspapers and was later made famous through Jefferson's use of it in his *Notes, on the State of Virginia* (especially the edition of 1800, Appendix 4). The exactness with which his speech was repeated at the conference must always be open to question, and, in spite of the credence given the charge by Jefferson, the truth of his accusation that Michael Cresap [*q.v.*] was the leader of the Yellow Creek massacre has been successfully challenged by later historians.

During the Revolution, Logan employed himself successfully in bringing in scalps and prisoners to the British at Detroit. As time went on, he became increasingly the ferocious and drunken savage, in pitiable contrast to the intelligent, capable, and friendly Indian of his earlier days. The testimony as to the manner of his death is conflicting, but it seems clear that he was killed by a nephew or cousin, probably in retaliation for a deed committed by him in a drunken rage.

[Brantz Mayer, *Tah-gah-jute; or Logan and Cresap* (1867); F. B. Sawvel, *Logan the Mingo* (copr. 1921), with some confusion of the deeds of Logan and his brother John Shikellamy; J. J. Jacob, *A Biog. Sketch of the Life of the Late Capt. Michael Cresap* (1826); Samuel Kercheval, *A Hist. of the Valley of Va.*, 4th ed. (1925); *Minutes of the Provincial Council of Pa.*, vol. VI (1851) pp. 35, 119, 216, vol. VII (1851), pp. 47, 51–52; *Pa. Archives*, ser. 1, vol. II (1853), pp. 23–24, 33–37, vol. IV (1853), p. 525.]   L. C. W.

LOGAN, JAMES HARVEY (Dec. 8, 1841–July 16, 1928), jurist, horticulturist, was the son of Samuel McCampbell and Mary Elizabeth (McMurty) Logan, both of Scotch ancestry and both natives of Kentucky. He was born near Rockville, Ind., the seventh of eight children. After graduating from Waveland Collegiate Institute in 1860 he taught school for a year at Independence, Mo., then started West as driver of an ox team for the Overland Telegraph Company. By the fall of 1861 he had made his way to California, where for a year he lived with his uncle, a physician, at Los Gatos. In December 1863 he commenced to read law at San Jose, in the office of C. T. Ryland, and in 1865 was admitted to the bar. Three years later he moved to Santa Cruz, where he became deputy district-attorney almost immediately, served from 1870 to 1880 as district attorney, and for the next twelve years was a judge of the superior court in Santa Cruz County. In 1892 he retired from office because of failing health.

Although he was comfortably successful in his profession, it was through his avocation that Logan attained his special distinction. In 1880 he started an experimental fruit and vegetable garden at his home in Santa Cruz. He was interested in producing a cross between the Texas Early blackberry and the wild California blackberry (*Rubus Vitifolius*) and planted a row of the wild berry bushes between a row of the Texas Early and one of Red Antwerp raspberries. By 1881 he had secured several hundred seedlings of the blackberry. When the fruit came, he found he had made a successful cross between the blackberries, producing a new variety which he named the Mammoth. Furthermore, he discovered one plant which resembled a raspberry more than a blackberry, and when the fruit ripened he found that it had a flavor and character all its own. This fruit, since known as the loganberry, he described as a true hybrid, believing it a cross between the Red Antwerp raspberry and the wild blackberry. He gave it to Professor Wickson of the University of California for free distribution. It is now extensively cultivated (by propagating cuttings) from British Columbia to California, and forms the basis of a substantial industry in canning and preparing fruit juice for the market. In 1916 evidence was reported tending to disprove the belief that the loganberry is a hybrid and to show that it is a true species (*Journal of Heredity*, November 1916), but in 1923 Judge Logan delivered an address reasserting his conviction that it is a hybrid (*Seventeenth Biennial Report of the Board of Horticulture of the State of Oregon*, 1923). He died at his home in Oakland, Cal., survived by his second wife, Mary Elizabeth Couson, whom he married Aug. 1, 1910, and by their daughter.

[Autobiographical material in R. D. Hunt, *California and Californians* (1926), V, 141ff.; *New Internat. Year Book*, 1928; *Literary Digest*, Nov. 25, 1916; *Country Life in America*, Sept. 1916; *San Francisco Chronicle*, July 17, 1928.]   M. P. S.

LOGAN, JOHN ALEXANDER (Feb. 9, 1826–Dec. 26, 1886), Union soldier, United States senator, was born on a farm in Jackson County, Ill. His father, Dr. John Logan, was of Scotch descent, an immigrant from the north of Ireland who settled first in Maryland, then in Missouri, and finally in Jackson County, Ill., near the present Murphysboro. His second wife, Elizabeth Jenkins, also of Scotch ancestry, was the mother of his eleven children. John, the eldest, received a broken education which included some study of law. After service as a lieutenant in the Mexican War, he continued his legal studies under his uncle, Lieut.-Gov. Alexander M. Jenkins, began practice, served in local offices and in the Illinois legislature, and married, on Nov. 27, 1855, Mary Simmerson Cunningham, the daughter of a comrade in the war. In 1858 he was elected to Congress from the eleventh Illinois district, as an anti-Lecompton Democrat.

Logan's spread-eagle oratory and contentious spirit, together with the abundant black hair that suggested Indian ancestry, made him a noticeable spokesman of the "Egyptian" counties constituting his district. He was sent to the Charleston convention of 1860 as a Douglas supporter, and was again elected to Congress that autumn. At intervals for the rest of his life he was forced to repel the calumny of having been at heart a Southern sympathizer; but he was able to bring to his vindication the testimony of Lucius Q. C. Lamar and the words of his numerous Union speeches in Congress (*Congressional Record, 49 Cong., Special Session of the Senate*, pp. 132, 330, Mar. 30, Apr. 19, 1881). When his Democratic associates from the South went home in the winter of 1861, he repeatedly avowed his determination to stand by the Union. In the spring he seized a musket and marched with a Michigan regiment to the battle of Bull Run; and when the special war session came to an end he hurried back to "Egypt" and raised the 31st Illinois Regiment, of which he was at once made colonel.

His military career was distinguished. He took his regiment into early action, had a horse shot under him at Belmont, was twice wounded, was made a brigadier-general after Fort Donelson, and a major-general after Vicksburg. In the fighting around Atlanta he commanded the XV Corps of the Army of the Tennessee; and upon the death of McPherson, July 22, 1864, he took command of that army. It was a matter of deep chagrin to him, and to his Illinois supporters, that, upon the recommendation of Sherman, Lincoln relieved him of this command. Logan believed that the discrimination against him was due to the West Point prejudice against a volunteer; but the fact was that Sherman mistrusted Logan's active political interests, which often took him from the field, and furthermore, as he later explained, although he considered Logan "perfect in combat," the latter "entertained and expressed a species of contempt" for the laborious preparations in logistics that a commander, to be successful, must carry on (*Report of the Proceedings of the 19th Annual Meeting, Society of the Army of the Tennessee*, 1887, p. 57).

Logan declined a permanent commission in the regular army and was discharged in 1865. He helped organize the Society of the Army of the Tennessee and the Grand Army of the Republic, of which he was three times president (*Proceedings of the First to Tenth Meetings . . . of the National Encampment, Grand Army of the Republic*, 1877, pp. 23, 29, 74); and he went back to Congress as a Republican, elected in 1866 as representative-at-large from Illinois. The Democratic counties of his old district now gave him a substantial majority as a Republican. He was reëlected in 1868 and 1870, and in 1871 was chosen senator from Illinois. He lost this seat in 1877, because of a coalition of Democrats and independents that gave it to David Davis [*q.v.*]; but he obtained the other seat by ousting R. J. Oglesby in 1879; and was chosen for a third term after a prolonged deadlock in 1885 (D. W. Lusk, *History of the Contest for U. S. Senator before the 34th General Assembly of Illinois*, 1885).

In the Senate Logan was a stalwart Republican who associated himself with all matters of veteran relief. His dislike for West Point and its graduates was never far beneath the surface. He clung to his job, for he had no other means of support; and when his defeat in 1877 threw him into poverty his wife was bitter because President Hayes did not provide him with an appointment (*Reminiscences of a Soldier's Wife*, p. 360). He was naturally a worker for the nomination of Grant in 1880, making every effort to establish the right of the Illinois convention to name the district delegates and to bind them to the unit rule; but he accepted Garfield and organized the western canvass. In 1884 he had some local support for the presidency, but was obliged to take the second place on the Republican ticket. He fought a vigorous campaign, knowing it to be a losing one, and in the outcome derived his mortification less from Cleveland's victory than from that of Hendricks, whom he believed to have been disloyal. The last months of his life were devoted to the compilation of his war book, *The Great Conspiracy: Its Origin and History* (1886), which is unimportant save as an expression of his views, and to the preparation of a ponderous manuscript published after his death under the title: *The Volunteer Soldier of America, With Memoir of the Author and Military Reminiscences from General Logan's Private Journal* (1887).

Logan was described as "clearly the most eminent and distinguished of the volunteer soldiers" of the Civil War (*Diary and Letters of Rutherford Birchard Hayes*, vol. IV, 1925, p. 302). He had conceived the idea of Memorial Day and inaugurated it on May 30, 1868; his last public utterance was a plea for every disabled "Union soldier who served in the army and has an honorable discharge" and for "Every Union soldier over sixty-two years old" (*Chicago Tribune*, Nov. 20, 1886). He died in Washington, D. C., survived by two children, and by his wife, whose intelligence and charm had always been valuable assets in his campaigns.

[G. F. Dawson, *Life and Services of Gen. John A. Logan as Soldier and Statesman* (1887), a revamped campaign biography, provided the basis for most of the material of the elaborate obituary in the *Chicago Tribune*, Dec. 27, 1886. Mary S. C. Logan, *Reminiscences of a Soldier's Wife; an Autobiog.* (1913), is affectionate and personal. Memorial addresses in Congress were printed as *Sen. Misc. Doc. No. 93*, 49 Cong., 2 Sess. See also: *Hist. of Jackson County, Ill.* (1878); *War of the Rebellion: Official Records* (Army); *Memoirs of Gen. Wm. T. Sherman* (2 vols., 1875); J. G. Blaine, *Twenty Years of Cong.* (2 vols., 1884–86); *Personal Memoirs of U. S. Grant* (2 vols., 1885–86); *Autobiog. of Oliver Otis Howard* (2 vols., 1907).]   F.L.P.

LOGAN, OLIVE (Apr. 22, 1839–Apr. 27, 1909), actress, journalist, lecturer, author, was the daughter of Cornelius Ambrosius [*q.v.*] and Eliza (Akeley) Logan. Cornelius Ambrose Logan [*q.v.*] was her brother. She was born in Elmira, N. Y., and when a little child was taken by her parents to Cincinnati, where she attended school. As the daughter of an actor, dramatist, and manager, she became interested in the stage at an early age, making her début in Philadelphia at the Arch Street Theatre, Aug. 19, 1854, under the management of John Drew and William Wheatley, as Mrs. Bobtail in *Bobtail and Wagtail.* Her stage appearances, however, were confined wholly to her younger years; the greater part of her professional life was actively spent in the writing of plays, books, newspaper articles, and in lecturing on woman's rights and other social and political subjects. She appears to have attempted the acting of a male character when she was less than eighteen years of age, for Joseph Norton Ireland (*post,* p. 653) notes that she appeared at the Broadway Theatre, Feb. 21, 1857, as one of the two Antipholi in *A Comedy of Errors,* with the brothers Placide as the two Dromios. She was also, according to the same authority, at the new Broadway Theatre in 1865, being described as a "valuable coadjutress" of Mr. Chanfrau in *Sam.* T. Allston Brown says that after having spent several years in France and England, she reappeared at Wallack's Theatre, New York, in 1864 in a play of her own composition called *Eveleen,* and that then, after a starring tour in the West and South she "reappeared in the New York boards at the Broadway Theatre under the management of her brother in law, George Wood, in November, 1865, in the play called 'Sam,' and for nearly one hundred consecutive nights played the same role to large and admiring audiences" (*post,* pp. 222 and 225).

By 1868 she had retired as an actress. Her record as a writer of plays comprises also *Surf,* *or Summer Scenes at Long Branch,* a comedy in five acts travestying fashionable life at a seaside resort, produced by Augustin Daly at his Fifth Avenue Theatre, New York, Jan. 12, 1870; *Newport,* produced at Daly's Theatre, New York, Sept. 17, 1879; and a dramatization of Wilkie Collins' novel, *Armadale.* Among her books are *Photographs of Paris Life* (1862), written under the pen name of "Chroniqueuse"; *Apropos of Women and Theatres* (1869); *Before the Footlights and Behind the Scenes* (1870); *The Mimic World* (1871); and *They Met by Chance* (1873), a society novel. None of them is of more than temporary interest. She was a woman of alert mind, a forceful personality, but she was erratic and had little ability to turn her talents in the direction of permanent success in the theatre, in literature, or in any profession. She was married three times: in 1857 to Henry A. De Lille (or Delille), from whom she was divorced in 1865; about 1872 to William Wirt Sikes [*q.v.*], a member of the American consular service at Cardiff, Wales, who died in 1883; and third to James O'Neill (not the famous actor of that name), who was some twenty years her junior. She and her last husband were known as Mr. and Mrs. James O'Neill Logan. Her last years were spent in poverty and were clouded by insanity, and she died in Banstead, England, while an inmate of an asylum.

[See J. N. Ireland, *Records of the N. Y. Stage,* vol. II (1867); T. Allston Brown, *Hist. of the Am. Stage* (1870); E. A. Dithmar, *Memories of Daly's Theatres* (1897); Wm. Winter, *The Wallet of Time* (1913), vol. I; J. F. Daly, *The Life of Augustin Daly* (1917); the *Sun* (N. Y.), Apr. 11, 1906, Feb. 26, Apr. 29, 1909; *Telegram* (N. Y.), and *N. Y. Tribune,* Apr. 11, 1906; *Chicago Chronicle,* Apr. 15, 1906. The date of birth is taken from *Who's Who in America,* 1899–1900.]   E.F.E.

LOGAN, STEPHEN TRIGG (Feb. 24, 1800–July 17, 1880), jurist, law partner of Lincoln, son of David and Mary (Trigg) Logan, was born in Franklin County, Ky., of Scotch-Irish and English ancestry. Much of the history of pioneer Kentucky may be read in the chronicles of his family. His grandfather, Col. John Logan, represented a Kentucky county in the legislature of Virginia and served in the Kentucky constitutional convention of 1799; his great-uncle, Gen. Benjamin Logan [*q.v.*], established a fort in Lincoln County in 1776 and took prominent part in the Indian wars of the Boone period. Stephen Trigg, his maternal grandfather, moved from Virginia to Kentucky in 1779 and was killed in 1782 in the battle of Blue Licks. The first thirty-two years of Logan's life were spent in Kentucky. He was educated at Frankfort, admitted to the bar before attaining his majority, served as deputy in the circuit clerk's office of Barren County, held the office of commonwealth's attorney of the Glasgow circuit, and practised law in Barren and adjoining counties until 1832. He then moved to Illinois, lived for a time on a farm in Sangamon County, gave up agriculture for the law, and made his home in Springfield. He soon became one of the foremost lawyers of the state. Elected in 1835 by the legislature as judge of the first judicial circuit of Illinois, he held this office until 1837, when he resigned to resume his law practice. He served in the state legislature for four terms (1842–48, 1854–56), and he was a prominent member of the Illinois constitutional convention of 1847, where he urged strict economy and opposed debt repudiation. Indorsing the obligations of a friend, he had become insolvent; but through personal thrift he paid all of his vicarious debt.

In 1841 he formed a partnership with Abraham Lincoln and for a time these two men, together with E. D. Baker, formed a group known as the "Springfield junto," their word being locally decisive as to the nomination of candidates in Whig conventions (A. J. Beveridge, *Abraham Lincoln,* 1928, I, p. 302). Lincoln owed much to his senior partner, for it was during the period of this partnership that Lincoln's serious practice of the law began. After the dissolution of the partnership late in 1844—a dissolution which has sometimes been attributed to political rivalry between the partners, though the evidence on this matter is insufficient—the two men remained warm friends. In 1848 Logan was the Whig candidate to succeed Lincoln in Congress; but, suffering from the unpopularity of Lincoln's attitude toward the Mexican War, he was defeated. In 1860 he served as a member of the Republican convention which nominated Lincoln, and in February 1861 he was one of the representatives of Illinois in the Peace Convention which assembled in Washington at the call of Virginia to avert the Civil War. In this convention he delivered a notable speech, striving hard to effect a compromise which might reunite the North and South. From this time, having acquired considerable means, he lived in comfortable retirement. He died in his Springfield home, July 17, 1880.

On June 25, 1823, Logan was married to America T. Bush of Glasgow, Ky. There were four sons and four daughters, of whom David (1824–1874) became prominent in Oregon politics, Mary (1831–1874) married Milton Hay of Springfield, and Sally (1834–1892) became the second wife of Ward Hill Lamon [*q.v.*]. Logan was small, thin and wiry, with an intellectual face surmounted by thick, reddish curling hair. "Though of ample means," says a contemporary (*Memoirs of Gustave Koerner,* 1909, I, pp. 478–79), "occupying a very fine residence surrounded by a large and beautiful park, his clothes were shabby. . . . I never saw him wear a necktie. He wore an old fur cap in winter and a fifty-cent straw hat in summer, baggy trousers, and a coat to match. Thick, coarse, brogan shoes covered his feet." It has been said that Lincoln once sought Logan's appointment as federal judge, at that time regarding him "as the most thorough and accomplished lawyer he had ever known" (*Memorials, post,* p. 61).

[See *Memorials of the Life and Character of Stephen T. Logan* (1882); *Encyc. of Biog. of Ill.,* vol. I (1892); *Chicago Legal News,* July 24, 1880; J. M. Palmer, *The Bench and Bar of Ill.* (1899), vol. I; J. G. Nicolay and John Hay, *Abraham Lincoln* (10 vols., 1890); A. J. Beveridge, *Abraham Lincoln* (2 vols., 1928); P. M. Angle, ed., *Herndon's Life of Lincoln* (1930) and *New Letters and Papers of Lincoln* (1930). As stated by Beveridge on the authority of Logan Hay (*op. cit.,* I, p. 446, note), Logan destroyed all the letters he had received from Lincoln.]   J. G. R.

LOGAN, THOMAS MULDRUP (July 31, 1808–Feb. 13, 1876), sanitarian and climatologist, was born in Charleston, S. C., son of Dr. George Logan, a navy surgeon, and Margaret White (Polk), a native of Delaware. The Logans, according to family tradition, were descended from Col. George Logan, scion of a Scottish noble family, who came from Aberdeen to Charleston in 1690. Thomas attended Charleston College and subsequently began the study of medicine with his father. He was graduated from the Medical College of South Carolina in 1828, commenced practice in Charleston, and after a year of study in London and Paris (1832–33), was appointed lecturer on materia medica and therapeutics in the Charleston school. While here he collaborated with Dr. Thomas L. Ogier in the preparation of two volumes of a *Compendium of Operative Surgery* which appeared in 1834 and 1836. He moved in 1843 to New Orleans, where he joined the medical staff of the Charity Hospital, transferring to the staff of the Luzenberg Hospital in 1847. Moving to California in 1850, he took up his residence in Sacramento, where he spent the remainder of his career.

For the next quarter century his name was identified with every movement for the physical, mental, and moral improvement of the community in which he had settled. He interested himself in climatic and hygienic conditions and during his first three years in the new state he contributed a series of articles on these subjects to Southern medical journals. He was an observer at Sacramento for the Smithsonian Institution for a number of years. To the *Annual Report* of the Institution for 1854 and 1855 he furnished articles upon climatology and meteorology of the Pacific coast region. Among his other writings worthy of note are the "History of Medicine in California" (*California State Medical Journal,* 1858); "Report on the Medical Topography, Meteorology, Endemics and Epidemics of California" (*Transactions of the Third Session of the Medical Society of the State of California,* 1858); "Report on the Medical Topography and Epidemics of California" (*Transactions of the American Medical Association,* vol. XII, 1859); "Mushrooms and Their Poisonings" (*Pacific Medical and Surgical Journal,* April 1868); and "Mortality in California" (*Transactions of the Medical Society of the State of California,* 1870–71). He was elected president of the State Medical Society in 1870, and in 1872, at its Philadelphia meeting, was chosen president of the American Medical Association. At the St. Louis meeting in the following year his presidential address was a scholarly paper on medical education and state medicine. When in 1870 the California State Board of Health was authorized, Logan became its permanent secretary. In this capacity he was especially interested in the improvement of school hygiene. His studies of the epidemiology of the state are particularly complete. He was an active advocate of a national board of health and he prepared a bill which was introduced into Congress with that end in view, but was not acted upon (*Second Biennial Report of the State Board of Health of California,* 1873). Though he is most widely remembered for his public health work, Logan was a competent practitioner and had a devoted following in his home city. He spent the summer of 1867 visiting the medical centers of England, France, and Germany. He was president of the Agassiz Institute of Sacramento and meteorologist of the State Agricultural Society of California. He was an honorary member of the Imperial Botanical and Zoological Society of Vienna. He died in Sacramento of pneumonia.

Logan married Susan, daughter of Judge John S. Richardson of Charleston, S. C. She died in 1864, and in the following year he married Mary A. Greely of Hudson, N. H. A son of his first marriage became a physician practising in Alabama; Gen. T. M. Logan [*q.v.*] was a nephew.

[*Charleston Medic. Jour. and Rev.,* Apr. 1876; *Western Lancet* (San Francisco), Feb. 1876; *Trans. of the Medic. Soc. of the State of Cal.,* 2 ser., VI (1876); J. M. Toner, in *Trans. Am. Medic. Asso.,* vol. XXIX (1878); H. A. Kelly and W. L. Burrage, *Am. Medic. Biogs.* (1920); G. W. Logan, *A Record of the Logan Family*

of Charleston, S. C. (1874; new ed., enl., by L. L. Morrill, 1923); *Sacramento Union,* Feb. 14, 1876.]
J. M. P—n.

LOGAN, THOMAS MULDRUP (Nov. 3, 1840–Aug. 11, 1914), Confederate general and capitalist, was born in Charleston, S. C., the tenth child of Judge George William and Anna D'Oyley (Glover) Logan and a nephew of Dr. Thomas Muldrup Logan [*q.v.*]. He was graduated from the South Carolina College in 1860, first in his class. The following year he served as a volunteer at Fort Sumter and then, aiding in the organization of Company A, Hampton Legion, was elected first lieutenant. After First Manassas (Bull Run) he was promoted captain. In spite of a wound received at Gaines's Mill in June 1862, he commanded his company at Second Manassas the following August. For "great bravery" at Sharpsburg (Antietam) in September, he was officially cited and promoted major. He then served in the campaigns of Micah Jenkins' brigade, particularly distinguishing himself in reconnaissance duty. In 1864, he was severely wounded. His daring leadership was rewarded by further promotions which in February 1865 culminated in his appointment as brigadier-general, the youngest then in the army. This promotion had been indorsed by Lee (Logan and Morrill, *post,* p. 55) as "the best appointment that can be made for this brigade" (M. C. Butler's). Transferred to Johnston's army, Logan led its last charge of the war, at Bentonville, N. C., in March 1865. When Johnston went to Sherman to surrender, Logan, "a slight, fair-haired boy," accompanied him; his youthful appearance made it difficult for Sherman to believe that he commanded a brigade.

A month after the surrender, Logan borrowed five dollars from a friend and on May 25, 1865, married Kate Virginia Cox, daughter of Judge James H. Cox of Chesterfield County, Va. He successfully managed a local coal mine and its railroad for a few years, and then practised law in and near Richmond. Shortly before 1878 he started upon his career of railroad organization by beginning to purchase the stock of the Richmond & Danville Railroad. In this venture he saw profit for himself after long waiting, but he was more concerned with the development of a great railroad, which would aid the growth of Richmond. In 1878 he organized a Richmond syndicate to buy the pool of the Richmond & Danville controlled by the Pennsylvania Railroad. This syndicate quietly purchased at a low price the Pennsylvania pool, and, securing a broad charter for a new corporation, the Richmond & West Point Terminal Company, built the Georgia Pacific from Birmingham to the Mississippi and bought several other Southern railroads. In less than two years the Terminal Company increased its trackage from 300 to over 2,000 miles. When Richmond & Danville and Terminal stocks were succumbing to a bear attack in Wall Street, Logan threw in $1,500,000 of his own money to protect them. About two years later he was aided by John D. Rockefeller in purchasing and disposing of the controlling share of these stocks, and made a profit of approximately $1,500,000. In 1894, the railway system which he had organized was given its present name, the Southern Railway.

About 1890 Logan bought control of the Seattle, Lake Shore & Eastern Railroad, which he soon sold at a large profit to the Northern Pacific. From about 1888 until his death, as president of the Gray National Telautograph Company, he worked despite great discouragement to adapt a new invention, the telautograph, to the market. He spent a fortune in the development of the machine; but only after his death did it prove its great usefulness. Logan was chairman of the Virginia Democratic Executive Committee in 1879 and of the Virginia Gold Democrat Party in 1896. He was an old-fashioned Southern host, a lover of good literature, an influential speaker and writer. A skilful though daring promoter, he carried into business the same capacity he showed on the battlefield. Although he probably lost several fortunes, after each disaster he returned to his enterprises with renewed courage. He died in New York City.

[Information obtained from W. P. de Saussure and other Richmond business associates of Logan; G. W. Logan and Lily Logan Morrill, *A Record of the Logan Family of Charleston, S. C.* (1923); *Richmond News-Leader,* Jan. 11, 1929; *War of the Rebellion, Official Records (Army)*; *Confed. Mil. Hist.* (1899), vol. V; *Who's Who in America,* 1914–15; M. J. Verdery, in *News and Courier* (Charleston), May 10, 1899; *Times-Dispatch* (Richmond) and *N. Y. Times,* Aug. 12, 1914.]

R. D. M.

LOGUEN, JERMAIN WESLEY (*c.* 1813– Sept. 30, 1872), bishop of the African Methodist Episcopal Zion Church, was born near Manscoe's Creek in Davidson County, Tenn., the natural son of a white resident, David Logue, and a slave mother, Cherry, who had been kidnapped in Ohio. The story of the experiences of Cherry and her family forms one of the blackest pictures of the slavery system. Growing up without schooling, with many hardships and few glimpses of the sunnier aspects of life, Jermain long planned to break away from slavery, but determined never to buy his freedom. Although his first attempt at escape failed, the sale of his sister aroused anew his resolution. The account of

his flight through Kentucky and southern Indiana (*c.* 1834–35), antecedent to the organization of the Underground Railroad, shows that the preliminary surveys for that system had been made and that a few lines already ran through the homes of Quakers as unerringly as railroads run through the large towns and cities. Jermain crossed from Detroit to Canada, making his way to Hamilton, Ont., in search of work. Writing to Frederick Douglass in May 1856 (see *The Rev. J. W. Loguen,* p. 339), he refers to this episode as "twenty-one years ago—the very winter I left my chains in Tennessee" and to himself as "a boy twenty-one years of age (as near as I know my age)." This statement furnishes the best available guide to the chronology of his early life.

In Canada, he learned to read, while by hard farm labor and thrift, in the face of great discouragement, he made a start towards competency. After two years as porter in a hotel at Rochester, N. Y., he was able to study at Oneida Institute, Whitesboro, where he received the only schooling he had. He then opened a school for colored children in Utica, and later one in Syracuse. At Busti, N. Y., in November 1840 he married Caroline Storum, a woman with some negro blood. Settling in Syracuse shortly afterward, he became one of the local managers of the Underground Railroad. He subsequently became an elder in the African Methodist Episcopal Zion Church, with successive pastorates (1843–50) in Bath, Ithaca, Syracuse, and Troy. He was presiding elder of the last-named district. He had begun to call himself Loguen, and through the persuasion of his Methodist friends he adopted Wesley as his middle name.

As a speaker against slavery he aroused much interest. Citizens of Cortland, N. Y., raised a fund to purchase his mother, but her master, Manasseth Logue, a brother of David, refused to sell her unless Jermain would buy his freedom also. His liberty imperiled by the Fugitive-slave Act of 1850, he left Troy and returned to the comparative safety of Syracuse, where his home again became an important station of the Underground Railroad. During the decade before the Civil War, he was a central figure in the activities of that organization, especially such as centered around his Peterboro neighbor, Gerrit Smith [*q.v.*]. In various ways he assisted some fifteen hundred fugitives. Indicted for participation in the "Jerry rescue" case (1851), he sought temporary refuge in Canada. Just before John Brown's raid on Harpers Ferry, Loguen went again into Ontario with John Brown, Jr., in behalf of the League of Liberty and possibly also to further plans of the elder Brown. In 1864, Loguen declined election as a bishop of his denomination, but accepted in 1868, and was assigned to the Fifth District (Alleghany and Kentucky conferences). After two years he was transferred to the Second District (Genesee, Philadelphia, and Baltimore conferences). In 1872 he was reëlected bishop and appointed to take charge of mission work on the Pacific Coast, but he died at Saratoga Springs, N. Y., before he could go to his field.

[The main source of information is *The Rev. J. W. Loguen, as a Slave and as a Freeman, a Narrative of Real Life* (t.p. 1859, but the book contains letters dated 1860); although it is written in the third person, its detailed information indicates autobiography. A manuscript note by a Syracuse genealogist in a copy at the Syracuse Pub. Lib. states that Loguen died in his sixty-third year, which would place his birth *c.* 1810. See also W. H. Siebert, *The Underground Railroad* (1898); J. W. Hood, *One Hundred Years of the African Meth. Episc. Zion Ch.* (1895); death notice in *N. Y. Tribune*, Oct. 1, 1872.]   W. H. A.

LOMAX, JOHN TAYLOE (Jan. 19, 1781–Oct. 1, 1862), jurist and teacher of law, was born on his father's plantation, "Port Tobago," Caroline County, Va., the fourth of eleven children of Thomas and Anne Corbin (Tayloe) Lomax. With both Dissenter and Cavalier ancestry, a descendant of John Lomax who came from England to Jamestown, Va., about 1700, he was by birth and breeding a member of the Tidewater aristocracy. Graduating in 1797 from St. John's College, Annapolis, he studied law and began practice in Fredericksburg. In 1805 he married Charlotte Belson Thornton, a member of a prominent Northumberland County family. From about 1810 to 1818 he practised in Richmond County and during the War of 1812 served as a militia officer for the lower counties of the Northern Neck. Returning to Fredericksburg, he attained eminence at the bar. Meanwhile the University of Virginia had been established, but, largely owing to the inadequate salary, a suitable professor of law had not been secured. After receiving a number of disheartening refusals the Board of Visitors in 1826 offered the place to Lomax. He accepted and became the first professor of law in the University.

Fervent and faithful in the study of the law, he taught its principles with a high sense of moral responsibility. To him a law school was something more than a trade school in which to gain the means of livelihood. During 1827–28, under the unique Jeffersonian system, unchanged until 1904, Lomax was chairman of the faculty and, incidentally, the only native American among its members. In 1830, however, the General Assembly unanimously elected him asso-

ciate judge of the circuit superior court of law and chancery, a position carrying a higher salary. Unfortunate investments had swept away the Lomax holdings during his father's later years, so for the sake of his family he regretfully resigned his professorship. He was assigned to the fifth judicial circuit, comprising his native Caroline and neighboring counties, and once more made his home in Fredericksburg, where he remained until his death. In 1848 he was appointed to a temporary court established to relieve the overburdened supreme court of appeals. In drafting the constitution of 1851, the convention set the age limit for judges at seventy; Lomax, then seventy, thus faced disqualification. On request of the bar of his circuit, however, the clause was eliminated and, judicial office becoming elective under this constitution, he returned to his post without opposition. He was the author of a *Digest of the Laws Respecting Real Property* (3 vols., 1839) and *A Treatise on the Law of Executors and Administrators* (2 vols., 1841). For many years he conducted a private law school in Fredericksburg and continued to influence legal education in Virginia. After twenty-seven years of faithful service on the bench the aged jurist resigned in 1857, despite a contrary plea from the bar. Although politically inactive, he was a student of public affairs and the gathering war clouds appalled him. When Virginia seceded, however, he followed his state. He died a few weeks before the defeat of Burnside at Fredericksburg.

Judge Lomax was stately and impressive in appearance, but with a simplicity of manner and a benevolence of face which endeared him to all. Although an Episcopalian since middle life he was too broad for strict sectarianism. A calm scholar rather than a dynamic teacher, he was a careful and analytical judge whose sense of right was instinctive.

[E. L. Lomax, *Geneal. of the Va. Family of Lomax* (1913); Joseph Lomax, *Geneal. and Hist. Sketches of the Lomax Family* (1894); P. A. Bruce, *Hist. of the Univ. of Va., 1819–1919* (1920–21), vols. II, III; L. L. Lewis (a grandson), in *Va. Law Reg.*, May 1896; E. W. P. Lomax, in *Green Bag*, Sept. 1897.]   T. S. C.

LOMAX, LUNSFORD LINDSAY (Nov. 4, 1835–May 28, 1913), Confederate soldier, nephew of John Tayloe Lomax [*q.v.*], was the son of Mann Page Lomax of Virginia, major of ordnance in the United States Army, and of Elizabeth Virginia Lindsay, a descendant of Capt. William Lindsay of Light-Horse Harry Lee's cavalry in the Revolutionary army. Born at Newport, R. I., he was educated in the schools of Richmond and Norfolk, Va., and appointed to the Military Academy at West Point in 1852.

He was graduated in 1856 with his lifelong friend, Fitzhugh Lee [*q.v.*], and as second lieutenant of cavalry did frontier duty in Kansas and Nebraska. He was serving as first lieutenant when Virginia seceded, and on Apr. 25, 1861, he resigned his commission and was appointed captain in the state forces of Virginia, serving first as assistant adjutant-general on the staff of Gen. Joseph E. Johnston. Later he was transferred to the Confederate Army as inspector-general on the staff of brigadier-general McCulloch in Van Dorn's army. After McCulloch's death he served as inspector-general with the rank of lieutenant-colonel on Van Dorn's staff until October 1862, when he was made inspector-general of the army in East Tennessee. He took part in battles in Arkansas, Mississippi, Louisiana, and Tennessee, and in 1863 was called to the eastern campaign as colonel of the 11th Virginia Cavalry. He participated in the raid into West Virginia with Jones's brigade, and in the campaign culminating in the battle of Gettysburg. On July 23, 1863, he was promoted brigadier-general, and his brigade was one of the principal factors in Fitz Lee's operations from Culpeper through the Wilderness campaign and the fighting around Richmond. On Aug. 10, 1864, he was made major-general and fought in the Valley campaign of Gen. Jubal A. Early. He was captured at the battle of Woodstock by a cavalry company but overcame his captors and escaped in a few hours. On Mar. 29, 1865, he was put in entire command of the Valley District of the Army of Northern Virginia. After the fall of Richmond he removed his troops to Lynchburg and when General Lee surrendered he tried to effect a juncture with General Echols in order to continue the struggle, but he finally surrendered his division with Johnston at Greensboro.

Immediately after the close of the Civil War Lomax bought a place near Warrenton, Va., and settled down to farming. He remained here until his election in 1885 to the presidency of the Virginia Agricultural and Mechanical College (now Virginia Polytechnic Institute), at Blacksburg. In 1899 he resigned this position and moved to Washington, where he took up the compilation, begun in 1880, of the Civil War records, published by the War Department under the title, *War of the Rebellion: Official Records of the Union and Confederate Armies*. He was engaged in this task until it was completed and then (1905) was appointed one of the commissioners of the military park at Gettysburg. To this work he gave enthusiastic service until his death, which took place at Washington. He **was** married, Feb. 20, 1873, to Elizabeth Winter,

daughter of Dr. Alban S. Payne and cousin of Gen. William H. Payne. Distinguished in manner and known for his great physical and mental vigor, he enjoyed the esteem and close friendship of leading men in both the Union and Confederate armies, and won the affection of those associated with him in his college work.

[The best sketch of Lomax is in *Forty-fifth Ann. Reunion, Asso. Grads. U. S. Mil. Acad.* (1914); family history is found in Joseph Lomax, *Geneal. and Hist. Sketches of the Lomax Family* (1894) and E. L. Lomax, *Geneal. of the Va. Family of Lomax* (1913); an interesting estimate of Lomax written to Gen. Stanley, U. S. A., by L. J. Perry, U. S. A., is in the possession of Mrs. Lomax. See also *Who's Who in America*, 1912–13; *War of the Rebellion: Official Records (Army)*; *Confed. Veteran* (Nashville), Sept. 1913; *Washington Post*, May 29, 1913. The sketch in *Confed. Mil. Hist.* (1899), vol. III, is notably inaccurate.]

J. E. W.

LONDON, JACK (Jan. 12, 1876–Nov. 22, 1916), writer, was born in San Francisco, Cal., the only child of John and Flora (Wellman) London. On both sides he came of nomadic pioneer stock. John London, of whose eleven children by a first marriage only the two youngest lived with him, was neither well-to-do nor destitute. He did many kinds of work, chiefly truck-gardening, first on one side and then the other of San Francisco Bay. Jack attended what schools were available, finally graduating from grammar school in Oakland. Before that time, financial troubles had forced John London to give up farming and to settle on the Oakland waterfront. Thereafter his poverty grew increasingly acute. Jack delivered newspapers, worked on an ice wagon, and set up pins in a bowling alley. For a year after graduation he worked in a cannery. During these years he read voraciously in the public library, chiefly books of romance, travel, and adventure.

The Oakland waterfront was a disreputable neighborhood. Jack London had a skiff which he sailed in the Estuary and on the bay and he knew the region intimately. When fourteen, he caroused with a runaway sailor and a harpooner on an opium-smuggling yacht. Already he had formed his lifelong passion for the sea, and wished to be a sailor. When fifteen, he bought the sloop *Razzle Dazzle* and turned oyster pirate. He won the title, Prince of the Oyster Pirates, chiefly by taking with him the girl called the Queen of the Oyster Pirates. For a year or so he sailed San Francisco Bay, robbing oyster beds, living a lawless, reckless life, full of danger and hard drinking. For a little while he joined the fish patrol as deputy. For a few weeks he was a hobo. Then he returned to the Oakland waterfront and spent most of his time loafing in saloons until he signed up, Jan. 12, 1893, on the *Sophie Suther-*

land, a sealer, as able-bodied seaman and boat-puller. After he had established his position on board by one fierce fight, he enjoyed the voyage, with its riotous visits to Japan before and after the seal hunt off the Siberian coast.

On his return to Oakland in the fall of 1893, he decided to settle down. He won a newspaper prize with an account of a typhoon near Japan, and did some other writing, a little of which appeared in a local paper. He worked in a jute mill, stoked a furnace; but as always rebelled against such monotonous labor. In the spring of 1894, an army of the unemployed, similar to Coxey's, appeared in Oakland. Jack London decided to join it, but arrived after it had been sent off to Sacramento. He followed and became a tramp, making his way eastward until at Council Bluffs, Iowa, he overtook Kelly's Army, only to leave it as soon as it reached Hannibal, Mo. As a hobo he roamed over the eastern part of the United States. In Niagara Falls he was arrested and sent to the Erie County penitentiary for thirty days. As soon as released, he worked his way back to Oakland, resolved to make a complete change in his manner of life.

For a year he attended high school, working as school janitor and doing odd jobs. In the high-school paper he published some of his experiences on the road. He read eagerly, being interested especially in sociology and popular science. Herbert Spencer influenced him definitely. He became a socialist and made soapbox speeches, for which he was arrested and gained some notoriety. He decided to go to college at once; after three months of unaided cramming he passed his entrance examinations, and in August 1896 entered the University of California at Berkeley. In January 1897 he left the university and took to writing, but sold none of his work. Forced to earn money, he got a job in the laundry of Belmont Academy, south of San Francisco. In the summer of 1897 he joined the gold rush to the Klondike, sailing July 25 and arriving in August at Dyea. He and his partners packed over Chilkoot Pass, made boats, and navigated rivers and lakes until on Oct. 9 they stopped for the winter on the Yukon near the Stewart River. When spring came, London was so ill with scurvy that he was forced to leave for the outside. He voyaged down the Yukon to St. Michael. Thence he worked his way as stoker to British Columbia and traveled steerage from there on. Before reaching home, he learned that his father had died.

Unable to get a job of any sort, he returned to writing and worked furiously. Early in December 1898 the *Overland Monthly* accepted a story of the Yukon, "To the Man on Trail," for five dollars. Later the editors offered to take all similar work at seven dollars and a half a story, and during 1899 London published eight stories in the magazine. Finding great difficulty in collecting the small sums due him from this and other periodicals, he was close at times to desperation. But when the *Atlantic Monthly* accepted "An Odyssey of the North" in July 1899 (published in January 1900) and Houghton Mifflin took the collected stories, *The Son of the Wolf* (published in 1900), he had arrived. During the five years 1899–1903 he averaged yearly two dozen contributions to periodicals—short stories, serials, juveniles, essays, articles, verses, newspaper hackwork. During the same years he published eight volumes, of which five—two novels and three collections of stories—dealt with the Klondike. The second of these novels, commonly thought his best book, brought him enormous and world-wide popularity : *The Call of the Wild,* a story of a dog who, taken to Alaska, reverts to type and runs with a wolf pack.

Meanwhile, with success, his private life had altered. From his high-school days until after his return from the Yukon, he had been in love with a girl whom he portrays as Ruth in *Martin Eden.* But on Apr. 7, 1900, he was married to Elizabeth Maddern. By this marriage he had two daughters, Joan and Bess, born in 1901 and 1902. Before this time he had made many acquaintances among Bohemians and socialists. In the fall of 1899 he met Anna Strunsky, and the two wrote each other long letters of intellectual discussion. In the summer of 1902 he went to London and spent several weeks in the slums of the East End, writing up his experiences in *The People of the Abyss* (1903). After a short visit to the Continent, he returned to California. Although he then wrote *The Call of the Wild* and became famous, this was a time of extreme depression and sense of futility, to which he later referred as "the long sickness." Perhaps domestic troubles were partly responsible ; he separated from his wife in the summer of 1903. In January 1904 he set off for the Russo-Japanese War as war correspondent for the *San Francisco Examiner,* but he returned in June. At once he was sued for divorce. The final decree was granted Nov. 18, 1905. The next day, in Chicago, he married Charmian Kittredge. He was on a lecture tour at the time ; having fulfilled his engagements and made a visit to the Caribbean, he established his home at Glen Ellen, Sonoma County, Cal., where he lived until his death.

In April 1907, he and Mrs. London set forth to sail around the world in a forty-five-foot yacht, the *Snark*. After visiting Honolulu, they cruised among the islands of the southern Pacific. Every one on board was extremely ill, with fever and other maladies. Jack London himself was stricken with a severe disease which he called "Biblical leprosy" and which he attributed to the tropic sunlight. Upon reaching Australia he was sick for six months. He abandoned the voyage and returned to California by way of Ecuador, getting home in July 1909. Thenceforth his chief interest was his ranch. He planned, and in part achieved, a magnificent patriarchal estate. The burning in August 1913 of his huge stone house, still unfinished, was a great blow to him. During his last years he took great pleasure in driving a coach with four horses, and in sailing his yawl, the *Roamer,* on inland bays and rivers. In 1912, returning from New York, he took passage round the Horn in a sailing vessel. In 1914 he went to Vera Cruz, Mexico, as war-correspondent. Toward the end of his life he made several pleasure trips to Honolulu. These years were clouded by a growing depression and lassitude. He was constantly ill with uremia and was warned to alter his diet and habits. He did not care enough for life, however, to follow this advice. On the morning of Nov. 22, 1916, he was found unconscious and died that evening.

In sixteen years Jack London published forty-three volumes and by 1933 seven more had been issued posthumously. Besides fiction, he produced volumes of socialistic and miscellaneous essays. Several of his books are directly autobiographical: *John Barleycorn* (1913) tells the story of his life with special reference to alcohol; *The Road* (1907) relates his experiences as a tramp; *The Cruise of the Snark* (1911) has to do with his voyage across the Pacific. *Martin Eden* (1909) is a semi-autobiographical novel dealing with the time when he was beginning to write. The rest of his fiction for the most part is mined direct from first-hand experience. Most important are the dozen or so volumes of short stories and novels laid in the Far North. Of less consequence are those laid in the South Seas. Among his sea stories the chief is *The Sea Wolf* (1904), for which he drew upon his adventures in the sealer, *Sophie Sutherland,* in 1893. Less intimately connected with his own life are his two novels of prize-fighting, *The Game* (1905) and *The Abysmal Brute* (1913), and his phantasies of the remote past and future.

Almost all his writing, whether it deals with the future, the past, prize-fighters, sailors, dogs, gold-seekers, Indians, tramps, or the proletariat, has to do with one motif—the primitive, and above all reversion to savagery. His insistence is constant upon the importance of brute force. Civilized beings are "mollycoddles" to be destroyed or regenerated through conflict with a savage environment. The title of one of his books, *The Strength of the Strong* (1914), announces his favorite theme. His first popularity he gained because the brutality in his stories shocked and thrilled his readers and because his highly colored and sometimes violent style excited them. He is still read as a master of swift and vivid action and adventure. In his art his chief debt is to Kipling. His European vogue he owes not only to his "Americanism" (in the tradition of Cooper, Harte, and Mark Twain) but also to his socialism. For all the prevalence of the "abysmal brute" in Jack London's writing, he himself was a man of abnormal sensitiveness both physical and emotional. His own life, it is true, was affected by his cult of the primitive, yet he must not be confounded with the tough, hardened supermen he portrays. He was generous and sympathetic; he accepted conventional duties for the most part, and supported many dependents. His extraordinarily keen feelings and intense sensibilities were his most striking traits. Everything about him, when he was at his best, from his lively blue eyes and brown curly hair to the quick play of his muscles, bespoke a man alert, ardent, and alive.

[Besides London's own works mentioned above, the principal source of information is Charmian K. London, *The Book of Jack London* (2 vols., 1921, with a bibliography), though it is vague, confused, and not wholly reliable. Some further information is contained in Rose Wilder Lane's journalistic and untrustworthy "Life and Jack London," *Sunset* (San Francisco) Oct. 1917–May 1918. For his life in the South Seas, see also Charmian K. London, *The Log of the Snark* (1915) and *Our Hawaii* (1917); and Martin E. Johnson, *Through the South Seas with Jack London* (1913). Georgia L. Bamford, *The Mystery of Jack London* (1931) was banned (see *Publishers' Weekly,* Dec. 12, 1931) because the author used copyrighted material without authorization. The *Overland Monthly* (San Francisco) contains many reminiscences and impressions of London, including those of Ninetta Eames, May 1900, and those in the London memorial number, May 1917 (see especially G. W. James, "A Study of Jack London in his Prime," pp. 361–99). For other recollections and criticism, see: H. M. Bland, article in the *Craftsman,* Feb. 1906; and C. H. Grattan, article in *Bookman,* Feb. 1929. The best critical study is by F. L. Pattee in *Sidelights on Am. Lit.* (1922), pp. 98–160. For the Russian view of London, see L. S. Friedland, article in *Dial,* Jan. 25, 1917. For the French view, see Régis Michaud, *Mystiques et Réalistes Anglo-saxons* (1918); E. Sainte-Marie Perrin, article in *Revue des Deux Mondes,* Sept. 1, 1922. For the German, see Frank Thiess, article in *Die Neue Rundschau,* Nov. 1927; Edgar Stern-Rubarth, article in *Deutsche Rundschau,* July 1927.]   T. K. W.

LONDON, MEYER (Dec. 29, 1871–June 6, 1926), socialist and labor leader, was born in the Russian-Polish province of Suwalki, but in his boyhood moved with his family to Zenkov in the province of Poltava. His mother, Rebecca Ber-son, came from a family of learned rabbis. His father, Ephraim London, was trained in Talmudic studies, but early became a free-thinker and social radical. He emigrated to New York in 1888, and the family followed in 1891. Meyer, the eldest of five sons, gave private lessons, worked in a library, studied law at night, and was admitted to the bar in 1898. His practice never became lucrative. He would not deal with clients whom he did not respect nor refuse his services to those who were unable to pay.

In 1896 the Socialist Labor party nominated him for the New York Assembly. Opposing the leadership of Daniel DeLeon [q.v.], he went over in 1897 to the Social Democratic party, newly organized by Eugene V. Debs [q.v.] and Victor L. Berger, and through the realignments of 1899 to 1901 he became one of the founders of the Socialist Party of America. In 1914 he was elected to Congress from the Ninth (later the Twelfth) district, and in spite of Democratic-Republican fusion was reëlected in 1916 and 1920 and only narrowly defeated in 1918. A gerrymander in 1921 made further election in that district impossible. During his three terms in Congress London advocated measures against lynching, better salaries for government employees, abolition of injunctions in labor disputes, prohibition of child labor, unemployment insurance, old-age pensions, maternity allowances, and nationalization of coal mines, and opposed the Fordney tariff, restriction of immigration, the property qualification for voting in Puerto Rico, intervention in Mexico, and increases of army and navy. He urged strict neutrality in the World War, and when the crisis came he voted against the declaration of war and the conscription and espionage laws and threw himself into a fight against profiteering and for defense of civil liberties. Savagely denounced for his lack of "war patriotism" and at the same time attacked by those extremists in his own party who later became Communists, he stedfastly followed what he thought the right course.

London was as active in the trade-union field as in politics. No man did more for the development of unions in the "needle trades." He served them as legal counsel, as adviser in matters of union policy, as spokesman in negotiations with employers, and as inspiring speaker in time of strike. His influence was felt in every clothing center in North America and, though strongest among the Jewish workers, it affected the whole labor movement. He sharply criticized the non-political and, as he deemed it, too conservative policy of the American Federation of Labor, yet his services were warmly acknowledged by Samuel Gompers and other Federation leaders. Besides the unions, he had much to do with the building up of the Workmen's Circle, a great mutual-benefit society with educational features.

London was wholeheartedly American, but he could not be indifferent either to his native land or to his race. In 1916 he wrote: "I deem it a duty of the Jew everywhere to remain a Jew as long as in any corner of the world the Jew is being discriminated against" (quoted by Rogoff, *post,* p. 118). It is fair to say, however, that only a sense of loyalty to those suffering under racial discrimination kept London from being in effect an assimilationist. He valued Jewish cultural tradition, but wished to see it become an element of the general culture. He strenuously combated Antisemitism and at the same time worked hard for the relief of Jewish sufferers. That he was respected by his opponents was shown by his election as chairman of the Jewish Relief Committee and by the large part he was able to play in getting the factions to work together in the Jewish Congress.

He always took a lively interest in the struggle against Tsarism and rendered invaluable services to the *Bund* and other Russian revolutionary organizations. The revolution in February 1917 filled him with hope, and he held that if the United States and the Entente Powers had dealt reasonably with the provisional government and the Russian people the Bolshevist *coup* in October could have been averted, the democratic uprising in Germany hastened, and the war brought to an earlier close. While strongly condemning Bolshevism or Communism in theory and practice, he as vigorously denounced the Allies' policy of intervention and blockade, both on general principles of humanity and because it rallied the Russian masses to the support of the Bolshevist régime. He died in the height of his powers, being fatally injured by a taxicab while crossing a New York street. His body lies in the Workmen's Circle plot of Mount Carmel cemetery, where memorial exercises are held annually. He was survived by his wife, Anna Rosenson, whom he married in 1899, and by their only child, a daughter.

Meyer London was of slight build and small stature, with thin features and bright blue eyes. His movements were quick and restless, and his face commonly wore a somewhat sardonic expression, which easily broke into a quizzical smile or hardened into grim resoluteness. His speeches in Congress were argumentative, with flashes of wit but with no attempt at oratorical grace. He spoke best in labor mass-meetings and conventions, especially when he had to meet opposition. On such occasions he made free use of a quaint folk-humor and his climaxes were often highly poetic. He was an unresting rather than a tireless worker. Saddened by the suffering he saw about him, often deeply hurt by hostile reactions for which his too impulsive frankness might be in part responsible, wearied by labors beyond his physical strength, he had fits of black melancholy, from which he emerged to throw himself into action with reckless abandon. He died poorer in worldly goods than many a mechanic, rich only in the love of the masses, which first found full expression at his grave.

[Harry Rogoff has written a life of London entitled *An East Side Epic* (1930). Materials for a much fuller biography are scattered through the files of Socialist, Labor, and Jewish periodicals (especially the *Arbeiter Zeitung, Jewish Daily Forward, N. Y. Call,* and *People and Worker*) from 1896 to 1926 and through the records of the 64th, 65th, and 67th Congresses. Character sketches appeared in the *Nation* (N. Y.) and the *Outlook,* June 23, 1926, and obituaries in all the New York papers. The present article is based partly on personal acquaintance with London, partly on information supplied by his widow and his brothers.]   A. L.

LONESOME CHARLEY [See REYNOLDS, CHARLES ALEXANDER, *c.* 1842–1876].

LONG, ARMISTEAD LINDSAY (Sept. 3, 1825–Apr. 29, 1891), military secretary and biographer of Gen. Robert E. Lee, was born in Campbell County, Va. His father, Col. Armistead Long, was a son of Armistead Long of Loudoun County, Va., and Elizabeth, daughter of Col. Burgess Ball; his mother was Calista Cralle of Campbell County. Long was graduated from West Point in 1850 and appointed brevet second lieutenant of artillery. After serving at Fort Moultrie and on the frontier, he was promoted first lieutenant in 1854 and stationed chiefly in Indian Territory, Kansas, and Nebraska until 1860. Shortly before the outbreak of the Civil War, he was in garrison at Augusta Arsenal, Ga., but in February 1861 was transferred to duty in the defenses of Washington, and on May 20, was appointed aide-de-camp to Gen. Edwin Vose Sumner, whose daughter, Mary Heron, he had married the year before. Because of the influence of his father-in-law as well as his own military ability, Long had much to hope for by remaining in the old army. Nevertheless, on June 10, 1861, he resigned his commission and offered his services to the Confederacy.

Following a short service in West Virginia, he was ordered, in the fall of 1861, to report to Gen. Robert E. Lee in South Carolina. He arrived in Charleston on the eve of the great fire and that night he and Lee fled together from a burning hotel, each clasping a baby in his arms. Thus Long was introduced to an intimate companionship with his chief which continued throughout the war. Shortly afterward, when Lee became commander of the Army of Northern Virginia, Long was appointed his military secretary with the rank of colonel, and served in that capacity until September 1863. Lee had chosen Long, whom he loved and trusted, for the most responsible position upon his staff. In September 1863 Long was promoted brigadier-general of artillery and during the subsequent Virginia campaigns he handled his guns with skill and vigor.

After the war he was appointed chief engineer of a Virginia canal company, but in 1870 he became totally blind as the result of exposure during his campaigns. While laboring under this disability, using a slate prepared for the blind, he wrote his *Memoirs of Robert E. Lee, His Military and Personal History* (1886). This volume contains the most intimate of the accounts of General Lee during the Civil War. Although the author was naturally influenced in his judgments by his close association with Lee, his book gives no evidence of narrow partisanship. The information obtained from personal recollections and from his careful wartime diary he substantiated by information and documents from other individuals who had been in Lee's confidence. In all, the work is one of the most valuable source books for the history of Lee and of the Civil War, and is a memorial to Long's courage and biographical skill. Prior to its publication he had contributed two articles, "Seacoast Defences of South Carolina and Georgia" and "General Early's Valley Campaign," to the *Southern Historical Society Papers* (vols. I, II, 1876, and vol. III, 1877, respectively). The latter article he revised in Volume XVIII (1890) of the same *Papers.* He died in Charlottesville, Va., where a few years after he had become blind his wife had been appointed postmistress by President Grant.

[A. L. Long, *Memoirs of Robert E. Lee*; information as to certain facts from Long's daughter, Mrs. Robert A. Brown; *Confed. Mil. Hist.* (1899), vol. III; *War of the Rebellion: Official Records (Army)*; G. W. Cullum, *Biog. Reg. Officers and Grads. U. S. Mil. Acad.* (3rd ed., 1891), vol. II; *Twenty-second Ann. Reunion Asso. Grads. U. S. Mil. Acad.* (1891); *Richmond Dispatch,* Apr. 30, 1891.]   R. D. M.

LONG, CHARLES CHAILLÉ [See CHAILLÉ-LONG, CHARLES, 1842–1917].

LONG, CRAWFORD WILLIAMSON (Nov. 1, 1815–June 16, 1878), anæsthetist and surgeon, the son of James Long, a cultivated Southerner, by his wife Elizabeth Ware, was born in Danielsville, Ga. His grandfather, Capt. Samuel Long, a Scotch-Irish Presbyterian born in the province of Ulster, settled in Pennsylvania about 1761 and later fought in the War of the Revolution. Crawford Long, who as a boy was studious, entered Franklin College (now the University of Georgia) at the early age of fourteen and was graduated in 1835, second in his class. After a year of teaching in the academy which his father had founded at Danielsville, he began to read medicine, first under a preceptor, later at Transylvania University, Lexington, Ky., and finally, in 1838, at the University of Pennsylvania, where in 1839 he received his medical degree. He then spent eighteen months in New York, where he gained the reputation of being a skilful surgeon. In 1841, owing to family difficulties, he was forced to return to Georgia and began to practise in the isolated village of Jefferson, Jackson County, where he obtained the clientele of his old preceptor, Dr. Grant. During idle moments and during horseback rides in the country necessitated by his rural practice Long read widely in general literature, developing a particular fondness for Shakespeare and Dickens. On Aug. 11, 1842, he married Caroline Swain, niece of Governor David Lowry Swain [q.v.] of North Carolina.

In the early forties the exhilarating effect of laughing gas was a subject much under discussion, and wandering charlatans gave demonstrations of its action to voluntary subjects [see G. Q. Colton]. In January 1842, after witnessing such a demonstration, several of Long's friends induced him to permit them to have a "nitrous oxide frolic" in his room. Unfortunately no nitrous oxide was available, but Long offered a substitute. Telling of the incident later, he said: "I informed them . . . that I had a medicine (sulphuric ether) which would produce equally exhilarating effects; that I had inhaled it myself, and considered it as safe as the nitrous oxide gas" (*Southern Medical and Surgical Journal,* December 1849). The young men inhaled the volatile gas and became hilarious, and many received more or less severe bruises. Long made the shrewd observation that the bruises were unaccompanied by pain; from this observation he inferred that ether must have the power of producing insensibility, and he decided to test it in his surgical practice. A few months later (Mar. 30, 1842) he administered sulphuric ether to a patient, James Venable, who, when completely anæsthetized, had removed from the back of his neck a small cystic tumor. This patient later testified that he experienced no pain, and a second operation, involving the removal of another similar tumor from the same man's neck, was performed by Long on June 6, 1842. On July 3, 1842, he amputated the toe of a negro boy

named Jack and on Sept. 9, 1843, he removed an encysted tumor from the head of Mrs. Mary Vincent. A fifth operation, the amputation of a finger, was carried out Jan. 8, 1845. Three other operations were performed before September 1846, making a total of eight. His experience with ether was not published, however, until December 1849, when, as a result of the controversy that had arisen over the claims of W. T. G. Morton [q.v.], Long described his first five operations in a short paper contributed to the *Southern Medical and Surgical Journal,* under the title, "An Account of the First Use of Sulphuric Ether by Inhalation as an Anæsthetic in Surgical Operations" (see also *Transactions of the Medical Association of Georgia,* April 1853). His apologia for his delay in publication may best be given in his own words: "I was anxious before making my publication, to try etherization in a sufficient number of cases to fully satisfy my mind that anæsthesia was produced by the ether, and was not the effect of the imagination, or owing to any peculiar insusceptibility to pain in the person experimented on . . . I determined to wait . . . and see whether any surgeon would present a claim to having used ether by inhalation in surgical operations prior to the time it was used by me." His claim was issued in modest terms, but, as Dr. W. H. Welch has remarked, "Long is necessarily deprived of the larger honor which would have been his due had he not delayed publication of experiments with ether until several years after the universal acceptance of surgical anæsthesia. . . . We need not . . . withhold from Dr. Long the credit of independent and prior experiment and discovery, but we cannot assign to him any influence upon the historical development of our knowledge of surgical anæsthesia or any share in its introduction to the world at large" (*post,* p. 9). He was ever modest in urging his claims, but in the year before his death, Dr. J. Marion Sims [q.v.] published in the *Virginia Medical Monthly* (May 1877) a paper recalling Long's statement made in 1849 and declared him to be the "first discoverer of anæsthesia."

In 1850 Long removed to Athens, Ga., where he immediately acquired a large surgical practice. In June 1878 he died in that city after a long and useful career as surgeon and general practitioner. An obelisk, given by Dr. L. G. Hardman, was erected at Athens in 1910 to the memory of the anæsthetist.

[Biographies and appreciations include H. H. Carlton, in *Trans. Medic. Asso. of Ga.,* vol. XXXII (1881); F. R. Packard, in *Alumni Reg.* (Phila.), Oct. 1902, portr.; L. B. Grandy, in *Va. Medic. Mo.,* Oct. 1893; L. H. Jones, in *Trans. Medic. Asso. of Ga.,* 1899. A critical discussion of Long's claim, with full quotations from important original documents, is given by H. H. Young, in *Bull. Johns Hopkins Hospital,* Aug.-Sept. 1897. See also W. H. Welch, *A Consideration of the Introduction of Surgical Anæsthesia* (n.d.), Ether Day address, Boston, 1908; R. M. Hodges, *A Narrative of Events Connected with the Introduction of Sulphuric Ether into Surgical Use* (1891); D. W. Buxton, in *Proc. Royal Soc. of Medicine* (London), vol. V, pt. 1, Section of Anæsthetics, Dec. 1911. The most exhaustive authority is *Crawford W. Long* (1928), a biography by his daughter, Frances Long Taylor, who has supplied certain additional information for this sketch.]

J.F.F.

LONG, JAMES (*c.* 1793–Apr. 8, 1822), military adventurer in Texas, was born in North(?) Carolina (*Lamar Papers,* I, 47), some time between Oct. 10, 1792, and Apr. 8, 1793, and as a child moved with his father to Rutherford, Tenn. Early failure as a merchant led him to complete his education and study medicine. During the War of 1812 he served as a doctor in Carroll's brigade, and saw action at New Orleans in 1815. Later that year he married Jane Wilkinson, niece of Gen. James Wilkinson [*q.v.*], and resigned from the army. In 1817, after attempts at medicine and farming, he became a merchant at Natchez, Miss.

Two years later his fellow townsmen, aroused by the treaty of Feb. 22, 1819, chose him to lead an expedition intended to open Texas to American settlement. He gathered three hundred men, mostly ruffians, and proceeded to Nacogdoches, where a republic was formed with Long as president of the supreme council and commander-in-chief. He declared independence, June 23, 1819 (*Niles' Weekly Register,* Sept. 11, 1819, pp. 31–32), and thereafter made provision for easy land sales and land bounties to soldiers and settlers. On Aug. 14 Eli Harris began to issue the weekly *Texas Republican,* the first Texas newspaper. Long intended an early march against Bexar, but because of the non-arrival of expected supplies he was compelled to send most of his force in four trading parties to the Trinity and Brazos rivers. About Oct. 10 culmination of negotiations with Jean Laffite [*q.v.*] took Long to Galveston, which he declared a port of entry. Laffite, as governor, was commissioned to outfit privateers. Meanwhile, the Spanish, having protested Long's presence to the United States, dispatched Perez from Bexar with several hundred troops to expel him. Perez routed Long's outlying parties, devastated east Texas, and drove Long's men on the lower Trinity to Bolivar Point. Long, forced across the Sabine, returned with provisions after the departure of Perez. Having issued a proclamation ordering his forces to gather at Bolivar, he coasted to New Orleans, where he enlisted Ben Milam and John Austin, and spent two months gathering supplies and men. In June

Long, again at Bolivar, decided that the republican cause would benefit by a new leader, and tendered the presidency to E. W. Ripley, who accepted but never assumed office. Long now proposed to free Texas by capturing La Bahia and Bexar, but his supporters required him to remain at Bolivar to await immigration, which his presence was expected to induce. About October 1820, Long and Ripley entered into alliance with Jose Trespalacios, a Mexican revolutionist, who secured formal recognition from juntas in Mexico (*Lamar Papers,* II, 93; *Niles' Weekly Register,* June 2, 1821, pp. 223–24), thus giving the enterprise the same status as movements in the interior. Trespalacios assumed command late in 1820, but little occurred until September 1821, when Iturbide's successes made action imperative. Trespalacios and Milam sailed for Mexico, and Long undertook a friendly visit to Bexar. Through misinformation acquired en route he was led to attack and capture La Bahia Oct. 4. When Perez arrived from Bexar Long refused terms but was soon forced to surrender with his fifty-two men. They were sent from Bexar to Monterey, and Long was allowed to proceed to Mexico City in March 1822. There he found Trespalacios in high favor, and was himself well received. Nevertheless, he became offended by Iturbide's monarchism, and shortly determined to settle his affairs and quit the country; but on Apr. 8 he was shot and killed by a sentry, ostensibly because of a misunderstanding concerning his passport. H. H. Bancroft (*History of the North Mexican States and Texas,* 1889, II, 51) contends that Long struck the sentry. Lamar (*Lamar Papers,* II, 119) and Milam (J. H. Brown, *History of Texas,* vol. I, 1892, p. 81) both claim that Long's death was an assassination, but Lamar holds Iturbide responsible, while Milam charges Trespalacios. The three theories are about equally tenable.

Long, though hot-headed and rather impractical, was extremely tenacious in the pursuit of his ideal, an Americanized Texas. His career may be regarded as an honest but ill-considered attempt to achieve by military force what the Austins were even then undertaking by peaceful colonization.

[*The Papers of Mirabeau Buonaparte Lamar,* here cited as *Lamar Papers,* esp. vols. I (1921), 30–53, and II (1922), 51–134, are the best source of material. Lamar gathered considerable information for a life of Long and completed part of the projected work. Portions of his account of Long's early life and activities through 1819 were first published in H. S. Foote, *Tex. and the Texans* (1841), I, 192–217. These are reprinted in *Lamar Papers,* vol. II, together with the body of Lamar's sketch and a conclusion compiled by the editors from Lamar's notes. The *Lamar Papers,* vol. I, contain also translations of several documents on the La

Bahia incident. Important references to Long's activities are to be found in *Niles' Weekly Reg.*, vols. XVI-XXII (1819–22). *Quart. of the Tex. State Hist. Asso.*, Oct. 1902, Jan. 1904, and *Southwestern Hist. Quart.*, Jan. 1913, July 1932, contain essential articles on the *Texas Republican*. Long's activities in Texas as a factor in negotiations concerning the ratification of the treaty of Feb. 22, 1819, may be traced in *Am. State Papers, For. Rel.*, IV (1834), 664–84. Most of the standard histories of Texas, esp. H. K. Yoakum, are inaccurate and inadequate in their treatment of Long after 1819. The detailed account in A. H. Abney, *Life and Adventures of L. D. Lafferty* (1875) is fictitious. The period given above for Long's birth is deduced from *Lamar Papers*, I, 48, II, 123: the date of his death, from *Lamar Papers*, II, 118, 121, and *The Austin Papers*, pt. I (1924), pp. 498, 505. Among guides showing the location of manuscript material, the most important is H. E. Bolton, *Guide to Materials for the Hist. of the U. S. in the Principal Archives of Mexico* (1913).]

B. F. L.

LONG, JOHN DAVIS (Oct. 27, 1838–Aug. 28, 1915), governor of Massachusetts, congressman, secretary of the navy, was born in the village of Buckfield, Me. His father, Zadoc, was descended from Miles Long who went to Plymouth, Mass., from North Carolina about 1770; his mother, Julia Temple (Davis) Long, was a descendant of Dolor Davis who came to Massachusetts from Kent, England, in 1634. Two influences shaped Long's boyhood, the village and his father. Without the village he would not have had his cheerful and tolerant philosophy, his shrewd but kindly understanding of human nature, and his dreams and poems of pleasant meadows and sunny blue skies. Without his father he would have had neither the ambition nor the discipline necessary for reaching the goals he attained. He was never satisfied with his schooling. His preparatory education at Buckfield and in the Academy of nearby Hebron, Me., seemed inadequate. In spite of a high scholastic rating, he considered his years at Harvard College (1853–57) both an educational failure and an unhappy personal experience. Likewise he believed that his legal training, picked up in law offices and during a term in the Harvard Law School, had left him poorly grounded in fundamentals and permanently handicapped. His real education must have been gained from his own insatiable eagerness for self-improvement. Typical is his translation into English blank verse of Vergil's *Æneid* (1879) during the winter he was serving as lieutenant-governor, in order to increase his own vocabulary.

After leaving Harvard he taught for two years in the Academy at Westford, Mass., but to Boston and to the law he was driven inevitably by what he called a desire to express "the consciousness of power" within him (*Journal, post*, pp. 117–18). In 1863 he wrote in his journal (*Ibid.*, p. 129): "Can such a man [as I] *succeed, get rich, acquire a reputation?*" The answer was triply in the affirmative. He was admitted to the bar in 1861 and after a year in Buckfield, returned to Boston, where he built up a lucrative practice. During his steady advance in his profession his home life was pleasant. He lived in the attractive village of Hingham, close enough to Boston for daily visits. On Sept. 13, 1870, he married Mary Woodward Glover of Hingham. She died in 1882 after bearing her husband two daughters, and on May 22, 1886, he married Agnes Peirce of North Attleboro, who bore him a son.

In politics Long was honest and something of a peacemaker rather than venturesome. If he desired reform it never led him either to leave his party or to prod it into traveling at an uncomfortable pace. After 1871, in which year he accepted a Democratic nomination for the legislature and ran (unsuccessfully) as an independent, he was steadfastly associated with the Republican party, accepting Blaine in 1884 and denouncing Roosevelt in 1912. He was elected to the legislature in 1875, held the speakership in 1876 and 1877, and rapidly ascended the ladder of party service until he reached the governorship, which he occupied for three annual terms, 1880, 1881, and 1882. His office was run efficiently and honestly, but it was in the main a routine administration. From 1883 to 1889 he sat in Congress, his committees—Shipping, Commerce, and Appropriations—indicating his main interests. Perhaps his most important speeches during this period of service were those on the whiskey tax, Mar. 25, 1884; on interstate commerce, Dec. 3, 1884; on silver coinage, Mar. 27, 1885; and on the French spoliation claims, Aug. 4, 1888. Some of his addresses were published under the title, *After-dinner and Other Speeches* (1895).

In 1897 William McKinley appointed him secretary of the navy. He was too wise to endeavor to master the intricacies of his department. "My plan," he wrote (*Journal*, p. 157), "is to leave all such [technical] matters to the bureau chiefs . . . limiting myself to the general direction of affairs . . . especially personal matters." Here his tactful manner did much to remove friction and to promote cooperation within the department. Again he opined that the cabinet officer "does not so much represent the Department before the people as he represents the people in the Department" (*Ibid.*, p. 195). The untarnished record of the navy in the war with Spain must in part be accredited to the secretary. He was closely associated with McKinley, was conservative and calm in judgment, and gave his department loyal support. Involved in the unhappy Sampson-Schley controversy, he conducted himself in a wholly creditable manner. He retired from the cabinet in 1902.

Much of his later life was devoted to writing, chiefly on naval affairs. He published a number of articles and books on the navy and the Spanish-American War, by far the most important of which is *The New American Navy* (2 vols., 1903). Some of his poems appeared in a little volume entitled *At the Fireside* (1905). In 1888 he had edited a campaign history, *The Republican Party, Its History, Principles, and Policies,* and, with others, he edited *The American Business Encyclopædia and Legal Adviser* (5 vols., 1913). To the *Proceedings of the Massachusetts Historical Society* (vol. XLII, 1909), he contributed "Reminiscences of My Seventy Years' Education." He also found time to advocate a number of reforms, including prohibition, woman's suffrage, world peace, and the abolition of the death penalty. He died in Hingham, Aug. 28, 1915.

[Long's journal from 1848 to 1915, filling twenty volumes in manuscript, has been made the basis of Lawrence Shaw Mayo's *America of Yesterday, as Reflected in the Journal of John Davis Long* (copr. 1923). See also tributes by J. F. Rhodes and W. R. Thayer, in *Proc. Mass. Hist. Soc.,* vol. XLIX (1916); W. R. Castle, Jr., in *Harv. Grads. Mag.,* June 1917; *Hist. of the Town of Hingham, Mass.* (1893), vol. III; Alfred Cole and Charles F. Whitman, *A Hist. of Buckfield, Oxford County, Me.* (1915); *Boston Transcript,* Aug. 30, 1915.]
P. H. B.

LONG, JOHN HARPER (Dec. 26, 1856–June 14, 1918), chemist, was born near Steubenville, Ohio, the son of John and Elizabeth (Harper) Long, both of Protestant Irish ancestry. Left an orphan at an early age, he made his home with an uncle in Olathe, Kan., and in 1877 graduated from the University of Kansas with the degree of B.S. An interest in chemistry fostered by the able and enthusiastic teaching of George E. Patrick, then a recent graduate of Cornell, led him to continue his studies in that science (1877–80) at the universities of Würzburg, Breslau, and Tübingen. At Tübingen, where he was a student of Lothar Meyer, he was granted the degree of D.Sc. in 1879. After serving as assistant, 1880–81, to W. O. Atwater [*q.v.*] of Wesleyan University, a pioneer in agricultural and food chemistry in the United States, he was appointed in 1881 to the professorship of chemistry in the Liberal Arts department of Northwestern University, and the next year was transferred to the chair of chemistry in the Medical School, a position which he held until his death in 1918. During its existence he taught also in the School of Pharmacy, of which he was dean from 1913 to 1917. He was married, Aug. 24,

1885, to Catherine Stoneman of Cedar Rapids, Iowa, by whom he had five children.

He was a fellow and vice-president of the American Association for the Advancement of Science, a member of the revision committee of the United States Pharmacopoeia, a member of the council on pharmacy and chemistry of the American Medical Association, president, 1903–04, of the American Chemical Society, and first president of the Institute of Medicine of Chicago. For a number of years he was consulting chemist for the State Board of Health of Illinois and the Sanitary District of Chicago, and it was largely his work in this capacity, confirmed by thousands of analyses on the oxidation of sewage by running streams, that led to the decision of the Supreme Court (Feb. 19, 1906) for the defendants in the case of *Missouri* vs. *Illinois and the Sanitary District of Chicago* (200 *U. S.,* 496), a question of sewage disposal which directly affected the future of Chicago. As a member of the Remsen "Referee Board" of consulting scientific experts appointed by the Department of Agriculture, he directed long and painstaking investigations, carried out in the Northwestern laboratories, on the influence of sodium benzoate, of copper, and of alum on the health of man (*United States Department of Agriculture Reports,* 88, 94, 97 and *Bulletin 103,* 1904–14). This work was of very great benefit in the later administration of the Food and Drugs Act.

A pioneer in the chemical phase of medical education, he found the existing texts inadequate and in an endeavor to supply the need, wrote a series of books which played an important rôle in his educational service: *Elements of General Chemistry* (1898), *A Text-book of Elementary Analytical Chemistry* (1898); *A Text-book of Urine Analysis* (1900); *Laboratory Manual of Elementary Chemical Physiology and Urine Analysis* (1894); *The Optical Rotating Power of Organic Substances* (1902), translated from the German of H. H. Landolt; *A Text-book of Physiological Chemistry* (1905). His research papers and reports in chemistry and biochemistry, numbering 109 titles, are listed in the memorial volume (Gault, *post*) and in the "Proceedings" of the American Chemical Society for 1919. His most important papers (1913–18) related to the action of digestive ferments, with special reference to those of the pancreas.

Long was a man of pronounced personality, a hard fighter for his convictions, but a fast friend, genial, and with a keen sense of humor. His interests were many-sided, and that characteristic, coupled with his capacity for work, enabled him to achieve great success in many lines. Modest and unassuming, he was a hater of cant, pretension, and slovenly work. As a scientific man he was rigidly accurate and dependable, and his conclusions were based upon all the evidence that could be brought to bear on the problem under investigation. He was conservative, but with that best kind of conservatism that is ready to accept new views when they become matters of fact and not mere speculation.

[F. B. Dains, in "Proc. Am. Chem. Soc., 1919," published as an appendix to the *Jour. Am. Chem. Soc.*, vol. XLI (Jan.–June, 1919); *John Harper Long, 1856–1918 . . . A Tribute from His Colleagues* (n.d.), ed. by Robert Gault; *Who's Who in America,* 1918–19; *Chicago Tribune,* June 15, 1918.]   F. B. D.

LONG, JOHN LUTHER (Jan. 1, 1861–Oct. 31, 1927), author, dramatist, was born at Hanover, Pa. He was admitted to the bar in Philadelphia, Oct. 29, 1881, and became a practising lawyer, but his bent was toward literature, and he wrote many short stories. One of these, "Madame Butterfly," published in the *Century Magazine* for January 1898 and later that year in a collection, attracted much attention. A little tale of the deserted Japanese wife of an American naval officer, it was touching in its simple tragedy and caught with seeming authenticity the Oriental atmosphere. As a matter of fact, the author had never been in Japan. His story and atmosphere were based on the observation of his sister, Mrs. Irwin Correll, the wife of a missionary. The details were carefully verified from her experience. More than one American actress sought the dramatic rights to this story, among them Maude Adams, but Long disposed of them to David Belasco, because Belasco proposed himself to dramatize the tale. He did so, and the play was produced as an after-piece to a comedy, at the Herald Square Theatre, New York, Mar. 5, 1900, with Blanche Bates as the little Japanese wife. The dramatization was entirely the work of Belasco, but he used much of the original dialogue, and had Long's assistance in the creation of atmosphere. The production was an immediate success, but the stage life of the play was soon to be indefinitely prolonged, because Puccini, the Italian composer, chose it for the libretto of what time has proved his most popular opera, *Madame Butterfly.* First produced in Milan, without success, it was sung in English translation in America at the Garden Theatre, New York, Nov. 12, 1906, and highly acclaimed. Since then it has gone into the repertory of every opera house, and the pathetic, wistful story of little Butterfly is known all over the civilized world, and seems likely to perpetuate Long's name for many years to come.

This collaboration with Belasco led to further work together, in which Long contributed the actual scenarios and dialogue of two plays, which were then worked over by the two men, and resulted in two dramas of distinction, marking, with *Madame Butterfly,* the best of Long's production. The plays were *The Darling of the Gods,* a romantic Japanese melodrama, produced in Washington, Nov. 20, 1902, with Blanche Bates and George Arliss in leading rôles, and *Adrea,* a tragedy of the late Roman Empire, produced in Washington, Dec. 26, 1904, with Mrs. Leslie Carter in the title part. The former play was the more successful on the stage, perhaps because of its exotic color, its thrilling situations, a certain strain of romantic mysticism, and superb acting. The latter play, however, had much tragic dignity, and represented on Long's part a prodigious amount of careful historical research (see his letters to Belasco, in William Winter, *post,* pp. 135–38).

These three plays represented the peak of Long's achievement in the theatre, or, indeed, in literature. He was not, by himself, a successful dramatist, but needed the technical skill of a collaborator in sympathy with his romantic conceptions to give them stage form. With E. C. Carpenter he wrote *The Dragon Fly* (produced in Philadelphia, 1905), and alone he wrote *Dolce* (produced by Mrs. Fiske in Philadelphia and then in New York in 1906), *Kassa* (produced in New York, Jan. 23, 1909, with Mrs. Leslie Carter in the leading rôle), and finally *Crowns* (produced at the Provincetown Theatre, Nov. 11, 1922). None of these plays was a success, nor exhibited the striking quality of romantic imagination Belasco had enabled his friend to release into the theatre.

Long's published prose works included *Madame Butterfly, Purple Eyes,* etc. (1898), *Miss Cherry-Blossom of Tôkyô* (1895), *The Fox-Woman* (1900), *The Prince of Illusion* (1901), *Naughty Nan* (1902), *Billy-Boy* (1906), *The Way of the Gods* (1906), *Felice* (1908), *Baby Grand* (1912), and *War, or What Happens When One Loves One's Enemy* (1913). He also wrote the text for several cantatas, and tried his hand at two opera librettos. With the passage of time, however, all these works have been largely forgotten, save only the story of *Madame Butterfly,* on which his fame will undoubtedly rest. He was married to Mary J. Sprenkle, and lived quietly in Philadelphia until his death, reticently avoiding the publicity which generally comes to successful writers.

[Wm. Winter, *The Life of David Belasco* (2 vols., 1918); *Who's Who in America,* 1926–27; *Green Room Book* (1909); J. H. Martin, *Martin's Bench and Bar of Phila.* (1883); obituaries in *N. Y. Herald Tribune,*

Nov. 1, 1927; *Evening Pub. Ledger* (Phila.), Oct. 31, 1927; *Phila. Record,* Nov. 1, 1927.]   W. P. E.

LONG, STEPHEN HARRIMAN (Dec. 30, 1784–Sept. 4, 1864), explorer and engineer, was born in Hopkinton, N. H., the son of Moses and Lucy (Harriman) Long. He graduated from Dartmouth College in 1809, and in 1814, following a period of teaching, he entered the army as a second lieutenant of engineers. After serving for two years as assistant professor of mathematics at West Point, he was transferred to the topographical engineers with the brevet rank of major and continued with this branch of the service throughout the remainder of his life. He was made major in 1838, and in 1861 became chief of the corps and colonel. In 1817 the War Department sent him West to examine the portages of the Fox and Wisconsin rivers and to explore the upper Mississippi. His account of this expedition appears under the title, "Voyage in a Six-oared Skiff to the Falls of St. Anthony in 1817" (*Collections of the Minnesota Historical Society,* vol. II, pt. I, 1860). Returning, a skilled explorer, he was assigned by Secretary Calhoun in 1819 to command the expedition to the Rocky Mountains. After selecting an encampment for his party, he returned to Philadelphia to spend the winter of 1819–20 with his bride, Martha Hodgkins, whom he had married on Mar. 3, 1819. Rejoining the expedition the following spring, he pushed westward along the Platte and South Platte, reaching the Rockies in July 1820 and discovering the lofty peak which bears his name. He did not penetrate the Front range but turned south to the vicinity of Colorado Springs, and headed east by way of the Arkansas and its tributaries, exploring a considerable section of the southwestern country, about which only vague and inaccurate geographical ideas had hitherto prevailed. A vivid narrative of the journey is given by Edwin James [*q.v.*] in *Account of an Expedition from Pittsburgh to the Rocky Mountains, Performed in the Years 1819 and '20* (2 vols. and atlas, 1822–23). In 1823 Long was assigned to examine the sources of the St. Peter's (Minnesota) River and the northern boundary of the United States to the Great Lakes. W. H. Keating [*q.v.*], who accompanied the party, prepared the *Narrative of an Expedition to the Source of the St. Peter's River, Lake Winnepeek, Lake of the Woods . . . Performed in the Year 1823* (2 vols., 1824).

From this time on, railroad routes supplanted Indian trails in Long's interest and activities. In 1827 he was assigned by the War Department to act as consulting engineer for the Baltimore & Ohio Railroad Company, and in association with Jonathan Knight [*q.v.*] he selected the route of the road. He later was president of its board of engineers. Continued friction with the management of the company led to his withdrawal from all official connection in 1830, but only after he had made a reputation as an authority in the new field of railway engineering (S. H. Long and W. G. McNeill, *Narrative of the Proceedings of the Board of Engineers of the Baltimore & Ohio Rail Road Company,* 1830). In connection with his theory of grades and curvatures, which appeared first in *Report of the Engineers, on the Reconnoissance and Surveys Made in Reference to the Baltimore and Ohio Railroad* (1828), and was afterward embodied in his *Rail Road Manual* (1829), he developed tables which obviated the need of all computations in the field. In 1834 he made a preliminary survey of possible railway routes between points in Georgia and Tennessee, which was followed by a period as chief engineer of the Atlantic & Great Western Railroad, 1837–40. Subsequently, he served as a consulting engineer for a number of railroad companies when not engaged in active military service. An outgrowth of this experience was his interest in bridge construction, on which he published a thin pamphlet in 1830 (*Description of the Jackson Bridge, Together with Directions to Builders of Wooden or Frame Bridges*). Six years later he obtained a patent on his method of bracing and counterbracing wooden bridges (*Description of Colonel Long's Bridges, Together with a Series of Directions to Bridge Builders,* 1836). A number of bridges in New England and elsewhere were constructed in accordance with his specifications. On duty at the mouth of the Mississippi River at the outbreak of the Civil War, he was called to Washington and advanced to the rank of colonel, retiring in 1863, and dying on Sept. 4 of the following year in Alton, Ill. His wife survived him; they had four sons and a daughter.

[C. C. Lord, *Life and Times in Hopkinton, N. H.* (1890); G. T. Chapman, *Sketches of the Alumni of Dartmouth Coll.* (1867); R. G. Thwaites, *Early Western Travels,* vol. XIV (1905), preface; H. M. Chittenden, *The Am. Fur Trade of the Far West* (1902); Edward Hungerford, *The Story of the Baltimore & Ohio Railroad* (1928), vol. I; W. T. Norton, *Centennial Hist. of Madison County, Ill., and Its People* (1912), vol. I; F. B. Heitman, *Hist. Reg. of the U. S. Army* (1890); *Minn. Hist. Bull.,* Nov. 1923.]
                                                    H. C. D.

LONGACRE, JAMES BARTON (Aug. 11, 1794–Jan. 1, 1869), line and stipple engraver, was born in Delaware County, Pa., the son of Peter Longacre and a descendant of early Swedish settlers. John F. Watson, the annalist of Philadelphia, discovered the talents of the boy and took him into his family as an apprentice in his bookstore. Later he placed Longacre with

George Murray, an engraver in Philadelphia, to learn the art of engraving, for which he displayed talent. He remained in Murray's establishment until in 1819 he set up in business for himself. He already was regarded as one of the best engravers in the country, and during his last years with his old employers, Murray, Draper, Fairman & Company, he had been engaged to engrave the portraits of Washington, Jefferson, and Hancock, on the facsimile of the Declaration of Independence published by John Binns in Philadelphia in 1820. This plate, thirty-five by twenty-five inches in size, was the largest engraving that had been made in the United States up to that time. John Vallance executed the other engraving on the plate. The finished production, which was the first correct facsimile of the document ever made, cost the publisher $9,000.

Soon after he had established himself in business, Longacre was commissioned to engrave many of the portraits for John Sanderson's *Biography of the Signers to the Declaration of Independence,* publication of which was begun in 1820. In 1826 he engraved some of the portraits of actors which accompanied the Lopez & Wemyss edition of the *Acting American Theatre.* His chief work as an engraver may be said to rest with the ambitious series of volumes, the first of its kind ever attempted in this country, known as *The National Portrait Gallery of Distinguished Americans.* In this publication he was associated with James Herring, of New York. It was a difficult undertaking, but between 1834 and 1839 four octavo volumes were published. Longacre engraved a number of the portraits, and some of the engravings were made from portraits he had painted from life. The *Portrait Gallery* was reissued several times and constitutes the engraver's principal claim to fame. His other work included engraved plates for annuals and illustrations for many of the juveniles issued by the American Sunday School Union in Philadelphia. He succeeded David Edwin [*q.v.*] as the best stipple engraver in the country, although he had developed an entirely different technique.

On Sept. 16, 1844, Longacre became chief engraver of the United States Mint, having succeeded Christian Gobrecht [*q.v.*]. During his occupancy of the office, he designed and engraved the first double-eagle, in 1849, the first three-dollar gold piece, in 1854, and the gold dollar struck at that time. He was also engaged in remodeling the coinage of the Republic of Chile, a work which he completed within two years of his death. Longacre died in Philadelphia on Jan.

1, 1869. Four days later a memorial meeting, attended by all the employees of the Mint, was held and honor was paid him through eulogies on his character and skill. In 1928 he was represented in the exhibition of one hundred notable American engravers held in the New York Public Library.

[Wm. Dunlap, *A Hist. of the Rise and Progress of the Arts of Design in the U. S.* (1834), vol. II; W. S. Baker, *Am. Engravers and Their Works* (1875); David McN. Stauffer, *Am. Engravers upon Copper and Steel* (1907); *Recollections of the Life of John Binns* (1854); F. C. Wemyss, *Twenty-Six Years of the Life of an Actor and Manager* (1847); J. T. Scharf and Thompson Westcott, *Hist. of Phila.* (1884), vol. II; *Hist. of the Longacre-Longaker-Longenecker Family* (n.d.), p. 75; excerpts from Longacre's diary for the year 1825 in the *Pa. Mag. of Hist. and Biog.,* Apr. 1905; G. G. Evans, *Illustrated Hist. of the U. S. Mint* (rev. ed., 1888); *Pub. Ledger* (Phila.), Jan. 5, 1869.]
J. J.

LONGFELLOW, ERNEST WADSWORTH (Nov. 23, 1845–Nov. 24, 1921), painter, was a son of Henry Wadsworth Longfellow [*q.v.*], and Frances (Appleton) Longfellow. His early surroundings, productive of frustrations and a sense of inferiority, may have been disadvantageous to him. He once wrote: "Any one who has had the misfortune to be the son of an illustrious parent knows how hard it is to be taken seriously by people" (*Random Memories,* p. v). His autobiography, witty, informing, opinionated, not always good-natured or charitable, is a document to interest psychologists. He was born at the Craigie House, Cambridge, whence his father walked to his modern language classes at Harvard. "The Castle-Builder" describes him as "a gentle boy, with soft and silken locks." His formal education began at a dame school facing the Washington Elm and was continued at Ambrose Wellington's school, Cambridge, and the Dixwell School, Boston. Not being proficient in languages, as his father notably was, but displaying good scholarship in mathematics, Ernest tried vainly for a West Point appointment. He was temperamentally inclined to it, and, contrary to the elder Longfellow's pacifist views, he had a life-long interest in military science. He entered the Lawrence Scientific School at Harvard College during the Civil War, in which he hoped to serve, but the conflict ended just before he was graduated in engineering in 1865.

When the Union armies were disbanded, engineers were numerous and Longfellow, perhaps mistakenly, felt that competition might be too keen in the profession for which he had been trained. Having seen much of art in his parents' home and elsewhere, and having shown ability in mechanical drawing, he decided to become an artist. With his uncle, the Rev. Samuel Long-fellow, he went to London, then proceeded to Paris, where he studied with Ernest Hébert, who found his draftsmanship good. Bohemian-ism never appealed to him and he had few Latin Quarter contacts. Returning to Boston, he opened in 1866 a studio in the Studio Building, Tremont Street, where he had as neighbors George Inness, Appleton Brown, and B. C. Por-ter. In the same year he inherited a fortune from the estate of his mother, who was burned to death in 1861. In May 1868 he was married to Harriet Spelman, the daughter of Israel Spel-man, and the following summer they went abroad. In Paris Longfellow studied with Leon Bonnat and in Rome, through G. P. A. Healy, painter of his father's portrait, he became one of Abbe Liszt's friends. Some years later (1876–78) he returned to France. This time he sought out Thomas Couture, whose work he had admired and from whom he received valuable instruc-tion. In 1879 he was elected a vice-president of the Boston Art Club. In that year he painted the portrait of his father which hangs at Bowdoin College. An earlier portrait, for which he had less regard, hangs at Craigie House.

As the years passed Longfellow and his wife usually spent winters in New York or abroad and summers at Magnolia, Mass. Possessed of ample means he had little incentive to commer-cialize his work. While his painting was al-ways well drawn and intelligently thought out, it has generally been thought cold and unsympa-thetic. He was also disadvantaged as an artist by feeling that in matters of art his own time was out of joint; a bitter tone toward his pro-fessional contemporaries often appears in his memoirs. He died at the Hotel Touraine, Bos-ton, after a long illness, and was buried from the Craigie House. His will, which left his collec-tion of paintings and $200,000 to the Boston Museum of Fine Arts, and the major part of his estate to his widow, specifically disinherited his nephews, H. W. L. Dana and Allston Dana, be-cause of "their socialistic and pacifist tenden-cies."

[*Random Memories* (1922) is Longfellow's informal autobiography. For a just if somewhat severe evalua-tion of his art works see Harley Perkins' review of the Longfellow Memorial Exhibition, Museum of Fine Arts, published in the *Boston Evening Transcript,* Jan. 17, 1923. C. H. Hawes described the Longfellow col-lection in the *Museum of Fine Arts Bulletin,* Dec. 1923. See also: Clara E. Clement and Laurence Hutton, *Art-ists of the Nineteenth Century and Their Works* (1879), vol. II; *Am. Art News,* Dec. 3, 1921; and the *Boston Herald,* Nov. 25, 1921.]   F. W. C.

LONGFELLOW, HENRY WADS-WORTH (Feb. 27, 1807–Mar. 24, 1882), poet, was born in Portland, Me. His first known an-cestor was Edward Longfellow, a man of prop-erty in Yorkshire early in the seventeenth cen-tury, whose grandson, William, settled in New-bury, Mass., about 1676, and married Ann Sew-all, a sister of Judge Samuel Sewall [*q.v.*]. Their grandson Stephen took two degrees at Harvard, and became teacher, town clerk, and clerk of the courts in Portland, Me. His son Stephen was a Massachusetts legislator and judge of the court of common pleas. The judge's son Stephen [*q.v.*], the poet's father, a Harvard graduate, was a distinguished lawyer in Portland, member of Congress, trustee of Bowdoin College, and president of the Maine Historical Society. The poet's maternal grandfather, Peleg Wadsworth [*q.v.*], was descended from Christopher Wads-worth, Englishman, who settled in Duxbury, Mass., before 1632. Peleg, a Harvard graduate, a general in the Revolution, and member of Congress, married Elizabeth Bartlett of Plym-outh; and through these grandparents the poet had descent from at least four of the Pilgrims, including John Alden, Priscilla Mullens, and Elder Brewster. His mother, Zilpah, a nervous invalid, was an intense lover of music, poetry, and nature.

Henry, the second child, was educated chiefly in private schools. He began to write early, the *Gazette of Maine,* Portland, publishing a poem by him on Nov. 17, 1820. (He denied that he wrote the doggerel about Mr. Finney and his turnip.) Entering Bowdoin College as a sopho-more, he graduated in 1825, fourth in a class of thirty-nine; Hawthorne was a classmate, but they were not intimate. While in college Long-fellow had many poems accepted by the maga-zines; and by his senior year he had set his heart on a literary career, writing to his father, "I most eagerly aspire after future eminence in literature." He planned to study at Harvard and then attach himself to a magazine; but soon after graduation he was offered a projected pro-fessorship of modern languages at Bowdoin, on condition that he study abroad, and therefore spent the years 1826–29 in France, Spain, Italy, and Germany. From 1829 to 1835 he was pro-fessor and librarian at Bowdoin, also preparing textbooks and contributing essays and sketches to the magazines. He married, Sept. 14, 1831, Mary Storer Potter of Portland, a beautiful and cultivated woman.

In 1835 Longfellow accepted the professor-ship of modern languages and belles-lettres at Harvard, and went abroad for a year to improve his knowledge of German and the Scandinavian tongues. In spite of the sudden death of his wife at Rotterdam in that year, he held to his course and made an extensive study of German literature before returning to America in 1836. At Cambridge, where he lodged in the Craigie House, Washington's former headquarters, his life settled into a pleasant routine. His college duties were heavy, for he had to prepare three lectures a week, besides supervising four native teachers and often taking the classes himself. But he went much into society, a jaunty figure immaculately clad; and he made many friends, the closest being Professor Cornelius C. Felton, Charles Sumner, George S. Hillard [*qq.v.*], and Henry R. Cleveland, who with the poet formed "The Five of Clubs," dubbed by outsiders "The Mutual Admiration Society." After 1837 his relations with Hawthorne were increasingly friendly; and at this time, as always, he kept up by letter his intimacy with George W. Greene [*q.v.*] of Rhode Island, whom he had met in Italy in 1828. During 1837-40 he contributed five articles to the *North American Review;* and in 1839 published *Hyperion,* a romance, and *Voices of the Night,* his first book of verse. The spring and summer of 1842 he spent mostly at Marienberg, a water-cure on the Rhine; but he formed a lifelong friendship with the German poet Ferdinand Freiligrath, visited Dickens and other men of letters in England, and wrote *Poems on Slavery* (1842) during the voyage home.

On July 13, 1843, he married Frances Elizabeth Appleton, the original of the heroine of *Hyperion,* whom he had met in Switzerland in 1836. She was now a woman of twenty-six, "of stately presence, of cultivated intellect, and deep, though reserved feeling" (Samuel Longfellow, *Life, post,* II, 1, 2). Her father, a Boston merchant, bought the Craigie House for the pair as a wedding present. The poet's life now flowed on for many years with full and placid tide. Six children were born to him, among them Ernest Wadsworth Longfellow [*q.v.*]. Lowell and Agassiz became his intimate friends. In the summer he found congenial society at Nahant, where he and his brother-in-law, Thomas Gold Appleton [*q.v.*], finally bought a cottage. In 1854 he resigned his professorship, which had grown increasingly irksome; and his life thereafter had more unity and peace—until tragedy suddenly engulfed him. On July 9, 1861, Mrs. Longfellow was sealing up packages of her daughters' curls; a match set fire to her dress, and, in spite of her husband's efforts to put out the flames, by which he also was badly burned, she died the next day. How deep was his wound is shown by the few words wrung from him after some weeks: "How can I live any longer!" is the second entry in his journal, on Sept. 12,

after a long gap. In a letter to George W. Curtis on Sept. 28, he says that although "to the eyes of others, outwardly calm" he is "inwardly bleeding to death." The persistence of his grief is revealed by "The Cross of Snow," written eighteen years afterwards. Next to the care of his children he found most solace in daily labor to complete his translation of Dante's *Divine Comedy.* While the work was slowly going through the press, in 1865, Lowell and Charles Eliot Norton aided in the last revision. "Every Wednesday evening," wrote Norton, "Mr. Lowell and I met in Mr. Longfellow's study to listen while he read a canto of his translation from the proof-sheet. We paused over every doubtful passage, discussed the various readings, considered the true meaning of obscure words and phrases, sought for the most exact equivalent of Dante's expression, objected, criticised, praised, with a freedom that was made perfect by Mr. Longfellow's absolute sweetness, simplicity, and modesty. . . . Almost always one or two guests would come in at ten o'clock, when the work ended, and sit down with us to a supper, with which the evening closed. Mr. Longfellow had a special charm as a host, the charm of social grace and humor" (*First Annual Report of the Dante Society,* May 16, 1882, p. 22).

In the poet's remaining years honors were heaped upon him. During a tour of Europe with his family, in 1868–69, he received the degree of LL.D. from Cambridge, and that of D.C.L. from Oxford; breakfasted or lunched with Gladstone, the Duke of Argyll, and other notables; was given a private audience by the Queen; visited Tennyson on the Isle of Wight; and met scholars and artists in Italy, including Liszt, who soon after set to music the introduction to *The Golden Legend.* To the Craigie House came distinguished visitors year after year—Froude, Trollope, Kingsley, Dean Stanley, Lord and Lady Dufferin, Salvini, Ole Bull, the Emperor of Brazil, and many others. He was more and more lonely, however; Hawthorne and Felton had died before his European tour; Agassiz and Sumner died in 1874; Lowell went abroad; Greene became feeble and depressed; yet Longfellow kept at work with calm cheerfulness. The summers he spent at Nahant, except for a week's visit each year with his sister in the old Portland home. On his seventy-second birthday the children of Cambridge gave him an arm-chair made of wood from the chestnut tree of "The Village Blacksmith." His next birthday was celebrated in the public schools of Cincinnati, and the following year many schools throughout the country observed the day. During the last three months of 1881 he was confined to his room by vertigo followed by nervous prostration, and never fully recovered. On Mar. 18, 1882, four schoolboys called, and he showed them the house with his usual courtesy. That afternoon he became ill, peritonitis developed, and six days later he died. He was buried at Mount Auburn. On Mar. 2, 1884, a bust of him was unveiled in Poets' Corner, Westminster Abbey.

Longfellow's gentleness, sweetness, and purity have always received due emphasis. Lord Ronald Gower's eulogy in 1878 is typical: "There is a kind of halo of goodness about him, a benignity in his expression which one associates with St. John at Patmos" (*My Reminiscence,* vol. II, 1883, p. 265). Other essential aspects of his personality have often been ignored, however. "Injustice in any shape he could not brook," said his sister of him as a boy; and he proved it as a young man when he hotly refused to accept an instructorship at Bowdoin instead of the promised professorship, and the corporation yielded to the indignant stripling. The sterner side of his nature showed itself at his Boston club one day: "Felt vexed at seeing plover on the table at this season, and proclaimed aloud my disgust at seeing the game-laws thus violated." The comments in his journal and letters are often severe. "The smokers turned my study into a village tavern with cigars and politics, much to my annoyance." "My ways of thinking are so different from those of most of the Bostonians that there is not much satisfaction in talking with them. ―― himself is an exception. He has a liberal, catholic mind, and does not speak as if he were the pope." "The American character seems often wanting in many of the more generous and lofty traits which ennoble humanity." "The fugitive slave is surrendered to his master . . . Dirty work for a country that is so loud about freedom as ours!" This critical edge he may have got from his father; from his mother he inherited nervous sensibility verging on disease. In boyhood he begged to have cotton put in his ears on Fourth of July, to deaden the sound of the cannon; his illness in 1842 was disorder of the nerves; in middle life he was sometimes "half crazed" with neuralgia; a medical examination in 1867 found his "bell-wires . . . out of order"; nervous prostration preceded the end. This sensibility caused restlessness, fretfulness, and depression. "I pray a benediction on drudgery. It . . . takes the fever out of my blood and keeps me from moping too much." "I know not in what littlenesses the days speed by; but mostly in attending to everybody's business but my own, and in doing everything but

what I most want to do. It frets my life out." Abnormal excitement appears in some entries. "It [Niagara] drives me frantic with excitement. . . . My nerves shake like a bridge of wire." More often his nervous delicacy gave delight. "It is raining, raining with a soft and pleasant sound. I cannot read, I cannot write, . . . but dream only." "Like delicious perfume, like far-off music, like remembered pictures, came floating before me amid college classes, as through parting clouds, bright glimpses and visions of Tyrolean lakes." "I have still floating through my brain that crowd of fair, slender girls, waving, like lilies on their stems, to the music as to a wind." He had a marked fondness for good dinners, choice wines, and fine clothes. An English traveler who met him at a reception in 1850 pictures him as "dressed very fashionably . . . almost too much so, a blue frock coat of Parisian cut, a handsome waistcoat, faultless pantaloons, and primrose-colored 'kids' set off his compact figure, which was not a moment still; for like a butterfly glancing from flower to flower, he was tripping from one lady to another, admired and courted by all" (quoted by Higginson, *post,* p. 279, from *The Home Circle,* London, October 1850). He had not yet begun to be St. John.

This artistic sensibility affected his modes of composition. He worked steadily, so far as moods allowed; but he could not twang off a lyric at will or mechanically grind out a long poem. "I was often excited, I knew not why; and wrote with peace in my heart and not without tears in my eyes, 'The Reaper and the Flowers, a Psalm of Death.' I have had an idea of this kind in my mind for a long time, without finding any expression for it in words. This morning it seemed to crystallize at once, without any effort of my own." "Why do no songs flit through my brain, as of old? It is a consolation to think that they come when least expected."

Longfellow's popularity in his later years was great, both at home and abroad. "No other poet has anything like your vogue," Hawthorne wrote from England in 1855. In London 10,000 copies of *The Courtship of Miles Standish* were sold the first day. Before 1900 his poems had been translated into German, Dutch, Swedish, Danish, French, Italian, Portuguese, Spanish, Polish, Bohemian, Hungarian, and Russian. In German thirty-three different translations had appeared, including eight of *Evangeline* and five of *Hiawatha*; in French, nine, including four of *Evangeline*; in Italian, twelve. The prices he received for poems show the growth of his fame: fifteen dollars for "The Village Blacksmith" in

1840; $3,000 for "The Hanging of the Crane" in 1874. Poe was hostile, but most American men of letters praised the new poet warmly. Bryant wrote of his "exquisite music" and "creative power." Motley found himself "more and more fascinated with Evangeline" and the hexameters "'musical as is Apollo's lute.'" Hawthorne wrote, "I take vast satisfaction in your poetry, and take very little in most other men's." Prescott thought the "Skeleton in Armor" and "The Wreck of the Hesperus" the best imaginative poems since "The Ancient Mariner." European criticism was also very favorable. Professor Philarete Chasles, of the College of France, wrote in 1851: "Longfellow seems to us to occupy the first place among the poets of his country" (*Études sur la littérature et les mœurs des Anglo-Américains au XIXᵉ siècle*, 1851, p. 299). *Blackwood's Edinburgh Magazine* said in February 1852: "In respect of melody, feeling, pathos, and that exquisite simplicity of expression which is the criterion of a genuine poet, Mr. Longfellow need not shun comparison with any living writer." The London *Spectator* (June 20, 1868) spoke of "the sweet and limpid purity, . . . and the thoroughly original conception and treatment, of his later poems, especially that which will doubtless live as long as the English language, 'Hiawatha.'"

Longfellow's writings belong to the Romantic Movement in its milder phases: they have nothing of the Storm-and-Stress mood, except in *Hyperion,* and nothing of Byron's or Shelley's spirit of revolt. He was a Victorian only in his moderation and decorum, which were a part of his Puritan heritage: social reforms, except the abolition of slavery, did not much interest him; and his Unitarian faith combined with his unspeculative nature to save him alike from the theological struggles of Tennyson, Arnold, and Clough, and from the paganism of Swinburne and Morris. His first prose model was Irving, soon succeeded by the florid German school. His poetic style may have owed its purity to Bryant, whose nature poems he imitated in youth, but it also has something of Goldsmith's soft grace and Keats's sensuous beauty. In his nature poetry as a whole he is more like Keats than Bryant or Wordsworth; but Wordsworth may have quickened his sympathy with children and with common men and women. "The Ancient Mariner" clearly influenced his ballads of the sea. From the Finnish *Kalevala* he got the metre of *Hiawatha*; and his use of hexameters, an innovation in American verse, was doubtless due to their success in German narrative poems. The strongest single foreign influence was that

of Goethe and the German romantic lyrists. Most of the prose works had only a passing value, but *Outre-Mer* and *Hyperion* are still worth reading for their pictures of European life in the early nineteenth century. The poems did a threefold service to American readers: they brought a sense of the beauty in nature and the lives of common people; they gave some feeling for Old-World culture; they handled American themes, especially Indian legends and colonial history, more broadly and attractively than had been done before in verse.

Didacticism is the charge most often brought against Longfellow's poetry. If this means merely that his purpose was to teach, he might well be content to stand with Dante, Spenser, and Milton. The true criticism is that his method is sometimes bald preaching, as in "A Psalm of Life," and sometimes silly symbolism, as in "Excelsior"; that at other times he pins a moral to incident or portrait which needs none, as in "The Village Blacksmith"; and that in general his way of presenting truth lacks the imagination, passion, and power of the great poets. But it is also true that most of his didactic poems are pleasing in form, and that the larger part of his poetry is not didactic at all but depicts various aspects of life for their own sake. His nature poems, such as "An April Day" or "Amalfi," are often purely sensuous; and those on the sea give with rare felicity a sense of its magic and its terror. His ballads are astir with spirited incident. In the delightful poems on children he anticipated Swinburne. His sketches of individuals show vivid appreciation of a wide range of human types—men of action, like the hero in "Victor Galbraith" or "Kambalu"; men of science, like Agassiz; poets, like Dante and Chaucer; ecclesiastics good and bad, like those in *The Golden Legend* and "The Monk of Casal-Maggiore"; women, like Evangeline, Priscilla, and the heroic mother in "Judas Maccabaeus." His sympathy with the joys and sorrows of "the common lot" is genuine and deep, as in "The Bridge" and "The Goblet of Life." The love scenes in *The Spanish Student, Evangeline,* and "The Courtship of Miles Standish" have delicate beauty although they lack warmth; and "Stars of the Summer Night," in the first named, is one of the best serenades in English. The joys of wine and social drinking are sung jollily in "King Witlaf's Drinking Horn" and with a connoisseur's discrimination in "Catawba Wine."

As interpreter of the Old World to the New, Longfellow still has no rival among American poets. Even now there is cultural charm in "Nuremberg," "The Belfry of Bruges," "Monte

Cassino," "Castles in Spain," and the translations from German, French, and Spanish. The spirit of the Northland and the Vikings lives in "The Saga of King Olaf." Much of the Middle Ages is in *The Golden Legend,* where, said Ruskin, the poet "entered more closely into the temper of the Monk, for good and for evil, than ever yet theological writer or historian" (*Modern Painters,* 1862, IV, 359). The translation of *The Divine Comedy,* although its line-for-line exactness sacrifices some lucidity and ease, first revealed Dante to numberless readers, and is still one of the great versions.

Longfellow's approach even to American life was through his library. The poems on slavery, although sincere enough, seem "literary" and slight for so terrible a theme. He knew the Indian almost wholly from books; but the more significant fact is that in the legends as recorded by Schoolcraft and others he rejected the darker and more primitive elements, making Hiawatha too much like a Christian gentleman—as Tennyson had begun to make King Arthur; yet "Hiawatha" paints delightfully the poetic phases of the Indian imagination, which are as real as Indian cruelty or treachery. *Evangeline* smells not only of the library but also of a "diorama" of the Mississippi that came to Boston while he was writing the poem; but the first part sketches beautifully the peaceful life of Acadia, with the heroine as its perfect center, and in the second part the interest is sustained largely by the broad pictures of Western scenery, although the poet had seen neither Acadia nor the West. "The Courtship of Miles Standish" conveys a neglected truth by its playful emphasis on the lighter side of the Pilgrims' doings; the grimmer aspects of Puritanism are painted black enough, though without dramatic power, in "John Endicott" and "Giles Corey of the Salem Farms." It is unnecessary to insist upon the truth and vividness of the pictures of American life in Longfellow's popular short poems. Admirable also are the less-known sonnets and poems on his friends, all representative American figures and drawn with the sure touch of the poet's maturity.

The later poems in general have more merit than is commonly recognized. They lack the freshness and easy sweetness of the earlier works; but the thought is broader and maturer, the style often has more distinction and strength. The most ambitious of these, *The Divine Tragedy,* is not a success either by itself or linked with *The Golden Legend* and *The New England Tragedies* in an attempt to depict the development of Christianity. "The Hanging of the Crane" and "The Masque of Pandora" are also

inferior. But no one knows Longfellow fully who is not familiar with the sonnets, some of which are among the best of the century; with "Morituri Salutamus," less buoyant than "Rabbi Ben Ezra" and less venturesome than "Ulysses," but more truthful than either in its statement of the mingled weakness and strength of old age; and with "Michael Angelo," in which the elderly poet and scholar moves thoughtfully in high regions of Italian art and character. Longfellow's fame will never again be what it was in his own century; but it remains to be seen whether, by the pure style and gracious humanity of his best poems, he will not outlast louder men, in popular favor.

The principal works published in book form during his lifetime appeared as follows: *Outre-Mer* (1835); *Hyperion* (1839); *Voices of the Night* (1839); *Ballads and Other Poems* (dated 1842, issued late in 1841); *Poems on Slavery* (1842); *The Spanish Student, a Play in Three Acts* (1843); *Poems* (1845); *The Belfry of Bruges and Other Poems* (dated 1846, issued in December 1845); *Evangeline* (1847); *Kavanagh, a Tale* (1849); *The Seaside and the Fireside* (dated 1850, issued in December 1849); *The Golden Legend* (1851); *The Song of Hiawatha* (1855); *Prose Works* (1857); *The Courtship of Miles Standish, and Other Poems* (1858); *The New England Tragedy* (1860); *Tales of a Wayside Inn* (1863); *The Divine Comedy of Dante Alighieri* (3 vols., 1865–67); *Flower-de-Luce* (title-page dated 1867, published in November 1866); *The New England Tragedies* (1868); *The Divine Tragedy* (1871); *Christus, a Mystery* (*The Divine Tragedy, The Golden Legend, The New England Tragedies,* 3 vols., 1872); *Three Books of Song* (1872); *Aftermath* (1873); *The Hanging of the Crane* (1874); *The Masque of Pandora, and Other Poems* (1875); *Kéramos and Other Poems* (1878); *Ultima Thule* (1880); *In the Harbor: Ultima Thule, Part II* (1882). The posthumous volume, *Michael Angelo,* appeared in 1883. A "complete" edition, *The Writings of Henry Wadsworth Longfellow,* in eleven volumes, was published in 1886.

[Two useful bibliographies are L. S. Livingston, *A Bibliography of the First Editions in Book Form of the Writings of Henry Wadsworth Longfellow* (p.p. 1908), and bibliog. by H. W. L. Dana, in *The Cambridge Hist. of Am. Lit.,* II (1918), 425–36. The most important biography is *Life of Henry Wadsworth Longfellow with Extracts from his Journals and Correspondence* (3 vols., 1891), by his brother, Samuel Longfellow [*q.v.*]. See also T. W. Higginson, *Henry Wadsworth Longfellow* (1902); "New Longfellow Letters," *Harper's Mo. Mag.,* Apr. 1903; E. S. Robertson, *Life of Henry Wadsworth Longfellow* (1887); G. R. Carpenter, *Henry Wadsworth Longfellow* (1901); G. L. Austin, *Henry Wadsworth Longfellow: His Life, His*

Works, His Friendships (1883), containing the early poems not republished in *Voices of the Night*; E. W. Longfellow, *Random Memories* (1922); Annie Fields, *Authors and Friends* (1896); E. Montégut, "Oeuvres de H. W. Longfellow," *Revue des Deux Mondes,* Oct. 15, 1849; F. Kratz, *Das deutsche Element in den Werken H. W. Longfellows* (2 vols., Wasserburg, 1901–02); A. Johnson, "The Relation of Longfellow to Scandinavian Literature," *Am. Scandinavian Rev.,* Jan. 1915; R. H. Stoddard, ed., *The Works of Edgar Allan Poe* (1884), vol. VI; J. R. Lowell, in *Atlantic Mo.,* Jan. 1859; O. W. Holmes, in *Ibid.,* June 1882; G. E. Woodberry in *Harper's Mo. Mag.,* Feb. 1903; T. B. Aldrich in *Atlantic Mo.,* Mar. 1907; P. E. More, *Shelburne Essays,* 5 ser. (1908); W. D. Howells, in *No. Am. Rev.,* Mar. 1907; Bliss Perry, in *Atlantic Mo.,* Mar. 1907; W. P. Trent, in *The Cambridge Hist. of Am. Lit.,* vol. II (1918); W. H. O. Smeaton, *Longfellow and his Poetry* (1919); H. S. Gorman, *A Victorian American: Henry Wadsworth Longfellow* (1926).]
W. C. B.

LONGFELLOW, SAMUEL (June 18, 1819– Oct. 3, 1892), teacher, clergyman, poet, philosopher, was the youngest son of Stephen [*q.v.*] and Zilpah (Wadsworth) Longfellow and was born in Portland, Me. His early boyhood was made happy by the enjoyment of imaginative literature and by his rare sensitiveness to the beauty of his seashore home where he rambled, botanizing and sketching. From the classes of the Portland Academy he went to Harvard College, where (1835–39) he stood high in studies and enjoyed many intimate friendships. In 1839– 40 he taught in a family school at Elkridge, Md., then returned to Cambridge, where he acted as college proctor, cultivated his love of music, and tutored young boys for college entrance. For the latter task he had unusual aptitude through his remarkable understanding and affection for the young and his power to kindle their moral aims.

Entering the Harvard Divinity School in 1842, he shared with a gifted group of students including Samuel Johnson, O. B. Frothingham, and T. W. Higginson an enthusiasm for the new thought of "Transcendentalism" as taught by Convers Francis, preached by Theodore Parker, read in the pages of Cousin, Emerson, Carlyle. Delicate health, a lifelong recurrence, made him spend the next year in Horta, Fayal, as tutor to the children of the American consul, Charles Dabney. Returning to the Divinity School in 1844 he clarified his ardent theistic conviction— essentially like Parker's though held with more philosophical precision—and in his freedom from dogma was satisfied with a reverential love of Jesus as "a living human friend . . . whose life is to be interpreted by our own deepest, holiest experience" (*Samuel Longfellow: Memoir and Letters,* p. 60). Before graduation he collaborated with Samuel Johnson in *A Book of Hymns, for Public and Private Devotion* (1846, 1848), which gave prominence to the new hymnody of Whittier, H. B. Stowe, Jones Very, and Theodore Parker.

On grounds of health he at first declined a settled pastorate but after temporary engagements in West Cambridge, Mass., and Washington, D. C., he was ordained to the Unitarian ministry in Fall River, Mass., Feb. 16, 1848. His spiritual discourse, his beautiful voice, together with the charm that made the children gather round him, won him high esteem, but discouraged by what he deemed inadequate success he withdrew, June 18, 1851, and spent a year in England and France as companion and tutor of a young student. Suspicion of his religious views, then deemed radical, delayed parochial appointment and he thought of serving as chaplain in prisons or reform schools, but in April 1853 he was summoned by the Second Unitarian Church in Brooklyn, N. Y., where his nature and talent came to full expression. He exalted the act of worship in the church, initiated a vesper service with more music and a meditative talk, and introduced in the Sunday School a manual of worship and a children's sermon. His *Vespers* (1859) contains his own beautiful vesper hymns. With equal stress on the social service of the church he sought to organize his parish for the study of social problems and to diffuse a love of art and literature. Another decline in health and some protest against his utterances concerning slavery led to his resignation in June 1860. After two years of extensive travel in Europe he returned to Cambridge, preaching (1867–68) to the congregation gathered by Theodore Parker, traveling abroad again in 1865 and 1868, writing powerful theological essays for the *Radical* edited by Sidney H. Morse. Once more he was a settled pastor, serving the Unitarian church in Germantown, Pa., from January 1878 to the summer of 1882 when he sought leisure for writing in Cambridge. He published in 1886 a two-volume biography of his brother, *Life of Henry Wadsworth Longfellow,* and in the following year he published a sequel, *Final Memorials of Henry Wadsworth Longfellow.* On Oct. 3, 1892, he died in Portland, Me.

Of the group ill named Transcendentalists he was the clearest and most methodic in thought and will be remembered for his discriminating argument and for the devout fervor and beauty of his hymns. A gentle and serene spirit, a man of social charm, he gave and received abundant love. In addition to the works already mentioned he published a book of poems, *Thalatta: A Book for the Seaside* (1853), in collaboration with T. W. Higginson; *A Book of Hymns and*

Tunes (1860, 1876); and *Hymns of the Spirit* (1864), with Samuel Johnson. A final collection, *Hymns and Verses,* was edited and published by Edith Longfellow in 1894.

[See Joseph May, *Samuel Longfellow: Essays and Sermons* (1894) and *Samuel Longfellow: Memoir and Letters* (1894); O. B. Frothingham, *Transcendentalism in New England: A Hist.* (1876); O. F. Adams, "Samuel Longfellow," *New Eng. Mag.*, Oct. 1894; J. W. Chadwick, "Samuel Longfellow," in S. A. Eliot, *Heralds of a Liberal Faith* (1910), vol. III; H. W. Foote, "The Anonymous Hymns of Samuel Longfellow," *Harvard Theol. Rev.*, Oct. 1917; J. H. Allen, *Sequel to "Our Liberal Movement"* (1897); *Christian Reg.*, Oct. 6, 13, 1892; *Daily Eastern Argus* (Portland), Oct. 4, 1892.]
F. A. C.

LONGFELLOW, STEPHEN (Mar. 23, 1776–Aug. 3, 1849), lawyer, congressman from Maine, fourth of the name, was born on his father's farm in Gorham, Me., whither his parents, Stephen and Patience (Young) Longfellow had fled on the destruction of Falmouth (now Portland) by the British in October 1775. His great-great-grandfather, William Longfellow, had settled in Newbury, Mass., about 1676. It is not surprising that he chose the law for his profession, since his grandfather, a graduate of Harvard College in 1742, was register of probate and clerk of the judicial court for York County, and his father, judge of the court of common pleas. Stephen entered Harvard in 1794, graduating in 1798, having been elected to Phi Beta Kappa. He immediately commenced the study of law with Salmon Chase of Portland, who had the most extensive practice of any lawyer in the county. On being admitted to the bar in 1801, he established himself in Portland, which with a population of 3,800 was already served by seven lawyers. By 1807 he had won recognition as one of the leading lawyers in the District of Maine. The volumes of Massachusetts and Maine reports show that he was engaged in a considerable number and a wide range of cases.

Longfellow was a representative in the Massachusetts General Court in 1814 and 1815, and, being a stanch Federalist, was chosen a delegate to the Hartford Convention in 1814. In 1816 he actively opposed measures then being taken for the separation of Maine from Massachusetts. The same year, as a presidential elector, he, along with others from Massachusetts, threw his vote to Rufus King. He represented Maine in the Eighteenth Congress (1823–25), where he opposed the great expenditures on internal improvements then under consideration. In 1826 he represented Portland in the state legislature. From 1811 to 1817 he was an overseer, and from 1817 to 1836, a trustee of Bowdoin College. He served as president of the Maine Historical So-

ciety in 1834. An attack of epilepsy in 1822 so weakened his constitution that he was forced gradually to relinquish a good part of his law practice. As a lawyer he was direct and forceful, depending not at all upon brilliant rhetoric or abstract arguments. At the same time he never forgot courtesy nor did he lose his wonted suavity of manner. He married, on Jan. 1, 1804, Zilpah, the daughter of Peleg Wadsworth [q.v.]. They had four daughters and four sons. Of the latter Henry Wadsworth and Samuel [qq.v.] are the best known.

[The sketch of Longfellow in Wm. Willis, *A Hist. of the Law, the Courts, and the Lawyers of Me.* (1863), is reprinted from the *Me. Hist. Soc. Colls.*, 1 ser., V (1857). See also Wm. Willis, ed., *Jours. of the Rev. Thos. Smith and the Rev. Samuel Deane* (1849), p. 384 note; S. E. Titcomb, *Early New England People* (1882); *Portland Daily Advertiser*, Aug. 6, 1849. The Me. Hist. Soc. owns two small collections of Longfellow papers.]
R. E. M.

LONGFELLOW, WILLIAM PITT PREBLE (Oct. 25, 1836–Aug. 3, 1913), architect, author, grandson of Stephen Longfellow [q.v.], was a son of Stephen and Marianne (Preble) Longfellow and a nephew of Henry Wadsworth Longfellow [q.v.]. He was born at Portland, Me. After graduating from Harvard College in 1855, he continued his studies in the Lawrence Scientific School at Harvard, winning the degree of S.B. in 1859. He then joined the staff of Edward Cabot, the Boston architect. In 1868–69 he served as secretary of the Boston Society of Architecture, making many pleasant and valuable professional contacts. For the following three years he was an assistant architect of the United States Treasury Department and took an active part in designing and constructing the Boston Post Office. Later, for one year, 1881–82, he served as adjunct professor of architectural design at the Massachusetts Institute of Technology. He had married in Boston, on May 26, 1870, Susan Emily Daniell, and for many years he and his wife had a residence adjacent to the Craigie House in Cambridge, in which his uncle lived. When school children of Cambridge planned to surprise the aging poet on his seventy-second birthday with a chair made from wood of the spreading chestnut tree over the familiar village smithy, Longfellow the architect was selected to design the chair.

Longfellow was of a reserved disposition, a clever amateur musician and a serious student of literature. His contributions to the progress of his profession were solid, not showy or spectacular. He was for a time director of the newly opened school of drawing and painting at the Boston Museum of Fine Arts; of the museum itself he became a trustee. He was the first editor of the *American Architect* during the years in which it was published in Boston. In 1893 he served on the jury of award of the architectural section of the World's Columbian Exposition. Increasingly in his later years he gave practically his whole time to writing on architectural subjects. Among his published works were *Abstract of Lectures on Perspective* (1889); *A Cyclopaedia of Works of Architecture in Italy, Greece and the Levant* (1895); *The Column and the Arch* (1899); and *Applied Perspective* (1901). His musical compositions, particularly his settings for some of Tennyson's poems, were creditable. He and his wife were accustomed to spend their summers on the Maine coast with his bachelor cousin, Alexander Wadsworth Longfellow, also an architect. His death occurred at East Gloucester, Mass., during a brief visit at the summer art colony. He left no children.

[There is a manuscript biographical note in the records of the School of the Boston Museum of Fine Arts. For printed sources see *Who's Who in America*, 1912–13; the *Am. Architect*, Aug. 13, 1913; *Boston Evening Transcript*, Aug. 4, 1913.]   F. W. C.

LONGLEY, ALCANDER (Mar. 31, 1832– Apr. 17, 1918), publisher and social reformer, was born in Oxford, Ohio. Between 1843 and 1846 his father, Abner Longley, a Universalist minister, was interested in a Fourierist phalanx at Clermont, Ohio, and the son early adopted Fourier's ideas. In 1852 he was connected with the North American Phalanx in Monmouth County, N. J., but left the Community, about 1854, to return to Cincinnati to be married. Shortly afterward, he joined his four brothers in establishing, at Cincinnati, a printing firm that specialized in reform literature. One of its publications, *The Type of the Times*, was partly in phonetic spelling. On his own account, Longley began in 1857 the publication of a small monthly, *The Phalansterian Record*. Although the firm of brothers seems to have been dissolved by 1860, he remained in Cincinnati as a printer and, in 1862, was a postoffice clerk there. His first attempts at organizing Utopian colonies were along the lines of producers' cooperation, but, after two or three short-lived ventures, he abandoned cooperation for communism. . In 1867 he and his family became probationary members of Icaria, the colony founded by Étienne Cabet in Iowa. Delighted as he was with the altruistic spirit of the Icarians, he, nevertheless, withdrew after a few months.

In January 1868, he began the publication in St. Louis of *The Communist,* devoted to the propagation of his own program of social reform and to communistic activities all over the country. At first it consisted of only four pages, and, although advertised as a monthly, it appeared somewhat irregularly. In 1885 he changed the name to *The Altruist,* under which name he continued it until May 1917. For almost fifty years, in the face of all sorts of difficulties and discouragements, he persisted in issuing his paper and in proceeding with designs for the organization of ideal communities. In the years 1868 to 1885 he made no less than five attempts to establish a communistic society in various parts of Missouri, but each failed within a comparatively short time. The weakness common to all his experiments was lack of capital. Immediately after the disruption of one colony he began his projects for another, and, as late as 1909, was planning still another communistic group at Sulphur Springs, Mo. A printer of the older type, who was typesetter, compositor, and pressman as well as editor, he worked at his trade, during the intervals between experiments, in the composing rooms of one or another of the St. Louis newspapers.

His program of social reform had nothing of the religious element characteristic of many American communistic experiments. He was an ardent believer in the equal rights and responsibilities of women. On marriage and the relations of the sexes his ideas were liberal but not radical. Under a capitalistic system he found that marriage was despotism, but he had no sympathy with the promiscuity of the Perfectionists or the celibacy of the Shakers. His colonists were to be "free and independent in the enjoyment of their affections and in the control of their own persons" (*Communist,* Jan. 1868, p. 3). Misinterpretation of this statement led him to state explicitly that he contemplated no innovation in sex relations that would be contrary to existing laws (*Ibid.,* Feb. 1868, p. 16). He became interested in the political means for the improvement of society and was an active member of the Socialist Labor party in St. Louis. In 1880 he brought together many of his theories on social reform in a book called *Communism: the Right Way and the Best Way for All to Live.* He also arranged, in 1878, a phonetic figure musical system, in which figures denoted the length of sound while the staff designated only the pitch, and he published *The Phonetic Songster and Simple Phonography* (n.d.).

He was married three times. On Nov. 19, 1854, he married Zelie Mottier, the daughter of John E. Mottier, a well-to-do grape grower of Cincinnati. Devoted to the ideals of communism, he used his wife's money for his various colonies, to feed the poor, and to help the unfortunate, even when it meant deprivation for his wife and their three children. At last, after about twenty years, she took the children and left him. His second wife, Genevieve, died, in 1891, soon after their marriage. About 1901 he married Susan Ella Jones of Paris, Ky., who was burned to death, on Jan. 11, 1907, in spite of his heroic attempts to save her from the flames of an exploded lamp. He died in Chicago at the home of his daughter.

[Information obtained from his daughter, Mrs. Justine M. Thrift of Washington, D. C.; from pamphlets, leaflets, and clippings in the St. Louis Public Library as well as from a relative through the courtesy of Irving Dilliard of St. Louis; from letters of Longley to the Oneida Community and clippings in the Oneida *Circular* scrapbook supplied by Mrs. S. R. Leonard of Oneida, N. Y. Published material includes *St. Louis Post-Dispatch,* Sept. 26, 1909; *Circular* (Oneida Community), June 14, 21, 1869; *Williams' Cincinnati Directory . . . 1862* (copr. 1862); Albert Shaw, *Icaria* (1884); W. A. Hinds, *Am. Communities,* revised ed. (1902), esp. pp. 351, 388; J. H. Noyes, *Hist. of Am. Socialisms* (1870); F. A. Bushee, "Communistic Societies in the U. S.," *Pol. Sci. Quart.,* Dec. 1905. Papers and letters are in the possession of his granddaughter, Mrs. Walter J. Cook, Colmar Manor, Brentwood Post Office, Md.]   P. W. B.

LONGSTREET, AUGUSTUS BALDWIN (Sept. 22, 1790–July 9, 1870), jurist, author, educator, was born in Augusta, Ga., and died in Oxford, Miss. His parents, William [*q.v.*] and Hannah (Randolph) Longstreet, of Dutch and French-English ancestry, migrated to Georgia from New Jersey about 1785. Until he was fifteen, he was dilatory in his studies, but after that time, inspired by the zeal of his friend George McDuffie, he was more faithful. From 1808 to 1810 he attended the academy of Dr. Moses Waddel [*q.v.*] in Willington, S. C., and in 1811, following the example of his friend John C. Calhoun, he entered Yale College. He finished his course there in 1813, and, still following Calhoun, entered the Litchfield (Conn.) Law School. Returning to Georgia late in 1814, he was married after about two years to Frances Eliza Parke, of Greensboro, where he had taken up his residence. She was wealthy and he was poor, but he was already a capable lawyer and he had to a phenomenal degree the gift of attracting friends and keeping them. He was in the state legislature in 1821, and from 1822 to 1825 was a judge of the superior court. In 1824, he offered himself for election to Congress, but soon afterward the death of his eldest child caused him to abandon all political ambition, and to turn from his hitherto skeptical attitude in religion to the devout Methodism of his neighbors.

He returned to Augusta to live in 1827, and there wrote a series of sketches called "Georgia Scenes," begun anonymously for the Milledgeville (Ga.) *Southern Recorder,* but soon transferred to his own paper, the Augusta *State Rights Sentinel.* These humorous, often crudely realistic compositions, dealing with life in Georgia as he knew it, were at once widely popular. The author silenced his misgivings relative to their frivolity by reminding himself of how valuable they would become as a source of history. In addition they are significant as being among the earliest manifestations in America of the type of literature which later produced such characters as Tennessee's Partner, Uncle Remus, and Huckleberry Finn. Longstreet first published the *Georgia Scenes* in book form (still anonymously) in Augusta in 1835, but in 1840 the firm of Harper & Brothers in New York gave them introduction under the author's name to a national body of readers which proved enthusiastic and persistent. They were frequently imitated, but scarcely equaled even by Longstreet himself, who in the same vein wrote many other stories and sketches, and also a novel, *Master William Mitten* (1864).

Literature was in Longstreet's mind always chiefly a means of diversion. His real interests were politics and religion. In his fervent advocacy of nullification as the proper course for the state of Georgia he established and edited a newspaper, the *State Rights Sentinel* (Augusta, 1834–36), but with the collapse of his hopes in this regard he felt himself driven for refuge to something that he could believe more dependable than democracy. In 1838 he became a Methodist minister, and in that capacity, with conspicuously good results, he presided (1839–48) over Emory College, newly founded in Oxford, Ga. In 1844 he went to New York to take part in the General Conference of his Church at which the denomination, after debating the propriety of slave-ownership among its bishops, divided into two branches. The disagreement centered about Bishop Andrew, of Oxford, and Longstreet took active part in the discussion through both speech and writing, publishing, in 1845, *Letters on the Epistle of Paul to Philemon, or the Connection of Apostolic Christianity with Slavery,* and two years later, *A Voice from the South* (1847). During 1849, he was president of Centenary College in Jackson, La., and from 1849 to 1856 of the University of Mississippi. Here his administration was successful, but his continued political activities, as evidenced primarily by his *Letters from President Longstreet to the Know-Nothing Preachers of the Methodist Church South* (1855), published by the Democratic State Central Committee, occasioned so much opposition that he determined to withdraw from public life.

He had barely retired with his family to his near-by plantation when he was invited (1857) to become president of the University of South Carolina. The opportunity was more than he could resist. The executive's position there was at that time most difficult, but he soon established his mastery. He was a vigorous proponent of secession, but when he saw war actually upon him—and, what was worse, upon his students—he had no longer any courage in his belief, and went about appealing frantically on all sides that something be done at once to hold off the terrible destroyer. From then on till the war's end he was a strenuous but sadly dismayed patriot. In 1865 he settled down again in Mississippi and wrote extensively to prove that the South had always been right and the North always wrong. His happiest companionship in his extreme age was with his son-in-law, L. Q. C. Lamar [q.v.]. As an author his distinction is more one of date than of quality; as a public character he possibly effected as much harm as he did good; but in everything he did he was sincere and throughout his life was animated by high motives.

[J. D. Wade, *Augustus Baldwin Longstreet* (1924), with a full bibliography; Edward Mayes, *Geneal. of the Family of Longstreet* (1893); O. P. Fitzgerald, *Judge Longstreet; a Life Sketch* (1891); F. B. Dexter, *Biog. Sketches Grads. Yale Coll.,* vol. VI (1912); *XIX Century* (Charleston), Feb., Aug., Oct. 1870.]

J. D. W.

LONGSTREET, JAMES (Jan. 8, 1821–Jan. 2, 1904), soldier, the son of James and Mary Anna (Dent) Longstreet and the nephew of Augustus Baldwin Longstreet [q.v.], was born of New Jersey stock in Edgefield District, S. C., but removed in early childhood to the vicinity of Augusta, Ga., where his father farmed until he died in 1833. The widow then resided at Somerville, Morgan County, Ala., from which state James Longstreet was admitted to West Point in 1838. He attended the academy with McDowell, Sherman, Halleck, Thomas, and Grant, and was graduated fifty-fourth in a class of sixty-two in July 1842. Brevetted second lieutenant of the 4th Infantry, he served at Jefferson Barracks, Mo., Natchitoches, La., and then with the 8th Infantry at St. Augustine, Fla. In the Mexican War, he was with Zachary Taylor until after the battle of Monterey and with Scott during the expedition to Mexico City. Wounded at Chapultepec and brevetted major, he continued in the army and in 1861 was a major (as of July 19, 1858) in the paymaster's department. Following his resignation (effective June 1, 1861) to join the Confederacy, he sought commission in the same department because, as he said, he had abandoned his aspirations for military glory; but his good reputation and rank in the "old army" won him commission as a Confederate brigadier-general, June 17, 1861.

Longstreet's admirable employment of his troops at First Manassas (Bull Run) and his skill in organization brought him promotion to the grade of major-general, Oct. 17, 1861, with command of a division under Joseph E. Johnston. He was with Johnston at Yorktown in the spring of 1862 and conducted the rearguard action at Williamsburg, May 5, 1862, when he enhanced his prestige; but at Seven Pines, May 31, his tardiness in taking position and his singular misinterpretation of his orders were material factors in the Confederate failure. During the Seven Days' Battles around Richmond (June 25–July 1, 1862), after Gen. Robert E. Lee assumed direction of the army, Longstreet moved promptly, did his full share of the fighting, and won Lee's entire confidence. Recent criticism of his action at Frayser's Farm, June 30, and in the pursuit of McClellan, July 2, is hardly justified by the evidence.

After the Seven Days, Lee placed more than half his infantry under Longstreet and on Aug. 13 sent him to reënforce "Stonewall" Jackson, who was near Orange Court House, confronting a new Federal army under Maj.-Gen. John Pope. In the first stage of the campaign of Second Manassas, which now opened, Longstreet was slow in crossing the Rapidan, but he later conducted with much skill his part of the difficult shift up the Rappahannock River, and on the morning of Aug. 29 he brought his troops into position on the right of Jackson, who had completed his famous march to Manassas Junction and had then stood on the defensive near Groveton to await reënforcements. Lee was anxious for Longstreet to assume the offensive that day, but Longstreet, always cautious and deliberate in attack, made repeated excuses for not doing so, and did not enter the action till Aug. 30, when the Federals were quickly routed. Examined in detail, Longstreet's reasons for not attacking on the 29th are certainly defensible and may be valid, but his general attitude showed for the first time that though he was vigorous and effective when his judgment approved the plans of his superior, he was slow to yield his own opinions and equally slow to move when he thought his commander's course was wrong. This was to become the greatest defect of his military character.

Longstreet did not indorse the expedition into Maryland in September 1862, but he fought well at Sharpsburg (Antietam) and was made lieutenant-general, Oct. 11, 1862, on Lee's recommendation. His various divisions were organized as the I Corps with which, on Dec. 13, 1862, he bore the brunt of the defensive fight at Fredericksburg. On Feb. 17, 1862, he followed Pickett's and Hood's division to southeastern Virginia to guard the roads to Richmond from the south and east. In this so-called "Suffolk campaign," he exercised his first semi-independent command, but without substantial achievement of any sort. Although his force equaled that of the Federals, he failed to seize the initiative and was content to employ his troops in collecting supplies from eastern North Carolina. Lee diplomatically urged him either to fight or to rejoin the Army of Northern Virginia, but at a distance from Longstreet and without precise knowledge of his difficulties, Lee refrained from giving him peremptory orders. The result was that Longstreet neither fought nor returned. The absence of two of his divisions from Charlottesville was the chief reason Lee could not follow up the victory won at Chancellorsville, May 2–3.

After the death of "Stonewall" Jackson, May 10, 1863, Longstreet was Lee's most distinguished lieutenant and seems to have taken it upon himself to be Lee's mentor. He advised that the campaign into Pennsylvania, which Lee was then planning, should be offensive in strategy but defensive in tactics, and in some way he got the mistaken idea that Lee made him a promise to this effect. The consequence was that, when Longstreet at the head of his corps joined Lee in front of Gettysburg on July 1, 1863, and learned that Lee intended to attack Meade, he was disappointed, perhaps disgruntled, and certainly filled with misgivings of failure. The story of Gettysburg, as it concerns the I Corps, is the story of Longstreet's slow, reluctant, and despairing acquiescence in orders he believed would bring disaster. He delayed action on July 2 till it was too late to execute Lee's plan to storm Cemetery Ridge before it was fully manned, and by that delay he made the attack of July 3 almost a military necessity. The disadvantages which convinced Longstreet that it was dangerous for Lee to assume the offensive were heightened by Longstreet's tardiness and lack of confidence (see Lee, Robert Edward).

Gettysburg virtually concluded Longstreet's service with the Army of Northern Virginia during the period of its major offensive operations. He was dispatched to Georgia in September 1863 and did admirably at Chickamauga, but

he was not successful in front of Knoxville, Tenn., in November, and later, isolated in eastern Tennessee, was so close to despair that he contemplated resignation. Aroused, however, by the danger of a Federal invasion of Georgia, he proposed several plans for an offensive in Tennessee and Kentucky. None of these was considered practicable by President Davis. Brought back to Virginia with his troops in April 1864 and stationed near Gordonsville by Lee, Longstreet arrived on the field on the morning of May 6 in time to rally Hill's corps in the second day's battle of the Wilderness. He at once organized an excellent counter-stroke, in the execution of which he was wounded. He returned to duty in November, participated in the later phases of the defense of Richmond and still had the remnant of his corps in good order when it was surrendered with the rest of the army at Appomattox on Apr. 9.

After the war, Longstreet became head of an insurance company and prospered for a time as a cotton factor in New Orleans, but he joined the Republican party, was ostracized in consequence, and turned to political office for a living. From 1869 till his death at Gainesville, Ga., he held a series of Federal appointments—surveyor of customs at New Orleans, postmaster of Gainesville, minister resident to Turkey, United States marshal for Georgia, and United States railroad commissioner. He was twice married: first, on Mar. 8, 1848, to Maria Louise Garland of Lynchburg, Va., who died Dec. 29, 1889; second, on Sept. 8, 1897, to Helen (or Ellen) Dortch, who survived him. In person he was slightly below middle height, broad-shouldered and somewhat heavy in his prime, and during the war was afflicted with a partial deafness that sometimes made him appear taciturn.

Longstreet's espousal of the Republican faith made him unpopular in the South and probably caused some post-bellum Southern writers to do him less than justice. The claims he made in his military autobiography, *From Manassas to Appomattox* (1896), and in his earlier contributions to *The Annals of the War* (1879) and *Battles and Leaders of the Civil War* (4 vols., 1887–88), aggravated the feeling against him. Despite these criticisms, his place in American military history is not difficult to fix. Essentially a combat officer, he did not possess the qualities necessary to successful independent command, and his skill in strategy was not great. His marching was apt to be slow and he was too much prone to maneuver and await attack; but once battle was joined, he displayed a cheerful composure, a tactical understanding, and a skill in handling his troops that made him an almost ideal corps commander.

[The first two chapters of Longstreet, *From Manassas to Appomattox* (1896), contain an autobiographical review, somewhat inaccurate as to dates, of his life prior to the Civil War. G. W. Cullum, *Biog. Reg. of the Officers and Grads. of the U. S. Mil. Acad.* (3 ed., 1891), contains all his assignments to duty prior to his resignation from the U. S. Army and an outline of his civil career after the war. He was painstaking in the preparation of his reports of battles, all of which appear in the *War of the Rebellion: Official Records* (*Army*). Much of his correspondence is published there also. His military correspondence during the last months of the war, not published in the *Official Records*, is in Lee's military papers. No biography of Longstreet has been printed, and the sketches in *Confed. Mil. Hist.* (1899), I, 660–63, and in similar works are perfunctory. His wife, Helen D. Longstreet, published *Lee and Longstreet at High Tide* (1904). For the Gettysburg controversy, see J. W. Jones, "The Starting of the Longstreet-Gettysburg Controversy," *Richmond Dispatch*, Feb. 16, 1896; Dunbar Rowland, *Jefferson Davis, Constitutionalist, . . .,* 1923, vol. IX, 531. See also Edward Mayes, *Genealogy of the Family of Longstreet* (1893); *Who's Who in America,* 1903–05; *Atlanta Constitution,* Jan. 3, 1904.]   D.S.F.

LONGSTREET, WILLIAM (Oct. 6, 1759– Sept. 1, 1814), inventor, was born near Allentown, Monmouth County, N. J., the son of Stoffel and Abigail (Wooley) Longstreet, and a descendant of Dirck S. Langestraet who emigrated from the Netherlands to New Netherland in 1657. William was educated in the country school near his home and early showed a marked mechanical skill. About 1780, either through a book which he secured or through local discussions of the work being done by Oliver Evans and John Fitch [*qq.v.*] in nearby communities, he became greatly interested in the steam engine. It is possible that he attempted the construction of an engine at this time, but the public ridicule to which he was subjected deterred him from working very seriously on such a project. After his marriage to Hannah Randolph of Allentown, N. J., in 1783, and the establishing of his own home in Augusta, Ga., he applied himself earnestly to the construction of a steam engine. With the financial aid of one Isaac Briggs, he had made such good progress by 1788 that on their petition, the General Assembly of Georgia, Feb. 1, 1788, passed an act securing to "Isaac Briggs and William Longstreet, for a term of fourteen years, the sole and exclusive privilege of using a newly constructed steam engine invented by them." With this protection Longstreet proceeded to build engines and apply them to useful work. He had already patented in Georgia the so-called "breast roller" of cotton gins, which was operated by horsepower and was of incalculable value to the growers of sea-island cotton. He then undertook the construction of steam-operated gins, but because of lack of

money he completed only a few. They were built and put into operation in Augusta but were almost immediately destroyed by fire. Commenting on this occurrence, the *Augusta Herald,* Dec. 23, 1801, concludes, "This accident seems to have been particularly unfortunate as the ingenious proprietor of the works had, we understand, the day before completed a new boiler which had, on trial, been found to equal his utmost expectations, and enabled him with a single gin and with a trifling expense of fuel, to give from 800 to 1000 weight of clean cotton per day." Longstreet also designed a portable steam sawmill, a number of which he erected and operated in various parts of Georgia; one of these, near St. Mary's, was destroyed by the British in 1812. His third application of steam power was to propel a boat. As early as 1790 he solicited, by letter, the aid of Gov. Edward Telfair in raising funds for such a purpose. The letter was published in the Savannah and Augusta newspapers but without avail. Sixteen years later, however, Longstreet succeeded in building a small steamboat which ran on the Savannah River against the current at the rate of five miles an hour. No record exists of the design of boat or engine, nor of the method of propulsion. He died in Augusta, Ga., and was survived by his wife and six children. Augustus Baldwin Longstreet [*q.v.*] was his son.

[T. G. Bergen, *Reg. in Alphabetical Order of the Early Settlers of Kings County, Long Island, N. Y.* (1881); Edward Mayes, *Geneal. of the Family of Longstreet* (1893); C. C. Jones, Jr., *Memorial Hist. of Augusta, Ga.* (1890); G. H. Preble, *A Chronological Hist. of the Origin and Development of Steam Navigation* (1883).]   C. W. M.

LONGWORTH, NICHOLAS (Jan. 16, 1782– Feb. 10, 1863), horticulturist, was born in Newark, N. J., of a Loyalist family whose property was confiscated during the Revolution. His parents were Thomas and Apphia (Vanderpoel) Longworth, and his uncle was David Longworth, the publisher of the early directories of New York City. His great-grandson was Nicholas Longworth [*q.v.*], the speaker of the House of Representatives. For a time he was a clerk in his elder brother's store in South Carolina but, returning to Newark because of his health, he began the study of law. About 1803 he moved to Cincinnati, a log village of eight hundred inhabitants, and continued his law studies in Judge Jacob Burnet's office. He married, in 1807, Susan Connor, widowed daughter of Silas Howell, by whom he had four children. The fee for his first case, the defense of an alleged horsethief, was two second-hand copper stills which he traded for 33 acres, later valued at $2,000,000. He offered $5,000, on time, for Judge Burnet's cow-pasture, was reproved for his foolhardiness, but saw his acquisition reach a valuation of $1,500,000. His practice of accepting land for fees soon involved him in extensive real-estate dealings. In 1850 he paid, next to William Backhouse Astor, the highest taxes on realty in the United States. He was patron of the sculptors, Hiram Powers and Shobal Vail Clevenger [qq.v.] and the donor of the site of the Cincinnati observatory. He seldom gave away money, but he offered the unemployed work in his stone-quarry on the Ohio and often deeded widows half the property their husbands had leased. A Whig and an attendant of the Presbyterian Church, he had little respect for politicians or preachers. He was active in the Cincinnati Horticultural Society and was, for some time, president of the Pioneer Association of Cincinnati.

Lawyer, millionaire, patron of the arts, he is one of the ablest horticulturists America has produced. By his experiments he succeeded in making the growing of grapes a commercial success. He imported thousands of European grapes but was unsuccessful until he obtained the native Catawba from John Adlum. In 1828 he produced marketable wine, retired from the law, and devoted himself to grape-culture and wine-manufacture. He had extensive vineyards and two large winehouses near Cincinnati. His sparkling Catawba and Isabella wines took many state agricultural society prizes, and a gift of wine to Longfellow inspired the poem, "Catawba Wine." The part he played in the cultivation of strawberries was equally interesting. Of the gardeners about Cincinnati, only Abergust, a German from Philadelphia, raised strawberries profitably. One day Abergust's son, sauntering through Longworth's strawberry patch, remarked that the crop would be poor as nearly all the plants were male. With this clue, Longworth soon discovered that, virtually, staminate and pistillate plants must be interplanted for successful culture. He informed Cincinnati's market growers, who soon took a leading position in strawberry production, published his discovery, and, when met with scepticism, precipitated, in 1842, the "Strawberry War," which he triumphantly waged against the foremost horticulturists of his time (Horticultural Review, June 1854, pp. 288–89). Longworth denied the value of hermaphrodite strawberries but, later, introduced one, the Longworth Prolific, found by a tenant. He also introduced the Ohio Everbearing Black Raspberry. He wrote numerous articles, which appeared in horticultural peri-

odicals and, in 1846, published A Letter from N. Longworth . . . on the Cultivation of the Grape, and Manufacture of Wine, also, on the Character and Habits of the Strawberry Plant (1846). He wrote the "Appendix Containing Directions for the Cultivation of the Strawberry" for the 1852 edition of Robert Buchanan's The Culture of the Grape.

[L. H. Bailey, Cyc. of Am. Horticulture, vol. II (1900); Charles Cist, Sketches and Statistics of Cincinnati (1851); C. F. Goss, Cincinnati, the Queen City (1912), vol. IV; L. H. Bailey, Sketch of the Evolution of our Native Fruits (1898); S. W. Fletcher, The Strawberry in North America (1917); Mag. of Horticulture, Apr. 1903; Ohio Arch. and Hist. Quart., Jan. 1923, p. 20; Archives of State of N. J., ser. 2, vol. I (1901); G. B. Vanderpoel, Geneal. of the Vanderpoel Family (1912); Cincinnati Daily Commercial, Feb. 11, 1863; World (N. Y.), Feb. 11, 1863, Feb. 25, 1895.]
H. D. H.

LONGWORTH, NICHOLAS (Nov. 5, 1869– Apr. 9, 1931), speaker of the House of Representatives, was born at Cincinnati, Ohio, the son of Nicholas and Susan (Walker) Longworth and the great-grandson of Nicholas Longworth [q.v.]. His father, his grandfather, and his great-grandfather were men of wealth, prominent in the business and cultural life of Cincinnati. Graduated at Harvard (B.A.) in 1891, he entered the Harvard Law School in 1892 but received his LL.B. degree from the Law School of Cincinnati College in 1894. Election to the Cincinnati board of education, in 1898, brought him into politics. He attracted the eye of George B. Cox [q.v.], the Republican boss of the city and, with his backing, won a seat in the state House from 1899 to 1901 and in the state Senate from 1901 to 1903. He then served in Congress, for the first Ohio district, from 1903 to 1913 and, again, from 1915 to his death in 1931. From 1923 to 1925 he was Republican floor leader of the House and was elected speaker of the Sixty-ninth, Seventieth, and Seventy-first congresses. As a young man of thirty-four he set resolutely to work to study the machinery of the House and to master the intricate details of parliamentary procedure. On his first committee, that for Foreign Affairs, he helped initiate legislation to provide buildings for embassies and legations abroad. In the Sixtieth Congress, he was placed on the ways and means committee, where, as a strong believer in the protective tariff, he came to exercise a commanding influence on tariff matters and, as chairman of the sub-committee on chemicals, paints, and oils, was one of the leaders in framing these important schedules in the 1922 tariff act.

When Frederick H. Gillett became a senator, in 1925, Longworth was elected speaker. A firm believer in responsible party government, he laid down three requisites for the efficient working of the House, strong leadership, adherence to a system of rules that permits a majority to function when necessary, and cooperation. Though a partisan Republican, he never tried to ride rough shod over the Democrats and the western radicals. So strong an impression did his fairness make on his colleagues, that, when he was reëlected speaker in 1927, Finis J. Garrett, the minority leader, told the House that the fitness he had already shown inspired entire confidence in the rectitude of his future administration of the great office. In spite of his party loyalty, he, at times, opposed a Republican president. He left the speaker's dais to take the floor in opposition to the naval program of Coolidge and helped to push the soldiers' loan bill through the House over the opposition of Hoover.

On Feb. 17, 1906, he married, at the White House, Alice Lee Roosevelt. The wedding was one of the most brilliant in the history of the capital. His rise to prominence, however, could be attributed neither to the accident of his birth nor to his marriage to the daughter of Theodore Roosevelt. In 1912, when Roosevelt broke with Taft, Longworth refused to follow. He supported Taft and was defeated that year for Congress.

Longworth will not rank as a great speaker, yet his place will be an honored one. He defended the prerogatives of the House and sought to enhance its prestige against the Senate; in a notable decision from the chair, he insisted that, in their comments on individual senators, House members observe the courtesies laid down in Jefferson's Manual, even though the presiding officer of the Senate had ruled that senators were free to indulge in personalities about members of the House (*Congressional Record,* 71 Cong., 2 Sess., pp. 8453–56). As a tactful mediator, he helped adjust many a dispute. He was a musician of real distinction, democratic in his social contacts, and possessed withal a geniality that won the hearts even of political opponents. He, his wife, and their little daughter, Paulina, enjoyed a position of importance in American life. He will be remembered as much for his personality as for his abilities as a presiding officer and parliamentarian.

[Sources of information include: *Cong. Record,* 72 Cong., 1 Sess., pp. 11171–78, 413–14; C. F. Goss, *Cincinnati, the Queen City* (1912), vol. IV; Harvard College Class of 1891, *Secretary's Report,* nos. IV, VI (1906–16?); *Scribner's,* Mar. 1928; *Review of Reviews* (N. Y.), Aug. 1926, Apr. 1925; *Am. Mercury;* Sept. 1931; *New York Times,* Apr. 10, 1931, Feb. 12, 1928; *New York Herald Tribune,* Apr. 10, 1931; *The Times* (London), Apr. 10, 1931. As this sketch goes to press publication is announced of *The Making of Nicholas Longworth* (1933), by his sister, Clara Longworth de Chambrun.]   O. M., Jr.

LONGYEAR, JOHN MUNROE (Apr. 15, 1850–May 28, 1922), capitalist, was born in Lansing, Mich., the son of Harriet (Munroe) and John Wesley Longyear, a congressman and jurist of some distinction. He was educated in the Lansing public schools, in the preparatory departments of Olivet College at Olivet, Mich., and of Georgetown College at Washington, D. C., and in Cazenovia Seminary at Cazenovia, N. Y. Forced by ill health, he sought outdoor employment and scaled and shipped lumber in the Saginaw Valley. In the spring of 1873 he joined an expedition into the Upper Peninsula of Michigan to examine and report on the widely scattered state mineral reserve lands. The steamer *Rocket* landed the party at Marquette, then with a population of about three thousand in an almost unbroken wilderness. The explorations proved so interesting to him that he decided to spend the next five years in an extensive study of the timber, water power, and mineral resources of the Upper Peninsula. He acquired an extraordinary knowledge of the country's resources, which helped him to become, in later years, the trusted agent and associate of capitalists.

The first large concern to appoint him its agent, in 1878, was the Lake Superior Ship Canal, Railway & Iron Company, now the Keweenaw Land Association, whose extensive holdings he continued to direct until his death. However, it is the opening and development of the Menominee and Gogebic iron ranges for which Longyear is best known. His magnetic survey of these regions in 1880 and 1881 led to unusual success in the development of iron and iron ore. By 1912 the Gogebic range was producing three million tons annually. In 1885 he investigated the possibility of valuable deposits in the Mesaba district of Minnesota and brought back findings that resulted in contracts made with the Wright & Davis Lumber Company, Ex-Governor Pillsbury, James J. Hill, and the United States Steel Corporation. In addition to all this he had a share in exploring and developing a high-grade bituminous coal deposit at Longyear City, on the Arctic island of Spitzbergen, which he continued to hold even after Norwegian bankers bought out all other interests during the World War. He also maintained an unflagging interest in the "Longyear Process" for utilizing low-grade ores, which is still in the course of development.

Among his many connections, he was president of a bank, president of a button company in Detroit, and joint owner of a score of large property holdings controlling some three million acres. He was also active in public affairs, a leader in the Michigan taxpayers' association, mayor of Marquette in 1890–91, and patron of education. He was a member of the board of control of the Michigan College of Mines for twenty-four years and was also a member of the corporation of the Massachusetts Institute of Technology. Among numerous contributions were gifts to hospitals, colleges, libraries, and high schools. In 1919 he helped establish a printing plant for the blind in Los Angeles, which became the printing department of the Braille Institute of America. For many years he was president of the Marquette County Historical Society and a member of many other organizations. He and his wife, Mary Hawley (Beecher) Longyear, whom he married on Jan. 4, 1879, founded the Zion Research Foundation of Brookline, Mass., and also presented to the Church of Christ, Scientist, in Boston, the park which separates it from Huntington Avenue.

[A large part of the material for this sketch was furnished by a daughter, Mrs. Carroll Paul, from the papers of the Longyear Estate, and from Longyear's own unpublished reminiscences; Mrs. Paul is the authority for the spelling of the middle name; see also papers of the Marquette County Historical Society; *Memorial Record of the Northern Peninsula of Mich.* (1895); A. L. Sawyer, *A Hist. of the Northern Peninsula of Mich.* (1911) vols. I, II; N. H. Dole, *America in Spitsbergen; the Romance of an Arctic Coal-mine* (1922) largely from material supplied by Longyear; *Mich. Hist. Mag.*, nos. 2–3 (1922); *A Biog. Sketch of J. Robert Atkinson* (copr. 1932) reprinted from *Cal. and Californians*, ed. by R. D. Hunt (1932); *Early Hist. of Mich. with Biographies*, comp. by S. D. Bingham (1888) for father's career; *Boston Transcript*, May 29, 1922.]
H. L. G.

LOOMIS, ARPHAXED (Apr. 9, 1798–Sept. 15, 1885), law reformer and congressman from New York, was born in Winchester, Litchfield County, Conn., a son of Thaddeus and Lois (Griswold) Loomis and a descendant of Joseph Loomis, who emigrated from England to Windsor, Conn., about 1639. His family removed, while he was a small boy, to Salisbury in Herkimer County, N. Y. Until he was about fourteen he worked on his father's farm and then became a district school teacher. By teaching in the winter and going to the academy at Fairfield, Conn., in the summer, he managed to acquire a good basic education. In 1818 he began to read law and was admitted to the bar in 1822, when he established himself in practice at Sacketts Harbor. He removed to Little Falls in 1825, where he lived for the rest of his life. On Oct. 5, 1831, he married Anne P. Todd, daughter of Stephen Todd of Salisbury.

In 1828 he became surrogate of Herkimer County and served until 1836; from 1835 to 1840 he was first judge of the county. Elected to Congress as a Democrat in 1837, he served in that body until 1839. He was elected to the state Assembly for the sessions of 1841 and 1842, where he became chairman of the judiciary committee and prepared a bill designed to improve the administration of justice. Gifted with the ability to speak well in public, he became widely known for his support of measures in behalf of law reform and was chosen to sit in the constitutional convention of 1846, where he took a prominent part in the proceedings, particularly in relation to the judiciary article. The constitution provided for the appointment by the legislature of a commission on practice and pleadings. The three commissioners appointed were Loomis, Nicholas Hill, Jr., and David Graham [*q.v.*]. Hill was not in harmony with the other two members and resigned. When David Dudley Field [*q.v.*] was appointed in his place, the commission was united in desiring an entire revision in the system of pleading and practice instead of various attempts at amendment. It rendered to the legislature six reports, in all, which remain a distinct contribution to the history of codification. The Code of Civil Procedure drawn up by it was duly enacted and went into effect July 1, 1848, but the commission continued until Dec. 31, 1849, the date of its final report.

Loomis was again a member of the state Assembly in 1853 and was a delegate to the state nominating conventions of 1861 and 1863. Afflicted with a progressive deafness, he retired more and more completely but exerted himself from time to time, nevertheless, to oppose such measures as the suspension of the writ of *habeas corpus* during the Civil War. In 1879 he published his own account of his activities for law reform in a pamphlet, *Historic Sketch of the New York System of Law Reform in Practice and Pleadings*. His reputation has been overshadowed by the fame of his co-worker, David Dudley Field; yet he rendered service of real importance and lasting value. His claim to a share in the credit for the work of the committee of 1848 has been set forth by John T. Fitzpatrick: "The Code of Procedure, as amended in 1849, is commonly referred to as the Field Code, from the common belief that David Dudley Field drafted the greater part. Field never denied this, but Arphaxed Loomis, one of the commissioners, presents a very good case to show that the work was jointly that of all three commissioners, none having a preponderating part" (*Law Library Journal*, Oct. 1924, p. 15).

[S. Croswell and R. Sutton, *Debates and Proc. in the N. Y. State Convention, for the Revision on the Constitution* (1846); W. G. Bishop and W. H. Attree, *Rept. of the Debates and Proc. of the Convention for the Revision of the Constitution of the State of N. Y.*,

1846 (1846); *Jour. of the Convention of the State of N. Y. . . . 1846* (1846); E. A. Werner, *Civil List and Constitutional Hist. of the Colony and State of N. Y.* (1889); *Memorial Proc. of the Herkimer County Bar, with a Few Obit. Notices on Death of Hon. Arphaxed Loomis* (1885); David McAdam and others, *Hist. of the Bench and Bar of N. Y.*, vol. I (1897); G. A. Hardin and F. H. Willard, *Hist. of Herkimer County, N. Y.* (1893); D. A. Alexander, *A Pol. Hist. of the State of N. Y.*, vols. II, III (1906–09); *Biog. Dir. of the Am. Cong.* (1928); E. S. Loomis, *Descendants of Joseph Loomis* (1908).]   A. S. M.

LOOMIS, CHARLES BATTELL (Sept. 16, 1861–Sept. 23, 1911), humorist, was born in Brooklyn, N. Y., son of Charles Battell and Mary (Worthington) Loomis, and brother of Harvey Worthington Loomis the composer. He was a descendant of Joseph Loomis of Braintree, Essex, England, who emigrated to Boston, Mass., in 1638 and by 1640 was living in Windsor, Conn. Charles attended the Brooklyn Polytechnic Institute, without graduating, and from 1879 to 1891 was engaged in clerical work chiefly in Brooklyn. On Feb. 14, 1888, he married Mary Charlotte Fullerton of Brooklyn, by whom he had two sons and a daughter. The illness of his eldest child led him in 1891 to leave the city and settle in the Battelle family home, Torringford, Conn., where his great-grandfather had lived. Having already contributed jokes and light verse to *Puck* and other periodicals, he soon found writing more profitable than chicken-farming, and turned definitely to it as a career. After 1899 the family usually spent the winters at Leonia or some other Jersey suburb, but each spring returned to Torringford. It was from the people around him—Connecticut Yankees, suburbanites, and some city folk—that Loomis drew the kindly, whimsical, everyday characters of his sketches. With a remarkable voice and irresistibly humorous manner—he was by general testimony one of the homeliest and most lovable of men—he also took up public reading, and by the late nineties his success in this field began to keep pace with his reputation as a writer. In 1905 he accompanied Jerome K. Jerome on a platform tour through the United States, and subsequently went with Jerome to England. With his audiences Loomis was always very effective, his funereal aspect, skill in impersonation, and quick but never caustic wit adding to his work a quality which in print is hardly conveyed. "His writings," remarks Jerome (*My Life and Times*, 1926, p. 254), as scattered through the magazines, "were mildly amusing, but that was all . . . until . . . he read them, when at once they became the most humorous stories in American literature. He made no gestures; his face, but for the eyes, might have been carved out of wood; his genius was in his marvelous voice." As a member of

the Salmagundi and Authors clubs of New York he was loved for his modesty and warm friendliness. He was in constant demand as an entertainer, possessing both as a reader and after-dinner speaker an unusual ability to sense the spirit of an audience and draw it to him with his first effort. His earliest published book was a collection of light verse, *Just Rhymes* (1899). His prose contributions to magazines were published from time to time in some fifteen volumes, the best of which, perhaps, are his *Cheerful Americans* (1903) and *A Holiday Touch* (1908). *A Bath in an English Tub* (1907) followed his stay in England, and *Just Irish* (1909) was the outcome of his visit to Ireland the next year. Death came at a hospital in Hartford, Conn., from cancer of the stomach, from which he had suffered for nine months. During this time he was writing some of his best work, a series of Irish fairy tales for the *Saturday Evening Post*, never collected in book form. It was as a platform humorist that Loomis won his chief title to fame. As such, in the view of Ellis Parker Butler (letter to A. F. Loomis), he was "the most important in his period, and far and away the funniest . . . the last of the great platform humorists and the link between the speaking and reading humorist and the printed humorist that later usurped public favor."

[Elias and E. S. Loomis, *Descendants of Joseph Loomis in America* (1908); *The Bookman*, May 1912; *Who's Who in America*, 1910–11; *Hartford Daily Courant*, Sept. 25, 1911; family sources.]   A. W.

LOOMIS, DWIGHT (July 27, 1821–Sept. 17, 1903), jurist and congressman from Connecticut, a descendant of Joseph Loomis of Braintree, England, who settled in the Connecticut colony, at Windsor, about 1639, and the second son of Mary (Pinneo) and Elam Loomis, a prosperous farmer, was born in the small town of Columbia, in Tolland County, Conn. He received a common-school education and attended the academies at Monson, Mass., and at Amherst, Mass. For a short time thereafter he taught in the Connecticut towns of Andover, Columbia, Lebanon, and Hebron. In 1844 he began to read law with John H. Brockway of Ellington and, in 1846, entered the law department of Yale College. The next year he was admitted to the bar and began practice in Rockville. In 1851 he was a member of the lower house of the state legislature. Five years later he was a delegate to the Philadelphia convention that nominated Frémont as Republican candidate for the presidency. In 1857 he was a member of the state Senate. From 1859 to 1863 he was a representative in Congress. During his first session, on June 16, 1860, he made a long speech, in which he upheld the rights of the House of Representatives against a supposed attempt on the part of the President to influence legislation. He was moved by such a strong feeling of animosity to Buchanan that, in closing his address, he remarked that, were the administration to collapse, a fitting funeral sermon might be preached on the theme—"With rapture we delight to see the cuss removed" (*Cong. Globe,* 36 Cong., 1 Sess., App., pp. 429–31). In advocating his favorite principles, opposition to a strong executive economy in public expenditures, and the desirability of a high tariff, he was restating the policies held by most Connecticut politicians of the first half of the nineteenth century, and in supporting the Union against secession, he was guided, for the most part, by motives of local or state interest.

In 1864 he became judge of the superior court of Connecticut, was reëlected in 1872, but did not finish his second term, for, in 1875, he was elected associate judge of the supreme court of errors, on which he continued to serve with distinction until he reached the age of retirement in 1891.

After he left the bench he moved to Hartford, where he devoted himself to various professional pursuits; from 1891 to 1893 he was an instructor in the Yale Law School; in 1895 he edited, with J. Gilbert Calhoun, *The Judicial and Civil History of Connecticut*; he acted as arbitrator in such disputes as those between the state, Yale University, and Storrs Agricultural College; and he served as a member of the state board of mediation and arbitration. Most of his attention, however, he gave to his duties as state referee, to which position the General Assembly appointed him in 1891. He was returning home from a hearing at Torrington, when he died suddenly near Waterbury. In November 1848 he married Mary E. Bill, who died in 1864 and, in May 1866, he married Jane E. Kendall.

[*Biog. Encyc. of Conn. and R. I.* (1881); *Conn. Reports,* vol. LXXVI (1904); *Encyc. of Conn. Biog.* (1919), vol. VI; *Representative Men of Conn.,* ed. by W. F. Moore (1894); J. R. Cole, *Hist. of Tolland County, Conn.* (1888); *Roll of State Officers and Members of Gen. Assembly of Conn. from 1776 to 1881* (1881); E. S. Loomis, *Descendants of Joseph Loomis* (1908); *Hartford Courant,* Sept. 18, 1903.]

J. M. M.

LOOMIS, ELIAS (Aug. 7, 1811–Aug. 15, 1889), mathematician and astronomer, was one of six children of Rev. Hubbel Loomis of Willington, Conn., and his wife, Jerusha Burt of Longmeadow, Mass. The father was a Baptist clergyman and a descendant of Joseph Loomis who emigrated from England to Massachusetts in 1638 and two years later was in Windsor,

Conn. As a young man Hubbel Loomis attended Union College for a time, and in 1812 Yale University conferred upon him the honorary degree of master of arts. Soon after the death of his wife in 1829, he joined the pioneers in what was then known as the West, settling in Illinois. Here he became vice-president of the state anti-slavery society and was one of the prime movers in establishing Shurtleff College. Before leaving New England he had personally attended to the preliminary education of Elias, his eldest son, who was admitted to Yale College at the age of fourteen and graduated in 1830.

After a year of teaching mathematics in Mount Hope Academy, near Baltimore, Elias entered Andover Theological Seminary in 1831, but two years later, receiving a call to his alma mater, abandoned his intention to become a minister and returned to Yale, where he taught Latin, mathematics, and natural philosophy. Here he found the opportunity to pursue further some work in astronomy in which he had been interested while in college. He devoted much attention to the study of the variations of the magnetic needle and with Professor Alexander C. Twining [*q.v.*] of West Point carried on a series of important observations (1834) to determine the altitude of shooting stars. With Professor Denison Olmsted [*q.v.*], he rediscovered Halley's Comet on its return to perihelion (1835) and again computed its orbit. In 1836 he was appointed to the professorship of mathematics and natural philosophy at Western Reserve College, then at Hudson, Ohio, and went abroad for further study in Paris (1836–37) under the direction of Arago, Biot, and others. There and in London he purchased the apparatus needed for the professorship awaiting him, and particularly the outfit for a small observatory. Returning to America in 1837, he assumed his duties at Western Reserve, where he remained until 1844.

From 1844 to 1860, except for one year (1848) at Princeton, he was professor of mathematics and natural philosophy in the University of the City of New York. Thence he went to Yale, succeeding Denison Olmsted, and there he remained until his death in 1889. In 1873 he was made a member of the National Academy of Sciences. He contributed to various scientific journals, notably the *American Journal of Science,* in which he published a series of papers on the aurora borealis (November 1859–September 1861) and a series of twenty-three papers with the general title "Contributions to Meteorology" (July 1874–April 1889). It was through his textbooks, however, that he exerted his greatest influence. These included works on natural philosophy, astronomy, meteorology, analytic geometry, and the calculus, besides other and more elementary subjects. From their sale he derived a comfortable fortune. His books were translated into Chinese and Arabic, and did much to make western mathematics known in the Orient. As a teacher he was possessed of unusual ability; Chief Justice Waite said of him, "If I have been successful in life, I owe that success to the influence of tutor Loomis more than to any other cause whatsoever" (Newton, *post*, p. 29). In his will he left $300,000 to Yale, the largest single donation received by his alma mater up to that time.

Loomis was interested in the history of his family and compiled a genealogy, *The Descendants of Joseph Loomis, Who Came from Braintree, England, in the Year 1638, and Settled in Windsor, Connecticut, in 1639,* first published in 1870, which went through three editions in his lifetime and was again revised in 1908. He was married, May 18, 1840, to Julia Elmore Upson, of Tallmadge, Ohio, who died in 1854. They had two sons, Francis Engelsby and Henry Bradford Loomis, each of whom established a scientific fellowship at Yale.

[*The Descendants of Joseph Loomis* (1908), revised by E. S. Loomis; H. A. Newton, *Elias Loomis, LL.D. . . . Memorial Address Delivered in Osborn Hall, Apr. 11, 1890* (1890), repr. in *Am. Jour. Sci.,* June 1890; *Obit. Record Grads. Yale Univ.* (1890); J. L. Chamberlain, *N. Y. Univ. . . . with Biog. Sketches* (1901–03); *Morning Journal and Courier* (New Haven), Aug. 16, 1889.]   D. E. S.

LOOMIS, ELMER HOWARD (May 24, 1861–Jan. 22, 1931), physicist, was born in Vermillion, Oswego County, N. Y., the son of Hiram Warren and Adaline Sabra (Sayles) Loomis. He was a descendant of Joseph Loomis of Braintree, Essex, England, who came to Massachusetts in 1638 and later settled in Windsor, Conn. Hiram Loomis was engaged in the insurance business, and was at one time a member of the New York legislature. He removed to Mexico, Oswego County, while Elmer was still young. The boy was prepared for college in an academy of that town, and in 1883 was graduated from Madison University (now Colgate). He taught physics and chemistry for seven years in Colgate Academy, Hamilton, N. Y., and while there, July 23, 1885, married Mary E. Bennett of Mexico. By this marriage he had two children who died in infancy, and a son, who survived him. In 1904 his wife died, and on Oct. 12, 1911, he married Grace Eaton Woods of Rochester, N. Y.

In 1890 he went to Germany for study. He began his work at the University of Göttingen and later transferred to the University of Strass-

burg, where he received, in 1893, the degree of doctor of philosophy. His dissertation, *"Ueber ein exacteres Verfahren bei der Bestimmung von Gefrierpunktserniedrigungen"* (*Annalen der Physik und Chemie,* Neue Folge, Band LI, no. 3, 1894), dealt with the lowering of the freezing points of solutions, and presented a critical study of the difficulties involved in making exact determinations of these important quantities, and with various improvements in the methods of observation. It was honored with a *summa cum laude.* On his return to America, he became in 1894 instructor in physics at Princeton University, and was later assistant professor and professor. He continued for some years to publish papers on the same general subject as that of his dissertation, in which he presented a great collection of measurements that were carried to the highest degree of exactitude which the nature of the problem permitted. In particular he proved that non-electrolytes in solution obey Raoult's law with great precision, and he made what may be considered a final determination of Raoult's constant. These papers appeared in the *Annalen der Physik* and the *Physical Review* (1896–1901). He was a fellow of the American Association for the Advancement of Science, and of the American Physical Society. In 1929 he retired from his professorship.

He was a man of strong philanthropic instincts, serving for years as a member of the Princeton board of health, and as a director of the New Jersey Sanitarium for Tuberculosis. His sympathy went out to the poor and the unfortunate, and he was always ready with labor and thought to contribute to their welfare. He amused himself in the later years of his life by collecting antique furniture, and he became an adept as a collector and restorer. His other hobby was the planting of shrubs and trees. Many of the streets of Princeton are lined with the trees which he planted.

[Elias and E. S. Loomis, *Descendants of Joseph Loomis in America* (1908); *Who's Who in America,* 1930–31; *Princeton Alumni Weekly,* Jan. 30, 1931; *Princeton Herald,* Jan. 23, 1931; *N. Y. Times,* Jan. 23, 1931; information as to certain facts from family, and personal acquaintance.]   W. F. M.

LOOMIS, MAHLON (July 21, 1826–Oct. 13, 1886), dentist, experimenter, pioneer in wireless telegraphy, was descended from Joseph Loomis, who came from England to Massachusetts in 1638 and later settled in Windsor, Conn. His father was Prof. Nathan Loomis, associated with Benjamin Peirce of Harvard in founding the *American Ephemeris and Nautical Almanac;* his mother was Waitie Jenks (Barber) Loomis. He was born in Oppenheim, N. Y., moved to Virginia with the family in the forties, and in 1848 went to Cleveland, Ohio, where he studied dentistry and taught school for a time. After a period as a traveling dentist he practised successively in Earlville, N. Y., Cambridgeport, Mass., and Philadelphia. On May 2, 1854, he patented a mineral-plate (kaolin) process for making artificial teeth, for which he also received a patent in England. He was married, May 28, 1856, to Achsah Ashley.

About 1860, he turned his attention to electricity. One of his early experiments was the forcing of growth of plants by buried metal plates connected to batteries. At about the same time he became interested in the electrical charges which could be obtained from the upper air by means of kites carrying metal wires. At first, he planned to use this natural source of electricity to replace batteries, and actually did so on a telegraph line four hundred miles long. From this experiment, by one step after another, he was led to the discovery that a kite wire sent aloft in one region would affect the flow of electricity to ground in another kite wire some distance away. In 1868 in the presence of members of Congress and eminent scientists, he carried on two-way "wireless" communication for a distance of eighteen miles between two mountain peaks in Virginia. From one peak, he sent up a kite and wire, connecting this to ground through a galvanometer. At once the galvanometer deflected, showing a steady passage of current to ground from the charged air stratum above. He then set up a similar outfit from a peak eighteen miles away. When ready to "send," he touched this second kite wire to ground; by this action he tapped the "aerial battery" and reduced the voltage of the entire charged stratum of air above, thus lessening the voltage available at the distant air-wire, and hence causing the galvanometer needle there to move to a smaller deflection. This change in deflection was a true telegraphic signal; Loomis had succeeded for the first time in "sending signals to a distance without wires." He interested a group of Boston capitalists in his discovery, only to lose their support in the "Black Friday" panic of 1869. Two years later, the promise of Chicago bankers to aid him likewise came to naught, owing to the great Chicago fire. In 1870 a bill incorporating the Loomis Aerial Telegraph Company was introduced into Congress; it passed the House in May 1872 and the Senate in January 1873, and was signed by President Grant, but it failed to provide the appropriation of $50,000 for which Loomis had hoped. Thereafter, he was unable to find anywhere the financial backing he needed for his experiments. He died in 1886 at Terre Alta, W. Va., heartbroken by what he deemed his failure.

Of Loomis' inventiveness there is no question. His brain teemed with ideas. Some were not altogether practical, such as replacing batteries by atmospheric electricity; some were eminently practical. His notebooks, in the Manuscripts Division of the Library of Congress, are filled with cryptic references and suggestions; on the other hand, he actually carried out many of his experiments, and his records of these are clear and eloquent. It was not until twenty-seven years after his experiment of 1868, however, that Marconi used this same air-wire in true Hertzian-wave communication, the modern "radio." Although Loomis produced sparks when he touched his kite wire to ground, and hence sent out electric waves, he had no means of detecting them. Had Branly brought out his coherer or Fessenden his electrolytic detector prior to Loomis' experiment, it would have been a simple matter to use one of these instruments instead of the galvanometer, and Loomis instead of Marconi might have been known as the father of radio. As it is, his distinction is, that of the long line of those who carried on experiments in wireless telegraphy, using the aerial, he was the first.

[Elias and E. S. Loomis, *Descendants of Joseph Loomis in America* (rev. ed., 1908); *Cong. Globe*, 41 Cong., 2 Sess., p. 5439, 42 Cong., 2 Sess., pp. 3667–70, 3687–88, 3 Sess., pp. 604–05, 631–32; Mary Texanna Loomis, *Radio Theory and Operating* (1925); E. S. Loomis, *Dr. Mahlon Loomis and Wireless Telegraphy* (1914); *The Candlestick* (Springfield, Mass.), Dec. 1910; W. J. Rhees, article in *Evening Star* (Washington), Nov. 18, 1899; "An American Pioneer in Wireless," (Baltimore) *Sun*, Sept. 7, 1930; Robert Marriott, "How Radio Grew Up," *Radio Broadcast*, Dec. 1925.]

G. H. C.

LOOP, HENRY AUGUSTUS (Sept. 9, 1831– Oct. 20, 1895), portrait and figure painter, was born at Hillsdale, N. Y. He was the son of George H. and Angelica M. (Downing) Loop and a descendant of Gerlach Leupp who emigrated to America from the Netherlands. He received his early education in a school for boys at Great Barrington, Mass. At the age of nineteen he went to New York City and began the study of his art under Henry Peters Gray, with whom he remained for about a year. About 1857 he went to Paris and continued his studies under Thomas Couture. Later he made independent preparations for his life work in the galleries of Rome, Venice, Florence, and other Italian cities. On his return to New York he was made a member of the National Academy of Design in 1861. In 1865 he married Jennette Shepherd Harrison of New Haven, Conn. (1840–1909), one of his most talented pupils. She became an accomplished portraitist and an associate of the National Academy. They had three daughters, one of whom, Edith, also became a portrait painter.

From about 1860 Loop was one of the most regular exhibitors in the annual exhibitions of the National Academy of Design for some thirty years. His genre and mythological subjects, though doubtless somewhat academic in conception and execution, were marked by grace, refinement, and a pleasant vein of sentiment, and were consequently popular. Among the most interesting of these performances were his "Undine" (1863), which was warmly praised by the critics of the time; his "Aphrodite," which was bought by Collis P. Huntington after being shown at the Centennial Exposition of 1876 in Philadelphia; his "Italian Minstrel," which appeared in the Paris Salon of 1868; and "Love's Crown," which was given to the Metropolitan Museum of Art, New York, in 1898, by his wife. This last-named piece represents a female figure clad in loose, flowing white draperies, and crowned with a wreath of flowers. Loop also found steady employment as a portrait painter, and among his sitters were Bishop Gregory T. Bedell of Ohio, Anson Phelps Stokes, J. M. Ward, Russell Sage, Hon. William G. Choate, Worthington Whittredge, and other well-known men. The artist went abroad again in 1867 for the purpose of visiting the principal Continental art centers and was away from home for a year and a half. With this exception his professional life was passed in New York, where for many years he had a studio on Madison Avenue. He was a member of the Artists' Fund Society and the Century Club. He died at Lake George in his sixty-fifth year.

[Sources include: Clara E. Clement and Laurence Hutton, *Artists of the Nineteenth Century and Their Works* (1879), vol. II; the *Art Jour.*, May 1876; *Evening Post* (N. Y.), June 3, 1863, Oct. 21, 1895. Information as to certain facts was supplied for this sketch by Loop's daughter, Miss Edith Loop.]

W. H. D.

LOOS, CHARLES LOUIS (Dec. 23, 1823–Feb. 27, 1912), clergyman of the Disciples of Christ, editor, college president, was born at Woerth-sur-Sauer, Lower Alsace. His father, Jacques George Loos, was French and had been a lancer in Napoleon's army; his mother, Katharina P. Kull, was German. The boy had thus the opportunity to learn two languages and, perhaps, varying political opinions; he adopted, however, his father's patriotic and religious views to the extent of favoring France and attending the Lutheran Church. Admiring Na-

poleon, the lad became, in opposition to the Bourbonists, a Republican, and afterward related how he helped in 1830 to sing the *Marseillaise* through the streets of his native town.

At the age of four he went to the academy in Woerth and continued his schooling there until the family emigrated to the United States in 1834, settling on a farm near Canton, Ohio. For the next few years he spent his time in farming, in acquiring an education in a new environment, and in pondering matters of religion. He was confirmed in the Lutheran Church in 1837, but the next year, having become convinced that the views of the Disciples of Christ were most satisfying, he joined that body and retained membership therein until his death. At sixteen he was teaching school; at seventeen he served as a lay minister in the church he had just espoused. Ambitious to advance in teaching and preaching, he entered Bethany College, Bethany, Va. (now West Virginia), in 1842. After graduation in 1846, he spent the following years as instructor in the preparatory department of the college, and in 1848 married Rosetta Erina Kerr. The year 1849 found him a preacher in Wellsburg, Va.; from 1850 to 1856 he held a pastorate in Somerset, Pa.; and for one year he served a congregation in Cincinnati (1856–57). Ministerial duties did not absorb all his energies: in Somerset he headed a Collegiate Institute from 1853 to 1856, and also founded and edited in 1851 *The Disciple,* a magazine which survived two years. When he moved to Cincinnati he became assistant editor of *The Christian Age.* Dividing his loyalties between church and school, Loos nevertheless preferred the latter, and from 1857 his occupation was largely educational. In that year he became president of Eureka College, Illinois, and in 1858 he accepted a call to the professorship of ancient languages at his alma mater. Here he remained until 1880, assisting in the editing of *The Millennial Harbinger* from 1865 to 1871 and widening his reputation as a classical scholar whose desire was to make scholarship an aid to piety. In 1880 this reputation resulted in an offer of the presidency of Kentucky University (now Transylvania College) and in that year he moved to Lexington to assume this position. For seventeen years he performed his duties with wisdom and tact, and after his resignation in 1897 he remained in the institution as professor of Greek.

The closing decade of his life found him respected as a personal friend of Alexander Campbell [*q.v.*] and as a scholar thoroughly familiar with his church's history and proficient in Hebrew, Latin, French, German, and Italian, as well as in Greek. Prominent in days of bitter controversy, he nevertheless pursued a career singularly free from disputes and antagonisms, a fact easily credited by one who examines the gentle features revealed in his photographs. He wrote no books, but his contributions to church papers exerted no little influence. He was concerned over the proper execution of the sacrament of baptism; he championed the rights of colored members of his church; he resented alleged efforts of the French Catholic Church to interfere in education. He is buried in the Lexington cemetery.

[W. T. Moore, *A Comprehensive Hist. of the Disciples of Christ* (1909); J. T. Brown, *Churches of Christ* (1904); *Biog. Cyc. of the Commonwealth of Ky.* (1896); A. W. Fortune, *The Disciples in Ky.* (1932); *Who's Who in America,* 1910–11; *Courier-Journal* (Louisville, Ky.), Feb. 28, 1912; files of *The Crimson* (Ky. Univ.); Charles Louis Loos's scrapbook, in library of Transylvania Coll.; information from acquaintances.]   G. C. K.

LOPEZ, AARON (1731–May 28, 1782), colonial merchant, was the son of Diego Jose Lopez; his mother was also "of the Lopez family." He was born in Portugal. On Oct. 13, 1752, he arrived in Newport, R. I., with his wife, who was the daughter of his half-sister Elizabeth, his daughter, and younger brother. An older half-brother named Moses had been residing in Newport since the middle forties. In Portugal the three Lopez brothers had lived openly as Christians but secretly as Jews. Aaron and his wife had been named Edward and Anna, but on coming to America they adopted Jewish names and were remarried according to Jewish ceremony. Apparently Aaron Lopez' beginnings as a merchant were exceedingly meager, for even by the period of the Seven Years' War he does not appear to have been at all active. It seems that he at first started, as did so many other merchants of the day, by buying, selling, and exchanging only in Newport and Providence. In 1756 he was in regular correspondence with Henry Lloyd of Boston. At this time, however, his chief interest was the spermaceti candle business in which he and Jacob Roderique Rivera were among the pioneers. By 1761 there were so many competitors in this whale-oil industry that the New England firms formed the United Company of Spermaceti Candlers and arranged price agreements.

Previous to 1765 the Lopez shipping was mostly coastwise, and the invoices usually listed boxes of candles. After 1765 Lopez attempted, in addition to his small business with London, to enter the Bristol trade on a large scale, a venture which proved most disappointing. Far more successful was his later search for new markets in the West Indies. His first factor, Abraham Pereira Mendes, was incompetent, but Mendes' successor, Capt. Benjamin Wright, gradually built up a lucrative trade. Markets in the Caribbean were poor until about 1770 when at last Lopez realized a number of profitable ventures and had so extended his commerce that his vessels could have been seen riding the bounding main to Jamaica, Hispaniola, Surinam, Honduras, Newfoundland, England, Holland, Spain, Portugal, Africa, the Azores and Canaries. The debt to his Bristol correspondent, Henry Cruger, Jr., in 1767 was £10,514 sterling, but by 1773 this enormous liability appears to have been practically erased. Lopez had learned the necessity of a multiform commerce, and by the seventies he had found prosperity. The years 1773 and 1774 had seen a tremendous increase in his shipping, but these were the last golden years for both the house of Lopez and the town of Newport. He was still pushing his trade in the West Indies, in Europe, Africa, and America. Indeed, he had even joined Francis Rotch of New Bedford in dispatching a fleet of thirteen whalers to the Falkland Islands. It may be said conservatively that by 1775 he had a complete or part ownership in over thirty vessels.

When the violence of the American Revolution finally broke, Lopez moved from Newport to Leicester, Mass. The war not only brought an abrupt end to his business ventures but left his accounts in utter chaos. In May 1782, while on a journey to Rhode Island with his wife and family, he stopped to water his horse at Scott's Pond near Providence and was accidentally drowned. The tragedy was a blow to his friends throughout the commercial world. Although in 1761 he was refused citizenship in Newport and was forced to go to Massachusetts for it, at the outbreak of the American Revolution no man in Newport was more highly respected. On his death, Ezra Stiles, pastor of the Second Congregational Church and later president of Yale College, recorded: "On the 28th of May died that amiable, benevolent, most hospitable & very respectable Gentleman, Mr. Aaron Lopez Merchant. . . . He was a Jew by Nation, was a Merchant of the first Eminence; for Honor & Extent of Commerce probably surpassed by no Mercht in America: He did Business with the greatest Ease & Clearness—always carried about with him a Sweetness of Behav. a calm Urbanity an agreeable & unaffected Politeness of manners. Without a single Enemy & the most universally beloved by an extensive Acquaintance of any man I ever knew. His beneficience to his famy [family] connexions, to his Nation, & to all the

World is almost without a Parallel" (*post*, p. 24). Lopez' first wife, who took the name Abigail, died in 1762, the mother of seven children. His second wife, Sarah Rivera, the daughter of Jacob Roderique Rivera, survived him and moved to New York. She was the mother of ten children, eight of whom lived to maturity.

[See the *Biog. Cyc. of R. I.* (1881); M. J. Kohler, "The Lopez and Rivera Families of Newport," *Am. Jewish Hist. Soc. Pubs.*, no. 2 (1894), and scattered references to Lopez in *Ibid.*, no. 27 (1920); Leon Huhner, "A Merchant Prince of Colonial New England," *Jewish Comment*, May 26, June 2, 1905; F. B. Dexter, *The Lit. Diary of Ezra Stiles, D.D., LL.D.*, vol. III (1901). Many Lopez letter books, ledgers, day books, shipping books, sailors' books, etc., are in the possession of the Newport Hist. Soc. A few Lopez manuscripts are in the Wetmore Collection of the Mass. Hist. Soc. Some of these have been printed in "Commerce of R. I.," *Mass. Hist. Soc. Colls.*, 7 ser. IX and X (1914–15). For a detailed account of the commerce of Lopez see the doctoral thesis at Brown University by B. M. Bigelow on "The Commerce Between Rhode Island and the West Indies Before the American Revolution."]   B. M. B.

LORAS, JEAN MATHIAS PIERRE (Aug. 30, 1792–Feb. 19, 1858), Roman Catholic prelate, was the tenth child of Jean Mathias and Étiennette (Michalet) Loras. Born at Lyons just as the Revolution in France was rushing toward its climax, he was but an infant held in his mother's arms when she pleaded with the tyrant Couthon for the life of her husband, a wealthy merchant and councilor of Lyons. Loras, however, was in the very first group to be guillotined in the Square des Terreaux. Young Jean Mathias received his early education at the hands of priests who sought the hospitality of his mother's home. In an old Carthusian house nearby he commenced his priestly studies. As a lad, he had visited the exiled and imprisoned Pius VI at Valence. In 1807 he entered the seminary of L'Argentière (Hautes-Alpes) and was ordained a priest in the Cathedral of Lyons by the Cardinal-Archbishop in 1817. He was immediately appointed president of the Petit Seminaire of Meximieux; and in 1824 he was promoted to the important office of superior of the seminary of L'Argentière. Having resigned in 1827 to act as pastoral missioner in the Lyons archdiocese, he met Bishop Michael Portier of Mobile, Ala., and decided in 1829 to accompany him to America. For seven years he labored in Alabama as pastor of the Cathedral of Mobile, superior of the newly founded Spring Hill College, and vicar-general of the young diocese.

Chosen in 1837 for the newly created bishopric of Dubuque (then in Wisconsin Territory) he was consecrated on Dec. 10 of the same year by Bishop Portier in the cathedral at Mobile. He

did not arrive in Dubuque until Apr. 19, 1839, having spent the intervening months in France seeking priests and funds for his American missions. His new diocese reached from the northern boundary of Missouri to the Canadian line and westward from the Mississippi River to the Missouri River. One priest he found in all that expanse—Father Samuel Charles Mazzuchelli [*q.v.*], the versatile and illustrious Dominican missioner—30,000 Indians, and a few widely scattered white settlements. Believing that the rich soil of the upper Mississippi Valley could be transformed into an agricultural empire, he strove sturdily and steadily to draw the Catholic immigrants from the crowded cities of the Atlantic seaboard. He himself went about among the immigrants of his wide diocese, by canoe and steamboat, in stage-coach and on foot, ministering and organizing. With the strategic eye of a general he picked church sites in new villages even before the arrival of Catholics; he organized schools; he evangelized the Indians; he brought in teaching and nursing sisterhoods; he induced a Trappist order of monks to erect a monastery near Dubuque; and he founded a college—a short-lived project but crowned with success while it endured. Offered an archbishopric in France by influential relatives if he would return to that country, he refused it emphatically; and roused by remarks of some French bishops, he wrote: "We have no martyrs of blood in the United States but many of charity."

He also participated actively in many public and civic movements. A firm total abstainer, he appealed to the Catholics to uphold temperance by voting for the Iowa Liquor Law of 1855. In May 1846 he and Bishop John Hughes [*q.v.*] of New York called on James Buchanan, then secretary of state, and succeeded in having President Polk appoint chaplains to serve the Catholic soldiers during the Mexican War.

[Louis de Cailly, *Memoirs of Bishop Loras, First Bishop of Dubuque, Iowa, and of Members of his Family from 1792 to 1858* (1897); J. F. Kempker, *Hist. of the Cath. Ch. in Iowa* (1887); published letters of Loras in *Acta et Dicta* (1907–08, 1916–18); John Ireland, in *The Cath. World*, Sept.–Oct., 1898; unpublished documents and letters in the archdiocesan archives of Dubuque and St. Louis.]   M. M. H.

LORD, ASA DEARBORN (June 17, 1816–Mar. 7, 1875), educational leader, was born at Madrid, N. Y. His father, Asa Lord, died when the boy was two years old, and his early education was directed by his mother, Lucretia (Dearborn) Lord, a woman of marked intelligence and an experienced teacher. After attending the district school he became a teacher at the age of seventeen. His further professional preparation he acquired while pursuing a course of study in the academy at Potsdam, N. Y. In 1837 he taught a private school at Willoughby, Ohio, and entered the sophomore class of Western Reserve College in 1838. The following year he was chosen as head of the Western Reserve Teachers' Seminary in the neighboring village of Kirtland, a position which he held for eight years. On July 21, 1842, he married Elizabeth W. Russell, who, herself, had a remarkable career, first, in helping her husband in his work for the blind and, after his death, as superintendent at Batavia, in his place, and as assistant dean at Oberlin College. While still principal of the seminary he attended lectures in the medical department of the neighboring Willoughby University. Though he obtained a diploma in 1846, he never entered upon regular practice.

At about the same time, influenced largely, it seems, by Henry Barnard, who visited Ohio in 1843 and again in 1846, he engaged in a variety of educational activities. In 1845 he gave instruction in what is usually considered the first teachers' institute held in Ohio, though he had, in 1843, organized and conducted a similar institution at Kirtland. During 1846 he began the publication of the *Ohio School Journal*, which he continued to publish until 1849, when it was combined with *The School Friend*. In 1847 he was appointed superintendent of schools at Columbus, Ohio, an office created largely through the influence of Henry Barnard and the first of its kind in the Middle West. In the process of classifying the pupils he was led to organize the first public high school in Columbus and one of the first in the state. While continuing to publish *The Ohio School Journal,* he also published *The Public School Advocate,* primarily in the interest of good understanding between the school board and the patrons of the public schools. Convinced, as was Barnard, of the importance of the interchange of ideas among teachers, he promoted the organization of the Ohio State Teachers' Association in 1847 and, from the first, took a leading part in its activities. When, in 1852, the association established, as its organ, *The Ohio Journal of Education* that became, in 1860, *The Ohio Educational Monthly,* he was elected its resident editor and served until 1855. In 1854 he resigned, temporarily, his superintendency in order to act as agent of the association. He resumed his work as superintendent in 1855, but the following year, became head of the Ohio Institution for the Education of the Blind. In this field of educational activity, to which he devoted the remainder of his life, he paid especial attention to training in the practical arts. Already qualified as a physician, he took up the study of theology and, in 1863, was licensed to preach by the Presbytery of Franklin. In 1868 he was called to be head of the new state school for the blind at Batavia, N. Y., where he died.

[The unpublished reminiscences of Lord by his daughter, Mrs. H. F. Tarbox of Batavia, N. Y.; Lord's address—"Twenty-five Years in the Schools of Ohio," delivered before the Ohio State Teachers' Association at Cleveland on July 1, 1863, of which an abridgment is published in the *Ohio Educational Monthly,* Sept. 1863; J. J. Burns, *Educational Hist. of Ohio* (1905); J. W. Taylor, *A Manual of the Ohio School System* (1857): *Am. Journal of Education,* Dec. 1866, Mar. 1859, June 1859, Sept. 1865.]   L. F. A.

LORD, DANIEL (Sept. 23, 1795–Mar. 4, 1868), lawyer, was born in Stonington, Conn., the only child of Daniel and Phebe (Crary) Lord. His father, a physician of ability but scholarly rather than practical, removed in 1797 to New York City, where he rendered devoted service in the yellow-fever epidemic of 1798, incidentally gathered data relating to that disease that, later, proved to be of great value, and soon thereafter abandoned his profession to become a druggist with a store in his house on Water Street. The boy, associating mostly with adults, matured early and enjoyed school, where he acquired, especially, a love of French that was a pleasure and resource to him all his life. In 1811 he entered Yale College as a Sophomore and graduated in 1814, second in his class. Having already decided on his profession, he spent a year at the law school in Litchfield, Conn., then entered the office of George Griffin, an eminent lawyer, and was called to the bar in October 1817. On May 16, 1818, he married Susan, the second daughter of Lockwood de Forest.

He spent a few years of discouragement in faithful application and thorough research, then his progress was rapid, and he attained a position of first rank in his generation. His absorption in the law was such that he declined all offers of public office and devoted himself wholly to his profession until two or three years before his death. One of his first important cases, that of *Aymar and Aymar* vs. *Astor* (6 *Cowen,* 266), led to a business connection with John Jacob Astor that was of great advantage to the young lawyer. Another early case, *Grover* vs. *Wakeman* (11 *Wendell,* 187), became a leading case on voluntary assignments in trust, and his victory made him a favorite lawyer for influential business men. He successfully conducted trials, involving large interests, that grew out of the fire of 1835 and of the panic of 1837, and he was intrusted with the case of *The Attorney General ex rel Marselus* vs. *The Minister and Elders of the Dutch Reformed Protestant Church of New York* (36 *N. Y.,* 452). Among the famous cases argued by him were *A. N. Lawrence and Others* vs. *The Trustees of the Leake and Watts Orphan House* (2 *Denio,* 577), both the John Mason will case (1 *Barbour,* 436) and the contest over the will of Anson G. Phelps (28 *Barbour,* 121, 23 *N. Y.,* 69), and *Charles Barnard and Others* vs. *Joseph Adams and Others* (10 *Howard,* 269) on general average. The Methodist Church case (*Bascom* vs. *Lane, Federal Cases,* case no. 1089), brilliantly argued, was followed by the *People of New York on the Relation of the Bank of Commerce* vs. *the Commissioners on Taxes for the City and County of New York* (2 *Black,* 620), and a series of prize cases, notably *The Schooner Crenshaw* (2 *Black,* 635).

From 1833 until his death he was an active member of the Brick Presbyterian Church. Among other addresses, he delivered July 30, 1851, the Phi Beta Kappa oration at Yale *On the Extra-Professional Influence of the Pulpit and the Bar* (1851). In 1861 he published a pamphlet on *The Legal Effect of the Secession Troubles on the Commercial Relations of the Country.*

[*Memorial of Daniel Lord* (1869); L. B. Proctor, *The Bench and Bar of N. Y.* (1870); F. B. Dexter, *Biog. Sketches of the Grads. of Yale College,* vol. VI (1912); E. J. de Forest, *A Walloon Family in America* (1914), vol. II; *N. Y. Tribune,* Mar. 6, 1868.]

A.S.M.

LORD, DAVID NEVINS (Mar. 4, 1792–July 14, 1880), merchant and theologian, was born at Franklin, Conn., the youngest but one of the sixteen children of Nathan and Mary (Nevins) Lord. At fifteen he went to work in New York, where a brother was established in business. After four years of city life he was advised by his physician to change his occupation and he returned to the country. Here he indulged a taste for studious pursuits and eventually entered Yale College, from which he graduated in 1817. With a view to entering the ministry he studied theology, but the loss of his voice and recurring ill health closed that calling to him, and in 1823 he again settled in New York, this time as an importer of dry goods. His business prospered until the great fire of 1835, in which he lost heavily; and the financial panic of 1837 played even greater havoc with his fortunes. Later an inheritance from his brother, Rufus, restored them temporarily, but soon this, too, was swept away.

In spite of the disasters in his career, Lord seems to have been a fairly skilful and sagacious

business man; but it is hardly to be doubted that his inclinations and ambitions lay in another direction. His theological researches were never given up. He followed a daily program of study in Biblical prophecy, interpretation, and symbolism. In 1848 appeared the first number of a quarterly review entitled *Theological and Literary Journal,* of which Lord was editor. In the thirteen years of this periodical's existence most of its articles were written by the editor and his brother, Eleazar [*q.v.*], one of the early presidents of the Erie Railroad. Both men were tremendously concerned with the meaning of scriptural prophecy, and it was not unusual to give seventy-five pages of the *Journal* to a book review or original article on that subject. David also made excursions into geology and questioned the scientific theory of stratification. Even the Darwinian hypothesis did not escape his challenge. Had he lived fifty years later he would undoubtedly have been classified as a Fundamentalist. The *Journal* expired in the first year of the Civil War, but its editor lived on to 1880. Among his published works are: *The Characteristics and Laws of Figurative Language* (1854); *Geognosy; or, The Facts and Principles of Geology Against Theories* (1855); *The Coming and Reign of Christ* (1858); *Visions of Paradise* (1867). In 1824 he married Eliza J. Lyon; there were no children.

[*Obit. Record Grads. Yale Coll.,* 1881, pp. 8–9; *N. Y. Tribune,* July 18, 1880.]

W.B.S.

LORD, ELEAZAR (Sept. 9, 1788–June 3, 1871), preacher, railway president, author, son of Nathan and Mary (Nevins) Lord, was born at Franklin, Conn. He received his early education in the district school, and at the age of sixteen left home to become a clerk at Norwich. In 1808 he began to prepare for college, studying with Rev. Andrew Lee, pastor of the Congregational church at Hanover (now Lisbon). In 1810 he entered Andover Theological Seminary, two years later he was licensed to preach by the Haverhill Association, and after supplying various pulpits for a year, he entered the College of New Jersey (Princeton) to complete his studies for ordination. Within a few months, however, serious eye trouble compelled him to give up his chosen calling, and he went to New York City, where three brothers were already established as merchants.

After travel in Europe, 1817–18, he commenced a notable business career. He was the founder and first president, 1821–34, of the Manhattan Fire Insurance Company, and first president (1833) of the New York and Erie Railroad

Company, which he served again as president in 1839–41 and 1844–45. Although his policy of locating the road in the Susquehanna Valley and his insistence on the six-foot gauge have been severely criticized, he is credited with having "tided the New York and Erie Railroad Company over some of its darkest days" (Mott, *post*, p. 460).

He early showed ability as a political lobbyist and in 1819, 1820, and 1823–24 visited Washington as a representative of the merchants of New York City to promote the then new idea of a high protective tariff. He published a book in 1829 entitled *Principles of Currency and Banking,* in which he advocated the "Free Banking System" later established in New York and other states. This was reprinted, with additions, under the title, *Credit, Currency, and Banking* (1834) and was followed by other publications in the same field. His *Six Letters on the Necessity and Practicability of a National Currency* (1862) attracted the attention of W. H. Seward, and Lord was summoned to the Capital to advise on the national fiscal policies, but it does not appear that he played any prominent part in the active measures by which the "Free Banking System" was actually established.

His interest in religious work was life-long. In 1815 he called the meeting which resulted in the formation of the New York Sunday School Union Society, which he served as secretary, 1818–26, and president, 1826–36. He devoted much time to organizing Sunday Schools and editing lesson material. He was also a charter member and active leader in the American Home Missionary Society; was its first secretary, and wrote its first report. He was a founder and a member of the council (1831–34) of the University of the City of New York, and a founder of Auburn Theological Seminary (1820). In addition to his other activities he gave such time as he could spare to writing. His earliest notable book was *A Compendious History of the Principal Protestant Missions to the Heathen* (1813). In 1825 he edited *Lemprière's Universal Biography* in two volumes, and, with his brother David Nevins Lord [*q.v.*] contributed to it some eight hundred sketches of American subjects. At the age of forty-eight he retired from many of his business pursuits and thenceforth, at Piermont, N. Y., overlooking the Hudson, devoted a large part of his time to literary work. Among the books he published during this period are: *Geological Cosmogony; or, an Examination of the Geological Theory of the Antiquity of the Earth* (1843); *The Epoch of Creation* (1851); *The Messiah: in Moses and the*

Prophets (1853); *Symbolic Prophecy* (1854); *A Historical Review of the New York and Erie Railroad* (1855); *Plenary Inspiration of the Holy Scriptures* (1857); *The Prophetic Office of Christ* (1859), and an *Analysis of the Book of Isaiah* (1861). He also contributed frequently to the *Theological and Literary Journal* edited by his brother David.

On July 12, 1824, he married Elizabeth, only daughter of Jeremiah H. Pierson of Ramapo, N. Y., and to them seven children were born. She died in 1833, and two years later, Dec. 31, 1835, he married Ruth, daughter of Deacon Eben Thompson, of East Windsor, Conn. He died at his home at Piermont.

[E. H. Mott, *Between the Ocean and the Lakes: A History of the Erie* (1899); unpublished biography of Eleazar Lord by his son; unpublished "Autobiography of Eleazar Lord, LL.D." in the handwriting of his son-in-law, Wm. H. Whiton, in the possession of his great-grandson, Henry D. Whiton, Esq., New York; obituary in *N. Y. Tribune*, June 6, 1871.]

H. A. M—n.

LORD, HENRY CURWEN (Apr. 17, 1866–Sept. 15, 1925), astronomer, was born in Cincinnati, Ohio, the son of Henry Clark and Eliza Burnet (Wright) Lord. His grandfather, Rev. Nathan Lord [*q.v.*], was president of Dartmouth College from 1828 to 1863, and his father, a prominent citizen of Cincinnati and at one time a railroad president. Henry studied at Ohio State University (1884–87), and then entered the University of Wisconsin, from which he graduated in 1889. At the latter institution he took part, as assistant, in the work of the Washburn Observatory.

After graduation he engaged for a short time in electrical work, but in 1891 he joined the faculty of Ohio State University, as assistant in mathematics and astronomy. On leave of absence in 1893, he was astronomer for the Alaskan Boundary Survey. He was promoted through the various ranks to a professorship in astronomy (1900). In the meantime, 1895, he had become director of the observatory which Emerson McMillin built and equipped. In connection with this enterprise, Lord was sent East to visit observatories and instrument makers. The building and complete equipment for instruction were the first considerations, but there were sufficient funds to warrant a $12\frac{1}{2}$-inch equatorial and a spectroscope for research. The spectroscope was designed by Lord, following the best features of the Lick and Potsdam instruments, and was built by him, as well as most of the other accessory apparatus, largely to minimize expense, but also, apparently, because of a fondness for mechanical work, in which he was skilled.

As a line of research he took up the measurement of the radical velocities of stars, feeling his way along in this new field as others were doing. He published careful and specific directions for focussing a telescope accurately on the slit of a spectroscope (*Astrophysical Journal*, May 1897), and a derivation of Scheiner's formula for the curvature of spectral lines (*Ibid.*, May 1897). In 1897 he adopted a suggestion of Keeler's and had a compound correcting lens made for use with the visual objective to flatten the color curve (*Ibid.*, August 1897). In 1898 he made his first detailed report on the radical velocities of stars (*Ibid.*, August 1898). His observing program was necessarily limited to the brighter stars because the telescope was small and the observatory was "located within the limits of a city of 150,000 population, where soft coal is used extensively." The preliminary probable error of 2 km. sec. was satisfactorily small. Distressed at his inability to photograph the faint iron lines in stars of type I, he developed a graphical comparison of the effects on the efficiency of spectroscopes resulting from the variation of any one of the several elements that enter into their optical design (*Ibid.*, April 1899). The final results of ten years of work on radical velocities was published in 1905 (*Ibid.*, May 1905) when he had decided to give up this line of research "in view of the optical giants at work in this branch of research today, and in further consideration of the fact that our sky . . . is yearly getting worse." In May 1900 he observed with the United States Naval Observatory eclipse expedition, using his spectroscope on a 4-inch telescope, and obtaining one of the early successful photographs of the flash spectrum. This he measured completely, discussing the identifications of the lines and the elevations to which the various gases rise in the sun's atmosphere (*Ibid.*, March 1901). He also published some observations of double stars (*Astronomical Journal*, Apr. 27, 1920). His optical studies included the testing of various kinds of glass for prisms; the statement and proof of a relation which must be satisfied in order that a symmetrical photographic doublet of four separated thin lenses may be free from the errors of achromatism and astigmatism (*Astrophysical Journal*, October 1913); and the formulation for the illumination of the field of a photographic doublet (*Monthly Notices of the Royal Astronomical Society*, Jan. 14, 1916).

He was the author of *The Elements of Geodetic Astronomy for Civil Engineers* (1904). This he printed himself on a hand printing-press. In 1898 he married Edith Lelia Hudson of Middleport, Ohio, by whom he had one child, a daughter.

[R. G. Thwaites, *The Univ. of Wis.* (1900); Alexis Cope, *Hist. of the Ohio State Univ.*, vol. I (1920); *Thirtieth Ann. Report of the Board of Trustees of the Ohio State Univ.* (1900); *Monthly Notices of the Royal Astronomical Soc.*, Feb. 12, 1926; *Who's Who in America*, 1924–25; *Ohio State Jour.* (Columbus), Sept. 16, 1925.]   R. S. D.

LORD, HERBERT MAYHEW (Dec. 6, 1859–June 2, 1930), financial administrator, was born at Rockland, Me., the son of Sabin and Abbie (Swett) Lord. He was a descendant of Nathan Lord of Kent, England, who settled in Kittery, Me., about the middle of the seventeenth century. Following a common-school education, he worked his way through Colby College, Waterville, Me., receiving the degree of A.B. in 1884. On leaving college his first work was that of teacher, but he soon entered newspaper work, writing editorials for papers at Rockland, Me., Denver, Col., and Cardiff, Tenn. His real career began in 1894, when he was appointed clerk of the committee on ways and means of the House of Representatives. This position he held until the outbreak of the Spanish-American War in 1898, when he resigned in order to offer his services to the War Department. These services were accepted and on May 17, 1898, he was appointed major and paymaster of volunteers, in which capacity he served until honorably discharged in order to accept appointment as captain and paymaster in the regular army, Feb. 5, 1901. He was promoted until he reached the rank of brigadier-general, July 15, 1919. Upon the entrance of the United States into the World War he was made assistant to Major-General Goethals, with the title of director of finance. In this capacity he supervised the disbursement of more than $24,000,000,000. In recognition of the ability with which he handled the many difficult and complicated problems connected with the financing of the war he was awarded the Distinguished Service Medal. Upon the reorganization of the army, July 1, 1920, he was made chief of finance and as such headed the newly created finance section of the War Department.

On June 30, 1922, he was retired from active service, and on July 1, he succeeded Gen. Charles G. Dawes as director of the budget, an office created by the Budget and Accounting Act of June 10, 1921. This position he filled until May 31, 1929, when he retired. About a year later he died at his residence in Washington, D. C. On Sept. 9, 1885, he married at Thomaston, Me., Annie Stuart, daughter of Shubael and Martha (Haskell) Waldo. He had three children, one of whom died in infancy. His religious affiliations were with the Christian Science Church; in politics he was a Republican.

Lord, undoubtedly, was one of the ablest financial administrators ever connected with the United States government. As director of finance of the War Department his responsibilities were heavy and were performed with great ability. As director of the budget, he had great responsibilities, not only in respect to the handling of the current work of his office, but in determining, during the early years of the bureau's history, the principles and procedures to be followed. Though compelled to oppose the demands of the spending services of the government for money, he did it in a way to elicit universal respect for his courage, his fairness, and his skill in meeting conflicting considerations.

[C. C. Lord, *A Hist. of the Descendants of Nathan Lord of Ancient Kittery, Me.* (1912); *Third Gen. Cat. of Colby Coll.* (1909); *Army and Navy Jour.*, June 7, 1930; *Who's Who in America*, 1930–31; *Evening Star* (Washington, D. C.), June 2, 1930; *N. Y. Times*, June 3, 1930; information as to certain facts from a son, Maj. Kenneth P. Lord.]   W. F. W.

LORD, JOHN (Dec. 27, 1810–Dec. 15, 1894), historical lecturer, was born in Portsmouth, N. H., the son of John Perkins and Sophia (Ladd) Lord. He was a descendant of Nathan Lord of Kent, England, who settled in Kittery, Me., about the middle of the seventeenth century. For the first ten years of his life his home was in Portsmouth, where he attended a Lancasterian School and was whipped, he says, at least once a day, until his "hand became as hard as a sailor's." In 1820 his father failed in business and moved to South Berwick, Me., in the academy of which town John prepared for college, without proving, however, a promising scholar. His uncle, Nathan Lord [*q.v.*], was president of Dartmouth College, and in 1829 he entered that institution, graduating in 1833 with an awakened interest in history and literature. Without feeling any particular call to the ministry apparently, he entered Andover Theological Seminary, from which he graduated in 1837. During these years of his education he contributed to his support by teaching school in various places, and while at Andover he had the temerity to undertake a lecture tour in New York State, his subject being the Dark Ages.

After he finished his course at Andover, his uncle, William Ladd [*q.v.*], president of the American Peace Society, offered him a position as agent for that organization. In this capacity he traveled, preached, and lectured for a year or more, his labors being brought to an end by a letter from his uncle, who stated that he did not wish longer to invest capital in unproductive property. A brief period of pastoral work was equally unsatisfactory in its outcome. After serving on trial as minister of the Congregational Church, New Marlboro, Mass., he was called to be its settled pastor. The call was not unanimous, however, for some were doubtful of his orthodoxy. An ecclesiastical council decided that it was inexpedient to ordain him. For a time he supplied the pulpit of the Second Presbyterian Church, Utica, N. Y.; but he soon decided that he was unfitted for the ministry and resolved to become an historical lecturer.

From 1840 to 1843 he lectured with encouraging success, chiefly in New England. In the latter year he went abroad, where he remained three years, lecturing acceptably in England and Scotland, gathering material in the British Museum, and in May 1846, at a country church near Brixton, marrying Mary Porter, an English woman, by whom he had a son and a daughter. He was now well launched on a career which he followed for many years, achieving considerable popularity and fortune. From 1852 to 1854 he was again in Europe. Upon his return he chose Stamford, Conn., as his permanent residence, later acquiring there six acres of land and building a home. In his lectures, as a rule, he portrayed history by grouping its events around a series of striking personalities. He made no pretense of originality, appropriating to his use the results of the best scholarship available. His characterizations were vivid and he spoke with fervor and conviction, his delivery being marked by numerous eccentricities. A professor of rhetoric once told him that "he succeeded by neglecting all rhetorical rules, and that if he had followed them he would have been a failure" (Twombly, *post,* pp. 217, 218). During his lifetime he delivered some six thousand lectures on many different topics. His books were popular and widely read, some of them being used as textbooks in schools and colleges. Among them are *A Modern History from the Time of Luther to the Fall of Napoleon* (1849); *The Old Roman World* (1867); *Ancient States and Empires* (1869); *The Life of Emma Willard* (1873); *Points of History for Schools and Colleges* (1881). Probably his best-known publication, however, largely a rewriting of his lectures and other works, is *Beacon Lights of History* (8 vols., 1884–96). His first wife died in 1860 and in 1864 he married Louisa Tucker, an English woman, whom he first met in Paris. Two years later she also died. Lord's death occurred in Stamford.

Lord

Lord

[C. C. Lord, *A Hist. of the Descendants of Nathan Lord of Ancient Kittery, Me.* (1912); G. T. Chapman, *Sketches of the Alumni of Dartmouth Coll.* (1867); *Andover Theological Seminary—Necrology, 1894–95* (1895); A. S. Twombly, "The Life of John Lord," in *Beacon Lights of Hist.*, vol. VIII (1896), based in part on Lord's manuscript "Reminiscences of Fifty Years"; *Boston Transcript*, Dec. 15, 1894.] H. E. S.

LORD, NATHAN (Nov. 28, 1792–Sept. 9, 1870), Congregational clergyman and college president, was born at South Berwick, Me., the son of John and Mehitabel (Perkins) Lord and a descendant of Nathan Lord of Kent, England, who settled in Kittery, Me., about 1652. He was educated at the local academy and at Bowdoin College, where he graduated in 1809. After two years as a teacher at Phillips Exeter Academy, he began the study of theology, completing his work in the seminary at Andover in 1815. In May 1816 he was ordained pastor of the Congregational Church at Amherst, N. H., and on July 24 of the same year he married Elizabeth King Leland of Saco, Me. His pastorate lasted twelve years and he was considered one of the ablest and most successful ministers in the state. Certain liberals, however, withdrew from membership in his church and formed a separate congregation.

In 1821 he was elected a trustee of Dartmouth College and in 1828, president. At this time conditions there were far from satisfactory, since the institution was still feeling the effects of its contest with the state in respect to its charter (1816–19). The new president assumed the task of rehabilitation with notable success and great improvements were soon in evidence; but his administration as a whole can hardly be considered noteworthy for financial or other material progress. He was not a pioneer in educational policy, although one innovation, the abolition of honors and prizes, introduced in 1830, attracted some attention—mostly unfavorable. He was an able executive and disciplinarian, however, and like his contemporary Mark Hopkins [*q.v.*] at Williams, a great teacher, whose character exercised a deep influence on students and associates. For many years he conducted courses in theology and ethics.

Intellectually, he represented a school which was rapidly passing, and his views on the great question of the day—slavery—eventually cost him his position. He had at first supported the Liberty Party, but soon after the Mexican War, an event which drove many other New Englanders into the anti-slavery movement, he became a decided supporter of slavery as an institution. His thesis was simple and logical. Slavery was sanctioned by the Bible, it was therefore divinely ordained and not to be ques-

tioned on political, humanitarian, or economic grounds. He had no sympathy with "a philosophy which makes happiness the end of living," or with "the sentiment and romance which had infected the descendants of the Puritans." His views on the question are well stated in *Letter of Inquiry to Ministers of all Denominations on Slavery* (1854), *A Northern Presbyter's Second Letter . . .* (1855), and in *A Letter to J. M. Conrad, Esq., on Slavery* (1859). The last-named first appeared in the *Richmond Daily Whig*, Richmond, Va., and denounced the recent raid at Harpers Ferry. *A True Picture of Abolition* (1863) subjected him to widespread censure, and in July 1863, the trustees, while refusing to remove him from office, expressed such disapproval that he felt obliged to resign. In a dignified statement he defended his views and denied the right of the board to impose any religious, political, or ethical test not authorized by the charter. In spite of the intensity of his views, however, he had what many men of his type have lacked, a genuine sense of humor and a large measure of tolerance and kindliness. Furthermore, he was fond of outdoor life, had athletic tastes and good health, and whatever he may have thought of ultimate human destiny, he enjoyed association with his fellows.

After retirement he spent his last years in Hanover, his friends having provided an annuity in recognition of his long and scantily remunerated services. His last publication, a letter to the alumni on the occasion of the college centennial in 1869, continues to emphasize his opposition to the current philosophy which stressed "the ability, not the weakness of man; his dignity, and not his sinfulness and shame; his rights, and not his duties; and the reorganization of society upon the basis of universal freedom, equality and fraternity."

[Many of his addresses, sermons, and papers were published in pamphlet form and the library of Dartmouth College has, it is believed, a complete collection of manuscript material dealing with his administration. See also C. C. Lord, *A Hist. of the Descendants of Nathan Lord of Ancient Kittery, Me.* (1912); J. K. Lord, *Hist. of Dartmouth Coll.* (1913); *Proc. N. H. Hist. Soc.*, vol. IV (1906); D. F. Secomb, *Hist. of the Town of Amherst, N. H.* (1883).] W. A. R.

LORD, OTIS PHILLIPS (July 11, 1812–Mar. 13, 1884), jurist and legislator, the second son of Nathaniel and Eunice (Kimball) Lord, was born in Ipswich, Mass., where his ancestor, Robert Lord, had settled when he emigrated from Ipswich, England, in 1631. In the early years of his education Otis was taught by his father; he was prepared for college in the grammar school of Ipswich and, in 1832, was graduated from Amherst College. The next year he

409

began to read law with Judge Oliver B. Morris of Springfield, then entered the Harvard Law School, and received the degree of LL.B. in 1836. He was admitted to the Essex County bar and practised in Ipswich, where he married Elizabeth Wise Farley on Oct. 9, 1843. In November of the next year he moved to Salem. The Whigs sent him to the lower house of the legislature for 1847 and 1848 and, the next year, to the Senate. So stanch was his party loyalty that he supported Webster even after the Seventh-of-March speech. In 1852 and 1853 he was again in the House, contending unsuccessfully for the speakership. When, in 1853, a constitutional convention was called to consolidate the recent alliance of Free Soilers and Democrats, he offered an obstinate resistance, as a leader of the Whig minority. The proposed constitution called for a popularization in the frame of government: judicial tenure was to be for ten years instead of life; juries were to determine the law as well as the facts; appointive offices were to become elective; voting was to be secret; and the payment of a poll tax was no longer to be a prerequisite. He spoke vehemently against these innovations (*Official Report, post,* especially I, 573–81; III, 187–88, 460–61, 510–11). A reaction set in; the constitution was rejected, and his prestige was enchanced by his "masterly exposition of the blunders, incongruities and iniquities of the rejected constitution" (*Boston Transcript,* Mar. 14, 1884). In 1854 he again sat in the House and became speaker in the last Whig legislature. After the decline of the Whigs he became a man without a party. He refused to support Frémont and, on Oct. 8, 1856, made a speech against him in Faneuil Hall (*Frémont's "Principles" Exposed,* 1856). In 1858 he was nominated for Congress by an independent group of old-line Whigs but was defeated. Two years later he lost as a Constitutional Unionist. In 1868 he declined the Democratic nomination.

In the meantime he became a leader at the bar. He was celebrated for his "thorough knowledge of the law and an impulsive force and vigor not always under rigid restraint" (*Proceedings of the Bar, post*). As a cross-examiner he proceeded, as he once said, "somewhat energetically." In 1859 he accepted appointment to the superior court and proved to be an able *nisi prius* judge. In 1875 he became an associate judge on the supreme bench of the commonwealth, where he sat until, in 1882, protracted illness obliged him to resign. It was a moot question whether in this case it was a step upward from bar to bench. "The tone of his mind was forensic rather than judicial. . . . His learning was not extensive,

and his temperament was always too impatient for much research, but he could recognize a distinction or detect a fallacy at a glance" (137 *Mass. Reports,* 593). "Whether his views were right or wrong, he saw them clearly and strongly; and such was his power of forcible expression, that there was at times danger that he might make the worse appear the better reason"; but he had the candor frequently "to yield his willing assent to a result which he had in the outset vigorously resisted" (*Ibid.,* 596).

[*Proc. of the Bar of the Commonwealth and of the Supreme Judicial Court . . . on the Death of Otis Phillips Lord* (1884); *Obit. Record of Grads. of Amherst College for . . . 1884* (1884); W. L. Montague, *Biog. Record of the Alumni of Amherst College* (1883); Asahel Huntington, *Memorial Address before the Essex Institute* (1872) reprinted from the *Hist. Colls. of the Essex Institute,* vol. II (1872); James Schouler, "The Mass. Convention of 1853," *Proc. of the Mass. Hist. Soc.,* ser. 2, vol. XVIII (1905); *Official Report of the Debates and Proc. in the State Convention Assembled May 4th, 1853 to Revise and Amend the Constitution of the Commonwealth of Mass.,* 3 vols. (1853); C. F. Adams, *Richard Henry Dana* (1890), vol. I; *Boston Transcript,* Mar. 14, 1884.]   C. F.

LORD, WILLIAM PAINE (July 1, 1839– Feb. 17, 1911), Oregon jurist and governor, was born in Dover, Del., the son of Edward and Elizabeth Paine Lord. He was educated in the schools of Dover and by private tutors, graduated from Fairfield College, New York, in 1860, studied law, and, at the outbreak of the Civil War, enlisted in the Union army, in which he rose to the rank of major. At the close of the war he entered the law school at Albany, from which he graduated in 1866, and was admitted to practice of law in New York. Military life, however, had a stronger appeal so he again joined the army, as a second lieutenant, with stations successively at Fort Alcatraz, near San Francisco, Fort Steilacoom, Washington, and, for four months, in Alaska. In the fall of 1868 he resigned his commission to take up the practice of law in Salem, the capital city of Oregon, where he served, in turn, as city attorney, state senator in 1878, justice of the state supreme court from 1880 to 1894, and governor from 1895 to 1899. He was married to Juliette Montague of Baltimore, Md., on Jan. 14, 1880.

His eight years as associate justice and his six years as chief justice of the supreme court were the most notable of his career. He made a reputation as one of the judges who have most influenced the jurisprudence of the state. The state bar association selected him, in 1914, as the greatest of Oregon's chief justices, and designated his picture for the frontispiece in the forty-second volume of *Corpus Juris* (1927). His judicial opinions, when read today, seem characterized by clearness of statement, close reasoning, convincing argument, and a humanitarian point of view, and he seems to have been less influenced by technicalities than other judges of his generation. His election as governor on the Republican ticket against Nathan Pierce, the candidate of the People's Party, was due in great measure to his personal reputation and popularity. As governor he recommended a policy of retrenchment and economy, the taxation of "all property liable to taxation," the self-support of the penitentiary, a school law "simple in its provisions and inexpensive in its arrangements," and such support of the state university as should lift it to "a plane where it may compete with similar institutions in other states" (*The Journal of the Senate . . . of Oregon . . . 1895,* 1895, pp. 57, 58 and *Ibid. . . . 1897,* 1898, App., pp. 25, 29). He condemned the practice of creating numerous administrative boards, as dividing executive responsibility and as increasing salaries of the governor and other state officers in violation of the limitations fixed by the constitution. The legislative assembly of 1895, however, spent most of the session in controversy over the election of a United States Senator and gave little attention to legislation, while that of 1897, known as "the hold-up" session, failed to organize because of the conflict over the senatorship. In 1899 he was appointed minister to the Argentine Republic, a position which he held until 1902, when he returned to Oregon to resume the practice of law. His last important public service was to compile and annotate *Lord's Oregon Laws* (3 vols., 1910).

[J. C. Moreland, *Governors of Oregon* (1913); Elwood Evans and others, *Hist. of the Pacific Northwest* (1889), vol. II; F. E. Hodgkin and J. J. Galvin, *Pen Pictures of Representative Men of Ore.* (1882); *Biennial Rept. of the Secretary of State of . . . Oregon . . . 1897–98* (1899); *San Francisco Call,* Feb. 18, 1911; *Daily Oregon Statesman* (Salem), Feb. 18, 1911.]
R. C. C.

LORD, WILLIAM WILBERFORCE (Oct. 28, 1819–Apr. 22, 1907), poet, clergyman, was born in Madison County, N. Y., the son of John Way and Sarah Bryant (Chase) Lord. After attending the Geneseo high school he entered the now defunct University of Western New York and graduated in 1837. There is reason to believe that the next four years were spent as a seaman on the Pacific in search of health (R. W. Griswold, *Poets and Poetry of America,* 1850, p. 467). He entered the Auburn Theological Seminary in 1841 but transferred to the Princeton Seminary for his senior year. In 1845–46 he held a Boudinot fellowship at the College of New Jersey (now Princeton), and for a short time thereafter he taught mental and moral science at Amherst. In 1848 he took orders as

deacon in the Episcopal Church, and two years later he was ordained priest. After holding a few minor posts in the South, including one at Baltimore where he served bravely in a deadly epidemic of cholera, he was made, in 1854, rector of Christ Church, Vicksburg, Miss.

In 1845 he had brought out a small volume, *Poems,* which Wordsworth praised in a letter to the author, but which Poe savagely attacked (*Broadway Journal,* May 24, 1845, p. 328). In the main the poems show, to use Poe's mildest phrase, "a very ordinary species of talent," but at least one of them, "On the Defeat of a Great Man," has found numerous admirers and is included with several others by Lord in Edmund C. Stedman's *An American Anthology* (1900). His later volumes were *Christ in Hades* (1851), an epic notable chiefly for its Miltonic echoes; and *André* (1856), an unacted tragedy, written in uninspired blank verse and showing but little dramatic sense.

When the Civil War broke out, Lord continued as rector of Christ Church and became chaplain of the 1st Mississippi Brigade. Throughout the siege of Vicksburg he worked tirelessly in his double capacity of chaplain and pastor. During the siege all his possessions were destroyed, including his library, which was reputed to be the largest and most scholarly private collection in the Southwest. When Vicksburg fell, Grant urged upon him a passport to St. Louis, where he would be free from danger. Far from accepting it, he pushed still further into the Confederacy in the pursuit of his calling. Shortly after the conclusion of the war, he assumed the rectorate of St. Paul's Church, Charleston, S. C. In 1871 he was back in Vicksburg, where he founded the Church of the Holy Trinity. In 1876 he was called to Christ Church, Cooperstown, N. Y., and there he served until his retirement from the ministry about 1883. At his death, which occurred in New York City, he was survived by his wife (formerly Margaret Stockton, whom he married Feb. 19, 1851), a son, and a daughter.

[*Gen. Biog. Cat. of Auburn Theological Seminary* (1918); *Princeton Theological Seminary Bull. Necrological Report,* Aug. 1908; *The Albany Ch. Record,* May 1907, p. 349; *The Church Almanac* and its successor, *The Am. Church Almanac,* 1850–1908; W. W. Lord, Jr., "A Child at the Siege of Vicksburg," *Harper's Mag.,* Dec. 1908, and "In the Path of Sherman," *Harper's Mag.,* Feb. 1910; *N. Y. Tribune* and *Sun* (N. Y.), Apr. 23, 1907.]
O. S. C.

LORILLARD, PIERRE (Oct. 13, 1833–July 7, 1901), merchant, sportsman, and breeder of race horses, was born in New York City, the son of Peter and Catherine (Griswold) Lorillard.

His family, originally of German stock, had been engaged for two generations in the manufacture of tobacco and snuff. In his youth Pierre distinguished himself in various sports—notably in shooting and yachting. As the owner of the schooner *Vesta* and the steam yacht *Radha* he made Newport a yachting center. Later he became a road driver of trotting horses in the days of Bonner and Vanderbilt. Taking up the breeding of trotters, he sent from his stables five or six peers of the road in their day. In 1873 he bought 1,200 acres of land at Jobstown, N. J., and established a famous stock farm known as "Rancocas." From there he began in 1878 to ship horses to run the principal English races. His Parole won the Newmarket Handicap, the City and Suburban Stakes, the Great Metropolitan Stakes, the Great Cheshire Stakes, and the Epsom Gold Cup. In 1879 he sent over Iroquois, winner of the Derby in 1881 and one of the greatest racers ever bred in America. Pontiac and several other horses from the "Rancocas" stables made heavy winnings at home and abroad. Lorillard became a "plunger" in betting. In 1898 he formed a partnership with Lord William Beresford on the English turf.

Since 1812 Lorillard's family had owned a tract of 7,000 acres in Orange County, N. Y. Pierre bought up the interests of the other heirs in this property, acquiring a clear title to the entire tract. His purpose was to establish a shooting and fishing club and to that end he enclosed 5,000 acres in wire fence eight feet high. Thus a game preserve was formed, containing deer, pheasants, and a trout hatchery (the lake on the domain had been stocked with black bass as early as 1860). The club was organized, the name Tuxedo Park adopted, and a clubhouse built. The plans were expanded to include a residential park, developed in accordance with the best engineering practice of the day, with modern roads, sewer and water systems. After his father's death Lorillard had bought the interests of his four brothers in the tobacco industry and had been unusually successful in expanding the business. His income from that source was exceptionally large. For the last six years of his life he lived abroad most of the time, a sufferer from Bright's disease, but he died in New York. He shared with the French Republic the cost of the Charnay archeological expeditions to Central America and Yucatan and for this benefaction he was admitted to the Legion of Honor. He had married, in 1858, Emily Taylor of New York. She with a son and two daughters survived him.

[Russel Headley, *The Hist. of Orange County, N. Y.* (1908), pp. 401–03; *Race Horses and Racing: Recollections of Frank Gray Griswold* (1925); W. S. Vosburgh, "*Cherry and Black*": *The Career of Mr. Pierre Lorillard on the Turf* (1916); *N. Y. Geneal. and Biog. Record*, Apr. 1877, p. 89; *Turf, Field and Farm*, July 12, 1901; *Tobacco* (N. Y.), July 12, 1901; *Sun* (N. Y.), July 8, 1901.]
W. B. S.

LORIMER, GEORGE CLAUDE (June 4, 1838–Sept. 7, 1904), Baptist clergyman, was born and received his early schooling in Edinburgh, Scotland. While he was still a child, his father died and his mother married W. H. Joseph, a theatrical manager. As a result, the boy's impressionable years were passed in the atmosphere of the theatre, and at the age of seventeen he became a professional actor and emigrated to the United States. While playing at Louisville, Ky., he had a religious experience which led him to abandon the stage for the ministry. After a period of study at Georgetown College, Kentucky, he was called to a church in Harrodsburg, Ky., where he was ordained in 1859. Pastorates at Paducah, the Walnut Street Baptist Church, Louisville, the First Baptist Church, Albany, N. Y., and the Shawmut Avenue Church, Boston, followed.

In 1873 he began the first of two pastorates at Tremont Temple, Boston, the scene of his real life-work. They were separated by a period of twelve years, however, which were spent in Chicago with the First Baptist Church (1879–81) which he freed from serious financial straits, and with the Immanuel Baptist Church (1881–91) where, under his leadership, the membership increased from 170 to 1,100. His health was impaired by his arduous and successful efforts to raise $400,000 to meet the conditions of a Rockefeller gift to that church, and returning East he began his second pastorate at Tremont Temple. Here he soon had the largest congregations in Boston and despite three disastrous fires the great institution flourished and grew. During this period he formed the habit of preaching every summer in London. In 1900 he declined the presidency of Columbian University, Washington, D. C., but in 1901 accepted a call to the Madison Avenue Baptist Church, New York City, with which he was connected until the time of his death at Aix-les-Bains, France, where he had gone for his health. On Feb. 26, 1859, he had married Arabelle D. Burford.

Lorimer was a man of magnetic personality, and an enthusiasm that was infectious. He was a popular preacher, but his discourses were carefully prepared and filled with the fruits of wide reading. His sermons, committed to memory at a single reading, were delivered in a voice of remarkable sweetness, compass, and power. He published a number of books, which deal chiefly with Christianity in relation to modern thought and social conditions. Among the more important are *Isms Old and New* (1881); *Jesus the World's Savior* (1883); *The People's Bible History* (1896); *Christianity and the Social State* (1898); *Christianity in the Nineteenth Century* (1900); the Lowell Lectures, Boston, delivered in 1900.

[William Cathcart, *The Baptist Encyc.* (1881); W. B. Burford, *Burford Geneal.* (1914); *The Watchman*, Boston, Sept. 15, 1904; *Outlook*, Sept. 17, 1904; *Boston Daily Globe*, Sept. 9, 1904.]   G. H. E—g.

LORIMIER, PIERRE LOUIS (March 1748–June 26, 1812), Indian trader, interpreter, Spanish commandant, founder of Cape Girardeau, Mo., was a native of Lachine, Canada, and is said to have been of noble blood. He accompanied his father in 1769 to the Miami River, and was established at a place called Pickawillany. Here he had a post known as "Loramie's" in what is now Shelby County, Ohio. He traded with various tribes of Indians and exercised great influence over them. He was an agent and interpreter for the British and his post became a rendezvous for them during the Revolutionary War. In 1778 during one of his raids he captured Daniel Boone. Raids by the Shawnee and Delaware Indians under Lorimier caused George Rogers Clark to attempt their extermination, and in 1782 he destroyed the post. Lorimier lost his stores, barely saving his life, and fled to Wapakoneta, Auglaize County, Ohio. In 1787 he was driven by his creditors to Spanish territory, where he settled near the present town of St. Mary's, Mo., and traded with the Indians in partnership with the commandant of Ste. Genevieve. Many Indians from the vicinity of his old post, who had been cowed by the Americans, were coaxed by Lorimier to his new home. They were welcomed by the Spaniards, who relied upon them for protection from the Osages and conferred upon them large tracts of land. Lorimier was appointed agent of Indian affairs and established their village at Apple Creek. He chose for himself the present site of Cape Girardeau, and in 1808 laid out this town from his own land grants. He was appointed captain of the militia and Spanish commandant of that district. After the Louisiana Purchase he was appointed by the United States government to be one of the judges of the court of common pleas. His Spanish land titles were rejected by the first board of land commissioners and were not confirmed until long after his death. Cape Girardeau did not emerge until 1840 from the cloud thus cast upon these grants.

Lorimier was called upon by the lieutenant-governors of Upper Louisiana to serve as interpreter to the chiefs of the several Indian nations and as conciliator. On many critical occasions he made perilous voyages, and through persuasion and gifts, kept peace and tranquillity in the country. He was given many concessions of land by the Spanish, and license to trade on the St. François, White, and Arkansas rivers. His first grant was for six thousand arpens, and his petition in 1799 for thirty thousand arpens was granted before the American occupation. In 1796 the first Americans came to his district and stimulated by his favor and encouragement others followed. His district became inhabited by the most intelligent farmers. Lorimier himself could neither read nor write but was undoubtedly a man of great natural ability. He spoke French, English, and several Indian languages with fluency. He had a beautiful signature and appended it to documents only after they had been read to him many times. He was a firm, brave, and successful commander, feared and respected by the Indians. His reputation for justice, both as an official and as a man, became firmly established. All his personal debts, even those made in gambling, were fully paid. He was twice married. His first wife was a half-breed of Shawnee and French blood named Charlotte Pemanpieh Bougainville. They had several children of whom one son was graduated from West Point. His second wife was Marie Berthiaume, also a half-breed Shawnee. He was a well-formed, handsome man, fond of dress and display. His profusion of hair was arranged in a long plait, fastened with ribbons, which he used as a whip for his horse while riding.

[Sources include Louis Houck, *The Spanish Régime in Mo.* (1909), vol. II, containing a transcript of Lorimier's journal for the years 1793–95; the same author's *Memorial Sketches of Pioneers* (1915) and *Hist. of Mo.* (1908), vol. II; F. A. Rozier, *Rozier's Hist. of the Early Settlement of the Miss. Valley* (1890); *Hist. of Southeast Mo.* (1888); *Jour. of Capt. Wm. Trent* (1871), ed. by A. T. Goodman; *The John Askin Papers*, vol. I (1928), ed. by M. M. Quaife; L. J. Kenny, "Geo. Rogers Clark in Ohio," *Ill. Cath. Hist. Rev.*, Jan. 1928; Census of St. Louis and Ste. Genevieve, 1787; original petitions for concession of land; Lorimier's will, dated Oct. 20, 1788; Ste. Genevieve archives. The last items are in the possession of the Mo. Hist. Soc.]   S. M. D.

LORING, CHARLES HARDING (Dec. 26, 1828–Feb. 5, 1907), naval officer, was born in Boston, Mass., the son of William Price and Elizabeth (Harding) Loring. He was a descendant of Deacon Thomas Loring of Axminster, Devonshire, England, who emigrated to America in 1634 and settled at Hingham, Mass. Charles received his early education in the public schools of his native city. Later, since technical schools were not established at that time, he became a machine-shop apprentice and thus began his career on a practical basis. On Feb. 26, 1851, he formally entered the navy by a competitive examination, in which he stood first in a group of fourteen.

During the next decade, he laid the foundation for his subsequent career, passing through the various naval grades and becoming chief engineer on Mar. 25, 1861. Among his assignments had been that of assistant to the engineer-in-chief, and as such he had had charge of the experimental work, particularly the testing of steam-engineering devices. The outbreak of the Civil War found him in active service, and he was first made fleet engineer of the North Atlantic station; later, he became general inspector of all the iron-clad steamers that were being constructed west of the Alleghanies, his duties including supervision over the famous "monitors."

After the Civil War, the question of supplanting simple with compound engines arose. In 1872 Loring and Charles H. Baker were appointed a board to consider this subject, and after an exhaustive study, they recommended the use of compound engines (*Report of the Secretary of the Navy*, 1873, pp. 120 ff.). For several years, Loring conducted thorough investigations in various phases of engineering details and the recommendations in his published reports have become standard engineering practice the world over. (See especially *Report of the Secretary of the Navy*, 1874, pp. 105 ff.) In 1881 he was a member of the "First Naval Advisory Board," significant because it brought about the abandonment of the old wooden naval ships and started work on the modern steel fighting ships. President Arthur in 1884 appointed Loring engineer-in-chief with the rank of rear admiral. The following year, he came into conflict with departmental politics and resigned this office. Thereafter he served on important experimental boards and contributed much to their researches up to his retirement from the navy on Dec. 26, 1890. During the Spanish-American War, he was recalled to active service and made inspector of engineering work in New York City.

He was well known throughout the engineering world and was president of the Engineers' Club of New York, and of the American Society of Mechanical Engineers (1891–92), the highest honor which his profession could offer him. In 1852 he married Ruth Malbon of Hingham, Mass., and they had one daughter. His death occurred at Hackettstown, N. J.

[C. H. Pope and K. P. Loring, *Loring Geneal.* (1917); *Jour. Am. Soc. Naval Engineers,* Feb. 1907; *Trans. Am. Soc. Mech. Engrs.,* vol. XXIX (1907); *Official Records of the Union and Confederate Navies in the War of the Rebellion*; L. R. Hamersly, *The Records of Living Officers of the U. S. Navy and Marine Corps* (5th ed., 1894); *Reg. of the Commissioned and Warrant Officers of the Navy of the U. S. and of the Marine Corps* (1907); *Army and Navy Reg.,* Feb. 9, 1907; *Army and Navy Jour.,* Feb. 9, 1907; *Who's Who in America,* 1906–07; *Brooklyn Daily Eagle,* Feb. 6, 1907.]
                                                                A. R. B.

LORING, CHARLES MORGRIDGE (Nov. 13, 1832–Mar. 18, 1922), national figure in civic betterment work, was born in Portland, Me., the son of Horace and Sarah (Willey) Loring and a descendant of Thomas Loring who emigrated to Hingham, Mass., in 1634. After his school days several trips to the West Indies in his father's vessels convinced him that this was not the calling he should follow and he set his face toward the West. After four years in a Chicago wholesale house he went to the little town of Minneapolis, Minn., in 1860, hoping the climate would be more suitable to his never too robust health. As merchant, miller, and dealer in real estate, he acquired what then passed for a considerable fortune. Merely as a successful business man he was not to be distinguished from others who utilized the opportunities of a new country. From the first, however, he exhibited a lively and intelligent interest in the civic problems of a community unhampered by fixed traditions. Politics as such did not attract him, although he held a minor office or two in his earlier years; his attention was drawn to the possibilities of enhancing the beauty and increasing the healthfulness of his city. He was active in the state horticultural society and in the forestry association, over each of which he was president for a time. In them his activities were only incidental to his major avocation—seeing that Minneapolis was provided with parks, playgrounds, and the like, laid out and equipped with consideration for future growth.

In 1864 Loring made his first definite move toward this goal when he persuaded a citizen to donate a small tract of land for a park. For years he struggled to secure the cooperation of a citizenry reluctant to spend money for anything that seemed to have no immediate practical utility. He saw them neglect many opportunities to acquire land cheaply for park purposes. Not until 1880 was any real step taken in the direction he desired to go; then a small sum appropriated by the city council permitted the improvement of a few acres donated several years before, and he not only supervised the laying out of paths and the planting of trees, but did much of the work with his own hands. In 1883 the state legislature, against the protest of the city council, created a board of park commissioners for Minneapolis and named Loring a member. Made president, he served in this capacity until 1890 when he failed of reëlection owing to a Democratic landslide. Elected again in 1892 he served a year and then resigned since the board contemplated purchasing land in which he had an interest. He was commissioner again from 1903 to 1906.

Whether or not on the board he labored incessantly for, and gave freely of his own means to, the cause, and before his death had the satisfaction of seeing Minneapolis equipped with a comprehensive system of parks, parkways, and playgrounds which form some of the principal attractions of the city. By his addresses, newspaper contributions, and ready advice he aroused dormant civic pride in many towns of the state. In Riverside, Cal., where he spent his winters from the early eighties until near the close of his life, he stimulated the same kind of betterments that he had in Minneapolis and it was through his efforts that Mount Rubidoux was made a scenic park and one of the first bird sanctuaries of the country, while the planting of thousands of trees about it was the direct result of his endeavors. Having become nationally known, he was consulted by people from all over the country and through the American Park and Outdoor Art Association, of which he was president in 1899 and 1900, he spread his gospel. While the whole Minneapolis park system was the outgrowth of his work and planning for the future, certain features peculiarly owed their origin to him. One of the last projects to receive his impress was the Victory Memorial Drive in the Grand Rounds which took form in accordance with his suggestions and to which he not only donated money to plant some six hundred trees dedicated to victims of the World War, but left a sum to provide for maintenance of the memorial. In his honor Central Park was renamed Loring Park. Loring was twice married: in 1855 to Emily Smith Crossman, who died in 1894, and on Nov. 28, 1895, to Florence Barton. He died at Minneapolis.

[Warren Upham and R. B. Dunlap, "Minn. Biogs.," *Minn. Hist. Soc. Colls.*, vol. XIV (1912); M. D. Shutter and J. S. McLain, *Progressive Men of Minn.* (1897); W. W. Folwell, *Hist. of Minn.*, vol. IV (1930); C. H. Pope and K. P. Loring, *Loring Geneal.* (1917); C. M. Loring, "Hist. of the Parks and Pub. Grounds of Minneapolis," *Minn. Hist. Soc. Colls.*, vol. XV (1915); *Minneapolis Tribune*, Mar. 19, 1922; birth record, Portland, Me.]   L. B. S.

LORING, EDWARD GREELY (Sept. 28, 1837–Apr. 23, 1888), ophthalmologist, who devised the first practical ophthalmoscope, was born in Boston, Mass., the second son of Judge Edward Greely and Harriet (Boott) Loring. He passed his boyhood in Boston and in Winthrop, where his father had a summer home, and there he acquired a fondness for boating which he retained through life. He prepared for college at the Boston Latin School and entered Harvard in 1857. At the end of his sophomore year, he went to Florence, Italy, and began the study of medicine. He spent three years between the clinics of Florence and Pisa, coming under the individual instruction of Dr. Grysanovski and, in anatomy, of Dr. Duranti of Pisa. Returning to Boston in 1862 he entered Harvard Medical School and received the degree of M.D. in 1864, taking the Boylston Prize on graduating with an essay on "The Causes of Exudation in Inflammation." He then became associated with Dr. Henry Willard Williams, Boston's pioneer ophthalmologist, as ophthalmic externe at the Boston City Hospital, and also followed the clinics at the Massachusetts Charitable Eye and Ear Infirmary. After a year of this training, he married, Jan. 3, 1866, Chevalita Jarves, a daughter of James Jackson Jarves [q.v.], and moved to Baltimore to begin practice. In another year he went to New York and became a partner of the noted ophthalmologist, Cornelius Rea Agnew. After six years he set up practice by himself and had a good and remunerative clientele. In 1883 his wife died and in 1886 he was married to Helen Swift, a niece of Judge Rapallo. He had no children by either marriage. On Apr. 23, 1888, when returning from the Hudson River, where he had superintended the fitting out of a yacht, he fell dead. A post mortem disclosed that the cause of death was coronary occlusion.

Loring had served as surgeon to the Brooklyn Eye and Ear Hospital, was one of the original staff of the Manhattan Eye and Ear Hospital and, at the time of his death, was surgeon to the New York Eye and Ear Infirmary. His greatest contribution to medicine was his improvement of the ophthalmoscope, an instrument for looking into the eye. The first ophthalmoscope, invented in 1847 by an English mathematician, Charles Babbage, consisted of a small plane mirror from the central portion of which the silvering had been removed. Through this hole the physician's eye looked into the eye of the patient, a light placed beside the patient's head being reflected by the mirror into the patient's eye. This was a rough affair, did not allow for varying refraction of the media of different eyes, and was hard to manipulate. Helmholtz in 1851 independently invented another ophthalmoscope, but Loring made the first practical instrument by gathering many little lenses on the edge of a disc behind the mirror that could be rotated by the forefinger to bring the lens best suited to the refraction of the eye under examination before the physician's eye (*Transactions of the American Ophthalmo-logical Society,* 1869, pp. 47–51). He brought out an improved form in 1874 which he demonstrated to the fifth international ophthalmological congress in New York two years later. His ophthalmoscope, though modified by many oculists, was in general use until, with the development of electric lighting, a small incandescent bulb was placed in the instrument and the eye ground illuminated by direct light. Loring wrote many papers on subjects connected with diseases of the eye. His *magnum opus* was his book entitled: *A Text Book on Ophthalmoscopy,* the first volume of which was published in 1886. The second volume, partially finished at his death, appeared in 1891, edited by his brother, Dr. Francis Boott Loring of Washington, D. C. Loring did much by his writings and by the perfection of the ophthalmoscope to place American ophthalmology on an equal footing with the best practice of the world.

[*Trans. Am. Ophthalmol. Soc.,* vol. V (1890), containing bibliography; *Am. Encyc. of Ophthalmol.,* vol. X (1917); *Hist. of the Boston City Hospital* (1906); *Boston Medic. and Surgic. Jour.,* May 3, 1888; J. J. Walsh, *Hist. of the Medic. Soc. of the State of N. Y.* (1907); *Medic. Record* (N. Y.), Apr. 28, 1888; C. H. Pope and K. P. Loring, *Loring Geneal.* (1917); *N. Y. Times,* Apr. 25, 1888.]   W.L.B.

LORING, ELLIS GRAY (Apr. 14, 1803– May 24, 1858), lawyer and anti-slavery advocate, was born in Boston, Mass., the only son of James Tyng Loring, an apothecary, who died in 1805, and Relief (Faxon) Cookson Loring. He was descended from Thomas Loring who emigrated to America in 1634 and settled in Hingham, Mass. From the Latin School, where he was distinguished for scholarship, and where he made Emerson's friendship, he went to Harvard College. He was a member of the class of 1823, attaining membership in Phi Beta Kappa, but he left in May 1823, when members of his class were dismissed for resistance to college discipline. Later he studied law and in 1827 he began a successful career at the bar. Troubled by the existence of slavery, he was "one of the little band who assembled, on the evening of January 1st, 1831, . . . to consider the expediency of organizing a New England Anti-Slavery Society" (the *Liberator,* June 4, 1858, p. 91). These twelve zealots were of divided counsel. Loring favored "gradualism" as opposed to Garrison's "immediateism." The constitution called for "immediate freedom," and Loring withheld his

signature. But by January 1833 he was holding office in the society.

There were many aspects to Loring's support of the abolition movement. Unlike Garrison, he had social prominence to lose: the movement cost him many clients and the friendly intercourse of leading Boston families. He gave decisive financial support, without which the *Liberator* could not have continued. On Oct. 29, 1827, he had married Louisa Gilman and together they made their home a center for anti-slavery workers, to whom other doors were closed. Here Harriet Martineau visited and observed the movement at close range. Loring opened his house to fugitive slaves as well and was perhaps the first lawyer to take a colored boy into his office to train him for the bar. More widely known abolitionists, as Dr. Channing, drew strength from his counsel. From his hand Wendell Phillips received his first anti-slavery pamphlet. Though he shrank from speaking in public, Loring could on occasion argue to good purpose, notably in the hearing before the legislative committee considering Gov. Edward Everett's suggestion that the abolitionists be repressed.

In anti-slavery as in other matters, Loring was of liberal but moderate views. He opposed third-party sentiment in the American Anti-Slavery Society and also Phillips' view that abolition must be sought either in blood or over the ruins of the church and the Union. In *An Address to the Abolitionists of Massachusetts on the Subject of Political Action,* printed about 1838, he sketched the tactics by which agitation should be conducted: by petitioning legislative bodies, by interrogating candidates publicly, and by using the suffrage. In his profession he was rather a chamber counsel than an advocate. His best-known argument was for the slave Med, brought to Massachusetts by her mistress (*Commonwealth* vs. *Thomas Aves,* 35 *Mass.,* 193). On *habeas corpus* proceedings Loring won against Benjamin R. Curtis. The case established the principle that a slave brought voluntarily by his owner into Massachusetts could not be removed from the state against his will. Justice Story wrote: "I have rarely seen so thorough and exact arguments as those made by Mr. B. R. Curtis, and yourself. They exhibit learning, research, and ability, of which any man may be proud" (W. W. Story, *Life and Letters of Joseph Story,* 1851, II, 235). In his petition for the pardon of Abner Kneeland, convicted of blasphemy, he made a splendid defense of free speech. For some years prior to his death he had withdrawn from public observation, being content that others should assume prominence in the movement he had helped to launch. He has sometimes been confused with his distant kinsman, Edward Greely Loring, United States commissioner, who was attacked by the abolitionists for the rendition of Burns, a fugitive slave.

[W. P. and F. J. Garrison, *Wm. Lloyd Garrison, 1805–1875* (4 vols., 1885–89), vols. I–III; A. H. Grimké, *Wm. Lloyd Garrison* (1891); Lindsay Swift, *Wm. Lloyd Garrison* (1911); W. H. Channing, *The Life of Wm. Ellery Channing, D.D.* (1880); Henry Wilson, *Hist. of the Rise and Fall of the Slave Power in America,* vol. I (1872); C. H. Pope and K. P. Loring, *Loring Geneal.* (1917); the *Liberator,* May 28, June 4, 18, 1858; *Boston Transcript,* May 25, 1858.]

C. F.

LORING, FREDERICK WADSWORTH

(Dec. 12, 1848–Nov. 5, 1871), author, journalist, was born in Boston, Mass., the first of three sons of David Loring, a cabinet maker, and Mary Hall Stodder, a native New Englander. The first Loring in America was Deacon Thomas Loring who came from Devonshire, England, and joined the Hingham colony in Massachusetts in 1634. Under the guidance of his mother, Frederick read and absorbed English literature and was well versed in Shakespeare at the age of seven. Though she died when he was eleven years old, she left an indelible mark upon her devoted son who inherited her sympathetic sensitiveness and intelligence. He was sent to Phillips Academy at Andover, Mass., and entered Harvard in 1866. Here he abhorred the exact sciences and used his pen to extravagance in ridiculing mathematical formulas. Only his unusual promise kept him within the pale. After the death of his friend Prof. Elbridge J. Cutler, which was the second great grief of his life, he was befriended by James Russell Lowell. He was a regular contributor to the *Harvard Advocate* and while at college showed a passion for the drama. He made friends of actors and dramatists. Miss Mazie Mitchel, dramatist, permitted him to revise an act of her play and had the play produced. During these years also, to assist a friend, he wrote *Wild Rose,* which was produced with success in Boston by George Selwyn.

After his graduation in 1870, Loring became assistant editor of the Boston *Saturday Evening Gazette.* Later he was connected with the *Boston Daily Advertiser* and *Every Saturday,* "a journal of choice reading." Meanwhile he contributed short stories as well as short poems to the *Atlantic Monthly,* New York *Independent,* New York *World,* and *Appletons' Journal.* A serial story, "Two College Friends," which appeared in *Old and New* (April, July 1871), was published in book form later in 1871. His best-known poem, "In the Church Yard at Fred-

ericksburg," first appeared in the *Atlantic Monthly* for September 1870. *The Boston Dip, and Other Verses* was published a year later. The publisher's advertisement quotes the *New York Tribune* as saying the poems were noticeable as "celebrating young love with a tenderness, flavored with a certain cool humor which might have been done by Thackeray in that fresh, earnest, enthusiastic stage of his literary career which he depicts in Arthur Pendennis."

In 1871 Loring was sent with the Wheeler Expedition as correspondent for *Appletons' Journal.* His reports, written always in a light and humorous vein, were interesting. Apparently safe from the many dangers he had experienced Loring took the Wickenburg and La Paz (Arizona) stage on his way home. The stage was attacked by Apaches and he was one of those killed.

[C. H. Pope and K. P. Loring, *Loring Geneal.* (1917); *Triennial Report of the Secretary of the Class of 1870 of Harvard Coll.* (1873); H. H. Bancroft, *Hist. of the Pacific States of North America,* vol. XII (1888), "Arizona and New Mexico"; T. E. Farish, *Hist. of Ariz.,* vol. VIII (1918); *Appletons' Jour.,* Dec. 9, 1871; the *Weekly Ariz. Miner,* Nov. 11, 1871; *Boston Daily Advertiser,* Nov. 14, 16, 1871; information from the Division of Vital Statistics for the state of Mass.]

F. W. S.

LORING, GEORGE BAILEY (Nov. 8, 1817–

Sept. 14, 1891), physician, agriculturist, political leader, was born at North Andover, Mass., the son of Bailey and Sally Pickman Osgood Loring and a descendant of Thomas Loring who emigrated to Hingham, Mass., in 1634. He attended Franklin Academy at North Andover and graduated from Harvard College in 1838, a classmate of James Russell Lowell. Four years later the Harvard Medical School awarded him the degree of M.D. After a few months of practice in his ancestral village he became a surgeon at the Marine Hospital at Chelsea, Mass. During his seven years of service in that institution he made an impression sufficient to win an appointment as commissioner to revise the marine hospital system of the United States. He left the hospital, however, in 1850, removed in 1851 to Salem, Mass., and thereafter devoted himself to agriculture and politics. He developed a stock farm which became widely known as "Loring Manor." He speedily made himself sufficiently useful in the Democratic party to receive the postmastership of Salem from the Pierce administration and held the office from 1853 to 1857. After this first step he skilfully made his two new interests play complementary rôles in furthering his personal advancement.

In 1856 Loring attended the National Democratic Convention as a member of the Massachusetts delegation. After 1861 he allied himself with the War Democrats. In a Fourth of July oration at Salem in 1862 he rejoiced that "all our desire is manifested in the Flag which we still call our own, and from which no star has been stricken by hand of ours." After this speech he steadily developed into a popular orator. His tall robust figure, his handsome face, and his dignified manner made him a notable figure at public gatherings. His oratory, as over-decorated as a Victorian interior, pleased the New England taste of his day. He never championed unpopular causes, and his orations—which he was careful to have printed—reflected the religious and political conservatism of his times. In 1864, chafing, perhaps, under the disadvantages of being a Northern Democrat in the changed situation brought about by the war, he publicly renounced his allegiance to his old party and became a Republican. The change of standards proved almost immediately advantageous. He served in 1866–67 as a member of the Massachusetts House of Representatives. He was chairman of the Republican state committee (1869–76) and was a delegate to the national conventions of that party in 1868, 1872, and 1876. He was president of the state Senate from 1873 to 1876 and representative in Congress for the next four years. When his constituency recalled him from Washington in the election of 1880, President Garfield saved his political fortunes by selecting him in 1881 for commissioner of agriculture, a post which he held until the inauguration of Cleveland.

Garfield's choice was excellent. Loring was sincerely interested in agriculture and was an intelligent leader in the contemporary efforts to improve husbandry, taking care, however, that his activities should aid in making him conspicuous. From 1860 to 1877 he represented the Essex Agricultural Society on the Massachusetts Board of Agriculture and served on the same board by appointment of the governor in the years 1888–90. In this capacity he did much to further the interests of the recently established Massachusetts Agricultural College and lectured on stock-farming in that institution from 1869 to 1872. In 1864 he founded the New England Agricultural Society and served as its president until 1889. He published in 1876 *The Farm-Yard Club of Jotham,* a curious volume intended to popularize discussions of agricultural subjects. The book is in part a loose narrative characterized by a somewhat sugary sentimentality and gives a romanticized picture of the rural life that Loring knew. The story is constantly interrupted by sensible essays on many aspects of hus-

bandry presented in the guise of papers read before the Farm-Yard Club. Late in life Loring disclosed even more intimately than in the volume of 1876 his attitude toward agriculture. He remarked of his former friend, Ralph Waldo Emerson: "His aesthetic love of nature, which made him rejoice in a bare hillside with stumps and briars . . . was in me a practical reality, which moved me as it did him, but with the addition of a farmer's consideration of the value of the scenes he loved. Nature to him meant God; to me it meant also the rule God gave man over the fowls of the air and the beasts of the field" (*A Year in Portugal,* p. 160). Such an outlook helps to explain why Loring, like his good friend Louis Agassiz, rejected Darwinism with "scorn and contempt."

In his latter years Loring's mind ranged over a variety of subjects. He wrote, among other things, *A Vindication of General Samuel Holden Parsons against Charges of Treasonable Correspondence During the Revolutionary War* (1888). In 1889–90 he tried his hand at diplomacy when he served as minister to Portugal under appointment by President Benjamin Harrison. His rambling travelogue, *A Year in Portugal,* was published in the year of his death, 1891. He died on Sept. 14 from heart disease following an acute attack of dysentery. He was twice married: on Nov. 6, 1851, to Mary Toppan Pickman, who died in 1878; and on June 10, 1880, to Anna (Smith) Hildreth, the widow of Charles H. Hildreth.

[L. H. Bailey, *Cyc. of Agric.,* vol. IV (1909); *Biog. Dir. Am. Cong.* (1928); C. H. Pope and K. P. Loring, *Loring Geneal.* (1917); the *Critic,* Sept. 19, 1891; *Boston Transcript,* Sept. 14, 1891; *N. Y. Times,* Sept. 15, 1891.]   R. H. G.

LORING, JOSHUA (Aug. 3, 1716–October 1781), naval officer, Loyalist, was born in Boston, the son of Joshua and Hannah (Jackson) Loring and the descendant of Thomas and Jane (Newton) Loring, who emigrated from Axminster, Devonshire, England, to Dorchester, Mass., about 1634 and, later, settled in Hingham, Mass. In his youth he learned the tanner's trade, being apprenticed to James Mears of Roxbury. About 1740 he married Mary Curtis, daughter of Samuel Curtis of Roxbury. When continual warfare between England and France made privateering attractive to many New Englanders, he became commander of a brigantine privateer, which was captured by two French men-of-war in August 1744. The next few months he spent as a prisoner in the Fortress of Louisburg. The outbreak of the French and Indian War again found him in the naval service. On Dec. 19, 1757, he was commissioned captain in the British navy. In 1759 he commanded naval operations on Lakes George and Champlain and, the next year, on Lake Ontario, and he is now usually referred to as Commodore Loring. He was severely wounded in 1760. He participated in the capture of Quebec by General Wolfe and the subsequent conquest of Canada by General Amherst. At the close of the war he retired on half pay and settled down at Jamaica Plain, Roxbury. Joshua Loring was one of the five commissioners of revenue and became a member of General Gage's council by a writ of mandamus. He was sworn in on Aug. 8, 1774. Gage's appointees were immediately subjected to the greatest pressure to induce them to resign. Writing under date of Aug. 30, John Andrews said, "Late in the evening a member waited upon Commodore Loring, and in a friendly way advis'd him to follow the example of his *townsmun* (Isaac Winslow who had already resigned). He desir'd time to consider of it. They granted it, but acquainted him, if he did not comply, he must expect to be waited upon by a larger number, actuated by a different spirit. His principal apprehension was that he should lose his *half pay*" (*Proceedings of Massachusetts Historical Society,* ser. 1, vol. VIII, 1866, p. 349).

Loring is said to have deemed the cause of his countrymen just, but he did not believe it could succeed. On the morning of the battle of Lexington, he left his home and rode into the British lines of Boston, remarking to a neighbor, "I have always eaten the king's bread, and always intend to" (Drake, *post,* p. 417). On Mar. 30, 1775, the Provincial Congress of Massachusetts denounced Loring and other irreconcilables as implacable enemies of their country. On Oct. 16, 1778, he was proscribed and banished by act of the General Court. His home at Roxbury was, for a while, the headquarters of General Nathanael Greene, and then a hospital for American soldiers. The passage of the confiscation act in 1779 made his property the possession of the state, for whose benefit it was eventually sold. Upon the evacuation of Boston, he went to England and was the recipient of a pension from the crown until his decease at Highgate. In 1789 his widow died at Englesfield, Berkshire County, England, where their son, Joshua Loring [*q.v.*], had settled after the Revolution.

[J. H. Stark, *The Loyalists of Mass.* (1910); E. A. Jones, *The Loyalists of Mass.* (1930); F. S. Drake, *The Town of Roxbury* (1878); Lorenzo Sabine, *Biog. Sketches of the Loyalists* (1864), vol. II; Justin Winsor, *The Memorial Hist. of Boston,* vols. II, III (1881); *Proc. Mass. Hist. Soc.* ser. 1, vol. VIII, ser. 2, vol. X (1866–96); *Colls. Mass. Hist. Soc.* ser. 4, vol. IX (1871); *Pubs. of the Colonial Soc. of Mass.,* vol. XVII

(1915); *Letters and Diary of John Rowe,* ed. by A. R. Cunningham (1903); C. H. Pope and K. P. Loring, *Loring Geneal.* (1917).]   J. G. V–D.

LORING, JOSHUA (Nov. 1, 1744–August 1789), Loyalist, was born at Hingham, Mass., the son of Mary (Curtis) and Joshua Loring [*q.v.*]. As a young man he served with the army; on July 11, 1761, he was commissioned ensign, became lieutenant on Aug. 1, 1765, and retired in 1768. For his military services he was granted 20,000 acres of land in New Hampshire. In 1769 he was appointed permanent high sheriff of Massachusetts and married, on Oct. 19 of the same year, Elizabeth Lloyd of Boston. He became a pew-holder in King's Chapel and a citizen of importance. He signed a protest against the solemn league and covenant issued by the committee of safety, and he was one of the one hundred and twenty-three who affixed their names to an address approving the course of Governor Hutchinson and presented it to him on the eve of his departure for England in 1774. He signed a similar address to General Gage the next year. One of the last official acts of Gage was to sign a proclamation of Oct. 7, 1775, appointing him sole vendue-master and auctioneer. When General Howe evacuated Boston, in March 1776, Loring went with the royal army to Halifax, and early the next year was appointed commissary of prisoners in the British army.

In the conduct of this office he made himself detested by the Whig leaders, who charged him with excessive cruelty in his treatment of prisoners. Ethan Allen complained of his murder of two thousand prisoners. Others affirmed that he charged for supplies furnished to prisoners long after they were dead, so that he must be "feeding the dead and starving the living" (Frank Moore, *Diary of the American Revolution,* 1860, vol. II, 210). Elias Boudinot, who occupied a corresponding position in the American army, accused him of neglect and ill-treatment, although he admitted that the situation had been very much worse before Loring became commissary. On Aug. 16, 1777, Boudinot sent to Washington Loring's memorandum denying these charges and pointing out the lack of interest in Congress for the welfare of those colonials who had been taken prisoner (Boudinot papers, *post*). The truth is not easy to discover. War is grim and conditions in the best military prisons are always bad enough. It is probable, too, that partisan feeling was responsible for some exaggeration. The letters of General Gold Selleck Silliman testify that Loring treated him with "complaisance, kindness, and friendship" (Thomas Jones, *post,* II, 425).

Banished from Massachusetts, he spent the last years of his life in Berkshire, England. One of his sons, Sir John Wentworth Loring, became a Vice Admiral in the British Navy and another son, Henry Lloyd Loring, was archdeacon of Calcutta.

[Transcripts of Elias Boudinot papers and the Washington papers in the Lib. of Cong.; J. H. Stark, *The Loyalists of Mass.* (1910); Lorenzo Sabine, *Biog. Sketches of the Loyalists* (1864), vol. II; E. A. Jones, *The Loyalists of Mass.* (1930); Thomas Jones, *Hist. of N. Y. during the Rev. War* (2 vols., 1879); F. S. Drake, *The Town of Roxbury* (1878); Peter Force, *Am. Archives*, ser. 4, vol. III (1840), col. 984; *Letters and Diary of John Rowe,* ed. by A. R. Cunningham (1903); H. W. Foote, *Annals of King's Chapel,* vol. II (1896); C. H. Pope and K. P. Loring, *Loring Geneal.* (1917).]   J. G. V–D.

LORING, WILLIAM WING (Dec. 4, 1818–Dec. 30, 1886), a soldier who fought under three flags, was descended from Thomas Loring who emigrated to America in 1634 and settled in Hingham, Mass. His father, Reuben Loring, a native of Hingham, moved to Wilmington, N. C., and there married Hannah Kenan. William was born in Wilmington but at an early age moved with his parents to Florida, where as a youth he fought with the 2nd Florida Volunteers against the Seminoles in engagements at Wahoo Swamp, Withahoochee, and Alachua, and at nineteen years of age, won for himself a second lieutenancy. He prepared for college at Alexandria, Va., attended Georgetown College, studied law, returned to Florida as a member of the state bar, and was elected to the state legislature for three years. He was appointed captain, Mounted Rifles, May 27, 1846, and major, Feb. 16, 1847, accompanying General Scott's expedition to Mexico and participating in the campaign from Vera Cruz to the capture of the city of Mexico (T. F. Rodenbough, *From Everglade to Cañon with the Second Dragoons,* 1875, pp. 140–41). He commanded his regiment at Contreras and led the fighting at Chapultepec where he lost an arm. For these acts of gallantry he was brevetted lieutenant-colonel, Aug. 20, 1847, and colonel, Sept. 13, 1847. He was promoted lieutenant-colonel in the regular army, Mar. 15, 1848, and the following year crossed the continent with his regiment in the van of the army of gold-seekers. After a march of some twenty-five hundred miles, he assumed command of the military department of Oregon, 1849–51. During the five years following he was stationed with his regiment in Texas, being promoted colonel, Dec. 30, 1856, and engaging hostile Indians in several skirmishes in New Mexico, 1856–58. In the latter year he marched his command into Utah, taking part during the years 1858–59 in the so-called Mormon War under

Gen. Albert Sidney Johnston (T. F. Rodenbough, *The Army of the United States,* 1896, pp. 200–01). Granted leave of absence thereafter, he spent a year traveling in Europe, Egypt, and the Holy Land, studying foreign armies. Returning to the United States, he commanded the Department of New Mexico during the years 1860–61, and although he was opposed to secession, he approved of state rights and resigned from the army on May 13, 1861, to join the Confederacy.

His ability as a military commander was promptly recognized by his appointment as brigadier-general on May 20, 1861. He was given a command in West Virginia but in December 1861 his army was included in Gen. "Stonewall" Jackson's command. He took part in Jackson's Valley campaign in 1862 but after a violent controversy with Jackson [see biography of Thomas Jonathan Jackson] he was detached and placed in command of the army in southwestern Virginia. Meanwhile he had been promoted major-general, February 1862. Late in 1862 he was transferred to the Southwest where he participated in engagements at Grenada, Miss., and Champion Hills (F. V. Greene, *The Mississippi,* 1882, pp. 100 ff., and *Personal Memoirs of U. S. Grant,* vol. I, 1885, p. 435). Thereafter he served as a corps commander in Georgia, Mississippi, and Tennessee, and was active in the battles of Franklin and Nashville, where he was second in command to Gen. John B. Hood (J. D. Cox, *The March to the Sea,* 1882, pp. 88–125). His last Civil War service was under Gen. Joseph E. Johnston in the Carolinas, where, in April 1865, he surrendered to Sherman.

For a time he engaged in banking in New York City but in 1869, in company with certain other officers of the late Confederacy, Loring entered the military service of the Khedive of Egypt with the rank of brigadier-general, first acting as inspector-general, and later, in the year 1870, assuming command of the defenses of the city of Alexandria and of all Egyptian coast defenses. In the years 1875–76 he took part in the Egyptian expedition against Abyssinia and participated in the important battle of Kaya-Khor. Promoted to the grade of general of division, he was elevated by the Khedive to the dignity of a Pasha, and decorated with the Egyptian orders of the Osmanli and of the Medjidie. In the year 1879, in company with other American officers, he was mustered out of the Khedive's service and returned to the United States, residing for a time in Florida and later making his home in New York City. He contributed articles to magazines and to the press and in 1884 published a book: *A Confederate Soldier in Egypt,* which gives an entertaining narrative of his ten years' service under the Khedive. He died in New York City in his sixty-eighth year of an acute heart attack. At the time of his death he had in preparation an autobiography, "Fifty Years a Soldier." He never married.

[In addition to sources cited see: F. B. Heitman, *Hist. Reg. and Dict. of the U. S. Army* (1903), vol. I; *Battles and Leaders of the Civil War* (4 vols., 1887–88); *War of the Rebellion: Official Records (Army)*; *Confed. Mil. Hist.* (1899), vol. XI; J. M. Morgan, *Recollections of a Rebel Reefer* (1917); C. H. Pope and K. P. Loring, *Loring Geneal.* (1917); *N. Y. Herald* and *World* (N. Y.), Dec. 31, 1886. The genealogy gives Loring's middle name as *Wallace.*]   C. D. R.

LOSKIEL, GEORGE HENRY (Nov. 7, 1740–Feb. 23, 1814), bishop of the Renewed Unitas Fratrum or Moravian Church, was born at Angermuende, Courland, Russia, the son of John Christian Loskiel, a Lutheran preacher. He studied theology at Halle and on Dec. 26, 1759, while he was still a student, joined the Moravian Church. On leaving the university he taught and filled various pastoral charges. He was married to Maria Magdalena Barlach of Volmer, Livonia, on June 27, 1771. In 1782 he was appointed superintendent of the mission in Livonia and agent for the Church in Russia. He occupied himself also for ten years, 1791–1801, with administrative and financial matters in connection with mission affairs. He was consecrated bishop on Mar. 14, 1802, and sailed almost immediately for the United States to take charge of the work in North America in place of John G. Cunow.

He reached the Moravian headquarters, Bethlehem, Pa., at a critical time in the history of the Moravian Church on the continent. The original establishments had been founded in 1742 on land purchased by funds advanced from the estate of Count Zinzendorf. The business depression of 1750, following the Treaty of Aix-la-Chapelle, had thrown Zinzendorf's affairs into bankruptcy and receivers had been appointed. At that time investments in the New World were looked upon with little favor, for France and England were on the brink of another war. As a consequence, in 1750 the entire establishment of the Moravian Church in the English colonies had been ordered to shift for itself in the belief that the investment was lost. This attitude on the part of the European authorities at Herrnhut continued until after the Revolution when, affairs in Europe having been rehabilitated, the receivers were discharged and the estate became a sustaining fund for the worldwide mission operations of the Church. By that time circumstances had altered the fortunes and possibilities of the Bethlehem group. The property had advanced in value, and the attention of the Herrnhut authorities was now riveted upon reëstablishing a connection that had been broken for a generation. It was too late, however, for such a backward movement, and Cunow, whom Loskiel replaced, had found himself in a generation that knew not the old times. On all sides he had been met with refusal when he proposed a return to the old paternalism and European control. As a consequence he gave up his task, and the suave and diplomatic Loskiel took his place.

For ten years this shrewd and clever scholar labored to bring about a compromise whereby the European and American interests might be separated. There was, on the part of the Bethlehem group, no denial of either the debt or the obligation to pay interest. Upon the basis of this acknowledgment, Loskiel proceeded to effect the desired result. From Pennsylvania to North Carolina, he jogged from station to station; and it is solely to his credit that at the conference of 1810 a scheme of adjustment was adopted, and that from it there emerged a successful plan of separation. There is no doubt that the anxieties incident to his strenuous efforts shortened his life. Although he was relieved of his duties in May 1811, the state of his health and the outbreak of war with England prevented his return to Europe, and he died at Bethlehem in 1814. His was a work that, necessarily, was performed without trumpets and drums. Hence history has often omitted his name from the list of those who have contributed to the creation of the American national spirit. Nevertheless he was the first of the Moravian bishops to visualize and strive for a new spirit of nationalization and to bring about, in those early days, a process of Americanization. He was the author of *Geschichte der Mission der Evangelischen Brueder unter den Indianern in Nordamerika* (1789), translated into English as *History of the Mission of the United Brethren among the Indians in North America* (London, 1794); and a devotional book, *Etwas für' Herz* (c. 1791).

[*Bethlehem Diary*, 1801–14, *Gemein Nachrichten*, 1802–12, and Loskiel's diary of his journeys, all MSS. in Bethlehem Archives; J. M. Levering, *Hist. of Bethlehem* (1892); E. W. Cröger, *Geschichte der Erneuerten Brüderkirche*, vol. III (1854); J. M. Hark, Introduction to *Extempore on a Wagon; A Metrical Narrative of a Journey from Bethlehem, Pa., to the Indian Town of Goshen, Ohio, in the Autumn of 1803* (1887).]   A. G. R.

LOSSING, BENSON JOHN (Feb. 12, 1813–June 3, 1891), wood-engraver, author, editor, son of John and Miriam (Dorland) Lossing, was born at Beekman, Dutchess County, N. Y. The family name descended from Pietre Pieterse Lassingh, a Dutch settler who came to Albany about 1658. John Lossing, a small farmer, died when his son was an infant, and the boy's mother died when he was about twelve years old. Attendance at the district schools for three years gave him the only formal education he was to receive. At thirteen he was apprenticed to a watchmaker at Poughkeepsie and his early life was hard. In spite of many obstacles, however, he found time for reading and study, especially in the field of history. When he was twenty-two years old he became a joint editor and proprietor of the *Poughkeepsie Telegraph,* the official Democratic newspaper of Dutchess County; later he was joint editor of a literary fortnightly called the *Poughkeepsie Casket.* From J. A. Adams, who drew illustrations for his periodical, he learned the art of engraving on wood. In 1838 he moved to New York City, where he established himself as a wood-engraver. From June 1839 to May 1841 he edited and illustrated the weekly *Family Magazine* for J. S. Redfield. In his leisure moments he wrote an *Outline History of the Fine Arts,* which appeared in 1840 as No. 103 of Harpers' Family Library.

In 1848 Lossing conceived the idea of writing a narrative sketchbook treating of scenes and objects associated with the American Revolution. Harper & Brothers advanced funds to enable him to carry out the project, which ultimately took the form of the *Pictorial Field Book of the Revolution,* in two large octavo volumes. In gathering material for this work the author traveled more than eight thousand miles in the United States and Canada, occasionally returning home with sketches from which he made drawings on the block for the engraver. The preparation of the book consumed about five years. It was published in parts, 1850–52, and gave Lossing a wide reputation. For the next thirty-five years he was a prolific writer and editor of books mostly on popular subjects in American history. His historical and biographical works comprise more than forty titles, including: *Our Countrymen, or Brief Memoirs of Eminent Americans* (1855); *The Hudson, from the Wilderness to the Sea* (*Art-Journal,* London, Jan. 1, 1860–Dec. 1, 1861; issued in book form in 1866); *The Life and Times of Philip Schuyler* (2 vols., 1860–73); *Pictorial Field-Book of the War of 1812* (1868); *Pictorial History of the Civil War* (3 vols., 1866–68, later editions entitled *Pictorial Field-Book . . .*); *Our Country* (2 vols., published in parts, 1876–78);

A Biography of James A. Garfield (1882); *History of New York City* (1884); *The Empire State* (1887). Among his many enterprises the *American Historical Record and Repertory of Notes and Queries,* a magazine which he edited in the years 1872–74, deserves mention. One of his best pieces of work was *A Memorial of Alexander Anderson, M.D., the First Engraver on Wood in America* (1872), a paper he read in 1870 before the New York Historical Society.

Although to the appraising eye of the twentieth century Lossing appears to have been primarily a successful popularizer of American history, his *Pictorial Field Book of the American Revolution* still commands respect. It was an original idea well executed, and the antiquarian of today turns to it for details which cannot be found elsewhere. Lossing was married first, June 18, 1833, to Alice, daughter of Thomas Barritt; she died in 1855, and on Nov. 18, 1856, he married Helen, daughter of Nehemiah Sweet. He made his home at "The Ridge," Dover Plains, N. Y., near the Connecticut boundary.

[G. W. Willis, in *Appletons' Jour.,* July 20, 1872, portr.; Nathaniel Paine, in *Proc. Worcester Soc. of Antiquity, 1891* (1892), with a list of Lossing's works; *Proc. Am. Antiq. Soc.,* n.s., VII (1891); F. L. Mott, *A Hist. of Am. Mags.* (1930); *Am. Ancestry,* vol. III (1888); C. E. Fitch, *Encyc. of Biog. of N. Y.,* vol. II (1916); J. H. Smith, *Hist. of Duchess County, N. Y.* (1882); *N. Y. Daily Tribune,* June 4, 1891.]
L. S. M.

LOTHROP, ALICE LOUISE HIGGINS (May 28, 1870–Sept. 2, 1920), social worker, was born in Boston. The daughter of Albert H. and Adelaide A. (Everson) Higgins, she was descended from Richard Higgins of Plymouth, a founder of Eastham, Mass. She was educated in local private schools and at twenty-eight entered the service of the Associated Charities as a worker in training. Her rare qualifications for social service were at once manifest, and when in 1900 she was entrusted with the secretaryship of a Charities district, she showed such qualities of leadership, such grasp of community problems that after but two years' experience, supplemented by a summer course at the New York School of Philanthropy, she was called to headquarters as general secretary. Upon her marriage, in 1913, to a Boston business man, William H. Lothrop, she resigned the secretaryship and was made a director of the society for life.

Alice Higgins was a breathing refutation of the old charge that organized charity is necessarily mechanized, formal, heartless. She was, as Dr. Samuel M. Crothers said, "not only a clear intelligence, but a great soul" (*The Family,* December 1920, p. 2). She interpreted family cases in terms of community needs, yet never lost sight of the individual. To the efficiency and sound judgment of the born executive and the swift-moving, original mind that pierced beyond conditions to underlying causes she added quick sympathies, perennial freshness of interest, buoyancy, and a stimulating faith in other people. For ten years she may be said to have animated the Associated Charities. Her influence went far beyond the society; for in practice as in her sixteen years (1904–20) of teaching in the Boston School of Social Work, she upheld her belief that interrelated social agencies should strengthen one another. Her support meant much to the medical-social group which began work in 1905 at the Massachusetts General Hospital under the leadership of Dr. Richard C. Cabot, and she did much to spread the modern medical-social viewpoint among Boston workers. She helped to shape important social legislation, including the provision for state inspection of charitable corporations and the Massachusetts mothers' aid law; she served on the Massachusetts Child Labor Commission, on tuberculosis boards, and in the Civic League. She was active in founding the American Association for Organizing Family Social Work, largely for the sake of the Boston society, some of whose directors could see no point in studying methods pursued in other places. Said she, "No movement so provincialized could live" (*Ibid.*, p. 16). She remained chairman of the executive and administration committees of the American Association from 1914 to her death.

In 1906, while the ruins of San Francisco still smoked, she entered on her first signal service in disaster relief. She spent some nine weeks in San Francisco, where, in cooperation with Lee Frankel and Oscar K. Cushing she organized rehabilitation practice which served as a model in later disasters. After the fires at Chelsea (1908) and Salem (1914), and the explosion at Halifax (1917), she showed herself an expert. It was she who after the Halifax explosion dispatched with the Red Cross contingent eye-surgeons whose prompt aid saved the sight of many gashed by flying glass. Her connection with the Red Cross began in 1916, when she developed plans for the Emergency Relief Unit of the Boston chapter. When America entered the war, she was the first division director of civilian relief to be appointed. She had to break new ground, and much that was vital in the success of Home Service to soldiers' families was due to her initiative. Dr. Crothers used to say, "We always knew where to find Mrs. Lothrop. It was where the need was greatest, the issue most

vital" (*Ibid.*, p. 2). She died at her home in Newtonville.

[K. C. Higgins, *Richard Higgins and His Descendants* (1918), and *Supp.* (1924); *Boston Transcript*, Sept. 3, 11, 1920; *Survey*, Sept. 15, 1920; Memorial number of *The Family* (organ Am. Asso. for Organizing Family Social Work), Dec. 1920.]   M. B. H.

LOTHROP, AMY [See WARNER, ANNA BARTLETT, 1820–1915].

LOTHROP, DANIEL (Aug. 11, 1831–Mar. 18, 1892), publisher, was born in Rochester, N. H., the son of Daniel and Sophia (Horne) Lothrop. Both his parents were of American descent for several generations; his father, descended from Mark Lothrop who was in Salem, Mass., in 1643, also numbered John and Priscilla Alden among his ancestors. Daniel was given a classical education to prepare him for college, but at fourteen was diverted to a business career when an elder brother asked him to take charge of his drug store while its owner studied medicine. The youthful manager found the Rochester store so profitable that in 1848 he opened others in Newmarket and Laconia. In 1850 he bought out a book store in Dover, N. H. Soon he introduced the sale of books into his drug stores and later made some small experiments in publishing. In 1856 he went West and established a drug store and a bank in St. Peter, Minn., which was then the capital of the Territory; but the transfer of the seat of government to St. Paul and the panic of 1857 caused the failure of both ventures.

After a period of inactivity, he returned East, and in 1868 established a publishing business in Boston. He had carefully matured his plans and determined that his policy should be to cater to the needs of Sunday-schools and to specialize in juvenile literature. He met with such success in this undertaking that, notwithstanding severe losses incurred in the famous Boston fire of 1872, he expanded his business in 1874 and again in 1887. He sought to choose the material he published for its interest as well as for its informative and edifying qualities, and though his Sunday-school books had the inevitable moral note, they usually contained things that appealed to the children themselves rather than the more solemn matter that their elders thought they ought to have. In addition to publishing works of such well-known writers as Edward Everett Hale, Thomas Nelson Page, and Margaret Sidney, he founded several popular juvenile periodicals, the best-known of which was *Wide Awake,* established in 1875 with Mary Mapes Dodge [*q.v.*] as a prominent contributor. The publishing house of D. Lothrop & Company became a leader in the field in which it specialized, and had a considerable influence on juvenile literature in America.

A prominent figure in the business life of Boston, Lothrop also took great interest in good government, and in 1880 founded the American Institute of Civics, an organization designed to spread a knowledge of politics and an interest in government. He married, first, on July 25, 1860, Ellen Morrill of Dover, N. H., who died in 1880; and, second, on Oct. 4, 1881, Harriett Mulford Stone, who wrote under the name of Margaret Sidney [see Lothrop, Harriett Mulford Stone]. He had one daughter by the second marriage.

[E. B. Huntington, *A Geneal. Memoir of the Lo-Lathrop Family* (1884); E. E. Hale, in *Lend a Hand*, Oct. 1892; J. N. McClintock, in *Bay State Monthly*, Dec. 1884; *Publishers' Weekly*, Mar. 26, 1892; *Boston Daily Advertiser, Boston Herald, Boston Transcript*, Mar. 19, 1892; *Boston Globe*, Mar. 20, 1892.]
S. G.

LOTHROP, GEORGE VAN NESS (Aug. 8, 1817–July 12, 1897), lawyer, minister to Russia, was born at Easton, Bristol County, Mass. His ancestor, Mark Lothrop, came to Massachusetts in 1643, settling first in Salem and then in Bridgewater. Howard Lothrop, father of George, served in both branches of the Massachusetts legislature and as member of the governor's council; his wife, George's mother, was Sally Williams, daughter of Edward Williams of Easton. George owed his middle name to his father's friend, C. P. Van Ness, at one time governor of Vermont. His early years were spent on his father's farm. He acquired his preparatory education at the Wrentham Academy and in a private school at Taunton. In 1834 he became a freshman at Amherst and in 1835 entered the sophomore class at Brown, where he graduated in 1838. Immediately after his graduation he went to Harvard to study law under Joseph Story and Simon Greenleaf. One year later, however, impaired health compelled him to give up his studies, and he removed to Prairie Ronde, Kalamazoo County, Mich., where his brother, Edwin H. Lothrop, was living on a farm. Here he practised farming with marked success. Outdoor life soon restored his health, and, after having studied law for a short time in Detroit, he was admitted to the bar (1843) and entered practice with D. Bethune Duffield, whose partner he presently became.

During his forty-odd years of practice before the Michigan supreme court he secured the invalidation of several laws as unconstitutional. Among these measures were an act providing for taking the vote of soldiers in the field (13 *Mich.*, 127) and acts authorizing municipalities

to aid in the building of railroads (20 *Mich.*, 452 and 23 *Mich.*, 499). He practised also in the federal courts, interesting himself especially in Admiralty law. In 1848 he became attorney-general of Michigan, but resigned three years later. In 1853 he accepted a position as recorder of Detroit. He was a Democrat, and in 1860 was a delegate to the convention at Charleston. From 1879 to 1896 he was president of the Detroit Bar Association. He was general solicitor for the Michigan Central Railroad for twenty-five years. In Detroit he acquired valuable property and in various parts of eastern Michigan he owned extensive farms. His real-estate holdings were valued at about $2,000,000 (*Sunday News-Tribune*, Detroit, July 28, 1895).

In May 1885 he was appointed minister to Russia by President Cleveland, who had met him at Buffalo the previous year and had been struck by his fine appearance and apparent ability. While he was stationed at St. Petersburg one of his daughters was married to a Russian baron. Returning to Michigan in 1888 on account of his health, he spent his last nine years in peaceful retirement at Detroit, where he died. On May 13, 1847, he had married Almira Strong, daughter of Gen. Oliver Strong of Rochester, N. Y. Of seven children born to them, two sons and two daughters survived their father. Lothrop was a man of irreproachable manners, modest, dignified, courteous, affable, a master of correct English, a painstaking scholar; for many years he was called the "leader of the Michigan bar."

[C. A. Kent, in W. D. Lewis, *Great American Lawyers*, VII (1909), 163–99; E. B. Huntington, *A Geneal. Memoir of the Lo-Lathrop Family* (1884); *Illustrated Detroit* (1891); G. I. Reed, *Bench and Bar of Mich.* (1897); Fred. Carlisle, *Wayne County Hist. and Pioneer Soc.: Chronography* (1890); Brown Univ. necrology in *Providence Daily Journal*, June 15, 1898; *Sunday News-Tribune* (Detroit), July 28, 1895, Apr. 4, 1897, and *Evening News* (Detroit), July 12, 1897.]
A. H.

LOTHROP, HARRIETT MULFORD STONE (June 22, 1844–Aug. 2, 1924), widely known under the pen name Margaret Sidney as a writer of books for children, was born in New Haven, Conn., the daughter of Sidney Mason and Harriett (Mulford) Stone. Her father was one of the earliest professional architects of that city, and her mother, the daughter of a prominent merchant. Harriett graduated from the Grove Hall School, New Haven, and early showed talent for writing both fiction and verse. Contributions to *Wide Awake*, begun in 1878, attracted attention, and in 1880 there appeared serially in that magazine a story which, published subsequently in book form, has given delight to thousands of youthful readers, *Five Little Peppers and How They Grew* (1881). For years it was one of the books for children in greatest demand. It was followed by a number of other somewhat less popular but widely read tales dealing with the fortunes of the Pepper family, together with many more narratives of interest to boys and girls. Their author had the gift of writing simply and naturally, of making very real the homely, everyday life of ordinary people, both on its serious and its amusing side, and an understanding of the mental operations of young and old which make her characters attractively human. Occasionally the didactic motive distorts the portrayals a little, but in general it does not much diminish the pleasurable impression of reality which one receives. The kindly, affectionate spirit in which the stories are written also contributes much to their charm. Among them may be noted *So As By Fire* (1881); *The Pettibone Name, a New England Story* (1882); *Hester and Other New England Stories* (1886); *A New Departure for Girls* (1886); *Dilly and the Captain* (1887); *How Tom and Dorothy Made and Kept a Christian Home* (1888); *Rob, a Story for Boys* (1891); *A Little Maid of Concord Town* (1898); *The Judges' Cave* (1900); *Sally, Mrs. Tubbs* (1903); *A Little Maid of Boston Town* (1910).

One of those whose interest was aroused by Miss Stone's earlier writings was Daniel Lothrop [*q.v.*], head of the publishing house of D. Lothrop & Company, and on Oct. 4, 1881, she became his second wife. The firm which he controlled specialized in juvenile literature, especially in the kind suitable for Sunday-school libraries, and the numerous books written by Mrs. Lothrop did much to give it success. She also contributed to young people's magazines and wrote verse for children which was popular. In 1883 the Lothrops purchased "Wayside," Hawthorne's old home at Concord, which they made their residence until Daniel Lothrop's death in 1892. Later Mrs. Lothrop acquired the nearby estate of Ephraim Wales Bull [*q.v.*], restored "Grapevine Cottage," and dedicated it as a memorial to its former owner, the propagator of the Concord grape. She was descended from colonial stock, and was active in patriotic societies. She founded the Old Concord Chapter, Daughters of the American Revolution, and in 1895 formed the Old North Bridge Society, Children of the American Revolution, the beginning of a national organization of which she was president until 1901, and honorary president until her death, when it had a membership of over 22,000. During the latter part of her life she spent her summers in Concord, and her winters at her home at Stanford University, Cal. She died at San Francisco in her eighty-first year.

[*Daughters of the Am. Revolution Mag.*, Sept. 1924; *Children of the Am. Revolution*, Sept. 1924; *Who's Who in America*, 1924–25; J. L. Swayne, *The Story of Concord Told by Concord Writers* (1906); G. B. Bartlett, *Concord, Historic, Literary and Picturesque* (15th ed., 1895); *Book News*, Oct. 1892; *Publishers' Weekly*, Aug. 9, 1924; *Boston Transcript, San Francisco Chronicle*, Aug. 4, 1924.]   H. E. S.

LOTHROPP, JOHN (1584–Nov. 8, 1653), clergyman, minister at Scituate and Barnstable in the Colony of New Plymouth, was the son of Thomas and Mary Lothropp (variously spelled) of Cherry Burton and Etton, Yorkshire. He was baptized at Etton Dec. 20, 1584. He matriculated at Queen's College, Cambridge, and received the degrees of bachelor of arts in 1606 and master of arts in 1609. After preaching at Bennington, Hertfordshire, and at Cheriton and Egerton, Kent, he renounced his orders because he could no longer conform to the ceremonies of the Church of England. He united with a congregation of non-conformists and separatists which met in and about London in 1624, and succeeded Henry Jacob as pastor of the group in 1625. This congregation was tracked down at the house of Humphrey Barnett, a brewer's clerk, in Blackfriars, Apr. 29, 1632, by Tomlinson, a pursuivant of Bishop Laud, and Lothropp and two-thirds of his congregation were arrested. He appeared before the Court of High Commission May 3 and May 8 and was committed to prison, where he remained for two years. During his imprisonment his wife died. Her name is unknown, but he married her prior to 1614, and she bore him eight children. He was liberated Apr. 24, 1634, on a bond to absent himself from all private conventicles and to appear before the Court of High Commission in Trinity Term (*Calendar of State Papers, Domestic Series, 1633–34*, 1863, p. 583). At the invitation of the settlers of Scituate in the Colony of New Plymouth to become their pastor (*Calendar of State Papers, Colonial Series, America and the West Indies, 1574–1660*, 1860, p. 194), and accompanied by some thirty followers, he fled to New England, where Winthrop recorded his arrival at Boston in the *Griffin*, Sept. 18, 1634. He proceeded immediately to Scituate, arriving there Sept. 27 and preaching twice on the following day. On condition that a church should be organized at Scituate, the church at Plymouth on Nov. 23 dismissed its members living at the former place. A church was gathered there Jan. 8, 1634/35, and Lothropp was chosen first pastor and ordained Jan. 19. Services were held in homes until a meeting-house was completed and dedicated in 1636. Soon after his arrival at Scituate, Lothropp took as his second wife a widow, Ann (surname unknown), by whom he had six children. He was admitted freeman of the Colony of New Plymouth June 7, 1637. With other freemen of Scituate he complained to the Court of Assistants of the Colony of scarcity of land at Scituate, Jan. 1, 1637/38, and he wrote to Governor Prence, Sept. 28, 1638, and again Feb. 18, 1638/39, asking for the grant of a new site. The Colony granted the group Seppekann or Rochester Jan. 22, 1638/39, but this tract proved unacceptable and Lothropp and more than half of his congregation removed to Barnstable, Oct. 11, 1639. A church was gathered there Oct. 31, 1639, and services held in dwelling houses until a meeting-house was erected in 1646. There Lothropp served as pastor until his death at the age of sixty-nine.

[J. and J. A. Venn, *Alumni Cantabrigienses*, pt. I, vol. III (1924), p. 104; *Reports of Cases in the Courts of Star Chamber and High Commission* (Camden Soc., 1886), ed. by S. R. Gardiner; E. B. Huntington, *A Geneal. Memoir of the Lo-Lathrop Family* (1884); *Winthrop's Journal* (2 vols., 1908), ed. by J. K. Hosmer; "Scituate and Barnstable Church Records," *New-Eng. Hist. and Geneal. Reg.*, July 1855, Jan. 1856; *Records of the Colony of New Plymouth in New England*, vols. I and III (1855), and vol. XII (1861); Samuel Deane, *Hist. of Scituate, Mass.* (1831); H. H. Pratt, *The Early Planters of Scituate* (1929); *Geneal. Notes of Barnstable Families*, vol. II (1890), rev. and completed by C. F. Swift; Nathaniel Morton, *New Englands Memoriall* (1669; 6th ed., with notes, 1855); Daniel Neal, *The Hist. of the Puritans* (first ed., 4 vols., 1732-38; 3 vols., 1837); Champlin Burrage, *The Early English Dissenters in the Light of Recent Research* (2 vols., 1912); John Lathrop, "Biog. of Rev. John Lothropp," *Mass. Hist. Soc. Colls.*, 2 ser. I (1814); W. B. Sprague, *Annals Am. Pulpit*, vol. I (1857); sketch by Alexander Gordon, in *Dict. Nat. Biog.*]

I. M. C.

LOTTA [See CRABTREE, CHARLOTTE, 1847–1924].

LOUCKS, HENRY LANGFORD (May 24, 1846–Dec. 29, 1928), agrarian politician, was the son of William J. Loucks (or Lux), of Luxemburg-German ancestry, and his wife, Anna York, born in Pennsylvania of Irish parents, who had gone soon after their marriage to Hull, across the Ottawa River from Ottawa, Canada. Here William Loucks engaged in general merchandising and here Henry was born. He was educated in the Canadian common schools. After reaching manhood, he engaged in mercantile pursuits in Canada, Michigan, and Missouri, and in 1884 settled upon a government homestead in Deuel County, Dakota Territory.

His settlement in Dakota came as the great boom was subsiding and the reaction was setting in. Economically the situation was difficult at the best; markets were distant, rates high, and prices low. Loucks, who possessed great vitality and public spirit, at once took up the cause of the farmers in a movement for the legal regulation of transportation rates, the prohibition of usury, and the exclusion of middlemen in marketing and purchasing. He became the leader and president of the Territorial and soon of the National Farmers' Alliance and assisted in organizing a number of cooperative business ventures, including fire and hail insurance and merchandising. He also established the *Dakota Ruralist* as the exponent of his economic views and published it for nearly a score of years.

At first, he and his associates, who generally affiliated with the Republican party, hoped to accomplish their objectives through the existing parties, but in 1890, at a joint convention of the Knights of Labor and the state Farmers' Alliance, of which he was then president, Loucks was named as candidate for governor. He was defeated, but succeeded in consolidating a large section of the farmers into a separate political party (at first known as the Independent, later identified with the People's or Populist party) that for a number of years was an important factor in affairs. He had an influential part in directing the fusion of Populists and Democrats which resulted in the election of James H. Kyle [*q.v.*] to the United States Senate in 1891. The following year he was president of the national convention of the People's party held in Omaha, and in November 1892 he was elected president of the National Farmers' Alliance and Industrial Union. He threw himself into the fight for the adoption of the initiative and referendum in South Dakota in 1898 and its success was conceded to have resulted from his efforts and finesse. From early in his career he devoted much energy to the promotion of temperance, and attained more than provincial reputation for his labors in that cause. In all his work for temperance and economic reform he was notable for kindly spirit, fairness to his opponents, and moderate temper. He was an acute debater, ingenious in method, and utterly imperturbable before violent attack. He published several works, the titles of which indicate the direction of his thought: *The New Monetary System* (1893); *Government Ownership of Railroads and Telegraphs* (1894); and *The Great Conspiracy of the House of Morgan and How to Defeat It* (1916).

In Canada, May 2, 1878, he married Florence McCraney, of an Irish family, and they became the parents of seven children. His death occurred at Clearlake, S. Dak., in his eighty-third year.

[Letters from Loucks's family and files of the *S. Dak. Ruralist,* 1888–1900, in Archives S. Dak. Dept. of Hist.; J. D. Hicks, *The Populist Revolt: A Hist. of the Farmers' Alliance and the People's Party* (1931); F. E. Haynes, *Third Party Movements Since the Civil War* (1916); F. G. Blood, *Hand Book and Hist. of the National Farmers' Alliance and Industrial Union* (1893); *Memorial and Biog. Record . . . S. Dak.* (1898); *Nation* (N. Y.), June 12, 1890; *National Economist* (Washington, D. C.), July 19, 1890; *N. Y. Times,* Dec. 30, 1928.]   D. R.

LOUDON, SAMUEL (*c.* 1727–Feb. 24, 1813), merchant, printer, and publisher, was born probably in Ireland of Scotch-Irish ancestry and emigrated to America some time before 1753. In October of that year he was proprietor of a store opposite the Old Slip Market in New York City, where his stock in trade included speaking trumpets, pots and kettles, powder and shot, and "a parcel of ready-made coats and breeches, in the newest fashion" (*New York Mercury,* Oct. 8, 1753). Four years later he had changed his location to Hunter's Quay and was calling himself a ship-chandler (*Ibid.,* Sept. 19, 1757). His correspondence with Philip Schuyler of Albany during the years 1769–74 shows that he was one of several who had invested money in the "Saratoga patent" in upper New York, seeking a profit by dividing it into lots and selling to Scotch immigrants. Another of his ventures, undertaken in 1771, is disclosed by an advertisement of "A Book Store just Opened" (*New York Mercury,* Dec. 23, 1771), with which he later combined "Samuel Loudon's Circulating Library" (Jan. 1, 1774).

Soon after the outbreak of the Revolution he began, Jan. 4, 1776, the publication of *The New York Packet and the American Advertiser,* a weekly newspaper. Stanch patriot though he was, he fell into disfavor with the radical Committee of Mechanics in the city when, in March, he started to issue *The Deceiver Unmasked; or Loyalty and Interest United,* written anonymously as an answer to Paine's *Common Sense.* He was warned not to publish the pamphlet and promised to proceed no further with it at that time. Nevertheless, on Mar. 19 his printing office was invaded and 1,500 impressions carried away and burned. (A pamphlet preserved in the New York Historical Society bears the inscription "This copy was saved.") Always a keen observer of his balance sheet, he bitterly bewailed this misfortune which, he said, represented a £75 loss. In an open letter "To the Public" (*New York Packet,* Apr. 11, 1776) he strongly avowed his patriotism and resented the affront to the freedom of the press at a time when the question of independence was still a debatable matter. The following week (Apr. 18, 1776) he advertised as "necessary at the present time for all families who have the good of their country at heart" a pamphlet, *Essays upon the Making of Salt-Petre and Gun-Powder,* just published by order of the Committee of Safety of the Colony.

The arrival of the British forces at New York necessitated the suspension of the *Packet* (Aug. 29, 1776) and the removal of Loudon's numerous family to a place of safety. After a brief period as a merchant in Norwich, Conn., he opened a store and printery at Fishkill, N. Y., and resumed publication of the *Packet,* Jan. 16, 1777. Regularity of issue was at times interrupted by shortage of paper, but he kept the news sheet going during the remainder of the Revolution. Furthermore, he was state printer and for a time postmaster at Fishkill. In the former capacity he printed the first constitution of the State of New York (1777), and also several issues of state paper money. The British gone, he moved back to New York City, reopened his printery, resumed publication of the *Packet* as a biweekly, and started again his bookshop and circulating library. Because of alleged sharp practice in connection with the issue of another batch of paper money for the state (1786), a rival newspaper editor said of him:

> "To good and evil equal bent,
> He's both a Devil and a Saint"
> (Shepard Kollock [*q.v.*], quoted by Wall, *post.*)

In 1786 he printed *Laws of the State of New York,* in one volume, also Noah Webster's short-lived periodical, the *American Magazine.* In 1792 the *Packet* became the *Diary or Loudon's Register.* By this time the founder's son Samuel was prominently connected with the paper.

Loudon was an elder in the Scotch Presbyterian Church, a member of the St. Andrew's Society, and an honorary member of the Society of the Cincinnati. He was twice married: first, Jan. 24, 1756, to Sarah Oakes, and second (before 1768), to Lydia Griswold, sister of Gov. Matthew Griswold of Connecticut. He had five sons and three daughters. He died near Middletown Point, N. J., in his eighty-sixth year.

[A. J. Wall, in *N. Y. Hist. Soc. Quart. Bull.,* Oct. 1922; "Loudon's Diary," in W. W. Pasko's *Old New York,* Nov. 1889; Isaiah Thomas, *The Hist. of Printing in America* (1810), vol. II; C. R. Hildeburn, *Sketches of Printers and Printing in Colonial N. Y.* (1895); M. E. Perkins, *Old Houses of the Antient Town of Norwich, 1660–1800* (1895); E. E. and E. M. Salisbury, *Family Hists. and Geneals.* (1892), II, 52; J. W. Francis, *Old New York* (ed. of 1866); files of *N. Y. Packet,* 1776–83, and of *The Diary,* 1792–95, also *N. Y. Gazetteer,* Jan. and Feb. 1786; letters of Loudon among the Schuyler Papers in N. Y. Pub. Lib., in Peck Lib., Norwich, Conn., in N. Y. Hist. Soc., and in private hands; *Jours. of the Provincial Cong. . . . of N. Y.* (2 vols., 1842); *N. Y. Gazette and General Advertiser,* Mar. 2, 1813.]   A. E. P.

LOUDOUN, JOHN CAMPBELL, Fourth Earl of (May 5, 1705–Apr. 27, 1782), British commander-in-chief in North America, was the son of Hugh, third earl, of Loudoun Castle, Galston, Ayrshire, and of his wife Margaret, only daughter of John Dalrymple, first Earl of Stair. Choosing to follow the military profession, he entered the Scots Greys as cornet in 1727, and by 1739 had become captain, with the army rank of lieutenant-colonel, in the 3rd Foot Guards. His interests were not confined to the army, however. Having succeeded to the title in 1731, he was elected in 1734 as a Scottish representative peer, and shared in the Scottish patronage by getting, in 1741, the governorship of Stirling Castle. In Ayrshire he improved his own estates by systematic and scientific planting, and encouraged the building of roads and bridges. The Royal Society elected him fellow in 1738. In 1743 he saw service in Flanders and after Dettingen became aide-de-camp to George II. Loyal to the king, as his family had ever been, he played an important part in the Jacobite rebellion of 1745, acting as adjutant-general to Sir John Cope, commanding later in the north of Scotland where the Young Pretender eluded him, and raising as colonel a regiment of Highlanders. This regiment was cut to pieces at Preston Pans; recruited again, it relieved Fort Augustus and was later reduced. In 1749 Loudoun became colonel of the 30th Regiment and in 1755 major-general.

A believer in the necessity of stern disciplinary measures to preserve colonial dependence on the royal prerogative, Loudoun readily accepted, in January 1756, the post of commander-in-chief of all forces in North America, offered him by the Duke of Cumberland with the approval of Fox and Halifax. At the same time he was appointed governor-general of Virginia, a sinecure post, and colonel-in-chief of the new Royal American Regiment. Administrative entanglements in London delayed his arrival at New York until July 23. There his candor and affability, his readiness to accept wise suggestions, his incessant attention to infinite detail (which was to undermine his health), and his direct methods of dealing, provoked favorable comment, at first, from such different men as Franklin and Hutchinson. His tasks were two: to mold the British army in North America into an efficient fighting unit, and to unite jealous and divided colonies in support of the war. Without the aid of an adequate staff, he organized the transportation, supply, and ranging services to function without direct colonial support. He took the preliminary steps in training the raw recruits of the army for wilderness warfare. Such work constituted his greatest achievement and gives him a place among the conquerors of Canada. In his relations with the colonies Loudoun was less successful. The British ministry had intended them to furnish, not only provincial troops, but recruits, funds, and quarters for the regular army. Loudoun's blunt insistence on his authority, accompanied often with deliberate outbursts of temper, led many colonial assemblies to fear military government, while Massachusetts almost refused him support. His campaigns were completely unsuccessful. Montcalm took Forts Oswego and William Henry in successive summers, and his own projected invasion of Canada by way of Louisbourg and the St. Lawrence failed. None of these disasters was wholly his fault, for he was a good soldier, if no genius. In December 1757 Pitt determined on his recall, less because he had not accomplished visible results than because Pitt refused to continue longer the extensive political and military authority he possessed.

Second in command of the British expedition to Portugal in 1762, Loudoun, after Tyrawley's resignation in June, acted as commander of British troops in the Peninsula until the following spring, and aided in turning back a Franco-Spanish invasion. There, as in America, he irritated the somewhat dilatory civil ministers by his tactless insistence upon conditions he deemed essential for the health of his troops. Lieutenant-general in 1758, governor of Edinburgh Castle in 1763, he became general in 1770, and colonel of the Scots Guards. He died unmarried at Loudoun Castle, and was succeeded by his cousin. Peter Wraxall in 1756 described him as "short, strong made & seems disposed & fit for Action," his countenance "full of Candor, his Eyes Sprightly & good Humoured."

[Original materials for Loudoun's American career are in the Loudoun Papers in the Henry E. Huntington Library, San Marino, Cal., in the Amherst, Chatham and various state papers in the Public Record Office, in the Newcastle, Bouquet, and Hardwicke Papers in the British Museum, in the Cumberland Papers in the Royal Archives, and in printed collections of colonial documents and correspondence for the period. Recent accounts of his command are by C. T. Atkinson, in *The Cambridge Hist. of the British Empire*, vol. VI, "Canada and Newfoundland" (1930); and by S. M. Pargellis, *Lord Loudoun in North America* (1933). A good general history is J. S. Corbett, *England in the Seven Years' War* (2 vols., 1907).]   S. M. P.

LOUGHRIDGE, ROBERT McGILL (Dec. 24, 1809–July 8, 1900), missionary and educator among the Creek Indians, came of Scotch-Irish people in South Carolina. He was born at Laurensville, S. C., but in his childhood, with his parents, James and Deborah Ann (McGill)

Loughridge, moved to the Alabama country. He was taught by the Rev. John H. Gray, with whom he afterward studied theology, and in the Mesopotamia Academy until he went to Ohio to attend Miami University, where he graduated in 1837. He entered the Princeton Theological Seminary, but, after one year there, he returned home to Eutaw, Ala., on account of his father's death. While he was teaching school and continuing his theological studies near their former territory, he became concerned for the Creeks who, deprived of their lands in Alabama and Georgia and moved to what is now Oklahoma, remained resentful and intractable. In 1836 the missionaries, who had worked among them for a few years with small success, had all left the country because of their opposition.

Nevertheless five years later Loughridge went there to find a place for work, armed with letters to the chiefs from the Presbyterian board of foreign missions and from the war department. On Apr. 9, 1841, he was licensed to preach. On Oct. 15 of the next year he was ordained by the Presbytery of Tuscaloosa, Ala., and in December, with his bride, Olivia (Hills) Loughridge, to whom he had been married on the sixth of the month, left Alabama to settle among the Creeks. He gained a grudging admittance and built a school at Coweta. There, in June 1843, he began teaching and preaching. Four years later the situation was greatly changed. The mission was prospering, and its founder was publicly called by a Creek chief "their friend Loughridge" (*Foreign Missionary Chronicle,* Aug. 1847, p. 243). In 1847 the Creek Council made an agreement with the Presbyterian board for joint support of the original school, now become a boarding-school, and of another one, to be established. This was opened in 1850, as a manual labor boarding-school at Tallahassee, and to it, especially, he devoted himself. Under his direction the mission continued to flourish. In 1855 he reported twelve missionaries at work, and the same year began, with *The Gospel According to Matthew,* the publication of his translations of the Gospels. By 1861 several hundred Creek men and women had received elementary and industrial education. Two churches had been organized and two Indian ministers trained. Schoolbooks and literature for religious instruction had been published in Muskokee, the principal Creek dialect. As early as 1845 he had published the first edition of *Muskokee Hymns,* based on the earlier work of John Fleming [*q.v.*] and the next year had published his *Translation of the Introduction to the Shorter Catechism.* He had acquired a commanding influence among

the Indians. Yet, at the outbreak of the Civil War, white men hostile to the mission were able to instigate the Indians to expel the missionaries.

From that time until 1880 he was minister of Presbyterian churches in several places in eastern Texas, among them Lagrange, Goliad, and Marlin. In 1881, he returned to his mission, which had been revived in 1866. From 1883 to 1885 he had charge of the Tallahassee school in a new building provided, at Wealaka, by the Creek council. Then he gave himself to preaching among the Indians and to completing his *English and Muskokee Dictionary,* which was published in collaboration with David M. Hodge in 1890. At the age of seventy-nine he had ended his work for the Creeks, in whose progress toward civilization he had played a great part. In 1888 he became minister of the Presbyterian church in Tulsa and in 1889 moved to Red Fork, I. T. For three years he had charge of both these churches. In 1892 he went to Waco, Tex., where he ministered to churches in the neighborhood until he was eighty-six years old and where he died. In September 1845 his first wife died and, on Dec. 4, 1846, he married, in Conway, Mass., Mary Avery, who died Jan. 20, 1850. On Oct. 15, 1853, he took as his third wife Harriet Johnson.

[*Necrological Report Presented to the Alumni Asso. of Princeton Theol. Sem. . . . 1901* (1901); information from the Rev. R. H. Lamb, Tulsa, Okla.; *Foreign Missionary Chronicle,* esp. Mar., July, Aug. 1847; *Foreign Missionary,* Feb. 1854; *Annual Reports of the Board of Foreign Missions of the Presbyt. Church* for 1850, 1855, 1867, 1881, 1883, 1885; *Minutes of the General Assembly of the Presbyt. Church of the U. S.* (1863–80); *Minutes of the General Assembly of the Presbyt. Church in the U. S. of America,* n.s., vols. XI–XV (1888–92).]   R. H. N.

LOUNSBURY, THOMAS RAYNESFORD (Jan. 1, 1838–Apr. 9, 1915), author and philologist, was born in Ovid, N. Y., the son of the Rev. Thomas and Mary Janette (Woodward) Lounsbury. He prepared for college in Ovid and entered Yale in the class of 1859. As an undergraduate he won prizes in English composition, debating, and public speaking, was elected to Phi Beta Kappa, and was one of the editors of the *Yale Literary Magazine.* A few months at home convinced him that life in a farming community was neither "mentally stimulating nor pecuniarily profitable," and he moved to New York City where he occupied himself writing for Appleton's *New American Cyclopædia.* On Aug. 9, 1862, he joined the Union army as first lieutenant of Company C in the 126th New York Regiment. His first adventures in the field terminated ingloriously at Harpers Ferry, where he was surrendered with nine thousand other men to General Jackson, by what he characterized as "an imbecility so hopelessly imbecile, as almost to reach the sublime in that department" (*Yale College Class of 1859: Decennial Record,* 1870, p. 64). He was exchanged in November and was on active service in Virginia until the close of the Gettysburg campaign. His impressions of Virginia in war time are recorded in a paper written in 1864 and subsequently published under the title, "In the Defenses of Washington" (*Yale Review,* April 1913). His regiment suffered heavily in the battle of Gettysburg, and he was one of seven officers who escaped uninjured. In August 1863 he was detailed to Elmira, N. Y., as adjutant-general of the draft rendezvous; and here he remained until mustered out of service in June 1865.

He taught Latin and Greek for some months in Lespinasse's French Institute on Washington Heights, New York, and was tutor in a private family at Milburn, N. J., for two years. During this period he pursued a rigorous course of reading and study, with particular attention to Anglo-Saxon and early English. In January 1870 he returned to Yale as instructor in English in the Sheffield Scientific School, and in the following year he married Jane D. Folwell, daughter of Gen. Thomas J. Folwell of Kendaia, N. Y. In 1871 he was made professor of English in the Sheffield Scientific School, and he continued to hold this chair until 1906. He was librarian of the Scientific School from 1873 to 1896, its representative on the university council from 1900 until the year of his retirement, and for many years a member of the standing committee in charge of the university library.

In teaching English literature in a scientific school, Lounsbury was more happily situated than might at first appear. Sheffield was still a new enterprise when he joined the faculty, and he had more freedom to deal imaginatively with a subject still under some suspicion than he would have had in an institution bound by the old academic traditions. He broke away from the formal teaching of rhetoric, took his students straight to the texts of the poets and prose writers, and taught them to recognize in literature the record of a life as real as their own. The principal interests of most of his students lay naturally in other directions, but he succeeded in making literature a permanent interest with a surprisingly large number of them. He brought to his classroom the hard common sense, the firm regard for fact, and the unshakable sense of values that distinguished his own scholarship; and the first object of his teaching was to assure himself that his pupils knew what they were talking about. That he did not flatter himself that he had been invariably successful one may infer from a passage in his life of Cooper. "We need not feel any distrust," he says, in speaking of Cooper's education, "of his declaration, that little learning of any kind found its way into his head. Least of all will he be inclined to doubt it whom extended experience in the class-room has taught to view with profoundest respect the infinite capability of the human mind to resist the introduction of knowledge" (*James Fenimore Cooper,* p. 7). Evidence that he was able to view with the same sardonic amusement the teacher's inevitable failure to hold the attention of his pupils at all times and seasons is to be found in the oft-told tale that he once exhorted a class, growing unusually restless toward the end of the hour, to bear with him a little longer, for he had a few more pearls to cast.

As a scholar, Lounsbury was recognized in Europe and America as one of the most eminent masters of his subject. He was one of the fifteen original members of the American Academy of Arts and Letters, and in 1896 he was made fellow of the American Academy of Arts and Sciences. His first book, an edition of Chaucer's *Parlament of Foules* (1877), was followed by a *History of the English Language* (1879, 1894, 1907), and *James Fenimore Cooper* (1882). His *Studies in Chaucer,* published in three volumes in 1892, was one of the most important works in the field to appear in the nineteenth century and remains one of the great classics of Chaucerian scholarship. Three volumes upon Shakespeare, grouped under the title *Shakespearean Wars* were published between 1901 and 1906. An increasing interest in questions of spelling, pronunciation, and usage manifested itself in a number of articles in the magazines, which were subsequently collected in book form under the titles *The Standard of Pronunciation in English* (1904), *The Standard of Usage in English* (1908), and *English Spelling and Spelling Reform* (1909). In April 1907 he was elected president of the Simplified Spelling Board. Four lectures delivered at the University of Virginia were published in 1911 under the title *The Early Literary Career of Robert Browning;* and *The Yale Book of American Verse,* an unusual anthology with a striking preface, appeared in 1912. His last work was left unfinished at his death and was published in the autumn of 1915 by Wilbur L. Cross, with the title *The Life and Times of Tennyson from 1809 to 1850.*

Lounsbury's style is pungent, forthright, and voluble. His books are entirely free from the affectation and arrogance of pedantry, and although they are sometimes too diffuse, their vitality is unfailing. Lounsbury taught and wrote and lived with an honest vigor that left upon all who met him an indelible impression of the man beneath the scholar. "His appearance was by no means academic," says Barrett Wendell; "rather his burly vigor bespoke the old soldier. . . . A tall man and a large, sandy-haired and bearded, with heavy-lidded eyes which troubled him in his later years, he might have looked ponderous, if he had been less alert" (*Proceedings of the American Academy of Arts and Sciences, post,* p. 833). Many hours, in the latter part of his life, were spent in a darkened room, and much of his writing was done in the evening without a light. His accurate and well-stored memory was of great service to him in these years. He once addressed a class of undergraduates, after his retirement, entertaining them for an hour with a running commentary upon Chaucer's *Nonne Preestes Tale.* The text was before him on the desk, and at the close of the hour, the instructor in the course asked him if he had been able to see it without difficulty. Lounsbury explained that he had not been able to see it at all but had not wanted the boys to know he was reciting the poem from memory. A simple and unpretentious manliness was the essence of his nature. He loved sport and he loved good talk. He was overtaken by death in the midst of a conversation with a friend, and collapsed in his chair with a half-smoked cigar between his fingers.

[Barrett Wendell, in *Proc. of the Am. Acad. of Arts and Sciences,* Sept. 1918; Brander Matthews, in *Proc. of the Am. Acad. of Arts and Letters,* no. IX (1916); R. H. Chittenden, *Hist. of the Sheffield Scientific School of Yale Univ.* (1928), vol. I; *Obit. Record of Yale Grads. 1914–15* (1915); *Yale College, Class of 1859: Decennial Record* (1870); *Hist. of the Class of 1859* (1914); *Yale Alumni Weekly,* Apr. 30, 1915; *N. Y. Times,* Apr. 10, 1915.]   R. D. F.

LOVE, ALFRED HENRY (Sept. 7, 1830–June 29, 1913), radical pacifist, son of William Henry and Rachel (Evans) Love, was born and spent his life in Philadelphia, Pa. As a high-school student he showed a bent for journalism, which later found expression in the periodicals which he edited. His marriage to Susan Henry Brown in January 1853 brought him into affiliation with the Society of Friends, although he did not at once become a formal member of a meeting. From 1853 until his death he was a package woolen commission merchant. When the Civil War came, many Quakers and almost all the members of peace organizations compromised with their principles and accepted the struggle. Unable to make this adjustment, Love defended his position in *An Appeal in Vindication of Peace Principles* (Philadelphia, 1862).

To support the war seemed to him both unchristian and inhuman, and he pointed to the danger of "becoming absorbed in the enthusiasm of the hour" and of floating along "on the swelling tide, forgetful that popular movements always should be watched, often even doubted." Though an active and thoroughgoing friend of the negro, Love did not believe that any great good could be achieved for him through war, which, he maintained, would not be a death-blow to "Slavery in its widest sense." He refused to sell his goods for army use, and his business suffered. In 1863 he was drafted, but he refused to serve or to procure a substitute. William Lloyd Garrison, the high-priest of non-resistance, having accepted the war, wrote to Love that he believed money could be paid in lieu of service "without any compromise of the peace or non-resistance principle" (manuscript "Anti-Slavery Letters Written by William Lloyd Garrison, 1861–65," vol. VI, Boston Public Library), but Love thought otherwise and maintained his position.

Since the American Peace Society had justified the Civil War, a handful of non-resistants felt the need for a new and thoroughly radical peace organization. Love assumed the leadership of this movement (*Address before the Peace Convention Held in Boston, Mar. 14 and 15, 1866*) which resulted in the formation of the Universal Peace Society, later the Universal Peace Union. Its platform was expressed in its motto, "Remove the causes and remove the customs of war! Live the conditions and promulgate the principles of peace." Until his death Love was president of the organization and responsible for its periodical. The society maintained close relations with European peace groups and came to number some ten thousand American adherents. It worked for a reconciliation between North and South, for a more humanitarian treatment of the Indian, for the rights of women, and for the abolition of capital punishment. It also labored for the peaceful adjustment of disputes, local as well as international. In the eighties Love became a pioneer in popularizing the idea of the arbitration of disputes between capital and labor, his own services as a mediator in strikes attesting his faith in the efficacy of pacific principles.

Love was not unknown to congressmen, secretaries of state, and presidents from Lincoln to Wilson. He urged party conventions and presidents-elect to mention international arbitration in their platforms and messages. He instigated delegations and petitions praying for the outlawry of war by constitutional amendment, for the negotiation of permanent treaties of arbitration, and for an international court. He was an uncompromising opponent of militarism in all its forms. Again and again he wrote vigorously if naïvely to the secretary of state and to foreign governments suggesting peaceful means for preventing a threatening war. His letters and cables on the eve of the Spanish-American war aroused such indignation among certain patriots that he was burned in effigy. His uncompromising pacifism seemed, in the opinion of certain moderate friends of the cause, to injure the peace movement by making it appear unpractical. As the cause became more realistic and scientific Love's work, which he carried on courageously against great odds, appeared to some of the new leaders sentimental and ineffective. Yet his service in keeping alive the high standard of pacifism in the dark, discouraging days during and after the Civil War, and in forcing the question upon skeptical politicians and an indifferent people, gives him a secure though minor place in the history of American idealism. Love's wife, two sons and a daughter, survived him.

[The above sketch is based largely on material in the periodicals which Love edited: *Bond of Peace, Voice of Peace,* and *The Peacemaker,* published in Philadelphia. Consult also: *Who's Who in America,* 1912–13; *A Brief Synopsis of Work Proposed, Aided, and Accomplished by the Universal Peace Union* (1912); the *Advocate of Peace,* Nov. 1913; *Friends' Intelligencer,* July 26, 1913; *Phila. Inquirer* and *Pub. Ledger* (Phila.), June 30, 1913. The "Miscellaneous Letters" in the Department of State contain many letters from Love.]

M. E. C.

LOVE, EMANUEL KING (July 27, 1850–Apr. 24, 1900), Baptist clergyman, was born in slavery near Marion, Perry County, Ala., the son of Cumby Jarrett Love and Maria Antoinette Love, both of African blood. His early life was one of hard work on a farm, but he was ambitious to learn and studied nights by torch light. Obtaining admission to Lincoln University in Marion in 1871, he remained only part of the year, but mastered most of the restricted curriculum. The following year he entered Augusta Institute, Augusta, Ga., where he led all his classes and graduated in 1877. During this period he was ordained to the Baptist ministry at Augusta, Dec. 12, 1875. For a time he had charge of his church at Marion and did some teaching at Augusta Institute and in negro public schools of Georgia. From 1877 to 1879 he was a missionary for the state of Georgia under joint appointment of the American Baptist Home Mission Society and the Georgia Mission Board, both organizations of white Baptists. On Oct. 30, 1879, he married Josephine Carter Leeks, and that year became pastor of the First African Baptist Church at Thomasville, Ga., which

throve under his leadership. For about four years, 1881–85, he was supervisor of Sunday-school mission work among the negroes of Georgia, under an appointment of the American Baptist Publication Society of Philadelphia. His most distinctive work and greatest influence came in his pastorate of the First African Baptist Church of Savannah, which he served from Oct. 1, 1885, until his death. This was probably the largest Baptist church in the world and the oldest negro Baptist church in the United States. He not only increased its membership, but broadened the scope of its work. In 1888 he published *History of the First African Baptist Church, from Its Organization, January 20th, 1788, to July 1st, 1888.* He was one of the organizers of the Baptist Foreign Mission Convention, of which he was president in 1889–91 and 1893, while at the time of his death he was president of the Georgia Negro Baptist Convention and editor of its organ, *The Baptist Truth,* which he had founded. He was especially interested in securing for the negro an education which would provide adequate leaders in church, state, and industry. When the Georgia State Industrial College was established, he was largely responsible for its location in Savannah and formulated the plan for raising the necessary money. He was among the prime movers in the founding of Central City College, which opened in 1899. Selma University, Selma, Ala., conferred upon him the degree of doctor of divinity in 1888. He was a man of native eloquence, with an ability to secure cooperation from whites as well as from members of his own race.

[Love's book, mentioned above; E. R. Carter, *Biog. Sketches of Our Pulpit* (n.d.); A. W. Pegues, *Our Baptist Ministers and Schools* (1892); W. J. Simmons, *Men of Mark* (1887); *Morning News* (Savannah), Apr. 25, 1900; information as to certain facts from a brother, Philip E. Love, M.D.]

W. H. A.

LOVE, ROBERTUS DONNELL (Jan. 6, 1867–May 7, 1930), journalist and author, was the second son among five children of the Rev. Dr. Thomas Shelby and Nancy Eveline (McFarland) Love. His grandfather, William Calhoun Love, was a Cumberland Presbyterian minister in eastern Tennessee and his father, taken as a child into Kentucky, was ordained in the same denomination, after which he assumed a charge at Irondale, in the Missouri Ozark foothills. Near this place Robertus was born on a rocky farm. His first literary effort was an "obituary poem" on a neighborhood girl, written at the age of fourteen. The next year his father was called to another pastorate and the family moved to Louisiana, Mo. Thereafter throughout the period of his schooling at McCune College, then situated at Louisiana, his favorite pastime was to lie outstretched on a bluff overlooking the Mississippi, with books of poetry ordered by mail from the East. He received the degree of A.B. in 1884 and after further study at Lincoln University, Illinois, he returned to Louisiana, Mo., to become at nineteen local editor of the Louisiana *Press,* with wages of five dollars a week. Ten months later he was city editor of the *Daily Journal,* Wichita, Kan., and his forty-three years of itinerant journalism had begun.

His career included virtually every duty connected with the writing side of newspapers, and took him into cities of varying sizes, scattered from coast to coast. He was editor of the *Press,* at Asbury Park, N. J., 1892–95; coast correspondent of the New York *Sun,* 1895; and founder of the *Asbury Park Daily Star,* 1896. He also established *Seashore Life* at Asbury Park, the first of several periodicals of which he was, as he said, "both founder and funeral director." From 1896 to 1899 he was managing editor of the *Day,* New London, Conn.; and he was reporter on the *St. Louis Post-Dispatch,* 1900–03. An early assignment on the *Post-Dispatch* was the Galveston hurricane (September 1900). When Mark Twain made his last visit to Missouri in 1902, Love accompanied him, and was fondly introduced as "my son." Another warm friendship he enjoyed was with Joaquin Miller. He had charge of press bureaus at the Louisiana Purchase, Lewis and Clark, and Jamestown expositions, in 1905 was editorial writer on the Portland *Oregonian* and columnist for the *Los Angeles Times*; and from 1906 to 1911 wrote and edited material for the American Press Association's "boiler plate." He returned to the *St. Louis Post-Dispatch* as feature writer, 1911–13; then wrote "Rhymes Along the Road" for the *St. Louis Republic,* 1913–16. He went to Oklahoma as Sunday editor of the Tulsa *Democrat,* 1917–18, and editor of the Ardmore *Ardmoreite,* 1918–20. After a period in Kansas City, Mo., 1921, on the editorial staff of the *Kansas City Post,* he returned to St. Louis where he was Sunday magazine writer, 1922–25, and literary editor, 1925–26, of the *Post-Dispatch*; then Sunday magazine writer, *St. Louis Globe-Democrat,* 1926–28, and literary editor thereafter until his death.

Love's topical newspaper verse found its way into many a Mississippi Valley scrapbook and his rhymes about the Ozarks attracted attention to the beauties of that then little appreciated region. He was the author of two books, *Poems All the Way from Pike* (1904), homely pieces on the Missouri meerschaum, old spellers, and the like, and *The Rise and Fall of Jesse James* (1926),

first printed in the *Post-Dispatch.* This latter work, a running story of Missouri banditry, resulted from a life-long interest in Middle-western outlaws. Picturing Jesse James as a product of his times, it was one of the first full-length studies of American desperadoes. The *Springfield Republican* (July 18, 1926) described it as "an admirable piece of research in the lighter style."

At thirty-four, Dec. 31, 1901, Love married Catherine Heck of Ruma, Ill., who was unable to walk for the last seventeen years of her life. She died in 1926, the union childless. Love's yearning to break away from journalism and devote himself entirely to other writing went unrealized. He died of pneumonia following an operation and was buried in Oak Grove Cemetery, near St. Louis, leaving unpublished "The Joy-Log of a Journalist," a ramblingly repertorial autobiography, befitting his roving and light-hearted life.

[Unpublished MS. of "The Joy-Log of a Journalist" in possession of Love's brother, Dr. William H. Love of St. Louis, who also supplied information; *Who's Who in America,* 1928–29; obituaries in the *St. Louis Post-Dispatch,* May 7, 1930, and the *St. Louis Globe-Democrat,* May 8; *Mo. Hist. Rev.,* July 1930; W. A. Kelsoe, *St. Louis Reference Record* (1928); *N. Y. Times,* June 6, 1926; *Saturday Review,* July 17, Sept. 11, 1926; *Book Review Digest,* 1926.]   I. D.

LOVEJOY, ASA LAWRENCE (Mar. 14, 1808–Sept 10, 1882), lawyer, companion of Marcus Whitman on his famous ride, founder of Portland, Ore., was the third son of Dr. Samuel Lovejoy and Betsey (Lawrence) Lovejoy, a sister of Abbott Lawrence |*q.v.*]. He was born and spent his boyhood in Groton, Mass. At sixteen he began work with a Boston mercantile house. Later he attended school again and then studied law. After his admission to the bar he moved to Sparta, Mo. (1840) and began the practice of law. In the spring of 1842 he joined Dr. Elijah White, United States Indian agent, on his way to Oregon, and was one of three men who recorded the experiences and discoveries of the trip. Dr. Marcus Whitman, head of the mission at Waiilatpu, where the party stopped in October 1842, persuaded Lovejoy to return with him to the states. Together the two men started on their arduous ride in November. Whitman finally reached Missouri in February by the southern route through Santa Fé, Mexico. Lovejoy stayed at Bent's Fort on the headwaters of the Arkansas River until the following July, when he joined Whitman and the emigrant train and returned to Oregon, settling at Oregon City. In this train he met Elizabeth McGary whom he married in 1845.

Lovejoy began the practice of law but took

an active part in public affairs. In 1844 he was chosen one of the eight members of the legislative committee of the provisional government, which remodeled the organic laws drawn up the year before. During the same year he held the office of attorney-general. In 1845 he was defeated as candidate for governor against George Abernethy but was elected mayor of Oregon City. Running against Abernethy again in 1847, he lost the election by only sixteen votes. In 1846 and again in 1848 he was sent to the provisional legislature. After the Whitman massacre, Lovejoy together with Jesse Applegate and Governor Abernethy pledged their personal credit to the Hudson's Bay Company for supplies to carry on war against the Indians. Lovejoy served as adjutant-general during the war. He was elected supreme judge in 1848 and held that position until the establishment of the territorial government in 1849. He was speaker of the House in the first territorial legislature, a member of the council in 1851–52, postal agent in 1853, and delegate to the lower house in 1854 and again in 1856. As one of the members of the convention of 1857, he took an active part in shaping the state constitution.

Lovejoy is remembered in Oregon as one of the founders of the city of Portland. He was a stockholder in the People's Transportation Company, which was organized in 1862, to promote a project for a portage at Oregon City. He was also a member of the Oregon City Woolen Manufacturing Company, which was incorporated in 1863, and a director of the Oregon Telegraph Company. He was interested in railroads and in 1847 acted as chairman of a public meeting called to memorialize Congress on the construction of a transcontinental line. Later he became one of the directors of the east-side Oregon Central Railway Company, which completed the first railroad through the Willamette Valley. In 1873 he moved to Portland where he remained until his death.

[*Hist. of the Pacific Northwest* (1889), vol. II; Jos. Gaston, *Portland, Ore.: Its Hist. and Its Builders* (1911), vol. I; H. W. Scott, *Hist. of the Ore. Country* (6 vols., 1924), especially vol. II; letters of Lovejoy describing the Whitman ride in W. H. Gray, *A Hist. of Ore.* (1870); O. W. Nixon, *How Marcus Whitman Saved Ore.* (1895); C. E. Lovejoy, *The Lovejoy Geneal.* (1930); H. H. Bancroft, *Hist. of Ore.*, vol. II (1888); *Morning Oregonian*, Sept. 11, 1882.]
R. C. C.

LOVEJOY, ELIJAH PARISH (Nov. 9, 1802–Nov. 7, 1837), the "martyr abolitionist," was born at Albion, Me., the son of a clergyman, Rev. Daniel Lovejoy, and Elizabeth (Pattee) Lovejoy, both of old New England stock. He graduated from Waterville (now Colby) College in 1826, taught school until May 1827, then emigrated to St. Louis, Mo., where he again taught school and for a short time edited a Whig newspaper. Determining to follow his father into the ministry he returned to the East in 1832 to attend the seminary at Princeton. He was licensed to preach by the Philadelphia Presbytery in April 1833 and went back to St. Louis as editor of the Presbyterian weekly for the far West, the *St. Louis Observer*. On Mar. 4, 1835, he married Celia Ann French, the daughter of a nearby planter. His editorial career began peacefully enough, but a spirit like his could not be peaceful long. Fired by the "expanding benevolence" that inspired his church in the early thirties, he enlisted his paper in the Presbyterian war against slavery, intemperance, and "popery." The border-states movement for the gradual abolition of slavery, so nearly successful in Kentucky and Virginia, had not extended to Missouri; and St. Louis, river port for the lower South, would hear no discussion of the subject. Protests multiplied, and rather than moderate his tone, in 1836 Lovejoy moved to Alton, Ill., twenty-five miles up the river.

At that time Alton was the most prosperous city in Illinois. Emigrants from New England and the Eastern states made up its population; and the doctrine Lovejoy had preached in St. Louis, the evil of slavery and its gradual emancipation, was their own as well. Abolitionism, as the doctrine of immediate emancipation then was called, Lovejoy had denounced in the strongest terms. But even as he left St. Louis for Alton his views were changing. At the next General Assembly, which he attended shortly before he moved to Alton (July 1836), the equivocating course of that body toward abolition petitions so angered him that with his own indignant pen he wrote the protest which the abolitionists published to the church. An abolitionist by conviction and sympathy, if not by affiliation, he returned to edit the *Alton Observer*.

At the outset he encountered misfortune. His press arrived from St. Louis on a Sabbath morning and Lovejoy's Sabbatarian convictions compelled him to leave it unguarded on the wharf. Some time during Sunday night it was dumped into the river. But the good citizens of Alton called a public meeting, unanimously condemned the outrage and—carefully expressing their disapproval of abolitionism—pledged the money for a new press. On his part Lovejoy expressed his gratitude and promised to edit his paper in the interest of the church alone. That promise he could not keep. Week by week his abolitionism crept into the columns of the *Observer*: reports of his local anti-slavery society; his abolition resolutions to the Presbyterian Synod; his correspondence with a score of fearless agitators here and there in the state; and even accounts of the progress of the cause in the nation. Finally, July 4, 1837, he printed a call for a meeting of the anti-slavery host at Alton to form a state auxiliary to the American Anti-Slavery Society; and after numerous delays the state society was organized on the 26th of October. Alton citizens were outraged. Mobs destroyed the *Observer* press again and yet again; but each time the Ohio Anti-Slavery Society sent another. Lovejoy wrote defiantly: "These mobs will cease as soon as some of the mobites are hung up by the neck, and not before. . . . Mercy no less than Justice calls for a summary execution of some of the wretches as an example to the rest."

After the founding of the state society the press was destroyed again, but news soon arrived that another press from Ohio was on the way. Lovejoy's friends caught his defiant spirit. Sixty young abolitionists from towns nearby assembled with arms in their hands, determined that this press should not go the way of the others. At a public meeting leading citizens implored Lovejoy to leave, but he replied that he was ready for martyrdom. The press arrived on Nov. 7 and was placed in a warehouse under guard. Merchants closed their stores and the whole city waited in dread for the night. An armed mob gathered in the darkness and stormed the warehouse, but the guard fought them back. Some of the mob tried to set the warehouse on fire, and Lovejoy, rushing out to prevent it, was shot dead.

[The chief source for Lovejoy's biography is the *Memoir of the Rev. Elijah P. Lovejoy* (1838), by Joseph C. and Owen Lovejoy. One of the armed band, Henry Tanner, reported the trials of the rioters, *The Alton Trials* (1838). His other later accounts are largely based on the *Memoir.* Edward Beecher's *Narrative of the Riots at Alton* (1838) is an honest but prejudiced account. Similar in the contrary direction is the account in Thos. Ford, *A Hist. of Ill.* (1854). Essential to an understanding of the story as part of the national anti-slavery agitation are the *Alton Observer,* 1836–37, the *Philanthropist,* 1836–38, and the *N. Y. Evangelist,* 1835–38. For Lovejoy's ancestry see C. E. Lovejoy, *The Lovejoy Geneal.* (1930).]   G. H. B.

LOVEJOY, OWEN (Jan. 6, 1811–Mar. 25, 1864), abolitionist and statesman, brother of Elijah Parish Lovejoy [*q.v.*], was born at Albion, Me., the son of the Rev. Daniel and Elizabeth (Pattee) Lovejoy. He attended Bowdoin College from 1830 to 1833, but did not graduate, and after studying at law and teaching school, he journeyed in 1836 to Alton, Ill., to prepare for the ministry under his brother. Elijah Lovejoy

had just begun active abolition propaganda and Owen speedily enlisted in the anti-slavery cause. In the growing excitement in Alton he stood steadfastly by his brother, and on the final tragic night after Elijah had been killed, Owen knelt beside his body and vowed "never to forsake the cause that had been sprinkled with his brother's blood." After completing his theological studies, he served as minister of the Congregational church at Princeton, Ill., for seventeen years. In January 1843 he married a widow, Eunice (Storrs) Dunham, who bore him seven children. He was a popular and devoted minister, but persistently kept his vow, never losing an opportunity to testify to the wrong of slavery. During the decade from 1840 to 1850 he spoke fearlessly for the cause wherever he could find a hearing, despite the Illinois state law prohibiting abolition meetings. Frequently he encountered violence, but his unflinching boldness and the memorable name he bore saved him from injury. His colleague in the Illinois agitation, Ichabod Codding, was an abler orator, but Lovejoy, more than any other man, advanced abolition sentiment in the state.

During the next decade, Lovejoy became increasingly influential; and in 1854, when the Republican organization began, he was elected to the state legislature to lead the forces of freedom. In Illinois the new party embraced anti-foreign "Know-Nothings" and Germans representing the hundred thousand foreign-born in Illinois, disgruntled Democrats and their enemies—old-line Whigs, and, feared by all, the Abolitionists. Lovejoy believed that only one man in Illinois could discipline this "rag-tag and bob-tail gang" into party organization, and that man was Abraham Lincoln. He urged Lincoln to lead the new movement, but Lincoln replied that the time was not yet ripe. He even tried to force Lincoln's hand by placing his name at the head of the state central committee for the Republican party. However, when Lincoln came to the Bloomington convention in 1856, it was Lovejoy who compelled the radicals to relinquish their abolition program and to accept Lincoln's conservative leadership. The same year Lovejoy was elected to Congress. There and in the Republican conventions at Pittsburgh and Philadelphia he was a radical leader; but in Illinois he was still Lincoln's henchman. When Lincoln stood for the Senate, Lovejoy put all his influence at his disposal. It was a dangerous gift. If Lincoln's opponents could "make Lincoln hang on Lovejoy's coat tails for Republican strength," the semblance of a bargain with Lovejoy would "choke Lincoln to death." Only Lovejoy's self-effacement prevented this catastrophe. Though he stumped the state in Lincoln's interest, he suffered Lincoln's repudiation of abolitionism gladly. While his contest with Douglas was lost, Lincoln thereby captured radical support, without losing his name for conservatism, for the presidential contest two years later.

In Congress Lovejoy assailed slavery and the South with a violence equaled only by Thaddeus Stevens and Sumner; but when Lincoln came to Washington, Lovejoy once more became his loyal supporter. To William Lloyd Garrison's attacks on Lincoln in 1862 he made fierce rejoinder, and to Thaddeus Stevens' proposals to treat the defeated South as a conquered province, he replied in the spirit of Lincoln's magnanimous reconstruction program. To him fell the honor of proposing the bill by which slavery in all the territories of the United States was abolished forever. He heard at last the Emancipation Proclamation, and died the next year. Lincoln wrote (J. G. Nicolay and John Hay, *Abraham Lincoln: Complete Works*, 1894, II, p. 527): "My personal acquaintance with him . . . has been one of increasing respect and esteem, ending, with his life, in no less than affection on my part. . . . To the day of his death, it would scarcely wrong any other to say he was my most generous friend."

[See the *Liberator*, 1862–63; the *Nat. Anti-Slavery Standard*, 1840–58; the *Philanthropist*, 1836–42; Albert J. Beveridge, *Abraham Lincoln* (1928); J. C. and Owen Lovejoy, *Memoir of the Rev. Elijah P. Lovejoy* (1838); T. C. Smith, *The Liberty and Free Soil Parties in the Northwest* (1897); C. E. Lovejoy, *The Lovejoy Geneal.* (1930); *Addresses on the Death of Hon. Owen Lovejoy, Delivered in the Senate and House of Representatives, on Monday, Mar. 28, 1864* (1864); *Cong. Globe*, 35 Cong., 1 Sess., pp. 752–54, 36 Cong., 1 Sess., App., pp. 202–07, 37 Cong., 2 Sess., p. 194; *N. Y. Tribune, Daily Ill. State Jour.* (Springfield), Mar. 28, 1864.]

G. H. B.

LOVELACE, FRANCIS (*c.* 1621–1675), second English governor of New York, was eighth in descent from John Lovelace, who founded Lovelace Place at Bethersden, Kent, in 1367. His father was Sir William (1584–1627) of Bethersden and Woolwich, son of Sir William, the elder, and Elizabeth Aucher. The family was only remotely related to the Lords Lovelace of Hurley. Francis' father was knighted by James I, on Sept. 20, 1609, and about 1610 married Anne, daughter of Sir William Barne, of Woolwich, and Anne Sandys, daughter of Edwin Sandys, archbishop of York in Elizabeth's reign, and sister of Sir Edwin Sandys of the Virginia Company and George Sandys the poet. The Barne and Sandys families were actively concerned in Virginia's colonization. In 1627 Francis' father was killed at the siege of the

Burse, or the Groll, in Holland, and his mother died about 1633. They had five sons and three daughters, of whom Richard (1618–1658), poet and Cavalier, was the eldest, and Francis, the third son. Both were bachelors. Two brothers, Thomas and Dudley, were in New York with their governor-brother. The eldest daughter, Anne, wife of the Rev. John Gorsuch, emigrated to Virginia with seven younger children about 1650.

Lovelace's immediate forebears were Royalists supporting the Stuarts. He himself served as a colonel for Charles I in the civil wars, and was active in Wales, where he was governor of Carmarthen Castle until it capitulated to Parliamentary forces in 1645. The death of his brother William in that siege was lamented in a poem written by Richard Lovelace, in *Lucasta*. For a while Francis and his brothers Richard and Dudley served Louis XIV on the Continent. In 1650, Francis seems to have gone to Virginia for two years, probably to accompany and aid his sister, Anne Gorsuch. After December 1652 he was an exile on the Continent with Charles II and his retinue; but in 1658 he was back in England aiding the Royalist cause. On Aug. 5, 1659, he was arrested and imprisoned in the Tower of London, but he was freed upon the Commonwealth's collapse. He is mentioned by Pepys in his *Diary,* as being in London on Dec. 16, 1662, and perhaps was then employed in the Admiralty. On May 14, 1667, he is referred to as "appointed Governor of New York," in an English warrant to the Ordnance (*Calendar of State Papers, Colonial Series, America and West Indies 1661–68,* no. 1480, p. 466), and the earliest reference to his appointment appears in a newsletter as of Apr. 12, 1667. While waiting to go to America he was, on June 13, 1667, commissioned as lieutenant-colonel in a regiment raised by Col. Sir Walter Vane, with the Duke of York's approval. The evidences all point to his selection as governor as a reward for his royalist services and because he had been before in English-America.

The treaty of Breda was proclaimed in New York in 1668. Lovelace arrived in March and for several months was familiarized by Gov. Richard Nicolls with the administration. Lovelace had been instructed to continue unabated the policies of government that were in operation. About the middle of August 1668, he assumed full control. It was a time of epidemic diseases and deaths were numerous. He took hold of the situation with concern. He instituted regular sessions of his executive council on Sept. 2, 1668, and its minutes, to July 11,

1673, were the first regular English council minutes recorded in New York. Since their publication in 1910 (see bibliography) it can no longer be justly charged that Lovelace was arbitrary or incompetent. He was a conscientious man, and in tolerance was the equal of his predecessor, from whom he had inherited unfulfilled promises, unsettled problems, and precedents in administration which the Duke of York required to be continued. This made him cautious rather than phlegmatic in what he undertook. Yet, in his five years in office, he transacted much business by himself, with his councilors, in the high court of assizes, or by commissions appointed by him and under his control. He not only watched over his vast territory, but entered into every phase of its needs and difficulties. His administration was harassed, internally and externally, by Indian troubles, boundary disputes, an insurrection in the Delaware country, a rebellion in New Jersey, and the incompatibilities of a mixed population of Dutch, English, Swedish, and other nationalities. He interested himself in better ferriage, roads, and transportation by land and water; and the regulation of trade and extension of commerce. He instituted the first merchants' exchange and the first haven master of the port. He promoted shipbuilding and himself owned a fine ship, *The Good Fame of New York*. He extended settlements and laid out new villages and townships, and by purchase for the Duke freed Staten Island from Indian control. He was tolerant toward religious sects, even to Quakers. He was interested in Indian missions and, though unsuccessful, made the first attempt to introduce the art of printing into the middle British colonies. He furthered the strengthening of fortifications and the raising of foot companies and troops of horse, keeping them in training. The drift whale, as well as sport fisheries, engaged his attention. His intercolonial activities, especially with New England, are outstanding, for he instituted the first continuous post road between New York and Boston, under a postmaster. It was while on a visit to Connecticut to promote this laudable object, that his vigilance lapsed, and he lost New York to a Dutch naval squadron, July 30–Aug. 9, 1673. Had he been at his fort and used all the meager resources he had, the capitulation could not have been prevented. The defenses of New York were not capable of withstanding an attack of a Dutch naval expedition, already encouraged by former triumphs. By the loss of New York Lovelace was impoverished and degraded. All his property was stripped from him, first by the Dutch, then by his countrymen, some for debts

to the Duke of York, others for unpaid property or mortgages, or other private debts in New York. Litigation over these debts continued many years. While traveling in the Mediterranean, in 1674, he was captured by Turks, taken to Algiers, and there stripped of his jewels and several hundred pounds. On being ransomed he returned to England, where he was pursued by the vindictiveness of the Duke of York, who claimed a debt of seven thousand pounds and was irritated by the loss of his proprietary province. In January 1675 he was imprisoned in the Tower, but he was released in April on security, on account of being "dangerously ill of a dropsy." Meanwhile he had been under examination, for the loss of New York, by a committee appointed by the King. His last months were spent in retirement at Woodstock, near Oxford, where he probably died in the latter part of 1675, as letters of administration were issued to his brother Dudley on Dec. 22 of that year. This administration was still unsettled in 1686, when Dudley died.

[The best account is J. H. Pleasants, "Francis Lovelace, Gov. of N. Y.," *N. Y. Geneal. and Biog. Record,* July 1920, which includes sketches of the brothers Thos. and Dudley Lovelace. The plantations of the Lovelaces on Staten Island are discussed by E. C. Delavan in "Col. Francis Lovelace and His Plantation on Staten Island," *Proc. Nat. Sci. Asso. of Staten Island,* Mar. 10, 1900, reprinted separately in 1902. See also: A J. Pearman, "The Kentish Family of Lovelace," *Archæologia Cantina,* vol. X (1876); Elizabeth Doremus, *Lovelace Chart* (n.d.); J. R. Brodhead, *Hist. of the State of N. Y.,* vol. II (1871); I. N. P. Stokes, *The Iconography of Manhattan Island,* vol. IV (1922); *Minutes of the Executive Council of the Province of N. Y.: Administration of Francis Lovelace, 1668–1673* (2 vols., 1910), ed. by V. H. Paltsits, with collateral and illustrative documents; E. B. O'Callaghan, ed., *Docs. Relative to the Colonial Hist. of the State of N. Y.,* vol. II (1858), vol. III (1853); Berthold Fernow, ed., *Docs. Relating to the Colonial Hist. of the State of N. Y.,* vol. XIII (1881), vol. XIV (1883), and *The Records of New Amsterdam* (1897), vols. VI and VII; "The Interment of Wm. Lovelace," *Am. Hist. Rev.,* Apr. 1904; *Calendar of State Papers, Colonial Ser., America and West Indies, 1661–68* (1880), *1669–74* (1889), *1675–76* (1893); *Calendar of State Papers, Domestic Ser., . . . 1673 . . . 1675* (1904); "The MSS. of H. S. Le Fleming, Esq., of Rydal Hall" (1890), *Hist. MSS. Commission: Twelfth Report,* App., pt. 7.]
V. H. P.

LOVELAND, WILLIAM AUSTIN HAMILTON (May 30, 1826–Dec. 17, 1894), pioneer Colorado merchant and railroad promoter, was born in Chatham, Mass. His parents, Leonard and Elizabeth (Eldridge) Loveland moved to Illinois in 1837, settling first in Alton and then in Brighton. The boy received as good an education as the district afforded. After attending the common schools, he was sent first to McKendree College and then to Shurtleff College, in Alton, but owing to ill health he did not complete his formal training. In 1847 he was lured from home to serve as wagonmaster in the Mexican War. Wounded, he returned to Illinois, but he had tasted the joy of adventure and in 1849 went to California. He mined in Grass Valley, traveled to Central America, and, in 1851, once more went home. A few years of mercantile life ended in another venture westward. In the spring of 1859 tales spread of rich finds of gold at Pike's Peak. Loveland sold out, packed a wagon-train with goods, crossed the plains, and reached Denver in June, at the time when everyone was hurrying to the newly discovered mines in the valley of Clear Creek. He promptly left Denver to open a store in Golden, a town at the foothill entrance to the mines. His wanderings were over; he settled down to become a prosperous merchant, a political leader, a builder of railroads, and one of the leading men of his generation in Colorado.

Loveland was always a keen man of business. He owned the largest general merchandise store in Golden, held mining properties in the nearby mountains, and invested in real estate. In 1878 he purchased the Denver *Rocky Mountain News,* a political as well as a business investment, and held it until 1886. In later life he was president of an ore reduction company and organizer of an electric railway between Denver and Golden. In politics he was a leader in the Democratic party. He was a member of the council of the territorial legislature from 1862 to 1870, and president of the abortive constitutional convention of 1865. Largely owing to his influence, Golden was the seat of the territorial government from 1862 to the end of 1867. Thereafter he was not so successful. He was Democratic candidate for the United States Senate in 1876 and 1879, and for governor in 1878, but he failed of election.

The spectacular struggle of his life was for railroad connections with the eastern states. Both Denver and Golden hoped to become the railroad center of the state. Loveland promoted the Colorado Central & Pacific Railroad Company which was to effect a connection between the Kansas Pacific and the Union Pacific, through Golden. Before that road was completed, Denver was connected with the Union Pacific at Cheyenne, and Golden lost in the race. In the late seventies the Colorado Central was absorbed by the Union Pacific. In December 1894 Loveland contracted pneumonia and died in Lakeside, a suburb of Denver. He was survived by his second wife, Maranda Ann Montgomery, whom he had married in Alton on Aug. 25, 1856. His first wife, Philena Shaw, whom he married in Brighton, Ill., on May 13, 1852,

died in 1854. Loveland's name is commemorated in that of a small town on the railroad which had been his pride.

[There is an unsatisfactory account of Loveland's life, taken by dictation from him July 24, 1886, in the Bancroft Library. For printed sources see Frank Hall, *History of Colorado* (4 vols., 1889–95) containing scattered references and a biographical sketch in vol. IV; J. B. and George Loveland, *Geneal. of the Loveland Family,* vol. II (1894), containing a sketch by Loveland's son; *Rocky Mountain News* and *Denver Republican,* Dec. 18, 1894.]   J. F. W.

LOVELL, JAMES (Oct. 31, 1737–July 14, 1814), school-master, politician, second son of John [*q.v.*] and Abigail Lovell, was born in Boston. He received his early training in the South Grammar School, of which his father was master, graduated from Harvard in 1756, took a post-graduate course the following year, then became usher in his father's school, a position which he held acceptably for eighteen years. Such was his scholarship that he delivered an oration in Latin in the chapel of Harvard College, Feb. 19, 1760, at the funeral of Henry Flynt, a long-time tutor in the college. On Nov. 24 of that year he married Mary Middleton, daughter of Alexander Middleton, a native of Scotland, and settled down to a life of uneventful usefulness as a trainer of young Bostonians. Ten years later he was chosen as the first orator to commemorate the Boston Massacre. The oration which he delivered (Apr. 2, 1771) placed him amongst the stanchest opponents of British measures respecting the colonies. The South Grammar School was closed by the British military authorities in April 1775, and following the battle of Bunker Hill James was arrested for spying and giving intelligence to the rebels and in 1776 was sent as a prisoner to Halifax. It happened that his father took up his residence in Halifax at about the same time, as a Loyalist refugee. After some delay, owing to the fact that some of Lovell's "billets," as he called them, fell into the hands of General Howe, an exchange was effected in the autumn of 1776, and Lovell returned to Boston "to the no small joy of the inhabitants" of that city.

Within a few days of his landing he was chosen as a delegate to the Continental Congress, taking his seat Feb. 4, 1777, at Baltimore. From the first Lovell took an active part in the proceedings of Congress, distinguishing himself at once for industry and zeal. Investigation of the conduct of Schuyler and conferences with Gates enhanced his conception of the prowess of the latter general, and partiality for Gates, which, after Saratoga, attained a degree of perfervid devotion, led him straight into the ranks of the critics of Washington. What part he may have had in the actual formation of the plot known as the Conway Cabal is not definitely known, but that he fomented it with all the power that was in him, is sufficiently evidenced by his letters to Gates and other intimate correspondents. Lovell surpassed all his colleagues in his vocabulary of sneers and sarcasm directed at Washington yet, like many another, in 1789 he could profess a pious devotion to the "demi-god"—and beseech him for an appointment to office.

Lovell's early appointment to the committee on foreign applications must have had no small share in shaping his subsequent course. Congress was besieged by a horde of French officers seeking commissions, and Lovell was one of the few members who knew French. "These Frenchmen have used me up quite," he wrote in June 1777, and his mood had not changed, when, a month later, he met Lafayette and sought vainly to chill the ardor of that young enthusiast. But the most far-reaching consequence of this episode was the distrust, mounting to fierce hostility, engendered in a large group in Congress toward Silas Deane [q.v.] who was in a measure responsible for the coming of the Frenchmen. The anti-Deane party, of which Lovell was one of the most rabid, were not able to destroy Franklin, but they succeeded in hounding the life out of poor Deane. As a member of the committee for foreign affairs, to which he was appointed May 26, 1777, Lovell probably achieved his greatest distinction, whether for better or for worse. The committee was neglected by Congress, and for months at a time Lovell was all that was left of it. Members came and members went, but Lovell stayed on, never once in five years so much as visiting his wife and children. Diligent to a fault, he kept his seat all day in Congress, then spent long hours at night "quill-driving," as he expressed it. Marbois described Lovell as "Homme de capacité, souple, insinuant . . . laborieux, intelligent," but little conversant with foreign affairs. Lovell, nevertheless, sought in the autumn of 1779 to be placed where he might catch Franklin's mantle when it should fall. He had already done what he could to loosen it. He was not a diplomat, though he was liberally gifted in intrigue and loved mystery and mystification. A useful member of Congress in many ways, serving on innumerable committees, sometimes taking high ground, he nevertheless vitiated his career by his intense partisanship.

For reasons that do not wholly appear Lovell quitted Congress in April 1782, apparently chagrined over the failure of so many of his cherished ambitions. He became receiver of continental taxes in Boston, then (in 1788) collector of customs for the state of Massachusetts, and on Aug. 3, 1789, was appointed naval officer for the district of Boston and Charlestown. This office he held for the remainder of his life. He died while visiting relatives at Windham, Me. His eldest son, also named James, made a creditable record as an officer in the Revolution and lived till 1850; his grandson, Joseph Lovell [q.v.], rose to be surgeon-general of the United States; and his great-grandson, Mansfield Lovell [q.v.], became a Confederate general.

[*Mass. Hist. Soc. Colls.*, 2 ser., I (1814), 3 ser., III (1833), 4 ser., IV (1858) ; *Colonial Soc. of Mass. Pubs.*, vol. XV (1925) ; *Essex Inst. Hist. Colls.*, July, Oct. 1876 ; Peter Force, *Am. Archives*, 4 ser. (6 vols., 1837–46), 5 ser. (3 vols., 1848–53) ; J. S. Loring, *The Hundred Boston Orators* (1852) ; Francis Wharton, *Revolutionary Diplomatic Correspondence of the U. S.* (1889), vols. I–IV ; S. A. Drake, *Old Landmarks and Historic Personages of Boston* (1873) ; E. C. Burnett, *Letters of Members of the Continental Cong.* (1921–) ; *Cat. of the Boston Pub. Latin School* (1886) ; *Columbian Centinel* (Boston), July 20, 1814 ; *Boston Gazette* and *Independent Chronicle* (Boston), July 21, 1814 ; Boston town records and records of births and marriages.]
E. C. B.

LOVELL, JOHN (Apr. 1, 1710–1778), schoolmaster, was born in Boston, Mass., the son of John and Priscilla (Gardiner) Lovell. Graduated from Harvard College in 1728, he was appointed an usher of the South Grammar or Latin School in Boston in the following year. In 1734 he became master of the school and continued to serve in that capacity until Apr. 19, 1775. Among the boys who came under his tutelage were Samuel Adams, Samuel Langdon, James Bowdoin, Robert Treat Paine, Andrew Oliver, John Lowell, John Hancock, Thomas Brattle, Jeremy Belknap, Francis Dana, Henry Knox, William Phillips, William Eustis, Christopher Gore, and Harrison Gray Otis. By his contributions to the *Weekly Rehearsal* (1731–35) Lovell won at least a local reputation as "a pleasing and elegant writer," and at the first annual town meeting held in Faneuil Hall, Mar. 14, 1742/43, he delivered a funeral oration upon Peter Faneuil, the donor. Toward the end of the address he exclaimed, "May Liberty always spread its joyful wings over this place!" But in another breath he added, "And may Loyalty to a King, under whom we enjoy this liberty, ever remain our character!" True to his invocation Lovell chose the British side in the American Revolution and left Boston with many other Loyalists and the British army in March 1776. He died at Halifax, Nova Scotia, in 1778. His son, James Lovell [q.v.], stanchly American, was carried to Nova Scotia in 1776 as a British prisoner but was exchanged in the fall and returned to Boston.

John Lovell was a severe teacher, but socially a humorous and agreeable companion. He was a member of a French Club, at the meetings of which "the whole conversation was to be in French" (*Diary and Letters of Thomas Hutchinson*, 1883, I, p. 47), and of the Fire Club (*Letters and Diary of John Rowe*, 1903, p. 36). Various members in the *Pietas et Gratulatio Collegii Cantabrigiensis apud Novanglos* (1761) are attributed to Lovell's pen, and he was also the author of "The Seasons, an Interlocutory Exercise at the South Latin School." By his contemporaries he was considered an excellent classical scholar and also a sound critic. A record of Lovell's intention to marry Abigail Green was filed in Boston on Apr. 10, 1735.

[J. S. Loring, *The Hundred Boston Orators* (1852), contains a good biographical sketch including specimens of Lovell's verse. H. F. Jenks's "Hist. Sketch" in the *Cat. of the Boston Pub. Latin School* (1886) is excellent and devotes a number of pages to Lovell, but should be supplemented by Robert F. Seybolt's "Schoolmasters of Colonial Boston," *Colonial Soc. of Mass. Pubs.*, XXVII (1930), 130–56, which lists many useful references to Lovell and his son James. See also Justin Winsor, *Memorial Hist. of Boston*, II (1881), 264–65; S. E. Morison, *Harrison Gray Otis* (1913), vol. I; and records of Boston births and marriages. Lovell's oration on Peter Faneuil was printed in 1743 and was reprinted in Caleb Hopkins Snow, *A Hist. of Boston* (1825), pp. 235–37. A portrait of Lovell by Nathaniel Smybert, a former pupil, is reproduced in Winsor's *Memorial Hist. of Boston* (1881), II, p. 401. The original is in the possession of Harvard University.]
L. S. M.

LOVELL, JOHN EPY (Apr. 23, 1795–May 3, 1892), educator, was born in Colne, Lancashire, England, the eldest child of John and Elizabeth (Epy) Lovell. His parents sent him to a private boarding-school at St. Ives, where in five years' time he finished at the head of his class. As tutor at the age of sixteen in the family of the Duke of Bedford he made the acquaintance of Joseph Lancaster, originator of the famous Lancasterian system of instruction, whereby a single teacher could instruct many by using the older pupils as teachers of the younger. This acquaintance was decisive for Lovell's further career. Through Lancaster's influence he shortly became principal of a Lancasterian school at Burr Rose, England, but after some years decided to try his fortune with the system in the United States. After attempts to establish himself in Philadelphia and in Baltimore, he finally started a school in New Haven, Conn., in 1822, which was immediately successful. In 1827, however, a rift in the community's support led him to accept an appointment to teach elocution in the Mount Pleasant Classical Institute at Amherst, Mass. The New Haven school languished during his absence and

in three years he was recalled. For the next quarter century this school, under his control, was the pride of the town and Lovell's personal popularity was unbounded. In fact, so successful was he that New Haven clung to the Lancasterian system long after other cities were adopting the more modern plan of graded schools. He published *Introductory Arithmetic* (1827) and *Rhetorical Dialogues* (1839). In 1857 he tendered his resignation to the New Haven Board of Education, assigning the burden of his textbook writing as the cause. The next few years he spent in completing a series of school readers, *Lovell's Progressive Reader* (5 vols., 1855–59), and in doing some private tutoring. Later he made his home with his daughter, and when she moved to Waterbury, Conn., about 1882, he accompanied her. Some time after 1890 he moved with her to Milwaukee, Wis., where he died.

Lovell's place in American educational history is almost identical with that of the Lancasterian system of instruction. His influence was never national in scope. Some of his books were known outside Connecticut, but it is doubtful if his reputation as a teacher extended thus far. He recognized his debt to Lancaster by dedicating to him his first publication, *Introductory Arithmetic*, and when, late in life, Lancaster was in want, Lovell was active in raising funds for him. Lovell's own peculiar success with the Lancasterian mode of instruction seems to have resided in his ability to infuse a highly mechanical system of instruction with the warmth of personal magnetism. Regarding his application of the system he wrote at length for the *Connecticut Common School Journal* (June 1840). His forte was elocution, and among his pupils were Henry Ward Beecher and Edwin Booth. It was in this field that he wrote his most successful book, *The United States Speaker* (1833).

One child survived his first wife, Harriet Fletcher, who died in 1835. Two children were born to him by his second wife, Minerva Camp, whom he married Mar. 29, 1845.

[*New Haven Daily Palladium, New Haven Evening Register*, and *New Haven Leader*, May 4, 1892; *Memories, Reminiscences, etc., in Verse of the Old Lancasterian School* (New Haven, 1897); information from Lovell's scrapbook in possession of his grandson, George Blakeman Lovell.]
J. S. B.

LOVELL, JOSEPH (Dec. 22, 1788–Oct. 17, 1836), surgeon-general of the army from 1818 to 1836, was born in Boston, Mass., the son of James S. and Deborah (Gorham) Lovell and the grandson of James Lovell [*q.v.*]. His early education was obtained from Boston schools, after which he entered Harvard College, graduating in 1807. He at once began the study of medicine under Dr. Ingalls of Boston, and was graduated from Harvard Medical School in 1811, in the first class to receive the M.D. degree. Prior to that time only the degree of M.B. had been awarded. On May 15, 1812, he entered the army as surgeon of the 9th Infantry. He was but twenty-four years old, but he was much better educated than most medical men of his day. He was soon put in charge of the general hospital at Burlington, Vt., which became known as a model. On June 30, 1814, he was appointed hospital surgeon and the next month he established a general hospital for 1,100 patients at Williamsville, N. Y. All of his work was of a quality to excite the admiration of his superiors and he won praise from Generals Wilkinson, Scott, and Brown. After the establishment of peace, Lovell continued in the service as hospital surgeon. In 1817, as chief medical officer of the Northern Department, he submitted to General Brown a paper discussing the causes of disease in the army. Naturally, in the total lack of any knowledge of bacteriology, the diseases were generally attributed to meteorological conditions, to insufficient clothing, and to insufficient or spoiled food. But Lovell also discussed medical administration, and he did it in such a way that this report, together with his excellent record, resulted in his appointment as surgeon-general in 1818 when the army was reorganized and a medical department established. He was at the time but thirty years old. He continued in office until his death. He did much to establish the new corps in public and official esteem. At one time Secretary of War Eaton advised Congress that "the Surgeon General of the Army might be dispensed with," but Lovell obtained permission to write a reply to be forwarded to Congress and as a result obtained a long-sought increase in his corps, instead of a reduction.

Immediately upon becoming surgeon-general, Lovell ordered all medical officers to submit quarterly reports of weather and of the incidence, prevalence, and causes of disease. From the medical reports were later compiled departmental reports of the greatest historical value. The weather reports form the historical beginning of the present Weather Bureau. He also rendered a positive service to the army and the country in continually inviting attention to the great evils of the alcoholism of that day, and in bringing about, as he did in greater measure than any other single man, the abolition of the rum ration. Finally he will be remembered for the encouragement and official assistance which he gave to William Beaumont [*q.v.*], in promot-

ing the latter's study of gastric physiology. After the Black Hawk War Lovell obtained another small increase in the size of his corps and he was seeking yet a third at the time of his death, which occurred on Oct. 17, 1836. Harvey E. Brown wrote of him (*post,* p. 157): "In all his relations, whether as christian philanthropist, profound scholar, skilful surgeon, experienced officer or true-hearted gentleman, he was one of whom the Medical Staff may always be proud and the memory of whose good life is written on every page of its history." Lovell survived his wife, Margaret (Mansfield) Lovell, and left a family of eleven children, one of whom was Mansfield Lovell [*q.v.*].

[H. E. Brown, *The Medic. Dept. of the U. S. Army* (1873); J. E. Pilcher, "Joseph Lovell, Surgeon General of the U. S. Army, 1818–1836," *Jour. Asso. Mil. Surgeons,* May 1904, and reprinted in Pilcher's *Surgeon Gens. of the U. S. Army* (1905); James Mann, *Medic. Sketches of the Campaigns of 1812, 13, 14* (1816); T. F. Harrington, *The Harvard Medic. School: A Hist.* (1905), vol. II; J. S. Myer, *Life and Letters of Dr. Wm. Beaumont* (1912); biography of Lovell's son in *Fifteenth Ann. Reunion, Asso. Grads. U. S. Mil. Acad.,* 1884; *Nat. Intelligencer* (Washington, D. C.), Oct. 19, 1836.]   P. M. A.

LOVELL, MANSFIELD (Oct. 20, 1822–June 1, 1884), soldier and civil engineer, was born in Washington, D. C., the son of Dr. Joseph Lovell [*q.v.*], surgeon-general of the army, 1818–36, and his wife, Margaret (Mansfield) Lovell. Having received an ordinary school education, he entered West Point at sixteen, graduating in 1842 and being commissioned second lieutenant, 4th Artillery. His army service was unremarkable prior to the Mexican War, during which he was commissioned first lieutenant in February 1847, brevetted captain for gallantry at Chapultepec in September, and was twice wounded. After the war he saw garrison service on the frontiers and in New York. In 1849 he married Emily, daughter of Col. Joseph Plympton. Resigning from the army in 1854, he secured employment in Cooper & Hewitt's Iron Works, Trenton, N. J. He became superintendent of street improvements, New York, in April 1858, and deputy street-commissioner in November, serving as such until his resignation in September 1861, to join the Confederate army. During the two years previous he had kept in touch with things military by teaching the old City Guard, a select organization, how to handle the guns of Fort Hamilton. That he was favorably remembered as a soldier is evidenced by a letter from Joseph E. Johnston to Jefferson Davis, recommending him as a possible division commander a month before he resigned his New York position. On Oct. 7, 1861, he was appointed a major-general in the Confederate army, and ordered to assume command at New Orleans. Before proceeding there, and afterwards, he protested against the divided command of land and sea forces. His garrison was none too large to withstand an attack, and in spite of strenuous efforts throughout the winter of 1861–62 to improve the defenses, he was hampered by requisition of the field armies for troops and guns. When Farragut appeared with his fleet in April 1862, Lovell had but 3,000 ninety-day men, not half of whom possessed muskets. For ten days he stood off the superior Federal fleet, but on Apr. 23 it passed the city, and he judged evacuation necessary to save the city from bombardment by naval guns. He withdrew his forces and all state and government property up the Mississippi, and prepared to defend Beauregard's rear against attack from the river. These dispositions were approved by Robert E. Lee; but Lovell was not entrusted with important command again until the battle of Corinth (Miss.), Oct. 3–4, when he commanded the I Corps and attacked on the Confederate right the first day. After the Confederate defeat, at Coffeeville on Oct. 5, he commanded the rearguard so skilfully as to draw praise from his opponent, Rosecrans.

Feeling had arisen regarding the loss of New Orleans, and in December 1862, Lovell was relieved of command. He took up the matter with the War Department (see *Correspondence between the War Department and General Lovell Relating to the Defences of New Orleans*, 1863), and secured the appointment of a military court of inquiry, which finally published its findings in November 1863, absolving him of blame for the loss of New Orleans, but mildly censuring him for minor faults incident to the evacuation (*Proceedings of the Inquiry Relating to the Fall of New Orleans*, 1864). No bitterness appears in the correspondence of this trying time, but the endeavors of his friends to obtain further commands for him failed. In a final effort to demonstrate his ability he served under Joseph E. Johnston as a volunteer staff officer in the summer of 1864.

Following the war, he returned to New York, and later, after a disastrous venture into rice-planting on the Savannah River, he took up civil engineering and surveying there, and was assistant engineer under Gen. John Newton in removing East River obstructions at Hell Gate. Lovell was courageous, and a good soldier, with a clear grasp of strategy, but it was his great misfortune to lose New Orleans through governmental ineptitude after he had repeatedly warned that it could not be held without unified command and the presence of ample garrison and sufficient long-range guns.

[G. W. Cullum, *Biog. Reg. Officers and Grads. U. S. Mil. Acad.* (3rd ed., 1891) ; G. W. Smith, in *15th Ann. Reunion Asso. Grads. U. S. Mil. Acad.* (1884) ; *War of the Rebellion: Official Records (Army)*, 1 ser. ; *Battles and Leaders of the Civil War* (4 vols., 1887–88), esp. vol. II ; M. J. Wright, *Gen. Officers of the Confed. Army* (1911) ; *War of the Rebellion: Official Records (Navy)*, 1 ser. ; M. F. Steele, *Am. Campaigns* (1909) ; *Confed. Mil. Hist.* (1899), vol. X ; *N. Y. Herald*, June 2, 1884.]
D. Y.

LOVERING, JOSEPH (Dec. 25, 1813–Jan. 18, 1892), for fifty years Hollis Professor of Mathematics and Natural Philosophy in Harvard College, was born in Charlestown, Mass., the son of Robert and Elizabeth (Simonds) Lovering. The Rev. James Walker [*q.v.*], afterward president of Harvard, aided him in various ways to fit himself for college. He graduated from Harvard as the fourth scholar in his class, in 1833. While a student in the Harvard Divinity School, he was also an assistant teacher of mathematics in the college, and in the year 1835–36 for a time conducted morning and evening prayers in the college chapel. These temporary engagements led to his appointment as lecturer in natural philosophy and in 1838 he was appointed to the Hollis professorship. The same qualities, mental, moral, and physical, that would have made him an impressive preacher made him, for his time, a much respected professor of natural science, and with respect a considerable measure of affection was mingled. At the same time, people were likely to smile when they mentioned him, for some of his rather infrequent remarks were witty and some of his unchanging ways were odd. He was highly praised by eminent men as a lecturer, stating the facts and laws of science with lucidity and grave oratorical effect, illustrating them by carefully prepared experiments. In the classroom, on the other hand, he seems to have followed in its most extreme form the then prevailing habit of setting for his students definite lessons to be learned and recited in the exact words of the textbook.

Despite the limitations of his experimental work, Lovering wrote a paper "On a New Method of Measuring the Velocity of Electricity" (*Proceedings of the American Association for the Advancement of Science*, vol. XXIV, 1876), describing a procedure which apparently he had devised. The method he employed gave no information of importance, but as evidence of the will of an old-fashioned teacher, in his sixty-second year, to break ground in what was for him a novel field of experimental research, it is of considerable importance. He also wrote various essays on scientific subjects, many notices of deceased scientific men, a number of addresses which he made as president (1880–92) of the American Academy of Arts and Sciences, and discussions of natural physical phenomena such as the aurora borealis and other atmospheric happenings. He produced, it appears, no books, but he did much editorial work, especially for the *Proceedings* of the American Association for the Advancement of Science of which he was permanent secretary from 1854 to 1873 and president for the year 1873. He was frugal in his way of life and not disposed to follow changing fashions. One of his pithy sayings, which had a peculiar pungency for his younger colleagues, was substantially this: "The reason why the undulatory theory of light is now universally accepted is that the people who formerly held the corpuscular theory are all dead." He married in 1844 Sarah Gray Hawes of Boston, and of this marriage came two sons and two daughters. Retiring in 1888, he lived till Jan. 18, 1892.

[B. O. Peirce, memoir in *Nat. Acad. Sci., Biog. Memoirs*, vol. VI (1909), with bibliography; *Memorials of the Class of 1833 of Harvard Coll.* (1883); *Proc. Am. Acad. Arts and Sci.*, n.s., XIX (1893); *Popular Sci. Monthly*, Sept. 1889; T. B. Wyman, *The Geneals. and Estates of Charlestown* (1879), vol. II; *Boston Transcript*, Jan. 19, 1892.]   E. H. H.

LOVETT, ROBERT WILLIAMSON (Nov. 18, 1859–July 2, 1924), orthopedic surgeon, was born in Beverly, Mass., the only child of John Dyson and Mary Elizabeth (Williamson) Lovett, his ancestry running back through mariners and merchants to early colonial days. His boyhood seems to have been somewhat restricted because of a natural parental solicitude for the last male of his line. The woolen business in which his father was engaged brought the family to Boston winters and the lad was prepared for college at two famous old schools, Chauncy Hall and Noble's. He received the degree of A.B. from Harvard College in 1881 and that of M.D. from the Harvard Medical School in 1885. After gaining surgical experience from an eighteen months' internship at the Boston City Hospital and from a four months' service at the New York Orthopædic Hospital, he began to practise in Boston. In 1895 he married Elizabeth Moorfield Storey, eldest daughter of Moorfield Storey [*q.v.*].

Becoming connected with the out-patient department of the City Hospital he was at length appointed visiting surgeon. Early interest in crippled children became a controlling passion, which slowly drew him away from general surgery, until in 1899 he resigned from the City Hospital. Thereafter the Boston Children's Hospital became his main clinic. The breadth of view which long surgical training had given him was now focused upon orthopedic surgery. He held many accessory appointments, was made chief surgeon of the Massachusetts Hospital School at Canton, and until his death was the guiding spirit in the development of the New England Peabody Home for Crippled Children. In 1912 he became head of the department of orthopedic surgery at the Boston Children's Hospital and succeeded Edward Hickling Bradford [*q.v.*] as the John Ball and Buckminster Brown Professor of Orthopædic Surgery at the Harvard Medical School.

A charter member of the American Orthopædic Association and of the Boston Surgical Society, he was elected to the presidency of both. He organized the Harvard Infantile Paralysis Commission and became its chairman in 1916. The states of New York, Vermont, and Massachusetts sought his aid in their fights against the ravages of this disease. Holding the commission of major during the World War, he was in charge of the training of medical officers in military orthopedic surgery. He was a fellow of the American Academy of Arts and Sciences, and of the American College of Surgeons, a member of the Société Internationale de Chirurgie, and honorary or corresponding member of British, French, and Italian orthopedic associations. His contributions to medical literature were voluminous. Among his more important monographs are *Diseases of the Hip Joint* (1891), *Lateral Curvature of the Spine and Round Shoulders* (1907), *The Treatment of Infantile Paralysis* (1916). He was co-author with Edward H. Bradford of the leading early textbook in his special field, *A Treatise on Orthopedic Surgery* (1890), and his crowning work, prepared in co-operation with his friend Sir Robert Jones, *Orthopedic Surgery*, appeared in 1923.

Wise counsellor of the Harvard Medical School, controlling spirit of the Boston Children's Hospital, eminent practitioner, subtle in approach, rarely polemic, quick of wit, often merry, this tall, spare aristocrat of medicine compelled men and women to work for him and with him and retained their loyalty. The controlling purpose of his life was to make contributions to his specialty which would outlive him. For this he successfully labored with an intensity which never dulled his intellect but proved his physical undoing. He was taken ill on a journey to England and died in Liverpool at the house of Sir Robert Jones. His wife and a daughter survived him.

[Sir Robert Jones in *British Medic. Jour.*, July 12, 1924; Harvey Cushing, in *Boston Medic. and Surgic. Jour.*, Aug. 14, 1924; R. B. Osgood, in *Jour. of Bone and Joint Surgery,* Oct. 1924; *Harvard Grads. Mag.,* Sept. 1924; *Boston Transcript, N. Y. Times,* July 3, 1924; information from widow and friends.] R. B. O.

LOVEWELL, JOHN (Oct. 14, 1691–May 8, 1725), Indian fighter, was born in that part of Dunstable, Mass., now lying within Nashua, N. H. He was the son of Anna (Hassell) and John Lovewell, who served under Captain Benjamin Church in the "Great Swamp Fight" of 1675. In 1724 he was the owner of a two-hundred-acre farm at Dunstable and had a wife, Hannah, and two children. When the town was attacked, his brother-in-law, Josiah Farwell, was one of the few who escaped out of the pursuing company, which was ambushed by the Indians. Soon afterward, Lovewell and others petitioned the Massachusetts government for a commission "to range . . . the woods . . . in order to kill and destroy their enemy Indians" (Fox, *post,* p. 110). The General Court granted two and a half shillings a day with a bounty for every male Indian scalp. After managing, with a force of thirty recruits, to kill one Indian and capture a boy on Dec. 10, 1724, he was able to raise a company of eighty-seven men for a second expedition. Taking a course along the Merrimac, past Lake Winnepesaukee and nearly to the White Mountains, they found a warm trail and, on Feb. 20, 1725, surprised and killed ten sleeping Indians. On Mar. 10 the company marched in triumph through the streets of Boston. He raised a third expedition with some difficulty because of the planting season and, advancing with forty-six men into the stronghold of the Pequawkets, on the site of Fryeburg, Me., he showed himself more daring than prudent. At Lake Ossipee he built a small fort and garrisoned it. With his force reduced to thirty-four, on May 8, he crossed the Saco just above where it enters what is now called Lovewell's Pond. Decoyed by an Indian, the company was ambushed by a band of Pequawkets, and, in the first fire of the enemy, he and several others were killed. The remainder of the force fought stubbornly throughout the day. At evening the Indians withdrew leaving the fallen bodies untouched.

Lovewell and his company were the subjects of balladry even before the full truth of the fight was known. The earliest version of the song was advertised under the title "The Voluntier's March" in the *New England Courant* for May 31, 1725, and, though no known copy has been preserved, is probably the same ballad as "Lovewell's Fight," which appeared in the February 1824 issue of *Collections, Historical and Miscellaneous,* edited by John Farmer and J. B. Moore, and followed closely the account of the

battle in Franklin's paper of May 24, 1725. The second known version, also called "Lovewell's Fight," was printed by Farmer and Moore in their issue for March 1824 and has usually been attributed to Thomas Cogswell Upham [*q.v.*], who was at that time a minister at Rochester, N. H.

[Frederic Kidder, *The Expeditions of Capt. John Lovewell* (1865) and *The Adventures of Capt. Lovewell* (1853), reprinted from the *New-England Hist. and Geneal. Register,* Jan. 1853; C. J. Fox, *Hist. of the Old Township of Dunstable* (1846); Francis Parkman, *A Half-Century of Conflict* (1892), vol. I; Thomas Symmes, *Lovewell Lamented* (1725) and *The Original Account of Capt. John Lovewell's "Great Fight,"* ed. by Nathaniel Bouton (1861); E. S. Stearns, *Early Generations of the Founders of Old Dunstable* (1911); *Hist. Sketches of Dunstable, Mass. Bi-Centennial Oration* (1873); G. L. Kittredge, "The Ballad of Lovewell's Fight" in *Biog. Essays; a Tribute to Wilberforce Eames* (1924); R. P. Gray, *Songs and Ballads of the Maine Lumberjacks* (1924).] A. I. D.

LOW, ABIEL ABBOT (Feb. 7, 1811–Jan. 7, 1893), merchant in the China trade, was born in Salem, Mass., one of a family of twelve children of Seth and Mary (Porter) Low. His ancestors had been natives of Massachusetts, the founder of the American line, Thomas Low, having settled in Massachusetts Bay in the first half of the seventeenth century. Low was educated in the public schools and at an early age became a clerk in the house of Joseph Howard & Company, engaged in the South American trade. In 1829 his father removed from Salem to Brooklyn, N. Y., and established himself as an importer of drugs and India wares, and the son worked in his employ for several years. In 1833, at the invitation of a relative, Low sailed to Canton, China, and became a clerk in the mercantile house of Russell & Company, the largest American firm in China. He soon acquired a thorough knowledge of the intricacies of foreign trade and in 1837 was admitted to the firm. Three years later, desirous of returning home, he engaged in a joint enterprise with a Chinese merchant which remitted both parties a handsome profit and enabled Low to enter into business in New York on his own account, thus laying the foundations of A. A. Low & Brothers. Low's firm very soon gained a prominent position in the trade in China tea and Japanese silk. Celebrated among their fleet of clipper ships were *The Houqua,* launched in 1844 and named after the Chinese mandarin who had engaged with Low in the joint enterprise, the speedy *Samuel Russell,* which gained a reputation for outstripping its rivals with ease, and *The Contest* and *Jacob Bell,* both destroyed by Confederate privateers, recovery for which was effected before the Joint High Commission at Geneva. Low's economic interests extended beyond the flourishing import business which

Low

his firm conducted. He actively participated in financing the first Atlantic cable and, together with Collis P. Huntington and others, was associated with the building of the Chesapeake & Ohio Railroad through West Virginia to the Ohio River and in the founding of Newport News, Va., and Huntington, W. Va.

Though an unusually powerful and eloquent speaker, and well equipped for public life, Low seems to have felt no desire to enter politics, in which field his father, in a modest way, and his son, Seth Low [q.v.], more spectacularly engaged. He by no means, however, held himself aloof from civic affairs. During the Civil War he was president of the Union Defence Committee of New York and of other war financing bodies. As president of the New York Chamber of Commerce from 1863 until his resignation in 1866, he voiced the hostility of New York business men to Great Britain's rôle in relation to the Confederate commerce destroyers (J. B. Bishop, *A Chronicle of One Hundred & Fifty Years— The Chamber of Commerce of the State of New York, 1768–1918,* 1918, p. 82). On his return to New York in 1867 from a voyage around the world he urged a policy of government subsidies for the American merchant marine (*Entertainment Given to Mr. A. A. Low by Members of the Chamber of Commerce . . . Oct. 8, 1867,* 1867, p. 26). Despite the conciliatory attitude which his son Seth demonstrated throughout his life in dealing with the labor problem, he himself was hostile to labor combinations (*Address by A. A. Low . . . May 3, 1866,* 1866, p. 9). After the Civil War he gave vigorous expression to the demands of the New York merchants for a resumption of specie payments (*Centennial Celebration of the Chamber of Commerce of the State of New York, Apr. 6th, 1868,* 1868, pp. 21–30). One of his last important public services was in rendering a report as commissioner of charities of Kings County on the bearing of the growth of urban population and unsanitary conditions on the increase of pauperism: Low was married on Mar. 16, 1841, to Ellen Almira, daughter of Josiah Dow of Brooklyn. Following her death, he married, on Feb. 25, 1851, his brother William Henry's widow, Anne, daughter of Mott Bedell. He was a Unitarian in religion and an exceptionally liberal patron of education and welfare work. He died in Brooklyn.

[See Benjamin R. C. Low, *Seth Low* (1925); W. G. Low, *Some Recollections for His Children and Grandchildren* (1909); A. L. Moffat, "Low Geneal.: The Descendants of Seth Low and Mary Porter" (1932), a copy of which is in the Lib. of Cong.; *Tribute of the Chamber of Commerce of the State of N.-Y. to the Memory of Abiel Abbot Low* (1893); *Brooklyn Daily Eagle,* Jan. 7, 1893.] R. B. M.

LOW, FREDERICK FERDINAND (June 30, 1828–July 21, 1894), governor, diplomat, banker, was born in that part of Frankfort which later became Winterport, Me. His father was a small farmer in the Penobscot Valley; the common school provided his education. At fifteen he was apprenticed to the East India firm of Russell, Sturgis & Company, Boston, and during the next five years he learned much about California and the Far East, where the firm operated. He also broadened his education by diligent attendance at the lectures given by the most distinguished men of the time at Faneuil Hall and the Lowell Institute. The expiration of his apprenticeship coincided with the amazing news from California in 1849. On Feb. 22 he embarked for the Isthmus of Panama, and after the usual hardships and delay, passed through the Golden Gate on the steamer *Panama* on June 4, 1849. He at once struck out for the mines and panned some gold on the south fork of the American River, but when the winter rains began he returned to San Francisco. Then began a successful business career as a merchant, first in San Francisco, then in the autumn of 1850 in partnership with his brother in Marysville, where he married Mollie Creed. In March 1854 he brought about a merger of almost all the inland steamship lines on the bay and the Sacramento River. This was followed by the establishment of a banking business in Marysville.

In 1861 he was nominated as a Union Republican for representative-at-large in Congress after the census of 1860 disclosed that California would be entitled to a third member. It was not until June 3, 1862, the day after a special act was approved granting the additional seat, that he was sworn into office. During the remainder of the session, until Mar. 3, 1863, he took little active part, but manifested his interest in revenue and banking bills and in California land titles. On retiring from Congress, he was persuaded by Secretary Chase to accept the post of collector of the port of San Francisco, but this position was soon terminated by his election as ninth governor of California. He was the first to serve for a four-year term (Dec. 10, 1863–Dec. 8, 1867). As governor he was respected for his sound judgment and fearlessness, and much credit is due him for the later founding of the University of California and for the preservation, from land grabbers, of the site of San Francisco's Golden Gate Park. He vetoed many objectionable bills and withheld his assent to others, and he pleaded for justice to the Chinese immigrants.

In December 1869 Low was appointed minister to China. During his four years in Peking (1870–74) the major incidents were the Tientsin massacre (1870), the attempt of the United States to secure a treaty with Korea, which resulted in naval operations in May 1871, and the long controversy over the audience question, which was partially won by the foreign representative in 1873. As minister, Low won the esteem of Chinese and foreigners alike. On returning to San Francisco he accepted the position of joint manager of the Anglo-California Bank (1874–91), the second in size on the Pacific Coast, and was also interested in many other business enterprises. He died there on July 21, 1894. While he could hardly be considered a remarkable political leader or diplomat, he held the respect of his contemporaries because of his good sense, honesty, courage, and friendliness.

[The best memoir of Low is that by E. T. Sheppard, to which is appended a biographical sketch compiled from the Low papers in the Bancroft Lib., in the *Univ. of Cal. Chronicle*, Apr. 1917. For his administration as governor see T. H. Hittell, *Hist. of Cal.*, vol. IV (1897); for his messages as governor see the *Journals* of the California Senate and Assembly, 1863–67. For his career as diplomat see Tyler Dennett, *Americans in Eastern Asia* (1922); and *Foreign Relations of the U. S.*, 1870–74. For an obituary, see the *San Francisco Chronicle*, July 22, 1894.]   P. J. T.

LOW, ISAAC (Apr. 13, 1735–July 25, 1791), New York merchant, member of the First Continental Congress, Loyalist, was born at Raritan Landing, near New Brunswick, N. J., the son of Cornelius, Jr., and Johanna (Gouverneur) Low, and a descendant of German, Dutch, and French settlers in New York in the seventeenth century. He moved to New York, built up a sizable fortune as a merchant, possessed wide commercial connections, and was financially interested in a slitting mill (P. Curtenius to Boston Committee of Correspondence, Aug. 26, 1774, Boston Committee of Correspondence Papers, New York Public Library, II, 381–85). He was married, on July 17, 1760, to Margarita, daughter of Cornelius Cuyler, mayor of Albany. In the pre-Revolutionary conflict he was an active Whig and was long to head merchants' committees in their efforts to obtain trade concessions from Parliament. He was a delegate to the Stamp Act Congress of 1765 and was chosen in 1768 to head a committee of inspection to enforce the non-importation agreement (C. L. Becker, *The History of Political Parties in the Province of New York, 1760–76*, 1909, p. 75). On the eve of the Revolution his liberal attitude brought down upon his head the condemnation of the more fanatical conservatives who held him to be "a person unbounded in ambition, . . . extremely opinionated," whose principles of government were "inclined to the republican system" (Jones, *post*, I, p. 35). Low served as chairman of the Committee of Fifty-one and was one of the five who drafted the proposals for a general congress to deal with non-importation.

As Low was essentially a moderate, his adherence to the cause of outright independence was doubted by shrewd observers. As early as 1773, he had, with Jacob Walton, opposed forcible resistance to the landing of the tea (Peter Force, *American Archives*, 4 ser., I, 1837, p. 254 note), and in the summer of 1774, John Adams, on his way to the First Continental Congress, was a breakfast guest at Low's elegant mansion on Dock Street. While favorably impressed by Low's "rich furniture for the tea table" and his beautiful wife, Adams was frankly skeptical. "Mr Low, the chairman of the Committee of Fifty-one," his *Diary* records, "they say, will profess attachment to the cause of liberty, but his sincerity is doubted" (C. F. Adams, *The Works of John Adams*, II, 1850, p. 350). Subsequent events proved the accuracy of this prediction. Elected a delegate from New York to the First Continental Congress (Force, *op. cit.*, pp. 305–30), he pursued a moderate course, was hostile to independence, and opposed the prohibition of all exports to the West Indies. Lee's demand for a bold front was met by an expression of fear on Low's part that Parliament might not yield and that therefore it would be wise "to provide ourselves with a retreat or a resource" (E. C. Burnett, *Letters of Members of the Continental Congress*, I, 1921, p. 64). Nevertheless, with the other conservative delegates from New York, he signed the Association.

In the end Low threw his own influence against independence. After the outbreak of hostilities in April 1775, he declined membership in the Provincial Convention of Apr. 20–22, and thus deliberately rendered himself ineligible for election to the Second Continental Congress. On sober second thought he accepted the chairmanship of the Committee of Sixty of Apr. 26, 1775, which called for an emergency Committee of One Hundred, which he again headed. In this capacity he sought to guide the action of the Provincial Congress which began its sessions in May. When the British took possession of New York, Low, unlike his brother Nicholas [q.v.], who embraced the colonial cause, remained and continued to give loyal support to the authorities. Chosen in 1775 president of the New York Chamber of Commerce, of which he was one of the founders, Low called a meeting of that body in 1779, which, attended by the Loyalist wing, expressed sympathy with the British cause (J. B. Bishop, *A Chronicle of One Hundred and Fifty Years: The Chamber of Commerce of . . . New York,* 1918, p. 29). Previous to the evacuation he was appointed by Sir Guy Carleton one of the board of commissioners for the settlement of debts due the Loyalists. He was named in an act of attainder of the state of New York of Oct. 22, 1779, and his property, including a tract of land in Tryon County, was confiscated. In 1783 he moved to England, where he died in Cowes, Isle of Wight, July 25, 1791. His only son, Isaac, became a commissary-general in the British army.

[See Lorenzo Sabine, *Biog. Sketches of Loyalists of the Am. Revolution* (ed. 1864), vol. II; M. J. Lamb, *Hist. of the City of N. Y.,* vol. I (1877); W. C. Abbott, *N. Y. in the Am. Revolution* (1929); *Biog. Dir. Am. Cong.* (1928); M. C. Nicoll, *The Earliest Cuylers in Holland and America and Some of Their Descendants* (1912); Thos. Jones, *Hist. of N. Y. During the Revolutionary War* (2 vols., 1879). The date of death is taken from the *Biog. Dir. Am. Cong.*]   R. B. M.

LOW, JOHN GARDNER (Jan. 10, 1835–Nov. 10, 1907), potter and painter, was a son of John and Hannah Gardner Low, of Chelsea, Mass. The father, a surveyor, and a prominent citizen, encouraged John to study art, of which he himself was a connoisseur. The younger Low accordingly was sent, in 1858, to Paris where he had three years at the ateliers of Thomas Couture and Constant Troyon. According to tradition he was somewhat wild as a student but he acquired a sound professional technique. His interest in pottery is said to have been aroused during his stay in France, but he returned to the United States purposing to be a painter and he engaged for several years in scenic and other decorative work. In 1866 Alexander William Robertson started at Chelsea, where clay is abundant, a pottery for manufacture of artistic wares. At this plant Low served an apprenticeship, learning all he could about glazing and firing, and conducting experiments of his own. About 1877, in partnership with his father, Low inaugurated a manufactory under the style of the Low Art Tile Works. Picturesquely situated under Powderhorn Hill the plant exemplified in architecture, fixtures, and output its founder's conception of a combination of utility and beauty. Some of Low's processes in tile making were original, as when by use of a specially devised screw he pressed upon unburnt clay leaves, grasses, ferns, and laces, which left their impress on the finished product. The works employed as head designer Arthur Osborne, an artist, whose creative ingenuity was similar to Low's. Later Low's son, John F. Low, entered the firm.

A kiln of tiles was first successfully fired at the Low Works in May 1879. In September following an exhibit of the tiles sent to the Cincinnati Industrial Exposition won a silver medal. In 1880 Low tiles were entered in competition with the well-established English potters at the Crewe, Stoke-upon-Trent, Exposition, held under royal auspices. Award of the gold medal to the American entrant created a veritable sensation in the Five Towns, and the occurrence naturally had wide publicity in the American press. Other prizes and medals followed. In 1882 by invitation an exhibit of Low tiles and plastic sketches was held at the rooms of the Fine Art Society, London. It was visited and commended by members of the royal family, by Sir Frederick Leighton, and by many other members of the Royal Academy.

The output of the Low Tile Works was extensive for about twenty years. It included, besides tiles and plastic sketches (the latter being ceramic portraits, figure compositions, and landscapes in low relief), such objects as paperweights, inkstands, clock cases, candlesticks, and especially tiling for soda fountains. In time, however, the activities of the Low Tile Works gradually lessened. In the last ten years of his life John G. Low resumed his painting in which his attainments were respectable. He was temperamentally an intense, positive man, but he was also constructive and public-spirited. He was long a member of the Chelsea park commission, and he held offices in the Allston and Paint and Clay clubs of Boston. In religion he was a Unitarian. He died after a brief illness and his remains were cremated for deposition at Mt. Auburn Cemetery.

[*J. and J. G. Low Art Tile* (1881); *Plastic Sketches of J. G. and J. F. Low* (1887); E. A. Barber, *The Pottery and Porcelain of the U. S.* (1909); *Art. Jour.* (London), Aug. 1882; *Am. Pottery and Glassware Reporter,* Sept. 9, 1880; *Vital Records of Chelsea, Mass., to the Year 1850* (1916); *Boston Transcript,* Sept. 3, 1880, Nov. 11, 1907; *Boston Herald,* Nov. 11, 1907; *Chelsea Citizen,* Nov. 16, 1907.]   F. W. C.

LOW, JULIETTE GORDON (Oct. 31, 1860–Jan. 17, 1927), founder of the Girl Scouts in America, was of Scotch descent, the daughter of Gen. William Washington Gordon and Eleanor (Kinzie) Gordon. Through her mother she was descended from John Kinzie [*q.v*]. She received her education in private schools in Staunton and Edgehill, Va., and in New York City. After her marriage on Dec. 21, 1886, to William Low of Wellesbourne House, Warwickshire, England, she divided her time between England, Scotland, and America, maintaining homes in all three countries. Through her friendship with

Sir Robert Baden-Powell, founder of the Boy Scouts, and his sister, founder of the Girl Guides in England, she became interested in the Scout movement. She organized her first group of Girl Guides in the valley of Glenlyon in Scotland. In that region girls left home at an early age in order to earn their living. Mrs. Low taught them to support themselves at home, in addition to teaching them camp lore. It was the following year, on Mar. 9, 1912, that she organized the first troop of Girl Guides in America in her home in Savannah, Ga. The organization gained favor rapidly, national headquarters were opened in Washington, D. C., and the name was changed to the Girl Scouts, as being more appropriate in America. Soon after the organization was established, the headquarters were moved to New York City. Mrs. Low gave unceasingly of her time and energy and private means to furthering the interests of the organization, and though handicapped by deafness, she interviewed people in many parts of the country in its behalf. Upon her retirement from the office of president, the national convention of the Girl Scouts gave her the title of Founder, and her birthday was made Scouts Founder's Day. From the first meeting, attended by eight leaders and eighteen girls, the organization, at the time of her death, had grown to one of more than 140,000 members with troops in every state in the Union.

Mrs. Low was a woman of broad culture and wide interests. She won her causes by her vitality, her disarming sense of humor, and her infallible charm. Though without formal training in art, she had a keen interest in the subject and was one of the organizers of the Savannah Art Club which she served as vice-president. She modeled several small figures which were cast in porcelain, one of them being the figure of her mother, said to have been the first white child born in Chicago, and which Mrs. Low presented to that city. The wrought-iron gates in the park in Gordonston, a suburb of Savannah, were also her handiwork and were presented by her in memory of her mother and father. Her last work was a bust of her grandfather, Gen. William Washington Gordon, the founder of the Central of Georgia Railway and the mayor of Savannah from 1832 to 1834. This was a gift to the city of Savannah, and although it arrived from England only a few days before her death, when she was very ill she completed the plans for its presentation.

[Anne Hyde Choate and Helen Ferris, *Juliette Low and the Girl Scouts* (1928); *Juliette Low: Founder of the Girl Scouts* (Savannah, Ga., 1927), a memorial; *Am. Girl*, Mar. 1927; *Savannah Morning News*, Jan. 18, 19, and 24, 1927; *Savannah Press*, Jan. 18, 1927.]
B. R.

LOW, NICHOLAS (Mar. 30, 1739–Nov. 15, 1826), New York merchant, land speculator, and legislator, was born near New Brunswick, N. J., the son of Cornelius, Jr., and Johanna (Gouverneur) Low. As a young man he was a clerk in the establishment of Hayman Levy, prominent New York pre-Revolutionary merchant, who assisted him in going into business on his own account. Low attained considerable prominence as a member of the important mercantile firm of Low & Wallace. He was likewise interested in finance and industry. In 1784 he was one of the committee appointed to receive subscriptions for stock of the Bank of New York and was elected a director in 1785 (H. W. Domett, *A History of the Bank of New York, 1784–1884*, 1884, pp. 9, 18, 28, 132). He was also a director of the branch of the Bank of the United States, and was associated in the enterprise known as the Society for Establishing Useful Manufactures at Paterson, N. J. (Low to Elisha Boudinot, Sept. 2, 1793, New York Public Library). Unlike his brother, Isaac [q.v.], who joined the Loyalist ranks at the outbreak of the Revolution, Nicholas espoused the cause of independence. He was elected to the Assembly and was a Federalist member of the state convention which met at Poughkeepsie in 1788 and adopted the federal Constitution.

In later life his chief interest was in the rôle of proprietor and land speculator. His real-estate transactions in New York City were conducted on an extensive scale and he was one of the city's most highly assessed property owners (J. G. Wilson, *The Memorial History of the City of New-York*, III, 1893, p. 151). He possessed extensive tracts of land in St. Lawrence, Jefferson, and Lewis counties in New York state. As an active Federalist he strongly supported the project for the Black River Canal and for a connection between Lake Champlain and the St. Lawrence (D. R. Fox, *The Decline of Aristocracy in the Politics of New York*, 1918, p. 156). He introduced extensive developments on his western New York lands, building a hotel and cotton factory in Ballston about 1810, and giving much attention to the settlement of his tracts, which included the sites of Adams, Watertown, and Lowville. In the summer of 1814, at seventy-five, he joined the "New York Hussars" to defend New York from possible bombardment by the British. He died in New York City at the age of eighty-seven. He had married, late in life, Alice Fleming, a widow, by whom he had three children.

[Low's real-estate transactions in New York City can be estimated from *Minutes of the Common Council of the City of New York, 1784–1831* (19 vols., 1917). His upstate land speculations are developed in F. B. Hough, *A Hist. of St. Lawrence and Franklin Counties* (1853), *Hist. of Lewis County, N. Y.* (ed., 1883), and *A Hist. of Jefferson County* (1854). The N. Y. Pub. Lib. has the land book, No. 2, of Nicholas Low relating to lands in New York City, Ballston Spa, Township No. 2 (Watertown), Township No. 7 (Adams), and Township No. 11 (Lowville), 1794–1862. A large collection of ancient deeds of the Nicholas Low estate, covering, in addition to these regions, Montgomery and Washington counties, as well as New York, is in the possession of Ruland & Benjamin, real-estate brokers, of New York City.]   R. B. M.

LOW, SETH (Jan. 18, 1850–Sept. 17, 1916), merchant, college president, youngest child of Abiel Abbot Low [*q.v.*] by his first wife, Ellen Almira (Dow) Low, was named after his paternal grandfather, who had left Massachusetts, where the Lows had dwelt from the seventeenth century, and moved to Brooklyn in 1829, setting himself up as a merchant. In his youth Low enjoyed the advantages of extensive travel, was educated in a private school, and completed his secondary studies at the Brooklyn Polytechnic Institute. He entered Columbia College with the class of 1870, earning the encomium of President Barnard, as "the first scholar in college and the most manly young fellow we have had here in many a year" (B. R. C. Low, *Seth Low,* p. 41). Reared in a home on Brooklyn Heights overlooking the New York harbor, he early acquired an enthusiasm for maritime trade evoked by the sight of his father's famous clipper ships. At the end of his senior year at Columbia, yielding to his father's wishes, he terminated a year's study of law and entered the establishment of A. A. Low & Brothers. He was employed in his father's warehouse from 1870 to 1875 and became a member of the firm a year later, supervising importations of raw silk from China, Japan, and France. On the retirement of the senior members four years later he succeeded with other junior partners to the business which was finally liquidated in 1887. On Dec. 9, 1880, he married Anne Wroe Scollay Curtis of Boston, the daughter of Justice Benjamin R. Curtis [*q.v.*] of the United States Supreme Court.

Low's efforts in behalf of civic reform were first enlisted in charitable work. In 1878 he organized and became the first president of the Bureau of Charities of Brooklyn. He first attained political prominence as president of a Republican Campaign Club organized in Brooklyn in 1880 to promote the election of Garfield and Arthur. The club, reorganized under the title of "The Young Republican Club," addressed itself to municipal reform and advocated the complete separation of local and national politics. The

mayoralty contest of 1881, the first under Brooklyn's new charter, was warmly contested. The Republican party was divided in allegiance between two contestants, Gen. Benjamin F. Tracy and Ripley Ropes. The former, in the interest of party unity, suggested that both candidates withdraw in favor of Low, who was then nominated and elected mayor of Brooklyn by a fair majority. He was renominated in the autumn of 1883 and reëlected by a close margin of votes in a hotly contested campaign against the Democratic nominee, Joseph C. Hendrix. A feature of his administration was the introduction of the merit system in the municipal service of Brooklyn, a reduction of the city debt, and a complete reform of the public-school system (*Fourth Annual Message of Hon. Seth Low, Mayor of Brooklyn,* 1885; *World,* New York, Sept. 2, 1897). Low, ever a stanch friend of civil service, stood for the separation of local and national politics and refused to use the patronage of the city for any party in the presidential campaign or in any other election. In refusing to support the candidacy of James G. Blaine in 1884, he maintained: "I am not a Republican mayor, as you say I am. I am Mayor of the whole people of Brooklyn" (*Seth Low,* p. 53). Casting his vote for Cleveland, Low never again received the whole-hearted support of the Republican organization.

In 1889, shortly after his retirement from active business, Low received a call to the presidency of Columbia College. He was not quite forty years of age when he accepted the office. His selection was symbolic of a new day, when the university administrator would not be a clergyman nor a professional scholar, but a broad-visioned executive. It was in the latter capacity that he was to render notable service to Columbia. At the beginning of his administration, which covered the years 1890–1901, he centralized graduate organization and established the University Council. Graduate and professional instruction was reorganized and widened considerably in scope. Teachers' College, Barnard, and the College of Physicians and Surgeons, among other institutions, were brought into association with the university. The most forward-looking step taken through his initiative was the purchase of the new site on Morningside Heights in 1892. Low made himself responsible for a library building on the new site which he contributed as a memorial to his father. In addition he established a number of trust funds for the encouragement of study and research (*A History of Columbia University, 1754–1904,* 1904, pp. 154–71).

Low's activities as president of Columbia did not preclude his participation in public affairs during this decade. He served on the board of the Rapid Transit Commission and assisted in drafting the charter for Greater New York. He was frequently selected to act as arbiter in labor disputes and aided generously in relief work, especially during the cholera epidemic of 1893. In 1899 he went as a delegate to the first Hague Conference. In 1897 he was nominated by the Citizens' Union for the first mayor of Greater New York. As in his vigorous Brooklyn campaigns, his keynote was the complete separation of municipal and national politics (*Seth Low's Great Speech at Cooper Union, Oct. 6, 1897*, 1897, pp. 3, 8). The failure of the Republican party to support him, coupled with the death of Henry George toward the end of the campaign, brought about his defeat by Robert Van Wyck of Tammany Hall. Low ran second, 50,000 votes ahead of Benjamin F. Tracy, Republican. In 1901, however, he was elected to the mayoralty of New York by a large majority on a reaction of public sentiment against the Tammany régime. His administration was distinguished as a brief era of civic reform. Patronage was checked and the civil service was developed. Through his efforts the first subway to Brooklyn and the Pennsylvania tunnel to Long Island were planned and the electrification of the New York Central within the city limits was effected. Notwithstanding this excellent record, he failed of reëlection in 1903.

From leadership in civic affairs Low turned to the farmer's cooperative movement, laying out a home and farm at Bedford Hills in Westchester County, N. Y., and organizing the Bedford Farmers' Cooperative Association. He firmly believed that the two major problems which America must solve were the negro and labor. In 1905 he became a member of the board of trustees of the Tuskegee Institute and two years later was elected chairman of the board, a position which he held until his death. During this period he actively cooperated with Booker T. Washington. In the last decade of his life, he devoted much of his time to securing more harmonious relations between capital and labor. In 1907 he became president of the National Civic Federation, and in the autumn of 1914 he was appointed by President Wilson a member of the Colorado Coal Commission for the investigation of labor difficulties in that state. In 1914, after a long membership in the New York Chamber of Commerce, he was elected president of that body. His service to the organization was as notable as that of his father as its president during the Civil War. His administration is associated with the organization of a committee on problems of shipments, the organization at Washington of the Bureau of War Risk Insurance, and with the movement for the rehabilitation of American shipping. His last important public service was rendered as chairman of the committee on cities of the New York constitutional convention of 1915, a position to which he was justly entitled. He had gained international recognition as an advocate of municipal self-government and executive responsibility, ideas which he elaborated upon at Lord Bryce's invitation in a chapter which he wrote for the first edition of *The American Commonwealth*, and in his *Addresses and Papers on Municipal Government* (1891).

In later years Low was portly in physical appearance; in manner, kindly and benevolent, but in public somewhat shy and reserved. He possessed a talent for merging himself in a cause and an unfailing acumen in the selection of experts. He was universally respected as the pattern of the scholar in politics. In religion he was an active Episcopalian. His death occurred at his home in Bedford Hills after a lingering illness.

[Benjamin R. C. Low, *Seth Low* (1925); *Columbia Alumni News*, Oct. 20, 1916; *Board of Estimate and Apportionment and Board of Aldermen: Joint Session in Memory of Honorable Seth Low . . . Sept. 25, 1916* (1916); A. L. Moffat, "Low Geneal.: The Descendants of Seth Low and Mary Porter" (1932), a copy of which is in the Lib. of Cong.; and the New York press of Sept. 18, 1916.]   R. B. M.

LOWE, CHARLES (Nov. 18, 1828–June 20, 1874), Unitarian clergyman, was born in Portsmouth, N. H., the son of John and Sarah Ann (Simes) Lowe. As a boy he attended Phillips Academy in Exeter, N. H., where his father had become manager of a cotton-mill. Entering Harvard College as a sophomore he graduated as salutatorian of the class of 1847. For a year he read law with Amos Tuck [*q.v.*] in Exeter, then he began the study of theology under the direction of the Rev. Andrew P. Peabody [*q.v.*] of Portsmouth, completing the course in the Harvard Divinity School (1849–51) while he served as tutor in the college of arts. In the spring of 1851 he became the colleague of the Rev. John Weiss in the Unitarian church of New Bedford, Mass., but two years later a serious malady of the lungs made him seek health in extensive travel in Western Europe and the Turkish Empire. After a winter semester, 1854–55, in the University of Halle under the theologians Erdmann and Tholuck he became in September 1855 the pastor of the North Church in Salem, Mass., but after nearly two years of ministry he was again obliged to resign. On Sept. 16, 1857, he was married to Martha A. Perry, daughter of Justus and Hannah (Wood) Perry of Keene, N. H., and settled on a farm near Salem. In February 1859, his health improved, he became pastor of the Unitarian church in Somerville, Mass., and during the Civil War he added to his pastoral care temporary service as army chaplain in 1863, as chairman of the Army Committee of the American Unitarian Association in 1864, and in behalf of the Freedmen's Aid Society in 1865. His sagacity and success in these activities led to another responsibility, a leadership in the effort to organize the autonomous, loosely related Unitarian congregations into a National Conference (April 1865) which would be composed of devout conservatives, who cherished recognition of Christ as a superhuman being, and younger innovators, some of whom were disinclined even to the name Christian since for them it necessarily implied the inherited system of authoritative dogma. In this difficult situation Lowe, now transferred from his parish to the office of executive secretary of the American Unitarian Association, served as a catalyst. His calm courage and frankness, his catholicity of mind, and his sweetness of spirit won divergent parties to unity. After six years of remarkably efficient administration he was too ill to continue the work and in 1871 again traveled abroad for his health. Returning in May 1873 he declined the pastorate of the First Church of Cambridge, and the presidency of Antioch College, but undertook the editorship of the *Unitarian Review and Religious Magazine,* planned to succeed the older *Monthly Religious Magazine.* A few months after he had taken over the work he sought the sea air of Swampscot, May 30, 1874, but immediately suffered the beginning of hemorrhages from which he died on June 20.

[Martha Perry Lowe, *Memoir of Chas. Lowe* (1884); *Memorial to Chas. Lowe* (1874), reprinted, with additions, from the *Unitarian Rev. and Religious Mag.,* July, Aug. 1874; S. A. Eliot, ed., *Heralds of a Liberal Faith* (1910), vol. III; the *Christian Reg.* (Boston), June 27, July 4, 1874; *Boston Transcript,* June 22, 1874.]   F. A. C.

LOWE, RALPH PHILLIPS (Nov. 27, 1805–Dec. 22, 1883), governor and chief justice of Iowa, was the son of Jacob Derrick and Martha (Per-Lee) Lowe, who conducted a tavern in Warren County, Ohio, where the boy early heard great issues discussed by Henry Clay and other distinguished guests. He worked on the farm and acquired enough preparation by 1825 to enter Miami University, from which he graduated in 1829. Estranged from his father on account

of his refusal to farm, he made his way to Ashville, Ala., where he taught school, read law, was admitted to the bar, and began to practise. After five years he returned to Ohio to open a law office in Dayton. In 1837 he married Phoebe Carleton and three years later removed to a farm near Bloomington, now Muscatine, Iowa. He quickly became active in public affairs and served in the constitutional convention of 1844. Defeated the following year as the Whig candidate for territorial delegate, he devoted himself to building up a successful practice, served as district attorney and, from 1852 to 1857, was judge of the first district. When, in 1858, he became the first governor under the constitution of 1857, he faced a serious situation. With no banking system of her own, Iowa was overrun with wildcat currency from neighboring states and was still experiencing the disastrous effects of the panic of 1857. She was deeply stirred, too, by the slavery issue. In cooperation with the able Seventh General Assembly, his administration put the new constitution into effect, established a banking system, enacted ample revenue laws, rescued the school lands and funds from fraud and waste, encouraged railway construction, created the state agricultural college, and placed the township and county government on a sounder basis. These measures together with good crops and good prices, in 1860, restored state prosperity. Yet when the time came for the nominating convention in June 1859 Samuel J. Kirkwood [*q.v.*] had so far established himself as the leader of the antislavery sentiment in Iowa that there was a general desire to make him the next governor. Lowe's record and character undoubtedly entitled him to a renomination, but he was not as popular as Kirkwood. His tolerance, gentleness, and dignity gave the appearance of weakness to what was, in reality, a sturdy, fearless character. In the interest of party harmony he reluctantly consented to go to the supreme bench while Kirkwood became governor.

He served on the bench until 1868, acting as chief justice in 1860 and from 1866–68. As a judge he was broad-minded, sympathetic, and intellectually honest. Being neither deeply read in the law nor thoroughly convinced of the efficacy of the law as a general rule of action he regarded equity as a higher law and rendered decisions that seemed to him just, even if not in strict accord with the technicalities of the law. When he left the bench he was interested in Iowa's "Five Per Cent Claim." He spent some years trying to collect about $800,000, in accordance with the agreement of the federal government to pay the states five per cent. of the proceeds of land sales in return for five years' exemption from state taxation on land sold by the government. In order to prosecute the claim more advantageously he moved to Washington, where he died without knowing that the Supreme Court had already decided against his suit. He was a member of the Presbyterian church and deeply interested in such phases of religious thought as the interpretation of Biblical prophecies and the question of the lost tribes of Israel. His faith in human beings continued to be strong throughout a varied and active life. A colleague wrote of him, that he "was a most credulous man, taking every man to be honest and true until convinced otherwise" (*Annals of Iowa*, Oct. 1893, p. 211).

[B. F. Shambaugh, *Hist. of the Constitutions of Iowa* (1902); E. H. Stiles, *Recollections and Sketches of Notable Lawyers and Public Men of Early Iowa* (1916); *Iowa Hist. Record*, Oct. 1891; *Annals of Iowa*, Oct. 1900; *Gen. Cat. of the Grads. and Former Students of Miami Univ.* (1910?); *Iowa State Register*, Dec. 23, 1883; *Washington Post*, Dec. 25, 1883.]

C. E. P.

LOWE, THADDEUS SOBIESKI COULINCOURT (Aug. 20, 1832–Jan. 16, 1913), aeronaut, meteorologist, and inventor, was born at Jefferson Mills, N. H., now known as Riverton, the son of Clovis and Alpha (Green) Lowe. As early as 1856 he became interested in ballooning as a means of investigating upper-air currents, and in 1858 he made his initial voyage, from Ottawa, Canada, in connection with the celebration of the laying of the first Atlantic cable. The following year he built an airship, named the *City of New York*. As the result of an ascension made in Philadelphia, June 1860, Prof. Joseph Henry [*q.v.*] of the Smithsonian Institution became interested in Lowe's experiments and furnished him with certain instruments. He himself invented a device for getting latitude and longitude quickly without a horizon, which he miscalled an altimeter. On Apr. 20, 1861, he left Cincinnati, Ohio, in a balloon and after traveling some nine hundred miles in nine hours, landed near Pea Ridge, close to the boundary between North and South Carolina. He was regarded as a Yankee spy, arrested, and was in some danger of mob violence; but a gentleman who had witnessed an ascent made by Lowe at Charleston, S. C., the previous year, identified him and vouched for him as a scientific investigator not connected with military matters. Lowe maintained that he was thus the first prisoner taken in the Civil War. He tells of his experiences in a chapter in *Navigating the Air* (published by the Aero Club of America, 1907). This voyage was made purely in the in-

terest of science. Lowe believed that aloft there were strong winds blowing from west to east and that advantage might be taken of their presence to carry a balloon from America to Europe. To satisfy Professor Henry, a test was made with a smaller balloon than the one intended for transoceanic purposes. Coal gas was used to inflate, and the trip as a whole was successful. The balloon moved west in the lower levels at the start, to the great delight of the doubters; but at a height of 7,000 feet, a reverse current carried it eastward. The average height was 16,000 feet and the greatest 23,000 feet.

Soon after the outbreak of the Civil War, Lowe went to Washington with a view to interesting the authorities in the use of balloons for observation purposes. On June 6, 1861, Secretary of War Cameron asked Professor Henry to report on the matter. On June 18, Lowe made an ascent, during which he sent to President Lincoln the first telegraph message from a balloon in air. On June 21, Henry reported to Secretary Cameron (*Official Records*, 3 ser. I, 283–84) that balloons would probably be of military value. Lowe was made chief of the aeronautic section and rendered valuable service to the Army of the Potomac from the battle of Bull Run to that of Gettysburg. He was the first in the country to take photographs from a balloon. For his services he was elected an honorary member of the Loyal Legion.

After the war, Lowe became interested in the manufacture of artificial ice and as early as 1866 had constructed a plant for this purpose. He is credited with making the first artificial ice for commercial purposes in the United States. The New York *Sun* (Dec. 21, 1868) described his equipment of a refrigerated steamer for the transportation of perishable meats, vegetables, and fruits from Galveston to New York. A shipment of fresh beef from Texas to New Orleans arrived there Dec. 10, 1868, on the steamer *Agnes*, in good condition, looking as if freshly slaughtered although killed five days earlier. A company was formed to transport perishable goods in refrigerating devices; but the company failed, leaving Lowe in debt.

Later he made several improvements in the manufacture of gas and coke. By building regenerative metallurgical furnaces (1869–72) he succeeded in producing gas and fuel. In 1873–75 he invented and built water-gas apparatus; and in 1897 he constructed the New Lowe Coke Oven system for producing gas and coke, the latter known as anthracite coke, and used in smelting furnaces. The grade of coke produced equaled the best European product. From 1891 to 1894, while he was living in California, he became widely known because of his construction of an inclined railway at Rubio Canyon on Echo Mountain. The peak near the well-known Mount Wilson was named Mount Lowe, and he equipped and maintained an observatory on the summit. On Feb. 14, 1855, he married Leontine A. Gachon of Paris, by whom he had three sons. He died at Pasadena.

[T. S. C. Lowe, *The Air-Ship City of N. Y.* (1859) and "Observation Balloons in the Battle of Fair Oaks," *Rev. of Revs.* (N. Y.), Feb. 1911; *War of the Rebellion: Official Records (Army)*; W. J. Rhees, "Reminiscences of Ballooning in the Civil War," *The Chautauquan*, June 1898; *Jour. of the Franklin Institute*, Feb. 1887; J. S. Brainard, in *The Californian Illus. Mag.*, Aug. 1892; G. W. James, in the *Arena*, Oct. 1907; editorial in the *Arena*, Nov. 1907; *A Biog. Album of Prominent Pennsylvanians* (3 ser., 1890); *Who's Who in America*, 1910–11; *N. Y. Herald*, Sept. 29, 1859; *Daily National Intelligencer* (Washington, D. C.), June 20, 1861; *Los Angeles Times*, Jan. 17, 1913; *Scientific American*, Jan. 25, 1913.]   A.M.

LOWELL, AMY (Feb. 9, 1874–May 12, 1925), poet and critic, the daughter of Augustus Lowell and Katharine Bigelow (Lawrence) Lowell, was born in Brookline, Mass., in the house in which she died. She was, as she said, "of thoroughgoing New England stock," and her forebears were men of positive character, a trait which she inherited. Her first American ancestor, Perceval Lowell (or Lowle), a merchant of Bristol and member of a family of Somerset gentry, came to Newbury, Mass., in 1639. His descendant, John Lowell, 1743–1802 [q.v.], was a member of the Provincial Congress which defied the authority of the Crown, and later a member of the Federal Congress. His son, in turn, John Lowell, 1769–1840 [q.v.], who called himself on occasion "the Boston Rebel," opposed the War of 1812, and affirmed England's right to impress American seamen. His son, John Amory, Amy Lowell's paternal grandfather, a cousin of James Russell Lowell, was a pioneer in the development of the cotton industry in New England, and with him was associated her maternal grandfather, Abbott Lawrence [q.v.], at one time minister to the Court of St. James's. Her father followed in his father's footsteps. She grew up, accordingly, in a family where the sense of tradition was strong, and in an atmosphere of comparative affluence.

She was the youngest of five children, of whom Percival Lowell [q.v.], the astronomer, and Abbott Lawrence Lowell, president of Harvard University, were the eldest. When eight years old she was taken to Europe for six months, "traveling at a fearful rate of speed" over England and the Continent. The overstimulation of her brain resulted in serious illness; her nights for months afterwards "were made horrible by visions of the iron virgin" of Nürnberg; and it was many years before she ceased to be afraid in the dark. Of a trip to California when she was nine the two details which stuck in her memory were "the lassoing of a horse in a corral, and the wild dash in a coach along the steep roads of the Yosemite." Except for these journeys her early life was spent entirely between Boston and Brookline. "Living at home in those days," she wrote, "was very simple. I was devoted to animals, and as we kept horses, cows and dogs, I had plenty of opportunity to gratify these tastes." Under an old family coachman, a one-time Newmarket jockey, she "learned to ride and drive in a fearless manner, to which training," she remarked, "I attribute a great many useful things." Her love of animals (which at one time extended to seven huge and notorious English sheepdogs) never left her, and it was rivaled by her affection for the immediate surroundings of her home. For three generations the men of her family had been lovers and planters of gardens. The garden of her poems had been planned entirely by her father, and in it still bloomed azaleas brought from France and given to "the Boston Rebel" for his greenhouse. Almost every detail of her home and every influence upon her childhood found expression later in her poems.

Her formal education was gained entirely in private schools. To her mother, however, who was an accomplished musician and linguist, she owed, as she said, far more than to her other teachers, especially her thorough grounding in French. In 1895, when she was twenty-one, her mother died; in 1896 she spent six months on the Continent; and in the winter of 1897 went up the Nile in a dahabiyeh. The overstrain of traveling once more brought on a nervous breakdown, and the winter of 1898–99 was spent on a fruit ranch in California, and the following summer in Devonshire. In 1900 her father died; she purchased the family place ("Sevenels") in Brookline; and at once identified herself with the municipal and educational interests of the town, and with the movement for better libraries through the state. But "about 1902," to use her own words, "I discovered that poetry . . . was my natural mode of expression. And from that moment I began to devote myself to it seriously, studying as hard as possible, and endeavoring to perfect myself in the art." There were trips to Europe again in 1905 (including Constantinople and Greece), in 1913, and in 1914 (when she was caught by the outbreak of the Great War); but from 1902 until her death the supreme interest of her life was her art.

She followed, however, the Horatian maxim, for eight years elapsed before her first published poem appeared (*Atlantic Monthly,* August 1910), and her first book, *A Dome of Many-Coloured Glass* (1912), was not published until two years later. Meantime, in 1911, she had translated Alfred de Musset's *Caprice,* and had taken the leading part herself at an amateur performance in Boston. During her visit to England in 1913 she met Ezra Pound; became associated with the Imagists, then just crystallizing into a school; and contributed to the first Imagist anthology, *Des Imagistes* (1914). On her return she made the authorized translation of Edmond Rostand's *Pierrot qui pleure et Pierrot qui rit,* given in Boston as an opera in February 1915. From her visit to England in 1914 she brought back the manuscript of *Some Imagist Poets,* an anthology of which three numbers were issued (1915, 1916, and 1917), the first with a Preface, not written by her, which defined the tenets of the group, and which she later elaborated in *Tendencies in Modern American Poetry* (below, pp. 239–48). In 1914 her second volume, *Sword Blades and Poppy Seed,* was published, and in it are to be found her first poems in *vers libre,* or, as she preferred to call it, "unrhymed cadence," the principles of which she defined in the Preface, and later in two noteworthy articles (*North American Review,* January 1917; *Dial,* January 17, 1918). The same volume also contained her first experiments in so-called "polyphonic prose," elucidated later in the Preface to *Can Grande's Castle.* Both the new techniques owed their suggestion to her intimate acquaintance with contemporary French poetry, and in 1915 appeared *Six French Poets: Studies in Contemporary Literature.* A third volume of verse, *Men, Women, and Ghosts* (1916), included, together with poems in the conventional meters, further experiments in the two new forms. *Tendencies in Modern American Poetry* (1917), a series of critical studies of six contemporary American poets, was followed in 1918 by *Can Grande's Castle,* a collection of four long pieces wholly in "polyphonic prose," of which the last, "The Bronze Horses," remains the most notable example. During these half-dozen years she was one of the storm-centers of an active controversy on both sides of the Atlantic over the new forms of verse. *Pictures of the Floating World* (1919), containing some of her most beautiful work, showed markedly the influence of her studies in Chinese and Japanese poetry; while in *Legends* (1921) she retold, using all the varieties of technique at her command, a dozen "Tales of Peoples which [she had]

loved," drawn from Peru, Yucatan, the North American Indians, China, Europe, England, and her own New England. In *Fir-Flower Tablets: Poems Translated from the Chinese* (1921) her interest in China reached its culmination. She collaborated in the enterprise with Mrs. Florence Ayscough, whose literal translations she turned into unrhymed English verse, preserving so far as possible the spirit of the originals. In 1922 she published anonymously *A Critical Fable* (later acknowledged), a spirited skit in rhymed couplets, in which she let herself go in a series of lively sketches of her fellow poets, and included a racy and vivid characterization of herself. This *jeu d'esprit,* however, was largely relaxation from a more arduous undertaking. In 1921 she had been invited to deliver a commemorative address at Yale University on the one hundredth anniversary of the death of Keats. Out of this grew her most important critical performance, *John Keats* (1925), which occupied almost without cessation the last four years of her life. It frankly essays to interpret Keats as "a new generation of poets and critics" saw him, and it owes its distinctive quality as a biography to the fact that in it one poet has relived, almost from day to day, another poet's life.

From 1915 until her death in 1925 she lectured and read from time to time, with a verve and brilliancy peculiarly her own, before audiences at Harvard, Yale, Columbia, and other universities, and before societies and clubs the country over. During the same period she expounded with skill and defended with vigor, in various periodicals, her own poetic creed and her technique. On the eve of a visit to England, during which she was to have lectured at Oxford, Cambridge, Eton, Edinburgh, and elsewhere, she was stricken with paralysis, and died without recovering consciousness. For many years she had endured unintermitted physical discomfort and often acute pain, and her achievements represent the triumph of an indomitable will. The legend that her death was hastened by hostile criticism of *John Keats* is as baseless as, in view of her militant character, it is absurd. At the time of her death three volumes of poems were in preparation. They were posthumously published—*What's O'Clock* in 1925, *East Wind* in 1926, *Ballads for Sale* in 1927—under the oversight of Mrs. Harold Russell, her literary executor and the "A. D. R." to whom, in *John Keats,* were dedicated all her poems. *Poetry and Poets: Essays* was published in 1930.

During the later years of her life Amy Lowell was the most striking figure in contemporary American letters. Like every one who, without shunning publicity, prefers his own road to the beaten track, she stirred the general myth-making faculty. Her serene independence of conventional opinion, which found its popular symbol in her frank addiction to cigars; her Elizabethan outspokenness; her choice of the hours from dark to dawn for work, and of the daylight hours for sleep; her insistence upon the elaborate paraphernalia which accompanied her travels; her Olympian detachment from all demands of punctuality—traits such as these inevitably kept her more or less picturesquely in the public eye. What the public eye, however, often failed to see was the vivid and powerful personality which dominated handicaps and resolved apparent inconsistencies. She had not the gift of physical beauty, except as spirit and intelligence animated every expression of a keen and finely modeled face. Grace of form had also been denied her, but her presence, on occasion, could be regal. She could be arrogant, even domineering; yet open-mindedness, willingness to learn, and generosity were among her most deeply ingrained qualities. Her insurgencies, when all is said, were intellectual; the bedrock was conservative. And in her paradoxes lay half the richness of her character. She was a brilliant and provocative talker, but her talk was seldom a monologue. She loved best the give and take between contending minds, and her flashing wit and quickness of repartee and often crisp finality of statement will always be associated with the great book-walled room in which she met her friends. Her mind was endlessly acquisitive; she had the instinct, though not the training, of a scholar; and her more ambitious poems and *John Keats* were the fruits of ardent and indefatigable study. In the end it was her eagerness of spirit which outran her bodily strength.

Her poems number more than six hundred and fifty titles, in eleven volumes. Collectively, they exhibit extraordinary catholicity of interests; an almost unrivaled command of the vocabulary of sensuous impressions; a "firm belief that poetry should not try to teach"; a corresponding emphasis on finished craftsmanship; and a passion for adventures in technique. In "unrhymed cadence" she perfected a new and (in skilled hands) effective instrument. "Polyphonic prose," on the other hand, proved too alien a visitant to domiciliate itself. She suffers, as she recognized herself (*A Critical Fable*, pp. 46–50), from her profusion. Her blaze of colors tends to draw attention from her thought and feeling; her "hurricaning" (as she called it), from her clarity and restraint. The final appraisal of her con-tribution belongs to later times, but in her best work she has left securely a body of verse of distinction and beauty.

[This biography is based upon Miss Lowell's autobiographical memoranda, written about 1917; upon information contributed by Mrs. Harold Russell; and upon the writer's personal knowledge. See also D. R. Lowell, *The Hist. Geneal. of the Lowells of America* (1899); *Who's Who in America*, 1924–25; Winifred Bryher, *Amy Lowell, a Critical Appreciation* (1918); *The Dial*, Nov. 2, 1918; *North Am. Rev.*, Mar. 1925; *Revue Anglo-Americaine*, Aug. 1925, Apr. 1929; *Saturday Rev. of Literature*, Oct. 3, 1925; *New Republic*, Nov. 18, 1925; *Bookman*, Mar. 1926; *Scribner's Mag.*, Sept. 1927; *Modern Language Notes*, Mar. 1928. The authorized biography, by S. Foster Damon, is in course of preparation.]   J. L. L.

LOWELL, EDWARD JACKSON (Oct. 18, 1845–May 11, 1894), historian, son of Francis Cabot and Mary Lowell (Gardner) Lowell, was born in Boston, Mass., where his father was actively engaged in business for more than fifty years. His paternal grandfather, Francis Cabot Lowell [*q.v.*], was a son of the second wife, and his maternal grandmother, Rebecca (Lowell) Gardner, a daughter of the third wife of Judge John Lowell, 1743–1802 [*q.v.*]. His uncle, John Lowell, 1799–1836 [*q.v.*], was the founder of the Lowell Institute. When he was nine years old Lowell was taken abroad by his father and placed in Sillig's school at Bellerive near Vevey, Switzerland. Later he attended the Latin school of E. S. Dixwell in Boston and entered Harvard College in 1863. While an undergraduate he wrote a good deal of verse, and he was Class Odist at Commencement, 1867. In January 1868 he married Mary Wolcott Goodrich, daughter of Samuel Griswold Goodrich [*q.v.*], who is best remembered by his pen name, Peter Parley. Lowell spent a year or two in business, and then studied law. Admitted to the bar in 1872, he opened an office in connection with Brooks Adams [*q.v.*], but after his wife's death in 1874 he gave up his practice and devoted himself to his three children and to study. In June 1877 he married Elizabeth Gilbert Jones, daughter of George Jones [*q.v.*], who was one of the founders and for many years the manager of the *New York Times*.

Going abroad in the summer of 1879, Lowell spent a number of years in Europe, where he became interested in the history of the German mercenaries used by Great Britain in America during the Revolution. In German archives he collected documents which enabled him to write to the *New York Times* in 1880–81 a series of letters on this subject. These were developed into a volume entitled *The Hessians and the Other German Auxiliaries of Great Britain in the Revolutionary War,* which appeared in 1884.

Shortly after it was published the author was elected a member of the Massachusetts Historical Society and of the American Academy of Arts and Sciences. In 1888 he contributed to Justin Winsor's *Narrative and Critical History of America* the chapter on "The United States of America, 1775–1782: Their Political Struggles and Relations with Europe." He had considered preparing a biography of Lafayette, but changed his plan, deciding instead to study conditions in France just before the French Revolution. He approached the subject without theory or prejudice and with a comprehensive interest. The book was published in 1892 under the title *The Eve of the French Revolution*. In it the author made clear his conviction that the great upheaval was due not to lack of prosperity among the French people but to France's consciousness "that her government did not correspond to her degree of civilization." He later undertook a study of the influence of the French Revolution in other countries, which was unfinished at his death.

For a number of years Lowell was treasurer of the American School of Classical Studies at Athens. In the winter of 1893 he visited the Mediterranean, then returned to America. A few months later he died, at Cotuit, Mass., his summer residence. His "strong social instincts and quick and comprehensive sympathy made him beloved by his contemporaries" (A. L. Lowell, *post*). In conversation he had a happy gift of aphorism which lent additional charm to his remarks. Guy Lowell [*q.v.*] was his son.

[Memoir by A. Lawrence Lowell, in *Proc. Mass. Hist. Soc.*, 2 ser., IX (1895) ; memoir by H. W. Haynes, in *Proc. Am. Acad. Arts and Sci.*, n.s., XXII (1895), with a list of Lowell's published writings ; *Harvard Coll. Class of 1867, Secretary's Report No. 10* (1897) ; *Harvard Grads. Mag.*, Sept. 1894 ; D. R. Lowell, *The Hist. Geneal. of the Lowells of America* (1899) ; *Boston Transcript*, May 12, 15, 1894.]   L. S. M.

LOWELL, FRANCIS CABOT (Apr. 7, 1775–Aug. 10, 1817), textile manufacturer, was born at Newburyport, Mass., the son of Judge John Lowell, 1743–1802 [*q.v.*], and his second wife, Susanna (Cabot) Lowell, and a half-brother of John Lowell, 1769–1840 [*q.v.*]. In 1776 his father moved to Boston and here Francis received his education, entering Harvard in 1789 at the age of fourteen. For lighting a bonfire in the college yard during his senior year he was "rusticated" to Bridgewater where he continued his studies under Rev. Zedekiah Sanger, but graduated with his class in 1793. In college he excelled in mathematics, an aptitude which in later years served him well and provoked the admiration of the great mathematician, Nathaniel Bowditch.

After leaving Harvard Lowell engaged successfully in importing and exporting in company with his uncle, William Cabot, until 1810, when ill health induced him to make a prolonged journey to the British Isles. This trip to England was fraught with great significance for the future of American industry. Impressed by the importance of manufacturing as a source of national wealth, he closely studied the textile machinery which he saw in Lancashire, and upon his return to America in 1812, determined to establish a cotton factory. The almost total cessation of commerce owing to the War of 1812 left him free to devote his entire time to this project. Interesting his brother-in-law, Patrick Tracy Jackson [*q.v.*], in the scheme, he formed the Boston Manufacturing Company, purchased land at Waltham, and busied himself during the winter of 1812–13 in designing and constructing with the aid of a mechanical genius, Paul Moody [*q.v.*], spinning machinery and a practical power loom. With little to aid him except recollections of observations in Europe and imperfect drawings, Lowell not only designed an excellent power loom but contributed such improvements to textile machinery as the double speeder and the method of spinning the thread directly through the quill. "I well recollect," said a leading stockholder, Nathan Appleton [*q.v.*], who had been invited by Lowell to view his new power loom, "the state of admiration and satisfaction with which we sat by the hour, watching the beautiful movement of the new and wonderful machine, destined as it evidently was, to change the character of all textile industry" (Appleton, *post*, p. 9). Another year was to pass before the factory was in complete operation, but when all the machinery was functioning the plant at Waltham was believed to be the first mill in the world which combined all the operations of converting raw cotton into finished cloth. "Although Messrs. Jackson and Moody," says Appleton, "were men of unsurpassed talent and energy in their way, it was Mr. Lowell who was the informing soul, which gave direction and form to the whole proceeding" (*Ibid.*, p. 15). Of a humanitarian turn of mind, Lowell was also interested in proper living conditions for his employees and his efforts at his Waltham mills had a salutary influence on the development of the New England textile industry.

Scarcely were the wheels turning in the new mill before the war with England came to an end, and the infant industry seemed destined to be submerged in a flood of cheap foreign goods. Lowell with others repaired to Washington, where he was influential in convincing Lowndes and Calhoun of the wisdom of incorporating in the tariff of 1816 a substantial duty on cotton cloth. The full realization of his plans he did not live to see. In ill health for some years, he died in Boston at the early age of forty-two. He had married, Oct. 31, 1798, Hannah Jackson (Feb. 3, 1776–May 10, 1815), daughter of Jonathan and Hannah (Tracy) Jackson, of Newburyport, who bore him three sons and a daughter. One of the sons, John, 1799–1836 [q.v.], was the founder of the Lowell Institute, while among his descendants through his other children were John, 1824–1897, Edward Jackson, Percival, Amy, and Guy Lowell [qq.v.].

[Nathan Appleton, *Introduction of the Power Loom, and Origin of Lowell* (1858), is the most authoritative source, while almost all that is known of the man is collected in a speech by his descendant F. C. Lowell, in *Exercises at the Seventy-Fifth Anniversary of the Incorporation of the Town of Lowell* (1901). See also Alfred Gilman, "Francis Cabot Lowell," in *Contributions of the Old Residents' Hist. Asso., Lowell, Mass.,* I (1879), 73–86; F. W. Coburn, *Hist. of Lowell and Its People* (1920), vol. III; D. R. Lowell, *The Hist. Geneal. of the Lowells of America* (1899); *Illus. Hist. of Lowell and Vicinity* (1897); *New-Eng. Palladium & Commercial Register* (Boston), Aug. 12, 1817.]
H.U.F.

LOWELL, GUY (Aug. 6, 1870–Feb. 4, 1927), architect, was born in Boston, of an old Boston family, the son of Edward Jackson Lowell [q.v.] and Mary (Goodrich) Lowell. He received his early schooling in Dresden and Paris, was prepared for college at Noble's School in Boston, and graduated with the degree of A.B. from Harvard in 1892. He next entered the department of architecture at the Massachusetts Institute of Technology, then flourishing under the leadership of the brilliant Frenchman, Despradelle, and followed a two-year course leading to the degree of B.S. in 1894. Feeling the need of European training, he sailed for France in 1895 and entered the Atelier Pascal of the École des Beaux-Arts in Paris. He received his diploma from the École in 1899 and almost immediately returned to America to practise. Meantime, in April 1898, he had married Henrietta Sargent of Brookline, Mass., daughter of Charles Sprague Sargent [q.v.].

In Paris, Lowell followed the regular course of the Beaux-Arts. His designs had the exuberance and the frequent lack of restraint so often observed in students' work in France. More important, he absorbed the logic and, above all, the inherent grasp of planning which is the especial glory of French architecture and the most useful asset in French architectural education. From the beginning of his practice in America, however, he showed that he was to abandon the flashy and exuberant detail that he had learned

in Paris and would return to the conservatism and refinement which has marked American architecture at its best. In America, he had immediate success. His social position and connections gave him unusual opportunities which his unusual gifts and thorough training enabled him to capitalize. That his success was largely due to his own ability, however, was proved by the fact that he in no wise feared competition with the most brilliant of his contemporaries. His work was extremely variegated. At Harvard he built Emerson Hall, the New Lecture Hall, and the President's House. He was the leading spirit of the architectural expression of Phillips Academy, Andover, Mass., where he designed many buildings and created one of the most inspiring ensembles in American scholastic work. His hand is seen in the Carrie Memorial Tower at Brown, in buildings at Simmons College, Boston, and at the State Normal School, Bridgewater, Mass. His designs for private residences —many of them of the most elaborate sort—are to be found in Massachusetts, in Maine, and on Long Island. At Piping Rock he designed one of the most attractive and simplest of country clubs, using a modified Dutch Colonial style indigenous to the district. His most notable single work was the New York County Court House, for which in 1913 he furnished the winning design, distinguished by its ingenuity of plan. The detail was severely classical and Lowell, to the end of his career, remained a confirmed classicist. Other public buildings which came from his office were the Museum of Fine Arts, Boston; the Cumberland County Court House, Portland, Me.; and the New Hampshire Historical Society, Concord, N. H.

His interest extended to landscape architecture and he designed not only gardens in connection with estates, but city gardens as well. Although his inspiration came undoubtedly from his studies in Italy, his work was never imitative nor offensively archeological. In the field of landscape architecture he published *American Gardens* (1902), *Smaller Italian Villas and Farmhouses* (1916), and *More Small Italian Villas and Farmhouses* (1920). His style was charming in its informality. He was an enthusiastic amateur photographer and largely illustrated his books with his own photographs. For a number of years he lectured on landscape architecture in the Massachusetts Institute of Technology.

During the World War he entered the American Red Cross with the rank of major and served principally in Italy. There his skill, tact, courage, and gift for organization enabled him to accomplish much, and his outspoken friendship for Italy gave courage to a country which received far less attention and sympathy in America than did the better-known and better-understood allies, Great Britain and France. For this service he was awarded the Italian War Cross, with two citations, the silver medal for valor, the Order of Mauritius and Lazarus, and the Order of the Crown of Italy.

He was a lover of music, painting, and sculpture, and had more than an amateur's knowledge of these arts. After the death of his cousin, Percival Lowell [q.v.], he was the sole trustee of the Lowell Observatory at Flagstaff, Ariz., and the responsibility gave him a new hobby—the grinding of lenses for telescopes. He was an enthusiastic yachtsman and participated in the international races at Kiel. His death occurred suddenly, at Madeira, while he was on a vacation with his wife. His body was cremated in Italy, and the ashes brought to the United States for burial.

[A. S. Pier, "Guy Lowell," in *Harvard Grads. Mag.*, June 1927; *Harvard Coll. Class of 1892, Necrology*, Report X, pt. II (1927); D. R. Lowell, *The Hist. Geneal. of the Lowells of America* (1899); *Who's Who in America, 1926–27*; *Am. Architect*, Feb. 20, 1927; *Arch. Record*, Apr. 1927; *Architecture and Building*, Mar. 1927; *Architecture*, Apr. 1927; *Bull. Boston Soc. of Architects*, Feb. 1927; *N. Y. Times*, Feb. 5, 1927.]
G. H. E—l.

LOWELL, JAMES RUSSELL (Feb. 22, 1819–Aug. 12, 1891), author, teacher, public servant, foremost American man of letters in his time, was born and died in the same house, "Elmwood," in Cambridge, Mass. His father, the Rev. Charles Lowell, for more than forty years minister of the West Church (Unitarian), Boston, was descended from Perceval Lowell (or Lowle) who emigrated in 1639 from England to settle at Newbury in the Massachusetts colony. Immediately back of Charles Lowell in descent were two John Lowells, graduates, like himself, of Harvard College, of which his father, Judge John Lowell, 1743–1802 [q.v.], was a fellow. From Harriet Brackett Spence, daughter of Keith and Mary (Traill) Spence of Portsmouth, N. H., the wife of the Rev. Charles Lowell, their poetic son received a sharply different strain of inheritance. Her forebears on both sides had come from the Orkney Islands; she herself, brought up in the Episcopal Church, in which one of her sons, Robert Traill Spence Lowell [q.v.], became a clergyman, was of a mystical strain, with a reputed gift of second sight and a contagious love of old ballads, proper to one not impossibly related to the hero of the ballad of Sir Patrick Spens. The spirit of this mother was, indeed, so sensitive that in her final years

it fell into a disorder that called forth her son's poem, "The Darkened Mind," ending with the sorrowful lines:

"Not so much of thee is left among us
As the hum outliving the hushed bell."

Through Lowell's boyhood and younger manhood, however, her influence played a vital part in the forming of the poet, even as the paternal strain fortified the future publicist.

After preparation at the classical school of Mr. William Wells in Cambridge he entered Harvard College. As an undergraduate he took his prescribed duties with a lightness that could meet only with disapproval from academic authorities. Promiscuous reading in the college library was not then encouraged, but without it he could hardly have formed those lasting friendships with books described in his paper on Landor. "It was," he wrote, "the merest browsing, no doubt, as Johnson called it, but how delightful it was! All the more, I fear, because it added the stolen sweetness of truancy to that of study, for I should have been buckling to my allotted task of the day. I do not regret that diversion of time to other than legitimate expenses, yet shall I not gravely warn my grandsons to beware of doing the like?" (*Latest Literary Essays*, p. 54). This tendency might have been overlooked, but at the end of his senior year came a concrete offense which could not escape punishment. In T. W. Higginson's *Old Cambridge* (1899, p. 157) and Ferris Greenslet's *James Russell Lowell* (p. 23) may be found good evidence for believing that Lowell's personal celebration of his election as class poet sent him to chapel one afternoon when he might better have gone to his room, for at the beginning of the service he rose in his place and bowed, with smiles, to left and right, as if in acknowledgment of the honor his classmates had paid him. On the ground of "continued neglect of his college duties" the faculty promptly rusticated him to the care and instruction of the Rev. Barzillai Frost in the neighboring town of Concord until "the Saturday before Commencement." Thus he was prevented from reading his own class poem, a young conservative's fling, both jaunty and grave, at causes and persons soon to enlist his sympathies. Here he is even found decrying:

"those who roar and rave
O'er the exaggerated tortures of the slave."

The poem is not included in his published works, but, filling thirty-nine generous pages of what has now become a rare pamphlet (*Class Poem*, 1838), it may be read as a truly promising and prophetic performance for the youth of nineteen who received his bachelor's degree with the Harvard class of 1838.

The few years of "finding himself" that followed immediately upon his leaving college were far from placid. He began the study of law, and, in spite of many uncertainties about its continuance, graduated at the Harvard Law School in 1840. An unhappy youthful love affair had made its contribution to the unsettled state of his mind. In 1866 he recalled this distressful time: "I remember in '39 putting a cocked pistol to my forehead—and being afraid to pull the trigger, of which I was heartily ashamed, and am still whenever I think of it" (*Letters*, II, 136).

It was not until he met and became engaged in marriage to Maria White, the gifted and beautiful sister of a classmate in Watertown, immediately adjoining Cambridge, that his future began to clarify itself. His prospects of self-support were so meager that their marriage had to be deferred for more than four years. Before it occurred (on Dec. 26, 1844) Lowell made his public beginnings as poet, editor, critic, and reformer. In poetry this period marked the appearance of *A Year's Life* (1841) and *Poems* (1844). The second volume contained several anti-slavery poems. Now Maria White was a devotee not only of poetry but of anti-slavery sentiments, and the happy "Band" of young people who became Lowell's intimates through his association with her was eagerly devoted to the reforms of the day, among which abolitionism ranked high. Thus the young conservative became something of a radical before he was twenty-five. As a critic of literature he printed his first book, *Conversations on Some of the Old Poets* (1845), the preface of which was dated one week before his marriage. Much of this volume had already appeared serially in the *Boston Miscellany*, edited by Nathan Hale, even as many poems in the two previous volumes had been printed first in periodicals. Though Lowell declared in later life, "I am a book-man" (see address on "The Place of the Independent in Politics," 1888, *Literary and Political Addresses*, p. 235), he might have said with equal truth, "I am a magazine man," for both as editor and as contributor he touched the periodicals of his time at an extraordinary number of points.

His first appearance as an editor was in connection with *The Pioneer: A Literary and Critical Magazine*, produced in the months of January, February, and March 1843, by Lowell and his friend Robert Carter as editors and proprietors. Whether through lack of support or through a failure of Lowell's eyesight which drove him to New York for treatment by a spe-

cialist, the venture was short-lived; but the three issues, containing contributions from Poe, Hawthorne, Whittier, and others whose names have endured, testify to Lowell's instincts and capacities as an editor. In an introduction to the first issue, setting forth the aims of *The Pioneer*, he wrote in a vein that seems contemporaneous today, even while it was prophetic of what was to befall Lowell himself: "We hear men speak of the restless spirit of the age, as if our day were peculiar in this regard. But it has always been the same . . . still the new spirit yearns and struggles and expects great things; still the Old shakes its head, ominous of universal anarchy; still the world rolls calmly on, and the youth grown old shakes its wise head at the next era."

Before completing this process himself Lowell was to live through some years of relative radicalism. Brought into the anti-slavery movement by his ardent young wife's enthusiasm for the cause and never himself counted one of its more violent advocates, he nevertheless identified himself completely with it by serving in Philadelphia for a few months immediately after his marriage as an editorial writer for the *Pennsylvania Freeman*, by continuing, on his return to Cambridge early in the summer of 1845, to write, in prose and verse, against slavery, and, within a year, by forming a connection with a New York publication, *The National Anti-Slavery Standard*, of which, two years later, in 1848, he became "corresponding editor."

Not in this quarter only did the sympathy and influence of Lowell's wife prevail with him. Her interest in reform was matched by her devotion to poetry, in which, besides the gift of appreciation, she possessed a graceful lyric faculty of her own. Their idyllic life together seemed fulfilled in the birth of their first child, Blanche, who died (in March 1847) when an infant of less than fifteen months, but lived on in lines among the best known of Lowell's shorter poems: "She Came and Went," "The Changeling," and "The First Snow-fall." A second daughter, Mabel, who survived him, was born in September 1847. A daughter, Rose, born in 1849, lived but a few months. A son, Walter, born in December 1850, died in Rome in April 1852. Before the end of the next year (Oct. 27, 1853) Mrs. Lowell, deeply affected by these losses, herself died. In 1855 a slender volume, *The Poems of Maria Lowell*, "privately printed" in Cambridge and thus offered rather to friends than to the general public, bore witness to Lowell's appreciation of his wife's poetic gift.

The year 1848, called by one of Lowell's biographers (Ferris Greenslet) his *annus mirabilis*, certainly justified that name, for during its course, besides a volume of *Poems by James Russell Lowell, Second Series,* he published *A Fable for Critics,* the first volume of *The Biglow Papers,* and *The Vision of Sir Launfal.* To his claims for consideration as a poet and critic, this output added the claims of a humorist and political satirist. Thus at twenty-nine he had made his challenge in all the fields of production in which his ultimate place among American writers must be determined. With regard to his poetry, there would be less dissent today from an opinion of Margaret Fuller's than there was either when she expressed it some three years before the *Fable for Critics* appeared or in the later decades of the nineteenth century. "His interest in the moral questions of the day," she declared, "has supplied the want of vitality in himself; his great facility at versification has enabled him to fill the ear with a copious stream of pleasant sound. But his verse is stereotyped; his thought sounds no depth, and posterity will not remember him" (*Papers on Literature and Art,* pt. II, 1846, p. 132). If posterity does not forget Margaret Fuller, it may be in part because Lowell included in his *Fable* such lines about an unmistakable "Miranda" as the following:

> "She always keeps asking if I don't observe a
> Particular likeness 'twixt her and Minerva."

As a humorist and satirist Lowell can hardly be considered apart from his qualities as a critic and political observer. In the *Fable for Critics* humor and criticism are more frankly and plentifully blended than anywhere else in his writings. The critical estimates of his contemporaries among American writers have in general proved surprisingly near to the verdicts of posterity. When he wrote about himself:

> "The top of the hill he will ne'er come nigh reaching
> Till he learns the distinction 'twixt singing and preaching,"

he forestalled what others may still say about a considerable portion of his poetic work. Nearly twenty years later he wrote in a letter to Norton (Aug. 28, 1865), "I shall never be a poet till I get out of the pulpit, and New England was all meeting-house when I was growing up" (*Letters,* II, 105). Nowhere more clearly than in the *Fable for Critics,* from its ingeniously rhymed title-page through its seventy-four pages of text in the first edition, does Lowell exhibit his facility in the twisting of words into all the shapes demanded by punning and verse-making. He was indeed an incorrigible punster in prose as well as verse. Even in a serious book review he was capable of applying to certain Shakespearian

commentators "the quadrisyllabic name of the brother of Agis, King of Sparta"—in which it took a Felton to recognize Eudamidas ("White's Shakespeare," *Atlantic Monthly,* February 1859, p. 244). This, for all its elaboration, has a neatness that justifies it—which cannot be said for all of Lowell's verbal pranks. Some of his ineptitudes became apparent even to Lowell after their first commission and were removed from later printings. Witness, for example, in the course of so serious and admirable a poem as "The Cathedral" (*Atlantic Monthly,* January 1870, p. 4), the miserable interchange with an Englishman at Chartres:

> " 'Esker vous ate a nabitang?' he asked;
> 'I never ate one; are they good?' asked I."

Such things are incredible, but there they are in the spontaneity of Lowell's first printing, subject to all such discount as the spirit of a period of ponderous jocosity will warrant, yet certainly dimming the luster to which he had so many valid claims as a wit and, in the eighteenth-century meaning of the term, a man of taste.

As the *Fable for Critics* illustrates, from several angles, one aspect of Lowell, so do *The Biglow Papers,* of which the first series appeared in the same year, 1848. Lowell's preoccupation with words is here displayed through the medium of dialect. Proud of his intimacy with the finer shades of the Yankee vernacular—"I reckon myself a good taster of dialects," he once wrote—he carried to an extreme of phonetic exactness his reproductions of the peculiarities of New England speech. To this somewhat elaborate vehicle of his humor another was added in the academic utterances of the Rev. Homer Wilbur, whose list of degrees in an imaginary college catalogue is one of Lowell's triumphs of fooling. Through the mingled prose and verse of this clergyman, the rustic Hosea Biglow, and other mouthpieces, Lowell delivered himself, in the first series of *Biglow Papers,* of trenchantly telling criticism of the national government in the conduct of the Mexican War, especially in relation to the possible extension of slavery. These articles, appearing in the periodical press before their assemblage between covers, produced a palpable effect upon public opinion and first gave to Lowell the place he was henceforth to occupy as a patriotic observer of political affairs whose opinions about them must be reckoned with. Nearly twenty years later the same medium of *Biglow Papers* stood ready to convey his sentiments on the Civil War—sentiments in which a distrust and dislike of England held a surprisingly large place for one who was to become one of the most acceptable of American ministers to Great Britain. Out of all the writings of James Russell Lowell, the two series of *Biglow Papers,* joining wit, highly skilful writing, and a passionate devotion to liberty and country, may be regarded as his most distinctive contribution to the literature of his time.

Between 1848 and 1853, the year of his wife's death, Lowell spent fifteen months (July 1851–October 1852) in Europe, ripening his powers by observation and study. The death of Mrs. Lowell a year after his return was a desolating blow, yet before and after it fell he busied himself with writing for magazines and with much intercourse with friends. It is significant that between 1849, when he brought out a two-volume edition of his *Poems,* and 1864, when his *Fireside Travels,* a volume of essays, appeared, he made no addition to the list of his published books. The decade ending in 1864 was nevertheless of great moment in his career. Early in its course, and immediately after his delivery (January 1855) of a series of Lowell Institute lectures in Boston on the English poets, he was appointed, in succession to Longfellow, Smith Professor of the French and Spanish Languages and Literatures, and professor of belles-lettres in Harvard College; and in 1857 he became editor of the *Atlantic Monthly,* of which the first number was issued in November of that year. In his teaching position the scholarly interests which he had long pursued as an amateur became professional interests, with the large by-product of critical writing which he was henceforth to produce. Through his editorship—four years with the *Atlantic Monthly* (1857–61), followed for several years beginning in January 1864 by an association with Charles Eliot Norton [*q.v.*] in the conduct of the *North American Review*—he not only found an outlet for his vigorous thinking on political matters and his appreciations of contemporary letters, but exerted a powerful influence in the direction of public thought and taste.

On Lowell's appointment to the Harvard professorship he went, alone, to Europe (June 1855–August 1856) for studies, especially in Germany and Italy, which should augment his qualifications for the teaching of European letters. He had left his only daughter, Mabel, in Cambridge at the home of his brother-in-law, Dr. Estes Howe, in charge of a governess, Frances Dunlap, whose admirable qualities of mind and character led to the fortunate repair of Lowell's shattered domestic structure through his marriage with her in September 1857. This was at the beginning of his second year of college teach-

ing, in which he continued without interruption for sixteen years. After two years' intermission (August 1872–July 1874) he took it up for four years more. Nominally he held the Smith Professorship from 1855 to 1886, when he became professor emeritus for the remaining six years of his life. In Barrett Wendell's *Stelligeri* (1893, pp. 205–17) a sketch of Lowell as a teacher of Dante to a small class in a college lecture-room or, still more personally, in his own study at "Elmwood," shows forth the informal method of the sympathetic, stimulating instruction which made him one of the most memorable influences with many college generations at Cambridge.

Through his identification with the infant *Atlantic Monthly* Lowell bore a leading part in a highly significant episode in the history of American letters. The remarkable group of writers in and about Boston at the middle of the nineteenth century—Emerson, Hawthorne, Whittier, Holmes, Longfellow, and others, who had flowered simultaneously with the Unitarian reaction from the extreme Calvinism of earlier New England—was really the fortuitous springing up of a band of neighbors of diverse gifts yet with much in common. The *Atlantic,* standing for liberal thought and speech on matters of politics, religion, and letters, provided them with a single mouthpiece and afforded that sense of solidarity which contributes to the formation of a "school." Lowell proved himself an admirable editor, not merely in such larger matters of *Atlantic* policy as his insistence upon securing contributions from Holmes as a "condition precedent" to his accepting the editorship, but in the minutiæ of editing, even with respect to emendations in poems by Emerson and Whittier. He gave evidence, moreover, by his own striking contributions in prose and verse to the pages of his magazine, that he should be counted also among its best contributors.

Lowell laid down his editorship of the *Atlantic* just about the time the Civil War was beginning, and began his association with the *North American Review* when, in January 1864, it was nearing its end. During the war, however, the *Atlantic* published several political papers from his pen, besides the second series of *Biglow Papers.* From 1864 till late in 1866 he contributed to the *North American Review* a series of vigorous prose papers, afterwards assembled with earlier articles, and one later, in his *Political Essays* (1888). To Lowell's passion for freedom there was allied, in all his feeling about the war and its consequences, the poignancy of the deaths of three beloved nephews at the front. No wonder that his writings about the issues of the times, whether in prose or in verse, glowed with a special fervor. No wonder that when it fell to him to produce the "Ode Recited at the Harvard Commemoration, July 21, 1865," in honor of the sons of his college who had given their lives in the war, he produced the poem which, by common agreement, represents him at his best.

The occasion itself was memorable. Phillips Brooks, then a young clergyman settled in Philadelphia, made a prayer which seemed to eclipse all other utterances of a day on which scholars and soldiers held the center of the stage. Lowell's Ode, written at white heat on the very eve of the celebration, after many fears that it would not "come," suffered grave disadvantages: it was delivered under a strain of weariness from presiding at a Phi Beta Kappa meeting on the day before, and from much sacrifice of sleep for a final copying of the lines; and it lacked the noble strophe relating to Lincoln, which was added after the poem was read. Like Lincoln's Gettysburg Address, it seems to have fallen far short of recognition as an outstanding event of the day: indeed, in two Boston newspapers of the next morning no mention of it is found in the long accounts of the exercises. New York papers did better. From the time of its reaching the general public with its Lincoln strophe, in the *Atlantic Monthly* for September 1865, it took the place which it has held ever since, in the front rank of poems proceeding from the war and preeminent in its expression of Lowell's exalted spirit of patriotism.

Closely related to Lowell's work as a teacher in Harvard College stands the changed proportion of critical to creative writing as he grew older. A volume of poems, *Under the Willows* (1869), and a single poem, *The Cathedral* (1870), followed, to be sure, upon his *Fireside Travels*; but in 1870 also appeared another volume of essays, *Among My Books*; in 1871 still another, *My Study Windows*; and in 1876, *Among My Books,* second series. Literary criticism was the substance of all these volumes. The topics, such as Dryden, Dante, Shakespeare, and other poets, English and American, were topics with which he dealt in the classroom. They lent themselves well to treatment also for such periodicals as the *Atlantic* and the *North American Review,* and to assemblage in book form when they sufficed for a new volume.

As a critic Lowell was highly rated in his day, but with the passing of the years his stature has diminished. In *The Romantic Revolution in America* (1927), V. L. Parrington has found him an exemplar of Bostonian Victorianism (p. 436), of the united dignity and con-

science of English liberalism and Cambridge Brahminism (p. 472), and has defined him as "a bookish amateur in letters, loitering over old volumes for the pleasure of finding apt phrases and verbal curiosities" (p. 461). An English student of his writings, John M. Robertson, calls him "a man primarily endowed with a great gift of copious literary expatiation, highly 'impressionistic,' and only under pressure of challenge analytic" (*North American Review,* February 1919, p. 256). W. C. Brownell, in his *American Prose Masters* (1909), alluding to Lowell's cleverness and personal charm, remarks: "Nothing is more envied in the living. Nothing finds prompter interment with their bones" (p. 277); and says of his critical work in general that it "will excel more in finding new beauties in the actual than in discovering new requirements in the ideal" (pp. 300–01). The upshot of Professor Norman Foerster's penetrating study of Lowell in his *American Criticism* (1928) is that he fell short of realizing his ambitions, "partly because his native force was inadequate, and partly because he was sucked into the current of his times" (p. 156). Nevertheless, every critic must acknowledge the breadth and alertness of his reading, the gusto and common sense that pervaded his prose writings, the exuberance of fancy and expression, the flow of humorous extravagance which he would have done well at times to check, the ardor, even the passion, of his feeling for his native land and its traditional ideals. To these qualities may be attributed his influence upon his contemporaries and the generation following.

The books that Lowell was still to write did not materially affect his place in American literature. Prose was decidedly to predominate over poetry. After 1876 two volumes of verse were published during his lifetime: *Three Memorial Poems* (1877), and *Heartsease and Rue* (1888); after his death appeared *Last Poems of James Russell Lowell* (1895). In prose— omitting pamphlets included also in collected writings—were *Democracy and Other Addresses* (1887), *Political Essays* (1888), and, after his death, *Latest Literary Essays and Addresses* (1891), *The Old English Dramatists* (1892), *Letters of James Russell Lowell* (2 vols., 1893), edited by Charles Eliot Norton, and *New Letters of James Russell Lowell* (1932), edited by M. A. De Wolfe Howe. Other posthumous publications were reprints or rescues of fugitive writings which had not seemed to him worthy of preservation.

As the literary and political essays included

in his earlier volumes had reflected his life as an editor and professor, so the later essays bore a recognizable relation to his later interests as a public servant. These began when, in 1876, he went as a delegate to the Republican National Convention, to bear his part in the defeat of Blaine and the selection of Hayes as a nominee for the presidency. Serving as a member of the Electoral College, after refusing solicitations to run for Congress, he adhered to Hayes, in the election contest with Tilden, on the clear ground that Hayes was the candidate he was chosen to support. For such party service men less qualified than Lowell for a diplomatic post have received their reward. His came in the spring of 1877, in the form of an invitation to assume the post of United States minister to Spain. His saying, "I should like to see a play of Calderon," accounted in part for the acceptance of this offer, but for nearly three years in Madrid—from the summer of 1877 to the spring of 1880—he enacted the rôle of minister with much credit to himself and his country, adapting himself well to the formalities of a ceremonious court, appreciating and appreciated by the cultivated society of Madrid, extending his knowledge of the Spanish language and literature, seizing a summer opportunity for visiting Turkey and Greece, yet sorely harassed in the third year of his mission by the serious illness of his wife. When he received notice in January 1880 that the President had nominated him minister to the Court of St. James's, his equipment for service there had greatly improved since he left home, and his immediate perception that his wife's health would probably be much the better for the change gave added reason for accepting the post.

Of Lowell in England, Henry James wrote characteristically that "some of his more fanatical friends are not to be deterred from regarding his career as in the last analysis a tribute to the dominion of style," and that "the true reward of an English style was be sent to England" (*Essays in London and Elsewhere*, 1893, pp. 45, 55). The reward would have seemed more fitting if in earlier years Lowell's antagonism to England and the English had not been so pronounced. During the Civil War, beyond expressing himself frankly as he did in the "Jonathan to John" verses in the *Biglow Papers*, he found it nearly impossible to write to a single English correspondent. In his essay on "New England Two Centuries Ago" (*North American Review*, January 1865), he alluded to our "English cousins (as they are fond of calling themselves when they are afraid we may do them a mischief)"; and "On a Certain Condescen-

sion in Foreigners" (*Atlantic Monthly*, January 1869) contains the remark, "Not a Bull of them all but is persuaded he bears Europa upon his back." When Lowell and the English came to know each other, the war was fifteen years in the past and there was as much inclination to forgive on the one side as to forget on the other. Lowell indeed performed a notable mission of good will, besides conducting to the satisfaction of all but certain Irish-Americans the delicate relations growing out of Fenian disturbances and carrying on the general work of the London legation. At private and public dinner tables, as on ceremonial and other occasions—such as his assuming the presidency of the Birmingham and Midland Institute (Oct. 6, 1884), when he delivered one of the best of his addresses, "Democracy"—his gift of informal and formal speech kept him in constant demand. In England, as in America, his friendships with the most interesting men and women of his time played a vital part in his life. In London, as in Madrid, his wife's health was a cause of grave anxiety, and on Feb. 19, 1885, she died. A few months later the newly elected President Cleveland appointed Edward J. Phelps to succeed Lowell in London, and in June 1885 he returned to private life, mainly in America. In his six remaining summers there were four visits to England, where his many associations caused him to feel greatly at home. It was really at home, however, at "Elmwood," on Aug. 12, 1891, that he died, in his seventy-third year.

From Lowell's writings in general his personality is clearly to be deduced—ardent, affectionate, whimsical, deeply serious. In the *Letters* edited by his friend Charles Eliot Norton his characteristics are revealed perhaps most clearly and consistently. If what seems a consciously "literary" quality in the letters causes a suspicion that ultimate publication was not wholly absent from Lowell's mind, such a suspicion may be dismissed. He was himself conscious of a tendency to write as if for more than a single reader. "It is a bad thing for one's correspondents, I find," he wrote to his daughter in 1869, "that one has been lecturing these dozen years" (*Letters*, II, 215). His letters indeed seem to have been much like his talk, in which he sparkled, perhaps as brightly as his Saturday Club colleague, Dr. Holmes, though with a superiority over that friend in the capacity of listener. One of his pet topics was the detection of a Jewish strain in unexpected quarters, and "to say the truth," wrote Sir Leslie Stephen, "this was the only subject upon which I could conceive Lowell approaching within measurable distance of boring" (Lowell's *Letters*, III, 336). His occasional speeches, like his *vers d'occasion*, abounded in felicities. In more serious speeches, of which his address (Nov. 8, 1886) at the 250th anniversary of the founding of Harvard University is an admirable example, he gave impressive utterance to his ripened wisdom.

Professor Norman Foerster, in an appraisal of Lowell (*American Criticism*, p. 150), states that he "stood forth among his contemporaries because of his accomplished versatility rather than because of high attainment." Lowell himself, in his essay on Carlyle, wrote that "real fame depends rather on the sum of an author's powers than on any brilliancy of special parts" (*My Study Windows*, p. 58). In special parts Lowell was abundantly brilliant, but the parts were so many and diverse—all of his writings being capable of separate or loosely connected magazine publication—that the effect of his work in its totality is inevitably diffused, and suffers in comparison with that of writers, perhaps of more limited abilities, who employed them with greater concentration. His *Biglow Papers,* a few of his poems, a few of his essays, seem forty years after his death to be compacted of the stuff of permanence. The great body of his work today offers its reward chiefly to the student of Lowell's time and of Lowell as an eminent figure of that period.

[The first important edition of Lowell's collected works was *The Writings of James Russell Lowell*, Riverside Edition (10 vols., 1890), to which vols. XI and XII, *Latest Literary Essays and Addresses* and *The Old English Dramatists*, ed. by C. E. Norton, were added in 1891 and 1892; the most comprehensive collection is *The Complete Writings of James Russell Lowell*, Elmwood Edition (16 vols., 1904), which includes the letters, ed. by Norton, in 3 vols. Citations in the foregoing article, except where otherwise indicated, are of the Elmwood Edition. Noteworthy collections of fugitive writings are *Lectures on English Poets* (printed for the Rowfant Club, Cleveland, 1897), being the Lowell Inst. Lectures of 1855, repr. from the *Boston Daily Advertiser*; *The Anti-Slavery Papers of James Russell Lowell* (2 vols., 1902), repr. from the *Pa. Freeman* and the *Nat. Anti-Slavery Standard*; and *Impressions of Spain* (1899), comp. from the Diplomatic Correspondence by J. B. Gilder, with introduction by A. A. Adee. Bibliographies include: L. S. Livingston, *A Bibliog. of the First Editions in Book Form of the Writings of James Russell Lowell* (1914); G. W. Cooke, *A Bibliog. of James Russell Lowell* (1906); and that comp. by Irita Van Doren for *The Cambridge Hist. of Am. Lit.*, II (1918), 544 ff. The main sources of biographical material are *Letters of James Russell Lowell* (2 vols., 1894), ed. by C. E. Norton and *New Letters of James Russell Lowell* (1932), ed. by M. A. DeWolfe Howe. The *Papers Relating to the Foreign Relations of the U. S.*, 1877–85, contain the record of his diplomatic career. See also H. E. Scudder, *James Russell Lowell* (2 vols. 1901); Ferris Greenslet, *James Russell Lowell* (1905); E. E. Hale, *James Russell Lowell and His Friends* (1899); E. E. Hale, Jr., *James Russell Lowell* (1899); A. L. Lowell, memoir in *Proc. Mass. Hist. Soc., 2 ser. XI* (1897); G. W. Curtis, *James Russell Lowell, An Address* (1892); A. H. Thorndike, "Lowell," in *The Cambridge Hist. of Am. Lit.*, vol. II (1918); J. J. Reilly, *James Russell Lowell as a Critic*

(1915); E. W. Emerson, *The Early Years of the Saturday Club* (1918); D. R. Lowell, *The Hist. Geneal. of the Lowells of America* (1899); *Letters of John Holmes to James Russell Lowell and Others* (1917), ed. by W. R. Thayer; W. D. Howells, *Literary Friends and Acquaintance* (1900).]

M. A. DeW. H.

LOWELL, JOHN (June 17, 1743–May 6, 1802), legislator, jurist, born at Newburyport, Mass., was the only son of the Rev. John and Sarah (Champney) Lowell. His father, pastor of the First Religious Society of Newburyport, was descended from Perceval Lowell (or Lowle), who emigrated from Bristol, England, to Newbury in 1639. John, after graduating from Harvard in 1760, studied law in the office of Oxenbridge Thacher, in Boston, and was admitted to the Massachusetts bar. Returning to his native town, he early took part in public affairs. In 1767 he was chosen to draft a report upon a letter from the selectmen of Boston concerning plans for resistance to obnoxious acts of Parliament. He was a selectman of Newburyport in 1771, 1772, 1774, and 1776; in April of the last-mentioned year he was delegate to a county convention called to prepare plans for a more equal representation of voters in the General Court, and in the following month he represented Newburyport in the Provincial Congress and was apparently a major in the militia.

In 1777 he moved to Boston and in 1778 represented that town in the General Court. In 1779–80 he was a delegate to the state constitutional convention. It has frequently been asserted, on the basis of a letter from his son, Rev. Charles Lowell, to Charles E. Stevens in 1856, that he was responsible for introducing into the declaration of rights the words "free and equal," which the courts later decided excluded slavery from the state. Since, however, the declaration was adopted practically as drafted by John Adams, and the phrase in question was similar to phrases used previously in the Virginia and Pennsylvania declarations, Lowell was probably not its author. He was decidedly in favor of abolishing slavery, however, and showed his sympathy with the negro on several occasions. (Deane, *post.*)

He was a member of the Continental Congress in 1782 and 1783, and in the former year was appointed one of three judges to hear appeals in Admiralty cases. In 1784 he was made a member of the Harvard Corporation, and served, with great benefit to the college, until his death. In 1784 also he was a member of the commission appointed to settle the boundary dispute between Massachusetts and New York. In 1789 he became a United States judge for the district of Massachusetts and in 1801 was appointed chief judge of the First Circuit (Maine, Massachusetts, New Hampshire, and Rhode Island) under the new organization of the United States courts. He was for many years president of the Massachusetts Agricultural Society, and contributed greatly to the establishment of the Botanic Garden at Cambridge. He was also one of the founders of the American Academy of Arts and Sciences (1780), and an occasional writer in verse and prose. Several distinguished men, one of whom was Harrison Gray Otis, began their legal careers in his office.

One of the most upright, capable, public-spirited, and cultured citizens of his state in his time, Lowell was the worthy progenitor of a notable family. By his first marriage (Jan. 3, 1767), to Sarah, sister of Stephen Higginson [q.v.], he was the father of two daughters and a son, John, 1769–1840 [q.v.]. His second wife, Susanna Cabot of Salem, whom he married May 31, 1774, bore him a daughter and a son, Francis Cabot Lowell [q.v.], for whom the city of Lowell is named. After her death he married, third, Rebecca (Russell) Tyng, widow of James Tyng of Dunstable and daughter of James and Katharine (Graves) Russell of Charlestown. Of this union there were three daughters and a son, Charles, who became the father of James Russell and Robert T. S. Lowell [qq.v.]. Judge Lowell died in Roxbury toward the close of his fifty-ninth year.

[Emory Washburn, *Sketches of the Judicial Hist. of Mass.* (1840); J. J. Currier, *"Ould Newbury"* (1896) and *Hist. of Newburyport, Mass.* (2 vols., 1906–09); Josiah Quincy, *The Hist. of Harvard Univ.* (1840), vol. II; D. R. Lowell, *The Hist. Geneal. of the Lowells of America* (1899); Charles Deane, "Judge Lowell and the Massachusetts Declaration of Rights," *Proc. Mass. Hist. Soc.,* XIII (1875), 299–304, and XIV (1876), 108–09.]   J.T.A.

LOWELL, JOHN (Oct. 6, 1769–Mar. 12, 1840), lawyer, political writer, was born in Newburyport, Mass., the son of Judge John Lowell, 1743–1802 [q.v.], and his first wife, Sarah (Higginson) Lowell. He was a half-brother of Francis Cabot Lowell [q.v.]. Entering Harvard in 1783, he graduated in 1786, and in 1789 was admitted to the bar. Brilliant and enthusiastic, he soon acquired a wide and lucrative practice. On June 8, 1793, he married Rebecca Amory. He ably represented Boston in the Massachusetts legislature from 1798 to 1800 (Lodge, *post,* p. 298). His active professional career ended in 1803, when, his health broken through overwork, he went abroad for a three-year rest. Already he had amassed a sufficient fortune to retire for the remainder of his life.

After his return to Massachusetts in 1806 he took an active part in the political controversies of the day, writing vigorous pamphlets and letters to the press, generally supporting the Federalist point of view, and opposing the Embargo, Madison, the "French alliance," and the War of 1812. An expression in one of his papers gained him the sobriquet of "the little Rebel" or "the Boston Rebel." He opposed the Hartford Convention because "it would not go far enough" (Pickering Papers, XXX, 325). Though he was consequently and with some justification (Lodge, *post,* pp. 128–29) regarded as a secessionist, he denied the allegation. His *Review of a Treatise on Expatriation by George Hay Esquire* (1814) is said to have been influential in persuading the government not to retaliate for the death of three British deserters captured in the Chesapeake affair (Greenwood, *post,* pp. 16–17). Henry Adams (*post,* VIII, 5) refers to him as "literary representative" of Timothy Pickering [q.v.], and their correspondence indicates that Pickering often dictated Lowell's political views (see particularly Pickering Papers, XV, 64 and XXX, 325). Because of his failure to sign his writings and his distaste for publicity it is difficult to estimate his importance. Unquestionably influential in New England, his pamphlets seem to have been generally unknown elsewhere (Pickering Papers, XXXVIII, 114).

From 1810 to 1822 he was a member of the Harvard Corporation; from 1823 to 1827, an Overseer. He was a founder of the Massachusetts General Hospital and the Provident Institution for Savings, as well as an early and influential member of the Boston Athenæum, Massachusetts Agricultural Society, Massachusetts Historical Society, and American Antiquarian Society. After his retirement he quietly gave both money and legal services to those in need. His religious articles were widely read; his contributions to the current controversy about the constitutions of the Massachusetts Congregational churches were considered valuable. His writing, clear, forceful, and carefully argued, was praised by such men as Edward Everett, John Jay, and John Marshall. He was a scientific farmer and cattle-breeder, a competent botanist, and a frequent contributor to the *New England Farmer.* On his Roxbury farm he had some of the finest greenhouses in the country, the first to be built on truly scientific principles. He loved farming, and "wanted only to be known as the 'Norfolk Farmer'" (D. R. Lowell, *post,* p. 58). The following titles are representative, among his many pamphlets: *Mr. Madison's War* (by a New England Farmer), issued in 1812; *Are You a Christian or a Calvinist?* (by a Layman), 1815; *An Address Delivered Before the Massachusetts Agricultural Society* (1818).

Through his son John Amory Lowell he was the grandfather of John Lowell, 1824–1897 [q.v.] and the great-grandfather of Percival [q.v.], Amy [q.v.], and Abbott Lawrence Lowell.

[F. W. P. Greenwood, *A Sermon on the Death of John Lowell, LL.D.* (1840) ; Pickering Papers (MSS.), in Mass. Hist. Soc. ; John Amory Lowell, "Memoir of John Lowell," *Proc. Mass. Hist. Soc., 1835–55,* 1 ser. II (1880) ; *Proc. Mass. Hist. Soc.,* 2 ser. XII (1899), 114 ; Edward Everett, *A Memoir of Mr. John Lowell, Jun.* (1840) ; D. R. Lowell, *The Hist. Geneal. of the Lowells of America* (1899) ; Theophilus Parsons, *Memoir of Theophilus Parsons* (1859) ; F. S. Drake, *The Town of Roxbury* (1878) ; H. C. Lodge, *Life and Letters of George Cabot* (1877) ; Henry Adams, *Hist. of the U. S.,* vol. VIII (1891) ; and *Documents Relating to New England Federalism* (1877) ; S. E. Morison, *Life and Letters of Harrison Gray Otis* (2 vols., 1913).]
G. S. J.

LOWELL, JOHN (May 11, 1799–Mar. 4, 1836), founder of the Lowell Institute, was born in Boston. His father, Francis Cabot Lowell [q.v.], was the pioneer of cotton manufacturing in the United States ; his mother, Hannah (Jackson) Lowell, was the daughter of the wealthy and locally esteemed Jonathan Jackson. Such aristocratic parentage brought wealth and social prominence to the son. His preparatory education was gained in the schools of Boston and Edinburgh, Scotland. He entered Harvard College in 1813, but the ill health which seems to have pursued so many youthful collegians of those days compelled his withdrawal two years later. Then came long voyages to India, partly for recuperation, partly for instruction in a phase of his father's business. In 1817 he returned to Boston and there began his business career. He gave little more attention to his affairs, however, than was necessary. His main interests were intellectual. He read widely and wisely, and rapidly acquired a large and well-selected library. Public affairs also attracted his attention ; he sat in the city council and in the state legislature. Here again, however, his interests were more philosophical than practical. John Lowell was an observer of life far more than an active participant in it.

The peaceful and conventional course of his life was rudely shattered when successive deaths in the years 1830 and 1831 deprived him of his wife, Georgina Margaret (Amory) Lowell, whom he had married in 1825, and the two children, both daughters, who had been born of this happy union. A settled existence in Boston henceforth became distasteful to him and he spent the remainder of his short life in travel. He died in Bombay, India, before he was thirty-seven.

The endowment of Lowell Institute is provided for in a will which Lowell drew up in 1832 and in a codicil added in 1835. New England, he observed, was a "sterile and unproductive land." Its prosperity depended on the moral qualities, the intelligence, and the information of its inhabitants. Motivated by this idea, he sought to provide free or practically free lectures of the highest type in all branches of human knowledge. He bequeathed half of his estate, amounting to approximately $250,000, for the establishment of a trust, and made intelligent stipulations for its administration and increase.

Lowell combined two dominant tendencies of the New England educational movement of his day : the "higher lecture for the average citizen," and provision for adult education. The Institute was so liberally endowed, and the trust has been so skilfully administered, that the best work of the world's leading scholars has been made accessible to Boston audiences and, through publication of the lectures, to a much larger reading public. In a sense also the Institute has been a patron of learning, since its liberal stipends have served as an encouragement to those who have been called to its lecture platform. In all respects the Lowell Institute stands as a foundation-stone in the cultural life of New England and as a happy monument to him who placed it there.

[The chief source of information is Edward Everett's excellent *Memoir of Mr. John Lowell, Jun.* (1840). See also Harriette Knight Smith, *The History of the Lowell Inst.* (1898) ; D. R. Lowell, *The Hist. Geneal. of the Lowells of America* (1899) ; Justin Winsor, *Memorial Hist. of Boston,* vol. IV (1881).]
P. H. B.

LOWELL, JOHN (Oct. 18, 1824–May 14, 1897), jurist, was born in Boston. His father, John Amory Lowell, was the son of John Lowell, 1769–1840 [q.v.] ; his mother, Susan Cabot (Lowell), was the daughter of Francis Cabot Lowell [q.v.]. From private schools he went to Harvard, graduating from the college with distinction in 1843 and from the law school in 1845. After studying in the office of Charles G. Loring, he was admitted to the Boston bar in 1846. Directly afterwards he spent a year abroad. His early practice, in association with his brother-in-law, William Sohier, chiefly concerned trust estates. He began practice alone in 1857. The panic and his family mill connections brought him into much litigation which made him a life-long expert in insolvency law. In 1853 he married Lucy Buckminster Emerson of Boston, daughter of George B. Emerson [q.v.] and his first wife, Olivia Buckminster, who was of New Hampshire stock. They had three sons and four daughters. In 1858 Lowell purchased a large farm at Chestnut Hill where he lived the rest of his life. Though he was a small man, not especially robust, his constant activity in walking about his land, planning its development, kept him free from any illness until shortly before his death. The beautiful grounds, with the pond, woods, and wild flowers, were by his tacit consent almost common property. From 1856 to 1860 he edited the *Monthly Law Reporter* (volumes XIX–XXII), assisted the last two years by S. M. Quincey. An article adversely criticizing the Dred Scott decision, by Lowell and Horace Gray, was published in the *Law Reporter,* June 1857, and reprinted as a pamphlet with the title, *A Legal Review of the Case of, Dred Scott* (1857).

In March 1865, President Lincoln appointed Lowell United States district judge for Massachusetts. Many of his most interesting opinions deal with marine controversies. These show a strong sense of practical situations and emergencies. "They smell of the sea; you can almost smell the tar, almost hear the wind rustling through the rigging" (*Proceedings of the Bench and Bar, post,* p. 23). The enactment in 1867 of a national Bankruptcy Act, after an interval of twenty years, gave him the opportunity to display his mastery of that field. His promotion in 1878 to be circuit judge for the first circuit transferred his work to the common law and patents. He disliked patent cases at first, but soon handled them with sound common sense and an acute perception of mechanical facts.

In his judicial opinions Lowell cited few cases. His wide knowledge of precedents took shape chiefly in a clear and orderly statement of principles. Every proposition was ultimately tested for its practical working value. He realized keenly the human factors of a case, and had a remarkable instinct for perceiving on which side real justice lay. One of the bar of his court said: "He would not, unless the law and the evidence compelled him, do what he thought was a practical injustice. And it seldom happened that he found himself so compelled. He had a marvellous talent for escaping from that difficulty" (*Ibid.,* p. 45). Consequently, some called him a wayward judge, independent to the verge of wilfulness in establishing justice. When he resigned his office in 1884, the merchants of Boston took the unusual course of giving him a public dinner in recognition of his able solution of commercial questions. They requested him to prepare a new bankruptcy act, that of 1867 having been repealed. His draft was printed but not adopted. He also wrote *A Treatise on the Law of Bankruptcy* (2 vols., 1899), which was completed after his death by his son, James A. Lowell, and is still useful, although much of the author's

knowledge was superseded by the Act of 1898.

After his retirement Lowell had a large practice. He did not quite cease to be a judge, for he was frequently selected as arbitrator or referee in important controversies. On the bench his uniform courtesy had often relieved a young practitioner of all embarrassment and aided him in the proper presentation of his case, and in later life his learning and experience were always at the service of younger members of the bar. He was an Overseer of Harvard, and had long service on the board of the Massachusetts General Hospital. In 1896 he became chairman of the commission to revise the Massachusetts tax laws.

He was a delightful conversationalist, who walked up and down as he talked. His fund of humor never failed even on the bench. A man of very strong likes and dislikes, he was consciously on guard to prevent their affecting his judicial action.

[*Judgments Delivered in the Courts of the U. S. for the Dist. of Mass.* (2 vols., 1872–77); *Proc. of the Bench and Bar of the Circuit Court of the U. S., Dist. of Mass., upon the Decease of Hon. John Lowell* (1897); T. K. Lothrop, in *Proc. Am. Acad. Arts and Sci.,* vol. XXXV (1900), and *Proc. Mass. Hist. Soc.,* 2 ser. XI (1897); D. R. Lowell, *The Hist. Geneal. of the Lowells of America* (1899); *Later Years of the Saturday Club* (1927), ed. by M. A. DeW. Howe; *Boston Transcript,* May 14, 1897. Judge Lowell's portrait hangs in the U. S. District Courtroom in Boston.]

Z. C., Jr.

LOWELL, JOSEPHINE SHAW (Dec. 16, 1843–Oct. 12, 1905), philanthropist and reformer, was born in West Roxbury, Mass., to a family of wealth and high traditions. Her father, Francis George Shaw, was esteemed for his learning, his integrity, and his wise administration of the fortune inherited from his merchant father, Robert Gould Shaw, of Boston. Her mother, a cousin of her father, was Sarah Blake Sturgis, daughter of Nathaniel Russell Sturgis, also a Boston merchant. When Josephine was three years old the family moved to Staten Island, which remained her home until 1874, when a New York residence became the center of her manifold activities. In 1851 her father took his family abroad and until she was twelve she was in school at Paris or Rome. A year in Miss Gibson's school, New York, and another in a Boston school completed her formal training, from which she probably gained less than from her association with her parents and the group of friends which they drew to the home. After 1856, when he married her sister Anna, George William Curtis [*q.v.*] was a member of the household, and Josephine frequented his library and was much influenced by him. Her diary, kept for a few months after the outbreak of the

Civil War, gives an excellent idea of her intellectual development and her qualities of character at this time, while it also describes the mingled feelings of the Northern group to which she belonged, as the war news came from day to day (Stewart, *post*, pp. 10–37). The war brought her the greatest sorrows of her life. On July 19, 1863, her brilliant young brother, Robert Gould Shaw, was killed at Fort Wagner, and on Oct. 19, 1864, less than a year after her marriage (Oct. 31, 1863), she lost her husband, Col. Charles Russell Lowell, a nephew of James Russell Lowell [*q.v.*]. Six weeks after his death a daughter, Carlotta Russell, was born to the young widow.

With the close of the war she interested herself in the Freedmen's Association, in local hospitals of New York, and in the work of the State Charities Aid Association. In connection with the last named she prepared a report on the methods, the scope, and the results of the administration of the poor law in West Chester County, with special attention to the old problem of the "sturdy beggar." The competence displayed in this report attracted the attention of Gov. Samuel J. Tilden, who in 1876 made her a member of the State Board of Charities, the first woman to be appointed to that board. During her thirteen years of service, she was concerned with the housing and reform of vagrants, and the care of delinquent women, the mental defectives, and the insane. Her reports on these and kindred topics, based on a wealth of information and a thorough familiarity with the history of poor law administration, were models of clarity and cogency. In 1889, convinced that the most effective attack on the problem of poverty was to be made by adjusting the difficulties between capital and labor, she resigned from the State Board to devote more of her energy to the improvement of industrial conditions.

Her most enduring monument, however, is the Charity Organization Society, which she founded and to which she gave unremitting service for twenty-three years. She was also one of the organizers of the Consumer's League and an active worker for civil service reform, municipal lodging houses, and many other good causes. Reports and addresses on such subjects constitute the bulk of her published work. Over forty of these have been printed, all characterized by insight and vigor. Of her other publications, the most important perhaps are *Public Relief and Private Charity* (1884) and *Industrial Arbitration and Conciliation: Some Chapters from the Industrial History of the Past Thirty Years* (1893). Her achievements are attributable to a rare combination of courageous idealism and practical common sense. Her judgment as to ways and means was never that of a fanatic but rather that of a sagacious person, who was willing to wait for results but never lost sight of the ultimate goal.

[W. R. Stewart, *The Philanthropic Work of Josephine Shaw Lowell* (1911) contains biog. sketch, extracts from reports, and list of writings ; see also *Charities and the Commons*, Dec. 2, 1905, Jan. 27, 1906 ; E. W. Emerson, *Life and Letters of Charles Russell Lowell* (1907) ; *Outlook*, Oct. 21, 1905.]   E. D.

LOWELL, PERCIVAL (Mar. 13, 1855–Nov. 12, 1916), astronomer, business man, and gifted writer, brother of Amy Lowell [*q.v.*], was born in Boston, Mass. His father was Augustus Lowell, a brother of John Lowell, 1824–1897 [*q.v.*] ; his mother, Katharine Bigelow (Lawrence), was the daughter of Abbott Lawrence [*q.v.*], United States minister to Great Britain in 1851. Lowell prepared for college at Noble's School and graduated from Harvard in 1876, distinguishing himself particularly in mathematics. After a year of travel in Europe and the East he returned to Boston. He rapidly became a force in the business world, taking an active part in the development of cotton-mills, trust, and electric companies.

The years 1883 to 1893 were spent in travel and writing in the Far East, chiefly in Japan. Soon after his arrival in Tokyo he was appointed counselor and foreign secretary to the special mission from Korea to the United States ; and at the conclusion of this mission he went to Korea as the guest of the government. His travels there are described in *Chöson—The Land of the Morning Calm* (1885). His *Soul of the Far East*, published in 1888, shows a remarkable insight into the Oriental mind. Lafcadio Hearn, in recommending this book to a friend, wrote: "Please don't skip one solitary line of it and don't delay reading it,—because something, much ! is going to go out of it into your heart and life and stay there !" (letter in G. M. Gould, *Concerning Lafcadio Hearn*, 1908, p. 116). Lowell's *Noto*, a delightful account of his rambles in Japan, appeared in 1891, and his interest in the strange rites of Shintoism, awakened by a trip up the sacred mountain of Ontaki, resulted in *Occult Japan*, published in 1895.

With all his other interests and activities he retained a keen taste for mathematics and astronomy. In a letter to Hector MacPherson he said that his interest in the latter study dated "from 1870, when I used to look at Mars with as keen an interest as now." In 1877 he spent many hours on his father's roof gazing at Mars with a 2-inch telescope, and his enthusiasm was fired anew in that year by Schiaparelli's announcement of the discovery of fine markings on Mars which the Italian astronomer called *Canali*. It was not until the early nineties, however, that Lowell's many-sided interests allowed him to devote his main energies and fortune to astronomy. Schiaparelli's eye-sight had failed and Lowell determined to carry on the work. Realizing that the first essential in planetary observation is good "seeing," he first investigated, with an admirable curb on his impatience, the steadiness and cloudlessness of the atmosphere in various parts of the world. "A large instrument in poor air," he said, "will not begin to show what a smaller one in good air will. When this is recognized . . . it will become the fashion to put up observatories where they may see rather than be seen" (*Mars,* p. v). His final choice as the site for his observatory was the mesa three hundred feet above the town of Flagstaff, Ariz., at an altitude of 7,200 feet, "far from the smoke of men." Isolation in an undeveloped country necessitated the gathering not only of a staff of observers, but also mechanics and carpenters to build the instruments, domes, machine shop, and houses, and laborers to build roads, cut the winter's supply of wood, and milk the cows. Lowell's own picturesque, rambling house, which he called the "Baronial Mansion," was built on the edge of the mesa where he could look through and over the age-old pines of the Conconino Forest, across a plain, to the San Francisco Peaks. "The Peaks this morning are white-laced from yesterday's storm, a white mantilla over their heads and shoulders," he wrote on one occasion (Leonard, *post,* p. 70).

Observation was begun on "Mars Hill" in 1894 with an 18-inch refractor. This was replaced two years later with a 24-inch. Since then, a 40-inch reflector and many smaller instruments and accessories have been added. Visual, photographic, and micrometric observations of Mars and their careful discussion are prominent in the three volumes of the *Annals of the Lowell Observatory,* vol. I (1898), vol. II (1900), vol. III (1905), and in many of the *Bulletins,* started in 1903. What Lowell saw was, in his own words, "over a geography not unakin to the Earth's . . . a mesh of lines and dots like a lady's veil." The gradually increasing conspicuousness of the markings in lower latitudes as the "wave of quickening" spread from the shrinking polar cap, the spectroscopic evidence of water-vapor, the color changes in the blue-green areas, all strengthened his conviction that Mars is the abode of intelligent life. Interest at the Observatory, however, was not long con-

fined to Mars. Mercury, Venus, and all the other planets as well as their satellites were subjected to the same careful study and measurement. Some of the most reliable values for diameter, oblateness, and rotation periods of planets and satellites were derived at the Lowell Observatory. New divisions in Saturn's rings were seen. Lowell was quite justified in stating in one of his lectures that the study of the solar system "is chiefly carried on at the present time by the observatory which I represent." It was not long, either, before members of the staff carried the campaign far out beyond the solar system, in the spectroscopic study of clusters and nebulae. Lowell himself contributed researches on the development of the solar system, the structure of Saturn's rings, and the problem of a trans-Neptunian planet. The discovery of Planet X in January 1930 was the direct result of his mathematical prediction.

His passionate interest in the planets embraced also the earth. "The planet Mars was the only rival to his botanical love. Study of the trees was his chief delight in his tramps afield." His letters are full of delightful records, such as: "May 13. Holly and Potentilla canadensis near the mullein patch. Radishes big enough to eat, *and eaten*" (Leonard, p. 76). There are also references to "Paint Brush Point," "Arrowhead Hills," and "Holly Ravine."

Lowell believed ardently that the results or scientific research should be made accessible to all, by voice and pen. He was a brilliant lecturer and his books on astronomical subjects are delightful reading. Among these are *Mars* (1895); *The Solar System* (1903); *Mars and Its Canals* (1906); *Mars as the Abode of Life* (1908); *The Evolution of Worlds* (1909); *The Genesis of the Planets* (1916). He was appointed non-resident professor of astronomy at the Massachusetts Institute of Technology in 1902. He received medals from the astronomical societies of France and Mexico and honorary membership in the Royal Astronomical Society of Canada. In 1908 he married Constance Savage Keith, of Boston. He died in his sixty-second year and was buried on Mars Hill, close beside the 24-inch telescope with which the work he started is being carried forward through his endowment.

[Louise Leonard, *Percival Lowell—An Afterglow* (1921); Hector MacPherson, "Percival Lowell, an Appreciation," *Observatory,* Jan. 1917; *Percival Lowell* (1917), pub. by the Lowell Observatory; R. G. Aitken, in *Pubs. Astronomical Soc. of the Pacific,* XXVIII (1916), 266–68; A. Fowler, in *Nature,* Nov. 23, 1916; *Popular Astronomy,* Apr. 1917; G. R. Agassiz, in *Proc. Am. Acad. Arts and Sci.,* vol. LII (1917); D. R. Lowell, *The Hist. Geneal. of the Lowells of America*

(1899); *Harvard College, the Class of 1876* (1926); *Ariz. Republican* (Phoenix), and *N. Y. Times*, Nov. 14, 1916.]   R. S. D.

LOWELL, ROBERT TRAILL SPENCE (Oct. 8, 1816–Sept. 12, 1891), Protestant Episcopal clergyman and author, was born in Boston, Mass. He was the son of Rev. Charles Lowell, a distinguished Unitarian clergyman, minister of the West Church, and of Harriet Brackett Spence. The fifth in a family of six children, he was the older brother by three years of James Russell Lowell [*q.v.*]. He began his education at the Round Hill School in Northampton, Mass., an institution founded by Joseph Green Cogswell [*q.v.*], who had been a tutor at Harvard and also librarian of the college, and was thus favorably known to the Lowell family. Cogswell seems to have made a profound impression on his young pupil, who years later dedicated to him a book of poems with "love and reverence." From Round Hill, Robert went to Harvard, where he graduated in 1833. He then went through a full course of medicine but, without taking a degree, abandoned his medical pursuits to go into business with his eldest brother. Three years later, however, he decided to enter the ministry of the Protestant Episcopal Church, in which his mother had been reared, and went to Schenectady, N. Y., to study for holy orders under Dr. Alonzo Potter, who had been rector of St. Paul's Church in Boston.

On the invitation of Bishop A. G. Spencer, young Lowell went in 1842 to Bermuda, where he was ordained deacon, and the next year (1843) was ordained priest and appointed domestic chaplain to the Bishop. Later he was transferred at his own request to Newfoundland, where he took a missionary post at Bay Roberts as representative of the English Society for the Propagation of the Gospel. On a trip home in 1845, he married, on Oct. 28, Mary Ann (Marianna) Duane, of Duanesburg, N. Y., by whom he had seven children. Shortly after his return to Newfoundland, he encountered a famine in which he suffered with his parishioners, and, broken in health, returned in 1847 to America after receiving the thanks of the Colonial Secretary. By appointment of Bishop G. W. Doane, he began a mission in a poor quarter of Newark, N. J., where he reëstablished and rebuilt a neglected church. In 1859 he became rector of Christ Church, Duanesburg, N. Y. In 1868 he was appointed professor of belles-lettres in Racine College, Wisconsin, but declined. After ten years' work among the farming people of Duanesburg, he accepted in 1869 the headmastership of St. Mark's School, Southboro, Mass. In 1873 he was made professor of Latin language and literature in Union College, Schenectady, N. Y., and remained in this position until 1879. He died on Sept. 12, 1891, just a month after the death of his more famous brother.

Robert Lowell was a delicate, sensitive, strangely rarefied soul. In his missionary experiences, at home and abroad, he displayed something of that robust quality which was characteristic of his family, but he had mystic elements which were all his own. The literary gift of the Lowells he shared; he wrote with facility and occasional distinction. Several of his books were the product of his varied personal experiences. Thus, *The New Priest in Conception Bay,* a story which appeared in 1858, contained vivid pictures of Newfoundland. This book, an excellent piece of work, was published by Phillips, Sampson & Company just as the senior partner died and the firm went into bankruptcy. It thus had a poor start, and though republished years later never enjoyed the popularity and fame it merited. A book for boys, *Antony Brade, a Story of a School* (1874), grew out of Lowell's experiences as headmaster of St. Mark's. His life at Schenectady suggested *A Story or Two from an Old Dutch Town* (1878). He published also *Fresh Hearts that Failed Three Thousand Years Ago, with Other Things* (1860), a volume of *Poems* (1864), and occasional verses, short stories, sermons, and addresses. His best-known poem, the spirited "Relief of Lucknow," appeared in the *Atlantic Monthly* (February 1858) under his brother's editorship.

[D. R. Lowell, *The Hist. Geneal. of the Lowells of America* (1899); *Memorials of the Class of 1833 of Harvard College* (1883); H. C. Scudder, *James Russell Lowell, A Biog.* (2 vols., 1901); *Appletons' Ann. Cyc. of 1891* (1892); *The Churchman*, Sept. 19, 1891; *Boston Transcript*, Sept. 14, 1891.]   J. H. H.

LOWERY, WOODBURY (Feb. 17, 1853–Apr. 11, 1906), lawyer, annotator and editor of law books, historian, collector of maps, was the only son of Archibald H. Lowery, merchant, and Frances Anstriss Woodbury, daughter of Levi Woodbury [*q.v.*]. Born in New York City, he spent several years with his parents in Europe, gaining an unusual cultural and linguistic equipment. He graduated from Harvard in 1875 and continued there two years more in the chemical laboratory, receiving in 1876 the degree of M.A. His thesis "On Parabrombenzyl Compounds" appears in the *Proceedings of the American Academy of Arts and Sciences* (n.s. vol. IX, 1877). Meanwhile, his parents had removed (1873) to Washington, D. C., where the young chemist now went seeking a place in the Smithsonian Institution or the Department of Agriculture. Failing in this he studied law at Columbian University (LL.B., 1880, LL.M., 1881), was admitted to the bar in 1881, and entered the firm of Baldwin, Hopkins & Peyton. Early in his practice, he took up legal editorial work and gave to it most of his time for fifteen years. His publications in this field include: *Patents, Copyright, and Trade-Marks* (1886), edited in collaboration with W. D. Baldwin, which is Volume XXV of Myer's *Federal Decisions*; volumes IV–XX of *Brodix's American and English Patent Cases* (1887–92); *Interference Proceedings in the United States Patent Office* (1891); and *Index-Digest to the Decisions of the Supreme Court of the United States in Patent Causes* (1897).

Following the example of his uncle, Charles Levi Woodbury, who from deliberate choice had remained a bachelor, he did not marry, finding the close companionship of his parents and his only sister Virginia all that his quiet, studious nature seemed to need. But now, in the space of a few months, his home circle was obliterated. His mother died in June 1895; in August his sister married, and went with her husband, José Brunetti, Duke de Arcos, to his post of Spanish minister to Mexico; his father died in April 1896. Lowery now abandoned the law and gave the remainder of his life, ten years, to historical work. On the advice of his uncle he chose for his field a synthetic treatment of Spain's policy in her North American possessions—the reasons for her preliminary success, her later apathy, her final decadence. He collected and studied indefatigably all printed sources. The Duke de Arcos aided in opening to him archives hitherto inaccessible. He traveled widely, spending many months in research in the archives and libraries of Mexico, Madrid, Seville, London, Paris, and Rome.

In 1901 appeared the first volume of the work which preserves his name: *The Spanish Settlements Within the Present Limits of the United States, 1513–61*; the second volume, devoted to Florida, 1562–74, was published in 1905. Authoritative criticism declares this work to combine in a rare degree accuracy of statement with charm of literary style. He was encouraged to make extensive notes for more volumes—never to appear. After a sudden illness of a few days, he died at Taormina, Sicily, Apr. 11, 1906. He left to the Library of Congress his manuscripts, such of his books as it might select, his 300 early maps, with an elaborate descriptive list of them which the Library published in 1912 as *The Lowery Collection*. In his memory his sister and her husband established at Harvard a fund of $20,000 in aid of historical research.

[A sketch by Lowery's sister, in P. L. Phillips, *The Lowery Collection*, with portrait, is the chief authority. See also the class records for the Harvard University class of 1875; *Harvard Grads.' Mag.*, June 1906; *Washington Post*, Apr. 15, 1906.]   F. W. A.

LOWNDES, LLOYD (Feb. 21, 1845–Jan. 8, 1905), governor of Maryland, was a member of a family which had been conspicuous in social and political affairs of Maryland from the days when his great-grandfather, Christopher Lowndes, emigrated from Cheshire, England, to settle at Bladensburg. Through Richard Lowndes, of Bostock House in Cheshire, he seems to have been related to the family of Rawlins Lowndes [*q.v.*], and he was the great-grandson of Edward Lloyd, governor of Maryland [*q.v.*]. He was born in Clarksburg, Va. (now W. Va.), where his father, Lloyd Lowndes, a successful merchant with large farming and lumbering interests, was living with his wife, Maria Elizabeth (Moore) Lowndes. After preparatory training at the Clarksburg academy the lad entered Washington College in Pennsylvania but transferred for the last two years to Allegheny College, graduating in 1865. He graduated from the law school of the University of Pennsylvania, two years later, and settled at Cumberland, in which city his father had opened a store. However, he was soon taking a prominent part in politics, and, shortly after his marriage, on Dec. 2, 1869, to his cousin, Elizabeth Tasker Lowndes, he abandoned law for the more congenial fields of finance and mining. He was also identified with the agricultural interests of his section. He acquired a controlling interest in many financial, mining, and milling enterprises throughout the state and, by virtue of such business experience, was able to contribute by his counsel to the stability and soundness of the state finances. His warm heart, gracious manner, and frank kindliness made him a charming companion and, with the means afforded by his wealth, made him the esteemed benefactor of many public and private undertakings. He was a member of the Emmanuel Episcopal Church of Cumberland, which he served as vestryman and faithful representative to the diocesan conventions for twenty years.

His first political venture was as Republican candidate for Congress in the Grant-Greeley campaign of 1872, in which he demonstrated his popularity by defeating his Democratic opponent with a reversal of about 3,200 votes. The youngest member in Congress, he proved by committee service that he was a worker rather than a talker and demonstrated his independence in defying his party by opposing the Civil Rights Bill. The large negro constituency in his district deserted him when he came up for reëlection, and his defeat silenced his political ambitions for over two decades, though he continued to influence Republican policies throughout the state. In 1895, however, at the solicitation of friends of both parties, he accepted the Republican nomination for governor and was the first Republican elected in thirty years. He administered the affairs of the state in a manner which elicited warm commendation from both parties, and, in spite of an unsympathetic legislature, he fulfilled his campaign pledges for reform. Especially notable were the creation of a state geological survey, a new charter for Baltimore city, and an excellent election law, drafted by the reform league, which greatly improved the conduct of Maryland elections. His nice sense of honor forbade his permitting his name to be considered for United States senator at either of the two legislative elections that occurred during his term, though he secretly cherished ambitions for the office. He failed of reëlection in 1899, partly because friendly Democrats felt that a change was imperative for the good of Baltimore. After his retirement, he continued to be intimate with national party leaders and to be the strongest figure of his party in the state. At the time of his sudden death he was regarded as the probable candidate for governor in 1908.

[Manuscript Letters in the possession of the family are still unavailable; date of death was taken from a copy of the death certificate in the files of the Congressional Joint Committee on Printing; for published sources see H. E. Buchholz, *Governors of Md.* (1908); J. T. Scharf, *Hist. of Western Md.* (1882), vol. II, esp. pp. 1448–50; J. W. Thomas and T. J. C. Williams, *Hist. of Allegany County, Md.*, 1923, vol. I; *Baltimore American*, Jan. 9, 1905; *Sun* (Baltimore), Jan. 9, 10, 1905; *Daily News* (Cumberland), Jan. 9, 1905; *News* (Frederick, Md.), Jan. 9, 1905.]   E.L.

LOWNDES, RAWLINS (January 1721–Aug. 24, 1800), president of South Carolina and leader in opposing the adoption of the federal Constitution, was born in St. Kitts, British West Indies. He was the grandson of Charles Lowndes who was probably a younger brother of Richard Lowndes of Cheshire, England, an ancestor of Lloyd Lowndes [*q.v.*]. He was the son of Charles Lowndes who emigrated, first, to St. Kitts, where he married Ruth, the daughter of Henry Rawlins, an influential planter. In 1730, on account of financial difficulties, the family went to Charleston, S. C., where the father died when Rawlins was about fourteen years old. The widow returned to St. Kitts, leaving her son in the care of Robert Hall, provost-marshal of the colony, whose careful guidance and extensive library served admirably for his education at law. The youth did not reach his majority before his

guardian died, in 1740, but nevertheless he was allowed to fill Hall's position temporarily and later was permanently appointed provost-marshal. In 1754 he resigned this position to practise law. In 1749 he had been elected to the legislature from St. Paul's Parish, and from 1751 until the Revolution he almost continuously represented St. Bartholomew's in that body, becoming speaker of the lower house, from 1763 to 1765, and, again, from 1772 to 1775. In 1770 he was chairman of a committee that reported a plan to establish eight free schools for the newly settled districts as well as to found a provincial college (Commons House Journal, Mar. 1, 1770). He made the motion, passed unanimously, to erect a statute of William Pitt in Charleston as a memorial to his efforts to obtain the repeal of the Stamp Act. In 1766 he was appointed associate judge of the court of common pleas and, in that capacity, espoused provincial and popular rights. He refused to enforce the use of stamp paper, defied the chief justice on the bench (Council Journal, Feb. 3, 1772), and, in a *habeas corpus* case of 1773, denied the right of the royal council to act as an upper house of assembly (McCrady, *Royal Government, post,* pp. 717–21). Not long afterward he was removed from the bench (Commons House Journal, Oct. 24, 1773).

As a conservative in temperament and conviction he opposed rebellion or separation from the Mother Country and deplored the trend of events after the break. Yet he continued to be bound by his devotion to his province and to the rights of her representative government. When the provincial congress was considering the appointment of delegates to the First Continental Congress, he favored sending delegates with strictly limited powers, who should be allowed to support only measures to obtain the repeal of Parliament's oppressive acts and the redress of grievances. In this way he hoped to place his colony in opposition to the more radical northern colonies, particularly in New England, which favored independence. When the South Carolina convention discussed granting money to continue the "American Association," he advised caution, and upheld the right of Parliament to legislate for the colonies. St. Bartholomew's sent him to both the provincial congresses of 1775, from which he was chosen a member of the Council of Safety, where he opposed the confiscation of the property of Loyalists leaving the colony. He was one of the committee of eleven selected to form a new constitution for the colony, although he was unfavorable to the idea, and, after the new government was established in 1776, was made a member of the legislative council. When, in 1778, radical changes were proposed in the constitution, the church, and the legislature, he opposed them vigorously, yet he accepted the presidency of the colony when John Rutledge vetoed the measures and resigned. His position weighed heavily upon him, the colony was threatened with a British attack, and he had personal griefs to occupy his attention. His health was affected, he had lost one son, and another was so seriously ill that he later died. Moreover dissatisfaction with his administration broke out in open strife. He asked Christopher Gadsden [q.v.], the vice-president, to act for him but with characteristic vigor continued his own activities by proposing strong measures to thwart the attack, which, however, did not occur during his administration. He declined re-election in 1779 and was the last president of South Carolina, for his successor took the title of governor. When the British captured Charleston in 1779 and overran the state, he quietly abandoned the struggle, retired to his plantation, and seems to have accepted British protection, though this is a matter of dispute.

After the end of the war he represented Charleston in the legislature. In the committee of the whole he opposed the ratification of the Constitution, though his constituents favored it, basing his opposition on the failure of that document adequately to guard the rights of minorities, on the excessive power given the Senate, and on the limitation of slave trade to twenty years. He closed his objections with the statement that he wished no other epitaph than, "Here lies the man that opposed the constitution, because it was ruinous to the liberty of America" (Jonathan Elliot, *The Debates of the Several State Conventions of the Adoption of the Federal Constitution*, 2 ed., vol. IV, 1836, p. 298). This was his last public appearance, for, though he was elected to the constitutional convention, he did not serve. He was married, on Aug. 15, 1748, to Amarinthia Elliott of Rantoules, Stono River, who died in January 1750. The following year, on Dec. 23, he celebrated his marriage to Mary Cartwright of Charleston, who bore him four daughters and three sons. Bereaved of his second wife in 1770, he married, in January 1773, Sarah Jones of Georgia, a girl of sixteen, whose third and youngest child was William Lowndes [q.v.].

[Journals of the Commons House and of the Council of S. C., through the courtesy of Prof. Robert L. Meriwether, Columbia, S. C.; a few letters in the Lib. of Cong.; G. B. Chase, *Lowndes of S. C.* (1876); Mrs. St. Julien Ravenel, *Life and Times of Wm. Lowndes* (1901); W. R. Smith, *S. C. as a Royal Province* (1903); Edward McCrady, *The Hist. of S. C. under*

the Royal Government (1899) and *The Hist. of S. C. in the Revolution* (1901); F. A. Porcher, "Christopher Gadsden," *S. C. Hist. Soc. Colls.*, vol. IV (1887); *S. C. Hist. and Geneal. Mag.*, July 1901, Oct. 1902, Apr. 1903, Apr. 1906, Jan. 1911, Jan. 1914, July 1915, Apr. 1920, July 1926.]
H. B–C.

LOWNDES, WILLIAM (Feb. 11, 1782–Oct. 27, 1822), congressman from South Carolina, was the son of Rawlins Lowndes [q.v.], who was prominent in the affairs of the province and state. When something over fifty years old Rawlins Lowndes married, as his third wife, Sarah, the sixteen-year-old daughter of Col. Charles Jones, of Georgia. Their third child was born at the Horseshoe Plantation in the parish of St. Bartholomew, Colleton County, S. C., and was christened William Jones, but he never used in any form his second baptismal name. In his seventh year he was placed in school in England and, while there, contracted an inflammatory rheumatism that weakened his health all through his life. Returning to South Carolina after three years, he studied in private schools, being especially interested in Latin, Greek, and French. He was early marked for his clear, luminous style of writing and speaking. On Sept. 16, 1802, he married Elizabeth, daughter of Thomas Pinckney [q.v.]. He practised law for a few years but soon gave this up for love of his plantation.

He identified himself with the Republican party, though his wife remained a strong Federalist, and, from 1806 to 1810, he served in the General Assembly. He was in close touch with Joseph Alston, Daniel Huger, Langdon Cheves, and John C. Calhoun. The original draft of the act of 1809 to amend the state system of representation in behalf of the upper country is in his handwriting. Strongly opposing the Embargo and Non-Intercourse policy of Jefferson, he was elected to the Twelfth Congress in 1810 along with Cheves and Calhoun, and these, with David R. Williams and others, formed the nucleus of a war party. In this Congress he served on the committee for commerce and manufactures and on that for military affairs and, in the Thirteenth Congress, as chairman of the committee on naval affairs. He had served, in 1807, as captain of a military company and regretted, in later life, that he had not given himself to a military career. He spoke in behalf of every motion to increase the military and naval strength of the country, and his service on the naval committee added to his reputation. In 1815 he was appointed chairman of the committee on ways and means and served for three years. He supported the creation of the second Bank of the United States, and he reported and, along with Calhoun, advocated the tariff of 1816, avowedly for protection. He was offered the position of secretary of war but declined. He was the author of the sinking fund act, under the operation of which the national debt was paid off in fourteen years. He supported Forsythe's bill of 1817 against privateering and in the next year supported the right of the executive to a free hand in investigating affairs in the South American republics. His speech of Jan. 30, 1819, expressing disapprobation of Andrew Jackson's course in the Seminole War is a fair sample of his style (*Annals of Congress,* 15 Cong., 2 Sess., cols. 912–22). He argued closely, without heat or passion, stated first the position of his opponent so fairly that John Randolph once said, "He has done that once too often; he can never answer that" (Ravenel, *post,* pp. 239–40), and then won his argument by logical statement. In this year, 1819, as chairman of a special committee on coinage, he submitted a classic report on the relative value of coins of different nations in relation to our own (*Annals of Congress,* 15 Cong., 2 Sess., cols. 788–96). The summer of 1819 he spent in European travel in a vain attempt to build up his failing health. In the Sixteenth Congress, 1819, he was appointed chairman of the Committee on Foreign Affairs, and in 1820 was the candidate of his party for speaker of the House. The debate on the Missouri question was the last important public work in which he was engaged. He spoke briefly in the beginning, as one of the conference committee, in favor of the compromise under which Missouri was allowed to make her own constitution. When Missouri offered her constitution at the next session, he was chairman of a committee of three to report on its acceptance. This report took the ground that Missouri was already a state, and he supported it by a speech so calm and dispassionate as to win approval from both sections in the midst of a frenzied debate. After this effort, his health compelled him to entrust the handling of the Missouri question to Clay.

In 1822 he was offered the mission to France but was compelled to decline this, as he had previously declined appointments to Turkey and to Russia. In December 1821, he had been nominated by the South Carolina legislature for the presidency. In this connection he made the statement, often quoted since, "The Presidency is not an office to be either solicited or declined" (Ravenel, *post,* p. 226). On May 8, 1822, he resigned his seat in Congress and again tried the effect of a sea voyage for his health. When six days out from Philadelphia he died and was buried at sea. Of striking height, over six feet six, he

was unusually slender and loose-limbed. Grave and dignified in bearing, he won such a position of leadership in the House that Henry Clay in his old age said, "I think the wisest man I ever knew was William Lowndes" (Ravenel, *post,* p. 239). He considered his part as one of the "War Hawks" in bringing on the "Second War for Independence" his greatest achievement.

[The most valuable of the Lowndes papers were destroyed in the Charleston fire of 1861; Mrs. St. Julien Ravenel's *Life and Times of William Lowndes* (1901) is the fullest account extant, dealing mostly with the personal side of his life; G. B. Chase's *Lowndes of South Carolina* (1876) is genealogical but contains a valuable sketch based on a life by Major Rawlins Lowndes, of which the manuscript was lost before publication; see also *Memoirs of John Quincy Adams,* ed. by C. F. Adams, vols. IV, V, VII, VIII (1875–76), and Mrs. St. Julien Ravenel, *Charleston* (1906).]

J. E. W.

LOWREY, MARK PERRIN (Dec. 30, 1828– Feb. 27, 1885), Baptist clergyman, Confederate soldier, educator, was born in McNairy County, Tenn., the ninth in a family of eleven children. His father, Adam Lowrey, who was born in Ireland, and his mother, Margaret Doss, of English descent, were of good stock but uneducated. When Mark was but a few years of age his father contracted cholera while on a trip to New Orleans, and died. Living in a comparatively newly settled country, his mother widowed and impoverished, he had practically no educational advantages. When he was fifteen he moved with his mother to the village of Farmington in Tishomingo County, Miss. Enlisting in the 2nd Mississippi Regiment, he went to Mexico in 1847, though his organization did not arrive in time to see active service in the Mexican War. Two years later he married Sarah Holmes, daughter of Isham Holmes, a farmer living near Rienzi, Miss. For several years he earned his livelihood as a brick-mason, but at the age of twenty-four he decided to enter the ministry. He was ordained by the Farmington Baptist Church in 1853 and until the outbreak of the Civil War held pastorates, served as missionary, and improved his education as best he could. It is said that he frequently boarded the district school teacher in order to learn from him at night.

Entering the Confederate army, he served for a while in the fall of 1861, as colonel of the 4th Regiment of sixty-day volunteers. The regiment suffered much from sickness and at the end of their term of enlistment the men were mustered out. In 1862 Lowrey raised and organized the 32nd Mississippi Regiment, of which he was elected colonel. He was wounded in the arm in the battle of Perryville, served with great distinction at the battle of Chickamauga, and was promoted to brigadier-general Oct. 4, 1863. He commanded a brigade in Hardee's corps, and later a division, until his resignation from the army, Mar. 14, 1865.

At the conclusion of hostilities he returned to Mississippi, where he served for a while as state missionary and did much to reorganize and revive churches that had suffered from the war. In 1873 he founded Blue Mountain Female Institute (later Blue Mountain College). This institution he served as president and as professor of history and moral science until his death. It exercised considerable influence in the field of education for women in Mississippi, and continued under the control of the Lowrey family until 1920, when it was taken over by the Mississippi Baptist Convention. From 1872 to 1876 Lowrey was a member of the board of trustees of the University of Mississippi. His prominence and influence in the Baptist denomination in his state are attested by the fact that he was president of the Mississippi Baptist Convention from 1868 to 1877. He fell dead in the railway station at Middleton, Tenn.

[MSS. in Am. Antiquarian Soc., Worcester, Mass.; *Southern Hist. Soc. Papers*, vol. XVI (1888); Dunbar Rowland, *Mississippi* (1907), vols. II, III; C. A. Evans, *Confed. Mil. Hist.* (1899), vols. VII, VIII; *War of the Rebellion: Official Records* (*Army*); J. L. Boyd, *A Popular Hist. of the Baptists in Miss.* (1930); L. S. Foster, *Miss. Baptist Preachers* (1895); *Commercial Appeal* (Memphis, Tenn.), Feb. 12, 1906; I. A. Buck, *Cleburne and His Command* (1908).]   C. J.

LOWRIE, JAMES WALTER (Sept. 16, 1856–Jan. 26, 1930), missionary to China, was born in Shanghai and died in Paotingfu. Missionary interests surrounded his boyhood. His grandfather, Hon. Walter Lowrie [*q.v.*], who had emigrated from Scotland about 1792, was the first secretary of the Board of Foreign Missions of the Presbyterian Church in the United States of America. One uncle, John Cameron Lowrie, had been a missionary to India; and another uncle, Walter Mason Lowrie, a missionary to China, had been killed in 1847 by pirates near Ningpo. His father, Reuben Post Lowrie, was a missionary stationed in Shanghai when the boy was born, and died there in 1860 when James Walter was less than four years old. After the father's death, his mother, Amelia Palmer (Tuttle) Lowrie, returned to the United States with her daughter and son. The boy studied at the Lawrenceville, N. J., high school and at Princeton University, receiving the degree of B.A. there in 1876 and that of M.A. in 1879. For three years (1877–80), he taught at Madison, N. J., and then entered Princeton Theological Seminary. The impulse towards missionary life had been his by inheritance; but quietly and characteristically he waited until he was convinced of his "call." On June 3, 1883, the year of his graduation from the Seminary, he was ordained by the Presbytery of New York and appointed a missionary of the Presbyterian Board to China.

For eight years he was stationed at Peking, laying the foundations for his unusual command of the Chinese language and taking an increasingly active part in mission work. A short interval (1892–93) in the United States ensued, during which he served as stated supply for a church in Longmont, Col. Returning to China, he became one of the founders of the mission station at Paotingfu. The next six years were an active and happy period. His evangelistic efforts were fruitful; and, always an intense home lover though he never married, he had his mother with him at Paotingfu, and his sister and her husband, Dr. B. C. Atterbury, were also members of the mission. While he was absent from the station in 1900 for the purpose of escorting to the coast his mother, who was returning for a time to America, the Boxer massacres occurred at Paotingfu. In after years his thankfulness for their escape was obviously tinged with regret that he had not been with his fellow Christians during those days. He at once plunged into the work nearest at hand. Joining the Allies at Tientsin, he accompanied them to Peking immediately after the relief of the beleaguered legations; and from Peking he was sent, as guide and interpreter, with the allied detachment which was dispatched to Paotingfu. The first intention of the allied officers was to raze that city as punishment for the massacres, and it was only Lowrie's courageous and incessant pleas that prevented its destruction. This unexpected example of Christian magnanimity profoundly impressed the Chinese, and their gratitude became a factor in the subsequent success of mission work in that place of the martyrs.

Honors began to come to him. In 1903 the Chinese Imperial Government made him a Mandarin of the fourth degree. In 1910 he was chosen as the first chairman of the China Council, the executive body on the field of the seven China missions of the Presbyterian Church in the United States of America. His headquarters were in Shanghai, but his duties led him far afield. His work was modestly and quietly done, but was effective in constructive and unifying results. Equally effective was his personal influence. A man of social graces and warm sympathies, he was the favorite guest in a multitude of homes. During his later years ill health and failing eyesight limited his activities; and he was deeply troubled by those whom he feared to be destroying the true foundations of Christianity. In 1925 he became honorary chairman of the China Council, and four years later he left Shanghai to spend his last days in Paotingfu. His death occurred after only a few months, however, and he was buried in the Paotingfu cemetery beside the grave of his mother.

[*Necrological Report of Princeton Theological Sem.*, 1930; *Who's Who in America*, 1918–19; W. T. Ellis, "Some Missionaries I Know," *Outlook*, Apr. 17, 1909; *China Council Bull.*, Feb. 5, 1930; records of the Board of Foreign Missions of the Presbyterian Church in the U. S. A.; *Chinese Recorder*, Mar. 1930; *N. Y. Times*, Jan. 29, 1930.]   H. Cl—s.

LOWRIE, WALTER (Dec. 10, 1784–Dec. 14, 1868), United States senator, missionary secretary, the son of John and Catherine (Cameron) Lowrie, was born in Edinburgh, Scotland. About 1792 his family came to Huntington County, Pa., and a few years later settled in Butler (then part of Allegheny) County. John Lowrie was an enterprising farmer, a stanch Presbyterian, and influential in his community. Walter was reared on the farm. He attended a subscription school and began to study the classics under Rev. John McPherrin with a view to entering the ministry. Despite his fervent desire to preach the Gospel, unforeseen obstacles made him change his plans, and in 1807 he went to Butler to teach school. There, attracted by the opportunities of public life, he was successively a clerk, member of the board of commissioners, and justice of the peace. He also opened a store in partnership with his brother. On Jan. 14, 1808, he married Amelia McPherrin, the daughter of his preceptor. In 1811–12 he served in the state House of Representatives and in 1812 was elected state senator as a Democrat, holding his seat until his resignation in 1819 to enter the United States Senate. His maiden effort in the Senate was a speech (Jan. 20, 1820) on the Missouri question in which he boldly announced that "if the alternative be . . . a dissolution of this Union, or the extension of slavery over this whole Western country, I, for one, will choose the former" (*Annals of Congress*, 16 Cong., 1 Sess., pp. 201–09). As a member of the committee on public lands, he opposed a revision of the land policy which would place it upon a cash rather than a credit basis, and otherwise championed the cause of land purchasers and Western settlers. He was also on the committees on roads and canals, accounts, finance, and Indian affairs. He was an ardent temperance advocate, and a founder of the congressional prayer meeting. After one term as senator he was secretary of the Senate from 1825 until 1836.

In 1836 Lowrie was elected corresponding sec-

retary of the Western Foreign Missionary Society, which a year later became the Board of Foreign Missions of the Presbyterian Church. Under his guidance, 1836–68, the organization grew from obscurity to a great missionary enterprise. He later declared that the sacrifices and self-denial involved in the post were the charms by which the office secured its incumbent. Invariably in close touch with all phases of the work, he corresponded extensively with missionaries abroad, solicited contributions for the cause, personally supervised the sending of household provisions and farm implements to the Indians, and frequently visited the Indian missions in the West. Three of his sons were foreign missionaries. James Walter Lowrie [*q.v.*] was his grandson. His first wife, by whom he had eight children, died in 1832, and two years later he married Mary K. Childs. He died in New York City.

[Lowrie edited his son's memoirs, *Memoirs of the Rev. Walter M. Lowrie, Missionary to China* (1849), which appeared in several editions and contains valuable material. John D. Wells, "The Hon. Walter Lowrie," in *The Record of the Presbyt. Ch. in the U. S. A.*, Apr. 1869, portrays his activities with the Board of Foreign Missions. See also J. A. McKee, *20th Century Hist. of Butler and Butler County, Pa.* (1909); *Hist. of Butler County, Pa.* (1895), ed. by R. C. Brown; *Ann. Reports of the Board of Foreign Missions of the Presbyt. Ch. in the U. S. A.*, 1838–68; *Presbyt. Mag.*, Mar. 1855; *Biog. Dir. Am. Cong.* (1928); *The Centennial of the Western Foreign Missionary Society* (1931), ed. by J. A. Kelso; *N. Y. Times*, Dec. 15, 1868.]   J. H. P.

LOWRY, HIRAM HARRISON (May 29, 1843–Jan. 13, 1924), for more than fifty years a missionary in China, was born on a farm near Zanesville, Ohio, the son of Hiram and Margaret (Speare) Lowry. In 1862 and 1863 he was in the Union army—for fourteen months in active service and then for several months in military hospitals as a patient. Entering Ohio Wesleyan University in 1864, he graduated from that institution in 1867 and during his senior year, Feb. 28, 1867, was married to Parthenia Nicholson. That same year he was ordained to the ministry of the Methodist Episcopal Church and, with his bride, sailed for China to join the mission of his Church at Foochow. In the spring of 1869 he was transferred to Peking. Here, together with L. N. Wheeler, he founded the Methodist mission in North China. Upon the retirement of Wheeler because of illness in 1873, Lowry became superintendent of the North China mission and served in this position for twenty years. During his tenure of office the mission expanded steadily in staff, in institutions, and in territory covered. It was a period when Protestant missions in China were growing rapidly, and when churches in Europe and America were augmenting their efforts abroad. Lowry proved to be an able, broad-minded, unselfish, and diligent administrator. He traveled extensively throughout the region which his colleagues were attempting to occupy and helped them meet the obstacles of their pioneer enterprises, including the acquisition of property in the face of local prejudice and opposition. During much of the time he was also the head of the school for the training of Chinese preachers, an institution which later became the Wiley College of Theology of Peking University.

By 1893 the North China mission had been so enlarged that it was erected into a Conference, and, accordingly, the office of superintendent passed. Lowry was, however, almost immediately made the head of Peking University, which had been begun by his mission. From December 1893 to June 1894 he was acting president and thereafter, president. He held the office during the years when education of a Western type was becoming popular in China, and he helped the institution to take advantage of the situation. In time—with the hearty cooperation of Lowry—the University, later to be known as Yenching, was reorganized to include the higher educational work of several of the Protestant denominations. After this federation was accomplished, Lowry, in 1918, became president emeritus. He served as acting president for a year longer, however, and was the head of Peking Academy, a secondary school of his mission, until his formal retirement from active life in 1922. For years he had struggled against ill health, but he lived to be well past eighty years of age. He died in Peking.

[*Ann. Reports* of the Missionary Soc. of the M. E. Ch. (after 1907, the Board of Foreign Missions of the M. E. Ch.) ; *Official Minutes, No. China Conference of the M. E. Ch.*, esp. for 1924, which contains biog. sketch ; *China Christian Advocate*, Mar. 1924 ; *China and Methodism* (1906) ; *Christian Advocate* (N. Y.), Jan. 24, 1924 ; *Who's Who in America*, 1922–23.]

K. S. L.

LOWRY, ROBERT (Mar. 10, 1830–Jan. 19, 1910), lawyer, Confederate soldier, governor of Mississippi, was born in Chesterfield District, S. C., the son of Robert and Jemimah (Rushing) Lowry, both of Scotch-Irish extraction. The family moved to Tennessee about 1833 and to Tishomingo County, Miss., in 1840. Robert's educational advantages were limited. In 1846 he went to Raleigh, Miss., to live with his uncle, Judge James Lowry, with whom he engaged in mercantile enterprises first at Raleigh and later at Brandon. On Sept. 9, 1849, he married Maria M. Gammage, of Jasper County, Miss. From about 1854 to 1859 he was in Arkansas, during which period he read law. Upon his return to Mississippi he practised law as a partner of Judge A. G. Mayers.

When the Civil War began he enlisted as a private in the Rankin Grays, but in August 1861 was elected a major of the 6th Mississippi Regiment, which was being organized at Grenada. He was twice wounded at the battle of Shiloh and in 1862 was commissioned colonel. He served with Gen. Joseph E. Johnston during the Vicksburg campaign. On the death of his superior officer, Brigadier-General John Adams, he was placed in command of the brigade and was commissioned brigadier-general, Feb. 4, 1865; he was with Gen. Joseph E. Johnston when he surrendered to Sherman on Apr. 26, 1865.

Returning to Mississippi, he served as state senator in 1865–66, and with Giles M. Hillyer was appointed by Gov. B. G. Humphreys on a commission, authorized by the legislature, to visit Washington and request President Johnson to release Jefferson Davis. In 1869 he was the Democratic candidate for the office of attorney-general but was not elected. In the campaign which resulted in the overthrow of the Carpet-bag government in 1876, he took an active part. In 1881 the adherents of Gov. J. M. Stone and Ethelbert Barksdale caused a deadlock in the state Democratic convention and Lowry was nominated as a compromise candidate for governor. The following campaign, which was the last in which the Republican party (under the name of Independent Party) put forward candidates for state offices in Mississippi, resulted in a victory for Lowry. He was renominated in 1885 and elected without opposition. During his term of office the local-option law was passed, the Industrial Institute and College for women at Columbus was established, and appropriations for public schools were increased. After retiring from the governorship he practised law at Jackson, Miss. In 1891, in collaboration with William H. McCardle, he published *A History of Mississippi*. He was a candidate for the unexpired term of United States Senator E. C. Walthall, who died in 1898, but failed of election. For seven years prior to his death he was state commander of the United Confederate Veterans. He died in Jackson and was buried in Brandon.

[*Official and Statistical Reg. of the State of Miss. Centennial Edition* (1917) ; Dunbar Rowland, *Encyc. of Miss. Hist.* (1902), and *Mississippi* (1907) ; Lowry and McCardle, *A Hist. of Miss.* (1891) ; *Confed. Mil. Hist.* (1899), vol. VII ; *Who's Who in America*, 1908–09, which is the authority for years of birth and marriage ; *Confed. Veteran*, Apr. 1910 ; *Vicksburg Herald*, Jan. 20, 21, 1910.]

C. J.

LOWRY, THOMAS (Feb. 27, 1843–Feb. 4, 1909), capitalist, was the son of Samuel R. Lowry, who emigrated from Ireland to Pennsylvania, married Rachel Bullock and, about 1834, settled in Illinois. Thomas was born in Logan County and reared under frontier conditions. He attended country schools and, after a journey through the West, began to read law, was admitted to the Illinois bar, and then settled in Minneapolis in 1867. Blessed with a likable personality, he had established a paying practice within two years and was becoming interested in business, especially in real estate. On Dec. 14, 1870, he married Beatrice Goodrich, who bore him a son and two daughters. Though the panic of 1873 affected him seriously, he not only extricated himself from the effects of the depression but was generally conceded to have been a large factor in helping Minneapolis weather the storm. Gradually his business interests so completely occupied his attention that he gave up the practice of law. In 1875 in order to salvage his land holdings he bought, with eastern financial aid, an interest in the Minneapolis Street Railway Company, a new corporation, abandoned because of the panic. Two years later he controlled a majority of its stock. During the next decade, getting little support at home and relying upon New York capital, he struggled with his traction company, which he would gladly have sold could he have found a purchaser (letter of Pliny Bartlett, *Minneapolis Journal*, Apr. 18, 1889). He began to acquire control of the St. Paul street railways in 1882 and 1883 and, in 1891, consolidated the systems of both cities in a holding company, the Twin City Rapid Transit Company, capitalized at more than twice the stock value of the two systems. During the period of consolidation the railways were electrified and the most serious labor disturbances of his career took place. In April 1889 the lines were paralyzed in a strike caused by a wage cut and by the requirement that operatives sign an "iron clad" agreement not to join a union. Public sympathy was with the strikers and futile efforts were made to induce Lowry to arbitrate; but he showed his understanding of human nature by keeping still until acts of violence alienated public support from the strikers, who gradually capitulated.

By 1890, having accumulated a comfortable fortune, he decided to retire from business and celebrated the event by a trip around the world. On his return he found he had been elected president of the Minneapolis, St. Paul and Sault Sainte Marie Railway, which he had helped to promote. Abandoning the idea of retirement, he not only continued his direct interest in the traction company and in the railroad, but engaged in numerous other activities. He helped found the North American Telegraph Company and the Minneapolis General Electric Company, was vice-president of a bank, and carried on his real-estate operations. At the same time he was active in several lines of civic endeavor, giving time and money to the public library, to parks, and to the church work of the Universalists. In 1901 he showed a lively interest for the first time in political matters by becoming a candidate for United States senator after the death of Cushman K. Davis. His defeat in the legislature offended him, and he never thereafter consented to be a candidate for any office. By 1905 his vigorous constitution had begun to show unmistakable signs of weakening. He spent the last years of his life in a vain search for health through the various resorts of the Southwest, and in writing *Personal Reminiscences of Abraham Lincoln* (1910), which is thirty-one pages of random notes.

[Isaac Atwater, *Hist. of the City of Minneapolis* (1893); *Hist. of Minneapolis,* ed. by M. D. Shutter (1923), vol. II; H. B. Hudson, *A Half Century of Minneapolis* (1908); *Compendium of Hist. and Biog. of Minneapolis,* ed. by R. I. Holcombe and W. H. Bingham (1914); *Hist. of Minneapolis,* ed. by Isaac Atwater and Hennepin County, ed. by Col. J. H. Stevens (1895); Eva Gay, *A Tale of the Twin Cities* (1889); H. K. Webster, "Lords of Our Streets," *Am. Illustrated Mag.,* Sept. 1905; *Minneapolis Jour.,* Apr. 18, 1889, Feb. 4, 1909.]
L. B. S.

LOY, MATTHIAS (Mar. 17, 1828–Jan. 26, 1915), Lutheran clergyman, was born in Cumberland County, Pa., of German parentage, the fourth of the seven children of Matthias and Christina (Reaver) Loy. After a bleak, poverty-pinched boyhood he was apprenticed in 1847 to the printing firm of Baab & Hummel at Harrisburg, was treated well by his masters, read several of the English classics, learned the rudiments of Latin and Greek at the Harrisburg Academy, was confirmed by the Rev. Charles William Schaeffer [*q.v.*], and began to think of a ministerial career. In 1847 he went west for his health and at Circleville, Ohio, was persuaded by the Rev. J. Roof to become a beneficiary student in the seminary (later part of Capital University) of the Joint Synod of Ohio at Columbus, where he had Christian Spielmann and Wilhelm Friedrich Lehmann as his teachers. He was influenced strongly by the writings of C. F. W. Walther [*q.v.*] and by several friends among the clergy of the Missouri Synod. His only pastorate was at Delaware, Ohio, 1849–65. On Dec. 25, 1853, he married Mary Willey of Delaware, who with five of their seven children survived him. Frail of body and often ill, Loy had a strong mind and a great capacity for work. As president of the Joint Synod 1860–78 and

1880–94, editor of the *Lutheran Standard* 1864–91, professor of theology in Capital University, 1865–1902, and president of the University, 1881–90, he dominated the Synod, which grew during his lifetime into an organization of national scope. He was a zealous student of the Lutheran confessions but had little knowledge of Biblical criticism or appreciation of its implications. He was a truculent controversialist, never forgetting that the Church Visible is also the Church Militant, and never giving his opponents time to forget it. In 1867 he refused to let the Joint Synod become a member of the General Council of the Evangelical Lutheran Church in North America and framed the questions about the "four points"—chiliasm, altar fellowship, pulpit fellowship, membership in secret societies—that afflicted so sorely the spokesmen of the General Council. In 1871, however, he carried the Joint Synod into the Synodical Conference. Ten years later he rejected Walther's doctrine of predestination, founded and edited the *Columbus Theological Magazine* (1881–88) to combat it, and of course withdrew the Joint Synod from the Synodical Conference. He was the author of twenty published hymns and of *The Doctrine of Justification* (1869; 1882); *Essay on the Ministerial Office* (1870); *Sermons on the Gospels* (1888); *Christian Prayer* (1890); *Story of My Life* (3rd ed., 1905); *The Augsburg Confession* (1908); *The Sermon on the Mount* (1909); and *Sermons on the Epistles* (1910). He shows to best advantage in his sermons, which are simple in language, earnest, and deeply felt. In 1902 an attack of angina pectoris compelled him to retire, but for eight years more he continued to write and to take pleasure in his garden, before softening of the brain set in. He died at his home in Columbus.

[Matthias Loy, *Story of My Life* (3rd ed., 1905); J. Julian, *A Dict. of Hymnology* (rev. ed., 1907); T. E. Schmauk, "Dr. Loy's Life and Its Bearings on the Lutheran Church in This Land," *Luth. Ch. Rev.*, Jan. 1907; P. A. Peter and Wm. Schmidt, *Geschichte der Allgemeinen Evang.-Lutherischen Synode von Ohio und anderen Staaten* (1908); G. W. Mechling, *Hist. Ev. Luth. District Synod of Ohio* (1911); C. V. Sheatsley, *Hist. Ev. Luth. Joint Synod of Ohio and Other States* (1919); *Who's Who in America*, 1914–15; *Lutherische Kirchenzeitung*, Feb. 6, 20, Mar. 6, 1915.]

G. H. G.

LOYD, SAMUEL (Jan. 31, 1841–Apr. 10, 1911), better known as Sam Loyd, composer of chess problems and puzzles, was born in Philadelphia, the son of Isaac Smith and Elizabeth (Singer) Loyd. The family moved in 1844 to New York, where Loyd attended the public schools until he was about seventeen. He studied to be an engineer; held a steam and mechanical engineer's license in New York, and is said to have had an editorial connection with the *Sanitary Engineer*. At one time he owned a printing office in Elizabeth, N. J., and at other times engaged in a variety of business enterprises.

As a youth, with his two elder brothers he frequented a chess club on University Place and there became acquainted with Miron H. Hazeltine, long chess editor of the *New York Clipper*. At that time the exploits of Paul Charles Morphy [*q.v.*] were causing a widespread interest in chess in America which resulted in the establishment of chess columns in many newspapers and journals. Loyd began composing chess problems in 1855, won first place in numerous contests, and as early as 1858 was recognized in Germany as the leading American problem composer. In 1860, the *Chess Monthly*, edited by Morphy and D. W. Fiske [*q.v.*], engaged him as problem editor. Fiske and Loyd collaborated in a form of literary anecdote resting upon some ingenious chess problem. These stories and problems have often been reprinted and the problems, which were Loyd's part, are recognized as the work of a genius. Another type of problem cultivated by Loyd places the chessmen upon the board to make a letter or numeral. Later Loyd himself wrote sketches and made problems or puzzles to fit the conditions. In chess problems he always defended the thesis, now generally accepted, that the position must be a possible one in play. To *American Chess-Nuts* (1868), edited by E. B. Cook, W. R. Henry, and C. A. Gilbery, he contributed many problems, and in 1878 he published *Chess Strategy*, a collection consisting mainly of his own work, in which the rather difficult classification of problems is attempted.

Loyd was abroad in 1867, participating, without notable success, as a player in the International Chess Tournament. In problem tournaments his greatest achievement was at the Centennial Exposition of 1876, when his various entries won first and second prize, as well as numerous minor prizes. In 1870 he married Addie J. Coombs of Utica, N. Y. About this time he originated a puzzle called "The Trick Donkeys," which sold literally in millions of copies. Later he developed "Pigs in Clover" and the 14-15 puzzle, both widely popular in Europe and America. The game "Parchesi" is also his invention. In 1896 he collaborated with his son Sam in a puzzle called "Get Off the Earth" or "The Disappearing Chinaman." About this time some newspapers and magazines began to introduce Sam Loyd puzzle columns, edited by father and son, who collaborated in the invention of the puzzles featured. The Loyd puzzles display remarkable ingenuity, particularly in the application of simple algebraic devices or old mathematical puzzles in such new garb as to conceal the source. The story devices applied by Fiske and Loyd to chess problems were developed with puzzles by the Loyds. Until his death in 1911, Loyd continued to make puzzle columns and advertising devices employing puzzles his source of livelihood.

[A. C. White, *Sam Loyd and His Chess Problems* (Leeds, 1913), and "Reminiscences of Sam Loyd's Family," *The Problem* (Pittsburgh), Mar. 28, 1914; W. P. Eaton, in *Delineator*, Apr. 1911; *Woman's Home Companion*, June 1911; *Am. Chess Bull.*, May, June 1911; *Sci. American*, Apr. 22, 1911; *Am. Mag.*, May 1911; *N. Y. Daily Tribune*, *N. Y. Times*, *Times-Democrat* (New Orleans), Apr. 12, 1911; *Brooklyn Daily Eagle*, Apr. 11, 12, 1911; information from Sam Loyd of Brooklyn.]   L. C. K.

LOZIER, CLEMENCE SOPHIA HARNED (Dec. 11, 1813–Apr. 26, 1888), homeopathic physician, feminist, was born at Plainfield, N. J., the daughter of David and Hannah (Walker) Harned. She studied at the Plainfield Academy, and at the age of sixteen was married to Abraham Witton Lozier, an architect and builder of New York City. Not long afterward his health failed, and she opened a school for girls which she conducted for eleven years. Through a brother, who was a physician, she became interested in the study of medicine, and after the death of her husband she entered, in 1849, the Rochester Eclectic Medical College. Later she attended the Syracuse Medical College, from which she graduated in 1853. She at once settled in New York City and in 1860 began to teach physiology and hygiene to a class of girl students in her own home. This class became the nucleus of the New York Medical College and Hospital for Women, a homeopathic institution which was formally established in 1863. After the conclusion of the Civil War she toured Europe to investigate hospital construction and administration and upon her return in 1867 reorganized her school and hospital, taking the title of dean and professor of gynecology and obstetrics. She was aided in her work by her daughter-in-law, Charlotte (Denman), first wife of A. W. Lozier, Jr., and after her death, by his second wife, Jeanne M. Lozier, both graduates of the medical school. A niece, Dr. Anna Manning Comfort, was also a valued lieutenant. The school and hospital, although small, flourished for many years, until with other minor institutions they were merged with the New York Homeopathic Medical College. Although Dr. Lozier is said to have performed a number of major operations, she wrote but little on medical subjects. One small pamphlet, *Childbirth Made Easy*, appeared in 1870. As a feminist, she was interested in most of the movements intended to improve the economic and social status of women. She was for five years president of the National Woman's Suffrage Association and was active in the New York City Suffrage League, the New York Sorosis, the Woman's Christian Temperance Union, of which she was a past president, and the National Working Women's League. She died of angina pectoris in her seventy-fifth year.

[*In Memoriam, Mrs. Charlotte Denman Lozier* (1870); *Eminent Women of the Age* (1868); H. A. Kelly and W. L. Burrage, *Am. Medic. Biogs.* (1920); *Evening Post* (N. Y.), Apr. 27, 1888.]   E. P.

LUBBOCK, FRANCIS RICHARD (Oct. 16, 1815–June 22, 1905), governor of Texas, Confederate soldier, second child and eldest son of Dr. Henry T. W. and Susan Ann (Saltus) Lubbock, was born in Beaufort, S. C. His ancestors on both sides were of English stock and prominent as planters, ship-owners, and merchants. The boy was educated in private schools until he was fourteen, when his father's death forced him to take a clerkship in Charleston. He later removed to Hamburg, S. C., and in 1834 went to New Orleans where he opened a drugstore. On Feb. 5, 1835, he married Adele Baron, a member of a French Creole family of New Orleans. In December 1836, he emigrated to Texas and opened a store, first in Velasco and later in Houston. In 1837 he became a clerk of the Texas Congress and was appointed comptroller of the Republic by President Houston, serving one year. He was again appointed comptroller in 1841, but resigned to look after the ranch he had acquired near Houston. For sixteen years he was district clerk of Harris County. Elected lieutenant-governor by the Democrats in 1857, he was defeated by Edward Clark in 1859, when Sam Houston was successful as the head of an independent ticket. Lubbock was a delegate to the Charleston convention of his party in 1860, and supported secession. In the summer of 1861 he defeated Edward Clark for the governorship.

At the beginning of his administration the treasury was empty, Texas bonds were unsalable, and the wild Indians were hostile. Lubbock exerted himself to strengthen the defenses and increase the resources of the state. At his suggestion the legislature raised a mounted regiment for frontier defense and in the spring of 1862 created a military board, composed of the governor, comptroller, and treasurer, to provide means for the defense of the state. The board sought to raise funds by selling a part of the United States "indemnity bonds" acquired through the sale of the Santa Fé region in 1850, and by the exportation of cotton through Mexico. It also established a state foundry and a percussion-cap factory, and contracted with private firms for the manufacture of arms for state troops, but these operations were only moderately successful. Lubbock had better success in developing a cloth and shoe factory at the state penitentiary. He supported the war measures of the Confederate government, maintained cordial relations with the military authorities, and endeavored by proclamations and public addresses to keep up the spirits of the people. At the close of his term he was commissioned colonel in the Confederate army, and served on the staff of General Magruder and then on that of General John A. Wharton in the campaign against Banks in Louisiana. In the summer of 1864 President Davis called him to Richmond as adviser on trans-Mississippi affairs. He was captured with Davis in May 1865, and was imprisoned for several months in Fort Delaware (*Southern Historical Society Papers*, March 1878).

After his release he returned to Texas, opened commission houses in Houston and Galveston, turned to ranching again, and lost everything in a beef-packery venture. He next became tax collector of Galveston. In 1878 he was elected state treasurer and held this office until he voluntarily retired in 1891. After the death of his first wife he married, in December 1883, Mrs. Sarah E. (Black) Porter; and twenty years later, on Aug. 12, 1903, he married Lue Scott. His *Six Decades in Texas, or Memoirs of Francis Richard Lubbock*, edited by C. W. Raines, was published in 1900. Though he was not possessed of extraordinary ability, he won and held public confidence. His last years were spent in Austin, where the bent form of the vivacious little old man, dressed on all important occasions in Confederate gray, was a familiar and popular figure.

[Lubbock's *Six Decades* (1900); *War of the Rebellion: Official Records* (*Army*); war-time files of Texas newspapers, especially the *Houston Telegraph*; *Southwestern Hist. Quart.*, Apr. 1924; *Confed. Mil. Hist.* (1899), I, 733–34; *Who's Who in America*, 1903–05; *Dallas Morning News*, June 23, 1905.]   C. W. R.

LUBIN, DAVID (June 10, 1849–Jan. 1, 1919), agriculturist, was born at Klodowa in Russian Poland, the son of Simon and Rachel (Holtz) Lubin. His father died in David's early infancy. His mother, who was left with six children, married again. About 1853 the family, after passing unharmed through a pogrom, fled to England and, in 1855, emigrated to the United States. David's boyhood was spent in the Ghetto of New York City and his formal education was that of the public grammar school. His mother, a resolute, high-tempered, energetic, and deeply religious woman, trained him so thoroughly in faith and morals that her influence persisted throughout his life. The boy learned the trade of goldsmith and jeweler. Going west at sixteen, he knocked about San Francisco and in 1868 was a member of a party of gold-hunters in Arizona. Returning east without having found gold, he met with failure as a traveling salesman. In 1874 he opened a small dry-goods store in Sacramento, Cal., in partnership with his half-brother, Harris Weinstock. Two principles, complete truth in the representation of articles for sale and a fixed price, dominated the enterprise. The idea of a fixed price was new in California. The principles, together with sound management, made the business an outstanding success. A mail-order department speedily grew into the largest mail-order undertaking on the Pacific Coast. In 1884, now prosperous, he fulfilled a promise to his mother by taking her on a pilgrimage to Palestine. In the Holy Land, he later remarked, "I was vividly reminded of the mission of my people" (Agresti, *post*, p. 71). He became a militant reformer, a minor Hebrew prophet. His passion "to render service in ways in which Israel is to serve" was directed by a restless and inquiring mind. He read much of economics, political science, and history, and was influenced particularly by Herbert Spencer and John Stuart Mill. His own ideal was abstract justice.

From his mercantile venture Lubin branched into fruit-growing in California. He promptly discovered that the policies of the railroads worked to the disadvantage of the small grower and to the undue profit of certain Eastern middle-men and he became one of the leaders of an agrarian revolt which caused the railroads to modify their practices and which eventuated in the organization of the fruit-growers. Soon he advanced from a provincial to a national point of view. He was a protectionist because he feared the results for America of competition with the low-paid labor of Europe. He argued that since the tariff could not protect the farmer, who was primarily an exporter, the system of protection worked an injustice to the agricultural group. By means of lectures and pamphlets he began an agitation for "equalization of protection." His proposal was to offset the protection afforded to manufacturers and industrial laborers by granting the producers of the staples a bounty on exports in the form of a government subsidy to reduce the cost of ocean carriage from shipping points to the foreign import markets. He won a following, but the dominant protectionists publicly sneered at the "crank" while privately one of their number tried to silence him by persuading him to accept a consulship. The country was not ready to carry the principle of protection to its logical limit.

In 1896 the intense and often irascible reformer parted from his first wife, Louisa Lyons, whom he had married in 1875, under circumstances which caused his physician to order a trip to Europe to ward off a breakdown. The journey caused Lubin to transfer the emphasis of his thought from the American husbandman to the farming classes of the world. Attending the International Agricultural Congress of 1896 at Budapest, he sketched in an address the rough outlines of a project that was to absorb his energies for the rest of his life. Convinced now that justice to the American farmer was impossible without justice to the husbandmen of the world, he proposed an International Institute of Agriculture in which could be pooled and made available that information concerning crops and other agricultural matters which would enable the husbandmen of any country to fight intelligently for their own interests. During the next twelve years he talked, wrote letters and pamphlets, and traveled widely seeking to win adherents to his plan. After a snub by the United States Department of Agriculture he laid his case before the governments of Europe. Great Britain and France ignored him, for his proposal seemed almost absurd in a day of intense nationalism. Victor Emanuel of Italy, however, was persuaded. Italian initiative resulted in the establishment in 1910 of the International Institute of Agriculture, the creation of a treaty ratified by forty-six nations. Lubin remained for the rest of his life the United States delegate to the permanent committee of the Institute. Success did not change his mood. He consciously tried to personify Israel fighting for mankind. "But there is a higher service ... and that is for the United States of the World. And I am happy to be an humble soldier and private in that army" (Agresti, *post*, p. 1). He died of influenza in Rome on Jan. 1, 1919. He had married, in 1897, Florence Platnauer. He was survived by his second wife and by eight children, three sons and five daughters.

[Signora Olivia Rosetti Agresti, a woman of marked ability who was familiar with European society, assisted Lubin in his long and difficult task of securing co-operation from European governments. Her book, *David Lubin* (1922), is the only important study. For other printed sources see R. D. Hunt, *Cal. and Californians* (1926), vol. IV; *Lit. Digest*, Feb. 8, 1919; *Outlook*, Jan. 15, 1919; *Am. Rev. of Revs.*, June 1919; *Overland Monthly*, Aug. 1919; *Sacramento Union, San Francisco Chronicle*, Jan. 3, 1919. Information as to certain facts was supplied for this sketch by Lubin's son, Simon J. Lubin, Sacramento, Cal.]   R. H. G.

LUCAS, ANTHONY FRANCIS (Sept. 9, 1855–Sept. 2, 1921), geologist, engineer, was born in Spalato, Dalmatia, Austria, the son of a ship-builder and ship-owner, Capt. Francis Stephen Luchich, and his wife, Giovanna Giovanizio, of Montenegrin descent. When Anthony was six years old his family removed to Trieste, Austria, where he received his primary education. At the age of twenty he graduated from the Polytechnic Institute, Gratz, and then entered the Naval Academy of Fiume and Pola from which he graduated in 1878. The following year he came to the United States to visit an uncle residing in Saginaw, Mich., and became so much interested in the lumber industry that he resigned from the Austrian navy, followed his uncle's example and changed his name to Lucas, and applied for American citizenship. His final naturalization papers were granted May 9, 1885. From 1879 to 1893 he engaged first in lumbering and then, as a consulting mechanical and mining engineer, with offices and residence in Washington, D. C., in mining activities in the West. In 1893 he accepted a position as mining engineer for a salt-mining company at Petit Anse, La. During his three years' service with this organization he became much interested in the occasional mounds of low elevation occurring in the Gulf Coastal Plain areas of Louisiana and Texas, and in 1896 he began privately the serious study of these so-called domes. In the course of this work, which involved prospecting with a diamond drill, he located a number of great deposits of rock salt and also studied the seepages of petroleum and sulphur from other domes. He came to the conclusion that these elevated areas were geological structures *per se*, distinct from the surrounding sedimentary deposits with which the elevation was encircled, and that the areas showing seepages on the surface were in reality natural reservoirs of petroleum. On the basis of this theory, he selected an elevated area known as Big Hill, now Spindletop, near Beaumont, Tex., leased 220 of its 300 acres, and then sought financial aid to undertake drilling for oil. Because of his unusual theory, for which there was no proof in any of the oil fields then existing in the world, Lucas could secure the aid of only the J. M. Guffey Petroleum Company of Pittsburgh, Pa., and that only by relinquishing the larger part of his interest in the undertaking. Operations were begun on Oct. 27, 1900, using a crude form of hydraulic rotary drill. After successfully overcoming discouraging difficulties with quicksand by devising a check valve (which he failed to patent) he struck oil at a depth of 1,139 feet on Jan. 10, 1901. Within twenty-four hours petroleum was gushing from the well at the rate of nearly a hundred thousand barrels a day—the largest oil well, by far, ever completed in the United States. The Lucas Gusher on Spindletop started a new era in the oil industry, but while Lucas, as the discoverer, became famous the world over, his own financial reward was negligible. He continued with the J. M. Guffey Petroleum Company for about a year and then in 1902 undertook petroleum exploration in Mexico for the Mexican Eagle Oil Company, Limited. In 1905 he returned to Washington, D. C., and resumed his consulting practice, which he continued until his death. He was a member of the American Institute of Mining Engineers, the Franklin Institute, and the American Electrochemical Society, and of the Engineers' Club, New York, and the Cosmos Club, Washington. On Sept. 22, 1887, he married Carolina Weed Fitzgerald, who with a son survived him.

[*Trans. Am. Inst. Mining and Metallurgical Engrs.*, vol. LXV (1921); R. S. McBeth, *Pioneering the Gulf Coast; A Story of the Life and Accomplishments of Capt. Anthony F. Lucas* (1918); *Who's Who in America*, 1920–21; *Mining and Scientific Press*, Sept. 17, 1921; *Evening Star* (Washington, D. C.), Sept. 2, 1921.]   C. W. M.

LUCAS, DANIEL BEDINGER (Mar. 16, 1836–July 28, 1909), jurist, author, "poet of the Shenandoah Valley," was born at "Rion Hall," near Charles Town, Va. (now W. Va.). He came of a family of distinguished soldiers. The first Lucas of which there is record, Robert, came from England and settled in Pennsylvania in 1679. Edward, a son of this Robert, moved on to the Shenandoah Valley of Virginia and settled near Shepherdstown; his grandson, William, built on one of the most beautiful spots of the Valley, "Rion Hall," where his son Daniel was born. The boy's mother, Virginia Bedinger, was a daughter of Daniel Bedinger, collector of the Port of Norfolk during John Adams' administration, a man of considerable poetic talent. Because of an injury to his spine during infancy, which kept him from more active amusements, Daniel spent much time in his father's excellent library, forming a taste for good literature and a desire to write poetry. After some schooling under private tutors in the home of Braxton Davenport at Charles Town he went to the University of Virginia where he excelled in oratory. Completing his course in 1854, he attended the law school of Judge John W. Brockenbrough at Lexington, Va., where he graduated with honors. In 1859 he began practising law at Charles

Town but moved the next year to Richmond. At the beginning of the Civil War he joined the staff of Gen. Henry A. Wise and took part in the Kanawha Valley Campaign; physical disability kept him from active service during the last years of the war. Toward the end of the war he courageously ran the blockade to help defend his classmate, John Yates Beall [q.v.], accused in New York of being a spy. Unable to return south he stayed in Canada where upon the surrender of Lee he published his best-known poem, *The Land Where We Were Dreaming*. The war over he returned to Charles Town. Barred from the practice of his profession by the test oath, he turned to literature and became co-editor of the Baltimore *Southern Metropolis*, in which magazine he published some of his poems. The same year he married Lena Tucker Brooke, grand-niece of Gov. Robert Brooke of Virginia.

In 1871 Lucas reëntered his profession and shortly became one of the most distinguished practitioners before the courts of West Virginia. A stanch Democrat of the Jeffersonian school he took a prominent part in the politics of the state. He was Democratic presidential elector in 1872 and 1876; elector at large on the Cleveland ticket in 1884; was elected to the legislature in 1884 and 1886; and was a member of the supreme court of appeals from 1889 to 1893, serving as president from Nov. 8, 1890, to Jan. 1, 1893. Because of ill health he was comparatively inactive during the last ten years of his life, spending the time quietly on his estate with his wife and only child, Virginia, who like her father was a contributor to several magazines. Lucas' volumes of poetry include, besides the first, *The Wreath of Eglantine* (1869), written in collaboration with his sister, and *Ballads and Madrigals* (1884). A collected edition of his poems, edited by Charles W. Kent and Lucas' daughter, was published in Boston in 1913 under the title *The Land Where We Were Dreaming*. His plays, three in number, are in blank verse. *The Maid of Northumberland* was published in 1884. *Hildebrand* and *Kate McDonald* were published posthumously in the *Dramatic Works of Daniel Bedinger Lucas* (1913). All three have to do with the Civil War in America, *The Maid of Northumberland* being perhaps the first play written in America on this subject. In two of the plays the author makes use of his blockade-running experiences at the time of the John Yates Beall trial. They are full of Shakespearian echoes, contain some excellent speeches, and some good descriptions of nature, but on the whole, Lucas the dramatist is inferior to Lucas the writer of lyrics. His poems are of different kinds—nature poems, love poems, narrative poems, poems of sentiment, poems dealing with the South and the war, and poems written for special occasions. They show the influence of Keats, Tennyson, and Poe. His prose works include *The Memoir of John Yates Beall* (1865), and *Nicaragua, War of the Filibusters* (1896). At the time of his death he was writing a life of Lincoln.

[*Who's Who in America*, 1908–09; J. E. Norris, *Hist. of the Lower Shenandoah Valley* (1890); G. W. Atkinson and A. F. Gibbens, *Prominent Men of W. Va.* (1890); G. W. Atkinson, *Bench and Bar of W. Va.* (1919); *Lib. of Southern Lit.*, vol. VII (1909); Lucy F. Bittinger, *Bittinger and Bedinger Families* (1904); *Univ. of Va., Its Hist., Influence, Equipment, and Characteristics* (1904), vol. I.]   F.M.S.

LUCAS, ELIZA [See PINCKNEY, ELIZA LUCAS, 1722–1793].

LUCAS, FREDERIC AUGUSTUS (Mar. 25, 1852–Feb. 9, 1929), naturalist, museum administrator, was born at Plymouth, Mass., the son of Augustus Henry and Eliza (Oliver) Lucas. The first eighteen years of his life were spent in his native town, where he received a common-school education and where his inherent fondness for natural history was given opportunity for expression. He writes that as a boy he was only second-rate at the ordinary boyish sports but that he did possess a more than average mechanical ability and skill at handling tools.

At the end of his second long voyage in a clipper ship, of which his father was captain, he found himself, at eighteen, confronted with the problem of what to do in life. He had a strong desire to become a taxidermist and collector of birds, and through Prof. J. W. P. Jenks of Pierce Academy, at Middleboro, Mass., a taxidermist of considerable ability, he became acquainted with the museum of that institution. Soon he secured a position in the Natural Science Establishment of Prof. Henry A. Ward [*q.v.*] at Rochester, N. Y., and for eleven years, 1871 to 1882, he was a member of that famous organization. There he had as laboratory associates men who were later to become leaders in various branches of natural-history work. There also he had ample opportunity for the development of his mechanical ability along many lines, although he specialized in the preparation and mounting of skeletons. In this work he developed such a high technique that in 1882 he was called to the United States National Museum in Washington as osteologist. Under the influence of Dr. George Brown Goode [*q.v.*] he developed so rapidly and so broadly that in 1902 he was simultaneously curator of comparative anatomy, acting curator of fossil vertebrates, in charge of biological exhibits, and in charge of the children's room. In 1904 he was called to Brooklyn as curator-in-chief of the Museum of the Brooklyn Institute of Arts and Sciences.

Here he found a museum in a somewhat chaotic state, with the exhibits unbalanced and a general lack of coordination. He gave his attention particularly to the natural-history department, and when he resigned the mark of his genius was left in the exhibition halls. His idea of a natural-history museum was that it should not be merely a collection of curious objects from various parts of the world but a teaching institution with the specimens cautiously selected, carefully installed, and instructively labeled. This idea he carried out first in the National Museum, then in Brooklyn, and finally in the great American Museum of Natural History in New York, to which he was called as director in 1911 and where he remained until his death. His influence on the museums of America was great and lasting.

As a field naturalist, he was given but few opportunities. There are only three major expeditions to his credit, but each one was carried out successfully. The first was to Funk Island for remains of the Great Auk, the second to the Pribilof Islands as a member of the Fur Seal Commission, and the last to a whaling station in Newfoundland for the great sulphur-bottom whale. His published writings, both technical and popular, comprise some 365, and the wide range of subjects covered indicates the breadth of his interest and activities. Probably his best-known works are two small volumes, *Animals of the Past* (1901) and *Animals before Man in America* (1902), and the articles contributed to Johnson's *Universal Cyclopædia*. On Feb. 13, 1884, he married Annie J. Edgar, by whom he had two daughters.

[T. S. Palmer, in *The Auk*, Apr. 1929; C. H. Townsend, in *Science*, Apr. 26, 1929; R. C. Murphy, in *Natural Hist.*, Mar.–Apr. 1929; *Who's Who in America*, 1926–27; *N. Y. Times*, Feb. 10, 1929; autobiography and bibliography entitled "Fifty Years of Museum Work," to be published (1933) by the Am. Museum of Natural Hist.]   W.G.

LUCAS, JAMES H. (Nov. 12, 1800–Nov. 9, 1873), banker, capitalist, railroad president, was born at Pittsburgh, the fifth son of John Baptiste Charles Lucas [*q.v.*] and Anne (Sebin), who came to America from Normandy in 1784. Appointed territorial judge and commissioner of land claims of upper Louisiana Territory in 1805, John Lucas moved with his large family to St. Louis, then "an untamed and unprogressive trading town." He commenced immediately to purchase large tracts of land in, and adjacent to, the town and to lay the foundation for a great fortune. The boy received his early education there under unsatisfactory conditions and was sent to St. Thomas' College, Kentucky, in 1814, and later, to Jefferson College, Pennsylvania. He then studied law under the direction of family friends in Poughkeepsie, N. Y., and in Litchfield, Conn., but with no desire to follow that profession. In 1823 he moved to Arkansas Territory, where he remained for thirteen years and had a varied experience. He was, successively, a school-teacher, a merchant, county clerk, a plantation owner, a lawyer, a probate judge, and a militia officer. Here, in May 1832, he married Mary Emilie Desruisseaux, a native of Cahokia, Ill., by whom he had numerous children. Upon his father's request, his four brothers having died, he returned to St. Louis in 1837 to assume the management of the family properties. By this time the "Lucas estate" comprised vast holdings in the city, together with plantations in several counties. With the economic transformation of St. Louis and its firm establishment as a commercial and industrial center, there came a phenomenal rise in land prices and in the value of the estate. The wealth thus acquired enabled Lucas to sponsor numerous enterprises. He early realized the vital need for better transportation facilities in the West, and with other wealthy and public-spirited men of the city he was instrumental in the organization of the Pacific Railroad in 1849, the first and most important line built in Missouri. He donated large sums for its construction, served as a director and twice as president, and assisted it in the recurrent financial crises which beset early railroad ventures. He founded the private banking house of Lucas, Simonds & Company, organized the St. Louis Gas Company, and was a director and large stock holder in a score of corporations. His interests extended to California, but the St. Louis property was the corner-stone. He was not content, however, merely to accumulate money, but was a generous patron of enterprises of an educational, cultural, and religious character. In politics he was a stanch Whig, and twice ran for office, serving one term, 1844–48, in the state Senate, and being defeated for the office of mayor of St. Louis in 1847. He was an effective exponent of the conservative business interests of his city. The grave conditions in Western finance occasioned by the panic of 1857 were successfully met by him, despite considerable losses; but the outbreak of the Civil War precipitated a crisis in the governmental and economic situation in Missouri. Lucas, in common with many business men, supported the Bell-Everett ticket, and in 1861 was opposed both to secession and to coercion of the South. He labored for compromise, and when that failed, steadily and resolutely supported the Union cause. During the critical and uncertain decade following the war, he was chiefly concerned with the economic restoration of St. Louis and in the administration of his estate. Following a long period of ill health he died a few days before the completion of his seventy-third year.

[J. T. Scharf, *Hist. of St. Louis* (1883); L. U. Reavis, *St. Louis: the Future Great City* (1875); *Mo. Hist. Soc. Colls.*, vol. III, no. 3 (1911); R. E. Riegel, *Story of the Western Railroads* (1926) and "Trans-Mississippi Railroads during the Fifties," *Miss. Valley Hist. Rev.*, Sept. 1923; H. L. Conard, *Encyc. of the Hist. of Mo.*, vol. IV (1901); *St. Louis Democrat* and *St. Louis Republican*, Nov. 10, 1873.]   T.S.B.

LUCAS, JOHN BAPTISTE CHARLES (Aug. 14, 1758–Aug. 29, 1842), congressman, jurist, was born in the ancient town of Pont-Audemer on the river Brille, in Normandy, France. His father was Robert Édouard Lucas, *procureur du roi*; his mother before her marriage was a Mademoiselle de l'Arche. He attended the Honfleur and Paris law schools, and in 1782 graduated from the law department of the University of Caen. For the next two years he practised law in his native town, and sometime during this period he married Anne Sebin.

In 1784 he emigrated to the United States and settled on a farm on the Monongahela River, a short distance above Pittsburgh, Pa. Here, in addition to agricultural pursuits, he devoted his time to the acquisition of the English language and to familiarizing himself with the history, constitution, and laws of his adopted country. During these early years in Pennsylvania he seems to have made some trading voyages down the Ohio and Mississippi rivers to New Madrid, in what was to become the state of Missouri. He soon gained the confidence of his neighbors and was elected to the Pennsylvania House of Representatives, where he served from 1792 to 1798. During the year 1794 he was also a judge of the court of common pleas in his district. He was elected to Congress as a Democrat from the Allegheny district, to succeed Albert Gallatin, and served from Mar. 4, 1803, until 1805, when, having been appointed United States judge for the northern district of Louisiana by President Jefferson, he resigned and removed to St. Louis. He served in this capacity until 1820 and was also a member of the commission for the adjustment of land titles in the territory from 1805 until its dissolution in 1812. At one time he was acting governor of Missouri Territory, and when the first state legislature met he was a candidate for the United States Senate.

It is probable that service on the commission for the adjustment of land titles directed the attention of Judge Lucas to the acquisition of real estate. When he came to St. Louis it was a small French frontier village, but he foresaw its future and possessed himself of all the land he could obtain. As a result he left to his heirs a large estate. Some time after the death of his wife, in 1811, he built a small stone house on what is now the corner of Seventh and Market streets, and here he made his home until his death.

He has been described as small in stature, and as a man of honor and of untiring industry. He was eccentric and irritable and frequently exhibited these defects while on the bench. His administration of the laws was excellent, for he understood the old French and Spanish titles as well as any man in the territory. During his later years he was very melancholy, due in large part to the fact that several of his sons met violent deaths. One of them, Charles, was killed in a duel with Col. Thomas Hart Benton [q.v.] in 1817. A surviving son, James H. Lucas [q.v.], was prominent in the commercial development of Missouri.

[*Biog. Dir. Am. Cong.* (1928); J. T. Scharf, *Hist. of St. Louis City and County*, vol. II (1883); F. L. Billon, *Annals of St. Louis in Its Territorial Days: from 1804 to 1821* (1888); W. B. Davis and D. S. Durrie, *An Illustrated Hist. of St. Louis* (1876); W. V. N. Bay, *Reminiscences of the Bench and Bar of Mo.* (1878); William Hyde and H. L. Conard, *Encyc. of the Hist. of St. Louis* (1899), vol. III; obituary in *St. Louis Daily New Era*, Aug. 30, 1842.]   M.J.W.

LUCAS, JONATHAN (1754–Apr. 1, 1821), millwright, was born in Cumberland, England, the son of John and Ann (Noble) Lucas. His mechanical genius is said to have been inherited from his mother's family, who were mill-owners in Whitehaven. On May 22, 1774, he married Mary Cooke; and the christenings of their five children are on record in St. Mary's Church, Egremont. After the death of his first wife, between 1783 and 1786, he married Ann Ashburn, of Whitehaven. About 1790, he came to Charleston, S. C., where he attracted attention by setting up a small windmill on the gable of a wooden store in King Street, where he lived. A passing rice-planter, learning that the maker of the mill was in needy circumstances and desired work, took him to Santee. There the system of flooding rice fields by action of the tide was coming into general use; but a large crop was considered a dubious blessing because of the difficulty of removing husks from the grain. Much was pounded out by hand in wooden mortars with pestles, a slave's task being from a bushel to a

bushel and a half a day. Crude mills turned by animals were in use: the pecker machine, which moved its pestle like the stroke of a woodpecker, and the cogmill, whose upright pestles were driven by a horizontal cog wheel. These could clean from three to six barrels a day. Lucas set up a new type of pounding-mill, probably at first moved by wind; but he is remembered for his water-mill, driven by a very large undershot water-wheel. He built the first on Peach Island Plantation for J. Bowman, who as late as 1810 owed him £1,500. For Andrew Johnston, on Millbrook Plantation, he built the first of his tide mills, which operated automatically with every ebb tide, day and night. In 1793, he built for Henry Laurens on Mepkin Plantation, Cooper River, an improved tide mill, with rolling screens, elevators, and packers. After the rice was threshed from the straw, it was lifted by the elevators (buckets on an endless belt) to a rolling screen in which it was freed of sand, and was then poured into a hopper above the millstones. A wind fan having blown away chaff, the milled rice passed into mortars where pestles weighing some two hundred pounds struck the grain from thirty to forty times a minute. It then went through a rolling screen to remove the flour, and after a winnowing fan had blown off the remainder of the chaff, the clean grain was placed in six-hundred-pound barrels by the packer. Three persons could manage such a mill, and, on a favorable tide, beat from sixteen to twenty barrels.

Assisted by his son, Lucas installed his mills throughout the rice region, some early ones being on the reserves of Mrs. Middleton, Gen. Peter Horry, and Col. Wm. Alston of Santee. He prospered, and in 1793 he bought at auction a plantation on Shem Creek in Christ Church Parish. There he made his home and built a combined rice and saw mill, called Greenwich Mills. Later, in partnership with two carpenters, he bought a large lot in Charleston, where afterwards the rice mills centered. In 1803 he acquired five lots in Mount Pleasant, and in 1804 he purchased fifty acres on Shute's Folly in Charleston harbor, where he is said to have built a windmill. In 1817 either he or his son Jonathan [q.v.] built in Charleston the first steam rice mill; but in all essentials the later rice mills adhered to his plans, and the rice industry owed as much to him as the cotton industry to Eli Whitney. On the afternoon of Apr. 2, 1821, his funeral was held at the residence of his son in Charleston, and he was buried in St. Paul's churchyard.

[John Drayton, *A View of S. C.* (1802); R. F. W. Allston, *A Memoir of the Introduction and Planting* of Rice in S. C. (1843) ; Year Book, City of Charleston, 1883. Charleston Courier, Apr. 2, 1821 ; Charleston Mercury, June 17, 1851 ; Southern Cabinet of Agriculture, Horticulture, Rural and Domestic Economy (Charleston, 1840) ; Charleston Mesne Conveyance Records ; family records ; epitaph.]   A. K. G.

LUCAS, JONATHAN (1775–Dec. 29, 1832), millwright and inventor, was born in England and christened in St. Mary's Church, Egremont, Cumberland, Feb. 26, 1775. His parents were Jonathan [q.v.] and Mary (Cooke) Lucas, both of Cumberland. As a lad of about fifteen years he came to South Carolina with his father, whom he assisted in building rice mills. In 1798 he bought a large tidewater lot in Cannonborough, Charleston, where he banked a mill pond and built a rice mill that attracted a considerable toll business. On July 18, 1799, he married Sarah Lydia Simons, daughter of Benjamin Simons of the Grove Plantation in Christ Church Parish. In 1801, on Middleburg Plantation, Cooper River, inherited by his wife from her father, he built a toll rice mill. On July 12, 1808, he patented a new type of machine for removing the husks from rice without pounding by pestles. This machine consisted of two vertical conical cylinders, turning in opposite directions, one within the other, the inner cylinder having a much higher velocity than the outer. The outer cylinder was faced with sheet iron punched like a grater; the inner was sometimes similarly faced, sometimes covered with fluted cork or other soft wood, and sometimes had sand or another scouring substance cemented to the surface. The rice passed into the space between the cylinders, which were usually about a half inch apart, though the inner cylinder might be moved up or down at will. From the cylinders it went to the rolling screen where the flour was sifted off, and finally it was polished by the brushing machine.

The South Carolinians preferred to keep the rice-pounding mills of the elder Lucas, but the new machine was a great success in England, which, with a duty of four dollars a tierce on clean rice, became a depot for heavy shipments of paddy or rough rice. In 1822, Jonathan Lucas the younger, at the invitation of the British government, returned to England; and in 1827, he and his son-in-law, Henry Ewbank, doing business in Mincing Lane, London, received a British patent for his invention. Rice-cleaning mills were eventually established at London, Liverpool, Copenhagen, Bremen, Amsterdam, Bordeaux, and Lisbon; and Jonathan Lucas amassed a large fortune.

At Hatcham Grove, his residence in Surrey, he became ill on Christmas morning, 1832, and a few days later died of what was called an ef-fusion of blood to the head. On Jan. 5, 1833, his body was placed in a vault in Camberwell Church, London. By his will, dated Oct. 7, 1831, but not recorded in Charleston until 1836, he appointed his sons-in-law as trustees to manage his plantations, negroes, and trading and other partnerships in Great Britain, America, or elsewhere, making provision for his adult and minor children and bequeathing to his widow all his real and personal property in South Carolina.

[Family papers in possession of T. S. Lucas, Society Hill, S. C., including records copied from St. Mary's Church, Egremont, and letter from Elizabeth Lucas, Dec. 1832; Charleston Mesne Conveyance Records; H. L. Ellsworth, A Digest of Patents Issued by the U. S. from 1790 to Jan. 1, 1839 (1840) ; S. C. Hist. and Geneal. Mag., Jan. 1917; Oct. 1924; R. F. W. Allston, A Memoir of the Introduction and Planting of Rice in S. C. (1843) ; Year Book City of Charleston, S. C., 1883; Charleston Courier, May 28, 1827.]   A. K. G.

LUCAS, ROBERT (Apr. 1, 1781–Feb. 7, 1853), governor of Ohio and territorial governor of Iowa, was born at Shepherdstown, Va. (now W. Va.), the son of Susannah (Barnes) and William Lucas, a Revolutionary soldier of some wealth. His early education was obtained largely from a private tutor, who instructed him especially in mathematics and surveying. When he was about twenty, he moved with his parents to the valley of the Scioto in the Northwest Territory, and in the new state of Ohio he became surveyor for Scioto County, justice of the peace, and an officer in the militia, in which he reached the grade of major-general. On Apr. 4, 1810, he married Elizabeth Brown, who died in 1812. In the War of 1812, after helping to organize a battalion of volunteers from his brigade of Ohio militia, he acted as a detached officer in the disastrous campaign of General Hull. During this time he kept a daily journal that has been published as The Robert Lucas Journal of the War of 1812 (edited by J. C. Parish, 1906, reprinted from Iowa Journal of History and Politics, July 1906). State politics engrossed his attention in the period following the war. He had been a member of the lower house in 1808 and 1809. In 1814 he was elected to the state Senate. On Mar. 7, 1816, he married Friendly Ashley Sumner and, about that time, moved to the newly organized Pike County, where he opened a general store at Piketon. He continued to represent his district in the state Senate until 1822 and, again, from 1824 to 1828 and from 1829 to 1830. In the session of 1831 and 1832 he served once more in the lower house. As a stanch supporter of Jacksonian politics he had become well known in Ohio and in 1830 was nominated for the governorship of the state. He was defeated but, two years later, was again nominated and was elected. During the presidential campaign of this year he attended the first national convention of the Democratic party and was given the honor of acting as its temporary and permanent chairman.

He served for two terms as governor of Ohio. His most notable service was the vigorous part he took in the acute controversy over the boundary line between the state of Ohio and the territory of Michigan, which led to the "Toledo War." After two years of retirement he was appointed, in 1838, by Van Buren as governor and superintendent of Indian affairs for the newly created territory of Iowa. He was fifty-seven years old, full of experience, intense in his convictions, and positive in his methods. The early part of his governorship was stormy because of the hostility of an ambitious young secretary of the territory and the opposition of a youthful and spirited territorial legislature that chafed at the limitations imposed by the absolute veto power of the governor. Again he found himself involved in a boundary dispute, the line between the state of Missouri and the territory of Iowa being at issue. In 1841 Harrison appointed John Chambers, a Whig, as governor of the territory, and Lucas retired to private life. His most conspicuous public service in the dozen years of life still left him was his participation in the convention of 1844 to form a constitution for the state of Iowa. His messages and proclamations and his public and private correspondence show him to have been a man of practical common sense and of seasoned wisdom in political matters, and, though stern and unbending in his policies, he was the type of executive greatly needed by the territory of Iowa in its initial period. He spent his last years for the most part on his farm near Iowa City, Iowa, and devoted much energy to the causes of temperance and public education, and to the encouragement of railroad projects. He was an ardent worker in the Methodist Church and spent a good deal of time writing religious hymns and verses. Although he had been a life-long Democrat he refused to vote for Franklin Pierce, and cast his ballot in the last year of his life for the Whig ticket.

[Collection of Letters and Papers of Lucas in the Lib. of the State Hist. Soc. of Iowa; *Executive Jour. of Iowa, 1838–41*, ed. by B. F. Shambaugh (1906); "Documents Relating to Governor Lucas," *Iowa Hist. Record*, April 1900; J. C. Parish, *Robert Lucas* (1907); Frederick Lloyd, "Robert Lucas," *Annals of Iowa*, Jan., Apr., July 1870; N. W. Evans, *A Hist. of Scioto County* (1903); T. S. Parvin, "The Quarrel between Gov. Lucas and Sec. Conway," *Annals of Iowa*, July–Oct. 1895.]   J. C. P.

LUCE, STEPHEN BLEECKER (Mar. 25, 1827–July 28, 1917), naval officer, was born in Albany, N. Y., the son of Vinal and Charlotte (Bleecker) Luce, who traced their ancestry back to English and Dutch colonists. His paternal ancestor, Henry Luce, is said to have settled on Martha's Vineyard in the last quarter of the seventeenth century. When Stephen was about eight years old the family moved to Washington, D. C. On Oct. 19, 1841, at the age of fourteen, he was appointed a midshipman as from the state of New York. He learned the rudiments of seamanship on the *North Carolina,* the *Congress,* and the *Columbus.* In March 1848 he was ordered to the Naval Academy, and in the following year, promoted to the rank of passed midshipman, he was ordered to sea again on the *Vandalia* and cruised in the Pacific until October 1852. After shore duty at Washington, during which he assisted in astronomical work, he joined the *Vixen,* May 1853, and the following year was ordered to the Coast Survey. Promoted to master and lieutenant in 1855, he was on the *Jamestown* until February 1860, cruising for much of the time along the Mosquito Coast. In March he was assigned to the Naval Academy as assistant to the commandant. Meanwhile, Dec. 7, 1854, he married Eliza Henley, a grandniece of Martha Washington. They had one son and two daughters.

Shortly before the firing on Fort Sumter, Luce was detailed to the *Wabash* as a watch officer, but his cruise was cut short by his detachment, at the urgent request of the superintendent of the Naval Academy, to become head of its department of seamanship. The Naval Academy, at that time, was at Newport, R. I., having been moved there because of the proximity of Annapolis to the war zone. In 1862 Luce was promoted to the rank of lieutenant commander. His tour of duty at the Academy marks the beginning of work which led to the publication of his book, *Seamanship* (1863). This supplied a great lack in text-books and became the standard treatise on the subject, passing through many editions. In October 1863 he was ordered to command the monitor *Nantucket*; later he took over command of the *Pontiac*; and in 1865, he was ordered to cooperate with General Sherman in the capture of Charleston. He next became commandant of midshipmen at Annapolis under the leadership of Admiral Porter, and on July 25, 1866, was promoted to the grade of commander. In 1869 he was detached, and until 1884 he was with the European Squadron (1869–72), on shore duty (1872–75), in command of the flagship *Hartford* (1875–77), of the training ship, *Minnesota* (1877–81), and of all apprentice ships (1881–84).

Luce was a "lean, wiry man of medium height, with thin features between iron gray sidewhiskers, a prominent hawk-like nose, thin lips and determined chin, and . . . piercing gray eyes" (J. M. Ellicott, in *United States Naval Institute Proceedings,* October 1924, p. 1616). He was good-humored, witty, shrewd, and, above all, inspiring. In the years following the Civil War, when the navy was in a deplorable condition, he believed in its future, and, determined, persistent, and unselfish, did as much perhaps as any one person to upbuild it. While his activities were varied, he directed his energies principally to raising the efficiency of the personnel. In 1873 he read a paper at the Naval Academy, entitled, "The Meaning of Our Navy and Merchant Marine," which appeared as the first paper in the initial number of the *United States Naval Institute Proceedings.* In this and subsequent publications he plead for a better training of seamen, both for the navy and for the merchant marine. Many of his suggestions were later adopted. During the periods when he was in command of training ships he put into operation numerous original methods, the success of which proved their value.

Appreciating as did few naval men of his day the great importance of tactics and strategy, he labored, in the face of no little opposition, to secure better training facilities for officers. It was his own practice, when opportunity offered, to put ships through the most intense and exacting tactical maneuvers, often to the extreme annoyance of their officers. Convinced of the need of officers being versed in naval methods he long advocated, though at first meeting not only indifference but ridicule, the establishment of an institution where they might pursue advanced studies. The army had schools for this purpose, but the navy's need of them had not been recognized. Finally, however, on May 30, 1884, Secretary Chandler appointed a board to make a report on the whole proposition of "post graduate" work for naval officers. Its report resulted in a general order dated Oct. 6, 1884, establishing the Naval War College, with Luce, who had received the rank of commodore Nov. 25, 1881, as the first president. The College was opened in Newport, R. I., and it was not long before Luce had secured as lecturer on tactics and naval history Capt. A. T. Mahan [*q.v.*], who also became a molding influence in the development of the institution. At first the college received poor support, both financially and professionally. Time proved its value, however, and eventually, together with technical war-game studies, it provided officers with instruction in history, for-

eign policy, international law, and higher command. Similar naval institutions in England, Japan, Germany, and France were patterned after Luce's ideas. The value of what he did for the education of officers is incalculable; as Admiral Fiske succinctly stated in the *Naval Institute Proceedings* (*post,* p. 1936), he "taught the navy to think." The building at the Naval Academy housing the department of seamanship was named in his honor.

In 1886 Luce was commissioned rear admiral and three years later was retired. He was the naval editor of Johnson's *Universal Cyclopaedia* and of Funk and Wagnall's *Standard Dictionary.* He also compiled a book of naval songs. He was a prolific writer, most of his articles appearing in the *Naval Institute Proceedings* and the *North American Review.* Professional reports of boards on which he served appeared in the reports of the Secretary of the Navy. From 1901 to 1910 he was on special duty at the War College. He died at Newport in his ninety-first year.

[B. R. Fiske, in *U. S. Naval Inst. Proc.,* vol. XLIII, no. 175 (Sept. 1917) and C. S. Alden, in *Ibid.,* vol. L, no. 262 (Dec. 1924); Albert Gleaves, *Life and Letters of Rear Admiral Stephen B. Luce* (1925); C. F. Goodrich, *In Memoriam: Stephen Bleecker Luce* (1919); *Who's Who in America,* 1916–17; L. R. Hamersly, *The Records of Living Officers of the U. S. Navy and Marine Corps* (6th ed., 1898); *Official Records of the Union and Confederate Navies in the War of the Rebellion*; obituaries in *Army and Navy Jour.* and *Army and Navy Reg.,* Aug. 4, 1917; *N. Y. Times,* July 29, 1917.]   A.R.B.

LUDELING, JOHN THEODORE (Jan. 27, 1827–Jan. 21, 1891), jurist, son of John and Françoise Lorette (de Salnavo) Ludeling, was born in New Orleans, but moved when a boy to Monroe, La. His mother was from Santo Domingo. Her father, a coffee planter, and most of his family were massacred in 1801 during the rebellion of the blacks under the leadership of Toussaint L'Ouverture. The future Mrs. Ludeling, then three years of age, escaped with her grandmother and reached a vessel which brought them to New Orleans. Here she was brought up by her grandmother, and here she married John Ludeling, an emigrant from France. After his death she married Bernard Hemken, and settled in Monroe. On July 18, 1839, when he was twelve years of age, John enrolled, as a Roman Catholic, in St. Louis University, St. Louis, Mo., which at that time drew more than half of its students from Louisiana. He attended until 1843, but neither he nor his brother, who enrolled at the same time, remained to complete the work for the bachelor's degree, which then required six years. His name appears in a very small roster of students of excellent conduct, and again in a long roll of diligent students, but he seems to have won no premiums for scholarship. While at the university both brothers were known by the name of their stepfather, Hemken, but John, at least, later took back the family name of Ludeling.

After leaving St. Louis University, he returned to Monroe, studied law in the office of Isaiah Garrett, was admitted to the Louisiana bar, and married Maria Copley, daughter of Enoch Copley. He early took the side of the North in the sectional controversy, joined the Republican party soon after its organization, and, although two brothers served in the army of the Confederacy, he remained a Union man. The Republican governor, H. C. Warmoth, appointed him chief justice of Louisiana, and he held the office from Nov. 1, 1868, to Jan. 9, 1877, through the bitter years of reconstruction. When he retired from the bench he returned to Monroe and associated himself with Talbot Stillman, and the connection continued until his death.

Ludeling was a man of indomitable courage and unshakable integrity, and was charitable in ways not published to the world. He was an able and successful lawyer, and he was also successful financially. He was instrumental in building the Vicksburg, Shreveport & Pacific Railroad, and served as its first president. It has been said that the Ludeling court was one of the best that Louisiana ever had. It failed to receive local credit, however, because it was Republican and in office during reconstruction days. Ludeling died at Killeden Plantation, his country home near Monroe. His funeral was conducted by Western Star Lodge No. 24, F. & A. M., and he was buried in the old City Cemetery, Monroe.

[Information from John T. L. Hubbard, attorney-at-law, Bridgeport, Conn.; Rev. Laurence J. Kenney, S.J., of St. Louis University; E. G. Courtney, Monroe, La., secretary of Western Star Lodge No. 24, F. & A. M.; and Judge Rufus E. Foster of New Orleans; H. P. Dart, "The History of the Supreme Court of Louisiana" and W. K. Dart, "The Justices of the Supreme Court," in 133 *La. Reports*, repr. in *La. Hist. Quart.*, Jan. 1921; L. C. Quintero in *Green Bag*, Mar. 1891; Wm. F. Fanning, *Memorial Volume of the Diamond Jubilee of St. Louis Univ.* (1904); *Times-Democrat* and *Daily Picayune* (New Orleans), Jan. 23, 28, 1891.]   M. J. W.

LUDLOW, DANIEL (Aug. 2, 1750–Sept. 26, 1814), merchant and banker, eldest child of Gabriel Ludlow by his second wife, Elizabeth (Crommelin), was born in New York City, where for over fifty years the Ludlows had been prominent merchants and distinguished citizens. He was a descendant of Gabriel Ludlow, grandnephew of Roger Ludlow [*q.v.*] and member of a Somerset family, who emigrated to New

York in 1694. At the age of fifteen the boy was sent to Holland to enter the counting-house of the great Amsterdam firm of Crommelin & Zoon, which had been founded by his maternal grandfather, Charles Crommelin. Here he learned the banking business and acquired a knowledge of the French, German, and Dutch languages. Returning to New York after four or five years, he joined his father as a general merchant and upon the latter's death in 1773 continued the business under his own name. After the Revolution, during which he remained loyal to the British Crown, Ludlow, with Edward Goold as partner, conducted a general importing business at 47 Wall St. This partnership was dissolved about 1790, and thereafter until 1808 Ludlow and his nephew, Gulian, under the firm name of Daniel Ludlow & Company, carried on the enterprise and built up the largest mercantile and importing trade in the city. In 1799 he was active in the organization of the Manhattan Company and was chosen its first president. This company was formed ostensibly to supply New York "with pure and wholesome water"; but apparently its real object was to establish a bank, since an inconspicuous clause in the charter permitted surplus funds to be used in any "monied transactions and operations" not inconsistent with state or national laws (*Laws of New York*, 1799, ch. LXXXIV). Though there were many complaints about the water supply, the Bank of the Manhattan Company, established on Sept. 1, 1799, at 40 Wall St., prospered under Ludlow's leadership and remains today one of New York's greatest financial institutions. The succeeding years were busy ones for the merchant banker, for in addition to his other activities he was appointed navy agent in 1801 and later he became a leading director of the Harlem Bridge Company.

Ludlow was also prominent socially. He had a summer home at Barretto's Point on the East River, whither he often conveyed guests in his four-in-hand equipage. An avenue and square in that locality, now part of the Borough of the Bronx, still retain the family name. Both at his country seat and at his large marble house at 54–56 Broadway he dispensed hospitality, keeping six or eight places set at table for unexpected guests. The unsettled trade conditions in Europe, culminating in the Berlin and Milan decrees, brought Daniel Ludlow & Company to bankruptcy, however, and in 1808 Ludlow was forced to sell both his city home and his country estate. As a matter of policy he resigned as president of the Manhattan Company, and shortly afterward moved to Skaneateles, N. Y., where he was an honored resident until his death. He was twice married: first, Oct. 4, 1773, to Arabella Duncan, who died in 1803; and later, to a Mrs. Van Horne. George Duncan and Gabriel George Ludlow [qq.v.] were his half-brothers.

[N. Y. Geneal. and Biog. Record, Jan., Apr. 1919; New-Eng. Hist. and Geneal. Reg., Apr. 1888; E. N. Leslie, Skaneateles: Hist. of its Earliest Settlement and Reminiscences of Later Times (1902); J. A. Scoville, The Old Merchants of N. Y., 3 ser. (1865); J. G. Wilson, The Memorial Hist. of the City of N. Y., vols. II–IV (1892–93); J. A. Stevens, Colonial N. Y. Sketches Biog. and Hist., 1768–1784 (1867); N. Y. City directories; Minutes of the Common Council of the City of N. Y. 1784–1831 (1917), vol. I; death notice in Evening Post (N. Y.), Oct. 6, 1814.]   A. E. P.

LUDLOW, FITZ HUGH (Sept. 11, 1836–Sept. 12, 1870), writer, was born in New York City, son of Rev. Henry G. and Abby (Wills) Ludlow. His father, a prominent abolitionist, was minister of the Spring Street Presbyterian Church, New York, from 1828 to 1837, and for many years pastor of a Presbyterian church at Poughkeepsie. After a bookish boyhood, studying largely at home under his father's guidance, Fitz Hugh Ludlow entered the junior class of the college of New Jersey (1854), but after the burning of Nassau Hall transferred to Union College, where he graduated in 1856. By classmates he is described as brilliant in conversation, genial, generous to a fault, of active physique, with finely chiseled features and most expressive eyes. One of his poems written at Union is still the college song. Before entering college he had become addicted to the narcotic hashish, and in December of his graduation year published "The Apocalypse of Hasheesh" in Putnam's Magazine. Parts of this article were incorporated into a volume, The Hasheesh Eater (1857), his most remarkable work. It was strongly influenced by DeQuincey, but showed original powers of imagination and style. The rest of his life was an almost constant struggle against hashish. He taught a year at Watertown, N. Y., then studied law in New York City under William Curtis Noyes. Though admitted to the bar in 1859, he never practised, and even during his studies was engaged largely in writing. In June 1859 he married Rosalie H. Osborne.

He was subsequently on the staff of the World and the Commercial Advertiser, and in 1861 contributed a serial, "The Primpenny Family," to Vanity Fair, edited by Charles Farrar Browne. During these and the following years he also furnished dramatic, art, and music criticism for the Evening Post and Home Journal, and wrote for Harper's publications; contributing to the Monthly, up to 1870, two poems and twenty

or more tales, clever but hardly memorable; to the Weekly (Jan. 14–Apr. 14, 1860), a continued story, "The New Partner in Clingham and Co., Bankers"; and to Harper's Bazar (May 30–Aug. 22, 1868), "The Household Angel," pronounced by a contemporary "a real work of genius amidst the usually rather vapid temperance literature" (Harper's Bazar, Nov. 12, 1870).

Ludlow and his wife were members of the literary circle of the Bayard Taylors, Stedmans, and Stoddards (Lilian W. Aldrich, Crowding Memories, 1920, p. 18). Stedman wrote of him: "He has talent enough for anything, and a heart as noble as native sunshine can make it" (Life and Letters of Edmund Clarence Stedman, 1910, I, 259). For his health, in 1863, he traveled overland to California, describing his journey in articles for the Atlantic Monthly which were later included in The Heart of the Continent (1870). His "Through-Tickets to San Francisco: A Prophecy," in the Atlantic for November 1864, correctly outlined the route of the first Pacific railway. In the West he met Mark Twain, who speaks appreciatively of Ludlow's favorable criticism. In 1864 he dramatized Cinderella for the New York Sanitary Fair, and coached the child performers. Two of his best stories were included in Little Brother; and Other Genre-Pictures (1867), which was republished in 1881. A vivid and powerful treatise on the effects of opium, "What Shall They Do to be Saved?", was published in Harper's Monthly, August 1867.

Ludlow's first marriage ended unhappily, and in December 1867 he was married again, to Maria O. Milliken, widow of Judge Milliken of Augusta, Me. Accompanied by his wife and his sister, he went to Switzerland, June 1870, in a final effort to recover his health, but died at Geneva in September of that year. His body was brought home to Poughkeepsie a year later for burial. Contemporary memoirs testify to the tragedy of Ludlow's life, in which a brilliant intellect and a character noble in many ways were ruined by a habit that broke down moral and physical strength.

[Article by F. B. Carpenter in N. Y. Mail, Dec. 1871 (clipping); Poughkeepsie News, Jan. 12, 1872; Atlantic Monthly, July 1870; Harper's New Monthly Magazine, Dec. 1870; material collected in the Union College library; L. J. Bragman, "A Minor De Quincey," Medical Journal and Record, Jan. 7, 1925; information from Hugh Sebastian, Esq., Ann Arbor, Mich., whose dissertation, "A Biographical and Critical Study of Fitz Hugh Ludlow," is in the Univ. of Chicago Library.]   A. W.

LUDLOW, GABRIEL GEORGE (Apr. 16, 1736–Feb. 12, 1808), Loyalist and president of

New Brunswick, was descended from Gabriel Ludlow, born at Castle Cary, Somerset County, England, who arrived in New York on Nov. 24, 1694, became a successful merchant, built and owned vessels engaged in the coasting trade, and obtained a royal patent for 4,000 acres on the west bank of the Hudson in what is now Orange County, then known as the Rockland Tappan tract. His son Gabriel married Frances Duncan and became the father of George Duncan Ludlow [q.v.], and of Gabriel George Ludlow. By his second marriage he was the father of Daniel Ludlow [q.v.]. On Sept. 3, 1760, Gabriel George (the subject of this sketch) married Ann Ver Planck and established himself at Hyde Park near Hempstead, Long Island, on an estate of 144 acres, which he valued at two thousand pounds sterling in his claim for damages before the Loyalist commissioners at Saint John in 1787. He was governor of King's College, colonel of militia, and justice of the peace in Queens County. During the Revolution he commanded the third battalion of De Lancey's Long Island brigade of loyal Americans, in which he held a colonel's commission at the close of the war. At various times his battalion was stationed at Brookhaven, Lloyd's Neck, and Flatbush on Long Island. He was included in the act of attainder passed by the legislature of New York on Oct. 22, 1779. His property was confiscated and sold for the benefit of the state.

In 1783, before the evacuation of New York by the British armies, he sailed for England. After a short residence there, he was given a grant of land at Carleton in the newly created province of New Brunswick. The royal instructions to Lieut.-Gov. Thomas Carleton named him a member of the first council of the province. He was sworn in on Nov. 22, 1784, and held the position until his death. He was also a member of the first city council of Saint John, was the first mayor of Saint John from 1785 to 1795, and was the first judge of the Vice-Admiralty Court from 1787 to 1803. After Carleton embarked for England in 1803, as senior member of the council, he administered the government of New Brunswick until his death, under the title of President of His Majesty's Council and Commander-in-Chief of the Province.

[Thomas Moffat Diary and a few letters of Samuel Culper in Lib. of Cong.; *Second Report of the Bureau of Archives for the Province of Ontario,* ed. by Alexander Fraser (2 pts., 1905); *Winslow Papers,* ed. by W. O. Raymond (1901); W. O. Raymond, "Loyalists in Arms," in *New Brunswick Hist. Soc. Colls.* no. 5 (1904) and "A Sketch of the Life and Administration of Gen. Thomas Carleton," *Ibid.,* no. 6 (1905); W. S. Gordon, *Gabriel Ludlow and his Descendants* (1919); Thomas Jones, *Hist. of N. Y. during the Revolutionary War* (2 vols., 1879); J. W. Lawrence, *Foot-Prints*

(1883), pp. 8–12; Henry Onderdonk, *The Annals of Hempstead* (1878); *The Orderly Book of the Three Battalions of Loyalists Commanded by Brig.-Gen. Oliver DeLancey* (1917); *The Judges of New Brunswick,* ed. by A. A. Stockton (1907), esp. p. 3; James Hannay, *Hist. of New Brunswick* (1909), vol. I; Lorenzo Sabine, *Biog. Sketches of the Loyalists* (1864), vol. II, incomplete and inaccurate.]   J. G. V–D.

LUDLOW, GEORGE DUNCAN (1734–Nov. 13, 1808), jurist, was the son of Gabriel and Frances (Duncan) Ludlow. At first an apothecary, he abandoned this venture, retired to his estate near Hempstead, Long Island, adjoining that of his brother Gabriel George Ludlow [q.v.], and studied law, in which profession he met with immediate success. In 1768 he became a member of the governor's council in the colony of New York. The next year, he was named by Governor Colden as one of the four justices of the supreme court of the colony. When, in 1778, the chief justiceship became vacant, he was disappointed at not receiving the vacant post and resigned. In order to appease the angry jurist, whose many friends were influential, the governor gave him the positions of master of rolls and of superintendent of police for Long Island, which together were of much greater pecuniary value than the chief justiceship. Like his brother Gabriel George Ludlow and his half-brother Daniel Ludlow [q.v.], he was a Loyalist during the Revolutionary troubles. He signed the address to General Howe upon his occupation of New York City and supported the administration of Gov. James Robertson. He barely escaped from the colonials who broke into his house and, in 1779, was attainted by the New York legislature and lost all his property by confiscation. On June 19, 1783, he sailed for England.

He was appointed by the Crown as the first chief justice of the new province of New Brunswick and became a member of the governor's council. He took his oath of office in the fall of 1784 and continued on the supreme bench until his death. He was not popular with all classes. James Glenie, a radical reformer elected to the lower house in 1791, described him as "the ignorant, strutting Chief Justice" (Hannay, *post,* I, 213). A disagreement of the court in a slave case of 1800 was anything but satisfactory. The chief justice believed that, as there was nothing contrary to slavery in the laws of the province, slaves might be held, and one other judge concurred. The remaining two judges held that as slaves could not be owned in England, slavery could have no legal existence in New Brunswick. Although his opinion was sustained by the King in council, he received much abuse for his decision of 1805 that there were no exclusive private fishing rights in navigable waters. In March 1808 he suffered a paralytic stroke, and he died at "Spring Hill," his estate of 1500 acres near Fredericton. He was survived by his widow Frances (Duncan) Ludlow, his cousin, whom he had married on Apr. 22, 1758, and by a son and two daughters.

[*The Judges of New Brunswick,* ed. by A. A. Stockton (1907); W. S. Gordon, *Gabriel Ludlow and his Descendants* (1919); W. O. Raymond, "Loyalists in Arms," *New Brunswick Hist. Soc. Colls.,* no. 5 (1904) and "A Sketch of the Life and Administration of Gen. Thomas Carleton," *Ibid.,* no. 6 (1905); Thomas Jones, *Hist. of N. Y. during the Revolutionary War* (2 vols., 1879); James Hannay, *Hist. of New Brunswick* (1909), vol. I; *Winslow Papers,* ed. by W. O. Raymond (1901); "Colden Papers," *N. Y. Hist. Soc. Colls.,* vol. X (1877); *New York during the American Revolution . . . from the MSS. now in the Possession of the Mercantile Lib. Asso. of New York City* (1861); Lorenzo Sabine, *Biog. Sketches of the Loyalists* (1864), vol. II, incomplete and inaccurate.]   J. G. V–D.

LUDLOW, NOAH MILLER (July 3, 1795–Jan. 9, 1886), actor, theatrical manager, author, was born in New York City, the son of John and Phebe (Dunham) Ludlow, and a descendant of Gabriel Ludlow who emigrated to New York in 1694. At an early age the boy was placed in a mercantile house. During the summer of 1813, after the death of his father, he went to live at his brother's home in Albany. He was irresistibly attracted to the stage and in Albany he became acquainted with some actors and was soon playing small parts. In the spring of 1815 he was engaged as a member of Samuel Drake's company, who were to travel to Kentucky, giving performances at towns along the way. By the middle of August 1815, they had reached Pittsburgh where they played until about the middle of November. Traveling by flat-boat down the Ohio River from Pittsburgh to what is now Maysville, Ky., thence by wagon, they arrived at Frankfort, after many thrilling experiences, and opened their season there in early December. After a barn-storming tour through Kentucky to Nashville, Tenn., Ludlow married there on Sept. 1, 1817, Mary (Maury) Squires (or Squire). He had left the Drake company in June of that year and had formed a partnership with two fellow actors. They took with them such members of their troupe as cared to go, and opened in New Orleans on Dec. 24, 1817. These were the first performances given in English in New Orleans by a professional company, according to Ludlow's autobiography.

For several years Ludlow traveled in the South, sometimes managing his own company, but more often acting under the management of others. In many towns in which he appeared, no professional performances had ever been given.

On June 29, 1826, he made his début in New York as Young Wilding in a one-night performance of *The Liar* at the Chatham Theatre. He reappeared in New York at a benefit at the Park Theatre on July 15, 1828, and in the fall of the same year his own company played at the Chatham. After this, he presented his company in Mobile, Louisville, Cincinnati, and St. Louis. In the fall of 1835 he formed a partnership with Sol Smith [*q.v.*] which lasted till 1853. During this partnership, Ludlow assisted in the management of theatres in Mobile, St. Louis, Cincinnati, and New Orleans, where the local stock companies supported as visiting stars at frequent intervals the famous actors of the day. Ludlow himself occasionally found time during this period to act. Some of his best-known parts were Rolando in *The Honeymoon,* Young Marlowe in *She Stoops to Conquer,* Scamper in *The Promissory Note,* and Doctor Pangloss in *The Heir at Law.* From 1853 until his death he lived in retirement in St. Louis, occasionally appearing at benefit performances and engaging in literary work. His book, *Dramatic Life as I Found It* (1880), is well known. He also compiled *A Genealogical History of the Ludlow Family* (1884) and wrote a "sketch or tale," "Manatua, or the Spirit of the Glen." As a player he is said to have been "unquestionably a general actor of considerable merit" (Ireland, *post,* p. 614). As a manager, with his partner, Sol Smith, he blazed the trail of the drama in what was then almost a wilderness.

[In addition to Ludlow's books mentioned in the text, see: W. G. B. Carson, *The Theatre on the Frontier* (1932); J. N. Ireland, *Records of the N. Y. Stage,* vol. I (1866); Mary C. Crawford, *Romance of the Am. Theatre* (1925); G. C. D. Odell, *Annals of the N. Y. Stage,* vol. III (1928); *Daily Picayune* (New Orleans), Dec. 3–10, 1846; *Mo. Republican* (St. Louis) and *St. Louis Globe-Democrat,* Jan. 10, 1886. The name of Ludlow's wife is spelled differently in the *Dramatic Life* and the genealogy.]   L. H. F.

LUDLOW, ROGER (fl. 1590–1664), colonial lawmaker, was baptized at Dinton, Wiltshire, England, Mar. 7, 1590, the son of Thomas and Jane (Pyle) Ludlow. The family, which was typical of the west country gentry, had first risen to prominence under Henry VIII. Of Roger's early life we know little beyond that he entered Balliol College, Oxford, in 1610, and two years later was admitted to the Inner Temple for the study of law. At the meeting of the General Court of the Massachusetts Bay Company held in London, Feb. 10, 1630, he was elected an Assistant of the company; and on Mar. 20 sailed from Plymouth on the *Mary and John,* known as "Mr. Ludlow's ship," arriving at Massachusetts Bay on May 30, where he became one of the founders of Dorchester and took an active part in the early government of the colony. In 1634 he was elected deputy-governor. The following year he threw in his lot with the colonists who were making settlements along the Connecticut River, and at Windsor, on Apr. 26, 1636, presided, under a commission from Massachusetts, over the first court held in Connecticut. He is credited with having drafted the Fundamental Orders adopted by the colony in January 1638/39 which, embodied with some additions and changes in the Charter of 1662, remained the basis of Connecticut government until 1818. In 1646 the General Court requested him "to take some paynes in drawing forth a body of Lawes for the gouernment of this Comõn welth"; the result was "Ludlow's Code" or "The Code of 1650," the first gathering together and codification of the Connecticut laws which had been enacted previous to that date.

Meanwhile, as a direct result of the Pequot war, and probably as part of a well-planned policy of expansion against the Dutch, Ludlow had, in 1639, planted a settlement at Fairfield, whither he removed and from which town he was annually elected for the next fifteen years either as magistrate or deputy-governor, and during the years 1651–53 as commissioner of the United Colonies of New England. In 1654, owing either to irritation at the refusal of the colonies to back up his proposed expedition against the Dutch at Manhattan or because of a tempting offer from the Cromwellian government for his services at home, he suddenly returned to England, and in the autumn of that year we find him in Dublin as a member of a distinguished commission for the hearing and determination of claims in and to forfeited lands in Ireland, which was then undergoing the rigors of the Cromwellian Settlement. This office, together with others of high honor, he held until the collapse of the Commonwealth in 1660. That he continued to reside in Dublin until 1664 (when he was seventy-four years of age) is evident from various documents. When or where he died is not known. His wife, Mary Ludlow, died in Dublin in 1664.

That Ludlow was of quick temper and blunt speech is amply attested; that these qualities seriously affected his career may be doubted—despite the statements of those early biographers who knew nothing of his life subsequent to 1654. That he was honest, capable, and public-spirited to a high degree is obvious from the esteem in which he was held by his contemporaries. His return to England may be interpreted in the same light as that of the Mathers and many an-

other who, from 1642 to 1659, left America to serve the Commonwealth in England, coming back later to reap fame in America; only Ludlow did his great work before he left and he did not, so far as is known, return.

[See H. F. Waters, *Geneal. Gleanings in England* (2 vols., 1901); J. M. Taylor, *Roger Ludlow, the Colonial Lawmaker* (1900); Elizabeth H. Schenck, *The Hist. of Fairfield*, vol. I (1889); R. C. Winthrop, *Life and Letters of John Winthrop* (2 vols., 1864–67); John Winthrop, *The Hist. of New England* (2 vols., 1853), ed. by Jas. Savage; H. R. Stiles, *The Hist. and Geneals. of Ancient Windsor, Conn.* (rev. ed., 1892); N. B. Shurtleff, *Records of the Gov. and Company of the Mass. Bay* (5 vols., 1853–54); Robt. Dunlop, *Ireland Under the Commonwealth* (2 vols., 1913); Jos. Foster, *Alumni Oxoniensis*, Early Series; C. H. Firth, *The Memoirs of Edmund Ludlow* (2 vols., 1894); J. H. Trumbull, *The Pub. Records of the Colony of Conn.*, vol. I (1850); W. A. Beers, "Roger Ludlowe," *Mag. of Am. Hist.*, Apr. 1882. In Taylor, *op. cit.*, Ludlow's signature appears with a final *e*, but this sketch has followed the spelling more commonly used.]   R. V. C.

LUDLOW, THOMAS WILLIAM (June 14, 1795–July 17, 1878), lawyer and financier, was born in New York City, the second son of Thomas Ludlow, a well-known architect. Both his father and his mother (Mary Ludlow, a first cousin of her husband) were members of an old and prosperous New York family, whose founder, Gabriel Ludlow, had emigrated to the city in 1694 from Somerset, England. The family was strongly Episcopalian, and Thomas William was a faithful and generous supporter of his church throughout his life. A precocious boy, at the age of sixteen he graduated in the class of 1811 from Columbia College, of which he was later trustee (1833–36). Thereafter, he studied law in the office of Martin Wilkins, a leader of the bar of that day, a study interrupted by a short service in the New York militia during the War of 1812. Quite as important in the formation of his character and his mind was his constant association at home and among family friends with the best that the city offered socially and intellectually. He early acquired a taste for archeology and became an enthusiastic numismatist.

Ludlow devoted himself to the general practice of law for but a short time. He soon became counsel for a number of wealthy corporations, among others the important Dutch banking house of Crommelin & Company, whose American representative he was. This work, the settlement of many large estates, and the management of his own extensive property filled all his time. His legal activities were increasingly subordinated to his operations as a financier. One of his earliest enterprises was the promotion of the New York Life Insurance and Trust Company, of which he was a trustee from its organization (1830) until his death. For long years he was a member of its committee on investments and in later life was one of its vice-presidents. He was also a founder of the New York Life Insurance Company (1845). For some years he was a trustee and, at the time of his death, vice-president of the National City Bank of New York. Like many other financiers of his day he took a lively interest in the development of railroads as promising fields for the investment of capital. In 1849 he helped to incorporate and to finance the Panama Railroad Company; he became its first president and was for some years one of its directors. Before it was completed he and two of his associates in the enterprise, J. W. Alsop and William H. Aspinwall [q.v.], shared with others in the promotion of the Illinois Central Railroad. He was also connected at an early date with the Harlem Railroad. His interest in all these enterprises appears to have been limited to their financial operations.

Aristocrat that he was, Ludlow was none the less a Jacksonian Democrat. Though on intimate terms with the leaders of his party, he refused to share in the conflicts of the political arena. He declined all political offices but, when his friend, President Van Buren, needed an able and trustworthy representative to place treasury notes in Europe during the depression of 1837–39, Ludlow cheerfully accepted the commission, which he carried out successfully. To the majority of New Yorkers of the ante-bellum period he was quite as much a social leader as a financier. His urbanity and charm, his high family connections, and his wealth placed him in the highest rank of New York society. In the pages of Philip Hone one frequently sees him dining with the élite of the city and on occasions entertaining admirably at his country home near Yonkers. His wife, Frances W. Morris, whom he married in 1828, died ten years before him. They had no children but adopted a son who was a namesake and distant relative of Ludlow. He died at Yonkers.

[A manuscript sketch of his life by W. S. Gordon has apparently served as a basis for later accounts, especially that which appears in W. K. Ackerman, *Hist. Sketch of the Ill. Central Railroad* (1890); see also *The Diary of Philip Hone* (1889), ed. by Bayard Tuckerman; *N. Y. Tribune*, July 19, 1878.]   P. D. E.

LUDLOW, WILLIAM (Nov. 27, 1843–Aug. 30, 1901), soldier, engineer, was the son of Gen. William Handy Ludlow, who distinguished himself in the Civil War, and Frances Louise Nicoll, of Islip, Long Island, a descendant of the royal secretary of New York after its transfer from the Dutch. Born at Islip on the original Nicoll

patent, the second child of a family of six children, William Ludlow received his early education at Burlington Academy, New Jersey, and the University of the City of New York (later New York University). In 1860 he entered the Military Academy at West Point, from which he graduated four years later. Plunged into the Civil War as chief engineer, XX Army Corps, he won the brevet of captain for gallant services in the battle of Peach Tree Creek, July 20, 1864. After participation in the siege and capture of Atlanta, and in General Sherman's campaigns, he was brevetted major, Dec. 21, 1864, for meritorious services in the Georgia campaign, and lieutenant-colonel, Mar. 13, 1865, for services in the Carolinas—a brilliant record for an officer less than a year out of the Military Academy. He was commissioned captain of engineers, Mar. 7, 1867, and became assistant to the chief of engineers until Nov. 10, 1872. During these years he was stationed at Staten Island and Charleston, S. C. From 1872 until May 1876 he served as chief engineer, Department of Dakota. During this period he made valuable surveys of the Yellowstone National Park (1873 and 1875), and of the Black Hills country (1874). His prophecy (report of Mar. 1, 1876) that the National Park would some day be thronged with visitors from all parts of the world has approached fulfilment.

Ludlow was on duty in Philadelphia from 1876 to 1882 in connection with river and harbor work, then served as engineer secretary of the Light House Board at Washington until March 1883, and was chief engineer of the Philadelphia water department from 1883 to 1886. In the last-named duty he reorganized and rejuvenated the city water system, which had fallen into a deplorable state of inefficiency. He was promoted major of engineers, June 30, 1882. On Apr. 1, 1886, he was appointed by the President engineer commissioner of the District of Columbia and was responsible for many improvements in the capital city. He was on several engineering duties from 1883 to 1893 and was military attaché at London from 1893 to 1896. He made a thorough inspection of the deep-water canals of Suez, Kiel, Corinth, and of those in Holland, and served from April to November 1895 as chairman of the Nicaragua Canal Board. He was promoted lieutenant-colonel of engineers, Aug. 13, 1895, and on Feb. 23, 1897, was placed in charge of river and harbor improvements in New York Harbor. His recommendations that the East River channel be deepened have since been carried out.

With the outbreak of war with Spain, Ludlow

was appointed brigadier-general of volunteers, May 4, 1898, accompanied Shafter's V Corps to Santiago-de-Cuba, and commanded the 1st Brigade in the attack on El Caney and in the subsequent investment of the city of Santiago. For meritorious services in this campaign he received written commendation from both Generals Shafter and Lawton (official reports, War Department). On Sept. 7, 1898, he was commissioned major-general of volunteers, and on Dec. 13, following, was made military governor of Havana. On Jan. 21, 1900, he was commissioned brigadier-general in the regular army. In discontinuing the Department of Havana, May 1, 1900, the secretary of war expressed high appreciation of Ludlow's services while governor, in the maintenance of order, the administration of the city government, and in greatly improved sanitary conditions in Havana. Early in 1900, he became president of the Army War College Board, and during the summer of that year, inspected the French and German military systems and methods of training. This duty completed, he was ordered, April–May 1901, to active duty in the Philippines, then in a state of insurrection; was on sick leave of absence until Aug. 30 of that year; and on that date, his constitution weakened by arduous labor, much of it in the tropics, he died at his daughter's home, Convent Station, N. J. In the year 1866 Ludlow had been married to Genevieve Almira Sprigg, of St. Louis, who with a daughter and two grandsons survived him. He was interred at Islip with military honors, from Trinity Church, New York; later his ashes were removed to Arlington Cemetery. A brave soldier, he achieved notable success as engineer, governor, and commander.

[For biographical data see G. W. Cullum, *Biog. Reg. . . . U. S. Mil. Acad.*, vols. III (1891), IV (1901), and V (1910); sketch by W. M. Black in *Thirty-third Ann. Reunion, Asso. Grads. U. S. Mil. Acad.* (1902); E. H. Nicoll, *The Descendants of John Nicoll of Islip, England* (1894); *N. Y. Times*, Aug. 31, 1901. The librarian of the U. S. Mil. Acad. has compiled a complete bibliography of Ludlow's writings which includes the reports of his western surveys and his reports as military governor of Havana.]   C. D. R.

LUDLOWE, ROGER [See LUDLOW, ROGER, fl. 1590–1664].

LUDWELL, PHILIP (fl. 1660–1704), colonial governor of Carolina, was the son of Thomas and Jane (Cottington) Ludwell, of Bruton, Somerset, England. According to Bishop Meade (*post*), he belonged to "an old and honorable family . . . the original of them many ages since coming from Germany." He emigrated to Virginia about 1660, acquired two estates, "Rich Neck" and "Green Spring," in James City Coun-

ty, and gave Bruton Parish its name. After serving as deputy for his brother, Thomas, who was secretary of the colony, he was made a member of the Governor's Council in March 1674/75. Later he held the office of secretary for a short time. During Sir William Berkeley's administration as governor, Ludwell was one of those who petitioned for the pardon of Nathaniel Bacon [*q.v.*], leader of the popular uprising known as Bacon's Rebellion, but when the disturbances were renewed, Ludwell espoused the cause of Berkeley and went with twenty-six armed men who captured Giles Bland and others implicated in the revolt. Because of his activities in this connection he was considered "rash and fiery" by the Lords of Trade and Plantations and deprived of his seat in the Council in 1679, but was reinstated the following year. In 1686–87 he led the resistance to levies made by the corrupt and unpopular governor, Lord Howard of Effingham. In consequence, charged with having "rudely and boldly disputed the King's authority," he was suspended from the Council and then dismissed. Though elected to the House of Burgesses in 1688, as a suspended councillor he was not permitted to take his seat. The following year he was sent to England to present the Burgesses' charges against Howard, and obtained a series of instructions to the governor which were favorable to the colony.

On Dec. 5, 1689, the Lords Proprietors of the Province of Carolina elected Ludwell "Governor of that part of our province . . . that lyes North and East of Cape Feare" (*Records,* I, 362). His commission gave him power to appoint a deputy governor; and he appointed two in succession, Thomas Jarvis and John Harvey, himself spending most of his time in Virginia. His immediate predecessor in office, Seth Sothell, had been guilty of every manner of abuse, public and private, but, although he was instructed to inquire into these abuses, Ludwell seems to have given little time to such investigation. On Nov. 2, 1691, his commission was altered to make him governor of the entire province of Carolina, and in 1692 he was given the hereditary title of cacique. While Ludwell was governor, Col. John Gibbs (said to be a cousin of the Duke of Albemarle) put forth a proclamation claiming the governorship and denouncing the incumbent as a "Rascal, imposter & usurp^r" and offering to do battle personally "as long as my Eye-lidds shall wagg" in any part of the King's Dominions, with "any of the boldest Heroe [*sic*] living in this or the next County" who should uphold Ludwell's title (*Records,* I, 363). Little attention was paid to the verbal vaporings of Gibbs; but when he seized two magistrates who were holding court, the Carolina colonists chased him back to Virginia.

According to F. L. Hawks, the historian of North Carolina, "Ludwell understood the character and prejudices of the people thoroughly; and, as he was possessed of good sense and proper feeling, he had address enough, by harmlessly humoring their prejudices, gradually to restore a state of comparative peace, without the surrender of any important principle" (*post*, II, 494). In 1694, however, the Proprietors recalled his commission, and he ultimately returned to England. He was twice married: first to Lucy Higginson, relict of Maj. Lewis Burwell and of Col. William Bernard, and second, to the widow of Governor Berkeley (Frances Culpeper), whose first husband, Samuel Stephens, had been governor of Albemarle in Carolina. Among the descendants of Philip Ludwell by his first marriage was Hannah Ludwell who married Thomas Lee and became the mother of Richard Henry, Francis Lightfoot, Arthur, and William Lee [*qq.v.*]. Ludwell died in England sometime after 1704, possibly after 1707. He was buried at Stratford-le-Bow.

[H. R. McIlwaine, *Minutes of the Council and Gen. Court of Colonial Va.* (1924); *Journals of the House of Burgesses of Va., 1659/60–1693* (1914); *The Colonial Records of N. C.*, vol. I (1886), ed. by W. L. Saunders; *Calendar of State Papers, Col. Ser., America and West Indies, 1677–80* (1896) and *1685–88* (1899); William Meade, *Old Churches, Ministers, and Families of Va.* (1857), II, 138–39; F. L. Hawks, *Hist. of N. C.*, II (1858), 492–95; Edward McCrady, *The Hist. of S. C. under the Proprietary Govt.* (1897); S. A. Ashe, *Hist. of N. C.* (1908), vol. I; *Va. Mag. of Hist. and Biog.*, Oct. 1893; E. J. Lee, *Lee of Va.* (1895).]

M. DeL. H.

LUDWICK, CHRISTOPHER (Oct. 17, 1720–June 17, 1801), superintendent of bakers in the Continental Army, philanthropist, was born at Giessen, in Hesse, formerly Hesse-Darmstadt, Germany, and was taught the trade of baker by his father. When he was fourteen he was sent to a free school and given the rudiments of an education. Being naturally of an adventurous disposition, at seventeen he enlisted as a soldier, fought against the Turks (1737 to 1740), and later took part in the seventeen weeks' siege of Prague. After the surrender, in 1741, he enlisted in the army of the King of Prussia, and shortly afterward, peace having been declared, was discharged and went to London. There he signed up as baker on an East Indiaman, and after three and a half years spent in India, returned to London in 1745. He visited his native town, where he learned that his father had died and left him his entire estate. It consisted principally of a freehold, which young

Ludwick converted into money—five hundred guilders. Back to London he hastened, his pockets filled; and when he reached his last shilling, once more he went to sea, this time as a common sailor. For the succeeding seven years (1745–52), he made voyages to the West Indies and to European ports. Desiring to quit the sea, he invested £25 in ready-made English clothing and in 1753 embarked for Philadelphia. Having sold the clothing there for four times its cost, he went back to London, where he spent nine months learning to bake gingerbread and make confectionery.

The following year he returned to Philadelphia, taking with him implements for the bakery which he soon started in Laetitia Court of that city. In 1755 he married Mrs. Catharine England, a widow. His business prospered, and he became a respected figure in the neighborhood, being alluded to as "The Governor of Laetitia Court." Frugal as well as industrious, at the time of the Revolution he was the possessor of nine houses, a farm in Germantown, and £3,500, Pennsylvania currency, at interest. He actively supported the war, on one occasion subscribing £200 for firearms, and in the summer of 1776 volunteering in the flying camp and refusing to draw either pay or rations. Upon his request, Congress gave him permission to visit the Hessian camp on Staten Island, disguised as a deserter. Once among the mercenaries, he reminded them that they were slaves, and invited them to follow him to Philadelphia, where they could live in comfort and in freedom. Hundreds of desertions followed, and the deserters were placed in Ludwick's charge by Congress, which voted him money for the purpose. His loyalty, integrity, and business ability were so highly regarded that on May 3, 1777, Congress, by a resolution, appointed him superintendent of bakers and director of baking in the Continental Army. He was everywhere known in the army and was permitted almost as much freedom as the Commander-in-Chief himself. Washington was very fond of him, addressed him as "old gentleman," and called him "my honest friend." He was frequently in private conference with Washington and often dined with him when large companies were present. He was always referred to as the Baker General, and was familiarly called "General," although his title was superintendent.

When the war was ended, Ludwick returned to find that his home in Germantown had been plundered by the British, and that he had scarcely any ready cash; but he would neither borrow money nor buy on credit. In 1785 Washington wrote what might be termed a certificate of character for him, attesting his patriotism and other virtues. His first wife died in 1795, and in 1798 he married Mrs. Sophia Binder. His private donations were large for one of his means. During the yellow-fever epidemic in Philadelphia, in 1797, he volunteered his services to bake bread for the stricken. In addition to bequeathing substantial sums to churches and various charities in Philadelphia, he left the residue of his estate to his executors to be used in providing free education for poor children; the entire fund to be given to such free schools as should be established before the lapse of five years after his death. He was buried in the yard of Trinity Lutheran Church, Germantown, Philadelphia.

[Benjamin Rush, *An Account of the Life and Character of Christopher Ludwick* (1831), which originally appeared in *Poulson's Am. Daily Advertiser* (Phila.), June 30, 1801; Henry Simpson, *The Lives of Eminent Philadelphians now Deceased* (1859); *Pa. Archives*, 1 ser. V (1853); J. F. Watson, *Annals of Phila. and Pa. in the Olden Time* (2nd ed., 1844), vol. II; *Jour. of the Continental Cong.*, vols. VII (1907), VIII (1907), X (1908), XIII (1909), XIX (1912); *Papers of the Continental Cong.*, No. 41, V, folios 175 and 230, No. 136, I, folio 113; *Poulson's Am. Daily Advertiser*, June 19, 1801.]   J. J.

LUELLING, HENDERSON (Apr. 23, 1809– Dec. 28, 1878), nurseryman, was born in Randolph County, N. C., of a Welsh family which had been in America for a number of generations. His father was Meshach Luelling, and his mother, whose family name was Brookshire, was of English extraction. Both the parents were Quakers. The elder Luelling was a physician, but combined the practice of his profession with the nursery business. The family moved to Greensboro, Ind., in 1825, and on Dec. 30, 1830, Henderson Luelling was married to Elizabeth Presnell, who had lived near his old home in North Carolina.

In 1837, he and his brother John went to Salem, Iowa, and started a nursery. Here he remained ten years, making numerous journeys to the East in search of the best varieties of fruit for his stock. Accounts of the Lewis and Clark expedition stirred in him a desire to see the Western country, and with the news of the beginnings of settlements in the Willamette Valley of Oregon, he conceived the idea of transporting across the plains by ox-team a small nursery stock, sufficient to start him in business there. He set about preparing for the adventure, and after much discouragement and delay he began the journey Apr. 17, 1847. With him were his wife and eight children, the eldest about thirteen; the youngest, named Oregon Columbia, was born shortly before they started. A friend, William Meek, accompanied the family. The

nursery stock, consisting of 800 to 1,000 young trees and shrubs, was planted in two long boxes, containing about a foot of soil, built to fit a wagon-bed. Racks were constructed about the cargo to prevent the trees being eaten by the cattle. The wagon was drawn by four yoke of oxen.

The journey across the two thousand miles of wilderness was one of hardships and hazards. The party with which the Luellings traveled was a small one, and on one occasion an Indian attack was averted only by the fact that one of the wagons was laden with living trees, which the Indians regarded as under the special care of the Great Spirit. The trees were tended and watered with the utmost care, and about half of the total number ultimately survived. At The Dalles the nursery stock was taken from the boxes, wrapped in bundles and transported down the Columbia by flatboat to a point opposite Fort Vancouver. Here the party remained for some time, while Luelling was seeking a place for his nursery. He chose a point near the present site of Milwaukee, a few miles south of Portland. It was already late in November, but the trees and shrubs were planted as soon as the ground could be cleared for them. They included apples, pears, quinces, plums, cherries, grapes, and the common berry-bushes, and were the first grafted fruit stock that had ever come to the Pacific Coast. The varieties had been selected with the greatest care. Luelling and Meek formed a partnership and the nursery throve. The settlers, of whom there were scarcely more than 5,000 in the whole Oregon country, eagerly purchased every tree offered for sale. In 1850, Seth Luelling, a brother of Henderson, arrived and joined in the enterprise.

A spirit of restlessness, however, increased perhaps by private misfortune, especially the death of his wife and his eldest daughter, who had married William Meek, soon started Luelling on a new venture. In 1854 he moved a part of his nursery stock to a point near Oakland, Cal., and began again. Here he prospered even more than in Oregon, and within five years he had accumulated a considerable fortune. Not content, a new adventure, the nature of which seems not to be recorded, took him, with two of his sons and their families, to Honduras, in a vessel purchased and equipped by himself. This venture ended disastrously, and he returned to California to engage again in the nursery business. He never regained what he had lost, and seems to have lived rather quietly for the remainder of his days, making his home in California. He died in San José, and was interred in Mountain View cemetery, Oakland. He was an uncle of Lorenzo Dow Lewelling [*q.v.*].

[J. R. Cardwell, *Brief Hist. of Early Horticulture in Ore.* (1906), and *Proc. of the Am. Pomological Soc.* (1913); S. A. Clarke, *Pioneer Days of Oregon Hist.* (1905), vol. II; Joseph Gaston, *The Centennial Hist. of Ore.* (1912), vol. I; H. K. Hines, *Illustrated Hist. of the State of Ore.* (1893); *Iowa Jour. of Hist. and Politics*, Oct. 1929; *Oakland Tribune*, Mar. 5, 1916; *Eighth Biennial Report of the Board of Horticulture of the State of Ore.* (1905); *Trans. of the Seventh Ann. Re-Union of the Oregon Pioneer Asso., 1879* (1880); *Trans. Ore. State Horticultural Soc.* (1910); H. W. Scott, *Hist. of Oregon* (1924), vol. III; *The Call* (San Francisco), Dec. 30, 1878.]   M. E. P.

LUFBERY, RAOUL GERVAIS VICTOR (Mar. 21, 1885–May 19, 1918), aviator, greatest American ace in the World War, was born in Clermont, department of Oise, France. His father, Edward, was a United States citizen, born in New York; his mother, Annette Vessières, was French. The latter died when Raoul was young, his father married again and went to the United States, and the child, with two brothers, was brought up by his grandmother. As a youth he worked in a chocolate factory at Blois and in a factory at Clermont-Ferrand. When he was about nineteen he started out to see the world and thereafter lived a roving life. He made his way to Algiers, then visited Tunis, Egypt, Turkey, the Balkans, and Germany, supporting himself by whatever work he was able to secure. In Constantinople he was a waiter in a restaurant; in Hamburg he found employment with a steamship company. In 1906 he appeared in Wallingford, Conn., where his father had established himself, but the latter, his second wife having died, had left his family there and gone to France. For two years Raoul worked in the silver shops of the town, and then set out for new adventures. Cuba was his first destination; later he was a baker in New Orleans and a hotel waiter in San Francisco. In the last-named place he enlisted in the United States Army and was sent to the Philippines. His term of service over, he went to Japan, from there to China, and finally to India, where for a time he was a ticket collector in the Bombay Railroad station. During all his wanderings he had never been more than a week out of work.

In Calcutta he met Marc Pourpe, a French aviator who was giving exhibition flights, and became his mechanic. The two were in France to secure a new machine when the World War began. Pourpe enlisted in the air service and Lufbery in the Foreign Legion, but he was shortly permitted to transfer to aviation and served as Pourpe's mechanic. When the latter was killed, December 1914, Lufbery determined to become a pilot. He was sent to the aviation

school at Chartres and after further training saw service as a pilot in the Voisin Bombardment Squadron 106. On May 24, 1916, having qualified as a *pilote de chasse,* he joined the *Escadrille Lafayette.* Fearless, and handling his plane with superb mastery and ease, he was soon cordially acknowledged by his comrades to be the best of them all. There was no love of the spectacular or heroic in him, only keen zest for flying and simple devotion to his work. "Above all the pilots who found themselves at Verdun," said his commanding officer, Captain Georges Thenault, "was Lufbery 'without fear and without reproach.' . . . His Spad was always the highest and every day he won new victories. He seemed to hardly care about having them confirmed. Calmly he reigned as sovereign lord in his chosen element and beat down his foes to accomplish his duty and not for the sake of glory" (*The Story of the LaFayette Escadrille,* 1921, translated by Walter Duranty, p. 152). While with the Escadrille he was officially credited with seventeen victories, though he undoubtedly brought down twice that number of planes, was awarded the *Croix de Guerre,* the *Médaille Militaire,* and the Military Medal (British), and was promoted to adjutant and decorated with the Legion of Honor.

On Jan. 10, 1918, he was commissioned major in the air service of the United States Army. On Jan. 28, he joined the 95th Aero Squadron, and was relieved a week later to go to the front at Villeneuve (Marne) to prepare the way for the 94th Squadron of the First Pursuit Group. The squadron arrived in March, but because machine guns were lacking could do no fighting. In April it began patrol duty in the Toul sector. On May 19 Lufbery went in pursuit of a German plane which had come over the lines. In the combat which ensued Lufbery's plane burst into flames and he jumped from a height of more than two thousand feet. His body was found in the garden of a house in the little town of Maron and was buried in the American Cemetery, Sebastopol Barracks. On July 4, 1928, it was removed to the Lafayette Escadrille Memorial at Villeneuve, near Paris.

[War Department Records; J. N. Hall and C. B. Nordhoff, *The Lafayette Flying Corps,* vol. I (1920); L. La Tourette Driggs, *Heroes of Aviation* (1918); P. A. Rockwell, *Am. Fighters in the Foreign Legion, 1914–18* (1930); *Hartford Courant,* May 21, 1918; *Hartford Times,* May 20, 1918.]   H. E. S.

LUKENS, REBECCA WEBB PENNOCK (Jan 6, 1794–Dec. 10, 1854), iron manufacturer, was born in Coatesville, Pa., the daughter of Isaac and Martha (Webb) Pennock. Her father was the founder of the Brandywine Rolling

Mill, the first mill in the United States for the manufacture of boiler plate. Rebecca received the education customarily accorded to young ladies of her time and in 1813 was married to Charles Lloyd Lukens, a physician, to whom she bore three children. After the death of her father, her husband assumed the management of the iron works, and when he died in 1825, in fulfilment of his wish she succeeded him as manager, thus becoming the first woman in the United States to engage in the iron industry. Employing a superintendent to direct the works and handle the employees, she herself assumed full control and management of the commercial end of the business. Among the difficulties confronting her was the problem of transportation. Her finished product had to be hauled by teams thirty-eight miles to Philadelphia or twenty-six to Wilmington, while her coal was carried from Columbia, a distance of more than forty miles. Her exceptional ability in marketing her product enabled her to enlarge the business. The boiler plates made in her plant became famous among engineers, and several shipments were made to England, where they were used in the building of some of the earliest locomotives. She died in Coatesville, Pa., leaving the business to be carried on by two sons-in-law, Abraham Gibbons and Dr. Charles Huston [q.v.]. Upon her death the name of the iron works was changed to Lukens Mills in her honor, and in 1890 the business was incorporated as the Lukens Steel Company.

[J. B. Pearse, *A Concise Hist. of the Iron Manufacture of the Am. Colonies up to the Revolution and of Pa. until the Present Time* (1876); J. M. Swank, *Hist. of the Manufacture of Iron in All Ages* (1884); Gilbert Cope and H. G. Ashmead, *Hist. Homes and Institutions and Geneal. and Personal Memoirs of Chester and Delaware Counties, Pa.* (1904), vol. I; G. P. Donehoo, *Pennsylvania: A Hist.* (1926), vol. VIII; J. W. Jordan, *Colonial Families of Phila.* (1911), vol. I; *Lukens Steel Company* (5th ed., 1924), a handbook; *The Friend,* Fourth Month 28, 1855; date of birth supplied from family Bible by C. L. Huston, Esq., Coatesville, Pa.]   J. H. F.

LULL, EDWARD PHELPS (Feb. 20, 1836–Mar. 5, 1887), naval officer, was born at Windsor, Vt., the youngest of the six children of Martin Lull. When Edward was nine his widowed mother moved to Milwaukee, Wis. After a brief schooling, he was apprenticed to learn printing, a calling that he abandoned when on Oct. 7, 1851, he entered the navy, through the favor of a former governor of Wisconsin. On graduating from the Naval Academy in June 1855, he was warranted midshipman and ordered to the *Congress* of the Mediterranean Squadron. In April 1858 he joined the *Colorado;* and later in that year the *Roanoke,* a few months before he was war-

ranted master. His studious habits led to his appointment in September 1860 as assistant professor of ethics and English at Annapolis, to the duties of which position were shortly added those of teacher of fencing, as he was an excellent swordsman. He was promoted lieutenant from Oct. 30, 1860. Desiring active duties he was on May 23, 1861, ordered to the *Roanoke* and on that vessel took part in the engagement at Hatteras Inlet. In September, against his own wishes and at the request of the superintendent of the academy, he returned to that institution as assistant to the commandant of midshipmen in charge of the *Constitution* and later was promoted commandant. On July 16, 1862, he was commissioned lieutenant commander and in June 1863 he took part as commander of the *John Adams* in the search off the Atlantic Coast for the privateer *Tacony.* In December he became executive officer of the *Brooklyn* and in that capacity participated in the battle of Mobile Bay. He remained in active service until the end of the war, commanding the captured ironclad *Tennessee,* the *Seminole* when she was blockading Galveston, and for a time the third division of the Mississippi Squadron.

After a period of service with the *Swatara* of the West India Squadron, Lull from 1866 to 1869 was attached to the Naval Academy, first as an instructor in mathematics, and later in Spanish. Following his promotion to the grade of commander on June 10, 1870, he had a varied experience as an explorer and surveyor. In 1870–71 he was in charge of the *Guard* of the Darien Surveying Expedition. In 1872–73 he commanded the Nicaragua Exploring Expedition and received the thanks of the department for the energetic manner in which he performed a laborious task. After serving on the Interoceanic Ship Canal Commission, and commanding the Panama Surveying Expedition, he was from 1875 to 1880 hydrographic inspector in the Coast and Geodetic Survey and was frequently employed in active surveying duties. When he left the survey he was highly commended by the superintendent. In 1880–81 he commanded the *Wachusett* of the Pacific Squadron and received the thanks of the department for his efficient services. On Oct. 1, 1881, he was promoted captain. In the following year he visited Nicaragua in the interest of the Provisional Interoceanic Canal Society and on his return was made equipment officer of the Boston Navy Yard. His last duty was as commandant of the navy yard at Pensacola.

The results of Lull's survey of Nicaragua were published in 1874 (*Senate Executive Document*

57, 43 Cong., 1 Sess., pp. 33–143) ; and those of his survey of Panama in 1879 (*Senate Executive Document 75*, 45 Cong., 3 Sess., pp. 7–52). He was the author of a *History of the United States Navy-Yard at Gosport, Va.* (1874), and joint-author of *Methods and Results: Table of Depths for Harbors on the Coasts of the United States* (1883). About 1863 Lull was married to Elizabeth F. Burton. His second wife, Emma Gillingham Terry, to whom he was married on Nov. 5, 1873, was a sister of Commodore Edward Terry.

[Record of Officers, Bureau of Navigation, 1846–88 ; H. V. Eddy, *The Lull Book* (1926) ; Stephen Terry, *Notes of Terry Families* (1887) ; *War of the Rebellion: Official Records* (*Navy*), 1 ser. XXI, XXII, XXVII ; *Army and Navy Jour.*, Mar. 12, 1887 ; *N. Y. Tribune*, Mar. 7, 1887 ; information as to certain facts from R. S. Lull.]   C.O.P.

LUMBROZO, JACOB (fl. 1656–1665), physician, planter, and merchant, was born in Lisbon of Portuguese-Jewish ancestry. His family removed from Portugal to Holland during his lifetime and he had a sister in the latter country with whom he corresponded. He emigrated from Holland to Maryland in 1656 and at once began the practice of medicine, being one of the first Jews to settle in that colony, and the first physician to practise there. The court records for 1657 and 1658 show that he obtained judgments for the payment of debts owed to him. In 1658 he had trouble with his fellow colonists on account of his religious views. Charged with blasphemy, he declared that he had only answered from the point of view of a Jew the questions put to him, and had said nothing scoffingly (*Archives of Maryland*, XLI, 203). He was ordered held for the next court. The penalty if he were convicted was death and the confiscation of goods ; but he was released under a general amnesty, proclaimed by Lieut.-Gov. Josias Fendall [*q.v.*] in honor of the proclamation of Richard Cromwell as Protector (*Ibid.*, p. 258). He was not subjected to any further annoyance, because he was recognized as an asset to the colony and probably because the fanatical element among the colonists lost the ascendancy. For the next five years little is known of him. During 1663 he served as a juror and on Sept. 10 of that year letters of denization were issued to him along with certain privileges which allowed him to take up land and become a planter. About this time he married a woman, Elizabeth by name, who had come to the colony in 1662, and who is believed to have been a Christian. He had for some time been engaged in commerce as well as agriculture, is known to have traded extensively with London merchants, and

in 1665 was commissioned to trade with the Indians. After 1663 he signed his name John. He was living as late as Sept. 24, 1665, but died before May 31, 1666. A son, John Lumbrozo, was born posthumously in June. The widow soon remarried and the son may have taken the name of his step-father, for the name Lumbrozo disappears abruptly and permanently from the records of the colony.

[*The Jewish Encyc.*, vol. VIII ; *Pubs. Am. Jewish Hist. Soc.*, no. 1 (1893), no. 2 (1894) ; *Archives of Md.*, vols. II (1885), XLI (1922), XLIX (1932).]   E.P.

LUMMIS, CHARLES FLETCHER (Mar. 1, 1859–Nov. 25, 1928), author, editor, was born at Lynn, Mass., the son of Henry and Harriet (Fowler) Lummis. His early education was received largely at home, his father being a minister and teacher. He studied at Harvard from 1877 to 1881, but did not receive his degree until 1906. From 1882 to 1884 he was editor of the *Scioto Gazette,* at Chillicothe, Ohio. In September of the latter year he started from Cincinnati on a walking trip to Los Angeles "for recreation and observation," arriving at his destination on Feb. 1, 1885, after covering a distance of 3,507 miles. In a cañon in Arizona on this trip he broke his arm but after setting the bone himself and binding it up in a rude sling he continued on his way. The day after his arrival at the end of his journey he entered the employ of the Los Angeles *Times* and served as city editor from 1885 to 1887. Overwork brought on paralysis, and in January 1888, with one arm hanging limp, he went to New Mexico to recuperate and for long periods lived among the Pueblo Indians in their villages, learning their customs, languages, folk lore, and folk songs, much of which material he incorporated later in books of history, fiction, essay, and verse. By 1891 he had recovered fully from his illness. In 1892, associated with Adolph Bandelier [*q.v.*], he took part in a two years' ethnological and historical expedition to Peru and Bolivia. Upon his return to Los Angeles in 1894, he founded and assumed the editorship of *Land of Sunshine,* a magazine devoted to the life and history of the Far West, continued later under the title *Out West.*

The decade of the nineties was a period of productive writing. In 1891 appeared *A New Mexico David* and in the following year *A Tramp Across the Continent,* describing his walking trip of 1884–85. In the same year he published *Some Strange Corners of Our Country.* In 1893 appeared the two books by which he is perhaps most widely known : *The Land of Poco Tiempo,* descriptive of the Southwest and its people, and *The Spanish Pioneers,* a historical account of the conquistadores and priests who played a conspicuous part in the fifteenth and sixteen centuries. Before the end of the century he had published *The Man Who Married the Moon* (1894), Pueblo folk tales; *The Gold Fish of Gran Chimú* (1896); *The King of the Broncos* (1897); *The Enchanted Burro* (1897); and *The Awakening of a Nation: Mexico of Today* (1898). In 1905 he became librarian of the Los Angeles Public Library serving until 1910 and building up in this period a fine collection of Southwest material. In 1911 he was stricken with blindness which was complete for many months but from which he fully recovered. One of his greatest achievements was the founding and building of the Southwest Museum in Los Angeles, an institution fostering the historical, archeological, and ethnological interests of the Southwest. To this work he gave much of his time and energy in his later years. He was the founder of The Landmarks Club and through many years was indefatigable in his efforts to preserve the Spanish missions and other historical relics of California and the neighboring states. He also interested himself in the songs of the Southwest and made phonographic records of more than five hundred early Spanish songs of the region and more than four hundred Indian songs in many languages. *Spanish Songs of Old California* (2 vols., 1823–28) and *Mesa, Cañon and Pueblo* (1925) reflect his ethnological and literary interests in these years.

The early Spanish and Mexican inhabitants and the native population of the region provide the personal content of most of Lummis' literary products. But he occasionally wrote on other phases of life, as for example *My Friend Will* (1911) which is a stimulating account of the psychological battle which he fought against paralysis and of his subsequent recovery. His first book was a collection of verses published in 1879 on real bark, bearing the title *Birch Bark Poems,* and the last book which appeared in his lifetime was a poetical volume entitled *A Broncho Pegasus* (1928). *Flowers of Our Lost Romance* was accepted by the publishers before his death but did not appear until 1929. His style was stirring and colorful, full of imagery and original and well-turned phrases. Although a pioneer in the study of the Southwest, he was a journalist rather than a scholar and he was more successful in his prose descriptions of strange people and places than he was in the field of verse or in that of history or archeology. Without doubt his greatest contribution was the service

he rendered in arousing interest in the non-American inhabitants and the half-known regions of the Southwest by his writings and lectures and by his organization and development of the Southwest Museum. He was married three times; to Mary Dorothea Roads, Apr. 16, 1880, to Eva Douglas, Mar. 27, 1891, and to Gertrude Redit, May 9, 1915.

[The main facts of his life are outlined by Lummis in *Who's Who in America,* and in a biographical record filled out and filed at the Los Angeles Public Library. Further autobiographical material is to be found in his writings. See also: Ben Field, article in *Overland Monthly and Out West Mag.,* July 1929; *Nation,* Dec. 12, 1928; *Harvard Coll. Class of 1881: Fiftieth Anniversary* (1931); *Harvard Grads.' Mag.,* Mar. 1929; Los Angeles *Times,* Nov. 26, 1928.]   J. C. P.

LUMPKIN, JOSEPH HENRY (Dec. 23, 1799–June 4, 1867), first chief justice of the supreme court of Georgia, was born on a plantation in Oglethorpe County, Ga., the seventh son of John and Lucy (Hopson) Lumpkin. His parents were among the numerous Virginians who had gone to middle Georgia immediately after the Revolutionary War. John Lumpkin prospered and had numerous progeny. His second son, Wilson Lumpkin [q.v.], became governor of Georgia. In his formative years Joseph had access to what was regarded as an unusual library and was thrown with the foremost men of the state, who were his father's frequent guests. At fifteen he entered Franklin College (later the University of Georgia) and when that institution was temporarily closed he went to the College of New Jersey, where he was graduated with honors in 1819. Returning to Georgia he studied law in the office of Thomas W. Cobb and upon his admission to the bar in 1820, entered the practice at Lexington, later moving to Athens where he made his home for the rest of his life. In February 1821 he was married to Callender C. Greve, a native of Edinburgh, Scotland. Many of his descendants attained prominence; two, Samuel and Joseph Henry Lumpkin II, became justices of the supreme court over which their grandfather was the first to preside.

Lumpkin was a successful practitioner from the beginning. His arguments were well reasoned and reflected scholarship and wide reading, but his forte was eloquence. His impressive figure, handsome features, and the resonant qualities of his clear and melodious voice added no little to the effectiveness of his utterances. He never sought public office and, with the exception of serving two terms in the state legislature (1824 and 1825) and assisting in framing the Georgia Penal Code in 1833, devoted his time to his profession until called to the bench. In 1844, his health having become somewhat impaired, he took a year's vacation in Europe. During his absence the General Assembly, heeding at last the constitutional mandate of 1835, passed the legislation necessary to establish a supreme court. Lumpkin was unanimously elected one of the justices, and his associates—Hiram Warner and Eugenius A. Nisbet—made him their chief. He presided over the court for more than a score of years and died in office. Soon after he was made chief justice a school of law was added to the University of Georgia and given his name. Here he lectured until the outbreak of the Civil War. He gave much thought to social and economic problems and in 1852 published a treatise, *The Industrial Regeneration of the South,* in which he urged the encouragement of manufacturing, primarily to give employment to the "poor whites" whose condition he deplored. (See *The South in the Building of the Nation,* vol. VII, 1909, p. 179.) In 1860 he was elected chancellor of the University of Georgia but declined to serve. He had also declined, a few years before, a position on the federal court of claims tendered him by President Pierce.

The task which confronted the first chief justice and his associates was made difficult by the fact that for more than seventy years the people of Georgia had tenaciously clung to a system of jurisprudence unique in English-speaking countries. Each judge of the superior (circuit) courts, bound neither by the decisions of his predecessors or his colleagues—and not always by his own—was the final arbiter of all litigation in his circuit. The people were not only satisfied with this form of judicature, they were aggressively antagonistic to courts of review that lived by correcting the errors of others and adhering to their own. Therefore, for the supreme court to survive, its judges were under the necessity not only of promulgating principles that would harmonize and make uniform the administration of law throughout the commonwealth; they also had to pronounce judgments the inherent justice of which would be apparent. That the first justices met these requirements to the satisfaction of the people is attested by an act of the legislature of 1858 which declared the decisions of the supreme court to be the law of the state having the same force and effect as acts of the General Assembly. Lumpkin had strong convictions against the tendency of courts to permit technical rules of practice to defeat justice. The scientific application of legal principles meant less to him than deciding a case on its merits. Nevertheless, a number of his decisions became widely followed precedents. His opinions were delivered orally and delighted his hearers. Many of

them as later—sometimes carelessly and hastily —reduced to writing are worthy of his reputation. But a large proportion of the more than two thousand that bear his name, in the judgment of so competent a critic as Chief Justice Bleckley, "afford no just ideal of his wonderful gifts. . . . Those who never saw and heard him cannot be made to realize what a great master he was."

[See memorial in 36 *Ga. Reports,* 1–42; sketch by Bernard Suttler in W. J. Northen, *Men of Mark in Ga.,* vol. II (1910); J. R. Lamar, "Hist. of the Establishment of the Supreme Court of Ga.," *Report of the Twenty-Fourth Ann. Session of the Ga. Bar Asso.* (1907); Walter McElreath, *A Treatise on the Constitution of Ga.* (1912); L. L. Cody, *The Lumpkin Family of Ga.* (1928); *Daily Intelligencer* (Atlanta, Ga.), June 6, 1867. Lumpkin's opinions are contained in volumes 1–35 *Ga. Reports.*]   B.F.

LUMPKIN, WILSON (Jan. 14, 1783–Dec. 28, 1870), Georgia statesman, son of John and Lucy (Hopson) Lumpkin, was born in Pittsylvania County, Va., second of eleven children. In 1784 when Wilson was an infant, the family moved to the Georgia frontier, where they became pioneers on Long Creek, in what became Oglethorpe County. Wilson was educated in the common schools of the county. He supplemented this scanty education by wide reading in history and public law during five years (1799–1804) while he assisted his father as clerk of superior court, worked on the farm, taught school, and studied law. In 1804, at the age of twenty-one, he was admitted to the bar and began practice at Athens, Ga. In the same year he was elected to the lower house of the Georgia legislature, where he served for the greater part of the next ten years. In 1814 he was elected to Congress but was defeated for reëlection in 1816. He then took up residence in Morgan County, west of Oglethorpe, where he intended to farm, but in the same year (1818) he was appointed a commissioner to run the lines of lands recently ceded by the Creek Indians to the state of Georgia. He began at this time that long and intimate connection with Indian problems in Georgia, in which field he rendered his most distinctive service. In 1819 he again went to the legislature, but he retired in 1821 to accept another appointment as Indian commissioner.

He was elected to Congress in 1826, serving through two terms (1827–31). Although reëlected for a third term in 1831, he resigned from Congress to run for the governorship and was successful. At this time the chief public question in Georgia was the removal of the Creek and Cherokee Indians from the state. In Congress, Lumpkin supported the vigorous governors, George M. Troup and John Forsyth, in their controversies with the federal government over Indian removals. As governor of Georgia for two terms (1831–35) Lumpkin was chiefly preoccupied with the problem of removing the Cherokees, settled by favorable treaty in 1835. In handling the Cherokee situation he maintained the vigorous state-rights attitude of his predecessors. In 1836 he was appointed Cherokee commissioner and was serving in this capacity when elected in November 1837 to fill the unexpired term of John P. King in the United States Senate. Retiring from the Senate in 1841 he devoted two years to the task of rehabilitating the affairs of the state railroad, the Western & Atlantic, then under construction, in which he had long taken interest. The southern terminus of this road (now Atlanta) was for a time called Marthasville, in honor of Governor Lumpkin's daughter. In 1843 he retired to his plantation, where he continued for years to exercise large public influence through his correspondence and friends. In the developing sectional controversy, 1845–60, he maintained extreme state-rights views. When secession came, his advanced age precluded participation in public affairs, but his sympathies were with secession and the Southern Confederacy. He died at Athens, Ga., in his eighty-eighth year. He had married, on Nov. 20, 1800, Elizabeth Walker, who bore him five sons and three daughters. She died in 1819 and on Jan. 1, 1821, he was married to Annis Hopkins, by whom he had four children. The Lumpkin family was distinguished for its jurists, among them being the brother of Wilson, Joseph Henry Lumpkin [q.v.], chief justice of the supreme court of Georgia.

[Lumpkin left a voluminous manuscript captioned "The Removal of the Cherokee Indians from Georgia," but in effect an autobiography, containing letters, speeches, and public papers, covering his entire career. In 1907 this was privately printed in 2 vols. by Wymberly De Renne. Other sources include: G. G. Smith, *The Story of Ga. People: 1732–1860* (1900); R. H. Shryock, *Ga. and the Union in 1850* (1926); J. F. Jameson, "Correspondence of John C. Calhoun," *Ann. Report of the Am. Hist. Asso. for the Year 1899* (1900), vol. II; U. B. Phillips, "Ga. and State Rights," *Ann. Report of the Am. Hist. Asso. for the Year 1901* (1902), vol. II; L. L. Cody, *The Lumpkin Family of Ga.* (1928); W. J. Northen, *Men of Mark in Ga.*, vol. II (1910).]   H. J. P., Jr.

LUNA Y ARELLANO, TRISTAN de (fl. 1530–1561), Spanish explorer, son of Don Carlos de Luna y Arellano, came from Castile to New Spain in 1530 or 1531 and served as captain and *maestre de campo* under Francisco Coronado on his New Mexico expedition, accompanying that leader on part of his Quivira journey. In 1548 he suppressed for viceroy Mendoza a dangerous Indian outbreak in Oaxaca. His wife was Isabel de Rojas, widow successive-ly of Juan Velázquez and Francisco Maldonado, "first conquerors." Their *encomiendas* were inherited by her children, and Luna hypothecated the properties to finance his Florida expedition. In December 1557 Philip II, fearful that the French would advance from their holdings in Newfoundland into his northern frontier, revoked previous orders forbidding the conquest of Florida and commanded its occupation. The viceroy, Luis de Velasco, chose his friend Luna as governor and captain-general of Florida and the Punta de Santa Elena (Port Royal). The task was to select a base on the Gulf, advance to an intermediate province, Coosa in Alabama, and thence press on and fortify the Punta to protect the north coast, assure the Bahama Channel freedom from pirates, and serve as a mission center from which to proselyte among the Indians.

The expedition, costing 300,000 *pesos* of the King's money and all Luna's fortune, comprised 500 soldiers and 1,000 colonists and servants. It sailed from San Juan de Ulúa on June 11, 1559, and, after a stormy voyage, reached Ochuse or Pensacola Bay, previously selected by Guido de Las Bazares, on Aug. 14. On Aug. 19 a terrific wind destroyed nearly all the ships and provisions, sealing the doom of the enterprise. Compelled to live off the country, Luna moved to Nanipacana on the Alabama River, sending a party under Mateo del Sauz to Coosa, fabulously opulent according to Soto's accounts. When the governor tried to lead his starving followers to Coosa his captains voted to return to the Gulf coast. At Ochuse Luna again tried, upon the suggestion received from Sauz, to reach Coosa; but his officers challenged his authority and judgment, averring that he, long a sick man, had lost his wits. Reports from them and the Dominican friars with the party led Velasco to relieve Luna by sending as governor Angel de Villafañe. An attempt under Luna's nephew Martin Doz and Diego Biedma to reach Santa Elena by sea failed because of storms; a second effort, under Villafañe himself, actually reached the region desired, but storm again wrecked the ships, driving the leader to Havana.

After being relieved on Apr. 8, 1561, Luna left Ochuse for Spain to petition the King to decide the suit his officers had brought for the purpose of defeating his commands, and to petition for reimbursement and restoration of his governorship. He was unsuccessful in this; nor did he inherit from his brother Pedro the title of mariscal of Castile; Pedro briefly outlived him, and the inheritance went to Carlos; Tristán died in poverty in Mexico city. His children, Carlos de Arellano and Juana de Ávalos, married into the Mendoza-Velasco family; their descendants, being members of the noble families of the counts of Santiago Calimaya and of the Valle de Orizaba, served in many important colonial offices.

[The best Spanish accounts of Luna in Florida are in Andrés González de Barcia, *Ensayo Cronológico para la Historia General de la Florida* (1723) and Agustín Dávila Padilla, *Historia de la Fundación y Discurso de la Provincia de Santiago de México* (1596). There are a few pages by J. G. Shea, in Justin Winsor's *Narrative and Critical Hist. of America,* vol. II (1886). See also Ricardo Ortega y Pérez Gallardo, *Historia Geneal. de las Familias mas Antiguas de Mexico* (1908), vol. II; Woodbury Lowery, *The Spanish Settlements Within the Present Limits of the U. S., 1513–61* (1901), and *The Luna Papers* (2 vols., 1928), edited and translated by H. I. Priestley.]   H.I.P.

LUNDIE, JOHN (Dec. 14, 1857–Feb. 9, 1931), engineer, inventor, son of James and Anne (Honeyman) Lundie, was born in Arbroath, Scotland. After graduation from the Dundee high school in 1873, he served for four years as a pupil in the office of the harbor engineer of the Port of Dundee, where he obtained some excellent training in civil engineering. Entering the University of Edinburgh, he graduated in 1880 with the degree of bachelor of science, having been first prize man in mathematical physics.

He then came to the United States and for four years was engaged upon railroad work in Oregon and Washington, including the building of Table Rock Tunnel, of which he was in charge. Going to Chicago, he engaged in private practice and later entered the employ of the city. In this capacity he made the preliminary survey of the Chicago Drainage Canal and designed several bridges. In 1890 he became engineer in Chicago for the King Bridge Company of Cleveland. This position he held for four years, during which time he erected numerous structures, including steelwork for some of the buildings of the Columbian Exposition. He then returned to private practice, during the course of which he laid out the first low-level drainage system for Chicago and was connected with water-supply projects for other places. While engaged upon work at Memphis, Tenn., he developed a method of determination of the yield of artesian wells. As a result of investigations regarding the use of electricity for the suburban travel of the Illinois Central Railroad came one of his principal achievements. After an entire year of research he enunciated the principle of "rapid acceleration" and the advisability of utilizing a high percentage of weight upon the driving wheels. From this work he prepared a thesis, "The Economics of Electric Train Movement," which he presented to the University of Edinburgh, from which he received the degree of doctor of science

in 1902. This thesis also established the Lundie formula for train resistance.

In 1898 he was called to New York City in connection with some heavy traction problems, and soon afterward began practice there. About this time he reported upon power handling of freight for the Central of Georgia Railroad and in the course of his investigation designed the first combined electric hoist and tractor, since called a telpher. He also designed and patented (Patent No. 687,569, Nov. 26, 1901) the Lundie Ventilated Rheostat, now in extensive use. In addition to a wide consultation practice upon railroad electrification problems in the United States, he was called to London to advise regarding the Metropolitan Underground system; and to Canada, on important electric railway work. In 1904 he reported to the General Electric Company upon water-power development and the use of electric power on the Isthmus of Panama, and at the same time directed the affairs of the Panama-American Corporation. In 1913 he designed and patented the Lundie Tie Plate (Patent No. 1,065,696, June 24, 1913), and later, a duplex rail anchor. Thereafter these inventions and their applications took much of his time and energy, requiring eventually the formation of the Lundie Engineering Corporation, of which he was president. He was now able to give more personal time to research and technical work, in which his greatest interest lay. In 1921 he became technical adviser to the United Central America Corporation. Although not in the best of health during the latter part of his life, he remained active in business up to the time of his death, which occurred in New York City. In 1906 he married Iona Oakley Gorham, who died in 1925; and in 1929, Mrs. Alice Eddy Snowden, widow of Dr. Albert A. Snowden.

[*Trans. Am. Soc. Civil Engineers,* vol. XCV (1931); *Specifications and Drawings of Patents Issued from the U. S. Patent Office,* Nov. 1901; *Official Gazette of the U. S. Patent Office,* June 24, 1913; *Who's Who in America,* 1930–31; *Engineering News-Record,* Feb. 12, 1931; *N. Y. Times,* Feb. 10, 1931.]   H. K. B.

LUNDIN, CARL AXEL ROBERT (Jan. 13, 1851–Nov. 28, 1915), optician and mechanician, was born at Venersborg, Sweden, third of the eleven children of Carl Fredrik and Ulrika Henrietta (Anderson) Lundin. During his childhood the family moved to Falun, where he was educated at the high school. He early showed an interest in things mechanical and in drawing, and after his course at Falun he served an apprenticeship of seven years at Stockholm as an instrument maker. Subsequently he went to Christiania, where he was employed by the instrument maker Olsen, his work being principally on chronometers. In Christiania he met Hilda Marie Hansen, his future wife, who was indirectly responsible for his later contact with the already famous firm of Alvan Clark & Sons, Cambridgeport, Mass., makers of telescopes. She came to America in October 1872 as governess in the family of the Norwegian consul at Boston and within less than a year he followed. Landing at New York in August 1873, he went immediately to Boston and soon found employment in nearby Newton as a skilled mechanic in work on fire-alarm apparatus. In a short time his unusual skill was brought to the attention of the Clarks and in November 1874 he became their chief instrument maker. With them and their successors he saw continuous service until his death forty-one years later. His ability and good judgment, combined with extreme patience and modesty, immediately won for him the closest confidential relations with each member of the firm. Finding himself now established in congenial surroundings, he married in April 1875, and began his residence at Cambridge. Here were born his two children, a daughter and a son.

From his earliest associations with the firm he was interested in its optical work and since he showed himself unusually gifted, Alvan Clark [q.v.] personally instructed him—and him alone —in the methods by which this talented family had attained success in making their famous telescope lenses. Though continuing his contact with the mechanical work, he was soon devoting so much of his attention to optical matters that, shortly, skill superior to his in this line was not to be found. With time his responsibilities increased until the failing health of Alvan G. Clark [q.v.], the last surviving member of the original firm, brought to him complete responsibility for all undertakings bearing the name of Clark. He did important work on the 30-inch lens for the Pulkovo Observatory in Russia, at that time the largest lens in existence, which was installed by him personally under special decree of the Russian government in 1883. The Clarks followed this lens with two others, each in turn of record-breaking dimensions, the 36-inch lens for the Lick Observatory (1887) and the 40-inch lens for the Yerkes Observatory (1896), in the production of which he took an important part and was specially designated to complete the latter in case Clark should be unable to finish the task. He completed the 24-inch lens for the Lowell Observatory (1895). He made the 16-inch lens for the University of Cincinnati (1904), the 18-inch for Amherst College (1905), and many smaller lenses, mirrors and optical parts. Dur-

ing these experiences he had devised and applied several important optical tests. Definite plans for large lenses were being delayed at the time of his death because optical glass could not then be obtained from Europe. In 1876 he received a medal from the authorities in charge of the Centennial Exhibition for the excellence of his "flats"; and in 1893, a diploma from the Columbian Exposition for excellence in the optical parts of engineering instruments. He was a fellow of the American Association for the Advancement of Science and a charter member of the Astronomical and Astrophysical Society of America (later, the American Astronomical Society). In 1905 he received from Amherst College the honorary degree of master of arts as "scientific expert in cutting and fashioning glasses of great telescopes."

With his patience and skill was combined an extreme sensitiveness. He was deeply disturbed by extravagance of any kind. Though modest in the expression of opinion, he held firmly to conclusions which had resulted from a rich experience. His solution of a problem was direct and through the application of simple devices. Instrumental astronomy in America is in debt to him for his generosity in placing his experience at the service of others—a generosity limited only by his being "unwilling to waste time on a poor telescope."

[*Nature*, Jan. 6, 1916; *The Observatory*, Feb. 1916; *Science*, Aug. 4, 1905, Dec. 17, 1915; *Popular Astronomy*, Jan. 1916; *Guide to Nature*, Jan. 1916; *Boston Transcript, Journal, Post, Herald*, and *Globe*, Nov. 29, 1915; family documents and personal acquaintance.]

J. M. P—r.

LUNDY, BENJAMIN (Jan. 4, 1789–Aug. 22, 1839), abolitionist, was born in Sussex County, N. J., the only child of Joseph and Eliza (Shotwell) Lundy, both Quakers. His great-grandfather, Richard Lundy, son of Richard Lundy who came from Devonshire to Philadelphia in 1682, was a Quaker minister and established several Friends' meetings in Pennsylvania and New Jersey. Benjamin Lundy received only elementary education, and the strenuous physical labor he undertook in youth is said to have injured his hearing. In 1808 he went to Wheeling, Va., to learn the saddler's trade, and there first came into contact with slavery, witnessing coffles of negroes passing through the town in the inter-state slave trade. In 1815, at St. Clairsville, Ohio, to which place he had removed, he organized an anti-slavery group known as "The Union Humane Society," and in January 1816 issued a circular letter urging the formation of anti-slavery societies with common name and constitutions, with machinery for correspondence and cooperative effort, and with general conventions for determining policies. In this suggestion may be seen the germ of the later national anti-slavery societies. He began soon to contribute to *The Philanthropist,* published by Charles Osborn at Mount Pleasant, Ohio, in which slavery was discussed, and eventually accepted Osborn's invitation to join him in the publication of the paper. This necessitated closing his saddlery, which had been financially profitable; accordingly, he loaded his stock of goods on a flatboat and took it to St. Louis, arriving there in the fall of 1819 at the time when the Missouri slavery question was everywhere under discussion. Lundy at once associated himself with the anti-slavery forces and contributed articles to the newspapers. During his absence from Ohio, Osborn sold *The Philanthropist,* and when Lundy returned to Mount Pleasant he began publication, January 1821, of a new paper, *The Genius of Universal Emancipation.* After but a few issues it was removed to Greenville, Tenn., where it was published until the summer of 1824, when Lundy removed it to Baltimore.

During the next decade he became deeply interested in the question of colonization of freed negroes, as a possible solution for the national problem. He spent much time trying to find suitable places for such colonies, journeying to Hayti in 1825 and again in 1829, to the Canadian province of Upper Canada in 1832, and to Texas three times, 1830–31, 1833–34, and 1834–35. While he was absent on his first visit to Hayti, his wife, Esther Lewis, whom he had married in 1815, died at Baltimore. In January 1827 he was assaulted by Austin Woolfolk, a Baltimore slave-dealer, as a result of critical comments in the columns of *The Genius* upon Woolfolk's business. In 1828 Lundy went on a six months' lecturing trip through the Northern states, in the course of which he met William Lloyd Garrison and sought his help in the publication of *The Genius.* Garrison at first declined, but in 1829 joined Lundy at Baltimore and became associate editor. His vitriolic pen quickly involved the paper in lawsuits, however, and he and Lundy separated; while growing opposition in Baltimore led to the removal of the paper to Washington. During 1830–31, when Lundy was absent from home to obtain subscribers, he carried part of his equipment with him and had the paper printed in local shops wherever he happened to be. Publication became more and more irregular until finally, toward the end of 1835, *The Genius* ceased to appear.

In the following August, Lundy began the publication in Philadelphia of *The National En-quirer and Constitutional Advocate of Universal Liberty,* the chief purpose of which seems to have been to expose what the editor regarded as slaveholders' plots to wrest Texas from Mexico. At this time he was in close touch with John Quincy Adams and doubtless supplied Adams with much of the information concerning the Texas situation which he used so effectively in his speeches in Congress. In 1836 Lundy also published his pamphlet, *The War in Texas,* which presented arguments against the annexation of Texas and was one of the most vigorous of the writings to appear in that controversy. He continued to publish *The National Enquirer* at Philadelphia until March 1838 when it was taken over by John G. Whittier and its name changed to *The Pennsylvania Freeman.* In May of that year Lundy lost all his papers and journals when a Philadelphia mob destroyed "Pennsylvania Hall," and in the following summer he left for Illinois where his family resided. There he associated himself with the local anti-slavery societies and reëstablished *The Genius,* twelve issues of which appeared before his death, after a brief illness, in August 1839. Though dated from Hennepin, the Illinois numbers of *The Genius* were printed at Lowell, Ill. Lundy was buried in a Friends' graveyard on Clear Creek, in Putnam County.

Cheerful in temperament, gentle and mild in manner, a keen observer of men and nature, as his writings show, he was ready to adapt himself to whatever conditions he encountered. He was a pioneer in the organization of anti-slavery societies and in the publication of an anti-slavery newspaper, and was the most active figure in the whole movement during the twenties, while his enlistment of Garrison brought to the abolitionist cause its chief figure in the later period.

[*The Life, Travels and Opinions of Benjamin Lundy* (1847), comp. by Thomas Earle "under the direction and on behalf of his children"; W. C. Armstrong, *The Lundy Family and Their Descendants of Whatsoever Surname* (1902); files of *The Genius of Universal Emancipation*; W. P. and F. J. Garrison, *Wm. Lloyd Garrison* (4 vols., 1885–89); G. A. Lawrence, "Benjamin Lundy—Pioneer of Freedom," in *Jour. Ill. State Hist. Soc.,* July 1913; "The Diary of Benjamin Lundy Written during His Journey through Upper Canada, January 1832," repr. from *The Genius,* with notes by Fred Landon, in *Ontario Hist. Soc., Papers and Records,* vol. XIX (1922); Fred Landon, "Benjamin Lundy, Abolitionist," in *Dalhousie Rev.,* July 1927.]

F. L.

LUNT, GEORGE (Dec. 31, 1803–May 16, 1885), author and journalist, son of Abel Lunt, a sea-captain, and Phoebe (Tilton) Lunt, was born at Newburyport, Mass., where his ancestor, Henry Lunt, had settled in 1635. He attended Phillips Academy at Exeter, N. H., and was graduated from Harvard College in 1824. While a student at Harvard he kept a district school at Groton, Mass.; later he was for several years the principal of the high school in his native town. After studying law in the office of Asa W. Wildes of Newburyport he was admitted to the bar in 1831. In the preceding year he had represented the town in the General Court. In 1835 and 1836 he was a member of the state Senate; in 1837 and 1841 he was in the lower house; and in 1847 was again elected representative, to fill the unexpired term of Caleb Cushing [q.v.], resigned. He removed to Boston in 1848, and the following year was appointed United States attorney for the district of Massachusetts, as a reward for his activity in the Whig convention that nominated Gen. Zachary Taylor for the presidency. Lunt held this office until 1853, when he resumed private practice. During this period of his life he appears to have enjoyed a considerable reputation as an orator and he made speeches on various occasions. Upon the dissolution of the Whig party he became a Democrat, and in 1857 assumed the editorship of the *Boston Daily Courier,* the leading Democratic newspaper in the city. In this capacity, dreading hostilities and the disruption of the Union, he opposed such policies as would tend to estrange the South, and thus during the years immediately preceding the war gained for himself the name of being a defender of "slavery and its attendant evils" (Hurd, *post,* p. xli). He continued in the editorship until 1863, when he retired and devoted his leisure to literature.

As early as 1826 he had published a volume of verse entitled *The Grave of Byron, with Other Poems.* This was followed by *Poems* (1839); *The Age of Gold, and Other Poems* (1843); *The Dove and the Eagle* (1851); *Lyric Poems, Sonnets and Miscellanies* (1854); *Julia: a Poem* (1855); and finally *Poems* (1884). His work included some translations from Vergil and Horace; it is filled with classical allusions and marked by dignity and a certain grace. In prose he produced *Eastford; or Household Sketches* (1855); *Three Eras of New England, and Other Addresses* (1857); *The Union* (1860); a pamphlet entitled *Review of McClellan's Campaigns as Commander of the Army of the Potomac* (1863); *The Origin of the Late War* (1866); and *Old New England Traits* (1873), as well as magazine articles and editorials. The last-named book gives a picture of Newburyport in the old days and incidentally throws not a little light on Lunt's childhood. In January 1877 he contributed "Recollections of Thackeray" to *Harper's Magazine.* During his later years he spent much time at Scituate, Mass. He became interested in the improvement of Scituate harbor, and it is

said that the work done on it by the federal government in the eighties and likewise the establishment of a life-saving station at the Third Cliff are attributable largely to his efforts and influence. As advocate or adversary of any cause he was independent and unyielding, but always honorable. His manner was a happy combination of simplicity and dignity. In religious matters he was an ardent Episcopalian. He was married three times: on Oct. 25, 1834, to Sarah Miles Greenwood of Newburyport; on Dec. 4, 1845, to Emily Ashton, then residing in Newburyport; and in 1864 to Adeline Parsons of Boston, sister of Thomas William Parsons [q.v.].

[*Boston Daily Courier,* May 24, 1885; *Boston Daily Advertiser,* May 18, 1885; *Boston Morning Journal,* May 19, 1885; Newburyport *Herald,* May 19, 1885; *Turner's Public Spirit* (Ayer, Mass.), May 23, 1885; D. H. Hurd, *Hist. of Essex County, Mass.* (1888), vol. I; J. J. Currier, *Hist. of Newburyport,* II (1909), 281, 513; *Old Scituate* (1921); T. S. Lunt, *A Hist. of the Lunt Family in America* (1914).] L. S. M.

LUNT, ORRINGTON (Dec. 24, 1815–Apr. 5, 1897), philanthropist, was born at Bowdoinham, Me., the son of William Webb Lunt, for some time a member of the state legislature, and his wife, Ann Matilda Sumner. He was descended from Henry Lunt, who emigrated from England and settled at Newburyport, Mass., in 1635. Orrington Lunt entered his father's store in his fourteenth year, became a partner when he was twenty-one, and was made clerk and treasurer of the town at twenty-two. His reputation for stability and integrity was established at this early day. On Jan. 16, 1842, he married Cornelia A. Gray, who became the mother of his four children. In this same year he moved to Chicago to seek a fortune. He engaged in business in a small way, but it was a time of financial depression and he found it difficult to get a start. In 1845 he began to buy wheat and in November he sold all the wheat he had accumulated in two storehouses and a large elevator. The transaction was so profitable that he was led to buy largely and rather recklessly, and in a year lost all he had made. He later said that he had learned two things by this experience: not to buy on speculation and not to go outside Chicago for his market; and he thought this wisdom had been cheaply bought. He soon reëstablished himself, and thenceforth had a permanent standing in the business world. He helped to project the Galena & Chicago Union Railroad, the first built from Chicago, which ran its cars from Chicago to Des Plaines in 1849; he was for two years its vice-president, and served as a director until the road was consolidated with the Chicago & Northwestern. In 1862, because his health was poor, he gave up active business life, and in 1865 he went abroad for two years with his family, traveling extensively in Europe and Asia.

A devout Methodist, Lunt had joined the Clark Street Church in Chicago as soon as he arrived in that city and he was identified with all the Methodist enterprises in the next generation. He had a pleasing countenance and in his later years a patriarchal appearance, and he was always characterized by a beautiful and benign disposition. He had a singing voice in his youth which maintained its sweetness even in old age. A shrewd and honest business man, he was much sought for as treasurer of important funds. When the Chicago fire threatened his offices he removed the valuable papers belonging to the institutions with which he was connected before he took care of his own. He was a trustee of the Chicago Young Men's Christian Association, president of the Chicago Bible Society, a member of the Committee of Safety and Finance during the Civil War, secretary and treasurer of the board of trustees of Northwestern University and also of Garrett Biblical Institute for many years.

Lunt and his friend and fellow trustee, John Evans [q.v.], were appointed on a committee to choose a site for the projected Northwestern University, but it was Lunt alone who waded through the swamp which lay between the road and the lake shore and discovered the ridges and hardwood groves along the lake which marked the site of the present university campus. The trustees purchased 379 acres at seventy dollars an acre. The city of Evanston, which they wished to call Luntville or Orrington, but which was finally named after John Evans, grew up about the university; Lunt moved his residence to Evanston in 1874 and was a foremost citizen until the day of his death. Orrington Avenue and the Orrington Lunt Library Building on the Northwestern campus preserve his name.

[*Biog. Sketches of the Leading Men of Chicago* (1876); A. D. Field, *Worthies and Workers of the Rock River Conference* (1896); A. H. Wilde, *Northwestern Univ., a Hist.* (4 vols., 1905); J. S. Currey, *Chicago: Its Hist. and Its Builders* (1912), vol. IV; T. S. Lunt, *Lunt: A Hist. of the Lunt Family in America* (1914); E. F. Ward, *The Story of Northwestern Univ.* (1924); *Chicago Daily Tribune* and *Chicago Times-Herald,* Apr. 6, 1897.]   D. A. H.

LURTON, HORACE HARMON (Feb. 26, 1844–July 12, 1914), jurist, the son of Sarah Ann (Harmon) and Lycurgus L. Lurton, a practising physician who later became a clergyman in the Protestant Episcopal Church, was born at Newport, Ky. His early education was with private teachers and, in 1859, he entered the old University of Chicago. His collegiate course

was interrupted by the Civil War and never completed, but by constant study and discriminating reading he became a man of learning and broad culture. In 1861, at the age of seventeen, he enlisted in the 5th (afterwards the 35th) Tennessee Infantry Regiment of the Confederate States Army and served as sergeant major until discharged in 1862 for physical disability. A few weeks later he enlisted in a Kentucky Regiment, was taken prisoner upon the surrender of Fort Donelson, confined at Camp Chase, from which he escaped in April 1862, and at once enlisted under Gen. John Morgan. During that general's raid into Ohio, he was captured and held a prisoner until early in 1865, when his mother appealed to Lincoln to parole him on account of his serious illness. After the war he graduated, in 1867, from the law school of Cumberland University at Lebanon, Tenn., where in September of the same year he married Mary Frances Owen, who bore him two sons and two daughters. He settled at Clarksville, Tenn., and practised law there until 1886, except that from 1875 to 1878 he served as a chancellor. He soon became known as a profound and successful lawyer. Strong in his convictions and a natural leader, he possessed unusual political sagacity, and, though he himself was never a candidate for any except judicial office, his counsel was always valued by his party and by his friends. From 1898 to 1910 he was professor in the law school of Vanderbilt University and, for the last five years of that time, he was dean of the law school. He was, for many years, a vestryman in the Trinity Episcopal Church of Clarksville.

In August 1886 he was elected as one of the justices of the supreme court of Tennessee and began a judicial career that ended only with his death. In January 1893 he succeeded to the chief-justiceship. Several months later, Cleveland appointed him United States circuit judge to succeed Howell E. Jackson whom Harrison had promoted to the supreme bench. He thus became a member of the circuit court of appeals for the sixth circuit, of which William Howard Taft was the presiding judge. After Taft resigned to become governor-general of the Philippines, Lurton was the presiding judge. During these years on the bench he became a close friend of Taft, who was so much impressed with his legal and judicial ability that, in December 1909, he offered him the appointment as associate justice of the United States Supreme Court. Such an appointment by a Republican president of a southern Democrat caused some surprise. Moreover, Lurton was sixty-six years old, a more advanced age than that at which any other justice had ever been appointed, but he was strong and vigorous and came to the Supreme Court with a longer experience on the federal bench than most of his predecessors. As a judge, his opinions were clear and accurate, as in the cases of the *City of Omaha* vs. *Omaha Water Company* (218 *U. S.*, 191–205) and *United States* vs. *Baltimore and Ohio Railroad Company* (231 *U. S.*, 280–98). He was devoted to the Constitution and to the established rules of law. Although he was aware of the changing conditions in modern life and thought, which demanded certain adjustments of governmental machinery, he had little sympathy with those who wished such adjustments to come by way of judicial interpretation. In 1911 he published an essay (*North American Review,* Jan. 1911) in which he expressed his faith in Montesquieu's system of divided powers and his belief that the opposite tendency led to "a substitution of government of men for a government of law" (p. 12). He was a member of the committee to revise the federal equity rules. In order to study the course of English experience he went to England in the vacation of 1911 and carried on some correspondence with the Lord Chancellor. The edition of *The New Federal Equity Rules* edited by James Love Hopkins (1913) was dedicated to him in recognition of this work. In December 1913 he was forced by ill health to absent himself from the court, but after a vacation in Florida he returned to his place in April 1914 and sat to the end of the session, when he sought rest at Atlantic City, where he died.

[U. S. Circuit Court of Appeals for the Sixth Circuit, *In Memory of Horace Harmon Lurton* (1914); J. T. Moore, *Tenn. the Volunteer State* (1923), vol. II; 237 *U. S. Reports*; *Who's Who in America*, 1914–15; *Outlook*, Jan. 1, 1910, July 25, 1914; *Current Literature*, Mar. 1910; *New York Times*, July 13, 14, 16, 1914; *Nashville Tennessean and the Nashville American*, July 13, 1914; *Evening Star* (Washington, D. C.), July 13, 1914.]   W.L.F.

LUSK, WILLIAM THOMPSON (May 23, 1838–June 12, 1897), obstetrician, was born at Norwich, Conn., the son of Sylvester Graham and Elizabeth Freeman (Adams) Lusk. His father was a great-grandson of John Lusk who emigrated from Scotland to Wethersfield, Conn., in 1788. After preliminary schooling under Rev. Albert Spooner in Norwich, at Charles Anthon's classical school in New York City, and at Russell's Military Academy, New Haven, he entered Yale College in 1855. Before the close of his freshman year, however, he was compelled to give up his studies because of an eye affection. After a brief experience in business he went to Geneva, Switzerland, to consult a famous oculist, and received such encouragement in regard to his condition that he resumed his studies, entering upon a medical course at Heidelberg in 1858. After two years there he spent a third year at the University of Berlin. Returning to America at the outbreak of the Civil War, he enlisted in the 79th New York Infantry Highlanders as a private and fought in a number of battles, including first Bull Run, Antietam, and Fredericksburg. He was several times commended for gallantry in action. During the draft riots in New York City he was a captain. In September 1863 he retired to the inactive list and the following winter entered Bellevue Hospital Medical College, graduating at the head of his class in 1864. After eighteen months of post-graduate study under Sir James Y. Simpson of Edinburgh and Karl Braun of Vienna, he undertook general practice at Bridgeport, Conn., for one year. In 1866 he accepted the offer of a junior partnership with Benjamin Fordyce Barker [*q.v.*] which lasted until 1873. During this period he was professor of physiology and microscopic anatomy at Long Island College Hospital, 1868–71; delivered a course of lectures in physiology at Harvard, 1870; and jointly with Dr. J. B. Hunter, edited the *New York Medical Journal*, 1871–73. In 1871 he accepted the professorship of obstetrics, diseases of women, diseases of infancy, and clinical midwifery at Bellevue Hospital Medical College, to succeed George T. Elliot, deceased. This chair he retained until his death. From 1889 he was president of the faculty, and in 1894 he was president of the American Gynecological Society. Among his numerous hospital appointments were those of gynecologist to Bellevue and St. Vincent's, obstetrical surgeon to Bellevue and the Emergency Hospital, consulting obstetrician to the Lying-In and Maternity hospitals and, earlier in his career, visiting physician to the Nursery and Child's Hospital and to the Charity Hospital. He contributed freely to periodical literature and at the International Medical Congress in 1876 read a paper upholding the germ origin of puerperal fever, which at that time had very few supporters (*Transactions of the International Medical Congress of Philadelphia, 1876,* 1877). Succeeding Fordyce Barker as the fashionable obstetrician of the day, he had a large private practice.

Lusk is known chiefly for his classic work, *The Science and Art of Midwifery,* which first appeared in 1882 and went through eleven printings in thirteen years. The author's familiarity with the German language and literature, old and recent, gave to the book all the authority and thoroughness of a German monograph. Considered the most learned textbook of the day in English, it was translated into French, Italian, Spanish, and Arabic. It could have survived the author's death had not his heirs always refused consent to any alteration of the original text in the interest of revision. Lusk was married twice: on May 4, 1864, to Mary Hartwell Chittenden, and in 1876 to Matilda (Myer) Thorn. Four of the five children of his first marriage survived him, the two sons attaining distinction in medicine and medical education, while a daughter of the second marriage married a well-known professor of gynecology.

[*War Letters of Wm. Thompson Lusk* (1911); sketch by a son, Graham Lusk, in H. A. Kelly and W. L. Burrage, *Am. Medic. Biogs.* (1920); *N. Y. Jour. Gynaecol. and Obstetrics*, Feb. 1892; *Am. Jour. Obstetrics*, July 1897; *British Gynaecol. Jour.*, Aug. 1897; *Medic. Record* (N. Y.), June 19, 1897; *Medic. News*, June 19, 1897; *N. Y. Medic. Jour.*, June 19, 1897; *Trans. Am. Gynecol. Soc.*, vol. XXIII (1898); *Trans. N. Y. Acad. of Medicine, 1896–1901* (1903); *Am. Gynecol. and Obstetrical Jour.*, Dec. 1907; *Medic. Pickwick*, July 1915; *Album Am. Gynecol. Soc.*, 1918; F. A. Virkus, *The Abridged Compendium of Am. Geneal.*, vol. I (1925); *N. Y. Tribune*, June 13, 1897.]   E. P.

LUTHER, SETH (fl. 1817–1846), carpenter and pioneer advocate of labor reforms, was born toward the end of the eighteenth century, probably in Providence, R. I. His ancestors may have been the Welsh Luthers who settled in Rhode Island about 1650, and founded there the first Baptist church in America. Of formal education he had but little. "For myself," he wrote, "I had no advantages but those of a common school, and that of a far inferior kind to those of the present day. . . . I am indebted for *what little I do know* to newspapers and books, and to a constant habit of observation" (*Address on . . . Avarice*, p. 38). In 1817 he made a trip down the Ohio River from Pittsburgh to Cincinnati. His travels took him "in and about 14 of the United States, including a visit to the frontiers of Upper Canada and East Florida" (*Ibid.*). Upon his return from his journeys he went to work as a carpenter, in Providence or Boston, or one of the mill towns that were growing so fast just before 1830. According to his own account, he lived for years "among Cotton mills, worked in them, traveled among them" (*Address to the Working-men*, p. 35).

He espoused the workingman's cause wholeheartedly. From the West he had brought back the democratic spirit of the frontier, and the class distinctions of New England irritated him. "You cannot raise one part of the community above another," he wrote, "unless you stand on the bodies of the poor" (*Avarice*, p. 42). His first pamphlet, *An Address to the Working-men of New England* (1832, 3rd ed., 1836), based on

speeches in a half-dozen towns and cities, was an attack on the abuses of the factory system. The author cited instances of children who worked twelve to fifteen hours per day and of their physical maltreatment; quoted factory regulations showing paternalistic control exercised by employers, and asserted that "the whole system of labor in New England, more *especially in cotton mills,* is a cruel system of exaction on the bodies and minds of the producing classes, destroying the energies of both" (p. 28). His conclusion may be questioned, since his temperament was not that of an impartial observer; nevertheless, although political leaders frowned upon the proposals of Luther and his fellow agitators and the newspapers gave them no support, the best educated and the most intelligent element of the community were sympathetic, and in 1842 Massachusetts enacted the first American child-labor law. In 1833 Luther published *An Address on the Right of Free Suffrage* (Sabin, *post*), and in 1834 *An Address on the Origin and Progress of Avarice.* The latter was a denunciation of political and religious as well as economic oppression. At its conclusion the author laid down the following program of reform: Universal equal education by means of manual labor schools supported at the public expense; abolition of all licensed monopolies; abolition of capital punishment and of imprisonment for debt; the entire revision or total abolition of the militia system; a less expensive system for the administration of justice; equal taxation for property; and an effective mechanic's lien law. His deadly sincerity, forceful language, grim humor, and biting sarcasm made his pamphlets valuable weapons in the labor movement. The General Trades Convention in Boston in 1834 selected him as one of its secretaries and a year later he helped draft a manifesto known as the *Boston Circular,* in favor of the ten-hour day, which, reprinted in Philadelphia, is said to have inspired a general strike. In 1835 he addressed the National Trades Union Convention upon the condition of women and children in cotton mills. The last mention which has been found of him is a record of his participation in a ten-hour convention in Manchester, N. H., in 1846.

[J. R. Commons and others, *A Doc. Hist. of Am. Industrial Soc.*, vols. VI, VIII (1910), X (1911), and *Hist. of Labour in the U. S.* (2 vols., 1918); R. T. Ely, *The Labor Movement in America* (1886); Edith Abbott, "A Study of the Early History of Child Labor in America," *Am. Jour. Sociology*, July 1908; S. M. Kingsbury, *Labor Laws and Their Enforcement* (1911); Joseph Sabin, *A Dictionary of Books Relating to America*, vol. X (1878).]   P. W. B.

LUTKIN, PETER CHRISTIAN (Mar. 27, 1858–Dec. 27, 1931), educator, composer, and conductor, was born in Thompsonville, Racine County, Wis., the youngest of six children of Peter Christian and Hannah Susanna Define (Olivarius) Lutkin. Both parents were born in Denmark. The father was interested in the violin as an amateur, but Peter was the only one of his children to display musical ability. Before the family moved to Chicago in 1869, the father was engaged in the wholesale grocery business in Racine, from which district he was elected to the Wisconsin legislature. The sudden death of both parents in 1871 threw the boy on his own resources. He obtained his education in the public schools of Chicago and in the choir school of the Episcopal Cathedral, where in 1869 he became alto soloist of the pioneer boy choir of the midwest. At the age of fourteen he became organist at the Cathedral, though as yet technically untrained, holding this position till 1881. In the meantime he began the study of piano with Mrs. Regina Watson, organ with Clarence Eddy, and theory with Frederick Grant Gleason. From 1879 to 1881 he was instructor of piano at Northwestern University in Evanston. For the next two years he was in Berlin studying organ with Haupt, piano with Raif, and theory with Bargiel (mostly at the *Hochschule für Musik*), winning a scholarship in the *Königliche Meisterschule für Composition* in October 1882. He also studied piano in the Leschetizky Piano School in Vienna (1883) and with Moszkowski in Paris (1884).

Returning to Chicago, Lutkin became organist and choirmaster at St. Clement's (1884–91) and at St. James's (1891–96). From 1888 to 1895 he was director of the theory department of the American Conservatory of Music. Meanwhile, in 1891, when the department of music of Northwestern University was organized, he was appointed professor of music and in 1897 became dean of the School of Music upon its organization. The development of this school into one of the important musical institutions of the country was one of the main achievements of his life. He became dean emeritus in 1928 but continued active as a teacher until a few weeks before his death. He was conductor of the Evanston Musical Club (1894–1919) and the Ravenswood Musical Club (1896–1904). In 1906 he founded the noted a cappella choir of the University, an organization which, of all his major activities, probably lay closest to his heart and for which he wrote most of his compositions for unaccompanied voices. These choral units made it possible for him to establish, with the financial aid of influential citizens, the Chicago North Shore Festival Association in 1908, of which he was the choral conductor until 1930. The first festival took place in May 1909. These annual festivals, among the best of their kind, exerted a large influence in developing the musical interests of Chicago.

Lutkin was one of the founders of the American Guild of Organists (1896) and was twice president of the Music Teachers National Association (1911–12 and 1919–20). His special interest from early manhood was in church music and until his death he kept the headship of the department of church and choral music of the School of Music, writing and editing many pamphlets on various phases of church music. He was also special lecturer on church music in the Western Theological Seminary (Chicago) and the Garrett Biblical Institute (Evanston), one of his lecture courses in the former being published as *Music in the Church* (1910). As a composer he wrote little outside the field of church music and part-songs. His best work displays a good understanding of contrapuntal writing and characteristic choral effects, particularly with unaccompanied voices. Among his best compositions may be listed the following: *Te Deum*, "Peace" (first given at the North Shore Festival, 1919), Communion Service in C, *Te Deum* No. 2 in B-flat, *Magnificat* and *Nunc Dimittis* in B-flat, and several anthems— "Christians, Awake," "Fairest Lord Jesus," and "What Christ Said." Lutkin died at Evanston in his seventy-fourth year. He was a man of simple, dignified bearing, of striking sincerity and kindliness, and with a delightful sense of humor. He was survived by his wife, Nancy Lelah Carman, whom he had married on Oct. 27, 1885, and by a son, Harris Carman Lutkin.

[*Who's Who in America,* 1930–31; article by Carl Beecher in *Northwestern Univ. Alumni News,* Feb. 1932; the *Diapason,* Apr. 1, 1930; Jan. 1, Feb. 1, Apr. 1, 1932; *Chicago Tribune,* Dec. 28, 1931; information as to certain facts from Mrs. Peter C. Lutkin.]

R. G. C—e.

LYALL, JAMES (Sept. 13, 1836–Aug. 23, 1901), inventor, manufacturer, was born in Auchterardar, Perth, Scotland, the son of Charles and Mary (Cooper) Lyall. When he was three years old his parents came to the United States and settled in New York City. Here Lyall was educated in the public schools and then went to work in his father's shop, making and mounting Jacquard looms. On the outbreak of the Civil War he enlisted in the 12th New York Infantry and served for a short time in the defense of the national capital. In 1863, while still in the service, he prepared a new substance for enameling cloth, and the government awarded him a large contract to supply enameled haversacks and knapsacks. Following the completion of this work, he and his brother William founded the firm of J. & W. Lyall, for the manufacture of looms and other cotton-making machinery. On Aug. 11, 1868, he obtained the basic patent on his positive-motion loom. This loom he further perfected with two additional inventions, patented July 4, 1871, and Dec. 10, 1872. Its special feature lies in the fact that the shuttle is not thrown as a projectile through the wedge-shaped space between the two sets of warp threads, but is positively dragged back and forth by an endless belt attached to the shuttle carriage, running first in one direction and then in the other. While this invention did not eliminate the flying-shuttle loom, it revolutionized the manufacture of cotton goods throughout the world; for it abolished the use of picking sticks, permitted great widths of fabric to be woven, and made it possible to unite several looms into one machine and weave a number of fabrics simultaneously.

Besides attending to the enormous business resulting from this invention, Lyall found time to make other improvements in textile machinery, including a new take-up motion for looms, patented in 1875 and 1877, and a cap press for compressing cotton on the shuttles. In the eighties he established mills for manufacturing cotton and jute goods. These included the Chelsea Jute Mills, New York; the Planet Cotton Mills, Brooklyn; the United States Corset Company, New York, which manufactured the first machine-made corsets in the world; and the Brighton Mills, established in New York and later moved to Passaic, N. J. He also patented, in 1888 and 1889, two improvements in the manufacture of jute binder twine. Between 1893 and 1896 he obtained five patents for a new kind of woven fabric for pneumatic tires and fire hose. Its peculiarity lay in the fact that both warp and filling threads were of the same length, thus overcoming the squirming tendency of hose or tires consisting of fabric woven with threads of unequal length. Finally, in 1897, he invented a "tubular wheel tire," the cotton fabric of which was made with a large number of warp threads and very few filling threads per inch. In 1869 the American Institute of New York awarded him a gold medal of honor for his positive-motion loom; and for subsequent inventions, a bronze medal in 1871 and a silver medal in 1873. He was married on Sept. 8, 1864, to Margaret Telford of Meredith Hollow, near Delphi, N. Y., and at the time of his sudden death in New York City he was survived by his widow and five children.

[*Textile World,* Sept. 1901; *Wool and Cotton Reporter,* Aug. 29, 1901; E. W. Byrn, *The Progress of Invention in the Nineteenth Century* (1900); *Who's Who in America,* 1901–02; *House Ex. Doc. No. 52,* 40 Cong., 3 Sess.; *Specifications and Drawings of Patents Issued from the U. S. Patent Office,* July 1871, Dec. 1872, Dec. 1875, June 1877, Jan. 1888, Aug. 1889, Sept., Oct. 1893, Mar., June 1896, Feb. 1897; *N. Y. Tribune,* Aug. 24, 1901.]
C. W. M.

LYDSTON, GEORGE FRANK (Mar. 3, 1857–Mar. 14, 1923), physician, was the son of George N. and Lucy A. Lydston, both descended from Scotch-English ancestors who had early emigrated to New England. As a recently married couple they went to California during the gold excitement of 1849 and there in Jacksonville, a mining village in Tuolumne County, their son was born. Following a childhood in these primitive surroundings he was sent to private schools, first in California and later in New York. His medical courses were taken at Bellevue Hospital Medical School in New York, where he graduated in 1879. After a year's service as interne in the New York Charity Hospital he was appointed resident surgeon to the State Immigrant Hospital at Ward's Island. He resigned this latter position in 1881 and moved to Chicago to practise his profession. The year following his arrival he joined the faculty of the recently organized College of Physicians and Surgeons.

For over twenty years he conducted courses in genito-urinary surgery and venereal diseases at that school, for nine years as lecturer, then as head of the department. His teaching was marked by that originality and independence of thought which characterized his whole career. He was always interested in the business management of medical practice. During his Chicago career he built up a large and select clientele and was said to have had the most lucrative practice of his time. From the time of his graduation Lydston was a prolific writer upon widely varying topics. Beginning in 1880 he contributed over one hundred articles to medical periodicals, mostly relating to his specialty. In addition he was the author of *Surgical Diseases of the Genito-Urinary Tract* (1899, 1904), *Diseases of Society* (1904), a work upon the problems of vice and crime, and *Impotence and Sterility* (1917). Of fiction, he wrote *Over the Hookah* (1896) and *Poker Jim* (1908). *Panama and the Sierras,* written in 1900, is a book of travel. He also wrote a play, *The Blood of the Fathers* (1912). He was especially interested in criminology and was a friend of Lombroso. For many years he was professor of criminal anthropology at the Kent College of Law. Many of his later contributions to medical literature were devoted to the possibilities of securing rejuvenation by gland transplantation.

Lydston was a man of aggressive personality and was frequently involved in controversy. He had a keen and satirical humor to which he gave full vent with tongue and pen. For years he acted the part of the bad boy of the medical profession, hitting right and left among the organized fraternity. He was in perpetual feud with the American Medical Association. Physically he was tall and powerfully built. He practised boxing and was interested in all athletics. He was surgeon of 2nd Illinois Infantry before and during the Spanish-American War. In his later years he spent much of his time in California, and in Los Angeles, he died of pneumonia. He was married to Josie M. Cottier of Chicago in that city in 1884.

[R. F. Stone, *Biog. of Eminent Am. Physicians and Surgeons* (1894); *Jour. Am. Medic. Asso.*, Mar. 17, 1923; *Am. Jour. of Clinical Medicine*, Apr. 1923; *Los Angeles Times*, Mar. 15, 1923; personal acquaintance.]
                                          J. M. P—n.

LYMAN, ALBERT JOSIAH (Dec. 24, 1845–Aug. 22, 1915), Congregational clergyman, author, was born in Williston, Vt., the first child and only son of Josiah and Mary L. (Bingham) Lyman. The family sprang from early colonial stock, the earliest progenitor in this country being Richard Lyman of High Ongar, Essex, who crossed the Atlantic in 1631 in the same ship, the *Lion,* which brought John Eliot, the famous apostle to the Indians, and the wife and the eldest son of Gov. John Winthrop. Josiah Lyman, a graduate of Williams College and a licensed preacher, was teaching school at Williston when his son was born. A few years later he removed with his family to Lenox, Mass. Albert early showed an aptitude for literary and scholarly pursuits, and he became a district school teacher at fifteen years of age; but his interests turned him to the ministry, and after a period of study in Williston Seminary, Easthampton, Mass., where he was graduated in 1863, he was licensed to preach. He determined, however, to obtain a thorough education. To this end he spent a year (1865–66) at the Chicago Theological Seminary, attended the Union Theological Seminary in New York, where he was graduated in 1868, was a resident licentiate at the Yale Theological School (1868–69), and on Sept. 7, 1870, was regularly ordained to the Congregational ministry in connection with his settlement as minister of the First Congregational Church of Milford, Conn.

In a long career of forty-five years, Lyman served only two parishes—the Milford church (1869–73), and the South Congregational

Church, Brooklyn (1874–1915). "For the best of reasons," says a distinguished associate, "might the South Church be called Dr. Lyman's, for it was his. For more than forty years he gave it all the wealth of his intellect and his heart." An active man, in a busy pastorate, he entered deeply and widely into the life of his city. He was an intimate friend of Henry Ward Beecher and of Richard S. Storrs, and succeeded the latter as president of the Brooklyn Academy of Arts and Sciences. In his religious views he represented the liberal wing of Orthodoxy, but he was never interested primarily in theological thought, and contributed little of importance to its development. It was his practical ability, attractive personality, and utter loyalty to his denomination which early lifted him to that position of leadership in American Congregationalism which he held through many years. Exceptional grace as a preacher made him a popular guest in college pulpits. He gave important courses of lectures at Hartford Theological Seminary, Bangor Theological Seminary, and Auburn Theological Seminary. He frequently preached and lectured abroad, in Scotland and in Switzerland; but his heart was always in his parish. Handsome in person, of warm sympathies, possessed of a genius for friendship, he was unrivaled in pastoral power. He was a lover of nature, and an indefatigable mountain climber, having the ascent of Mont Blanc to his credit. His published works, mostly volumes of sermons and lectures, are: *Preaching in the New Age* (1902), *A Plain Man's Working View of Biblical Inspiration* (1907), *The Christian Pastor in the New Age* (1909), *Underneath Are the Everlasting Arms* (1910), *The Three Greatest Maxims in the World* (1911), *The Mystery of Jesus* (posthumous, 1916). He was twice married: on June 1, 1870, to Ella Stevens, of Brooklyn, who died in 1893; and on June 26, 1902, to Elizabeth Hills, of Philadelphia.

[E. A. Lyman, *A Sketch of the Record of the Descendants of Daniel Lyman and Sally Clapp of Easthampton, Mass.* (1923); Lyman Coleman, *Geneal. of the Lyman Family in Great Britain and America* (1872); *A Service in Memory of the Reverend Albert Josiah Lyman, D.D.* (1915); *The Congregationalist*, Sept. 2, 1915; *The Congreg. Year Book* (1915); *Brooklyn Daily Eagle*, Jan. 13, 1899, Aug. 23, 1915; papers and records in possession of Dr. Lyman's family.]
                                          J. H. H.

LYMAN, BENJAMIN SMITH (Dec. 11, 1835–Aug. 30, 1920), geologist, mining engineer, was the son of Samuel Fowler and Almira (Smith) Lyman and was born in Northampton, Mass. He was descended from Richard Lyman who emigrated to America in 1631, settling first in Charlestown, Mass., and later in Hartford, Conn. In his native city he prepared for college and entered Harvard University with the class of 1855. During the first year after graduating he tried his hand at school-teaching and the mercantile business but his greatest interest, he soon discovered, was in neither of these occupations but in geology. In 1856, therefore, he became an associate of Peter Lesley [q.v.], his uncle by marriage, and spent two field seasons in topographical and geological survey work in eastern Pennsylvania. During the intervening winter he taught school in Philadelphia. In 1858 he joined the Iowa State Geological Survey as assistant geologist but resigned within a year and went abroad for further study in his profession. From 1859 to 1861 he attended the Imperial School of Mines in Paris, France, and during 1861 and 1862 he attended the Royal Academy of Mines at Freiberg, Germany. Returning to the United States late in 1862 he established his residence in Philadelphia and opened an office as a consulting mining engineer. From 1863 to 1865 his principal work was that of surveying coal lands in and around Cape Breton, Nova Scotia, and also in gold mining in California; between 1865 and 1870 he undertook general geological and topographical work in many sections of the United States. In 1870 he was appointed mining engineer in the public-works department of the government of India and devoted that year to studying and preparing a report on the Punjab oil lands.

Upon returning to the United States in 1871 Lyman carried on his private practice until 1873 when he was made general geologist and mining engineer for the Japanese government. During the succeeding seven years in Japan he made both topographical and geological surveys of the major part of the Japanese Empire, the results of which were published in governmental reports. In the course of this work he discovered many of the coal and other mineral deposits of Japan and upon the completion of the survey he was prevailed upon to remain in Japan to assist in the development of several of these deposits. He returned to the United States early in the eighties and settled for a time in his boyhood home in Massachusetts. In 1887 he again took up his residence in Philadelphia and became assistant geologist for the state of Pennsylvania and served in this capacity until 1895. Thereafter he was privately engaged in geological researches not only in the United States but in Europe, India, China, and the Philippines as well. He was the author of 150 papers on geological subjects and wrote on a number of other subjects. Many of

his articles were published in the *Transactions* of the American Institute of Mining Engineers and in the *Proceedings* of the American Philosophical Society and of the American Association for the Advancement of Science. His first professional paper was *Bourinot Coal Claims and Lands, Cape Breton* (1865). His other published writings include: *General Report on the Punjab Oil Lands* (1870); *Geological Survey of Japan* (1878); and *Against Adopting the Metric System* (1897). In 1864 Lyman became an advocate of vegetarianism and in 1917 published *Vegetarian Diet and Dishes* which has enjoyed a wide circulation. He held but one political office during his long career, namely, that of common councilman for Northampton, Mass., in 1885–86. He was a member of twenty-three technical and scientific societies, a fellow of the American Association for the Advancement of Science, and an honorary member of the Mining Institute of Japan. He died unmarried in Philadelphia and was buried in Northampton.

[*Who's Who in America*, 1920–21; *Report of the Secretary of the Class of 1855, Harvard Coll.* (1865); *Apocrypha Concerning the Class of 1855 of Harvard Coll.* (1880); Lyman Coleman, *Geneal. of the Lyman Family in Great Britain and America* (1872); M. L. Ames, *Life and Letters of Peter and Susan Lesley* (2 vols., 1909); G. P. Merrill, *The First One Hundred Years of Am. Geology* (1924); *Science*, Sept. 10, 1920; *Engineering and Mining Jour.*, Sept. 11, 1920; *Pub. Ledger* (Phila.), and *N. Y. Times*, Aug. 31, 1920.]
C. W. M.

LYMAN, CHESTER SMITH (Jan. 13, 1814– Jan. 29, 1890), astronomer and physicist, was born at Manchester, Conn., the son of Chester and Mary (Smith) Lyman. His father was a farmer and descendant of Richard Lyman who came to America from England in 1631. Chester attended the district common-school at Manchester, performed the farm boy's usual routine of chores, and spent a large part of his playtime in his father's tool shop. Before he was thirteen he had made several of the simple astronomical instruments that he found described in James Ferguson's *Astronomy*. When he was sixteen he decided to enter the ministry and taught the district school at Manchester two winters (1830–32) to obtain funds to prepare for college. He then attended the Ellington Academy for twelve months and entered Yale University in 1833. At Yale he took several prizes in composition and translation, was an originator and an editor of the *Yale Literary Magazine*, and was assistant to the professor of natural philosophy. This last position gave him the opportunity to use the observatory, where he spent most of his leisure. Upon graduation (1837) he became superintendent of the Ellington Academy. In September 1839 he entered

Union Theological Seminary and the next year returned to Yale to attend the theological school. In February 1843 he became pastor of the First Church (Congregational) at New Britain, Conn., from which position he resigned in 1845 because of ill health. He then traveled for his health and in the next five years was successively missionary, school teacher, and surveyor in Hawaii, and surveyor and gold digger in California. The journal he kept during his travels (published as *Around the Horn to the Sandwich Islands and California, 1845–50,* 1924) and the letters that he wrote to the *American Journal of Science and Arts* (September 1848 to January 1850) are detailed accounts of his travels and work, as well as interesting records of life in those places at that time. The letter published in the issue of September 1848 is said to be the first credible account of the discovery of gold in California to be received in the East and was widely copied by the press. His name appears on the first list of trustees for the proposed College of California (S. H. Willey, *A History of the College of California,* 1887, p. 5).

Lyman returned to New Haven in April 1850 and on June 20 of the same year was married to Delia Williams Wood. He was then employed for some time in preparing definitions of scientific words for an edition of Webster's *Dictionary.* In 1859 he became professor of industrial mechanics and physics in the Sheffield Scientific School at Yale. In 1871 the professorship was modified to include only physics and astronomy and after 1884 included only astronomy. While at Yale, Lyman invented the first combined transit and zenith instrument for determining latitude by Talcott's method (*American Journal of Science and Arts,* July 1860); an apparatus for demonstrating the theory of wave motion (*Ibid.,* May 1868); a pendulum apparatus for describing Lissajon's acoustic curves; and improvements in clock pendulums and escapements. The wave motion apparatus was patented and manufactured by Ritchie & Son of Boston and was widely sold to schools and colleges. In astronomy, Lyman was actively interested in the Yale Observatory, of which he was a manager, and there in 1866 he made the first satisfactory observation of Venus as a delicate ring of light when very near the sun in inferior conjunction (Agnes M. Clerke, *A Popular History of Astronomy During the Nineteenth Century,* 2nd ed., 1887, p. 302). He was a vice-president of the American Association for the Advancement of Science (1874) and president of the Connecticut Academy of Arts and Science (1859–77). He died at New Haven.

[*Record of the Class of 1837 in Yale Univ.* (7th ed., 1887); J. L. Chamberlain, *Universities and Their Sons,* vol. III (1899); Lyman Coleman, *Geneal. of the Lyman Family in Great Britain and America* (1872); *Am. Jour. of Sci. and Arts,* Mar. 1890; *Sidereal Messenger,* Nov. 1890; *Popular Sci. Monthly,* Nov. 1887; *Morning Jour. and Courier* (New Haven), Jan. 30, 1890.]   F. A. T.

LYMAN, JOSEPH BARDWELL (Oct. 6, 1829–Jan. 28, 1872), agriculturist, was born at Chester, Mass., the son of Timothy and Experience (Bardwell) Lyman and a descendant of Richard Lyman who emigrated to New England in 1631. After graduating from Yale in the class of 1850 he taught school for three years, first in Cromwell, Conn., then in Mississippi. In June 1853 he went to Nashville, Tenn., where, until he moved to New Orleans early in 1855, he studied law and again taught school. In 1856 he graduated from the law department of the University of Louisiana and for the next five years practised law in New Orleans. On July 14, 1858, he was married to Laura Elizabeth Baker. Upon the outbreak of the Civil War he enlisted as a private in the 1st Louisiana Cavalry. Taken prisoner at London, Tenn., in September 1863, he was sent to the military prison at Louisville, Ky., from which he was released later in the month upon taking the oath of allegiance to the United States. He spent some months in Massachusetts, farming part of the time, then moved to New York City in 1864 to engage in journalism. In 1865 he published *Resources of the Pacific States.* His various writings brought him to the attention of the New York press and in 1867 he became agricultural editor of the New York *World.* From December 1868 to August 1869 he was also managing editor of *Hearth and Home.* In 1868 he had published some of his observations on Southern husbandry in *Cotton Culture,* and in 1869, in collaboration with his wife, he published *The Philosophy of Housekeeping.* In the latter year he became agricultural editor of the *New York Weekly Tribune.* The nationwide circulation, particularly among farmers, of this paper gave him an opportunity to exercise considerable influence on agricultural development.

In New York City Lyman was a member of the American Institute, a group of agricultural experts who met periodically to discuss questions of all sorts coming from farmers from all over the nation. These discussions he summarized in clear and simple language for his *Tribune* readers. He was conscientious and diligent rather than brilliant, and he gave as patient attention to letters requesting the most elementary information as to those dealing with the most interesting of contemporary questions. He constantly impressed upon American farmers the necessity of sustaining home manufactures, of diversifying their products, and of supporting every movement by which the power of association could be employed for the public good. Much of his time during 1871 he spent in supervising the building of a house at Richmond Hill, Long Island. He had barely moved his family into the new home when he died of smallpox on Jan. 28, 1872, and was buried the same day. He left six children.

[*Biog. Record of the Class of 1850 of Yale Coll.* (1877); *Obit. Record of Grads. of Yale Coll.* (1872); A. B. Booth, *Records of La. Confed. Soldiers and La. Confed. Commands* (3 vols. in 4, 1920); *Thirty-second Ann. Report of the Am. Inst. of the City of N. Y.* (1872); Lyman Coleman, *Geneal. of the Lyman Family in Great Britain and America* (1872); the *Cultivator and Country Gentleman,* Feb. 8, 1872; *N. Y. Tribune,* Jan. 29, 1872.]   R. H. G.

LYMAN, PHINEAS (1715–Sept. 10, 1774), provincial general, was born near Durham, Conn., the second son of Noah and Elizabeth Lyman and a descendant of Richard Lyman who emigrated to America in 1631. Renouncing the weaver's trade he had learned, Phineas prepared for and entered Yale, graduated in 1738, was elected tutor, and began to study law. In 1742 he resigned his tutorship, in October married Eleanor, only daughter of Col. Timothy Dwight of Northampton, and moved to Suffield, where he became prominent at the bar, in the local militia, and in town government. Through his efforts Suffield, in 1749, joined Connecticut, and he represented the town as deputy in the colonial Assembly until 1752, then acted as assistant until 1759. During the Seven Years' War, in which Lyman, as commanding officer of the Connecticut troops, served eight campaigns, and won the reputation of being the ablest and most trustworthy provincial general in the northern colonies, he succeeded in gaining the approval of his British superiors at the same time that he aided, through his high political position, in maintaining the independence of his colony. His military career contains few brilliant feats, but dull work conscientiously done. In 1755, as major-general and second in command of the Lake George expedition, he shared with Johnson the honors of defeating the French under Dieskau. In 1756 he associated with the moderates in the provincial-regular dispute over military rank; as commander of the garrison at Fort Edward, which he had laid out as Fort Lyman the previous year, he followed the suggestions and orders of his superiors in matters of camp discipline and sanitation. In 1757 he was with Webb, and in 1758 he was leading one column at the lower end of Lake George when Lord Howe [*q.v.*], leading another, was killed. He accompanied Amherst the following year against Crown Point, and later commanded at Ticonderoga. There, over the construction work that his provincial troops were engaged upon, he conducted with Amherst a close, friendly correspondence that shows him to have been earnest, responsible, grateful for favors and flattery, and proud of his trust. In 1760, after serving at Montreal, he commanded the construction work at Fort Ontario. He was again in New York the next year and in 1762, arrayed in "the finest Coat ever seen at New York," he sailed to join Albemarle at Havana as commander of all the provincial troops on that expedition.

In the third and last period of his life Lyman became known as one of the chief projectors of western colonies. Having Amherst's support, he first hoped to settle discharged provincial soldiers on lands east of Lake Champlain; but after 1763, when he went to England as agent for his own company of "Military Adventurers," and for the remaining subscribers to Samuel Hazard's colonization scheme of 1755, he planned a series of colonies along the Mississippi, and especially a large one of his own at the mouth of the Ohio. The unfavorable attitude of the ministry to western colonization, and the uncertainty of British politics prevented any of his various schemes from succeeding, although in 1770 he obtained 20,000 acres near Natchez. In 1772 he returned home, with a pension, but broken in health and disappointed. He served two further terms as deputy, and when the inclusion of Dartmouth in the ministry seemed to promise favorable action on his last petition for a new colony, "Georgiana," he reorganized the Adventurers, and left for the west. A change of policy defeated this project, too, and he obtained only squatters' rights. Soon after his arrival at Natchez, he died, leaving his wife and surviving children to continue his ill fortune.

[Lyman Coleman, *Geneal. of the Lyman Family in Great Britain and America* (1872); Wm. Fowler, *Hist. of Durham, Conn.* (1866); H. S. Sheldon, *Documentary Hist. of Suffield* (1879); Timothy Dwight, *Travels in New Eng. and N. Y.* (1823), I, 271–81, III, 349–58; *Commissary Wilson's Orderly Book . . . 1759* (1857), ed. by J. W. DePeyster; *Gen. Orders of 1757, Issued by the Earl of Loudoun and Phineas Lyman* (1899), ed. by W. C. Ford; C. J. Hoadly, *The Pub. Records of the Colony of Conn.,* vols. IX–XIV (1876–87); "The Wolcott Papers," *Conn. Hist. Soc. Colls.,* vol. XVI (1916); "The Fitch Papers," *Ibid.,* vols. VII and XVIII (1918–20); C. W. Alvord, *The Miss. Valley in British Politics* (2 vols., 1917); C. W. Alvord and C. E. Carter, "The New Régime, 1765–67," *Ill. State Hist. Lib. Colls.,* vol. XI (1916); F. B. Dexter, *Biog. Sketches of the Grads. of Yale Coll.,* vol. I (1885), and *The Lit. Diary of Ezra Stiles* (3 vols., 1901); *Acts of the Privy Council of England, Colonial Ser. . . . 1766–83* (1912).]   S. M. P.

LYMAN, THEODORE (Feb. 20, 1792–July 18, 1849), author, mayor, philanthropist, father of Theodore Lyman, 1833–1897 [q.v.], was born in Boston, Mass., a descendant of Richard Lyman who emigrated to New England in 1631. He was the second son of Theodore Lyman, a wealthy merchant, and the latter's second wife, Lydia Williams, niece of Timothy Pickering. The boy prepared for college at Phillips Exeter Academy and graduated from Harvard in 1810. Believing that he would pursue a career in letters, he spent the years until 1819 chiefly in study and travel, establishing European contacts, and accumulating a library. His first published efforts, two small books and several articles of travel and description, grew out of these years. He returned to Boston in 1819 and two years later married Mary Elizabeth Henderson of New York. In 1823 he published *A Short Account of the Hartford Convention* and in 1826 *The Diplomacy of the United States,* enlarged and republished in two volumes in 1828.

Lyman's political activities, which began almost immediately upon his return to Boston, were greatly affected by his inheritance and social position. His father had been of the Essex Junto, the family was related to Pickering, and the elder Lyman's intimate friend, Harrison Gray Otis, was still a candidate for office. Consequently Lyman was inescapably bound to that small group of die-hard Federalists who were vainly endeavoring to prevent the disintegration of the party. From 1820 to 1825 he sat in the state legislature in steadfast opposition to the Republicans. In 1823 he actively supported Otis in the latter's unsuccessful campaign for governor. In 1824 he fought against the elevation of John Quincy Adams to the presidency. Gradually he emerged as the leader of a silk-stocking group in uncompromising opposition to the Adams wing of the Republican party. This enmity, the disappearance of Federalism as a party, and the hope that Calhoun would come to control the movement, influenced Lyman to throw his support to Jackson in the election of 1828. Jackson was already receiving in Massachusetts the support of a popular and democratic following built up by Henshaw, and with this faction Lyman brought his aristocrats into a union that had little in common except hostility to Adams. The Lyman group worked heroically in the canvass. They established in August 1828 a newspaper, the *Jackson Republican* (merged in December 1828 with the *Evening Bulletin*). In the course of the campaign Lyman wrote an editorial (Oct. 29, 1828) which so infuriated Webster as to result in a suit of criminal libel. The trial was

celebrated, but the jury could not agree on a verdict and the case was later dropped.

After the election of Jackson, Lyman continued in active support of him, but the patronage went to the Henshaw faction and Lyman grew lukewarm. The disaffection of Calhoun and Jackson's attack on the Bank completed the alienation, and Lyman in course of time became a Whig. But the currents remained confused. In 1831 Lyman ran for mayor of Boston with the support of anti-Jacksonian elements. He was defeated. Two years later he ran again, supported by Henshaw and the (Jacksonian) *Boston Post* although he was far from being a Jacksonian at this time, and triumphed over the National-Republican and Anti-Masonic candidates. He ran again in 1834 and was reëlected, thus serving as mayor throughout 1834 and 1835. His administration was able but undistinguished. The one noteworthy event was the mobbing of Garrison. Lyman's conduct during this riot was bitterly assailed by abolitionists, but it seems now that he acted with courage and discretion.

The later years of Lyman's life were devoted to philanthropy. There was in Boston a Farm School, a private charity intended to rescue morally exposed children. Lyman was called to the board of managers of this school and was thus introduced to the problem of reformatory schools. Consequently when the Massachusetts legislature appropriated in 1846 the sum of $10,000 for the purpose of establishing at Westborough a state-owned reformatory for juvenile offenders, Lyman greeted the venture with the greatest satisfaction. The amount appropriated, however, seemed to him inadequate, and he therefore acted promptly to insure the institution ample funds for a successful start. Between the founding date and his death in 1849 Lyman gave the school $22,500 and in his will there was a further bequest for $50,000. This financial aid was the vital factor in establishing the school on a strong foundation of usefulness. Lyman also bequeathed $10,000 to the Boston Farm School and a like sum to the Horticultural Society of Boston.

[Contemporary newspapers are important for Lyman's political career. Other sources include: *Memorial Biogs. of the New-Eng. Historic Geneal. Soc.,* vol. I (1880); J. H. Benton, Jr., *A Notable Libel Case: The Criminal Prosecution of Theodore Lyman, Jr., by Daniel Webster* (1904); *Proc. Mass. Hist. Soc.,* vol. XIX (1882); Lyman Coleman, *Geneal. of the Lyman Family in Great Britain and America* (1872); W. P. and F. J. Garrison, *Wm. Lloyd Garrison, 1805–1879,* vol. II (1885); Theodore Lyman, III, *Papers Relating to the Garrison Mob* (1870); A. B. Darling, *Pol. Changes in Mass., 1824–48* (1925); *Ann. Reports of the Trustees of the State Reform School at Westborough, 1848–52*; *Reports of the Boston Asylum and Farm School, 1835,*

1836, 1839, 1845, 1847, 1852; *Am. Jour. of Educ.*, Mar. 1861; *Boston Daily Atlas*, July 19, 1849.]   P. H. B.

LYMAN, THEODORE (Aug. 23, 1833–Sept. 9, 1897), zoölogist, was born in Waltham, Mass., the son of Theodore Lyman, 1792–1849 [*q.v.*], a man of broad culture and varied interests, and Mary Elizabeth Henderson. He was reared in a home of affluence and culture and in his early youth was instructed by private tutors. In 1855 he was graduated from Harvard College, and at the time of his graduation he stood fourth in his class. He was attractive in physical appearance, of great personal charm, with a keen intelligence and sense of humor. During the years immediately following his graduation he worked under the tutelage of Louis Agassiz in the Lawrence Scientific School, joined an expedition of scientific research in Florida waters, took the degree of B.S. in 1858, and began the publication of papers on Ophiurans. In 1859 he was elected one of the original trustees of the Museum of Comparative Zoölogy, and somewhat later treasurer. "His rare common sense," wrote George R. Agassiz, "acted as a balance wheel in its somewhat hectic development" (S. E. Morison, *Development of Harvard University, 1869–1929*, 1929, p. 405). For the next score of years he wrote numerous articles on the Ophiuridae, which appeared in the publications of learned societies, and he came to be recognized as an authority on the subject.

From 1861 to 1863 Lyman was abroad in the pursuit of his scientific work and securing collections for the Museum. The outbreak of the Civil War did not seem to stir him greatly. He was opposed to the abolitionists and did not vote for Lincoln in 1860. The progress of the war, however, awakened his interests and a letter from General Meade whose acquaintance he had made on the Florida research expedition, inviting him to be a member of his staff, offered him an opportunity for service in the Unionist cause. He was commissioned as volunteer member of the staff of Governor Andrew, serving without pay, and in the autumn of 1863 joined Meade's headquarters with the rank of lieutenant-colonel. As personal aide-de-camp of the General he served bravely and efficiently at the battles of the Wilderness, Spotsylvania, and Cold Harbor. He was present at the siege of Petersburg and at the surrender of Lee at Appomattox. His letters to his wife covering this period (*Meade's Headquarters, 1863–65: Letters of Col. Theodore Lyman from the Wilderness to Appomattox*, 1922, selected and edited by George R. Agassiz) furnish valuable information on these campaigns. Upon his return to civil life he read before the Military Historical Society of Massachusetts of which he was a member numerous papers on phases of these operations.

In 1866 Lyman became chairman of the newly established Fisheries Commission of Massachusetts and in 1884 president of the American Fish Cultural Association. He was elected Overseer of Harvard College in 1868. Founder of the Reform Club, he was elected to Congress in 1882 on the issue of civil-service reform on an independent ticket, but he failed of reëlection largely because of the disappearance of the reform issue, and because of the beginning of the malady which was to make him a helpless invalid for the last dozen years of his life. He died at his summer home in Nahant. He had married, on Nov. 28, 1856, Elizabeth Russell, daughter of George Robbert Russell, a successful merchant of Dorchester, Mass. Besides numerous articles written for scientific societies, he contributed a short biography of his father to the *Memorial Biographies of the New-England Historic Genealogical Society* (vol. I, 1880) and published *Papers Relating to the Garrison Mob* (1870) in vindication of the action of his father who was mayor of Boston at the time of the riots.

[Henry P. Bowditch, memoir in *Nat. Acad. Sci., Biog. Memoirs*, vol. V (1905), with bibliography; C. F. Adams, memoir in *Proc. Mass. Hist. Soc.*, 2 ser. XX (1906); remarks occasioned by Lyman's death in *Ibid.*, 2 ser. XII (1899); M. A. DeWolfe Howe, *Later Years of the Saturday Club* (1927); *Boston Transcript*, Sept. 10, 1897.]   H. M. V.

LYNCH, ANNA CHARLOTTE [See BOTTA, ANNA CHARLOTTE LYNCH, 1815–1891].

LYNCH, CHARLES (1736–Oct. 29, 1796), soldier, planter, and justice of the peace after whom the term "Lynch Law" appears to have been named, was born at "Chestnut Hill," his father's estate near the present site of Lynchburg, Va. He was the eldest son of Charles Lynch, a Virginia burgess who had emigrated from the north of Ireland as an indentured servant, and who had married Sarah, daughter of Christopher Clark the indenter. The early death of his father left whatever intermediate education Lynch received in the hands of his Quaker mother, but nothing is known specifically of his life until 1755, when, on Jan. 12, he married Anna Terrell (spelled variously). Settling on his patrimonial lands in the newly formed Bedford County, Lynch rapidly became a man of wealth and importance. He took the oath of office as justice of the peace in 1766. The following year he was "disowned" by the Quakers "for taking solemn oaths" (J. P. P. Bell, *Our Quaker Friends of Ye Olden Time*, 1905, p. 147). In 1769 he became a member of the House of Burgesses, continuing as such until the Revolution. He signed the Williamsburg protests of 1769 and 1774 against English taxation, served in the Virginia constitutional convention of 1776, and was a member of the Virginia House of Delegates until January 1778. Already a member of the Burgesses' committee of trade, Lynch played an important part in the mobilization of the state's resources for war. On Feb. 24, 1778, he was recommended for the office of colonel of militia; and in 1781 he was dispatched by Governor Jefferson to the assistance of General Greene in North Carolina (H. R. McIlwaine, *Official Letters of the Governors . . . of Virginia*, II, 1928, *passim*). With his volunteer regiment, he participated in the battle of Guilford Court House and continued with Greene until the surrender of Cornwallis at Yorktown, after which he resumed his duties as justice of the peace. He later served inconspicuously in the Virginia Senate between May 1784 and December 1789.

The disrupted state of the courts in Bedford County during the Revolution early led to the formation of an extra-legal court "to punish lawlessness of every kind" (J. E. Cutler, *Lynch-Law*, 1905, p. 27). With Lynch as the presiding justice, convictions by this court were frequent and were followed by summary whippings. In 1780 when Cornwallis' success seemed probable, a Loyalist conspiracy was discovered in Bedford County; and, as the General Court had been dispersed, Lynch's impromptu court tried and sentenced the conspirators. Two years later Lynch and his companions were exonerated by the Assembly, on the ground that their acts, though not "strictly warranted by law," were "justifiable from the imminence of the danger" (W. W. Hening, *The Statutes at Large . . . of Virginia*, XI, 1823, p. 135). Though remembered now chiefly on account of the connotation of the term "Lynch Law," Charles Lynch, a man of considerable public spirit and broad-mindedness, was of at least minor importance in the economic development of Virginia. He died at his estate on the Staunton River, leaving three sons. The city of Lynchburg was named for his younger brother, John.

[J. T. McAllister, *Va. Militia in the Revolutionary War* (1913); T. W. Page, "The Real Judge Lynch," *Atlantic Monthly*, Dec. 1901; H. C. Featherston, "The Origin and Hist. of Lynch Law," *Green Bag*, Mar. 1900; E. G. Swem and J. W. Williams, "A Reg. of the Gen. Assembly of Va.," *Fourteenth Ann. Report of the . . . Va. State Lib.*, 1916–17 (1917); Margaret C. A. Cabell, *Sketches and Recollections of Lynchburg* (1858); R. H. Early, *Campbell Chronicles and Family Sketches* (1927).]　　　　　　　　　　J. C. W.

LYNCH, JAMES DANIEL (Jan. 6, 1836– July 19, 1903), Confederate soldier, author, was born in Boydton, Mecklenburg County, Va., the scion of a family well known in the early history of Virginia. He was prepared for college in an academy near his home, and in 1855 entered the University of North Carolina, where he remained for three years. In 1860 he moved to Mississippi and became instructor in Greek and Latin in the Franklin Academy at Columbus. In February of the following year he was married to Hettie M. Cochran of West Point, Miss., and the same year, upon the outbreak of the Civil War, he volunteered his services to the Confederacy. After serving as a private for a year, during which time he took part in the Shiloh campaign, he returned to Columbus and organized a company of cavalry, of which he was elected captain, and returned to the front. On June 30, 1864, while leading a charge at Lafayette, Ga., he was severely wounded. He was subsequently captured in a skirmish near Rome, Ga., but managed to make his escape by jumping from a moving freight car at night. During the closing months of the war he was connected with the Niter and Mining Department of the Confederacy and was stationed at Selma, Ala.

After the war Lynch engaged for several years in farming near West Point, Miss., then took up the practice of law at Columbus. He was soon forced to abandon the practice of law, however, owing to an impairment of his hearing, brought on by the wound received during the war. He accordingly turned to the profession of letters for a living. In 1879 he published a volume entitled *Kemper County Vindicated, and a Peep at Radical Rule in Mississippi*; and this was followed in 1881 by *The Bench and Bar of Mississippi*, a volume of biographical sketches of prominent jurists in his adopted state. In 1884 he moved to Texas, making his home at Austin for several years. There he collected the materials for the most important of his prose works, *The Bench and Bar of Texas* (1885). He also published at various times a number of poems. The best known of them are "The Clock of Destiny," "The Siege of the Alamo," and "Columbia Saluting the Nations," the last of which was selected by the World's Columbian Commission in 1893 as America's salutation to the visiting nations at the World's Fair in Chicago. Lynch spent his declining years at Sulphur Springs, Tex., and there prepared for the press two volumes: "The Industrial History of Texas" and "A History of the Territory Indians," neither of which has been published. He was a gentleman of the old school, kindly, chivalrous, unpretentious, but impulsive. He died at Sulphur Springs, Tex., and is buried there.

[The chief authority on the life of Lynch is Dabney Lipscomb, "James D. Lynch of Miss., Poet Laureate of the World's Columbian Exposition," *Miss. Hist. Soc. Pubs.*, vol. III (1900). The author used also a scrapbook, compiled by Lynch's wife, now in the possession of their daughter, Mrs. J. O. Creighton, Austin, Tex.]
K. C.

LYNCH, JAMES MATHEW (Jan. 11, 1867–July 16, 1930), labor leader, was born at Manlius, N. Y., the son of James and Sarah (Caulfield) Lynch. He attended the Manlius public school until his seventeenth year, when he became a "printer's devil" in the office of the Syracuse *Evening Herald*. In August 1887, at the end of his apprenticeship, he joined the Syracuse Typographical Union, of which he soon afterward became secretary, later vice-president, and in 1889 he was elected to the presidency, an office in which he served for two terms. He also served for seven terms as president of the Syracuse Central Trades and Labor Assembly. In November 1898, on his election as first vice-president of the International Typographical Union, he moved to Indianapolis. On June 28 of the following year he married Letitia C. McVey, of Syracuse. In 1900 he was elected to the presidency of the I.T.U. and was reëlected for each of the six following biennial terms. His administration was marked by great energy and exceptional executive ability. Under his leadership the union won for its members the eight-hour day (1906–08), established an old-age pension system, enlarged and improved the Union Printers' Home at Colorado Springs, provided for the better education of apprentices, virtually doubled its membership, and greatly strengthened its financial position.

In 1913 Lynch was appointed by Governor Sulzer commissioner of labor of New York, but the Senate rejected the nomination. A few months later he was reappointed, this time by Governor Glynn, and the nomination was confirmed. On Jan. 8, 1914, he resigned the presidency of the I.T.U. He then returned to Syracuse, where he established his home, though his official duties for the next seven years kept him for the greater part of his time in Albany. In 1915, when the Department of Labor was merged in the Industrial Commission, he was appointed by Governor Whitman one of the five members of the new body, and in 1919 he was reappointed by Governor Smith. In 1916 he was an unsuccessful candidate, on the Democratic ticket, for the place of delegate at large to the state constitutional convention. At the opening of Governor Miller's administration, in 1921, the commission was reorganized and he was legislated out of office. During this period he exerted himself actively in behalf of a rigorous enforcement of the labor laws and gave particular attention to the condition of women wage-earners and to the movements for health insurance and old-age pensions. On leaving office he became president of the American Life Society, a mutual insurance company, but after a year's service became dissatisfied and resigned. In 1924 he was again elected president of the I.T.U., but was defeated in 1926. In June 1929 he was appointed by Governor Roosevelt a member of the Old Age Security Commission, which drew up the old-age pension bill later enacted. From some time in 1927 he had been ill, and in the fall of 1928 suffered an attack of heart disease. He continued at work, however, until toward the end of June 1930, when he was taken to St. Joseph's Hospital, in Syracuse, where three weeks later he died. His wife, six sons, and three daughters survived him. He was buried in the Catholic Cemetery at Fayetteville.

Lynch was a large man, and his bulky figure, with his round, bald head and jovial, bespectacled face, was a familiar sight at many labor and social-reform gatherings. He traveled extensively, was a member of many fraternities, and was widely known. Though genial and expansive in manner, he had a good share of pugnacity and when defending a cause which he had at heart was a doughty antagonist. His services as a public speaker were eagerly sought, for though not an orator he talked with clearness and force and with a thorough understanding of his subject. He wrote many articles for the press, and during his last year edited a Syracuse labor paper, the *Advocate*. His social philosophy was that of a conservative trade-unionist, and he was influential in the councils of the American Federation of Labor. Though active in forwarding social legislation, he was not interested in general schemes of social reconstruction or in projects for independent political action. He was generally recognized as one of the ablest of the labor executives and of the public officials intrusted with the care of the wage-earners' interests.

[*Who's Who in America*, 1922–23; files of the *Typographical Jour.* (Indianapolis), especially the issue of Aug. 1930, containing articles by M. P. Woods and Frances Perkins; *Am. Labor Legislation Rev.*, Sept. 1930; *Inland Printer* (Chicago), Aug. 1930; *N. Y. Times*, July 17, 1930; various controversial pamphlets issued by printers' organizations in 1924 and 1926; information from Jerry R. Connolly, Syracuse, N. Y.; recollections of the writer.]
W. J. G.

LYNCH, PATRICK NEESON (Mar. 10, 1817–Feb. 26, 1882), Roman Catholic bishop of Charleston, S. C., was born at Clones, Ireland. At the age of one he emigrated with his parents, Conlan Peter and Eleanor McMahon Lynch, to

Cheraw, S. C. Manifesting a desire to study for the priesthood, he was sent to the College of the Propaganda, in Rome, later received the degree of doctor of divinity, and was ordained on Apr. 5, 1840, by the Cardinal Prefect. He became successively rector of St. Mary's Church, Charleston (1845), rector of the Cathedral (1847), and vicar-general (1850). Upon the death of the Rt. Rev. Ignatius Reynolds, he was consecrated bishop, at Charleston, by the Most Rev. F. P. Kenrick (Mar. 14, 1858). His episcopal ring, a gift, had once been worn by Cardinal Ximenes. He proved not only a successful administrator but also a forceful preacher and writer who had profited by experience gained as professor of theology and editor of the *United States Catholic Miscellany*. The coming of Ursuline Sisters, invited to establish an academy in the diocese, aroused much non-Catholic opposition. This slowly disappeared, however, and Lynch reported favorably upon conditions when he attended the ninth council of the province of Baltimore in 1858. At the opening of the Civil War he was ministering to ten thousand Catholics. But a disastrous fire which swept Charleston on Dec. 11, 1861, destroyed the Cathedral, the bishop's residence, and other ecclesiastical structures, causing a loss of $180,000. Undaunted, the bishop erected temporary chapels and found time to intervene in behalf of Federal prisoners sent south from the battlefields of the war.

During 1863, Lynch went to Rome bearing a letter from Jefferson Davis expressing the desire of the Confederacy for peace. Pius IX replied, Dec. 3, 1863, by saying: "May it please God at the same time to make the other peoples of America and their rulers, reflecting seriously how terrible is civil war, and what calamities it engenders, listen to the inspirations of a calmer spirit, and adopt resolutely the part of peace." This was widely taken to imply an indorsement of the Confederacy. The Holy See promptly denied such intention, however, pointing to the fact that it had no diplomatic relations with the Confederacy. Shortly afterward, Sherman's army marched into the Carolinas, and much remaining Catholic property was destroyed. When peace had been signed, Lynch, still abroad, petitioned Secretary of State Seward for permission to return, pleading his kindness to Federal prisoners. The request was granted, Jan. 12, 1866, and the Bishop arrived to find his diocese in ruins and his scattered priests discouraged. He therefore visited many cities in the North for the purpose of collecting alms and was so successful in this as well as so instrumental in promoting better feeling between North and South

that he was widely termed "ambassador of good will." His imposing figure (he was more than six feet in height) and his eloquence enforced respect. Once again he went to Rome, attending in 1869 the Vatican Council where he upheld the dogma of papal infallibility. He died in Charleston and is buried there.

[Diocesan archives, Charleston; J. G. Shea, *Hist. of the Cath. Ch. in the U. S.*, vol. IV (1892); F. X. Reuss, *Biog. Cyc. of the Cath. Hierarchy in the U. S.* (1898); J. H. O'Donnell, *The Cath. Hierarchy of the U. S., 1790–1922* (1922); Elizabeth Lynch, *The Lynch Record* (1925); the *News and Courier* (Charleston), Feb. 27, 1882; the *Irish-American* (N. Y.), Mar. 11, 1882; Lynch's middle name is sometimes spelled *Nieson* or *Niesen*. The spelling given in this sketch follows Shea, *op. cit.*]   G. N. S.

LYNCH, ROBERT CLYDE (Sept. 8, 1880–May 12, 1931), physician, was born in Carson City, Nev., the only child of William Mercer Lynch and Minerva Ann Maitlen, the former of English-Bohemian, the latter of English descent. When the son was three years old, the family moved to New Orleans, La., the father, who was an assayer, having been transferred from the Carson City to the New Orleans Mint. The family so completely adapted itself to the strange but sympathetic environment that the son always felt himself to be a native of the city. He was educated at McDonogh School, Number 9, at the Warren Easton Boys' High School, and at the Tulane University of Louisiana, receiving from the latter, on Apr. 29, 1903, the degree of M.D., with special honors. Immediately after graduation he proceeded to Natchitoches, La., where he began the practice of medicine under almost frontier conditions, being sometimes compelled to spend the whole day in the saddle in order to make the rounds of his patients. Before he left this community he had so far overcome difficulties as to have succeeded in organizing a little hospital, the staff consisting of himself and one nurse.

Upon his return to New Orleans, in January 1906, he began intensive preparation for his specialty at the local Eye, Ear, Nose, and Throat Hospital. In August of that year he was married to Amanda Cecile Genin, a member of an old French Louisiana family. From September 1906 until April 1907 he rounded out his special training in Europe, under the direction of distinguished specialists in London, Paris, Vienna, and Freiburg. For three years he practised independently, then he became associated with Dr. A. W. De Roaldes, at that time surgeon-in-charge of the Eye, Ear, Nose, and Throat Hospital. After the death of his senior, Lynch was appointed to his position at the hospital. In 1924 he was made acting surgeon-in-chief and in

1930, surgeon-in-chief. In these capacities he proved himself an unusually able administrator. During this period and until his death, he was also consultant in otolaryngology at the Touro Infirmary. For the period of the Great War, he served as a contract surgeon, in the capacity of medical examiner in the aviation corps.

In 1911 Lynch was appointed to the faculty of the post-graduate school of medicine of Tulane University. From this date until the time of his death he served his university in various capacities as professor of rhinology and otolaryngology, in both the undergraduate and graduate schools of medicine, as well as on various administrative committees which directed advanced study in the medical sciences. Here, too, he won respect for his administrative talent and for his high ideals of medical education. In his specialty he won particular distinction for his improvement of suspension laryngoscopy, for his outstanding contributions to operative treatment of cancer of the larynx, and for his development of the radical frontal sinus operation, now known as the "Lynch operation." He was the first to make successful moving pictures of the larynx and the vocal cords. Some twenty-five articles dealing with his contributions he published in medical journals. In 1924 he was president of the American Bronchoscopic Society and at the time of his death he was chairman of the otolaryngological section of the American Academy of Ophthalmology and Otolaryngology. He was admired as a great surgeon, demonstrator, and teacher, and was loved for his personal qualities. He died, in the prime of life, from injuries received in an automobile accident, near Richmond, Ky.

[The article is based upon information from Lynch's widow, Mrs. Amanda Genin Lynch, and upon the records of Tulane University. For printed sources see: obituary and bibliography of Lynch's writings in *Laryngoscope*, May 1931; *Times Picayune* (New Orleans), and *New Orleans States*, May 13, 1931.]   M. ten H.

LYNCH, THOMAS (1727–December 1776), planter and member of the Continental Congress, was a member of the third generation of the family in America. Jonack Lynch, his grandfather, emigrated from Ireland to South Carolina shortly after the first settlement of that colony. His youngest son, Thomas, discovered a method of cultivating rice on the alluvial lands periodically flooded by the tides. He took out grants for large tracts of tidal areas on the North and South Santee rivers and laid the basis of a fortune which he bequeathed to his son. Thomas Lynch, son of Thomas Lynch by his second wife, Sabina Vanderhorst, was born in St. James Parish, Berkeley County, S. C. He gave early prom-

ise of interest in public affairs, and for several terms was the representative of the Parish of of St. James, Santee, in the House of Commons of the provincial Assembly (1751–57, 1761–63, 1765, 1768, 1772). He was an ardent advocate of resistance to the encroachments of Crown and Parliament. With Christopher Gadsden and John Rutledge [qq.v.] he represented South Carolina in the Stamp Act Congress (1765) which convened in New York City. Denying the jurisdiction of Parliament, Lynch opposed sending any remonstrance to that body. Subsequently, however, he was chairman of the committee which drafted a petition to the House of Commons. He was a member of the General Committee (1769–74) and of the First and Second Continental congresses (1774–76). Silas Deane, in a letter to his wife, described Lynch as he appeared in Congress: "He wears the manufacture of this country, is plain, sensible, above ceremony, and carries with him more force in his very appearance than most powdered folks in their conversation. He wears his hair strait, his clothes in the plainest order, and is highly esteemed" (Burnett, *post*, I, 18). Since he favored non-importation as the measure best calculated to bring the British government to terms, the merchant group opposed his candidacy for Congress, but he was one of the delegates selected by a popular convention in Charleston, and the selection was subsequently ratified by the provincial congress. In the early part of 1776, a stroke of paralysis incapacitated him from further participation in public affairs. He recovered sufficiently to attempt to make his way homeward in company with his son, but at Annapolis, Md., a second stroke ended his life. He was buried in St. Anne's Churchyard, Annapolis.

Thomas Lynch was married, probably on Sept. 5, 1745, to Elizabeth Allston, and in March 1755 he was married a second time, to Hannah Motte, daughter of the treasurer of South Carolina. He had one son, Thomas [q.v.], and three daughters, one of whom, Elizabeth, became the mother of James Hamilton [q.v.] of Nullification fame. Lynch's widow subsequently married Brigadier-General William Moultrie [q.v.].

[Josiah Quincy, *Memoir of the Life of Josiah Quincy, Jun.* (1825), pp. 108, 112–13; E. C. Burnett, *Letters of Members of the Continental Cong.*, vol. I (1921); A. S. Salley, Jr., *Marriage Notices in the S. C. Gazette and Its Successors* (1902) and *Marriage Notices in the S.-C. and Am. General Gazette* (1914); *S. C. Hist. and Geneal. Mag.*, July 1916; references in bibliog. of Thomas Lynch, Jr.]   J. G. V–D.

LYNCH, THOMAS (Aug. 5, 1749–1779), signer of the Declaration of Independence, only son of Thomas [*q.v.*] and Elizabeth (Allston) Lynch, was born in Prince George's Parish, Winyaw, S. C. He received a good academic education at the Indigo Society School, Georgetown, then went to England where he completed his education at Eton and Cambridge and studied law at the Middle Temple (1764–72). In 1772, he returned to South Carolina. Having acquired a distaste for the law, he persuaded his father to permit him to abandon that profession. This task was easier because his father had formed the design of introducing him to public life. To promote this object, he presented him with Peach Tree plantation in St. James Parish on the North Santee. The young man now married Elizabeth Shubrick (May 14, 1772) and settled down as a planter. Being the only son of a wealthy and influential father, he was elected to many important civil offices. He was a member of the first and second provincial congresses (1774–76), of the constitutional committee for South Carolina (1776), the first state General Assembly (1776), and the Second Continental Congress (1776–77). On June 12, 1775, the provincial congress elected him one of the captains in the 1st South Carolina Regiment. He accepted the command, somewhat in opposition to the wishes of his father, who offered to use his influence to obtain him a military appointment of higher rank. In July he went into North Carolina to recruit his company. During this service he contracted bilious fever which made him a partial invalid for the remainder of his life.

On Mar. 23, 1776, the General Assembly of South Carolina, organized under the constitution which young Lynch had cooperated in drafting, elected him to the Continental Congress as a sixth delegate in order that he might care for his father, whose health had given way. His own health was too feeble to permit continued activity in public concerns, but he was present and voting when the Declaration of Independence was adopted and shortly afterward affixed his signature to that document. He did not remain long in Congress, for his health began to decline with alarming rapidity. The elder Lynch had experienced a temporary recovery and his physicians hoped he might live to reach Carolina. Father and son began the journey homeward by easy stages, but the father died on the way. The younger Lynch reached his native state, but in a physical condition which did not promise a long continuance of his own life. After more than two years of illness, with the hope of possibly regaining health, he and his wife took passage for the West Indies toward the close of 1779, expecting to board a vessel there for the south of France. The ship on which they sailed was never heard of again and it is probable that all on board were lost.

[A. S. Salley, Jr., *Delegates to the Continental Cong. from S. C. 1774–89, with Sketches of the Four who signed the Declaration of Independence* (Bull. 9, S. C. Hist. Commission, 1927); John Sanderson, *Biog. of the Signers to the Declaration of Independence,* vol. V (1824); E. A. Jones, *Am. Members of the Inns of Court* (1924); *Biog. Dir. Am. Cong.* (1928); A. S. Salley, Jr., *Marriage Notices in the S. C. Gazette and Its Successors 1732–1781* (1902), *Marriage Notices in the S–C. and Am. General Gazette* (1914), *Marriage Notices in S. C. Gazette and Country Journal (1765–1775)* and in the *Charleston Gazette* (1904); "Journal of Mrs. Ann Manigault, 1754–1781," in *S. C. Hist. and Geneal. Mag.,* vol. XX (1919); *S. C. Hist. and Geneal. Mag.,* Jan. 1927.]   J. G. V–D.

LYNCH, WILLIAM FRANCIS (Apr. 1, 1801–Oct. 17, 1865), naval officer, was born in Norfolk, Va. In his *Naval Life; or, Observations Afloat and on Shore,* published in 1851, which is partly autobiographical, he states that he was early left motherless, that his father was occupied with care of property, and that he welcomed eagerly his appointment as midshipman (Jan. 26, 1819). His first cruise was in the *Congress* to Brazil, thence to China, and around the world. Next he was in the *Shark* on the African coast, then for two years under Porter hunting pirates in the West Indies. He was made lieutenant on May 17, 1828, and commander, Sept. 5, 1849. Following service in the Gulf during the Mexican War, Lynch, who was both an earnest Christian and a lover of adventure, planned the exploring expedition to the River Jordan and the Dead Sea with which his name was afterward chiefly associated. With official support, he left New York in the storeship *Supply,* and after a steamer trip from Smyrna to Constantinople for a firman from the Porte, finally disembarked, Apr. 1, 1848, at Acre. Thence, with the five officers and nine seamen of his party, he proceeded to the Sea of Galilee, dragging overland his two large metal boats, one of iron and one of copper, for navigation of the Jordan. The trip down river to the Dead Sea he made in eight days, Apr. 10–18, accompanied by a caravan on shore, and encountering very real dangers and hardships from the innumerable rapids and hostile Arab tribes. After three weeks of sounding, sketching, and scientific study, the party returned overland through Palestine, and was back in New York at the close of 1848. Though there had been earlier expeditions, Lynch's was the most successfully executed and most productive of scientific results. His *Official Report of the United States Expedition to Explore the Dead Sea and the River Jordan* was published by the Naval Observatory in 1852, and his more popular *Narrative of the United States Expedition to the River Jordan and the Dead Sea* (1849) went through several editions. In 1851 he published his *Naval Life,* before-mentioned, a curious medley of tales, descriptions, and sea experiences. In 1853 he was on the west African coast, reconnoitering for another exploring expedition there (see his report in the *Report of the Secretary of the Navy* for 1852, pp. 329–89), which was not carried out. He was promoted to captain, Apr. 2, 1856.

When the Civil War came his sympathies were with the South, and he was made captain, first in the Virginia, and later (June 10, 1861) in the Confederate navy. He commanded the Aquia Creek batteries on the Potomac, May 30 and June 1, 1861, during their bombardment by Union gunboats; and thereafter, in charge of North Carolina naval defenses, commanded the nine small gunboats that opposed the Union expedition against Roanoke Island. Hopelessly inferior, his "mosquito flotilla" lost two boats in the action of Feb. 6, 1862, and the next day retreated to Elizabeth City, where on the 10th they were completely destroyed by Northern vessels. Capt. W. H. Parker, who served in this campaign, tells of spending the evening before the Roanoke Island battle talking with Lynch of books and reading. "He was," says Parker, "a cultivated man and a most agreeable talker ... I never served under a man who showed more regard for the comfort of his officers and men" (*Recollections of a Naval Officer, 1841–1865,* 1883, p. 228). Lynch was in charge of naval forces around Vicksburg from March to October 1862, and then until September 1864 was in command of ships in North Carolina waters, including the *North Carolina* and the ironclad *Raleigh.* The latter crossed the Wilmington bar on May 7, 1864, and drove off the blockaders, but went aground and was irreparably damaged on her return. Lynch also commanded at Smithville, N. C., during the attacks on Fort Fisher. He died in Baltimore six months after the war ended. His wife, according to J. F. Cooper (*Lives of Distinguished Naval Officers,* 1846, p. 145), was Virginia, daughter of Commodore John Shaw. According to the same writer, he had two children.

[In addition to references in the text, see J. T. Scharf, *Hist. of the Confederate States Navy* (1887), biog. sketch, p. 277; *War of the Rebellion: Official Records (Navy)*; J. C. Thom, "The American Navy and the Dead Sea," *U. S. Naval Inst. Proc.,* Sept. 1926; *Baltimore Weekly Sun,* Oct. 21, 1865.]   A. W.

LYNDE, BENJAMIN (Oct. 5, 1700–Oct. 5, 1781), jurist, was born in Salem, Mass., the son of Benjamin and Mary (Browne) Lynde. He

was a descendant of Simon Lynde of London who emigrated to New England in 1650. The elder Benjamin was a lawyer and served as chief justice of the superior court of the province of Massachusetts. The son graduated from Harvard in 1718 and received the degree of A.M. in 1721. After studying law for a brief period in the office of his uncle, Samuel Browne, he accepted the post of naval officer at Salem. Political differences with Gov. William Burnet [*q.v.*] led to his resignation in 1729. He was active in local affairs, being repeatedly elected moderator of town meeting and town treasurer, and representing Salem in the General Court from 1728 to 1731. On May 25, 1737, he was chosen by the General Court a member of the Council, and, barring a brief period, served continuously thereon for over a quarter of a century. In the same year he was appointed an agent to adjust the boundary dispute between New Hampshire and Massachusetts, and in 1739, to determine the boundary between Rhode Island and Massachusetts. Meanwhile, he had launched upon a judicial career, for on June 28, 1734, he was appointed special judge of the inferior court of common pleas for Suffolk County, and on Oct. 5, 1739, was made one of the standing judges of the same court for Essex County. The death of his father in 1745 created a vacancy on the bench of the superior court, and he was appointed, Jan. 24, 1746, associate justice. In 1766 the propriety of having judges serve as councillors was questioned by the House of Representatives, ostensibly on the ground that membership in the council hampered their administration of justice, but really because the House desired to place at the Council board members more friendly to the popular interest. Lynde was reluctant to be drawn into the controversy and on May 28 his resignation from the Council was announced.

The most noteworthy incidents in his career as a justice of the superior court were two. He was on the bench when the legality of the writs of assistance was argued in 1761; and in 1770, when Thomas Hutchinson [*q.v.*], the chief justice, was obliged to occupy the executive chair, on the departure to England of Gov. Francis Bernard [*q.v.*], Lynde presided over the trial of the British soldiers involved in the Boston Massacre. The latter duty demanded great firmness and courage, since the mob was crying for vengeance upon the red-coats. Hutchinson accuses Lynde of timidity in the face of the popular clamor, alleging that Lynde twice offered his resignation in order to avoid trying the cases (J. K. Hosmer, *The Life of Thomas Hutchinson,* 1896, p. 196). A portion of Lynde's charge to the jury has been preserved (*Diaries, post,* pp. 228–30), and attests his thorough knowledge of the law and his earnest desire to deal justly with the defendants. Upon Hutchinson's appointment to the governorship and "as the result of strong political and other influences" (*New-England Historical and Genealogical Register,* October 1886, p. 349), Lynde was commissioned, Mar. 21, 1771, chief justice of the superior court. His tenure was brief. On Jan. 15, 1772, owing to a dispute regarding payment of judges' salaries by the Crown, and because he felt too old to ride the circuit, he resigned, accepting the less onerous post of judge of probate for Essex County, his last public office.

On Nov. 1, 1731, Lynde was married to Mary (Bowles), widow of Capt. Walter Goodridge and a descendant of John Eliot. He was the owner of considerable real estate, including part of Thompson's Island in Boston harbor, a mansion in Salem, and a fine summer residence near Castle Hill, which he built in 1748 and where he dispensed generous hospitality. Among his many public benefactions were the gift of a fire engine to his native town and a set of English statute books to the state. On one occasion he devoted his salary as town treasurer to the advancement of education. He was an active member of a society to obtain employment for poor people in Boston, and a ruling elder of the First Church, Salem. A diligent scholar, he was keenly interested in the genealogy of his family and the history of his section. His death occurred at Salem from the effects of the kick of a horse.

[Lynde's legislative and judicial career may be studied in the manuscript legislative journals of the General Court and the manuscript records of the superior court, Boston. Consult also Emory Washburn, *Sketches of the Judicial Hist. of Mass.* (1840); *Hist. Colls. of the Essex Institute,* Aug. 1861; *The Diaries of Benj. Lynde and of Benjamin Lynde, Jr.* (1880), ed. by F. E. Oliver; W. T. Davis, *Hist. of the Judiciary of Mass.* (1900).]
E. E. C.

LYNDE, FRANCIS (Nov. 12, 1856–May 16, 1930), novelist, was born in Lewiston, N. Y., the son of William Tilly and Elizabeth (Need) Lynde. Though both of his parents were born in Canada, his father at Whitby and his mother in Montreal, the family had come from the United States. The immigrant ancestor on his father's side was Deacon Thomas Lynde, a member of the Massachusetts Bay Colony, who settled in New England in 1634. When Francis was four years old his parents moved to Kansas City, Mo., where he spent his boyhood and attended the public schools. At the age of fifteen, he returned to the East and endeavored by work in the cotton-mill at Suncook, N. H., to earn money for an advanced education. Discouraged

by the severe toil and long hours, he found employment in a railroad machine-shop as a machinist's helper, won advancement, and went to California in 1876, becoming master mechanic in the shop of the Southern Pacific Railroad at Tulare by the time he was twenty-one. Subsequently, he was appointed chief clerk to the general-passenger agent of the Union Pacific Railroad, and thereafter held various executive appointments in Western roads. At the age of thirty-five he was traveling-passenger agent for the Union Pacific with headquarters in New Orleans.

Here he made the acquaintance of Maurice Thompson [*q.v.*], to whom he confided his earnest desire to become a writer. Encouraged by the successful author to make a trial, he sent a story to the *Century Magazine,* and when it was rejected set himself the task of learning how to write successful fiction, using his constant travels as a source of material. His first article to be accepted dealt with the process of manufacturing artificial ice. He composed it in the writing-room of a hotel in Baton Rouge and sent it to the *Youth's Companion.* Continuing to write, in 1893 he felt justified in giving up his position with the railroad company and devoting his whole time to literary work.

In 1891 he had moved to Chattanooga, Tenn. To secure solitude for his writing, he purchased a part of the Craven Farm on Lookout Mountain, the scene of severe fighting in the Civil War. There he constructed, chiefly with his own hands, a comfortable stone dwelling which he called "Wideview," and which remained his home until his death. In this congenial environment he wrote diligently, producing a large number of magazine articles, short stories, and books. The first of his novels of American life, "A Question of Courage," was published in *Lippincott's Magazine* in 1894. Of some thirty-five novels the most popular have been, perhaps, those that like *David Vallory* (1919) and *The Wreckers* (1920) were based upon his railroad experience in the West. Others were tales of pioneer adventure and five were specifically stories for boys. Among the best of his later books were *Blind Man's Buff* (1928) and *Young Blood* (1929). In 1926, his work was recognized by the degree of Litt.D. from the University of the South at Sewanee.

Lynde was twice married: first, in 1874, to Marietta Williams, who bore him two sons; and second, Jan. 17, 1888, to Mary Antoinette Stickle of Denver, Colo. Of this union there were four children, of whom two daughters, with their mother, survived him. He was a member of the Protestant Episcopal Church and for a number of years was lay reader in charge of a mission at St. Elmo near his home. He is described as straight and slender, auburn-haired, fond of walking, and skilful with his hands. His death occurred at "Wideview" after an illness, and he was buried in Forest Hills Cemetery, Chattanooga.

[E. Y. Chapin, "Literary Figures of Chattanooga," *Chattanooga News,* Apr. 9, 1930, and sketch in *Lib. of Southern Lit.* vol. XVII (1923); *Who's Who in America,* 1930–31, containing a list of Lynde's books; *Chattanooga News,* May 16, 1930; *Chattanooga Daily Times,* May 17, 1930; unpublished personal reminiscences by Mrs. Francis Lynde.]   J.C.F.

LYNDS, ELAM (1784–Jan. 8, 1855), prison administrator, was born in Litchfield, Conn. While he was still an infant, his parents moved to Troy, N. Y., where he learned the hatter's trade. In 1808 his name appeared among the lieutenants of Lieut.-Col. Adam Yates's regiment from Rensselaer County and by 1812 he had risen to major's rank as aide-de-camp of the commander of the 8th Infantry Division. He entered the federal service Apr. 30, 1813, as captain in the 29th Infantry and was honorably discharged June 15, 1815. When the Auburn state prison was established in 1817, he became its principal keeper and four years later he succeeded to the agentship of the prison, only to be forced out in 1825 because of certain scandals arising from his severe disciplinary methods. His executive ability, however, caused him to be placed that same year in charge of the construction and management of the new Mount Pleasant state prison— now Sing Sing. After four years, during which he employed only prison labor, the institution was completed. In 1838, he was again called to Auburn, and once more he aroused such public indignation by his disciplinary measures that he was compelled to resign in 1839 under circumstances which included a grand jury indictment. This episode did not deter the board of inspectors of Sing Sing from engaging him a few years later (1843) as principal keeper, but his experience in that position was short-lived, for in 1844 he was removed on charges of cruelty and misappropriation of state property. Apparently he held no other public office until his death in South Brooklyn a decade later.

Lynds is regarded by some penologists as the creator of the so-called Auburn system, with its solitary confinement of prisoners during the night, its labor in silence in the common workshops during the day, and its lockstep. It is certain that the order and system which impressed the visitor to his prisons were the product of the mailed fist. He was a great believer in the lash, which he considered the least harmful and the

most efficient of all disciplinary means, and he so inculcated this belief into his staff that their excesses, which on at least two occasions hastened the death of a prisoner, caused him the loss of his positions. The interview with him which G. A. de Beaumont and Alexis de Tocqueville published in 1833 (*Du système pénitentiaire aux États-Unis*..., Paris, 1833, pp. 336–41) pictures him as a man of undoubted courage, an autocrat who brooked no interference from political superiors, whose philosophy of punishment was as rigid as his backbone. All prisoners were to him cowards, who should be "tamed" and bent to submission. The interviewers reported as characteristic a story they had heard at Sing Sing. When Lynds learned that a certain prisoner had threatened to kill him, he called that individual into his bedroom, made him shave him, and sent him away saying, "I knew you wanted to kill me, but I despised you too much to believe that you would ever have the courage to do it. Alone and unarmed, I am still stronger than all of you."

[Brief biographical note, with rare portrait, in F. G. Pettigrove, "The State Prisons of the United States under Separate and Congregate Systems," in vol. II, pp. 27–67, of C. R. Henderson, *Correction and Prevention* (1910); Henry Hall, *The Hist. of Auburn* (1869); John Luckey, *Life in Sing Sing State Prison, as Seen in a Twelve Years' Chaplaincy* (1860); *A Letter from John W. Edmonds, One of the Inspectors of the State Prison at Sing Sing to General Aaron Ward, in Regard to the Removal of Captain Lynds as Principal Keeper of That Prison* (1844); *Actes du Congrès pénitentiaire international de Rome, Novembre 1885,* vol. III, pt. II (1888), pp. 275–77; *Mil. Minutes of the Council of Appointment of the State of N. Y., 1783–1821* (1901), II, 993, 1364; F. B. Heitman, *Hist. Reg. and Dict. U. S. Army* (1903), vol. I; *N. Y. Times,* Jan. 9, 1855.]   T. S.

LYON, CALEB (Dec. 8, 1821–Sept. 7, 1875), politician, art and literary connoisseur, son of Caleb and Mary (duPont) Lyon, was born at Lyonsdale, Lewis County, N. Y. His father's family had lived in New England for six generations; his mother was the daughter of Major Jean Pierre duPont, nephew and aide of General Montcalm. Caleb received an excellent education at the regular public school of Lyonsdale, a boys' school in Montreal, and Norwich University, Northfield, Vt., where he graduated in 1841. He entered politics at an early age. On Jan. 20, 1847, he was nominated and on Feb. 15 confirmed, as United States consul at Shanghai (*Journal of the Executive Proceedings of the Senate of the United States of America, 1845–48,* 1887, pp. 182, 184, 194), but he never reached China, and resigned his position within a year. He did get as far from home as California, however, and there served as an assistant secretary of the constitutional convention of 1849. In accordance with the wish of the real designer, Maj.

Robert Selden Garnett, Lyon was credited with designing the State Seal of California, adopted by the convention in 1849 (*Governmental Roster ... State and County Governments of California,* 1889, pp. 191–94).

He soon returned to New York, where he was elected to the state Assembly for the session of 1851, but he did not take an active part in its proceedings. In November 1852, he was elected to the Thirty-third Congress as an independent supported by the Whigs. While there he showed a marked interest in the debates. His most important speeches were on naval and territorial questions. He advocated an increase in the navy, and urged larger subsidies for American shipping lines to enable them to compete with the British as carriers of the mails. He opposed the abrogating of the Missouri Compromise in 1854 and the sanctioning of polygamy in Utah. His congressional speeches were filled with literary quotations, historical and classical allusions, statistics, innumerable adjectives, and witty personal remarks that called forth frequent laughter.

At the close of this Congress, he retired to private life until he was appointed (Feb. 26, 1864) second territorial governor of Idaho, which office he held until April 1866. The one act of his administration that seemed important to the people was the moving of the capital from Lewiston to Boise, but there were others of a more beneficial character that caused less comment. A polished misfit in a country of mining camps, he amazed, amused, and antagonized the people of Idaho by his "weird and fantastic" official utterances, and by his insistence on cleanliness and formal dress. As superintendent of Indian affairs in the Territory, he failed to account satisfactorily for about $50,000 of an appropriation, but he died before the congressional investigation of the matter took place.

The last years of his life were spent in retirement at Rossville, Staten Island, and at the time of his death he was preparing a book on the ceramics of the Revolutionary period. His own collection of pottery contained many valuable pieces from Europe and Asia, and a good-sized group of American pieces of historical interest. His wife, Anna, whom he had married about 1842, survived him until 1881.

[*Lyon Memorial,* vol. I (1905); *Biog. Dir. Am. Cong.* (1928); J. R. Browne, *Report of the Debates of the Convention of California on the Formation of the State Constitution* (1850); H. T. French, *Hist. of Idaho* (3 vols., 1914); W. A. Goulder, *Reminiscences* (1909); J. H. Hawley, *Hist. of Idaho* (1920), vol. I; F. B. Hough, *Hist. of Lewis County, N. Y.* (1883); W. J. McConnell, *Early Hist. of Idaho* (1913); *Catalogue of the "Governor Caleb Lyon Collection of Oriental and Occidental Ceramics" ... to be Sold at Auction* (1876);

Green-Wood Cemetery Records, lot 2244, sec. 94, authority for date of birth; *N. Y. Times,* Sept. 9, 1875.]
M. L. B.

LYON, FRANCIS STROTHER (Feb. 25, 1800–Dec. 31, 1882), Alabama congressman, bank-commissioner, was born in Stokes County, N. C., where his father, James Lyon, a Virginian by birth, owned a large tobacco plantation. His mother was Behetheland (Gaines) Lyon, daughter of James Gaines, a Revolutionary soldier and member of the North Carolina convention which ratified the Constitution of the United States. Francis Strother Lyon was educated in the schools of North Carolina and when he was seventeen years old left the state to make his home with his mother's brother, George Strother Gaines [*q.v.*], Indian agent at St. Stephens, Ala. Lyon's handwriting, which was remarkable for its neatness and legibility, procured him employment as clerk in the bank at St. Stephens and before long he was clerk of the court as well. He read law and was admitted to the bar in 1821. A year later he became secretary of the state Senate and held that position for eight years. On Mar. 4, 1824, he married Sarah Serena Glover. In 1833 he was elected state senator, served three years, and in 1835 was elected to Congress as a Whig. He represented the Mobile district in the Twenty-fourth and Twenty-fifth congresses and then resumed his law practice.

Lyon was a popular lawyer. He often sacrificed a fee to settle disputes between neighbors out of court. Whenever he appeared before a jury, although he was not an eloquent pleader, he was acknowledged to be a dangerous opponent. His hair, which had turned white early in life, gave him an appearance of venerable kindliness which predisposed the jury in his favor. Added to this was his skill in cross-examination, which he conducted with such suave courtesy and careful politeness that his opponents' witnesses often became his own before they were aware of it. Although he was one of the busiest lawyers in Alabama and managed several large plantations and other interests, he always found time for public service and, in a day when good dogs and guns were a necessary part of every man's life, possessed the best in the state.

His greatest public service was rendered in connection with the liquidation of the Bank of the State of Alabama. This institution had been organized as a bank of issue in 1823. From the beginning it was poorly managed. By 1844 it had become hopelessly involved and the state refused to renew its charter. Liquidation was a long and difficult process. Lyon was appointed member of a commission created to close up the affairs of the bank and in 1847 was made sole commissioner with extraordinary powers to collect debts, take up depreciated state bonds, ascertain assets, adjust, extend, renew or exchange securities in such ways as would best serve the interests of the state. He was also to conduct all litigation arising from the liquidation of the bank and to arrange for the payment of the interest and the principal of the public debt. Rarely has a state entrusted such large powers to one man. By shrewd management and untiring vigilance he saved Alabama from bankruptcy and many of the bank's creditors from ruin.

Although Lyon had been elected to Congress by the Whigs, as he came to accept the necessity of secession he drifted into the Yancey wing of the Democratic party. He was chairman of the state Democratic committee in 1860 and a delegate to the Charleston convention. Elected to the Provisional Congress of the Confederacy, he declined to serve, but was elected to the first Congress of the Confederate States and served throughout the Civil War. Most of his fortune was lost through heavy subscriptions to the cotton loan. Throughout the Reconstruction period he was a vigorous supporter of the rights of the state against the national government and he took an active part in the constitutional convention of 1875 which drafted the constitution designed to restore white supremacy. This was his last important public service. He died at Demopolis, Ala., in his eighty-third year.

[J. M. L. Curry, *Hon. Francis Strother Lyon as Commissioner and Trustee of Ala.* (printed in 1889 for private circulation), is the best account but somewhat rare; see also T. M. Owen, *Hist. of Ala. and Dict. of Ala. Biog.* (1921), vol. IV; *Biog. Dir. Am. Cong.* (1928); and obituary in *Daily Register* (Mobile), Jan. 2, 1883. J. G. Baldwin has an interesting character sketch in *The Flush Times of Ala. and Miss.* (1853) but strangely enough writes of Lyon as "Honorable Francis Strother."]

H. F.

LYON, HARRIS MERTON (Dec. 22, 1883– June 2, 1916), author, was born at Santa Fé, N. Mex. His mother was Mary (Merton) Lyon, successively a cook in a railroad hotel, a "bawler out" for a loan shark, a private detective, and an insurance agent; his father, apparently, he never knew. In spite of the severity of the mother's struggle for existence, she managed to put her son through a Texas high school and to send him to the University of Missouri, where, supporting himself by casual employment and some newspaper writing, he graduated in 1905. His college years appear to have been happy. Having a good linguistic sense, he worked hard at Latin and fairly reveled in modern French literature, especially in the work of the symbolists and naturalists. He enjoyed hunting and various

field sports, entered into correspondence with William Marion Reedy [*q.v.*], and for a short time was theatrical reporter on the Houston, Tex., *Post*. As was inevitable with a young man seething with literary ambition, he quickly made his way to New York, where, in the spring of 1906, he was doing minor assignments for the *Broadway Magazine* when Theodore Dreiser became its editor. Under Lyon's rough, surly exterior Dreiser discerned an honest, sensitive mind and an unusual talent for writing; and as soon as he could he put Lyon on the staff of the magazine. He remained with the *Broadway* through two reorganizations and modifications of its name, and, when it became *Hampton's Magazine* in 1909, was made dramatic critic and a director of the concern. The owner sent him to Europe to interview Dr. Frederick A. Cook at Copenhagen and to visit Paris and gave him other opportunities. For a few years, during which he married and bought a farm in Winsted, Conn., he lived in a hectic, uncertain prosperity, was somewhat bemused by the rush and glitter of metropolitan life, lived beyond his income, and overestimated his security and influence. With the suspension of *Hampton's Magazine* in 1912 this prosperity came to an abrupt end, and the remaining four years of his life were marked by poverty, the bitterness of frustrated ambition, and the rapid progress of a fatal disease of the kidneys. Though he continued to write with furious energy, the market for his stories had vanished. To *Reedy's Mirror* in 1914–15 he contributed, probably without pay, an excellent series of essays under the general title, "From an Old Farmhouse," and he also did some work for a motion-picture company on the Pacific coast. His place in American literature depends on two volumes of short stories, *Sardonics* (1908) and *Graphics* (1913). The first was dedicated, significantly enough, to the memory of "the Norman master," and the second to Joseph Conrad. They were issued by obscure publishing houses and received little notice, but they contain some of the best short stories ever written by an American. In sharpness of observation, in deft, sympathetic characterization, and in the concentration and poetic quality of his language Lyon displayed literary power of a high order. At the time of his death he was practically forgotten, and he has been neglected since; but among his fellow writers he has always been admired.

[*Who's Who in America*, 1910–11; *N. Y. Times*, June 4, 1916; editorial comment, *Reedy's Mirror*, June 9, 1916; Alexander Harvey, "Harris Merton Lyon," *Ibid.*, June 23, 1916; Carl Sandburg, "No Regrets," *Ibid.*, Aug. 4, 1916; Theodore Dreiser, "De Maupassant, Junior," *Twelve Men* (1919); portrait, *Bookman*, Mar. 1909, p. 6.]

G. H. G.

LYON, JAMES (July 1, 1735–Oct. 12, 1794), psalmodist, Presbyterian minister, was born in Newark, N. J., the son of Zopher and Mary Lyon, and a descendant of Henry Lyon who emigrated to America in 1649 and settled first in Milford, Conn., and then in Newark. His father died in 1744. On July 18, 1750, by order of the court of Essex County, he was given as guardians Isaac Lyon and John Crane. He attended the college of New Jersey (later Princeton) and was mentioned as the composer of the music for the class ode, presented at the graduation exercises in 1759. In May 1760 he was in Philadelphia taking subscriptions for a projected collection of hymn tunes, probably printed in 1761, which came out under the title *Urania*. It is likely that it was he who brought out in 1763, through William Dunlap in Philadelphia, *The Lawfulness, Excellency and Advantages of Instrumental Musick in the Public Worship of God,* an exposition urging Presbyterians to relax their hostility to instrumental music. Having been licensed to preach, he was ordained by the synod of New Brunswick in 1764 and the next year was settled at Halifax, N. S. There and at Onslow, N. S., he supported himself with difficulty. Finally in 1771 he went in search of a better parish. In Boston he met a member of the committee charged with getting a preacher for the newly founded town of Machias, Me., and in the spring of 1772 he accepted a call to that place with a salary of £84 and £100 as a settlement.

Lyon preached at Machias (except for two intermissions, 1773 and 1783–85) until he died. He was an ardent supporter of the Revolution and in 1775 he outlined in a communication to General Washington plans for the conquest of Nova Scotia with whose places and people he was well acquainted. This elicited a "polite reply" in which the feasibility of the project was not denied. During three years of the Revolution Lyon received no salary but later he was awarded £1,000 in back pay. To eke out an income he operated for a time a salt distillery on Salt Island near Machiasport. His health began to fail in 1793 and he died in the following year. At Machias he retained his interest in music, but his fame rests chiefly upon *Urania,* which must have been conceived while he was in college. Its purpose was to "Spread the Art of Psalmody, in its Perfection, thro' our American Colonies" (*Pennsylvania Journal,* May 22, 1760). It was reported that the first edition had "ruined the publisher," but this was evidently malicious for in 1767 the work went into a second edition. As a composer Lyon possessed respectable but

not extraordinary technical accomplishments. His best piece is the "Hymn to Friendship" which contains some fairly beautiful passages to prove that the writer had innate musical ability. He may have written music during his Machias pastorate, but so far as is known no music of that period survives. He was twice married: on Feb. 18, 1768, to Martha Holden of Cape May, West Jersey, and on Nov. 24, 1793, to Sarah Skillen, in Boston.

[O. G. T. Sonneck, *Francis Hopkinson . . . and James Lyon, Patriot, Preacher, Psalmodist, 1735–1794* (1905); F. J. Metcalf, *Am. Writers and Compilers of Sacred Music* (1925); G. W. Drisko, *Narrative of the Town of Machias* (1904); Geo. Hood, *A Hist. of Music in New Eng.* (1846); *Lyon Memorial,* vol. II (1907); *Columbian Centinel* (Boston), Nov. 15, 1794.]

F. W. C.

LYON, JAMES BENJAMIN (Apr. 21, 1821–Apr. 16, 1909), manufacturer of pressed glass, was born at Pennsylvania Furnace, Pa., the son of John and Margaret (Stewart) Lyon. His grandfather had come to Pennsylvania from Enniskillen, Ireland, in 1763. James entered Jefferson College, Canonsburg, Pa., in 1837, but left without graduating. In 1841 he began working for his father in the iron works of Lyon, Shorb & Company. Six years later he obtained a position with a bank at Hollidaysburg, Pa., but gave it up when he found that his health suffered from indoor work.

On Jan. 1, 1849, under the name of Wallace, Lyon & Company, he started the manufacture of glass. Three months later fire destroyed the entire plant, but he put it into operation again, and in 1851 bought his partner's interest, incorporating the business as James B. Lyon & Company, with William B. David and Alexander P. Lyon as his associates. In 1852 he purchased the old O'Hara glassworks and increased its furnace capacity threefold. Although when he entered the industry, as he himself said, he "did not even know what glass was made of," he obtained a knowledge of the chemistry of the subject from a Boston chemist, and being of a practical and inventive turn of mind, developed a number of new methods and processes, which he refused to patent. He also introduced into glass-making the use of natural gas as a fuel.

Although pressed glass had been made in America since 1827, Lyon was the first to make it the chief output of his factory. He originated most of his beautiful patterns himself, and produced work fully equal in merit to the more famous Sandwich glass manufactured on Cape Cod. Indeed, the founder of the Sandwich plant, Deming Jarves [*q.v.*], wrote of the product of Lyon's firm: "To such a degree of delicacy and fineness have they carried their manufacture, that only experts in the trade can distinguish between their straw stem wines, and other light and beautiful articles made in moulds, and those blown by the most skilled workmen" (*post*, p. 94). In 1867 Lyon was chosen by the National Flint Glass Manufacturers' Association to represent the United States at the Paris Exposition, where his products were awarded a diploma and a bronze medal.

He was interested in education and was one of the incorporators of the Pittsburgh Female College, now the Pennsylvania College for Women. He was also the leading spirit in the organization of the Pittsburgh School of Design. On Oct. 3, 1850, he married Anna Margaret Lyon, a third cousin, and they had three daughters and four sons. In 1893 he sold his business to the United States Glass Company, of which he became treasurer. He retired in 1904 and died, following an attack of pneumonia, at the age of eighty-eight.

[Deming Jarves, *Reminiscences of Glass-Making* (2nd ed., 1865); *Lyon Memorial*, vol. III (1907); R. M. Knittle, *Early Am. Glass* (1927); *Mag. of Western Hist.*, Feb. 1886; *Nat. Glass Budget*, Apr. 24, 1909; *Pittsburgh Dispatch*, Apr. 16, 1909; *Pittsburgh Post*, Apr. 17, 1909.]   A. I.

LYON, MARY (Feb. 28, 1797–Mar. 5, 1849), educator, was born in Buckland, Mass., the sixth of eight children. She had in her veins good old New England blood; among her ancestors were Lieut. Samuel Smith, who sailed for the new world in the *Elizabeth* in 1634, and Rev. Henry Smith, who came from England a few years later. Her father, Aaron Lyon, was a man beloved in the community, a good neighbor, and devoted to his home and children. His death when his daughter Mary was less than seven years old left the mother, Jemima (Shepard) Lyon, with the responsibility of a large family and slender means with which to meet it.

It was a merry, light-hearted young girl, however, who grew up among the hills, in many ways not different from other girls, but outstripping them all in the quickness of her mind and by her passion for learning. Her education was mainly in the academies at Ashfield and Amherst, terms interrupted by periods of teaching. Her extraordinary mental quickness and her zeal for study are shown in the familiar story of her mastery of the English grammar in four days and of the Latin in three. It is not surprising that she was not satisfied with the terms in the Ashfield and Amherst academies and that in 1821 she was eager to go to the seminary at Byfield, which the Rev. Joseph Emerson [*q.v.*] had made famous by his championship of education for women. She was then twenty-four and in those days

it was a thing unheard of for a woman so old to go to school. But she went, and the two terms there gave her a new inspiration for learning, not for acquirement simply, but for service. Thirteen years of teaching followed, three in the academy at Ashfield, of which she was associate principal, and ten with Zilpah Grant at Londonderry, N. H., and Ipswich, Mass.

During these thirteen years, Mary Lyon became more and more impressed with the importance of establishing a seminary for women which should not be dependent "upon the health or life of a particular teacher, but, like our colleges, be a permanent blessing to our children and to our children's children." At first, it was her hope and that of Zilpah Grant that the seminary at Ipswich might be put on a permanent basis, but when she saw that this hope was not likely to be realized, she began to think of a new project, in a different field.

On Sept. 6, 1834, a few gentlemen met with her in Ipswich, "to devise ways and means for founding a permanent female seminary, upon a plan embracing Miss Lyon's favorite views and principles." These "views and principles" had grown more definite, during the months of deliberation, and among them was the hope that the seminary would be "like our colleges, so valuable that the rich will be glad to avail themselves of its benefits, and so economical that people in very moderate circumstances may be equally and as fully accommodated." This interest in the girls of moderate means became a vital part of her plan. "Indeed," she wrote, "it is for this class principally, who are the bone and sinew and the glory of our nation, that we have engaged in this undertaking."

The months between Sept. 6, 1834, and Nov. 8, 1837, were a critical period in the history of the higher education of women. With indomitable spirit Mary Lyon faced indifference and antagonism, difficult to comprehend in this later day. In the effort to raise the amount necessary to establish the seminary, she was indefatigable; but although she was the mainspring of all the effort, she kept herself in the background as much as possible, "pushing forward a few gentlemen of independence and repute who would yet do what she wanted them to do," a task truly requiring "a nice diplomacy." On Oct. 7, 1836, she wrote: "I have indeed lived to see the time when a body of gentlemen have ventured to lay the corner stone of an edifice which will cost about $15,000, and will be an institution for the education of females. Surely the Lord hath remembered our low estate. This will be an era in female education."

On Nov. 8, 1837, Mount Holyoke Seminary was opened, at South Hadley, Mass. In order to bring the opportunities of the school within the range of girls of moderate means, each student had assigned to her some definite household task, but there was no attempt to teach housework. "However important this part of a woman's education," the founder insisted, "a literary institution is not the place to secure it." There was no preparatory department; the course of study covered three years—junior, middle, and senior—with a curriculum based on that followed at Amherst College.

The brief span of Mary Lyon's life after the opening of Mount Holyoke is difficult to realize, so much was accomplished in the twelve years before her death. The growth of the seminary in numbers, as well as in strength and popularity, was steady; the second year four hundred applicants were turned away for lack of room. The main building, accommodating eighty students, was completed and a south wing added. Landscape architects proving too costly, the students brought from home plants and shrubbery, the beginning of the lovely seminary gardens. The original curriculum, including mathematics, English, science, philosophy, and Latin, was expanded by the addition of the modern languages and music, with the hope that Greek and Hebrew and more music might come in the future. The regular instructors were women, their courses supplemented by lectures from the faculties of Williams and Amherst.

Mount Holyoke's claim to priority in the higher education of women is based not only on the curriculum but also on the fact that it was the first institution "where the buildings and grounds, the library and apparatus" were "pledged as permanent contributions to the cause of female education," the permanency of the institution being an essential part of the plan. Mary Lyon's contribution to educational theory is better appreciated today than in her own age. She believed in physical as well as intellectual and spiritual training; in adding music, English, and the sciences to the curriculum; in concentrating attention upon a few subjects. Her contribution to the education of women was threefold: first, the opening to them of the highest educational opportunities; second, the conviction that these opportunities should be used as a preparation for service; third, the conception of such education as the development of all the powers of the individual.

[*The New-England Hist. and Geneal. Reg.*, Apr. 1849; *The Power of Christian Benevolence, Illustrated in the Life and Labors of Mary Lyon* (1851), comp. by Edward Hitchcock; S. D. L. Stow, *Hist. of Mount Hol-*yoke Seminary, South Hadley, Mass., during its First Half Century, 1837–87 (1887); *Lyon Memorial*, vol. I (1905); Beth Bradford Gilchrist, *The Life of Mary Lyon* (1910); Thomas Woody, *A Hist. of Women's Education in the U. S.* (2 vols., 1929); unpublished letters and diaries in the possession of Mount Holyoke College.]				M. E. W.

LYON, MATTHEW (July 14, 1750–Aug. 1, 1822), soldier, politician, pioneer, and entrepreneur, was born in County Wicklow, Ireland, and emigrated to America in 1765. He is known to have worked out the cost of his passage by three years' service to Jabez Bacon of Woodbury, Conn., and Hugh Hannah of Litchfield. About 1771 he married a Miss Hosford of Litchfield, niece of Ethan Allen. Removing to Vermont in 1774, he purchased lands at Wallingford, and resided there for three years. A born forester and pioneer, possessing natural qualities of leadership, he was soon prominent in the turbulent border country of Lake Champlain. He took part in the incessant Hampshire Grants dispute and the early organization for revolutionary action, followed Ethan Allen at Ticonderoga, and served as adjutant of a Vermont regiment under Montgomery in the early stages of the Canadian campaign. In 1776 he was again in service as a lieutenant near the Canadian border, when the indiscipline of his command, characteristic of the Revolutionary army, led to his being cashiered by General Gates. That this action was probably unjustified was evidenced by his reinstatement and distinguished service during St. Clair's retirement in 1777 and the subsequent operations around Saratoga.

He resigned from the army after Burgoyne's surrender and thenceforth took a prominent place in the civil and military affairs of Vermont, being promoted to the rank of colonel in the militia, serving as secretary to the governor and Council, and representing Arlington in the legislature. He was probably in touch with the leaders of the Haldimand intrigue although not a principal in that affair. His share in the operations of the council of public safety and those of the court of confiscation is not clear. In 1785 he was impeached for failure to deliver the records of the latter body, although proceedings were soon dropped, apparently through fear of unpleasant disclosures. His first wife died in 1782 and a year later he married Mrs. Beulah (Chittenden) Galusha, a daughter of Gov. Thomas Chittenden. In 1783 he moved to Fair Haven and became the leading business man of the locality, opening ironworks, manufacturing paper from basswood, establishing a printing-press, and getting out ship-timber for the Lake Champlain-Montreal trade. When the great party struggle of the next decade began he was in an established position. "I had wealth, high political standing, an established character and powerful connections attached to me by long riveted confidence, as well as matrimonial affinity, to throw in the scale" (McLaughlin, *post*, p. 500). This statement is important in view of Federalist slanders creating the impression that Lyon was an ignorant, uncouth demagogue of the frontier.

Following the admission of Vermont to the Union, Lyon was an unsuccessful candidate for both the federal Senate and House, but he was elected to the latter body in 1797. New England had as yet furnished few Republicans to Congress and the Vermont member was immediately an object of unfriendly curiosity, heightened by his vigorous objections to the current practice of waiting on the president with a reply to the annual message (*Annals of Congress,* 5 Cong., 1 Sess., col. 234). He was mercilessly lampooned by Cobbett (*Porcupine's Works,* 1801, VI, 16–17, 168–71) and the whole Federalist press was soon in action. On Jan. 30, 1798, he spat in the face of Roger Griswold [*q.v.*] when the latter made an insulting reference to his military record, and, on Feb. 15, Griswold assaulted him with a cane. These, the first and probably the most famous personal encounters on the floor of the House, with the subsequent investigations, serve to enliven the dreary pages of the *Annals* for several weeks. Lyon escaped expulsion but endured an incredible amount of scurrility and abuse, the whole affair showing in unequaled fashion the intense bitterness of party spirit at the time.

He was now a marked man and the newspapers were carefully watched for material that would render him liable to prosecution under the Sedition Act, which he had manfully opposed on the floor. Actionable matter was discovered in a letter of his, published in the unfriendly *Vermont Journal* on July 31, 1798. Prosecution followed and on Oct. 9, 1798, Lyon was sentenced to serve four months in jail at Vergennes and to pay a fine of one thousand dollars. (The report of the trial is in *The Debates and Proceedings of the Congress . . .,* 16 Cong., 2 Sess., pp. 478–86, Dec. 1820.) This stupid prosecution, of doubtful legality, combined with grave suspicion of jury-packing, had the natural result. Lyon was reëlected by an overwhelming majority and on release enjoyed a triumphal progress to Philadelphia. In 1840 a bill was passed, refunding the fine to his heirs (*Congressional Globe,* 26 Cong., 1 Sess., pp. 410–14, 478). During his second term he continued a vigorous opposition to the Adams administration, resisted the tampering of agents of Burr during the presidential

contest in the House, and, on the withdrawal of his colleague Lewis R. Morris, cast the decisive vote of Vermont for the election of Thomas Jefferson. Then followed his famous letter to "Citizen John Adams" (McLaughlin, pp. 397–406) which is a valuable index to the sentiment of the day, although history has revised the contemporary estimates of both men.

Lyon had already decided to move West and after a preliminary journey went with a considerable colony of relatives and associates to Eddyville, Ky., in 1801. There his career was in many respects a repetition of that in Vermont. Eddyville became a prosperous business center and Lyon was soon a political power in Kentucky, serving a legislative term in 1802 and being elected for a further period of congressional service extending from 1803 to 1811. These years served to bring out Lyon's best qualities as a vigorous speaker and debater, who displayed elements of statesmanship sufficient to refute the earlier slanders. In fact, his repeated clashes with John Randolph on the Yazoo question and his vigorous denunciation of the Embargo and the foreign policies of President Madison brought him into friendly relations with some of his old enemies. He became a friend and correspondent of Josiah Quincy [*q.v.*], and took advantage of the fact to urge the Massachusetts leader not to endanger the Union in the critical days of 1814. In his speeches in Congress Lyon's ingrained love of democracy constantly crops out. He denounced the tyranny of the House rules, the speaker's appointment of committees, the centralizing tendencies to which the Jeffersonians had resorted, the arbitrary government of the western territories, the growth of executive prerogative, and the congressional caucus. He argued for the protection of infant industries with a vigor worthy of Henry Clay, even suggesting the possibility of using slave labor in the industrial development of the South and West (*Annals of Congress,* 11 Cong., 1 Sess., cols. 122–26, 163, 183, 185; 11 Cong., 2 Sess., cols. 1900–03).

His vigorous opposition to the policies leading to the War of 1812, together with neglect of his "fences" in an attempt to recoup heavy losses incurred by the Embargo, led to his defeat for election to the 12th Congress. His business suffered during the war and on Jan. 16, 1817, he wrote: "I am reduced to dependence on my children" (McLaughlin, p. 496). He was always on good terms with President Monroe, who soon found a federal office for him, and in 1820 Lyon went to Arkansas as factor to the Cherokee Nation. He was soon in politics, being defeated as congressional delegate in the first territorial election but succeeding in the second; he died at Spadra Bluff, Ark., before taking his seat. In his seventy-third year he had performed a three-thousand-mile journey on a flatboat to New Orleans and return. A vigorous blast of his against the extravagance and degeneracy of the times in general and of Washington society in particular was posthumously published in *Niles' Weekly Register,* Dec. 7, 1822; this was a typical utterance of the Republican stalwart of 1798. In many ways his career was symbolic of national progress and "this national growth which I almost idolize," as he once put it in the course of debate. He was typical both of the northern frontiersmen and "the men of the Western waters," but with a shrewd business ability which, uninterrupted by politics, might well have made him an early American merchant prince. The loss of his autobiography, said to have been destroyed by mice in a Kentucky garret, undoubtedly deprived the country of an entertaining and valuable historical document.

[J. F. McLaughlin, *Matthew Lyon: The Hampden of Congress* (1900), though eulogistic, is valuable for certain aspects of Lyon's career and contains some important correspondence and reminiscences. See also *Records of the Council of Safety and Governor and Council of the State of Vt.,* vols. I–III (1873–75), with a biographical sketch of Lyon, vol. I, pp. 123–28; *State Papers of Vt. Volume Three. Jours. and Proc. of the Gen. Assembly ...* (4 vols., 1924–29); Pliny H. White, *The Life & Services of Matthew Lyon* (1858); A. N. Adams, *A Hist. of the Town of Fair Haven, Vt.* (1870); R. H. and Lewis Collins, *Hist. of Ky.* (1874), II, 491–92; Elizabeth A. Roe, *Aunt Leanna, or Early Scenes in Ky.* (1885), a tale by Lyon's daughter which has some sketches of the family life.]   W. A. R.

LYON, NATHANIEL (July 14, 1818–Aug. 10, 1861), soldier, son of Amasa and Keziah (Knowlton) Lyon, was born at Ashford, Conn. His father was a descendant of William Lyon who settled in Roxbury, Mass., in 1635; his mother was a niece of Thomas Knowlton [*q.v.*]. At Ashford, Lyon received a common-school education and a Puritan upbringing. He entered the United States Military Academy and graduated in June 1841, being commissioned second lieutenant of infantry, and assigned to the 2nd Regiment, which was already fighting the Seminoles in Florida. He was next ordered to the quiet post of Sacketts Harbor on Lake Ontario. While here he became deeply interested in national politics, and unbosomed himself by writing (1844) that the sending of troops to the Texas frontier bore the earmarks of "madness and folly." Nevertheless, two years later he was ably doing his bit at Vera Cruz, Cerro Gordo, and Mexico. He was commissioned first lieutenant during this campaign and captain in 1851. For several years he was on frontier duty in

California. Between 1854 and early 1861 he was stationed, most of the time, in "Bleeding Kansas."

Impressed with his experiences in Kansas, and Washington, D. C. (during a leave of absence), Lyon wrote a series of political articles (1860–61) for the *Manhattan* (Kan.) *Express,* wherein he bitterly condemned Douglas, called President Buchanan a "blue-eyed old hypocrite," and praised Lincoln and the Republican party. He felt that no state could withdraw from the Union short of revolution, and that in case of attempted secession "discreet measures of coercion" should be used. Nevertheless, he was opposed to disturbing slavery where it already existed, and even approved the enforcement, "in good faith," of the Fugitive-slave Law. After his death some of his papers were gathered into a volume, *The Last Political Writings of Gen. Nathaniel Lyon* (1861).

The most critical epoch in his career opened when he was assigned (Feb. 6, 1861) to the St. Louis Arsenal. Here he was not only efficiently alert in all military matters, but was in constant conference with Francis Preston Blair, Jr. [*q.v.*] and other Republican leaders. After Lyon had questioned the zeal of his superior officer, Gen. W. S. Harney [*q.v.*], and had threatened to throw the Arsenal ordnance officer into the Mississippi if he weakened toward the Southerners, and after Blair had exerted pressure at Washington, Lyon was made a brigadier-general and placed in supreme command (May 1861) of the Union forces in St. Louis. Among his important acts immediately thereafter were the seizure of Camp Jackson and the arming of volunteers. On June 12, Sterling Price and Gov. Claiborne F. Jackson [*q.v.*], in a final effort at compromise, met Blair and Lyon for a conference at the Planters' Hotel. Although it was expected that Blair would lead the discussion for the Union, it was Lyon who took control. Proving himself a master of the issues involved, he dominated the entire four-hour conference. His final conclusion was, "This means war."

The next day he sent Colonel Franz Sigel with a small force directly into southwest Missouri, while he, with some two thousand regulars, pushed up the Missouri River, took Jefferson City June 15, and captured Boonville two days later. The state forces retreated to southwest Missouri and Lyon turned in pursuit, reaching Springfield July 13. After fruitless efforts to obtain reënforcements he decided (Aug. 9) to attack the main forces of the enemy, camped ten miles southwest on Wilson's Creek. The combined effective state and Confederate troops in this battle totaled slightly over ten thousand, while Lyon's regulars and others numbered 5,400. At night Lyon sent Sigel with 1,200 men to attack, early the next morning, the enemy's extreme right wing, while he, with 4,200 troops, fell upon the rear of their left. Initially successful, Sigel was later surprised and routed, and thus a probable Union victory was turned into defeat. After about five hours of courageous and able fighting Lyon was killed at the head of his troops. The entire North mourned his death and he immediately became a national hero and martyr. In spite of the defeat at Wilson's Creek, his brilliant work had done much to hold Missouri for the Union. The volunteer private soldiers did not like him because, among other things, "he had no compliments or kind words for anybody, and talked to his soldiers as he did to a mule." Nevertheless, they had that respect for him which all soldiers feel toward an officer who understands his business.

[James Peckam, *Gen. Nathaniel Lyon and Mo. in 1861* (1866) and Ashbel Woodward, *Life of Gen. Nathaniel Lyon* (1862), are eulogistic. Other sources are: "The Diary of Private Ironquill," in N. L. Prentis, *Kan. Miscellanies* (1889); *Springfield* (Mo.) *Leader*, Sept. 29, 1928; *War of the Rebellion: Official Records* (*Army*), 1 ser., vol. I; *Report of the Joint Committee on the Conduct of the War*, pt. 3 (1863); T. L. Snead, *The Fight for Mo.* (1888); W. E. Smith, "The Blairs and Fremont," *Mo. Hist. Rev.*, Jan. 1929; *The Lyon Monumental Asso.* (1871), comp. by E. H. E. Jameson; W. F. Switzler, *Switzler's Illus. Hist. of Mo.* (1879); J. G. Nicolay and John Hay, *Abraham Lincoln* (10 vols., 1890); R. J. Rombauer, *The Union Cause in St. Louis in 1861* (1909); Allan Nevins, *Frémont* (1928); L. U. Reavis, *The Life and Mil. Services of Gen. Wm. Selby Harney* (1878); Galusha Anderson, *The Story of a Border City During the Civil War* (1908); G. W. Anderson, *Life and Character of Gen. Nathaniel Lyon* (1863), an address; files of St. Louis newspapers, Feb.–July 1861, and esp. *Daily Mo. Democrat*, Aug. 14, 1861; *Lyon Memorial*, vol. I (1905); G. W. Cullum, *Biog. Reg. Officers and Grads. U. S. Mil. Acad.* (3rd ed., 1891), vol. II.]   H. E. N.

LYON, THEODATUS TIMOTHY (Jan. 23, 1813–Feb. 6, 1900), pomologist, was born at Lima, N. Y., the son of Timothy and Mary (Davis) Lyon and a descendant of Richard Lyon who settled in Fairfield, Conn., in 1649. His father, a millwright, architect, and farmer, removed from New York state to Plymouth, Mich., in 1828, when the boy was in his sixteenth year. The son had attended the village school in Lima and in the West had the varied experiences of frontier life. For a time he carried the mail to outlying points on horseback. In 1834 he returned to Lima, attended school for a summer, then taught at Conesus, 1834–35, and at Penfield, 1835–36. He went west again to Plymouth in 1836 and engaged in milling, farming, and fruit-growing. Two years later he was married to Marilla, daughter of William S. Gregory of Plymouth. He was active in pioneer railroad

construction and for several years was president of two of the roads which eventually became a portion of the Pere Marquette Railway system. About 1844 he established a nursery, collecting varieties of trees from surrounding orchards. He soon learned that the local varietal nomenclature was badly confused. He became interested in the study of fruit varieties and assembled a large collection of apples. He made intensive study of their identity and nomenclature, publishing from time to time articles in the *Michigan Farmer* and other periodicals of the region. The accuracy of his published descriptions interested Charles Downing who was then engaged in the revision and enlargement of *The Fruits and Fruit Trees of America* which his deceased brother, Andrew Jackson Downing, had first published in 1845. Through the correspondence which developed with Downing and other pomologists of that epoch, as well as through his published articles, he soon came to be regarded as "the most critical and accurate of American pomologists" (Bailey, *post*, p. 1586).

In 1874, when the development of the then new "fruit belt" of western Michigan was in progress, he removed to South Haven, where he spent the remainder of his life. He took charge of a nursery there, which, though not financially successful, constituted an important factor in the rapid development of the orcharding of the region because of the accuracy and honesty of varietal description and the trueness to name of the stock grown and sold for planting. Lyon's particular interest in the study and appraisal of fruit varieties was such that he consistently devoted more time and energy to it than to the development of a nursery business. In 1876 he was elected president of the Michigan Pomological Society (after 1880 the Michigan Horticultural Society) and served actively until 1893, when he became honorary president. His "History of Michigan Horticulture" was published in the *Seventeenth Annual Report of the ... State Horticultural Society* (1887). In 1889 the collection of fruit varieties which he had assembled on his own property at South Haven was taken over by the state board of agriculture as the nucleus of the South Haven substation of the Michigan Experiment Station. He was in charge of this station from 1889 until his death, issuing frequent published reports for the guidance of the fruit growers of the state. As chairman of the committee on revision of catalogue of fruits of the American Pomological Society from 1889 to 1897, he initiated and developed as an agent of the division of pomology of the United States Department of Agriculture, the card catalogue of fruits which later, as further enlarged by W. H. Ragan, became the basic fruit-variety reference list of the Department. Lyon was one of the most eminent of the self-taught pomologists of the nineteenth century and deserves recognition for his efforts at clarifying pomological nomenclature and for his insistence upon the accurate description and honest appraisal of varieties of fruits.

[L. H. Bailey, *Standard Cyc. of Horticulture*, vol. III (1915); C. W. Garfield, "Theodatus Timothy Lyon," *Hist. Colls., Colls. and Researches . . . Mich. Pioneer and Hist. Soc.*, vol. XXIX (1901), and memorial address in *Thirtieth Ann. Report . . . of the State Horticultural Soc. of Mich.* (1901); *Lynn Memorial*, vol. II (1907); *Detroit Free Press, Detroit Jour.*, Feb. 7, 1900; personal acquaintance.]   W. A. T.

LYON, WILLIAM PENN (Oct. 28, 1822–Apr. 4, 1913), legislator, jurist, was born of Quaker parents at Chatham, Columbia County, N. Y. His father, Isaac Lyon, was descended from Thomas Lyon who was born in England about 1621 and died in Connecticut. His mother, Eunice (Coffin) Lyon, was descended from Tristram and Dionis Coffin, English Quakers who emigrated to America in 1642 and settled in Nantucket. William was the third child in a family of ten children. The father conducted a small country store for some years but suffering financial reverses moved with his family to the town of Hudson (later Lyons), Walworth County, Wis., in 1841. William grew up in a community in which the Quaker tradition was predominant. He attended a district and select school, but his formal education, meager as it was, he supplemented by extensive reading. Under the guidance of his mother, who seems to have been a woman of great wisdom and unusual foresight, he began the study of law by reading Blackstone's *Commentaries,* Cowan's *Treatise,* and Chitty's *Pleading.* He studied in the law offices of Judge George Gale and Judge Charles M. Baker and was admitted to the bar of Walworth County in the spring of 1846. He was at once elected a justice of the peace and later town clerk. His income was sixty dollars for the first year. On Nov. 18, 1847, he was married to Adelia Caroline Duncombe, daughter of Dr. E. E. Duncombe of St. Thomas, Ontario. He later practised law at Burlington and Racine, served as district attorney of Racine County, 1855–58, and was a member of the Assembly as well as its speaker for two terms, 1859–60.

In September 1861 he entered military service as captain of Company K, 8th (Eagle) Regiment of Wisconsin Volunteers. In 1862 he was commissioned colonel in the 13th Wisconsin. He saw much hard service, participated in many battles and engagements, and served throughout his enlistment with credit and distinction. Shortly after his discharge he was breveted a brigadier-general of the United States volunteers to date from Oct. 26, 1865. In the spring of 1865, while he was still in the service, he was elected judge of the first judicial circuit, then second in importance to the fourth circuit, which included Milwaukee County. Upon his return to Racine, he entered upon his duties as circuit judge and five years later (1871) he was appointed justice of the supreme court to fill the unexpired term of Byron Paine. He was elected to the same office in 1871, 1877, and 1883, and served until his voluntary retirement on Jan. 1, 1894. For the last two years he was by virtue of seniority, chief justice. Although at the time of his retirement Lyon had passed three score and ten years, he was two years later called to serve as a member of the state board of control, governing penal and charitable institutions, and served in that capacity for seven years. Upon his retirement his services were commended by Gov. Robert M. LaFollette. He passed his declining years with his son and daughter at Edenvale, Cal., where he died in the ninety-first year of his age. A perusal of his career leaves one with a distinct impression that he lacked almost entirely the dramatic instinct. It never occurred to him to set the stage, or in any way seek to win public acclaim. He was modest, of a gentle but firm spirit. Perhaps no public man in the history of the state had fewer enemies or was more generally beloved and respected.

[Clara Lyon Hayes, *Wm. Penn Lyon* (1926), reprinted from the *Wis. Mag. of Hist.*, Sept. 1925–July 1926; Adelia C. Lyon, *Reminiscences of the Civil War* (1907), compiled from Lyon's correspondence and other papers; 154 *Wis. Reports*, xxviii–xl; P. M. Reed, *The Bench and Bar of Wis.* (1882); J. R. Berryman, *Hist. of the Bench and Bar of Wis.* (2 vols., 1898); J. B. Winslow, *The Story of a Great Court* (1912); *Lyon Memorial*, vol. III (1907); *Mag. of Western Hist.*, Apr. 1887; the *Wis. State Jour.* (Madison), Apr. 4, 5, 1913.]
                                                                            M. B. R.

LYONS, PETER (1734/35–July 30, 1809), Virginia jurist of Irish ancestry, was presumably born in County Cork to John and Catherine (Power) Lyons. Nothing is known of his schooling: the supposition that he attended Trinity College, Dublin, is erroneous. According to family tradition he was persuaded by his maternal uncle, James Power, of King William County, Va., to emigrate to America. It is known that he studied law under Power and was licensed to practise in the county courts of Virginia on Feb. 5, 1756. Succeeding to the profitable practice of his uncle, he rose rapidly in his profession; and having moved to Hanover County, he attained there "an unrivalled reputation for legal learning" (William Wirt, *Sketches of*

the Life and Character of Patrick Henry, 1817,
p. 16). He was plaintiff's attorney in the celebrated "Parsons' Cause" when the Rev. James
Maury brought suit for the recovery of the part
of his salary lost through the "two penny act" of
1758. Lyons, arguing the nullity of an act which
had never received the royal sanction, won the
case on a demurrer. A jury was chosen to assess the damages, and Patrick Henry, having
become counsel for the defense when the case
was already lost, so far succeeded in stirring the
latent prejudices of the jury that damages of one
penny were awarded.

Daniel Call states that "in the contest with
Great Britain" Lyons "took part with the colonies, and was a friend to the revolution" (4 Call,
Va. Reports, xix), but he seems to have seen no
active service. In 1779 he was appointed judge
of the general court of Virginia, and in the same
year, by virtue of this position, became a judge
of the court of appeals. He was one of the first
five judges in the reorganized court of December 1788 and on the death of Edmund Pendleton
in 1803 became its second president. Among the
most important cases argued during his connection with the court was one limiting the independent pardoning powers of the lower house,
and another, as a result of which the church lost
its glebe lands. Though Lyons continued as
president of the court until his death, ill health
prevented his active connection with it after 1807.

The portrait of Lyons by Thomas Sully in the
supreme court room at Richmond shows a man
past middle age, of clear, rounded features and
benevolent appearance. He was not a brilliant
man but was a close student of the law and enjoyed a reputation for unvarying impartiality.
He was twice married, first to his cousin, Mary
(Catherine?) Power, and secondly to Judith
Bassett. He died at "Studley," his home in Hanover County.

[David J. Mays, "Peter Lyons," *Proc. Thirty-Seventh Ann. Meeting: The Va. State Bar Asso.,* 1926, pp.
418–26, is the best account of Lyons' life and contains
full bibliographical information. Some letters of Lyons
to his grand-daughter, of little biographical value, are
printed in *Tyler's Quart. Hist. and Geneal. Mag.,* Jan.
1927. Call's sketch (cited above) gains in authority
what it lacks in length and perspective.]   J. C. W.

LYSTER, HENRY FRANCIS LE HUNTE
(Nov. 8, 1837–Oct. 3, 1894), physician, was born
at Sander's Court, County Wexford, Ireland, to
the Rev. William N. and Ellen Emily (Cooper)
Lyster. The father, an Episcopal clergyman,
graduate of Trinity College, Dublin, had already
been to America, where in 1833 he built St. Peter's Church at Tecumseh, Mich., the first church
of his denomination in Michigan. He brought

his family to America in 1838. The son received
his preliminary education in private schools in
and about Detroit, graduated in arts at the University of Michigan in 1858 and in medicine
from the medical college of the university in
1860. At the outbreak of the Civil War he was
commissioned assistant surgeon of the 2nd Michigan Volunteer Infantry, subsequently becoming
surgeon of the 5th Michigan. He served in the
Army of the Potomac from the battle of Bull
Run to Appomattox, mainly as an operating surgeon. He was at one time acting medical director of the III Army Corps.

Returning to Detroit at the close of the war he
quickly became one of the leading physicians
and surgeons of the state. In 1868 he was appointed lecturer on surgery in the University of
Michigan which position he filled for two years.
From 1888 to 1890 he was professor of theory
and practice of medicine and clinical medicine
at the same school. The travel involved in going
from Detroit to Ann Arbor compelled him to
give up his teaching connection with the university. He was one of the founders and served as
president of the faculty of Michigan College of
Medicine. After its fusion in 1885 with the Detroit Medical College, when the Detroit College
of Medicine was formed, he served as professor
of the practice of medicine and of clinical diseases of the chest until 1893. At different times
he was connected editorially with the *Peninsular
Journal of Medicine* and the *Detroit Clinic.* His
professional writings appear in these journals
and in the *Transactions of the State Medical Society.* He was appointed in 1873 a member of
the original State Board of Health and served
eighteen years, taking particular interest in the
protection of water supplies. His genius for organization gave him a prominent part in the
founding of the Detroit Academy of Medicine,
the Wayne County Medical Society, and the
Michigan State Medical Society. For years he
was medical director of the Michigan Life Insurance Company.

Though he came out of the Civil War with
an unusual surgical experience and a reputation
as a skilful operator, he continued to the end as
a family practitioner, a conscientious attendant
upon whatever patient called upon his skill and
counsel. This exacting service took its toll of
his health and his last years were marked by invalidism from pernicious anemia from which he
died. Throughout his career he was in the forefront of every movement in his city and state that
had to do with the physical or moral welfare of
the community. In his chosen vocation he was
an example of the honor and generosity which

mark the ideal man of medicine. He was always a student and in his later years his fund of learning and his gift for logical expression made him one of the most accomplished public speakers in Detroit. Personally he was tall and of spare build, with dark hair and clear blue eyes. He was married in Washington, D. C., on Jan. 30, 1867, to Winifred Lee Brent, daughter of Capt. Thomas Lee Brent of Stafford County, Va. His wife and five children survived him.

[H. A. Kelly and W. L. Burrage, *Am. Medic. Biogs.* (1920); *Trans. Mich. State Medic. Soc.,* vol. XIX (1895); B. A. Hinsdale, *Hist. of the Univ. of Mich.* (1906); *Cyc. of Mich.: Hist. and Biog.* (1900); *Detroit Tribune,* Oct. 5, 1894; information as to certain facts from Lyster's son, Col. Wm. Lyster, U. S. A.]
                                              J. M. P—n.

LYTLE, WILLIAM HAINES (Nov. 2, 1826–Sept. 20, 1863), soldier, poet, was born in Cincinnati, Ohio. He was descended from a family distinguished for its martial spirit. His great-grandfather, William, a captain in the French and Indian War and a colonel in the Revolution, moved from Cumberland County, Pa., to Kentucky in 1779. His son, William, generally called General, settled in Ohio. Robert, the father of William Haines Lytle, was for many years an influential political leader, a representative to Congress from the Cincinnati district, and, during President Jackson's administration, surveyor-general, an office which his father had once held. From his mother, Elizabeth (Haines), William probably inherited his poetic strain. When sixteen years old he graduated from Cincinnati College. His military predilections made him desirous of entering West Point, but his family urged him to select law as a profession. Accordingly, he entered the law office of his uncle, E. S. Haines, where he remained for five years. Upon the outbreak of the Mexican War, he deserted his books and entered the service as first lieutenant of the 2nd Ohio Infantry. For ten months he was in active service, and at the close of hostilities had attained the rank of captain. At the conclusion of the war he began practising law as a member of the firm of Haines, Todd & Lytle. In 1852 and again in 1854 he was elected to the state legislature on the Democratic ticket. During part of this time he was speaker of the House. He was an unsuccessful candidate for lieutenant-governor in 1857 and the same year Gov. Salmon P. Chase appointed him major-general in command of the first division of the Ohio Militia.

The period of Lytle's greatest literary activity was during the years between the Mexican and Civil wars; and although his military record during the latter conflict was distinguished, his national fame rests upon his poetical writings. His best known poem, the lyric "Anthony and Cleopatra," is a "passionate glorification of love and war" (Randall and Ryan, *post,* V, 72). Its publication in the *Cincinnati Commercial,* July 29, 1858, brought the author instant recognition. It has long remained a popular favorite because of its "melody, dramatic vividness, and bold imagery." Among his other poems are, "Popocatepetl," "Jacqueline," "Macdonald's Drummer," "Volunteers," "Farewell," and "Sweet May Moon." A collection, *Poems of William Haines Lytle,* was published in 1894, and reprinted in 1912.

Upon the outbreak of the Civil War Lytle organized and established Camp Harrison at Cincinnati. In June 1861 he was appointed colonel of the 10th Ohio Infantry. He was twice severely wounded, first at Carnifex Ferry, Sept. 10, 1861; and later, at Perryville, Oct. 8, 1862, on which occasion he was left upon the field for dead. Recovering from his wound, he was paroled and permitted to return home. His gallantry at Perryville won for him the congratulations of Secretary Stanton, and, upon his exchange, Lytle was promoted to the rank of brigadier-general. On the second day of the battle of Chickamauga, he was severely wounded while leading a charge and died shortly afterwards. His funeral in Cincinnati, Oct. 22, 1863, was one of the most impressive of the war and reflected the high esteem in which he was held by friend and foe.

[E. O. Randall and D. J. Ryan, *Hist. of Ohio* (1912), vol. V; memoir by W. H. Venable in *Poems of William Haines Lytle* (1894, 1912); W. H. Venable, *Beginnings of Literary Culture in the Ohio Valley* (1891); Emerson Venable, *Poets of Ohio* (1909); *The Biog. Cyc. and Portrait Gallery . . . of the State of Ohio,* vol. I (1883); Whitelaw Reid, *Ohio in the War* (1868); *Cincinnati Daily Commercial,* Oct. 23, 1863.]   R. C. M.

LYTTELTON, WILLIAM HENRY (Dec. 24, 1724–Sept. 14, 1808), colonial governor, author, was the sixth son of Sir Thomas Lyttelton, bart., and Christian Temple, daughter of Sir Richard Temple, bart., of Stowe, Buckinghamshire. After attending Eton College and Saint Mary Hall, Oxford, he was called to the bar at the Middle Temple in 1748 and represented the borough of Bewdley, Worcestershire, in Parliament from December of that year until February 1755, when he was appointed governor of South Carolina.

Arriving in Charleston in 1756, he found awaiting him the task of arranging for the care of the unfortunate Acadians who had been deposited there, over one thousand strong. Some of these people he settled in the town, binding them out or placing them in suitable occupations.

Others he scattered over the province with any families who were willing to receive them as bond servants. The principal problem that confronted him as governor, however, was presented in 1759 as a result of Cherokee raids on the frontier. In that year he held a conference with the Cherokee chiefs, who seem to have desired peace; but contrary to the advice of his more experienced lieutenant-governor, William Bull [q.v.], he planned a punitive expedition against the tribe, broke off the conference, and detained the chiefs who had attended under the pledge of safe conduct, forcing them to accompany his army on its march to Fort Prince George. There, in a second conference with the Cherokees, it was agreed that these chiefs should be held as hostages until the Indians responsible for the murders on the frontier were surrendered. Unfortunately for Lyttelton's plans, smallpox broke out in his army, which gradually dispersed, leaving him practically alone except for the garrison at the fort. Under these circumstances he returned to Charleston in January 1760. After his departure the Indians, who had been greatly enraged by what they deemed his treachery in detaining their chiefs, killed the commander and some of his men and attacked the fort. In revenge the garrison turned on the Indian hostages and murdered them. The result was renewed Indian war and further ravages on the frontier.

The full force of this catastrophe was not felt by Lyttelton, for in April he sailed for Jamaica to assume the governorship, then considered the choicest of colonial appointments. Here he came into conflict with the Council and Assembly for interfering with their commitments of offenders. His action was bitterly denounced by the Assembly in July 1766 and Lyttelton himself represented as a tyrant (Edwards, post, II, 347–53; Bridges, post, II, 105–09). In October of that year he was appointed ambassador to Portugal. Returning home in 1771, he lived an active life and received many honors, being raised first to the peerage of Ireland and subsequently to that of Great Britain, as Lord Lyttelton, baron of Frankley. He wrote "An Historical Account of the Constitution of Jamaica," which was prefixed to the new edition of *The Laws of Jamaica* issued in 1792, and in 1793 was published as an appendix to Bryan Edwards' *History, Civil and Commercial, of the British Colonies in the West Indies* (I, 250–60). In 1803, he printed *Trifles in Verse* for private circulation. He was married June 2, 1761, to Mary, eldest daughter of James Macartney of County Longford, and on Feb. 19, 1774, to Carolina, daughter of John Bristow of Quiddenham, Norfolk. He had two sons, one by each marriage. He died at Hagley in 1808.

[Sketch by J. M. Rigg, in *Dict. Nat. Biog.*, with bibliography; Maud Wyndham, *Chronicles of the Eighteenth Century, Founded on the Correspondence of Sir Thomas Lyttelton and His Family* (2 vols., 1924); Edward McCrady, *The Hist. of S. C. under the Royal Govt.* (1889); Alexander Hewat, *An Hist. Account of the Rise and Progress of the Colonies of S. C. and Ga.* (2 vols., 1779); David Ramsay, *The Hist. of S. C.* (2 vols., 1809); W. R. Smith, *S. C. as a Royal Province* (1903); Edwards, *ante*; G. W. Bridges, *The Annals of Jamaica*, vol. II (1828); *Gentleman's Mag.* (London), June 1761, Oct. 1766, Feb. 1774, Sept. 1808.]

H. B–C.

MAAS, ANTHONY J. (Aug. 23, 1858–Feb. 20, 1927), Roman Catholic priest and educator, son of John and Elizabeth (Peetz) Maas, was born at Bainkhausen, Westphalia. He attended private schools at Hellefeld and Stockum (1869–74) in preparation for the gymnasium of Arnsberg, where he studied until about 1877, when he emigrated to the United States. He immediately sought entrance into the Society of Jesus; and after satisfying the scrutiny of the superior of the mission, Charles Charaux, he was admitted to the novitiate at West Park, N. Y., Apr. 9, 1877. At Frederick, Md., he continued the study of the classics and Hebrew before taking the philosophical course (1880–83) at the College of the Sacred Heart, Woodstock, Md. After a year's teaching of Latin and Greek to scholastics, he returned to Woodstock for theology (1884–88). He was ordained in 1887. A tried man of marked ability, he was assigned to an instructorship in scripture (1891–1902) and Hebrew (1885–1902) and to the custodianship of the rich library at Woodstock (1888–1902). These labors were interrupted in 1893, when he was ordered to Ignatius Loyola's own Manresa in Spain for the third year of his novitiate, or tertianship. In 1894, with intensified zeal, he returned to his chair at Woodstock.

Here he remained as prefect of studies (1897–1905) and as rector and consultor of the province after 1907, save for a leave of absence (1905–07) during which he was an editor of the *Messenger of the Sacred Heart*. In June 1910 he was delegate to the congregation of procurators at Rome. Two years later, under the rule of obedience (Oct. 4, 1912), he was appointed provincial of the Maryland-New York province with direction over 872 priests, scholastics, and lay brothers as well as authority over a dozen universities and colleges and a number of other institutions belonging to the Society. During his tenure of six years, he proved a benevolent ruler who was far more stern with himself than with his men; and the Society of Jesus prospered accordingly. As ex-provincial, from 1918 until his death he was instructor of tertians at St. Andrews-on-the-Hudson, except for a term in Rome (1923), where he aided in the revision of the *Institute* of the Society.

Through his publications, Maas had an influence which reached beyond the confines of his society. He contributed essays to the *American Catholic Quarterly Review,* to *America,* and to the *Ecclesiastical Review,* in which he edited the department of scripture; he was the author of about a hundred sketches and articles in the *Catholic Encyclopedia,* and wrote several books, including *The Life of Our Lord Jesus Christ* (1891), *Enchiridion ad Sacrarum Disciplinarum Cultores* (1892), *A Day in the Temple* (1892), *Christ in Type and Prophecy* (2 vols., 1893–96), and a *Commentary on the Gospel of St. Matthew* (1898).

[*Am. Cath. Who's Who* (1911); *Who's Who in America,* 1926–27; annual Catholic directories; *The Cath. Encyc. and Its Makers* (1917); *N. Y. Times,* Feb. 21, 1927; and material furnished from the Woodstock archives.]   R. J. P.

MABERY, CHARLES FREDERIC (Jan. 13, 1850–June 26, 1927), chemist, son of Henry and Elizabeth A. (Bennett) Mabery, was born at New Gloucester, Me., and died at Portland, Me. His early education was received in the public schools of Gorham, Me., and in Kent's Hill Academy. After graduation from the academy he taught for five years in schools of his native state. In 1873 he studied chemistry in the summer school of Harvard University and in the fall enrolled in the same institution for intensive study in chemistry under Josiah P. Cooke [*q.v.*]. Three years later he graduated from the Lawrence Scientific School with the degree of B.S. Continuing at Harvard as a graduate student, he received the degree of Sc. D. in 1881. During this time and also for two additional years he was an assistant in chemistry and supervised the work in chemistry in the Harvard Summer School. On Nov. 19, 1872, he married Frances A. Lewis of Gorham, Me.; they had one child, who died in infancy. He was appointed instructor in chemistry at the Case School of Applied Science, Cleveland, Ohio, in 1883, and the next year he became professor, retaining this rank until he retired in 1911.

After his retirement he continued investigations which he had long been carrying on. They dealt principally with petroleum, though he did considerable original work in organic chemistry, water analysis, and electric smelting. He published nearly sixty papers on petroleum chiefly in the *Proceedings of the American Academy of Arts and Sciences, American Journal of Science, American Chemical Journal, Journal of the American Chemical Institute,* and *Journal of Industrial and Engineering Chemistry.* His work on petroleum includes both theoretical studies of the geo-chemical evidence of the origin of petroleum and its relation to coal and asphalts, and practical investigations of lubrication and lubricants. About twenty-five papers deal with the composition of petroleum from the principal oil fields of the world. This comprehensive work, especially the analytical testing, was conducted with much skill and sagacity and as a result he became an authority on petroleum, particularly on questions concerning the proportion of sulfur and the identification of hydrocarbons in different oils. In electro-chemistry he published seven papers (some jointly with the Cowles brothers). One was "On the Electric Furnace and the Reduction of the Oxides of Boron, Silicon, Aluminum and Other Metals by Carbon" (*Proceedings of the American Association for the Advancement of Science, 1885,* pp. 136–40). Others dealt with various products from the electric furnace. All gave information on its construction and application at a time when such knowledge was helpful in solving initial problems in electric smelting. His four papers on water chemistry were a definite contribution to the vexatious question of municipal water supply. The fifteen papers on organic chemistry, which were published from 1877 to 1884, deal mainly with certain organic acids, *e.g.,* uric, propionic, and acrylic, and their halogen substitution products. Throughout his career he was deeply interested in chemical education, and he delivered twelve public addresses devoted to methods and problems of teaching chemistry.

[Information from Case School of Applied Science, Cleveland, Ohio; *Who's Who in America,* 1926–27; *Harvard Coll.: The Class of 1876: Tenth Report, June 1926* (1926); *Industrial and Engineering Chemistry,* news ed., July 10, 1927; *Portland Press Herald,* June 27, 1927.]   L. C. N.

MABIE, HAMILTON WRIGHT (Dec. 13, 1845–Dec. 31, 1916), editor, critic, and in his earlier years a lawyer, was born in Coldspring, N. Y., near West Point, the son of Levi J. Mabie, a business man engaged in the lumber, and later in the boot and shoe, industry, and his wife Sarah (Colwell) Mabie. He came of mingled Scotch and English blood on his mother's side and of French Huguenot on his father's. The American progenitor of the family was Sergeant Gaspard Mabille, who was driven from his estate at Névy, in Anjou, after the St. Bartholomew's Day Massacre. The name was Americanized to Mabie within a few generations after

Sergeant Mabille settled in New York state. Hamilton Mabie grew up in Coldspring, Buffalo, and Brooklyn, where his parents lived at various times during his youth. Prepared for college by a private tutor, he was ready for entrance at sixteen but, being held back a year on account of his youth, he occupied the interval reading law in the office of a Brooklyn attorney. During his four years at Williams College, where he was a member of the class of 1867, he occupied his leisure chiefly in reading. After graduating he returned to the law, received the degree of LL.B. from Columbia in 1869, and was admitted to the New York bar in the same year. For eight years he practised with fair success, though with no great enthusiasm; later he admitted that he read more poetry than law. After his marriage on Oct. 11, 1876, to Jeannette Trivett, daughter of the Rev. Robert Trivett, of Poughkeepsie, he began to think more definitely of a career in letters and in time determined to gratify his literary tastes while retaining his law practice.

Through Edward Eggleston, then at the height of his fame, Mabie in 1879 became a member of the staff of the *Christian Union,* renamed in 1893 the *Outlook,* and thus began his lifelong association with Lyman Abbott. He never joined another staff, though he was for a time contributing editor of the *Ladies' Home Journal* and helped to edit the Library of the World's Best Literature. He began his work for the *Christian Union* as editor of a department of church news, but he revealed critical talent and was soon made literary editor. Gradually he also began to read manuscripts and write editorials. In 1884 he became associate editor, a post which he occupied with the *Christian Union* and from 1893 until his death with the *Outlook.* He had already begun to write stories for children, and his series of *Norse Stories Retold from the Eddas,* originally published in the *Christian Union,* appeared in book form in 1882. In 1888 he moved to Summit, N. J., where a great deal of his journalistic work was done. During the years that followed, he poured forth books in rapid succession, including *My Study Fire* (1890); *Essays in Literary Interpretation* (1892); *Nature and Culture* (1896); *Books and Culture* (1896); *The Life of the Spirit* (1899); *William Shakespeare: Poet, Dramatist, and Man* (1900); *Works and Days* (1902); *Introductions to Notable Poems* (1909); *American Ideals, Character and Life* (1913); and *Japan To-Day and To-Morrow* (1914), the two last an outcome of his Carnegie lectureship in Japan in 1912–13. In this difficult task of explaining the intellectual and spiritual phases of American life to Orien-

tals, he was admirably successful. Among his most charming books were the series of *Myths* (1905), *Legends* (1906), *Heroes* (1906), and *Heroines that Every Child Should Know* (1908).

In 1915 Mabie suffered a sharp recurrence of writer's cramp which had occasionally afflicted him, and he was forced to dictate. In December he was stricken with dilatation of the heart at the University Club in Philadelphia and was never again able to resume active work. He died a year later, of pneumonia developing from cardiac asthma, and was buried in the Sleepy Hollow Cemetery at Tarrytown. Both in his personal life and in his criticism, he was remarkable for a peculiar gentleness and serenity. On this his college mates, his editorial associates, and his friends alike commented. He was influential, through his writings and his lectures, in fostering the development of literary culture in the United States, but he did not personally look forward to a truly national literature "until we have certain fundamental ideas universally held, and a deep and rich national experience in which every man in every section of the country shares" (*Bookman,* New York, December 1895). He was actively interested in education and social betterment and served various organizations. He was first secretary of the National Institute of Arts and Letters and a member of the American Academy of Arts and Letters. A special room in Williams College Library perpetuates his memory.

[The chief authority for Mabie's life is Edwin W. Morse, *The Life and Letters of Hamilton W. Mabie* (1920). There are several articles in periodicals, including an obituary by Lyman Abbott in the *Outlook,* Jan. 10, 1917, and a review of Morse's book in *Ibid.,* Nov. 17, 1920. Report of the 35th Anniversary of the Class of 1867, Williams College, contains a sketch and there are articles in the *Williams Alumni Rev.,* Jan., Apr. 1917. Mabie summarized his own critical views in an interview in the *Bookman* (New York), Dec. 1895, written by James MacArthur. An interpretive editorial in the *Springfield Republican,* Jan. 2, 1917, was probably written by his friend Solomon Bulkley Griffin. Some authorities give Mabie's birth date as Dec. 13, 1846. The date given in this sketch is correct according to Mrs. Hamilton W. Mabie.]   J. B.

McAFEE, JOHN ARMSTRONG (Dec. 12, 1831–June 12, 1890), educator, clergyman, was the eldest of nine children of Joseph and Priscilla (Armstrong) McAfee, who on their wedding trip had emigrated from Kentucky to Marion County, Mo. Joseph was descended from one of three McAfee brothers who joined other pioneers in establishing the first permanent settlement near Harrodsburg, Ky. Until of age, McAfee worked on his father's farm and obtained most of his education by his own efforts. The day's work done, he often lay studying before an open fire which supplied his light. Few books were available, and his self-tuition included little more than classical and American history and elementary science. His schooling began when, at twenty-one, he left home, hiring a substitute for the farm. After seven years' study, interrupted by several periods of school-teaching and other activities for self-support, he was graduated from Westminster College in Fulton, Mo., in 1859. At once he entered upon the educational career which continued until his death. After teaching at Ashley, Mo., from 1867 to 1870, he was successively connected with Pardee College at Louisiana, Mo., 1867–70, and with Highland College at Highland, Kan., 1870–75. In these colleges he was interested in plans for offering students means of self-help. In 1875 he cooperated with Col. George S. Park in founding Park College, which he served as president until his death. Here he offered an education to all worthy young persons of small or no financial resources.

This self-help plan, which remained the outstanding mark of Park College for many years after McAfee's death, was less to train artisans than to reduce student expense and to inspire service. McAfee's leading emphasis was on intellectual and spiritual discipline in preparation for religious leadership. He sought to develop the character resources of the growing West. He also fostered preparation for missionary service; of Park College graduates a notably large number have become foreign missionaries. Though he attended no theological school, McAfee was early ordained a Presbyterian minister and later received the honorary degree of D.D. from Westminster College, Mo. He married, Aug. 23, 1859, Anna W. Bailey. Of their five sons and one daughter, each for some years shared in the teaching or administrative work of Park College. As a preacher, McAfee was ardent and positive; as an educator, a determined classicist and advocate of traditional views; as an administrator, he was essentially practical.

[The author used an unpublished biographical manuscript, written by Jos. E. McAfee. For printed materials see the latter's memoir, "My Father," in the *Bull. of Park Coll.*, Jan. 1926; Neander M. Woods, *The Woods-McAfee Memorial* (1905); Theodore Roosevelt, *The Winning of the West*, vols. I and II (1889); C. A. Phillips, *A Hist. of Educ. in Mo.* (1911); *Presbyt. Jour.*, June 26, 1890.]   P.P.F.

McAFEE, ROBERT BRECKINRIDGE (Feb. 18, 1784–Mar. 12, 1849), Kentucky politician and historian, was born in the Salt River settlement in what is now Mercer County, Ky. He was of Scotch-Irish stock, a grandson of James McAfee who came to Pennsylvania in 1739 and later moved to western Virginia; his parents, Robert and Anne (McCoun) McAfee, were among the earliest settlers in Kentucky. His father had explored that region in 1773 and 1774, and had been sergeant-at-arms of the Transylvania Convention in 1775. Beginning at the age of five, young Robert attended various local schools and was evidently a proficient pupil. During 1795–97 he was a student in Transylvania Seminary. In 1798 he became aroused over the Alien and Sedition Acts and determined to become a politician. For a year he was an usher at Mahan's School, Danville, but in 1800 he began the study of law under John Breckinridge, 1760–1806 [*q.v.*], one of his guardians and the Jeffersonian leader in Kentucky. After being admitted to the bar in 1801 (too young, he decided), he had to borrow money to buy law books, and his practice (in Franklin County) was so small that he paid his debts by surveying land. He took part in local politics, becoming a leading member of the "Republican Society" and a captain of militia. He continued to read much, in philosophy, theology, and rhetoric. He wrote both poetry and prose, and some of his historical articles and other pieces were published in newspapers. In 1807 his growing practice enabled him to marry Mary Cardwell.

During the War of 1812, he volunteered as a private, was later second lieutenant, and in 1813 organized a mounted company in R. M. Johnson's regiment, which reinforced Harrison at Fort Meigs and took an important part in the battle of the Thames. There McAfee was wounded. In 1816 he published a *History of the Late War in the Western Country* (reprinted 1919), based on his own journal and on the correspondence of Harrison, Shelby, and other participants. The larger and more valuable part of the book is devoted to the operations in Indiana and on the Lakes. He endeavored to be fair, he said, but in his Preface confessed to "a natural attachment to his country and hostility to her enemies according to their deserts."

Resuming legal practice, he rose in politics to be a member of the state House of Representatives (1819) and state senator (1821). Supporting the relief of debtors and the new and more popular court of appeals, he was in 1824 elected lieutenant-governor by the Relief, or New Court, party. In 1825, the lower house passed a bill to abolish the new court, but the measure was defeated for the time by McAfee's deciding vote in the Senate. Later, as a member of the lower house (1830–33), he opposed reckless expenditures for internal improvements. He was a member of the first National Democratic Convention (1832), and the following year President Jackson appointed him chargé at Bogotá, New Granada (1833–37). He was later state senator (1841) and president of the board of visitors of the United States Military Academy (1842). After living in retirement for some years, he died on his farm in Mercer County.

[McAfee MSS. in the Ky. State Hist. Soc., including "History of the Rise and Progress of the First Settlements on Salt River" (*Reg. Ky. State Hist. Soc.*, Jan.–July 1931), "The Life and Times of Robert B. McAfee" (*Ibid.*, Jan.–Sept. 1927), and "The McAfee Papers" (*Ibid.*, Jan.–Sept. 1928); M. C. Weaks, *Calendar of the Ky. Papers of the Draper Collection of MSS.* (Pubs. State Hist. Soc. of Wis., Calendar Ser., vol. II, 1925); W. E. Connelley and E. M. Coulter, *Hist. of Ky.* (1922), vol. II; Lewis and R. H. Collins, *Hist. of Ky.* (2 vols., 1874); *The Biog. Encyc. of Ky.* (1878); N. M. Woods, *The Woods-McAfee Memorial* (1905); *Ky. Yeoman* (Frankfort), Mar. 22, 1849.]   W. C. M.

MACALESTER, CHARLES (Apr. 5, 1765– Aug. 29, 1832), merchant, son of Charles and Isabella (MacQuarrie) Macalester, was born at Campbeltown, Argyllshire, Scotland. He attended the schools of his native town, receiving a thorough grounding in the fundamentals, but at an early age went to sea as a foremast hand. Before he was twenty-one he came to America, settling in Philadelphia, and was naturalized in 1786, soon after reaching his majority. He continued to follow the sea, however, and for the next eighteen years commanded merchant vessels sailing from the port of Philadelphia. Usually he also acted as supercargo and in this capacity achieved a considerable reputation as a trader. With an increase in his fortune, he became owner of the vessel in which he sailed, and in the course of time, one of the leading merchant traders of his day. In the late years of the century, when privateers were seriously hindering commerce, he armed one of his vessels, the *George Barclay*, with twenty guns and manned it with a hundred seamen, and, thus equipped, made voyages with a rapidity and safety which further enhanced his reputation. Shortly after 1800, he designed a vessel, the *Fanny*, which was constructed for him by one of the ablest of the Philadelphia ship-builders, and proved to be the fastest merchant vessel of the day. Her first voyage, from Philadelphia to Cowes in the Isle of Wight, was accomplished in seventeen days, which was then a record.

In 1804 Macalester retired from the sea but continued in the shipping trade, with headquarters in Philadelphia. His vessels sailed to China, India, and the Dutch East Indies, as well as to European ports. In 1825 he planned to retire from all business, but was persuaded to accept the presidency of the Insurance Company of the State of Pennsylvania, which was then in financial difficulties. In two years he had restored the or-

ganization to a profitable basis, but he continued as president until he died. He was also a director of the Bank of North America. A loyal Presbyterian, he was a founder of the Mariner's Church of Philadelphia and of the Marine Bible Society. He was a promoter and vice-president (1813–25) of the St. Andrew's Society. By his wife, Ann Sampson, he had a number of children, among them Charles Macalester [*q.v.*].

[Henry Simpson, *The Lives of Eminent Philadelphians Now Deceased* (1859); S. N. Winslow, *Biogs. of Successful Phila. Merchants* (1864); *An Hist. Cat. of the St. Andrew's Soc. of Phila. with Biog. Sketches of Deceased Members, 1749–1907* (1907); C. H. Browning, *Americans of Royal Descent* (1891); *Poulson's Am. Daily Advertiser* (Phila.), Aug. 31, Sept. 4, 1832.]   J. H. F.

MACALESTER, CHARLES (Feb. 17, 1798– Dec. 9, 1873), financier, was born in Philadelphia, Pa., the son of Charles [*q.v.*] and Ann (Sampson) Macalester. His father was a prosperous merchant and ship-owner. The boy received a good education, at Grey and Wylie's School in Philadelphia, and during the War of 1812 entered his father's business. In 1821 he moved to Cincinnati, Ohio, where he engaged in a mercantile venture of his own. Returning to Philadelphia some years later, he soon became prominent in commercial circles there and in 1834, 1835, and 1837 was appointed a government director of the second Bank of the United States. In 1835 he became a member of the firm of Gaw, Macalester & Company, bankers. Various political appointments were tendered him at different times, all of which he declined, preferring the independence of private life. In 1842 he visited England and there became acquainted with the American banker, George Peabody of London. He served for years as Peabody's agent and correspondent in Philadelphia and later as one of the trustees of the Peabody Education Fund.

Through shrewd purchase of real estate in Philadelphia and western cities, particularly Chicago, he accumulated a large fortune, of which he gave liberally to various charities. Chief among the objects of his philanthropy, perhaps, was the Philadelphia Presbyterian Hospital, of which he was one of the founders. In 1873 he gave a piece of property in Minneapolis, Minn., for the establishment of an institution of higher learning which the trustees named Macalester College. He was a director of the Fidelity Insurance, Trust & Safe Deposit Company, and of other corporations, was a manager of and contributor to the Philadelphia Orthopaedic Hospital, and president of the St. Andrew's Society from 1864 until the year of his death. He was twice married: first, in 1824, at

Cincinnati, to Eliza Ann Lytle, and second, in 1841, to Susan Bradford Wallace. There were two children by the first marriage. In 1849 he retired from business and occupied himself with his private affairs and various trusts and executorships. He died suddenly from heart disease in Philadelphia.

[*In Memoriam—Charles Macalester* (privately printed, 1873); *Jour. of the Exec. Proc. of the Senate, 1829–37* (1887); Henry Hall, *America's Successful Men of Affairs*, vol. II (1896); C. H. Browning, *Americans of Royal Descent* (1891); *An Hist. Cat. of the St. Andrew's Soc. of Phila.* (1907); J. L. M. Curry, *A Brief Sketch of George Peabody and a Hist. of the Peabody Educ. Fund* (1898); H. D. Funk, *A Hist. of Macalester Coll.* (1910); *Press* and *Public Ledger* (both of Phila.), Dec. 10, 1873.]   J.H.F.

MACALISTER, JAMES (Apr. 26, 1840–Dec. 11, 1913), educator, was born in Glasgow, Scotland, son of John and Agnes Robertson MacAlister. In early childhood he lost his father and, with his widowed mother and two older sisters, went to live with his paternal grandfather, a man of strong character, an elder in the Presbyterian Church, engaged in business in Glasgow. After the grandfather's death the family emigrated to Wisconsin in 1850. James MacAlister's early schooling was obtained in Scotland; his three years of college training at Brown University, where he graduated in 1856. After leaving college he taught school in Milwaukee, Wis. Here, also, after graduation from the Albany Law School in 1864, he practised law. On June 24, 1866, he was married to Helen Lucretia Brayton. His success as a student of public affairs and as a speaker led to his absorption in the cause of education. In 1873 he was appointed superintendent of the public schools of Milwaukee. Thereafter he devoted himself to education.

When Philadelphia sought to reorganize its public-school system it chose as leader the notably successful Milwaukee superintendent. In 1883 he undertook the task of introducing progressive ideas into what was then a very conservative community. The contagious enthusiasm and skilful address which had won Milwaukee enlisted the interest of Philadelphia. He frequently lectured on modern education. Addressing the Modern Language Association at the University of Pennsylvania in 1887 he proposed that the writings of Dante, Cervantes, Shakespeare, and Goethe be added to a curriculum which had hitherto recognized only the ancient classics. He developed a program of industrial training in the schools. One of the earliest educational monographs issued by the New York College for the Training of Teachers under the editorship of Nicholas Murray Butler (vol. III, no. 2, March 1890) was by MacAlister:

"Manual Training in the Public Schools of Philadelphia." When he resigned in 1890, the Philadelphia *Press* declared that he had transformed the schools through his "energy, tact, industry, enthusiasm, ability, and unflexible pertinacity."

He resigned to become president of the newly established Drexel Institute of Art, Science, and Industry. The main building was dedicated Dec. 17, 1891, in the presence of Thomas A. Edison, Andrew Carnegie, J. Pierpont Morgan, and many educational and public officials, by Chauncey M. Depew. The first classes were held in 1892. A happy association with Anthony J. Drexel and his friend George W. Childs was ended by the death of Drexel in 1893 and that of Childs shortly after. The well-founded movement went on under MacAlister's guidance with the help of other friends. In addition to the courses which included among others the then undeveloped fields of electrical engineering, business, domestic economy, and library science, a powerful influence was exerted among students and the general public by the museum of industrial art, the picture gallery, and the organ recitals and other concerts. The success of the institution drew visitors from all over the world. The founder of the Armour Institute, Chicago, consulted MacAlister, as did the founder of Pratt Institute. He enjoyed friendships at home and abroad based upon a common enthusiasm for practical education, literature, and the fine arts. While the Drexel Institute building was being erected he studied technical education in Europe. He frequently visited London and Edinburgh, always returning with delight to Philadelphia or to his summer cottage in Rhode Island. His wife, who died in 1898, shared his joy in a hospitable home. One who gave himself so completely to students, colleagues, friends, and the public found little time for writing. He lectured at Drexel Institute, Johns Hopkins, the Harvard Summer School, and at many educational association meetings. He was an Officier d'Académie Français, trustee of the University of Pennsylvania (1885–97), and a member of the Committee of Fifty for the Investigation of the Liquor Problem (1897–1900). In 1913 his health had declined so seriously that he resigned in June. He was then made president emeritus of Drexel Institute. On his way to Bermuda in December he died of heart failure at sea.

[*Who's Who in America*, 1912–13; *Hist. Cat. of Brown Univ., 1764–1914*; R. B. Beath, *Hist. Cat. of the St. Andrew's Soc. of Phila.*, vol. II (1913); *Pub. Ledger* (Phila.), Dec. 13, 1913; publications of the Drexel Institute; information as to certain facts from MacAlister's daughter, Miss MacAlister.]   D.A.R.

McALLISTER, CHARLES ALBERT (May 29, 1867–Jan. 6, 1932), marine engineer, shipping official, was one of the outstanding advocates of the merchant-marine revival after the World War. He was born in Dorchester, N. J., the son of William and Abigail Ann Shute McAllister. His father, a ship-builder, had emigrated from Scotland and later established a shipyard on City Island in the Bronx, New York City. There Charles first became acquainted with naval architecture. To study marine engineering, he attended Cornell University where he received the degree of mechanical engineer in 1887. He spent the next five years as a draftsman, at first with the Cramp yards in Philadelphia and then with the navy. He helped to design the boilers for the *Oregon* and for other vessels of the new navy. For the next quarter century he was an engineer officer in the Revenue-Cutter Service. Appointed second assistant engineer on June 30, 1892, he was promoted to first assistant engineer on June 6, 1895. During the Spanish-American War he served in the navy as engineer officer on the *Pennsylvania* in the Pacific. On Apr. 13, 1902, he became chief engineer of the Revenue-Cutter Service where he exerted great influence. He is credited with suggesting the legislation approved on Jan. 28, 1915, combining the Revenue-Cutter Service and the Life-Saving Service into a single organization known as the Coast Guard. On Mar. 9, 1916, he became engineer-in-chief of the new service with a rank equivalent to that of commander in the navy and served in that capacity until his resignation on July 12, 1919.

He left the service to become vice-president of the American Bureau of Shipping at the instance of his friend, Stevenson Taylor, whom he succeeded as president upon the latter's death in 1926. Before McAllister's death the organization was registering ninety per cent. of the American merchant marine eligible for classification. In his new capacity, McAllister took a leading part in the agitation for governmental support of the American merchant marine. The Bureau brought him into contact with all the principal ship-builders and ship-owners, while his years at Washington had given him exceptional contacts with legislators, officials, and journalists. He made almost weekly trips from New York to Washington, testified at congressional merchant-marine hearings, and did much to facilitate the passage of the Jones-White Merchant Marine Act of 1928. His last efforts were to secure an appropriation of $125,000,000 to build a hundred new fast steamships for the merchant marine. He served with distinction as a delegate to the International Conference on Safety of Life at Sea in London in 1929 and, as chairman of the Shipping Board's committee on fuel conservation, was active in introducing the use of pulverized coal for economy. He was the author of two books on marine engineering and wrote numerous popular and technical articles on the merchant marine. McAllister was married to Adelaide Kenyon of Chicago on Mar. 6, 1907. He died at his home on Park Avenue in New York City.

[The principal source is the memorial number of the *Bull. of the Am. Bureau of Shipping*, Mar.–Apr., 1932, containing obituary notices, resolutions and personal messages. See also: *Who's Who in America*, 1930–31; *Jour. Am. Soc. Naval Engineers*, Feb. 1932; *Marine Engineering and Shipping Age*, Feb. 1932; *Marine Rev.*, Feb. 1932; *Cornell Alumni News*, Jan. 21, 1932; *N. Y. Times*, Jan. 7, 1932.] R. G. A—n.

McALLISTER, HALL (Feb. 9, 1826–Dec. 1, 1888), lawyer, son of Matthew Hall [*q.v.*] and Louisa Charlotte (Cutler) McAllister, was born in Savannah, Ga. He was named for his father but seems to have dropped the first name, Matthew, after he left college. In May 1846, he entered Yale College with the class of 1849 but withdrew during his sophomore year, in July 1847, studied law in Savannah, was admitted to the bar, probably in January 1849, and soon afterward sailed for California with his cousin, Samuel Ward. He arrived in San Francisco on June 4, 1849, in company with W. M. Gwin and Joseph Hooker [*qq.v.*], and he immediately engaged in law practice. In September he became second lieutenant of the California Guards, a military company organized to assist in the maintenance of law and order. Upon the arrival, in 1850, of his father and brother, Samuel Ward McAllister [*q.v.*], the three McAllisters formed a law partnership that continued until Ward's withdrawal and the father's elevation to the bench. As assistant to Horace Hawes, in 1850, he was active in apprehending and bringing to trial and conviction, before the unofficial court that had been set up, a band of desperate characters first known as the Hounds and later as the Regulators. The organization and methods of the vigilance committee the next year, however, seem not to have enlisted his approval or cooperation.

His courtly manners and popular personality, his character, and intellectual abilities soon brought him a large and lucrative law practice. He seems to have eschewed politics throughout most of his career. In 1860, however, he was one of sixty-five signers of an address to California Democrats declaring their support of the Breckinridge ticket. He did not confine his talents to any particular kind of legal practice. One

McAllister

of his best-known cases was the defense of Adolph Spreckels for shooting M. H. de Young, the owner of the *San Francisco Chronicle*. He was most at home before a jury, where his sense of humor often led him to inject into his arguments doggerel of his own composition. When trying a case, he habitually took down the testimony of witnesses himself, in spite of the fact that the court stenographer was doing this at the same time. Although not remarkable as a speaker, he had a convincing way with a jury, growing out of the thorough preparation and mastery of his cases. His name constantly appears in the seventy-odd volumes of California's supreme court reports published during his lifetime, beginning with the case of *Payne* vs. *The Pacific Mail Steamship Co.* in the first volume. Resolutions adopted by the bar association of San Francisco shortly after his death declared that he had tried more cases, won more verdicts, and received larger fees than any other California lawyer of the period (*Morning Call*, San Francisco, Mar. 24, 1889). Two of his most important victories were the judgments, for the plaintiff, in *Charles Lux et al.* vs. *James B. Haggin et al.* (69 *Cal.* 255–454), which involved irrigation projects and riparian rights in California and, for the defendant, in *Ellen M. Colton* vs. *Leland Stanford et al.* (82 *Cal.* 351–412), which involved the relations of trustee and beneficiary. This was his last great case. The actual trial lasted for many months in the lower courts, and his argument required seventeen days for delivery. Two years after his death, the California supreme court sustained his victory in the trial court.

In the summer of 1888 he became ill and went to Europe for several months in the hope of recovery. Returning in November, he died a month later of a brain tumor, at his country estate "Miramonte" in Ross Valley, near San Rafael, and was buried from Trinity Episcopal Church in San Francisco. He was survived by his wife, Louisa Clemence (Hermann) McAllister, the daughter of Samuel Hermann of San Francisco, and by four children, three daughters and a son. McAllister street in San Francisco was named in his honor and his bronze statue stands near the city hall.

[O. T. Shuck, *Bench and Bar in Cal.* (1888) and *Hist. of the Bench and Bar in Cal.* (1901), pp. 417–21; J. C. Bates, *Hist. of the Bench and Bar in Cal.* (1912); Z. S. Eldredge, *Hist. of Cal.* (copr. 1915), vol. III; T. H. Hittell, *Hist. of Cal.*, vols. II, III, IV (1885–97); H. H. Bancroft, *Popular Tribunals* (2 vols. 1887); M. F. Williams, *Hist. of the San Francisco Committee of Vigilance of 1851* (1921); *An Account of the Meetings of the Class of 1849 of Yale College . . . 1852* (1852); Ward McAllister, *Society as I Have Found It* (copr. 1890); M. C. McAllister, *Descendants of Archibald*

McAllister (1898); W. J. Davis, *Hist. of Political Conventions in Cal.* (1893); *Morning Call* (San Francisco), June 24, 1885, Dec. 2, 4, 8, 1888, Mar. 24, 1889; *San Francisco Chronicle*, Dec. 2, 8, 1888.] P. O. R.

McALLISTER, MATTHEW HALL (Nov. 26, 1800–Dec. 19, 1865), jurist, was born at Savannah, Ga., the great-grandson of Archibald McAlister, who emigrated from Scotland before 1730, acquired a large tract of land in the Cumberland Valley, owned a gristmill and a smith shop, and was one of the organizers of the First Presbyterian Church of Carlisle, Pa. His father, Matthew McAllister, a graduate of the College of New Jersey in the class of 1779, was a lawyer of some eminence whom Washington appointed district attorney for the southern district of Georgia. His mother was Hannah (Gibbons) McAllister, a sister of William Gibbons of Georgia [*q.v.*]. In June 1817 the son entered his father's college, where he did not distinguish himself academically and left college in October 1818. He prepared himself for the law and was admitted to the bar about 1820. For twenty-nine years thereafter he practised his profession in Savannah with great success. He was married to Louisa Charlotte Cutler of New York City, grand-daughter of Esther (Marion) Mitchell, the sister of Gen. Francis Marion and the aunt of Julia Ward Howe [*qq.v.*]. In 1827 he was appointed United States district attorney for the southern district of Georgia. His first noteworthy activity in politics came in 1832, when he appeared as an outstanding defender of the Union under the constitution and the opponent of nullification. From 1834 to 1837, he served in the Georgia Senate, in which he was a prominent and influential member. He was instrumental in bringing about the establishment, in 1846, of the Georgia supreme court for the correction of errors. Until 1840 he seems to have been identified with the National Republicans and, later, with the Whig party; but, after the nomination of Harrison for the presidency, he bolted that party and appealed to other state-rights Whigs to join the Democratic party. On July 4 of that year he made an *Address to the Democratic-Republican Convention of Georgia* (1840) which set forth his principles with a good deal of clarity. Although a coastal rice planter and a member of the most exclusive social aristocracy in the state, he soon became one of the three or four Democratic leaders in Georgia. In 1845 he ran for governor but was defeated by a close vote. During this campaign, he was denounced by opponents as an "aristocrat who has no sympathy with the people," and as belonging to "that class in Savannah known as

546

the 'Swelled Heads' who think the up-country people no better than brutes" (Shryock, *post,* p. 115). He was several times elected mayor of Savannah and, in that office, acquired some reputation as a protector of the colored people. In 1848 he was a delegate-at-large to the Democratic National Convention at Baltimore, supported the nomination of Lewis Cass, and campaigned in Tennessee for the Cass ticket. Early in 1850 the state legislature elected him one of the state's two delegates-at-large to the Nashville convention, but he declined the honor. Later that year, he moved with his family to California and practised law with his two sons Hall and Ward [*qq.v.*] in San Francisco. In 1853 he returned to Georgia during a legislative deadlock over the election of a United States senator. There he was nominated for the senatorship by his friends and received 93 out of 111 votes necessary to a choice.

In 1855 Pierce appointed him to be the first United States circuit judge in California. The character and variety of his judicial decisions is apparent from the volume of *Reports of Cases in the Circuit Court of the United States for the District of Columbia* (1859) reported by his son, Cutler McAllister. In those years he rendered many important decisions affecting the title to lands in California acquired under Mexican grants, notably, *United States* vs. *Andres Castillero,* in which the decision of his court was sustained by the United States Supreme Court (23 *Howard,* 469). Owing to impaired health, he resigned from the bench in 1862. Three years later he died in San Francisco, being survived by his wife, a daughter, and five sons. He was buried from the Episcopal Church of the Advent. His death evoked eulogies from the bench and bar of more than ordinary earnestness and impressiveness.

[Information from the secretary of Princeton University; O. T. Shuck, *Representative and Leading Men of the Pacific* (1870) and *Hist. of the Bench and Bar in Cal.* (1901); R. H. Shryock, *Ga. and the Union* (1926); *Federal Cases,* vol. XXX (1897), p. 1383; Ward McAllister, *Society as I Have Found It* (copr. 1890); M. C. McAllister, *Descendants of Archibald McAllister* (1898); State of Ga. Department of Archives and Hist., *Georgia's Official Register, 1927* (1927); L. E. Richards and M. H. Elliott, *Julia Ward Howe* (1915), vol. I; *Daily American Flag* (San Francisco), Dec. 20, 25, 1865.]   P. O. R.

McALLISTER, SAMUEL WARD (Dec. 1827–Jan. 31, 1895), New York society leader, son of Louisa Charlotte (Cutler) and Matthew Hall McAllister [*q.v.*], was born in Savannah, Ga. His father, at one time an officer of the Georgia Hussars and, afterward, a leader of the Savannah bar and federal circuit judge in California, was famous for his hospitality and enter-

tained many of the reigning wits and beauties of his day. When Ward, as he was usually called, was about twenty he visited New York, where he spent some time under the social patronage of a maiden relative, who introduced him into the fashionable circles of the city. After her death, he returned to Savannah and passed his bar examination. In 1850 he and his father joined his brother, Hall McAllister [*q.v.*], at San Francisco in order to establish a law firm. By 1852 he had made a comfortable fortune and in the autumn of that year returned to New York. The next year he married Sarah T. Gibbons, the daughter of a Georgia millionaire then living in Madison, N. J. They had one daughter and two sons. He bought "Bayside Farm," near Newport, R. I., and began his career as a society man. He initiated his campaign with several years' residence abroad, where he everywhere managed to form distinguished social connections and perfected himself in the arts of the finished host. On his return to the United States, he spent his winters in New York and Savannah but made Newport his home for nine months of the year. Always restless and feverishly active, he began at once to convert the sleepy old town of Newport into the gilt-edged, multi-colored scene he loved. The modest country picnic under his practised hand became a *fête champêtre* with music, floral decorations, dancing, banqueting, and exquisitely iced champagne. Beginning thus with successes at Newport he had, by the late sixties, made himself the arbiter of the New York social world and, as such, maintained his position with a diplomatic skill worthy of a higher aim. Yet, in his own belief, a social career was an end sufficient in itself because Society, as he saw it, tended to elevate and refine life and to stimulate all the higher arts that satisfy esthetic wants. His chief triumphs in the New York social world were the organization of the "Patriarchs" and the choosing of the "Four Hundred." As a protest against the powers of exclusion held by a few very rich men, in 1872, he banded together the oldest New York families, whose approval of any social aspirant should be final. The heads of the families so honored were called "Patriarchs," and they gave subscription balls for which regular invitations became a warranty of social position. The "Four Hundred" was a group of more casual origin. Mrs. William Astor, in planning her ball of Feb. 1, 1892, found that the ballroom would not accommodate all those upon her list. He undertook to cut the list and afterward boasted in the Union Club that there were "only about four hundred people in New York Society." The phrase was given publicity and the whirlwind of controversy that followed made it an idiom of the language. In 1890 he brought out his book, *Society as I Have Found It,* a curious mélange of reminiscence, good dining, servant management, and social etiquette and diplomacy. His many vanities and affectations laid him open, at times, to extravagant ridicule. Yet even those whom his militant individualism annoyed acknowledged his charm of manner and his amiability and freedom from malice, throughout a life devoted to maintaining the balance of his little throne in a glittering world that "smiles and smiling kills."

[Ward McAllister, *Society as I Have Found It* (copr. 1890); F. T. Martin, *Things I Remember* (1913); M. C. McAllister, *Descendants of Archibald McAllister* (1898); *N. Y. Times,* Feb. 2, 16, 1892, abstracted in I. N. P. Stokes, *Iconography of Manhattan Island,* vol. V (1926), pp. 2008–09; *N. Y. Tribune,* Feb. 1, 1895; *New York Times,* Feb. 1, 1895.]

E. M. H.

MCALPINE, WILLIAM JARVIS (Apr. 30, 1812–Feb. 16, 1890), civil engineer, was born in New York City, the eldest son of John and Elizabeth (Jarvis) McAlpine. His paternal grandfather, Donald McAlpine, was an officer in the famous "Black Watch"; his mother was a granddaughter of Abraham Jarvis [q.v.], second Protestant Episcopal bishop of Connecticut. John McAlpine, who was a millwright and mechanical engineer with a large practice, desired his son to enter the engineering profession with a view to carrying on his own business. Accordingly, after completing his elementary education at private academies in Newburgh and Rome, N. Y., William, then fifteen, was apprenticed to John B. Jervis [q.v.], a civil engineer.

He served under Jervis as pupil, assistant, and resident engineer for eight years, showing remarkable aptitude and developing rapidly. In 1836, he succeeded his preceptor as chief engineer of the eastern division of the Erie Canal. After several years' service in this capacity, he became chief engineer of the government dry dock in Brooklyn. This was a project of the first magnitude, and, because the foundations had to be laid on a deep layer of quicksand, forty feet below tide level, one of extraordinary difficulty. McAlpine handled the construction in a masterly manner, and by the successful completion of the work definitely established himself as one of the leading engineers of his time. As state engineer and railway commissioner of New York from 1852 to 1857, he made studies on comparative costs of rail and water transportation which achieved international recognition. He served as chief engineer of the Erie Railroad 1856–57, of the Chicago & Galena (later Northwestern), 1857, and of the Ohio & Mississippi, 1861–64;

and as consulting engineer to many others. He prepared plans and reports on water supply systems for Chicago (1851–54), Brooklyn (1852), Buffalo (1868), Montreal (1869), Philadelphia (1874 and 1884), San Francisco (1879), New York (1882), Toronto (1886), and many smaller cities. As chief engineer of the Third Avenue drawbridge over the Harlem River, New York (1860–61), he did pioneer work on the design and sinking of the caissons for the piers. Later he acted either as chief engineer or consulting engineer for a number of the greatest bridge projects of the time, including the Eads bridge over the Mississippi at St. Louis (1865), the Clifton suspension bridge at Niagara (1868), and the Washington bridge over the Harlem in New York City (1885–88). He was superintendent of construction of the New York State Capitol at Albany in 1873, a project of great magnitude and difficulty; and later, as engineer of parks for New York City, he built the famous boulevard, Riverside Drive. At the time of his death he was actively engaged upon plans for the "Arcade Railway"—a project for providing an underground rapid transit system for New York City and also second level streets under some of the congested thoroughfares. The scheme was one of remarkable ingenuity and in many respects far ahead of its time, but opposition of abutting property owners and legal and financial difficulties forced its abandonment.

McAlpine enjoyed wide professional recognition in England and Continental Europe, where he was consulted on many important projects, including the Manchester Ship Canal, a proposed railway to India, and improvement of the navigation of the Danube River near the "Iron Gate." He was the first and for many years the only American honored by membership in the British Institution of Civil Engineers, and was elected president of the American Society of Civil Engineers, 1870, and honorary member, 1889.

McAlpine was a prolific writer on technical subjects. Besides reports upon the various projects with which he was connected, he contributed to the *Transactions of the American Society of Civil Engineers* a number of original papers (perhaps the most important being "The Foundations of the New Capitol at Albany, N. Y.," in vol. II, 1874) and many detailed discussions. Possibly his most notable contribution to technical literature was his paper on "The Supporting Power of Piles," published in the *Minutes of Proceedings of the Institution of Civil Engineers* (vol. XXVII, London, 1868), which won him the Telford Medal. He also published in book form a work entitled *Modern Engineering* (1874).

McAlpine was one of the last great general practitioners of civil engineering, and was the recognized dean of the profession when he died. He was married on Feb. 24, 1841, at Watervliet, N. Y., to Sarah Elizabeth Learned (*Daily Albany Argus,* Feb. 26, 1841). His death occurred at New Brighton, Staten Island.

[*Proc. Am. Soc. Civil Engineers,* vol. XVIII (1892); *Minutes of Proc. of the Inst. of Civil Engineers* (London), vol. C (1890); *Engineering News,* Feb. 22, Mar. 8, 1890; *Engineering and Building Record* (N. Y.), Feb. 22, 1890; *Engineering and Mining Jour.* (N. Y.), Feb. 22, 1890; *Engineering* (London), Mar. 7, 1890; *N. Y. Tribune,* Feb. 18, 1890; personal acquaintance.]
               J. I. P.

MCANALLY, DAVID RICE (Feb. 17, 1810–July 11, 1895), Methodist clergyman, educator, journalist, was born in Grainger County, Tenn. Like his father, Charles, local preacher, sheriff, surveyor, who weighed 360 pounds and was married twice, the son was above the average in size and the husband of two wives. His mother was Elizabeth, daughter of the Rev. Rice Moore; and his wives were Maria Thompson and Julia Reeves. His early education, which was scanty, was received in a country school and in a private academy. Admitted on trial to the Holston Conference of the Methodist Episcopal Church in 1829, for fourteen years he served charges in Tennessee, North Carolina, and Virginia. In spite of the fact that he himself had not been privileged to go to college, he was elected in 1843 to the presidency of the East Tennessee Female Institute, and as administrator and by the publication of tracts and newspaper articles he served in that position effectively. His interest included not only the denominational institution of which he was head, but the common-school system as well; and for a number of years he was connected with Horace Mann [*q.v.*] and other prominent educational leaders in an effort to improve it. In 1851 he was chosen editor of the *St. Louis Christian Advocate,* and the next year he was chairman of the convention which founded Central College, Fayette, Mo., and cooperated with Enoch M. Marvin [*q.v.*] and others in raising what was then considered a good endowment for such an institution.

He continued as editor of the *Advocate,* with slight intermissions until his death. As a journalist, two aims seem to have been in his mind: first, through the arrangement and presentation of news of the week to acquaint his readers with the march of events; and second, by editorial exposition to ground those same readers in "sound doctrine." When the Civil War broke out, he strove diligently to allay excitement. In a series of editorials during April and May 1861, under such titles as "The Times," "The Duty of Chris-

tian Men," "The Time for Prayer," he warned his people of "the magnitude of the rebellion" and the "unprecedented unanimity of the South." His advice to the men of Missouri was to remain at home, cultivate friendly relations, and pray for a restoration of peace. Unfortunately, his straightforward account of the events of the conflict led to his arrest as an enemy of the Federal government, and for months he lay in the Myrtle Street Military Prison in St. Louis.

In addition to his editorial work, he wrote the following books: *Life and Times of Rev. William Patton* (1858); *The Life and Times of Rev. Samuel Patton* (1859); *The Life and Labors of Rev. E. M. Marvin* (1878); a biography of Mrs. Laura Ramsey; and *History of Methodism in Missouri* (1881). He was not a scholar, but his intimate touch with men and public affairs over a long period enabled him to present first-hand information. His primary interest was in the Church, and to that he gave greatest space; but in some of the volumes there are chapters devoted to an interpretation of the life and thought of the period. Sixty-six years a preacher, five times a delegate to the General Conference, more than forty years editor, "probably no man had more to do with fixing the ideals and customs of Missouri" than did he.

[*Christian Advocate* (Nashville), July 18, 1895; *Minutes of the Ann. Conferences of the M. E. Church, South* (1895); R. N. Price, *Holston Methodism,* vol. III (1908); M. L. Gray and W. M. Baker, *The Centennial Vol. of Mo. Methodism* (1907); J. B. McFerrin, *Hist. of Methodism in Tenn.* (3 vols., 1869–73); W. M. Leftwich, *Martyrdom in Mo.,* vol. I (1870); W. S. Woodward, *Annals of Mo. Methodism* (1893); Wm. Hyde and H. L. Conard, *Encyc. of the Hist. of St. Louis* (1899), vol. III; *Knoxville Daily Jour.,* July 13, 1895; *St. Louis Republic,* July 12, 1895.]   R. W. G.

MCARTHUR, DUNCAN (Jan. 14, 1772–Apr. 28, 1839), congressman and governor of Ohio, was born in Dutchess County, N. Y., the son of John and Margaret (Campbell) McArthur, natives of the Scotch Highlands. His mother died when he was very young, and in 1780 his father, who was poverty-stricken, moved to the neighborhood of Pittsburgh. McArthur somehow learned to read and write, but his youth was spent in farming or as a driver of transalleghany pack-trains. In 1790 he enrolled for service against the Indians and took part in Harmar's campaign and in other expeditions. During the winter of 1792–93 he was a salt-boiler at the licks near Maysville, Ky. In the spring he joined a surveying party under Nathaniel Massie, which penetrated the Scioto valley to the region of Chillicothe. When the Indians in the region became excited, he served two years observing their movements as a ranger. In March 1795, he was again associated with Massie and learned surveying. In

February 1796 he married Nancy McDonald and settled with her on a farm near the recently founded village of Chillicothe. He rapidly amassed property by shrewd buying and locating of Virginia land warrants that were issued to Revolutionary soldiers. Unquestionably he could drive a hard bargain, and his enemies charged that he was unscrupulous. His subsequent life was embittered by constant litigation over land titles. By 1804 he was considered the wealthiest land holder in the Scioto valley. In that year he was elected to the Ohio House of Representatives. The next year he was elected to the state Senate, where he served eight consecutive terms, and in the session for 1809–10 he was the speaker.

In 1806 he was elected a colonel of the militia. In February 1808 he became a major-general, and he held this rank in the spring of 1812, when the Ohio militia marched for Detroit. Upon the reorganization of the Ohio volunteers, he was elected colonel of one of the three militia regiments under Hull's command. He took a noteworthy part in the campaign. On arriving at Detroit he urged Hull to attack Malden immediately, led a raid that penetrated some thirty miles into Canada, and was acting as an escort for a supply train at the time of Hull's surrender, when his troops were included in the terms of Hull's capitulation. He was later a principal witness at Hull's court martial. He returned to Chillicothe from Detroit with reputation unimpaired and was elected to Congress in the autumn of 1812. He did not qualify, however, and on Apr. 5, 1813, shortly after he had been informed of the exchange of the prisoners taken at Detroit, he resigned to undertake active service in the regular army, to which he had been appointed brigadier-general in March. His first activity was to raise volunteers for the assistance of Harrison, who was in danger from Proctor. He then undertook the defense of Fort Meigs. During the campaign that ended at the battle of the Thames he was stationed at Detroit. Following that battle he was placed in command of the troops at Sacketts Harbor on Lake Ontario. He criticized Harrison because of his inactivity during the winter of 1814 and his correspondence with the Secretary of War and with General Cass has been severely criticized (Goebel, *post*, p. 194). On Harrison's resignation in May 1814, he succeeded to the command of the army in the Northwest. Save for one spectacular raid in Upper Canada, nothing important was achieved in his period of command.

Following the war he served as a member of several commissions for treaty-making with the Indians. He was frequently a member of the state legislature, in the lower house for three sessions, 1815–16, 1817–18 when he was speaker, and 1826–27, and in the upper house for three sessions, 1821–22, 1822–23, and 1829–30. He made himself unpopular by supporting the United States Bank when it was bitterly attacked by the legislature in 1817. In 1822 he was elected to Congress, where he served inconspicuously. In 1830 he was elected governor by a narrow margin over Robert Lucas, a Jackson man. In 1832 he chose to run for Congress rather than for re-election as governor but was defeated by a single vote by William Allen, who later married his daughter, Effie. In 1830 he met with a serious accident from which he did not fully recover. He died at his home "Fruit Hill" near Chillicothe.

[McArthur Papers in Lib. of Cong.; some letters in Ohio State Lib.; files of the Cong. Joint Committee on Printing; John McDonald, *Biog. Sketches of General Nathaniel Massie, General Duncan McArthur* (1838); L. S. Evans, *A Standard Hist. of Ross County, Ohio* (1917), vol. I; *Hist. of Ross and Highland Counties, Ohio* (1880); W. A. Taylor, *Ohio Statesmen and Hundred Year Book* (1892); D. B. Goebel, *W. H. Harrison* (1926); F. P. Weisenburger, *Ohio Politics during the Jacksonian Period* (1929); "The Bounty Lands of the Am. Revolution in Ohio," a typewritten dissertation by W. T. Hutchinson in the Lib. of the Univ. of Chicago.]

W. T. U.

McARTHUR, JOHN (May 13, 1823–Jan. 8, 1890), architect, known as John McArthur, Jr., was born in Bladenock, Wigtownshire, Scotland. He is said to have come to America in his childhood, perhaps in the care of his uncle, John McArthur. He was subsequently apprenticed to this uncle, who was a carpenter in Philadelphia. Being of a studious habit and earnestly desiring a knowledge of architecture, he devoted his evenings to acquiring instruction in drawing and design at the period when the Franklin Institute afforded opportunity through a course of lectures by Thomas U. Walter [*q.v.*]. It is said that McArthur declined his uncle's offer of means to obtain a liberal school education because he preferred to pursue his technical studies in the special field to which he aspired. As apprentice and later as foreman and superintendent of works he gained practical experience and promotion when such progressive advancement was highly regarded as the path to master craftsmanship. The influences under which he acquired the principles of design developed a classical taste which, joined with strict regard for utility and fitness, thereafter marked his architectural accomplishments.

In his twenty-sixth year (1848) while serving as superintendent of works with his uncle, he won, in competition with established architects, the first premium for a design of a new building for the House of Refuge at Philadelphia. He subsequently served as architect for the successive enlargement of the institution during his lifetime. Thus established in his profession, he planned numerous important public and private buildings, including the once famous Continental, Girard, and LaPierre hotels, Dr. David Jayne's granite business block and his marble residence, the Public Ledger Building, and George W. Childs's mansion, besides buildings for Lafayette College at Easton, the State Asylum for Insane at Danville, Pa., and others. During the Civil War he was employed by the United States government in the erection of hospitals and was architect of the naval hospitals at Philadelphia, Annapolis, and Mare Island. He twice declined the office of supervising architect of the United States Treasury Department, but superintended the erection of the post office at Philadelphia.

Judged by the standard of popular taste and architectural practice during the period of his career, his work exhibited sound construction and in design compared favorably with that of his contemporaries. It is claimed that his crowning achievement was the Philadelphia City Hall or Public Buildings, for which competitive designs were submitted in 1869. Although the structure has not escaped criticism, this criticism has been due primarily to the controversy its location involved and to the prolonged period of construction which brought it into conflict with changing fashions in design, and with the higher buildings which now surround it. It was at the time one of the two largest public buildings in the United States and was considered unique for its originality and the merit of its sculptural work and adornment. In his personal and professional career McArthur has been described as a worthy successor of Latrobe, Mills, Strickland, Haviland, and Walter [qq.v.], self-trained architects who were famed in their day. He died at Philadelphia, survived by his wife, Matilda (Prevost) McArthur, by two sons and two daughters.

[Joseph Jackson, *Early Phila. Architects and Engineers* (1923) ; Charles Morris, *Makers of Phila.* (1894) ; *The City Hall, Phila.: Architecture, Sculpture and Hist.* (1897) ; *The Twenty-first Ann. Report of the House of Refuge of Phila.* (1849), and later reports ; *The Biog. Encyc. of Pa. of the Nineteenth Century* (1874) ; obituary in *Public Ledger* (Phila.), Jan. 9, 1890.]
H. W. S—s.

McARTHUR, JOHN (Nov. 17, 1826–May 15, 1906), manufacturer and soldier, born at Erskine, Scotland, was expected by his parents, John and Isabella (Neilson) McArthur, to fulfill the bright promise of his parish school days and enter the Presbyterian ministry. He pre-

ferred his father's smithy, however, and one year after his marriage in 1848 to his neighbor, Christina Cuthbertson, he emigrated to America, joining his brother-in-law, Carlile Mason, in Chicago. After McArthur had gained a little capital by several years' work for a Chicago boiler-maker, he became Mason's partner (1854–58) in the ownership of the successful Excelsior Iron Works, "making steam boilers, engines, and iron work of every description." From 1858 to 1861 McArthur conducted the business alone.

During these years he rose from 3rd lieutenant to captain of the Chicago Highland Guards, and in May 1861 he was at Cairo, as colonel of the 12th Illinois Infantry. Drilling, Kentucky reconnaissances, and railway patrol filled the rest of the year, and by its close he commanded the 1st Brigade of the 2nd Division. From Fort Henry (February 1862) until the war ended, his troops were frequently on special duty. Grant found the tall, brawny, tight-lipped Scot both "zealous and efficient," a plain man who won his superiors' confidence and his soldiers' love. "Meritorious service" at Donelson made him a brigadier-general (Mar. 21, 1862), and at Shiloh, although wounded, he commanded his division after Gen. W. H. L. Wallace was killed. He effectively led the 6th Division, Army of the Tennessee, through the hard fighting around Corinth and Iuka. In the Vicksburg campaign, under General McPherson, his men were often detached for emergency service to McClernand's, F. P. Blair's, or Sherman's command. Grant requested his promotion, but McArthur had no political influence at Washington and his advance to higher rank was retarded.

From the early autumn of 1863 to Aug. 1, 1864, he was post commander of Vicksburg. For two months thereafter he protected Sherman's line of communication about Marietta, Ga., and was then ordered to Missouri to oppose General Price. In December, he was rushed to Nashville and here, on the 16th, his military career reached its climax. Not unwillingly yielding to his impatient troops, and with only the silent sanction of his superior, Major-General A. J. Smith, he charged the opposing heights, crushed Hood's left wing, and turned the battle of Nashville into a Confederate rout. On Thomas' recommendation, McArthur was brevetted major-general. Thereafter, until he was mustered out, Aug. 24, 1865, he served under Major-General E. R. S. Canby in the Alabama campaign and was stationed at Selma during the summer.

For twenty years after the war, McArthur suffered a series of reverses. Efforts to revive his foundry business failed. The Chicago Fire darkened his term as commissioner of public works (1866–72), and while he was postmaster of Chicago (1873–77), $73,000 of post-office funds disappeared in a bank crash. Bowing to a court decision, he used most of his fortune to make good this loss. Another of his ventures, the Chicago and Vert Island (Lake Superior) Stone Company, succumbed to two successive ship disasters in the early eighties. About 1885 he retired from business, but continued to take an active interest in the Presbyterian Church, the St. Andrew's Society, the Grand Army of the Republic, and the Loyal Legion. He died of paralysis and was buried in Rose Hill Cemetery, Chicago. He was the father of seven children. In 1919, a bust of General McArthur was unveiled on the Vicksburg battle-ground.

[Interview with a son, J. N. McArthur, Chicago, who possesses a MS. by J. N. Warrington entitled "McArthur Genealogical Tables and Family Record"; Chicago Directories, 1850 ff.; G. L. Paddock, "The Beginnings of an Illinois Volunteer Regiment in 1861," in *Military Essays and Recollections* (comp. in 1894 by Ill. Commandery, Mil. Order of the Loyal Legion of the U. S.), II, 258 ff.; *Mil. Order of the Loyal Legion . . . Commandery of the State of Ill., Circular No. 22,* series of 1906; *Who's Who in America,* 1906–07; T. B. Van Horne, *Life of Maj. Gen. George H. Thomas* (1882), pp. 324 ff.; *War of the Rebellion: Official Records (Army)*; *Sunday Times-Herald* (Chicago), Feb. 17, 1901; *Chicago Chronicle,* Oct. 6, 1903; *National Tribune* (Washington), July 8, 1906, and Oct. 26, 1916; *Chicago Daily News,* Aug. 26, 1906; *Chicago Tribune,* Oct. 16, 1919; *British-American* (Chicago), Sept. 27, 1919, and Chicago newspapers of the period May 15–26, 1906.]
W. T. H.

MACARTHUR, ROBERT STUART (July 31, 1841–Feb. 23, 1923), Baptist clergyman, editor, author, was born at Dalesville, Quebec, the eleventh child of Archibald and Margaret (Stuart) MacArthur. His parents had left the Highlands of Scotland in quest of religious freedom. His father was a stanch Covenanter; his mother, a devoted Baptist. After preparatory studies at the Canadian Literary Institute at Woodstock, Ontario, MacArthur went to Rochester, N. Y. He graduated from the University of Rochester in 1867 and from the Rochester Theological Seminary in 1870. In due time he became an American citizen. Ordained to the Baptist ministry in New York City in 1870, he served as pastor of the Calvary Baptist Church there for forty-one years. During his pastorate the membership increased from 200 to 2,300, a beautiful edifice was erected, and large contributions were made to benevolence. MacArthur was an eloquent speaker and was in constant demand as a preacher and lecturer. His preaching was exegetical and evangelical, marked by style and adornment, copious allusion, and spiritual discernment. His sermon, "What think ye of Christ," was translated into nine languages. His

two volumes entitled *Quick Truths in Quaint Texts* (1895, 1907) have been the sources for many a sermon. Though conservative in his theological point of view, he was able to present his ideas in a way that appealed to the modern mind. Throughout a five-decade preaching career, he missed preaching only one Sunday on account of illness. He made it a rule to visit every member of his church every year. This pastoral service was the laboratory of his pulpit ability.

MacArthur was an enthusiastic Baptist and promoted the interests of that denomination in three continents. He was a correspondent of various Baptist periodicals, editor for a time of the *Baptist Quarterly Review* and the *Christian Inquirer,* and was the author of more than a score of popular homiletical books. From 1881 to 1913 he acted as trustee of the New York Baptist Union for Ministerial Education. In 1911 he left his New York City pastorate when he was unanimously elected president of the Baptist World Alliance. In this capacity he visited Russia to secure the Czar's permission to erect a Baptist theological seminary at St. Petersburg, but the outbreak of the World War cancelled the provisional imperial consent. He also attended the centennial of Baptist missions in Burma. The growth of the ritual of worship in the Baptist Church is due in part to his promotion of a rather stately and formal service in his own church and the publication of addresses and books concerned with liturgy. His homiletical works include *The Attractive Christ and Other Sermons* (1898) and *The Old Book and the Old Faith* (1900). MacArthur was married, on Aug. 4, 1870, to Mary Elizabeth Fox, the daughter of the Rev. Norman Fox, for some years a member of the New York legislature. He died at Daytona Beach, Fla., within an hour after he was stricken with acute indigestion.

[*Who's Who in America,* 1922–23; *Annuals of the Northern Bapt. Convention,* 1907–23; Annual Sessions of the Baptist Congress, 1882, 1885, 1892, 1901; the *Baptist,* Mar. 10, 1923; the *Watchman-Examiner,* Mar. 1, 1923; *N. Y. Times,* Feb. 25, 1923.]
C. H. M.

McARTHUR, WILLIAM POPE (Apr. 2, 1814–Dec. 23, 1850), hydrographer, naval officer, was born at Ste. Genevieve, Mo., the son of John and Mary (Linn) McArthur. Appointed midshipman in the United States navy (Feb. 11, 1832) at the request of his uncle, Dr. Lewis Fields Linn [*q.v.*], later United States senator from Missouri, he spent several years in the South Pacific station and then attended the naval school at Norfolk. He commanded one of the vessels in the expedition to the Everglades during the second Seminole War (1837–38) but was severely wounded and sent to the naval hospital at Norfolk, where the energetic convalescent courted and married on May 3, 1838, Mary Stone Young, daughter of the hospital superintendent. In 1840 he was ordered to the brig *Consort,* which had been detailed to the United States Coast Survey, and during the next year he participated in the survey of the Gulf coast and was promoted to lieutenant (1841). Continuing in the Coast Survey, he was appointed by Alexander Dallas Bache [*q.v.*] in the autumn of 1848 to the command of the hydrographic party sent to make the first survey of the Pacific Coast. Arriving at Panama, McArthur found the isthmus overrun with lawless Americans and at once became the head of an effective vigilance committee. He then took command of the *Humboldt,* which lay at the island of Taboga without a captain and overloaded with emigrants, and sailed her to California. There he selected Mare Island as the most suitable location for a navy yard and sailed northward along the coast in the schooner *Ewing.* His pioneer work on the West coast, including a preliminary survey and a successful reconnaissance of the coast from Monterey to the Columbia River, was carried out in spite of mutiny, desertion, and McArthur's recurring attack of malignant fever. The results of the survey were published in 1851 by the United States Coast Survey (*Notices of the Western Coast of the United States*). McArthur died from an acute attack of dysentery as the *Oregon* was entering Panama Harbor on the return voyage.

[See *Senate Executive Doc. 1,* 30 Cong., 2 Sess.; *Senate Executive Doc. 5,* 31 Cong., 1 Sess.; *House Executive Doc. 12,* 31 Cong., 2 Sess.; and Lewis A. McArthur, "The Pacific Coast Survey of 1849 and 1850," *Quart. of the Oregon Hist. Soc.,* Sept. 1915. For the memorial meeting of the U. S. Coast Survey, see the *Daily Nat. Intelligencer* (Washington, D. C.), Jan. 10, 1851, and App. No. 40 of *Senate Executive Doc. 3,* 32 Cong., 1 Sess.]   F. E. R.

MACAULEY, EDWARD YORKE [See Mc-CAULEY, EDWARD YORKE, 1827–1894].

McAULEY, JEREMIAH (*c.* 1839–Sept. 18, 1884), reformed criminal, "apostle to the lost," was born in Ireland. His father was a counterfeiter who found it expedient to leave for parts unknown while Jerry, as he was always called, was an infant. He was brought up by a Roman Catholic grandmother whose head he frequently made a target for missiles as she knelt in prayer, for which impudence, upon arising, she was accustomed to curse him vigorously. He never went to school, was harshly treated, and grew up in idleness and mischief. When thirteen years of age he was sent to New York, where he made his home with a married sister until, confident

that he could live by his own wits, he took lodgings on Water Street. Here, in association with other criminals he became a river thief, boarding vessels at night and stealing whatever he could take away. At nineteen he was arrested for highway robbery, and, though innocent of the charge, was convicted and sentenced to Sing Sing for a term of fifteen years and six months. A Sunday morning talk given by a reformed criminal, Orville Gardner, better known as "Awful" Gardner, started him on the road to conversion. In 1864, having served more than seven years of his sentence, he was pardoned, and left prison determined to lead a sober and righteous life; but temptation was too strong for him and he reverted to evil ways. With others he began buying stolen goods of sailors; then, compelling them to join the army through fear of arrest, collected the bounty. After the war he was engaged in river thieving and in disposing of stolen and smuggled goods. It was profitable business, but he spent all his gains in riotous living. His conscience was never quiet, however, and through the influence of Water Street mission workers he was again, and this time permanently, converted.

Having secured honest employment, he was one day sitting at his work when, he says, "I had a trance or vision . . . and it seemed as if I was working for the Lord down in the Fourth Ward. I had a house and people were coming in. There was a bath, and as they came in I washed and cleansed them outside, and the Lord cleansed them inside." He interested others in the realization of his dream, a little money was raised, and on Oct. 8, 1872, he opened a mission at 316 Water Street. For nearly ten years, often persecuted by the vicious and not always supported by the police, he ministered to the fallen. His wife, Maria, who also had been rescued from a life of degradation, was his devoted colaborer. Scores were converted, and knowledge of the mission was carried by sailors and others to distant quarters of the world. It was incorporated as the McAuley Water Street Mission in 1876, and a three-story brick building erected for its work. In 1882 McAuley founded the Cremorne Mission on West Thirty-second street, which he conducted until his death. He also began in June 1883 the publication of a journal, *Jerry McAuley's Newspaper,* which contained accounts of mission meetings and testimonies of converts. An autobiographical sketch dictated by him, entitled *Transformed, or the History of a River Thief,* appeared in 1876, and was widely circulated. During his later years he suffered from consumption, which was the cause of his comparatively early death. He was buried in Woodlawn Cemetery.

[*Jerry McAuley, His Life and Work* (1885), ed. by R. M. Offord, with introduction by S. Irenæus Prime; 5th ed. (1907) entitled *Jerry McAuley, An Apostle to the Lost,* with additions; S. H. Hadley, *Down in Water Street* (1902); Helen Campbell, *The Problem of the Poor* (1882); *N. Y. Observer,* Sept. 25, 1884; *N. Y. Times, N. Y. Tribune,* Sept. 19, 22, 1884.]   H. E. S.

MCAULEY, THOMAS (Apr. 21, 1778–May 11, 1862), Presbyterian clergyman, educator, was born in Ireland, possibly at Coleraine, the son of Thomas A. and Eliza J. (Warden) McAuley. During a debate in the General Assembly of 1837 he stated that he had been a missionary on the frontier as early as 1799 (E. H. Gillett, *History of the Presbyterian Church in the United States of America,* 1864, II, 505). Except for this hint, his early life is altogether obscure. His missionary activity seems to have preceded his entrance to college, for he graduated from Union, Schenectady, N. Y., in 1804, having given his residence at the time of his enrolment as Salem, N. Y. He remained at the college for some years, serving as tutor (1805–06), lecturer in mathematics and natural philosophy (1806–14), and professor of these subjects (1814–22). In 1819 he was ordained by the Presbytery of Albany and in 1822 became pastor of the Rutgers Street Church, New York City. A warm-hearted Irishman whose conversation was full of racy humor, a fluent and ardent preacher, and a faithful pastor, he was popular personally and successful in his ministry. He took an active part in the affairs of the denomination and was moderator of the General Assembly in 1826. In 1827 he was elected president of Transylvania University, Kentucky, but declined (Robert Peter, *Transylvania University,* 1896, p. 156), accepting, however, a call to the Tenth Presbyterian Church, Philadelphia. Here he served until 1833 when he returned to New York and took charge of the Murray Street Church, which later moved to Eighth Street.

Unlike most Presbyterian ministers of his race, McAuley aligned himself with the new-school party, and was one of its leaders in the memorable General Assembly of 1837 at which the old-school adherents took action which resulted in a division of the Church. He was also present at the convention held in Auburn, N. Y., that same year, when the Auburn Declaration "stating the 'true doctrines' of the new-school men over against the 'errors' charged on them in the old-school memorial" was drawn up. Two years earlier he had taken part in the founding of Union Theological Seminary, originally known as the New York Theological Seminary,

and his name heads the list of the original directors elected Nov. 9, 1835. He was subsequently chosen the first president of the institution, and professor of pastoral theology and church government. He rendered valuable service for four years, resigning in 1840. In 1845 he also resigned his pastorate, and his later life was spent in retirement. The degree of LL.D. was conferred upon him by Dublin University.

[*A Gen. Cat. of the Officers, Grads. and Students of Union Coll., 1795–1868* (1868); *Gen. Cat. of Union Theolog. Sem.* (1919); E. F. Hatfield, *The Early Annals of Union Theolog. Sem.* (1876); G. L. Prentiss, *The Union Theolog. Sem. . . . . Hist. and Biog. Sketches of Its First Fifty Years* (1889); S. J. Baird, *A Hist. of the New School* (1868); *N. Y. Times,* May 13, 1862; information from James Brewster, Librarian of Union Coll.]   H. E. S.

MCBRYDE, JOHN McLAREN (Jan. 1, 1841–Mar. 20, 1923), agriculturist, college president, the son of John and Susan (McLaren) McBryde, Scotch immigrants who came to America about 1820, was born in Abbeville, S. C. His father, a prosperous cotton factor and merchant, gave his son the best education the South then afforded. Prepared in the village academy, he was admitted to the sophomore class of the South Carolina College, where, inspired by the lectures of John and Joseph Leconte [*qq.v.*], he developed a love of science that determined his life work. From Columbia he went to the University of Virginia in 1859, and left there in January 1861 to become a soldier of the Confederacy. Joining a volunteer company from Abbeville, he was stationed first on Morris Island. Mustered out, he volunteered for service in Virginia, and was with Beauregard at the first battle of Manassas. In 1862 he served with the cavalry on James Island, and thence, stricken with typhus fever, was invalided home. Unfit for military service, he entered the Treasury Department at Richmond and at the age of twenty-two was appointed chief of a division of the War Tax Office. He married Cora Bolton, daughter of James and Maria (Harrison) Bolton of Richmond, on Nov. 18, 1863. To this union six children were born.

At the close of the war he began farming near Charlottesville, Va., where through reading and private study he learned to apply scientific methods to agriculture. His enthusiasm and gift for leadership soon drew others to him and he organized farmers' clubs, before which he presented the results of his studies and experience. Through his addresses and articles in the newspapers he became well known as an agriculturist and in 1879 was called to the chair of agriculture in the University of Tennessee. His first report, published in 1880, marks an epoch in the history of scientific agriculture in the South.

In 1882 he accepted a chair in the South Carolina College, just then beginning to recover from the horrors of the war. Soon afterward, he was elected president and in that capacity reorganized the College and expanded it into a university along modern lines. As the director of experiment stations in different sections of the state he supervised the planting and fertilization of cotton and other crops. His experiments and reports gave an impetus to the revival of agriculture in South Carolina and had a lasting influence on methods of farming throughout the South. Though offered the directorship of the Agricultural Experiment Station in Texas and the presidency of the University of Tennessee, he chose to remain in the service of his native state.

Unfortunately, however, during the political disturbances in South Carolina in the nineties the University was reduced to a college and the agricultural department, in which his heart was engaged, was removed to Clemson. Therefore, when offered the presidency of the Virginia Agricultural and Mechanical College and Polytechnic Institute, at Blacksburg, he accepted, and in September 1891 took charge of a moribund school with a faculty of ten instructors and a student body of less than a hundred. In sixteen years he created a high-grade polytechnic institute with sixty teachers and more than seven hundred students. He had numerous flattering offers, including the assistant secretaryship of agriculture under Cleveland (1893) and the first presidency of the University of Virginia, but refused to leave his post. As a member of the board of directors of Sweet Briar Institute he organized the new school on a broad basis and outlined its policy. In June 1907 having tendered his resignation, he was made president emeritus of the Virginia Polytechnic Institute and granted the degree of Doctor of Science. In 1912 the University of South Carolina awarded him the McMaster Medal in recognition of his distinguished services to the state. He died in New Orleans.

Few other college executives in the South have rendered longer and more faithful service or have contributed to the cause of education along so many different lines. Six feet tall, erect, with keen gray eyes and kindly smile; calm, dignified, courteous towards high and low alike; gentle yet firm, McBryde had a charm of manner that captivated every one. He was an accomplished musician, a fine horseman, a keen sportsman, and an elegant gentleman of the old school. He inspired both faculty and students with con-

fidence and enthusiasm and developed an *esprit de corps* that contributed to the healthy, permanent growth of every institution with which he was connected.

[*Bull. Univ. S. C.*, no. 31 (July 1912), pt. II; *Bull. Va. Polytechnic Inst.*, Jan. 1908; *Who's Who in America*, 1922–23; *Men of Mark in Va.*, vol. III (1907), portr.; D. C. MacBryde, *MacBryde (McBryde—Macbride) of Auchinnie Parish . . . Wigton, Galloway, Scotland* (1931); MSS. in possession of the author and the family; *Times Picayune* (New Orleans), Mar. 21, 1923.]

C. W. D.

McBURNEY, CHARLES (Feb. 17, 1845–Nov. 7, 1913), surgeon, was born in Roxbury, Mass., the son of Charles and Rosine (Horton) McBurney. His father, an immigrant from the North of Ireland, was of Scotch extraction; his mother came from Bangor, Me., and was of old native stock. Their son was named Charles Heber, but after graduation from college apparently never used his middle name. He received his preliminary education at the Roxbury Latin School and at private institutions, graduated (A.B.) from Harvard in 1866, and was granted the doctor's degree in medicine at the College of Physicians and Surgeons, New York, in 1870. For the next eighteen months he was an interne at Bellevue Hospital, then followed postgraduate studies in Vienna, Paris, and London, giving special attention to surgery. On his return, he settled in New York and began his surgical career as assistant demonstrator (1873–74) and demonstrator (1875–80) of anatomy at the College of Physicians and Surgeons, under the ægis of the well-known surgeon Henry B. Sands. In 1874, he became junior associate in private practice of Dr. George A. Peters. This relationship continued until the retirement of Peters ten years later.

McBurney's first important hospital appointment was that of visiting surgeon at St. Luke's in 1875. This he retained until 1888 when he resigned to become visiting surgeon at Roosevelt Hospital. In the meantime (1882–88) he had served in the same capacity at Bellevue Hospital. He was made instructor in operative surgery at the College of Physicians and Surgeons in 1880, promoted to professor of surgery in 1889, and in 1892 became professor of clinical surgery. In 1907 he resigned and was made professor emeritus.

Late in the eighties of the nineteenth century antiseptic surgery had developed to such an extent that it became practicable to operate with safety in the abdominal cavity. McBurney had the merit of being one of a small group who led in both 'the diagnosis and the treatment of appendicitis. In the *New York Medical Journal* for Dec. 21, 1889, he published a paper entitled "Experience with Operative Interference in Cases of Disease of the Vermiform Appendix," in which he first described his diagnostic tender pressure point known thereafter throughout the world as "McBurney's point." His other gift to surgery, "McBurney's incision," a later development (1894), was characterized by his mode of exposing the appendix without cross section of the fibers of the abdominal muscles. In 1892, with money donated to Roosevelt Hospital by William J. Syms, McBurney planned and carried out the construction of an elaborate private operating pavilion which became one of the novel medical institutions of the city. He contributed "Surgical Treatment of Appendicitis" to F. S. Dennis' *System of Surgery* (vol. IV, 1896), and for *The International Text-book of Surgery* (2 vols., 1899), edited by J. C. Warren and A. P. Gould, he wrote "Technic of Aseptic Surgery" and "Surgery of the Vermiform Appendix." For about ten years after 1897 he was occupied with his extensive private practice and his work at Roosevelt, but in 1907 his health failed and he retired to his country seat at Stockbridge, Mass., where for several years he was an invalid. In June 1913 his wife died, and five months later his death occurred at the home of a sister in Brookline, Mass. According to his friends, McBurney was not of a scientific bent of mind; he was not classed as a brilliant operator, and he wrote little; yet he was regarded as one of the world's great surgeons. His interests outside his profession were limited to sports—shooting, fishing, and golf, of which he was an early devotee. He was married on Oct. 8, 1874, to Margaret Willoughby Weston. Two sons and a daughter survived him.

[*The Thirteenth Secretary's Report of the Class of 1866 of Harvard College* (1916); *The College of Physicians and Surgeons, a Hist.* (n.d.) ed. by John Shrady; H. A. Kelly and W. L. Burrage, *Am. Medic. Biogs.* (1920); *An Account of Bellevue Hosp. with a Cat. of the Medic. and Surgic. Staff, 1736–1894* (1893), ed. by R. J. Carlisle; *Medic. Jour. and Record*, Feb. 20, 1924; *Surgery, Gynecol. and Obstetrics*, Mar. 1923; *N. Y. Medic. Jour.*, Nov. 15, 1913; *Medic. Record*, Nov. 15, 1913; *Jour. Am. Medic. Asso.*, Nov. 15, 1913; *Boston Medic. and Surgic. Jour.*, Nov. 20, 1913; *Lancet*, Nov. 22, 1913; *N. Y. Times*, Nov. 8, 1913.]   E. P.

McBURNEY, ROBERT ROSS (Mar. 31, 1837–Dec. 27, 1898), Young Men's Christian Association secretary, was born of Scotch-Irish parentage at Castle-Blayney, Ulster, Ireland. His father, a prominent anti-Catholic leader, was a physician and surgeon: his mother, *née* Ross, was an ardent Methodist and the first of Dr. McBurney's three wives. She died when Robert was six years old. Early religious training gave him a relish for church singing and

hymnody and a zest for Christian service. He came to America in his eighteenth year (1854), a poor immigrant, and found employment as a clerk in a hat-establishment, which position he held until the business failed at the beginning of the Civil War.

McBurney early interested himself in religious work for young men and boys in New York City, becoming, in 1856, a leader of noon prayer-meetings at the North Dutch Church on Fulton Street. In 1852 an organization similar to the Young Men's Christian Association founded in London by George Williams in 1844 was organized in New York City, and after it had passed through a decade of volunteer leadership, McBurney was elected in 1862 as its employed officer at a salary of five dollars a week. He had a genius for friendship as well as sagacity and high intelligence, and succeeded in enlisting many prominent New Yorkers in the work of the Association. Leaving it for a brief period in business in 1864, he was called back in April of the following year.

After attending his first International Convention in Philadelphia, in 1865, McBurney realized the extent of the work of the Young Men's Christian Association throughout the United States and Europe, and the scope and variety of its activities. A survey was made of the needs of young men in New York and, as a result, a building was erected at a cost of $487,000, with adequate equipment for games, gymnasium, library, and meeting rooms, and with a central control which made the secretaryship an important office. The erection of this building, with its unified activities, marked an epoch in Young Men's Christian Association history. By the year 1868 there were five hundred Associations in the United States, all looking increasingly for leadership to the New York branch. Here for twenty-five years McBurney's study, "The Tower Room," heard every tale of human joy and tragedy, and in it he laid the plans which have been creative in the life of the Association.

From 1887 to 1898 McBurney was metropolitan secretary in New York City. Owing to his energy the railroad branch was established in 1887; the Bowery building purchased, athletic grounds and a boat house leased, and the Harlem building completed in 1888; the French branch opened, and student work organized in 1889; the Mott Haven railroad rooms and the Washington Heights branch opened in 1891; the Madison Avenue railroad building in 1893; the Lexington Avenue student building in 1894; the West Side building in 1896; and the East Side building partially erected in 1896.

The membership had grown in thirty-six years from 151 to 8,328, with a daily attendance of 5,670.

McBurney's outstanding contributions to the Association movement were the conviction that the work should be carried forward by young men for young men; the creation of a varied program, including games, gymnasium, libraries, education, trade classes, as well as evangelism; the development of specialized foreign work; the organization of the International Convention; the development of national supervisory agencies of help and counsel; training for leadership; the creation of the physical directorship; assistance in the founding of the training school for Young Men's Christian Association workers at Springfield, Mass., but greatest of all, the creation and development of the general secretaryship. The formative influence exercised by him upon the subsequent development of the Association in North America and throughout the world was profound, exceeding that of any other man. He was never married, and died at Clifton Springs, N. Y.

[L. L. Doggett, *Life of Robert R. McBurney* (1925) and *Hist. of the Young Men's Christian Assos.* (cop. 1922); R. C. Morse, *Hist. of the North Am. Young Men's Christian Assos.* (cop. 1913), and *My Life with Young Men* (1918); *Robert R. McBurney: A Memorial* (cop. 1899), ed. by R. C. Morse; *N. Y. Times,* Dec. 28, 1898.]
G. R. S., Jr.

McCABE, CHARLES CARDWELL (Oct. 11, 1836–Dec. 19, 1906), Methodist Episcopal bishop, popularly known as Chaplain McCabe because of his Civil War services, was born in Athens, Ohio, the son of Robert McCabe, whose grandfather, Owen, came to Pennsylvania from County Tyrone, Ireland, and whose father, Robert, in 1813 migrated to Ohio. Charles's mother, Sarah, daughter of Cuthbert Cardwell Robinson, was brought by her parents to the United States in 1822 from Kildwick, Yorkshire, England. She was a woman of literary tastes and an occasional contributor to the *Ladies' Repository.* From her Charles got his good looks and poetical imagination; from his father's family he derived his singing ability and persuasive eloquence. Both parents were devout Methodists. When he was about fifteen the family moved to Chillicothe, Ohio and then to Burlington, Iowa. For a short time he took charge of a farm in Mount Pleasant, belonging to his father, and then became clerk in a store at Cedar Rapids. He early displayed the characteristics which later gave him popularity and power, personal magnetism, bold initiative, glowing optimism, unfailing good humor, capacity for leadership, ability as a speaker, and a rich barytone voice which he could use in song with great effect. Since he was also evangelically religious, people were sure he was called to the ministry, and with a view to fitting himself for this work, in 1854 he entered the preparatory department of Ohio Wesleyan University. He never graduated, however, though later the college made him an alumnus of the class of 1860. He had an acquisitive mind and read widely, but he was not a student; he was a person of feeling and action rather than of thought; his natural gifts determined his career. For days he would be away from college assisting at revival meetings. His health soon broke down and his schooling ceased. For two years he was principal of the high school in Ironton, Ohio. Here, July 6, 1860, he married Rebecca Peters. In 1860 he joined the Ohio Conference of the Methodist Church.

While at his first appointment, Putnam, now a part of Zanesville, Ohio, he became chaplain of the 122nd Regiment of Ohio Volunteers, and that he might perform all the functions of a clergyman, he was ordained elder, Sept. 7, 1862. His work in connection with the war made him nationally known. On June 16, 1863, while remaining behind at Winchester to care for the wounded on the field, he was taken prisoner. For four months his optimism and song made him the life of Libby Prison. His experiences there he afterward told over and over again throughout the country in his famous lecture, "The Bright Side of Life in Libby Prison." He was broken by fever when freed by exchange of prisoners, but upon his recovery entered the service of the Christian Commission for which by his eloquence and song he raised large sums of money. His singing did much to popularize the "Battle Hymn of the Republic."

So great was his ability to persuade people to give that it destined him to be a money-raiser and promoter for much of the remainder of his life. After the war he was pastor at Portsmouth, Ohio, and agent for Ohio Wesleyan University, for which he secured $87,000. For sixteen years (1868–84) he was assistant corresponding secretary of the Board of Church Extension, and was largely responsible for its remarkable success. In this capacity he wrote to Robert Ingersoll his famous reply to the latter's assertion that churches were dying out all over the land: "We are building more than one Methodist church for every day in the year and propose to make it two a day!" In 1884 the General Conference elected him corresponding secretary of the Missionary Society. He at once sounded the slogan, "A Million for Missions." The goal was reached, and a new one set. Perhaps the most popular of American Methodists, in 1896 he was elected bishop. In December 1902, he became chancellor of the American University, Washington, D. C. Strenuously active almost to the close of his career, he died in New York of cerebral hemorrhage soon after completing his seventieth year, and was buried in Rose Hill Cemetery, near Chicago.

[F. M. Bristol, *The Life of Chaplain McCabe* (1908); *Christian Advocate* (N. Y.), Dec. 27, 1906; *Zion's Herald*, Dec. 26, 1906; *Phila. Inquirer*, Dec. 20, 1906; Julia Ward Howe, *Reminiscences* (1899); Florence H. Hall, *The Story of the Battle Hymn of the Republic* (1916).]   H. E. S.

McCABE, JOHN COLLINS (Nov. 12, 1810–Feb. 26, 1875), Episcopal clergyman and antiquarian, was born in Richmond, Va., of substantial Scottish and Irish descent, son of William and Jane (Collins) McCabe, and grandson of James McCabe who distinguished himself under Montgomery at the storming of Quebec. Denied the opportunity of much formal schooling, he largely educated himself, developing his youthful talent for speaking by active attendance upon a Richmond debating society and writing copiously for the newspapers and local magazines. He originally intended to prepare for the bar and read law for about a year, but the press of domestic circumstances altering his plans he entered the Farmer's Bank of Richmond, where he remained for a number of years. On Oct. 28, 1848, he was ordained to the priesthood of the Episcopal church by Bishop William Meade, having taken deacon's orders two years earlier. From his first parish, Isle of Wight County, where he was rector of the old brick church near Smithfield, he was called to historic St. John's in Hampton. During his pastorate here he served as chairman of the state yellow-fever committee when the plague ravaged Norfolk and its environs. From 1856 to 1859 he was rector of the Church of the Ascension in Baltimore, and then of St. Anne's Parish, Anne Arundel County, Md., until 1861, when he gave up his charge, "ran the blockade," and joined the Confederate army as chaplain of the 32nd Virginia Regiment. In 1862 he was transferred from field service to become chaplain-general to the Confederate military prisons of Libby and Castle Thunder in Richmond, remaining in this office until the close of the war and winning the affection of the Federal prisoners by his many kindnesses to them. Afterward he had charges at Bladensburg, Md., and Middletown, Del., before settling in Chambersburg, Pa., where he died.

During his lifetime McCabe enjoyed considerable local reputation as a man of letters, and is said to have commanded a high price for his writings, although his only publication in book form was the juvenile collection of periodical pieces and verses called *Scraps* (1835). He was a frequent contributor to the *Southern Literary Messenger* while Poe and, later, John R. Thompson were its editors. Poe not only gave him literary advice and encouragement, but was himself apparently attracted by McCabe's individuality, genial manners, and lofty character, for their professional relations rapidly developed into intimacy. He also lectured on literary or historical subjects, delivered numerous memorial addresses, wrote for the newspapers and the church journals, and composed occasional lyrics, several of which possess real merit; but the bulk of this work was ephemeral and perhaps his chief service to posterity grew out of his antiquarian interests, opportunity for the indulgence of which was supplied by his pastorates in tidewater Virginia. A recognized authority on the colonial beginnings and subsequent growth of the church in his native state, he made abstracts from the parish registers for an "Early History of the Church in Virginia" and published in the *Church Review* sketches of many of the parishes embodying the results of his scholarly genealogical and historical investigations, ultimately transferring his manuscript to Bishop Meade for use in writing the latter's *Old Churches, Ministers and Families of Virginia* (2 vols., 1857). McCabe was twice married: first, to Emily Hardaway and, second, Aug. 7, 1838, to Eliza Sophia Gordon Taylor, widow of John Rutledge Smith of South Carolina. William Gordon McCabe [*q.v.*] was a son of the second marriage.

[Lyon G. Tyler, *Men of Mark in Va.* (1907), III, 233–34; Armistead C. Gordon, *Memories and Memorials of Wm. Gordon McCabe* (1925), I, 14–27, and *passim*; *Public Opinion* (Chambersburg, Pa.), Mar. 2, 1875.]   A. C. G., Jr.

McCABE, WILLIAM GORDON (Aug. 4, 1841–June 1, 1920), schoolmaster and author, was born in Richmond, Va., of distinguished stock, son of the Rev. John Collins McCabe [*q.v.*] and Eliza Sophia Gordon Taylor. After graduating (1858) with highest honors from Hampton Academy, he was for a time tutor in the Selden family of "Westover" before entering the University of Virginia in the autumn of 1860. Here his time was short, for on the day that Virginia seceded he left the University for Harpers Ferry with a student company, and until Johnston's surrender, after Appomattox, remained a soldier of the Confederacy, rising, throughout a succession of major campaigns, from private to captain of artillery, and by his courage, gallantry, and determination winning the admiring affection of his men and of his battalion commander Pegram. In October 1865 he opened the University School at Petersburg, Va., and continued it there for thirty years before removing it to Richmond. From its founding it maintained a reputation for the highest standards of scholarship; and there were few who ever left its doors without having gained from association with the bright-eyed, fiery-souled little headmaster a love of truth and a noble code of living. An inspiring leader and a gifted administrator, McCabe was also known, partly through the textbooks which he edited, as a brilliant Latinist. When in 1901 he closed the school and retired, it was with a fame as a teacher second to none in America; he had previously declined professorships in several leading colleges or universities, and when the movement for an executive head for the University of Virginia was inaugurated, which was not put into effect until several years later, a majority of the Board of Visitors favored his election as its first president. During his school period he continued the writing career which he had begun while in his teens with contributions to the *Southern Literary Messenger,* and achieved enviable distinction as editor and author. His poems, mostly written in war time, have found a place in various anthologies; the foremost English and American magazines published his essays on literary and military topics; he edited sundry works; he composed historical and biographical papers, including many for the publications of the Virginia Historical Society, of which he was long president; and he was an eloquent and charming orator, his frequent occasional addresses—many of them championing the cause of his beloved Confederacy—compounding the same wit and solid information and sureness of touch that lent grace and point to his writings. Over and above the offices which he held, however, above his honorary degrees, his illustrious friendships, and above his scholastic achievements, it was the personal human side of McCabe "that was his most meaning and attractive possession" (A. C. Gordon, *Virginian Portraits,* 1924, p. 121). He had a genius for friendship, and wherever he went, into whatever company, he was a welcome guest. His extensive travels and wide experience, his knowledge of what was best in books and in people, his gift as a story-teller, combined with his courtesy, sincerity, and generous sympathy, his warm heart and intellectual independence, to make him a typical example of the cultured old-school Virginian. He married, Apr. 12, 1867, Jane Pleasants Harrison Osborne; she died in 1912, and he married, second, Mar. 16, 1915, the daughter of his boyhood schoolmaster, Gillie Armistead Cary.

[Armistead C. Gordon, *Memories and Memorials of Wm. Gordon McCabe* (2 vols., 1925); L. G. Tyler, ed., *Men of Mark in Va.* (1909), vol. III; P. A. Bruce, *Hist. of the Univ. of Va.* (5 vols., 1920–22); obituary notices in the Richmond, Va., newspapers.] A. C. G., Jr.

McCAFFREY, JOHN (Sept. 6, 1806–Sept. 26, 1881), Catholic educator and theologian, was born at Emmitsburg, Md., and rarely wandered from there during a long lifetime. At the age of thirteen, he entered the preparatory department of Mount St. Mary's College at Emmitsburg and progressed through the college and seminary. A deacon in 1831, he refused in a spirit of humility to undertake the duties of priesthood until 1838 when he was ordained by Archbishop Eccleston. As a teacher in the preparatory school, as a prefect of discipline, as professor of moral theology in the seminary, as vice-president, as pastor of the neighboring church, as rector from March 1838 until his resignation in August 1872, as professor of Latin literature, and as a member of the governing council until his death, McCaffrey served the Mount with the unswerving loyalty of one whose heart and soul were entwined with the fortunes of the institution. At that time Mount St. Mary's was one of the two leading Catholic seminaries, and a nursery of innumerable priests and no small proportion of the hierarchy. Upon all these ecclesiastics, McCaffrey left a definite impression. He was a sound theologian, who spoke with an old-fashioned exactness of rhetoric save when in ordinary conversation he fell with a degree of pride into the Maryland vernacular. He was also a classical enthusiast, and an encyclopedic source of information concerning men and events in the history of the Church in America. A courtly figure, deeply religious but somewhat Puritanical, he was accorded the right to rule, and rule he did with a stern and unyielding discipline. He might well maintain that "I am the college" for he governed quite free from the nominal responsibility to the various archbishops of Baltimore.

McCaffrey had no episcopal ambitions, though few vacant sees were filled from 1840 to 1860 for which his name was not on the list of nominees. He refused actual appointments to the bishoprics of Savannah and Charleston, and probably to Natchez, as he declared: "Here I am fully as useful as if I held a crozier." As early as 1853 he had been honored by the hierarchy when his predecessor in the rectorship, Archbishop Purcell, laid the corner-stone of McCaffrey Hall. In 1860 he attracted attention when he petitioned the Maryland legislature to forbid the sale of liquor to minors. A Southerner and state-rights advocate, he was a devotee of Calhoun and an open sympathizer with the South during the war as were several members of the faculty and a majority of the students to the annoyance of such outstanding alumni as the unionist bishops Hughes, Purcell, and McCloskey. He was a link between John Carroll and later times, but his contribution was as intangible as that of the usual great teacher, for aside from an occasional sermon or lecture he published little—a eulogy of Charles Carroll, an oration in commemoration of the landing of the "Pilgrims of Maryland," a discourse on Bishop Bruté, a sketch of Bishop Dubois, an essay on classical education, and *A Catechism of Christian Doctrine* (1865) which was widely used in elementary classes in Christian doctrine. His merits were extolled by Bishop F. S. Chatard at the obsequies over which Archbishops Gibbons and Corrigan presided as his remains were interred in the college cemetery near those of his priest-brother, Thomas McCaffrey.

[E. F. X. McSweeny, *The Story of the Mountain* (2 vols., 1911); *Sadliers' Cath. Directory* (1882), p. 63; sketch by Bishop Richard Gilmour in *Cath. Universe* (Cleveland), Oct. 6, 1881; obituaries in the *Sun* (Baltimore), Sept. 27, 30, and *N. Y. Freeman's Jour. and Cath. Reg.*, Oct. 8, 1881.]   R. J. P.

McCAINE, ALEXANDER (*c.* 1768–June 1, 1856), clergyman, controversialist, leader in founding the Methodist Protestant Church, was a native of Ireland. When about twenty years of age he came to the United States, landing at Charleston, S. C. Soon, under the preaching of a Methodist missionary, he professed conversion and determined to enter the Methodist ministry. Bishop Asbury became acquainted with him and was favorably impressed with his training and gifts. He was admitted on trial to the Methodist Conference, meeting at Charleston in 1797, and two years later was received into full membership. His early preaching circuits were in the Carolinas and Virginia. In 1806 he withdrew from the active ministry to educate his children. On the death of his wife in 1815, at Bishop Asbury's solicitation, he reëntered the active ministry, but again withdrew in 1821 and became the head of a flourishing boys' school in Baltimore. Though not a member of the General Conference of 1820, he was elected secretary of that body, a recognition of his ability and training.

At this period an attempt was being made on the part of some to introduce into the government of the Methodist Episcopal Church a larger degree of democracy, by securing lay representation in the Conferences and the election, rather than the appointment, of presiding elders. Those advocating these changes were called "Reformers" and they were particularly active in the vicinity of Baltimore, Nicholas Snethen and Alexander McCaine being the two most prominent leaders. McCaine offered strong arguments in favor of reform, ably setting forth his views in *The History and Mystery of Methodist Episcopacy* (1827); *A Defence of the Truth* (1829); and *Letters on the Organization and Early History of the Methodist Episcopal Church* (1850), published originally in the Boston *Olive Branch*. The reformers established a paper called *Mutual Rights* (1824), to which McCaine frequently contributed. His contention was that the Methodist Episcopal organization never had the sanction of John Wesley, and that episcopacy had been "foisted upon the Methodist societies." When the General Conference of 1828 refused to pass reform legislation, numerous churches split over the issue and in 1830 a convention of reformers was held in Baltimore and there organized the Methodist Protestant Church, which in four years had a membership of 26,387. In this new branch of Methodism McCaine was active as a writer and critic until the end of his life. During his latter years he lived with his children in South Carolina and Georgia, his eldest son being a physician at Lott's, S. C. He died at the home of his daughter, Mrs. James M. Brett, in Augusta, Ga.

Soon after the formation of the Methodist Protestant Church slavery became an issue of prime importance. Its General Conference in 1842 refused to legislate on the subject and recommended that each Conference make its own regulations. Numerous objections were raised to this proposal and some withdrew from the Church, but McCaine, among others, became an active advocate of slavery and wrote a pamphlet in its defense, entitled, *Slavery Defended from the Scripture Against the Attacks of the Abolitionists* (1842). In 1843–44 he carried on a controversy on the same subject in the *Western Recorder*. He was a striking figure, with majestic head and clearly cut features. As a preacher he was endowed with great native eloquence. He despised shams, was impetuous in his defense of what he thought was the truth, and was bold to bluntness in dealing with personalities, a characteristic which often laid him open to criticism.

[E. J. Drinkhouse, *Hist. of Meth. Reform and Meth. Protestant Church* (1899); T. H. Colhouer, *Sketches of the Founders of the Methodist Protestant Church* (1880); A. H. Bassett, *A Concise Hist. of the Meth. Protestant Church from its Origin, with Biographical Sketches* (1877); *The Meth. Mag. and Quart. Rev.*, Jan., Apr., July 1830; *Daily Constitutionalist* (Augusta, Ga.), June 3, 1856.]   W. W. S.

McCALEB, THEODORE HOWARD (Feb. 10, 1810–Apr. 29, 1864), jurist and educator, third son of David and Matilda (Farrar) Mc-

Caleb, was born in Pendleton District, S. C. His great-grandfather, William McCaleb (or McKillip, as the name was originally spelled), after taking part in the battle of Culloden, 1746, in behalf of "Bonnie Prince Charlie," fled to Ireland for refuge and in 1747 emigrated to South Carolina. His grandfather, William McCaleb, served as captain in the American Revolutionary army, was a member of the South Carolina convention that ratified the federal constitution, and in 1797 moved to the Spanish province of West Florida and settled in the Natchez district. His father, David McCaleb, was high sheriff of Pendleton District, S. C., and moved to Mississippi Territory in 1802. Theodore McCaleb was educated by private tutors at "Cold Springs Plantation," Claiborne County, Miss., and at Phillips Exeter Academy and Yale College. He is said to have withdrawn from Yale before completing his work there and to have begun to study for the ministry. But after pursuing theological studies for a year, he decided to become a lawyer and began to study law in 1830 in the office of Rufus Choate in Salem, Mass. In 1832 he moved to New Orleans and succeeded to the large law practice which his older brother, Thomas, who died in that year, had built up during the fourteen years he had resided there. Among his clients was the eccentric John McDonough of New Orleans.

In 1841, when he was only thirty-one years old, he was appointed judge of the United States District of Louisiana by President Tyler. In 1846 Congress passed an act dividing Louisiana into two districts and making his court the one for eastern Louisiana, presumably to get rid of him because of his stanch Whig politics; but if that was the case, President Polk rose above partisanship and appointed him to succeed himself. He remained in this office until January 1861, when, notwithstanding his Union sentiments, he decided to throw in his lot with the Confederacy on the secession of Louisiana from the Union. Meanwhile he had launched upon an academic career. He was one of the original members of the law-school faculty of the University of Louisiana, now Tulane University, and served as professor of admiralty and international law from 1847 to 1864. He also served as president of the collegiate faculty from 1850 to 1862. He was a distinguished linguist and even understood several Indian dialects. At one time he is said to have welcomed the Choctaw chief, Billy Bowlegs, to New Orleans in behalf of the mayor of that city in the chief's own language. He was famed for his oratory, his most noted addresses being those delivered on the oc-

casions of the dedication of the Lyceum at New Orleans, the death of his friend, Henry Clay, the unveiling of the Clay monument in Canal Street in New Orleans, and the death of S. S. Prentiss. He was a most liberal entertainer and was host to many foreigners of distinction, including Thackeray, Macready, Châteaubriand, and De Tocqueville. He was married to Agnes Bullitt, daughter of William and Octavia (Pannell) Bullitt of New Orleans, in 1832. They had five daughters and one son. He died and was buried at "Hermitage Plantation," Mississippi, which had been bequeathed to him by his uncle, Jonathan McCaleb.

[This sketch is based upon brief biographical sketches in Thos. M'Caleb, *The La. Book* (1894); *Biog. and Hist. Memoirs of La.* (1892), vol. II; *La. Sunday Rev.* (New Orleans), Dec. 23, 1894; J. S. Whitaker, *Sketches of Life and Character in La.,* . . . *Principally from the Bench and Bar* (1847); and upon data supplied by the authorities of Phillips Exeter Academy, Yale Univ., and Tulane Univ., and by Dr. James F. McCaleb of "Byrnmore Plantation," Carlisle, Miss., who has in his possession numerous documents pertaining to the McCaleb family.]   E. M. V.

McCALL, EDWARD RUTLEDGE (Aug. 6, 1790–July 31, 1853), naval officer, was born at Beaufort, S. C., the son of Hext and Elizabeth (Pickering) McCall. On losing his father at an early age, he was placed under the care of a guardian, who, when the boy showed a preference for a seafaring life, directed his studies in preparation for that calling. Appointed a midshipman on Jan. 1, 1808, McCall, after a period of duty at the Charleston naval station, was ordered to the *Hornet,* on which vessel he in 1811 became acting master. Early in that year he joined the *Enterprise,* and at the outbreak of the War of 1812 was serving on her as acting lieutenant. On her successful engagement with the *Boxer,* off the coast of Maine on Sept. 5, 1813, he was next in rank under Lieut. William Burrows [*q.v.*], her commander, and when early in the action Burrows fell mortally wounded, McCall took command and brought the prize into Portland. Recognition of McCall's share in the victory came from the residents of Charleston, S. C., who gave him a sword, and from the South Carolina legislature which appropriated money for the purchase of one. On Jan. 6, 1814, Congress expressed its appreciation of his gallantry by voting him a gold medal. In the previous year the Senate had confirmed his appointment to a lieutenancy.

After serving on the *Ontario,* McCall in the years 1815–17 made a cruise on the *Java* of the Mediterranean Squadron. On his return home he did duty at navy yards and shore stations at Charleston, Baltimore, Philadelphia, and elsewhere, and once, following his promotion as a master-commandant in 1825, he went to sea. This was in 1830–31 as commander of the *Peacock* of the West India Squadron. In March 1835 he was commissioned captain and thereafter he was on waiting orders until his death, which occurred at his residence in Bordentown, N. J. He had married Harriett McKnights of that city.

[Record of Officers, Bureau of Navigation, 1815–53; T. Wyatt, *Memoirs of the Generals, Commodores, and Other Commanders Who Distinguished Themselves in the Am. Army and Navy during the Wars of the Revolution and 1812* (1848), pp. 257–60. Theodore Roosevelt, *The Naval War of 1812* (1882); *Charleston* (S. C.) *Courier*, Aug. 10, 1853; information from Mr. D. E. Huger Smith, Charleston, S. C.]   C. O. P.

McCALL, JOHN AUGUSTINE (Mar. 2, 1849–Feb. 18, 1906), insurance official, was born at Albany, N. Y., a son of John A. and Katherine (MacCormack) McCall. His parents were of Irish descent. Compelled in early life to support himself, he found work with an Albany agency of the Connecticut Mutual Life Company and at twenty-one obtained a clerkship in the New York state department of insurance, where he won rapid advancement, becoming in 1876 deputy superintendent and examiner of fire, life, and accident companies doing business in the state. In that capacity he attracted attention by the energy and thoroughness with which he exposed the illegal practices of insurance officials. Insurance men of good standing and the business community generally were so favorably impressed by young McCall's activities and methods that in 1883 his appointment as superintendent was urged upon Gov. Grover Cleveland by men of both political parties. When the nomination was made and unanimously confirmed, Cleveland was heartily commended by the press. By this time McCall's knowledge of the insurance field and of insurance problems had been widely advertised. It was not to be expected that the state could long retain his services. Among the life insurance companies of New York City the Equitable was the first to offer him an attractive bid. It created a comptrollership for him and in 1885 he resigned his state office and went to the metropolis to accept double the salary that the state had paid him. Seven years' service as comptroller of the Equitable seems to have enhanced his reputation and popularity among insurance men. He was described at that time as a man of magnetic, vigorous personality, affable and kindly in all the relations of life.

In 1892 the New York Life Insurance Company, ranking in prestige with the Equitable and the Mutual Life, was falling behind its rivals in the race for business as a result of internal dis-

sensions. New blood was needed and the trustees' choice of an executive to succeed William H. Beers was McCall. The business record of the New York Life under McCall's administration seemed indeed to justify the faith of the trustees in calling him to the presidency. The company's business increased amazingly within a few years. The whole organization developed new life. In the twelve years ending in 1904 the income from all sources more than tripled, while the company's investments at the close of that period (nearing $325,000,000) were more than one hundred and thirty per cent. greater than at the beginning. This prosperity was in great part due to McCall's initiative and energy. But in spite of this brilliant showing, the year 1905 opened ominously. The disclosure of serious disagreements among the Equitable's officers was followed by rumors of unsound conditions in the "Big Three" companies and a public demand for an investigation, which was met by the appointment of the so-called Armstrong committee of the New York legislature and the retention of Charles Evans Hughes as chief counsel. Called as witnesses before this committee McCall himself and Vice-President George W. Perkins testified as to the use of the company's funds in political campaigns and in lobbying. When the New York Life's trustees declined to take the responsibility for these irregularities, McCall resigned the presidency and voluntarily obligated himself to make good $235,000 that had been advanced to Andrew Hamilton of Albany. To do this he had to transfer to the company his life insurance and a costly residence at Elberon, N. J. Within a few months he died of cancer of the liver. He was survived by his wife, Mary (Horan) McCall, whom he had married at Albany in 1870, and by two daughters and five sons.

[Obituaries in the New York newspapers of Feb. 19, 1906; M. C. Harrison, *N. Y. State's Prominent and Progressive Men*, vol. I (1900); *Testimony taken before the Joint Committee of the Senate and Assembly . . . of N. Y., to Investigate . . . Life Insurance Companies* (1906), vols. II and III; B. J. Hendrick, *The Story of Life Insurance* (1907); J. M. Hudnut, *Hist. of the N. Y. Life Insurance Company, 1895–1905* (1906); L. F. Abbott, *The Story of Nylic* (1930), pp. 149–51, 178–88; H. S. Beardsley, "The Despotism of Combined Millions," the *Era Mag.*, Nov. 1904, Oct. 1905.]   W. B. S.

McCALL, SAMUEL WALKER (Feb. 28, 1851–Nov. 4, 1923), congressman and governor of Massachusetts, was born in East Providence, Pa., the sixth of the eleven children of Henry and Mary Ann (Elliott) McCall. Two years after he was born, his parents removed to Mount Carroll in northern Illinois. His father was able to take with him eight or nine thousand dollars in gold, which he invested in land and in the manufacture of plows and farming tools. When the panic of 1857 brought financial reverses, the family moved to a farm near the town and again prospered. From the public schools the boy went to Mount Carroll Seminary, then in 1867 to New Hampton Literary and Biblical Institution at New Hampton, N. H., and three years later to Dartmouth College, where he graduated in the class of 1874 with high rank. He began the study of law in Nashua, N. H., went a year later to Worcester, Mass., where he was admitted to practice in 1875, and then opened an office in Boston. At Lyndon, Vt., May 23, 1881, he married Ella Esther Thompson, who had been a fellow student at New Hampton and was the daughter of Sumner Shaw Thompson, a railroad builder and manager. The newly married couple made their home in Winchester, a suburb of Boston, where they reared their five children. In 1887 his district elected him to the General Court. In his first session he introduced the act that practically ended imprisonment for debt in Massachusetts by abolishing the system of fees and giving jurisdiction to an established court in poor debtor cases. In 1888 he bought an interest in the *Boston Daily Advertiser* and became its editor-in-chief for two years. Reëlected to the state legislature that year he became chairman of the judiciary committee and took a leading part in the effort of the legislature to force the supreme court to give its opinion of certain questions on laws relating to public schools. He served two years as a ballot law commissioner and returned to the House for the session of 1892, where he obtained the passage of an act designed to regulate the use of money at elections.

In the autumn of 1892 he was elected to Congress, where his course so commended him to his constituents that he was easily reëlected nine times, thus rounding out an even twenty years of congressional service. Fortunately for him, he represented a district that thought more of independence of judgment than of party regularity, for, although in general loyal to the broad principles of the Republican party, he did not hesitate to take a bold stand in opposition to such policies as his judgment could not approve. He supported the measures in favor of the gold standard and advocated civil-service reform, but he disapproved of the annexation of the Philippines, urged moderation in fixing tariff rates, and opposed rigid control of the railroads, fearing that such a measure as the Hepburn Act concentrated too much power in the federal government and opened the way to public ownership. He did not speak often, but when he did take the

floor he commanded the attention and respect of the House by the force of his argument and the scholarly nature of its presentation. Both in and out of the House his discussion of such constitutional questions as arose was masterly. A firm believer in the established order and a convinced individualist, he opposed any development that he thought paternalistic. He regretted the aggrandizement of the central government at the expense of state and local prerogatives and, in the height of Roosevelt's popularity, he pointed out the dangers of executive encroachment. In 1902 he took the occasion of the centennial celebration at Dartmouth to discuss Daniel Webster's theories on the struggle of liberty against executive power (*Daniel Webster,* 1902). His retirement from the House, although his district would have been glad to have him stay indefinitely, may have been due to a well-warranted ambition to go to the Senate, and presumably the same consideration played some part in his declining to become president of Dartmouth College. He was a candidate for the Senate in the election of 1913, and he had strong support but in the end failed of a majority. Esteem for him, however, brought him back to the political arena the following year, as the nominee for governor. He could not, on the first trial, defeat the popular Democratic incumbent but succeeded in the following year and served as chief executive from 1916 to 1918 inclusive. As Republican governor in the war period he supported Wilson, and he advocated the ratification of the Versailles Treaty. The exceptional feature of his administration was the constitutional convention he led in obtaining, the first in more than sixty years. His public service ended with the dedication of the Lincoln Memorial at Washington in 1922, for which he was largely responsible and to which he had given much care as a member of the commission that had it in charge.

Throughout his busy life he found time for study and writing. His *Thaddeus Stevens* (1898) and *The Life of Thomas Brackett Reed* (1914), both of which appeared in the American Statesmen Series, are good examples of his readable style. Lectures at Columbia and at Yale were printed as *The Business of Congress* (1911) and *The Liberty of Citizenship* (1915). Various addresses on other than official topics have been published, and in the year before his death appeared his final volume, *The Patriotism of the American Jew.*

[L. B. Evans, *Samuel W. McCall* (1916); *Proc. Mass. Hist. Soc.,* vol. LVII (1924); C. H. Thompson, *A Geneal. of Descendants of John Thomson* (1890); *Boston Transcript,* Nov. 5, 1923; *New York Times,* Nov. 5, 6, 7, Dec. 3, 1923.]   R. L.

McCALLA, BOWMAN HENDRY (June 19, 1844–May 6, 1910), naval officer, was descended from John M'Calla who emigrated from Scotland in 1747, having received from the Crown a grant of land in Northumberland County, Pa.; his grandfather, Auley M'Calla, commanded a regiment of New Jersey militia in the Revolution. Bowman was born in Camden, N. J., the son of Auley and Mary Duffield (Hendry) McCalla. His parents died when he was a boy, and he was cared for by older sisters. At thirteen he was placed in Nazareth Hall, the Moravian boarding school at Nazareth, Pa. On the breaking out of the Civil War he wanted to join the army, but being thwarted in this desire because of his youth, he turned his attention to the navy and entered the Naval Academy on Nov. 30, 1861. Three years later he was graduated, fourth in a class of thirty-four. His first assignment was to the steam sloop *Susquehanna* of the Brazil Squadron. Later orders sent him to various ships of the South Atlantic, South Pacific, and European Squadrons, and then to shore duty at the Naval Academy. Meanwhile he had been commissioned lieutenant, Mar. 12, 1868, and lieutenant commander, Mar. 26, 1869. On Mar. 3, 1875, he was married to Elizabeth Hazard Sargent, daughter of Gen. Horace Binney Sargent of Boston. McCalla was made commander on Nov. 3, 1884. His first command was the *Enterprise* on the European Station (1887–90). He was known for his "advanced ideas" on naval administration, but in sharp contrast with his later success he seems at this time not to have been happy in carrying out his policies. At the end of the cruise several charges were brought against him. That of striking with the back of his sword an unruly sailor resulted in his being tried by court martial and convicted. The sentence was suspension for three years and loss of numbers. The next year (1891), however, the Secretary of the Navy returned him to duty; and a few years later, when he had been advanced seven numbers for heroic and distinguished services during the Spanish-American War, he fully recovered what he had lost.

His conspicuous service in the navy began with the Spanish-American War. For nearly a year he had been commanding the cruiser *Marblehead*. In this vessel he directed the gallant affair of cutting the cables off Cienfuegos, Cuba. Later he had charge of landing the first battalion of marines at Guantanamo, and led the forces that drove back the Spaniards. Continuing in command, he superintended the landing of great quantities of supplies, made an enviable reputation for sanitation, and also won the confidence

of the Cubans. On Aug. 10, 1898, he was promoted to the rank of captain. In the Philippine insurrection he took part in the restoration of order. He received the surrender of the provinces of Cagayan and Isabela, northern Luzon (December 1899), and turned them over to the army. He was then commanding officer of the *Newark,* and as such did important work the following year in China. When the American and other legations in Peking reported that they were threatened by the Boxers, McCalla in Tientsin took the initiative in urging the officers of the several powers to go to Peking and post additional guards. On their return, when train service was interrupted and the naval officers and consuls could agree on no plan of action, it was McCalla who proposed, even if the troops of other nations remained behind, to set out for Peking. An allied expedition was organized and made the attempt, but on reaching Lang-fang, forty miles from Peking, was obliged to turn back. In the fighting against heavy odds that followed, McCalla, commanding the American force, had the honor of leading the van and in course of the operations was wounded three times. For his efficient service and gallantry he was highly commended by Sir Edward Seymour, R. N., commanding the expeditionary forces. McCalla's last command was the Mare Island Navy Yard. He had been promoted, Oct. 11, 1903, to the rank of rear admiral, and was retired in 1906 for age. He died at Santa Barbara, Cal.

[Admiral McCalla left in manuscript "Memoirs of a Naval Career," which is in the possession of his son-in-law, Capt. Dudley Knox, Washington, D. C. For published material see *Army and Navy Register*, May 7, 1910; *Report of the Secretary of the Navy* (1900); L. R. Hamersly, *The Records of Living Officers of the U. S. Navy and Marine Corps* (7th ed., 1902); J. D. Long, *The New American Navy* (2 vols., 1903); *Who's Who in America*, 1910–11; *Los Angeles Times*, May 7, 1910.]

C. S. A.

McCALLA, WILLIAM LATTA (Nov. 25, 1788–Oct. 12, 1859), Presbyterian clergyman, controversialist, was born in Jessamine County, Ky., near Lexington, the son of Dr. Andrew and Martha (More) McCalla. He was a descendant of James McCalla, who was in Pennsylvania as early as 1732, and a grandson of William, who was a captain in the Revolutionary War. Andrew McCalla, a physician, was noted for his good works and was one of the projectors of Fayette Hospital, later the Eastern Lunatic Asylum (Lewis and R. H. Collins, *History of Kentucky*, 1874, II, 195). William received his early education chiefly at home. Various accounts of his career say that he graduated from Transylvania University, but the records of the institution do not corroborate this statement. He studied theology privately. In 1813 he was examined by the West Lexington Presbytery but his licensure was delayed. A strong supporter of the War of 1812, he became involved in an altercation with Rev. James Blythe, who held different political views. McCalla arraigned him before his presbytery on various charges, among them that Blythe had threatened to oppose the licensure of such a firebrand as himself. The case was referred to the Synod, and Blythe, having made some acknowledgments, was acquitted. (See *Case of McCalla Against Blythe, Tried Before the Synod of Kentucky in September, 1814,* 1814.) Soon afterward, apparently, McCalla went to Ohio, for he was commissioned chaplain in the army from that state, Apr. 29, 1816, and served until Apr. 14, 1818 (F. B. Heitman, *Historical Register and Dictionary of the United States Army,* vol. I, 1903, p. 653). In 1819 he was settled over a Presbyterian church in Augusta, Ky., where he remained until 1823.

For the next twenty years his ministry was in or near Philadelphia, during which time he became one of the most conspicuous figures in the Presbyterian body. He was pastor of the Eighth, or Scots' Church (1824–35). On Apr. 20, 1836 he assumed charge of the Fourth Church, but dissension arose because of his uncompromising preaching and strict construction of the constitution of the Church, and he and his friends withdrew and were recognized as the Assembly Church, with which he remained, except for a period of travel, until 1842. From Apr. 16, 1850, to May 31, 1854, he was pastor of the Union Church. Intervening years were spent in travel and in serving several small Pennsylvania churches. Tall and of commanding presence, gifted with fluency of speech, he was an effective preacher and debater. He had Scotch-Irish tenacity and pugnaciousness, and a bitter tongue which kept him in a turmoil all his life. Philadelphia was a hotbed of theological disturbance, and McCalla, a militant leader of the old-school party. He also waged vigorous warfare with those outside his denomination. He debated the subject of eternal punishment with Abner Kneeland [*q.v.*]; on two occasions he argued publicly with Alexander Campbell [*q.v.*] over modes of baptism; and on these and other theological questions he had vigorous controversies with opponents of less prominence. A number of these debates are preserved in printed form. He also published: *A Correct Narrative of the Trial of the Rev. Albert Barnes* (1835); *Review of Dr. Boardman's Address Against Kossuth* (1852); and *An Argument for Cleansing the Sanctuary,*

. . . Being in Opposition to the Prevailing System of Allowing Ungodly and Irresponsible Trustees to Manage Church Property, and Non-communicants to Vote at Church Elections (1853). Of adventurous disposition, he spent some time roughing it in Texas, and recorded his experiences in *Adventures in Texas, Chiefly in the Spring and Summer of 1840* (1841), a curious miscellany of narrative, broad humor, religious sentiment, and defense of the morals of the Texans, along with several appendices, including a manual of procedure for church tribunals.

His last years were spent in the South, where he preached in St. Louis, doing missionary work among the boatmen and slaves, and on plantations in Mississippi and Louisiana. He died and was buried in the latter state, apparently near what was then known as Bayou Bidal Church. His wife, whom he married Mar. 30, 1813, was Martha Ann, daughter of Gen. Samuel Finley of Chillicothe, Ohio.

[*The Presbyt. Hist. Almanac . . . for 1861* (n.d.); Alfred Nevin, *Encyc. of the Presbyt. Ch. in the U. S. A.* (1884), *Hist. of the Presbytery of Phila.* (1888); Robert Davidson, *Hist. of the Presbyt. Ch. in the State of Ky.* (1847); E. H. Gillett, *Hist. of the Presbyt. Ch. in the U. S. A.* (1864); W. P. White and W. H. Scott, *The Presbyt. Ch. in Phila.* (1895); T. L. Montgomery, *Encyc. of Pa. Biog.,* XIV (1923), 246–47.] H. E. S.

McCALLUM, DANIEL CRAIG (Jan. 21, 1815–Dec. 27, 1878), engineer, military director of railroads during the Civil War, was the son of a Scottish tailor. Born in Johnston, Renfrewshire, Scotland, he came as a boy with his parents to Rochester, N. Y., where after an elementary education he became a carpenter and builder, and eventually an architect and engineer. Settling for a time in Lundy's Lane, N. Y., he married Mary McCann. In the year 1851 he originated and patented a form of bridge described in *McCallum's Inflexible Arched Truss Bridge Explained and Illustrated* (1859). This invention in time brought him a large revenue, and thereafter, he specialized more or less in bridge construction. About 1852 he moved to New York and associated himself with Samuel Roberts, constructing engineer of High Bridge over the Harlem River; in 1855–56 he was general superintendent of the New York & Erie Railway. During 1858–59, as president of the McCallum Bridge Company, he devoted most of his time to railway bridges, especially in the West and as far south as the Panama Railroad; and for a while he acted as consulting engineer for the Atlantic & Great Western Railway.

Less than a year after the outbreak of the Civil War, Secretary Stanton appointed him military director and superintendent of railroads in the

United States (Feb. 11, 1862), with extraordinary war powers to seize and operate all railroads and equipment necessary for the successful prosecution of the war. He was commissioned colonel and given the position of aide-de-camp on the staff of the commander-in-chief. Beginning with a single Virginia railway about seven miles in length, his administrative control was extended until it embraced 2,105 miles of railroad as far south as the Division of the Mississippi; his construction corps, which was gradually expanded from 300 to 10,000 men, built or rebuilt some 641 miles of railroad and twenty-six miles of bridges; 419 locomotives and 633 cars were under his management; and expenditures for labor, materials, and upkeep reached a total of nearly $40,000,000. His most important achievement in this period was probably the supplying of General Sherman's army, during the Atlanta campaign, with rations, forage, and munitions. He transported supplies for 100,000 men and 60,-000 animals from a supply base 360 miles distant, over a single-track railroad which was constantly subject to destructive raids by an energetic enemy. On Sept. 24, 1864, McCallum was brevetted brigadier-general, and on Mar. 13, 1865, major-general, for meritorious services during the war. His report, "United States Military Railroads," appeared in 1866 as part of *House Executive Document No. 1* (39 Cong., 1 Sess.). After the close of hostilities McCallum was for a time inspector of the Union Pacific Railroad, but eventually retired to private life and with his wife and three sons made his home in Brooklyn, N. Y. He died after a year of ill health, and was buried in Mount Hope Cemetery, Rochester, N. Y. A large, powerfully built man, with a strict disciplinary temperament, McCallum was of a cheerful and genial disposition and wrote poetry as a diversion. A volume of his verse, *The Water-Mill and Other Poems*, was published in 1870.

[*N. Y. Times, N. Y. Herald*, Dec. 28, 1878; *Sun* (N. Y.), Dec. 29, 1878; McCallum's writings mentioned above; *War of the Rebellion: Official Records (Army)*; C. R. Fish, "The Northern Railroads, April, 1861," *Am. Hist. Rev.*, July 1917, with additional references; F. B. Heitman, *Hist. Reg. U. S. Army* (1890); for bridge patent, *Sen. Ex. Doc. 118, 32* Cong., 1 Sess.]

C. D. R.

MACCAMERON, ROBERT (Jan. 14, 1866–Dec. 29, 1912), figure and portrait painter, was born in Chicago, Ill., the son of Hattie and Thomas MacCameron, who had been residents of Long Island. When their son was barely a year old, the parents moved to Necedah, Wis. The artist's childhood and early manhood were spent there, surrounded by wild forest in which he played with Indian children, learning to be a woodsman and an expert rifle shot. Although his father was moderately well off, the locality offered little in the way of formal education, and in his later years MacCameron used to say that he never had more than one year of schooling. He acquired, however, a magnificent physique from working in the woods. At the age of fourteen he commanded a man's wage—$2.50 a day and board—as a lumberjack. Chance acquaintance with a French drawing teacher awakened his interest in art and gave him an opportunity to develop his talent. He saved his wages until he was able to go to Chicago, where he studied art at the Young Men's Christian Association.

Successful in making a living as an illustrator in Chicago and later in New York, he went to London at the age of twenty-two and obtained employment with a publication called *The Boy's Own*. His commercial success here enabled him to move on to Paris, where his ability soon won him entrance to the École des Beaux Arts. Here he studied under Jean Léon Gérôme, and after Gérôme's death, was helped along by Collin and James McNeill Whistler. His life in Paris was not easy, however; he achieved some recognition, but little money, and was often on the verge of starvation. In July 1902, he married Louise Van Voorhis of Rochester, N. Y. A son was born in 1904 and a daughter in 1906. Fortunately, things took a turn for the better with him at this time. In 1904 he received his first public recognition in the form of honorable mention at the Salon des Artistes Français. In 1906 he won the third-class medal, at the Salon, with a picture called *"Les Habitués."* The following year he painted *"Groupe d'Amis,"* popularly known as "The Absinthe Drinkers," which was purchased by the Corcoran Gallery of Washington, D. C. It was not a pleasant picture, but was thought to be technically excellent, showing a rich and luminous color scheme. "The Last Supper," painted in 1900, was an attempt to dramatize the spiritual significance of a religious theme.

MacCameron was always interested in the poor and destitute, claiming that his "peasant background," the product of his childhood in a small western town, gave him a sympathy with the common man which most artists could not feel. He was anxious that his painting have social influence. In "The People of the Abyss," named after Jack London's novel, he attempted to portray the mystical aspect of human squalor and suffering. "MacCameron was at his best," wrote a critic some years after his death, "when his brush, incisive and remorseless as a knife at a clinic, laid bare the misery and hopelessness of that portion of humanity which heredity or misfortune had submerged and deadened and de-formed" (*American Art News,* Apr. 26, 1924). According to the same critic, "The Undercurrent," "Waiting for the Doctor," and "Don Quixote" were notable among his pictures. During his last years MacCameron made his success in portraiture. After long residence abroad he returned to America in 1912 (as a chevalier of the Legion of Honor and a royal knight of La Mancha), to paint the portraits of the wealthy Goelet family. He died suddenly in New York of heart disease, in December of that year. A memorial exhibit of his work was held in New York in 1913.

[Sources of information include C. H. Caffin, "Some New American Painters in Paris," *Harper's Mag.,* Jan. 1909 ; *Who's Who in America,* 1912–13 ; *Am. Art Annual,* vol. X (1913) ; Briggs Davenport, "The Making of a Salon Picture," *Harper's Weekly,* Feb. 8, 1913 ; *Am. Art News,* Jan. 4, 18, 1913, Apr. 26, 1924 ; *N. Y. Evening Sun,* Nov. 24, 1912 ; *N. Y. Times,* Dec. 30, 1912, and Jan. 5, 1913 ; *Atlanta Constitution,* June 1, 1924. Several accounts of MacCameron, including the obituaries in New York papers, give his name as Robert Lee MacCameron, but the middle name does not appear in *Who's Who in America* or in the catalogues of the Nat. Acad. of Design, of which he was an associate.]
R. H.

McCANN, ALFRED WATTERSON (Jan. 9, 1879–Jan. 19, 1931), journalist, pure-food crusader, was born in Pittsburgh, Pa., the son of Michael McCann, a printer and engraver of Irish birth, and Maria Watterson, whose ancestors had come to Pennsylvania in 1762. During his youth he suffered from an ailment that he believed was remedied by proper diet. This experience marked the beginning of his life-interest in food. After attending Mount St. Mary's College, Emmitsburg, Md., he was graduated from Pittsburg College of the Holy Ghost (now Duquesne University) in 1899, remained there as an instructor in English, mathematics, and elocution, and studied nutrition in his spare time. He was soon engaged to write advertisements for various food concerns, including Francis H. Leggett & Company. In 1912, when Harvey W. Wiley [*q.v.*] resigned from the government service, McCann became impatient of pure-food reform through federal action and turned to newspaper propaganda, outlining his program in a full-page article, "The Pure Food Movement," in the New York *Globe* for Oct. 24, 1912. He was able to arouse public interest by his bitter personalities, his unearthing of startling news, and his torrent of catchy phrases. During the next ten years he wrote for the *Globe* series after series of sensational articles against manufacturers who used coal tar dyes, bleaches, inert fillers, and injurious preservatives, and against public officials who condoned such abuses. The *Globe* pro-vided him with a laboratory and stood behind him in the ensuing law suits. He took part in many inquiries such as that into the food at Ellis Island (September 1913), the milk supply of New York City (1919), and the egg supply (1921). In 1913 he published *Vital Questions and Answers Concerning 15,000,000 Physically Defective Children* and *Starving America.* In 1917 he produced a war emergency food book, *Thirty Cent Bread,* which urged the advantages of using cornmeal, of dehydrating instead of canning fruits and vegetables, and of killing off grain-consuming steers. These suggestions were the basis of an article in the *Forum* (October 1917) severely criticizing the United States Food Administration. He insisted continually on the value of the mineral salts in food in *This Famishing World* (1918; revised as *The Science of Eating,* 1919) and in *The Science of Keeping Young* (1926). After publishing a violent anti-evolution book, *God—or Gorilla* (1922), he received the degree of LL.D. from Fordham University. His *Greatest of Men—Washington* (1927) was a laudatory volume written to inspire young people. He wrote for the New York *Evening Mail* after the *Globe* suspended publication in 1923, and established the Alfred W. McCann Laboratories, Inc., in New York, whence issued a stream of indorsements of special brands of everything from chickens to cigars. In 1928 he began to broadcast food talks over the radio. He died of a heart attack Jan. 19, 1931, just after an hour of broadcasting. His wife, Mary Carmody, whom he married in 1905, and four of their five children survived him.

[*Pittsburg Coll. of the Holy Ghost,* 1901–02 (catalogue) ; *Who's Who in America,* 1930–31 ; letter from John B. Harvey, registrar of Duquesne Univ., Pittsburgh, June 23, 1931 ; *N. Y. Times,* Aug. 31–Sept. 13, 1913, July 3, 1925, Jan. 20, 21, 23, 27, 1931 ; portrait in *World's Work,* Oct. 1923 ; H. T. Finck, *Girth Control* (1923).]
M. W. G.

McCANN, WILLIAM PENN (May 4, 1830–Jan. 15, 1906), naval officer, was born in Paris, Ky., the son of James Harvey and Jane R. (Lowrey) McCann. From the latter's mother, Nancy Penn, he derived his middle name. The McCann family had come originally from near Wigtown in Scotland, where the name was spelled McKeand. William entered the navy as a midshipman in 1848 and served on the *Raritan* both in the Gulf of Mexico and in the South Pacific. Then, after nine months of instruction at Annapolis, he went again to the Pacific for three years on the *Independence.* He was promoted to passed midshipman, June 15, 1854, and to lieutenant, Sept. 16, 1855.

When the Civil War broke out, McCann, who

had taken part in the Paraguay expedition on the *Sabine,* was at Vera Cruz on the same ship. He went in this vessel to the relief of Fort Pickens and to the Charleston blockade, where the *Sabine* rescued the crew of the *Governor* of the Port Royal expedition. He was made lieutenant commander, July 16, 1862, and during that year was on the York and James rivers in the thick of the Peninsular campaign as executive, and frequently as commander of the *Maratanza.* She fought at Malvern Hill and also captured the *Teaser,* on which were the Confederate plans for the defense of Richmond. The next year McCann commanded the *Hunchback* in the attack on New Bern, N. C., and Washington, N. C. In November 1863, he received command of the fast 5-gun propeller *Kennebec* and served thirteen months off Mobile. His assistance in the destruction of the *Ivanhoe* under the guns of Fort Morgan secured him the favorable notice of Farragut. In the battle of Mobile Bay the *Kennebec* was lashed to the *Monongahela,* and was at close quarters with the *Tennessee,* for the latter scraped across the *Kennebec's* bow, set her on fire with a shell, and otherwise severely punished her.

After the Civil War McCann did duty at the Naval Academy, was promoted to commander, July 25, 1866, commanded the *Tallapoosa,* and held navy-yard and inspection posts till he was made a captain, Sept. 21, 1876, and was sent to command the *Lackawanna* in the North Pacific. On Jan. 26, 1887, he attained the rank of commodore. He had charge of the naval forces in Chile in 1891 and secured the surrender of the *Itata,* a ship that attempted to bring arms from the United States to the insurgents. When the insurgents refused him the use of the American cable, McCann had it cut several miles off shore. He retired in 1892. His death occurred at his home in New Rochelle, N. Y., and he was buried at Arlington. He was married in New York City, Jan. 31, 1867, to Mary Elizabeth Vulte. Schley, who was on the *Baltimore* with him in Chile, refers to him as "much beloved for his sterling qualities of heart and head" (*Forty-five Years Under the Flag,* 1904, p. 214).

[The Navy Department has the logs of the ships on which McCann served, his official dispatches, the record of his assignments, and a sketch he made of the battle of Mobile Bay. The best account of the *Itata* affair is by Osgood Hardy in the *Hispanic-American Hist. Rev.,* May 1922. See also, *Official Records of the Union and Confederate Navies in the War of the Rebellion*; L. R. Hamersly, *The Records of Living Officers of the U. S. Navy and Marine Corps* (7th ed., 1902); *Army and Navy Jour.,* Feb. 9, 1867, record of marriage; Jan. 20, 27, 1906; *Who's Who in America,* 1906–07; N. Y. *Sun,* Jan. 16, 1906.]

W. B. N.

McCARREN, PATRICK HENRY (June 18, 1847–Oct. 23, 1909), politician, was born in East Cambridge, Mass., the son of Owen and Mary (McCosker) McCarren. Both parents were born in County Tyrone, Ireland. They removed from East Cambridge to Williamsburgh, now a part of Brooklyn, N. Y., where young McCarren attended school until he was seventeen. He then learned the cooper's trade and worked in sugar refineries along the waterfront. He made friends easily, became a natural leader in the district, and at the age of twenty-one was made a member of the Democratic general committee of Kings County. Hugh McLaughlin [*q.v.*], Brooklyn Democratic boss since 1857, recognizing his value, had him nominated and elected to the state Assembly in 1881. He was twice reëlected, and in 1889 was advanced to the state Senate, of which, except for the years 1894–95, he remained a member until his death. In that body his influence was felt in the committee room, and he is reported to have expressed the opinion that it was "only once a century that a vote was changed by argument on the floor" (*Brooklyn Eagle,* Oct. 23, 1909). In 1897 he served on the Lexow committee to investigate the trusts and his minority report dissenting from that of the majority with respect to the American Sugar Refining Company gave him a reputation as the friend of trusts in a period when they were distinctly unpopular. He was chairman of the committee which managed the campaign of Van Wyck against Roosevelt for governor in 1898, and, though the shouting was all on the colorful Colonel's side, McCarren's remarkable marshaling of the opposition forces made the race exceedingly close. Having first served as one of McLaughlin's ablest lieutenants, McCarren overthrew the veteran Brooklyn leader of forty-six years' standing when, in 1903, he defied orders by supporting McClellan for mayor and carried Brooklyn for his candidate. He thus allied himself temporarily with boss Charles F. Murphy [*q.v.*] of Tammany, but almost immediately declared that the Brooklyn Democracy would maintain its independence. During the remainder of his life he fought desperately and successfully to keep Murphy from securing control of Brooklyn. Frequently, McCarren held the balance of power between Tammany and the upstate democracy, and he used it in 1904 to support Parker rather than Hearst for the presidential nomination, and again in 1906 when he threw the Brooklyn vote to Hughes as against Hearst for governor, thereby furnishing the margin by which the former was elected. Almost immediately, however, he plunged into a spectacular legislative campaign against Hughes's reform program and came close to wrecking it.

Few men were more bitterly attacked in the New York press by innuendo and caricature than McCarren; yet men who believed him an evil influence in public life liked him personally. His genius for tactical management was unquestioned and many stories are told of how he escaped from tight corners when he seemed defeated. A little over six feet in height, spare, and slightly stooped, with an unusually long head, and a habitual grim expression on his face, he was a figure of which cartoonists made the most. The loss of his wife, Kate Hogan, and their five children seemed to have imparted a fatalistic turn to his philosophy. He solaced himself by wide reading; by the study of law—he was admitted to the bar after he was forty-three years old; by indulgence in various forms of gambling, notably the race-track, of which he was passionately fond; and by politics, which also he seemed to have enjoyed chiefly for the game's sake.

[R. B. Smith, ed., *Hist. of the State of N. Y.* (1922), vol. IV; scrapbooks of the Hughes Administration, compiled by Hughes's secretary, R. H. Fuller (190 vols.; in N. Y. Public Library); *Brooklyn Daily Eagle,* Oct. 23, 1909; *N. Y. Times,* Oct. 23, 1909; information from David Hogan, nephew and former secretary of McCarren, and from Mrs. Anastasia McCarthy, a niece.]   O. W. H.

McCARROLL, JAMES (Aug. 3, 1814–Apr. 10, 1892), journalist, poet, dramatist, inventor, was born at Lanesboro, County Longford, Ireland. Emigrating to Canada at the age of seventeen, he settled in or near Toronto and almost at once began writing for the newspapers and magazines. By 1845 he had become editor and proprietor of the *Peterborough Chronicle,* and an active force in local politics. For his skill in influencing public opinion, he was rewarded by sinecures in the Customs service at Coburg and Niagara in the years 1849 and 1851 respectively, and in 1854 by appointment to the surveyorship of the port of Toronto. In the meantime he had settled at Coburg where in addition to his other activities he taught music. He was an accomplished flutist and upon occasion went on tour. In the course of these travels he met most of the celebrities in the concert field. It was at this time that his reputation as a technician and composer won him the post of music critic for the *Toronto Leader* and the *Toronto Colonist.* He contributed also to the Quebec *Morning Chronicle.* In view of his other interests, his literary output must have been considerable. Very little of his work appeared in book form, however, and of these writings the best are the *Terry Finnegan Letters* (1864), a series of humorous sketches done in the Irish dialect. Typical exam-

ples of his work in the drama are *The Adventures of a Night* (1865) and *Almost a Tragedy, A Comedy* (1874), both of them patterned upon the well-made play of the Scribe-Dumas school. At the same time, McCarroll was writing a great deal of verse in the whimsical, sentimental, highly imaged style of Clarence Mangan and Tom Moore. An occasional poem he sent to Oliver Wendell Holmes for criticism, but no collected edition appeared until 1889 (*Madeline and Other Poems*) and by that time McCarroll, after a few years of journalistic gypsying in northern New York state, had permanently settled in New York City. Here he became associated with *The People's Cyclopedia of Universal Knowledge* and *The American Cyclopædia,* and latterly he served on the editorial staff of *Humanity and Health* and contributed articles of a scientific character to *Belford's Magazine.* Linked with his talents for music and letters was an interest and ingenuity about mechanical things. At the time of his death he was negotiating the sale of patents upon his inventions: an improved elevator and a fire-proof wire gauze, but before the sales were closed he was seized with pneumonia and died after a short illness of nine days. He was very much a man of his own time. His associates knew him as a choice and merry spirit and a true Irish gentleman of the old school.

[*Belford's Monthly,* June 1892; prefatory sketch by C. L. Hildreth in *Madeline and Other Poems*; *Specifications and Drawings of Patents Issued from the U. S. Patent Office,* Mar., May 1882, Apr. 1883, Dec. 1884; *N. Y. Tribune,* Apr. 11, 1892.]   E. M. H.

McCARTEE, DIVIE BETHUNE (Jan. 13, 1820–July 17, 1900), medical missionary, educator, diplomat, was born in Philadelphia, the eldest of the ten children of Robert and Jessie (Bethune) McCartee, both of Scotch descent, though the Bethunes were originally French Huguenots. His mother was a sister of George W. Bethune [*q.v.*], and had some reputation as a poet. Divie spent his childhood in New York, where from 1822 to 1836 his father was pastor of the Irish Presbyterian Church. From early childhood he read widely, gaining much knowledge of law and theology from his father's library. In 1829 a course of popular lectures aroused in him an enthusiasm for science, to which he devoted his spare time thereafter. Prepared in private schools, he entered Columbia when only fourteen, but, disliking the classical course, left after the junior year to study medicine in the University of Pennsylvania. He graduated in 1840 and did post-graduate work while seeking appointment as a missionary. Designated to China by the Presbyterian Board in 1843, he arrived in Hong Kong early in the following year. While awaiting a vessel to the north he taught a few weeks in the Morrison School, having as one of his pupils Yung Wing, who was destined to be the first Chinese graduate of an American college.

Reaching Ningpo in June 1844, he founded a hospital and aided his colleagues in starting schools and evangelistic work. In 1853 he married Joanna M. Knight. To his other activities he added consular duties until a regular consulate was established in 1857. When the Taiping rebels were overrunning Eastern China, and it seemed necessary to secure their pledge not to molest Americans or their property, Flag Officer Stribling, in 1861, requested McCartee to accompany him to Nanking on this errand. Owing in no small part to McCartee's command of Chinese, the mission was successful. The same year, on account of his health, he went to Japan for a vacation, and later, to Chefoo to live. From 1862 to 1865 he served as vice-consul there. Returning to Ningpo in 1865, he might have remained permanently but for opposition by colleagues to some of his plans, which led to his transfer (1872) to Shanghai and, shortly thereafter, to his resignation from the mission to join the consular staff in Shanghai as interpreter and assessor in the mixed court.

Soon after this, when the Japanese government liberated certain coolies on their way to virtual slavery in the Peruvian ship *Maria Luz,* en route from Macao to Peru, McCartee suggested to the Nanking viceroy an embassy to thank Japan and repatriate the unfortunates. He was invited to accompany this embassy as a secretary and acquitted himself with distinction. Through Dr. Guido Verbeck's recommendation, he was detained in Tokyo to become professor of law and science in the Imperial University and joint curator of the botanical gardens. He was in this congenial position during five crucial years of Japan's metamorphosis and won Japanese confidence. He returned to his old consular position in 1877, but soon reappeared in Tokyo as secretary to the new permanent Chinese legation. In the strain between the two countries over the Loochoo Islands, in 1879, he was able from researches into Japanese—having by that time mastered the Japanese language also—to enlighten General Grant, whom China had invited to mediate; also to confute the more radical Japanese propaganda by a series of articles entitled *"Audi Alteram Partem."* Furthermore, he suggested a compromise, the division of the islands; but first Japan and then China refused to accept it. His relations with both sides helped to avert a break during the crisis. After his term

was ended, he spent some time in America and Hawaii. From 1885 to 1887 he was counselor to the Japanese legation in Washington. He was then reappointed by the Presbyterian Board and sent to Tokyo, where he engaged in executive and literary duties until a few months before his death, which occurred at San Francisco.

[*A Missionary Pioneer in the Far East* (1922), ed. by Robert E. Speer, contains McCartee's memoirs. See also David Murray, "Divie Bethune McCartee," *N. Y. Observer,* July 17, 1902; H. W. Rankin, "A Short Study in Heredity: Influence of Ancestry upon the Life of Dr. D. B. McCartee," *Ibid.,* Oct. 30, 1902; *Missionary Review of the World,* Apr. 1906; *San Francisco Chronicle,* July 20, 1900; State Dept. Archives.]

W. J. H.

McCARTHY, CHARLES (June 29, 1873– Mar. 26, 1921), political scientist and publicist, was born in Brockton, Mass. His mother, Katherine O'Shea, of scanty education but strong mentality, had been a domestic servant in Brockton, when she married John McCarthy, an engine-tender in a shoe-factory, a man of some self-education and, like his wife, a native of Ireland and an ardent Fenian. She maintained a lodging and boarding house, patronized by young Irish and English shoe-workers of various shades of political and sociological belief. Charles sold newspapers, ushered in a theatre, and worked on docks and coasting vessels. At nineteen, having succeeded in entering Brown University, he supported himself by working as a stage carpenter and scene-shifter. Although of meager build and weighing under 135 pounds, he quickly won a distinguished place in inter-collegiate football. After receiving, in 1896, the degree of Ph.B. from Brown, he spent a year at the University of Georgia. In 1899 he made his way to the University of Wisconsin and became a graduate student in political science. In 1901 he obtained the Ph.D. degree and married Louise Howard Schreiber, of Madison, who bore him one daughter. The next year his thesis *The Anti-Masonic Party* (1903) won the Justin Winsor prize of the American Historical Association.

The field of his activities, in the two decades that followed, presents an approximate cross-section of the liberal sociological and economic thinking that was being translated into political action and legislation. With his magnetic vitality, vivid speech, and ready pen he generally was able to enlist an influential following and to maintain the interest of a wide public. He organized in the State House at Madison, for the use of legislators, the first official reference library and bill-drafting bureau in the United States, which he served as director until his death. From 1905 to 1917, he conducted seminar

McCarthy

courses on legislation in the university. In 1912 he published *The Wisconsin Idea,* which, in spite of the faults of hasty preparation and too great emphasis on German influence, was a valuable attempt to describe the development of the state. *An Elementary Civics* (1916) written with Flora Swan and Jennie McMullin was designed as a textbook for the training of pupils in the upper grammar grades. Throughout his career he extended the scope of his teaching by addresses and by numerous magazine articles. He collected material and made contacts with legislators and writers, which helped him to influence the adoption of progressive legislation in Wisconsin and elsewhere. By adapting methods of the "correspondence schools" he brought about the creation of a new type of state university extension service for carrying instruction into remote rural homes. With the help of John R. Commons and others, he effected the establishment of part-time education for youths, of continuation schools for adults, and of special schools for apprentices, still the most advanced system in America of education for workers. He was an early national exponent of farmers' cooperation for purchasing and marketing; he influenced the growth of the state system for regulating rates, service, and practices of railroads and public utilities, wherein Wisconsin was then the pioneer among the states; and he actively advocated such steps in municipal government as budget reform and the commission form of administration. He was among the first, in writings and addresses, to undertake to organize public support for special training for public service in schools and universities. Throughout these activities he maintained a dynamic touch with contemporary legislative problems everywhere, being in personal contact with successive American presidents, with national party leaders, through whom he pushed new legislative ideas into party platforms, and also with foreign statesmen and publicists, by whom he was frequently consulted. In 1914 and 1915 he served as the first director of the United States Commission on Industrial Relations, appointed by President Wilson. After the United States entered the World War, he rendered important service to his state in the administration of the draft law and to the nation as an assistant in the food administration. In 1918 he campaigned unsuccessfully in the Democratic primaries for nomination for United States senator. After about three years of failing health he died in Prescott, Ariz.

[Personal acquaintance; memoranda and letters in McCarthy's files; Horace Plunkett, "McCarthy of Wis.," *Nineteenth Century,* June 1915; *New Republic,* Apr. 27, 1921; *Yale Review,* Nov. 1907; *Irish Homestead,*

McCartney

Apr. 9, 1921; *American School,* May 1921; *Wis. Lib. Bulletin,* Apr.–May, 1921; *Wis. State Journal* (Madison), Mar. 27, 1921.]   L. B. W.

McCARTNEY, WASHINGTON (Aug. 24, 1812–July 15, 1856), educator, mathematician, lawyer, born in Westmoreland County, Pa., was early left an orphan, dependent upon his own resources. After attending the common-schools until he reached the age of eighteeen, he entered Jefferson College at Canonsburg, Pa., from which he graduated with high honors in the class of 1834. In 1835 he became professor of mathematics in Lafayette College, Easton, Pa., but after a year was recalled to Jefferson as professor of mathematics and modern languages, resuming his chair at Lafayette, however, in 1837. Here, for most of the time until 1846, he taught mathematics, natural philosophy, and astronomy. On Apr. 18, 1839, he was married to Mary E. Maxwell of Easton. In 1843 he resigned his professorship to practise law, but resumed his connection with the college the following year. In 1844 he published *The Principles of the Differential and Integral Calculus,* which was widely used as a textbook. Because the trustees of Lafayette would not increase his salary from $600 to $800 a year, he relinquished his professorship again in 1846, although the students protested vigorously and offered to make good the difference themselves. From 1847 to 1852 he was a trustee of the college, and professor of mental and moral philosophy from 1849 to 1852.

These academic distinctions were attained outside of McCartney's chosen career, which was in the legal profession. Having studied law while teaching, he was admitted to the bar in 1838. From 1846 to 1848 he was deputy attorney-general for Northampton County. His bent for educational activities led him in 1844 to open a law school, in which, he announced, he would offer both the usual legal subjects and "an ample course in history," "the whole being designed to furnish a liberal system of legal instruction" (Easton *Democrat and Argus,* Sept. 10, 1846). McCartney's *Origin and Progress of the United States,* a textbook, or series of lectures, on United States history, was published in 1847. The school was so successful that in 1854 it was incorporated by the legislature as The Union Law School, but being a one-man institution it expired with its founder. In 1851 McCartney was elected president judge of the third judicial district of Pennsylvania.

Besides his work as teacher, lawyer, and judge, he engaged in many other activities. He delivered public lectures on such general topics as "How to Read a Book" as well as on the subjects of his special studies, and he was active in the formation of the Easton Lyceum in 1842. As an industrious member of the school board and an enthusiast for free education he was influential in the establishment of the Easton High School. At the time of his death a local editor wrote: "Perhaps no man in the borough had a closer relation to all its vital interests. . . . Without aspiring to leadership in anything, he was ever designing schemes to benefit his fellowmen" (Easton *Daily Express,* July 17, 1856). Living before the age of specialization, McCartney explored most of the fields of knowledge that then interested the scholarly mind. He was described as a learned theologian and as an accomplished linguist who, after mastering the common ancient and modern languages, took up the study of Russian. When he died, at the age of forty-four, he left unpublished a work on evidence and papers on other legal subjects and on logic, rhetoric, optics, and various mathematical topics.

[F. B. Copp, *Biog. Sketches of Some of Easton's Prominent Citizens* (1879); *The Biog. Encyc. of Pa.* (1874); S. J. Coffin, *Record of the Men of Lafayette* (1879); D. B. Skillman, *The Biog. of a Coll.: Being the Hist. of the First Century of the Life of Lafayette Coll.* (1932); Joseph Smith, *Hist. of Jefferson Coll.* (1857); J. F. Stonecipher, *Biog. Cat. of Lafayette Coll.* (1913).]   D. L. M.

McCAULEY, CHARLES STEWART (Feb. 3, 1793–May 21, 1869), naval officer, was born in Philadelphia, the son of John and Sarah (Stewart) McCauley and the nephew of Commodore Charles Stewart [*q.v.*], under whom he first served after receiving his appointment as midshipman in January 1809. During the War of 1812 he took part in a gunboat attack on the *Narcissus* in Hampton Roads and in the defense of Craney Island, and served in the *Jefferson* on Lake Ontario. He was made acting lieutenant in September 1813, and lieutenant in December 1814. After the war he saw much service in the Mediterranean, in the *Constellation* and the *United States.* In 1822 he obtained a furlough to make a voyage to the East Indies. After his return to the navy in 1825 he filled several minor positions at shore stations and in 1826–29 was attached to the *Boston* of the Brazil Squadron. In March 1831 he was made a master commandant and three years later commanded the *St. Louis* of the West India Squadron. His first important sea duty after reaching the grade of captain, December 1839, was performed in 1841–44 as the commander of the *Delaware,* 74 guns, of the Brazil Squadron. From 1846 to 1849 he was commandant of the Washington navy-yard; and from 1850 to 1853, commander-in-chief of the Pacific Squadron, whose cruising grounds at that time extend-

ed from the west coast of the two Americas to the 180th meridian. In 1855 as temporary commander of the home squadron, McCauley performed his most notable, as well as his last, sea service. This was the delicate mission of guarding American interests in Cuban waters, where a Spanish frigate had caused alarm by asserting the right of visitation and search. His successful efforts were commended by President Pierce.

On July 25, 1860, McCauley was made commandant of the Norfolk navy-yard, a position which, in the spring of the following year, entailed much responsibility. After the secession of Virginia, when the yard was threatened by the Confederates, he ordered its guns spiked and its ships scuttled and abandoned it without making a defense. This disaster ended his professional career. In 1862 he was retired with the rank of captain and in 1867 he was promoted commodore on the retired list. A select committee of the Senate that inquired into his conduct at the Norfolk yard reported that it was highly censurable. Feeling that his honor had been wounded and his professional reputation tarnished unjustly by the government, he fell into a melancholy that probably hastened his death, which occurred at his residence in Washington, D. C. On Oct. 25, 1831, he was married in Washington to Leila E. Dickens. Edward Yorke McCauley [*q.v.*] was his nephew.

[Record of Officers, Bureau of Navigation, 1809–71; *Army and Navy Jour.,* May 29, 1869; *Senate Report No. 37,* 37 Cong., 2 Sess.; *Official Records of the Union and Confederate Navies in the War of the Rebellion,* 1 ser.; *Diary of Gideon Welles* (1911), vol. I; *Sunday Morning Chronicle* (Washington), May 23, 1869.]   C. O. P.

MACCAULEY, CLAY (May 8, 1843–Nov. 15, 1925), Unitarian clergyman, missionary, publicist, was born in Chambersburg, Pa., the son of Isaac H. and Elizabeth (Maxwell) MacCauley. Descended from Scotch-Irish ancestors, he early decided to join the Presbyterian ministry, and at fourteen began his studies by reading aloud from books on science, theology, and philosophy to a blind pastor who repaid him with lessons in the classics. At sixteen he entered the sophomore class at Dickinson College, but after hearing Lincoln speak at Harrisburg withdrew from college to enlist. This enlistment was canceled because the lad was still a minor, and MacCauley transferred to the College of New Jersey (Princeton). He enlisted again in 1862, suffered a wound in the knee at Fredericksburg, was promoted to a second lieutenancy in February 1863, was captured by "Stonewall" Jackson, and, on his twentieth birthday, was committed to Libby Prison. He was paroled home, reëntered the college at Princeton, and after graduating in 1864 joined the United States Christian Commission, in which he served until the conclusion of the Civil War.

He then enrolled at Western Theological Seminary, Allegheny, Pa., and, on the removal of his parents to Illinois, transferred to the Presbyterian Theological Seminary of the Northwest (later McCormick), from which he was graduated in 1867. The following month he married Annie Cleveland Deane, daughter of Dr. Josiah and Annie (Everett) Deane of Bangor, Me., and as a licentiate of the Old School Presbytery of Chicago, began his first charge, at Morrison, Ill. His liberal views, however, aroused opposition to his ordination which caused him to refuse a call to continue in the Morrison pastorate and led to the revocation of his license to preach. In 1868, at the urgent suggestion of Charles Carroll Everett and Robert Collyer [qq.v.], he entered the Unitarian ministry. After serving charges in Detroit, Rochester, and Waltham, Mass., he resigned in 1873 to study philosophy and theology at Heidelberg and Leipzig. He returned to America in 1875, and from 1877 to 1880 was pastor of the First Unitarian (now All Souls') Church, Washington, D. C. Resigning this charge because of ill health, he was commissioned by the United States Bureau of American Ethnology to study the Indian tribes east of the Mississippi. His report on "The Seminole Indians of Florida" was published in the Bureau's *Fifth Annual Report, 1883–84* (1887). He also deposited in the Bureau's archives an extensive list of Seminole words and phrases and an analysis of the Seminole verb construction. After visits to the south of Europe and the American Northwest, he settled in Minnesota, where from 1883 to 1889 he gave his time to preaching, writing, and lecturing. During part of this period (1885–86) he was pastor in St. Paul, and during part, was editor of the Minneapolis *Commercial Bulletin.*

After the death of his wife, in April 1887, he applied for foreign-missionary service, and from 1889 until his retirement in 1920 was a member or director of the Unitarian mission in Japan. His furlough years, a brief intermission from 1901 to 1904, and the period from his retirement until his death, from abscess of the stomach, at Berkeley, Cal., were all spent in lecturing and in writing for the promotion of better relations between the United States and Japan. In addition to his missionary work in Tokyo, he edited the Japanese Unitarian magazine, *Shūkyo* ("Religion") from 1890 to 1895, and, during much of his residence in Japan was correspondent for the *Boston Transcript.* He was vice president and acting president of the Asiatic Society of Japan, 1910–16; vice president of the International Press Association, a Tokyo journalists' club, 1915–16; president of the American Peace Society of Japan, 1916–19. He was twice decorated by the Emperor, being awarded the Order of the Rising Sun in 1909, and the Order of the Sacred Treasure in 1918, and in 1920 he received the Red Cross Service badge.

Throughout his career MacCauley was a prolific writer. In addition to lectures, sermons, and contributions to periodicals, he published a number of books, including *Christianity in History* (1891), issued in both English and Japanese; *An Introductory Course in Japanese* (1896; 2nd ed., 1906); *Thought and Fact for Today* (1911), issued in both English and Japanese; and *The Faith of the Incarnation* (1913). In 1897 he contributed an article on Japanese literature to the *Library of the World's Best Literature,* edited by Charles Dudley Warner, and in 1899 he published, with an introduction, a translation of the Japanese classic *Hyaku-nin-issiu,* or "Single Songs of a Hundred Poets" (*Transactions of the Asiatic Society of Japan,* vol. XXVII, pt. 4, December 1899). From the days of his postgraduate study in Germany he had been influenced by the philosophy of Krause, and his last considerable publication was a pamphlet, *Karl Christian Friedrich Krause: Heroic Pioneer for Thought and Life, A Memorial Record,* issued in the spring of 1925. Two volumes, the autobiographical *Memories and Memorials* (1914) and *Looking Before and After: Some War Time Essays* (1919), contain reprintings of a number of fugitive articles.

[*Who's Who in America,* 1924–25; *Japan Advertiser* (Tokyo), Dec. 8, 1925; *Boston Transcript,* Nov. 17, 1925; *Christian Register,* Nov. 26, Dec. 10, 1925; portrait in *Trans-Pacific* (Tokyo), Dec. 12, 1925.]

H. E. W.

McCAULEY, EDWARD YORKE (Nov. 2, 1827–Sept. 14, 1894), naval officer, Egyptologist, nephew of Charles Stewart McCauley [q.v.], was born in Philadelphia, Pa., but spent his boyhood in Tripoli, where his father, Daniel Smith McCauley, a former naval lieutenant, was United States consul. His mother, Sarah (Yorke) McCauley, died in 1830. By 1840 Edward could speak five languages and had navigated his father's yacht from Tripoli to Malta. Appointed a midshipman in 1841, he cruised in the Mediterranean in the *Fairfield* till 1845, when he was ordered to the new naval school at Annapolis. During the Mexican War he served on the coast of Africa, and then returned to Annapolis till sent to the Mediterranean in the *Constitution* in 1849. From 1852 to 1855 he served on the *Powhatan* in the Orient, and he was with M. C. Perry [*q.v.*] on his second visit to Japan, when the treaty was signed. In 1852, as a lieutenant on the *Niagara*, he assisted in laying the Atlantic cable. Ill health, however, and perhaps his marriage, Jan. 28, 1858, to Josephine McIlvaine Berkeley of Virginia, caused him to resign and enter business in St. Paul, Minn.

With the outbreak of the Civil War he volunteered (May 1861), and subsequently spent nearly two years on the west coast of Florida, between Tampa and Appalachicola, where, in spite of an attack of yellow fever, his zeal was said by the squadron commander to have made his ship, the ferry boat *Fort Henry*, "the terror of the coast for fifty miles." His chief exploit was a launch expedition (armed only with howitzers and rifles) to capture vessels at Bayport, where he attacked enemy rifle pits and a small battery with considerable damage to the enemy and the burning of one vessel. He was commissioned lieutenant commander July 16, 1862. In 1863 he was sent to the Bahamas in the *Tioga* in a vain search for the *Florida*. During the last year of the war he commanded the *Benton* on the Mississippi, and operated between Grand Gulf and Natchez to prevent illegal movement of cotton and the escape of Confederate leaders to Texas. After the Civil War McCauley served as fleet captain in the North Atlantic Squadron, at the Portsmouth and Boston navy yards, as head of the department of French at the Naval Academy, as commander of the *Lackawanna* in the Pacific, and finally as superintendent of the Naval Asylum, Philadelphia. Having been promoted commander (1866), captain (1872), and commodore (1881), he was made a rear admiral in March 1885 and retired in 1887.

The environment of his early life had given him a keen interest in the languages and thought of the peoples of the Levant, and in his later days he made an especial study of Egypt, where his father had served as consul in the forties. Elected to the American Philosophical Society, Philadelphia, in 1881, he presented, that year, as his first contribution to its *Proceedings*, "A Manual for the Use of Students in Egyptology" (vol. XX, published in 1883). Some two years later he published a dictionary of Egyptian hieroglyphics (*Transactions of the American Philosophical Society*, n.s., vol. XVI, pt. 1, 1883). He died at his summer home, "The Mist," on Canonicut Island, Narragansett Bay, after a painful illness, bravely borne.

[Official papers and letter books in possession of the Navy Dept.; Persifor Frazer, in *Proc. Am. Philosophical Soc.*, vol. XXXIV (1895); L. R. Hamersly, *The Records of Living Officers of the U. S. Navy and Marine Corps* (4th ed., 1890); *Official Records of the Union and Confederate Navies*, I ser., II, XVII, XXVI; John Mullaly, *The Laying of the Cable, or the Ocean Telegraph* (1858); *Army and Navy Jour.*, Sept. 22, 1894; *The Press* (Phila.), Sept. 15, 1894. Throughout most of his active career McCauley spelled his name as given above, but toward the end of his life began to write it Macauley.]   W. B. N.

McCAULEY, MARY LUDWIG HAYS (Oct. 13, 1754–Jan. 22, 1832), Revolutionary heroine, better known as Molly Pitcher, was the daughter of John George Ludwig Hass (or Has), who apparently dropped his last name some time after coming to America. One of the sturdy German peasants who emigrated from the Palatinate in 1730 (I. D. Rupp, *A Collection of Thirty Thousand Names of German ... Immigrants in Pennsylvania*, 1856, p. 16), he acquired a small dairy farm near Trenton, N. J., where Mary was born. In 1769 she went, as a servant in the family of Dr. William Irvine, to Carlisle, Pa. There she married John Caspar Hays, on July 24, 1769 (*Pennsylvania Archives*, 2 ser. II, 133). On Dec. 1, 1775, her husband enlisted in the 1st Pennsylvania Regiment of Artillery, served one year, and in January 1777 joined the 7th Pennsylvania Regiment (*Ibid.*, X, 614, XI, 176). Molly Hays remained for some time in Carlisle, then returned to her parents' home to help them, and to be near her husband. At the battle of Monmouth, June 28, 1778, John Hays was detailed to the artillery. It was a terrifically hot day, and Molly, who was on the field, went back and forth from a well, carrying water to the exhausted and wounded. This won for her the sobriquet of "Molly Pitcher." Her husband fell, overcome by the heat. Molly stepped into his place beside his cannon, and filled it ably and heroically for the rest of the battle. After the war she and her husband returned to Carlisle. Some years after the death of John Hays in 1789, she married George McCauley, a union which proved unhappy. Molly obtained a livelihood by scrubbing, caring for children, and similar tasks. The General Assembly of Pennsylvania took notice of her services during the Revolution, passing on Feb. 21, 1822, "An act for the relief of Molly M'Kolly" which directed that she be paid forty dollars immediately and an annuity of the same amount (*Acts of the General Assembly of the Commonwealth of Pennsylvania*, 1821–22, p. 32). Molly was described by contemporaries as a short, thick-set woman, of rather rough appearance and brusque manner, but industrious and kindly. Her grave was marked in 1876 and in 1916 by monuments, and she is also depicted on the monument commemorating the battle of Monmouth.

[The accounts of Molly Pitcher's life are varied and conflicting. Several of them are summarized in W. S. Stryker, *The Battle of Monmouth* (1927), ed. by W. S. Myers, but Stryker's own account has errors in dates. J. B. Landis, "An Investigation into the American Tradition of a Woman Known as 'Molly Pitcher,'" in *Jour. Am. Hist.*, vol. V (1911), no. 1, p. 83, attempts to clear up the confusion. Other good accounts are: E. W. Biddle, *Hist. Address at the Unveiling of Molly Pitcher Monument* (1916), and J. A. Murray, *Contributions to the Local History of Carlisle, Pa.*, no. 2 (1902), which quotes obituaries from Carlisle papers of January 1832.]

V. R.

McCAUSLAND, JOHN (Sept. 13, 1836–Jan. 22, 1927), Confederate soldier, was the son of John McCausland, an emigrant from Tyrone County, Ireland, who became a successful merchant in Lynchburg, Va., married Harriet Kyle, the daughter of an old friend, and moved to St. Louis, Mo., where his son was born. After receiving his preparatory education at Point Pleasant, Mason County, Va. (now W. Va.), the boy entered the Virginia Military Institute and graduated there in 1857, first in a class of twenty-three. He studied at the University of Virginia the next year and then returned to his alma mater as assistant professor of mathematics. He was present with the detachment of cadets at the execution of John Brown at Charles Town. Upon the secession of Virginia he was sent by Robert E. Lee to the Kanawha Valley to organize a regiment of volunteers for the Confederacy. Commissioned colonel of the 36th Virginia Regiment, he was assigned to the division of John B. Floyd and was stationed in western Virginia until his command joined, in the latter part of 1861, the army of Albert Sidney Johnston in Kentucky. Commanding a brigade of Virginians at the siege of Fort Donelson, he displayed daring courage, and, before the surrender, escaped with his brigade. From April 1862 to June 1864 his brigade was a part of the department of West Virginia and engaged in several battles in southwestern and western Virginia. The chief duties of this Confederate force were to protect the Virginia and Tennessee Railroad and the saltpeter works at Saltville from Federal raids and, by constantly harassing the enemy, to detain a large body of Federals in western Virginia.

Promoted to brigadier-general on May 24, 1864, and given command of a brigade of cavalry, he opposed Hunter's army in the Valley of Virginia during the summer of 1864. Confronted by superior forces, he delayed Hunter's advance upon Lynchburg until the arrival of Early's army, despatched by Lee to hold this strategic place. In recognition of his services the citizens of Lynchburg presented him with a golden sword and memorialized him as the savior of Lynchburg. In Early's counter offensive

in the Valley of Virginia his brigade played a conspicuous part; his brilliant attack upon the flank of Lew Wallace's position at Monocacy resulted in the rout of the enemy; and he led his soldiers into the outskirts of Washington, D. C. On July 30, 1864, in retaliation for the destruction of property by Hunter's army in the Valley, he burned Chambersburg, Pa., under specific orders from Early, and after the refusal of its citizens to pay a levy of $100,000 in gold. Participating in the subsequent engagements in the Valley between the forces of Early and Sheridan, he finally joined Lee's army and took part in the retreat to Appomattox, where he and his brigade, refusing to surrender, cut their way through the Federal lines to safety.

After the war, on account of bitter feeling against him in West Virginia, he spent two years in Europe and Mexico, but returned to Mason County, W. Va., to spend the remainder of his life. He acquired a tract of about 6,000 acres, which he drained and developed. He was survived by one daughter and three sons.

[*War of the Rebellion: Official Records (Army)*, esp. 1 ser., vol. XXXVII, pts. 1, 2; *Confederate Military Hist.*, ed. by C. A. Evans (1899), vols. II, III; J. A. Early, *A Memoir of the Last Year of the War of Independence* (1866); M. P. Shawkey, *West Va.* (1928), vol. V; *Nation*, Feb. 9, 1927; *News* (Lynchburg), Jan. 25, 1927; *Wheeling Register*, Jan. 24, 1927.]

W. G. B.

McCAW, JAMES BROWN (July 12, 1823–Aug. 13, 1906), physician, editor, teacher, and Confederate medical officer, was born at Richmond, Va. He was a descendant of James McCaw, a Scotch surgeon who emigrated from Wigtownshire, Scotland, to Virginia in 1771 and settled near Norfolk. His son, James Drew, was a pupil of Benjamin Bell of Edinburgh and graduated from the medical school of Edinburgh University. Returning to Richmond he practised there until his death. Dr. William Reid McCaw, son of the last-named and also a Richmond practitioner, married Ann Ludwell Brown and was the father of James Brown McCaw. Having received his premedical education from Richmond Academy, James studied medicine in the University of the City of New York, where he was a pupil of Valentine Mott. He graduated in 1843, returned to Richmond, and soon became a leader in his profession. He was a founder and charter member of the Medical Society of Virginia, and a member and once president of the Richmond Academy of Medicine. From April 1853 to December 1855 he was an editor of the *Virginia Medical and Surgical Journal*. The name of the publication was then changed to *Virginia Medical Journal*, and McCaw was co-editor from January 1856 to December 1859. In

1858 he became professor of chemistry in the Medical College of Virginia.

His military service began with his enlistment in a cavalry troop, in which he was serving when Gen. Joseph Johnston asked for hospitalization for 9,000 men of his army. Surgeon-General Samuel P. Moore, who had but 2,500 beds at his disposal, went to see McCaw and they selected the site and name of Chimborazo Hospital. Early in 1862 it was opened. Eventually there were 150 wards, each 100 x 30 feet. Five large hospitals, or divisions, each consisting of thirty wards, were organized. A surgeon with forty or fifty assistant surgeons had charge of each, and all were under the supervision of Mc-Caw. In addition to the buildings for wards, there were 100 Sibley tents for convalescents, and such service buildings as ice houses and Russian baths. Chimborazo was the largest hospital of the Civil War, the next largest being Lincoln Hospital in Washington. Seventy-six thousand patients were treated there. In view of the poverty of the Confederacy in subsistence, clothing, and medicines, and of what was generally accomplished by the practice of the day, the results achieved at Chimborazo were considered good. In 1864 McCaw became editor of the *Confederate States Medical Journal,* the only medical periodical published under the Confederacy, fourteen numbers of which were issued.

After the war McCaw resumed private practice, teaching, and writing. He took up again his work as a professor of chemistry in the Medical College of Virginia, and in 1868 became professor of the practice of medicine, which position he held until 1883. He was also dean of the college for twelve years and later president of the board of visitors. In April 1871 he became one of the editors of the *Virginia Clinical Record,* of which three volumes were published. In 1845 he married Delia Patteson; nine children were born to them, three of whom entered the medical profession. McCaw was a man of striking presence and forceful but genial personality. He was fond of music and was for many years president of the Mozart Society of Richmond. He died at Richmond.

[F. H. Garrison, "Dr. James Brown McCaw," *The Old Dominion Jour. of Medicine and Surgery,* Aug. 1906; J. R. Gildersleeve, "Hist. of Chimborazo Hospital, Richmond, Va., and Its Medical Officers during 1861–1865," *Va. Medic. Semimonthly,* July 8, 1904; *Ibid.,* Aug. 24, 1906; *British Medic. Jour.,* Sept. 8, 1906; H. A. Kelly and W. L. Burrage, *American Medic. Biogs.* (1920); *Times-Dispatch* (Richmond), Aug. 14, 1906.] P. M. A.

McCAWLEY, CHARLES GRYMES (Jan. 29, 1827–Oct. 13, 1891), soldier, of Scotch-Irish ancestry, was born in Philadelphia. His father

was Capt. James McCawley, United States Marine Corps, son of a leading merchant of Philadelphia who emigrated from Ulster County, Ireland, in the eighteenth century; his mother was Mary Eliza Holt, of Norfolk, Va., whose father was mayor of that city for some years. Young McCawley attended school in Abington, Montgomery County, Pa., and later, at the Moravian school, Nazareth. After the death of his father in 1839, he entered business in New Orleans with his uncle, William McCawley; attended night school; and on Mar. 3, 1847, received appointment as second lieutenant in the Marine Corps.

He sailed immediately for Vera Cruz, joined Scott's army, and participated in the storming of the castle of Chapultepec and capture of the city of Mexico. For gallantry in battle, he was brevetted first lieutenant, Sept. 13, 1847. From 1848 to 1861, he served at sea and at various stations, being promoted first lieutenant, Jan. 2, 1855, and captain, July 26, 1861. After the beginning of the Civil War, he joined the battalion of marines at Bay Point, S. C. In May 1862, he commanded the detachment of marines which hoisted the national colors over the Norfolk navy-yard, and in August of the same year he saw service with the South Atlantic Squadron, landing at Morris Island, S. C., and taking part in the bombardment and occupation of Fort Wagner and Fort Gregg. In the night attack on Fort Sumter by the naval forces under Rear Admiral J. A. Dahlgren, Sept. 8, 1863, Captain McCawley's command of marines, which had volunteered for the hazardous duty, cooperated in a gallant but unsuccessful boat-maneuver, losing nearly one-third of its number in killed, wounded, and missing (*Official Records of the Union and Confederate Navies in the War of the Rebellion,* 1 ser. XIV, 622–23). For gallant and meritorious services in this action, McCawley received the brevet of major. He was promoted major, June 10, 1864, and lieutenant-colonel, Dec. 5, 1867. In June 1871 he was ordered to command the Marine Barracks at Washington, and to superintend recruiting. Five years later, Nov. 1, 1876, he was made colonel-commandant of the Marine Corps. His retirement from active service, by operation of law, occurred Jan. 29, 1891, and the following March, a stroke of paralysis led to his last illness and death, at Rosemont, Pa., where he had sought to regain his health. He was buried in the old churchyard at Abington, Pa.

McCawley was married in St. John's Church, Washington, March 1863, to Elizabeth Colegate (d. 1867), daughter of James Colegate, and grand-daughter of Rev. James Laurie, who emigrated from Scotland in 1800. He was married a second time, in 1870, to Elise Alden Henderson of Philadelphia, a niece of Admiral James Alden, United States Navy, who survived him, as did also two sons by his first marriage.

[L. R. Hamersly, *The Records of Living Officers of the U. S. Navy and Marine Corps* (4th ed., 1890); *Mil. Order of the Loyal Legion of the U. S. Commandery of the State of Pa., Circ. No. 18,* series of 1891; M. A. Aldrich, *Hist. of the U. S. Marine Corps* (1875); R. S. Collum, *Services of the Marines During the Civil War* (1886); *Public Ledger* (Phila.), Oct. 15, 1891.]   C. D. R.

McCAY, CHARLES FRANCIS (Mar. 8, 1810–Mar. 13, 1889), mathematician, actuary, brother of Henry Kent McCay, was born at Danville, Pa., the son of Robert and Sarah (Read) McCay and great-grandson of Donald McCay who came to the United States in 1758 from the Isle of Skye. He attended Jefferson College and was graduated in 1829. For a year, 1832–33, he taught mathematics, natural philosophy, and astronomy at Lafayette College, Easton, Pa., then for twenty years, 1833–53, he was at the University of Georgia at Athens. He was the author of a text on differential and integral calculus and was noted for the vigor, originality, and "modernism" of his teaching. His retirement from the University of Georgia was occasioned by a "disagreement" which he and the brothers John and Joseph L. Le Conte had with the then chancellor of the university, Alonzo Church [*q.v.*]. From 1848 to 1855 he served as actuary of the life department of the Southern Mutual Insurance Company of Athens, Ga. His connection with that company ceased when its life business was transferred to the Southern Mutual Life Insurance Company of Columbia, S. C., in 1855. While in Athens, he also acted as agent for the Mutual Life Insurance Company of New York (1846–53).

In December 1853 McCay was elected professor of mathematics at South Carolina College (later the University of South Carolina) at Columbia. In 1855 he became president. His career there was stormy, but despite some of his eccentricities, he was regarded as one of the most remarkable men on the faculty at the time. In 1859 he proposed a bill for the Georgia legislature which was passed and signed by the Governor, making effective for valuation purposes in Georgia his Southern Mutual Mortality Table. This was said to have been the first adoption of a life-insurance valuation table by any of the states. His connection with South Carolina College ceased in 1857 and he later entered the insurance business in Augusta, Ga. There he was also cashier, then president, of a bank. He accumu-

lated a modest fortune and in 1869 he gave $1,000 to the University of Georgia for a collection of books on the Civil War.

On Dec. 18, 1848, McCay established an agreement with the Girard Trust Company of Philadelphia, whereby an original sum of $337.35, with additional contributions to $2,000, was to be invested and its proceeds reinvested until the amount should equal the state debt of Pennsylvania, at which time the fund was to be used to extinguish the debt. About 1906 his children heard about the trust accidentally, and instituted suit to test the validity of the "elaborate and somewhat fantastic scheme, impossible of accomplishment." Judge J. B. McPherson in the United States Circuit Court (Eastern District of Pennsylvania) rendered an opinion in the case, directing the payment of $21,000 to the McCay heirs, on the ground that the trust violated the Pennsylvania statute against perpetuities (171 *Fed. Reporter,* 161). On appeal, the decision was affirmed (179 *Fed. Reporter,* 446). On Aug. 5, 1879, the board of trustees of the University of Georgia signified their willingness to accept from McCay the sum of seven thousand dollars in bonds, which sum by successive reinvestment would by 1970 amount to about $1,000,000 and then be used to pay the salaries of the faculty. The fund is now valued at more than one hundred thousand dollars. The trustees' committee said in 1880: "After all our arguments and persuasions, the donor could not be induced to change his purpose!"

McCay removed from Augusta to Baltimore in 1869. In 1886 he suggested to President Garrett of the Baltimore & Ohio Railroad the formation of the Employees Relief Association of which he became actuary, serving without pay through the remainder of his lifetime. He was also actuary of the relief fund for the clergy of the Southern Presbyterian Church, and of the Maryland Insurance Department from its formation in 1871 until his death. He acted as consulting actuary to a number of life insurance companies at various times between 1848 and 1889, achieving the high regard of insurance officials in this country and abroad. In 1875 he passed upon the validity of the mortality statistics of the Mutual Life Insurance Company of New York for the period 1843–73. He prepared what is believed to have been the first "select and ultimate" table of life-insurance mortality in the United States (1887). This table was based upon the combined experience of the Mutual Life (New York), Mutual Benefit Life (Newark), and Connecticut Mutual Life (Hartford) insurance companies. McCay was married, on

Aug. 11, 1840, to Narcissa Harvey Williams, the daughter of William and Rebecca Harvey Williams of Georgia. He died in Baltimore in 1889.

[E. L. Green, *A Hist. of the Univ. of S. C.* (1916); Maximilian La Borde, *Hist. of the S. C. Coll.* (rev. ed., 1874); E. M. Coulter, *College Life in the Old South* (1928); *Hunt's Merchants' Mag.,* Jan. 1850, Apr., May, July 1860, Feb. 1861; *The Internat. Insurance Encyc.,* vol. I (1910), somewhat inaccurate; the *Spectator,* June 23, 1887; *Weekly Underwriter,* Mar. 16, 1889; *Baltimore American,* Mar. 14, 1889; *Baltimore Underwriter,* Mar. 20, 1889; *Pittsburgh Dispatch,* July 2, 1906; *Macon Telegraph,* Oct. 30, 1907; *Atlanta Constitution,* Feb. 17, 1929; personal communications.]
E. W. K.

McCAY, HENRY KENT (Jan. 8, 1820–July 30, 1886), Confederate soldier and jurist, was born in Northumberland County, Pa., the son of Robert and Sarah (Read) McCay. His name was pronounced McCoy. He received an elementary education in Pennsylvania and in 1839 was graduated from the College of New Jersey. Soon afterward he removed to Georgia, where his elder brother, Charles Francis McCay [*q.v.*] was a member of the faculty of the University of Georgia. He taught school at Lexington in Oglethorpe County for two years, studied law in the office of Joseph Henry Lumpkin [*q.v.*], and was admitted to practice in 1842. In the same year he married Catherine Hanson and removed to Americus in southwest Georgia. There he formed a partnership with George H. Dudley, which lasted for seven years. Then he became a law partner of Willis A. Hawkins. Like himself these two partners later became associate justices of the state supreme court. His first appearance in politics appears to have been as a member of the state Democratic convention of 1860, which split on the question of indorsing the action of those members of the Georgia delegation who had seceded from the recent Charleston national convention. He was among the minority that declined so to indorse the seceders and refused to recognize the pending Richmond convention called by the bolters from the Charleston convention. This action seems to place him on the conservative side of the issues that were leading to war. On the outbreak of the Civil War he entered the army. On June 15, 1861, he became second lieutenant of Company A in the 12th Georgia Regiment, was wounded at Alleghany, Va., in December, and was promoted to be captain and assistant quartermaster the next February. He resigned, but late in the war he was in command of a brigade of state troops at the defense of Atlanta.

On the reconstruction issues he took the unpopular course and joined the Republican party. He has been classified, by a contemporary, as belonging in the small group of honest Georgians who thought the best interests of the state would be served by cooperation with Congress (Avery, *post,* p. 375). As a member of the constitutional convention of 1868 he has been given credit for some of the best features of the new constitution. On the coming into power of the Republican régime with Rufus B. Bullock as governor, he was appointed associate justice of the state supreme court. He served for seven years, resigned in 1875, and resumed the practice of law in Atlanta. On Aug. 4, 1882, he was appointed judge of the district court of the United States for the northern district of Georgia. He died in office.

[Letter from his grandniece, Mrs. Mark Sullivan, Washington, D. C.; I. W. Avery, *The Hist. of the State of Ga.* (1881); *Men of Mark in Ga.,* ed. by W. J. Northen, vol. III (1911); H. W. Thomas, *Hist. of the Doles-Cook Brigade* (1903); *War of the Rebellion: Official Records (Army),* 1 ser., vol. V; *Atlanta Constitution,* July 31, Aug. 1, 2, 1886.]
R. P. B.

McCLAIN, EMLIN (Nov. 26, 1851–May 25, 1915), lawyer and teacher, was born in Salem, Columbiana County, Ohio. His father, William McClain, and his mother, Rebecca (Harris) McClain, were natives of Pennsylvania, and Quakers, the former of Scotch-Irish and the latter of English descent. Emlin entered the State University of Iowa in 1867, completing both the scientific and classical courses in four years, in addition to studying music and indulging in amateur theatricals. He then did graduate work for a year in the classics and German. He thus earned the degree of Ph.B. in 1871 and that of A.B. in 1872. Entering the University law school, he completed the course there with honors and the degree of LL.B. in 1873. He began practice in Des Moines, but neither trial work nor a two-year view of politics in Washington (1875–77), where he served as secretary to a United States senator and as clerk of a Senate committee, interested him, and in 1881 he returned to the University as a professor of law. There he remained until 1901, becoming vice-chancellor of the law department in 1887, and chancellor in 1890. While acquiring an exceptionally wide reputation as a teacher, he also retained close touch with practitioners. From 1889 onward he was active in the American Bar Association, serving as a member of its section on legal education and of its committees on classification of the law and on uniform state laws. In various years he was one of Iowa's commissioners on uniform state laws and came to be recognized as the leading authority on the statutory law of the state. In 1894 he took a prominent part in reviving the defunct state bar association.

It was not surprising, therefore, that he was

twice elected a justice of the supreme court, serving for twelve years (1901–13), and as chief justice in 1906 and 1912. As a judge he profited by the exceptional knowledge of legal principles and their history, the training in legal analysis, and the warning against extreme technicality which he had acquired in years of teaching; but his general attitude toward law remained conservative. He was neither a reformer nor a blind adherent to precedent. As one of his colleagues said, "his best work was done in cases involving the application of old principles to new conditions"; on the other hand, "he believed that justice, as administered by the courts, was not morality, and that justice under the law was all to which any man was entitled" (*Proceedings, post*, p. 63). While on the bench he continued to lecture in the Law College; and upon leaving the court he accepted a professorship in Stanford University, returning to Iowa, however, in 1914 to serve as dean.

He was a man of prodigious industry. He published *Annotated Statutes of Iowa* (2 vols., 1880, with a supplement in 1884), which by statute of 1882 was given the authority of an official compilation in all courts of Iowa as evidence of law; *A Digest of the Decisions of the Supreme Court of Iowa* (2 vols., 1887, with later supplements) and *McClain's New Iowa Digest* (4 vols., dated 1908–09 but all issued in 1909), the former prepared by him alone, the latter merely edited by him; *Annotated Code and Statutes of the State of Iowa* (2 vols., 1888; 2nd ed., rev., 1889, with a supplement in 1892), which was treated by courts and legislature as authoritative; *Outlines of Criminal Law and Procedure* (1883; 2nd ed. 1892); *A Selection of Cases on the Law of Carriers* (1893; subsequent editions of altered content and titles, 1894, 1896, 1914); *A Treatise on the Criminal Law* (2 vols., 1897), his most ambitious textbook; *A Selection of Cases on Constitutional Law* (1900; 2nd ed. 1909); *Constitutional Law in the United States* (1905; 2nd ed. 1910); monographic articles in the fields of carriers, insurance, and constitutional law for several legal encyclopedias; and about twoscore miscellaneous articles, addresses, and syllabi of legal courses. His editions of the statutes supplanted the official edition of 1873 and served as official until the Code of 1897 was prepared by a commission of which he was a member. His fellows largely deferred to his judgment and knowledge; his arrangement and system of annotation were adopted; his prior annotations were purchased and embodied in the work; and he continued them in official supplements.

His mind was systematic, independent, and highly intelligent. Its fullness in the field of law is attested by his writings. He was also interested throughout life in history and problems of government, and had catholic tastes in literature. His sincerity, modesty, tolerance, and warm-heartedness constituted a gift for friendship which, coupled with his wide intellectual interests, led him, despite his professional industry, into an active social life. Though he remained a Quaker, he supported the local Congregational Church. On Feb. 19, 1879, he married Ellen Griffiths of Des Moines, and was survived by two sons and one daughter.

[H. E. Deemer, "Emlin McClain; 1851–1915," in *Proc. of the Twenty-first Ann. Session of the Iowa State Bar Asso.* (1915); Jacob Van der Zee, "Emlin McClain," in *Iowa Law Bulletin*, Nov. 1915, pp. 157–79, and Eugene Wambaugh, "Emlin McClain: a Great Teacher of Law," *Ibid.*, pp. 180–82; *Am. Law School Rev.*, Nov. 1915; *Who's Who in America*, 1914–15; *Register and Leader* (Des Moines), May 26, 1915.]

F.S.P.

McCLELLAN, GEORGE (Dec. 23, 1796–May 9, 1847), anatomist, surgeon, and founder of the Jefferson Medical College, Philadelphia, was born in Woodstock, Conn., the son of James and Eunice (Eldredge) McClellan. He came of Scottish ancestry. He received his early education at the Woodstock Academy, of which his father was principal, and in 1812 he went to Yale where he graduated in 1816. He entered the office of Dr. Thomas Hubbard of Pomfret, Conn., but after a year moved to Philadelphia where he became a pupil of John Syng Dorsey and entered the medical school of the University of Pennsylvania. He was a brilliant student and received the appointment of resident student in the hospital of the Philadelphia Almshouse. Here he showed great zeal in performing autopsies and in operating on the cadavers. He graduated in medicine in 1819, his thesis being entitled "Surgical Anatomy of Arteries." He began practice at once and soon acquired an enviable reputation, particularly in surgery. Not content with practice alone, he began also to teach. In those days private schools in medicine were in fashion, and from them the teachers were often chosen for chairs in the regular colleges. In 1821 he founded an institution for diseases of the eye and ear, which continued for four years. He also taught anatomy and surgery, for the former having a private dissecting room. In a few years he had the most successful private school in Philadelphia.

Having developed a large private following, he began to plan for the establishment of a new medical school. The proposal to found such an institution was not popular with the University of Pennsylvania and every effort was made to block the project. But McClellan was a fighter and did not give up although he was subjected to abuse and ostracized by part of the Philadelphia profession. The bitterness of this controversy affected him for the rest of his life. The influence of the University was sufficiently strong to block all attempts to secure an independent charter for the proposed new school from the legislature, but McClellan found a way to solve the difficulty by having the trustees of Jefferson College at Canonsburg, Pa., establish a medical department in Philadelphia, hence the name Jefferson Medical College. The college was opened in 1825 but when the time came for the granting of degrees in 1826, the legal difficulties had not been completely overcome. Driving to Harrisburg, a distance of one hundred miles, in less than twenty-four hours, he secured the authority giving the new institution power to grant the degree in medicine. In 1838 the medical department of the college was given a separate charter and continued as an independent institution. McClellan served as professor of surgery in the college from its beginning until 1839, and as professor of anatomy from 1827 to 1830. Students were attracted to the institution and by 1836 the enrolment had reached 360, but dissensions developed and in 1839 the trustees dissolved the faculty. There is some evidence that McClellan was given an opportunity to apply for reappointment but apparently he took no notice of it. He promptly engaged in the establishment of the "Medical Department of Pennsylvania College" in connection with Pennsylvania (later Gettysburg) College at Gettysburg. The school had fair success and continued until the Civil War.

One of McClellan's achievements of consequence was his establishment of a clinic with the opening of the Jefferson Medical College. He had conducted a clinic of his own and apparently referred these patients to the college clinic. Though naturally the facilities were meager his early attempt to bring medical students into contact with patients is notable. As a surgeon he had the reputation of being a bold and skilful operator. The operation for the removal of the parotid gland, which he did a number of times, was especially noteworthy. He was keen, ambitious, energetic, and always interesting, but his impulsive disposition excited opposition and enmity. His projected work on surgery, *Principles and Practice of Surgery,* which he did not live to complete, was published by his son in 1848. As a teacher he was brilliant rather than thoughtful, and notoriously unsystematic. Gross said that he "lacked judgment, talked too much, and made everybody his confidant" (*Autobiography,* II, p.

251). McClellan was married in 1820 to Elizabeth Brinton. He died suddenly in his fifty-first year. Gen. George B. McClellan [*q.v.*] was his son, and George McClellan, 1849–1913 [*q.v.*], his grandson.

[S. G. Morton, article in *Summary of the Trans. of the Coll. of Physicians of Phila.,* vol. II (1849); W. Darrach, *Memoir of Geo. McClellan* (1847); G. M. Gould, *The Jefferson Medic. Coll.: A Hist.* (1904), vol. I; S. D. Gross, *Lives of Eminent Am. Physicians and Surgeons of the Nineteenth Century* (1861), and *Autobiography* (2 vols., 1887); C. W. Bowen, *The Hist. of Woodstock, Conn.* (1926–32), vols. I and IV; *Pa. Inquirer and Nat. Gazette* (Phila.), May 10, 1847.]
T. M.

McCLELLAN, GEORGE (Oct. 29, 1849–Mar. 29, 1913), anatomist and physician, was born in Philadelphia, Pa., the son of Dr. John H. B. McClellan, an anatomist and surgeon, and the grandson of Dr. George McClellan, 1796–1847 [*q.v.*], for whom he was named. His mother was Maria Eldredge. He attended school in Philadelphia and later took the arts course at the University of Pennsylvania, graduating in 1869. In 1870 he was graduated from the Jefferson Medical College and began practice, devoting himself particularly to anatomy and surgery. Two years later he went abroad for a year, working with Hyrtl of Vienna. His fondness for anatomy had been evident in his student days and the influence of Hyrtl determined him to specialize in that branch of medical science. His methods and approach to anatomical problems were those of his preceptor. On his return to Philadelphia in 1873 he resumed practice and soon began to give private courses in anatomy and surgery. He was appointed to the staff of the Philadelphia and Howard hospitals, and in 1881 he founded the Pennsylvania School of Anatomy and Surgery in which he taught with great success until 1898. Interested in the study of anatomy as related to art, he was appointed professor of artistic anatomy at the Pennsylvania Academy of the Fine Arts, where he taught from 1890 till his death in 1913. In 1906 he was appointed professor of applied anatomy in the Jefferson Medical College, which position he also held with distinguished success until his death.

McClellan's monumental work, *Regional Anatomy,* published in two volumes in 1891 and 1892, went through four editions in the United States and was translated into French. The illustrations were remarkable in that they were made from photographs which he had taken and had colored himself. Another notable work, *Anatomy in Relation to Art* (1900), grew out of his work in anatomy in the Academy of the Fine Arts. His unusual ability in illustrating his lectures by drawings on the blackboard contributed greatly to his powers as a teacher. This talent, and his skill and facility as a dissector, made a lasting impression upon his students. He taught anatomy both as a science and as a subject which the medical student should be able to use. The recognition of his standing by the appointment to a professorial chair in his own college came late. No one ever questioned that it was well deserved. By nature he was tenacious and somewhat dour, with an impetuous temper. Probably only a few really knew him intimately and much of what seemed a stern outlook on life served to cover a sensitive nature. His death occurred in March 1913, from a rare condition, thrombosis of the abdominal aorta. He was survived by his wife, Harriett (Hare) McClellan, whom he had married in 1873.

[J. C. Da Costa, memoir in *Trans. Coll. of Physicians of Phila.*, 3 ser. XXXVI (1914); H. A. Kelly and W. L. Burrage, *Am. Medic. Biogs.* (1920); the *Independent*, May 29, 1913; *Pub. Ledger* (Phila.), Mar. 30, 1913.]
T. M.

McCLELLAN, GEORGE BRINTON (Dec. 3, 1826–Oct. 29, 1885), soldier, was born in Philadelphia, the third child and second son of Dr. George McClellan, 1796–1847 [*q.v.*] and Elizabeth (Brinton) McClellan. The family had come from Scotland to New England early in the eighteenth century. His great-grandfather, Samuel McClellan, served through the Revolutionary War with the Connecticut militia, and reached the grade of brigadier-general. In the Civil War, several members of the family were in service. His younger brother, Arthur, was one of his aides-de-camp; a first cousin, Carswell McClellan, was on the staff of General Humphreys; another first cousin, Henry Brainerd McClellan [*q.v.*], was chief of staff to the Confederate generals Stuart and Hampton, and wrote a biography of Stuart.

McClellan attended preparatory schools in Philadelphia, and entered the University of Pennsylvania in 1840, but left there upon appointment as cadet at West Point in 1842. He graduated in 1846, as No. 2 in his class, and was assigned to the Engineers. Joining a company of sappers and miners that was being organized at West Point for service in Mexico, he assisted in training it, and went with it to Matamoros. In January 1847 the company formed part of the column that marched from the Rio Grande to Tampico, and was charged with the road and bridge construction. It then became a part of General Scott's command, landed with the first troops at Vera Cruz, and served throughout his campaign. McClellan at once attracted attention, and was often mentioned in dispatches. He received the brevet rank of first lieutenant for service at Contreras and Churubusco, and of captain for Cha-

pultepec. (*The Mexican War Diary of George B. McClellan*, edited by W. S. Myers, was published in 1917.) He returned with his company to West Point in 1848, and for three years served there as assistant instructor in practical military engineering. During this time, he translated the French regulations on the bayonet exercise and adapted them to use in the American service; his regulations were tested in the company, and in 1852 were adopted for the army. He also became an active member of a group of officers formed for the study of military history.

In the summer of 1851 he was relieved from duty at West Point and assigned as assistant engineer for the construction of Fort Delaware. In March of the next year, however, he went with the expedition of Capt. R. B. Marcy to explore the sources of the Red River, in Arkansas (*Senate Executive Document No. 54, 32 Cong., 2 Sess.*). This duty was completed in July. He acted as chief engineer on the staff of Gen. Persifor F. Smith until October, and then took up river and harbor work in Texas. The next spring he was placed in command of an expedition to survey a route for a railway across the Cascade Mountains, which occupied him until the end of the year. His route did not ultimately prove the best; but Jefferson Davis, then secretary of war, was so much pleased with his work that he directed him to continue his study of railways, and report on the practicability of construction on the line selected (*House Executive Document No. 129, 33 Cong., 1 Sess.; Senate Executive Document No. 78, 33 Cong., 2 Sess.*). This study being completed, Davis sent him to report upon Samana Bay, in Santo Domingo, as a possible naval station (*House Executive Document No. 43, 41 Cong., 3 Sess.*).

An increase in the regular army was made in 1855, and McClellan was appointed a captain in one of the new regiments of cavalry, resigning his commission as first lieutenant of engineers. He never joined his regiment, for in April 1855 he was detailed as a member of a board of officers to study the European military systems. The board spent a year in Europe, visiting most of the principal countries as well as the theatre of operations in the Crimea. McClellan was to observe particularly the engineers and cavalry, as well as to make a special study of the Russian army at large. The board arrived too late to see much of active operations in the Crimea, but was able to make a very complete study of the siege of Sevastopol. McClellan's reports are most excellent (*Senate Executive Document No. 1, 35 Cong., Special Sess.*). In submitting them, he made numerous recommendations for improvements in the American service; notably, he proposed a new type of saddle, modeled on the lines of the Hungarian. This was adopted. Alterations in the McClellan saddle have been few and slight, and the specifications of 1929 reverted very nearly to his original design. In January 1857 he resigned his commission to become chief engineer of the Illinois Central Railroad. The next year he was made vice-president, in charge of operations in Illinois; and in 1860 he became president of the Ohio & Mississippi Railroad, with his residence in Cincinnati.

At the outbreak of the Civil War his services were sought by both New York and Pennsylvania. He started for Harrisburg to consult with Governor Curtin, but stopped in Columbus to inform Governor Dennison as to conditions in Cincinnati. Here he was tendered appointment as major-general of Ohio Volunteers, with command of all the Ohio forces, militia and volunteer. He accepted, a special act was hastily passed by the legislature, empowering the Governor to appoint to this office one who was not an officer of the militia, and he entered upon his duties the same day, Apr. 23, 1861.

By reason of the rioting in Baltimore, mail connection with Washington was uncertain, and states in the Ohio and Mississippi valleys had to act largely on their own initiative. The work of organizing, equipping, and training the troops fell chiefly upon McClellan, under state authority only. On May 13, however, he received appointment (dated May 3) as a major-general in the regular army, and was placed in command of the Department of the Ohio, including the states of Ohio, Indiana, and Illinois, and later certain portions of western Pennsylvania and Virginia. During this period Grant called upon him, to ask for employment on his staff or with troops. McClellan happened to be absent, and before his return Grant had been offered an Illinois regiment; so the interesting experiment, McClellan in command with Grant as chief of staff, was never tried.

McClellan's refusal to support the neutrality of Kentucky, when called upon by Simon B. Buckner [q.v.] to do so, had great influence in keeping that state in the Union. Western Virginia was chiefly Unionist in sentiment. To control this territory for the South, troops from eastern Virginia occupied Grafton, the junction point of the two branches of the Baltimore & Ohio Railroad. McClellan sent troops, which regained possession of the railways. This action led to further concentrations of troops on both sides and to the campaign of Rich Mountain, in which McClellan personally commanded, and by

means of which that region was cleared of Confederate troops and kept in the Union.

This success, just before McDowell's defeat at Bull Run, led to McClellan's appointment to command the Division of the Potomac, which included McDowell's department south of the river and Mansfield's in the city of Washington. He reached Washington on July 26, and found the troops in utter confusion. He plunged into his work with great energy, soon brought his command under discipline, and began reorganization and training. Spirit at once improved, and the army gained rapidly, both in strength and in efficiency. In a few months the troops became tired of inactivity and were anxious to take the offensive. McClellan, however, overestimating the strength of the enemy and underrating his own condition, refused to move. Meanwhile, his relations with General Scott became more and more strained. In November, Scott retired and McClellan became general-in-chief in his stead; this led to further delay, while he studied his enlarged problems.

The President began to exhibit impatience. Not only did he feel that the army was strong enough for a move, but the financial situation, with the increasingly unfavorable rate of exchange, convinced him that some military risk was preferable to certain bankruptcy. McClellan's plan was, not to move frontally upon the Confederate force at Manassas, and thence upon Richmond, but to transport his army by water to the lower Rappahannock or to Fortress Monroe, and advance on Richmond from the east. To this Lincoln demurred, fearing that Washington would not be sufficiently protected. Finally, on Jan. 27, 1862, the President issued his General War Order No. 1, prescribing an advance of all the armies on Feb. 22, and on the 31st his Special War Order No. 1, requiring that the move of the Army of the Potomac should be upon Manassas (*Official Records, Army,* 1 Ser., V, 41). This brought matters to a head. McClellan again urged his own plan, and Lincoln consented to a move by way of Fortress Monroe, but reluctantly and doubtfully, imposing conditions in regard to the security of Washington. The Confederate force at Manassas was withdrawn to the Rappahannock early in March, somewhat relieving this anxiety. A few days later the Army of the Potomac began embarking at Alexandria. McClellan, having taken the field with it, was relieved as general-in-chief and left only that army, reporting, as did the other independent commanders, direct to the secretary of war. Jackson's activity in the Shenandoah Valley now caused renewed alarm, and McDowell's corps and other troops intended for the expedition were held back for the defense of Washington.

Advancing from Fortress Monroe, McClellan encountered the Confederates at Yorktown and approached the lines there by regular siege operations, which delayed him for a month. He then moved up the Peninsula toward Richmond. Upon his urgent representations that he was outnumbered, McDowell's corps was ordered to march by way of Fredericksburg to join him; but Jackson's renewed activity caused these orders to be countermanded. Finally, over McDowell's protest, the corps was withdrawn from the Army of the Potomac and constituted a separate command. On the Chickahominy there was another long delay. Heavy rains had set in; the streams were up, and the roads almost impassable. The first troops to cross had heavy fighting at Seven Pines and Fair Oaks on May 31 and June 1; a position almost at the gates of Richmond was occupied and entrenched, and work was begun on bridges to bring the rest of the army across. Meanwhile, lingering hopes of McDowell's arrival made McClellan reluctant to relinquish his hold on the left bank of the river, where he expected to effect the junction.

Instead of McDowell, Jackson came. Having drawn as many Union troops as possible to the Valley, he had secretly moved his own force out by rail, and come down to join the army at Richmond. Upon his approach, on June 26, Lee launched a powerful attack upon the part of McClellan's army on the left bank of the river, and defeated it at Gaines's Mill. The bridges, just finished and ready to take that wing to the right bank for an attack upon Richmond, had to be used to bring supports across, the other way; and then, the immediate emergency having been met, to take them all back to the right bank, not now for an advance, but for a flank march to the James. The Confederate pursuit was finally checked at Malvern Hill on July 1, ending the Seven Days' Battles, and the army established itself at Harrison's Landing. McClellan, in his dispatches, attributed his reverses to lack of support from Washington, and insisted, as he had throughout the campaign, that he was outnumbered. He still contemplated a further offensive, south of the James, but he demanded for it a greater reinforcement than the President—or Halleck, who became general-in-chief late in July—was willing to provide. Finally, on Aug. 3, the Army of the Potomac was ordered withdrawn. McClellan established his headquarters at Alexandria. His troops, as they arrived, were detached from him and assigned to General Pope's Army of Virginia.

After Pope's defeat at Manassas, McClellan was again called upon to reorganize the army and prepare the defense of Washington. Orders from General Halleck to this effect reached him on Sept. 1; the next morning the President called upon him in Washington and personally requested him to undertake the task. He immediately rode out to meet Pope, took over the command from him, and went on to join the retreating troops, who received him with enthusiasm. Their spirits rose, and they forgot their defeat. Lee did not pursue in the direction of Washington, but moved toward the upper crossings of the Potomac. McClellan assembled the incoming troops at Rockville and Leesburg, assuming personal command for an advance, although his orders were simply to provide for the defense of Washington. Pending further information of the enemy, he directed his right upon Frederick, and kept his left on the Potomac. On the morning of Sept. 13 he learned, through a copy of one of Lee's orders which fell into his hands, that the Confederates were much scattered. He moved to take advantage of this, but too slowly; Lee succeeded in concentrating, and was able to avoid destruction in the battles of South Mountain and the Antietam. After these battles, McClellan did not press, and Lee accomplished the withdrawal of his army across the Potomac. McClellan did not follow until late in October. Early in the month he had been ordered by Lincoln to give battle, and on Oct. 13 he was asked by the President: "Are you not overcautious when you assume that you cannot do what the enemy is constantly doing?" (*Official Records*, 1 Ser., Vol. XIX, Pt. I, pp. 11, 13). At Warrenton, on Nov. 7, he received an order to turn over his command to General Burnside and to proceed to Trenton, N. J., to await orders. He was never again employed in the field. In 1863 he prepared a report covering his period of command of the Army of the Potomac (published as *House Executive Document No. 15*, 38 Cong., 1 Sess.).

In 1864 he was nominated as the Democratic candidate for the presidency. The country seemed weary of the war, and the leaders of the Democratic party thought they could see an opportunity to win on a platform calling for immediate cessation of hostilities. McClellan seemed the logical candidate. He could be represented as a victim of the injustice of the administration—a general who had accomplished much and would have accomplished more if he had been fairly treated. He accepted the nomination, although it placed him in a most embarrassing position; he had always stood for vigorous prosecution of the war, and had recently reaffirmed this attitude in an oration at West Point. In his letter of acceptance he tried to harmonize the inconsistency, but without conspicuous success. On election day he resigned his commission in the army. The returns showed that he had carried only New Jersey, Delaware, and Kentucky, with 21 electoral votes against Lincoln's 212.

The next three years he spent abroad. Upon his return he was placed in charge of construction of a new type of steam war-vessel, designed by Edwin A. Stevens of Hoboken, and being built with money left for that purpose in his will. The funds were exhausted before the ship was completed, and the project was abandoned in 1869. He was invited to become president of the University of California in 1868, and of Union College in 1869, but declined both offers. In 1870 he was appointed chief engineer of the New York City Department of Docks, but resigned in 1872. In 1871 he declined appointment as comptroller of the city. From January 1878 to January 1881 he served as governor of New Jersey. He was married in 1860 to Ellen Mary Marcy, and had two children, a daughter and a son. His wife was the daughter of his old commander in the Red River exploring expedition, Randolph B. Marcy [q.v.], who served later as his chief of staff. He died of heart trouble, at Orange, N. J., Oct. 29, 1885.

McClellan was slightly under the middle height, but very squarely and powerfully built, with exceptional strength and endurance. His features were regular and pleasing, his hair and moustache red. His tastes were quiet and scholarly. An excellent linguist, he knew and used all the principal languages of western Europe, ancient and modern. Not only did he always keep up military study, but he was well informed in current literature, particularly that dealing with archeological research and exploration. He spent much time abroad, chiefly in Switzerland, and interested himself in mountain climbing.

As a soldier, he fell barely short of conspicuous success. He took the best of care of his men and had the happy faculty of inspiring confidence and loyalty. His knowledge and comprehension of military affairs was great, and he was able to select from foreign systems features that were appropriate to the American service, and adapt them to its requirements. His ideas of organization, strategy, and tactics were clear and sound. But he was never satisfied with what he had, nor willing to make the best of an imperfect tool. He could always see wherein he might make improvements, given time; and he took the time, at the expense of losing his opportunities. He could not be content with a plan that took into account

all apparent factors, and trust to the inspiration of the moment to take care of the unforeseen; his plan must be complete. His reasoning powers carried him up to contact with the enemy; at that moment, when an independent will entered the problem, he became hesitating. Knowing accurately his own numbers, and knowing also the weaknesses and defects of his own force, he allowed for these and discounted the numbers. For the enemy's strength, he accepted too readily the estimates of his intelligence service, directed by Allan Pinkerton [q.v.], and these estimates were usually too high. Further, not knowing the enemy's troubles, he failed to make the discounts. Hence he always believed himself outnumbered, when in fact he always had the superior force.

While he had seen much field service, he had never held even the smallest command in war, until he conducted the operations in West Virginia as a major-general. Except for the campaign in Mexico, his only knowledge of warfare was gained at Sevastopol, and the siege technique observed there controlled his action in the Peninsula. In the Antietam campaign he showed that he was beginning to learn to attack. Under a good teacher—had there been such a teacher —he might have mastered the lesson. He probably came to the supreme command too early. In his *Own Story* he hints that such was the case. But at the time, possibly through a half recognition of his deficiencies, he expressed the utmost confidence, and always took the attitude that his superiors, through ignorance or jealousy, were not properly supporting him. Thus his successes were only half successes; at the same time, his failures were not disasters. Lee, who should have known, set him down as the best commander who ever faced him (R. E. Lee, Jr., *Recollections and Letters of General Robert E. Lee*, 1924, p. 416). But Lee saw the deficiencies, too; he once remarked, half seriously, when he learned that Burnside had taken command, that he regretted to part with McClellan, "for we always understood each other so well. I fear they may continue to make these changes until they find someone I don't understand" (*Battles and Leaders*, III, 70).

[*McClellan's Own Story* (1887) is a poorly constructed book and unsatisfactory in that it assumes the defensive throughout. Everything printed about him during or soon after the war is partisan. John G. Barnard, *The Peninsular Campaign and Its Antecedents* (1864), is a military analysis, sharply critical of McClellan. An excellent example of contemporary defenses of him is G. S. Hillard, *Life and Campaigns of George B. McClellan* (1864). Later and more dispassionate writings are P. S. Michie, *General McClellan* (1901), and Francis W. Palfrey, *The Antietam and Fredericksburg* (1882). See also G. W. Cullum, *Biog. Register of the Officers and Grads. of the U. S. Mil.*

Acad. (3 ed., 1891); *War of the Rebellion: Official Records (Army)*; "Report of the Joint Committee on the Conduct of the War," *Senate Report No. 108*, 37 Cong., 3 Sess.; memoir by Gen. W. B. Franklin in *Seventeenth Annual Reunion of the Asso. of the Grads. of the U. S. Mil. Acad.* (1886); J. G. Nicolay and John Hay, *Abraham Lincoln* (10 vols., 1890); Emory Upton, *The Mil. Policy of the U. S.* (1904); *Battles and Leaders of the Civil War* (4 vols., 1887–88); G. C. Gorham, *Life and Public Services of Edwin M. Stanton* (2 vols., 1899); *Diary of Gideon Welles* (1911), vol. I; J. H. Stine, *Hist. of the Army of the Potomac* (1892); G. T. Curtis, "McClellan's Last Service to the Republic," *North American Rev.*, Apr., May 1880; *Army and Navy Journal*, Oct. 31, Nov. 7, 14, 1885. Col. John R. Meigs Taylor, of Washington, has furnished recollections of conversations with his grandfather General Meigs, which have thrown light upon some of McClellan's relations with the administration.]   O. L. S., Jr.

McCLELLAN, HENRY BRAINERD (Oct. 17, 1840–Oct. 1, 1904), Confederate soldier, educator, was born in Philadelphia, Pa., of distinguished Scotch-Irish and English ancestry. His parents were Dr. Samuel McClellan and Margaret Carswell (Ely), both of Connecticut families. His great-grandfather, Gen. Samuel McClellan, commanded the 5th Brigade, Connecticut Militia, in the Revolutionary War; his maternal grandfather, Rev. Ezra Stiles Ely, moved to Philadelphia and donated part of the land for Jefferson Medical College, of which Dr. Samuel McClellan and his brother, Dr. George McClellan, 1796–1847 [*q.v.*], were the founders.

Henry McClellan was graduated from Williams College in August 1858 when not yet eighteen years old. He had already determined to enter the ministry, but since he was so young his family decided that he should teach for a few years. Consequently, for the next two and a half years he tutored in a private family in Cumberland County, Va., and here, under the influence of older persons, acquired a firm belief in state's rights. Only a short time before his death he laughingly declared that he was still a rebel, reconstructed but absolutely unrepentant. In 1861 he entered the Confederate army as a private in the 3rd Virginia Cavalry. He was handicapped not only by his lack of military training but by his Northern birth and affiliations. Three of his brothers served in the Federal army, while his first cousin, Gen. George B. McClellan [*q.v.*], was twice commander of the Army of the Potomac. Despite these obstacles he rose in two years, at the age of twenty-three, to the position of assistant adjutant-general and chief of staff of the cavalry of the Army of Northern Virginia. In 1862–63 he was adjutant of the 3rd Virginia Cavalry and from 1863 to the end of the war he served, with the rank of major, as assistant adjutant-general and chief of staff, first to Gen. J. E. B. Stuart and then to Wade Hampton.

Some important items regarding McClellan's military career may be gleaned from the *Official Records*. In his report of the engagement at Kelly's Ford, Va., Mar. 17, 1863, Fitzhugh Lee "particularly commended" him for his gallantry (*Official Records*, 1 ser. XXV, pt. 1, p. 62). Reporting the engagement at Fleetwood, June 9, 1863, Stuart wrote that McClellan "displayed the same zeal, gallantry, and efficiency which has on every battlefield, in the camp, or on the march, so distinguished him as to cause his selection for his present post" (*Ibid.*, XXVII, pt. 2, p. 685). Again, after the Bristoe (Va.) campaign in October 1863, Stuart reported McClellan as having been at his side "night and day" and that he was "greatly indebted" to McClellan "for the clearness with which orders and dispatches were transmitted" (*Ibid.*, XXIX, pt. 1, p. 453). After Stuart was wounded at Yellow Tavern, McClellan went to the bedside of his dying chief, who gave him his bay horse as a final evidence of his esteem. Two days later, May 14, 1864, McClellan was assigned to duty at Lee's headquarters and, on Aug. 11, 1864, was made assistant adjutant-general and chief of staff under Wade Hampton. He served under Hampton in his subsequent campaigns, including that with Johnston's army in the Carolinas. McClellan was notified that his commission as lieutenant-colonel had been issued, but since he did not receive it until after Lee's surrender, he modestly disclaimed the rank.

After the close of the war, he resided for some years in Cumberland County, Va. In 1870 he became principal of Sayre Female Institute, Lexington, Ky., which he conducted successfully until shortly before his death. He was the author of *The Life and Campaigns of Major-General J. E. B. Stuart* (1885), still the standard biography. In preparing this work he was aided by former high officers in the Union army, by Stuart's family, and by surviving Confederate associates. It contains much valuable source material, including in the appendix the personal war records of the officers and men in several Virginia cavalry regiments; it has been translated into German and is used as a source book by students of cavalry tactics and Civil War history. McClellan was married on Dec. 31, 1863, to Catherine Macon Matthews of Cumberland County, Va., and was survived by several children.

[H. B. McClellan, *The Life and Campaigns of Gen. J. E. B. Stuart* (1885); *War of the Rebellion, Official Records (Army)*; *Who's Who in America*, 1903–05; Cleveland Abbe and J. G. Nichols, *Abbe-Abbey Geneal.* (1916); M. S. Beach, *The Ely Ancestry* (1902); information from Miss Margaret E. McClellan, Lexington, Ky.]   R. D. M.

MCCLELLAN, ROBERT (1770–Nov. 22, 1815), scout, Indian trader, was born near Mercersburg, Pa., the son of a pioneer farmer, also named Robert. He had little schooling, but he became an expert woodsman and hunter. His first employment was that of a pack-horseman in the transport of goods. In 1790, at Fort Gower, on the Ohio, he joined the army as a spy, or ranger, and in the following year went to Fort Washington (Cincinnati) and later to Fort Hamilton, where he again found work as a pack-horseman. On the arrival of Wayne's army he was engaged as a scout, serving throughout the campaign of 1794–95 and distinguishing himself by a series of daring exploits which won for him the rank of lieutenant. In the summer of 1799 he journeyed south and at New Orleans was stricken with yellow fever. On his recovery he went to Philadelphia, where on account of wounds suffered in Wayne's campaign he was awarded a small pension and where for a time he was employed in the quartermaster's department. Sent to the Illinois country on official business in 1801, he shortly afterward resigned and entered the Indian trade.

In 1807 McClellan and Ramsay Crooks led an expedition toward the upper Missouri. On meeting Ensign Pryor's party returning from its defeat by the Arikaras they turned back to a point near Old Council Bluffs and established a trading post. They again started upstream in 1809 but were halted by a Sioux tribe and compelled to erect another establishment for trade. On the retirement of Crooks from the partnership early the following year, McClellan continued alone, but on being robbed by the Sioux he became disheartened and started for St. Louis. At the mouth of the Nodaway he found Crooks in the winter camp of Hunt's Astoria party and at once joined the Pacific Fur Company. He accompanied the expedition the following spring, arriving in Astoria, ragged, ill, and emaciated, in January 1812. In March he withdrew from the company, and in June started eastward with Stuart's party, which reached St. Louis, after extreme hardships and privations, Apr. 30, 1813. A month later he was imprisoned for debt. In January 1814, with a stock of goods furnished by a friend, he opened a store in Cape Girardeau, Mo., but ill health compelled his return to St. Louis the following summer. He found a home on the farm of Abraham Gallatin, and it was probably there that he died. He was buried on Gen. William Clark's farm, where his tombstone was unearthed in 1875. Though of slight physique, McClellan was in his prime a man of great strength and agility, and pioneer annals credit him, while

a scout in Wayne's army, with many amazing athletic feats. His courage is well attested by the inscription on his tombstone, thought to have been written by Clark: "Brave, honest and sincere; an intrepid warrior, whose services deserve perpetual remembrance."

[See: Jas. McBride, *Pioneer Biog.* (1871), vol. II; Stella M. Drumm, "More About Astorians," *Quart. of the Ore. Hist. Soc.*, Dec. 1923; Washington Irving, *Astoria* (1836); H. M. Chittenden, *The Am. Fur Trade of the Far West* (1902); John Bradbury, *Travels in the Interior of America* (1817, 2nd ed. 1819); H. M. Brackenridge, *Views of La., Together with a Jour. of a Voyage up the Mo. River in 1811* (1814); J. L. Finafrock, "Robt. McClellan," *The Kittochtinny Hist. Soc. . . . Papers*, vol. IX (1923). By Irving the name of McClellan is erroneously spelled M'Lellan, and by Chittenden, McLellan.]   W. J. G.

MCCLELLAND, ROBERT (Aug. 1, 1807– Aug. 30, 1880), congressman, governor of Michigan, secretary of the interior, was born at Greencastle, Pa., the son of Dr. John McClellan (*sic*) and Eleanor Bell McCulloh. He graduated from Dickinson College in 1829 and was admitted to the bar at Chambersburg in 1831. After practising for a year in Pittsburgh he migrated to Monroe, Mich., in 1833, where four years later he married Sarah E. Sabine of Williamstown, Mass. Michigan was about to become a state and McClelland was active in organizing the new government and the Democratic party. He served in the constitutional convention of 1835 and in the legislature, 1838–43; in the last-named year he went to Congress, to which he was twice reelected. At Washington he was interested in commerce and foreign affairs, and enjoyed the friendship of Wilmot and of Lewis Cass. He was in close association with the former and supported the "Proviso" to his later embarrassment. He became Cass's chief Michigan lieutenant and aided him considerably in his presidential campaign in 1848.

McClelland retired from Congress in 1849 and after participating in the constitutional convention of 1850 was twice elected governor (1850, 1852). During this period he labored to heal the party schism of 1848 by abandoning his support of the Wilmot Proviso and successfully urging the Michigan Democracy to indorse the compromise measures of 1850. His success in Michigan, his activities at the national Democratic convention of 1852, and especially his close association with Cass, attracted attention outside of Michigan, and when President-Elect Pierce sought a representative man from the Cass faction for his cabinet he invited McClelland to become secretary of the interior.

McClelland found his four-year-old department badly organized and set himself to produce order. His four bureaus, land, Indian, pension, and patent, were scattered over Washington and their work was behindhand. He instituted new regulations requiring more effort from his clerks, classified them under a recently enacted law, and in due time was able to report a coherent and efficient service. He struggled to reduce the corruption and waste that clung persistently to the land, Indian, and pension bureaus and his strictness improved conditions in these respects without adding, however, to the popularity of the Pierce administration. He urged that pensions be given only to the indigent. The Indians he favored placing upon reservations, as quickly as possible, so that they might be taught the arts of civilization. Money payments to them should be stopped, he argued, and their annuities settled in goods. As to the public lands, he was at first much interested in grants to the states to be used for railroad purposes and favored a Pacific railroad constructed by the aid of land subsidies from the federal government, but as the railroad interests became more importunate and brought to bear upon Congress what the Pierce administration considered improper pressure, he withdrew his support from projects for this form of aid. The land system itself he thought needed no improvement, and like the dominant element in his party he opposed homestead legislation. None of his major recommendations was adopted by Congress, however; the value of his service to his department lay in his ability to produce system, order, and honesty. As a member of Pierce's cabinet he belonged with Marcy and Guthrie to the more conservative wing and joined the former in advising the President to follow a neutral policy in Kansas.

In 1857 McClelland returned to Michigan, settling down in Detroit to twenty-three years of legal practice. He returned to public service briefly in 1867 as a member of the Michigan constitutional convention. In personality he was always plain and unprepossessing; his manners were somewhat brusque and forbidding; and he was regular and painstaking in his mode of life to an extent which in his later years became proverbial among his neighbors.

[A brief manuscript biography is in the possession of McClelland's grandson, R. McClelland Brady, Santa Barbara, Cal.; a few of his papers are in the Lib. of Cong., his family have a few, and a number of the letters he received from Cass are in the Burton Coll., Detroit Pub. Lib. See also Alfred Nevin, *Men of Mark of Cumberland Valley, Pa.* (1876); *Am. Biog. Hist. of Eminent and Self-Made Men . . . Mich. Vol.* (1878); *Pioneer Colls.—Report of the Pioneer Soc. of the State of Mich.*, IV (1883), 454–57; *Evening News* (Detroit), Aug. 30, 31, 1880; *Detroit Free Press*, Sept. 1, 1880.]
R. F. N.

McCLERNAND, JOHN ALEXANDER (May 30, 1812–Sept. 20, 1900), congressman and Union soldier, the son of John A. and Fatima McClernand, was born near Hardinsburg, Ky., and moved to Illinois when a small boy. His father died probably in 1816 and John, the only child, attended village school at Shawneetown, helped support his mother, and read law in a local office. He was admitted to the bar in 1832, but the Black Hawk War, Mississippi River trading, and the editorship of the *Gallatin Democrat and Illinois Advertiser* temporarily diverted him from his profession. As an assemblyman between 1836 and 1843, his political acumen and expansive eloquence, fortified with many allusions to the classics, quickly gained him prominence. Ever a stanch Jacksonian, he hated Abolitionists and supported sound money and extensive internal improvements. He married Sarah Dunlap of Jacksonville, on Nov. 7, 1843, and removed to that town eight years later. In Congress from 1843 to 1851 and from 1859 to 1861, although courting war with foreign powers for territorial gain, he urged conciliation and the popular sovereignty panacea during crises over slavery extension. He figured prominently in the tumultuous speakership contests of the first sessions of the Thirty-first and the Thirty-sixth congresses and shared in framing the compromise measures of 1850. He broke with Douglas in 1854, but they worked together for peace and the Union six years later. His wife having died he married his sister-in-law, Minerva Dunlap, probably on Dec. 30, 1862.

Following the first battle of Bull Run he proposed a resolution in the House to spend men and money without stint to restore the Union, and when the resolution was adopted he, himself, already a colonel of militia, left Congress to accept a brigadier-general's commission. While post commander at Cairo on reconnaissance in Kentucky and at Belmont, his vigor and bravery won Grant's approval; but at Fort Henry, despite orders, he failed to block the Confederate retreat and, after the fall of Fort Donelson, angered his superior by virtually crediting the victory to his own division, the 1st. Nevertheless, he was a major-general after Mar. 21, 1862, outranked in the West by Halleck and Grant alone. Ambitious and untactful, he resented dictation, disliked West Pointers, and never forgot his political fences in Illinois. He wrote of his decisive rôle at Shiloh to Lincoln and to Halleck, criticizing Grant's strategy and protesting assignments to duty inconsistent with his rank. He sought to supplant McClellan in the East, and, warning Lincoln that a closed Mississippi meant dangerous discontent in the upper valley, was authorized in October 1862 to raise a large force in the Northwest for a river expedition against Vicksburg. At Sherman's suggestion and unauthorized by Grant, he and his thirty thousand, with Porter's ironclads, reduced Arkansas Post on Jan. 11, 1863, and thereby gained the congratulations of Lincoln and Governor Yates of Illinois. Grant tartly ordered him to return to Millikens Bend and, over his protest, dissolved the Mississippi River expedition and assigned him to command the XIII Corps. For three months he supervised the making of roads, levees, and canals on the peninsula opposite Vicksburg. Although Charles Dana, war department observer in the field, repeatedly advised Stanton to remove him, he led the advance across the Mississippi at the end of April 1863. Grant charged him with tardiness at Grand Gulf and Champion Hills and with half of the heavy losses before Vicksburg on May 22. When he, without Grant's authorization, furnished the press with a congratulatory order, extolling his men as the heroes of the campaign, Grant, eagerly supported by Sherman and McPherson, ordered him to Illinois on June 18, 1863. Here, ever popular, and unbroken in spirit, he rallied the people to a renewed support of the war, and Governor Yates besought Lincoln on the eve of Gettysburg to give him the eastern command. When the President refused to call a court of inquiry, McClernand warned him that he would publish a severe indictment of Grant (*War of the Rebellion: Official Records, post*, 1 ser., XXIV, pt. 1, pp. 169–86). In early February 1864 he regained command of the XIII Corps, then scattered from New Orleans to the Rio Grande. For three months he contended with bad weather and water, shifting sands, an elusive enemy, a dwindling corps, and his own thwarted ambition. Hardly had he left his headquarters on Matagorda Island in late April to participate in the Red River expedition, than acute sickness forced him to return to Illinois. He resigned his commission on Nov. 30, 1864.

He served as circuit judge of the Sangamon district from 1870 to 1873, as a member of the state Democratic central committee, as chairman of the National Democratic Convention in 1876, and on the Utah commission under Cleveland. He died of dysentery in Springfield, where he had lived since some time before the Civil War. He was survived by his wife and four children.

[A few letters in the Chicago Hist. Soc. Lib. and in the McCormick Hist. Asso. Lib. in Chicago; *Ill. State Jour.* (Springfield), Oct. 19–Nov. 16, 1859, Aug. 8, Oct. 10, 31, 1860, Apr. 24, June 5, Aug. 7, Oct. 2, 1861, May 21, Aug. 6, Sept. 3, 10, Oct. 8, Nov. 19, 26, Dec. 31, 1862, Mar. 18, July 1, 1863, Feb. 3, 1864; *Ill. Weekly State Jour.* (Springfield), Dec. 31, 1862; J. M. Palmer, *The Bench and Bar of Ill.* (1899), vol. I; *Hist. of Sangamon County, Ill.* (1881); T. C. Pease, *Illinois Election Returns* (1923); *Jour. of the Ill. State Hist. Soc.*, Oct. 1923–Jan. 1924, Jan. 1929; *War of the Rebellion: Official Records (Army)*, 1 ser., III, VII, X, pts. 1, 2, XVI, pt. 2, XVII, pts. 1, 2, XXII, pt. 2, XXIV, pts. 1, 3, XXXIV, pts. 1–3, LI, pt. 1, LII, pt. 1; *Battles and Leaders of the Civil War* (1887), vols. I, III; John Fiske, *The Mississippi Valley in the Civil War* (1900); *Personal Memoirs of U. S. Grant* (1885), vol. I; *Memoirs of Gen. W. T. Sherman*, 2nd ed. (1886), vol. I; *Ill. State Register* (Springfield), Feb. 24, 1843, Nov. 10, 1843, Sept. 20, 1900.]   W. T. H.

McCLINTOCK, EMORY (Sept. 19, 1840–July 10, 1916), mathematician, actuary, was born at Carlisle, Pa., the son of the Rev. John M'Clintock [*q.v.*], a clergyman and educator, and Caroline Augusta Wakeman, a descendant of John Wakeman, treasurer of the New Haven Colony, 1655–59. At the age of fourteen he entered Dickinson College, leaving in 1856 to enter Yale. A year later he transferred to Columbia where he was graduated with high honors in 1859, being at once appointed to a tutorship in mathematics. A year later he went to Paris for the purpose of studying chemistry, spending the following year at Göttingen. From 1863 to 1866 he served as vice-consul at Bradford, England, and in the latter year he took a position with a banking firm in Paris. He continued his interest in mathematics, and particularly in the special field of actuarial science. He returned to America in 1868 to accept an appointment as actuary in the Asbury Life Insurance Company of New York. In 1871 he was called to a similar position with the Northwestern Life Insurance Company of Milwaukee, remaining there for eighteen years. In 1889 he became actuary of the Mutual Life Insurance Company of New York and continued with the organization in this capacity until 1911, when he became consulting actuary. Meantime (1905) he became a member of the board of trustees and one of the vice-presidents.

In the general reorganization of the American life-insurance companies in 1905–06 McClintock's grasp of the insurance problem was at once manifest, and his recommendations did much to reëstablish the position of these American companies in the United States. He was for many years the recognized leader in actuarial circles in this country, being one of the founders of the Actuarial Society of America (1889) and later (1895) its president. He was also a fellow of the Institute of Actuaries of Great Britain (1874), a corresponding member of the Institut des Actuaires Français, and of the Association d'Actuaires Belges, and a member of the permanent committee of the International Congress of Actuaries. In the domain of pure mathematics he was hardly less interested. He was one of the founders of the New York Mathematical Society, its second president (1891), and one of the leaders in transforming this organization into the American Mathematical Society (1894), and in establishing its *Bulletin* and *Transactions*. To both of these periodicals he contributed numerous articles. In his articles on the calculus of enlargement in the *American Journal of Mathematics* (June 1879, January 1895) he attempted to coördinate in a new way certain special fields of mathematics. For his work in actuarial science and in pure mathematics he received several honorary doctorates and was elected an honorary fellow of the American Academy of Arts and Sciences. McClintock's first wife was Zoe Darlington, of Yorkshire, England, by whom he had one son, Maj. John McClintock, for a time military attaché in the legation at Vienna. His second wife was Isabella Bishop of New Brunswick, N. J.

[T. S. Fiske, article in the *Bull. of the Am. Math. Soc.*, May 1917, with bibliography; Wm. A. Hutcheson, article in the *Trans. Actuarial Soc. of America*, vol. XVII, 1916, and discussion of article in *Ibid.*, vol. XVIII, 1917; *Weekly Underwriter*, July 15, 1916; *N. Y. Times*, July 12, 19, 1916.]   D. E. S.

M'CLINTOCK, JOHN (Oct. 27, 1814–Mar. 4, 1870), Methodist Episcopal clergyman, educator, and editor, was the son of John and Martha (M'Mackin) M'Clintock, both of whom were born in County Tyrone, Ireland. The younger John was a native of Philadelphia, where his father carried on a retail dry-goods business. He received his early schooling under Samuel B. Wylie [*q.v.*], also an Irishman, and a noted classicist. When he was fourteen years old he became a clerk in his father's store, and two years later, bookkeeper in the Methodist Book Concern, New York. While here he was converted, and began to consider entering the ministry. In 1832 he enrolled as a freshman at the University of Pennsylvania and completed the required course in three years. During the latter part of it he had preached regularly, and in April 1835 had been admitted on trial to the Philadelphia Conference of the Methodist Episcopal Church and appointed to Jersey City. His health broke down in 1836, and he was obliged to relinquish his charge. Thereafter he suffered from a recurrent throat trouble, and was never physically strong.

Turning now to the educational field, he accepted an assistant professorship of mathematics at Dickinson College, Carlisle, Pa., and in 1837 was made full professor. He remained with this institution for twelve years, being transferred to the chair of classical languages in 1840. While there he published some widely used textbooks,

A First Book in Latin (1846) and *A First Book in Greek* (1848), both in collaboration with George R. Crooks [*q.v.*]. They were followed by *A Second Book in Greek* (1850), and *A Second Book in Latin* (1853). With Charles E. Blumenthal he prepared a translation of Neander's *Das Leben Jesu Christi,* issued in 1848 under the title, *The Life of Jesus Christ in Its Historical Connexion and Development.* Improvement in his health enabled him to preach more frequently, and on Apr. 19, 1840, he was ordained elder by Bishop Elijah Hedding [*q.v.*]. When in 1847 two slave-owners from Maryland came to Carlisle to recover some runaway slaves, M'Clintock endeavored to see that the legal rights of the latter were respected. Before the matter was settled, a riot occurred and he and a number of negroes were arrested on the charge of instigating it. Excitement ran high and the feeling against him was strong, but a jury acquitted him.

In 1848 he resigned his professorship and became editor of the *Methodist Quarterly Review,* to which office the General Conference of that year elected him. For this position he was now well fitted. Having an acquisitive mind and a studious disposition, he had become "the most universally accomplished man American Methodism had produced" (J. M. Buckley, *A History of Methodists in the United States,* 1896, American Church History Series, V, 528). During the eight years he conducted the *Review* he made it a scholarly exponent of the best Christian thought, and under him it became, for the first time, self-supporting. Twice in this period he went abroad for the benefit of his health. In 1851 he was elected president of Wesleyan University, and in 1855, president of Troy University, both of which honors he declined. He published in 1855 *The Temporal Power of the Pope,* an exposition of the Ultramontane theory of the relation of church and state. Two years before, with Dr. James Strong [*q.v.*], he had begun the now well-known *Cyclopædia of Biblical, Theological, and Ecclesiastical Literature,* upon which ambitious undertaking he spent much time for the rest of his life. Three volumes only were published before his death, the first in 1867.

His connection with the *Review* terminated in 1856 and with Bishop Matthew Simpson [*q.v.*] he went abroad as delegate to the British Wesleyan Conference, and the conference of the Evangelical Alliance at Berlin. Upon his return he became pastor of St. Paul's Church, New York, where he soon ranked among the ablest preachers of the city. In 1860 he was appointed pastor of the American Chapel, Paris. During the Civil War, by speeches, writings, and personal contacts, he was a potent influence in removing misapprehensions abroad, and through the *Methodist,* of which he was a corresponding editor, in disseminating correct information at home. It is reported that President Lincoln declared him fitted for the position of minister to France (Buckley, p. 528). He again became pastor of St. Paul's Church, New York, in 1864, but ill health soon compelled him to resign. From 1864 to 1866, as chairman of a committee appointed by the General Conference, he was busily engaged in putting into operation an elaborate scheme for the celebration of the centenary of American Methodism. In accordance with the desire of Daniel Drew [*q.v.*], in 1867 he became the first president of Drew Theological Seminary, but less than three years later death brought his career to a close. His publications included *Sketches of Eminent Methodist Ministers* (1854), and *History of the Council of Trent, from the French of L. F. Bungener* (1855). After his death *Living Words: or Unwritten Sermons Reported Phonographically* (1871), and *Lectures . . . on Theological Encyclopaedia and Methodology* (1873), appeared. He was married first, in 1837, to Caroline A. Wakeman; Emory McClintock [*q.v.*] was their son. In October 1851, he married Catharine W. Emory, widow of his friend, Rev. Robert Emory.

[G. R. Crooks, *Life and Letters of Rev. John M'Clintock, D.D., LL.D.,* (1876); E. S. Tipple, *Drew Theological Seminary, 1867–1917* (1917); C. F. Himes, *A Sketch of Dickinson College* (1879); F. L. Mott, *A Hist. of Am. Magazines, 1741–1850* (1930); *Methodist Review,* July 1894, Nov. 1917; *Methodist,* Mar. 12, 1870; *N. Y. Times,* Mar. 5, 1870.]   H. E. S.

McCLINTOCK, OLIVER (Oct. 20, 1839–Oct. 10, 1922), merchant and political reformer, was born in Pittsburgh, Pa., the eldest of seven children of Washington and Eliza (Thompson) McClintock. He was a descendant of Scotch ancestors who came to Pennsylvania from Ireland in 1740. His grandfather engaged in Conestoga wagon freighting between Philadelphia and Pittsburgh and ran a blacksmith shop and ferry at Fort Pitt. Washington McClintock entered the business of his father-in-law, Samuel Thompson, who manufactured uniforms in the War of 1812 and established a carpet and drygoods store in Pittsburgh. In 1844 the firm became W. McClintock & Company. Oliver received a good education in local academies and graduated from Yale in 1861. He served as a corporal in the 15th Pennsylvania Emergency Militia during Lee's invasions, and was also a member of the subsistence committee which fed 500,000 Federal troops as they passed through Pittsburgh. He

was taken into his father's business in 1862, but shortly established a separate store, which merged with the parent company in 1864 as Oliver McClintock & Company. His brothers, and later two of his sons, were admitted to the firm, which attained a position of leadership in the mercantile life of the city and was finally dissolved on Apr. 1, 1914, after 106 years of activity by three generations.

McClintock was a prime mover in many civic enterprises. He was an elder of the Presbyterian Church, first president of the Pittsburgh Young Men's Christian Association (1866), a trustee and president of the board of Western Theological Seminary and of Pennsylvania College for Women. In 1883 he and his brother-in-law, Albert H. Childs, founded Shadyside Academy; and his sons were members of its first graduating class. He was long an official of the Chamber of Commerce and at his death was its oldest member. When the city government collapsed during the railroad-strike riots of 1877, McClintock acted for two weeks on the Emergency Public Safety Committee authorized by a mass meeting. He was a founder and director of the Civic Club of Allegheny County, and was active in such national and state bodies as the American Civic Association, National Civil Service Reform League, National Municipal League, Ballot Reform Association, and Indian Rights Association of Pennsylvania.

In the 1880's and '90's Pittsburgh was in the grip of a political ring led by Christopher L. Magee [*q.v.*], which distributed long franchises to utilities, let bids for public works at exorbitant prices, and generally battened on public moneys under cover of legal forms. A small group of citizens, inspired by McClintock and David D. Bruce, had for years vainly fought the public-works corruption in and out of court. In 1895 they aroused enough public sentiment to organize a Citizens' Municipal League, and campaigned to beat the ring in the election of February 1896. McClintock was a member of the executive committee of five, which nominated for mayor George W. Guthrie [*q.v.*], an able Democratic lawyer. The Magee machine was hampered by a factional fight with the state boss, Senator Matthew S. Quay [*q.v.*], and Guthrie actually won a majority; but he was fraudulently counted out and denied a recount by the courts. In 1902 McClintock again led a Citizens' Party, which partially broke the hold of the Magee ring. In 1906 the independents succeeded in electing Guthrie mayor, and a great exposé of councilmanic iniquity followed. McClintock secured in 1907 the passage of a state civil-service law for second-class cities (Pittsburgh, Scranton). In 1910 the veteran reformer threw his influence into the fight for a new city charter which replaced the corrupt and inefficient two-chambered council, elected by wards, with a small council of nine, elected at large on a non-partisan ballot. McClintock himself never sought public office. His tireless efforts for good government were attended by ridicule, threats, and boycotts of other business men. He said that he met his greatest discouragement in the cowardice and civic apathy of prosperous citizens. He attributed his reforming zeal to a hatred of autocracy inherited from his Revolutionary and Scotch-Irish ancestors. Lincoln Steffens, writing in *McClure's Magazine* in 1903, said of him: "This single citizen's long, brave fight is one of the finest stories in the history of municipal government."

McClintock was married, June 7, 1866, to Clara Courtney Childs of Pittsburgh. He had three sons and three daughters, all of whom survived him.

[G. I. Reed, *Century Cyc. of Hist. and Biog. of Pa.* (1904), vol. II; J. N. Boucher, *A Century and a Half of Pittsburgh and Her People* (1908), vol. I; G. T. Fleming, *Hist. of Pittsburgh and Environs* (1922), vol. IV; Lincoln Steffens, "Pittsburg: A City Ashamed," *McClure's Magazine*, May 1903; *Yale Univ. Obit. Record*, 1923; *Who's Who in America*, 1922–23; *Pittsburgh Post, Pittsburg Dispatch*, Oct. 11, 1922; notes of family.]   K. M. G.

McCLOSKEY, JOHN (Mar. 10, 1810–Oct. 10, 1885), Roman Catholic prelate, first American cardinal, was the son of Patrick and Elizabeth (Harron) McCloskey, recent immigrants from County Derry, Ireland. He was born in Brooklyn, N. Y., where his father was a clerk in the firm of H. P. Pierrepont and Company. Receiving his first lessons from an English actress, the boy learned to speak with a precision and perfect enunciation of which in later life he was proud. In New York, he attended Thomas Brady's classical school and St. Patrick's Church, where he attracted the attention of Rev. John Power, Pierre Malou, S. J., and the philanthropic merchant, Cornelius Heeney, who on the death of McCloskey's father became the boy's guardian. Entering Mount St. Mary's College, Emmitsburg, Md., in 1821, he completed both the preparatory and collegiate courses, graduating in 1828. After spending a year on his mother's Westchester farm, he returned as a seminarian to Mount St. Mary's where he came into contact with such influential ecclesiastics as Dubois, Bruté, Hughes, and Purcell, and was recognized as a cultured gentleman rather than an ascetic or a scholar.

Ordained by Bishop Dubois at old St. Pat-

rick's (Jan. 12, 1834), he was selected as an assistant at the cathedral and chaplain at Bellevue Hospital, and later received an appointment in the new seminary at Nyack. When this institution was burned, McCloskey was permitted to attend the Gregorian University at Rome (1835–37), where he made influential friends. Well traveled, fluent in French and Italian, and conversant with the mind of the Church, he returned to New York as rector of St. Joseph's Church in Greenwich. By prudent forbearance, he won the hostile trustees who would have closed the church doors upon him. In 1841, he was given additional duties as a teaching rector of St. John's College, Fordham. Two years later, on the application of Bishop John Hughes [q.v.] for a coadjutor, he was recommended by the bishops in a provincial council at Baltimore to Pope Gregory XVI, who forthwith named him titular bishop of Axiern with the right of succession to New York.

On Mar. 10, 1844, he was consecrated at St. Patrick's, Mott Street. While retaining his pastorate, he was chiefly engaged in visitations, ironing out difficulties in various parishes, toning down the opposition of certain pastors to Bishop Hughes, and winning over the aristocratic Catholics, whose ways he understood. While not openly involved in the nativist troubles or the school controversy, he was a conservative, dependable counselor upon whom the more virile Hughes learned to rely. The two bishops were decided opposites in character, yet they worked in perfect harmony. With the growth of the New York diocese, Buffalo and Albany were created separate sees, and McCloskey was given charge of the latter (May 21, 1847).

Though he took no part in politics, he was on intimate terms with Horatio Seymour, Erastus Corning, Rufus King, Thurlow Weed, and the Van Rensselaers. No doubt his work merited promotion, yet when he was elevated by Pius IX to the archbishopric of New York on the death of Hughes in 1864, there was a prevalent feeling that he had made use of consequential friends in Rome. Not until 1902 was it known that he had written to Cardinal Reisach beseeching that he, as physically frail, be spared the possible appointment and that M. J. Spalding or John Timon [qq.v.] be honored. His installation (Aug. 27, 1864) pleased the war administration in Washington, however, as well as the clergy and prominent laity of the archdiocese, who were relieved that the strenuous days of Hughes were over. Hence, he commenced his administration under the happiest auspices, although he always gracefully insisted that he was but reaping the fruits of his predecessor's labor. He retained the old council of priests, and there was no noticeable break with the past save in the method of conducting affairs. In 1866, he attended the Second Plenary Council of Baltimore, where he preached the opening sermon. In agreement with its deliberations, he silenced the Fenians by a letter of admonition read from all diocesan pulpits (Mar. 2, 1866), in which he counseled against wild schemes of freeing Ireland and invading Canada. Renewing work on St. Patrick's Cathedral, which had been discontinued during the war, he was so successful in collections and in obtaining furnishings during his frequent European journeys that the cathedral was ready for dedication on May 25, 1879. Compromising old administrative differences with the religious, he gave equal encouragement to Paulists, Franciscans, Dominicans, Augustinians, and Jesuits, as well as to the various communities of nuns. Deeply interested in eleemosynary institutions, he wheedled liberal donations for them from the increasingly large class of prosperous Catholics. In the Vatican Council, he considered the declaration of infallibility inexpedient, since the papacy was generally recognized as having the authority involved, but on the final ballot (July 18, 1870) he voted in the affirmative. For his hesitancy he was criticized by the ultramontane James A. McMaster [q.v.] of the *Freeman's Journal*. None the less, he gained rather than lost influence in Rome.

Pius IX preconized McCloskey in the same public consistory (Mar. 15, 1875) in which Archbishop Manning of Westminster was elevated to the cardinalate. There was almost universal approval in the United States, for even in non-Catholic circles national vanity was gratified that an American citizen had become a prince of the Church. McCloskey had made few enemies and had always worn his honors becomingly. Dignified in manner, benignant, confiding, and easily accessible, he held both the love and the respect of his priests and people. The investiture (Apr. 27) was a brilliant function. Three years later he journeyed to Rome, but was too late for the conclave which elected Pope Leo XIII, from whom he formally received the ring and red hat. In 1880 his work was lightened by the appointment of Bishop M. A. Corrigan [q.v.] as coadjutor; though until his golden jubilee (1884), he actively managed his great diocese himself. His last year was spent in quiet retirement at St. Vincent's-on-the-Hudson. His obsequies at St. Patrick's Cathedral (Oct. 25, 1885), presided over by Cardinal Gibbons, bore a national character.

[J. M. Farley, *The Life of John Cardinal McCloskey* (1918), *Hist. of St. Patrick's Cathedral* (1908), and notes on McCloskey's life in U. S. Cath. Hist. Soc., *Hist. Records and Studies*, vols. I, II (1900–01), and in *Cath. Encyc.*, IX (1910), 485; J. J. Walsh, *Our Am. Cardinals* (1926); R. H. Clarke, *Lives of the Deceased Bishops of the Cath. Ch. in the U. S.*, vol. III (1888); J. T. Smith, *The Cath. Ch. in N. Y.* (1905), vol. I; Louis Teste, *Préface au Conclave* (1877); Catholic Directories; *Celebration of the 50th Anniversary or Golden Jubilee of . . . Cardinal McCloskey* (1884); James Gibbons, *Funeral Oration on His Eminence John Cardinal McCloskey* (1885); M. A. Corrigan, *Words Spoken at the Month's Mind of his Eminence Cardinal McCloskey* (1885); J. G. Shea, *The Hierarchy of the Cath. Ch. in the U. S.* (1886); *N. Y. Times, N. Y. Tribune,* Oct. 10, 1885; *Donahoe's Mag.,* Jan. 1886; *N. Y. Freeman's Jour.,* May 7, Aug. 13, 1864.]
                                                    R.J.P.

McCLOSKEY, WILLIAM GEORGE (Nov. 10, 1823–Sept. 17, 1909), Roman Catholic prelate, was born in Brooklyn, N. Y., where he received his early schooling. His father, George, was a dairy farmer and long trustee of St. James's Church. In 1835, the boy was enrolled in Mount St. Mary's College, Emmitsburg, Md. Later he studied law in New York prior to his entrance into the seminary at Mount St. Mary's, where he served as a prefect and teacher and received his master's degree. Ordained by Archbishop Hughes, Oct. 6, 1852, he was assigned as an assistant to his brother George, pastor of the Church of the Nativity, New York. A year later he was recalled to Emmitsburg as a teacher of Latin, scripture, and moral theology. In 1857 he was promoted to the directorship of the seminary, and in that capacity became known in clerical circles as a man of distinguished appearance and some administrative ability. Two years later, when the American College in Rome was established, the American hierarchy submitted a list of fifteen candidates for the rectorship, from which the cardinals of the Sacred College of the Propaganda, with the assent of the Holy Father, selected McCloskey (Dec. 1, 1859). The selection was well received and McCloskey proved an excellent rector. Under his guidance the enrolment of students increased greatly, indicating that he had the confidence of the American bishops who furnished the seminarians. Tact was essential in the Civil War days, when the students separated into northern and southern factions. Then too there were financial difficulties as the war economies dwarfed diocesan allocations. Nevertheless, the institution was in a flourishing condition when McCloskey resigned to accept the bishopric of Louisville, left vacant by the death of Bishop Peter J. Lavialle.

Consecrated by Cardinal Count August de Reisach of Munich in the college chapel (May 24, 1868), McCloskey is said to have been the first American so consecrated in Rome. For forty-one years he ruled the Louisville diocese which, during that time, saw an increase of from eighty to 200 priests and from sixty-four to about 165 churches, of which a large number had schools attached. He introduced into the diocese the Passionists, the Benedictines, the Priests of the Congregation of the Resurrection who managed St. Mary's College, and the Brothers of Mary, as well as the Sisters of Mercy and the Franciscan Sisters for elementary schools and academies. As early as 1869 he established Preston Park Seminary, over which his brother George (died, 1890) later presided as rector. In no work was he more concerned than in the charitable and reformatory institutions of the Sisters of the Poor and of the Good Shepherd. This interest led him to translate from the Italian a *Life of St. Mary Magdalen* (1900). He won a place of influence as a figure in the Vatican Council and in the Plenary Council of Baltimore (1884), as an active proponent of Catholic education, and as the oldest member of the hierarchy at the time of his death. With a pontifical requiem mass by Archbishop Moeller [*q.v.*] and a eulogy by Bishop Denis O'Donaghue, at the Cathedral of the Assumption, he was buried in the cemetery of the Sisters of Charity at Nazareth, Ky.

[*Cath. Encyc.*, IX (1910), 388; E. F. X. McSweeny, *The Story of the Mountain* (2 vols., 1911); J. G. Shea, *The Hierarchy of the Cath. Ch. in the U. S.* (1886); H. A. Brann, *Hist. of the Am. College of the Roman Cath. Ch. of the U. S., Rome, Italy* (1910); *N. Y. Freeman's Journal*, Jan. 7, Mar. 3, 1860; obituaries in *The Record* (diocesan organ) and *Louisville Courier-Journal*, Sept. 17, 18, 1909.]   R.J.P.

McCLURE, ALEXANDER KELLY (Jan. 9, 1828–June 6, 1909), editor, lawyer, legislator, son of Alexander and Isabella (Anderson) McClure, was born in Sherman's Valley, Perry County, Pa., of Scotch-Irish descent. He was reared on his father's farm, educated at home, and at the age of fifteen was apprenticed to a tanner. At the same time he learned the printing trade in the office of the *Perry County Freeman,* where he absorbed Whig political principles. In the late forties he edited and published the *Juniata Sentinel* at Mifflintown. In 1849 he was commissioned colonel on the staff of Governor Johnson, and in the following year he was appointed deputy United States marshal for Juniata County. In 1852 he became part owner of the *Franklin Repository,* published in Chambersburg, and shortly afterward he secured full control. Under his direction it became one of the influential newspapers in the state. After failing of election as the Whig candidate for auditor-general in 1853, he turned his attention to law. He was admitted to the bar in 1856 but continued to devote most of his time to the *Repository.* He took

particular interest in the organization of the Republican party and was a member of the state convention that met in Pittsburgh in the summer of 1855. In 1860 he was a member of the Pennsylvania delegation to the Republican National Convention which was committed to Simon Cameron for the presidency. When it became evident that two-thirds of the delegates from the other states were in favor of William H. Seward, Curtin and McClure succeeded in switching the Pennsylvania vote from Cameron to Lincoln. McClure was elected chairman of the Republican state committee and in this office perfected a complete political organization in every city, county, township, and precinct in the state. Following a campaign of unprecedented aggressiveness Andrew G. Curtin was elected governor and later Lincoln swept the state by a large majority.

After a term in the state House of Representatives in 1858, McClure was elected in 1859 to the state Senate. There he was spokesman for Pennsylvania's war governor, and as chairman of the Senate committee on military affairs he was active in support of both state and federal governments for the preservation of the Union. In 1865 he was again in the House of Representatives. At the request of President Lincoln, he accepted a commission as assistant adjutant-general of the army and placed seventeen regiments in the field. In 1868 he became a resident of Philadelphia. He opened a law office and immediately became active in civic affairs. He was a delegate-at-large to the Republican National Convention that nominated General Grant in 1868. Differing with the dominant Republican leadership in 1872 he became chairman of the Pennsylvania delegation to the Liberal Republican national convention which nominated Horace Greeley for the presidency. He gave further evidence of political independence by running as a Citizen's candidate, with Democratic indorsement, for the state Senate in the West Philadelphia district, and after a bitter contest was sworn in. In 1874 he was the Citizen's-Democratic candidate for mayor of Philadelphia, making his canvass upon charges of gross corruption in the city administration, but he was defeated. In response to a demand for a newspaper to support the independent forces in Philadelphia, McClure in conjunction with Frank McLaughlin on Mar. 13, 1875, established the *Times* which became a well-known newspaper in the country. McClure was a man of impressive appearance and was in demand as a speaker on public occasions. He was twice married, first to Matilda S. Gray, on Feb. 10, 1852; and second to Cora M. Gratz, on Mar. 19, 1879. His later years were largely devoted to literary work, his books including *Three Thousand Miles through the Rocky Mountains* (1869); *The South: Its Industrial, Financial and Political Condition* (1886); *Abraham Lincoln and Men of War Times* (1892); *Our Presidents and How We Make Them* (1900); *To the Pacific and Mexico* (1901); *Col. Alexander K. McClure's Recollections of a Half Century* (1902); and *Old Time Notes of Pennsylvania* (2 vols., 1905). He edited *Famous American Statesmen and Orators* (6 vols., 1902).

[In addition to McClure's books see: *Encyc. of Contemporary Biog. of Pa.* (1893), vol. III; H. H. Hain, *Hist. of Perry County, Pa.* (1922); *Who's Who in America,* 1908–09; J. A. McClure, *The McClure Family* (1914); the *Press* (Phila.), June 7, 1909.]   L. C. P.

McCLURE, ALEXANDER WILSON (May 8, 1808–September 1865), clergyman, editor, author, was born in Boston, Mass., the youngest son of Thomas and Mary (Wilson) McClure. His maternal great-grandfather was the Rev. John Morehead, the first Presbyterian minister of Boston. He prepared for college at the Latin School, spent two years at Yale, and then transferred to Amherst where he graduated in 1827. After his graduation at Andover Seminary in 1830 he began to preach at the First Congregational Church at Malden, Mass., but was not ordained till Dec. 19, 1832. His pastorate continued till 1843 when he resigned on account of failing health. When he went to Malden, the church was weak and on the point of dissolution, but under his wise and courageous leadership it revived and he left it in a flourishing condition. Going as acting pastor to a Presbyterian church in St. Augustine, Fla., he accomplished a remarkable evangelistic work among the soldiers garrisoned there. In 1847 he returned to Boston and edited the *Christian Observatory* till 1850, at the same time acting as assistant editor of the *Puritan Recorder.* He also again served his old church in Malden from 1848 to 1851. At the close of the latter year he became pastor of the Dutch Reformed church on Grand Street in Jersey City, N. J., remaining a member of that denomination for the rest of his life.

In 1855 he became secretary of the American and Foreign Christian Union, an organization for carrying on Protestant work in Europe and other countries. In the first year of his secretaryship he served as pastor of the chapel in Rome maintained by this society, and it was largely through his efforts that the Paris chapel, an evangelical and unsectarian place of worship for American residents, was established. During his secretaryship he was also the editor of the monthly magazine, the *Christian World,* and

other publications of the Union. At the end of 1857 he retired on account of ill health and died at Canonsburg, Pa., after several years of inactivity. In addition to numerous religious and theological articles in various periodicals, McClure was the author of *The Life Boat; an Allegory,* a tract of wide circulation; *Lectures on Ultra-Universalism* (1832); *Lives of the Chief Fathers of New England* (1846), of which Volume I was "The Life of John Cotton" and Volume II "The Lives of John Wilson, John Norton and John Davenport"; and *The Translators Revived* (1853), consisting of biographical sketches of the translators of the King James version of the Bible. He was also a joint author of *The Bi-Centennial Book of Malden* (1850).

McClure accomplished a vast amount of work in spite of frail health. He was a man of wide and varied knowledge, a brilliant writer and preacher, formidable in debate and outspoken against what he considered to be evil. He had abounding wit, a deeply religious nature, and his life was rich in numerous friendships. In theology he was thoroughly evangelical and deeply attached to the standards of the Dutch Reformed Church. But he worked in sympathetic cooperation with all other evangelical denominations, regarding them as equally members of the Church of Christ. He married Mary Brewster Gould of Southampton, Mass., by whom he had eight children.

[*Christian World,* Nov. 1865, p. 349; *Biog. Record of the Alumni of Amherst Coll. During its first Half Century, 1821–71* (1883); *Boston Recorder,* Nov. 10, 1865; E. T. Corwin, *A Manual of the Reformed Church in America, 1628–1878* (3d ed., 1879), p. 373; Jacob Abbott, *The Corner-Stone* (1834), pp. 320–31; J. A. McClure, *The McClure Family* (1914). The date of McClure's death is given in the Amherst *Biog. Record,* cited above, as Sept. 17, 1865. Other sources give Sept. 20.]   F. T. P.

McCLURE, GEORGE (c. 1770–Aug. 16, 1851), soldier, was born near Londonderry, Ireland, son of Finla McClure, and a descendant of Scotch immigrants to Ireland. He relates that from his fourth to his fifteenth year he attended school under "cruel and tyrannical" pedagogues; that he then learned the carpenter's trade; and that at the age of twenty he emigrated to America (McMaster, *post*). He landed at Baltimore, and after working as a carpenter there and at Chambersburg, Pa., about 1793 went to Bath, Steuben County, N. Y., in a region which was then just being opened to settlement. Here he soon became a merchant. He studied the Seneca dialect in order to trade more successfully in furs; he erected a distillery, a flour mill, and a mill for making woolen yarn; he speculated in land; he built boats for lake and river traffic and conducted cargoes of flour, lumber, and cattle down the Susquehanna to Baltimore, or to Columbia, Pa., and thence overland to Philadelphia. On Aug. 20, 1795, he married Eleanor Bole of Derry, Pa., and after her death, Sarah Welles (1808). He held various civil offices and rose in the militia to the rank of brigadier-general (*Military Minutes of the Council of Appointment of the State of New York,* vol. I, 1901, pp. 411, 651, 843).

In the fall of 1812 his brigade was called into service by Gen. Alexander Smyth [*q.v.*], and McClure was one of a group of militia officers who protested in writing against Smyth's dilatory tactics. In the fall of 1813, when the expedition against Montreal under Gen. James Wilkinson [*q.v.*] was in preparation, McClure was ordered again to the Niagara frontier to command a detachment of militia and to defend the frontier in the absence of the regular troops. He established his headquarters at Fort George, on the Canadian side of the Niagara River at its mouth, and indulged a propensity for the writing of bombastic proclamations. When Wilkinson definitely abandoned the campaign against Montreal (Nov. 13), the British turned their attention to the Niagara. Meanwhile, the terms of enlistment of McClure's volunteer troops were expiring; the War Department inexcusably neglected to reënforce him; and by Dec. 10 he had only 100 men at Fort George to face 500 advancing British. Upon the advice of a council of his officers he determined to abandon the fort; and the nearby village of Newark, once the capital of Upper Canada, was given to the flames. The reason advanced by McClure for this wanton act of destruction was that it would deprive the enemy of winter quarters; he also appealed to a letter from Secretary of War John Armstrong, which had authorized the officer commanding at Fort George to destroy the village if necessary for the defense of the fort. This letter did not cover McClure's act, and in view of the fact that all the barracks, as well as tents for 1,500 men, were left standing, his plea that he was destroying winter quarters was without merit. That the burning of Newark was generally disapproved on the American side is indicated by the hostile reception accorded McClure in Buffalo. His popularity must have been still less after Dec. 30, when the British burned Buffalo and Black Rock in retaliation for the destruction of Newark. McClure returned to his home in Bath and did not again appear on the Niagara frontier. His conduct at Newark was disavowed by his superior officer, General Wilkinson, in a letter to Sir George Prevost. That his popularity at home

did not suffer seriously is indicated by his appointment as sheriff of Steuben County in 1815 and his three elections as representative of the county in the legislature. About 1834 he removed to Elgin, Ill., where he died. Politically, he is described as having been "a staunch freesoiler, a radical temperance man, and a firm believer in the future glory of the United States" (McMaster, *post,* p. 113).

[M. F. Roberts, *Hist. Gazetteer of Steuben County, N. Y.* (1891); G. H. McMaster, *Hist. of the Settlement of Steuben County, N. Y.* (1853), containing a brief autobiog. narrative of McClure's early life; Ernest Cruikshank, *The Documentary Hist. of the Campaigns upon the Niagara Frontier in 1812–14* (9 vols., 1896–1908); L. L. Babcock, "The War of 1812 on the Niagara Frontier," *Buffalo Hist. Soc. Pubs.,* vol. XXIX (1927); Henry Adams, *Hist. of the U. S. of America,* vol. VII (1891).] J.W.P.

McCLURG, ALEXANDER CALDWELL (Sept. 9, 1832–Apr. 15, 1901), bookseller, publisher, Union soldier, a first cousin of Joseph W. McClurg [*q.v.*], was the son of Alexander and Sarah (Trevor) McClurg. His paternal grandfather, Joseph, of Scotch-Irish descent, was involved in the Irish troubles of 1798 and fled to the United States, settling in Pittsburgh, whither his family followed him. Here he established what was probably the first iron foundry in that place, his son Alexander being associated with him in this and other business ventures. At the time of Alexander Caldwell's birth his parents were living in Philadelphia. When he was eight years old they returned to Pittsburgh, where he received his early education. At seventeen he entered Miami University, Oxford, Ohio, graduating from that institution four years later. Returning home, he entered the law office of Walter H. Lowrie, then chief justice of the Pennsylvania supreme court, but deserted the law after one year because of failing health and of declining interest in the legal profession. In 1859 he went to Chicago and became a clerk in the house of S. C. Griggs & Company, then the largest bookstore in the West.

At the commencement of the Civil War he enlisted as a private in a company recruited in Chicago which, however, was disbanded because the state quota was full. In 1862, with two others, he organized the Crosby Guards, mustered into the service, Aug. 27, 1862, as Company H of the 88th Illinois Volunteer Infantry. A few days later, much to his surprise, he was unanimously elected to the captaincy of his company, notwithstanding his complete inexperience and his small physical stature. At a second election, necessitated because of faulty procedure in the first, his selection was confirmed, again unanimously. His regiment received its baptism of fire at the battle of Perryville, Ky., Oct. 8, 1862. McClurg's conduct in the field, and his marked executive ability, brought him to the notice of his corps commander, Gen. Alexander McDowell McCook, who, in May 1863, detailed him as acting assistant adjutant-general of the corps. In August 1864 he was assigned to General Baird's division as assistant adjutant-general and chief of staff. Soon afterward, he was invited by General Sheridan, then commanding a division in the same corps, to join his staff, but declined. When Sheridan went to the Army of the Potomac he renewed the invitation but McClurg again declined it. He served through the Chickamauga and Chattanooga campaigns with great distinction, being frequently mentioned in dispatches and winning recognition as one of the ablest staff officers in the western army. Gen. J. C. Davis recommended his promotion to the rank of lieutenant-colonel for especial gallantry at the battle of Jonesboro, and made him chief of his staff. Continuing in this position, he participated in the campaigns of Sherman's army from Atlanta to the sea, ending in the battle of Bentonville, N. C., Mar. 19, 1865. His account of this engagement, in the *Atlantic Monthly* (September 1882), entitled "The Last Chance of the Confederacy," is regarded as a notable military narrative. He was mustered out in Chicago, Sept. 9, 1865, with the brevet rank of colonel, afterwards raised to brigadier-general, and despite the fact that Sherman, Thomas, and other officers urged him to enter the regular army, he returned to his former occupation in Chicago.

In April 1866 he purchased an interest in the firm of S. C. Griggs & Company. A disastrous fire, two years later, wiped out his capital, but the creditors were paid in full and the firm reëstablished itself in a new location on State Street, where three important book-dealers occupied adjoining premises, locally known as Booksellers' Row. Here the great fire of 1871 interrupted the thriving business. In the reorganization that followed, S. C. Griggs sold his interest to his partners and in 1886 McClurg became the principal owner. In 1880 the firm began publication of the *Dial* (Chicago). The Old English Book Department, a project originated by McClurg in 1877, developed into an important specialty, in part by reason of the interesting group of bibliophiles who foregathered there and whose lucubrations Eugene Field [*q.v.*] celebrated and imaginatively expanded as the proceedings of the "Saints and Sinners" corner in the "Sharps and Flats" of the Chicago *Morning News*. A third fire, in 1899, led the senior partner, long a confirmed invalid and frequently absent in search of

health, to contemplate withdrawal from active business; but devotion to his firm, and a characteristic concern for the welfare of his large staff, prevailed over his inclination. His health continued to fail, however, and his death, of Bright's disease, occurred Apr. 15, 1901, at St. Augustine, Fla.

He was married, Apr. 17, 1877, to Eleanor, daughter of Judge Nelson Knox Wheeler of New York City. Two sons were born to them. McClurg was a booklover and reader as well as a bookseller, and, withal, a lively hater of the cheap and trashy, both in the contents and the makeup of books. A fluent and entertaining writer, he contributed numerous addresses to the proceedings of the many organizations to which he belonged and several articles to the magazines. A portion of his manuscript memoirs, left uncompleted at his death, was published under the title, "The American Volunteer Soldier," in Mabel McIlvane's *Reminiscences of Chicago During the Civil War* (1914). It presents a vivid account of his enlistment and early army experiences.

[*A Sketch of the Origin and Hist. of the House of A. C. McClurg & Co.* (privately printed); *Hist. of Allegheny County, Pa.* (1889), pt. II, pp. 295–96; A. T. Andreas, *Hist. of Chicago*, vol. III (1886); John Moses and Joseph Kirkland, *Hist. of Chicago* (1895); *Memorials of Deceased Companions . . . Commandery of . . . Ill., Mil. Order of the Loyal Legion of the U. S.* (1901); *Soc. of the Army of the Cumberland, Thirtieth Reunion* (1901); *War of the Rebellion, Official Records* (*Army*); *Who's Who in America*, 1899–1900; Newton Bateman and others, *Hist. Encyc. of Ill. and Hist. of Morgan County* (1906); *Dial* (Chicago), May 1, 1901; *Chicago Daily Tribune*, Apr. 16, 1901; personal acquaintance.]   C. B. R.

McCLURG, JAMES (*c.* 1746–July 9, 1823), physician, officer of the Revolution and delegate to the Philadelphia convention of 1787, was born near Hampton in Elizabeth City County, Va. His father, Dr. Walter McClurg, was superintendent of the Hampton Small Pox Hospital, which was probably one of the first hospitals of its kind in America. After thorough preparation James was sent to the College of William and Mary and graduated in 1762 with an unusually excellent scholastic record. He then studied medicine at the University of Edinburgh, graduating M.D. in 1770. His inaugural essay at Edinburgh, "De Calore," gave him an admirable reputation among his scientific friends. He devoted several years to post-graduate medical studies in Paris and London and while in London published his *Experiments upon the Human Bile and Reflections on the Biliary Secretions* (1772), which aroused for its author considerable notice and was reckoned a valuable contribution to the science of medicine, being translated into several languages. He returned to Virginia in 1773 but seems to have had no prominent part in the preliminary controversies of the Revolution. During the war he was active as a surgeon in the Virginia militia and is referred to frequently in the official records as physician-general and director of hospitals for the state. On May 22, 1779, he was married to Elizabeth Selden, daughter of Cary Selden. In the same year he was appointed professor of anatomy and medicine at the College of William and Mary but in 1783 the chair was discontinued and it is uncertain whether he did any teaching. By the latter year he had probably removed to Richmond, where he made his home for the rest of his life. He was ranked as one of the most eminent physicians in the state, was president of the state medical society in 1820 and 1821, and was honored by the dedication of Volume I of the *Philadelphia Journal of Medical and Physical Sciences* for 1820.

McClurg's political career may be said to have begun in 1782–83 when Madison advocated, but did not bring about, his appointment to succeed Livingston as secretary of foreign affairs for the United States. In 1787, after Patrick Henry and Richard Henry Lee had declined to serve in the Philadelphia Convention, McClurg was selected to complete the Virginia delegation. His activities in the Convention centered in the advocacy of a life tenure for the executive and a federal negative on state laws. The McClurg motion for life tenure for the executive received the votes of four of the ten states then represented, though part of its support was probably due to the hope that provision for a stronger executive might be made through the medium of compromise. McClurg insisted that the executive be kept as far from legislative control as possible and his efforts to make the executive independent of its rival branch undoubtedly were rewarded in the provisions for the administrative branch in the completed constitution. His only political services of consequence after the federal convention were rendered as a member of the executive council for Virginia during the early years of Washington's administration. According to Madison McClurg's talents were of the highest order but he was modest and unaccustomed to exert them. Possibly his interest in his profession precluded any pronounced ambition toward a political career.

[See J. B. McCaw, *A Memoir of Jas. McClurg, M.D.* (1854); H. A. Kelly and W. L. Burrage, *Am. Medic. Biogs.* (1920); Jas. Thacher, *Am. Medic. Biog.* (1828), vol. I; W. C. Blanton, *Medicine in Va. in the Eighteenth Century* (1931); Max Farrand, *The Records of the Fed. Convention* (3 vols., 1911); H. D. Gilpin, *The Papers of Jas. Madison* (3 vols., 1842); W. P. Palmer and Sherwin McRae, *Calendar of Va. State Papers*, vols. I, V, and VI (1875–86); "McClurg Descent," *Wm. and Mary Coll. Quart.*, Jan. 1893; *Richmond Enquirer*, July 11, 1823; auditor's account book for Virginia during the Revolution.]   F. H. H.

McCLURG, JOSEPH WASHINGTON (Feb. 22, 1818–Dec. 2, 1900), congressman, governor of Missouri, a first cousin of A. C. McClurg [*q.v.*], was born in St. Louis County, Mo. His grandfather, Joseph, came to the United States from Ireland as a refugee in 1798, his family, including Joseph Washington McClurg's father, also named Joseph, following later. The second Joseph married Mary Brotherton, a native of St. Louis County, Mo. Their son, orphaned at an early age, was reared by relatives in Pittsburgh, Pa. He attended school in Xenia, Ohio, and for two years (1833–35) was a student at Miami University, Oxford, Ohio. He then taught for a year or more in Louisiana and Mississippi; later he was admitted to the bar in Texas and practised law there. From 1841 to 1844 he was deputy sheriff of St. Louis County, having married in the former year Mary C. Johnson. In 1849 he was living in Hazelwood, Mo., at which time he joined the California gold seekers, in charge of a caravan of twenty-four ox teams. Back in Missouri again in 1852, McClurg, with two partners, established a large wholesale and retail mercantile business at Linn Creek, which was increasingly prosperous.

Upon the outbreak of the Civil War he immediately took a strong stand for the Union. He organized, equipped (at considerable financial loss), and commanded a home-guard unit, called the Osage Regiment of Missouri Volunteers. Later, he became colonel of the 8th Cavalry, Missouri Militia, but resigned this position in 1862 when he was elected to Congress, in which he served practically three full terms. Though opposed to slavery in principle, he did not liberate the slaves which his wife had inherited until shortly before Lincoln's Emancipation Proclamation. Of great significance for his future political career was the fact that in the House he became an ardent disciple of Thaddeus Stevens [*q.v.*], the bell-wether of radicalism. Moreover, his bitter attacks upon his congressional colleague, Francis P. Blair [*q.v.*], a leading conservative Unionist, endeared him to the hearts of all Missouri radicals. In 1868 McClurg resigned his seat in the House to run for governor of Missouri on the Radical Republican ticket.

Because of the military and strictly partisan enforcement of the noted test oath and registry law, enacted by the legislature in 1865–66, McClurg was elected by a majority of nearly 20,000. During the campaign, at the polls, and throughout his administration, the spirit and the principles of Thaddeus Stevens and the carpetbaggers were logically and proudly set forth in the public utterances and policies of McClurg and his advisers. Their aim was not only to disfranchise the "rebels," but also so to control the election machinery as to render the loyal Union Democrats and the Liberal Republicans powerless. The *St. Louis Dispatch,* in an admittedly partisan broadside (July 17, 1868), asserted that "McClurg is the embodiment of all that is narrow, bigoted, revengeful, and ignorant in the Radical party." If he was ignorant, it was only in the sense that he did not comprehend the shortsightedness of the radical policies. He was, in fact, less a leader than a follower. Such radicals as Charles D. Drake [*q.v.*] and others long since forgotten really dominated the party of which McClurg was the nominal head. The controversies relating to negro and white suffrage claimed the major share of his attention during the two years he was in office. With the test oath and the registry law on the shelf in 1870, he was overwhelmingly defeated for the governorship. The memory of the proscriptions which he sponsored was largely responsible for the fact that Missouri remained in the Democratic column for over thirty years.

After his term as governor he lived at Linn Creek and engaged in various business enterprises. In 1885 he moved to Lebanon, where he lived until his death, except for the years 1889 to 1893, when he was register of the Federal Land Office at Springfield.

[*Gen. Cat. of the Grads. and Former Students of Miami Univ., 1809–1909* (n.d.); G. G. Avery and F. C. Shoemaker, *The Messages and Proclamations of The Governors . . . of Mo.,* vol. IV (1924); T. S. Barclay, "The Liberal Republican Movement in Mo.," *Mo. Hist. Rev.,* Oct. 1925–Oct. 19, 1926; *Pictorial and Geneal. Record of Greene County, Mo.* (1893); *Hist. of Laclede and Camden Counties, Mo.* (1889); *Kansas City Times,* Sept. 4, 1870; *St. Louis Dispatch,* July 17, 1868; *St. Joseph Herald,* Dec. 10, 1869; *Columbia Statesman,* July 24, 1868; *N. Y. Times,* Apr. 24, 1872; *Booneville Weekly Eagle,* May 21, 1870; *Mo. Democrat,* Oct. 1, 1869; *Jefferson City Peoples' Tribune,* Sept. 7, 1870; *St. Louis Globe-Democrat* and *St. Louis Republic,* Dec. 3, 1900; *Booneville Weekly Advertiser,* Dec. 21, 1900.]
H. E. N.

McCOMAS, LOUIS EMORY (Oct. 28, 1846–Nov. 10, 1907), Maryland congressman, senator, jurist, was born near Williamsport, Md., the second child of Frederick C. and Catharine (Angle) McComas. The family was of Scotch-Irish origin, the founder of the American line having settled in Harford County, Md., early in the eighteenth century. McComas' paternal grandfather, Zaccheus, fought in the War of 1812 and subsequently entered the Methodist ministry, holding charges in Baltimore and Williamsport. His maternal grandfather, Henry Angle, of

Pennsylvania origin, was a prosperous Washington County farmer. After an unsuccessful attempt at storekeeping in Springfield, Ill., his parents returned to Maryland where the father engaged first in agriculture and then in the hardware business. Louis McComas received his elementary education in Williamsport, after which he attended St. James College in Maryland and Dickinson College in Pennsylvania, graduating from Dickinson with high honors in 1866. He then began to read law in an office at Cambridge, Md., completed his studies under Judge R. H. Alvey of Hagerstown, was admitted to the bar in 1868, and practised law in the latter city until 1892. On Sept. 23, 1875, he married Leah Humrichouse of Baltimore. To them two daughters were born.

McComas' political career opened with his unsuccessful candidacy as a Republican for a seat in the Forty-fifth Congress. Entering the lists again some years later, he was chosen representative in the Forty-eighth Congress and served four terms, 1883–91, retiring following his defeat for reëlection to the Fifty-second Congress. During these years he developed into an able parliamentarian. His membership on the committee on coinage, weights, and measures and on those on appropriations and ways and means gave him a keen insight into currency and credit problems and several of his speeches on those subjects were used as campaign documents. Through his efforts, Antietam battlefield was placed under governmental control. He is also said to have framed the effective section of the contract labor law ("An act to prohibit the importation and migration of foreigners and aliens under contract or agreement to perform labor in the United States, its Territories, and the District of Columbia") passed in the Second Session of the Forty-eighth Congress. He gained national attention by procuring the passage of a private pension bill over President Cleveland's veto.

In 1892 McComas attended the Republican Convention in Minneapolis as delegate-at-large from Maryland and, being named secretary of the Republican National Committee, served in that capacity during the presidential campaign of 1892. In November of the same year President Harrison appointed him associate justice of the supreme court of the District of Columbia, which position he held until 1899 when he was elected senator from Maryland. During his six years in the upper chamber, he served as chairman of the committee on education and labor and as a member of various other committees. He played a prominent part in drawing up the organic laws of Puerto Rico and the Philippines, was an active supporter of civil-service reform, favored anti-trust legislation, made the Naval Academy his special charge, and took an active interest in the beautification of Washington. In 1900 and 1904 he again represented Maryland as delegate-at-large at the Republican conventions. From 1897 to 1901 he was lecturer on the law of contracts and evidence at the Georgetown University Law School and thereafter lecturer on international law and American foreign relations. For a quarter of a century he served as a trustee of Dickinson College.

McComas retired from the Senate in March 1905 and in July was appointed justice of the court of appeals of the District of Columbia by President Roosevelt. In July 1907, some years after his first wife's death, he married Mrs. Hebe Harrison Muir, the widow of Judge Upton Muir of Kentucky. He was stricken with pneumonia while on his way to Europe with his bride, returned home in feeble health after some weeks in an English hospital, and died of heart failure a month later. Affable and obliging, though possessed of marked judicial dignity, McComas was greatly admired and respected by his constituents, colleagues, and students.

[J. T. Scharf, *Hist. of Western Md.* (1882), vol. II; T. J. C. Williams, *A Hist. of Wash. County, Md.* (1906), vol. II; *Biog. Dir. Am. Cong.* (1928); *Who's Who in America*, 1906–07; the *Evening Star* (Washington), Nov. 11, 1907; the *Sun* (Baltimore), Nov. 11, 1907; Dickinson Coll. records; Georgetown Univ. records; private information.]   L. J. R.

McCOMB, JOHN (Oct. 17, 1763–May 25, 1853), architect, was the son of John and Mary (Davis) McComb. His father, son of James who came to America from Scotland, via North Ireland, in 1732, was born in Princeton, N. J. After his marriage, Apr. 27, 1761, he resided in New York, acting as architect and builder. His best-known work included the Brick Church, 1767, the North Dutch Church, 1769, and the New York Hospital, of which the cornerstone was laid in 1773. Upon the outbreak of the Revolution he took his family to Princeton, where he was made quartermaster in the Continental Army in 1777. He returned to New York in 1783 and was made a City Surveyor on Mar. 16, 1784. He was also influential in the founding of the General Society of Mechanics and Tradesmen in 1785. On his death in New York City, in 1811, he left three children, John and Isaac, both architects, and Elizabeth, who was an amateur artist of some skill.

The younger John was born in New York. He seems to have received the greater part of his culture and professional knowledge from his father, whose assistant he became in 1783. At some time prior to 1790 he made an extended tour of Europe and in that year began his independent career with an engagement to design the façade of Government House in New York (McComb MSS.). From that time on he became one of the busiest of the New York builders and architects. Among his public buildings were three lighthouses, the Montauk (1795) and the Eaton's Neck Light (drawings dated 1798), both still in use, and the Cape Henry Lighthouse (1791), now a national monument to the landing of Captain John Smith. Castle Garden in the Battery, New York, was designed and built by him (Account Books in New York Historical Society). On Oct. 4, 1802, the competition for the New York City Hall was decided by the award of a premium to the design submitted by McComb and Joseph F. Mangin [*q.v.*]. After some conferences and the curtailing of the original drawings, McComb was appointed architect to superintend the construction, and he was in sole charge of the detailing and execution of the design until its completion in 1812. During this period he also designed the New York Free School House (1808), the Hubert Street Fort (1808), Washington Hall, home of the Washington Benevolent Association (1809–12), and subsequently used as a hotel and assembly rooms, Queens Building, Rutgers College (cornerstone laid Apr. 27, 1809), the building of the Society of Mechanics and Tradesmen on Park Place (1802–03), and Alexander Hall of Princeton Theological Seminary (1815).

His most important church was St. John's Chapel on Varick Street (cornerstone laid Sept. 1, 1803), which he did in partnership with his brother Isaac. He was also the architect of the Cedar Street Presbyterian Church (1807), the Murray Street Presbyterian Church (1811–12), and the very beautiful Bleecker Street Presbyterian Church (1825). In 1822, he altered the interior and designed and built a new spire for the Brick Presbyterian Church, originally built by his father. Of his numerous houses, that for John Coles, on Whitehall Street, deserves mention for its size. "The Grange," designed for Alexander Hamilton, still stands in a new location as the rectory for St. Luke's Church, Convent Avenue and 141st Street, New York City. In 1817, on the resignation of B. H. Latrobe [*q.v.*] as architect of the United States Capitol, he was mentioned for the post, and on Dec. 5, 1817, his friend the elder James Renwick [*q.v.*] wrote him from Washington to find out, unofficially, if he would accept it (E. S. Bulfinch, *The Life and Letters of Charles Bulfinch*, p. 207;

Glen Brown, *History of the United States Capitol,* 1900–02, I, 55; Collingwood papers).

McComb was married, Dec. 15, 1792, to Elizabeth, daughter of James Embree Glean. By this marriage he had two children, a son and a daughter. His wife died June 3, 1817, and on June 24, 1821, he married Mrs. Rebecca Rockwell, a widow, who survived him. He was street commissioner of New York City from 1813 to 1821. On Dec. 31, 1816, he was made an Academician of the American Academy of Fine Arts, and in 1818, president of the General Society of Mechanics and Tradesmen. He was a trustee of the Brick Presbyterian Church, 1816–25, and deacon from 1827 until his death. His carefully kept account books reveal alike his generosity and his painstaking attention to detail. In general, his architectural work shows excellent taste, careful study, a refined sense of detail, and well illustrates the persistence of American Colonial tradition, with strong British influence, into the nineteenth century. The French character of the New York City Hall is so exceptional that it is probably to be accounted for by the connection of Joseph François Mangin with its original design.

[Manuscript biography by a great-grand-daughter, Mrs. Helen A. Collingwood, and notes of the family (copies in N. Y. Hist. Soc. and N. Y. City Hall); drawings and papers in the possession of Mrs. Collingwood; McComb Papers and Drawings and Ebenezer Stevens Papers, N. Y. Hist. Soc.; I. N. P. Stokes, *The Iconography of Manhattan Island* (6 vols., 1915–28); *Minutes of the Common Council of the City of N. Y.* (1917), vols. VII–XII; W. H. S. Demarest, *A Hist. of Rutgers Coll.* (1924); Morgan Dix, *A Hist. of the Parish of Trinity Ch. . . . N. Y.,* vol. II (1901); Thomas Earle and C. T. Congdon, *Annals of the Gen. Soc. of Mechanics and Tradesmen of the City of N. Y., 1785–1880* (1882); *National Advocate* (N. Y.), June 4, 1817, June 30, 1821; *N. Y. Herald,* May 27, 1853.] T. F. H.

McCONNEL, JOHN LUDLUM (Nov. 11, 1826–Jan. 17, 1862), author, was born in what was then Morgan but is now Scott County, Ill., the son of Murray and Mary Mapes McConnel. His father was a self-made pioneer lawyer who served in both branches of the state legislature and in the Black Hawk War, and was appointed by President Pierce one of the auditors of the United States Treasury, a post which he held for about five years. The eldest son John studied law under his father and at the Transylvania law school, from which he was graduated in 1843 in a class of twenty-nine. He enlisted for service in the war with Mexico and before leaving the rendezvous of his company at Alton, Ill., he was made first lieutenant. After the battle of Buena Vista, where he was wounded, he became captain in the 1st Illinois Volunteers. Returning to Jacksonville, he took over his father's practice, but he was as much interested in creative writing

as in his professed deity, the law. His first works were melodramatic novels. *Grahame: or Youth and Manhood* (1850) is an improbable tale which leaves the modern reader quite out of sympathy with any of the characters or situations. *Talbot and Vernon* (1850), a tale of love intrigue and the war in Mexico, with some excellent descriptions of that region and of court scenes in the West, and *The Glenns: A Family History* (1851), interesting for the author's pictures of the Southwest and the turbulent society of frontier Texas, throw valuable light on the social history of the period. *Western Characters: or Types of Border Life in the Western States* (1853) is a valuable descriptive volume which portrays the picturesque figures of the frontier. At the time of his premature death in 1862 he was engaged in a study to be entitled "History of Early Exploration in America," treating especially the work of the early Roman Catholic missionaries. Shortly after his return from Mexico in 1847, McConnel was married to Eliza Deniston of Pittsburgh. She, with two children, survived him.

[G. M. McConnel, "Some Reminiscences of My Father, Murray McConnel," *Jour. of the Ill. State Hist. Soc.,* Apr. 1925; Newton Bateman and others, *Hist. Encyc. of Ill. and Hist. of Morgan County* (1906); C. M. Eames, *Hist. Morgan and Classic Jacksonville* (1885); *Daily Ill. State Jour.* (Springfield), Jan. 28, 1862; family records.] D. A. D.

McCOOK, ALEXANDER McDOWELL (April. 22, 1831–June 12, 1903), soldier, came of a Scotch-Irish family known as "the fighting McCooks" from the fact that his father with eight sons and the five sons of his uncle saw distinguished service in the Union forces during the Civil War. His paternal grandfather, George McCook, emigrated from Ireland about 1780 and settled in Canonsburg, Pa., whence he subsequently moved to Carroll County, Ohio. Daniel and John, in the second generation, also settled in Ohio and here, in Columbiana County, Alexander was born to Daniel and Martha (Latimer) McCook. He was the fifth of nine sons, of whom one died in infancy. He graduated from the United States Military Academy in 1852, thirtieth in a class of forty-seven members, and was commissioned lieutenant in the 3rd Infantry. After service at frontier posts and field duty against hostile Utes and Apaches, in 1858–61 he was assistant instructor in infantry tactics at West Point. The day that President Lincoln called for volunteers, he was commissioned colonel, 1st Ohio Volunteers, and in the action at Vienna, Va., on June 17, and at Bull Run, July 21, 1861, was commended for coolness and good conduct.

He commanded a brigade in Kentucky until

January 1862, and a division in the Army of the Ohio until the end of June of that year, and distinguished himself at Corinth, Nashville, and Shiloh, receiving the brevets of lieutenant-colonel and of colonel. Promotion to the grade of major-general of volunteers followed, July 17, 1862, and during the operations of the Army of the Ohio in northern Alabama, Tennessee, and Kentucky, McCook commanded the I Army Corps at Nashville and in the battle of Perryville, Ky. (Oct. 8, 1862). For distinguished service in the latter engagement, he was brevetted brigadier-general, United States Army. After the organization of the Army of the Cumberland, he commanded the XIV and later the XX Corps with distinction, serving in the battle of Stone River, the advance on Tullahoma, and the battle of Chickamauga. He received blame for the disaster to the Union forces at Chickamauga and was relieved from command, Oct. 6, 1863, but a court of inquiry, convened at his request, exonerated him from responsibility. He was on duty with the defenses of Washington until October 1864, commanded the District of Eastern Arkansas until May 1865, and served with a joint committee of Congress, investigating Indian affairs, until October of the same year. For gallant and meritorious services in the field throughout the war he received the brevet of major-general, United States Army, Mar. 13, 1865.

In post-war army reorganization, McCook was appointed lieutenant-colonel, 26th Infantry, at the age of thirty-seven years, and again saw arduous frontier service. In 1874–75 he was acting inspector-general and from 1875 to 1881, aide-de-camp to Gen. William T. Sherman. He was promoted colonel, 6th Infantry, Dec. 15, 1880, and after protracted duty in the West and a period in command of the Infantry and Cavalry School at Fort Leavenworth, Kan., was promoted brigadier-general (1890) and major-general (1894). He was retired from active service for age, Apr. 22, 1895. In May 1896 he represented the United States at the coronation of Nicholas II as Czar of Russia, and in September 1898 was a member of the commission appointed to investigate the conduct of the War with Spain. He died at Dayton, Ohio. McCook was twice married: on Jan. 23, 1863, to Kate Phillips of Dayton, Ohio, who died in 1881, and on Oct. 8, 1885, to Annie Colt of Milwaukee, who survived him, as did three daughters by his first marriage.

[J. H. Wilson, biographical sketch in *Thirty-fifth Ann. Reunion, Asso. Grads. U. S. Mil. Acad.* (1904); J. H. Woodward, *Gen. A. McD. McCook at Stone River* (1892); *Battles and Leaders of the Civil War* (4 vols., 1887–88); *Personal Memoirs of U. S. Grant* (2 vols..

1885–86); *Personal Memoirs of P. H. Sheridan* (2 vols., 1888); *War of the Rebellion: Official Records (Army)*; Whitelaw Reid, *Ohio in the War* (1868), I, 806–09, severely critical of McCook's work at Perryville, Stone River, and Chickamauga; Henry Howe, "The Fighting McCooks," in *The Scotch-Irish in America, Proc. and Addresses of the Sixth Cong.* (1894); G. W. Cullum, *Biog. Reg. U. S. Mil. Acad.* (3rd ed., 1891); *Who's Who in America*, 1901–02; *Army and Navy Jour.*, June 20, 1903; *Ohio State Jour.* (Columbus), June 13, 1903.]

C. D. R.

McCOOK, ANSON GEORGE (Oct. 10, 1835–Dec. 30, 1917), Union soldier, congressman, publisher, was born in Steubenville, Ohio, a first cousin of Alexander McDowell McCook [*q.v.*] and the second son of Dr. John McCook, a native of Canonsburg, Pa., and of Catharine Julia (Sheldon) of Hartford, Conn. He was brought up in the town of Lisbon (then New Lisbon), Ohio. At the age of fifteen he left school and went to Pittsburgh where he was employed in a drugstore. After two years in Pittsburgh he taught school at a little crossroads town near Lisbon and worked as transitman on a local railway. When news of the discovery of gold in California reached the Middle West, he went overland to the coast with a party taking cattle across the plains. For the next five years he lived as a miner and businessman in California and Nevada. Upon his return to Ohio in 1859 he read law in the office of his cousin, George W. McCook of Steubenville, law partner of Edwin M. Stanton. The following year he was admitted to the bar.

McCook belonged to the famous "fighting McCooks" of Ohio. He, with his father and four brothers, was at that time a War Democrat, and upon the outbreak of the Civil War the five sons, among whom were Edward M., Henry C., and John James McCook [*qq.v.*], entered the military or naval service of the United States. Anson George organized a company of infantry at Steubenville and on Apr. 17, 1861, was commissioned captain in the 2nd Ohio Volunteers. He rose successively through the grades of major, lieutenant-colonel, and colonel of the same regiment, and when it was mustered out he became colonel of the 194th Ohio Volunteers. In March 1865 he was brevetted brigadier-general of volunteers "for meritorious services." During the war he took part in many engagements, including the battles of Bull Run, Perryville, Stone River, Chattanooga, Lookout Mountain, Missionary Ridge, Kenesaw Mountain, and Atlanta. He was also in the Shenandoah campaign which preceded the surrender of Lee at Appomattox.

Upon his honorable discharge at the close of the war he returned to Steubenville, where from 1866 to 1872 he was assessor of internal revenue. In 1873 he moved to New York and was admitted to practice in the courts of that state. Political honors soon came to him in his new domicile, and in 1876, 1878, and 1880 he was elected to the national House of Representatives from the eighth congressional district of New York. His congressional record was creditable but not outstanding. In 1884 he was chosen secretary of the United States Senate, a position which he retained until August 1893. Two years later he was appointed chamberlain of the City of New York by Mayor William L. Strong and served until the expiration of the latter's term of office in 1897.

When he removed from Ohio to New York, McCook became interested in the *Daily Register* (later the *New York Law Journal*) and was for many years its editor. He was also president of the New York Law Publishing Company and a member of many organizations. In May 1886 he married Hettie B. McCook, a daughter of his cousin and law preceptor. A son and a daughter were born to them. McCook died at the age of eighty-three at his home in New York.

[*N. Y. Times*, Dec. 31, 1917; *N. Y. Law Jour.*, Jan. 2, 1918; *Who's Who in America*, 1916–17; Whitelaw Reid, *Ohio in the War* (1868), I, 974; *War of the Rebellion: Official Records (Army)*, 1 ser., XX, XXIII, XXX–XXXII, XXXVIII, XXXIX, XLVI, LII; *Biog. Dir. Am. Cong.* (1928); Henry Howe, "The Fighting McCooks," in *The Scotch-Irish in America, Proc. and Addresses of the Sixth Cong.* (1894).]   H. J. C.

McCOOK, EDWARD MOODY (June 15, 1833–Sept. 9, 1909), Union soldier, minister to Hawaii, governor of Colorado Territory, was born at Steubenville, Ohio, of a family which gave many famous soldiers to the Civil War. A brother of Anson George, Henry Christopher, and John James, and a first cousin of Alexander McDowell McCook [*qq.v.*], he was the eldest son of Dr. John McCook, a physician, and Catharine Julia (Sheldon). Educated in public schools at Steubenville, he went to Minnesota when he was sixteen, and in the gold rush of the year 1849 went on to Colorado, where he practised law. In 1859, he represented his district in the legislature of Kansas Territory, and when Kansas became a state he was a leader in the organization of the Territory of Colorado. Upon the fall of Sumter, he joined the Kansas Legion in Washington, and in recognition of his success in carrying dispatches to General Scott through unfriendly Maryland lines, was appointed a lieutenant of cavalry. During the southern campaigns of 1862–63 he made a brilliant record, being brevetted first lieutenant for gallant services at Shiloh, captain for services at Perryville, Ky., major for his conduct at Chickamauga, and lieutenant-colonel for cavalry operations in East Tennessee. He was appointed brigadier-general of volunteers, Apr. 27, 1864, and commanded the cavalry of the Army of the Cumberland. His most brilliant exploit of the war was performed during the Atlanta campaign when he prevented the reinforcement of General Hood, then shut up in Atlanta. Sweeping with his cavalry in the rear of the city, he destroyed the Confederate transportation trains, cut railroads leading south, captured many prisoners, and finally made his way back to rejoin the main Union army at Marietta, Ga. At the close of the war he received the brevets of brigadier-general, United States Army, and major-general of volunteers in recognition of his record.

After the close of hostilities he acted as military governor of Florida, until June 1865. On May 9, 1866, he resigned his military commission, and until 1869 was United States minister to Hawaii. During his term in this office he negotiated a treaty of commercial reciprocity. In 1869 President Grant appointed him governor of the Territory of Colorado. As governor, he organized a school system, encouraged the building of railroads, secured the opening up of vast mineral and agricultural lands by the transfer of the troublesome Ute Indians to Utah, and was instrumental in the building of water-works for the city of Denver. He was unpopular in Colorado, where he was regarded as an office-seeker trading upon his military reputation; enemies charged him with participation in Indian frauds. At the request of the people of the territory Grant did not reappoint him in 1873, but in January 1874, after McCook had declined the office of postmaster general, the President renominated him for the governorship, and six months later the appointment was ratified by one vote. Early the next year he resigned.

After his retirement from public life, McCook had financial interests in many great enterprises in Colorado and the West, and at one time he was the largest real-estate owner and tax-payer in the Territory. Later, his investments extended to European telephone syndicates and to rich mines in Mexico. He was an early advocate of woman's suffrage. McCook was married twice: first, in 1865 to Mary Thompson of Peoria, Ill., grand-daughter of Charles Thompson, secretary of the Continental Congress, and after her death, which occurred in 1874, to Mary McKenna of Colorado. He died of Bright's disease in Chicago and was buried at Steubenville, Ohio.

[*Who's Who in America*, 1908–09; Henry Howe, "The Fighting McCooks," in *The Scotch-Irish in America, Proc. and Addresses of the Sixth Cong.* (1894); H. M. Cist, *The Army of the Cumberland* (1882) and J. D. Cox, *Atlanta* and *The March to the Sea* (both 1882), in Campaigns of the Civil War, vols. VII, IX, X; *Battles and Leaders of the Civil War*, vols. III,

IV (1888) ; *Mil. Order of the Loyal Legion of the U. S., Commandery of D. C., War Papers, 29* (1898) ; Frank Hall, *Hist. of the State of Col.,* vols. I, II (1889–90) ; *Daily Rocky Mountain News* (Denver), for 1874, esp. June 20 ; *Rocky Mountain News* and *Denver Republican,* Sept. 10, 1909 ; *Inter Ocean* (Chicago), Sept. 10, 1909.]   C. D. R.

McCOOK, HENRY CHRISTOPHER (July 3, 1837–Oct. 31, 1911), Presbyterian clergyman, naturalist, third son of Dr. John McCook and Catharine Julia (Sheldon), was born at New Lisbon, Ohio. His father was of Scotch-Irish and his mother of New England descent. A brother of Anson George, Edward Moody, and John James, and a first cousin of Alexander McDowell McCook [*qq.v.*], he belonged to that branch of the family which gave rise in the army to the expression "the fighting McCooks." He received the degree of A.B. in 1859 from Jefferson College, Canonsburg, Pa. Although attracted to the law at first, he changed to theology and studied at the Western Theological Seminary, Pittsburgh, in 1860–63. He was ordained to the Presbyterian ministry in Steubenville, Ohio, in 1861, but in July of that year, the Civil War having begun, he resigned his charge (the Presbyterian Church at Clinton, DeWitt County, Ill.), and volunteered. He raised two companies and part of a third, and served as first lieutenant in the 41st Illinois Volunteers and later as chaplain of that regiment, 1861–62. In 1863–64 he preached at Clinton, Ill., and from 1864 to 1869 was engaged in city mission work in St. Louis. In 1870 he became the pastor of the Tabernacle Presbyterian Church in Philadelphia, and remained in this post until 1902, when he resigned on account of ill health. During the Spanish-American War he was very active in hospital and relief work.

McCook was primarily a clergyman, but he was also an ardent naturalist. In 1873 he began to study spiders ; later he became interested in ants, and all through his active life, from 1876 to 1909, he published from time to time technical papers of much value, the majority of them relating to either spiders or ants. He also wrote many semi-popular papers and several books. One of the best-known of his books was *Tenants of an Old Farm: Leaves from the Note Book of a Naturalist* (1885). His last popular work was entitled *Ant Communities and How they are Governed, a Study in Natural Civics* (1909). Most of his more technical papers were published in the *Proceedings* of the Academy of Natural Sciences of Philadelphia and the *Transactions* of the American Entomological Society. Two articles, "Mound-Making Ants of the Alleghanies, Their Architecture and Habits" (*Transactions of the American Entomological Society,*

November 1877) and *The Natural History of the Agricultural Ant of Texas* (1879), brought him prominently to the attention of the entomological world. A later paper entitled *The Honey Ants of the Garden of the Gods and the Occident Ants of the American Plains* (1882), based on original field observations, made during a visit to the West, was widely read. This and his earlier papers showed him to be a keen observer, and his publications continue to be highly regarded.

His most notable work was a large, three-volume quarto called *American Spiders and Their Spinning Work: A Natural History of the Orb-Weaving Spiders of the United States with Special Regard to Their Industry and Habits.* The first volume, issued in 1889, relates to "Snares and Nests"; the second (1890), to "Motherhood and Babyhood, Life and Death"; and the third volume (1893) is composed of "Biological Notes, Descriptions of Species." The work is admirably illustrated, containing 853 text figures and forty colored lithographic plates of 913 figures. It was printed privately in an edition of 250 copies. McCook's published bibliography contains 101 titles. Of these writings eleven are verses and hymns, two are tracts, sixty are scientific papers, and the rest include addresses, sermons, teaching outlines, and stories. Among his non-scientific writings are *The Latimers— A Tale of the Western Whiskey Insurrection* (1897), *The Flag at Cedar Creek—A Ballad for the War of the Union* (1907), *Lincoln and His Veterans, a Centenary Ode* (1909), *Quaker Ben —A Tale of Colonial Pennsylvania in the Days of Thomas Penn* (1911), and *Prisca of Patmos— A Tale of the Time of Saint John* (1911). He married in 1860 Emma C. Herter, who died in 1897. In 1899 he married Mrs. Eleanor D. S. Abbey.

[P. P. Calvert, bibliographical account, in *Entomological News,* Dec. 1911 ; *Jour. Presbyt. Hist. Soc.,* McCook Memorial Number, Dec. 1911 ; *Ohio Archaeol. and Hist. Soc. Pubs.,* vol. VI (1900) ; *Press* (Phila.), Nov. 1, 1911.]   L. O. H.

McCOOK, JOHN JAMES (Feb. 2, 1843–Jan. 9, 1927), Protestant Episcopal clergyman, educator, was born in New Lisbon, Ohio, fifth and youngest son of John, a physician, and Catharine Julia (Sheldon) McCook, and brother of Edward Moody, Anson George, and Henry Christopher [*qq.v.*], and Roderick S. McCook. Alexander McDowell McCook [*q.v.*] was his first cousin. He attended Jefferson (now Washington and Jefferson) College, 1858–60. At the outbreak of the Civil War he was reading law in Steubenville, Ohio. His four brothers and an uncle, Daniel McCook, with his eight sons, enlisted in the service of the Union and made a record that gave them the name of "the fighting McCooks." As a lad of eighteen, John James helped to organize a company which was mustered into the 1st Regiment of Virginia Volunteers. He rose from private to be second lieutenant, served throughout McClellan's West Virginia campaign, and was later attached to McClellan's headquarters as acting assistant-quartermaster. Declining a permanent staff appointment, he entered Trinity College, Hartford, Conn., from which he was graduated in 1863. He studied a few months in the College of Physicians and Surgeons in New York and then transferred to the Berkeley Divinity School, graduating in 1866. In that year he was admitted to deacon's orders in the Protestant Episcopal Church and, on June 7, married Eliza Sheldon Butler of Hartford. After a year in St. John's Church, East Hartford, he was ordained priest (1867) and became rector of St. John's Church, Detroit, Mich., but returned in 1868 to the church in East Hartford which he served thenceforth until his death in 1927. In 1883 he began forty years of teaching as instructor of Latin in Trinity College. In 1886 he was made professor of modern languages. At different times he taught German, French, Italian, and Spanish, finally specializing in German.

Though voluntarily carrying more than the usual quantity of class work and active in building up his East Hartford church and a summer congregation in Niantic, he took vigorous part in civic affairs. In 1890 he was chairman of a "Committee to Confer with the Selectmen in the Matter of Outdoor Alms in the Town of Hartford." The *Report* submitted in 1891 led to a reform of abuses. In the years following, McCook started a movement to establish a state reformatory for youthful delinquents and in 1895 was appointed chairman of the first commission of the Connecticut Reformatory. After agitating for some time against the prevalent bribing of voters, he became in 1901 chairman of a nonpartisan committee which, with the cooperation of the two major political parties, succeeded in putting a stop to the practice in Hartford. In 1901, also, he was elected a member of the high-school committee of Hartford, on which he served until 1915, the last two years as chairman.

In his civic activities he always sought exact knowledge, especially of a statistical character, and thus found matter for a number of publications. His most considerable contribution is the *Report of the Special Committee on Outdoor Alms* (1891), referred to above, of which he was the author although his name does not appear on the title page. The report is broader than

the title indicates, since indoor relief is also considered and the Appendix contains material on methods followed in other places. At the time of issue it was the most informing American publication on official poor-relief. From 1892 to 1901 he published articles on venal voting, tramps, the saloon, and pauperism, in the *Forum*, the *Independent, Charities Review,* and *Journal of Social Science.* The most entertaining of these papers are the "Leaves from the Diary of a Tramp" which appeared in the *Independent* at intervals between Nov. 21, 1901, and June 26, 1902. All his papers are well-written and interesting because of their concrete detail, but his writings do not reveal the dynamic personality of the man and the deep impression which he ¬made on those who knew him personally.

[Henry Howe, "The Fighting McCooks," in *The Scotch-Irish in America, Proc. and Addresses of the Sixth Cong.* (1894); *Who's Who in America,* 1926–27; *Trinity College Bulletin—Necrology,* 1926–27; *Hartford Courant* and *Hartford Times,* Jan. 10, 1927; *Trinity Tripod,* Jan. 14, 1927.]

G. A. K.

McCORD, DAVID JAMES (January 1797– May 12, 1855), editor and agitator, was born in St. Matthew's Parish, S. C., the son of Russell and Hannah (Turquand) McCord. His grandfather, John McCord, emigrated from Ireland and about 1750 acquired lands and the ferry on the Congaree known afterwards by his name. David McCord left the South Carolina College in his senior year (1813–14). He studied law and was admitted to the bar in Columbia in 1818. With his partner, H. J. Nott [*q.v.*], he began a series of reports on cases in the state courts (*Reports of Cases . . . in the Constitutional Court,* 2 vols., 1820–21), and, after the dissolution of the partnership in 1821, he continued the series (*Reports of Cases . . . in the Constitutional Court,* I, II, 1822–23; *Reports of Cases in the Court of Appeals,* III, IV, 1826–30; *Chancery Cases,* I, II, 1827–29). In 1822 he became the partner of W. C. Preston. His editorship of the *Columbia Telescope* began in 1823, at the time that Dr. Thomas Cooper [*q.v.*] was leading the agitation of the tariff question in South Carolina. McCord agreed with him; the *Telescope* became the most violent of all the nullification papers, and the editor himself one of an influential group of state leaders in Columbia. In 1832 he was elected to the House of Representatives. After their victory in 1833 the nullifiers determined to clinch their doctrine of state sovereignty by forcing the oath of allegiance upon all state officers. This harsh business, from which the chief leaders shrank, he took in hand, and one of his distinguished opponents afterwards declared him "about the bitterest politician" with whom he had been acquainted (O'Neall, *post,* II, 510). His service in the legislature continued until 1837, when he was elected president of the Columbia branch of the Bank of the State (*Miller's Planters' and Merchants' Almanac,* 1837–41). He lost his position in 1841 because of his support of the Whig party in the preceding year. The death of Dr. Cooper in 1839, after he had edited five volumes of the *Statutes at Large of South Carolina* (1836–39), resulted in McCord's assignment to the task, and the remaining five volumes, including an elaborate index, were completed in three years more.

At various other times he served as intendant of Columbia, as trustee for the South Carolina College, and as trustee for the new state hospital for the insane. A year after the death of his first wife, Emmeline Wagner of Charleston, he married on May 2, 1840, Louisa Susanna Cheves, the gifted daughter of Langdon Cheves [*qq.v.*]. "Lang Syne," her plantation in St. Matthew's Parish, became their home, although they later built a house in Columbia, where they resided for a part of each year. He also owned cotton-land in Alabama, which he sold before his death. During this period of his life his unchanged political and economic principles found expression in a number of able articles or reviews in the *Southern Quarterly Review* (Apr. and Oct. 1846—reviews of Polk's message and Calhoun's report; initialed reviews, Oct. 1847, Apr. and Jan. 1850). Hot-tempered, impulsive, but frank, cheerful, and a lover of good company, he lacked neither friends nor enemies. He was small but well built and, refusing all challenges, met insults instantly with fist or cane.

[Notes and copies of a few letters in the possession of Mrs. John Bennett, Charleston, and David McCord Wright, Savannah; McCord's will in the Richland County Courthouse; J. B. O'Neall, *Biog. Sketches of the Bench and Bar of S. C.* (1859), vol. II; M. LaBorde, *Hist. of the S. C. College* (1859), pp. 451, 286; J. M. Fraser, "Louisa C. McCord," *Bulletin of the Univ. of S. C.,* no. 91 (1920); Dumas Malone, *The Public Life of Thomas Cooper* (1926); J. P. Carson, *Life, Letters, and Speeches of James Louis Petigru* (1920); E. J. Scott, *Random Recollections* (1884), pp. 56–57.]

R. L. M—r.

McCORD, LOUISA SUSANNA CHEVES (Dec. 3, 1810–Nov. 23, 1879), woman writer of the ante-bellum South, was born in Charleston, S. C., the daughter of Langdon Cheves [*q.v.*] and Mary Elizabeth (Dulles) Cheves. Her ancestors were of Scotch, Irish, and Huguenot extraction and represented the best element in South Carolina society. Her father gave her the education usual to girls of her day, sending her to Grimshaw's School in Philadelphia, and later employing M. and Mme. Picot, French émigrés,

to instruct her in languages before her presentation to Philadelphia and Washington society. He further allowed and encouraged her to study mathematics and other unusual branches under the tutor instructing her brothers. But the greatest educational influence she received was the society of her father and his eminent friends, and at an early age she became interested in questions pertaining to her state and to the South. In 1840 she was married to David James McCord [*q.v.*], a distinguished lawyer. They lived at "Lang Syne," her plantation near Fort Motte, S. C., and here she spent her busiest and most fruitful years. The care of the plantation and its several hundred negroes took most of her time, but she found leisure for translating and writing political and economic reviews and essays and poetry.

In 1855 her husband died, and for two years she sought solace in traveling through Europe. Upon her return she settled in Columbia, S. C., and lived there nearly all of her remaining years. During the Civil War her means, time, and sympathy were devoted to the cause that her state had espoused. In 1861 she became president of the Soldier's Relief Association and in the same year president of the Lady's Clothing Association, in which capacity, from her own funds, she armed and clothed the company under her son, Capt. Langdon Cheves McCord. Upon the death of her son at the battle of Second Manassas, she devoted herself to nursing, feeding, and clothing the soldiers in the military hospital housed in the dormitories of the South Carolina College in Columbia. After the Civil War, her family broken, her means diminished, and her dreams shattered, she retired to Charleston, dying there in November 1879. She was buried in Magnolia Cemetery.

Although her heroic labors during the Civil War overshadow the rest of her achievements, her writings are notable contributions to Southern literature. In 1848 she published a translation from Frédéric Bastiat's *Sophismes Économiques.* It influenced all of her subsequent political thinking. Her essays, contributed to various Southern journals, polemic, satiric, and always clear and coherent, were conservative, proslavery, and pro-Southern. Her ideal was a South with Southern culture, classic learning, and with economic independence based upon slavery and cotton. Her attitude toward slavery was that of the aristocratic Southern planter, an attitude expressed in the statement: "Christian slavery, in its full development, free from the fretting annoyance and galling bitterness of abolition interference, is the brightest sunbeam which Omniscience has destined for his [the negro's] existence" (the *Southern Quarterly Review,* January 1853, p. 120). *My Dreams,* her only volume of poetry, does not exhibit the vigorous style or maturity of thought of her essays. *Caius Gracchus,* a five-act blank-verse drama based upon the death of Gracchus, contains many of the poet's personal convictions but never rises above the average of the type of closet drama in vogue in the Victorian period.

[In addition to Mrs. McCord's writings see Jessie M. Fraser, *Louisa C. McCord* (1920), which is Bull. of the Univ. of S. C., no. 91; G. A. Wauchope, *The Writers of S. C.* (1910); Mary T. Tardy, *The Living Female Writers of the South* (1872); *Lib. of Southern Lit.,* vol. VIII (1907); W. P. Trent, *Wm. Gilmore Simms* (1892); *News and Courier* (Charleston), Nov. 27, 1879.]
R. D. B.

McCORMACK, JOSEPH NATHANIEL (Nov. 9, 1847–May 4, 1922), physician and sanitarian, was born on a farm near Howard's Mill, Nelson County, Ky. His father, Thomas McCormack, was a native of County Fermanagh, Ireland. His mother, Elizabeth Brown, was of a Pennsylvania family which migrated to Kentucky. He attended the local schools until the age of thirteen, after which he worked on the farm and in a store operated by his father. In 1868 he matriculated in the medical department of the Miami University at Cincinnati, which gave him the degree of M.D. in 1870. He was valedictorian of his class and delivered a thesis upon the physical and mental equality of man and woman. After an interneship in the Cincinnati General Hospital he returned to his father's home in Nelson County, Ky., for practice. In 1875 he moved to Bowling Green.

Here, during an epidemic of yellow fever in 1878–79, he attracted the attention of Gov. Luke P. Blackburn [*q.v.*], himself a physician, with the result that McCormack was appointed to the State Board of Health shortly after its formation in 1879. He had been a general practitioner with a leaning toward surgery, in which branch he was quite expert. The new appointment, however, focused his interest on the problems of public health, particularly those of the rural districts of his native state. When he was appointed secretary of the state board in 1883, he found it necessary to abandon his private practice. During the thirty years of his tenure of this office he was responsible for many noteworthy reforms. In the legislature of 1882 he caused the introduction of the state's first medical practice act, which failed of passage until the session of 1888. He drafted the state's first sanitary code and was a potent influence in its enactment into law. He followed this achievement with a state-wide campaign of education upon sanitary measures which led to a much-needed reorganization of the Kentucky State Medical Society and of its constituent county societies. The success of these activities gave McCormack a national reputation in public-health work. In 1892 he was made a member of the International Quarantine Commission. He was a member of the National Conference of State Boards of Health (1888–94) and of the National Conference of State Licensing and Examining Boards (1899).

His most notable service to the medical profession as a whole was his chairmanship (1899–1913) of the committee on organization of the American Medical Association. His ability as an organizer was recognized by the president, Dr. Charles A. L. Reed of Cincinnati, who found the organization in dire straits from an unworkable constitution and internal dissension. McCormack and his colleagues after a year's work brought in a draft of a new constitution and a plan for the rehabilitation of the society. These were presented at the St. Paul meeting in 1901 and adopted after a prolonged debate. It then became McCormack's function to put through the committee's plan by bringing all eligibles into the society and making them subscribers to its journal. To further these purposes he journeyed from state to state and even from county to county. It is said that he delivered his address, "The New Gospel of Health and Long Life," in a majority of the counties of the United States. As a result, the membership of the society was greatly increased, the subscriptions to the journal multiplied sixfold, and the erection of a permanent home for the association in Chicago was made possible. He was a member of the House of Delegates of the Association (1902–07) and of its Council of Health and Public Instruction (1910–13). He resigned from the Association work in 1913 and from the Kentucky state board the same year, but was retained as state sanitary inspector. In the meantime he had been instrumental in the erection and equipment of a model office and laboratory building in Louisville for the State Board of Health. In this building hangs an oil portrait of him, a gift of the medical profession of the state.

He died in Louisville, his home after 1913, from a cerebral hemorrhage. An ardent advocate of cremation, he directed that such disposal be made of his body. Physically he was above medium height, slight of build in his younger years but taking on more weight in later life. He was notably courteous and dignified, with a gift of persuasion in any cause that he advocated. Many honors came to him. He was made president of the state medical society in 1884 and was elected a member of the state legislature in 1912. In 1888 he received the personal thanks of President Cleveland for his work in the cholera epidemic. He was married in Bowling Green, to Corinne Crenshaw of Glasgow, Ky., on Sept. 14, 1871. A son, Dr. A. T. McCormack, succeeded him on the state board when he resigned in 1913.

[*Ky. Medic. Jour.* (Bowling Green), Jan. 1923, contains a symposium upon the life and work of McCormack by L. S. McMurtry, D. M. Griffith, J. C. W. Beckham, A. T. McCormack, and others; and prints his address on "The New Gospel of Health and Long Life." See also *Jour. Am. Medic. Asso.*, May 13, 1922, portrait; H. A. Kelly in H. A. Kelly and W. L. Burrage, *Dict. Am. Medic. Biog.* (1928); *Courier-Journal* (Louisville), May 5, 1922.]   J. M. P—n.

McCORMICK, CYRUS HALL (Feb. 15, 1809–May 13, 1884), inventor, manufacturer, and philanthropist, the eldest son of Robert [*q.v.*] and Mary Ann (Hall) McCormick, was born on "Walnut Grove" farm, Rockbridge County, Va., and died in Chicago. His formal education was limited, and it was not until he was twenty-two that his latent inventive ability became fully evident. In the spring of 1831 he invented and took out a patent for a hillside plow of original design. As the harvest of that year approached his father again attempted to perfect a reaping machine, an idea upon which he had been engaged spasmodically for twenty years. Following his father's final abandonment of the problem, Cyrus decided to undertake its solution. Avoiding Robert McCormick's mistakes, he constructed a crude machine, designed upon entirely different principles, and tried it upon ripe wheat at "Walnut Grove." Encouraged by the result, he built another implement with added parts and in the latter part of July gave a successful public trial on late oats in the field of John Steele. The seven fundamental principles contained in this reaper, the divider, reel, straight reciprocating knife, fingers or guards, platform, main wheel and gearing, and the front-side draft traction, together with their peculiar combination, have proved essential to reaping machinery down to the present day.

In 1832 McCormick introduced improvements and exhibited his machine on several farms near Lexington. It attracted the attention of the editor of the *Lexington Union,* whose commendation (Sept. 14, 21, 28, 1833) was echoed in Edmund Ruffin's *Farmers' Register* (October 1833), and thence in several New York periodicals. During the same year McCormick invented and patented a self-sharpening horizontal plow. In April 1834 the *Mechanics' Magazine* of New York City, published notice of a reaper invented by Obed Hussey [*q.v.*] in 1833. This caused McCormick to warn Hussey of the priority of his own invention (*Ibid.,* May 1834); and on June 21, 1834, he took out a patent. Not sufficiently satisfied that his machine was capable of meeting all the varied conditions of harvest, he decided against placing it on the market. Although he spent some time perfecting his reaper and giving exhibitions during the next few years, he was mainly engaged in the business of making iron. The panic of 1837 and other handicaps spelled the doom of the Cotopaxi iron furnace, leaving him and his father greatly in debt. McCormick now turned seriously to the exploitation of his reaper, and after making further improvements began its commercial manufacture. Early construction took place chiefly at "Walnut Grove" but he sold rights to build the reaper in various sections of the state beginning with 1843. He awoke to the possibilities of sale throughout the country in 1844 and, after a trip through the North and West, arranged for manufacture at Brockport, N. Y., Cincinnati, and other western points. His licensees, less careful than the workers at "Walnut Grove," turned out machines made of inferior materials, poorly assembled. To save the good reputation of his reaper, McCormick resolved to concentrate all manufacture in one place, under his own direction. With clear vision, in 1847, he erected his factory in Chicago, then an insignificant lakeport, and closed other manufacturing contracts as quickly as possible. By 1850 he had succeeded in building up a national business.

Obed Hussey was his first rival. Beginning with 1843 the two men were frequently competitors in the fields and elsewhere, each winning his share of public favor. The fact that McCormick's machine was better designed for reaping and Hussey's for mowing was not appreciated in the early years. Hussey's belated recognition of this fact came too late to maintain him in competition. Eventually his invention became the basis of the modern mower. McCormick had succeeded in convincing the public of the value of his reaper by the time his original patent expired in 1848. The basic principles of his implement now became public property and, although he was partially protected by patents for improvements taken out in 1845 and 1847, a flood of competition ensued. In 1847 McCormick and Hussey were the only manufacturers in the business. By 1850 there were at least thirty rivals and by 1860 over a hundred. Unable to cope with the situation, Hussey sold his patents in 1858 and retired. McCormick in this crisis showed himself so resourceful and fought with such courage that he retained his place as the pioneer inventor and manufacturer of reaping machines. He continued to improve his reaper up to the time of his death. A mowing attachment was added in the fifties. In the sixties and later, McCormick machines were foremost in presenting such developments as the automatic self-raking device, the hand-binding harvester, the wire-binder, and the twine-binder. After 1860 McCormick gave little time to actual invention, but employed skilled mechanics and engineers to make improvements. He also bought new and promising inventions, for which he was always seeking. In an effort to obtain the benefit of his unexpired patents, McCormick's rivals employed skilful patent lawyers to combat reissues, to find fault in the loose wording of specifications, and thus to secure advantages to which they were not entitled. Political influence was brought to bear upon the Patent Office and Congress. The press was resorted to in an effort to prejudice public opinion. When all else failed, patents were frequently infringed. McCormick battled to the last in defense of his rights and for this reason was constantly in litigation. Eminent lawyers, such as William H. Seward, Abraham Lincoln, Edwin M. Stanton, Reverdy Johnson, Judah P. Benjamin, and Roscoe Conkling, were engaged as counsel for or against him. McCormick outfought and outlasted two generations and lived to lead a third. As soon as his reaper was well established in his own country he seized the opportunity offered by the first great world's fair in London, in 1851, to introduce it into Europe. His brilliant success in the field, before an international jury and under most unfavorable circumstances, made him world-famous overnight. The London *Times* (Aug. 12, Sept. 27, 1851) announced that the machine, if it fulfilled its promise, was worth the whole cost of the exhibition; and McCormick was awarded the Council Medal. Although other manufacturers quickly followed him abroad, he continued to win the major prizes at subsequent world fairs at Paris, London, Hamburg, Lille, Vienna, Philadelphia, and Melbourne between 1855 and 1880. The French, particularly appreciative of his services, made him a chevalier and later an officer of the Legion of Honor and in 1879 elected him a member of the French Academy of Sciences as having done more for agriculture than any other living man. In spite of this recognition, Europe was slow to adopt the new labor-saving machines; McCormick received little financial return for his effort abroad, but he did lay the foundation for the foreign business enjoyed by his successors.

McCormick's invention and development of the reaper constitute his chief title to fame. With the advent of the reaper, for the first time the farmer felt secure about his crops. They could be cut whenever they were ready, in a much shorter time than heretofore, with less labor, less cost, and a greater yield. Since the machine could not operate well in fields strewn with rocks, stumps, and other obstructions, agriculturists soon began to clear their lands and put them in better shape for cultivation. The reaper facilitated the rapid settlement of vacant lands by a large emigrant population moving westward. Labor released from the fields by its use helped to build up urban and industrial enterprises. The success of the machine greatly stimulated the invention and adoption of other improved agricultural implements. The reaper also proved an important factor in the Civil War, since it enabled the North to maintain a large force at the front, to feed both them and the civilian population, and in addition to export large quantities of grain to Europe. The income from this trade tended to relieve the tremendous financial strain upon the government. McCormick was not only a pioneer in the invention and evolution of reaping machinery, but also in the creation of modern business methods. He was among the first to introduce the use of field trials, guarantees and testimonials in advertising, cash and deferred payments for merchandise, and to promote the invention and use in his factory of labor-saving machinery designed to insure mass production. A man of vision, great force of character, and boundless energy, he possessed the unusual combination of inventive ability and practicality. More than most men, he was able to convert his creative ideas into reality.

On Jan. 26, 1858, McCormick married Nancy Maria, daughter of Melzar Fowler of Jefferson County, N. Y. Seven children were born to them. Mrs. McCormick, who possessed a practical mind, keen perception, and rare charm, proved an efficient aid to her husband in his career. McCormick, by nature deeply religious, was keenly interested in the Presbyterian church. Attracted by the views of Nathan L. Rice, he induced him to assume the pastorate of his church and later made him editor of the *Presbyterian Expositor,* a religious paper which McCormick acquired (1860) to aid in bringing about a peaceful solution of the difficulties between the North and the South. In 1859 he endowed four professorships in the Presbyterian Theological Seminary of the Northwest, which in 1886 was named McCormick Theological Seminary. The *Expositor* was discontinued at the outbreak of the Civil War, but in 1872 McCormick bought the *Interior* (later known as the *Continent*) and, installing W. C. Gray as editor, made it the leading Presbyterian paper in the West. Following the War, McCormick consistently advocated the reunion of the Presbyterian church in the North and South. He joined the Democratic party in Virginia in the forties, and after 1857 took an active part in its councils until his death. He understood both sections and was deeply disturbed by the rising conflict over the question of slavery. Coincident with the acquisition of the *Expositor,* he bought the *Chicago Times* in 1860, and published it for a year in the hope of influencing the Democratic Party toward a peace policy. He used his influence for Douglas at Baltimore, and later for Breckinridge, and during the War supported the peace efforts of Greeley. McCormick was abroad from 1862 to 1864. Upon his return in the fall of 1864 he ran for Congress on the Democratic ticket against John Wentworth, but was defeated. He served as chairman of the Democratic state central committee in Illinois in 1872 and 1876. McCormick was a director of the Union Pacific prior to the Crédit Mobilier scandals; he displayed much interest in the expansion of the railroads and in the Nicaragua Canal; he made large investments in gold, silver, and copper mines. An advocate of free trade, he was one of the organizers of the Mississippi Valley Society which aimed to promote trade relations between England and the Mississippi Valley. In an endeavor to reestablish the institutions of the South after the War, in 1866 he made gifts to the Union Theological Seminary at Hampden-Sidney, Va., and to Washington College at Lexington, Va. As late as 1880 he served as president of the Virginia Society in Chicago.

[R. G. Thwaites, *Cyrus Hall McCormick and the Reaper* (1909); H. N. Casson, *Cyrus Hall McCormick, His Life and Work* (1909); W. T. Hutchinson, *Cyrus Hall McCormick: Seed-Time, 1809–1856* (1930); L. J. McCormick, *Family Record and Biography* (1896); Edward Stabler, *A Brief Narrative of the Invention of Reaping Machines* (1854); M. F. Miller, *The Evolution of Reaping Machines* (1902); Cyrus McCormick, *The Century of the Reaper* (1931); R. B. Swift, "Who Invented the Reaper?" in *Implement Age,* Apr. 15, 1897; L. J. Halsey, *A Hist. of the McCormick Theol. Seminary . . .* (1893); contemporary agricultural and scientific periodicals, proceedings of agricultural organizations, newspapers, reports of World Fairs, court records, McCormick family papers, and records of McCormick Reaper companies in Lib. of McCormick Hist. Asso., Chicago, Ill.]   H.A.K.

McCORMICK, JOSEPH MEDILL (May 16, 1877–Feb. 25, 1925), journalist, United States senator, was born in Chicago, Ill., the son of Robert Sanderson McCormick [*q.v.*], diplomat, and Katharine Van Etta Medill, the daughter of the editor of the *Chicago Daily Tribune,*

Joseph Medill [*q.v.*]. Brought up under the influence of his maternal grandfather, Medill McCormick imbibed at an early age an aggressive Americanism, though as a result of several years abroad he acquired a competent knowledge of foreign languages and learned to appreciate European points of view. After attending preparatory school at Groton, Mass., he became a student at Yale, and upon his graduation in 1900 returned to Chicago where he entered upon his career as newspaper editor and publisher. Beginning as police reporter for the *Tribune* at a salary of three dollars a week, he served in various capacities until by 1908 all departments of the paper were under his management. With the outbreak of revolt in the Philippines in 1901, he was sent to the seat of the disturbance as a special correspondent for the paper, and after participating in the Samar campaign he traveled about the Far East for several months. During this period he also became associated with Charles A. Otis in the ownership of the *Cleveland Leader* and the *Cleveland News.*

Actively entering into politics in 1908, McCormick became an ardent follower of Theodore Roosevelt, and in the Progressive revolt of 1912, served as a member of the National Campaign Committee, having complete charge of the Western headquarters of the Progressive party and using all the resources of the *Chicago Tribune.* Much against his will, he was elected during the same campaign to the lower house of the Illinois state legislature and in 1914 was reëlected. At this time he led the remaining Progressive recalcitrants back into the Republican party, for in the face of threatening war in Europe he believed that party harmony should prevail. In 1916 he was elected congressman at large from Illinois and served in the Sixty-fifth Congress until 1919, when he took his seat in the Senate. He had definitely imperialistic leanings, although he rejected the extreme position of the *Tribune,* then under the control of his brother. Throughout his senatorial career he was a bitter opponent of the League of Nations and the Versailles Treaty. He stood squarely in his opposition to any entangling alliance, although in 1923 as a member of the committee on foreign relations he admitted the value of a World Court. In domestic affairs he sponsored the McCormick-Good bill, providing for the creation of the Bureau of the Budget, which was vetoed by President Wilson in June 1920, but passed in virtually the same form in the next session and became law in June 1921. He also encouraged the proposed "Great Lakes to Gulf waterway" and favored the child-labor amendment. One of his last acts in the Senate was his effort toward securing the ratification of the Isle of Pines treaty.

In the Republican primary campaign of 1924, McCormick was defeated by Charles S. Deneen. He died in Washington, D. C., on Feb. 25, 1925, only a few days before his term of office was over. He was a vivid person, ambitious and hard-working, and eager for a real knowledge of the matters with which he dealt. In 1917, while still a member of the House of Representatives, he journeyed to the Western front, and again in 1920 and 1924 he was in Europe seeking additional knowledge on the foreign situation. He was survived by his wife, Ruth Hanna, the daughter of Marcus Alonzo Hanna [q.v.], whom he had married on June 10, 1903.

[*Who's Who in America*, 1924–25; *Yale Univ.: Obit. Record of Grads. Deceased During the Year Ending July 1, 1925* (1925); *Current Opinion*, Dec. 1916; the *Independent*, Nov. 22, 1924; the *Nation*, Mar. 11, 1925; L. J. McCormick, *Family Record and Biog.* (1896); *Cong. Record*, 68 Cong., 2 Sess., pp. 5087–89; obituaries in the Chicago newspapers, Feb. 25–27, 1925; *Chicago Tribune* clipping department.]   T. E. S.

McCORMICK, LEANDER JAMES (Feb. 8, 1819–Feb. 20, 1900), manufacturer, philanthropist, the son of Robert [q.v.] and Mary Ann (Hall) McCormick, was born on "Walnut Grove" farm, Rockbridge County, Va., and died in Chicago. He was educated in an old-field school and also received instruction from private tutors. As a boy he manifested much interest in mechanics and when he grew older aided his father and his brother Cyrus Hall McCormick [q.v.] in the construction of reapers in the blacksmith shop at "Walnut Grove." Cyrus engaged Leander to sell, set up, and repair reapers in Virginia in the early forties, and in 1847 brought him to Cincinnati to superintend the manufacture of a hundred reapers at the foundry of A. C. Brown. In 1849 Leander moved to Chicago, where he took charge of the manufacturing division of the McCormick factory, under contract on a salary basis, for one year. From 1850 to 1859 he held the same position on salary. In the latter year Cyrus McCormick gave a share of the profits of the reaper business to Leander and also to another brother, William S. McCormick. This gift was confirmed by contract and the name of the firm was changed from C. H. McCormick to C. H. McCormick & Brothers. Under this arrangement Leander continued to supervise the manufacturing department. Upon the expiration of the contract in 1864 it was renewed for a further period. The death of William in 1865 necessitated a change in the firm, and it was known as C. H. McCormick &

Brother from 1866 to 1874, when it became C. H. and L. J. McCormick. In 1879 Leander was made vice-president of the McCormick Harvesting Machine Company. He retired from active participation in the reaper business in 1881 and ten years later sold out his interest to his nephew, Cyrus H. McCormick.

Leander McCormick introduced a number of minor improvements in the McCormick machines, took out several patents jointly with employees of the engineering division, and was a factor in helping to build up the successful business so closely connected with the name of the family. Because of differences in temperament and opinion, relations between him and Cyrus McCormick were strained long before he retired from the family business; in his *Memorial of Robert McCormick* (1885) he sought to gain for his father, rather than his brother, credit for the invention of the reaper. (For the entire controversy, see Hutchinson, *post*, ch. v.) From 1891 to 1900 he devoted his attention to extensive real-estate holdings acquired in the course of his long residence in Chicago. Being much interested in art, he assembled a notable collection of paintings at his home. In 1874 he gave to the University of Virginia a refractor telescope, built by Alvan Clark [q.v.]. This gift was followed by another, of $18,000, for an observatory, which was named for the donor. In 1896, after years of research, he published a McCormick genealogy under the title, *Family Record and Biography*. On Oct. 22, 1845, he married Henrietta Maria, daughter of John Hamilton of Rockbridge County, Va. Four children were born of this union.

[W. T. Hutchinson, *Cyrus Hall McCormick: Seed-Time, 1809–1856* (1930); *Who's Who in America*, 1899–1900; *Daily Inter Ocean* (Chicago), Feb. 21, 1900; *Farm Implement News* (Chicago), Feb. 22, 1900; *Alumni Bulletin of the Univ. of Va.*, May 1900; Collections of the McCormick Hist. Asso. Lib., Chicago; references cited in bibliography of Cyrus Hall McCormick.]   H. A. K.

McCORMICK, MEDILL [See McCORMICK, JOSEPH MEDILL, 1877–1925].

McCORMICK, RICHARD CUNNINGHAM (May 23, 1832–June 2, 1901), journalist, politician, business man, was born in New York City, the eldest of the seven children of Richard Cunningham and Sarah Matilda (Decker) McCormick. He was of Scotch-Irish ancestry, a descendant of Hugh McCormick who emigrated from Londonderry to Dauphin County, Pa., before 1735. His father, a liberally educated man and for many years a journalist, gave him a classical education in the private schools of the city with a view to his entering Columbia College. His health, however, was not particularly good, and the family decided that it would be better for him to travel. He spent most of 1854 and 1855 in Europe and Asia. He was in the Crimea during the war and while there acted as correspondent for the *Morning Courier and New York Enquirer* and other New York journals. Later he published accounts of his travels and experiences in the Crimea under the titles *A Visit to the Camp before Sevastopol* (1855), and *St. Paul's to St. Sophia* (1860). Soon after his return to America he became editor of the *Young Men's Magazine,* holding the position from 1857 to 1859. During the same period he contributed to various periodicals and lectured frequently. In 1861–62 he was in Washington and with the Army of the Potomac as correspondent for the New York *Evening Post* and the *Commercial Advertiser*. His description of the battle of Bull Run was considered one of the best journalistic accounts printed.

On returning from Europe, McCormick had enthusiastically entered the movement for the formation of the Republican party. His antislavery opinions and the interest he had shown in 1856 secured him a prominent part in the campaign of 1860, when he became a member of the Republican state committee. During this campaign his friendship with both Lincoln and Seward began. In 1862 he was the defeated Republican nominee for the first congressional district of New York. Shortly after he was appointed chief clerk of the Department of Agriculture. In March 1863 he was appointed secretary of the newly organized Arizona Territory, an office which he held until Apr. 10, 1866, when he was appointed governor. In 1869 he was elected territorial delegate to Congress and held the office through three successive terms, but he declined renomination in 1874.

When he went to Arizona he took with him a small printing outfit and started the *Arizona Weekly Miner,* a publication supposed by some to have been devoted to furthering his own political ambitions (Farish, *post,* III, p. 46). Whatever these were, his ambitions for Arizona were intelligently and earnestly put before the government and the people. During his terms as secretary and governor, he was continually active in urging the construction of roads and railroads in order to improve communication between Arizona and New Mexico and California, the development of agriculture along with mining, the development of an educational system, and the intelligent treatment of both the friendly and hostile Indians in the territory. While in Congress, he spoke convincingly in favor of sharp and immediate punishment of the unneces-

sarily brutal Indians, such as the Apaches, and of the advisability of paying the friendly tribes on the reservations for work actually done instead of pauperizing them by gifts outright. He also advocated more government roads and surveys for the territory, restriction of wanton killing of the buffalo, conservation of the forests, and the development of irrigation. In 1876 he was appointed commissioner to the Centennial Exposition in Philadelphia. The following year he was offered the mission to Brazil and in 1879 that to Mexico, both of which he declined. In 1878 he was appointed commissioner general for the United States to the Paris Exposition. At the Exposition he was made a commander of the Legion of Honor. On returning to America, he retired from public life and entered business in New York, but resided at Jamaica, Long Island, where he served as president of the board of education and later as president of the local board of managers of the State Normal and Training School. He became interested in several western mining enterprises. From Apr. 12, 1892, until his death he was a trustee of the Citizens' Savings Bank of New York. In 1886 he ran for Congress but was defeated by the Democratic candidate. In 1894 he ran again and was elected, but refused renomination on account of ill health. He died in Jamaica a few hours after he had suffered a stroke of apoplexy. He was twice married: on Oct. 1, 1865, to Margaret G. Hunt, of Rahway, N. J., who died in 1867; and on Nov. 11, 1873, to Elizabeth Thurman of Columbus, Ohio.

[T. E. Farish, *Hist. of Ariz.* (8 vols., 1915–18) ; H. H. Bancroft, *Hist. of Ariz. and N. M.* (1889) ; S. R. De Long, *The Hist. of Ariz.* (1905) ; R. E. Sloan, *Hist. of Ariz.* (1930), vol. I ; *Biog. Dir. Am. Cong.* (1928) ; L. J. McCormick, *Family Record and Biog.* (1896) ; *Ariz. Weekly Miner,* 1864–69 ; *Young Men's Mag.,* 1857–59 ; the *Evening Post* (N. Y.), July 22–24, 1861 ; *Brooklyn Daily Eagle,* June 3, 1901.]   M. L. B.

McCORMICK, ROBERT (June 8, 1780–July 4, 1846), inventor, the youngest son of Robert and Martha (Sanderson) McCormick, was born and died at "Walnut Grove," Rockbridge County, Va. He was the grandson of Thomas McCormick who emigrated from Ulster in 1734 and settled first in Lancaster County and later in Cumberland County, Pa., where he made a name for himself as a weaver and an Indian fighter. The elder Robert McCormick settled in Juniata County, Pa., in 1755. In July 1779 he moved to the Valley of Virginia and purchased a tract of land lying partly in Rockbridge and partly in Augusta County, which he called "Walnut Grove." Later he fought in the Revolution. His son Robert was educated in a private school in the neighborhood and instructed at home in the strictest tenets of the "Seceder" branch of the Presbyterian church. On Feb. 11, 1808, he married Mary Ann Hall, daughter of Patrick Hall, who was also of Scotch-Irish descent. McCormick, who was medium in height, slight in physique, quiet and reserved in manner, and dreamy, displayed a wide range of interest. Mary Ann Hall was tall and robust, vivacious, possessed of great energy, and extremely practical. Both were deeply religious and noted in the community for integrity of character.

Although interested in music and astronomy, McCormick chiefly distinguished himself by the invention of a number of agricultural implements, designed to lighten the labor of the husbandman. In 1830 and 1831 he invented and took out patents on a hempbrake, gristmill, and a hydraulic machine. About this time he also invented a blacksmith bellows. In 1834 he produced a threshing machine. Although he built a number of his various machines in the blacksmith shop at "Walnut Grove" and sold them to the farmers and planters in the vicinity, his inventions never became commercially valuable. He was interested in too many devices and lacked the patience and perseverance to develop any of them to the point of practicality. Most important perhaps were his attempts to devise a power implement for reaping grain, extending intermittently over more than twenty years. His first reaping machine is said to have been produced as early as 1809 and in the course of years he experimented with several different types of apparatus. The most ingenious of these was a machine, completed in 1831, which consisted of a number of sickles projecting horizontally from a wooden bar. On top of the bar were placed an equal number of vertical cylinders with long spikes. In action the cylinders were designed to revolve, the spikes thrusting the grain across the edges of the sickles. The continued revolutions of the cylinders, aided by a series of leather bands studded with nails, discharged the severed grain to one side in swath. This implement cut straight grain fairly well but proved useless where the stalks were inclined or fallen and the discharging apparatus threw the grain to one side in a tangled mass. Discouraged, McCormick thereupon abandoned the problem.

If he accomplished nothing else, however, his efforts served as the inspiration for one of the world's great inventions, the reaper, devised that same year by his son, Cyrus Hall McCormick [q.v.]. In 1836 Robert and Cyrus built an iron furnace which they called Cotopaxi. Following the panic of 1837 the enterprise failed and threw Robert heavily into debt. In this crisis Cyrus

McCormick turned to his reaper and Robert McCormick began to manufacture it on a contract basis. By 1845 he had won back his financial independence. The next year he caught a severe cold which resulted in his death a few months later. Among his children were William S. and Leander James McCormick [q.v.], both of whom were associated with their elder brother in the development of the reaper.

[The best printed source is W. T. Hutchinson, *Cyrus Hall McCormick: Seed-Time, 1809–1856* (1930). L. J. McCormick, *Memorial of Robert McCormick* (1885), and R. H. McCormick and J. H. Shields, *Robert McCormick, Inventor* (1910), seek to credit the invention of the reaper to Robert rather than his eldest son. See also L. J. McCormick, *Family Record and Biography* (1896); and references cited under Cyrus Hall McCormick. The Collections of the McCormick Hist. Asso. Library, Chicago, contain much material.] H. A. K.

McCORMICK, ROBERT SANDERSON (July 26, 1849–Apr. 16, 1919), diplomat, was born in Rockbridge County, Va., the eldest son of William Sanderson and Mary Ann (Grigsby) McCormick, and grandson of Robert [q.v.] and Mary Ann (Hall) McCormick. His father (1815–1865) inherited the paternal homestead in 1846 but three years later moved to Chicago and joined his two brothers, Cyrus Hall and Leander J. McCormick [qq.v.], in the manufacture of reaping machines. Robert S. McCormick was educated at the preparatory department of the University of Chicago and at the University of Virginia. He inherited from his father not only a liberal fortune but much of his attractive personality and sound business ability. He early decided on a diplomatic career, but not until April 1889 did he obtain the appointment of second secretary of legation at London under Minister Robert T. Lincoln, which position he held for two years. On Feb. 18, 1892, he was appointed resident commissioner in London for the World's Columbian Exposition at Chicago in 1893. He had a difficult task to overcome the indifference and prejudice against participation that existed at that time in England, arising out of the ill feeling engendered by the McKinley tariff. McCormick's public addresses in various parts of the country, particularly that in London before the Society of Arts giving a scholarly review of British trade developments and an analysis of existing trade relations between the two countries, undoubtedly led to the success of his mission. After returning to Chicago from London he served for several years on the Public Library board. He was an ardent collector of books and specialized in Napoleonic biographies and etchings.

On Mar. 7, 1901, President McKinley appointed him minister to Austria, and on May 27, 1902, when the post was raised to an embassy, McCormick became the first American ambassador to Austria-Hungary. On Sept. 26, 1902, President Roosevelt appointed him ambassador to Russia. While there he aided in gaining entrance to Russia for the Associated Press which made possible a lifting of the veil that had hidden events in Russia from the rest of the world. He also succeeded in obtaining from the Russian government recognition of passports granted by the United States to its Jewish citizens. During the Russo-Japanese War he handled the interests of Japan in Russia, and for this the Japanese government decorated him with the first class of the Order of the Rising Sun; while in recognition of his services to Russia during the War the Emperor Nicholas conferred on him the Order of St. Alexander Nevsky. On Mar. 8, 1905, McCormick was promoted to the ambassadorship of France. This change was welcome to him as he had spent much of his earlier life in Paris and had a wide acquaintance there. The Russian climate having undermined his health, he was compelled to resign and left his post on Mar. 2, 1907. The French government as a mark of appreciation of his services conferred on him the grand cordon of the Legion of Honor. He died at his home in Chicago on Apr. 16, 1919, from pneumonia. He was married on June 8, 1876, to Katharine Van Etta Medill, daughter of Joseph Medill [q.v.]. They had two sons, Joseph Medill McCormick [q.v.], who became United States senator for Illinois, and Robert Rutherford McCormick.

[*Who's Who in America*, 1918–19; L. J. McCormick, *Family Record and Biog.* (1896); the *Chicago Tribune* and *N. Y. Times*, Apr. 17, 1919; records in the appointment section of the Department of State.] A. E. I.

MCCORMICK, SAMUEL BLACK (May 6, 1858–Apr. 18, 1928), Presbyterian clergyman, educator, was born in a rural district of Westmoreland County, Pa. His father, James Irwin McCormick, a classical scholar and well-known physician, was a grandson of John McCormick who came to America from Ireland in 1788; his mother, Rachel Long (Black), was a granddaughter of George Long, a captain in the Revolutionary War. Prepared by his father he entered Washington and Jefferson College and graduated with highest honors in 1880. During the next two years he taught Greek at his alma mater, served as an instructor in nearby Canonsburg Academy, and studied law. He was admitted to the Allegheny County bar in 1882 and on Sept. 29 of that year married Ida May Steep of Washington, Pa. Two sons and two daughters were born of this union.

In 1883 he removed to Denver, Colo., where he engaged in the practice of the law for four years, but, finding the legal profession an inadequate field for the realization of his aspirations, he decided to give his life to the Christian ministry. Returning to Pennsylvania, he entered the Western Theological Seminary in Allegheny from which he was graduated in 1890, meanwhile serving intermittently as an instructor in the Western University of Pennsylvania. Ordained (1890) by the Presbytery of Allegheny, he began his active ministry in the Central Presbyterian Church of that city. After four years he was called to the First Presbyterian Church of Omaha, Nebr., which he served three years. In 1897 he accepted the presidency of Coe College, Cedar Rapids, Iowa, where for seven years he grappled with problems of endowment, curriculum enrichment, faculty building, and the awakening of community interest in the rapidly growing institution.

His success in college administration earned for him an invitation to the chancellorship of the Western University of Pennsylvania, a dormant old college in Allegheny with a small group of recently affiliated professional schools in Pittsburgh. Intense loyalty to his native state made his acceptance inevitable. Here for sixteen years (1904–20) he wrought out his enduring monument, a modern university. He organized an educational program based on the obligations of the institution to the community; he purchased a new campus in the civic center of Pittsburgh and constructed modern buildings thereon; he secured appropriations from the state legislature for buildings and for maintenance; he had the name of the institution changed to University of Pittsburgh (1908) in order to win greater local interest and support and to characterize more accurately its field of service; he raised the scholastic standards, coordinated and integrated the constituent schools, secured the endowment of the Mellon Institute of Industrial Research, and created schools of education and economics and a summer session. In 1920 he was retired from active service with the title of chancellor emeritus. With an undiminished interest in public affairs he continued to write, speak and preach until, after a brief illness from pneumonia, he died at his home in Coraopolis Heights near Pittsburgh.

McCormick was a man of strong friendships and intense loyalties. While small of stature, he had tremendous energy and an active imagination. Neither his labors nor his reputation were limited to the field of his professional duties. He was a member of the committee of the General

Assembly of the Presbyterian Church for the revision of the confession of faith; and a director of the Carnegie Foundation for the Advancement of Teaching, of the Western Theological Seminary, and of the Pittsburgh Chamber of Commerce.

[*Who's Who in America*, 1899–1927; *Reports of the Chancellor of the University of Pittsburgh*, esp. 1910–20; *The Pitt Weekly*, Apr. 1928; *The Carnegie Foundation for the Advancement of Teaching, Twenty-third Ann. Report* (1928); *Univ. of Pittsburgh Bull.*; *The Celebration of the One Hundred and Twenty-fifth Anniversary* (1912); *Biog. and Hist. Cat. of Washington and Jefferson Coll.* (1902); *A Century and a Half of Pittsburg and Her People* (1908), vol. III, ed. by J. W. Jordan; *Pittsburgh Record*, June 1928; *Pittsburgh Post-Gazette*, Apr. 19, 1928.]   W.G.C.

McCORMICK, STEPHEN (Aug. 26, 1784–Aug. 28, 1875), inventor and manufacturer, was born at Auburn, in Fauquier County, Va., the son of John and Elizabeth (Morgan) McCormick and a kinsman of Robert McCormick [*q.v.*]. His paternal ancestors emigrated from Ulster, Ireland, to Pennsylvania and thence moved to Virginia. He did not take kindly to his father's suggestion that he study law but sought a more congenial occupation in inventive activities. One of his first enterprises was to improve the shape of the nether millstone on a water-power gristmill, thereby increasing its productivity. He next became interested in the development of a practical iron plow and by 1816 had invented, manufactured, and put into use a cast-iron plow, superior to that invented earlier by Charles Newbold. He took out his first patent Feb. 3, 1819, and followed it with subsequent patents on January 28, 1826, and December 1, 1837. His plow, made of detachable parts, consisted of an especially designed cast-iron mould board to the bottom of which was fastened an adjustable wrought-iron point. In practice, this implement decreased the draft, deepened the furrow, and pulverized the soil more thoroughly. The introduction of the principles of replacement and standardization of parts made the iron plow a practical invention and also aided in the development of manufacturing processes. When Lafayette visited the United States in 1824, McCormick presented him with one of his plows. Lafayette lent it to the Royal Central Agricultural Society of France which on May 17, 1826, highly commended its principles.

At first McCormick manufactured his plows in small numbers on the farm at Auburn and marketed them in the vicinity. Coincident with the grant of his second patent in 1826, he began an active campaign to introduce his plow into Virginia and other Southern states. He designed some twelve types intended to cover the needs of every variety of plowing. Still main-

taining the factory at Auburn, he established factories at Leesburg and Alexandria, Va. The product from these factories was sold directly to consumers or through the agency of the firm of McCormick & Minor in Richmond. Supplementing his personal activities, McCormick arranged for the construction of his plows with several Virginia iron furnaces on a license fee basis. Other iron furnaces of the state began to pirate his invention as early as 1827, manufacturing and selling his plow on an extensive scale in violation of his patent rights. He also had to contend with a claim of infringement of his patent by another inventor, Gideon Davis, who sued him but eventually compromised the case out of court.

McCormick's plows were manufactured chiefly between 1826 and 1850, when they were widely used in Virginia and to a less degree in other Southern states. The production figures available show that five thousand and forty were made and sold at the furnaces of William Weaver and Jordan & Irvine between 1827 and 1839, and that as many or more were made by a dozen other Virginia iron furnaces in the same period. McCormick wrote in 1830 that Benjamin Blackford, a Virginia iron manufacturer, was paying him annually between $1,200 and $2,000 in license fees, the royalty on each plow usually being seventy-five cents or less. McCormick's most widely known contemporary was Jethro Wood of New York, who took out a patent for his cast-iron plow some seven months later than McCormick's patent of the same year, and subsequently built and sold his plows in the Northern states. With Wood, McCormick shares the honor of the introduction of the cast-iron plow into the United States. McCormick married Sarah Barnett of Fauquier County in February 1807. She died in 1814, leaving three children, and on Feb. 29, 1816, he married Elizabeth M. Benson of Stafford County, Va., by whom he had nine children. He was a devoted "Old School" Presbyterian and a stanch Democrat. In character he was said to have been honest, candid, and fearless. Retiring from business in his later years, he died at the age of ninety-one and was buried on his old farm at Auburn.

[L. J. McCormick, *Family Record and Biog.* (1896); H. L. Ellsworth, *A Digest of Patents Issued by the U. S.* (1840); the *Am. Farmer* (Baltimore), July 28, Nov. 10, 1826, Oct. 24, Nov. 7, 1828; *Farmers' Reg.* (Shellbanks, Va.), Oct. 1834; *Farmers' Reg.* (Petersburg, Va.), Feb. 1836; *New Eng. Farmer* (Boston), Jan. 20, 1826, and correspondence and records in the Colls. of the McCormick Hist. Asso., Chicago, Ill.]   H.A.K.

McCOSH, ANDREW JAMES (Mar. 15, 1858–Dec. 2, 1908), surgeon, was born at Belfast,

Ireland, son of Rev. James McCosh [*q.v.*], then professor of logic and metaphysics at Queen's College, and Isabella Guthrie, the daughter of Dr. Alexander Guthrie of Edinburgh. In 1868, following his call to the presidency of the College of New Jersey, James McCosh moved his family to Princeton. Andrew was educated at the local schools and at the college, where he was graduated in 1877. He was athletic, played on the football team for three of his undergraduate years, and developed a superb physique. In 1880 he received the degree of M.D. from the College of Physicians and Surgeons, New York, and after serving an internship for eighteen months at the Chambers Street Hospital, where he had unusual facilities for studying casualties, he spent some time in Vienna under the renowned surgeon Billroth. Returning to the metropolis he entered practice in 1883 as junior associate of T. Gaillard Thomas, a gynecologist, with whom he remained for eleven years. By all precedent he should himself have become known as a gynecologist, but he refused to limit his surgical activity in any way and while he was a master of gynecological surgery he remained in his affiliations and practice a general surgeon. In 1887 he was made an attending surgeon to the Presbyterian Hospital, a position he retained until his death; he was at the same time one of the professors of surgery at the New York Polyclinic, from its inception until 1895, and he was also professor of clinical surgery at the College of Physicians and Surgeons. In 1903 he was made president of the medical board of the Presbyterian Hospital. His premature death resulted from an injury received in a runaway accident.

As a surgeon McCosh had few equals, and while he published no major work on surgery he wrote papers which covered every department of major surgery—abdominal, gynecological, urological, thoracic, and neurological. The records of the Presbyterian Hospital show that during the twenty-one years of his surgical connection with that institution he had operated sixteen hundred times for appendicitis alone. His papers on peritonitis, one of which was read before an International Congress at Brussels, attracted unusual attention. He collaborated with M. Allen Starr, the neurologist and a classmate, in a work entitled *A Contribution to the Localisation of the Muscular Sense* (1894). For many years he spent his summers abroad for the joint purpose of taking a vacation and of keeping in touch with European surgery. At a late period in his career he began the custom of holding monthly sessions at his office for the benefit of his junior hospital associates. His interests outside of the profession were limited largely to philanthropic and sociological activities. He never married.

[*N. Y. Medic. Jour.*, Dec. 5, 1908; *Medic. Record*, Dec. 5, 1908; C. A. McWilliams, "Master Surgeons of America," *Surgery, Gynecology, and Obstetrics*, June 1923; H. A. Kelly and W. L. Burrage, *Am. Medic. Biogs.* (1920); H. F. Osborn, *Fifty Years of Princeton '77* (1927); *Princeton Alumni Weekly*, Dec. 9, 16, 1908; *N. Y. Tribune*, Dec. 3, 1908.]   E. P.

McCOSH, JAMES (Apr. 1, 1811–Nov. 16, 1894), college president, was born within a mile of the river Doon, about ten miles from its mouth on the bay of Ayr, the region which had passed through stirring scenes in the days of Wallace. He was the son of Andrew and Jean (Carson) McCosh. At the early age of thirteen he entered Glasgow University. After a notable record there he finished his academic career at Edinburgh University, receiving the degree of master of arts in March 1833. The following year he became a licensed preacher of the Established Church of Scotland and was successful in his pastorates at the Abbey Chapel, Arbroath; and, later, at Brechin. While he was at Brechin the historic controversies arose in the Established Church of Scotland between the conservatives and the more liberally inclined. McCosh courageously allied himself with his colleagues who protested against the intolerable burdens and restrictions placed upon them by the technical demands of the state. This group, committed to the logic of their convictions, left the Established Church in a body, facing the total loss of all of their emoluments and without financial resources or assurance of support. The result was the establishment of the Free Church of Scotland. This action of McCosh was characteristic of his whole life, the following of his convictions in scorn of results. It was a noble company of patriots and churchmen, of which he was a member, led by the great Thomas Chalmers, the most conspicuous preacher, scholar, and philanthropist in Scotland.

At the University of Edinburgh McCosh had come under the influence of the philosophy and personality of William Hamilton, who stimulated his interest in philosophical studies. With a singular independence of thought, however, young McCosh soon began to react in opposition to the many negations of Hamilton and to find himself in closer sympathy with the Intuitionism of Reid and the Scottish school. In the intuitive powers of the human mind as expressed in the fundamental principles of that school, he became, at length, a firm believer. In 1843 John Stuart Mill's *System of Logic* appeared. To McCosh it seemed to evolve a view of nature that excluded the supernatural from the course of the world. Mill's philosophy and its growing influence called forth McCosh's first book, *The Method of the Divine Government, Physical and Moral* (1850). This brought him into public notice at once in the philosophical world and eventually led, through Lord Clarendon, to his appointment to the chair of logic and metaphysics in Queen's College, Belfast.

The sixteen years at Belfast (1852–68) mark a most productive period of McCosh's work. During it he published *Typical Forms and Special Ends in Creation* (1855), in collaboration with George Dickie; *The Intuitions of the Mind Inductively Investigated* (1860); *The Supernatural in Relation to the Natural* (1862); and *An Examination of Mr. J. S. Mill's Philosophy; Being a Defence of Fundamental Truth* (1866). His *Intuitions* presented the fundamental doctrines of the Scottish school, namely, that there are certain constitutional principles in the human mind which determine the form of its experience, and at the same time guarantee the objective authority of its fundamental beliefs. He maintained that our intuitions have their beginning in simple cognition, where they take on singular and concrete forms, and then pass into the realm of our higher judgments and beliefs, where they become universal and necessary principles. He did not, however, rest their authority alone, or even mainly, on experience, but appealed to certain marks by which they become accredited, namely, self-evidence, necessity, and catholicity. With him self-evidence held the main and unique place. He affirmed, moreover, that the intuitive principles bear intrinsic evidence which substantiates their claims, and that they are the chief grounds on which the negations of Kant and Hamilton are to be refuted and a positive philosophy constructed. Hamilton's *Lectures on Metaphysics and Logic* called forth, in 1865, Mill's *An Examination of Sir William Hamilton's Philosophy*. McCosh attacked vigorously Mill's position, his sensational psychology, his empirical logic, his utilitarian ethics, his negative metaphysics, and his skeptical attitude towards religion. The *Examination of Mr. J. S. Mill's Philosophy; Being a Defence of Fundamental Truth* is one of the most convincing statements concerning the principles of the Intuitional philosophy in opposition to pure Empiricism.

McCosh's reputation was extending rapidly in Ireland, Scotland, and England, and echoes of it reached American shores. In 1868 President John Maclean, of the College of New Jersey, Princeton, resigned. McCosh was immediately suggested as his successor, and the board of trustees unanimously called him to assume the office,

exactly one hundred years after the calling of his fellow countryman, John Witherspoon [*q.v.*], from Edinburgh to the same position. During his labors at Princeton McCosh continued to publish many works, among which the most important were *The Laws of Discursive Thought, Being a Text-book of Formal Logic* (1870); *Christianity and Positivism* (1871); *The Scottish Philosophy, Biographical, Expository, Critical, from Hutcheson to Hamilton* (1875); *Realistic Philosophy Defended in a Philosophic Series* (2 vols., 1887); a two-volume work, *Psychology* (1886, 1887); and another metaphysical treatise entitled *First and Fundamental Truths* (1889), the latter being in large measure a revised edition of his *Intuitions*.

Throughout all his philosophical writings, McCosh led up to his philosophy of religion, in which he presented the fundamental arguments for theism and expressed his belief in the divine origin and government of the world. One of his most conspicuous contributions to philosophical and theological discussions during his early years at Princeton was in connection with the subject of evolution. Although brought up in the conservative theology of Scotland, he had an open and ever-deepening mind. In the early seventies he stood out almost alone among the ministers of the United States, in defense of the doctrine of evolution. No one would have been more astonished and perplexed by the trial in Tennessee in which William Jennings Bryan figured, than McCosh would have been. In an age when the discussion was just starting, he insisted that the doctrine of evolution was not directly, or by implication, a denial of God; but that the program of evolution magnified the wonder and mystery of the process of creation.

When McCosh became president of the College of New Jersey it was at low ebb. After the Civil War, few students came from the South, formerly the chief recruiting ground; the attendance was small and the financial affairs of the institution were in a most critical state. The new president proved an able administrator, and his twenty years in office constitute a memorable period in the history of the college. His plans were well conceived and the power of his personality commanded enthusiastic support at all times. Eminent and well-qualified instructors were added to the faculty; a wisely balanced system of elective studies and of graduate work was instituted; schools of science, philosophy, and art were organized; fellowships and other means for stimulating research were provided; additions to scientific equipment were made; and buildings, the beauty and effective arrangement of which revolutionized the appearance of the campus, were erected.

As a teacher, also, McCosh had rare gifts. In his classes in psychology and the history of philosophy he succeeded in awakening in the students a unique interest in the subjects taught, and discussions there stimulated were carried on outside of the classroom. From time to time he held meetings in his library, to which he invited men of distinction in various philosophical fields to read papers and to lead in discussion. Admission into this inner circle was regarded by all the students as a highly prized privilege.

Throughout his life at Princeton McCosh was most ably aided, and at critical moments guided, by his wife, Isabella Guthrie McCosh, whom he had married on Sept. 29, 1845. She was a daughter of Alexander Guthrie, an eminent physician known throughout the length and breadth of Scotland, and a brother of the distinguished Rev. Thomas Guthrie, who had been intimately associated with McCosh in opposition to the Established Church of Scotland. A woman of personal charm, unusual mental capacity, and a heart overflowing with sympathy for all who needed help, she carried on labors of goodwill and mercy among the students and in the community. There was never a student ill but she immediately heard of it and would herself go to his room with comfort and encouragement. She took upon herself the function of a visiting nurse and, naturally, was beloved by all of the student body. To honor her memory an infirmary bearing her name was erected upon the college campus in 1892. A son, Andrew James McCosh [q.v.], was a distinguished surgeon.

McCosh resigned as president and was made emeritus in 1888, his death occurring at Princeton six years later. That the present and future of the college rest upon the foundations which he laid is being increasingly recognized as time brings a fuller understanding of the value of his labors.

[W. M. Sloane, *The Life of James McCosh* (1896), contains autobiog. material and complete bibliog. of McCosh's writings; see also the *Nation*, Oct. 8, 1896; *Princeton Coll. Bull.*, Feb., June 1895; F. L. Patton, "James McCosh: a Baccalaureate Sermon," in *Presbyt. and Reformed Rev.*, Oct. 1895; sketch in F. B. Lee, *Geneal. and Memorial Hist. of the State of N. J.* (1910), vol. I, reprinted in *Memorial Cyc. of N. J.*, vol. I (1915); *Disruption Worthies* (1881); M. A. DeW. Howe, *Classic Shades* (1928); *N. Y. Times, N. Y. Tribune*, Nov. 17, 1894.]   J. G. H.

McCOY, ELIJAH (Mar. 27, 1843–Oct. 10, 1929), negro inventor, was born in Canada, the son of George and Mildred (Goins) McCoy, both natives of Kentucky. He seems to have engaged in mechanical work at an early age and soon developed inventive talent, which he applied almost exclusively to the field of automatic lubrication of machinery. About 1870, at which time he was a resident of Ypsilanti, Mich., he began experimenting with lubricators for steam engines, and after two years of labor, June 23, 1872, he received patent No. 129,843. Probably he had an experimental machine-shop of his own, and as each of his ideas was perfected he made a partial or total assignment of his rights to the invention, thereby obtaining sufficient money to continue with his work. Thus his first patent was assigned outright to William and S. C. Hamlin of Ypsilanti; his second he retained for himself; while his third and fourth, granted May 27, 1873, and Jan. 20, 1874, respectively, were assigned to S. M. McCutchen and E. P. Allen, also of Ypsilanti. Between 1872 and 1876 McCoy obtained six patents for lubricators and one for an ironing table, the latter on May 12, 1874. For a period of six years thereafter his inventive work apparently ceased. Meanwhile, he moved to Detroit, and there from 1882 to 1926 he continued his activities. During this period forty-four patents were granted him, all but eight of which pertained to lubricating devices. McCoy is regarded as the pioneer in devising means for steadily supplying oil to machinery in intermittent drops from a cup, thus obviating the necessity of stopping a machine to oil it. His lubricating cup was in use for years on stationary engines and locomotives of the great railways of the West, on the engines of steamships on the Great Lakes, on transatlantic liners, and on the machinery of many factories. Other patents which he secured included those for the following devices: steam dome for locomotives, June 16, 1885; scaffold support, June 4, 1907; valve and plug-cock, June 30, 1914; vehicle wheel tire, Oct. 2, 1923; and a rubber heel, Nov. 10, 1925. About 1920 he organized the Elijah McCoy Manufacturing Company in Detroit and assigned to his company an improved airbrake lubricator, which he patented that year. Some time after 1926 his health began to fail. He was apparently alone in the world, his wife having died, and in 1928 he was committed to the Eloise Infirmary, Eloise, Mich., where he died about a year later. He was buried in Detroit.

[B. T. Washington, *The Story of the Negro* (1909), vol. II; *Jour. of Negro Hist.*, Jan. 1917; Patent Office Records; H. E. Baker, *The Colored Inventor* (1913); D. W. Culp, *Twentieth Century Negro Literature* (1902); *Negro Year Book . . . 1921–22* (1922); vital record, Eloise Infirmary, Eloise, Mich.]   C. W. M.

McCOY, ISAAC (June 13, 1784–June 21, 1846), Indian agent and missionary, was born near Uniontown in Fayette County, Pa. His father, William McCoy, was a clergyman and his mother a devout Christian woman, who early instilled in her son those religious principles that were later to shape his life. About 1790 he removed with his parents to Kentucky, where he received a limited education in the public schools. His conversion occurred in his seventeenth year, and in 1803 he married Christiana Polke, a young woman with religious convictions and missionary spirit, who bore him thirteen children and remained throughout his life his devoted fellow worker. In 1804 the young couple removed to Vincennes, Ind., and the following year to Clark County, Ind. Here McCoy was licensed by the Baptist Church to preach, and a little later he was ordained as pastor of Maria Creek Church. He remained for eight years making some short missionary tours but in 1817 was appointed missionary to the Indians in the valley of the Wabash. He labored for many years among the western Indians and in 1828 was appointed as member of a commission to arrange for the removal of the Ottawa and the Miami westward. Becoming convinced that the welfare of the Indians demanded their removal from the influence of the whites, he began agitation for a plan to remove the Indians east of the Mississippi to the region beyond that river and to form an Indian state. In 1827 he published *Remarks on the Practicability of Indian Reform* to set forth his ideas of the situation. Having visited Washington and obtained approval of his plans from John C. Calhoun, secretary of war, he accepted in 1830 an appointment as surveyor and agent to assist the Indians in their migration westward. Acting in this capacity, he aided the Indians in selecting new reservations in the West, surveyed their boundaries, and helped them to remove to their new homes. Assisted by his sons, Dr. Rice McCoy and John Calvin McCoy, he surveyed or had surveyed most of the Indian reservations in Kansas and the Cherokee Outlet in Oklahoma. He visited the present state of Oklahoma several times and lived for a time with his family at Union Mission in the Cherokee country.

In spite of his labors as missionary, surveyor, and United States Indian agent, he found time to write a *History of Baptist Indian Missions,* published in 1840, and numerous pamphlets on Indian affairs including several numbers of the *Annual Register of Indian Affairs within the Indian Territory,* which he published from 1835 to 1838. His plans for an Indian state never materialized, though he went so far as to survey a tract of land near the Ottawa Mission in Kansas as a site for the capital of the proposed Indian government. In 1842 he became first corre-

sponding secretary and general agent of the Indian mission association at Louisville, Ky., where he died.

[Diary and correspondence in 38 vols. in possession of the Kan. Hist. Soc.; letters in Congregational House Lib. in Boston; W. N. Wyeth, *Isaac McCoy* (1895); *Kan. State Hist. Soc. Colls.,* vols. II, IV, IX, X, XII, XVI (1881–1925); A. H. Abel, "The Hist. of Events Resulting in Indian Consolidation West of the Mississippi," *Am. Hist. Asso. Rept. . . . 1906,* vol. I (1908); J. B. Thoburn, *A Standard Hist. of Okla.* (1916), vol. I; L. B. Hill, *A Hist. of the State of Okla.* (1908), vol. I.]   E. E. D.

McCOY, JOSEPH GEATING (Dec. 21, 1837–Oct. 19, 1915), pioneer cattleman, was born in Sangamon County, Ill., the son of David McCoy, a Virginian who moved to Illinois in 1815, and Mary (Kirkpatrick) McCoy of Kentucky. He went to the district school and, from 1857 to 1858, to the academical department of Knox College. On Oct. 22, 1861, he married Sarah Epler of Pleasantplains, Ill., and the same year entered the cattle business. In 1867 he left the prosperous farm in Illinois and went west with the hope of getting beef from the southwest to the northern and eastern markets, where there was a great scarcity. He found in Texas vast herds of cattle, which had been increasing for many years. Cut off from the markets, they were of so little value as to be neglected and permitted to roam the plains at will. Notwithstanding the failures of others, he moved swiftly toward success. He favored the plan of driving the cattle to some shipping point, but the railroads would take no part in his seemingly impracticable scheme. He was ridiculed, and some persons even thought him crazy. He chose for his shipping-point Abilene, Kan., on the Kansas Pacific Railway and bought the whole town site with about 480 acres for $2,400. There he built a three-story hotel and constructed his own stockyards. He hired surveyors, laid out and marked a trail across the prairies from Abilene to Corpus Christi, Tex., and arranged facilities for pasture and water. By advertising and by personal contact he persuaded ranchers to drive their herds to Abilene. The first drive passed over this trail in September 1867, and by the end of the year 35,000 cattle reached Abilene and were shipped east. Following that year a very great movement of live stock took place. Ten millions of cattle are said to have reached the market over this trail. Notwithstanding lack of faith in the project, the Kansas Pacific Railway agreed to give him one-eighth of the freight on each car of cattle shipped. After the second year the sum of $200,000 was due him on this account. The company repudiated the contract on the ground that it was improvidently made, since such large shipments had not been anticipated. He surrendered his contract on a promise of another one, but the company never kept its promise. He sued for the amount due him, which he collected several years later, but the failure to receive the new contract cost him dearly. He served as mayor of Abilene and received many commissions from the federal government. His report on the live-stock industry, as director of that branch of the 11th U. S. Census, attracted large capital to meet production in the grazing regions.

Rival interests finally diverted the trade from Abilene, but he followed the industry. He established the cattle drives to Cottonwood Falls, to Wichita, and helped open the famous Chisholm Trail. He went to Wichita in May 1872. In 1881, operating from Wichita, he served as agent for the Cherokee Nation in collecting their land revenues. He lived for a time in Oklahoma, where he took part in political conventions. A stanch Democrat, he was nominated for Congress in 1890 but failed of election. With a reputation for honesty and character, he was probably, for a generation, the best-known man in southern Kansas. He was the author of *Historic Sketches of the Cattle Trade* (1874) and was the original for the character thinly disguised as Joe McCoyne in Emerson Hough's *North of 36* (1923). He was well known in Kansas City, where he lived for a time and where he died. He was survived by one son and two daughters.

[Letter from his daughter, Dr. Florence L. McCoy, Wichita, Kan.; autobiog. material in *Historic Sketches of the Cattle Trade* (1874); *Kansas Mag.* (Wichita), Dec. 1909; *Portrait and Biog. Album of Sedgwick County, Kan.* (1888); *Parsons' Memorial and Hist. Lib. Mag.*, ed. by Mrs. Augustus Wilson (1885); S. O. Henry, *Conquering our Great Am. Plains* (copr. 1930); *Chronicles of Okla.*, Sept. 1929; *Kan. City Star*, Dec. 3, 1911; *Kan. City Jour.*, Oct. 20, 1915.]   S. M. D.

MACCRACKEN, HENRY MITCHELL (Sept. 28, 1840–Dec. 24, 1918), Presbyterian clergyman, educator, was born at Oxford, Ohio, the eldest son of the Rev. John Steele and Eliza Hawkins (Dougherty) Welch MacCracken. His great-grandfather, Henry MacCracken of Sunbury, Pa., fought in the Revolution, and was killed by Indians in 1780. On his mother's side, he was descended from the English Col. Charles Hawkins, who was killed at the siege of Gibraltar in 1704. John Steele MacCracken was a minister of the Reformed Presbyterian Church, and his wife had established and conducted for several years in Oxford a female seminary, which was the forerunner of the Oxford College for Women, later merged in Miami University.

In 1857 Henry graduated from Miami. Following his graduation, he was principal of an academy in Cedarville and superintendent of schools in South Charleston, Ohio. In his twenty-first year, along with his teaching of the classics in the local high school, he began the study of theology in the seminary of the United Presbyterian Church, Xenia. After two years here he spent a year in Princeton Theological Seminary. On Nov. 7, 1863, he was ordained and became pastor of the Westminster Church, Columbus, Ohio. In 1867–68 he was in Europe, where he devoted a portion of the time to study in the universities of Tübingen and Berlin. Upon his return, he assumed the pastorate of the First Presbyterian Church, Toledo, which he served until 1881. On July 2, 1872, he married Catherine Almira Hubbard, daughter of the Rev. Thomas Swan Hubbard, of Rochester, Vt., by whom he had four children. His chief literary work during this period was *The Lives of the Leaders of Our Church Universal* (3 vols., 1879), a translation of Ferdinand Piper's *Die Zeugen der Wahrheit*, with the lives of American religious leaders added.

The year 1881 marks his definite turn from pastoral to educational activity. In that year he became chancellor of the Western University of Pennsylvania, at Pittsburgh, and professor of philosophy. During his three years as head of this institution he accomplished its removal from the heart of Pittsburgh to Allegheny, where it was to remain until its return to a new site in Pittsburgh. In 1884 he went to the University of the City of New York (now New York University) as professor of philosophy. A year later, he was made vice-chancellor, and from that time on the actual administration of the institution was in his hands. On the resignation of Dr. John Hall in 1891, MacCracken succeeded him as chancellor.

In the twenty-five years that it was under his direction, the University experienced a complete transformation. The University College, with the school of engineering, was removed to University Heights. On the old site at Washington Square a ten-story structure was erected, the upper floors to be used by certain University divisions; the remainder to be rented for business use, thereby producing an income for educational purposes. A graduate school and school of pedagogy and commerce were established. The loosely related Medical College was brought under direct control of the university council and given new strength and vitality by union with the Bellevue Hospital Medical College. The School of Law was likewise brought under full University control. The ambulatory encircling the main group of buildings at University Heights was designated as the Hall of Fame for

Great Americans, and a plan was elaborated by which this was to be made a shrine of patriotic remembrance. These advances were made only with the greatest difficulty, and brought into full play the dominant elements of the Chancellor's character, his active and creative imagination, his courage and tenacity of purpose, and his resourcefulness in finding ways to ends deliberately chosen.

On the completion of his seventieth year, in 1910, he resigned the chancellorship, and received from the University the designation of chancellor emeritus. He continued to the end of his life his membership in the university council, with special service as committeeman of the Hall of Fame. In the year following his retirement he made a tour of the world, the immediate fruit of which was an address on *Urgent Eastern Questions* published in 1913.

His interest in religious activities continued, with occasional preaching, to the end of his life. He was not an active participant in the doctrinal dissensions of the time, though by no means indifferent to them. For years he was an active member of the American Institute of Christian Philosophy, founded by Dr. Charles F. Deems. He became its president in 1900, and brought it into close working relations with New York University. His most important contribution to the Institute's proceedings, "Kant and Lotze," published in *Christian Thought* (November, December 1885), gives some indication of his philosophical position. He was also associated with Howard Crosby and Charles H. Parkhurst in the Society for the Prevention of Crime. His annual reports and occasional addresses give a general view of his thought and work, particularly "A Metropolitan University," in *The Christian at Work* (May 5, 11, 1892), and his state convocation address of 1904, *University Problems in the Metropolis.* His death, after a brief illness, occurred at Orlando, Fla.

[J. L. Chamberlain, *Universities and Their Sons: N. Y. Univ.* (1901); *Henry Mitchell MacCracken: In Memoriam* (1923); T. F. Jones, *N. Y. Univ. 1832–1932* (1933); *Who's Who in America,* 1916–17; *N. Y. Times,* Dec. 25, 1918.]   E. E. B.